Lecture Notes in Computer Science   **10918**

Commenced Publication in 1973
Founding and Former Series Editors:
Gerhard Goos, Juris Hartmanis, and Jan van Leeuwen

More information about this series at http://www.springer.com/series/7409

Aaron Marcus · Wentao Wang (Eds.)

Design, User Experience, and Usability

Theory and Practice

7th International Conference, DUXU 2018
Held as Part of HCI International 2018
Las Vegas, NV, USA, July 15–20, 2018
Proceedings, Part I

 Springer

Editors
Aaron Marcus
Aaron Marcus and Associates
Berkeley, CA
USA

Wentao Wang
Baidu Inc.
Beijing
China

ISSN 0302-9743   ISSN 1611-3349   (electronic)
Lecture Notes in Computer Science
ISBN 978-3-319-91796-2   ISBN 978-3-319-91797-9   (eBook)
https://doi.org/10.1007/978-3-319-91797-9

Library of Congress Control Number: 2018944301

LNCS Sublibrary: SL3 – Information Systems and Applications, incl. Internet/Web, and HCI

Printed on acid-free paper

This Springer imprint is published by the registered company Springer International Publishing AG
part of Springer Nature
The registered company address is: Gewerbestrasse 11, 6330 Cham, Switzerland

Foreword

The 20th International Conference on Human-Computer Interaction, HCI International 2018, was held in Las Vegas, NV, USA, during July 15–20, 2018. The event incorporated the 14 conferences/thematic areas listed on the following page.

A total of 4,373 individuals from academia, research institutes, industry, and governmental agencies from 76 countries submitted contributions, and 1,170 papers and 195 posters have been included in the proceedings. These contributions address the latest research and development efforts and highlight the human aspects of design and use of computing systems. The contributions thoroughly cover the entire field of human-computer interaction, addressing major advances in knowledge and effective use of computers in a variety of application areas. The volumes constituting the full set of the conference proceedings are listed in the following pages.

I would like to thank the program board chairs and the members of the program boards of all thematic areas and affiliated conferences for their contribution to the highest scientific quality and the overall success of the HCI International 2018 conference.

This conference would not have been possible without the continuous and unwavering support and advice of the founder, Conference General Chair Emeritus and Conference Scientific Advisor Prof. Gavriel Salvendy. For his outstanding efforts, I would like to express my appreciation to the communications chair and editor of *HCI International News*, Dr. Abbas Moallem.

July 2018

Constantine Stephanidis

HCI International 2018 Thematic Areas and Affiliated Conferences

Thematic areas:

- Human-Computer Interaction (HCI 2018)
- Human Interface and the Management of Information (HIMI 2018)

Affiliated conferences:

- 15th International Conference on Engineering Psychology and Cognitive Ergonomics (EPCE 2018)
- 12th International Conference on Universal Access in Human-Computer Interaction (UAHCI 2018)
- 10th International Conference on Virtual, Augmented, and Mixed Reality (VAMR 2018)
- 10th International Conference on Cross-Cultural Design (CCD 2018)
- 10th International Conference on Social Computing and Social Media (SCSM 2018)
- 12th International Conference on Augmented Cognition (AC 2018)
- 9th International Conference on Digital Human Modeling and Applications in Health, Safety, Ergonomics, and Risk Management (DHM 2018)
- 7th International Conference on Design, User Experience, and Usability (DUXU 2018)
- 6th International Conference on Distributed, Ambient, and Pervasive Interactions (DAPI 2018)
- 5th International Conference on HCI in Business, Government, and Organizations (HCIBGO)
- 5th International Conference on Learning and Collaboration Technologies (LCT 2018)
- 4th International Conference on Human Aspects of IT for the Aged Population (ITAP 2018)

Conference Proceedings Volumes Full List

1. LNCS 10901, Human-Computer Interaction: Theories, Methods, and Human Issues (Part I), edited by Masaaki Kurosu
2. LNCS 10902, Human-Computer Interaction: Interaction in Context (Part II), edited by Masaaki Kurosu
3. LNCS 10903, Human-Computer Interaction: Interaction Technologies (Part III), edited by Masaaki Kurosu
4. LNCS 10904, Human Interface and the Management of Information: Interaction, Visualization, and Analytics (Part I), edited by Sakae Yamamoto and Hirohiko Mori
5. LNCS 10905, Human Interface and the Management of Information: Information in Applications and Services (Part II), edited by Sakae Yamamoto and Hirohiko Mori
6. LNAI 10906, Engineering Psychology and Cognitive Ergonomics, edited by Don Harris
7. LNCS 10907, Universal Access in Human-Computer Interaction: Methods, Technologies, and Users (Part I), edited by Margherita Antona and Constantine Stephanidis
8. LNCS 10908, Universal Access in Human-Computer Interaction: Virtual, Augmented, and Intelligent Environments (Part II), edited by Margherita Antona and Constantine Stephanidis
9. LNCS 10909, Virtual, Augmented and Mixed Reality: Interaction, Navigation, Visualization, Embodiment, and Simulation (Part I), edited by Jessie Y. C. Chen and Gino Fragomeni
10. LNCS 10910, Virtual, Augmented and Mixed Reality: Applications in Health, Cultural Heritage, and Industry (Part II), edited by Jessie Y. C. Chen and Gino Fragomeni
11. LNCS 10911, Cross-Cultural Design: Methods, Tools, and Users (Part I), edited by Pei-Luen Patrick Rau
12. LNCS 10912, Cross-Cultural Design: Applications in Cultural Heritage, Creativity, and Social Development (Part II), edited by Pei-Luen Patrick Rau
13. LNCS 10913, Social Computing and Social Media: User Experience and Behavior (Part I), edited by Gabriele Meiselwitz
14. LNCS 10914, Social Computing and Social Media: Technologies and Analytics (Part II), edited by Gabriele Meiselwitz
15. LNAI 10915, Augmented Cognition: Intelligent Technologies (Part I), edited by Dylan D. Schmorrow and Cali M. Fidopiastis
16. LNAI 10916, Augmented Cognition: Users and Contexts (Part II), edited by Dylan D. Schmorrow and Cali M. Fidopiastis
17. LNCS 10917, Digital Human Modeling and Applications in Health, Safety, Ergonomics, and Risk Management, edited by Vincent G. Duffy
18. LNCS 10918, Design, User Experience, and Usability: Theory and Practice (Part I), edited by Aaron Marcus and Wentao Wang

19. LNCS 10919, Design, User Experience, and Usability: Designing Interactions (Part II), edited by Aaron Marcus and Wentao Wang
20. LNCS 10920, Design, User Experience, and Usability: Users, Contexts, and Case Studies (Part III), edited by Aaron Marcus and Wentao Wang
21. LNCS 10921, Distributed, Ambient, and Pervasive Interactions: Understanding Humans (Part I), edited by Norbert Streitz and Shin'ichi Konomi
22. LNCS 10922, Distributed, Ambient, and Pervasive Interactions: Technologies and Contexts (Part II), edited by Norbert Streitz and Shin'ichi Konomi
23. LNCS 10923, HCI in Business, Government, and Organizations, edited by Fiona Fui-Hoon Nah and Bo Sophia Xiao
24. LNCS 10924, Learning and Collaboration Technologies: Design, Development and Technological Innovation (Part I), edited by Panayiotis Zaphiris and Andri Ioannou
25. LNCS 10925, Learning and Collaboration Technologies: Learning and Teaching (Part II), edited by Panayiotis Zaphiris and Andri Ioannou
26. LNCS 10926, Human Aspects of IT for the Aged Population: Acceptance, Communication, and Participation (Part I), edited by Jia Zhou and Gavriel Salvendy
27. LNCS 10927, Human Aspects of IT for the Aged Population: Applications in Health, Assistance, and Entertainment (Part II), edited by Jia Zhou and Gavriel Salvendy
28. CCIS 850, HCI International 2018 Posters Extended Abstracts (Part I), edited by Constantine Stephanidis
29. CCIS 851, HCI International 2018 Posters Extended Abstracts (Part II), edited by Constantine Stephanidis
30. CCIS 852, HCI International 2018 Posters Extended Abstracts (Part III), edited by Constantine Stephanidis

http://2018.hci.international/proceedings

7th International Conference on Design, User Experience, and Usability

Program Board Chair(s): **Aaron Marcus, USA** **and Wentao Wang, *P.R. China***

- Sisira Adikari, Australia
- Claire Ancient, UK
- Jan Brejcha, Czech Republic
- Silvia De los Rios Perez, Spain
- Marc Fabri, UK
- Chao Liu, P.R. China
- Judith A. Moldenhauer, USA
- Jingyan Qin, P.R. China
- Francisco Rebelo, Portugal

- Christine Riedmann-Streitz, Germany
- Kerem Rizvanoglu, Turkey
- Elizabeth Rosenzweig, USA
- Patricia Search, USA
- Marcelo Márcio Soares, Brazil
- Carla G. Spinillo, Brazil
- Manfred Thüring, Germany
- Xuemei Yuan, P.R. China
- Paul Michael Zender, USA

The full list with the Program Board Chairs and the members of the Program Boards of all thematic areas and affiliated conferences is available online at:

http://www.hci.international/board-members-2018.php

HCI International 2019

The 21st International Conference on Human-Computer Interaction, HCI International 2019, will be held jointly with the affiliated conferences in Orlando, FL, USA, at Walt Disney World Swan and Dolphin Resort, July 26–31, 2019. It will cover a broad spectrum of themes related to Human-Computer Interaction, including theoretical issues, methods, tools, processes, and case studies in HCI design, as well as novel interaction techniques, interfaces, and applications. The proceedings will be published by Springer. More information will be available on the conference website: http://2019.hci.international/.

General Chair
Prof. Constantine Stephanidis
University of Crete and ICS-FORTH
Heraklion, Crete, Greece
E-mail: general_chair@hcii2019.org

http://2019.hci.international/

Contents – Part I

Usability and User Experience Evaluation Methods and Tools

DUXU in Software Development

Contents – Part II

GUI, Visualization and Image Design

Multimodal DUXU

Mobile DUXU

Contents – Part III

DUXU and Children

DUXU in Automotive and Transport

DUXU, Culture and Art

DUXU Case Studies

Design Thinking, Methods and Practice

Exploration of New-Generation Human Computer Interface Based on Participatory Design Strategy

Danni Chang[1(✉)], Carman Lee[2], and Lo Kwok Leung[2]

[1] Shanghai Jiao Tong University, Shanghai, China
dchangl@sjtu.edu.cn
[2] Hong Kong Polytechnic University, Hong Kong, China

Abstract. This study researched the next-generation human computer interactions. In particular, brainwave computer interaction (BCI) is emphasized. To investigate BCI, two stages are included: interface development to develop a BCI game, and interface evaluation with a series of user experiments to test user experience. For both stages, participatory design is adopted as the essential principle to involve potential users to provide their expectations and insights on possible application scenarios of BCI in daily life, help define the requirements, assist in concept screening and user experience investigation. In particular, a prototype with hardware (including brainwave computer chipsets and Bluetooth module) and software (i.e., a PC Tetris game developed by Labview) was developed. The physical part is to collect users' neural signals, and such signals will be used to control the game. A group of participants were involved to play the game, and interviews based on game experience questionnaire was constructed to identify participants' experience on BCI and also other traditional interfaces. Through results analysis, it can be concluded that BCI shows obvious strength which is more immersive, attractive and enjoyable. Therefore, BCI could be promising to enhance user experience and bring more fun to task completion.

Keywords: Human computer interaction · Brain computer interaction
Participatory design · User experiment

1 Introduction

With the massive influx and advancement of technologies, computer system has become a powerful tool to support human beings to complete tasks more easily and facilitate the realization of some challenging tasks. As a result, human computer interaction (HCI) which defines the two-way information transfer between human and computer (intelligent machine or systems) has become an important part of our life [1]. Lots of applications of human computer interface can be observed, for example, using multi-touch function to control the smartphone, using keyboard to operate the computer, using voice to control light switch. Therefore, HCI has become pervasive in our daily life. Diverse interaction ways are emerging, and different interfaces are accordingly developed.

© Springer International Publishing AG, part of Springer Nature 2018
A. Marcus and W. Wang (Eds.): DUXU 2018, LNCS 10918, pp. 3–13, 2018.
https://doi.org/10.1007/978-3-319-91797-9_1

Although modern human computer interface had gone through many notable achievements, continuous improvements are still needed [2]. On one hand, due to the rapid development of new technologies, the techniques applied in existing interfaces for computing, communication or display may become a bottleneck for the development of new human computer interfaces. It indicates that new interfaces should be developed along with the advancement of technologies. On the other hand, the dynamically changing and rapidly increased user requirements put forward the necessity to continuously optimize user experience, enhance user satisfaction and improve the interface to be as natural as possible. For such reasons, new generations of human computer interface need to be developed.

Existing widely adopted interaction ways include multi-touch, eye-tracking, voice recognition and control, gesture (e.g., head gesture, hand gesture) sensing and control, keyboard/mouse/joystick input. Besides, new interaction ways are emerging. For example, the technologies of virtual reality (VR), augmented reality (AR), mixed reality (MR) and brainwave control. Among them, the brainwave control, which allows users to communicate or control external devices using brain signals rather than the brain's peripheral nerves or muscles, really extends human capacity to interact with external environment [3]. It has attracted more and more research interest in healthcare and entertainment areas. Considering the applications of brain computer interfaces are still limited, it will be emphatically studied in this work.

Therefore, this study is intended to (i) investigate into brain computer interactions (BCI); and (ii) compare the brainwave computer interface with traditional human computer interface. To emphasize and ensure user satisfaction, the participatory design strategy is adopted during the development, test and evaluation of brainwave computer interfaces, as well as the comparison between different interfaces.

2 Related Works

2.1 Existing Human Computer Interactions

Human computer interaction has been pervasive in our daily life. However, human computer interaction is too wide, and specific interaction manners can vary from muscle level to neuro level. Roughly, existing HCI can include such types:

1. Eye tracking: This interaction is to capture human gazes and the moving path of fixations and use eye motion data to perform certain tasks [4]. Actually, eye-tracking has been widely applied in design activities. For example the user study for graphic design, package design, and supermarket layout design often rely on eye tracking. It has been widely demonstrated that eye tracking can be useful and effective to assist in design evaluation [5]. Besides, eye tracking is also used as input manner, such as eye tracking on-screen keyboard.

2. Speech recognition: This technology is to recognize and translate spoken language as input data. A lot of popular applications have already come out and become useful in our daily lives [6, 7], for example, the voice search in google map, Siri developed by Apple, and automatic translation tools. Moreover, more and more intelligent systems involve speech recognition, like intelligent transportation system

(e.g., vehicle-mounted system based on voice control) and smart home (e.g., voice-activated devices, light and conditioner).

3. Gesture sensing: This interaction is to recognize and interpret human gestures via mathematical algorithms [8]. Gestures can include bodily motion of head, hands or legs and also emotions from face. Nowadays, gesture recognition has been widely considered. Diverse motion capture systems (e.g., leap motion, Kinect) have been used in human factor analysis. In addition, gesture sensing is essential for virtual reality, augmented reality and mixed reality (e.g., Google Daydream, Microsoft HoloLens, HTC Vive), which greatly facilitate product design and simulation and help enhance user experience of entertainment products.

4. Brain control: Brain computer interaction is neural-control or mind-control. It collects electroencephalography waves, event or evoked related potentials, or the neuronal electrical pulse signal as inputs to perform certain tasks [9, 10]. It can be generally classified into invasive and non-invasive types. The invasive type implants microelectrodes into human brain and has been explored in medical area, for example, to help the patients with brain damage to control their body or artificial limb. The non-invasive type can detect electroencephalography waves and has been explored in intelligent manufacturing, for example, to try to use brain to control robot arm. In fact, brain computer interface (BCI) is a kind of direct and fast communication between human and computer, and can greatly extend human capacity to control external devices; therefore it has been regarded with huge potential and deserves further development. SAMSUNG Company had already started up a project about how to control the tablet by using neuro-signals. Nonetheless, the applications of brain computer interface in daily life are still limited.

Based on the analysis of existing interactions, BCI shows obvious advantage and potential, for example, to allow paralyzed people to control prosthetic limbs with their mind, to allow a mute person to have their thoughts displayed and spoken by a computer, and to allow gamers to control video games with their minds. It endows human with more direct and stronger communication with external environment. However, research about BCI technology is till at the beginning stage, and the user experience during such interaction process needs to be studied scientifically. Therefore, the further exploration of BCI is worthwhile.

2.2 Participatory Design

Participatory design (PD) is a way to achieve user-centered design. It aims to involve all stakeholders (e.g. employees, partners, customers, citizens, end users) in the design process to help ensure the result meets their needs and is usable to different facets. Users are especially valuable stakeholders and often crucial participants in product design process. The original tenets of PD were applied in a workplace context, but over the years, PD has expanded into new domains and contexts, partly owing to technological developments, for example, social media, healthcare, and exhibition [11]. Therefore, participatory design has evolved into a wide approach to apply to design in general.

For human computer interaction, users' requirements and experience are especially important, since users' responses are direct embodiment of the quality and effect of the interaction. To ensure that the exploration of BCI fully considers users' desire and feeling, PD is utilized in this study to assist in the development of BCI product and also user experiments.

In summary, BCI is a promising interaction way; however, there are still some issues which need further exploration: (i) current applications are still limited and more application scenarios especially to serve people in daily life are expected; and (ii) the scientific investigation of user experience on BCI is deficient. Therefore, this work is intended to explore possible use of BCI to improve people's task completion process, and investigate user experience on such interaction way.

3   Research Framework

As shown in Fig. 1, this study mainly consists of 2 main stages: interface development to develop a prototype brainwave computer interface which is suitable for casual users to complete certain tasks and interface evaluation to test the user experience on the prototype interface and further compare BCI with traditional interfaces. For both stages, participatory design is adopted as the essential principle to involve potential users to help define the interface requirements, perform concept screening and design evaluation and contribute to usability test. Therefore, this study is a user-centered exploration of the brainwave computer interaction.

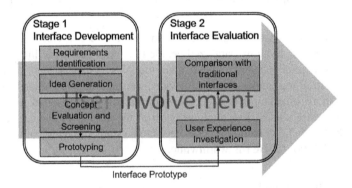

Fig. 1. Overall research framework

More specifically,

1. Interface Development: Considering that existing BCI is often applied in medical area and not suitable for casual use, a brainwave computer interface (including hardware and software) will be developed. For this purpose, user requirements will be collected to identify promising new application scenario of BCI in daily life. Based on user expectation, design concepts will be generated and screened

according to users' evaluation. The selected design will be further developed into physical prototype.

2. Interface Evaluation: To test and evaluate the prototype BCI, participants are recruited to use the prototype. Several rounds of interviews are conducted to collect their experience in order to evaluate the performance of the developed BCI prototype. Moreover, participants are invited to perform the same tasks by using keyboard, and a statistical comparison between BCI and keyboard is executed.

4   Interface Development and Evaluation

In this section, a human brainwave computer interface is developed, and then user experience on such interaction way is examined.

4.1   Interface Development

Generally, the development process follows Fig. 2, which can be divided into two parts, hardware and software. They both started from idea generation, screening and evaluation. For software, it continued with coding and layout design, and for hardware, it continued with product planning and prototyping.

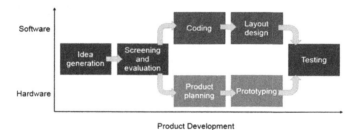

Fig. 2. Interface development process

Firstly, target users are involved to provide their expectations on the next-generation human computer interface. The promising new interfaces are compared, and BCI is emphasized. To extend the current applications of BCI to be more attractive and convenient to use in daily life, entertainment activities, which are also users' interest where they want to try BCI to serve them, are focused. In particular, PC game is selected as the application scenario, and a BCI-based PC game will be developed accordingly.

For hardware part, the sensors which can detect human brainwaves are considered. Through comprehensively considering the cost, technical functions, required development efforts and back up support, the brainwave computer chipsets ThinkGearAM, which can output Attention/Meditation Values, EEG Power Band Values and Raw wave values, is selected. Subsequently, a Bluetooth module, which enables the brainwave computer chipsets to be connected to computer, is employed. To make the brainwave computer chipsets easy to wear by users, a headphone is used. Bluetooth module is connected with ThinkGearAM, and these two parts are attached to the headphone (Fig. 3). Then the semi-completed product is connected to the computer.

For software part, a LabVIEW-based program is developed to make the hardware useable. For this end, a Tetris game is developed as the tasks for users to complete and control using the brainwave hardware. Three output signals, i.e., attention, mediation and blink strength, are used to control the game (Fig. 4). Attention is used to control the block to move to the right. Mediation is to control the block to move to the left. Blink strength is to control the block to turn 90° anticlockwise. By using these three controls, users can play game by neural signals to control the moving of the block and have fun.

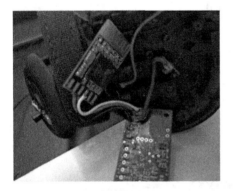

Fig. 3. Hardware part

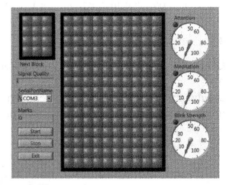

Fig. 4. Software part (Tetris game developed by Labview)

Therefore, the prototype BCI consists of hardware and software. Hardware is to collect human signals (i.e., attention, mediation and blink), and software is to use such signals to control the game.

4.2   Interface Evaluation

To evaluate the BCI game, two kinds of user experiments are conducted. One is to investigate users' experience on BCI game, and the other is to research the difference between BCI and traditional interfaces.

User Experience Investigation

To test the BCI game, a group of participants will be involved to play the game. Afterwards, an interview will be performed based on user experience questionnaire. The questionnaire is developed by referencing game experience questionnaire (GEQ) which is introduced by IJsselsteijn et al. [12]. Two main parts are included: gaming experience and post-game experience. For gaming experience, there are total seven dimensions and thirty questions. Those dimensions are competence, immersion, flow, tension, challenge, negative affect and positive affect. For post-game experience, there are total four dimensions and seventeen questions, and the dimensions are positive experience, negative experience, tiredness and returning to reality. Five-point Likert scale is used to collect players' opinions on each item, where 5 means that the players is totally agree with the statement and 1 means that players is totally disagree with the statement.

Comparison Study

Besides the developed BCI game, the traditional interaction ways are also tested. For PC games, keyboard and mouse are commonly used interfaces to implement operations; therefore, the Tetris game is also played by participants by using keyboard to control the motion of the blocks.

For both experiments, the same group of players are tested. In this primary study, there are 10 females and 10 males. All of them are 18–25 college students, who are familiar with computer and game operations. Moreover, the gender difference is often considered, so that experiments are conducted to compare the experience between female and male users. The general experiment plan is shown in Table 1. For the experiment process, participants are briefed about background information first, and then invited to play the Tetris game. After the game, they are required to complete the game experience questionnaire, and then an in-depth interview is conducted according to the questionnaire.

Table 1. Experiment groups

Experiment group	Descriptions
Group 1	Interviewers play game with BCI
Group 1.1	Male interviewers play game with BCI
Group 1.2	Female interviewers play game with BCI
Group 2	Interviewers play game with keyboard
Group 2.1	Male interviewers play game with keyboard
Group 2.2	Female interviewers play game with keyboard

5 Results and Discussion

In this section, the reliability and validity test of the user experiments are performed. Then the detailed results to reveal the user experience on BCI and the difference between BCI and keyboard are provided and discussed.

5.1 Reliability and Validity Test

Reliability test is used to ensure the stability and consistency of the questionnaire. There are always measurement errors when filling the questionnaire, and these errors may be due to the respondents' personal bias, environmental factors and measurement models. In order to reduce the effects caused by these errors, Cronbach's Alpha is adopted. If the value of Alpha is equal or more than 0.7, it is believed that the questionnaire have a high reliability.

Validity test is used to verify whether the questionnaire can measure the problems which researchers want to measure. For this project, factor analysis is used to calculate the validity. If the value of KMO is equal or more than 0.6, it is believed that the questionnaire is valid.

SPSS is used in the result analysis. It helps in analyzing reliability and validity. Through analysis, all the question items fulfil the reliability and validity requirements, so this game questionnaire is stable, consistent, and can effectively help researchers measure the problems.

5.2   Results Analysis

The independent T-test was also performed by SPSS, and results are presented in the Tables 2 and 3 below.

Table 2. Results of independent T test of GEQ part 1: Game experience

Dimensions	Group	Mean	Standard deviation	Mean difference	T value	P value
Competence	G 1	3.7800	0.26675	1.930000	26.724	0.000
	G 2	1.8500	0.18209			
	G 1.1	3.6600	0.16465	−0.24000	−2.207	0.041
	G 1.2	3.9000	0.30185			
	G 2.1	1.8200	0.17512	−0.06000	−0.728	0.476
	G 2.2	1.8800	0.19322			
Immersion	G 1	3.9500	0.66689	2.67500	16.337	0.000
	G 2	1.2750	0.30240			
	G 1.1	3.8500	0.62583	−0.20000	−0.661	0.517
	G 1.2	4.0500	0.72457			
	G 2.1	1.3000	0.25820	0.05000	0.361	0.723
	G 2.2	1.2500	0.35355			
Flow	G 1	3.8800	0.32053	2.20000	23.452	0.000
	G 2	1.6800	0.27067			
	G 1.1	3.9600	0.37476	0.16000	1.124	0.276
	G 1.2	3.8000	0.24944			
	G 2.1	1.7400	0.25033	0.12000	0.991	0.335
	G 2.2	1.8800	0.28983			
Tension	G 1	2.8667	0.39589	1.20000	10.987	0.000
	G 2	1.6667	0.28613			
	G 1.1	3.0000	0.38490	0.26667	1.562	0.136
	G 1.2	2.7333	0.37843			
	G 2.1	1.7333	0.26294	0.13333	1.044	0.310
	G 2.2	1.6000	0.30631			
Challenge	G 1	3.8125	0.24164	2.13750	26.369	0.000
	G 2	1.6750	0.27023			

(*continued*)

Table 2. (*continued*)

Dimensions	Group	Mean	Standard deviation	Mean difference	T value	P value
	G 1.1	3.8000	0.28382	−0.02500	−0.225	0.824
	G 1.2	3.8250	0.20582			
	G 2.1	1.7250	0.24861	0.10000	0.820	0.423
	G 2.2	1.6250	0.29463			
Negative affect	G 1	1.4125	0.23333	−1.80000	−22.446	0.000
	G 2	3.2125	0.27236			
	G 1.1	1.3750	0.27003	−0.07500	−0.709	0.487
	G 1.2	1.4500	0.19720			
	G 2.1	3.1750	0.26484	−0.07500	−0.605	0.553
	G 2.2	3.2500	0.28868			
Positive affect	G 1	3.9500	0.37205	1.20000	10.883	0.000
	G 2	2.7500	0.32363			
	G 1.1	4.0400	0.24585	0.18000	1.087	0.291
	G 1.2	3.8600	0.46236			
	G 2.1	2.8600	0.31340	0.22000	1.579	0.132
	G 2.2	2.6400	0.30984			

Based on the results, it can be found that (i) for general difference between BCI and keyboard, significant difference exists; in particular, BCI is more difficult to use and needs more concentration; however, it is also more interesting, immersive and attractive to users, compared with keyboard; (ii) for difference between female and male users playing with BCI, it can be found that there is no much significant difference, except competence (including questions: This game is tricky; It takes time to learn how to play; I cannot easily finish the game; I can find the goal of this game in a short time; I feel a sense of accomplishment). It can be an interesting research topic to further study the different brain control performance between players with different genders.

Table 3. Results of independent T test of GEQ part 1: Post-game experience

Dimensions	Group	Mean	Standard deviation	Mean difference	T value	P value
Positive experience	G 1	4.0400	0.24794	1.35000	17.560	0.000
	G 2	2.6900	0.23819			
	G 1.1	3.9200	0.23476	−0.24000	−2.427	0.026
	G 1.2	4.1600	0.20656			
	G 2.1	2.7000	0.23570	0.02000	0.183	0.857
	G 2.2	2.6800	0.25298			
Negative experience	G 1	2.1900	0.51698	−1.08000	−6.023	0.000
	G 2	3.2700	0.61310			
	G 1.1	2.2400	0.42999	0.10000	0.423	0.677
	G 1.2	2.1400	0.61137			

(*continued*)

Table 3. (*continued*)

Dimensions	Group	Mean	Standard deviation	Mean difference	T value	P value
	G 2.1	2.8200	0.41580	−0.90000	−4.856	0.000
	G 2.2	3.7200	0.41312			
Tiredness	G 1	3.9500	0.35909	1.85000	12.192	0.000
	G 2	2.1000	0.57583			
	G 1.1	3.9000	0.45947	−0.10000	−0.612	0.548
	G 1.2	4.0000	0.23570			
	G 2.1	1.9000	0.61464	−0.40000	−1.618	0.123
	G 2.2	2.3000	0.48305			

Based on the results, it can be found that (i) for general difference between BCI and traditional keyboard, there exists significant difference between them; In particular, BCI increases user satisfaction, has less negative affect, but is more tiring; (ii) for difference caused by genders, it can be found that female users have more positive experience with BCI games, and there is no significant difference regarding negative affect and tiredness.

In summary, based on T-test statistical analysis, the results show that there is significant difference between keyboard and brainwave control. In details, it can be indicated that BCI is more challenging to use, thus it may make users tired and frustrated compared with keyboard. However, keyboard is boring, and brainwave control is more interesting and enjoyable. In addition, BCI can make users more immersed in the game and obviously increase user satisfaction. Therefore, it can be reached that brainwave computer interface is very promising to enhance user experience and bring more fun to task completion process; however, some obstacles such as the difficulty to use and the tiredness of use should be overcome.

6   Conclusion

In summary, this study provides an exploration of new-generation human computer interfaces through an analysis of different types of human computer interfaces. An emphatic investigation of brain computer interface is performed. A BCI-based game is developed, and a series of user experiments have been conducted to reveal user experience on BCI and also compare BCI with traditional interfaces. The advantages of BCI regarding the attraction and fast response have been identified, and the limitations regarding the use challenge and required effort have also been revealed.

However, there are still some limitations of this work. For example, the size of participants can be further extended. The comparison study mainly considers keyboard and can include more interaction types, such as eye tracking and virtual reality which also attract much research interest. Therefore, in future study, a larger–scale user experiments will be performed, and more new human computer interactions will be compared and studied.

Acknowledgement. This work is supported by Shanghai Pujiang Program (17PJC054) and also received funding from Shanghai Jiao Tong University.

References

1. Card, S.K., Moran, T.P., Newell, A.: The Psychology of Human-Computer Interaction. Taylor & Francis, Routledge (1986)
2. Dix, A.: Human–computer interaction, foundations and new paradigms. J. Vis. Lang. Comput. **42**, 122–134 (2017)
3. Wolpaw, J.R., Birbaumer, N., McFarland, D.J., Pfurtscheller, G., Vaughan, T.M.: Brain–computer interfaces for communication and control. Clin. Neurophysiol. **113**(6), 767–791 (2002)
4. Nakano, Y.I., Conati, C., Bader, T.: Eye Gaze in Intelligent User Interfaces. Springer, London (2013). https://doi.org/10.1007/978-1-4471-4784-8
5. Khalighy, S., Green, G., Scheepers, C., Whittet, C.: Quantifying the qualities of aesthetics in product design using eye-tracking technology. Int. J. Industr. Ergon. **49**, 31–43 (2015)
6. Chan, K.Y., Nordholm, S., Yiu, K.F.C., Togneri, R.: Speech enhancement strategy for speech recognition microcontroller under noisy environments. Neurocomputing **118**, 279–288 (2013)
7. Liu, Z.-T., Wu, M., Cao, W.-H., Mao, J.-W., Xu, J.-P., Tan, G.-Z.: Speech emotion recognition based on feature selection and extreme learning machine decision tree. Neurocomputing **273**, 271–280 (2018)
8. Neiva, D.H., Zanchettin, C.: Gesture recognition: a review focusing on sign language in a mobile context. Expert Systems with Applications, 31 January 2018. https://doi.org/10.1016/j.eswa.2018.01.051. ISSN 0957-4174
9. McFarland, D.J., Wolpaw, J.R.: EEG-based brain–computer interfaces. Current Opin. Biomed. Eng. **4**, 194–200 (2017)
10. Williamson, J., Murray-Smith, R., Blankertz, B., Krauledat, M., Müller, K.-R.: Designing for uncertain, asymmetric control: interaction design for brain–computer interfaces. Int. J. Hum.-Comput. Stud. **67**(10), 827–841 (2009)
11. Halskov, K., Hansen, N.B.: The diversity of participatory design research practice at PDC 2002–2012. Int. J. Hum.-Comput. Stud. **74**, 81–92 (2015)
12. IJsselsteijn, W.A., Poels, K., de Kort, Y.A.W.: Measuring the experience of digital game enjoyment. In: Spink, A.J., Ballintijn, M.R., Bogers, N.D., Grieco, F., Loijens, L.W.S., Noldus, L.P.J.J., Smit, G., Zimmerman, P.H. (eds.) Proceedings of Measuring Behavior 2008, Maastricht, The Netherlands, 26–29 August 2008

Spatial and Service Design: Guidelines Defining University Dormitories

Luisa Collina(✉), Peter Di Sabatino(✉), Laura Galluzzo(✉),
Claudia Mastrantoni(✉), and Maddalena Mazzocchi(✉)

Politecnico di Milano, Milan, Italy
{luisa.collina,peterarthur.disabatino,
laura.galluzzo}@polimi.it,
claudia.mastrantoni@hotmail.com,
maddalena.mazzocchi@mail.polimi.it

Abstract. This paper contributes to the discussion about relationships between spatial and service design and how these two disciplines can interact and influence each other to achieve more complexity, capability and synergy in in a specific case such as university dormitories. Dormitories, university campuses, and schools, can be considered as *urban community hubs* through which synergistic relations between the institution and the surrounding neighborhood take place. The paper investigates how dormitories can, starting with the contribution of the students, perform strategic actions in the socio-cultural and civil regeneration of urban contexts. The aim is to delineate the various interactions and effective synergies, especially in relation to the most vulnerable and marginalized facets of the community, looking at the students' dorm as places of *social cohesion*. The methodology is related to community-centered design using for example co-design tools to present relationships between spatial and service design particularly through the context of a collaborative design studio and the technical department of Politecnico di Milano.

Keywords: Service design · Spatial design · Community hub

1 Introduction

Spatial design and service design are combined to achieve more complexity and synergy in the specific context of the university dormitory. The student dorms are considered as community hubs and places of social cohesion, creating powerful relationships.

Combining service and spatial design primarily means putting into practice a holistic, co-creative, and *human-centered approach*. It also involves using and, at the same time, understanding customers' behavior (students, staff, and community members in this case) to create and to refine new emergent typologies [1–3].

Nowadays, design is changing from a craft-oriented discipline into one that is more robust and multidisciplinary, connected with social environments, products, services, systems and brands [4, 5].

© Springer International Publishing AG, part of Springer Nature 2018
A. Marcus and W. Wang (Eds.): DUXU 2018, LNCS 10918, pp. 14–26, 2018.
https://doi.org/10.1007/978-3-319-91797-9_2

"Service design aims at designing services that are useful, usable and desirable from the user perspective and efficient, effective and different from the provider perspective" [1].

This paper describes a project undertaken at Politecnico di Milano's School of Design (PoliMi); its main goal is to understand how place, space and experience can be effective and memorable components of a comprehensive service and system design approach.

In this regard, the PoliMI employed many activities to try to answer these questions and to achieve this goal. In particular since 2007, the *Conservation and Building Services* department of the Politecnico di Milano, which is responsible for the planning and coordination of the faculty building development, has undertaken a complex project aimed at raising its level of hospitality, mainly through accommodation for international and PhD students, but also, visiting professors, and more generally, for the university community as a whole.

The project's final goal is the construction of around 1109 new residences. Although these answer the guests' basic needs, they do not fulfill the quality standards for services, functionality, furnishing and graphics. This failing is particularly evident in the common areas. Hence, the research is taking place in three locations with a special focus on public and communal spaces, and producing way-finding and overall communications and media, in relation to the existing and the yet-to-exist products, services, systems and environments.

"Institutions of higher learning are looking for student housing designs that create greater opportunities for students to interact with each other, thereby fostering a closer sense of community" [6].

Current research and design projects in existing dormitories projects need to provide a consolidating character of recreational, collective and gathering functions that are typical of many international university campuses and residences. These places are ideal contexts for experimentation and implementation of innovative communication projects for the student guests, through sustainable activities with the local neighborhood, and strategic projects at the center of university investments [7].

2   Co-design Experience Among the *Conservation and Building Services* Department and the *Polimi Desis Lab*

An innovative and multidisciplinary method for the building of dormitory relations with neighborhoods is the use of co-design tools, which can improve the relations between spatial and service design approaches: "Co-design offers a flexible portfolio of soft system methodologies which ensure that the voices of the key actors and stakeholders are heard and integrated into the system being designed. This participation in the design process is essential to maximize the satisfaction of all parties involved in service use or provision".

"Co-designing our services could be the next critical evolution of service design to ensure the sustained integration of human and natural ecologies for our cities" [8].

The active players in this research are two main figures, one is a research group from the Design Department of Politecnico di Milano, *Polimi Desis* Lab - Design for Social Innovation and Sustainability - a laboratory research about design for social innovation and sustainability, strategic and service design, and methods and tools of co-design. On the other side there is the *Conservation and Building Services* department of the Politecnico di Milano, which has been designing and overseeing the students' dormitories for the university for many years.

The main output of this working collaboration is the creation of a guideline manual for the students' dorms, using the strengths of service design combined with *conservation and building services* and applied to the environments of the dormitories and local context.

Investment in the last few years has led PoliMi to double of the number beds in their student residences, and demonstrates the centrality of the theme in the policies of development and modernization of the Italian and international universities. Faced with the mere quantitative growth that has characterized the last decade, the important challenge today is to overcome a pure 'assistance and receptive' concept of student housing and to foster a proactive role in the processes of social and cultural regeneration of the given urban contexts. The dorms become a sort of engine and hub in this context and enter into a mutually beneficial relationship with the local neighbourhood and community.

The aim of the research is to design the guidelines for the implementation of services for the residents inside the dormitories and to ensure the desired internal and external environmental improvements.

Three dormitories have been examined, designed and prototyped, and will become the models for future dormitories. In particular, guidelines must include a *communication system* that will be universally comprehensible and able to recognize the needs of all cultures. They must be able to propose improvements and greater relevance to the products, services, systems, spaces, environments, and experiences inside and outside the dorms.

3   Educational Trial: Spatial and Experience Design Studio

A consistent part of the design research is based on in-the-field interventions, such as undertaken in the graduate-level design studio held within PoliMi's PSSD degree program, and driven by a Human Centered Design Approach. Using the potential of creativity, it was possible to co-create with the students in the dorms and the students in the design studio. This trial was mainly focused on a studio that has worked with the existing and yet to existing products, services, systems, environments, and was experienced at the given context in a sort of prototypical manner with a particular focus on public/communal spaces, way-finding, and overall communications and media. The latter would include things like: the communication between the administration and the students' dorm through various platforms to provide information about security, maintenance, energy consumption; possibilities coming out of the neighbourhood; and sharing new events with the local community.

The students in the studio offer techniques, methods, tips, and worksheets to guide participants through a process that gives a voice to the dormitory's community and allows their wishes to help guide the creation and implementation of solutions, resulting in several scenarios of use having been designed through such processes.

The studio was composed of forty students from all around the world, including Turkey, Bulgaria, Italy, Thailand, Greece, India, Iran, Colombia, Austria, China, Egypt, Serbia, Spain, Germany, Mexico, Perù, Portugal, Scotland and Malaysia. The class was divided into eleven working groups, creating an interdisciplinary mix of thinkers, makers and doers. Students come from diverse educational backgrounds including interior, product, communication design, engineering and architecture, and created a great combination for the design challenge. All the students tried to see space, feel space, and imagine the space, also worked to understand the scale and sense of the existing environments. They quickly demonstrated the ability to manipulate and create the new or modified environments in relation to their research and direct interaction with the internal dormitory community and local external community.

During the last phase of the studio there was a specific focus on how environment and experience design can merge to create prototyping ideas using co-design sessions where students from the studio have engaged dormitory students and staff. Several tools and methods have been integrated to develop the strategy, for example, journey maps, relational maps, customer journey maps, storyboards, etc. A journey map, for example, can help to visualize a process from the beginning to the end and easily allow the entire flow of an experience to be imagined. At the end, all the designers organized all the information gained during the research phase, and they were then able to visualize patterns, and unpack the context in which were working.

The educational trial continued with the activation of two internship for two studio students in the *Polimi Desis Lab* at Politecnico di Milano. They were asked to develop in particular the overall communication inside the dormitories as a guideline manual for the future student dorms.

Together with the *wayfinding project*, three other communication guidelines components were developed: a *Welcome kit*, as a tool to set the dormitory and the local context in relationship with all the rules and procedures when first checking in; a *digital platform* focussed on the virtual communication between the students and the administration, and also among the students themselves; a *series of videos* for rules and regulations, and also to engage the local neighbourhood with dormitory life (Fig. 1).

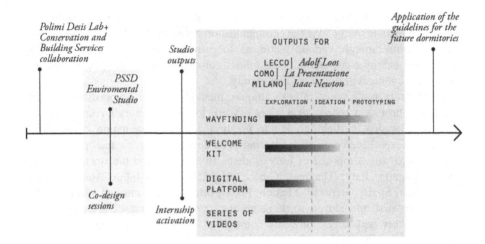

Fig. 1. Timeline of the research project and possible future developments.

4   Tangible and Intangible Practices and Level of Interactions Between the Dormitory Inhabitants and Their Context of Use

Design for Sustainability means shifting consumption from physical products to *product service systems* and *dematerialized services* [9, 10].

In the dormitory, design process, different tangible or intangible levels of interaction between the environment/space and service were able to be identified, and participatory actions were created that are "characterised by the process of exchanging services and benefits aimed at building relationship involved within service" [11, 12].

As a *tangible touchpoint*, focusing on various issues surrounding the "communicative" aspect of the research, different levels have been defined as to how to communicate directions (wayfinding), services and activities throughout the dormitory. Internal communication should be universally comprehensible, and can also be visual in nature, as well as using written language. The goal to define a *universal visual language* is mainly because (at least in the Italian context) that 85% of the dorm residents are from abroad. We're not talking only about "signs and pictograms" but also about awareness and procedural communication: to include overall information, procedures and rules, including also safety and security.

How do the dorm's residents interact and communicate with each other? Where do they interact together? It is important at this stage to talk about "internal" communication, and to define in particular the quality of *communal areas*. The communication and definition of limits of the *multi-functional areas* inside a dormitory residence is crucial. It is also important to promote *social engagement* through furniture, aesthetic scenarios and clear wayfinding graphics. These multi-functional places can be defined as *transitional spaces*: "Students need spaces that allow them to transition from social to private modes based on their individual personality type and learning style, often oscillating between these needs multiple times in a given day or week" [13].

We can consider as an *intangible touchpoint* the space between inside and outside, among the dorms' inhabitants and neighborhood sphere, and how these shared contact actions are shaped in environments that we usually define private, but now have to be characterized with a public space.

These landscapes can be reconfigured to transform "territories of refuge for diversity" into "theatres of strong dynamics" [14]. "The citizen of the diffuse urban realities, can rightly be defined as increasingly a wanderer, with multiple identities, fragile in real relationships behaviours, tending more and more towards the virtual but, at the same time, co-operative and participatory", that's why the citizen is always looking for emotional places that are able to support performances destined to transform and change functions [15]. We can call these environments "Heterotopian places: those spaces which have the particular characteristic of being connected to all the other spaces, but in such a way are able to suspend, neutralize or invert the set of relationships which they designate, reflect, or mirror" [16].

Therefore, the main design goal is to create a dialogue between individuals (students) and the surrounding community (neighborhood), trying to create new quality solutions and bring them to fruition; the generation design and manifestation of significant events and activities can include not only the neighbourhood, but the entire city.

5 University Dormitories as Community Hubs and Places of Social Cohesion

For university students, moving to college and into a dorm means experiencing a new sense of independence and personal responsibility. "On-campus residences embody a culture that is uniquely social, encouraging casual interactions in an environment focused both on learning and socializing. But most of the time the design of most dormitories does not reflect this cultural and social experience. The academic potential of the student residence is too often overshadowed by its social amenities" [13].

Many dormitories develop social actions starting from the idea of the *sustainable campus* to extend the dialogue with some more peripheral districts through the involvement of university residences.

Looking at schools, campuses and university residences, understood as portions of cities that traditionally relate to a practice of well-defined users (students, faculty and staff), today means trying to develop a model of fruition and integration in a context that can innovate not only the image but also the activities of the campuses themselves in the city; and design has been recognized as a powerful innovation driver. Thus, design methods and tools, currently, have also been applied in new fields, and "one of them is *social innovation* which is aimed at developing new ideas and solutions as response to social needs" [17].

University dormitories can, starting also from the students' contribution, perform strategic actions in the socio-cultural and civil regeneration of urban contexts mainly starting from impactful interactions and synergies, especially in relation to the most vulnerable and marginal aspects of the community. The student's dormitory can be conceived and designed as community hubs.

Significant and sustained relationships between the students' residence and the surrounding area are able to create multiple types of beneficiaries. Students in particular can benefit from the opportunity to develop social relations between themselves and the local community. They are able to access resources and services, and they can also be the promotors of synergy with the local community.

University dormitories are sometimes located in marginal areas, not necessarily far away from the city center, but which are immerse in fragile territories where different conditions of urban weakness are present. These conditions may include vulnerability of the social groups who live there, a low quality and dilapidation of the dwellings and public spaces, and an under-funding of resources and services. Additionally, there may be a concentration of problematic services, difficulties in the mobility, and low accessibility to the urban opportunities.

Isolation and exclusion are two important issues, due to the predominant component of *Bonds* and *Social Capital*. The latter "is generally defined and measured at the interpersonal, community, institutional, or societal levels in terms of networks (*bridging*) and norms of reciprocity and trust (*bonding*) within those networks" [18].

Gentrification is another issue that could result from the influx of university students in cities or medium-sized or small neighborhoods, and can bring the risk of a possible upheaval for the local community who lives in the district [19]. There is also potential damage to the rental market, and conversion of the commercial fabric and local services to become only for the benefit of the student population. The marginalisation of the original inhabitants can be a risk inherent to the processes of may be called *Studentification*. This term "emphasises the residential concentration of higher education students in distinct enclaves of the university town" [20].

The dormitory project aims to create, define and test the piloting actions and guidelines for the design of the environment and of the communication system acting on the internal and the external community of residences, in order to mitigate the *Studentification* process with the settlement of dorms in urban areas.

In the most progressive research, at the European level at least, we can talk about the *Community Hub* referring to those best practices of re-generation of different urban contexts. Dormitories need to be conceived and designed as inclusive and promoting social cohesion, open to different social groups and urban populations (young, elderly, immigrants, city users, professionals and NEET), together with the particular feature of being flexible spaces for usability and for the activities that they host. These can include services and activities catering to different spheres of the everyday life (leisure and free time, training and work, care and social services, culture and creativity) by ensuring a greater openness within spaces and an effective solution for welcoming new users. And lastly dormitories "should leverage living spaces into something more academically productive, socially dynamic, and culturally rich. Great residence halls have the potential to make the student experience more successful, memorable, meaningful, and satisfying" [13].

6 Services and Wayfinding Communication for Dormitories' Residents: Three Specific Case Studies in Milan

What is the role of the designer and how can the different levels of the project communicate effectively? Today, designers are considered to be facilitators who are able to understand the needs of the different users and translate them into useful services, environments or products. In order to achieve this aim, different methods are used; and particularly when there is the possibility possibility of designing *with* people, *co-design* and *co-creation* methods are applied. *Co-design* refers to the collaboration with communities when the final result developed by professionals, while *co-creation* requires the presence of the users throughout the design process [21].

The continuous intervention and exchange between the external local context in which the dormitory is situated and the internal concerns, increases the level of complexity and scalability of the overall project, allowing the use of different tools and methods to best express it.

The designer should approach this kind of project using a service design mind-set, this means taking into consideration and understanding the system and its actors using a holistic approach [1]. Indeed, the internal and external modes of communication imply a series of different artefacts that are mutually dependent.

So far, the creation of the *toolkit* described in this paper has involved different aspects of the internal and external communication.

Referring to the former, the creation of an adequate wayfinding system has been conducted over a period of six months. The project has involved three Politecnico dormitories: *Adolf Loos* in Lecco, *La Presentazione* in Como and *Isaac Newton* in Milan. Among them the first two had already some guidelines to follow, while the last was a blank canvas, a starting point for the future wayfinding guidelines.

At the time of the inspection, the dormitory in Lecco already had vinyl signage indicating both the room numbers and the intended use of some of the shared areas. These were burgundy, which was the colour of a temporary structure on the exterior of the building. Thus, the design choice used the pre-existing colour and the original graphics on the doors, which meant that only the new mounting boards had to be newly produced.

La Presentazione dormitory in Como represented another particular case: here there is no presence of signs but the function of each area is signified through the use of a specific colour: red for the common areas, orange for the cooking and dining areas, and yellow and dark grey for the sleeping areas. After having developed a material and colour board, dark grey was also selected as the colour for the mounting boards' background. Intervention was only partial in these two dorms, but the design of the different mounting boards made them traceable to the third. Therefore, the *Isaac Newton* dorm in Milan represented the starting point to design new guidelines for future dormitories. With its white and grey walls and the absence of any kind of signage, it has presented a significant challenge but also the perfect blank canvas on which to start the wayfinding project.

After having studied all the existing services inside the dorms, a series of pictograms was created, as well as two different typologies of mounting boards, *directional* and *indicators*, for a total of thirteen different boards, each with a specific and studied graphic grid. Beyond these last guidelines in Milan, a chromatic palette was used to characterize each floor. Here colours can also permeate all the different spaces, giving them personality and helping to outline and define multifunctional areas that still don't have an identity.

The creation of the *wayfinding* guidelines involves not only technical skills but also a sort of sensibility and capability to understand the user and the internal movement of the dorm. Designing a single mounting board may appear easy, but, on the contrary, many aspects need to be taken into consideration, the most important one being to what extent these graphics are universally comprehensible (Fig. 2).

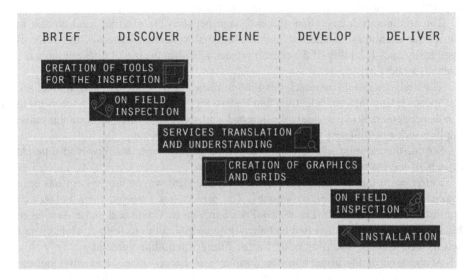

Fig. 2. All the tools and actions during the design process developed in the project.

7 Designing Narratives for Service and Communication Linking Students and Citizens

When the dormitory comes into contact with the neighbourhood via its spaces and services, additional complications arise. In this phase, a powerful tool assisting the designer to bring consistency to the system is the creation of *stories*. Actually, a service design script shares common elements with storytelling [22]. The use of *primary* and *secondary personas* helps to create an understanding of the user, and it is just as important as it is in a story to depict all the characters.

In design and narrative it is equally important to understand the context, the final aim, and the motivation that leads a user/character towards it. In this sense, designers assume the double role of *storyteller* and of *story-listener* and, thus, they become able to listen and translate innovative movements that are taking place in society [23]. The narration of this kind of story may exploit not only technologies but also *tangible spaces* where the personalities of dorm and neighborhood intersect.

Therefore, nowadays, digital storytelling is gaining more and more ground with the creation of experiences that involve both virtual and physical channels. The first step is-deep research directly with both dorm students and people from the neighbourhood, and a consequent creation of a narrative world.

Together with the *wayfinding* project, explained in the previous section, the other three communication guidelines components of the project are: a *welcome kit*, a *digital platform* and a *series of videos*:

- the *welcome kit* can be considered an artefact that is between the dorm and the neighborhood. First, it provides information about the rules and procedures to be followed inside the structure of the dorm but it is also used to give a taste of the external environment the students will find.
- the *digital platform* is an intangible touchpoint that, for some shared contents, may intersect with the *welcome kit*. Three different typologies of user interact within it: institution, in order to send out communications; students, in order to organize internal events or to share thoughts and ideas; neighborhood in order to participate in all kinds of events that may occur in the *transitional spaces*.
- the *series of videos* may be inserted in the *digital platform* or in an independent *YouTube channel*. The contents of the videos differ depending on the topic. One typology should be more instructive in terms of dorm regulations, paperwork and helpful tips. The other should be more narrative, connecting life inside the neighborhood with the one inside the dorm (Fig. 3).

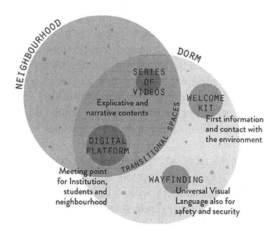

Fig. 3. Diagram of outputs and guidelines of the research in the transitional and multifunctional spaces.

While designing for dormitories the designer should be able to create a coherent narrative that is able to permeate both the spaces and the different media that can enrich and complete the entire experience. The design of this kind of system resembles a play, where the public is invited to actively participate in the development of the narration

[24]. Every neighborhood has its own identity that has changed over the years and is still changing; similarly, dormitories host students with different cultures, backgrounds and stories. The extraordinary association between these two offers a great opportunity to create a narrative world intended to involve both sides. This exchange should be bilateral: as the students are introduced to the neighborhood so the neighborhood should be aware of the presence of a multicultural and active presence in its territory. This enables the creation of a collective memory and a shared story, where dormitories and neighborhood meet.

8 Conclusion

These last scenarios help us to imagine how positive the relationship between the university dormitory and the urban environment could be, and how powerful dynamics can be established with the surrounding neighbourhood.

The positive synergies that are created between different populations can help to change peripheral areas by avoiding gentrification and ensuring a collaborative bottom-up process using co-design and co-creation methods to develop an improved environment. Co-designing the space-service allows a close collaboration between all the stakeholders involved in the design process and a variety of professionals who have hybrid research and design skills.

As mentioned, we can have different actors and facilitators in the project, like students, designers, professionals, community members, etc., but also actors coming from simultaneous formations and many types of culture: disciplinary culture, corporate culture, ethnic culture, worldview, mindset, etc. [25].

Wayfinding is used as a way to facilitate guests' permanence and to indicate the correct environmental destination and usage, but multimedia elements are also employed as a touchpoint between the tangible and intangible aspects of our research in creating new scenarios. "Sharing experiences through stories is emerging in various professions as a powerful way to exchange and consolidate knowledge. Research suggests that sharing experiences though narrative builds trust, cultivates norms, transfers tacit knowledge, facilitates unlearning, and generates emotional connections" [26].

In the future, we can imagine an evolution of the tools and methods allowing co-design as a common language to support and facilitate the many varieties of cross-cultural communication, and these will be highly appreciated [25]. We can also imagine services for dormitories able to understand and develop new dynamics and rich places, spaces and experiences, that will be powerful and memorable components of a comprehensive new environment, system and graphic design approach.

The next steps of the research project at PoliMi are to put into practice all the guidelines that have been designed until now, and use them to design another four dormitories in Milan. Two of these will be completely new and the other two are old buildings that have been used in the hospitality sector for many years.

Finally, the results of the achievements will be monitored; and we anticipate an evolution of the tools that will promote an integrated design between spatial design and design for services.

References

1. Mager, B., Sung, T.J.: Special issue editorial: designing for services. Int. J. Des. **5**(2), 1–3 (2011)
2. Polaine, A., Løvlie, L., Reason, B.: Service Design: From Insight to Inspiration. Rosenfeld Media, Brooklyn (2013)
3. Stickdorn, M., Schneider, J., Andrews, K., Lawrence, A.: This is Service Design Thinking: Basics, Tools, Cases, vol. 1. Wiley, Hoboken (2011)
4. Friedman, K.: Towards an integrative design discipline. Creating break-through ideas: the collaboration of anthropologists and designers in the product development industry. Westport, Conn, Bergin and Garvey (2002)
5. Muratovski, G.: Design and design research: the conflict between the principles in design education and practices in industry. Des. Principles Pract. Int. J. **4**(2), 377–386 (2010)
6. Fabris, P.: 6 Trends steering today's college residence halls. Building Design + Construction. https://www.bdcnetwork.com/6-trends-steering-todays-college-residence-halls
7. ISCN International Sustainable Campus Network. https://www.international-sustainable-campus-network.org/about/purpose
8. Fuad-Luke, A.: Co-designing services in the co-futured city. In: Service Design: on the Evolution of Design Expertise. Lahti University of Applied Sciences Series, A Research Reports, pp. 101–120 (2012)
9. Balcioglu, T.: The Role of Product Design in Post-Industrial Society. Middle East Technical University, Faculty of Architecture Press, Ankara (1998)
10. Charter, M., Tischner, U.: Sustainable Solutions: Developing Products and Services for the Future. Greenleaf Publishing Limited, Austin (2001)
11. Tung, W.F., Yuan, S.T.: A service design framework for value co-production: insight from mutualism perspective. Kybernetes **37**(2), 226–240 (2008)
12. Kuosa, T., Westerlund, L.: Service design: on the evolution of design expertise (2012)
13. Gensler Research: Remaking Student Living, Lores (2016). https://www.gensler.com/research-insight/gensler-research-institute/remaking-student-living
14. Gilles, C.: Manifeste du Tiers paysage. Collection L'Autre Fable, ED Sujet/Objet, Paris (2004)
15. Lega, E., Piccinno, G.: Spatial Design for In-between Urban Spaces. Maggioli Editore (2012)
16. Foucault, M.: Of other Spaces: Utopias and Heterotopias. In: Leach, E. (ed.) Rethinking Architecture, London (1997)
17. Hillgren, P., Seravalli, A., Emilson, A.: Prototyping and infrastructuring in design for social innovation. CoDesign **7**(3–4), 169–183 (2011)
18. Perkins, D., Hughey, J., Speer, P.W.: Community psychology perspectives on social capital theory and community development practice. Commun. Develop. **33**(1), 33–52 (2002)
19. Borlini, B., Memo, F.: Il Quartiere nella Città Contemporanea. Bruno Mondadori (2008)
20. Smith, D.P.: Studentification: the gentrification factory? Gentrification in a global context, p. 73 (2004)
21. Freire, K., Sangiorgi, D.: Service design and healthcare innovation: from consumption, to co-production to co-creation. Nordic Service Design Conference, Linkoping, Sweden (2010)
22. Gruen, D., Rauch, T., Redpath, S., Ruettinger, S.: The use of stories in user experience design. Int. J. Hum.-Comput. Interact. **14**(3–4), 503–534 (2002)
23. Bertolotti, E., Daam, H., Piredda, F., Tassinari, V.: Story-listening. The pearl diver. The designer as storyteller, pp. 20–21 (2016)

24. Rizzo, A.: Translation as artistic communication in the aesthetics of migration: from nonfiction to the visual arts. Ars Aeterna **9**(2), 53–70 (2017)
25. Sanders, E.B., Stappers, P.J.: Co-creation and the new landscapes of design. CoDesign **4**(1), 5–18 (2008)
26. Sole, D., Wilson, D.G.: Storytelling in organizations: the power and traps of using stories to share knowledge in organizations. LILA Harvard Univ. **53**(3), 1–12 (1999)

Design Theory and Methodology in HCI: Applying CPM/PDD to UCD

Jan Conrad[1(✉)], Christian Koehler[2], Dieter Wallach[1,3], and Tobias Luedeke[4]

[1] University of Applied Sciences Kaiserslautern, Kaiserslautern, Germany
jan.conrad@hs-kl.de
[2] htw saar Saarland University of Applied Sciences, Saarbrücken, Germany
christian.koehler@htwsaar.de
[3] Ergosign GmbH, Saarbrücken, Germany
dieter.wallach@ergosign.de
[4] csi entwicklungstechnik GmbH, Neckarsulm, Germany
tobias.luedeke@csi-online.de

Abstract. The development of human computer interfaces is a complex, multifaceted process with many soft influencing factors and boundary conditions. In addition to other approaches, the user-centered design has proved to be a meaningful and suitable model to support the development of interactive systems. Also, in design theory and methodology, a research field that investigates similar processes for the area of mechanical engineering, a large number of models have been investigated. This paper applies the Characteristics-Properties Modelling/Property-Driven Development (CPM/PDD) to User Centered Design (UCD). It explores the mapping of the two models to obtain support and insights for the selection of techniques and metrics for the development of interactive systems. For this purpose, this paper first describes CPM/PDD and discusses why it is particularly suitable for the considerations made here. After a short description of the UCD, the paper explores touch points and maps the two models to each other. A small case study shows the possible application and offers a starting point for further research.

Keywords: User centered design · CPM/PDD · Design theory
HCI · AI

1 Introduction

Different approaches exist to describe the design and development process of human computer interfaces (HCI). A very common approach is the human-centred design standard ISO 9241-210 of the International Organization of Standardization [1]. Wallach and Steimle describe a similar approach with the focus on collaborative projects [2]. Another famous representative is the Usability Engineering Lifecycle by Mayhew [3].

An area that considers the development and design process of technical products from the mechanical engineering and engineering design viewpoint is the field of design theory and methodology (DTM). In this regard, there exist also several different

© Springer International Publishing AG, part of Springer Nature 2018
A. Marcus and W. Wang (Eds.): DUXU 2018, LNCS 10918, pp. 27–39, 2018.
https://doi.org/10.1007/978-3-319-91797-9_3

ways to describe the used procedures and processes. The development of the internet of things (IOT) and internet of everything (IOE) increases the interdisciplinary nature of products and thus also of the human computer interfaces.

This paper takes up a methodology of the DTM and proposes an application to the HCI design and development process to gain new insights and a deeper understanding by opening a new perspective.

2 The Field of Design Theory and Methodology

The field of DTM became an independent research area after WWII [4]. It combines a large number of different approaches, some of them incompatible to each other. Based on scientific findings, the objective is to determine how much designing can be systemized and automated and to develop concepts which make the activity teachable and trainable [4].

In the variety of approaches available, some have emerged as particularly popular. Weber gives a good overview in [5] and some of the most remarkable theories should also be mentioned here. Suh introduced a model called "Axiomatic Design" in 1990 [6]. Suh basically describes the design process as mapping from a functional space to a physical space. Another approach from the research field of artificial intelligence is John Gero's "function behaviour structure model" [7]. In Europe and especially in the German-speaking countries, VDI guideline 2221 and the fundamental works of Pahl and Beitz play an outstanding role as a general framework and summary for design guidelines [8, 9]. The approach to product and process modelling this paper is based on is called Characteristics-Properties Modelling/Property-Driven Development, or CPM/PDD. It is based on the differentiation of product characteristics and properties. In the late 1990s, it resulted from mechanical design project work at Saarland University. It is particularly suitable for integrating existing models, methods and tools [10]. Its versatility has already been demonstrated in several research projects such as the approach of cost-driven development [11] the engineering change management [12] or the capturing of design knowledge [13] by means of CPM/PDD. For this reason, it appears to be especially appropriate for the intended purpose and was chosen as the basis for this paper.

3 Characteristics-Properties Modelling/Property-Driven Development

This section explains briefly the Characteristics-Properties Modelling/Property-Driven Development (CPM/PDD) approach. The concept of CPM represents a product model and PDD presents the process of developing and designing products based on CPM. The most significant feature is the differentiation in characteristics and properties of a product:

- Characteristics (C) cover all the items of a product that can be directly determined and influenced by the designer. These are for example the geometry, structure, shape, spatial configuration and material consistency [14].
- Properties (P) describe "the product's behaviour" [14]. They cannot be directly determined and influenced by the designer (e.g. weight, safety, aesthetic properties, usability), only indirectly through modifications of the characteristics.

This distinction is also applied in other approaches; the special point is that it is the focus of CPM/PDD's considerations [10].

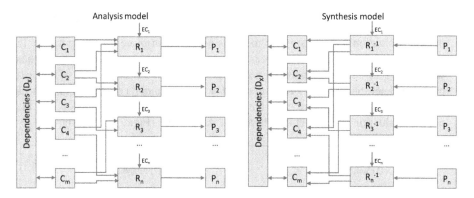

Fig. 1. Analysis and synthesis in the CPM model [14]

The links between characteristics and properties are represented by relations. They can be read in two directions. In the analysis direction (R), characteristics are known and the product's properties are derived (Fig. 1 left). In the synthesis direction (R^{-1}), properties are known/required and the product's characteristics are established (Fig. 1 right). In addition, Dependencies (D) respect potential constraints on the characteristic side and External conditions (EC) represent the context in which (analytical as well as synthetically) statements are valid.

PDD describes the product development process based on the CPM product model. Weber depicts the iteratively conducted 4 development steps in [10] as follows:

1. The product development process starts with a requirement list (Fig. 2 top left). In the PDD approach, this is basically a list of required product properties (PR_j). Starting from this, the first step of product development is a synthesis step: The product developer selects one of the required properties (in the case of a new design, usually the functional properties) and determines some essential characteristics (design parameters) of the solution (C_i) using suitable synthesis methods (R_j^{-1}), for example in the form of a sketch. Alternatively, existing (partial) solutions can also be used (e.g. solution patterns).
2. The next step is an analysis step (Fig. 2 top right). Based on the characteristics of the solution defined at this point, the properties (P_j, actual properties) are determined or predicted. Suitable analytical methods (R_j) are required for this purpose.

This analysis should include not only the examination of those properties which were the starting point of the previous synthesis step, but if possible all (relevant) properties. This is not always possible in early phases because there may not be enough characteristics defined at this stage.

3. In step 3 (Fig. 2 bottom left), the actual properties (P_j) are compared with the target properties (PR_j) and the individual deviations are determined (ΔP_j).

4. The individual differences (P_j) between the actual and target properties determined in the previous step are of relatively little benefit to the further process progress. However, they are the basis for an overall evaluation. The product developer must identify the most important problems of the current state of development and decide on how to proceed. This means that he must select the properties to be considered in the next cycle from synthesis, analysis, determination of individual deviations, overall evaluation and put suitable methods and tools in place for this purpose. In early stages of the development process, it is a possible strategy to take the properties with the greatest deviation between actual and target as the starting point of the next cycle. In later phases the situation is not so clear, under certain circumstances complex evaluation methods may have to be used. In any case, the results of the overall evaluation are the actual "driver" of the process (Fig. 2 bottom right).

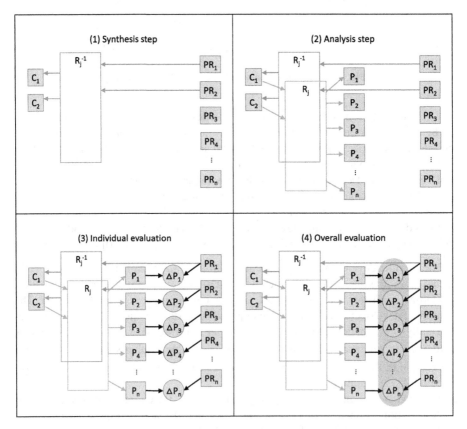

Fig. 2. The four steps of a PDD process iteration [10, 14]

The modeling of both, the product and the process is a major advantage of the CPM/PDD compared to most other models, which mostly focus on the process model. Among other things, this simplifies software support [10].

4 Processes in HCI

As mentioned in the introduction, there are also numerous procedural models for the design and development process in the field of HCI. The international standard 9241 210 [1] is the basis for many user-centered design methods. The aim of the User-Centered design is to design "products that have a high degree of usability" [15]. This includes a usable, manageable, efficient and effective realization of the user requirements. The user-centered design outlines the phases during the entire lifecycle of a design and development. It focuses on a good understanding of who will use the product by proposing four phases to go through in the design of each interactive system:

1. Understanding and specifying the context of use
2. Specifying the user requirements
3. Producing design solutions
4. Evaluating the design.

To realize a human centred approach in accordance to the ISO guideline, the development process should ensure to follow the principles below [1]:

- The design is based upon an explicit understanding of users, tasks and environments
- Users are involved throughout design
- The design is driven and refined by user-centred evaluation
- The process is iterative
- The design addresses the whole user experience
- The design team includes multidisciplinary skills and perspectives.

Together with the four design phases, these principles of UCD bring several dependencies into the development process. Figure 3 shows the ISO development process and its interdependences. It is complemented with the development results for each of the phases proposed by the International Usability and User Experience Qualification Board (UXQB) [16]. However, the UCD process does not specify precise methods for each phase. Therefore, the approach is very appropriate for the investigations in this paper.

In addition to this model, there are numerous other possibilities for the representation of the design and development. Due to its widespread use, this model will form the basis for further considerations.

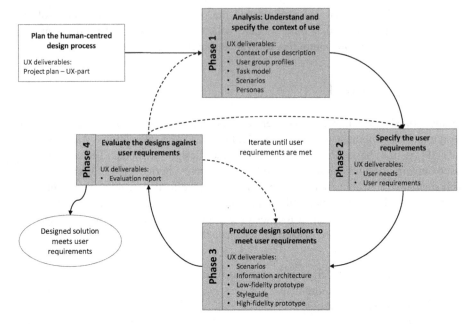

Fig. 3. Interdependence of human-centred design activities [1, 16]

5 Bringing CPM/PDD and UCD Together

In the development of interactive products, the requirements are usually not directly realizable. For this reason, the CPM/PDD model is particularly suitable in this context, since it describes a procedure for getting from the properties to the characteristics of a human-machine interface. In this chapter, the phases of the UCD are mapped to the steps of the PDD process. In the following explanations only a single iteration of the UCD or PDD is considered, in a real development process these steps are of course repeated several times until a finished product is obtained.

The first step *project planning* of the UCD is excluded, since it does not represent any of the recurring, iteratively incrementally executed phases of the process.

UCD starts by analyzing the context of use (phase 1 of the UCD) and specifying user requirements (phase 2 of the UCD). Output of these phases are the properties required (PR), the starting point for the PDD as shown in Fig. 4.

Phase 3 of the UCD is the creation of solutions that meet the user requirements. According to CPM/PDD, these solutions represent characteristics, i.e. the elements that can be directly influenced. The design solution is therefore a set of concrete characteristics and the "produce" is the synthesis step for determining characteristics (Fig. 5).

The fourth phase in UCD is the evaluation of a design against the user requirements. This evaluation corresponds to the analysis step in PDD. It is important that this step has no relation to the analysis of the context of use (phase 1 of the UCD) but refers explicitly to the evaluation of the design.

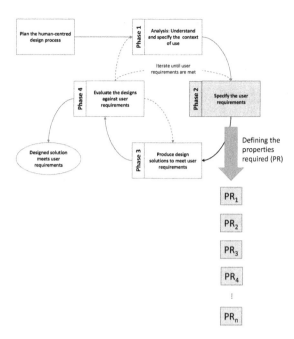

Fig. 4. Phase 1 and 2, defining the properties required

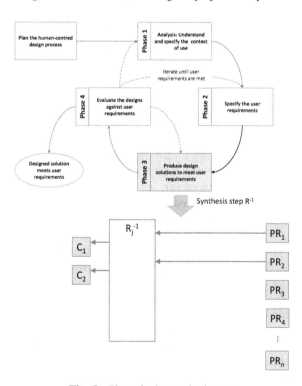

Fig. 5. Phase 3, the synthesis step

As a result of this analysis, properties of the solution emerge that can be compared individually with the required properties in the next step (Fig. 6).

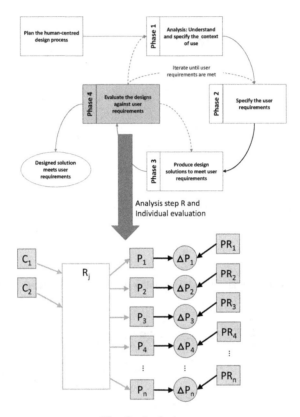

Fig. 6. Analysis step

The last step of PDD is the overall evaluation. Since this step is the actual driver of the development process, it is decided here whether the process is finished or not. If the user requirements are fulfilled, the process is terminated. Otherwise, depending on the result, a new iteration starts with phase 1, 2 or 3 (Fig. 7).

The mapping above shows that the four phases of both models cannot be mapped one to one. In phases 1 and 2, UCD focuses on analyzing the context and specifying user requirements. The aspect of the requirements analysis is not considered in the PDD process until a first version of the properties required, i.e. the user requirements, exists. In the course of the process, however, these are further developed, refined and in some cases discarded.

The representation of the relations R and R^{-1} is an interesting complement to the UCD. In particular, the method selection and execution of the synthesis as well as the analysis are presented in UCD rather implicitly and can be described more precisely with the help of PDD.

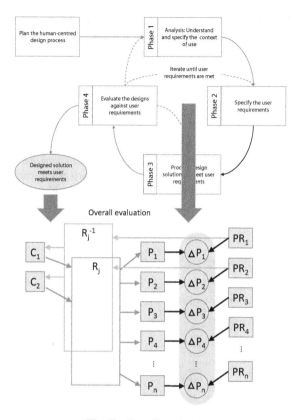

Fig. 7. Overall evaluation

The evaluation of the results of an iteration (phase 4) is mapped in PDD more fine-grained. Here, the analysis, i.e. the determination of properties from the previously defined characteristics, as well as the comparison of the evaluation results with the required properties are considered separately.

A particularly interesting aspect is the consideration of the overall evaluation in PDD. In a development iteration, the evaluation phase is followed by a decision as to whether to jump into one of the preceding phases 1–3 or whether the level of development is assessed as sufficient. This very important step is only implicitly represented in the UCD, although the underlying decision making is quite complex. In the PDD it is mapped as an overall evaluation. But in this context, the following steps are only displayed implicitly. In this field, following UCD and CPM results in a better clarity of the individual steps and a clearer overview of all steps.

6   Applying the Approach

To provide a case study of how to use the approach, excerpts from an example provided by UXQB are applied to the process described in the previous chapter. The proposed outcomes of each phase are already mentioned in Fig. 3. For the context of use description, these can be user group profiles, task models, scenarios and personas [17]. From this the user requirements can be defined. An example of derived user requirements for a calendar app is given in Table 1.

Table 1. Example for User requirements [17]

As-is scenario	Derived user requirements (i.e. Properties Required)
Mr. Smith leaves home as late as possible. His wife doesn't like this, but he is rather relaxed about it. The calendar in his notebook and smartphone contains the travel plan for each of the three days (Tuesday, Wednesday, Thursday)	• PR1: The user must be able to recognise in the system how long the ride to the train station or airport will currently take • PR2: The user must be able to recognize that the point of time has come when he must leave • (…)

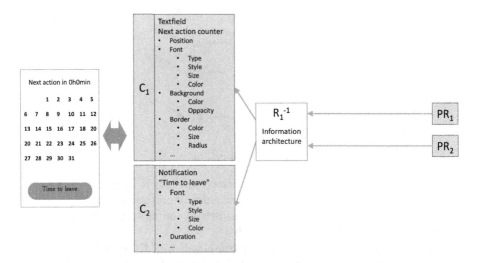

Fig. 8. Synthesis step example

Starting with these properties required, a synthesis step is conducted to define characteristics of the resulting user interface (Fig. 8).

The next step is the selection of a suitable analysis procedure for the respective maturity level and scope. In this example, a usability test was assumed. The result for each property is compared with the corresponding user requirement (Fig. 9).

The last step *Overall Evaluation* checks whether the properties fulfill the user-requirements adequately and which step of the UCD is the next (Fig. 10).

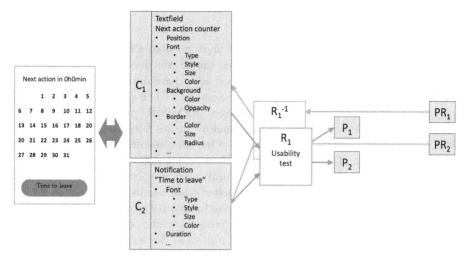

Fig. 9. Analysis step example

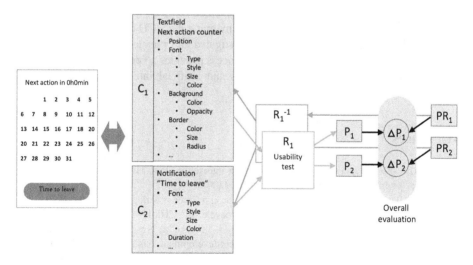

Fig. 10. Overall evaluation example

In ongoing studies, the design and development of IOT devices, as well as the limitations and benefits of the proposed combination of CPM/PDD and human centred design are investigated. As this example illustrates, the complexity of the presentation quickly becomes quite high. Depending on the application, a problem in a real development project will not be realizable without software support. In addition, parts of the CPM model described in Chap. 1.2 have not been considered in this example. These are the external conditions and dependencies, for example.

7 Conclusion and Future Work

This paper offers a first exploration of the application of CPM/PDD to the UCD process. It has shown that the two approaches can be combined very well. However, there is no one to one mapping since the approaches have different focal points. But this feature results in the strength of the combination. UCD focuses on the process of analysing users and determination of user-needs. CPM/PDD provides a clear framework for the evaluation part and process control. In this way, the method may be helpful to the practice development process of human computer interfaces.

The combination of UCD and CPM/PDD can support the collaboration in interdisciplinary development teams (e.g. mechanical engineering, software engineers, UX designer) by driving the process through customer requirements. In future work it may be the starting point for the development of interdisciplinary products like IoT devices.

The mapping of the models offers among other things the possibility to carry out a structured allocation of supporting tools and metrics in the design process.

Identifying and evaluating suitable user requirements is the central strength of the user-centered approach. On that basis, specific methods for the relations synthesis and analysis can be proposed via CPM/PDD. The preparation of catalogues and tables to support the process is part of current research. A very promising use is the integration of the UX Metrics Table as analysis tool, presented in [18].

The development of software support for mapping the UCD process in combination with CPM/PDD is also currently being investigated and pursued.

Last but not least, this modeling of the process provides a very good preparation for the application of deep learning algorithms and artificial intelligence to the design process.

References

1. ISO 9241-210: Ergonomics of human-system interaction. Part 210: Human-centred design process for interactive systems. ISO, Geneva (2008)
2. Steimle, T., Wallach, D.: Collaborative UX Design. dpunkt.verlag, New York (2018)
3. Deborah, J.M.: The usability engineering lifecycle. In: CHI 1999 Extended Abstracts on Human Factors in Computing Systems, pp. 147–148. ACM, New York (1999)
4. Weber, C.: Modelling products and product development based on characteristics and properties. In: Chakrabarti, A., Blessing, L.T.M. (eds.) An Anthology of Theories and Models of Design, pp. 327–352. Springer, London (2014). https://doi.org/10.1007/978-1-4471-6338-1_16
5. Weber, C.: CPM/PDD—an extended theoretical approach to modelling products and product development processes. In: Proceedings of the 2nd German-Israeli symposium. Fraunhofer-IRB-Verlag, Stuttgart, pp. 159–179 (2005)
6. Suh, N.P.: The Principles of Design. Oxford University Press, New York (1990)
7. Gero, J.S.: Design prototypes—a knowledge representation schema for design. AI Mag. **11** (4), 26–36 (1990)
8. VDI-Guideline 2221: Systematic approach to the design of technical systems and products. VDI, Düsseldorf, 1987. English version of VDI-Guideline 2221 (1986)

9. Pahl, G., Beitz, W.: Engineering Design. Springer, Heidelberg (2007). https://doi.org/10. 1007/978-1-84628-319-2. (1st edn. 1983, 3rd edn. 2007; all English editions translated and edited by Wallace, K., Blessing LTM) (1983/2007)
10. Weber, C.: Produkte und Produktentwicklungsprozesse abbilden mit Hilfe von Merkmalen und Eigenschaften – eine kritische Zwischenbilanz (Keynote-Beitrag). 23. DfX-Symposium, Bamberg, 04.–05.10.2012. In: Krause, D., Paetzold, K., Wartzack, S. (eds.) Design for X – Beiträge zum 23. DfX-Symposium Oktober 2012. TuTech Innovation GmbH, Hamburg, 2012, pp. 25–62 (2012)
11. Deubel, T.: Anforderungs-, kosten- und wertgetriebene Steuerung des Produktentwicklungsprozesses. Dissertation Universität des Saarlandes, Schriftenreihe Produktionstechnik Bd. 39, Saarbruecken (2007)
12. Köhler, C.: Technische Produktänderung – Analyse und Beurteilung von Lösungsmöglichkeiten auf der Basis einer Erweiterung des CPM/PDD Ansatzes. Dissertation Universität des Saarlandes. Schriftenreihe Produktionstechnik Bd. 45, Saarbruecken (2009)
13. Conrad, J.: Semantische Netze zur Erfassung und Verarbeitung von Informationen und Wissen in der Produktentwicklung. Dissertation Universität des Saarlandes, Schriftenreihe Produktionstechnik Bd. 49, Saarbruecken (2010)
14. Conrad, J., Köhler, C., Wanke, S., Weber, C.: What is design knowledge from the viewpoint of CPM/PDD? In: Proceedings of DESIGN 2008, Faculty of Mechanical Engineering and Naval Architecture, University of Zagreb, vol. 2, pp. 745–752 (2008)
15. Notes on User Centered Design Process (UCD). https://www.w3.org/WAI/EO/2003/ucd. Accessed 02 Apr 2018
16. CPUX-F – Curriculum and Glossary. http://uxqb.org/wp-content/uploads/documents/ CPUX-F_EN_Curriculum-and-Glossary.pdf. Accessed 02 Apr 2018
17. CPUX-UR Public Example Test. http://uxqb.org/wp-content/uploads/documents/CPUX-UR_EN_Public-Test-Questions.pdf. Accessed 02 Apr 2018
18. Wallach, D., Conrad, J., Steimle, T.: The UX metrics table: a missing artifact. In: Marcus, A., Wang, W. (eds.) DUXU 2017. LNCS, vol. 10288, pp. 507–517. Springer, Cham (2017). https://doi.org/10.1007/978-3-319-58634-2_37

Are Game Design and User Research Guidelines Specific to Virtual Reality Effective in Creating a More Optimal Player Experience? Yes, VR PLAY

Heather Desurvire[1(✉)] and Max Kreminski[2(✉)]

[1] User Behavioristics + University of Southern California,
Los Angeles, CA 90230, USA
heather@userbehavioristics.com
[2] University of California at Santa Cruz, Santa Cruz, CA 95064, USA
mkremins@ucsc.edu

Abstract. Virtual reality (VR) presents new usability, human-computer inter-action, and playability challenges for developers, user-experience researchers, and designers. In addition to facing the traditional challenges, developers and researchers of VR games and VR experiences must contend with issues of physicality (including physical activity and physical discomfort), spatiality, and new or intensified physiological, psychological, and social considerations. However, many existing resources intended to help designers and game-user researchers work through usability and playability issues do not address these VR-specific challenges. This paper introduces the Virtual Reality PLAY (VR PLAY) guidelines, a set of guidelines intended to help developers, designers, and user researchers create more usable and playable VR games and experiences by optimizing the user and player experience for virtual reality.

Keywords: Player experience · Heuristics · Game principles · VR PLAY
GAP · PLAY · Game design · Game-user research · Game usability
Virtual reality

1 Introduction

The VR PLAY guidelines have been created to assist in evaluating and designing an improved virtual reality (VR) user experience. They are based on experience with previous VR development and design; multiple research sessions on consumer VR games and other playful or creative VR experiences; a review of existing research in the field of VR; and discussions with colleagues who study VR. Based on our success in developing and utilizing design principles for use by researchers and designers of AAA games to optimize the player experience, we developed an understanding of some of the unique challenges of VR not covered by previous work. This motivated the creation of the VR PLAY guidelines.

© Springer International Publishing AG, part of Springer Nature 2018
A. Marcus and W. Wang (Eds.): DUXU 2018, LNCS 10918, pp. 40–59, 2018.
https://doi.org/10.1007/978-3-319-91797-9_4

The VR PLAY guidelines are intended to assist designers and game-user researchers of VR games when working through usability and playability issues that are unique to, or intensified by, VR. The guidelines can be found on a public site, https://userbehavioristics.squarespace.com/vr-play. They consist of five categories: Usability, Playability, VR Immersion, Creative VR, and New Player Experience. Each guideline contains a short summary suggesting a principle that designers and researchers may use to gain insight into their own games; a longer explanation of the reasoning and principles behind the guideline; and examples of existing VR games and software that adhere to or violate the guideline, demonstrating how the guideline may be used. This paper introduces the guidelines, describes how they were developed, and presents a study that lends support to the validity of the guidelines as a design tool.

In our study, the guidelines were introduced to the designer of an existing VR experience developed for the Vive VR system. The experience was sponsored by and developed for Steelcase in conjunction with the Mobile & Environmental Media Lab at the University of Southern California. After being introduced to VR PLAY, the designer created a revised version of the experience. Each player in the study was exposed to two versions of the VR experience: Version A (designed without use of the guidelines) and Version B (designed with the guidelines in mind). We conducted interviews with the designer to evaluate his understanding of the VR PLAY guidelines, and we performed a side-by-side evaluation of player experiences in the two versions to determine if the guidelines had a significant positive impact on the designer's understanding of player-experience issues and the usability and playability of the revised design. These findings support the utility of the VR guidelines in improving the player experience.

The study identified many useful principles. These included UI design, spatiality, physicality, and some playability components. Most of these were specific to VR and not found in other guidelines. Two guidelines concerning the halo effect and VR ethics were found to be not directly actionable but nevertheless helpful to the designer in an advisory context. In addition, several guidelines—especially those concerning challenge, pace, and intermediate and long-term goals of the game—were not applicable in this study. These guidelines pertained to specific gameplay experiences not present in the current study's VR design. To evaluate these guidelines, the authors plan to conduct a study with a VR game that includes the relevant gameplay experiences.

Altogether, the study found the guidelines to be significantly useful when evaluating the usability and playability of existing games and when designing and optimizing the player experience in new VR games.

1.1 Motivation for VR PLAY

Virtual reality is an emerging medium with significant potential to enrich experiences in fields ranging from games and entertainment to health and creativity tools. As VR technology becomes increasingly accessible and affordable, the medium is undergoing a process of rapid expansion.

VR experiences, in comparison to traditional game console and computer player experiences, pose several unique usability and playability challenges. The increased immersion has the potential to accentuate the negative and positive aspects of an experience, for instance by inducing physical discomfort or motion sickness [34] even as the higher fidelity of the experience instills in players a greater sense of satisfaction and delight [1]. In addition to considering all the usability and playability issues already known to exist in other digital games, designers of VR experiences must contend with issues of physicality (including physical activity and physical discomfort), spatiality, and new or intensified psychological and social phenomena [15]. Moreover, users and players of VR software and games are impacted by these new issues in a variety of ways. Some players may find they are especially sensitive to certain novel issues while for other players these very same issues may pass entirely unnoticed.

Usability and playability in video games are well-studied subject areas. There are resources [2, 6–8, 21] available to designers who want to improve the usability and playability of their game designs. Despite the growing popularity of VR, however, few of these resources have been designed with VR in mind. As a result, designers and evaluators of VR games and other VR play experiences have largely been left to their own devices in dealing with some of the novel challenges posed by VR.

To address such issues, we have created the VR PLAY guidelines. These guidelines for usability and playability can be used in two ways: as a set of heuristics against which existing VR games and play experiences can be evaluated, and as a design tool intended to inform the development of new VR games. To demonstrate the effectiveness of these guidelines as a design tool, we have employed them in a case study involving the revision of a work-in-progress playful VR experience.

1.2   Development of VR PLAY

In developing the VR PLAY guidelines, we drew on existing research in usability and playability for games and other software and on research in VR itself, including physical, psychological, social, and ethical perspectives on VR. We also conducted our own user research on VR games, have extensive experience with player research on VR games, and gleaned further information from discussions with other VR researchers. We divided the information we collected into several categories, each of which we concluded the guidelines should represent.

GAP and PLAY Principles. The Game Approachability Principles (GAP) [6, 14] and the Playability Principles (PLAY) [7] are two sets of heuristics or principles pertaining to general game usability and playability. The GAP heuristics deal primarily with issues of new-player experience and the processes by which players learn how to play a new game. The PLAY heuristics are broader in scope, encompassing a wide variety of issues that range from enduring play and player motivation to usability and user interface design. Both sets of principles have proven useful in our own research on over 60 games with AAA clients over the last several years, and countless other companies have used them successfully too. They have also been taught to over 150 students at the University of Southern California, one of the top universities that offer interactive media and games as a major. The students report using them in their own work now, including work for AAA publishers and indie studios.

VR PLAY Guidelines. Due to their generality, both the GAP and the PLAY heuristics are largely platform agnostic. Consequently, most of the advice they offer is applicable to VR. At the same time, however, these principles do not specifically address usability or playability issues that are unique to VR. Thus, adherence to these principles could be described as "necessary but not sufficient" for designers who wish to create positive player experiences in VR. In assembling the VR PLAY guidelines, we chose to include adapted and consolidated versions of the most important GAP and PLAY heuristics to highlight the general usability, playability, and new-player-experience issues that are likely to have the greatest impact on VR games.

Presence. One advantage of VR experiences over traditional video games and other software is the user's or player's increased sense of presence: the subjective perception that they are physically present in the virtual environment [5, 22]. Several forms of presence have been proposed, including social presence [10] and behavioral and cognitive presence [11, 24]. Presence can also be measured in several ways [3, 12, 17, 24, 27, 29, 34].

Presence is a key element of immersion, as more coherent experiences—in which multiple aspects of the experience, such as visuals and audio, work together to create the illusion of a "real" continuous world—are generally perceived by players as more immersive overall. Players who experience a heightened sense of presence feel that their experiences in the virtual environment are more "real" and thus more enjoyable when the experience itself is a positive one. They may also feel that their actions are more meaningful or consequential. As a result, creating and maintaining a sense of presence can be an important tool for improving the player experience in VR and non-VR games alike.

Embodiment. A factor closely related to presence is embodiment: the extent to which the player in a virtual environment identifies with the body of the player character and feels as though they are truly inhabiting it. Embodiment of the player character can be facilitated in a variety of ways, including by allowing the player to observe the way their actions directly map to equivalent actions by the player character (e.g., in a virtual mirror) [30]. Embodiment of certain characters may also pose ethical concerns, such as when a player inhabits the body of a character who commits violent actions [19].

Embodiment, like presence, is a key element of immersion. It can serve to further engage players in the experience by presenting them with the opportunity to embody characters they find particularly compelling. Many players find it enjoyable to engage in role-playing by temporarily taking up some of the attitudes and decision-making strategies of the character they are currently embodying, rather than maintaining their own real-life perspective during gameplay. In this sense, embodiment can be seen as a key contributor to player delight [2].

Ethics. Due to the heightened sense of presence and embodiment, VR environments often feel more similar to the real world than virtual environments in traditional video games. This greater sense of reality is accompanied by increased ethical issues [9, 19, 30]. For instance, research has shown that playing a first-person shooter game with a realistic gun-replica controller rather than a traditional mouse can lead to heightened levels of aggression in players [16]. Because players in VR experiences may experience "bleed" between the real and virtual worlds to a greater degree than players of traditional video games, it is especially pressing that designers of VR experiences take ethical aspects into consideration [2].

An especially acute example of an ethical issue related to VR can be found in the interaction between VR and post-traumatic stress disorder (PTSD). Due to their perceived "reality," VR experiences may trigger PTSD flashbacks, causing players to suddenly and unexpectedly relive their memories of past traumatic events. Since a player who is experiencing a PTSD flashback may not have the presence of mind to remove the VR headset or otherwise disengage with the VR experience, it may be necessary to provide an in-game safe space where players can recover. However, for the same reasons that VR experiences may act as triggers, they may also be applied to the treatment of PTSD in the form of exposure therapy taking place in a VR environment [26].

Physicality. Unlike traditional video games, which generally do not require high levels of physical activity or exertion, VR experiences often involve a significant degree of physical activity. Designers of VR experiences must consider the players' physical comfort; their physical ability to perform the actions that the game asks of them; their need for breaks or cooldown time between periods of intense physical activity; and their differing physical traits and capabilities, including physical fitness, height, and physical disability [21, 33]. For instance, since VR games often require players to exert themselves physically, it is possible for a VR game to ask players to perform physical feats that are beyond their actual capabilities. If players are not conditioned for intense physical activity, but the game encourages them to keep playing anyway, players who are not aware of their own physical limits may find themselves taking on more than they can handle in terms of physical exertion. Simultaneously, physical activity can be used to increase player immersion by giving them the sensation that they are performing the same physical actions that the player character performs in the game world—for instance, physically wielding a motion controller as if it were a gun or a sword to control a weapon of this type in the game.

Organization into Categories. We organized the information gathered from these resources into five broad categories: Usability, Playability, VR Immersion, Creative VR, and New Player Experience. We synthesized the information in each category to create between 4 and 9 specific guidelines, for a total of 33 guidelines across all five categories. Each guideline includes an overall explanation of a principle for designers to follow, followed by examples of the principle being adhered to and violated. This way, it demonstrates the outcome both with and without the principle. The finalized VR PLAY guidelines were then published on a website to be easily accessible for designers.

2   Procedure

2.1   Study Design

We created a study with two phases to test the impact of the VR PLAY guidelines on the design of an example VR experience.

In Phase 1, a designer without prior knowledge of the guidelines created an initial version, Version A, of the VR experience. He was then introduced to the guidelines and given a period in which to revise the VR experience using the guidelines. This culminated in the design of Version B of the same experience.

In Phase 2, a user study was conducted to identify which of the two versions adhered more closely to the VR PLAY guidelines, and which was closer to an optimal player experience overall. Both versions were evaluated on all five of the top-level criteria addressed by the guidelines. This user study followed a within-subject design and included eight players, all of whom played through both Version A and Version. The order in which each player went through these versions was counterbalanced to randomize any order effects.

2.2   Hypotheses

Within this study, we tested two hypotheses: Hypothesis A and Hypothesis B. Hypothesis A was that the designer's overall understanding of issues related to VR experience, user experience, and player experience would improve between Version A and Version B. This could be determined by examining the designer's impressions of user- and player-experience issues through the interviews and surveys, as well as by comparing the number of guidelines that were adhered to and violated in Version A and Version B. Note that the designer had to complete Version A as their best effort at creating an optimal player experience.

Hypothesis B was that Version B would consequently contain fewer violations of and more adherences to the VR PLAY guidelines than Version A across all five of the categories. Thus, we also predicted that Version B would be closer to an optimal player experience overall.

2.3   Phase 1. VR Experience: Designer Study

The existing VR experience that was revised within this case study is known as the "Tracked Chair" experience because it makes use of VR spatial tracking to create a virtual counterpart of a physical (real-world) office chair. The virtual chair is co-located with and follows the movements of the physical chair, meaning that a participant who is wearing a VR headset can see and sit down in the chair. This experience was constructed for the Vive platform and makes use of a Vive controller to track the location of the physical chair.

In the Tracked Chair experience, the participant must first "unveil" the chair by removing a virtual cloth covering. Then, they must sit in the chair and make use of several virtual interface elements: a set of virtual screens attached to the chair that can be displayed and hidden at will and a button that can change the color of the virtual chair.

The Tracked Chair experience was one entry in a larger series of VR experiences created within a University of Southern California research lab in cooperation with industry partners at the furniture company Steelcase. The experiences in this series adapt existing industrial design processes at Steelcase into a fictional future world in which virtual and augmented reality technologies have become deeply integral to the

Steelcase design process. The Tracked Chair scene portrays a final "unveiling" or "presentation" stage in the design process in which a finished furniture design is presented to a larger audience (outside the original design team) for the first time. Altogether, this series of experiences forms an "immersive design fiction" intended to inspire innovative thinking about the potential future of industrial design. This immersive design fiction uses VR to "realistically" portray a vision of the future that would currently be thought of as science fiction, allowing designers to directly interact with simulated mockups of futuristic design tools and social practices that could not otherwise be realized today [20].

Preliminary Interview with Designer. The designer of the existing VR experience had no prior exposure to usability or playability guidelines of any kind. We conducted a preliminary interview with the designer to discover what kinds of changes he already intended to make to the design, and whether he believed a set of VR-specific usability and playability guidelines would aid him in making these revisions.

Exposure to VR PLAY Guidelines. We then introduced the designer to the VR PLAY guidelines and provided him with a brief explanation of how the guidelines could be applied. To gauge any change in his perception of the guidelines' potential utility, we asked him several additional questions. Then, we instructed him to spend a week revising his existing design with the guidelines in mind.

After Exposure to VR PLAY Guidelines; Before Revisions. Immediately after being introduced to the guidelines, but before having a chance to apply them to the revision process, the designer stated that he could now think of many specific improvements he wanted to try. Many of these potential improvements made reference to ideas or language drawn from individual guidelines; in particular, while continuing to talk about "feedback" (using terminology introduced by guideline A1, Provide Feedback), he began to adopt terminology from other guidelines, framing several of the improvements using terms like "demonstration" (E4, Build Self-Efficacy through Demonstration & Practice); "knowledge transfer" (A5, Build on Real-World Knowledge + E1, Design for Knowledge Transfer); "goals" (B4, Provide Clear Goals); and "error prevention" (A2, Prevent Player Error) for the first time. He found these guidelines especially helpful because they gave him the vocabulary he needed to discuss issues he had noticed in some form already but did not previously know how to coherently express.

After Revisions. After a week-long revision process incorporating the guidelines, the designer rated Version B as 2.5 (where 1 = totally unlike the desired player experience and 5 = exactly like the desired player experience) in closeness to the desired player experience, noting that there had been substantial improvement over Version A, but that he would still not want to present Version B as a "finished" product. He rated the usefulness of the guidelines as 5 overall (where 1 = not useful and 5 = very useful), while rating their usefulness for the specific tasks (a) and (b) at 4.5 and 5, respectively. Overall, he felt that the guidelines had been especially useful in inspiring ideas for changes, but that the limited timeframe of the revision process meant that "if I went into

Unity [the game design tool] again for five minutes with the guidelines, I'm sure I'd come up with a whole bunch of other stuff to address." He also stated that he intends to use the guidelines from the very beginning of the design process when working on virtual reality projects in the future.

The designer's rating of his own understanding of how to use the guidelines dropped slightly, from 5 to 4.5 (where 1 = no understanding and 5 = complete understanding). He suggested, however, that this was because his initial assessment was over-optimistic, and that he still "definitely understood how to use them" overall. The guidelines, in his mind, discussed problems that "everyone [designing for virtual reality] deals with," and that—although it sometimes took a bit of searching—he was able to identify at least one applicable guideline for every design problem he encountered during the revision process.

Debriefing Interview with Designer. At the end of the revision process, we met with the designer to conduct a debriefing interview. The purpose of this interview was to develop an understanding of his design thinking and to gather evidence regarding whether and how his thinking had changed as a result of exposure to the VR PLAY guidelines. The designer was asked about any changes he made to the design, his use of the guidelines during the revision process, how useful he perceived the guidelines to be, and why he found them useful.

Overview of Designer and Design Portion of the Study. Altogether, the designer's involvement in the study can be summarized as a sequence of several distinct steps:

- Initial interview and survey (before exposure to guidelines)
- Design of Version A
- Initial exposure to VR PLAY guidelines
- First post-exposure interview and-survey (immediately after exposure to guidelines)
- Design of Version B (with access to guidelines)
- Second post-exposure and -survey (after finishing the design of Version B)

2.4   Phase 2. User Study Prep

Following the revision process, two versions of the designer's VR experience existed. To determine what impact the VR PLAY guidelines had on the revisions that were made, we used the guidelines to conduct a comparative heuristic evaluation of the two versions [13, 23].

User Study of Tracked Chair Experience. To test whether the guidelines resulted in significant improvements to the overall usability and playability of the VR experience, we conducted a user study. We recruited eight participants with levels of VR experience ranging from none to experienced.

To acclimate participants to the experience of being in a VR environment, each participant was first given a few minutes in an empty VR world. This was intended to mitigate any first-time-experience issues, including difficulties with the Vive controllers. Participants were then instructed to play through Versions A and B of the VR experience. To minimize (counterbalance) order effects, odd-numbered participants played through Version A first while even-numbered participants played through

Version B first. After playing through both versions, each participant took part in a debriefing interview and filled out a survey about their experiences.

Hypotheses. Our first hypothesis (H:A) was that, after working with the guidelines for a week, the designer would have a greater overall understanding of user- and player-experience issues. This hypothesis was supported by the interviews with the designer and by the comparative heuristic evaluation of Versions A and B. In later interviews (both immediately after being introduced to the guidelines and after an entire week of working with the guidelines), the designer began to use terminology from the guidelines to articulate a more sophisticated understanding of the reasons for certain player-experience issues, and how these issues could potentially be solved. Additionally, Version B was found to contain substantially more instances of adherence to the guidelines and fewer violations of the guidelines than Version A. (Version A had 43 instances of adherence and 28 violations; Version B had 79 instances of adherence and 15 violations.) This suggests that the designer understood the guidelines, internalized them, and successfully applied them to the design revision process.

Our second hypothesis (H:B) was that Version B would contain fewer violations of and more adherences to the VR PLAY guidelines than Version A across all five of the issue categories (Usability, Playability, VR Immersion, Creative VR, and New Player Experience) that the guidelines address, and, thus, that Version B would be closer to an optimal player experience overall. This hypothesis was mostly supported by the comparative heuristic evaluation of the two versions, which found that Version B performed better (i.e., had more instances of adherence and fewer violations) than Version A in four of the five categories (Playability, VR Immersion, Creative VR, and New Player Experience). The one exception to this hypothesis was in the Usability category, which saw a decline in both the total number of adherences and the total number of violations from Version A to Version B; this is believed to be largely the result of a bug in Version B that was absent from Version A and had a negative impact on usability but was not part of the intended revisions to the design. (See Table 2 for the exact changes in total numbers of adherences and violations across each category from Version A to Version B.)

Analysis of User Study. Players went through the experience one at a time, observed by three coders. The coders took notes on what happened during the players' time in each version of the experience, which they then used to identify VR PLAY guidelines that had been adhered to and/or violated. To ensure inter-rater reliability, all coders were experienced in using the VR PLAY guidelines and were given the same guidelines on how to code the player experience.

Each coder submitted a single set of data, documenting how many players had experienced each guideline being adhered to and/or violated within each version of the VR experience. These sets of data were then aggregated by taking the mean, median, and mode of each value. Since there was little variance between these values, we report only the means (see Table 1).

Table 1. VR PLAY adherences and violations, Version A vs. Version B (Dark gray = clear improvement from A to B; light gray = all zeros/not applicable) N = 8 Players.

	VERSION A		VERSION B	
	Adherences	Violations	Adherences	Violations
A. Usability	*21 [A1, A5, A8]*	*8 [A1]*	*18 [A1, A5]*	*7 [A2, A5, A7]*
A1. Feedback	8	8	14	0
A2. Error prev	0	0	0	2
A3. Burden	0	0	0	0
A4. Status	0	0	0	0
A5. Real-World	5	0	4	2
A6. Review	0	0	0	0
A7. UI	0	0	0	3
A8. Navigation	8	0	0	0
B. Playability	*3 [B1]*	*3 [B4]*	*11 [B3, B6]*	*1 [B4]*
B1. Control	3	0	0	0
B2. Challenge	0	0	0	0
B3. Engage	0	0	8	0
B4. Goals	0	3	0	1
B5. Variety	0	0	0	0
B6. Social	0	0	3	0
C. VR Immersion	*11 [C5, C7]*	*4 [C3]*	*15 [C1, C7]*	*4 [C3]*
C1. Presence	0	0	7	0
C2. Embody	0	0	0	0
C3. Side Effects	0	4	0	4
C4. Comfort	0	0	0	0
C5. Safe Space	3	0	0	0
C6. Inclusion	0	0	0	0

C7. Obstruct	8	0	8	0
C8. Halo Effect	0	0	0	0
C9. Ethics	0	0	0	0
D. Creative VR	**8 [D1]**	**1 [D3]**	**8 [D1]**	**0 [N/A]**
D1. Empower	8	0	8	0
D2. Social	0	0	0	0
D3. Phase	0	1	0	0
D4. Inspiration	0	0	0	0
E. NPE	**0 [N/A]**	**12 [E5, E6]**	**27 [E1, E4, E5, E6]**	**3 [E1, E3]**
E1. Transfer	0	0	3	1
E2. Sandbox	0	0	0	0
E3. Scaffolding	0	0	0	2
E4. Practice	0	0	8	0
E5. Integrate	0	4	8	0
E6. Stepwise	0	8	8	0
Total	**43**	**28**	**79**	**15**

3   Analysis

3.1   Highly Impactful Guidelines

List of Impactful Guidelines. The data show an especially clear improvement from Version A to Version B in adherence to the following specific guidelines.

A1. Provide Feedback. Four out of eight players experienced violation of this guideline in Version A, reporting that the buttons used to deploy screens around the chair were either too subtle to notice (a slight shift in color from gray to black) or occurred out of the player's line of sight (as players looked down at the buttons to use them, they missed the screens appearing and disappearing around the chair). These violations were absent from Version B, which used gestures to deploy and hide the screens. Some supplementary feedback, such as bursts of confetti on successful completion of certain actions, was added to Version B, increasing player delight.

B3. Encourage Player Engagement. In Version B, all players (8/8) found that exploration was rewarded with new and engaging feedback that did not appear in Version A. Two interactions that players found especially engaging in Version B were swiping to remove the cloth covering from the chair and spinning the chair to "calibrate" it, neither of which were present in Version A.

C1. Create a Sense of Presence. Version B adds several features that highlight the physicality of the virtual environment, including the two interactions discussed under B3. In addition to encouraging player engagement, these improvements helped to create a sense of physical presence in the world.

E4. Build Self-efficacy through Demonstration and Practice. Version A contained no demonstration of any of the mechanics players needed to use to interact with the chair. Version B demonstrated how to use all these mechanics, showing a transparent "ghost" version of the Vive controller repeatedly acting out the motions the player would need to perform. This made players substantially more confident in the knowledge that they were performing the actions "correctly."

E5. Integrate Tutorial with Gameplay. Version A did not make any explicit attempt to teach players how to interact with the various mechanics. Version B added introductory text and demonstration for several of these mechanics and integrated them smoothly with gameplay, alternating sections of explanatory scaffolding with sections in which players could freely practice with the mechanics they had learned so far.

E6. Teach Mechanics One Thing at a Time (Stepwise Learning). Version A of the experience introduced several new interactions in quick succession (revealing the chair, interacting with it as a mixed physical/virtual object, sitting in it, and using the buttons to raise and lower screens) without pausing to explain any of them in further detail. Version B, on the other hand, clearly separated these steps by displaying introductory text each time a new interaction was introduced.

What Does This Mean? The clear improvements in adherence to these guidelines between Version A and Version B indicate that the designer both understood and internalized the principles of usability and playability that these guidelines introduce. He was successfully able to use the guidelines to revise Version A's design for improved player experience in Version B.

3.2   Guidelines Not Applicable

List of Non-applicable Guidelines. Several of the guidelines were not applicable to this design and, as such, were not observed to be violated or adhered to during the user study. These included the following:

A3. Avoid Burden on Memory. Neither Version A nor Version B required players to remember things they had learned for more than a few minutes at a time, and there were relatively few things to remember in both versions. As such, players had no difficulty remembering the things they did need to recall, and no hints were needed to mitigate burden on memory in either version.

A4. Show Player Status and World State. In both versions, all elements of player status and world state were immediately visible in the virtual environment at all times. The VR experience did not keep track of any hidden, intangible, or abstract elements of status or state (such as a health bar, score, or inventory). As such, the visualization of these abstract elements did not pose any usability or playability concerns.

A6. Let Players Review What They've Learned. As with guideline A3, there was little for players to review in either version. Both versions were only a few minutes long, and players had no difficulty remembering how to use the few mechanics they needed to remember, even without any kind of review.

B2. Ramp Up Challenge Gradually. Unlike many games, neither Version A nor Version B featured any kind of scaling difficulty. There were no enemies for players to defeat, scores for players to earn, or time limits on players' exploration of the virtual environment.

B5. Support a Variety of Players. The brief duration of the experience and relatively simple mechanics present in both Version A and Version B ensured that most players would be able to play without difficulty.

C2. Facilitate Embodiment of Character. Neither Version A nor Version B attempted to show or tell players whom they were playing as. However, players did not seem to notice or comment on this, possibly suggesting that they did not notice, or mind the fact, that they did not know whom the player character was meant to be, or they might have assumed it was themselves.

C4. Keep the Player Comfortable. Player discomfort was not a significant issue in either version, due to the limited duration of the experience and the relative ease of performing the few physical gestures required. Neither version required any kind of strenuous physical exertion on the part of the players.

C6. Provide a Safe Space. Since neither version of the experience gave players the impression they were under any kind of threat, the entirety of both experiences could be seen as a safe space. Players could stop playing at any time without exiting the experience and would suffer no negative repercussions within the virtual world for doing so.

C8. Be Aware of the First-Time Halo Effect. Players will often be wowed by the VR experience, even if the interface and/or game is poorly designed, so their perception at first-time play is likely to be more positive than with more experience in VR. Therefore, a player's unusual enthusiasm is to be discounted as first-play enthusiasm. This guideline is primarily advisory in nature and does not make any specific suggestions about how the final experience should work. As such, instances in which it is adhered to or violated are not visible in the observation of player behavior. Instead, one must ask designers or observe the design process directly to determine whether this guideline was adhered to or violated.

C9. Design Ethically. To design ethically means, for example, to beware of triggering events in a person, such as triggering a PTSD event, without an escape area. Like guideline C8, this guideline is primarily advisory in nature. Instances of adherence to or violation of this guideline are not directly visible in the observation of player behavior.

D2. Facilitate Performance and Social Creativity. Neither version of the experience offered players the opportunity to perform for any kind of in-world audience. In addition, the experience was not primarily intended to facilitate creative expression, so player expression of creativity was sharply limited within both versions.

D4. Provide Creative Inspiration. As with guideline D2, neither Version A nor Version B was primarily intended to facilitate creative expression, and both versions sharply limited player expression of creativity. As such, it would not make sense for this experience to provide players with creative inspiration.

E2. Provide a Safe Place to Learn (Sandbox). As with guideline C6, neither Version A nor Version B ever gave the players the impression they were under any kind of threat. At no point were there significant negative consequences for any player action, meaning that players could stop to practice at any point without suffering any negative consequences.

What Does This Mean? Most of the guidelines that were found to be not applicable to this design are associated with game-like features, such as overarching goals, status, and scores. Due to this, these will likely be more applicable to games as opposed to the Tracked Chair experience. Their limited applicability to this design is primarily a consequence of the fact that this design lacks certain common game mechanics to which these guidelines apply.

Two of these guidelines, however, represent a special case: guidelines C8, Be Aware of the First-Time Halo Effect, and C9, Design Ethically. Both guidelines are advisory in nature. Rather than making concrete, directly actionable statements about the qualities of a successful game, they simply recommend that designers educate themselves about and remain aware of certain potential pitfalls during the design process. Thus, adherence to or violation of these two guidelines cannot readily be determined through observation of player behavior. In the future, it may be desirable to rewrite these guidelines using more action-oriented language or move them into a supplemental resource separate from (but attached to) the main guidelines list.

3.3   Player Perception of Changes Between Versions A and B

Usability. Due to the short time (one week) allotted for revisions, Version B contained several bugs that impeded the functionality of key features. None of these bugs were present in Version A. When players were asked to compare the usability of Versions A and B, they made frequent references to these bugs in their descriptions of the usability issues they encountered. As such, it is not possible to make a reliable direct comparison between player usability ratings for the two versions. However, observation of their experiences with the two versions demonstrated that, excepting the issues introduced by the bugs, players generally found Version B easier to use. In particular, the players who were least impacted by the bugs seemed to find the gestural controls in Version B intuitive, and all players (even those impacted significantly by the bugs) were immediately able to intuit that the gestures in Version B could be reversed to perform inverse actions.

Delight. In addition, players clearly felt that Version B was more delightful than Version A overall, with 6/8 players stating that B was more delightful than A. Players commonly cited the increased feedback, the physicality of the cloth-removal gesture, and the overall sense that completing objectives felt more "rewarding" in Version B as reasons for this preference.

Comfort. According to their responses, most players (5/8) felt that both versions were equally comfortable to use, with no significant differences between Versions A and B in terms of physical comfort. However, there was a slight preference among some players for Version B; 2/8 players said they felt B was more comfortable (as the surrounding environment appeared to be physically open rather than enclosed), while only one player felt A was more comfortable (as she felt the gestural interactions with the chair in B could become physically tiring after a while). This player's preference in particular underscores the importance of principle C5, Provide a Safe Space: VR experiences that ask players to perform physically demanding tasks as a regular part of play should provide a safe in-world place where players may physically rest.

3.4   Categories of Each Guideline Adhered to and Violated

The guidelines are divided into five categories: Usability, Playability, VR Immersion, Creative VR, and New Player Experience (see Table 2). We hypothesized that, for each of these categories, Version B would violate fewer of the guidelines and/or adhere to more than Version A. This was found to be true for four categories (Playability, VR Immersion, Creative VR, New Player Experience and Usability). (See Table 2 for the exact changes in total adherences and violations in each category from Version A to Version B.)

Table 2. Changes in VR PLAY adherences and violations by category from Version A to Version B

	Δ # Adherences	Δ # Violations
Usability	−3	−1
Playability	+8	−2
VR immersion	+4	±0
Creative VR	±0	−1
NPE	+27	−9

By far the most significant improvements were seen in the New Player Experience category, with 27 additional instances of adherence to the guidelines and 9 fewer instances of violation. This can largely due to the substantial improvements that were made to the new-player experience in Version B, which added a variety of features intended to teach players how to use the mechanics at their disposal. No such features were present in Version A, which left players almost entirely to their own devices in attempting to learn how to play.

The Usability category, meanwhile, was the only category to see an overall decline from Version A to Version B: although it had 1 fewer violation in Version B, it also had 3 fewer adherences. This can largely be explained by the impact of a bug introduced in Version B—due to the brief period (one week) allotted for the second iteration—that made certain gesture-based interactions in Version B function unreliably. For the players impacted by the bug, this had a substantial negative effect on the usability of Version B in comparison to Version A. Since the introduction of the bug in Version B was not deliberate but did have a definite impact on usability, it is not possible to judge whether the guidelines would have been shown to have a net positive effect on usability from Version A to Version B if the bug had not occurred.

4 Conclusion

4.1 Impact of the VR PLAY Guidelines

Between Versions A and B of the VR experience considered in this case study, a comparative heuristic evaluation found that Version B—the version created after the designer was introduced to the VR PLAY guidelines—violated fewer of these guidelines (28 versus 15 total violations for Versions A and B, respectively) and adhered to more (43 versus 79 total adherences). This indicates that the designer was successful in applying the guidelines to the revision process and confirms both Hypothesis A (that the designer's understanding of usability and playability principles increased with exposure to the guidelines) and Hypothesis B (that Version B would contain fewer violations of and more adherences to the guidelines than Version A).

Impact on the Designer. The results of the side-by-side heuristic evaluations of Version A and Version B suggest that the designer both understood and internalized the guidelines and was able to successfully leverage his understanding to improve the usability and playability in the revised design. In addition, his statements in interviews suggest that he acquired an expanded vocabulary for discussing usability and playability issues from his time spent with the guidelines as he continued to use terminology he learned from the guidelines in his interview responses, even after the end of the revision process.

In his own words, the designer felt that the guidelines were especially helpful as a tool to help him generate solutions to problems he was already aware of but did not yet know how to address. He also expressed a particular desire to use the guidelines again on VR projects in the future—this time ideally "from the very beginning" of the design process, and he rated the guidelines as 5 on a five-point scale (where 1 = not useful and 5 = very useful).

Impact on Version B as Experienced by Players. When surveyed, 6/8 players found Version B more delightful than Version A. This suggests that the changes made by the designer when working with the guidelines resulted in significant improvements to the overall enjoy-ability of the VR experience.

Due to the short playtime of the VR experience and the limited amount of physical activity required, players generally did not feel that physical comfort was an issue for them in either version. Consequently, 5/8 players expressed that the versions were approximately equal in terms of physical comfort. However, 2/8 players did express a slight preference for Version B over A while only 1/8 players expressed a slight preference for Version A in terms of comfort.

4.2   Which Guidelines Are Most Impactful?

Between Version A and Version B, we found a clear and significant improvement in adherence to several specific VR PLAY guidelines, including A1, B3, C1, E4, E5, and E6.

Notably, three of these highly impactful guidelines are from Category E (New Player Experience). This speaks to the potential significance of improvements in new-player experience relative to improvements in other areas: because Version A of the VR experience contained little to no guidance for new players, the addition of even relatively minimal guidance in Version B was a basic issue, yielding substantial improvements in overall player experience for relatively little investment in time and effort on the designer's part.

The absence of any guidelines from category D (Creative VR) from this list may be accounted for by the sharply limited nature of the creative expression possible within this VR experience. As the VR experience was not intended as a creative tool, players had few opportunities to exercise their creativity, limiting the applicability of creativity-specific guidelines. This leads us to conclude that some guidelines have more impact for some applications than for others.

Given the positive effects of the guidelines, we have evidence they are helpful in increasing the user experience.

4.3   Guidelines Not Applicable

Several guidelines, meanwhile, were found to be not applicable to the VR experience evaluated in this study. These guidelines included A3, A4, A6, B2, B5, C2, C4, C6, C8, C9, and D2.

The majority of these guidelines were not applicable because the VR experience being evaluated did not contain certain common game mechanics to which these guidelines apply. For instance, the experience did not include any form of ramping up the challenge or difficulty, did not track any kind of score, and took place over a very short span of time, limiting the applicability of guidelines pertaining to certain kinds of experiences and games. Almost all these guidelines would thus be applicable to games of different types.

Two of the guidelines that were not applicable stand apart from the others that were attributed to more game-like features not present in the current study. The guidelines C8, Be Aware of the First-Time Halo Effect, and C9, Design Ethically, are advisory in nature and do not make use of directly actionable language, instead merely recommending that designers keep certain potential pitfalls in mind during the design process. Adherence to and violation of these advisory guidelines thus cannot be determined directly from observation of player behavior, making it difficult to apply these guidelines in an evaluative capacity. This might be addressed in the future, see below.

4.4   Next Steps

In order to evaluate the utility of the guidelines that were found to be not applicable in this VR experience study, we intend to perform follow-up studies that apply the VR PLAY guidelines to other types of VR games and experiences where they might be applicable. Candidates include strategy games, physical games (including exercise games), action games, first-person shooter games, and horror games. These game varieties include mechanics that were not present in the VR experience evaluated by this study, increasing the likelihood that the specific guidelines will be applicable to these other games.

The "advisory" guidelines C8 and C9 are potential candidates for future revision and reevaluation. They might be rewritten to use more actionable language, making it possible to evaluate whether they have been adhered to or violated directly through observation of player behavior. Alternatively, they could be moved to a supplementary appendix attached to the main guidelines list but not presented as equivalent in form and purpose to the other guidelines.

Acknowledgements. We want to gratefully thank all the brilliant and hardworking interns of User Behavioristics, including Jordan Klein, Laura Doumad, Clerisse Cornejo, Shing-Hoi Lau, and Eva Wierzbicki, and colleagues and reviewers such as Dennis Wixon, Charlotte Wiberg, and Katherine Isbister, who provided helpful comments on previous versions of this paper. The authors also gratefully acknowledge the support from Scott Fisher and Joshua McVeigh-Schultz of the Mobile & Environmental Media Lab at the University of Southern California and Donna Flynn, Mark Baloga, and Paul Noll from Steelcase Corporation, who partnered with us on their Tracked Chair VR experience.

References

1. Basdogan, C., Ho, C.H., Srinivasan, M.A., Slater, M.: An experimental study on the role of touch in shared virtual environments. ACM Trans. Comput.-Hum. Interact. 7(4), 443–460 (2000)
2. Bowman, S.L.: Bleed: The Spillover Between Player and Character. Nordiclarp.org (2015). https://nordiclarp.org/2015/03/02/bleed-the-spillover-between-player-and-character/
3. Chastine, J.W., Nagel, K., Zhu, Y., Yearsovich, L.: Understanding the design space of referencing in collaborative augmented reality environments. In: Proceedings of Graphics Interface 2007, (GI 2007), pp. 207–214. ACM, New York (2007)
4. Chung, J., Gardner, H.J.: Measuring temporal variation in presence during game playing. In: Spencer, S.N. (ed.) Proceedings of the 8th International Conference on Virtual Reality Continuum and its Applications in Industry, (VRCAI 2009), pp. 163–168. ACM, New York (2009)
5. Crawley, D.: Introduction to Bayesian Statistics, April 2015. https://venturebeat.com/2015/04/18/were-not-talking-about-what-vr-is-doing-to-our-eyes-and-our-brains/. Accessed 18 Aug 2015

6. Desurvire, H., Wiberg, C.: Master of the game: assessing approachability in future game design. In: CHI 2008 Extended Abstracts on Human Factors in Computing Systems, (CHI EA 2008), pp. 3177–3182. ACM, New York (2008)
7. Desurvire, H., Wixon, D.: Game principles: choice, change & creativity: making better games. In: CHI 2013 Extended Abstracts on Human Factors in Computing Systems, (CHI EA 2013), pp. 1065–1070. ACM, New York (2013)
8. Dimopoulos, Y., Moraitis, P., Amgoud, L.: Characterizing the outcomes of argumentation-based integrative negotiation. In: Proceedings of the 2008 IEEE/WIC/ACM International Conference on Web Intelligence and Intelligent Agent Technology, (WI-IAT 2008), vol. 2, pp. 456–460. IEEE Computer Society, Washington, DC (2008)
9. Fink, P.W., Foo, P.S., Warren, W.H.: Obstacle avoidance during walking in real and virtual environments. ACM Trans. Appl. Percept. 4(1), Article no. 2 (2007)
10. Greef, P.D., Ijsselstijn, W.A.: Social presence in a home tele-application. Cyberpsychol. Behav. 4(2), 307–315 (2004)
11. Hayhoe, M.M., Ballard, D.H., Triesch, J., Shinoda, H., Aivar, P., Sullivan, B.: Vision in natural and virtual environments. In: Proceedings of the 2002 Symposium on Eye Tracking Research & Applications, (ETRA 2002), pp. 7–13. ACM, New York (2002)
12. Hung, Y.H., Parsons, P.: Assessing user engagement in information visualization. In: Proceedings of the 2016 CHI Conference Extended Abstracts on Human Factors in Computing Systems, (CHI EA 2017), pp. 1708–1717. ACM, New York (2017)
13. Jeffries, R., Desurvire, H.: Usability testing vs. heuristic evaluation: was there a contest? SIGCHI Bull. 24(4), 39–41 (1992)
14. Kajiyama, T.: Botanical data retrieval system supporting discovery learning. In: Proceedings of the 1st ACM International Conference on Multimedia Retrieval, (ICMR 2011). ACM, New York (2011). Article 36
15. Kerse, D., Regenbrecht, H., Purvis, M.: Telepresence and user-initiated control. In: Proceedings of the 2005 International Conference on Augmented Tele-Existence, (ICAT 2005), pp. 239–240. ACM, New York (2005)
16. Kim, K.J., Biocca, F., Jeong, E.J.: The effects of realistic controller and real-life exposure to gun on psychology of violent video game players. In: Proceedings of the 5th International Conference on Ubiquitous Information Management and Communication, (ICUIMC 2011). ACM, New York (2011). Article 49
17. Lehtinen, V., Hänninen, R., Toivonen, V., Oulasvirta, A., Kuuva, S., Saariluoma, P.: Developing a rapid questionnaire-based metric for experience of form. In: Norros, L., Koskinen, H., Salo, L., Savioja, P. (eds.) European Conference on Cognitive Ergonomics: Designing beyond the Product—Understanding Activity and User Experience in Ubiquitous Environments, (ECCE 2009). VTT Technical Research Centre of Finland, VTT, Finland (2009). Article 4
18. Lobel, A., Granic, I., Engels, R.: Stressful gaming, interoceptive awareness, and emotion regulation tendencies: a novel approach. Cyberpsychol. Behav. Soc. Netw. 17(4), 222–227 (2014)
19. Madary, M., Metzinger, T.K.: Real virtuality: a code of ethical conduct Recommendations for good scientific practice and the consumers of VR-technology. Front. Robot. AI 3, 3 (2013)
20. McVeigh-Schultz, J., Kreminski, M., Prasad, K., Hoberman, P., Fisher, S.S.: Immersive Design Fiction: Using VR to Prototype Speculative Interfaces and Interaction Rituals within a Virtual Storyworld (in process)
21. Mueller, F., Isbister, K.: Movement-based game guidelines. In: Proceedings of the SIGCHI Conference on Human Factors in Computing Systems, (CHI 2014), pp. 2191–2200. ACM, New York (2014)

22. Nesbitt, K.V.: Modelling human perception to leverage the reuse of concepts across the multi-sensory design space. In: Stumptner, M., Hartmann, S., Kiyoki, Y. (eds.) Proceedings of the 3rd Asia-Pacific Conference on Conceptual Modelling, (APCCM 2006), vol. 53, pp. 65–74. Australian Computer Society, Inc., Darlinghurst (2006)

23. Nielsen, J.: Enhancing the explanatory power of usability heuristics. In: Adelson, B., Dumais, S., Olson, J. (eds.) Proceedings of the SIGCHI Conference on Human Factors in Computing Systems (CHI 1994), pp. 152–158. ACM, New York (1994)

24. Nunez, D., Blake, E.: Cognitive presence as a unified concept of virtual reality effectiveness. In: Proceedings of the 1st International Conference on Computer Graphics, Virtual Reality and Visualisation, (AFRIGRAPH 2001), pp. 115–118. ACM, New York (2001)

25. Pätsch, G., Mandl, T., Hacker, C.W.: Using sensor graphs to stimulate recall in retrospective think-aloud protocols. In: Proceedings of the 5th Information Interaction in Context Symposium, (IIiX 2014), pp. 303–307. ACM, New York (2014)

26. Rothbaum, B.O., et al.: Virtual reality exposure therapy for PTSD Vietnam veterans: a case study. J. Trauma. Stress **12**(2), 263–271 (1999)

27. Schloerb, D.W.: A quantitative measure of telepresence. Presence: Teleoper. Virtual Environ. **4**(1), 64–80 (1995)

28. Shin, J., An, G., Lee, K.: Integration of a precise indoor position tracking algorithm with an HMD-based virtual reality system. In: Proceedings of the 2nd ACM International Workshop on Immersive Media Experiences, (ImmersiveMe 2014), pp. 23–26. ACM, New York (2014)

29. Slater, M., Steed, A.: A virtual presence counter. Presence: Teleoper. Virtual Environ. **9**(5), 413–434 (2000)

30. Souza, C.S., Leitão, C.F.: Semiotic engineering methods for scientific research. HCI Synth. Lect. Hum.-Cent. Inform. **2**(1), 1–222 (2009)

31. Turpin, A., Scholer, F., Mizzaro, S., Maddalena, E.: The benefits of magnitude estimation relevance assessments for information retrieval evaluation. In: Proceedings of the 38th International ACM SIGIR Conference on Research and Development in Information Retrieval, (SIGIR 2015), pp. 565–574. ACM, New York (2015)

32. Yee, N., Bailenson, J.N., Rickertsen, K.: A meta-analysis of the impact of the inclusion and realism of human-like faces on user experiences in interfaces. In: Proceedings of the SIGCHI Conference on Human Factors in Computing Systems, (CHI 2007), pp. 1–10. ACM, New York (2007)

33. Yoo, S., Parker, C., Kay, J.: Designing a personalized VR exergame. In: Tkalcic, M., Thakker, D., Germanakos, P., Yacef, K., Paris, C., Santos, O. (eds.) Adjunct Publication of the 25th Conference on User Modeling, Adaptation and Personalization (UMAP 2017), pp. 431–435. ACM, New York (2017)

34. Von Mammen, S., Knote, A., Edenhofer, S.: Cyber sick but still having fun. In: Proceedings VRST 2016 of 22nd ACM Conference on Virtual Reality, pp. 325–326. ACM, New York (2016)

35. Witmer, B.G., Singer, M.J.: Measuring presence in virtual environments: a presence questionnaire. Presence: Teleoper. Virtual Environ. **7**(3), 225–240 (1998)

Establishment of Design Strategies and Design Models of Human Computer Interaction Interface Based on User Experience

Chao Gong[⊠], Yue Qiu, and Bin Zhao

Beijing Institute of Technology, Beijing, China
1484445636@qq.com

Abstract. Taken into consideration people's demand for access to information in nowadays society, the paper carries a systematic analysis and a detailed study of designing human-computer interaction interface by theoretical analysis and integration thereof combined with practical experience. The paper puts forward reasonable and practical design strategies, establishes relatively complete and systematic software interface design models, and makes rewarding suggestions on the future of software interface design.

First, the paper delves into the subject of the interactive process, human, namely users, and sets up the model of user analysis. The essay studies and analyzes relevant design strategies based on the users' perceptive, cognitive, emotional ability towards information and the characteristics of the user experience in the process of human-computer interaction, proposes design strategies of human-computer interaction interface based on users' perception, cognition, emotion of information and the characteristics of the user experience. Also, user-centeredness is established as the fundamental research ideology. Then, characteristics of information identification in software interaction interfaces are summarized. Principles of interface design for information representation and recognition is proposed, and the subject of the design of software interaction interface is determined. Further, the paper presents specific methods in which designs can be implemented. It develops a systematic model of the integral design of the software interface, summarizes principles of software interface design based on the characteristics of interface. The integral design model mainly comprises of the following phases: demand analysis, implementation, testing and evaluation. It puts forward the demand of "iteration" throughout the designing process. What is more, the optimization theory of "three transformation and fusion" of software interaction interface design is proposed. Last but not the least, the paper puts forward the goals of future software interface design, that is, "generalization", "intelligentization" and "actualization" and raises relevant opinions and suggestions thereof. The research provides a practical and valuable reference for software interaction interface design in the future.

Keywords: User experience · Design implementation model · Design strategy
Optimization theory

© Springer International Publishing AG, part of Springer Nature 2018
A. Marcus and W. Wang (Eds.): DUXU 2018, LNCS 10918, pp. 60–76, 2018.
https://doi.org/10.1007/978-3-319-91797-9_5

1 Introduction

Nowadays, new technologies can transmit massive amounts of information to each and every corner of the world in a very short period of time, with all possible aspects of human activities the manifestations of interaction of information. At this age and time, the carrier of information becomes the interactive platform for all kinds of activities of human and begins to partake in human cognition, human behavior and human communication [1]. This is gradually changing the way people live. Under the impact of the massive amounts of information, people's forms of life gradually transform from material to non-material society. A form of society that centers around the interaction of information, provides information services and produces information technology gradually takes form, steering design from the static, single and materialized modeling design to the dynamic, complex, dematerialized information design. Design patterns change from the one-way output to the two-way interactive communication [2].

After the entry into the non-material society, the way that people cognize information has changed with the revolution of the transmittal of information. The application of interactive technology leads to equality and freedom of relationships involved in information interaction and breaks down the limitations of time and space in the transmittal of information. Nowadays, harmonious information interaction is a great vision that people have for information acquisition and recognition. Scientific, efficient and systematic software interface design has become the ultimate goal interface of interface designers. Satisfaction of users' physical, psychological and behavioral demands, characteristics of user experience, and realization of rapid, accurate, efficient and comfortable acquisition and identification of information by software interfaces have become a necessity of the society (Fig. 1).

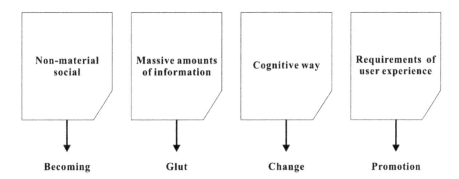

Fig. 1. Background about software interface design

2 User-Centered Software Interface Design Strategy

The most fundamental requirement for designing software interaction interfaces is to understand the subject of the information interaction process, namely, the users. In the initial stage of the interface design life cycle, users' demands should make the basic motive and the ultimate purpose of the design strategy [3]. In the process designing and developing the interface, the researching into and understanding of users should be considered as the basis for various design decisions. At the same time, the principle of evaluation for each phase of interface design should also be derived from the user's feedback of demand. Therefore, the research and analysis of human as users is the core of the whole process of software interaction interface design and evaluation.

2.1   Characteristics of User Experience in Software Interaction Interface Design

User experience is the emotion or mood that users experience in specific temporal, spatial and environmental conditions. The characteristics of user experience are as follow [4] (Fig. 2).

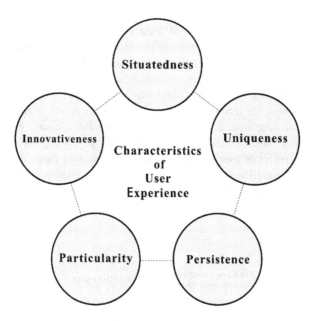

Fig. 2. The characteristics of user experience

Situatedness. User experience is closely related to a specific situation. In different situations, users have different feelings. With time and situation different, the same interaction can produce different effects in terms of experience.

Uniqueness. User experience is closely related to users' individual physical characteristics. Different users may have completely different experience towards the same interaction.

Persistence. User experience can be conserved, accumulated and persisted in the continuous interactions that the users performed with the interface. When the expected goal of interaction is fulfilled, the whole experience does not end. Instead, the interaction gives the users a feeling of fulfillment and realization.

Particularity. User experience has its own unique characteristics. Each experience, spreading over the whole interaction process, is different from another.

Innovativeness. Interactive experience does not only derive from the spontaneous feelings of users. Users need to be stimulated in diversified and innovative ways.

2.2   User's Perception, Cognition, Emotion of Information

Perception is at the beginning of users' understanding and identification of information in the process of information interaction. The cognitive activities of users for more advanced and more complex information are generated on the basis of perception [5]. The users' perception, which is directly correlated with the representation of information and methods of interaction in the design of software interaction interface, is quite superficial. Designers should fully consider the characteristics of users' organs of perception and the process in which the perception is processed. Attention should be paid to the following:

- Designers should fully consider the mutual influences, the compensation effects, and the association of different means of perception. Designers should fully consider the significance and the priority of information, and choose different ways to represent different information according to the attributes thereof, so as to achieve orderly and effective communication of information on the interface.
- When the same receptor receives strong and continuous stimulation of the same information from the interface, the experience of the user towards the message transmitted from the interface changes, impeding information to be identified. This kind of perceptual adaptation is mainly reflected in the application of color and sound stimuli of information representation.
- Sensitivity of the user's same receptor to the stimulation of information in different interfaces changes in intensity and nature. To some extent, the users' perception of contrast is an illusion. This can affect the user's information identification, so designers should reasonably design the interface, guided by the content of information and users' demand, to meet users' demand for perceived contrast.
- Lack of certain feeling or inadequacy of certain function of the user may lead to the enhancement of the faculty of other sensory organs, compensating for the perception. Designer should employ ways of representation that certain user groups are familiar with to increase the interactivity of the interface.
- Human's perception can be enhanced and developed through daily life and work. With some special training, one person's ability of perception and cognition to such an extent that an average person is unlikely to be level. Designers should enhance the usability of the interactive interface by selecting the methods of interaction and information representation to adjust to the actual conditions of these users.

The user experience can be very complex in the process of information interaction, and the emotions of users towards the surrounding conditions also impact the user's information cognition process [6]. Positive emotions allow the user to think about things in a more imaginative way and enable them to identify complicated information. When the user is relaxed, the identification of the information may be easier. Users' emotions relate to their own physical conditions, but also relate to the design in which transmittal of information is achieved on the interface. The two factors greatly impact users' the ability to identify information and the effect thereof, thereby affecting the interaction between the users and the computer [7]. Designers should fully consider the users' emotional factors and create an interactive interface environment that can improve the user's positive reactions. Only in this way can the interaction be more successful and effective.

2.3   User-Centeredness as the Basic Design Strategy

The user-centered design is an important part of the whole software interaction interface design process. It should always be followed rigorously and implemented effectively [8]. User-centered design should take into account: repeated designing, timely acceptation of feedbacks from users, effective communication among team members, as well as coordination and balance of potential problems. In general, the principle of user-centered design is a practical, effective guarantee for software interaction interface design (Fig. 3).

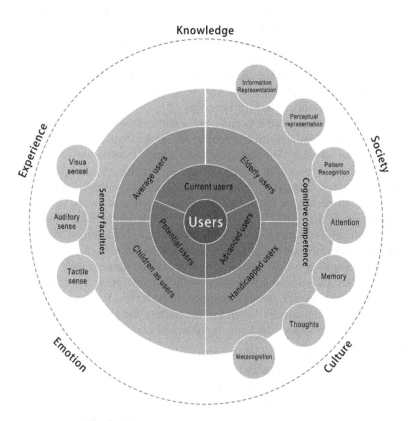

Fig. 3. The user research model for user analysis

The principle of user-centered design should be combined into the whole process of designing and developing software interface, which include: analysis of user's background, determination of user's demand for information, designing and implementation, testing and evaluation, and improvement of the design based on users demand, integration of user-centered design principle with other design activities; identification of individuals or organizations in the user-centered design process and the scope of support they can provide; establishment of effective mechanism of feedback and methods of communication in the process of user-centered design process; alternation of the design or incorporation of the feedback into the appropriate phase of the entire software interaction interface design. The following figure illustrates the user research model for user analysis:

User-centered interface design should effectively make available users' access to information and inspire users to learn. It is a principle that should be carried out through the whole life cycle of software interface designing [9]. The following design strategies can be employed to ensure implementation of the principle:

Actively Foster User Participation. Users' participation provides valuable sources of information on users' background, users' demand, possible ways of interactions, and users' patterns of cognition. The nature of user participation should be consistent with the design requirements of different phases of design. This approach, in which the actual users participate in the evaluation of the design, enhances the user's acceptance and satisfaction of the product.

Appropriately Distribute Interactive Behaviors. Designers should specify which behavior in the interface should be done by the users and which should be done by the computer. These design decisions determine the degree to which information is automatically or manually identified. The distribution of interaction behaviors depends on a number of factors, such as, faithfulness of information transmittal, the speed thereof, the accuracy thereof and flexibility of giving feedback, etc.

Repeatedly Design in a Reasonable Way. Repeated design should be combined with the user's active partaking. Users' feedback, which minimizes the risk of the interface not meeting the demand of the user for information, is a very important factor. The method of repeated design should be combined with other design methods to achieve the completeness of interactive interface design.

Emphasize the Application of Multi-disciplinary Knowledge. User-centered interactive interface design requires guidance from and application of knowledge of a wide variety of subjects. A multi-disciplinary design team does not necessarily need to be packed with people, but its team composition needs to meet the diversity requirements of interface system design, so that reasonable design schemes and effective trade-offs can be realized.

3   Design Strategy of Software Interaction Interface Based on Information Identification

3.1   The Categories and Features of Information in the Software Interfaces

In the design of software interaction interfaces, the information can be divided into: first-time information, second-time information and third-time information [10]. The information can also be divided into: digital information, textual information, image information and sound information. These types of information can be transformed and expressed through effective design methods (Table 1).

Table 1. Characteristics of information in software interactive interface design [11]

Characteristics	Specific manifestation thereof in software interaction interface
Authenticity	If the information objectively and faithfully reflects the real world
Differentiation	Information should be differentiated according to the categories of users on the interface
Identification	Information should be designed visually, thereby identifiable in ways that are visual, comparative and indirect etc.
Transformability	Information needs to be transformable from one form of representation into another form of representation
Storability	Information can be stored by computer memory
Treatability	Computer software system has the function of information processing
Transitivity	Information can be perceived and transmitted by users' sensory system
Compressibility	The same piece of information can be described with different amount of information
Timeliness	Information is a valuable resource. It is effective and usable
Participatory	Information is diffusive and transmissible, thereby sharable

In the design of software interaction interfaces, information has the following characteristics:

3.2   Design Principles Based on Information Identification in Software Interface

Easiness to be Perceived. Designers should choose reasonable, effective and easily perceivable ways to convey information according to the content of the information. Having information on the interface that is easy to perceive is the key. This is not sufficient for but a requisite to a good software interface design.

Understanding of Habits. Users often perceive and understand the information conveyed based on past experience and habitual expectations. Good interface design should accept and adopt the habits that users tend to keep. The way in which certain information is conveyed should be consistent with other ways in which the information may be represented at the same time or with the way in which the information is expressed most recently.

Proper Recurrence. In a design, the information appearing more than once tend to be understood correctly by the user. This is especially true when the same piece of information is expressed in many different ways at the same time. However, redundancy is not simply repeating the same things.

Distinguishability. Similar representations of certain information easily lead to confusion. Designers need to use distinguishable elements to express and handle information. For certain representations of information that may lead to confusion, designer should create some particularity in the way that each piece of information is represented. Deletion of information representation of similar characteristics and emphasis on different characteristics help make information distinguishable.

4 Principles and Strategy of Software Interaction Interface Design

In the process of software interface design, the whole design process must be an integral totality with each and every phase closely connected, instead of with each phase existing separately. The whole design process must be based on demand analysis, which is the prerequisite and foundation of the interface design. The whole design process should focus around the user's acquisition of information, which is the goal of the interface design. The entire design process should be iterative so as the design can be improved. The demand analysis module is the foundation of the whole process of software interaction interface design. The design and implementation module is the key to realize the design whereas the testing and evaluation module is the effective guarantee for the success of the interface design. Designers should abide by the following principles so that the design of the interface is well guided.

4.1 Application of the Principle of Visibility of the Interface

Principle of Being Visually Pleasant. The employment of visual elements should be able to stimulate users' visual sensory organs accordingly. Designers should give full consideration to users' the physiological and psychological reaction to visual stimuli, thereby reasonably maneuvering the display elements such as category, shape, size and color, etc.

Principle of Reasonable Layout. Complex and various visual information should be reasonably divided and orderly arranged so that users have a sense of completeness towards the interface. The simplest, most stable and the most wholistic arrangement of information should be adopted to help users understand and identify the structure and content of the information on the interface.

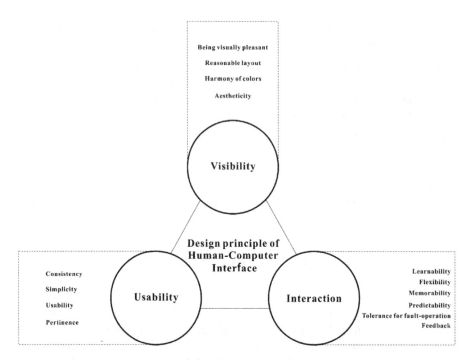

Fig. 4. Principles and strategy of software interaction interface design

Principle of Harmony of Colors. Designers should be familiar with the attributes of colors, fully grasp the influence of colors on users' physiology, psychology and emotion status, and understand the representation and association of colors. Designers need to ensure the conformity of the aesthetic tendency of the user with the stimulation that the color of the information incurs, to ensure the conformity of the content of information interface on the interface with the stimulation that the color of the information incurs, to ensure the conformity of the function of information with the stimulation that the color of the information incurs, and to ensure unity of structural organization of the information on the interface with the stimulation that the color of the information incurs.

Principle of Aesthetics. The aesthetics of the interface depends on the designer's artistic taste and his or her designing ability. Beautiful interface design provide users with a comfortable interactive environment, which will effectively boost users' information cognition and increase their sense of satisfaction.

4.2 Application of the Principle of Interactivity of the Interface

Principle of Learnability. This principle makes the interactive interface almost intuitive. Only when the function intuitive, the operation simple and the status clear, can the user understand upon first sight and master upon first attempt. The interactive interface should provide users with operational rules and basic concepts that are very easy to learn, learning methods of many varieties, tools for relearning and ways for users to familiarize themselves with the elements of the interaction.

Principle of Flexibility. Flexibility is an important manifestation of the interactivity of software interface. Flexible software interaction interfaces can be used in a variety of environments and they acclimate themselves to a wide variety of demands of the users. Users should be allowed to determine how they would like to interact with the computer based on their respective needs. The design should adapt to users' language, culture, knowledge, experience, as well as the user's perception, feeling and cognition ability. Interactive interface enables users to process information in accordance with their preferences and allows users to introduce their own way of representation onto the interface. In this way, a personalized interactive mode of the user can take form.

Principle of Memorability. This can be used to boost the efficiency of users' information interaction. It means the interface being easy to learn to use and operate. Designers should place specific informational objects in a fixed position. Also, designers should logically categorize visual information if they use graphics or symbols to express it. If the designer uses a variety of ways to convey information, users will choose the way to perceive the information based on their personal preference, which will strengthen the user's long-term memory.

Principle of Predictability. Predictable representations of information is considerably easy for users to perceive. The results of its representation can be predicted by users. Predictable representation of information engenders a sense of security and makes the process of user interaction more effective. This sense of security will encourage users to explore some unfamiliar ways of interaction on the interface, thereby enhancing the usability of the interface. The predictability of interactive interfaces can be enhanced by the utility principle of the interface. In the meantime, familiarity can also increase the predictability of the information on the interface.

Principle of Tolerance for Fault-Operation. This helps prevent the user from fault operations and make room for the erroneous operations, preventing critical information from being destroyed on the interface. Designers should remind users of the possible consequences of their actions; gives tips on possible operation for users' negligence and omission; allows the users to withdraw an already-executed command; gives interpretations for users' mistakes and help users to correct mistakes. It is also possible to extend the fault situation for a period of time so that users have enough time to decide what should be done. Also, correction of a fault operation should be conducted without altering the current state of the user interaction.

Principle of Feedback. Feedback information should be expressed in a consistent way. Feedback should be used as an auxiliary means for the training of the users and should be designed according to the users' expected level of knowledge. The types and expressions of the feedback provided should be in accordance with the user's needs and characteristics thereof; The interface should provide timely information feedback and so on.

4.3   Principle of Usability of the Interface

Principle of Consistency. Multiple components and the design objectives of interaction of multiple components need to be unanimous. The same kinds of software should be designed consistently in terms of style. When users perform interactive behavior in relation to different types of elements, the patterns of interaction need to be consistent accordingly. This requires the designer to keep all the select menus, the input and output of commands, the representations of information and other functions of the interface consistent in style. In the design of interface, the consistency of diction of certain information should be kept; the consistency of methods of operation should be maintained; the consistency of layout of interface should be maintained; the consistency of representation of information should be maintained; the consistency of the response to certain information should be kept. Only by keeping the interface design consistent can the interface be more usable.

Principle of Simplicity. Interactive interface should be compact, making it easy for users to understand information, to learn, memorize and to predict the functions and effects of the interface. However, simplicity does not always mean simplification. Simplification often leads to a mediocre interface design, which should be avoided. A simple and compact design can accomplish complex tasks in a reasonable way.

Principle of Usability. Information on the interface should be expressed in a way that is easy for users to comprehend and to read. These ways of representations include: demonstration of control of functions, methods of operation; display of results of information and the current status; display of tips, helpful information, erroneous operation etc. The realization of functions of interactive interface should be simple, convenient and effective. The interface ought to convey the exact information to the users and reveals the status of interaction to the user in a timely manner in the interaction process, so that the user do not feel confused.

Principle of Pertinence. The designer must know who the users are and fully understand the user's intentions, the technology the users master and their existing experience. The designers need to get hold of what the users want. Different types of users and environments make different requirements for the software interface. The emphasis of software interaction interface design should vary accordingly.

5   Establishment of Software Interaction Interface Design Model Based on User Experience

5.1   Establishment of Systematic Research Methods and Implementation Model of Software Interaction Interface Design

In the process of software interface design, the keys are: participation of typical users in the whole design cycle, (a must to ensure that the designer can understand the needs of the user interface for interaction design in a timely manner); appropriate guidelines and principles in the re-design process to ensure the feasibility and effectiveness of the design; Repeated usability testing to guarantee the usability of the design. Considering the foregoing, the model that the paper proposes mainly consists of four parts: demand analysis, interface implementation, testing and evaluation, and in-time iteration. The model as shown in Fig. 4.

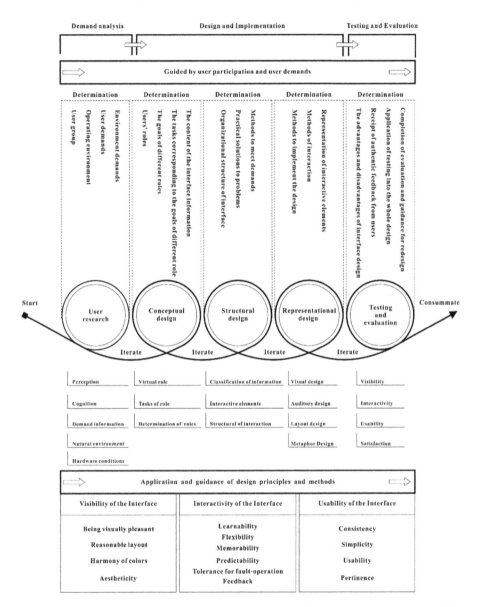

Fig. 5. Systematic research methods and implementation model of software interaction interface design

Demand analysis is the stage where research into possible users and environment of the software interaction interface is conducted. The purpose of this stage is to specify the requirements of the design of interactive interfaces. The problem to be solved by the demand analysis module is to clarify the environment in which the software interface is used; to pinpoint the user group that make use of the software interaction interface; to identify the requirements that conditions that the software interaction interface is used imposes on the design; to bring clear of the users' requirements for the design of software interaction interface; to make explicit all the factors that impact the design of software interaction interface (Fig. 5).

The implementation of interface design is composed of three parts: conceptual design, structural design and representational design. For conceptual design, designers primarily need to determine the roles for the virtual users, and set the tasks and goals for the roles. For structural design, the main task is to determine the methods of interaction for the interface and to create specific elements of interaction. The purpose of this stage is to ensure the feasibility of the conceptual design and the realization thereof to a feasible framework or a prototype. Representational design, mainly concerns the final display of information demanded by the users on the interface, include: the representation of visual and auditory information and layout design thereof, the use of colors and metaphors on the interface, etc. The problems need to be solved in the design and implementation module are: determination of the roles of the virtual users guided by the demand analysis; determination of the goals and tasks of different roles; classification of different types of demands for information and establishment of the framework and prototype of the interface; determination of the methods of interaction that the interface adopts; determination of the content and methods of the representation of interface design.

The Final phase, the testing and evaluation phase is the phase where each part of the interface and its totality go through testing and evaluation of usability. The purpose of this phase is to clarify how this design is better than other designs, to get authentic feedback from users, and to apply the usability testing to the whole design process. The problems to be solved by the testing and evaluation module are: Formation of the visual evaluation results of the interactive interface and employment thereof to guide the redesigning process; Formation of the interactivity evaluation results of the software interface and employment thereof to guide the redesigning process; Formation of the usability evaluation results of the software interface and employment thereof to guide the redesigning process; Formation of the user satisfaction evaluation results of the software interface and employment thereof to guide the redesigning process.

Iteration at any time among the former three phases, is the process where the designers find problems, discover demands and perform repeated design in a timely manner. The purpose of this phase is to remedy the flaws in the design and to optimize the final scheme. The problems need to be solved in the iteration module is to find the problems existing in each stage of the whole design process; to adjust and redesign in a timely manner; to discover new demands for the design that appear at any time during the design process, and to tinker of redesign in time.

5.2   Optimization Theory of Software Interface

Software Interface Design Should Transform from "Endurable" to "Intelligent" to Achieve the Fusion of Human and Machine. Users' operation of computers, using software with interactive interface in its inchoate stages, is conducted in a considerably passive way. The operation is realized by the users' constant adaption to the computer. Users are required to understand all existing functions and ways of interaction on the interface and to go through a long period of time of learning so as to operate the computer. The representation, the transmission and response of information were limited to the computer's scope of capacity of realization its functions and the range of ability of the software interface possesses. It was impossible to consummate the interaction in accordance with the users' needs. Users have been enduring this.

The new generation of software with interactive interface should offer means of information acquisition and recognition corresponding with the user's demands, and the users are going to become the real subjects of the interactive process. Therefore, the design of interactive interface should transform from "endurable" to "intelligent". To achieve harmonious human-computer interaction, it does not only simply take the adaptation of the computer to human's needs, but also the organic fusion of human and computer, that is, the mutual aid of the two in complement. Only by doing so, can the accessibility of information transmittal and the fusion of computer and human be truly achieved.

Software Interface Design Should be Changed from "Chaos" to "Orderly" to Achieve the Fusion of Art and Technology. Nowadays, to meet the needs of the people to improve their lives, products of functionality multiply rapidly. Similarly, complicated technical functions are listed on the interface of software in order to meet the demands of users to materialize many functions. The rise of complicated additional functions makes the software interface appear to be chaotic.

To deal with these chaotic situation, designers are required to make use of simple and compact design methods and interaction design to compensate for the chaos caused by complex functions on the interface. It allows users to get the "essential" information they need from the interface, rather than the accumulation of repressed, chaotic, non-prioritized information. This requires the design to transform from "chaotic" to "orderly". The user's demands for various functions are real. Nevertheless, the "orderly" design is a practical requirement of the design of software interfaces. In order to achieve various functions in an "orderly" design, designers should strive to realize an fusion of art and technology, which is also the fundamental requirement for the design of diversified software interaction interfaces in the future.

Software Interface Design Should Realize the Transformation from "Shape" to "Soul" to Achieve the Fusion of Material and Spirit. Various forms of software interfaces exist and designers should not only treat these interfaces as the realization of functions or the artistic effects thereof, i.e. the representation of "the shape". The interface design should also meet users' demands for spiritual and emotional experience, to assist users to obtain and identify information accurately, namely response to "the soul". This is also the requirement by modern users on interface design.

The interface that meets the spiritual and emotional demands of users should put particular emphasis on o researching into the psychological features of users' emotional activities. Designers should consider the changing patterns of users' psychological and emotional status and pay attention to their spiritual inclination. Designers should make sure that users feel as free, safe, friendly, comfortable and pleasant as possible in the process of interaction and make possible a sense of accomplishment and satisfaction derived from the interaction, so as to make users resonate with the interactive behaviors, thereby realizing the design's transformation from "shape" to "soul".

Humans are animals with rich psychological activities and emotions. People have demands of a higher level, that is, the psychological, spiritual and emotional demands, in the process of human-computer interaction. Therefore, the future design of software interaction interfaces should realize the fusion of users' material and spiritual needs (Fig. 6).

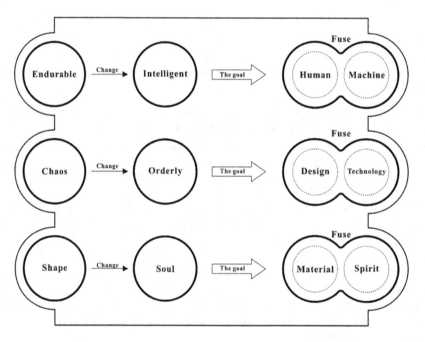

Fig. 6. The optimization theory of "three transformation and fusion" of software interaction interface design

6   The Trend of Software Interaction Interface Design Based on User Experience

Nowadays, the ubiquity of human-computer interaction systems increases the speed of people's communication to such an extent that used to be beyond imagination. The keys to future software interface design are: the application of new technology, the improvement of the users' ability to perform information interaction between the computer, the fully realization of the software interface to meet the various needs of users, so as to achieve the ultimate purpose of harmonious interaction. Therefore, the design of future software interaction interfaces should be more universal, intelligent and authentic.

The design of future software interfaces should fully consider its universality. Designers should take into consideration of the universality of the software interface design and cater to the needs of different groups of users. The design of software interaction interfaces is not only relevant to the display of the interface or to the feeling that it gives the user, but also relevant to the creation of peculiarity and design of intelligence. Designers should familiarize the interactive interfaces with the users, make them understand the users' needs, recognize the users' language, facial representation and body movements, etc.; The software interfaces should be able to adjust themselves to a user or a task by altering its working status [12]. Designers should make use of the users' multiple sensory faculties and channels of behavior to enable interaction thereof with the computer system in parallel and non-precise ways in order to improve the naturality and efficiency of human-computer interaction and ultimately realize better usability, effectiveness and naturalness of software interface [13]. Ideal environment for interactive interfaces should transcend the realistic conditions, and should immerse the users in multi-dimensional space of information. Relying on their own perception and cognition to acquire information from the interface from all aspects and in every possible way, the users will exert their voluntary initiative as the core of interaction, thus come the natural, reasonable and effective solution for problem and acquisition of information.

7   Conclusion

In this paper, we study and integrate the systematic research methods of the design of interactive interfaces based on user experience in the process of human-computer interaction, making up for the systematic and methodical defects in the researches based on design principles of software interface design. After theoretical analysis combined with practical experience, a thorough analysis of design of software interactive interface in the process of human-computer interaction is proposed. Based on the research content put forward, reasonable and feasible design strategies are proposed. A relatively complete and systematic software interface design model is established. Also, the optimization theory of "three transformation and fusion" set up for software interface design come into being. The essay puts forward opinions on and suggestions for the future of software interface design. Interactive interfaces in the future will be more closely adapted to people's natural way of work and life. Natural and efficient software interaction interface design is the major demand of future users.

References

1. Xiang, C.: What Does Information Mean—Information Science and Humanistic View. Anhui Education Publishing Housse, Hefei (2002)
2. Yu, X.: Research on interactive design of nonmaterial society. J. Shenzhen Univ. Ed. Humanit. Soc. Sci. **23**, 107–109 (2006)
3. Vredenburg, K., Isensee, S., Righi, C.: User-Centered Design: An Intergrated Approach. Prentice Hall, Upper Saddle River (2001)
4. Luo, S., Zhu, S.: User Experience and Innovative Design of Products. Mechanical Industry Press, Beijing (2011)
5. Lohse, G.L.: A cognitive model for understanding graphical perception. Hum.-Comput. Interact. **8**, 353–388 (1993)
6. Wang, A.: Cognitive Psychology, 1st edn. Peking University Press, Beijing (1992)
7. Norman, D.A.: Emotion and design: attractive things work better. Interact. Mag. **ix**(4), 36–42 (2002)
8. Shneiderman, B.: User Interface Design - Effective Human-Computer Interaction Strategy, 3rd edn. Electronic Industry Press, Beijing (2004). Trans. by G. Zhang et al.
9. Salvendy, G.: Human-Computer Interaction: User-Centered Design and Evaluation. Tsinghua University Press, Beijing (2003). Trans. by J. Dong
10. Shneiderman, B.: Designing the User Interface, Strategies for Effective Human-Computer Interaction. Addison-Wesley, Reading (1998)
11. Zhen, L.: Information Identification Technology. China Machine Press, Beijing (2006)
12. Druin, A.: Cooperative inquiry: developing new technologies for children with children. In: Proceedings of CHI 1999, pp. 592–599, Pittsburgh, PA, 15–20 May 1999. ACM, New York (1999)
13. Maybury, M.T., Wahlster, W.: Intelligent user interfaees: an introduetion. In: Maybury, M.T., Wahlster, W. (eds.) Readings Intelligent Interfaees, pp. 1–13. MorganKaufmann, SanFraneiseo (1998)

Analysis on Dimensional Design and Its Application

Qunye Gu and Guangshuai Zhang[✉]

Shandong University of Art & Design, No. 1255th, No. 1th Road, Science Park,
Changqing District University, Changqing campus, Jinan, Shandong, China
zgsl981@qq.com

Abstract. Modern design methods include computer-aided design, optimization design, reliability design, etc., and are with solid theory foundation. Modern design methods can be applied to solve some practical problems encountered in projects, and can improve product design and quality, thus promoting design development.

With the rapid development of Internet technology, the whole process of design activities are added with new features in terms of expression, communication and spreading means, embodying the concept of modernism, while existing design system has been unable to meet the demands of the new era. The main purpose of this paper is to build a new design system to serve the world view of the Internet era by putting forward the concept of the Dimensional -Design, and analysing real cases.

Keywords: Dimensions · Dimensionality · Interaction · Carrier
Technology · Dimensional design

1 Definition of Dimensions

1.1 Broad Definition of Dimensions

Dimensions refers to the multiple index of unknowns, commonly used to refer to dimensionality or independent spaces. Multiple exponents of unknowns is called dimensions, such as in mathematics the n-th power of a number can be called the n-th dimension of the number; or in physics, the meta-spaces can be called the meta-dimensions. So the dimensions refer not just to the number of squares in mathematics.

1.2 Dimensions Culture

ACGN originated in the mid-to-late 1990s and is an acronym for Animation, Comic, Game and Novel. Later the concept of Dimensions was introduced into ACGN works to refer to the fantasy world and the collection of other fantastic elements. For example, the world where magic or bullets exist is often referred to as "warp dimension world", or simply "warp dimension."

Cospa refers to the two-dimensional plane in ACGN culture. It is a term for imaginary worlds in Animation, Comic, Game and Novel (Fig. 1).

© Springer International Publishing AG, part of Springer Nature 2018
A. Marcus and W. Wang (Eds.): DUXU 2018, LNCS 10918, pp. 77–90, 2018.
https://doi.org/10.1007/978-3-319-91797-9_6

Fig. 1. Cospa comics works

The Three Dimensions is the dimensions where we exist, that is, the real world, including image or video works made from real-world people and things, such as live-action movies, TV dramas, and live-action photographs.

2.5-Dimensions refers to the collection of things "between cospa and three dimensions". It is abstract and covers various elements which can mainly be categorized into two types: three dimensions elements shown by using cospa elements, such as games and animations; and cospa elements shown by using three dimensions elements, such as Garage Kits, Voice Actor, Cosplay, Doll Outfit, etc. (Figs. 2 and 3).

Fig. 2. Garage Kits

In summary, dimensions culture can be understood from the aspect of dimensionality: 1-dimension means straight line or linear space; cospa means planes; 3-dimensions menas real and three-dimensional spaces; and also some concepts such as 2.5-dimensions are extended from the above foundations.

Fig. 3. Cosplay

1.3 Application of Dimensional Design

Although there are other words to substitute "dimensions" in language, the word "dimensions" popularized since it's widely used by certain groups. Dimensional concept in design area is referred to as Dimensional Design, which is a dimensionality concept but differs from that in dimensions culture or in the broad sense of dimensions.

We shall firstly come to a systematic understanding of the concept of "dimensionality":

Dimensionality is the number of the abstract concepts of "connection" of things, so the premise of this concept is that everything is relative. The connections one thing has to others constitutes its changing dimensions. In mathematics, dimensions is the number of parameters needed to describe a mathematical object under certain conditions (Fig. 4).

a[0]
a[1]
a[2]
a[3]
a[4]

一维数组

a[0][0]	a[0][1]	a[0][2]	a[0][3]	a[0][4]
a[1][0]	a[1][1]	a[1][2]	a[1][3]	a[1][4]
a[2][0]	a[2][1]	a[2][2]	a[2][3]	a[2][4]
a[3][0]	a[3][1]	a[3][2]	a[3][3]	a[3][4]
a[4][0]	a[4][1]	a[4][2]	a[4][3]	a[4][4]

二维数组

Fig. 4.

The physical dimensionality is extended from the space concept: 0 dimension is a point with no length; 1 dimension is a line with only length; 2-dimensions is a plane with area formed by the length and width (or curve); 3-dimensions adds height to 2-dimensions and has volume. The dimensions in dimensions culture is closer to the physical dimensions in meaning (Fig. 5).

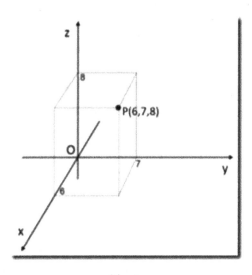

Fig. 5.

From a philosophical point of view, the way people observe, think, and describe things are known as the philosophical dimensions; for example, people may observe and think about the "design" thing from dimensions of "content, domain and method", or from the "carrier, form and space" of design.

When we come back to the concept of dimensional design, from the philosophical point of view and by combining with the current situation and development of today's design industry, we can divide its dimensions into content, interaction, carrier and technical means. The "thinking point of view" that divide design by using current elements is dimensional design.

2   Concepts in Dimensional Design

2.1   Dimensionality of Dimensional Design

The dimensionality of dimensional design is the "thinking point of view" from which the design elements are divided. In the following I shall explain the dimensionality of dimensional design through the development process of the design industry.

Modern design can be broadly divided into visual design, art design and product design. Design of the poster, 3D model animation, product, etc. in the early stage concentrates on the physical content of the object itself, which is the physical dimension of design, or can be defined as one-dimensional design.

With the development of science and technology, the dimensionality of dimensional design continues to expand, and enters the multi-design era, no longer confined to physical contents. Taking game design as an example, the designers need to design interactive patterns in addition to physical contents such as scenes and characters in the game. Interactive patterns may be the type of games, such as fighting games or shooting games; or interactive means such as interacting through a handle or a touch screen. These are the man-machine interaction dimensions of dimensional design, which requires the common realization of the two dimensions of vision and interaction, and thus can also be called cospa design.

Game design also includes carrier design. For example, game machine used to be the carrier of electronic games, which was then substituted by computers and mobile terminals as the hardware technology developed. This is the carrier dimension of dimensional design.

In face of fierce competition, the game design process also applied a variety of technical means: from the early stand-alone games to Internet games; augmented reality games and virtual real-world games emerged as graphics technologies developed; big data is being used in increasingly more large games with the development of computing and storage technologies. This is the technical dimension of dimensional design.

2.2   Concepts of Dimensional Design

3D animation technology is the emerging technology with the development of computer hardware and software technologies. It is the use of 3D model animation software to create a virtual world. It is mainly used in the dimension of physical content design, with main applications of video animation, advertising effects, virtual simulation, etc. It's called one-dimensional design from the perspective of dimensional design (Fig. 6).

Fig. 6. 3D animation

Mobile internet is an emerging technology after the Internet and mobile communication technologies are developed independently and then merged together. Nowadays, the mobile Internet is stronger than the Internet of mobile products. The mobile Internet is mainly applied in the man-machine interaction or technology dimensions, with main applications of mobile APP, mobile payment, WAP, two-dimensional code, navigation, location services, etc.

The design of mobile Internet generally involves two cross modules of functional design and information design. Functional design is broken into user interface (UI), content design and interaction design. Information design covers databases, artificial intelligence and big data. Overall, however, the mobile Internet-based products are designed based on two dimensions of functionality and information, which is thus called cospa design (Fig. 7).

Fig. 7. VR equipment

Virtual Reality (VR) uses modern advanced technology with computer technology as its core to create a verisimilar virtual environment that integrates vision, sound and tactile sense. Users can interact with virtual objects through the necessary input and output devices, and get immersive experience. This kind of computer-generated virtual environment can be a representation of a particular objective world, or can be a purely fictional world (Fig. 8).

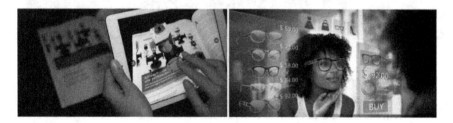

Fig. 8. AR application

Augmented Reality (AR) is also known as mixed reality. It uses computer technology to apply virtual information to the real world, where the real environment and virtual objects are superimposed and exist in real time on the same screen or in space. It is a real-time technology that not only shows the real world information, but also displays virtual information simultaneously. The two kinds of information complement each other. The goal of this technology is to set up a virtual world in the real world on the screen. AR is mainly used in the dimensions of man-machine interaction and technology, with main application areas of education, games, medical treatment, restoration of historic sites, cultural relics protection, advertising and so on.

VR and AR are mainly used in the dimensions of man-machine interaction and technology in dimensional design. VR content includes animation, video, artificial intelligence, databases and the Internet, and thus is called three-dimensional design (Fig. 9).

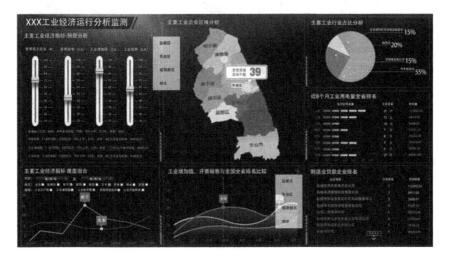

Fig. 9.

"Big Data" is a kind of information asset that needs new processing models to provide decision-making power, insight and process optimization capabilities to adapt to massive, high growth and diversified business. The key of big data technology is not to master the huge data information, but to process these data to make them meaningful. In other words, if big data is likened to an industry, then the key to making such an industry profitable is to increase the "processing power" of the data and "add value" to the data through "processing." Big data is mainly used in the dimension of technology, with application areas of education, healthcare, military, e-commerce, etc. (Fig. 10).

AI (Artificial Intelligence) is a comprehensive system developed through the interpenetration of computer science, cybernetics, information theory, linguistics, neurophysiology, psychology, mathematics and philosophy; it's a branch of science that trys to understand the underlying mechanisms of human intelligence and realize it on machines. Since ancient times, humans have had the idea of a smart machine that can assist or even surpass human beings to complete tasks that need to be done through self-thinking.

AI and big data are not only used in the dimensions of information, content and carrier design, but also in autonomous learning, data analysis, prediction and thinking, which is higher level of dimensional design.

Fig. 10.

2.3   Industry Application of Dimensional Design

As an important part of traditional Chinese culture, traditional Chinese medicine (TCM) is based on graphic and specimen samples, such as Compendium of Materia Medica. Chinese medicine literature and records have always relied on text, picture books graphics, physical models, herbs specimen, etc. With the development and application of digital media technologies, the forms of TCM are enriched, and multimedia forms such as video recording and sound recording have appeared. Important progress has been obtained in TCM industry design. With the continuous expansion of the dimensions of dimensional design, medical digital forms are also being enriched.

Our technical team developed a TCM digital platform during 2016–2017, which gives full play to the multidimensional design thinking in content, information, technology, big data and artificial intelligence.

In the project, we firstly designed (one-dimensional) graphics, sound and texts of Chinese medicine. Then we collected images and sorted out feature points through compilation of texts, two-dimensional scanning, picturing, camera shooting, etc. Then we selected typical herbs to build virtual digital models for them through 3D scanning, digital engraving, 3D modeling, sectional design, etc.

We also set up a TCM application software, which put user data and medicinal herb data on Internet through database, server and customer end. Thus two dimensional design of medicinal herbs introduction and physical features is completed.

We also applied AR and VR technologies on TCM to provide more intuitive and convenient interactive experience, breaking the constraints of traditional communication. In augmented reality and virtual space, multi-dimensional product experience is provided. In addition, we are trying to make machines learn to identify the characteristics of medicinal herbs through the analysis of big data, and finally being able to identify the authenticity of medicinal herbs to achieve a higher level of design and application.

Our technical team conducted comprehensive analysis after we got the topic and found out that identification of the herbs and their products was the greatest challenge for TCM application as well as for the system. With the rapid development of computer technology and three-dimensional image processing technology, people are expecting a tool that can effectively identify herbs for the purpose of both scientific research and daily life.

According to the concept of dimensional design, we need first of all design the physical contents of Chinese medicine. We collected literatures, pictures and materials of Chinese medicine and input them into the system to form a data base. Then we used 3-D model animation technology to generate virtual herbs on the computer or mobile terminal, so that customers can view the appearance and internal structure of the herbs. The growth process of the herbs can also be demonstrated through animation. All those graphics and animations are to provide data support for follow-up machine identification of Chinese herbs (Fig. 11).

With the support of data base, we need some interactive means to identify and display Chinese herbs. From the perspective of man-machine interaction in dimensional design, the traditional methods of planar and passive reading should be improved. In our system, users can view the appearance and internal structure of traditional Chinese herbs through mouse or touch screen, or learn the growing process of the herbs through animation display by clicking the hot spot area, or get more direct and convenient interactive experience through AR and VR technologies. In addition, the system's image recognition module can get images of the herbs through the mobile camera terminal to determine whether they are authentic (Fig. 12).

From the perspective of carrier of dimensional design, the system involves terminal carriers of computer, mobile terminal, AR/VR equipment, etc.; the 3-D identification system is carried on computers, which is divided into the client end (the 3-D identification and display system) and the management end (the management platform). The image recognition system is carried on mobile terminals, which owns big data and artificial intelligence as back-office support.

From the perspective of technology of dimensional design, the system involves technologies of big data, artificial intelligence and computer graphics and image technology. After the image system of herbs or herb products is established, the machine can learn by itself to improve its identification capability. The graphics system combines mobile Internet technology, big data, artificial intelligence technology, etc. to obtain ingredients and ratio of extract of each drug; which can help the system provide optimum mixture ratio according to specific physique condition of customers and drug content.

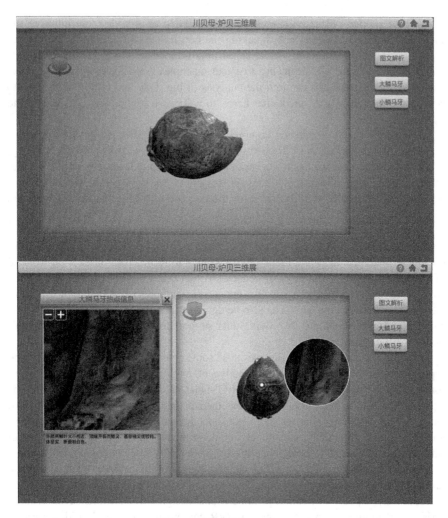

Fig. 11.

In addition, the AR and VR modules are also applied in the system. With AR technology, TCM knowledge is displayed in a stereoscopic way in augmented reality; the data base of which is obtained by scanning illustrations or pictures in Chinese medical textbooks by using mobile terminals. With VR technology, users can use wearable devices such as HTC Vive or VR helmet to experience the processing of Chinese herbal medicines through the handle.

The digital TCM system breaks the limitations of traditional methods such as plane and passive reading by using computer, mobile terminal and VR equipment as carriers, and adopting mobile Internet technology, 3D model animation technology, man-machine interaction technology, big data and artificial intelligence technology. It has played an important role in TCM application and laid solid foundation for the inheritance and popularization of TCM.

Fig. 12.

2.4   Meaning of Dimensional Design

The concept of dimensional design can be applied in various industries, to form a new multi-dimensional design system. Combined with the concept of "thinking angle" mentioned above, these new multi-dimensional conceptual designs are collectively referred to as dimensional design. The concept of dimensional design is a breakthrough in multi-design framework under the Internet environment and is an interpretation of design in terms of content, interaction, carrier and technical means.

With the development of new media technologies, more technical elements are being incorporated in dimensional design. The traditional design system is represented by technologies such as mobile Internet, AR, VR, man-machine interaction, big data and AI. The hardware and technical means are an important guarantee for dimensional design.

Future virtual world formed by Internet shall own complete system of world view, which is different from the physical world in terms of expression, communication and other aspects. A new design system is to be built to serve the online world view. In the future, the boundary between virtuality and reality will become increasingly vague, and dimensional design emerges as the times require. In the future, design will cover more dimensions and design languages will also be diversified. They will be more enriched in voice, audition, interaction, immersion and artificial intelligence.

Dimensional design, a parallel existence of traditional design, is a new mode of design thinking, and will no longer be subject to traditional constraints of discipline, tools, performance, industry, etc. It shall be broader, more diversified, intelligent and cross-dimensional.

References

Julier, G., Qian, F.: The Culture of Design, 3rd edn. Yilin Press, Beijing (2015)

Brynjolfsson, E., McAfee, A., Yongjun, J.: The Second Machine Age - How will Digital Technology Change Our Economy and Society. China Citic Press, Beijing (2016)

Wang, W.: Leap Motion Man-Machine Interaction Application Development. Xi'an University of Electronic Science and Technology Press, Xi'an (2015)

Greenberg, C., Yubing, S.: Art & Culture. Guangx i Normal University Press, Guangxi (2015)

Kelly, K., Yan, L.: What Technology Wants. Electronics Industry Press, Beijing (2016)

Analysis and Design for Mobile Applications: A User Experience Approach

Zhao Huang and ZhuoYu Tian$^{(\boxtimes)}$

School of Computer Science, Shaanxi Normal University, Xi'an 710119,
People's Republic of China
{zhaohuang, zhuoyutian}@snnu.edu.cn

Abstract. Mobile applications development has brought the new opportunities for businesses to market their brands and products through a new channel. Such a channel encourages an increasing number of users engaging in mobile applications. However, the challenge of designing "useful" mobile applications still remains. To date, only few studies have been done on the identification of user experience features on mobile applications design. To this end, this study aims to provide a systematic review of mobile applications analysis and design, exploring main design features from a user experience perspective. Three design dimensions, namely usability, functionality and aesthetic design have been focused on in the study. The results imply that current mobile applications design needs to be further improved to meet users' experience. The major contribution is to propose a systematic analysis of mobile applications for business managers and designers.

Keywords: Mobile applications · User experience approach · Aesthetic design

1 Introduction

With the rapid development in mobile and wireless technologies, an increasing number of users engage in mobile applications (apps). Users are now able to customize their mobile platforms with applications that suit their needs [1]. This trend, not only changes and impacts on the way of users' living and thinking, but also brings huge opportunities to business to define their mobile marketing. Mobile applications have generated intensive interest within business due to the high user engagement and the positive image that a brand transfers through applications [2]. It has been proved that the use of mobile applications has a positive persuasive impact increasing interest in the brand. In contrast to other forms of advertisements, mobile applications are welcomed as "useful," which suggests that they may be one of the most powerful forms of advertising yet developed [3]. Mobile applications design varies from business to business in terms of strategies, goals and feature designs etc. The qualities of mobile applications also differ significantly from one to one. How can these businesses get on the right track of designing their mobile applications? Some studies have been conducted in brand experiences, which are not related to mobile applications; some have been carried out on user satisfaction of mobile applications in specific domains, such as government and location based service. However, to date, no research has been done

© Springer International Publishing AG, part of Springer Nature 2018
A. Marcus and W. Wang (Eds.): DUXU 2018, LNCS 10918, pp. 91–100, 2018.
https://doi.org/10.1007/978-3-319-91797-9_7

on the identification of the framework and user experience features which can be of use to businesses developing their mobile applications.

To this end, this research aims to provide a systematic review of mobile applications analysis and design, identifying main constructs and features in mobile applications design from a user experience perspective. To be more specific, three dimensions in the user experience design, namely usability, functionality and aesthetic design have been addressed in order to develop more user-centered mobile applications. Our main contribution is to propose a systematic analysis of mobile applications for business managers and designers. The different criteria (usability features, functional features, aesthetic features) proposed in this research can be used as a guidance in the development of mobile applications.

This paper is structured as follows. In Sect. 2 we provide some background on user experience design, and discuss usability, functionality and aesthetic design in mobile applications. In Sect. 3 we present our research method and develop associated evaluation criteria. We then detail our data analysis and discussion in Sect. 4. Finally, our conclusion, implications and limitations are detailed in Sect. 5.

2 User Experience Design

User experience (UX), a buzz word in the field of Human-Computer Interaction (HCI), can be understood as a consequence of a user's internal state, the characteristics of the designed system and the context within which the interaction occurs [4]. User experience is crucial for the product designers to enhance user satisfaction and foster user interaction [5]. In this study, a number of features necessary for designing effective mobile applications are reviewed and categorized mainly from the field of HCI. Tables 1, 2 and 3 present relevant dimensions of UX design and their detailed design features from the literature review. Three main dimensions are focused on: functionality, usability, and Aesthetic design. Each dimension has its detailed design features.

Table 1. Usability dimension

UX design dimension	Design feature	Description	Refs
Usability	Navigation	To clearly show current position To clearly show exit button To support cancellation and redo To make process design meet users' needs	[5, 9, 12]
	Learnability	To support user learning capability To explain and guide for complex interaction	[13]
	Standard and consistency	To present information in consistent and standardized form To keep consistent color scheme	[14]
	User language	To use user understandable language To use short and direct language	[15]

Usability is one of most important design dimension for mobile application design [6]. According to the ISO [7], usability refers to the effectiveness, efficiency and satisfaction with the extent to which a mobile application can be used by the specific users to achieve specific goals in the specific context of use. Since mobile application usability differs from mobile device usability, the former has been importantly addressed for mobile application interface design, which is related to how ease of use and user-friendliness. Ease of use refers to the degree to which users perceive that using the particular system can achieve their performance [8]. User-friendliness is about the perception of aesthetic design in terms of mobile application interface [9]. Many studies use multiple features to explain mobile application usability design. For example, Zhang and Adipat [10] explain that mobile application usability should be learnability, efficiency, memorability, error, satisfaction effectiveness, comprehensibility and learning performance. Helander and Khalid [11] describe usability dimension in aspects of simplicity; support; accessibility; visibility; reversible action; feedback and personalization. In their explanation, simplicity refers to using simply functions; support is about maintaining user in control; accessibility and visibility may be implied by making objects accessible and visible; reversible action is to provide undo functions at all times; feedback is to provide visible comment mechanism after services, and personalization is related to allow user to customize interface.

Functionality is a critical factor in mobile application design because it is about the quality of mobile application being functional [16]. Functionality commonly refers to a set of functions and properties that satisfy users' requirements in the completion of their tasks, and contains a number of sub design elements including navigation, Accuracy [17], Suitability [14] and security [18]. Navigation refers to ability to guide user movement; accuracy is the ability to provide the right results with the required degree

Table 2. Functionality dimension

UX design dimension	Design feature	Description	Refs
Functionality	Search function	To provide search function To build indexes of data	[16]
	Response time	To offer accurate feedback To provide timely feedback for user action	[20]
	Control	To use user familiar controls To place aside the controls which may result serious consequences To reuse same controls over pages To show accurate control status To use clear and effective text on controls To allow user to control flow, reduce use of the system mandatory	[17, 21–23]
	Data preservation	To make function work without errors To minimize error occurrence	[18]
	Content relevance	To offer relevant information or content	[14]

of precision; suitability refers to the ability to have the adequate functions for the required tasks; and security is to prevent unauthorized access to services or data. Indeed, mobile applications are composed of functional (e.g., search function, tracking function) or non-functional (e.g., information presentation, information structure) components. Both functions and services constitute the basis for user interaction [19]. With a higher level of functionality, users can better use mobile applications, which can lead to a greater performance in interacting with information and services [6].

Aesthetics design has a long historic tradition in the research literature, and has been considered as a core property of mobile application design. It has been the subject of discussions by researches, such as beautiful objects incorporate proportion, harmony, and unity [15], and designers for example universal elements of beauty are order, symmetry, and definiteness [24]. Huang and Benyoucef [25] argue that aesthetics design provides the first impression of information systems. Users usually judge an aesthetics quickly because before other cognitive processes take place, preconscious judgements based on visual design elements are already made. The issues of aesthetics were raised by Wells et al. [9] whose aim is to discover the relationships between different design dimensions and perceived attractiveness through systematic manipulations of visual stimuli. Such relationship is further explored by Hoehle and Venkatesh [6], who claim that aesthetics design closely relates to user performance, level of usage and perceived quality of information systems. For example, by designing more aesthetic and identifiable icons, users can search for information and services more efficiently [9]. Moreover, providing rich visual graphics can increase overall quality of mobile applications, which in turn may attract user attention and support their task completion [6]. Accordingly, aesthetics design in mobile applications should be emphasized on a number of sub design features, including text, color, format, icon and multimedia.

Table 3. Aesthetic dimension

UX design dimension	Design feature	Description	Refs
Aesthetic design	Text	To make a layered text arrangement To improve readability To use list appropriately	[9, 13]
	Color	To make color scheme meet product features and characteristics of the target user groups To use limited color	[26]
	Format	To make proper spacing To distinct layers To use proper font size To use line spacing, alignment, indentation	[9, 27]
	Logo	To make logo appearance in each main page	[19]
	Icon	To make icons easy to understand To indicate clear, accurate information To make icons matched the overall style	[23, 24]
	Multimedia	To use meaningful multimedia effects To make multimedia style matched overall style To use animation properly	[28, 29]

3 Research Method

In order to better understand the design for mobile applications in this study, a heuristic evaluation was used on 45 branded applications developed by top 11 Fast Moving Consumer Goods (FMCG) brands. We believe it is a sector close to daily consumers.

In order to conduct the evaluation, we have developed the evaluation criteria of each dimension of user experience design (see example in Table 4). The criteria are adapted and refined from the literature review presented in the previous section.

Table 4. Evaluation criteria development

UX design dimension	Design features	Evaluation criteria
Usability	Navigation	App indicates current position
		App shows exit button at all times
		App provides cancellation and redo at any time
	Learnability	App reduces user memory load
		App offer clear user action feedback
		App provides guidance for complex interaction
	Language	App uses short and clear user language
		App employs understandable language
	Standard and consistency	App keep content expression consistent and standardized
		App uses consistent color scheme
Functionality	Search function	App makes search function available
		App allows users to search information in their own way
	Structure	App provides clear content structure
		App makes function shortcut available
		App places key content in a easy read location
	Control	App allows user control flow, reduce use of the system mandatory
		App process design meets needs of users task execution
		App place the controls in logical order
		App uses user familiar controls
		App reuses same controls over pages
		App provides clear text on controls
		App shows accurate control status
	Response time	App delivers timely feedback to users
		App provides accurate feedback
Aesthetic design	Text	App arranges text in a hierarchical way
		App ensures images corresponding to the context
		App uses list appropriately
	Color	App uses proper color scheme to meet user needs
		App utilizes limited color
	Format	App offers proper spacing
		App uses distinct layers
		App uses use proper font size
		App uses line spacing, alignment, indentation
	Logo	App makes icons easy to understand
		App provides logo on each page
		App makes icons style matched the overall style
	Multimedia	App uses appropriate and meaningful multimedia effects
		App makes multimedia style matched the overall style

Two coders conducted the content of branded applications. The coding categories were reviewed and discussed by both coders. Each item was coded with 0 and 1, while 1 is implied that the app has achieved the design criteria. Unclear items were clarified during the coding procedure. 45 branded applications were coded together and non-disagreement was found among the coders.

4   Results and Discussion

Understanding mobile applications design in terms of usability and the factors affecting user experience is crucial for the mobile applications designers to enhance customer satisfaction. Our results found a number of weak user experienced design features in selected 45 mobile applications. Among them, the weak design features that have been commonly found on the target mobile applications include "key information being not placed in a central location on the page", "inconsistent display format on each page" and "the absence of search functionality" (Fig. 1).

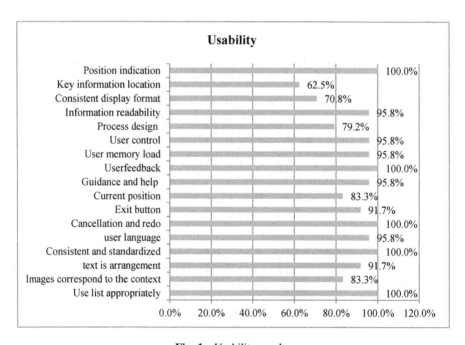

Fig. 1. Usability results

To be specific, central location is a focal point where it is used to emphasize the key element of a page. Since information or subject is presented in such a location, it makes the information or subject stand out and controls the users' gaze, drawing attention to the main area of the page. However, failure of presenting information in an easy read location may impact mobile applications content readability, which may take users more time to get important information (Fig. 2).

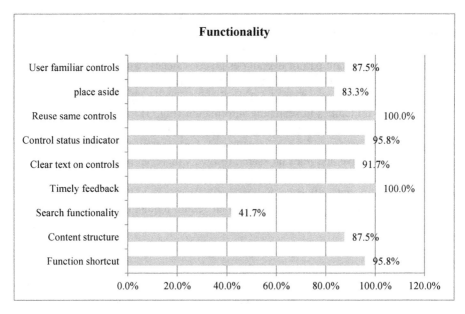

Fig. 2. Functionality results

Display format consistency is used to establish unity across pages of mobile applications, strengthening visual subject recognition and reducing layout clutter. It helps users understand that information visually provided is organized and presented in

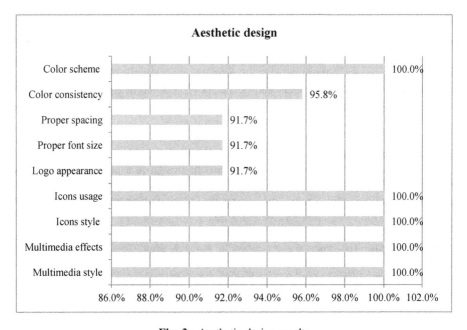

Fig. 3. Aesthetic design results

the same way throughout the applications. As such, after the initial experience with the mobile applications, consistent display format enables users to easily locate information to meet their needs. As indicated by Agarwal and Venkatesh [13], consistent display form an important part of overall design consistency, which may lead to better user performance and lower error rates. Conversely, failure of information presentation with consistent format may affect visual continuity of the mobile applications, which may cause users difficulties in searching information (Fig. 3).

Another weak user experience design feature is the absence of search function. The search engine is used to retrieve information. A high search capability can generate precise, comprehensive and relevant search results, which can help users easily locate the target object. Conversely, the lack of search engine or search engine with weak searching capability may influence the search effectiveness, so that users may feel it is difficult to find useful information to meet their search requirements.

5 Conclusion

Mobile applications development has brought challenges and opportunities for businesses to market their brands and products through a new channel. Traditional companies shall move towards this new culture facing together evolving technologies, changing user behaviors, and new marketing paradigm and strategies. To overcome these challenges, this study conducts a user experience approach to analyze mobile applications design, especially focusing on usability, functionality and aesthetic design dimensions. The results found a set of common weak design features on the target mobile applications, include "key information being not placed in a central location on the page", "inconsistent display format on each page" and "the absence of search functionality". Moreover, the particular design issues have been also identified on the mobile applications. It suggests that current mobile applications need to improve their design quality to meet the users' needs, supporting them to achieve their desirable outcomes. The major contribution is to propose a systematic analysis of mobile applications for business managers and designers. The different criteria (i.e. usability features, functional features, aesthetic features) proposed in this research can be used as a guidance in the development of mobile applications.

However, these are some limitations in this study. First, this study only addresses a user perspective, which may provide a limited viewpoint from the business side. Further study may consider the mobile applications design in aspects of brand goals and business strategies. Second, two coders are invited to conduct the content of branded applications, which may limit our results. More participants may be involved in order to provide more comprehensive results.

Acknowledgments. This study was supported by research grants funded by the "National Natural Science Foundation of China" (Grant No. 61771297), and "the Fundamental Research Funds for the Central Universities" (GK201803062, GK200902018).

References

1. Kortum, P., Sorber, M.: Measuring the usability of mobile applications for phones and tablets. Int. J. Hum. Comput. Interact. **31**, 518–529 (2015)
2. Hutton, G., Rodnick, S.: Smartphone opens up new opportunities for smart marketing. ADMAP **44**(11), 22–24 (2009)
3. Bellman, S., et al.: The effectiveness of branded mobile phone apps. J. Interact. Mark. **25**, 191–200 (2011)
4. Hassenzahl, M., Tractinsky, N.: User experience-a research agenda. Behav. Inf. Technol. **25**(2), 91–97 (2006)
5. Treiblmaier, H.: Web site analysis: a review and assessment of previous research. Commun. Assoc. Inf. Syst. **19**(1), 39 (2007)
6. Hoehle, H., Venkatesh, V.: Mobile application usability: conceptualization and instrument development. MIS Q. **39**(2), 435–472 (2015)
7. Venkatesh, V., Ramesh, V.: Web and wireless site usability: understanding differences and modeling use. MIS Q. 181–206 (2006)
8. Kumar, V., Mukerji, B., Butt, I., Persaud, A.: Factors for successful e-government adoption: a conceptual framework. Electron. J. E-govern. **5**(1) (2007)
9. Wells, J.D., Parboteeah, V., Valacich, J.S.: Online impulse buying: understanding the interplay between consumer impulsiveness and website quality. J. Assoc. Inf. Syst. **12**(1), 32 (2011)
10. Zhang, D., Adipat, B.: Challenges, methodologies, and issues in the usability testing of mobile applications. Int. J. Hum. Comput. Interact. **18**(3), 293–308 (2005)
11. Helander, M.G., Khalid, H.M.: Modeling the customer in electronic commerce. Appl. Ergon. **31**(6), 609–619 (2000)
12. Adipat, B., Zhang, D., Zhou, L.: The effects of tree-view based presentation adaptation on mobile web browsing. Mis Q. 99–121 (2011)
13. Agarwal, R., Venkatesh, V.: Assessing a firm's web presence: a heuristic evaluation procedure for the measurement of usability. Inf. Syst. Res. **13**(2), 168–186 (2002)
14. Tan, F.B., Tung, L.L., Xu, Y.: A study of web-designers'criteria for effective business-to-consumer (B2C) websites using the repertory grid technique. J. Electron. Commer. Res. **10**(3), 155 (2009)
15. De Wulf, K., Schillewaert, N., Muylle, S., Rangarajan, D.: The role of pleasure in web site success. Inf. Manag. **43**(4), 434–446 (2006)
16. Dou, W., Lim, K.H., Su, C., Zhou, N., Cui, N.: Brand positioning strategy using search engine marketing. Mis Q. 261–279 (2010)
17. Seffah, A., Donyaee, M., Kline, R.B., Padda, H.K.: Usability measurement and metrics: a consolidated model. Softw. Qual. J. **14**(2), 159–178 (2006)
18. Sarker, S., Wells, J.D.: Understanding mobile handheld device use and adoption. Commun. ACM **46**(12), 35–40 (2003)
19. Kang, S.H.: The impact of digital iconic realism on anonymous interactants' mobile phone communication. In: CHI 2007 Extended Abstracts on Human Factors in Computing Systems. ACM (2007)
20. Verhagen, T., van Dolen, W.: The influence of online store beliefs on consumer online impulse buying: a model and empirical application. Inf. Manag. **48**(8), 320–327 (2011)
21. Jokela, T., Koivumaa, J., Pirkola, J., Salminen, P., Kantola, N.: Methods for quantitative usability requirements: a case study on the development of the user interface of a mobile phone. Pers. Ubiquit. Comput. **10**(6), 345–355 (2006)

22. Gebauer, J., Shaw, M.J., Subramanyam, R.: Once built well, they might come: a study of mobile e-mail, University of Illinois at Urbana-Champaign. College of Business Working Paper 07-0117 (2007)
23. Kurniawan, S.: Older people and mobile phones: a multi-method investigation. Int. J. Hum. Comput. Stud. **66**(12), 889–901 (2008)
24. Huizingh, E.K.: The content and design of web sites: an empirical study. Inf. Manag. **37**(3), 123–134 (2000)
25. Huang, Z., Benyoucef, M.: Usability and credibility of e-government websites. Govern. Inf. Q. **31**(4), 584–595 (2014)
26. Lowry, P.B., Vance, A., Moody, G., Beckman, B., Read, A.: Explaining and predicting the impact of branding alliances and web site quality on initial consumer trust of e-commerce web sites. J. Manag. Inf. Syst. **24**(4), 199–224 (2008)
27. Huang, Z., Benyoucef, M.: From e-commerce to social commerce: a close look at design features. Electron. Commer. Res. Appl. **12**(4), 246–259 (2013)
28. Hong, W., Thong, J.Y., Tam, K.Y.: Does animation attract online users' attention? The effects of flash on information search performance and perceptions. Inf. Syst. Res. **15**(1), 60–86 (2004)
29. Hess, T.J., Fuller, M.A., Mathew, J.: Involvement and decision-making performance with a decision aid: the influence of social multimedia, gender, and playfulness. J. Manag. Inf. Syst. **22**(3), 15–54 (2005)

The Application of Human-Computer Interaction in Smart City Planning and Design

Yanlin Liu[1,2(✉)]

[1] Tianjin University, No. 92 Weijin Road, Nankai District, Tianjin, China
liuyanlin269@163.com
[2] University of Jinan, No. 336, West Road of Nan Xinzhuang,
Jinan, Shandong, China

Abstract. Base on the features of smart cities planning, the principles of the application of human – computer interaction has been discussed. This paper also present the details of the application of HCI on the multiple aspects of smart cities planning as well as the development prospect of human-computer interaction technology in urban planning.

Keywords: Human-computer interaction · Smart cities · Urban planning

A smart city is a new concept relating to urban construction and development formed in the course of urbanization and informatization with the development of a country. With the rapid development of technology of Internet, Internet of things and cloud computing, construction of smart cities represents the general trend, which exerts a profound influence on planning and design of modern cities. On the basis of mass data of urban information, planning of a smart city requires real-time information feedback to adjust its planning scheme properly during design and ensure rationality, feasibility and efficient management of planning of the smart city. Based on mutual effects of humans and computers, human-computer interaction of effective communication has an extensive application prospect in respect of planning of smart cities.

1 Brief Introduction of the Development of Human-Computer Interaction

Human-Computer Interaction (HCI) refers to the technology realizing interrelation and mutual effects between humans and computers via the human-computer interface. After rapid development for nearly thirty years, HCI has been transformed from interrelation with keyboards and mice into human-computer interaction through technology of touch control, multimedia and virtual reality. It seems that the current HCI has been converted from computer-centered interaction into human-centered interaction.

2 Application Principles of HCI in Planning of Smart Cities

Planning of smart cities not only includes traditional urban planning, but absorbs numerous elements of communication and information. Supported by modern technology of communication and information, planning of smart cities involves overall

A. Marcus and W. Wang (Eds.): DUXU 2018, LNCS 10918, pp. 101–111, 2018.
https://doi.org/10.1007/978-3-319-91797-9_8

Fig. 1. Smart cities (source: the author)

Fig. 2. Human-computer interaction (source: the author)

construction goals of smart cities, region optimization and perfection of detailed construction indicators etc. Thus it can be seen that unlike traditional urban planning, planning of smart cities requires HCI to present real-time design results (Fig. 1). In this way, it is convenient for designers to deal with problems and can enhance participation of decision-makers and even the public in design of smart cities. During application of HCI and planning of smart cities, the following basic principles should be observed.

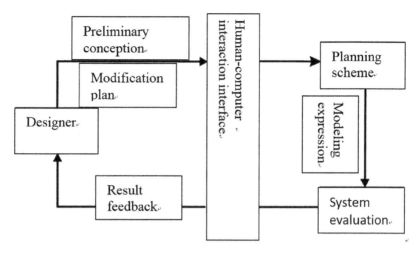

Fig. 3. The process of HCI application in urban planning (source: the author)

2.1   Aim: Efficient, Equal and Harmonious Urban Function

Against the background of the booming technology of communication and information, the concept of smart cities was put forward to enhance the efficiency of urban operation, strengthen fairness and balance in the process of urban development, improve comprehensive function of cities and realize the harmonious development of cities by applying the information technology to urban construction, management and operation. HCI is one of the core contents realizing natural, harmonious and efficient combination of humans and computers and one of the outstanding characteristics of the future development of computer systems and applications. Therefore, introduction of HIC into planning of smart cities can form an efficient interaction mode of top-level and global planning in a virtual environment, so that efficient, equal and harmonious urban function can be achieved.

2.2   Orientation: Service-Oriented Cities with a Standard, Open, Systematic and Secure Information Platform

On the basis of mass data, planning of smart cities involves every aspect of modern cities. Hence, by establishing a standard and open platform, unified modular planning of various functions and contents of smart cities can be carried out to set up a comprehensive platform system of shared information of smart cities, which guarantees the overall operation of a service-oriented city. In addition, planning of smart cities should attach great importance to information security of sharing platforms. The establishment of sound monitoring, management specifications and corresponding punishment measures is an important guarantee for information security and function of service-oriented smart cities. The combination of HCI and information service systems of smart cities can realize integration of various modules quickly on a unified system platform and feedback about fitness and mutual effects among different modules to achieve systematic management of smart cities in a virtual environment, real-time feedback of result states of management control and modification of the information platform system. Moreover, in terms of information security, through simulation of security vulnerabilities with HCI, real-time evaluation and feedback of their influences can be realized to provide an important basis for perfection of the security system of an information platform and formulation of related laws and regulations.

2.3   Final Objective: Enhance Participation of the Public and Meet People's Needs

Through HCI, planning of smart cities can present planning effects from multiple perspectives in real time, which allows designers, city managers and even the public to evaluate the planning effects. As a result, planning of smart cities is closely related to the public through barrier-free interaction and high participation of the public, so that it can meet needs of different people, improve people's quality of life and surroundings to the utmost extent (Fig. 4).

Fig. 4. The intelligent city of the general public (source: the author)

3   Application of HCI to Planning of Smart Cities

Since the emergence of smart cities, there have been many related successful cases. According to analysis of typical cases, it was found that planning of smart cities has its characteristic objectives and principles. On the basis of established urban planning, urban construction, economic strength and social development, corresponding planning of a smart city is carried out. In this way, the planning is really operable and relevant objectives of planning can be realized smoothly. In general, planning of smart cities includes planning of infrastructure construction of communication and information, information platform systems of smart cities and support systems of smart cities. Next, application of HCI to planning of smart cities is discussed from these three aspects.

3.1 Application of HCI in Respect of Planning of Infrastructure Construction of Communication and Information

If planning of smart cities digresses from relevant infrastructure support, the planning will become a mere formality. At present, all successful smart cities are equipped with corresponding urban infrastructure and resource environments with certain development of technology of Internet, Internet of things, cloud computing, IT, intelligent analysis and AI etc. For example, as the example of new smart cities, Hangzhou has the first comprehensive information covering network system if integration of three networks, which is a network of modern communication applying various technical means such as high-capacity stored-program control exchange, fiber-optical communication, data communication, satellite communication and wireless communication. All parts of the infrastructure relating to communication and information were gradually built in accordance with the planning of a smart city. In the face of enormous planning and engineering of a smart city, depending on a traditional design team only can leads to high human costs and poor interaction during design etc. Hence, in addition to elimination of drawbacks mentioned above, application of HCI to planning of smart cities can achieve objectives of design efficiently, harmoniously and pellucidly.

Planning of infrastructure construction of communication and information for a smart city requires planning of an all-round perception terminal system, high-speed fiber broadband, wireless networks and mobile communication networks and a cloud data processing center. Due to powerful ability of design interaction, HCI can be well applied to fields above.

In terms of planning of an all-round perception terminal system, standardized identification systems, video monitoring terminals of city management, position sensing terminals of moving objects and environmental monitoring terminals etc. can be realized rapidly, efficiently and economically through HCI. For instance, through HCI, coverage of video terminals can be realized in a virtual city environment in the system of video monitoring terminals to discover and remove blind angles of monitoring quickly and achieve the optimal layout of a monitoring network. In this way, operational efficiency and management capability relating to urban management, public safety, transportation and emergency response to urban emergencies can be greatly improved (Fig. 2).

Planning of high-speed fiber broadband, wireless networks and mobile communication networks supports and ensures efficient operation of terminals of all-sided perception. Real-time optimization of layout of communication networks can be realized through application of HCI. Party and government offices and major enterprises and public institutions can design TB-level and highly reliable all-fiber transmission networks and access high-speed wireless networks, that are mainly constituted

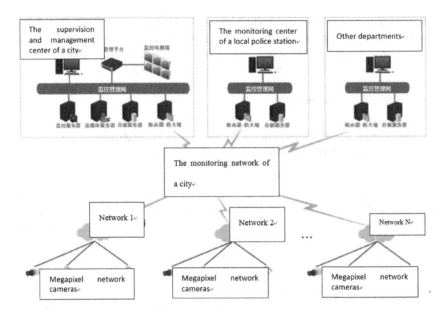

Fig. 5. A design sketch of integrated application of video terminals of a smart city (source: Baidu)

by wireless broadband and mobile Internet, in other regions. On the basis of transmission of the system of terminals of all-sided perception. Simulation and real-time feedback of carrying capacity of comprehensive business and differentiated network service capability can be conducted through HCI to optimize planning of information and communication networks (Fig. 5).

In addition, the cloud data processing center of a smart city is the core technology in planning of smart cities and supports storage, processing, exchange and backups of information. Therefore, introduction of HCI into the planning helps to realize rational urban spatial layout by the cloud data processing center of a smart city and multi-center interactive cloud data centers, ensuring operational efficiency and information security and adjusting planning effects on the whole.

3.2   Application of HCI in Respect of Information Platform Systems of Smart Cities

A smart city requires an information platform system according with its basic hardware facilities of communication and information. Moreover, the system is of strong compatibility and can attain standardization, modularization and integration of mass data from different management and service departments and various physical locations of a city. Various departments of a city, including departments of management, operation and social public service, can realize seamless connection to the urban information platform by establishing standardized module interfaces to greatly enhance construction effects and reduce construction costs of a smart city.

The planning of an information platform system of smart cities cannot do without HCI. As it involves the whole city and society, it needs the government's leadership, participation of the whole society and standardization and modularization of data. If its system is not reasonable, corresponding transformation often has great impacts with considerable quantities. Therefore, the introduction of efficient and natural HCI helps to realize urban modernization and a smart environment.

3.2.1 Application of HCI to Planning of Information Modules of Urban Management

Planning of an information platform system of smart cities primarily involves hardware infrastructure and modules of operation management of this city. Traditional hardware infrastructure construction and operation and management of a city often need to make physical models for repeated demonstration and modifications by decision-makers of several departments, resulting in poor interaction and high costs. However, HCI of virtual reality can offer real-time multi-angle presentation of large-scale scenes in construction areas and integrate data bases of different departments of urban management, including water resources, greening, urban smart grids and fire safety of the city. By design operation of simple objects, multi-level feedback of the planning is extracted in line with administrative rules of various departments (such as requirements relating to plot ratios and fire safety etc.). Besides, a shared linkage database can be built with other departments of social management, such as departments of health, industry and commerce, transport and public security etc. to realize seamless connection of management links in the process of city operation. It even can carry out simulation run to discover security vulnerabilities in real time and enhance emergency response capacity of a city (Fig. 6).

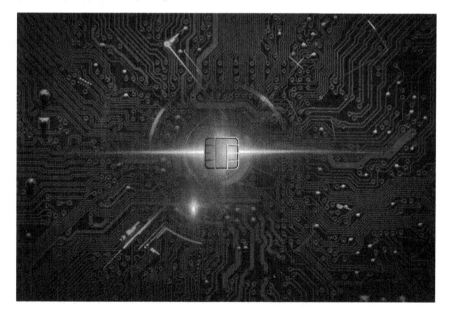

Fig. 6. The application of human-computer interaction in the information module of urban planning and design management (source: Baidu) (Color figure online)

3.2.2   Application of HCI to Planning of Modules of Social Public Service

Planning of modules of social public service is designed to satisfy people's needs of good life and a bright development prospect. It involves fields relating to people's livelihood and enterprise development, such as education, health, community life and industrial information service. As planning of modules of social public service targets common people of different backgrounds, the introduction of HCI into it is necessary. In terms of modules of social public service for education, education resources databases for people with different educational backgrounds can be built and corresponding usage platforms can be established through HCI. For example, during design of service modules for teaching staff, simple text reminders and input interfaces should be used to achieve concise and efficient usage of modules of educational service; during design of service modules for students and ordinary citizens, sound and text reminders, voice control of input interfaces can be added for easy and quick operation of educational service modules.

In terms of other aspects of social life, such as domestic service and equipment maintenance, a corresponding resource library for life service can be built. People's basic medical insurance information and corresponding medical records can be connected to medical service and public health service. An interactive linkage database about traffic information and meteorological service should be created for public travel. An industrial information service platform should be established to release information about industry associations and research institutes. During application of HCI to design of these modules, the latest platform of virtual reality can be utilized to conduct real-time deduction (Fig. 3). Through deduction of operation of an information platform by integrating different service modules in different ways, compatibility of different modules can be analyzed rapidly to carry out real-time optimization design (Fig. 7).

Fig. 7. A design sketch of real-time deduction by technology of virtual reality (Source: Holograph is not in sci-fi now)

3.2.3   Application of HCI to Planning of Modules for an Information Platform of Characteristic

Industries of a City

Since the introduction of the concept of smart cities, various cities in China have set off a craze of construction of smart cities, such as Smart Nanjing, Smart Shenzhen and Smart Foshan. However, with incomplete evaluation and unreasonable planning of some cities, these cities only introduced technology of Internet of things and cloud computing etc. into various fields, leading to a roundabout way of construction of smart cities. Hence, construction of a smart city should be closely related to development characteristics of cities, where characteristic advantaged industries of the city should be highlighted and key points of construction of the smart city should be 6 / 7 identified. In recent years, many cities in China have carried out related planning to build smart cities including Healthy Chongqing, Ecological Shenyang and Digital Nanchang etc. In general, planning of relevant modules of information platforms combining with strategic needs of development of cities' characteristic industries is an important part of construction of a smart city.

Each city has its specific competitive industries. For example, a tourist city can integrate information about tourist attractions, hotels and restaurants, transportation and tour guide service with a module. In addition, this module can connect to both scenic spots and electronic ticket enterprises. As a result, real-time information of passenger flows can be updated in scenic spots and electronic ticket enterprises can provide more channels of ticket information for tourists by connecting to networks of tourism information. A city featured by commercial trade can build a unified service platform of trade information data integrating information relating to domestic and foreign markets, investment promotion, international finance and real-time business news etc. During planning of this platform, introduction of HCI can realize real-time analysis of development needs of competitive industries, evaluation of interaction of competitive industries and other industries to constantly adjust modules within the system and optimize the service information system of characteristic industries.

3.2.4   Application of HCI to Planning of Modules for an Information Platform of Urban Operation and Management

With the development of China's comprehensive strength, the government points out the direction of urban construction and development in the national development strategy, namely construction of smart cities. The government plays a leading role in construction and operation of a smart city and gives full play to the basic role of market forces in allocating resources. Therefore, it is crucial to build modules for information platforms of urban operation and management. Good planning and application of modules can realize humanized, intelligent and rational management of urban operation and management. As the brain of urban operation, the module for information platforms of urban operation and management involves administrative examination and approval, civil society security service, comprehensive HR management service, community affair service, corporate information sharing service and enterprise business cooperation service etc. As the information platform of urban operation and management is a high-level module, some of its services often need to use databases of other service modules. Thus, HCI is necessary in planning of this module. Multimodal interaction of HCI, even multimodal 3D interaction, can be well applied to planning of this module, where imprecise interaction with computers via multiple interaction models is feasible. Through multiple interaction models, designers exploit the advantage of semantic expression with perception models to the full. In combination with multi-database multithreading parallel computing ability, it can greatly improve the interactive efficiency in design, avoiding frequent switching of input and output channels in the course of design (Fig. 8).

Fig. 8. The application of human-computer interaction in the management information platform of urban planning and design operation (source: Baidu)

3.3   Application of HCI to Design of Support Systems of Smart Cities

Construction and operation of a smart city requires a corresponding support system involving systems, mechanisms, regulations, safety and social ethics etc. The whole society should take part in the establishment of the system guided by the government. As a result, the design of this system should be in line with interests of all orders of society. The introduction of HCI into the design can help us understand real intentions of participants quickly and effectively and integrate relevant feedback information, which is an important part of top-level design of smart cities.

4   Conclusion

A smart city stands for an urban form integrating various core systems of urban operation through technology of communication and information. Planning of smart cities is based on mass information relating to life of people, industrial development, and social management and requires both professional intelligence and participation of the public. In the course of planning, introduction of an AI system and application of HCI make abstract information specific and intuitive, which greatly enhance efficiency and naturalness of design. With the development of HCI, application of latest technology of multimodal interaction, dynamic 3D imaging interaction and interaction of virtual reality to planning of smart cities can greatly improve rationality of a design strategy and authenticity of design effects.

References

1. Du, S.: Top-level planning of smart cities. Intell. Build. **8**, 32–35 (2016)
2. Wang, P., Yang, J., Wei, F., et al.: Brief analysis on the development process and patent outline of human-computer interaction. China Invent. Pat. **5**, 39–43 (2013)
3. Cheng, D., Shen, H.: Planning of smart cities: planning contents. Intell. Build. City Inf. **8**, 88–93 (2013)

A UX-Driven Design Method for Building Gamification System

Bing Ning[(⊠)]

Beijing Institute of Fashion Technology,
Yinghua East Street 2, Beijing, Chaoyang, China
gxynb@bift.edu.cn

Abstract. Gamification is an efficient design strategy to enhance user experiences. 'Design' is based on the actual needs, 'Game' creates virtual experiences, 'Gamification' is a program that takes the real needs as the goal and the game system as the framework. The program builds a real and virtual mixed product service system. This paper presents a user experience driven three-level design method on gamification system, which corresponds user experiences in three levels of nature, process, and interface. In this paper, some examples are presented to verify the applicability of the design method on gamification system. It is foreseeable that gamification will be an important means of creating the full user experience combined the virtual and real world.

Keywords: Gamification · Design method · User experience · Service system

1 Introduction

Gamification as a concept known and familiar to people is in 2010 [1, 2]. Till now, gamification is keeping high attention google trends (Fig. 1). It is mentioned in many areas, examples in the gamification.cc website cover education [3, 4], health [5], commerce [6], government, public services [7] and more. Some firms like SAP AG, [8, 9] Microsoft, IBM, Nike, LiveOps, Deloitte, and others have started using gamification in various applications and processes [10].

However, as gamification continues to be practiced in many fields, more and more criticism have been raised about gamification. Ian Bogost boldly claims "gamification is marketing bullshit," [13]. Game designers like Jon Radoff and Margaret Robertson have criticized gamification as excluding elements like storytelling and experiences and using simple reward systems in place of true game mechanics [11, 12]. Gamification practitioners [13, 14] have pointed out that while the initial popular designs were in fact mostly relying on simplistic reward approach, even those led to significant improvements in short-term engagement [15]. This was supported by the first comprehensive study in 2014, which concluded that an increase in gamification elements correlated with an increase in motivation score, but not with capacity or opportunity/trigger scores. [16, 17] These criticism show that gamification is not easy, and many results have not achieved the desired results.

© Springer International Publishing AG, part of Springer Nature 2018
A. Marcus and W. Wang (Eds.): DUXU 2018, LNCS 10918, pp. 112–124, 2018.
https://doi.org/10.1007/978-3-319-91797-9_9

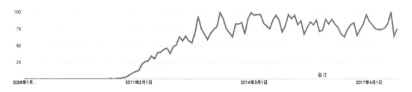

Fig. 1. Gamification in Google trends

For the emerging field of gamification, it is necessary and urgent to study how to correctly understand gamification and to effectively use the methods and principles of gamification. Some scholars and designers have done a lot of useful and enlightening work. For example, Janaki Kumar [18] has put forward 5 steps player centered design method. Philipp Herzig [19] has researched on the development process. (rethinking gamification). Martin Böckle et al. [20] have put forward a design framework for adaptive gamification applications. Benedikt Morschheuser et al. [21] have proposed one model of the gamify method for designing gamification.

This paper presents a user experience driven gamification system design method. This method builds a gamification system from three levels which respectively corresponds to the three levels of user experience to create the whole experience for users. And we use three examples of this method to prove the effectiveness of it.

2 The Relationship Among Gamification, Game and Design

On May 9, 2011, the U.S. National Arts Foundation, affiliated with the U.S. federal government, officially announced that "video game is an art form" [22]. Video games are the "ninth art" [22] accepted after the eight major art forms such as painting, sculpture, architecture, music, poetry (literature), dance, drama, and film. Besides the concept that video game is an art form, there are many concepts about "games," and here we can get some inspiration from several classic definitions. Well-known game designer Sid Meier believes that "the game is a series of interesting choices" [23]. This definition illustrates the game's interactive, systematic, entertaining attributes. "Playing games is a voluntary attempt to overcome all unnecessary obstacles" [24]. This definition is made by Bernard Sutz, a famous philosopher. This definition defines the real and emotional value of the game. The game is more focused on the creation and satisfaction of the virtual emotions, in the extreme sense, the game is a bit like spiritual opium. A game is a closed, formal system, that engages players in the structured conflict, and resolves in an unequal outcome. The concept game is made by Tracy Fullerton [25], Prof. of the University of Southern California. The definition of this game is from the game design perspective. It is also a significant reference for game designers.

Design is focused on solving problems [26]. Design is to discover the way things should be. So, design has Pragmatism DNA. IDEO [27], the famous design company, has a concept of design: design is system methodology; design is seeking a combination of rational and sensual solutions; design is people oriented.

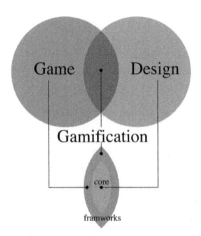

Fig. 2. The relationship among gamification, game and design

The "game of work", published by Coonradt [28] in 1984, explores the impact of game elements on work practices, refining five elements of interest over work: a clear goal, a sound scoring system, and timely feedback, highly free personal play space, (coach) continuous mentoring. In "Actional Gamification," Chou [29] proposed the octalysis framework as a design framework of a gamification, proposing that the principle of gamification is to optimize people's motivation. And consider gamification as a combination of game design, game motivation, motivation psychology, behavioral economics, UX/UI, technology platforms, and profit-driven business systems. The game has all of the above, except for the commercial system that drives ROI. The definition of gamification in "for the win" by Werbach and Hunter [30] is the use of game elements and game design techniques in non-game contexts. This definition is universal, and this definition focuses more on the differences between games and gamification. The understanding of this definition needs to be based on a clearer understanding of the game.

Based on past gamification studies and author's understanding, the essence of gamification design is user-centered, serving the needs of the user's real life, which is consistent with the nature of the design. Gamification focuses on shaping the user experience, which is similar to the game's emotional satisfaction. In the sense of speaking, gamification is an interdisciplinary field of design and games. It is a newer design mode with the characteristics of game thinking and design thinking. This paper, from the design point of view, gives the understanding of gamification (Fig. 2).

That is, gamification is an effective design strategy to enhance user experience. Gamification is a design pattern based on the actual needs and the game system. This model builds a product and service system that integrates the real environment and the virtual situation. Among them, user behavior is the core driving force of gamification system.

3   An UX-Driven Design Method for Gamification

The principle of gamification is to optimize people's motivation - "actionable gamification" Chou [29]. In my opinion, the goal of a gamification system is consistent with user motivation, and its cornerstone is the core value and need of what we want to serve our users. When designing and building a gamified system for user services, our core principle is to fulfill the real requirements of the users and to create an unexpectedly emotional experience for the users.

3.1   Overview

This paper presents a three-level gamification system design methods (Fig. 3), and the construction of gamification service system is divided into three levels: goal, rules, and tools.

Fig. 3. Gamification design system

Goal: Based on the actual needs of users, reconstructing the goal of gamification, and giving users value-added experience of emotional experience.

Rules: With user behavior as the core, building the rules of a gamification system, which form an independent and virtual reality integration system. Gamification rules include user role rules, user behavior rules, achievement rules, relationship rules, feedback rules and so on.

Tools: User behavior data tools, user attributes (results) data tools, user experience data tools, user relationship data tools. PBLs (points, badges, and leaderboards) are popular gamification tools.

Gamification is a valid design strategy to enhance user experience, with the goal of building value-added experiences for users. In this gamification design system, the purpose of gamification system is consistent with the core value essence of user experience. The rules correspond to the process of user experience, and the tools construct the user interface and feedback. The three levels of the gamification system together create the integrity of the user experience.

3.2   Three Levels of the System

Gamification system can be built by following steps. The primary question of gamification is whether the solution to the problem can form a stand-alone system, which is formed by goal, rules and tools.

Goal
First of all, the goal of gamification is equivalent to the heart of the gamification system, which is the core issue after the establishment of the gamification system.

The goal is to determine the basis of the actual needs of users, and is consisted with the user's real life. Different from the game, the purpose of the gamification is to meet the exact needs of users, which is the fundament of gamification. But user needs are not necessarily functional, or more than functional. Second, the goal of gamification system is rebuilt on users' real needs. In the gamification system, the user's internal motivation can be maintained and stimulated, without alienation, that is the key to the goal of gamification system.

Gamification differs from other design methods in that gamification requires connecting real-world needs with virtual emotions and balancing the two. Games is to satisfy people's emotional needs in the virtual world. Different from games, gamification will adopt the method of virtual construction in the real world to meet practical needs and bring more emotional satisfaction to users.

Fig. 4. Nike "Unlimited Stadium"

2017, Nike's award-winning interactive marketing project "Unlimited Stadium" (Fig. 4) has the application of the gamification design strategy. In the playground, runners can compete with the best "self" through interactive digital walls. In this gamification design, the best "self" represents the recording and reproduction of the player's athletic data through service system of Nike. The gamification of the contest represents the spirit of "continuously surpassing oneself" and is in harmony with the goal of sports and fitness, which gives Nike users great physical and mental satisfaction. In the "Unlimited Stadium," the virtual reality of the game and the real needs of fitness are the perfect blend of both, leaving everyone with a feeling of eagerness.

Rules

Second, the rules of gamification constitute the framework of the gamification system, which is the essential condition for the system to operate.

Rules are the epitaxial layers of the target. The rules not only construct the system but also guide the user's behavior, which is the intrinsic motivation for the normal operation of the system. User behavior is the driving force behind the gamification system. For example, gamification about fitness will take users' daily number of exercise steps and calories burned as the core value of the game, and user fitness behavior becomes the core driving force of the game. The goal of gamification design is to allow users to pass Data recognize your fitness behavior and adjust your behavior to a goal of developing good fitness habits. However, for the user's fitness behavior, using that gamification rules design, different products have different design strategies, the user experience is also different.

Another example of gamification design, we take children's smart product design on learning habits as an example, Realistic needs are to help the newly enrolled children, develop their habits of finishing school bags. It is his behavioral goal that children must put the learning kit of the next day into their schoolbag. The core rule of gamification system is that the behavior of packing up a school bag is transformed into the action of pet feeding, and the formation of habits is transformed into the growth of pets. Through the gamification of design, it is hoped that children can get a sense of accomplishment from this routine, from tedious work into a kind of emotional accumulation. Everyday boring behavior becomes meaningful and sense of mission.

The "gamification" behavior that virtual scenarios offer is important, and this is an opportunity to bring about a lasting lifestyle change. After experiencing the initial obstacles and difficulties, users enjoy the benefits of a new behavioral paradigm instead of always treating the gamified design experience as "play once again". Gamification designed to create a user experience beyond expectations, which guides users to recognize the nature of the real needs, mobilize the user's intrinsic motivation, and form new sustainable and beneficial behavior.

Tools

Finally, gamification tools can be looked like the surface of the gamification system, which is closely related to the user's perception and feedback and more concentrated on the user interface.

Gamification tools is a cluster of data and information, which is the external appearance of user's behavior index, the result of user's behavior, the feedback and the presentation of relationship. The familiar PBL (Point, Badges, Leaderboards) is the representative tool.

3.3 Relationship Between Gamification System and User Experience (UX)

It is an era of experience. For products and services, how to get beyond the expectations of the user experience is the ultimate standard design.

The term user experience was first widely recognized as being proposed and promoted by user experience designer Donald Norman in the mid-1990s. The ISO 9241-210 standard defines the user experience as "people's perceptions and responses to products, systems or services that are used or expected to be used." In simple terms, the user experience is "whether this thing is easy to use and convenient to use." Therefore, the user experience is subjective, and its effect is focused on practical application. The ISO-defined supplemental explanation is as follows: User experience, which is the user's entire experience before, during and after using a product or system, including emotion, beliefs, preferences, cognitive impressions, physical and psychological responses, behaviors and achievements And other aspects. User experience has three levels: nature, procedure, and UI, which Corresponds to the three levels of the gamification system (Fig. 5).

First, the goal of gamification systems is to enhance the user experience. The core of gamification is not functional design, which is to create the emotional process of users in the process of service. Emotion analogy is one of the critical methods. Also, gamification design has a natural affinity for the user, and the amusement and story-telling of the gamification design are especially useful in attracting the junior user. Final, data-driven service design opens up a vast space for gamification. Advances in sensor technology and information technology have enabled many of the features not available in the past to be achieved. In particular, they are used to digitize information about people's daily behaviors, such as sports data, sleep data, attitude data, and real-time recording and analysis of social relation data. The data is more conducive to people to understand the theme, to provide users with more specific experience of products and services. The digital mirror in the real world is becoming more and more complete and precise.

Gamification naturally seems to connect UX in the virtual digital world and the real digital world together. The future has been coming.

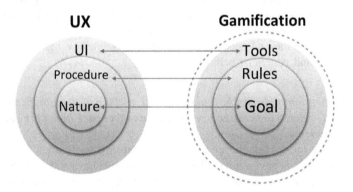

Fig. 5. Corresponding relationship between gamification system and UX

4   Method Applications

4.1   Gamification on Theme Event: The Food Design Workshop of South Korea and China

Project Description: This is a cross-border cultural exchange workshop project, which is attended by more than 50 college students from Beijing Institute of Fashion

Technology and the University Sangmyung University in South Korea (Fig. 7). The purpose is to increase the awareness and exchange of cultures among young people in China and South Korea through the redesign of traditional cuisine by them and transfer of each other's heritage and understanding of their own culture. In our case of gamification, the form of independent activity is often self-contained, and it is more amenable to gamification if it is relatively easy and requires more communication. For the cultural exchange workshop, the design of the gamification system is "Gourmet Market". In the "Gourmet Market" system, we have goals, rules, and tools, as shown in (Fig. 6) (Tabel 1):

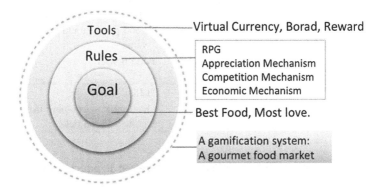

Fig. 6. The gamification system of food design workshop

It is worth mentioning that the integration of realistic space and virtual space (food market), the integration of realistic behavior (cooking, tasting, evaluation) and virtual achievements (points and lists) are prominent in this food market system. There is also a value relationship between the value of the virtual currency of the gamification tool in the system and the actual money.

Fig. 7. Some parts of the food design workshop

Table 1. Gamification plan of food design workshop

System: a gourmet food market	Aims	Best food, best love	
	Rules	1. RPG	Each group is both cooker and customer
		2. Appreciation mechanism	• Customers give "LIKE" • Cookers can't get their own "LIKE" • Give "LIKE" back to back
		3. Competition mechanism	No.1 on "LIKE" board get the reward
		4. Economic Mechanism	• Each member only has three free food tickets to buy food • One ticket worth 1000 Korea yuan • Food price should be equal to its value
	Tools	1. Virtual currency	Food tickets
		2. Board	"LIKE" board
		3. Reward	Grand prix——coming from the income of food tickets

4.2 Gamification on Product Service: An Intelligent Products to Guide Children's Habits

Project Description: The users of this smart interactive product are children and parents who have just entered primary school. The purpose is to help children adapt to their new life as soon as possible by developing their habit of organizing school bags. Through research, the habit of packing up a school bag belongs to the daily routine, repetitive work. Children do well no reward, but once the error often has unpleasant experiences; parents may also need to spend extra time to make up for the consequences. Therefore, this design is very beneficial for children and parents. But apart from the realities, because of the NFC technology solution, children must trigger smart hardware on a one-shot basis, with extra time burden on them.

Finally, pet-based gamification system (Fig. 8) design strategies, of which a critical consideration is that gamification of feeding practices make inherent and meaningful redundancy of the technical solutions. Besides, gamification (feeding pets) gives children a sense of accomplishment and initiative in picking up bags. Parents through APP information feedback can also quickly get children to pack the situation. The pet's 5-day workday sleeping and 2-day weekend awake design, but also do not take up children's time to avoid over-gamification.

As can be seen from the Fig. 9, gamification solution forms a relatively independent closed system, and the system is based on the user's behavior as a driving force. Users' behavior is recorded, presented, and feedback in the form of data in system. It is also the essential condition for the establishment of a gamification system.

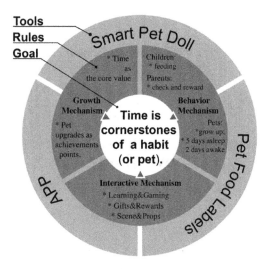

Fig. 8. Pet-fed gamification system of children's smart product

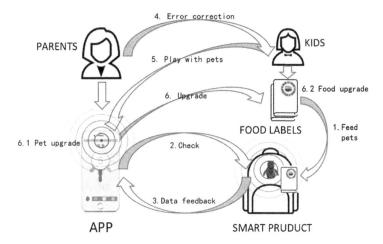

Fig. 9. User behavior closed loop in gamification system

4.3 Gamification on Education: Class on Designing Board Game

Gamification programs are also often used in the field of learning, and there are many devoted discussions about gamification learning. In this use of tabletop course, learning process introduces gamification of the design method. The independence of a single class and the nature of subject content make it easier to be a stand-alone system suitable for using gamification design strategies.

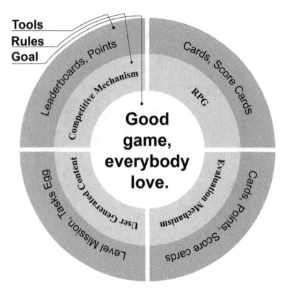

Fig. 10. Gamification system of board game design course

Project Description: In the gamification system of this course (Fig. 10), the goal is a good game, everybody loves. The purpose of the course is to convey the core idea of game design, that is, the evaluation of the game is based on the player experience, and the game design must iterate through the feedback of the players. Throughout the course, the main rules of gamification include: RPG (student is both designer and player); evaluation mechanism (player has the right to comment on the work); user-generated content (course has progressive tasks, but also random tasks Egg); competition mechanism (players divided ethnic groups, there are points list and the corresponding reward). Tools for the learning gamification are the card, task egg, scorecard, points, list, dice and so on. Also, randomness is also repeatedly applied in the gamification system, such as tribal groups, the task of publishing egg, lottery decision evaluation object and other parts.

Some parts of the course are as follows:

The above three cases are the verification of the design method of gamification system, involving activities planning, exceptional product services, learning areas. However, the three-level gamification system design method has universal guiding significance on how to adopt the gamification design strategy for all kinds of areas. Following the four steps, building system, creating goals, setting rules, and creating tools, users should get experience more than expected in the gamification system. In particular, an excellent gamification design system does not happen in one go, and like every design and game, one gamification system requires constant iteration based on users' feedback (Fig. 11).

Fig. 11. Some sections of the board game class gamification

5 Conclusion

In summary, gamification is an efficient design strategy to enhance user experience. Gamification is a design pattern that takes the real demand as a goal and the game system as a frame. This model builds a product service system that integrates real and virtual situations. Among them, user behavior is the core driving force of this gamification system.

For gamification, the first task is to build an independent system concept that takes user behavior as the intrinsic driving force and user behavior data information to run within the system. Secondly, designing system in order of goal, rules, and tools in sequence, and during the process integrating and balancing actual needs and virtual scenarios to provide the user with an unexpectedly emotional experience.

It is foreseeable that with the development of the digital society, gamification will permeate all aspects of life. Let people experience digital life and work efficiency commission at the same time, bring more experience and happiness.

References

1. Gamification at Google Trends. Google Trends. (http://www.google.com/trends/explore#q=gamification). Accessed 25 Nov 2012
2. Zichermann, G., Cunningham, C.: Gamification by Design: Implementing Game Mechanics in Web and Mobile Apps. O'Reilly Media, Inc., Sebastopo (2011)
3. Hamari, J., Shernoff, D.J., Rowe, E., et al.: Challenging games help students learn: an empirical study on engagement, flow and immersion in game-based learning. Comput. Hum. Behav. **54**, 170–179 (2016)
4. Herger, M.: Gamification Facts & Figures. Enterprise-Gamification (2012). http://enterprise-gamification.com/index.php/facts
5. Hamari, J., Koivisto, J.: Working out for likes: An empirical study on social influence in exercise gamification. Comput. Hum. Behav. **50**, 333–347 (2015)
6. Takahashi, D.: Website builder DevHub gets users hooked by 'gamifying'its service. VentureBeat, 25 August 2010
7. The Speed Camera Lottery. TheFunTheory. http://www.thefuntheory.com/speed-camera-lottery-0. Accessed 07 July 2015
8. Herger, M.: OINK OINK! Welcome to the SAP Gamification Cup! Enterprise-Gamification.com, 27 July 2011. http://enterprise-gamification.com/index.php/component/content/article/3-examples/6-oink-oink-welcome-to-the-sap-gamification-cup

9. Herger, M.: Gamified Manufacturing. Enterprise-Gamification.com, 2 November 2011. http://enterprise-gamification.com/index.php/manufacturing/47-gamified-manufacturing

10. Silverman, R.: Latest Game Theory: Mixing Work and Play—Companies Adopt Gaming Techniques to Motivate Employees. Wallstreet Journal, 2 November 2011. https://www.wsj.com/articles/SB10001424052970204294504576615371783795248

11. Radoff, J.: Gamification, 16 February 2011. https://web.archive.org/web/20110219171239/, http://radoff.com/blog/2011/02/16/gamification/. Radoff.com. http://radoff.com/blog/2011/02/16/gamification/. Accessed 19 Feb 2011

12. Robertson, M.: Can't Play Won't Play. Hideandseek.net. http://www.hideandseek.net/2010/10/06/cant-play-wont-play//

13. Bogost, I.: Forthcoming. "Why gamification is bullshit." In: Walz, S.P., Deterding, S. (eds.) The Gameful World: Approaches, Issues, Applications. MIT Press, Cambridge

14. Zichermann, G.: Lies, Damned Lies and Academics. Gamification.co. http://gamification.co/2011/08/10/lies-damned-lies-andacademics/

15. Herger, M.: Gamification is Bullshit? The academic tea-party-blog of gamification. Enterprise-Gamification.com. http://enterprise-gamification.com/index.php?option=com_content&view=article&id=18:gamification-is-bullshit-the-academic-tea-party-blogof-gamification&catid=4:blog&Itemid=251&lang=en

16. Herger, M.: Gamification facts & Figures. Enterprise-Gamification.com. http://www.enterprise-gamification.com/mediawiki/index.php?title=Facts_%26_Figures

17. Michie, S., Van Stralen, M.M., West, R.: The behaviour change wheel: a new method for characterising and designing behaviour change interventions. Implement. Sci. **6**(1), 42 (2011). https://doi.org/10.1186/1748-5908-6-42. http://www.implementationscience.com/content/6/1/42

18. Lister, C., West, J.H., Cannon, B., Sax, T., Brodegard, D.: Just a fad? Gamification in health and fitness apps. JMIR Serious Games. **2**(2), e9 (2014). https://doi.org/10.2196/games.3413. http://games.jmir.org/2014/2/e9

19. Kumar, J.: Five steps to enterprise gamification. UX Mag. **1**, 2013 (2013)

20. Böckle, M., Micheel, I., Bick, M., et al.: A design framework for adaptive gamification applications. In: Proceedings of the 51st Hawaii International Conference on System Sciences (2018)

21. Morschheuser, B., Hamari, J., Werder, K., et al.: How to gamify? A method for designing gamification (2017)

22. Gee, J.P.: Why game studies now? Video games: a new art form. Games Cult. **1**(1), 58–61 (2006)

23. Juul, J.: Introduction to game time/time to play: an examination of game temporality. First Pers. New Media Story Perform. Game 131–142 (2004)

24. Meier, K.V.: Triad trickery: playing with sport and games. J. Philos. Sport **15**(1), 11–30 (1988)

25. Fullerton, T., Swain, C., Hoffman, S.: Game Design Workshop: Designing, Prototyping, & Playtesting Games. CRC Press, Boca Raton (2004)

26. Jonassen, D.H.: Toward a design theory of problem solving. Educ. Technol. Res. Dev. **48**(4), 63–85 (2000)

27. Kelley, T.A.: The Art of Innovation: Lessons in Creativity From IDEO, America's Leading Design Firm. Broadway Business, Saskatoon's (2001)

28. Coonradt, C.A.: The Game of Work. Gibbs Smith, Layton (2007)

29. Chou, Y.: Actionable Gamification: Beyond Points, Badges, and Leaderboards. Octalysis Group, Fremont (2016)

30. Werbach, K., Hunter, D.: For the Win: How Game Thinking Can Revolutionize your Business. Wharton Digital Press, Philadelphia (2012)

Impact of Display Clutter on User Experience

Svetlana Ognjanovic[✉]

Chair of Cognitive Science, ETH Zurich, Zurich, Switzerland
svetlana.ognjanovic@gess.ethz.ch

Abstract. In human-technology interaction display properties are an integral part of a successful achievement of user goals. To assess display properties different approaches have been taken. Besides design and visualization research, displays also play a central role in Human Factors and Ergonomics, as well as in Usability and User Experience research. In Human Factors and Ergonomics research, Display Clutter is usually associated with the abundance of irrelevant information on a screen. Depending on the definition of clutter, poor display organization, or performance and attentional costs of the user are considered as clutter as well. In User Experience research display properties are divided into instrumental (e.g., usability, utility) and non-instrumental (e.g., visual aesthetics) qualities. The present paper puts the Display Clutter and the User Experience concept in relation. It becomes obvious that the two approaches pursue a similar goal, thus an optimal user-interaction with a technical system. From a theoretical point of view, however, there are clear differences. Also, from a methodological perspective, some measurement techniques, which include the computational quantification of the screen, are unique to Display Clutter. Nevertheless, user performance measures and user ratings are employed in both Display Clutter as well as in User Experience research. It is discussed how display clutter can influence users' experience on several levels: Instrumental (i.e., pragmatic) and non-instrumental (i.e., hedonic), from an objective system property perspective as well as subjectively perceived user perspective.

Keywords: Display clutter · Usability · User experience · Visual aesthetics

1 Introduction

When is a display perceived as cluttered? And what constitutes a good User Experience with a digital system? Both questions are relevant when it comes to the evaluation of new or existing user interfaces, but they are rarely asked together. Display Clutter and User Experience come from two separate lines of research with very little overlap. Both concepts imply though that there is a system display and a user; the interaction with that system will determine how cluttered the system is perceived and what experiences it produces. A display may appear cluttered to some users, but not so cluttered to others. Also, the user experience with a display may be very positive for some users, but frustrating for others. In both cases it can be assumed that we have to consider system properties, the physical and social context of system usage, as well as the target user with its characteristics and expectations. At the same time, it seems that the perspective on the user interaction, which is taken with the Display Clutter approach as

© Springer International Publishing AG, part of Springer Nature 2018
A. Marcus and W. Wang (Eds.): DUXU 2018, LNCS 10918, pp. 125–140, 2018.
https://doi.org/10.1007/978-3-319-91797-9_10

opposed to Usability and User Experience approach is a different one. Therefore, it needs to be determined how display clutter appears and how it can influence the user experience with a system. This will help to better understand the interplay between objectively given display properties and their subjective perception.

In the present paper, the aim is to systematically describe the research concepts of Display Clutter, Usability and User Experience (UX) and to demonstrate how they can be related to each other. For that, first Display Clutter will be defined in some detail, then the components of User Experience will be defined, and finally the expected impact of display clutter on user experience will be elaborated.

2 Display Clutter

The concept display clutter has been used in data-rich domains (e.g., aviation, radiology), where the system operator has to interact with multiple sources of information simultaneously in an effective and efficient way. Display clutter is usually associated with negative effects that the amount and arrangement of information can have on user performance. Among researchers and across different domains, there is no agreement yet on a distinctive definition for display clutter [1]. In order to structure the available research in a meaningful way, it will be differentiated between display-based and user-based aspects of clutter, and finally looked at clutter as a self-reported measure or perceived display clutter.

2.1 Display-Based Aspects

The first three clutter approaches, i.e. display density, layout, and target-background approach, do not include the user to define the level of clutter. The determination of clutter in that case can be based on image processing algorithms or some specific design principles.

Display Density Perspective. The display density approach, a widely accepted view of display clutter, relates display clutter to the high number of entities on a screen, [e.g., 2–4]. This concept is commonly referred to the set-size effect in psychology; the set-size effect is based on abstract experimental stimuli and it is related to the increase in search time with the increase in the number of distractors, or set size, on the screen [5, 6]. Wickens and colleagues [7] also call it "numerosity clutter", to point out the connection to the set size effect and the respective hindering of selective attention. The display density perspective is regarded as an extension of the set-size effect, which makes it applicable to real-life displays.

Since in real-life displays the number of information entities can be hardly measured manually, image processing algorithms are usually applied. They segment the screenshots of displays based on pre-defined criteria and provide one or several numeric values, which refer to the level of clutter. One rather basic clutter density measure is to calculate the percentage of pixels that was used to present graphical or text information on a website; whereas the background elements are not factored into the calculation [8]. Other algorithms are based on clusters (polygon objects or line vertices), which can identify the areas of an image (e.g., map image, display screen-shot) that are more cluttered than others. The output of such more complex image-processing algorithms is usually either a single numeric value (e.g., for edge density) or multiple numerical values that refer to several metrics (e.g., feature congestion, and subband entropy, both from Rosenholtz et al. [9]).

Display Layout Perspective. The display layout approach reflects the arrangement and structure of display entities, their nature and color in addition to density of entities [e.g., 10]. In their review of display clutter, Moacdieh and Sarter [1] distinguish between two broad factors of the display layout perspective: The organization of the information and the consistency of several design features.

Display Organization. According to Moacdieh and Sarter [1], a display is badly organized, thus cluttered, when a "logical or conceptual grouping" is missing, there is "absence of symmetry", and/or a target is masked or obscured. Wickens and colleagues [7] define this type of clutter as "disorganizational grouping" by referring to the lack of structure in the search field. Also, high entropy is expected to diminish the target predictability and is referred to display organization [9]. And finally, perceptual crowding has been related to clutter [e.g., 11, 12]. The perceptual crowding effect appears when the target on a screen is closely surrounded by distractors and the visual search is therefore expected to be slowed down.

Consistency. The lack of consistency with respect to different features on a display element, such as color, luminance, contrast, orientation, can also lead to increased clutter. Wickens and colleagues [7] define this category "heterogeneous clutter." It refers to non-target background features including their color, shape, and size.

Different types of image processing algorithms have been published that can account for the organization and consistency of display entities. Among the most cited algorithms for display clutter is the measure developed by Rosenholtz et al. [9]. It includes three aspects of clutter: Feature congestion, subband entropy, and edge density. Feature congestion includes the variability of three key features in a display: Color, orientation, and luminance; it is based on the statistical saliency model developed by Rosenholtz [13]. Subband entropy includes the grouping of entities by similarity and proximity and it refers to the predictability of individual parts of a scene, or their redundancy; the more there is redundancy in a display, the less clutter. Edge density was originally developed by Mack and Oliva [4] and it is based on the assumption that humans' attention is drawn to edges. A high number of edges is therefore associated with an increase in clutter in terms of high variability in the display; the number of edges can also be associated with the number of distinct regions.

Target-Background Similarity Perspective. Higher variability of features can lead to higher clutter, but what if the color of a target is the same as the color of a distractor or even of the background? According to the target-background or target-distractor similarity approach, display clutter appears due to the similarity of display elements that will compete for system users' attention. In radar domains, this clutter definition is very relevant because of its applicability to their use cases [1].

To capture this type of clutter, various image processing algorithms have been published that distinguish between the target and the background and quantify the similarities based on features like contrast, luminance, and structure [14, 15]. Some of these measures also incorporate the objective abilities of the human visual system in detecting differences of visual cues. Chu and colleagues [16], for example, developed a clutter metric, that refers to the contrast sensitivity function of the human visual system. The metric measures similarities between the target and the background in the frequency domain: The easier the human visual system is expected to notice the differences between the target and background, the lower the clutter is assumed to be.

The above mentioned, display-based aspects of clutter all refer to objectively measurable display properties where the context and the user are not completely captured. However, the lastly described image-processing algorithm that is based on human visual perception abilities is a step towards the target user of a system.

2.2   User-Based Aspects

Although objectively measured display properties can predict some interaction characteristics with a system, such as search time or detection rate, they cannot define the ideal middle ground between too much and too little information. From an objective perspective, more information will often be regarded as more clutter even though some additional information may be meaningful for a particular task or a certain user group. User-based aspects of clutter concern the physical and social context of the user as well as the resulting performance and attention costs during display interaction.

Task-Irrelevance Perspective. The task-irrelevance approach takes the user's perspective and defines display clutter as the amount of information presented on the screen that is irrelevant to the task at hand. Alexander and colleagues [17] make a distinction between "visual density" and "information density"; the visual density refers to the property of the display and the information density to the usage context, and the amount of task-relevant information on the screen. Furthermore, a distinction has been made between global and local clutter, where global clutter refers to the density of the entire display of interest and local clutter to density of the task-relevant area of the display [e.g., 12, 17].

Performance and Attentional Cost Perspective. This aspect of clutter not only includes the task, but also the respective characteristics and outcome of user interaction. Especially in human factors and ergonomics, the performance and attentional costs are central for determining the quality of the interaction. In addition to display properties and context, user characteristics will have a significant influence on an efficient and effective user performance. Users' experience of clutter can have various origins, either any of the display-based factors, or user based-factors (e.g., task difficulty, workload, or missing user knowledge). Rosenholtz and colleagues [18] for example, characterized clutter as "the state in which excess items, or their representation or organization, lead to a degradation of performance at some task" (p. 761).

Performance measures that have been mostly associated with display clutter are task effectiveness (e.g., task accuracy) and the efficiency of visual search. While the operationalisation of effectiveness is domain specific, the visual search paradigm is clearly defined and usually includes a present or absent target and the respective reaction time until the target is either found or the search is stopped. Moacdieh and

Sarter [1] note that the impairment of visual search is a central aspect to study when investigating the sources of display clutter. A rather new measurement technique in connection with display clutter assessment is the eye-tracking method. Since eye-tracking is a continuous measurement with a rather high data resolution (i.e., 30–1000 Hz, depending on the eye-tracking device), fine grained data analysis can be conducted. For local visual search assessment, one common eye-tracking metric is the time between the first fixation on the area of interest (AOI) that contains the target and the moment when the target is found. To investigate the global search across the whole display, measures about gaze location and spread (total fixations, fixations on certain areas), about directness (scanpath ratio), and about duration (mean fixation duration) have been used [e.g., 19]. Several studies showed a delay in visual search that was associated with clutter [8, 12, 20, 21]. Kim and colleagues [22], for example, varied several dashboard display design features and investigated their impact on driving performance and divided attention. Their findings show that low clutter (i.e., density perspective), and contrast of size could improve driving performance, especially of elder participants. Color variation, however, did not have the expected positive effect; only in the design condition where the dashboard included color elements and fills, some performance support was observed.

Based on the performance perspective, the amount of clutter can be varied to determine its effects on user performance. This approach can help to find the ideal middle-ground between too much and too little information on the display. At the same time, it is not clear, which display properties exactly deteriorated users' performance. Therefore, in addition to the continuous eye-tracking measures, it is beneficiary to complement the evaluation by asking participants to report their clutter experience. This allows for an additional perspective on clutter and also provides clues on how clutter influences users' perception of a system.

2.3   Perceived Display Clutter

Subjective measures have been widely used to characterize display clutter. They not only reflect display properties, thus bottom-up factors, but also top-down factors, such as user expertise or workload [e.g., 23–25]. Naylor [24], for example, showed that pilots with more experience provided higher clutter ratings than pilots with less experience. This result was seen as an indication of experienced pilots' higher discrimination abilities. In another aviation study, pilots' contrast sensitivity and the extension of their useful field of view (UFOV) were examined and they were asked to rate the overall clutter of the system on a scale from 0 to 20. The results revealed that user characteristics were related to clutter ratings. Thus, pilots with higher contrast sensitivity gave higher clutter ratings. Also, pilots with a higher UFOV performance gave lower clutter ratings [26]. Similarly, Kim and colleagues [22] found lower clutter ratings for lower workload conditions, which was related to the severeness of weather conditions in their flight simulation.

To assess the overall display clutter, different rating scales have been used, ranging from 7-point Likert scales up to 20-point scales [1]. Also, some researchers developed multi-dimensional scales to enable a more fine-grained clutter analysis. Kaufmann and Kaber [26], for example, developed a four-dimensional scale (clarity, similarity, density, and dynamics) that they validated in several studies and found to be highly correlated with their overall measure of clutter based on a 20-point Likert scale [23, 27].

Perceived display clutter has been correlated with both image-processing metrics as well as with performance measures; and for both comparisons significant correlations were found [e.g., 9, 19]. Furthermore, it was shown that some variability in performance could be captured with self-reported measures as opposed to with image-processing algorithms [19]. Moacdieh and Sarter [1] noted, however, that there was some uncertainty about what the participants exactly assess when asked to rate the display clutter. It may as well be that participants weight the different aspects of clutter differently than researchers intended, or that they are even biased by how aesthetically pleasing the particular display appears to them. Such additional perspectives on display clutter may be addressed with new and validated research tools or possibly with an extended view on users' experience with complex systems.

Display clutter definitions can be divided into display-based and user-based categories. Display-based approach includes display density, layout, and target-background similarity perspectives, and is usually associated with objectively measurable display properties. User-based approach refers to task-irrelevance as well as to performance and attentional cost perspectives. In that case, the optimal user task performance is considered. Finally, perceived display clutter was described that takes the subjective target users' perspective and allows for the assessment of additional, for the user interface relevant factors (e.g., design ratings, cognitive workload, expertise effects).

For the purpose of giving an overview on the different display clutter aspects, the definitions were described distinctively. In reality, various display clutter aspects are used in combination. This allows for a wider coverage of the negative effects of display clutter and the respective assessment of the quality of user interaction. However, it was also noted that the perceived display clutter measures might benefit from an extended view on users' experience; hence, a distinction between pragmatic display clutter ratings and hedonic (i.e., visual aesthetics) ratings may help to account for possible biases that existing clutter scales encounter.

3 Usability and User Experience

In Usability and User Experience research, perceived system aesthetics has been an integral variable of interest. Also, previous research on information design shows some connections between clutter aspects on the one hand and usability and user experience on the other. Tufte [28], for example, referred to the unnecessary visual information in charts and graphs, that has the potential to lead to confusion, as "chart junk." He recommended to avoid this type of information. Similarly, Nielsen's [29] ten usability heuristics include the heuristic "less is more", in which he proposes to avoid extraneous design features and irrelevant information. The "keep it short and simple" (KISS) principle (also known as: "Keep it simple, stupid"), alike, stated by the aircraft designer "Kelly" Johnson, urges designers to avoid unnecessary complication [30].

In the following, the concepts of Usability und User Experience will be described and some potential relations to Display Clutter will be outlined.

3.1 System Usability and Aesthetics

Hassenzahl [31] distinguished between 'pragmatic' and 'hedonic' system qualities. Mahlke [32] later referred to those qualities as 'instrumental' and 'non-instrumental' and showed that they were perceived as independent.

Instrumental qualities are related to system utility (i.e., user needs) as well as usability [33, 34]. Usability describes the quality of interaction between a user and a system in a particular context. ISO 9241-11 [35] defines usability as the extent to which users can accomplish a given task effectively, in a reasonable amount of time and effort (i.e., efficiently), as well as to their satisfaction. To capture the effectiveness and efficiency of a user interface different performance metrics (e.g., task success, accuracy, errors, time-on-task) have been used. For satisfaction measures, subjective judgments have been usually collected based on single item Likert-scale referring to general satisfaction or multi-dimensional scales [36].

Non-instrumental qualities are defined as a combination of aesthetic, symbolic, and motivational aspects [37]. Aesthetic aspects include visual aesthetics (colors, shapes), haptic quality, and acoustic quality. Symbolic aspects are distinguished in communicative and associative dimensions. And motivational aspects describe the ability of a system to stimulate the user to interact with it. The non-instrumental quality of visual aesthetics has been widely discussed and emphasized as a sensory input that leads to overall system judgment [32, 38].

The above described system usability and aesthetics are comparable with display-based aspects of clutter.

3.2 Perceived Usability and Aesthetics

As mentioned earlier, participants, when asked to rate display clutter, may evaluate the more pragmatic system qualities together with visual appeal of a display. To avoid this possible bias in usability, research a distinction is made between perceived usability and perceived aesthetics. The subjective perspective to the system usability is called perceived usability. It is usually evaluated with 7-point rating scales [e.g., 39]. For perceived visual aesthetics, some validated scales are used that cover several design features; in the following, especially one of these scales will be discussed in some detail and related to display clutter.

To capture perceived aesthetics of websites Lavie and Tractinsky [40] developed a scale, which consists of two dimensions "classical aesthetics" and "expressive aesthetics". "Classical aesthetics" refers to qualities that are typically associated with aesthetic design, such as pleasant, clean, clear, or symmetrical. "Expressive aesthetics" represents perceptions of creativity and originality, and includes items like sophisticated, special effects, and fascinating. The researchers found that both dimensions of aesthetics, but especially the "classical aesthetics", were highly correlated with perceived usability.

Lavie and colleagues [41] validated their aesthetics scale in three experiments with data-rich electronic maps. In their first experiment, they used 11 diverse electronic maps downloaded from various websites. Participants were asked to first examine each map and answer a content-related question, and then to evaluate each map. Based on the results, they refined the scale and also concluded that "expressive aesthetics" was not appropriate for map representations. In the second experiment, they varied the clutter level (i.e., defined as the amount of data) of electronic maps, along with the abstraction level and color schema. The experimental setup included a tracking system (left monitor), a navigation system (right monitor), and on-line questionnaires. In the tracking system participants were asked to maintain the distance of a blue square as close as possible to a moving target "X" by using a steering wheel. The navigation system, on the second monitor, displayed a map with a floating red dot cursor, which represented the location of the participant. At the bottom of the navigation screen navigation questions appeared referring to the locations relative to the cursor. By using arrow buttons on the steering wheel, the participants responded to these questions. For the on-line questionnaires, the other two tasks were halted, so the participants could fill out the perceived aesthetics and usability questionnaires on the navigation screen. Dependent measures were perceived aesthetics and usability of maps, as well as performance, response time, and accuracy. The study was able to validate the revised aesthetics scale. Furthermore, the results showed that the clutter level had a significant influence on both subjective judgments and behavioral performance: Maps with less details (i.e., low clutter) lead to higher perceived usability and aesthetics, and to better performance. Interestingly, the color variations only had an influence on some behavioral measures (response times and accuracy), but not on the perceived usability and aesthetics. The authors discuss the possibility that participants might have attributed the color to the salient cursor, which especially in the condition where the map was grey and the cursor red, assisted participants' performance. In the third experiment, the findings from the second experiment were confirmed; color only had an influence on objective measures and at the same time an interaction between color schema and cursor type appeared. The authors concluded that the results referring to color schemas might be specific to navigation tasks with maps and the color characteristics they chose might not have been distinguishable enough.

The reported study nicely connected the mostly accepted clutter approach (i.e., display density perspective) with usability measures and was able to show significant clutter effects on perceived usability as well as on perceived aesthetics. Furthermore, it revealed some design challenges with respect to color schema variations.

The Visual Aesthetics of Website Inventory (VisAWI) is a validated instrument, which measures the perceived aesthetics by including Colors as a parameter [42]. The other three parameters are Simplicity, Diversity, and Craftsmanship. The authors demonstrated that Simplicity highly correlated with "classical aesthetics" and Diversity correlated with "expressive aesthetics", while Colors and Craftsmanship explained additional facets of perceived visual aesthetics.

3.3 User Experience

Putting the different aspects together, that were discussed above, on the one side the objective system properties (clutter, usability, aesthetics) and on the other side the subjectively perceived usability and aesthetics, and the resulting user behavior (e.g., performance, visual search), a more complete picture of users' experience during system interaction can be drawn. Furthermore, it has been shown that not only perceived qualities play a central role in user's experience, but also the caused emotions, which the user encounters during system interaction, such as frustration, joy, or physiological reactions [43]. In ISO 9241-210 [44] User Experience (UX) is defined as "a person's perceptions and responses that result from the use or anticipated use of a product, system or service." Since this definition is rather broad, various theoretical approaches define UX in more detail.

The pragmatic/hedonic model of user experience by Hassenzahl [45] distinguishes between the two dimensions pragmatics and hedonics. Pragmatics refers to the achievement of "do-goals" and hedonics to the achievement of "be-goals" (e.g., "being special", "being competent"). When assessing the two dimensions, the focus of pragmatics is on utility and usability in association with a task; the focus of hedonics is on the user motive of owning and using a particular product, which can derive from "stimulation" (e.g., novelty and change), "identification" (e.g., relatedness), and "evocation" (e.g., symbolizing). His model of UX not only incorporates hedonic and pragmatic perceptions, but also relies on experiential aspects, such as global evaluation (i.e., actual experience), time (i.e., product perception can change over time), situated relevance (e.g., hedonics can be relevant in one situation, but irrelevant in another), and modes (i.e., user's general state goal and action-mode). Hassenzahl's model is regarded as a reductionist model of UX with the premise to make UX measureable and manageable.

Roto [46] refers to the hedonic/pragmatic model of UX from Hassenzahl [45], but also points out the importance of expected UX and long-term UX, and how they can relate to the UX during interaction.

Thüring and Mahlke [43] developed a theoretical framework based on empirical data, that consolidates different aspects of UX, the CUE model (Components of User Experience, see Fig. 1).

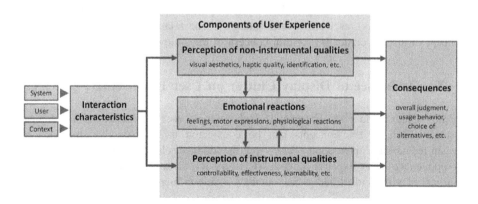

Fig. 1. Components of user experience (CUE model) by Thüring and Mahlke [43]

Influencing factors are system properties, user characteristics, and context. These interaction characteristics have a direct influence on the perception of instrumental and non-instrumental qualities. At the same time, emotional reactions are affected by both quality perceptions.

The later version of the CUE model was extended by including a bi-directional relationship between emotions and perceived user qualities [47, 48]. It is therefore assumed that emotions can also have an influence on perceived qualities. All three components have an impact on the consequences of user experience, such as overall judgment and usage behavior.

The CUE model has been used as a theoretical basis for several studies. The input variables (system, user, and context) provide the basis for the derivation of independent variables, the components (both classes of perception and emotions) are the basis for the derivation of dependent variables and their operationalization. Most often varied features in such studies were usability and visual aesthetics of a system [e.g., 48].

The variety of products or technical systems studied in User Experience (UX) research in general seems very broad. According to literature review by Bargas-Avila and Hornbæk [49], 64% of UX research has been applied to "leisure usage", 18% to "work" products, and 18% to "mixed" products. Based on these numbers the authors assume that with the shift from usability research to the more holistic UX approach the focus of the products most researchers study also changed. It has to be mentioned though that there are some exceptions, where UX research addresses experiences in the workplace [50–53].

With regard to the concepts of Display Clutter and User Experience, it seems obvious that there are several similarities between them. At first glance, what distinguishes them the most are the fields of application. Display Clutter has been associated with data-rich domains in Ergonomics and Human Factors (e.g., aviation, radar research), whereas in User Experience research more "everyday life" products have been more dominant test objects.

User Experience definitions described above, are associated with many different constructs that play a role before, during, and after the interaction with a product. The most interesting aspects for the present paper are system properties (i.e., objective usability and aesthetics) and perceived system qualities (i.e., perceived usability and perceived aesthetics), as well as their interplay. The relation of these aspects to the concept of display clutter is a central concern of the following elaboration.

4   The Influence of Display Clutter on User Experience

Display Clutter and User Experience both refer to user interaction with technical systems. Each of the concepts can be considered as a distinctive approach to human-technology interaction. Based on the defined clutter perspectives and the Components of User Experience model (CUE model) the touch points between the two approaches will be identified as well as the possible influence of display clutter on the user experience.

Display clutter definitions can be divided into two main categories: Display-based and user-based factors. In the following, the two factors will be directly related to instrumental and non-instrumental qualities of the CUE model. Table 1 summarizes their expected relationship.

Table 1. Impact of clutter on the two components of user experience

Types of clutter/System qual.	Instrumental (pragmatic)	Non-instrumental (hedonic)
Display-based	Objective usability	Visual design
User-based	Perceived (subj.) usability	Perceived aesthetics

4.1 Display-Based Factors

Display-based factors refer to display properties solely, without considering the context of the display and the user. Display-based factors include the density perspective of clutter, the layout perspective, as well as the target-background similarity perspective. The layout perspective has two sub-groups: Display organization (e.g., logical or conceptual grouping, symmetry) and consistency (e.g., color, luminance, contrast, orientation).

Display-Based Clutter Influences the Instrumental Quality "Objective Usability". When comparing those perspectives with the system properties defined in the CUE model, it becomes obvious that most of the display-based clutter perspectives (i.e., density, organization, target-background) are comparable to instrumental qualities, except for consistency. Since instrumental qualities include technical features, self-descriptiveness, and controllability, they are expected to be influenced by the amount of information shown on a screen as well as with the logical organization of information.

Display-Based Clutter Influences the Non-Instrumental Quality "Visual Design". Consistency refers to design features that have no direct relation to display content. Therefore, they match very well with the non-instrumental qualities in the CUE model that also include visual aesthetics of the system input. The Visual Aesthetics of Website Inventory (VisAWI) from Moshagen and Thielsch [42] identified four parameters of visual aesthetics: Simplicity, Diversity, Colors, and Craftsmanship. Most of them, and especially the first three facets, seem to be represented in display-based clutter. It can be assumed that display-based clutter features influence visual design.

The main differences between the two concepts appear in the way the display properties are measured. The display-based factors of clutter are usually determined by some image-processing algorithms, while the instrumental and non-instrumental display qualities either refer to objective usability measures or to some design guidelines. The touch point here could be the origin of the design guidelines that might be of some analytical nature as well. Furthermore, an additional dimension that covers the user perspective, known as perceived aesthetics in UX research, would be beneficial for cluttered system properties as well. It would test the existing visual design assumptions with target users and complement the existing objective approaches. Seckler and colleagues [54], for example, show the benefits of strictly distinguishing between objective design factors and users' visual aesthetics perception.

4.2   User-Based Factors

The user-based clutter factors refer to the two perspectives of clutter: task-irrelevance and to performance and attentional costs.

User-Based Clutter Influences the Instrumental Quality "Perceived Usability". With the user-based approach, the degree of display clutter is being inferred from its performance costs. Since it also includes context, task, and user characteristics, that approach is directly comparable with the usability aspect of instrumental qualities from the CUE model. Besides, interaction characteristics (e.g., reaction time, time on task, error rate) that address performance are an integral part of instrumental qualities as well, in addition to subjective ratings (e.g., satisfaction, general usability perception). The task-irrelevance perspective of clutter can to some extent be related to the utility aspect of instrumental qualities; if the displayed information is not relevant for the task at hand, it is more likely that the 'user needs' cannot be accomplished with the system. On the contrary: It distracts and ties up resources, which can be seen in the interaction characteristics and thus reduces the subjective usability (along with the objective usability). Therefore, user-based clutter will have a negative influence on the perceived usability.

The measurement of this type of clutter is almost the same or very similar to the typical usability performance measures. The only difference might be the fact that in the domains where display clutter is evaluated, the visual search performance can be a central variable of interest. Therefore, visual search tasks and their measurement will be found more often in display clutter research than in usability research.

4.3   Perceived Display Properties

Perceived display clutter is usually based on either general subjective clutter judgment (i.e., one item Likert-scale) or on a multi-dimensional scale. In both cases the evaluation is targeting perceived display properties. The question now is, whether it has some similarities with the perceived aesthetics ratings.

User-Based Clutter Influences the Non-instrumental Quality "Perceived Aesthetics". To some extent the clutter rating can refer to self-descriptiveness of the display, which is a part of usability. The focus of the judgment though will remain on the display properties and will not include user satisfaction with the display. The clutter rating can also include the visual appearance of display, such as color combination and contrast. Therefore, it is assumed that perceived display clutter will influence perceived aesthetics.

In the preceding chapter the attempt was to highlight the possible relationship between display clutter and User Experience and to especially elaborate on how display clutter can influence the user experience. The result is a two-by-two matrix that outlines the relationship between display-based and user-based clutter with instrumental and non-instrumental system qualities.

5 Conclusion

The contribution has shown where aspects of clutter and UX overlap and complement each other. Furthermore, it was described how clutter manifests itself in (objective) system properties and negatively influences aspects of UX (i.e., perceived usability and perceived aesthetics). From a theoretical point of view, the display clutter concept as well as the UX concept have their advantages as well was weaknesses, which is why they complement each other very well.

The positive aspect about the different display clutter perspectives, and especially the display-based factors, is the possibility of defining display properties and varying them based on objective design and statistical attributes (in image-processing algorithms). The User Experience approach, on the other side, captures the user interaction in a more complementary way by varying system properties and looking at users' behavior, users' system perception as well as users' emotional reactions. Furthermore, the User Experience concept is based on a theoretical framework that makes the choice of appropriate research methods easier. A rather negative aspect about Display Clutter is the missing theoretical framework that researchers could refer to. The definition of clutter seems to vary by domain and by research project.

From a methodological point of view, it will be beneficial to assess the influence of display-based and use-based clutter on the subjectively perceived usability and the perceived aesthetics. This will help to approach the challenge of finding an ideal middle ground between too much and too little information, and manage the negative influences of clutter. The perceived clutter measurement could be as well extended by including multi-dimensional user perceptions (in addition to display properties) to get a more complete picture of user interaction with a complex system. Moreover, for future research existing validated scales from UX research can be used or extended as showcased by Lavie and colleagues [41].

As a consequence, from a practical design point of view, it is essential to strive for avoiding clutter and to be aware of its negative implications to users' experience.

References

1. Moacdieh, N., Sarter, N.: Display clutter: a review of definitions and measurement techniques. Hum. Factors **57**(1), 61–100 (2014)
2. Tullis, T.S.: The formatting of alphanumeric displays: a review and analysis. Hum. Factors **25**, 657–682 (1983)
3. Ververs, P.M., Wickens, C.D.: Head-up displays: effect of clutter, display intensity, and display location on pilot performance. Int. J. Aviat. Psychol. **8**, 377–403 (1998)
4. Mack, M.L., Oliva, A.: Computational estimation of visual complexity. In: Paper presented at the 12th Annual Object, Perception, Attention, and Memory Conference, Minneapolis, MN (2004)
5. Wolfe, J.M.: Guided search 2.0: a revised model of visual search. Psychon. Bull. Rev. **1**, 202–238 (1994)
6. Palmer, J.: Set-size effects in visual search: the effect of attention is independent of the stimulus for simple tasks. Vis. Res. **34**, 1703–1721 (1994)

7. Wickens, C.D., Hollands, J.G., Banbury, S., Parasuraman, R.: Engineering Psychology and Human Performance, 4th edn. Pearson Education, Upper Saddle River (2013)
8. Grahame, M., Laberge, J., Scialfa, C.T.: Age differences in search of web pages: the effects of link size, link number, and clutter. Hum. Factors **46**, 385–398 (2004)
9. Rosenholtz, R., Li, Y., Nakano, L.: Measuring visual clutter. J. Vis. **7**(2), 1–22 (2007)
10. Shneiderman, B., Plaisant, C., Cohen, M., Jacobs, S.: Designing the User Interface: Strategies for Effective Human-Computer Interaction, 5th edn. Prentice Hall, Upper Saddle River (2009)
11. Tullis, T.S.: Screen design. In: Helander, M. (ed.) Handbook of Human-Computer Interaction, pp. 377–411. North-Holland, Amsterdam (1988)
12. Beck, M.R., Lohrenz, M.C., Trafton, J.G.: Measuring search efficiency in complex visual search tasks: global and local clutter. J. Exp. Psychol. Appl. **16**, 238–250 (2010)
13. Rosenholtz, R.: A simple saliency model predicts a number of motion popout phenomena. Vis. Res. **39**, 3157–3163 (1999)
14. Moore, R.K.: Masked target transform volume clutter metric for human observer visual search modeling (Doctoral dissertation). Available from ProQuest Dissertations and Theses database (UMI No. 3400193) (2009)
15. Xu, D., Shi, Z., Luo, H.: A structural difference based image clutter metric with brain cognitive model constraints. Infrared Phys. Technol. **57**, 28–35 (2012)
16. Chu, X., Yang, C., Li, Q.: Contrast-sensitivity-function-based clutter metric. Opt. Eng. **51**(6), 067003 (2012)
17. Alexander, A.L., Stelzer, E.M., Kim, S.-H., Kaber, D.B.: Bottom-up and top-down contributors to pilot perceptions of display clutter in advanced flight deck technologies. In: Proceedings of the Human Factors and Ergonomics Society 52nd Annual Meeting, pp. 1180–1184. Human Factors and Ergonomics Society, Santa Monica (2008)
18. Rosenholtz, R., Li, Y., Mansfield, J., Jin, Z.: Feature congestion: a measure of display clutter. In: Proceedings of the SIGCHI Conference on Human Factors in Computing Systems, pp. 761–770. ACM Press, New York (2005)
19. Neider, M.B., Zelinsky, G.J.: Cutting through the clutter: searching for targets in evolving complex scenes. J. Vis. **11**(14), 7 (2011)
20. Beck, M.R., Trenchard, M., van Lamsweerde, A., Goldstein, R.R., Lohrenz, M.: Searching in clutter: visual attention strategies of expert pilots. In: Proceedings of the Human Factors and Ergonomics Society 56th Annual Meeting, pp. 1411–1415. Human Factors and Ergonomics Society, Santa Monica (2012)
21. Goldberg, J.H., Kotval, X.P.: Computer interface evaluation using eye movements: methods and constructs. Int. J. Ind. Ergon. **24**, 631–645 (1999)
22. Kim, S.-H., Prinzel, L.J., Kaber, D.B., Alexander, A.L., Stelzer, E.M., Kaufmann, K., Veil, T.: Multidimensional measure of display clutter and pilot performance for advanced head-up display. Aviat. Space Environ. Med. **82**, 1013–1022 (2011)
23. Kaber, D., Kim, S.-H., Kaufmann, K., Alexander, A., Steltzer, E., Hsiang, S.: Modeling the effects of HUD visual properties, pilot experience and flight scenario on a multi-dimensional measure of clutter. Langley Research Center, Hampton (2008)
24. Naylor, J.: The influence of dynamics, flight domain and individual flight training & experience on pilot perception of clutter in aviation displays (Master's thesis) (2010). http://repository.lib.ncsu.edu/ir/handle/1840.16/6103
25. Alexander, A.L., Kaber, D.B., Kim, S.-H., Stelzer, E.M., Kaufmann, K., Prinzel III, L.J.: Measurement and modeling of display clutter in advanced flight deck technologies. Int. J. Aviat. Psychol. **22**, 299–318 (2012)

26. Kaufmann, K., Kaber, D.B.: The influence of individual differences in perceptual performance on pilot perceptions of head-up display clutter. In: Proceedings of the Human Factors and Ergonomics Society 54th Annual Meeting, pp. 70–74. Human Factors and Ergonomics Society, Santa Monica (2010)
27. Kaber, D.B., Alexander, A., Kaufmann, K., Kim, S.H., Naylor, J.T., Entin, E.: Testing and validation of a psychophysically defined metric of display clutter (Final Report: NASA Langley Research Center Grant. NNL06AA21A). NASA Langley Research Center, Hampton, VA (2009)
28. Tufte, E.: The Visual Display of Quantitative Information, 2nd edn. Graphics Press, Cheshire (1983)
29. Nielsen, J.: Heuristic evaluation. In: Nielsen, J., Mack, R.L. (eds.) Usability Inspection Methods. Wiley, New York (1994)
30. Rich, B.R.: Clarence Leonard (Kelly) Johnson: 1910–1990: A Biographical Memoir, p. 13. National Academies Press, Washington (1995)
31. Hassenzahl, M., Kekez, R., Burmester, M.: The importance of software's pragmatic quality depends of usage modes. In: Luczak, H., Çakir, A.E., Çakir, G. (eds.) Proceedings of the 6th International Conference on Work With Display Units (WWDU 2002), pp. 275–276. Ergonomic Institut für Arbeits- und Sozialforschung, Berlin (2002)
32. Mahlke, S.: User Experience of Interaction with Technical Systems: Theories, Methods, Empirical Results, and Their Application to the Design of Interactive Systems. VDM Verlag, Saarbrücken (2008)
33. Shackel, B.: Usability - context, framework, design and evaluation. In: Shackel, B., Richardson, S. (eds.) Human Factors for Informatics Usability, pp. 21–38. Cambridge University Press, Cambridge (1991)
34. Nielsen, J.: Usability Engineering. Academic Press, San Diego (1993)
35. ISO 9241-11: Ergonomic requirements for office work with visual display terminals (VDTs) – Part 11: Guidance on usability. International Standardization Organization (ISO), Geneva (1998, 2015)
36. Lindgaard, G., Dudek, C.: What is this evasive beast we call user satisfaction? Interact. Comput. 15(3), 429–452 (2003)
37. Mahlke, S., Lemke, I., Thüring, M.: The diversity of non-instrumental qualities in human-technology interaction. mmi interaktiv 13, 55–64 (2007)
38. Hassenzahl, M.: Aesthetics in interactive products: correlates and consequences of beauty. In: Schifferstein, H.N.J., Hekkert, P. (eds.) Product Experience. Elsevier, Amsterdam (2007)
39. Kirakowski, J.: The software usability measurement inventory: background and usage. In: Jordan, P.W., Thomas, B., Weerdmeester, B.A., McClelland, I.L. (eds.) Usability Evaluation in Industry, pp. 169–178. Taylor & Francis, London (1996)
40. Lavie, T., Tractinsky, N.: Assessing dimensions of perceived visual aesthetics of websites. Int. J. Hum Comput Stud. 60(3), 269–298 (2004)
41. Lavie, T., Oron-Gilad, T., Meyer, J.: Aesthetics and usability of in-vehicle navigation displays. Int. J. Hum Comput Stud. 69(1), 80–99 (2011)
42. Moshagen, M., Thielsch, M.T.: Facets of visual aesthetics. Int. J. Hum Comput Stud. 68(10), 689–709 (2010)
43. Thüring, M., Mahlke, S.: Usability, aesthetics and emotions in human–technology interaction. Int. J. Psychol. 42(4), 253–264 (2007)
44. ISO 9241-210: Ergonomics of Human-System Interaction – Part 210: Human-Centred Design Process for Interactive Systems. International Standardization Organization (ISO), Geneva (2010)

45. Hassenzahl, M.: The hedonic/pragmatic model of user experience. In: Law, E., Vermeeren, A., Hassenzahl, M., Blythe, M. (eds.) Towards a UX Manifesto – Proceedings of a Cost-Affiliated Workshop on HCI 2008, pp. 10–14 (2007)

46. Roto, V.: User experience from product creation perspective. In: Law, E., Vermeeren, A., Hassenzahl, M., Blythe, M. (eds.) Towards a UX Manifesto – Proceedings of a Cost-Affiliated Workshop on HCI 2008, pp. 31–34 (2007)

47. Minge, M., Wagner, I., Thüring, M.: Developing and validating and english version of the meCUE questionnaire for measuring user experience. In: Proceedings of the 60th Annual Meeting of the Human Factors and Ergonomics Society 2016, pp. 2056–2060. Sage Publications, New York (2016)

48. Minge, M., Thüring, M.: Hedonic and pragmatic halo effects at early stages of user experience. Int. J. Hum Comput Stud. **109**, 13–25 (2018)

49. Bargas-Avila, J.A., Hornbæk, K.: Old wine in new bottles or novel challenges: a critical analysis of empirical studies of user experience. In: Proceedings of the SIGCHI Conference on Human Factors in Computing Systems, pp. 2689–2698. ACM, May 2011

50. Burmester, M., Zeiner, K.M., Laib, M., Hermosa Perrino, C., Queßeleit, M.-L.: Experience design and positive design as an alternative to classical human factors approaches. In: Beckmann, C., Gross, T. (eds.) INTERACT 2015 Adjunct Proceedings, pp. 153–160. University of Bamberg Press, Bamberg (2015)

51. Harbich, S., Hassenzahl, M.: Beyond task completion in the workplace: execute, engage, evolve, expand. In: Peter, C., Beale, R. (eds.) Affect and Emotion in Human-Computer Interaction. LNCS, vol. 4868, pp. 154–162. Springer, Heidelberg (2008). https://doi.org/10.1007/978-3-540-85099-1_13

52. Lu, Y., Roto, V.: Evoking meaningful experiences at work–a positive design framework for work tools. J. Eng. Des. **26**(4–6), 99–120 (2015)

53. Zeiner, K.M., Laib, M., Schippert, K., Burmester, M.: Identifying experience categories to design for positive experiences with technology at work. In: Proceedings of the 2016 CHI Conference Extended Abstracts on Human Factors in Computing Systems, pp. 3013–3020. ACM, New York (2016)

54. Seckler, M., Opwis, K., Tuch, A.N.: Linking objective design factors with subjective aesthetics: an experimental study on how structure and color of websites affect the facets of users' visual aesthetic perception. Comput. Hum. Behav. **49**, 375–389 (2015)

Improving Value-Awareness Through Storytelling in User Experience Design

Qiong Peng[1,2(✉)], Jean-Bernard Martens[2], and Xiaoying Tian[1]

[1] Department of Culture and Art,
Chengdu University of Information Technology, Chengdu, China
pengqiongsjtu@gmail.com
[2] Department of Industrial Design, Eindhoven University of Technology,
Eindhoven, The Netherlands

Abstract. Value has been one of the topics in HCI and design field with various definitions from perspectives. Values are in essence related to experience because they are personal perception and assessment on objects, products, or services. Hence, it makes sense to involve values in user experience design and make values as one of the design goals. However, values are usually easy to take for granted but hard to work with in design practices. This paper proposed a storytelling-value approach with the aim to improve awareness of values in user experience design. It was based on storytelling methodology that emphasizes scenario-based envisioning and the results from a focus group which involved user experience designer in to discuss values in UX design. A co-design workshop was conducted as a support for improvement of the approach. It is promising to optimize this storytelling-value approach in the future since most of the participants showed their positive attitudes not only to the necessity in methods development but also to the acceptance of this approach.

Keywords: Values · Value awareness · Storytelling · User experience

1 Introduction

Value has been long considered in HCI and design field, and many approaches or tools have been developed to explore and support value creation, especially in product and service innovation. It is generally defined and discussed from economic and moral perspectives, such as customer value, value proposition design [1] emphasising on creating product and service that customer wants, and value-sensitive design [2] focusing on designing to support moral values of human wellbeing. Researches in participatory design are paid attention to values-led inquiry in support of participants' values [3, 4]. As value is defined as one of the constructs of user experience [5] and value is also characterized as an experience [6], it makes sense to involve value in the consideration of user experience design and make value as one of the user experience design goals. The majority of the adoption in user experience design is the combination of user experience and business models to pursue value creation, for instance, the value design method [7]. However, though these approaches stress on values creation, there is a lack of research on awareness of values from designers' perspective. Meanwhile, the

© Springer International Publishing AG, part of Springer Nature 2018
A. Marcus and W. Wang (Eds.): DUXU 2018, LNCS 10918, pp. 141–152, 2018.
https://doi.org/10.1007/978-3-319-91797-9_11

design methodology for value in user experience design process has not been made explicit to be effectively and easily adopted. Practitioners in user experience design cannot yet fully appreciate the benefits and importance of value creation in early design stages since they mostly separate values from experience and forget to consider about values due to lacking value awareness. Hence, the lack of value awareness results in a lack of clear understanding of how to work with value. There is obviously a need for such practical or operational approaches. In this paper, we present a research on an approach based on storytelling which emphasize improving value awareness by understanding and foregrounding of value in storytelling process from designers' perspective. The goal of this research was to provide visions that enhance UX designers' awareness of values to bridge the gap between designers' intention and users' needs fulfilment, then to improve user experience design.

In this paper, we first reviewed relevant literature on value both within and outside design field. Next, a focus group was held by involving UX designers to collect their opinions on values in their user experience design practices to gain insights into the approach development. Then, we presented the storytelling-value approach and gathered feedback for improvement. Finally, we considered several specific aspects of future work.

This research is experimental yet grounds on a literature study and exemplary application. It provides a direction for user experience designers to take value into account in the design process. The value awareness also indicates that value in user experience design should be viewed as a holistic system, not only focusing value creation, but also laying equal emphasis on other aspects like value delivery, value perception and value realization.

2 Related Work

Values are wildly discussed in design from many different perspectives. What values are involved in design? Whose values are at issue? How to work with values? How to decide users' feedback of values? All the questions should be comprehended by designers. Values usually refer to wealth, loyalty, equality, justice etc. However, there is no common definition of value in HCI [8] as researchers pointed out. A value is a shared idea about people's beliefs of something in desirability, goodness [9] or worth. Generally speaking, there are three main perspectives in HCI and design field: economic values, human values and user values of products. From economic perspective, values are usually interpreted with money like return and investment, referring to the economic worth objects [10], products or services. Human values are another thread which include moral values such as right, autonomy, privacy, etc. and non-moral values pertinent to ownership, property, etc. User values of products, similar to customer values, usually focus on usability which indicates the desired benefits of a product [11].

The literatures concerning value in design are the methodologies of value-centric design [12, 13] and value-driven design [14]. Value-centric design has been popular based on the background of Donald Norman's proposition of considering users in design [15] which lays the foundation for user-centred design methodology. It requires designers not only to know what values should be considered but also to understand whose values are at issue. Friedman et al. made a notable contribution to understanding and accounting for values by introducing value-sensitive design (VSD) [2, 11]. She defines value with an extended meaning as "what a person or group of people consider important in life" [10]. Value-sensitive design as a theoretically grounded approach supports designers to keep an eye toward values in design process from three aspects: conceptual investigation, empirical investigation and technical investigations [2]. Conceptual investigation helps to answer some basic questions, such as what values and whose values should be taken into account. Empirical investigation focus on human context and technical investigations involves consideration of technologies. Friedman and her colleagues also developed value scenarios as "a technique to envisioning systemic effect of new technologies" [16] and the envisioning cards as "a toolkit for catalysing humanistic and technical imaginations" [17] to make value-sensitive design method more operational by envisioning techniques. Because value-sensitive design approach roots in social-technical analysis, it takes account of the human values with attention to importance in human life such as right, privacy, and autonomy, which seems separating value from user experience. However, it is worth mentioning that its envisioning section implies the possible directions of talking about values in an imaginational style which is in accord with our proposed storytelling method.

Values are much studied in participatory design (PD) since PD which involves end-users as participants into design process has an inherent focus on values. Value-led inquiry [3, 4] proposed by Iversen et al. is used in participatory design (PD) for designers to engage with human values. It has been proved positively to promotes the value awareness of the participants in PD. Though it highlights the emergent and dynamic properties of value in dialogical process, it regards values separately from experience, while experience as proposed by Hassenzahl as dynamic, subjective and context-dependent [18] shares the some of the same properties with values. Others about value in design are mostly from design management perspectives which combine business value and customer value into design, for instance, Bussracumpakorn, C studied different values perceived by customers to demonstrate the significant role of design is value creation [19]; the proposition of emotional value creation through co-prototyping [20]; a model quantifies and visualises design values within service design industry from customers' perspective [21]; the value design method was proposed by Gultekin et al. to assist designers to integrate user insights, business insights and stakeholder expectations in design process [7]. It seems that attention is paid to value creation in most of the current researches.

Literatures of user values also indicate that values sometimes be confused with universal usability. Usability mostly refers to the product's characteristics especially in performance, including utility, ease of use, easy to learn, easy to recover from errors, etc. [22]. While user values not only depend on users' perception of the performance and quality of a product, but also are influenced by the goals and contexts, etc. Through the interaction between users and the product, experience changes over time, and values do the same.

Values in design are substantially users' measures of products' worth in particular contexts. Users engage in value-seeking by interaction with products based on their expectations. They would experience values through the mental process including value expectation—value perception—value realization. Values are generic experience and work as one construct of user experience [5]. Helkkula et al. characterized values as an experience [6] from the perspective of phenomenology. Values are always connected to values experience or experience of values. Though values differ individually and culturally, the temporal, dynamic and contextual features of values in accordance with other ordinary user experiences makes it reasonable to be discussed by storytelling which potentially helps people to interpret and make sense of experience as well. Storytelling is a narrative methodology offering illustrations of past and current experience and imagination of future through stories. It supports to explore user experience and values in various contexts. Hence, it makes sense to involve values in user experience design and make values as one of the design goals.

3   Research Methods

In order to facilitate UX designers to work with value in user experience design process, a focus group was conducted to collect their opinions on value in the context of user experience design including definitions of values, what values they take into account when designing, and how they involve values in design activities. The whole process was recorded into audio documents and analysed. The results of the focus group provided insights to develop our storytelling method to support UX designers think about values. The framework of the storytelling-value approach was proposed and developed through co-design with designer in a workshop.

4   A Focus Group

In the focus group, 15 designers (60% male and 40% female) were involved in to share their viewpoints about values. The participants including Ph.D.'s (46.7%), master students (40%) and undergraduate students (13.3%) were working or ever worked for user experience design. Their experience in UX design (60% of them have experience more than three years, 6.7% less than one year, and 33.3% between one year to three years) was reported by themselves in an information sheet before the starting the focus group discussion. All of them believed that they had the experience working with value (here we indicated the working with value by not only involving values but also just thinking about them based on their own definitions). During the focus group, participants discussed and shared their opinions of values based on user experience design context. The audio record of the focus group was transcribed verbatim and individual quotes were extracted and labelled. Three researchers involved in the analysis of the quotes and coding process.

The results of the focus group can be summarized into three aspects: First, all of the participants believed that a need for the methodology or tools to support value in user experience design probably exits, because it seems not as expected to involve values in design practice. The examples of their opinions like: "I think about values of my design from my own perspective and I am not quite sure whether the users will get it." "I worked with value mostly by giving functionalities to the products or improving usability". "The values depend on the feedback of the users and I can only confirm them after the testing. How can I know that earlier?" Secondly, their discussion about values in UX design mostly referred to users' assessment of owing, using and experience products. For instance, more than half of the participants believed values mean goals achievement or needs fulfilment after using the products. Thirdly, though the participants have their own definitions on values which are quite different, some similar key words were selected such as "quality", "functionality", "useful", "good usability", "good experience", etc. The mentioned values in user experience design mainly focused on the topics such as user, experience, using, products and the related quotes were categorized into two main clusters (shown in Table 1): product-inherent values which refers to opinions about the products as the output of user experience design including functional and aesthetic ones, and personal values that were related to values

Table 1. The clustering of the quotes about values in user experience design

Category	Sub-category	Quote no.	Examples
Product-inherent values	Functional values	38	Good performance Use advanced technology Usefulness Good usability Achieve goals Meet needs …
	Aesthetic values	27	Beautiful Nice look Nice colours Good interface design …
Personal values	Emotional values	36	Satisfied Happy after using Enjoy myself when using Simple to use Interesting Flow …
	Social values	8	Get respect More socially connected Get recognition Helpfulness …
	Cultural values	6	Culture symbolic Cultural colours and icons Expressing cultural features …

endorsed by individuals about personal aspects. The product-inherent values are the ones that more focus on product itself, generated and perceived by users directly from encountering and interacting with products. While the personal values include both moral values and non-moral values, as categorized into three sub-categories: emotional values, social values and cultural values. The clustering helped us to get a sense of the values that are involved in user experience design. We used these identified values in the development of the storytelling-value approach.

5   Storytelling-Value Approach Introduction

Based on the literature and the results of the focus group, we proposed that user experience designers can work with value in storytelling followed by the two sections: Analyse by storytelling and Envision by storytelling (shown in Fig. 1). For UX designers, what to design and how to design are the two important questions needed to be considered even before starting design. We made design for the future based on past and current situations or problems, and storytelling facilitate us to figure out the problems, analyse the design opportunities and envision the design. However, Values can be taken into account from different perspectives and purposes in different stages of UX design. They are not designed directed, but embedded inherently in the designed products and experienced by users through perception by encountering and interaction, and ex post realization. Hence, UX designers should think about and deal with values from a holistic point of view by taking users into consideration. There are three phases in the relationship between users and products: before using—in using—after using. Before using, users possibly have already got the expected values, while from designers' perspectives, these values are related to users' needs and should be considered as the intended values and the delivered values when designing. In the analysis phase of the storytelling, they can analyse what values that users need and can be converted into the intended values, then they can decide what to design and how to involve values in to deliver the intended values based on their design assumptions, like improving human welfare by the products or services, or just simply design to solve a problem in the daily life. In envisioning phase, UX designers can envision in storytelling and these future scenarios in storytelling offer designers vivid illustrations about the value perception and realization by users.

The proposed Storytelling-Value Approach is based on the story construction part (see Fig. 2) of the Integrated Storytelling Method [23] we introduced before. The Integrated storytelling method provides a framework of storytelling methodology to support user experience design. This storytelling-value approach is an extension which more focuses on value awareness. Based on the same five stages: Setting—Development 1—Climax—Development 2—Ending, more attention is paid to the later three stages. In climax in the storytelling process, the problems emerging and developing into conflicts are analysed under the same conflict analysis principle, which stresses the comparison of the basic needs of users and reality. Values are usually indicated by these needs. The analysing and envision phases are highlighted and detailed in the stages from climax to ending as Fig. 3 shows.

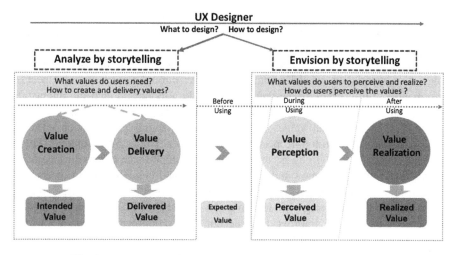

Fig. 1. The two sections of the value consideration in UX design

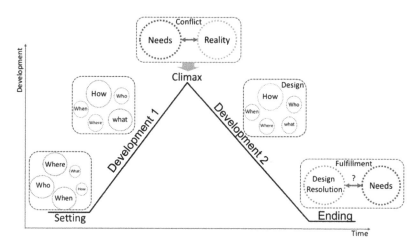

Fig. 2. The five stages of the storytelling-value approach

Value awareness would be improved by detailing the storytelling procedure. It also helps to solve the problems of the integrated storytelling method that it seems too general to be applied by designers in design practice. The stage of Development 2 in storytelling actually involves the envisioning of the design and interaction between users and the products. The needs list works as a guideline which helps designers to decide what the product it will be and what values the product would deliver. The product design referring to physical features, functionality etc. an be envisioned in

Design stage. While in the Interaction stage, designers can envision the scenarios when users interact with the product. User use the proposed product in the specific context and they can perceive the functional values such as good quality, advanced technology, usefulness, ease of use, etc., the aesthetic values such as beautiful or fashionable form design, nice material etc. as well as emotional values through perceiving the aspects of performance, utility, usability, aesthetics, etc. of the product through the interaction. Users would experience the value realization continuously in the Impact stage after the interaction. The emotional values like satisfaction, happiness, frustration, etc., the social values like recognition, respect, trust and cultural values like symbolic features are usually realized through users' realization of the importance or significance of the product. The value perception and realization differ individually because users have their definitions and opinions of these values, and not every user would experience all of the values in the five categories. However, for designers, it is important to take them into account in order to improve their design by promoting fulfilment of the user values. Another aspect which should not be neglected is that values as an experience would be dynamic over time, and storytelling provides opportunities for designers to envision what would happen and value changes along the timeline.

The storytelling-value approach works as a guideline to provide designers an overview of the values which possibly should be considered when designing based on user's needs. A check-list is suggested as a support to make concrete design strategies or decisions as shown in Fig. 4 as an example.

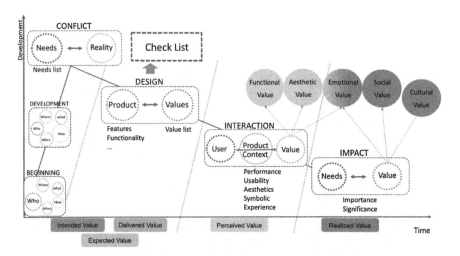

Fig. 3. The framework of value awareness

Check List		
Values	**Value Details**	**Design Strategies**
Functional	Performance Quality ...	Advanced technology, Good Structure design Simple operation ...
Aesthetic	Beautiful Fashionable ...	Nice color, Amazing shape Interface design ...
Emotional	Satisfied Happiness ...	fulfill the task quickly, easily Simple interaction ...
Social	Respect Recognition Environmentalism ...	Cool form, Social connection, sharing Environmental materials ...
Cultural	Symbolic Well-being ...	Symbols, Colors for special culture ....
Others	...	

Fig. 4. An example of the check list to support design strategies

6   Co-design Workshop

This storytelling-value approach was developed through co-design with design students. The workshop based on a real design project which was related to user experience design, and all the participants worked together to generate and develop design ideas guided by this approach. The initial framework of the proposed storytelling-value approach was put on the wall so that everyone could see it and worked based on it. Values were reminded and discussed when we made generation of the design ideas. The whole process was video recorded which was used to support analysis afterwards and all the participants were encouraged to report the problems or their opinions when necessary by thinking-aloud during the process. Some design ideas were generated and discussed and the output was presented in text, sketches and storyboards. A questionnaire including participants' basic information and the questions about acceptance from both utility and usability aspects. The results of the co-design workshop firstly showed the positive attitudes in acceptance of the approach itself. All the participants believed that it did improve their awareness of values in user experience design, and help them to make a holistic consideration of design by analysing both the user needs and values and envisioning in the storytelling process. Participants' opinions of the approach design not only referred to utility and usability but also involved something else in, such as advices on the adoption of the approach in workshops, time consideration and visual presentation, etc. The feedback had been used in the iteration design of the approach.

7 Discussion

In this paper, we presented the storytelling-values approach and its background as well as co-design improvement. This is primarily a concept paper with limited empirical illustration using interpretive research methods. We endeavoured to contribute to user experience design by combining storytelling and values into discussion. The narratives and scenario-based nature of storytelling benefits storytelling as a good way to express and discuss user experience including values. Through the positive feedback form the co-design workshop also indicated that this approach is potentially in improving value awareness for user experience designer because they usually forget or not mention it when design, this approach is still in its infant stages and needed to be improved. It seems to more appropriate to adopt the approach in ideation phase since storytelling method takes advantage of envisioning in scenarios.

Like all studies, the present research has certain acknowledged limitations. First, there were limited number of participants in both focus group and co-design workshop. All the participants involved are from universities, without any UX designers externally working in design companies. The difference in working environment probably influence their opinions on values since UX designers in companies should also take time, cost, available resources etc. into account when they make design. They may also view values from more practical perspectives which we did not get only from our participants.

Secondly, the storytelling-value approach was proposed with the aim to improve value awareness in design. In fact, value awareness is necessary during the whole design process, especially in real design projects which involve more factors from economical aspects or practical aspects in companies. we only tried to adopt it in ideation phase of UX design and it also seemed to be more suitable in early stages of design.

At last, the evaluation of the application of this approach is not clear. Participants gave feedback by their self-report on value awareness. Whether the awareness has been improved and how much it is increased is still confusing. Values as an experience change over time, and people who use this approach also experience the same dynamic change in their values in the approach. Therefore, in order to facilitate UX designers work with value, it is imperative to deal with all the limitations to make it more pragmatic in design practice.

8 Conclusion

In this paper, we introduced the storytelling-value approach which was developed to help improving awareness of value in user experience design. Values are important in user experience design because values are an experience, and they should be considered from a holistic point of view so that user experience would be improved by enhancement of value awareness. Our highlight of value awareness means that values should be considered in UX design process. The co-design workshop provided insights into design optimization. In the next phase of our research, we will examine the application of this approach in more design practice.

Acknowledgements. The research reported in this paper was supported by the 2017 project (WLWH17-23), 2016 project (2016Z036) and 2014 project (GY-14YB-13) of Sichuan Province Education Department of China. It is also part of the PhD research. Thanks to all who were involved in this research.

References

1. Osterwalder, A., Pigneur, Y., Bernarda, G., Smith, A.: Value Proposition Design: How to Create Products and Services Customers Want. Wiley, London (2014)
2. Friedman, B., Kahn, P., Borning, A.: Value sensitive design: theory and methods. University of Washington Technical report, pp. 02–12 (2002)
3. Leong, T.W., Iversen, O.S.: Values-led participatory design as a pursuit of meaningful alternatives. In: Proceedings of the Annual Meeting of the Australian Special Interest Group for Computer Human Interaction, New York, NY, USA, pp. 314–323 (2015)
4. Iversen, O.S., Leong, T.W.: Values-led participatory design: mediating the emergence of values. In: Proceedings of the 7th Nordic Conference on Human-Computer Interaction: Making Sense Through Design, New York, NY, USA, pp. 468–477 (2012)
5. User experience evaluation. Wikipedia. https://en.wikipedia.org/wiki/User_experience_ evaluation
6. Helkkula, A., Kelleher, C., Pihlström, M.: Characterizing value as an experience: implications for service researchers and managers. J. Serv. Res. **15**(1), 59–75 (2012)
7. Gultekin, P., Bekker, T., Lu, Y., Brombacher, A., Eggen, B.: Combining user needs and stakeholder requirements: the value design method. In: Markopoulos, P., Martens, J.-B., Malins, J., Coninx, K., Liapis, A. (eds.) Collaboration in Creative Design, pp. 97–119. Springer, Cham (2016). https://doi.org/10.1007/978-3-319-29155-0_6
8. Rotondo, A., Freier, N.G.: The problem of defining values for design: a lack of common ground between industry and academia? In: CHI 2010 Extended Abstracts on Human Factors in Computing Systems, New York, NY, USA, pp. 4183–4188 (2010)
9. Haralambos, M., Holborn, M., Heald, R.: Sociology: Themes and perspectives. HarperCollins Publishers, New York (2004)
10. Friedman, B.: Value-sensitive design and information systems. Interactions **3**(6), 16–23 (1996)
11. Gilmore, D.J., Cockton, G., Churchill, E., Kujala, S., Henderson, A., Hammontree, M.: Values, value and worth: their relationship to HCI? In: CHI 2008 Extended Abstracts on Human Factors in Computing Systems, pp. 3933–3936 (2008)
12. Cockton, G.: A development framework for value-centred design. In: CHI 2005 Extended Abstracts on Human Factors in Computing Systems, New York, NY, USA, pp. 1292–1295 (2005)
13. Cockton, G.: Value-centred HCI. In: Proceedings of the Third Nordic Conference on Human-Computer Interaction, New York, NY, USA, pp. 149–160 (2004)
14. Collopy, P.D., Hollingsworth, P.M.: Value-driven design. J. Aircr. **48**(3), 749 (2011)
15. Donald, N.: The design of everyday things. Doubled Curr., 9 (1988)
16. Nathan, L.P., Klasnja, P.V., Friedman, B.: Value scenarios: a technique for envisioning systemic effects of new technologies. In: CHI 2007 Extended Abstracts on Human Factors in Computing Systems, pp. 2585–2590 (2007)
17. Friedman, B., Hendry, D.: The envisioning cards: a toolkit for catalyzing humanistic and technical imaginations. In: Proceedings of the SIGCHI Conference on Human Factors in Computing Systems, pp. 1145–1148 (2012)

18. Hassenzahl, M.: Experience design: technology for all the right reasons. Synth. Lect. Hum. Cent. Inf. **3**(1), 1–95 (2010)
19. ADMC16 - Conference Proceedings - Design Management Institute. http://www.dmi.org/page/ADMC2016Proceedings
20. Miettinen, S., Rontti, S., Jeminen, J.: Co-prototyping emotional value. In: 19th DMI: Academic Design Management Conference Design Management in an Era of Disruption London, pp. 2–4 (2014)
21. Nam, K.W., Carnie, B.W.: The value of design for customers in the service industry: contributions and measurements. In: Design Management in an Era of Disruption: Proceedings of the 19th DMI, pp. 1365–1399 (2014)
22. Nielsen, J.: Usability Engineering. Elsevier, Amsterdam (1994)
23. Peng, Q., Matterns, J.-B.: Enhancing user experience design with an integrated storytelling method. In: Marcus, A. (ed.) DUXU 2016. LNCS, vol. 9746, pp. 114–123. Springer, Cham (2016). https://doi.org/10.1007/978-3-319-40409-7_12

Empowering Lesbian, Gay, Bisexual, and Transgender (LGBT) People with Codesign: A Critical Evaluation Through the Lens of Simplicity

Guilherme C. Pereira$^{(\boxtimes)}$ and M. Cecilia C. Baranauskas

State University of Campinas (UNICAMP), Campinas, SP 13083-852, Brazil
colucci.guilherme@gmail.com, cecilia@ic.unicamp.br

Abstract. LGBT people struggle with challenges and risks provoked by prejudice. We approached this issue with a critical socially-aware methodology, where interested parties engaged in participatory activities to conceive a mobile application aiming to empower this group. To conceive a product to act on such a complex issue as oppressions is challenging and demands sensible decisions from ideation to design. In this paper, we discuss how Maeda's laws of simplicity underlined such decisions throughout the construction process and present an evaluation of simplicity by HCI experts. The evaluation suggests our product meet the simplicity framework and also provides guidelines for future redesigns.

Keywords: LGBT · Simplicity in design · Critical theory

1 Introduction

HCI subdomains are increasingly taking into account approaches towards emancipation. Bardzell and Bardzell [3] define emancipatory HCI as "research or practice oriented toward exposing and eradicating one or more forms of bondage and oppression." Participatory Design (PD) is a traditional emancipatory branch, with roots in the political concerns of Scandinavian workers facing the insertion of computers in the workplace. It focuses on the knowledge about an issue from people whose lives are affected by it.

LGBT people are historically an oppressed group in most of Western societies, facing violence in physical, verbal, legal, and affective forms, among others. Such struggles are faced by LGBT people in current Brazilian society, as well. The country is home to half of the killings of transgender women in the world [10] and to 1 death of a LGBT person each 27 h [4]. Not only the numbers themselves are alarming, but also the cruelty present in such crimes, which often include sexual abuse, torture, and mutilation. One emblematic case was the killing of Dandara dos Santos in Fortaleza, a travesti beaten to death by men in a street of the city of Fortaleza, who later posted the video online in Facebook in February, 2017. Although such characteristics seem remarkable signs of hate crimes based on gender identity or sexual orientation, Brazilian law lacks specific definitions of LGBT-phobia causing such incidents to

© Springer International Publishing AG, part of Springer Nature 2018
A. Marcus and W. Wang (Eds.): DUXU 2018, LNCS 10918, pp. 153–164, 2018.
https://doi.org/10.1007/978-3-319-91797-9_12

blend with the country's high homicide rates. Congressmen also make harder for such law to be made, since the country is also facing a rise of political conservativeness and religious influence in politics.

The project where this work is inscribed aims to develop a novel system to support LGBT people and provide them with means to survive and empower themselves. In order to do this, we adopted a socially-aware approach, based on PD and Organizational Semiotics (OS). The result of the activities is a new Android mobile application called LGBTrust, which articulates formal and informal aspects of the fight against LGBTphobia strengthening a group of users constituted of people and partner institutions.

The fight against LGBTphobia is inherently complex – it involves immediate defense against life-threatening events, education to raise (self-)awareness, and support to collective action. When developing a system to tackle it, one risks embedding such relations in bewildering interactions or neglecting some component in a simplistic product. John Maeda [8] developed a framework to study simplicity in "design, technology, business, [and] life." The framework is based on 10 laws ranging from straightforward design principles to "deep" conceptual aspects, from information presentation to the dialectic simplicity-complexity relationship.

This work discusses the design rationale of LGBTrust through the lens of simplicity laws. Section 2 provides the theoretical foundations needed to comprehend the work. Section 3 details our codesign instance, from recruitment to evaluation. Section 4 discusses how simplicity underlined the application design, drawn upon an evaluation by HCI experts. Finally, we discuss our findings and possible future directions in Section.

2   Theoretical Foundations

2.1   Philosophical Stance

Scientific works are based on a set of assumptions that shape how the scientist sees the world. In his seminal work, Kuhn [6] names such sets "science paradigms." One can think about paradigms in terms of ontology (how one regards reality), epistemology (how one regards knowledge), and axiology (how one regards values). For each of these, a subjectivist or an objectivist stance might be taken. While the former might assume that reality is universal, fully apprehensible, and not influenced by personal values, the latter regards reality as a personal construct, shaped by our subjective experiences and values as well.

Ponterotto [9] summarizes four major paradigms according to such aspects: positivist, post-positivist, constructivist-interpretativist, and critical-ideological. It must be stressed that these classifications intend to guide decisions and to explain core characteristics of each approach, but in practice the paradigms contributions are often blended. More important than to automatically adopt a fixed set of such contributions is to be able to coherently adopt the stances more suited to the specific quest.

In this project, our assumptions fit better in the critical-ideological paradigm. In our view, reality is framed and constructed by socio-historical processes and collective interaction. Therefore, what we can learn from it is dependent of our own feelings, culture, and values. Furthermore, the dynamics of power in society creates oppressed or disenfranchised groups, whose emancipation or empowerment is the purpose of science development.

2.2   Socially-Aware Computing (SAC)

In order to achieve our critical goals, we adopted a codesign methodology, defined as "the action of jointly working with people, using diverse artifacts (…) to clear up meanings they build to what a product may become, engender a shared vision about the product and involve the parties, especially the most interested (…) in the design process." [1] Codesign is the core of the SAC framework [2], which aims to articulate knowledge and experience from diverse interested parties into a socially meaningful artifact.

SAC is rooted in the theory of OS [7]. In OS, an organization is seen as an information system (IS) composed by three nested layers (each one is an information system by itself). The most external layer is the informal IS, comprised by the organizational culture, values, beliefs, expectations, commitments, and others. The middle layer is the formal IS where bureaucracy instantiates the previous layer into norms, rules, laws, and regulations. The inner layer is the technical IS where materials and artifacts mediate processes in the previous ones. This scheme is depicted at Fig. 1 in the form of the "semiotic onion" (SO). In SAC, (co)design activities are intended to "peel" the onion carrying social knowledge to a novel technology which will, in turn, affect and influence the outer layers.

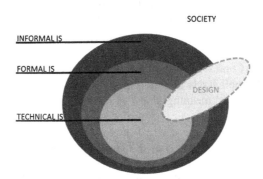

Fig. 1.   (Co)design activities and their inscription in the SO.

In SAC, different interested parties meet in workshops where they engage in PD activities to collectively construct artifacts which will guide the system development. Due to this, it can be named a "semioparticipatory" approach. From the point of view of the critical-ideological paradigm, OS theory is compatible with the assumed onto-logical and epistemological stances, since it advocates for a reality constructed by responsible agents' actions and experienced with the mediation of signs [7], following the tradition of Peircean semiotics. The participatory approach is also suited to lessen our own biases' influence and to carry meaningful knowledge from people affected by LGBT-phobia.

2.3 Maeda's Laws of Simplicity

The laws of simplicity (LOS) were first published in a homonymous book by John Maeda [8], where he presents a framework of simplicity ranging from design to life. The laws might be grouped in three sets of recommendations: laws 1–3, laws 4–6, and laws 7–9, spanning from "basic" simplicity immediately applicable in design to "deep" simplicity, which approaches more subjective or complex conceptual aspects. Law 10, "the one," is a summary of the others. Next, we present a brief explanation of the 10 laws.

Law 1 (Reduce) says that "the simplest way to achieve simplicity is through thoughtful reduction." This reduction is guided by the SHE acronym: shrink, hide, and embody. Law 2 (Organize) states that systems components must be organized to make it seem fewer by implementing another acronym, SLIP: sort, label, integrate, and prioritize. It is related to information visualization and also mental categorization processes as described by Gestalt theory. Law 3 (Time) also uses the SHE acronym to balance the tradeoff between reducing the time spent in a task as well as the feeling of spending time in a task.

Law 4 (Learn) says that "knowledge makes everything simpler." It also has an acronym, BRAIN: "Basics are the beginning; Repeat yourself often; Avoid creating desperation; Inspire with examples; Never forget to repeat yourself." It also advocates for the culturally-aware use of the relate-translate-surprise functions of design, which should first create a sense of familiarity in the person interacting through a translation of this familiarity in a service or component, and, ideally, insert a little surprise. Law 5 (Differences) stresses the dependence between simplicity and complexity – one needs the presence of the other, ideally in a rhythmical way where one is enhanced instead of cancelled out. Law 6 (Context) closes the medium simplicity set stating that "what lies in the periphery of simplicity is definitely not peripheral." It highlights the tradeoff between the boringness and meaningfulness of familiarity and the thrill and danger of being lost.

Law 7 (Emotion) stresses the need of provoking emotion, even though it might require a move towards complexity. Law 8 (Trust) deals with the balance between the ease obtained by what the system knows about you and the control resulting from what you know about the system. Law 9 (Failure) highlights there might be "flaws" in the framework – some things could (or should) never be made simple.

Finally, Law 10 (The One) summarizes everything: "simplicity is about subtracting the obvious and adding the meaningful." The 10 laws are also directly related to each other – emotions might aid learning, which reduces time to perform other activities; context provide situatedness in the differences dynamics; and so on.

3 Codesign Activities

3.1 Recruitment

The recruitment for SAC activities was made online, via calls for participation in Facebook groups dedicated to LGBT issues. The posts called participants interested in the subject or engaged in social activism to join a research aiming to develop a novel mobile application to fight and prevent LGBTphobia. In order to achieve a balanced stratified sample, volunteers were randomly picked from the interested groups. The final group of participants was comprised of 24 people[1]: 3 genderqueers (1 bisexual, 1 pansexual and 1 homosexual), 1 homosexual transgender man, 2 transgender women (1 heterosexual and 1 bisexual), 5 cisgender heterosexual women, 2 cisgender hetero-sexual men, 4 cisgender bisexual women, 2 cisgender bisexual men, 1 cisgender les-bian, and 4 cisgender gay men.

3.2 Overview

The activities were split into two phases – Organization and Context Analysis, which aimed to understand the LGBTphobia context experimented by participants and its relations with technology, and Codesign, which involved techniques to create and evaluate the application. Each workshop was named after a relevant character for the LGBT community, chosen by participants at the end of the meeting. Besides in-person meetings, volunteers could also engage in online warm-ups available through the Consider. It website, a public online debate tool. In these warm-ups, one or two ideas emerged in a workshop were explored prior to the next one. Not all volunteers engaged in both forms of contribution, but every one joined at least one activity, virtual or not.

In the first workshop, Alan Turing, volunteers and researches met for the first time and participated in a storytelling activity, where experiences related to LGBT issues and activism were shared. In the next workshop, David Bowie, two systems were explored (the Espaço Livre app, which intends to create a map of homophobia in Brazil, and the website of the Federal Chamber of Deputies) and discussed in terms of how they (could) aid the fight against LGBTphobia. The third workshop, Ellen Page, bridged both phases by analyzing the network behind a prospective system and listing interested parties using a stakeholder diagram and their respective issues on the application.

In the fourth workshop, Dandara, the concept of the system was constructed after brainwriting and braindrawing activities. The paper prototype was transformed into a digital prototype for evaluation in workshop Cássia Eller. Finally, open issues on the features conceived for the application were discussed in workshop Laerte. Two eval-uations were performed – an evaluation of simplicity with HCI experts and an eval-uation based on cultural values in the last workshop, Freddie Mercury.

---

[1] All participants signed a consenting term approved by an ethics committee. Certificate of Presentation for Ethical Consideration: 58185916.3.0000.5404.

3.3 LGBTrust

The resulting application was named LGBTrust after Laerte workshop. It aims to build a safe environment for people to collectively articulate pillars of the fight against LGBTphobia, such as education, protection, empathy, and sociability. Its main features are:

- An information portal, with news, external links, and other content related to LGBT issues
- The share of experiences, which could be 3 types: mobilizations (collective engagements such as manifestations, meetings, events, etc.), stories (personal narratives intended to relief emotional pain, motivate people going through similar issues, etc.), and reports of violence or prejudice episodes.
- A panic button, which sends a pre-configured message to pre-defined contacts and nearby users via SMS or notifications push.
- A ask for help section where people can directly reach registered partners such as NGOs and activists to ask for assistance in ongoing issues.

4 An Analysis of Simplicity

The evaluation of simplicity took place in between Laerte and Freddie Mercury workshops. The group of HCI experts was composed by UNICAMP students and teachers. 9 participants joined the activity. An application installer was made available in a cloud storage and participants were instructed to download and install it. Then, participants were distributed in 3 groups and instructed to navigate the application according to a scenario assigned to each one. Scenario 1 was a person in need of orientation after witnessing or experiencing a discrimination episode; scenario 2 was a person willing to share an experience or goal related to LGBT issues with other people; and scenario 3 was a passerby who had identified an imminent danger nearby. For each scenario, a task was defined to introduce users to the application; after finishing the task, participants were free to explore other interactions. The tasks were, respectively, to register and ask for aid to partners, to register and share an experience, and to login and ask for help. A debriefing was realized in the end.

4.1 Navigation and Structure

In the braindrawing activity, a map screen was defined as the landing page, containing the panic button in an easy to access area and buttons to the main features. In the final version, general navigation is performed in two bars: a top one containing the application logo, the panic button, a help button, and an icon for a general menu, and a bottom bar with icons to the information portal, timeline, map, ask for help, and profile pages. The evolution of the landing page is shown in Fig. 2.

Experts' feedback pointed out that although it is easy to master the use of the application, in accordance to Law 4 (Learn), this multi-menu navigation was onerous. In order to improve it, some suggested removing items of the bottom bar, following

Law 1 (Reduce), and grouping the panic button with the others, according to Law 2 (Organize). However, these recommendations were not consensually agreed. For instance, the repositioning of the panic button might violate Law 8 (Trust), by making it easier to be triggered by accident. Also, the bottom navigation bar as-is allows one-click access to all core functionalities of the application. By hiding these features, one might misbalance the embodiment of qualities stated by Law 1 (Reduce) and the background awareness required by Law 6 (Context).

Nevertheless, one suggestion was consensual – the removal of the help button in the top bar. When clicked, the help button displayed an overlay window with information about the currently displayed page. Experts pointed out that the button could be hidden in the main menu pursuing Law 1 (Reduce), also preventing a violation of Law 2 (Organize), due to the presence of multiple components with the label "help." Instead of this navigation-aware help, the first-access tutorial could be reformulated to provide a global vision of the application, still contributing to Law 4 (Learn) and avoiding user to feel directionless, according to Law 6 (Context).

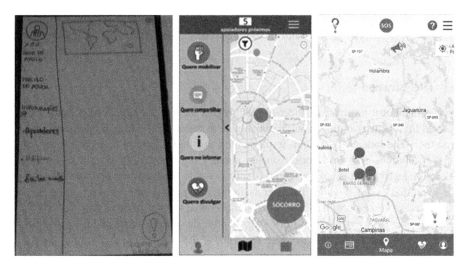

Fig. 2. From left to right, screenshots of the landing page in the paper and digital prototypes and evaluated application.

4.2   Share of Experiences

In the Laerte workshop, two alternative exploration tools were planned for user content: a map and a timeline. The presence of hate content in social media boosted debates on security concerns such as malicious people tracking targets, exposition of personal data, and prejudice broadcast. Such debates resonate with Law 8 (Trust) and resulted in mechanisms such as the possibility of reporting and anonymously creating content.

The timeline similarity with Facebook news feed was said to contribute to Law 4 (Learn) and its layout was highlighted by comments in Law 2 (Organize). In the map screen, each type of content was represented by an icon figure, proposed in the first digital prototype (a raised fist for mobilizations, a speech balloon for stories, and a loudspeaker for reports). In the version presented for evaluators, no identification was presented in the timeline, which was also criticized according to Law 2 (Organize). The different kinds of content were also mentioned as a contribution to Law 6 (Context).

New content could be created in the timeline screen, by fulfilling a form requiring the type of content, a place, a date and time, a summary, a description, identifier tags, and whether it should be anonymous. The form was also mentioned to violate Law 1 (Reduce), while some Android chosen components such as date/time and location pickers were praised for contrasting a complex data with a simple interaction in terms of Law 5 (Differences). In order to simplify the form, it was suggested to transform the radio buttons containing the type of content in different floating buttons which could be shown when the main one is clicked and to display it also in the map screen.

Other concerns around Law 8 (Trust) were discussed during the workshops – since the panic button might alert nearby users, it is necessary to prevent a false sensation of security when triggering it. Thus, a button was added in the map screen to display how many users were nearby. This button would also be hidden in the floating button in this screen.

4.3   Registration

Hate content also motivated concerns about registration. After Laerte workshop, it was defined that the registration would be available in two ways – after an invitation and as a partner. The latter was still not implemented for the evaluation. For the former, one must receive an invitation code from an already registered user via e-mail or SMS. Then, the registration is a 4 step process split in 4 different screens: first, the user insert the invitation code; if valid, the user is invited to provide the phone number to be associated with the account; then, the system sends a second phone code via SMS and asks the user to insert it in the third step; finally, the user is requested to provide full name, e-mail, password, and to agree to terms of use.

Experts mentioned the registration was too lengthy to complete due to its many steps, violating Law 3 (Time). Registering in the application is a sensible issue in the perspective of Law 8 (Trust), since it must assure as much as possible that the user is real, identifiable, and well-intentioned. It is an example of application of Law 9 (Failure), since the verification is inherently complex and impossible to be fully simplified without losing the security expectations. However, it is possible to simplify its current form according to some given suggestions. Firstly, the system could retrieve phone number or e-mail information automatically from the code generation, not needing to ask the user to insert it. The system could also detect SMS receiving and instantly validate the phone code. The perception of time could also be softened by providing a "big picture" of the process via a progress bar or the unlocking of options in a one-screen multistep form.

4.4 Help Calls

The application provides two ways of asking for help – through a panic button and a contact form with partners. For the panic button, the main concern during the workshops was to provide a fast mean to access it – resembling Law 3 (Time) – and to avoid mistakenly triggers – resembling Law 8 (Trust). Besides placing it in the top bar, a chronometer was added to the panic screen – until the chronometer finishes, the user would be able to hit the "cancel" button and stop the panic call. The first debated version of the other kind of help placed it as another type of user content and allowed users to ask and offer help among them. Again, Law 8 (Trust) was somewhat approached since some raised the concern about malicious or unprepared people attending the calls. It was decided to put users in contact only with registered partners, resembling Law 9 (Failure) by considering such activity too complex to be simplified by a direct contact between users.

The overall simplicity of both screens was mentioned while discussing Law 5 (Differences) due to its contrast with the complexity of user generated data. Also, the chronometer used along the panic button was complimented according to Law 3 (Time) and the exhibition of a list of registered partners in a separate tab also according to Law 8 (Trust).

The headline "Preciso de ajuda" (Portuguese for "I need help") in the call for aid screen was criticized for being confusing with the intention of asking help via the panic button. While some experts suggested merging both, others pointed the need of the panic button to be easier to trigger and a separate icon and suggested it was more an issue of labeling, approaching Law 2 (Organize). Others mentioned the absence of a third way of asking for help, which was not urgent as a panic call, but also not so sensitive to depend on a trusted partner, as an oversimplification violating Law 9 (Failure).

Observations were also made regarding what happens after the panic call is triggered. In its current version, the application displays a pop-up window informing the call was sent to user's contacts. Some experts argued that it violates Laws 6 (Context) and 9 (Failure) for not showing the user whom the request was sent to, neither providing ways to tell when the call was accidentally triggered. Suggestions included to display the list of contacts in the panic screen (it is currently displayed only in the profile page), to manually select who should receive the call, and to display notifications as people receive the message. While the two first suggestions might increase context awareness, they could also violate Law 1 (Reduce) by adding extra information arguably meaningless in a moment of desperation. Furthermore, Law 3 (Time) would also be affected. A possible middle ground would be to have a single notification opened in a sort of "panic state," allowing more complex interactions such as to cancel the call or to share current location but not adding complexity to the trigger itself.

4.5 General

When evaluating Law 7 (Emotion), the application was considered comfortable and suitable for the sentimental background when sharing experiences or asking for help. However, the design was criticized for not directly evoking emotions, for instance, using emojis. The application aesthetics was praised, including icon and color choices. When summarizing the findings in Law 10 (The one), experts mentioned the distribution of features along the screens, the sensation of security, and the ease of use.

The overall averages of grades given by HCI experts for laws 1–10 were, respectively, 3.4, 3.5, 3.9, 4.1, 4.0, 4.5, 4.0, 4.1, 3.5, and 4.4. The grades are depicted in Fig. 3.

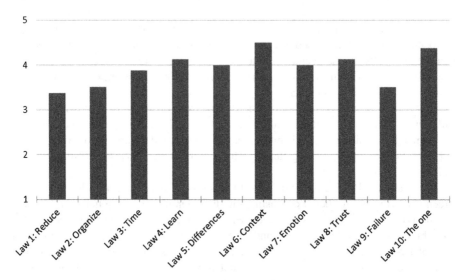

Fig. 3. Average of grades for each LOS.

5 Discussion

All LOS received grades above 3, with Law 10 (The one) exceeding 4, which suggests the application has successfully achieved the goal of simplicity. The most frequent compliments regarded the application layout, the safe environment it provides, its ease of use, and the articulation of multiple parts of a complex context. As of the most recurring drawbacks, we highlight the (over) complexity of forms, the confusing contextual help, and the misleading labeling of help calls.

No detailed presentation of the application was given prior to the evaluation and just one HCI expert in the group also joined the workshops process. While the lack of familiarity arguably privileged an impartial view of the application, it also opened room to conflicting suggestions – for instance, one participant mentioned it should be possible to share more types of content, besides the available. Thus, the analysis and debriefing of observations also required filtering the comments so that concerns, values, and interests developed in workshops were not overwritten by "outsiders'" contributions. Consequently, the results of the evaluation are somewhat constrained in technical comments. The contribution of HCI experts who also are part of the codesign cycle could be further explored in other works.

Even though the LOS could be applied in other domains, as reflected in Maeda's book subtitle - "design, technology, business, life," they are more common in design contexts. Due to the long timespan of workshops, we preferred to make just one meeting for final evaluation and focus it on cultural values rather than adapting the framework for a general audience. Therefore, subjective reflections on the critical role of simplicity were assigned to the leading researchers rather than the subjects themselves. We believe the involvement of subjects would require some training, since the association of laws titles and statements is not always immediate and might be confusing even for experts (e.g. Law 9 (Failure) which was incorrectly regarded as bugs-related by one evaluator). It must be noted that Maeda brings plenty examples not related to design in his book. Future works might further explore the contribution of non-technical participants of the codesign cycle in evaluating simplicity as well.

Since oppressions are multifaceted and often intertwined [5], the fight against them is inherently complex. The LOS were a proper framework for evaluating and reflecting on the application in such context, specially due to its stress of the relation between complexity and simplicity. The "deep simplicity" set shaped features in terms not only of what could be done, especially using Law 9 (Failure) but also what should be done, raising concerns around privacy, comfort, and autonomy. Finally, it must be noted that a future redesign does not imply in an end point to the process. The production of new signs via interaction with and through the application favors the concept of perpetual beta rather than final versions.

6   Conclusion

Such as other social concerns, the fight against prejudice is complex because it involves multiple parties, with different interests often intertwined with other kinds of oppression. In this work, we analyzed the development of a novel application using the lens provided by Maeda's LOS. An evaluation with experts was also performed, not only raising successful instances or violations of Maeda's laws, but also suggesting possibilities for the redesign cycle. Moreover, we verified the LOS potential influence in the conception and ideation of social applications, adding to its most direct use in design. Ongoing work in this project involves analyzing cultural aspects in the LGBTrust, as perceived by the involved people using it.

Acknowledgements. This work is funded by CNPq, #308618/2014-9 and CNPq, #132272/2016-4. We also thank the study volunteers and the colleagues from InterHAD for their valuable participation in the evaluation of simplicity and knowledge contribution throughout the project.

References

1. Baranauskas, M.C.C., Martins, M.C., Valente, J.A.: Codesign de redes digitais. Penso, São Paulo (2013)
2. Baranauskas, M.C.C.: Social awareness in HCI. Interactions **21**(4), 66 (2014)

3. Bardzell, J., Bardzell, S.: Humanistic HCI, 1st edn. Morgan and Claypool Publishers, San Rafael (2015)
4. GGB (Grupo Gay da Bahia): Assassinato de LGBT no Brasil: Relatório 2015 (2016). https://goo.gl/Hq5qZO. Accessed April 2017
5. Kincheloe, J.L., McLaren, P.L.: Rethinking critical theory and qualitative research. In: Denzin, N.K., Lincoln, Y.S. (eds.) Handbook of Qualitative Research, pp. 138–157. SAGE, Thousand Oaks (1994)
6. Kuhn, T.: A estrutura das revoluções científicas. Perspectiva (1998)
7. Liu, K.: Semiotics in Information Systems Engineering. Cambridge University Press, Cambridge (2004)
8. Maeda, J.: The Laws of Simplicity. Design, Technology, Business, Life, 1st edn. The MIT Press, Cambridge (2006)
9. Ponterotto, J.: Qualitative research in counseling psychology: a primer on research paradigms and philosophy of science. J. Couns. Psychol. 52(2), 126–136 (2005)
10. TransgenderEurope.: Trans murder monitoring 15. TGEU Transgender Europe (2015). https://goo.gl/OoYrdY. Accessed April 2016

Educational Digital Games: A Theoretical Framework About Design Models, Learning Theories and User Experience

Michelle Pereira de Aguiar[1,2(✉)], Brian Winn[3], Matheus Cezarotto[1],
André Luiz Battaiola[1], and Péricles Varella Gomes[2,4]

[1] Federal University of Paraná (UFPR), Curitiba, Brazil
`michelle.aguiardg@gmail.com,`
`matheus.cezarotto@gmail.com,`
`ufpr.design.profe.albattaiola@gmail.com`
[2] Positivo University (UP), Curitiba, Brazil
`periclesgomes@gmail.com`
[3] Michigan State University (MSU), East Lansing, USA
`winnb@msu.edu`
[4] Pontifícia Universidade Católica do Paraná (PUCPR), Curitiba, Brazil

Abstract. This article presents a study on design models for Educational Digital Games, taking into account learning theories, game design models, game elements and user experience. Through a theoretical framework the research seeks to understand the different perspectives involved in these models, considering the interdisciplinary character of the developer teams and their target users. The aim of the research is to identify similarities, differences, and gaps between the models investigated. Thus, a literature review was conducted and four models for analysis were identified. As a method, both a comparative and a qualitative analysis of these models were used, based on a data analysis spiral combined with an analysis protocol. The analysis sought to identify pedagogical approaches, instructional design aspects and other elements involved in the design process. Game elements and user experience were also considered relevant for the analysis. As a result, this research presents a hybrid model which complements the analyzed models, using the investigated framework as a structural basis to assist developers and content specialists when designing educational digital games for teachers and students, according to the learning objectives and the theme addressed in the game. Finally, this article presents a brief analysis of the results obtained and considers how the present study may contribute to future investigations.

Keywords: Educational Digital Games · Game design models · User experience

1 Introduction

The experience of the professionals involved in the design of digital games is an important factor in the design of games, since each professional has a personal perception of their activity. Both the literature and practical observations show that this

© Springer International Publishing AG, part of Springer Nature 2018
A. Marcus and W. Wang (Eds.): DUXU 2018, LNCS 10918, pp. 165–184, 2018.
https://doi.org/10.1007/978-3-319-91797-9_13

type of product is often developed by interdisciplinary teams composed of professionals with different backgrounds and experiences. This situation becomes even more complex when designing Educational Digital Games (EDG) due to the additional complexity this media presents: the game must be fun and teach specific content.

The development of a successful educational game requires the combination of different types of expertise (e.g. different design models and different instructional design methods). This often causes a lack of structural unification during the design and development processes [1]. It is therefore necessary to identify a model which combines the main aspects used in these processes. In order to do so, this article presents a comparative study between game design models, which despite their qualities still lack the desired structural unification of the different elements of the design process.

According to the literature game design involves two perspectives: the designer's perspective and the player's perspective. This premise represents the basis of the MDA model – Mechanics, Dynamics and Aesthetic [2]. The DPE model – Design, Play, and Experience [1], was proposed as an expanded structure of the MDA model, adding aspects of learning, storytelling, user experience, gameplay and technology. Such an approach allows for new reflections and alternatives to improve the design of educational games, as observed in the DDE model – Design, Dynamics, and Experience [3]. This model offers a more detailed description of the components of the design process. The LDGM model – Learning Games Design Model [4, 10], is also considered. This model focuses on the collaborative design process between game developers and content specialists.

These models were analyzed using a comparative method. The qualitative nature of this method has made it possible to identify similarities, differences, and gaps in these models, taking into account the following aspects: (a) learning theories and instructional design approaches, (b) relevant perspectives, (c) elements of user experience, and (d) game elements. Each model uses their own diagrams to explain their processes. These diagrams were thoroughly analyzed so as to identify their visual components, and a hybrid model combining the main aspects of each model has been proposed.

The hybrid model preserves both the player's (learner) perspective and the designer's perspective, as observed in the models analyzed. However, the hybrid model also takes into account the perspective of the content specialist, since the designer has influence over the design of the game but not over the content. Also, the teacher's perspective was added to the player's (learner) perspective given that the process of designing the user experience involves not only the primary users (learners) but also the secondary ones (teachers). Hence, the hybrid model takes into account both the development team and the different game users, and how they relate to one another. For instance, the teacher influences the choice of the game to be played by the learner and how the elements learned through play, both in and outside the classroom, will be used. Thus, the teacher's perspective is an aspect that must be considered by developers and content specialists in the development of educational games.

In summary, the design of educational games benefits from a hybrid model. Such a model elucidates the relationships between the members of the developing team and their perceptions of the game design process, providing an interdisciplinary approach to this type of project. Further, this model[1] emphasizes the instructional design and user experience aspects that must be considered in order to enhance the player's experience.

2 The Pedagogical Approach to Educational Digital Games

Games can help players develop self-control and build knowledge and skills related to everyday life situations. Such practice requires attention, intelligence and psychological resistance, all of which must be well managed by the player [7]. These claims are especially related to the pedagogical approach of Educational Digital Games (EDG). Therefore, it should be noted that although game-based learning is not a new concept, much still needs to be investigated about this subject, especially in relation to the design process of educational games.

2.1 Overview of the Learning Theories Directed at EDG

The educational process involves central categories of experiential and spontaneous education, which results in learning. Intentional or purposeful education, on the other hand, corresponds to the determination and organization of learning in specific environments such as school, through specific media. From this context, we have identified theoretical references associated with the construction of these media and which use a pedagogical approach which shows how to best direct learning in EDG.

Outdated approaches such as the behaviorist model are still used in pedagogical practices and in media tools to support learning, despite their noted decline in education research. Thus, in order to identify the main pedagogical approaches which implicitly or explicitly support teaching practices, an overview of the learning theories was consulted and combined with the other authors considered here, in order to identify an approach with a focus on EDG (Fig. 1):

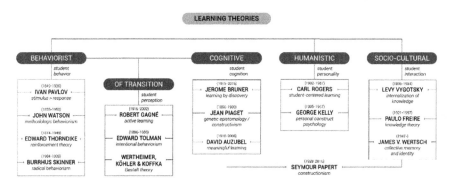

Fig. 1. Learning theories overview

---

[1] The hybrid model proposed here is part of the first author's doctorate research. It is an exploratory contribution and still needs to be validated. The model aims to be an auxiliary tool to help in the early phases of EDG prototyping.

Five main learning theories were identified. Firstly, the **behaviorist theory**, whose theorists were governed by the individual's behavior conditioning. Secondly, the **theories of transition between classic behaviorism and cognitivism**, whose thinkers were guided by the individual's actions and perceptions. Thirdly, the **cognitive theory** which focused on the individual's cognition and on the acquisition of new meanings. Fourthly, the **humanistic theory** which was based mainly on the personality of the individual. Finally, the **sociocultural theory** which focused on the individual's interactions.

The diagram above (Fig. 1) draws from the constructionist epistemology, which shares genetic epistemology premises and emerges from the Constructivism. It is believed here that the individual can use tools to construct their own knowledge and to facilitate this process [12, 13]. It should be noted that one of the tools used in this approach is the computer.

In order to complete the pedagogical approach presented in this section, it was necessary to understand the types of learning based on a revised version of Bloom's Taxonomy [1, 18], and supported by a structured classification concerned with the definition of some instructional theories connected with instructional design. In this context, three types of learning were alluded to: cognitive, psychomotor, and affective. Thus, the types of learning and their characteristics must be considered when designing an EDG learning situation, and during the planning of the pedagogical content of the game. This will lead to learning derived from a global experience [1].

Game-based learning is also guided by motivational models [19]. Both intrinsic and extrinsic motivation play an important role in learning situations, as they prompt the use of game elements in learning solutions. Thus, the content related in this section aims to assist the analysis of EDG-oriented game design models, as well as the structuring of learning situations proposed in educational projects which make use of instructional design to delimit the strategic conduction of learning during the process.

2.2 Instructional Design as a Strategic Approach to EDG

Instructional design is embedded in the area of educational technology. It encompasses a set of activities, identifying the learning needs to be designed, developed, and evaluated [20]. Therefore, it makes use of learning-oriented strategies, which allow the student to build skills and knowledge. Such strategies must be learned and demonstrated after the interaction with the proposed activity, according to the learning objectives [22]. Hence, it is important to recognize guidelines which help the composition of these objectives, according to the pedagogical approach adopted.

The realization of instructional design at the individual learning level depends on some characteristics desirable to instructional events, most of which are based on cognitive theories of learning. These instructional events define the processes involved in the act of learning which are activated internally by the student. This allows the student to pass from one stage to another and achieve the skill established as a learning objective. Thus, the processes presumed to occur during any learning act use instructional design as a checklist, to verify whether or not the student needs support in learning a task [15] (Table 1):

Table 1. Instructional events and their relation to learning processes [15].

Instructional event	Relation to learning process
1. Gaining attention	Reception of patterns of neural impulses
2. Informing learner of the objective	Activating a process of executive control
3. Stimulating recall of prerequisite learning	Retrieval of prior learning to working memory
4. Presenting the stimulus material	Emphasizing features for selective perception
5. Providing learning guidance	Semantic encoding; cues for retrieval
6. Eliciting the performance	Activating response organization
7. Providing feedback on performance correctness	Establishing reinforcement
8. Assessing the performance	Activating retrieval; making reinforcement possible
9. Enhancing retention and transfer	Providing cues and strategies for retrieval

However, a distinctive characteristic of the strategic management of the instructional design process is the conception and implementation of the proposed educational solutions. This can occur at three different levels: (i) **macro**, to establish a common direction for all learning experiences intended for the project; (ii) **meso**, to structure specific learning programs; and (iii) **micro**, to develop study units from a fine design [21]. In this sense, it is believed that the intended level in this research is related to the macro level, since EDG design seeks to explore learning experiences.

Thus, the instructional design approach has a practical and organizational character. This can be seen in the way it manipulates the information to be received, assimilated, and used by the student from their contact with EDG. The importance of this fact is also noted in the design models consulted, as reported in the next section.

3   The Design of Educational Digital Games

The design process involves managing knowledge which has been acquired, combined, transformed and incorporated. It is an iterative process and encompasses different disciplines. Moreover, the design process goes beyond simple visual results, influencing decision-making [23]. Thus, during the design process, it is important to promote dynamization and facilitate communication between the members of the team [24]. It is essential that the team fully understand the interdisciplinary aspects involved in the design process.

3.1   The Interdisciplinary Character of the Team in the Design of EDG

The different disciplines involved in the development of EDG make use of different areas of expertise in the design process. Thus, the organizational hierarchy of the team has a typical structure, which is usually based on the interactions between producers, content specialists, designers, programmers, and artists [25].

This study considers the EDG design process as an interdisciplinary process, since it combines different types of knowledge, which interact with each other, transcending the limits of their related areas [26]. During the EDG design process the team must share information, results, and methods, focusing on the continuous learning process based on a collaborative relationship between different but integrated areas of expertise [27].

The Interdisciplinary Team and the Different Perspectives Involved
The composition of the team may vary according to the requirements of the EDG to be developed. The ideal team, however, would consist of the following professionals [10, 24, 25]:

- Production manager: focuses on process management to ensure the filing of the documents developed and that deadlines are met.
- Instructional designer: focuses on management and quality of the instructional content; acts as project leader and makes final decisions.
- Content specialist: focuses on content and learning objectives. This professional knows the content in depth and has enough experience to teach it.
- Educator: focuses on the learning. This professional has classroom experience and fully understands the needs of the teacher and the student.
- Developers: focus on the game according to their areas of expertise. Similarly to artists, programmers, designers, writers and producers, developers give shape to the game.
- Assessor: focuses on the overall quality of the game; identifies problems, measures results, and refines the product.

Hence, each member of the team plays a distinct role during the design process and each contributes to the process according to their area of expertise. However, regardless of their expertise, every member of the team is involved in the following stages of the process [4, 10]:

- Refinement of the learning objectives according to the skills and knowledge that the student must present during the game, as well as understanding of how the student can demonstrate the required knowledge or behavior change.
- Ensuring that the content is appropriate to the game environment.
- Conducting of formative tests to ensure the educational usability and effectiveness of the game.
- Development of ideas and supplementary learning materials during the game development.

Such an approach ensures that the educational objectives of the EDG are achieved, and that the interdisciplinary nature of the team fulfills its function, by sharing information and results throughout the process. It also promotes collaborative work, integrating the different perspectives and disciplines involved.

3.2   Games and UX Elements of EDG

Game Elements

The term "game" refers not only to a specific activity, but to all images, symbols and tools necessary to the activity [7]. All these elements are specific components to be communicated between the development team members during the design process. Thus, these elements are grouped according to their respective characteristics as follows [19, 28]:

- Dynamic: combines elements that give consistency and regular patterns to the player experience. It is implicit in the game and supports both rules and conceptual elements such as constrictions, emotions, storytelling, progression and system relationship.
- Mechanic: corresponds to mechanisms that configure the actions in play – e.g. "verbs" – and that change the game such as challenges, luck, cooperation and competition, feedback, resources acquired, rewards, negotiations, turns, and winning states.
- Components: correspond to the specific ways which qualify and execute the dynamics and mechanics represented conceptually in the game, such as achievements, badges, avatars, collections, combat, "boss fights", unlocked contents, donation, score, levels, points, research and exploration, social graphs and virtual properties.
- Storytelling: corresponds to the sequence of events which take place during the game and can occur in a linear, branching or emergent way. It includes all the narrative elements of the game (e.g. the game's premise, characters' stories, environment), and it is based on a main concept, prompting the game experience.
- Technology: corresponds to the tools, media and interactions that make the game possible, such as software, game engine or another technological apparatus. It is essential for the development of the other elements in the game.

The game elements help define the experience to be experienced by the player during the game [19]. Thus, the planning of these elements must be carried out together, according to the game experience proposed.

User Experience Elements for Games

The user experience (UX) corresponds to the general effect created by the interactions and to the individual's perceptions when using a product. It refers not only to what the individual actually does but also to the impact caused by the interaction through an interface [6, 16]. Thus, in design practice, the UX must ensure that every aspect of this experience has been planned and is intentional, because all possibilities for each action and expectation must be predicted in the composition of the experience [16].

Specially in the practice of game design, the UX is based on two main elements [17]: (a) **graphic interface**, visibly available to the user on the device screen and its peripherals, and composed of common controls (buttons and menus) and Heads-Up Displays (HUD[2]); and (b) **interaction**, experienced by the player via the interface.

---

[2] HUD is one of the graphic elements available on the screen which can transmit information to the user, such as energy bars, scores, maps, etc. [17].

The interaction depends largely on the graphic interface, which should be carefully planned so that it can be fully explored by the player, offering them a positive experience during the game [17].

Game interaction also depends on other elements of the player's experience [29]. Thus, taking into account elements of user experience[3] non-game and their experience during the game, the interaction can be planned based on the following elements of the player's experience (Fig. 2):

Fig. 2. The elements of player experience [29]: authors' adapted model

The initial layer of the player experience (Fig. 2) is **motivation**, which corresponds to the reasons for the player to start a game and to play it until the end. The main elements of motivation are (a) interest, which is generated in the short-term by the user's initial attraction for the product and gives them pleasure during the interaction; and (b) rewards, whose intrinsic characteristics sustain the player's interest in the long-term experience and can affect their involvement in the game.

The second layer presents **meaningful choices**. These define how the structure and the rules of the game allow the player to make decisions, and as such influence the results of the game. Here two factors are considered: (a) **tactics**, which are short-term tactical decision-making, and (b) **strategy**, which requires from the player the ability to anticipate future moves in each turn.

Balance measures how the game elements have been combined to create a challenging, fair and balanced system. It covers short-term aspects and the most basic game interactions whose effects are perceived more quickly. It also covers long-term aspects, such as the player's participation in turns that unfold throughout the games and whose effects are constructed according to the player's progress.

The **usability** layer is responsible for the planning of all interface elements and considers specific elements of the game experience. In this sense, usability should facilitate the player's perception of their own actions and of the goals to be achieved. This situation should give the player a sense of control over their short-term experience and allow them to master the game over time.

---

[3] Specific UX model designed for the web by Garrett [16] consisting of five layers divided between the product functionalities and its information.

Finally, the last layer relates to the **aesthetic**[4] aspects of the game, which are the interface elements which are visible to the player. The game aesthetic is guided by the following two factors: (a) sensorial factor, which in the short-term corresponds to the user's direct sensory experience with the game, from images, characters, and game controllers, for example; and (b) contemplative factor, which in the long-term corresponds to the narrative of the game and the way it unfolds during the game.

It is important to mention that although the pleasure factor (UX) and the fun factor (game UX) emerge from this model (Fig. 2), they cannot be directly projected. Thus, these factors may contribute to the game experience if the layers of the player experience are adequately addressed [29]. Another important point to consider is the player experience in EDG. This, however, still needs to be further explored in future studies, according to the learning theories adopted by the content specialists during the design process.

3.3 Design Models for Educational Digital Games

Game design must be guided by a brief description of the player's intended experience during the gameplay. In general, this process relies on design documents which guide the project from start to finish. Such documents direct the professionals involved in the different stages of the game development [24]. Thus, from the several models identified in the literature, this study has selected the following ones for the design of digital games: MDA (Mechanics, Dynamics, and Aesthetic) [2], DPE (Design, Play, and Experience) [1], DDE (Design, Dynamics, and Experience) [3] and LGDM (Learning Game Design Model) [4, 10].

This context was delimited so as to identify the relationships between developers, content specialists and other stakeholders in each model. This strategy has led to a consensus with regard to the perspectives involved and all the relevant aspects of the product development (EDG). The relationship between these models and theories offers an analytical and complementary framework that aims to become a more robust model for EDG design.

Mechanic, Dynamics, and Aesthetic: The MDA Framework [2]

The MDA framework offers a formal approach, and thus contributes to the understanding of the games and bridges the gap between developers and players. This framework makes use of game techniques to clarify and strengthen the iterative design process, whose goal is to set aesthetic objectives, the design of the dynamics, and the mechanics established to achieve these objectives.

MDA's first layer corresponds to the **Mechanics** (M). This layer contains a description of the specific components of the game as actions, behaviors and control mechanisms. From the designer's perspective, the mechanics create the dynamic behavior of the game system and, consequently, the aesthetic experiences of the player. The second layer is the **Dynamics** (D), which comprises a description of the system behavior in relation to the mechanics and the results during the gameplay. The dynamics

---

[4] The term "aesthetic" is used here according to Ferrara [29], but its adequacy is discussed throughout this article since it relates to the game appearance design.

create aesthetic experiences that are determined by the player's average progression time during the game. The third and final layer of the MDA framework is the **Aesthetic** (A). Here the emotional responses to be evoked in the player during the game are described. From the player's perspective, the aesthetic layer defines the tone of the game (originated in the game dynamics) and, eventually, the operable mechanics.

According to this framework, the designer creates the game for the player to play, and thus considers the player's perspective during the design process (Fig. 3):

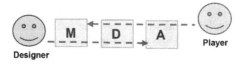

Fig. 3. The MDA framework [2].

Each category is directly related to the designer's and player's perspectives. Thus, when designing for the player, the designer is in a better position to propose a directed experience. Any small change made in any of these categories can result in a progressive effect, as one category can affect the other.

This framework has been widely used and criticized in the game design field. According to the DDE framework [3], for example, MDA neglects many aspects of game design. It also incorrectly uses the term "aesthetic". Nevertheless, MDA is a useful approach for this study, as it is a relevant model in the game design area.

Design, Play, and Experience: The DPE Framework [1]
The DPE model was proposed as an expansion of the MDA framework [2]. Its application would assist in the development of EDG, as well as guide the discussion on some semantic barriers identified among the development team in particular. This framework presents objective language to be used when discussing design, methodology and EDG (Fig. 4):

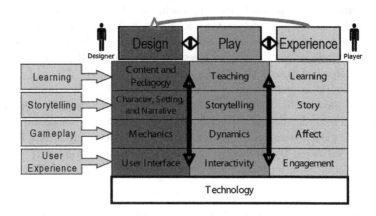

Fig. 4. The DPE framework [1].

This model preserves the perspectives of the designer and the player, both presented in the MDA framework [2]. However, the DPE framework adopts the graphic representation of an iterative design process between the Design (D), Play (P), and Experience (E) layers, and each one of these layers can be influenced by the other (Fig. 4). This structure is supported by technology and the game design process depends on the available technology.

The Learning layer allows the designer to plan how the pedagogical content should be taught in-game and how this content should direct the learning derived from a global experience. The second layer contains the Storytelling, which presents two contexts: (1) the designer's story, constructed for the game and used to promote engagement and convey content; and (2) the player's story, which corresponds to the experience resulting from the projected narrative, the player's interaction and their choices. The design decisions related to the narrative are influenced by the intended results.

The Gameplay expanded layer differs from the original MDA model [2] and replaces the Aesthetic category with the affect idea. This layer defines the actions of the player and their consequences, and is divided into three parts: mechanics, dynamics and affect. It is up to the designer to define what affects to induce in the player. To do so, the designer must consider every fun aspect of the game and understand the particular aspects that derive from the fun experience on the part of the player. Experience is the deepest layer of this structure, from the player's perspective. This layer aims to create means to achieve the desired learning outcomes. In this sense, the designer develops a game whose environment can involve the player and promote a significant immersion in the game experience. The Technology available is at the base of this framework. This layer influences the design process since the beginning, as it can either facilitate or hinder the project. Some design choices depend more on technology than others. For example, the user experience is most influenced by the technology, as the player experience depends heavily on technology.

The DPE framework is based on the idea that games are more effective for engaging students, giving them a more active role in the learning process. This framework considers three perspectives of the EDG[5] development process: (1) academic, which focuses on the theories related to education, pedagogy, communication theories, etc.; (2) content specialist, which focuses on a specific content; and (3) game designer, which focuses on creating involvement and entertainment during the game. However, only the designer's and the player's perspectives are graphically represented in the model's structure (Fig. 4).

Design, Dynamics, and Experience: The DDE Framework [3]

The DDE framework is based on other models such as the Elemental Tetrad – MTDA + N (Mechanics, Technology, Dynamics, Aesthetics and Narratives) Framework[6] [28], the DPE framework [1], and other models in the gamification area which take into account the gaps and incongruities of the MDA framework [2]. Accordingly,

---

[5] It is important to clarify that in the DPE framework [1] Educational Digital Games (EDG) are considered serious games.

[6] This model was proposed by Paul Ralph and Kafui Monu, and it combines the MDA framework and the Elemental Tetrad [3].

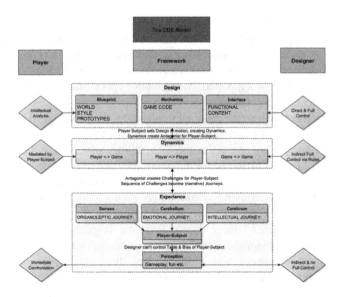

Fig. 5. The DDE framework synthesis [3].

the DDE model covers the entire development process, including the elements of the actual game production and the eventual journey of the player. As a result, this approach has a rather extensive structure, whose synthesis based on keywords is presented in Fig. 5.

The DDE framework offers Design, Dynamic and Experience as the main categories of the model. These are however, presented as separate layers and preserve both the designer's and the player's perspectives. The Mechanics layer – reminiscent from the MDA model [2] – is more specific in this model and delimits the entire architecture of the game, the technology and other elements of the game's operational system. However, in the DDE model the mechanics layer has been incorporated into the Design category, along with the subcategory Blueprint, which conceptually defines the game world, and the subcategory Interface, which defines the elements of the system which interact with the player.

In relation to the MDA model [2], the Dynamic category has undergone less intervention in the DDE model, and focuses on defining what occurs in the game according to the mechanics established by the design. It considers the unpredictability of the dynamics due to the different behaviors involved between the different types of players. The Experience category, on the other hand, was designed to suppress the controversy caused by the inaccurate use of the term "Aesthetic" (emphasis added by the authors [3]) in the MDA framework. The Experience category was discussed at length and presented through the player's configuration as player-subject. This term is used by Sicart [30] to define the act of playing, since it is not exactly the player who acts in the game, but a subset of himself through a character and the projection of its senses, emotions (cerebellum), and its mental journey (cerebrum), all of which rule the player's experience in play.

Also in relation to the MDA model [2], the DDE framework has added new sub-categories and replaced others. This model deeply examines the player's perspective. The authors of the DDE model admit that the model is still under development and may undergo changes in the future. Nevertheless, the present study considers that the DDE model as it stands is visually confusing and does not provide valid arguments for the criticisms it makes to the MDA [2] and DPE [1] frameworks. In addition, although the DDE model briefly addresses some aspects related to learning in the EDG design, this is not its focus, and the way learning issues are discussed may not be appropriate, particularly in its critique of the DPE model [1]. Yet, its contribution to the Experience category is relevant to the research reported here.

Learning Games Design Model: The LGDM Framework [4, 10]

This model was designed according to a specific approach to EDG which was developed by instructional designers from the Learning Games Lab[7] for the collaborative development of educational multimedia. This specific approach to the creation of EDG was intended to promote collaborative work between the members of the development team from the beginning of the design process. In this approach, everyone was responsible for both the game design and the intentioned educational outcomes. This joint action aimed at understanding the content, refining the educational objectives, and adjusting these objectives to the game mechanics. Based on these premises, the Learning Games Design Model (LGDM) has been proposed. The model considers the implications of such an approach for a more effective EDG development, and demonstrates its application through a case study (Fig. 6):

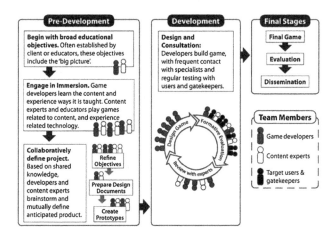

Fig. 6. The LGDM framework [4, 10].

The LGDM model integrates content specialists, learning experts, stakeholders (teachers and students) and the creative team. This design process has a cohesive team and is divided into three stages [4, 10]:

---

[7] The Learning Games Lab at New Mexico State University (NMSU) in Las Cruces, NM focuses on the study and development of educational multimedia [4, 10].

1. Pre-Development: team building and sharing of overall educational goals. At this phase the entire team is immersed in the educational content, traditional educational approaches used for teaching content, and any games considered relevant.
2. Development: active creation of the game by the team through an intense collaborative process. Formative tests should be conducted so as to preserve every aspect of the game design.
3. Final stage: summative evaluations should be conducted before the game is distributed and publicized.

The design process adopted by the team follows more closely with this model, when compared to previous ones. However, the LGDM visually demonstrates that all those involved in the process have actively participated since its inception. However, this situation does not always occur in the practice, since the participation of the content specialists and the stakeholders is minimal in many real teams [33]. Nevertheless, the LGDM model is relevant to this research, since it provides notes that can significantly assist the objectives defined herein, despite the identified limitations.

3.4   Design Model Analysis Directed at the EDG Design

The comparative-qualitative analysis conducted here was developed during the reading of the materials, according to the research problem and the characteristics identified in this reading. The analysis was a cyclical process in which it was often necessary to redo readings, revisit theories, and re-evaluate decisions made during the formation of the categories of analysis. As a result, the research has generated an analytical table, the narrative of the research, and the hybrid model based on the analyzed material.

Analysis Protocol
The spiral model of data analysis [31] has been adapted to the theme and research specifics, so as to support the analysis protocol, as shown in Fig. 7.

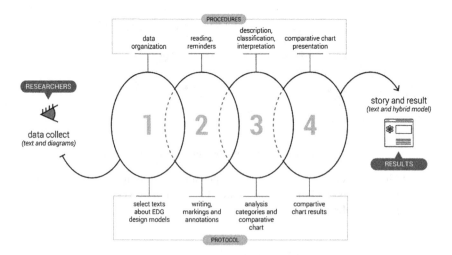

Fig. 7. Spiral of the data analysis and the analysis protocol.

The data collection (cycle 1) occurred during the reading of relevant papers and publications in the area, and the material collected was organized according to the following selection criteria (Table 2): (a) recognized in the game area and the academic environment; (b) presenting relevance and possible adherence to EDG development; (c) presenting a visual synthesis which allows the visualization of the model; and (d) presenting the different perspectives involved in the design process.

Table 2. Data organization and selection criteria.

Data collection		Criteria			
Model	Source	(a)	(b)	(c)	(d)
MDA [2]	Literature review	●	◉	●	◉
DPE [1]	Literature review	●	●	●	◉
DDE [3]	Literature review	◉	◉	◉	◉
LGDM [4]	Systematic literature review[a]	◉	●	●	●

● = yes | ○ = no | ◉ = partially
[a] The first three models originated from the literature review conducted throughout this study. The last model was identified during a more systematic literature review, conducted by the first author of this paper during her doctoral research.

Cycle 2 was the most extensive period of the analysis. It was during this cycle that the analytical reading of the texts which made up the theoretical framework of the research and of each model was conducted. This procedure was accompanied by notations, flagged whenever some strong and relevant information was identified.

Cycle 3 was dedicated to answering the research question and consisted of the following: (a) description, which included a report on each model through a synthesis text; (b) classification, which implied the breakdown of the elements of analysis according to the research question; and (c) interpretation, which included the organization of the data in a comparative table.

Finally, cycle 4 was dedicated to the presentation of the comparative table created during cycle 3 and whose protocol provided the discussion of the results, as reported in the next section.

Comparative Table Elements

The comparative table was designed according to the research question and draws on the theoretical framework on which the interpretation and analysis of the models described here are based, taking into account the following aspects (Table 3):

In order to analyze the **learning theories (LT)** and **the instructional design (ID)** involved in the models, a theoretical framework (Sect. 2) was used to identify how these items were dealt with in the EDG design models. Regarding the **perspectives involved**, we sought to identify how the perspectives beyond those of the designer and the player were treated, based on the framework presented in Sect. 3.1. Thus, this study considered the following perspectives as the main ones for the analysis: developer,

Table 3. Comparative table of the game design models.

Model	LT and ID	Perspectives	UX elements	Game elements
MDA [2]	○	D + P	●	●
DPE [1]	●	D + P	●	●
DDE [3]	○	P + D	●	●
LGDM [4]	◉	D + CS + P + T	●	◉

● = yes | ○ = no | ◉ = partially | D = designer | P = player | CS = content specialist | T = teacher

player, content specialist and teacher. It also sought to analyze the **elements of the user experience (UX)** presented in the models, considering the factors involved in the game interface (Sect. 3.3).

The analysis of the **game elements** investigated how and when each model handled the configuration of these elements during the design process. This was the most general aspect of the analysis and it was included to help identify possible differences or innovations in the way the game design is conducted. The theoretical framework of this aspect of the analysis is described in Sect. 3.2.

Discussion

Learning theories (LT) and instructional design (ID) approaches were identified only in the DPE [1] and the LGDM models [4, 10]. The DPE learning planning relied on the transition theories (Bloom's Taxonomy) and on humanistic theories (active learning), and the direction of the instructional design in this model was guided by the events of instruction. The LDGM, on the other hand, focused on collaborative instructional design, and did not explain the learning theories involved. However, this model contemplated learning aspects at all stages of the design process, since the educational objectives were its priority [4].

As regards the **perspectives involved**, only the LGDM model [4, 10] presented the perspectives sought in the present study. In the DPE model [1], for example, the framework itself did not describe the perspective of the content specialist nor the teacher's. The content specialist was briefly mentioned in some of the readings, and in interviews conducted in the GEL Lab[8], it was identified that these professionals would be considered in the process as needed as part of the design team, and were usually consulted when their expertise was required.

When analyzing the **elements of UX**, the MDA framework [2] considered this aspect from the player's experience point of view. This model's approach was supported by the formal decisions about the gameplay impacts on the player experience. The DPE framework [1], on the other hand, considered the elements of UX a category between the designer and the player perspectives, as in the MDA framework. Thus, according to the DPE model the design of the experience should optimize the learning outcomes and the fun-related factors, according to the layers established in this model [1].

---

[8] These interviews were conducted by this paper's first author with the resources provided by CAPES – "Foundation within the Ministry of Education of Brazil (…) to coordinate efforts to improve the quality of Brazil's faculties and staff in higher education through grant programs" [11].

The analysis of the UX elements in the DDE framework [3] was quite extensive. The model critically discussed the terminologies used in the MDA [2] and brought the term "player-subject" to the fore. In the LGDM [4, 10] model, the analysis of these elements during the course of the development stage was somewhat implicit. "Design and consultation" sections were planned, in which all perspectives involved took part in an iterative cycle to plan the game design, formative assessments and expert's reviews.

As for the **game elements**, the MDA framework [2] focused on delimiting these elements according to the gameplay, although these elements were not visually presented in the diagram. The DPE [1] diagram, on the other hand, visually represented these elements, focusing on storytelling and gameplay, similar to the DDE [3], which implicitly related these elements to its three categories. The LGDM [4] diagram did not specify at which point in time the game elements were delimited, but it made reference to the preparation of the design documents in the pre-development stage, and thus referred to their design.

These analyses showed that all the models, to a greater or lesser degree, used the perspectives involved, the elements of UX and the game elements, considering that the pedagogical and instructional approaches were not limiting factors. However, only the LGDM model [4, 10] took into account all the perspectives considered relevant in this study to the development of EDG. LGDM was also the only model to clearly present in its diagram the design process stages. The other models, although they also referred to iterative design processes for game development, did not clearly present them in their diagrams. The analysis presented here showed that there are more similarities between these models than differences and, therefore, it was concluded that the models can be complementary to each other, justifying the hybrid model proposition.

3.5 Proposed Hybrid Model for the EDG Design

Based on the results of the analysis a hybrid model is proposed (Fig. 8):

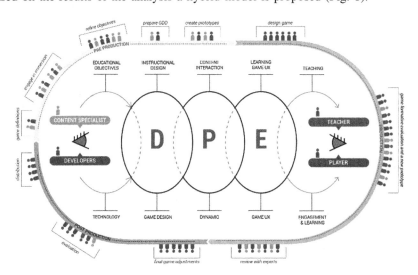

Fig. 8. Hybrid model of the EDG design.

Relevant aspects to EDG development were considered when creating this model. We have chosen to maintain the categories Design, Play and Experience of the DPE framework [1]. However, the DPE layers have been redistributed between these categories and the perspectives involved. Following the DDE framework [3], we considered the dynamic as part of the Play category. Following the MDA framework [2], we preserved the designer's and the player's perspectives, also presented in the DPE and DDE models. The stages of the design process were then inserted into the hybrid model based on the LGDM [4, 10] structure, signaling the performance of each perspective involved in this process.

The proposed model suggests a number of modifications based on the theoretical framework and on the objectives of this study. First, the content specialist's perspective is to be considered, along with the developer's perspective – which includes not only the designer but the development game team – while the teacher's perspective is to be added to that of the player. A further recommendation was inspired by the DPE [1] and the LGDM [4, 10] models and refers to the perspectives involved. The hybrid model visually relates the content specialist to the educational goals, and the developers to the technology aspects of the game. The teacher is related to teaching, and the player to the engagement and the learning through the EDG.

As for the iterative feature of the design process emphasized by all models, the hybrid model presents it as a cycle involving the three main categories, the relevant perspectives, and other related factors. Although based on the LGDM [4, 10] model, the resulting model differs from it in that it refers to its design process stages as: pre-production, production, and post-production [24, 25, 33]. Although the terminology has changed, the procedures adopted by the LGDM stage process are maintained.

Base on the research objectives, in what relates to the pedagogical approach and the learning theories involved, the hybrid model predicts its definition by the content specialists in the pre-production stage, although the model does not show these aspects in the diagram. As for the game elements, this model also predicts their definition during the pre-production stage, relating them to the game design subcategory, inserted in the Design category. The development of these elements is divided into categories and are constantly reviewed during the design process. Finally, the model associates fun aspects with engagement as an element predicted from the player perspective.

It should be highlighted that this model is the result of a research that sought to identify the fundamental aspects of EDG development. The model is a work in progress and requires amendments to be carried out in further research. The model will also be validated by representatives of all perspectives involved in the EDG design process.

4   Final Considerations

The framework reported here has led to the proposition of a hybrid model that is still under development. We believed that the framework between the analyzed models and the resulting model can be replicated and tested through an experiment in further research. With this, we hope to obtain results that allow the interpretation of collaborative situations among the team, both in the formation of concepts and in the negotiation of meanings. Such results would make a valuable contribution to the EDG design process.

Despite their limitations, the results of the analysis have provided relevant observations for the development of EDG. The results obtained during the comparative analysis and demonstrated in the proposition of the resulting hybrid model, also proved to be satisfactory with regards to the research focus and objectives. Yet, it must be noted that this study is part of an ongoing doctoral research. The final results will be presented later according to the schedule provided by the author.

Acknowledgements. We are thankful to CAPES [11] for funding part of the research reported here.

References

1. Winn, B.: The design, play, and experience framework. In: Handbook of Research on Effective Electronic Gaming in Education, vol. 3, pp. 1010–1024. ISR, New York (2009)
2. Hunicke, R., Leblanc, M., Zubek, R.: MDA: a formal approach to game design and game research. In: Proceedings of the AAAI Workshop on Challenges in Game AI (2004)
3. Walk, W., Görlich, D., Barrett, M.: Design, Dynamics, Experience (DDE): an advancement of the MDA framework for game design. In: Korn, O., Lee, N. (eds.) Game Dynamics, pp. 27–45. Springer, Cham (2017). https://doi.org/10.1007/978-3-319-53088-8_3
4. Chamberlin, B., Trespalacios, J., Gallagher, R.: The learning games design model: immersion, collaboration, and outcomes-driven development. Int. J. Game-Based Learn. (IJGBL) **2**(3), 87–110 (2012)
5. Svinicki, M.D.: New directions in learning and motivation. New Dir. Teach. Learn. **80**, 5–27 (1999)
6. Buley, L.: The User Experience Team of One. Roselfeld, New York (2013)
7. Caillois, R.: Os jogos e os homens: A máscara e a vertigem. Edições Cotovia, Lisboa (1990)
8. Cortella, M.S.: A escola e o conhecimento: fundamentos epistemológicos e políticos, 10th edn. Cortez, Instituto Paulo Freire, São Paulo (2006)
9. Ostermann, F., Cavalcanti, C.J.H.: Teorias de Aprendizagem, 1st edn. Evangraf, UFRGS, Porto Alegre (2011)
10. Chamberlin, B., Trespalacios, J., Gallagher, R.: Bridging research and game development: a learning games design model for multi-game projects. In: Gamification in Education: Breakthroughs in Research and Practice, pp. 66–88. IGI Global, Hershey (2018)
11. Institute of International Education: What is CAPES? In: IEE.org (2018). https://www.iie.org/Programs/CAPES. Accessed 19 Jan 2018
12. Papert, S.: A máquina das crianças: repensando Escola na Era da Informática. Artes Médicas, Porto Alegre (1994)
13. Papert, S.: Logo: computadores e educação, 2nd edn. Brasiliense, São Paulo (1986)
14. Moreira, M.A.: A teoria da aprendizagem significativa e sua implementação em sala de aula. UnB, Brasília (2006)
15. Gagné, R.M., Briggs, L.J., Wager, W.W.: The events of instruction. In: Principles of Instructional Design, 4th edn. Harcourt Brace Jovanovich College Publishers, San Diego (1992)
16. Garrett, J.J.: The Elements of User Experience: User-Centered Design for the Web and Beyond, 2nd edn. New Riders, Berkeley (2011)

17. Menezes, F.M., Silva, I.C.S., Frosi, F.O.: Game User Experience (UX): Explorando a Teoria da Diegese. In: SBC, Proceedings of SBGames 2017. XVI SBGames, São Paulo, SP, Brazil, 2–4 November 2017

18. Ferraz, A.P.C.M., Belhot, R.V.: Taxonomia de Bloom: revisão teórica e apresentação das adequações do instrumento para definição de objetivos instrucionais. Gest. Prod. São Carlos **17**(2), 421–431 (2010)

19. Alves, F.: Gamification: como criar experiências de aprendizagem engajadoras: um guia completo: do conceito à prática, 2nd edn. DVS Editora, São Paulo (2015)

20. Kenski, V.M.: Design instrucional para cursos on-line. Senac, São Paulo (2015)

21. Filatro, A.: Design instrucional na prática. Pearson Education do Brasil, São Paulo (2008)

22. Filatro, A.: Design instrucional contextualizado: educação e tecnologia, 2nd edn. Senac São Paulo, São Paulo (2007)

23. Mozota, B.B., Klöpsch, C., Costa, F.C.: Gestão do design: usando o design para construir valor de marca e inovação corporativa. Bookman, Porto Alegre (2011)

24. Schuytema, P.: Design de games: uma abordagem prática. Cengage Learning, São Paulo (2014)

25. Chandler, H.M.: Manual de produção de jogos digitais, 2nd edn. Bookman, Porto Alegre (2012)

26. Cardona, F.V.B.: Transdisciplinaridade, Interdisciplinaridade e Multidisciplinaridade. In: WebArtigos, 19 March 2010. goo.gl/tnFHpb. Accessed 7 May 2017

27. Tavares, S.O., Vendrúscolo, C.T., Kostulski, C.A., Gonçalves, C.S.: Interdisciplinaridade, Multidisciplinaridade ou Transdisciplinaridade. In: 5° Interfaces no fazer psicológico: Direitos humanos, diversidade e diferença. UNIFRA, Santa Maria (2012)

28. Schell, J.: The Art of Game Design: A Book of Lenses. Elsevier, Burlinton (2008)

29. Ferrara, J.: Playful Design: Creating Game Experiences in Everyday Interfaces. Rosenfeld Media, New York (2012)

30. Sicart, M.: The Ethics of Computer Games. MIT Press, Cambridge, London (2009)

31. Creswell, J.W.: Investigação Qualitativa e Projeto de Pesquisa: escolhendo entre cinco abordagens. Sage Publications, São Paulo (2013)

32. Games for Entertainment & Learning Lab, College of Communication Arts and Sciences, Michigan State University (2017). http://gel.msu.edu. Accessed Sep 2017

33. de Aguiar, M.P., Battaiola, A.L., Kistmann, V.: Gestão do design de jogos digitais: um estudo de caso em uma produtora paranaense. In: P&D 2016: Congresso Brasileiro de Pesquisa e Desenvolvimento em Design, UEMG, Belo Horizonte (2016)

Co-design of a Virtual Training Tool with Emergency Management Stakeholders for Extreme Weather Response

Jaziar Radianti[1(✉)], Santiago Gil Martinez[2], Bjørn Erik Munkvold[1], and Morgan Konnestad[3]

[1] Centre for Integrated Emergency Management (CIEM),
University of Agder, Kristiansand, Norway
{jaziar.radianti,bjorn.e.munkvold}@uia.no
[2] Centre for eHealth, University of Agder, Kristiansand, Norway
santiago.martinez@uia.no
[3] Multimedia and e-Learning, University of Agder, Kristiansand, Norway
morgan.konnestad@uia.no

Abstract. Emergency services usually prepare for the most frequent or predictable types of disasters, such as fires. However, preparation for complex, unpredictable disaster scenarios is infrequent, probably because of high resource demand and difficulty of covering dynamic training needs of multiple stakeholders. The use of serious game techniques as the core of simulated or virtual training tools opens for new ways of training and learning in emergency and crisis scenarios. However, the number of virtual training tools customized to specific disaster or crisis scenario that address needs of diverse user groups is limited. Existing tools are often tailored with a particular geographical setting and local threats, requiring an extensive adaptation outside the pre-defined settings. This paper describes the co-design process aimed at the creation of an emergency and disaster virtual training tool prototype linked to a Norwegian context. Two co-design workshops were run involving local emergency management actors. The general setting included an extreme weather scenario because of its high probability of occurrence and societal impact. The first workshop was used to gather end-user requirements for the training tool, explore the current gaps in the training practices, information needs and elements to improve training on decision making. In the second workshop, we focused on scrutinizing the detailed design, user interface, training use-case and learning points. Finally, we ran a small-scale usability testing of the initial prototype using SeGUE (Serious Game Usability Evaluator) instrument. The results of the prototype activities and the testing are reported in this paper.

Keywords: Emergency management · Co-design · Training tool
Extreme weather · User testing · SeGUE · Serious game

© Springer International Publishing AG, part of Springer Nature 2018
A. Marcus and W. Wang (Eds.): DUXU 2018, LNCS 10918, pp. 185–202, 2018.
https://doi.org/10.1007/978-3-319-91797-9_14

1 Introduction

Evidence shows that emergency management training and exercising of plans and standard procedures can significantly improve the efficiency of collaboration between responders in the field and in emergency operation center [1], together with disaster response in general. The training is generally designed as middle- to large-scale field drills, or as a tabletop exercise with graded-difficulty challenges. The use of serious game techniques as the core of simulated or virtual training tools opens for new ways of training and learning in emergency and crisis scenarios [2]. However, available virtual training tools that address the needs of diverse user groups, such as disaster and emergency managers, first-responders and civilians, are limited and potentially costly. Emergency and rescue services are generally well-trained for the most frequent or predictable types of disasters, such as fires [3, 4]. The problem arises in complex, unpredictable disaster scenarios where it is challenging to cover the dynamic training needs of the user groups involved. In addition, the locality factor, i.e., the tie that the most frequent or likely disasters have to particular areas, regions or countries, may interfere with how stakeholders learn about the risks faced in other geographical areas, making training tools that did not take into account this factor rather ineffective in particular contexts. Thus, when designing a training tool for emergency and disasters, one of the key steps for successful training is to include all stakeholders' needs and factors that may positively influence their learning.

This paper describes the co-design process [5] carried out for the development of a virtual training tool linked to the Norwegian context. Co-design refers to a cooperative design process where researchers and end-users together generate potential solutions for a defined problem. This method has already been used in the emergency management domain [6–9], as an iterative approach with participants representing various stakeholders whose degree of participation varied depending on user needs and the stage of the design process. Our co-design process aimed at the creation of an emergency and disaster virtual training tool prototype called "Operation Tyrsdal" [10].

Two workshops were run in the University of Agder (UiA), Norway, with representatives of stakeholders involved in an emergency/disaster scenario in Norway. The workshops were based on an extreme weather scenario, considered to have both high probability and high societal impact. Stakeholder representatives comprised local emergency services, i.e., police, firemen, emergency manager from a city of 90 000 inhabitants, volunteer organization, hospital and the county administration. In addition, researchers with expertise in co-design processes, emergency management, disaster e-health, and multimedia were part of the research team. The first workshop gathered end-user requirements for the training tool. We explored current gaps in the training practices, information needs and elements to improve training of decision making. In the second workshop, we focused on scrutinizing the detailed design, user interface, training use-case and learning points. The testing part focused on the design evaluation of the virtual training prototype with valuable feedback from non-real emergency responders. We included the findings from the second workshop into the prototype development, and will scale it up on a later phase into a complete virtual training testing with responders.

This paper is divided into 6 sections. Section 2 presents our literature review on co-design methods. Section 3 describes briefly the co-design method used in this article and the testing method of the prototype. Section 4 elaborates the prototype's evolutions and its features. Section 5 reports the testing results, received feedback and discussions. Section 6 concludes the paper, with implications for future work.

2   Literature

Co-design is generally defined as a cooperation process between users and designers. It has been exercised in different contexts, such as art and design, architecture or information and communication technology. The underlying purpose is to cooperatively design an artefact for a specific problem statement, context of use or desire [11]. The term artefact comprises a wide range of possibilities, from a building to sophisticated technology solution. The common principle is that the representation of that artefact will be crafted and presented by co-designers with paper-based props, arts and crafts, developed in a technology-free environment.

Historically, co-design was initially developed in the Nordic countries [12] with the aim of enabling industry employees to take part in the decision and control of their production means. Ever since, co-design has been used in information and communication technology to transform end-users into active contributors of a technology solution design for and with them [5]. It is precisely end-users of a technology solution who expressed and describe their needs with their own voice. In this way, end-user representatives meet in the same space and time, to create a shared understanding, selection and prioritization of needs that will be later transferred into functional and non-functional requirements and look and feel of the desired system solution.

Co-design has been used in different ways and areas, such as building community participation in community strategy [13], governance [14] and developing regions [15]. Common to all of them was the recruitment, consent and interaction of user group representatives. End-user represents the person who is intended to use the outcome of the co-design process, such as a technology solution. In technology contexts it is common to present a problem-scenario that users need to get acquainted to, and in some cases, solve. In this case, the aim of the co-design process is how and what users choose, express and decide in order to solve or improve the situation described in the scenario [5]. It will be same participants who will explained by their words, what they mean and want at the end of such process.

There are examples in the literature showing co-design and similar methods, such as participatory design [7] co-creation [16], user-centred design [17], all of them used to design technology solutions involving end-users. There are also examples of studies with end-users in disaster and crisis management scenarios. For instance, community participation in the form of a collaborative action-research method by the Tasmania fire service to transform community education [18]; governance to solve policy issues on tension between the government agencies and local companies [14]; and a study of technological solutions in the domains of communication, microfinance and education in developing regions, such as India and Uganda [15]. More specifically, usability engineering principles have been described regarding crisis and disaster management

[19]. However, the involvement of end-users in the co-design process of tools for disaster management is still scarce. There are several factors that may explain it. The recruitment of end-users who are usually employees require extra resources. More importantly, the unpredictability and complexity of disasters and crisis may hinder the appropriate selection of what groups are involved. Nevertheless, the probability of error, such as in communication and coordination processes, may increase the need for training and familiarity of user groups involved through a co-design process of a training tool.

3 Research Design

3.1 Co-design Methodology

The co-design process allowed to obtain results in each of the workshops. In this work, we have carried out two workshops, interviews and two development cycles using the Scrum method. In the first workshop, we identified several key game elements related to possible training scenarios, such as extreme weather, passengers trapped in a ship fire, flood, landslide/avalanche, loss of power and telecommunications infrastructure, and life-threatening violence. Several suggestions for content and feedback in the game were presented by the participants, such as: information that concerns responders, conducting responsibility, closeness, equality and cooperation principles, actionable information, consequences of a choice, and best practice feedback in the game on an unknown situation. The following factors were suggested as training purposes: cooperation, understanding of information flow, understanding of the role of decision makers, establishing appropriate situation descriptions, coordination and taking care of personnel.

For the game setting, the extreme weather and weather data were ranked as "relevant". Scores as learning rewards and people saved were proposed as game incentives. Based on this discussion, we narrowed down the topic, and selected the extreme weather scenario for the training game, theme was mentioned by all stakeholders.

Some ideas from the first workshop were used in the prototype. The prototype included activities that were iteratively implemented using the Scrum method, consisting of seven bi-weekly iterative sprints (work cycles). The high-level requirements for the game were: focus on one, realistic scenario, concentrate on the individual experience, focus on managing resources and with dilemma situations, use local language (to enable user testing with local responders) and finally the game had to be playable from a laptop. We limited our target to Windows machines for availability purposes. The main game engine used for the development work was Unity, which allows to port the game into multiple platforms when required.

The co-design process occurred also in the Scrum processes, as we did test the developed tool especially after the 5th Sprint. Figure 1 shows the screenshot of the development of the same feature from 3rd Sprint to 7th Sprint. The human icon on the upper left represents the involvement of users or stakeholders during the development stage which was only started at Sprint 5. In the 1st and 2nd Sprints, the user interface did not reach a sufficient level of development to be shown to the testers.

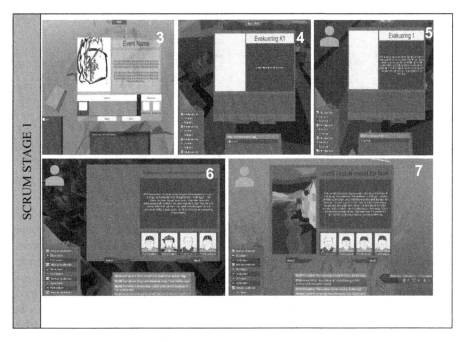

Fig. 1. Scrum and sprints examples of the prototyping process

In the 2nd workshop, we explored various themes such as information flows, information needs of different stakeholders, and elicited the detailed user interface. The stakeholders also suggested some alternative designs that could be useful for the training purpose. The stakeholders were exposed to more information on the developed prototype. This action provided them with a more concrete experience on the expected output of the project and allowed them to adapt the requirements and suggestions more systematically.

One of the suggestions mentioned in the 2nd workshop was that the tool should fully interplay in the entire crisis organizations to enable learning about the work methods of other parties, as today emergency responders work in a "silo" mode, or sit in their own "glass-bowl". In other words, a role-play type Virtual Training Tool (VTT) has been proposed where someone from each response unit can play, change role (login as another organization), and do a joint evaluation afterwards. In this way, each actor can learn about "outside" perspectives.

They also engaged in the workshop on eliciting elements required for the user interface. Figure 2 depicts the diagram shown in a presentation from a workshop participant on elements required in the training tool user interface. The full requirements as the results from the 2nd workshop have been documented in [20]. The results from the discussion were used as a basis for the 2nd Scrum process. In this stage, we set new requirements, such as that we wish to be able to split the visual information into different screens.

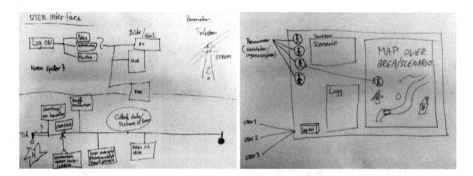

Fig. 2. Suggestions of user interface elements presented by end-users

The players could be more than one (preferably multiplayer), playing through networked computers, and including a map showing events and deployed resources. One of the split screens displayed a control room view. We also listed some requirements that are suitable to have, such as the possibility to combine the game with real data such as weather data, being able to simulate agents (flow of people), and have smaller events such as a tree falling over or power black-out. The last three can be considered as "nice to have" features, as in the second workshop the stakeholders suggested that information available for players is adequate if detailed visualization cannot be achieved. This was a basis for working in the 2nd Scrum process that consisted of 5 sprints. The results of the 1st and 2nd Scrum are presented in Sect. 4. However, the testing stage only covers the results from the 1st Scrum process.

3.2 Testing Methodology

The testing was held in a controlled environment where we conducted small-scale testing of the initial prototype. Moreno-Ger et al. [21] argue that prototype usability testing is especially important when the system is to be used by people who are not familiar with how to interact with new technologies, and that the usability issues are crucial. Heuristic methods with experts [22], video-assisted usability testing [22], task allocation [23], diagnostic evaluations [24], performance evaluations [24], subjective evaluations [25] and many other techniques, including the procedure suggested by the ISO 13407 [26] on the human design processes for interactive systems SUS Scale [27], SUMI [28], CSUQ [29] and USE [30], are among the possible methods to use in the user satisfaction survey.

Which appropriate method(s) to use is depending upon different conditions such as time and resources available, the possibility for direct access to the end users or any limitation in their skills and expertise, and the stage of the product development. Also, there is not a single method that alone could satisfy the testing purpose. For instance, Moreno-Ger et al. [21] point out that heuristic instruments do not always identify all the pitfalls in a design, while the prototype evaluation could fail to identify comprehensively all of the stumbling points in a design.

Currently, we do not consider that the "Operation Tyrsdal" product is in the "*Test and Measure*" stage, or even in the "*Release*" stage. It is not in the "*Planning/feasibility*" stage either, but rather lies between the "*Design*" and "*Implementation*" stage, where the "prototype evaluation" technique [31] or interface design pattern [32] methods could be relevant. The latter approach puts emphasis on making the end-user participants aware of design pattern examples, encouraging them to express interaction concepts in terms of design patterns, and reviewing the final results of requirements. While the former requires the testers to provide their impressions of a page design, which has also been implemented in our co-design process.

As we target the evaluation that can provide the impressions on the look and feel of the developed user interface, and identify potential barriers when interacting with the developed product, we adapted the simplified version of the SeGUE procedures [21] for testing our VTT prototype described in Sect. 4. This is a structured method to analyze a prototype play session where the evaluators can annotate events as they try to identify issues and stumbling points. This predefined set of event types is necessary to facilitate the annotation process as well as to provide structure for the posterior data analysis. Ideally, we need to have a design of the play session, selection of the testers, performance and recording of the play session, application of the instrument and annotation of the results and reconciliation of the results.

SeGUE's framework suggests two dimensions as the basis for evaluation: *the system dimension* and *the user dimension*. The *system dimension* covers the functionality, layout, gameflow, content, technical error, and other events that have no categories or are not applicable. The *user dimension* entails learning, reflecting, satisfied/excited, mildly frustrated, frustrated, confused, annoyed, unable to continue, non-applicable, commenting and other perceptions not covered by the abovementioned categories.

The testers of the developed SG was a group of six male and two female university students, with age ranging between 24–26 years old (Fig. 3), as it was designed as a small-scale test. As mentioned earlier, we treated the game as in the "Design" and "Implementation" stage, and thus considered the use of non-real emergency responder participants to be sufficient. Regarding the number of the testers, the literature suggests that five users should be enough to detect 80% of the usability problems, as an increased number of testers do not necessarily yield new information [21]. Thus, we

Fig. 3. Testing activities

concluded to have a more than adequate number of testers. Intentionally, the testers had never seen the game before, as they were expected to be able to play based on the tutorial included in the beginning of the gameplay.

As background information on the testers, five participants play game, while one rarely plays and another does not play games. The following games within different genres were listed as the most frequently played: *Diablo 2* (action role-playing game), *Heroes 3* (strategy game), *Stardew Valley* (farming simulation role-playing), *World of Warcraft* (massively multiplayer online role-playing game), *Overwatch* (multiplayer shooter game), *the Binding of Isaac* (action adventure) *and the Sims* (life simulation game). In addition to having experience from playing well-known games, all the testers had multimedia education as a background which added to their credibility and judgement during the testing. We also had a facilitator and observers that helped during the testing, and lead the discussion and debriefing process after the game testing. In this test seven participants delivered the questionnaires.

The SeGUE instrument was used for the usability evaluation, and was expressed as a questionnaire combining multiple choices and open questions. Our questionnaire to cover all aspects of "Event categories for the system dimension" and "Event categories for the user dimension" that were derived from the Operation Tyrsdal game [21]. Although it is suggested to use video recording and annotation from the multiple reviewers, we considered it unnecessary in our case as it was a less complex game, with approximately 30 min gameplay. The testers filled out the questionnaire and had a debriefing discussion with feedback to us. In the next section, we present the prototype results, while the testing results are reported, analyzed and discussed in Sects. 5 and 6 respectively.

4 Prototype Results

We developed two prototypes as seen in Figs. 4 and 5. The game was inspired by the big storm "Synne" that occurred in Eigersund on the west coast of Norway in December 2015, where continuous heavy rain caused significant evacuation of inhabitants. However, Synne is not the only extreme weather that has occurred in Norway. Between 1994 to 2017, there were at least 76 registrations of extreme weather by the Norwegian Meteorological Institute (MET). Since October 1995, MET provides names to each extreme weather to facilitate the communication between authorities, the public, media and other relevant actors. This practice is also recommended by the World Meteorology Organization [33].

Typical characteristics of extreme weather that will lead to warning and preparedness due to the risk of extensive damage or danger to life are: strong wind, heavy rainfall, storm tide and waves. The Synne extreme weather fulfilled these criteria, where the flood reached "red level warning" – the highest of four flood alert levels. The flooding supposedly exceeded the level of a 200-year flood. An escalating crisis over several days, such as Synne, offers a unique case to learn about managing a sequence of tight events over a longer period with limited resources. In "Operation Tyrsdal", the time and place are fictional, but some elements such as the plots, stories, and sequence of events were modified from series of events during the storm Synne.

PROTOTYPE STAGE 1

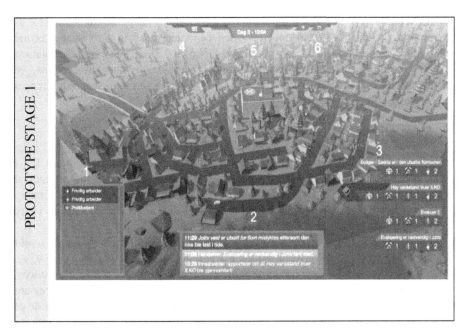

Fig. 4. The graphical user interface in Prototype 1

PROTOTYPE STAGE 2

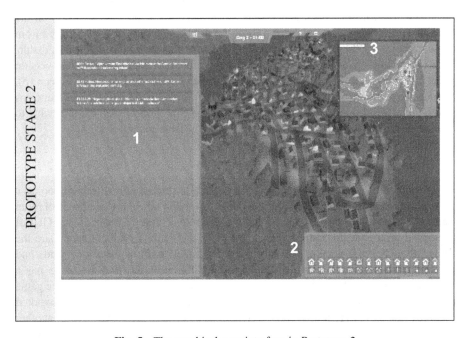

Fig. 5. The graphical user interface in Prototype 2

The technology used for developing the tool is Unity as the game engine and C# as programming language. We developed two sets of requirements in the first and second prototype. The requirement in each stage was extracted from the feedback obtained during the co-design workshops and the Scrum process. In the next sub-sections, we describe briefly the game mechanics, requirements, and the similarities and differences between the two prototypes.

4.1   Prototype 1

Prototype 1 was produced from the 1st Scrum (Fig. 4). The game was meant for a single scenario acting as On-Scene-Commander, and concentrated on the individual experience. The game platform was made for machines with Windows operating system, but in the future it would be possible to port the game to other systems as Unity supports multiple platforms.

The main background in the Graphical User Interface (GUI) is the game world showing the location of the area hit by the extreme weather. In the GUI in Fig. 4, we can see the dashboard that consists of a set of resources (the police, the health services, the firefighters and the volunteers) (1). In this screenshot, most of the resources are deployed and appear as symbols of each unit with the tracking bars in the right side of the screen (3). The main dashboard (2) is the area where the player will get the notification on an event. In the bottom right area, there are tracking bars that can be used for tracking all the resources deployed in different event locations in the game world (3). We also had an action report button (4) that would log all players' decisions and interaction with the event and resources. Initially, we had included a quiz in the game, and the action report would also show the right and wrong answers selected from multiple choice by the player. However, this feature was then considered as a disturbance for the immersion of the game and was therefore removed from the final version of the first prototype. The time counter is seen in the upper middle of the screen (5), showing the game world time, while (6) is a button for the game setting. The game has a tutorial that will pop-up as a user starts playing. The tutorial will tell the user what to do with all different events and buttons in the GUI of the game.

4.2   Prototype 2

In the second prototype, the player(s) had the option to run the virtual training tool as a single player or as two players, where the other player can take a role as a control room operator in addition to the On-Scene-Commander role. Figure 5 illustrates the GUI of the second prototype for a single player. Most of the game world's elements are the same, although some detailed visual objects are added such as electricity grids and some detailed buildings. The main tangible UI differences are that the game has a bigger notification dashboard (1), resources dashboard (2), and a mini-map of the game world (3). At the current stage, the design focused on the two-players networked machines. The notification dashboard (1) and the map (3) will be available in another screen so that it is less crowded compared to the single player's GUI. This version still needs improvement, such as how to not block the view to the game world. Hence, the testing in this paper focused on the first prototype version.

5   Testing Results and Discussions

The summaries of the testing results can be seen in Tables 1 and 2. Table 1 shows the participants' judgement of different features or elements in the game user interface, rating the features from "very good" to "very poor". As it can be seen below, most features were judged as "neutral" which can be seen from the pie diagram icon or the color intensity of the neutral column. We focus here on the elements that were judged as "very good", "good", "poor" or "very poor". We noticed that approximately half of the participants evaluated the tutorial (57.1%), text-size (42.9%), game color (42.9%) and information in the dashboard as "good". While the poorest rated feature was "Deploying volunteer", rated as "very poor" by 42.9% of the participants. As a background information, the volunteer resources were not immediately visible to the players, unless they clicked on a small volunteer button, deploy them, and return to the main resource dashboard. This procedure was subject for extensive comments and discussions (See Discussion section).

However, not all results are consistent with the evaluation of the players' game experience presented in Table 2. Here, the answers are more distributed among "satisfied/excited", "mildly frustrated", "frustrated", "confused" and "annoyed". The positive consistent answer on the game features as in Table 1 are "Textsize in the Dashboard" and "Tutorial", i.e. 85.7%, and "Setting button" in addition.

Table 1. The tester's rating of various graphical user interface elements

Feature	Rating (%)				
	Very good	Good	Neutral	Poor	Very Poor
Deploying Volunteer	0.00	0.00	28.57	28.57	42.86
Resource Tracking Bars	0.00	0.00	57.14	14.29	28.57
Resource Dashboard	0.00	0.00	57.14	28.57	14.29
Action Report Functionality	0.00	0.00	71.43	28.57	0.00
Deploying Resources	0.00	0.00	100.00	0.00	0.00
Volunteer Button	0.00	14.29	71.43	0.00	14.29
Tutorial	0.00	57.14	42.86	0.00	0.00
Speed of Information in the Dashboard	14.29	0.00	57.14	14.29	14.29
Notification Dashboard	14.29	14.29	42.86	28.57	0.00
Setting Button	14.29	14.29	71.43	0.00	0.00
Information in the Dashboard	14.29	28.57	28.57	28.57	0.00
Textsize in the Dashboard	14.29	42.86	28.57	14.29	0.00
Game Color	14.29	42.86	28.57	14.29	0.00

Some players were particularly "frustrated" (37.5%) when deploying the volunteers, and "confused" with the usage of the volunteer button (37.5%). Information in the dashboard (i.e. event notifications appearing in the dashboard) caused them to be "frustrated" (42.9%) and "mildly frustrated" (28.6%), respectively. While the impressions of the notification dashboard were divided equally with opposite opinions between "exciting/satisfied" (42.9%) and "confused" (42.9%). The reasons for these results are discussed further, after presenting some more results.

Table 2. Results of the game experience

Feature	Expressed Feeling (%)				
	Satisfied/ Excited	Mildly frustrated	Frustrated	Confused	Annoyed
Deploying Volunteer	12.5	12.5	37.5	25.0	12.5
Volunteer Button	12.5	25.0	12.5	37.5	12.5
Information in the Dashboard	14.3	28.6	42.9	14.3	0.0
Resource Tracking Bars	18.2	27.3	27.3	27.3	0.0
Action Report Functionality	25.0	25.0	12.5	12.5	25.0
Resource Dashboard	37.5	12.5	37.5	12.5	0.0
Speed of Information in the Dashboard	42.9	0.0	28.6	14.3	14.3
Notification Dashboard	42.9	14.3	0.0	42.9	0.0
Deploying Resources	44.4	33.3	11.1	11.1	0.0
Textsize in the Dashboard	57.1	28.6	14.3	0.0	0.0
Game Color	85.7	0.0	0.0	0.0	14.3
Setting Button	85.7	0.0	0.0	0.0	14.3
Tutorial	85.7	14.3	0.0	0.0	0.0

At the end of the session, we asked participants to describe their impression of the overall game which gave encouraging results (Fig. 6). The users saw the value of learning (71.4%), which is basically a process where the user figures out how to perform an action that was unclear before (learn to play), or when the user is actively engaging in consuming content (learn content). While in the detailed questions (Tables 1 and 2) there were some frustrations, annoyance and technical problems, from a macro perspective, actually none (0%) were frustrated, annoyed or unable to continue the game, as they were actually learning (71.4%), reflecting (28.6%) and satisfied/ excited (57.1%).

Even though half of the participants were satisfied and learning, some of them in general were also confused (42.9%). The following discussions and feedback can help explain the results shown in Tables 1 and 2, as well as in Fig. 6.

The sources for the quite good scores on satisfaction, excitement and learning come from several reasons. The testers found the overall game play to be good, because of the fact that the game met the expectations or criteria of the player such as what function should do what. The necessary buttons were easy to find, and worked as

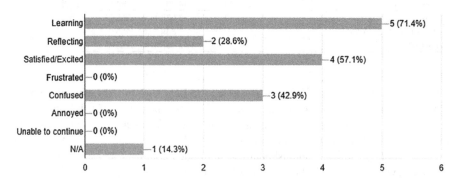

Fig. 6. The participants' impression on the overall game prototype

expected, although there are functions that are not yet there. Some of the users liked the game color and responded that it was not annoying for the eyes. However, the experience with the game color was not uniform as one tester considered the graphics to be a bit dark, making it sometimes difficult to track the vehicles in the game world.

On the clarity, understandability and helpfulness of the tutorial, the users considered that it was good because it was informational. The testers appreciated the tutorial since it covered all the necessary information in the beginning of the game. Text and images in the tutorial help but it should be less visible and hidden in a button such as a question mark icon, representing ask for help. If a player understood the gameplay, he/she can then skip the tutorial, and only press this button when more detailed information is needed. In other words, the players considered the tutorial to be functional, with clear responses and good explanations on what action to do in the game. By large, in Table 1 the tutorial is rated between good (57.1%) and neutral (42.9%), but 85.7% of the testers are mostly satisfied (Table 2).

Positive comments mentioned by the participants were that the test was fun and interesting. The game had a good information flow and was easy to use, and the camera tracking of the game world was satisfying. One participant thought the game to be promising, when the events and graphical user interface are handled seriously.

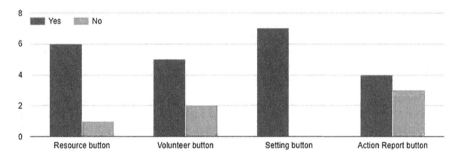

Fig. 7. Evaluation of all types of buttons in the game

The confusion, frustration and annoyance originated from several reasons. Some buttons were not intuitive, such as the volunteer button. In the current version, when a player needed to activate the volunteers, he/she needed to click a very small button for volunteers and send them to the main resources dashboard. The testers did not see the point in why the volunteers should be hidden, and why they are not easily accessible like the other resources such as the police, fire brigade and health service personnel. This issue was addressed and confirmed by several testers, as represented by this statement: "Switching between the worker/volunteer tabs was very annoying; please keep the buttons static". A user had an experience where some buttons did not function as expected. Figure 7 show the testers' results when they were asked whether the buttons functioned correctly.

The information in the notification-dashboard of the game was frustrating because it had a lot of lag (please consult Fig. 4 on features discussed from here onward). One player had difficulties to scroll down, so that the list of events was not findable. On the other hand, the events appear too fast, causing the player to miss some events that required actions and response. Notifications were not easy to read instantly, especially when several events happened almost simultaneously. One player claimed to lose a couple of events just because of getting several "all workers back" and "work finished" notifications almost simultaneously as a new event that needed an action popped-up on screen.

One player had trouble with the resource button (See Fig. 7), i.e. when the players should pick the right personnel to handle the events they had to click the resource button several times. From the developer perspective, it has to do with design, where the resource button is supposed to only be clicked once. If the player is used to do double clicks before something happens in other games or applications, then the picked resource would be returned to the dashboard, and only the third click would make the player succeed in selecting rescue personnel. Conversely, the right-hand event status/tracking bars were deemed confusing as well, as they stayed on screen until all personnel returned regardless of the mission status.

Some players were confused about where to find the place of an event in the game world. The players should look at the flow of new incoming events, but at the same time the players were busy with reading the information card on an event that came earlier, in order to take the correct action. A tester suggested to use the game world more actively, for example with arrows that point to off-screen events.

Regarding feedback on the game improvement, many have to do with the game's GUI and functionalities. For example, one user suggested adding different lights such as night and day and "what time it is" in the game. Variations on the weather such as sun, rain and storm would make the game more realistic and alive than just a plain condition with a set of events that occur.

Instead of dividing the notifications into the right-hand bar and center panel, a player suggested to have these two unified. Readability would also be improved if the continuous flow of messages was dropped, and instead presenting mission cards that showed a quick overlook of the event: status, resources sent, time left, etc. without the need to click through to another window. As the game already have a good system of readable icons, the game should not have to rely on as much text as the current status.

On the topic of returning personnel, the players had no idea of how to find out how long time would personnel take to return. The testers suggested to have a simple timer next to the personnel's name which would help users. One player suggested to add the Civil Defense as it is also considered a part of the Norwegian Crisis Management system, and therefore should be included.

To sum up, we have implemented the user testing to detect usability barriers and problems, perceptions of the user interface, and user experience when playing the game. These elements were evaluated both from negative experience such as frustrated, annoyed; technical difficulties as well as positive experience such as exciting experience, opportunity for learning and reflecting. The overall results indicated that the subjects tended to rate the game prototype as positive, as seen in Fig. 6. However, it is not the good or bad judgement that is the main focus in this user testing part, but how much the testers could reveal various usability problems, and providing alternative solutions and feedback on future improvement. At this point, we consider the testing result to be adequate as a departure point for the further enhancement of the VTT Operation Tyrsdal.

6 Lessons Learned

The selected methodologies for game development and testing have provided new understanding on the current status of the work and the results of these methodologies can be a basis for producing a final "Serious crisis management game". The co-design approach has helped us to define what elements are important when developing a serious game for crisis management so that it is more realistic than merely relying on the literature. The results of the SeGUE instrument application to our prototype testing have not only helped us to identify improvement points as addressed in Sect. 5, but also gave knowledge in what way the user felt frustrated, annoyed or experienced barriers, and on elements that they found exciting. Some comments also provide a hint on possible technical issues that need to be solved. The lessons learned from our research for both co-creation and game testing methods are as follows:

On the co-creation methodology:

- The co-creation with stakeholders can help sharpening the project goals, for example in our co-design process, a tool that enables learning on the different emergency response organizations' working methods which will benefit from the training of local actors.
- The flexibility in the elicitation process is important as sometimes there were borderline-interrelated themes supposed be discussed in two sessions, but then these "borderline" topics had fully covered already in one session. In other words, we used less time than planned in a particular topic. On the other hand, some areas can be challenging and require more time to discuss than initially planned for.
- The audio-video recording was very useful for extracting the most relevant information from the workshop, especially requirements specification.

On the game testing methodology:

- The players brought their own devices for the game testing. We experienced a mismatch between the testers' machines and the game. Half of them have Mac machines while the prototype was designed for a Windows platform, assuming porting to multiple platforms would be trivial for later expansion. But this problem was solved quickly by running the testing in two sessions, which was no problem at all as the game highlights the individual experience. However, it required some extra time. For this type of testing, having extra machines as back-up would be recommended. An alternative would be to port the game to more than one platform.
- The total time available for the discussion and debriefing was limited as the testers were also asked to fill out questionnaires. Time allocation for the discussion should be longer and a bit flexible. This would allow a facilitator to ask more detailed questions, and to stop whenever not more new information can be obtained or reaching a saturation point.
- The suggested SeGUE technique uses annotated video during the testing, while we only observed the participants' activities, and took notes in the discussion. Game experience on different aspects of the game was not so easy to be identified even if video recording was used, as the testers were busy solving the tasks in the game. The questionnaire really helped to elicit the user's game experience. However, video recording is useful when extensive discussion is planned for the testing.

7 Conclusions

This paper presents our work on the development of a serious game for crisis management of extreme weather events. The game prototype was developed through a co-design process. The paper also describes the co-design methodology, i.e. workshops and the usability tests that are fit for a product that is still in the prototype or implementation stage. The workshops have resulted in a set of requirements that is then used for prototyping activities. For the usability testing, we adapted the SeGUE or "Serious Game Usability Evaluator" instrument, by focusing on "Event categories for the system dimension" and "Event categories for the user dimension". The players substantially contributed to detecting usability problems in the Operation Tyrsdal game. Such information was very relevant for the future game development, to make the game playable by the end users, and used for reflection and learning.

The limitation of this study is that we conducted usability testing at the game implementation stage, and not at final or release stage. In addition, the testers were not end users (crisis responders), but qualified for evaluating the graphical user interface and expressing the experience and technical barriers during the testing. We did not implement the video annotation technique to supply the usability test process, which can be a future improvement on the methodology part. When the game is considered a final product, we will involve the first responders to implement a more comprehensive usability testing, combining the SeGUE method with standard user satisfaction questionnaires and the eye-tracking usability technique.

Acknowledment. The KriseSIM project is supported by Aust-Agder Utviklings og Kompetansefond and Sparebanken Sør, Norway. We thank the emergency management stakeholders in Sørlandet, Norway, for fruitful discussions of the KriseSIM project, and all volunteers who tested the game. This project has been approved by Norwegian Data Protection (NDS), Project No. 54141. We are grateful to Mattias N. Tronslien, Max Emil Moland, Christian A. Kulmus, Kristoffer K. Thomassen who worked on the prototype.

References

1. Ford, J.K., Schmidt, A.M.: Emergency response training: strategies for enhancing real-world performance. J. Hazard. Mater. **75**(2), 195–215 (2000)
2. Linehan, C., et al.: There's no 'I' in 'Emergency Management Team:' Designing and evaluating a serious game for training emergency managers in group decision making skills. In: Proceedings of the 39th Conference of the Society for the Advancement of Games & Simulations in Education and Training. Innovation North-Leeds Metropolitan University (2009)
3. Fanfarová, A., Mariš, L.: Simulation tool for fire and rescue services. Proc. Eng. **192**, 160–165 (2017)
4. Wang, B., et al.: BIM based virtual environment for fire emergency evacuation. Sci. World J. **2014**, 1–22 (2014)
5. Martinez, S., Isaacs, J., Fernandez-Gutierrez, F., Gilmour, D., Scott-Brown, K.: Building bridges between user and designer: co-creation, immersion and perspective taking. In: Di Bucchianico, G., Kercher, P. (eds.) Advances in Design for Inclusion, pp. 117–129. Springer, Cham (2016). https://doi.org/10.1007/978-3-319-41962-6_11

6. Cinderby, S., Forrester, J.M.: Co-designing possible flooding solutions: participatory mapping methods to identify flood management options from a UK borders case study. J. Geograp. Inf. Sci. **1**, 149–156 (2016)
7. Hughes, A.L.: Participatory design for the social media needs of emergency public information officers. In: ISCRAM (2014)
8. Munkvold, B.E.: Diffusing crisis management solutions through living labs: opportunities and challenges. In: Information Systems for Crisis Response and Management Conference, Rio de Janeiro, Brazil (2016)
9. Petersen, K., et al.: Designing with users: co-design for innovation in emergency technologies (2015)
10. Radianti, J., Tronslien, M.N., Moland, M.E., Kulmus, C.A., Thomassen, K.K.: A crisis management serious game for responding extreme weather event. In: Dokas, I.M., Bellamine-Ben Saoud, N., Dugdale, J., Díaz, P. (eds.) ISCRAM-med 2017. LNBIP, vol. 301, pp. 131–146. Springer, Cham (2017). https://doi.org/10.1007/978-3-319-67633-3_11
11. Sanders, E.B.-N., Stappers, P.J.: Co-creation and the new landscapes of design. Co-design **4**(1), 5–18 (2008)
12. Bødker, S.: Creating conditions for participation: conflicts and resources in systems development. Hum.-Comput. Interact. **11**(3), 215–236 (1996)
13. Leicestershire: Working Together to Build Great Communities: The Leicestershire Communities Strategy 2017-21, Leicestershire County Council (2017)
14. Hill, R., et al.: Workplace learning in the New Zealand apple industry network: a new co-design method for government "practice making". J. Workplace Learn. **19**(6), 359–376 (2007)
15. Ramachandran, D., et al.: Social dynamics of early stage co-design in developing regions. In: Proceedings of the SIGCHI Conference on Human Factors in Computing Systems. ACM (2007)
16. Prahalad, C.K., Ramaswamy, V.: Co-creation experiences: the next practice in value creation. J. Interact. Mark. **18**(3), 5–14 (2004)
17. Vredenburg, K., et al.: A survey of user-centered design practice. In: Proceedings of the SIGCHI Conference on Human Factors in Computing Systems. ACM (2002)
18. Middleton, P., Leahy, B.: Bushfire ready neighbourhoods: from informed and aware to engaged and prepared. In: Disaster Resilience: An Integrated Approach. Charles C Thomas Publisher, Springfield (2017)
19. Mentler, T.: Applying usability engineering to interactive systems for crisis and disaster management. In: Proceedings of the 14th ISCRAM Conference, Albi, France (2017)
20. Radianti, J., et al.: Co-designing a virtual training tool for emergency management. In: Information Systems for Crisis Response and Management Conference, Rochester, NY, USA (2018)
21. Moreno-Ger, P., et al.: Usability testing for serious games: making informed design decisions with user data. Adv. Hum.-Comput. Interact. **2012**, 4 (2012)
22. Nielsen, J.: Usability inspection methods. In: Conference companion on Human Factors in Computing Systems. ACM (1994)
23. Sujan, M., Pasquini, A.: Allocating tasks between humans and machines in complex systems. In: Proceedings of the 4th International Conference on Achieving Quality in Software (1998)
24. Sweeney, M., Maguire, M., Shackel, B.: Evaluating user-computer interaction: a framework. Int. J. Man Mach. Stud. **38**(4), 689–711 (1993)
25. Nielsen, J.: Guerrilla HCI: using discount usability engineering to penetrate the intimidation barrier. In: Cost-Justifying Usability, pp. 245–272 (1994)

26. ISO 13407: Human-centred design processes for interactive systems. ISO, Geneva (1999)
27. Brooke, J.: SUS-a quick and dirty usability scale. Usability Eval. Ind. **189**(194), 4–7 (1996)
28. Kirakowski, J., Corbett, M.: SUMI: the software usability measurement inventory. Br. J. Edu. Technol. **24**(3), 210–212 (1993)
29. Lewis, J.R.: IBM computer usability satisfaction questionnaires: psychometric evaluation and instructions for use. Int. J. Hum.-Comput. Interact. **7**(1), 57–78 (1995)
30. Bevan, N.: Measuring usability as quality of use. Softw. Qual. J. **4**(2), 115–130 (1995)
31. Gray, W.D., Salzman, M.C.: Damaged merchandise? A review of experiments that compare usability evaluation methods. Hum.-Comput. Interact. **13**(3), 203–261 (1998)
32. Tidwell, J.: Common Ground: A Pattern Language for Human-Computer Interface Design (1999). http://www.mit.edu/~jtidwell/common_ground.html
33. MET. Norske ekstremvær får navn, 28 January 2018. http://www.met.no/vaer-og-klima/farevarsel-og-ekstremvaer/norske-ekstremvaer-far-navn

Redefining the Customer Centricity Approach in the Digital Age

Christine Riedmann-Streitz[(⊠)]

MarkenFactory GmbH, Frankfurt am Main, Germany
christineriedmann-streitz@markenfactory.com

Abstract. When user experience (UX) issues in information and communication technology are investigated, the application context is usually determined by situations where people use and interact with software systems. In this position paper, we address the specific application context where users are also in the role of customers, although they might not be the one who "bought" the product or service. Customer is here defined in the more general term as the key stakeholder. The paper explores the relationship between the notion of "user-centric" design and the notion of "Customer Centricity", a concept that has been around in marketing and business already in the so called pre-digital era. Companies agree that the customer should be in the focus of their business. But they do not really follow the core idea of Customer Centricity. This results in the Customer Centricity Paradox: The more data about the individual customer are available at the touch of a button, the more he (In this paper, the term 'he' is used for simplifying reasons, but it refers to all genders.) is reduced to a set of data points and serves only as a means to an end. He is not in the focus, he is the product. For this reason, Customer Centricity needs to be rethought and redefined. We introduce and propose the Activity-oriented Customer Centricity (ACC) approach. If companies do not want to turn the Customer Centricity approach against their customers, then they must follow the ACC approach as in the concept of Humane Customer Centricity.

Keywords: Customer Centricity · Hybrid Brand · User brand experience
User experience · Design thinking · Job to be done
Human-Centered Design (HCD) · Activity-Centered Design (ACD)
Activity-oriented Customer Centricity (ACC) · Humane Customer Centricity

1 Introduction

When user experience (UX) issues in information and communication technology are investigated, the application context is usually determined by situations where people use and interact with software systems on mobile or stationary devices or interact within a smart environment, e.g., searching for information, navigating websites, using software packages, engaging in social media and other communication activities. In this position paper, we address the special application context where users are in the role of customers at the customer touch points, e.g., ordering items in an online shop. Thus, an additional dimension is to be considered when discussing user experience issues, i.e. the experience as a customer. The paper explores the relationship

© Springer International Publishing AG, part of Springer Nature 2018
A. Marcus and W. Wang (Eds.): DUXU 2018, LNCS 10918, pp. 203–222, 2018.
https://doi.org/10.1007/978-3-319-91797-9_15

between the notion of "user-orientation" or "user-centric"[1] design and the notion of "Customer Centricity", a concept that has been around, especially in the marketing and sales domain, for a long time and independently of digitalization.

Customer Centricity has become a buzzword with no real focus; this was also caused by the fact that there is no uniform definition [3]. It is regarded as a concept, mission statement, process, marketing and sales or corporate strategy. Therefore, it is also not surprising, that the term "customer" is not defined in this context resulting in a wide range of interpretations of who the customer is. Usually, the customer is seen as "a person who buys goods or services from a shop or a business" [4]. This person could be an individual (end customer, B2C) or a business (B2B). It is important to recognize, that the customer is not necessarily the user. It is not unusual, that one person (e.g., wife, mother, child) buys a product or service for someone else who uses the product (husband, baby, aged parents). Customer relationships exist also within a company, between departments as e.g., IT and marketing. In this paper, we argue for the necessity to rethink the Customer Centricity approach in the context of digitalization.

Customer Centricity puts the customer at the center of attention – due to the simple fact, that he is the one who should buy the product or service. Consequently, there is hardly any company that does not concentrate on the customer. Statements like "we focus on the customer", "we put customers first" are found in all corporate guidelines and internal employee guides.

Usually, the concept "customer orientation" is used in processes such as sales, innovation and marketing and is concerned with activities "taken by a business to support its sales and service staff in considering client needs and satisfaction their major priorities" [5]. Corporate culture, i.e. a company's culture (beliefs, ideas) as well as the impact of this culture on how business is done and how its employees behave, has played only a minor role in the past. But even where customer orientation is explicitly anchored in the corporate vision and guidelines, it is often based on a technology-driven approach. Corresponding to the goal, however defined, of putting the customer at the center of attention, there are different interpretations of what it means to "understand" the customer and how to manage the relationship via a CRM system (Customer Relationship Management). Data were needed already in the past for the CRM system. But now, given the new tools and possibilities that come with an increased digitalization, a new level of competition was triggered: Who can collect the most and the best data? Who can track and monitor a customer's behavior in more detail and draw more precise predictions? The focus is on mainly technology-driven approaches to Customer Centricity.

---

[1] In ISO 9241-210 the notion "human-centered design" replaces the former "user-centered design" to emphasize that it "also addresses impacts of stakeholders not just typically considered as users." It is "an approach to interactive system developments that aims to make systems usable and useful by focusing on the users, their needs and requirements, and by applying human factor/ergonomics, and usability knowledge and techniques. The approach enhances effectiveness and efficiency, improves human well-being, user satisfaction, accessibility and sustainability; and counteracts possible adverse effects of use on human health, safety and performance" [1]. This shift from user-related design to human-related design goes back to Krippendorff [2].

The issue to be discussed in this position paper is, how can the existing approaches of "user-orientation" and "Customer Centricity" be adapted and combined to provide a new perspective in the context of digitalization, employing and using but not surrendering to technology, by proposing a Humane Customer Centricity, where the customer is still in the loop and in control as well as valued by the companies. If these conditions are not fulfilled, then people allow that technology, invented by mankind, is taking over and controlling them. Hence, in the Customer Centricity approach we introduce and emphasize (Sect. 6.1), customers are defined in the more general term as key stakeholders. According to Freeman and Reed [6], the customer as stakeholder is also considered to be a person for whom the company should be responsible.

2 Selected Factors of Customer Centricity

In this section, we discuss selected relevant factors which help to understand the current notion of Customer Centricity and how to adapt it to new challenges:

- Strategic starting points for new business opportunities
- UX
- Design Thinking
- Brand

2.1 Strategies for Business Opportunities

There are several strategic starting points for innovation and business success (Fig. 1). The "market-centric" approach is the attempt to identify hitherto unnoticed gaps and niches in the market to step in and squeeze out competition. In the digital age, the availability of new technologies (i.e. 3D printing, AR, VR, beacons, blockchain) triggers new product ideas and promotes a "technology-centric" approach. The

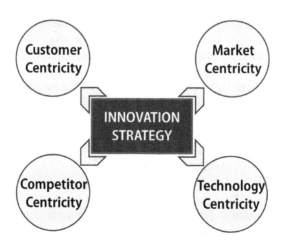

Fig. 1. Strategic Starting Points for New Business, (innovation, new products or services). (Source: Graphics by Riedmann-Streitz [7] following Müller [8])

"competition-centric" approach searches for a better market position in the existing industry with the main competitor of a company as its benchmark. Ultimately, every new offer and every successful innovation must also meet the conditions of Customer Centricity. The term "customer" could refer to the B2B-customer (here, the customer as decision-maker decides and buys for potential resellers or re-users), the B2C-consumer, and rarely to the user of the offer (who might not be the same person who purchases the offer). This approach is of high importance because the customer (and the user in the end) is the one who pays, after all. So finally, Customer Centricity is crucial for the development of successful innovation and it determines the success of a company.

2.2   The Role of UX

UX refers to the experience of the user and emphasizes, that for satisfying a user of a product or service it is by far not enough to offer him only a product that works. To enhance satisfaction, all aspects and elements of interaction with the product or service must be taken into account: accessibility, usability (e.g., intuitive operation), functional factors (e.g., functional design), emotional factors (e.g., pleasure, attractive design). The role of UX becomes more important, when the majority of processes and communication takes place in a digital context. Users are often also customers (with some limitations in B2B). Thus, taking customer orientation seriously, customer experience is a decisive factor. Therefore, UX is also key to shape the way how a product or service is perceived by the customer. (In multi-level-distribution channels it is important to notice, that the needs of buyer, reseller, final customer and user can vary enormously.)

2.3   The Role of Design Thinking

Design thinking is a creative method for designers which involves aspects outside the pure design context e.g., from societal and business sectors. It was David and Tom Kelley [9] who synchronized the basic design processes with the relevant aspects of business strategies, resulting in what is called "design thinking". It became the core principle of the design consultancy IDEO [9]. Their work for Apple and other well-known brands made design thinking popular. In this approach, the actual user is in the focus. The process of innovation (in the context of product development) was completely rethought and restructured with the overall goal of creating successful "breakthroughs" by putting the user in the focus of all activities. According to Burmester [10] design thinking "aims to develop innovative and creative solutions for complex problems ... to find a solution that satisfies the needs of users, is technically feasible and economical", whereas the "goal of human-centered design is to guarantee a high usability and user experience of a product".

The current hype about design thinking is strengthened by the effort to gain successful products by taking into account the customer and his needs. As a problem-solving approach it should lead to the development of new ideas and innovation that convince as many customers as possible. This leads to the (theoretical) conclusion that new offers must be convincing – not in the eyes of the company, but first and foremost in the eyes of the customer.

2.4   The Role of Brands

Customer Centricity needs a consignor, the company (industry, media, NGOs, service or others), and an addressee (customer, user). The relationship is reciprocal. The identity of the consignor, the company, is characterized by the company's brand. Analogous to the insight of Watzlawick et al. [11]: "One cannot *not* communicate", it is impossible not to be perceived as a brand. Therefore, it does not matter whether the company has a strong brand, is a hidden champion or a "no name". The company's brands (corporate, employer, product, service, personal brand) always provide the specific framework for the customer experience (Fig. 2). The design of Customer Centricity is shaped by a company's brand (attitude, promises, values) which is offering rational as well as emotional experiences and benefits. Thus, it is inevitable to talk about brands in the context of this paper.

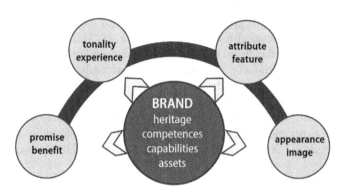

Fig. 2. The main Elements of the Brand Identity. (Source: Graphics by Riedmann-Streitz [7] following Esch [12])

Furthermore, a strong brand, in addition to successful innovation, is the key value driver of sustainable profitability - a goal that every company has set itself to remain viable. Thus, Customer Centricity also aims at strengthening the brand's image and increasing the value of a company.

In the digital era, millions of similar products and services are accessible at the touch of a button. For the customer this freedom of choice is no longer manageable when too much unweighted information is available. Strong brands offer valuable orientation in complex situations with their signal effect and set of values. Thus, brands are most valuable for companies as well as for people in their role as customers [7].

Today, customers and society in general expect corporate responsibility. Customers tend to buy products from brands they are familiar with and showing brand promises and brand values they can identify themselves with. The requested corporate or brand responsibility goes far beyond the responsibility for a specific product. It is expected that companies accept responsibility for the short-term and long-term impact of their decisions and actions. This becomes an important driver for brand relevance. People want companies to take over the responsibility and to provide value-based orientation in an increasingly complex and volatile environment, in a world in which confidence in public institutions and politics decreases. The younger the generation, the more pronounced is the desire to make the favorite brand play an important role in shaping a future worth living in, make the world a better place and solve the world's major problems [7]. While these goals might be very ambitious and hard to meet by the companies, these expectations exist and play a role in the customer behavior.

2.5   The Role of UX in Brand Relevance

"Understanding the customer" is one key to success. The fit between brand and customer is a matter of identification and identity. Identification and identity is based on content, culture and values, provided by the brand (and its company). There is a close correlation between brand relevance, brand promise, customer benefit and a company's success. But there is a problem of increasing significance: Over 70% of the brands worldwide, over 90% of the brands in Europe are simply irrelevant to people. Customers would not miss these brands if they did not exist tomorrow [13]. Most of the brands have lost their relationship with their customers. This situation will become even more explosive in the digital era. Companies - inspired by the possibilities of big data – evaluate the relationship with stakeholders primarily as an economic factor. They use people as a source of data instead of checking the customer and societal benefit the brand offers. In the long run, brands cannot be successful without loyal customers, who will trust and recommend them. Both, the customer's and the user's perception and experience of the brand and its products is crucial for customer loyalty and brand relevance. UX plays a major role in the perception and relevance of a brand.

3   Related Work

Before we propose a new approach to Customer Centricity, it is useful to provide a selected overview about related work in this area.

3.1   The Reason Why of Customer Centricity

Peter Drucker stated: "The aim of marketing is to know and understand the customer so well that the product or service fits him and sells itself" [14]. Recognizing that economic success is based on satisfied, loyal customers, customer satisfaction has become a central business purpose. This is one aspect which Drucker [15], among others, repeatedly pointed out. Drucker reminds us also that the success of a company is due to the customer's willingness to spend his money on a given product or service.

3.2   Customer Centricity in the Context of the Hedonic and Pragmatic Model of UX

Hassenzahl [16] developed a model of UX with two dimensions (hedonics and pragmatics), which are interesting for the further development of Customer Centricity, especially with respect to the motivational aspect of purchase decisions. Hassenzahl's model "assumes that people perceive interactive products along two different dimensions. *Pragmatics* refers to the product's perceived ability to support the achievement of 'do-goals', such as 'making a telephone call', 'finding a book in an online-bookstore', 'setting-up a webpage'. In contrast, *hedonics* refers to the product's perceived ability to support the achievement of 'be-goals', such as 'being competent', 'being related to others', 'being special'" [16]. The hedonics approach "calls for a focus on the Self", here "more general human needs beyond the instrumental come into play, such as a need for novelty and change, personal growth, self-expression and/or relatedness" [16]. The customer evaluates the product individually and sets "its utility and usability in relation to potential tasks" [16]. What Hassenzahl describes here can be applied not only to interactive products, but to products and services in general.

His differentiation between hedonic and pragmatic aspects has its analogy in the emotional and rational dimensions of a brand. And we find this idea of two-sided goals (here: "do-goal" and "be-goal") also in the proposal of Christensen [17] (described in Sect. 3.3) who argues from a very different direction, namely that of innovation.

Another theory that should be mentioned in this context is the CUE Model by Thüring and Mahlke [18]. It addresses identification (see Sect. 2.5) as a hedonistic aspect, but in contrast to Hassenzahl it puts more emphasis on emotion in the context of UX. In an updated version by Minge and Thüring [19] it describes the interdependencies between hedonic and pragmatic qualities and specifies "product loyalty" as one main UX consequence, which can be interpreted as a reference to brand (loyalty). The questionnaire resulting from the more elaborated meCUE 2.0 model [20] for the first time questions people about their experience of a product or service.

3.3 Customer Centricity is about "Jobs to be done"

Clayton Christensen has become known widely for his research and work on the problem that even successful companies cannot be sure that their success will continue in the future [17, 21]. From the perspective of a company's ability to innovate, he developed new important aspects of Customer Centricity. In September 2016, Christensen (et al.) [22] warned of a major misunderstanding. His comments refer to the fact that most of the innovation still fail and that the comprehensive knowledge of the customer companies gained by big data is leading many companies in the wrong direction: "After decades of watching great companies fail, we've come to the conclusion that the focus on correlation - and on knowing more and more about customers - is taking firms in the wrong direction. What they really need to home in on is the progress that the customer is trying to make in a given circumstance - what the customer hopes to accomplish. This is what we've come to call the job to be done" [22].

3.4 From HCD to ACD: Human-Centered Design Considered to be Harmful

We find reflections like those of Christensen in another area, that of design, from another widely respective thinker: Don Norman. His work on "Emotional Design" [23], "The Design of Future Things" [24], "The Design of Everyday Things" [25] gained worldwide attention. He expressed a very skeptical view at Customer Centricity from a design perspective. Norman wrote in his much-debated essay on "Human-Centered

Design Considered Harmful" (we refer here to his jnd.org blog [26] and quote only those aspects relevant for our topic, the text goes far beyond that): "Human-Centered Design has become such a dominant theme in design that it is now accepted by interface and application designers automatically, without thought, let alone criticism. That's a dangerous state - when things are treated as accepted wisdom." He states that "some of the fundamental principles of Human-Centered Design" (HCD) need to be reconsidered and argues for the term "Activity-Centered Design" (ACD). Why? To know your user is one of the core principles of HCD as well as of Customer Centricity. But, according to Norman: "Even companies that pride themselves on following human-centered principles still have complex, confusing products." But even with products or designs that work well, Norman mentions the automotive industry and everyday objects as kitchen utensils, we have to find out: Why do they work well? "People all over the world manage to learn them - and manage quite well." Some of those products were designed by design teams, others evolved during generations as some of the kitchen tools. "But even for those devices created by formal design teams, populated with people whose job title was 'designer', these designers used their own understanding of the activities to be performed to determine how the device would be operated. The users were supposed to understand the task and to understand the designers' intentions" [26]. Hassenzahl, too, criticizes the typical designer's viewpoint: For a designer the UX key elements are "product features" and "intended product character", whereas for the user the UX key elements are "apparent product character" and the situational consequences of use, i.e. experiences as "appeal", "pleasure", "satisfaction" [27].

3.5   Customer Centricity – but who is the "Customer"?

The interdependence between a company and its customers is a fact that is often underestimated and not well respected in common business practice. The question of who the customer is can be answered differently. Has anyone ever asked how the customer sees himself? "We are not seats or eyeballs or end users or consumers. We are human beings - and our reach exceeds your grasp. Deal with it." is a summary statement in front of the Cluetrain Manifesto [28] published in 1999 by Searls, et al. They formulated 95 theses on the company-customer relationship in the emerging time of online markets and the World Wide Web in general. In 2015, they found themselves forced to rewrite the manifesto, now with 121 theses [29]. In retrospect, it becomes apparent how far-sighted the theses written in 1999 were. In the meantime, the balance of power has been reversed by digitalization.

4   Customer Experience must be Seamless

The future will be seamless. Riedmann-Streitz [7] addressed this aspect under the topic "Seamless Gateways". "Digitalization creates a new complexity and superposition of communication and distribution channels and realities. The challenge for brands is to change from one channel into the other and from physical reality to virtual reality and back avoiding inconvenient interfaces for the customer" [7]. Online giants such as

Amazon® and Zalando have shown this in an impressive way. Both are successful brands that started in the digital world and had a high global impact on our private life and the economy in general. A few years ago, they extended their business into the real physical world by opening their own brand shops, so that people can experience the brand world physically and join likeminded customers. Amazon® opened bookstores in the US. Zalando opened fashion shops, e.g., in Germany.

"The future lies in the seamless shopping experience" [7]. This seamless shopping experience is a demand-oriented contact at the touch point, where the customer is currently located, whether mobile, at home, out-of-home, desktop or in-store. This seamlessness has more than just a technical component, although it is supported by new digital technologies such as AR, VR or beacons. It becomes a central issue and convenience factor as the transitions between the real and virtual worlds are fluid; for decision-making, purchasing and delivery processes the customer seamlessly changes the medium. Focusing on the needs of the stakeholders ultimately enables the brands to create a seamless environment. Seamlessness goes beyond the hitherto existing cross-media strategies and the customer journey cannot longer be regarded as linear. Also, both online and offline should be synchronized and orchestrated. Furthermore, seamlessness presumes the consistency of messages and appearance in all channels. To avoid any dissonances and disruptions there should be one consistent concept of Humane Customer Centricity for both worlds. Inconsistencies have a negative effect, since they lead to cognitive dissonance and damage the brand's image.

Accordingly, brands must be developed into "Hybrid Brands" [7]. The ACC approach consciously integrates the real and virtual worlds in a hybrid world - with a seamless customer experience focusing on the needs of the customer/user. Online and offline channels complement each other, as well as mobile, desktop and in-store. Hybrid Brands are characterized by using the advantages from all realities and channels in terms of targeted use of communication and distribution. They connect the best of both worlds - physical and digital reality for people (society) and the user - to a very special brand USP (unique selling proposition).

5 The Customer Centricity Paradox

Customer Centricity is vital. This leads most companies to follow the principle: "The customer is king" – which became a core principle of modern marketing. The concept of Customer Centricity is based on the relationship between a company and its customer (existing and potential ones). Relationships are established by communication through all kinds of communication channels. In the so-called "customer journey" the customer is attracted by a brand, decides to put it into his so-called "relevant set" and finally decides to buy this product and not the other branded product. If he does this frequently, he becomes a key customer – and is at the heart of business interests. Marketing experts are warning [30] not to be customer-friendly, but customer-centric, which means to focus on the "best" (i.e. the most valuable) customers. Here, big data play an important role in identifying these customers. Regular loyal customers are the backbone of corporate success. Ultimately, the brand as well as the company only exists because many loyal customers are willing to pay their money for products of that brand.

Looking back, in the pre-digital era, it was a kind of a winking agreement and mutual understanding between a company and the educated customer that the individual's desire to buy is fueled by attractive brands with exciting brand experiences. The customer should get the feeling: "the company understands me". His buying and recommendation behavior supports the profit and image growth of the company which in return reassures the customer and makes him proud "to be part of it".

Digitalization now offers new possibilities causing a disruptive change in the methods of Customer Centricity. Under the umbrella of Customer Centricity, many companies try to collect as many data as possible for a better understanding of the customer's needs. Customer Centricity promises to strengthen market share, profitability and customer perception - and significantly higher sales. This appraisal is strengthened by the suppliers of digital tools and services. Quite often a fatal mix-up takes place: collecting, aggregating and clustering a huge amount of data does not necessarily imply a better understanding of customers, their motives, decision rationale and overall consumption patterns. Following the logic of big data, the use of algorithms results in correlations and probabilities by recommending "customers who bought this item also bought", "is often bought together", "other customers are also interested in", "your most recently viewed articles and special recommendations - inspired by your browsing history", "discovered for you" and so on [7]. Correlations are often confused with causal relationships. Consequently, today, "we do not lack correlations, but we do lack sustainable conclusions with visionary decisions" [7]. This mix-up results in producing a variety of marketing activities to trigger the customer instead of looking for high qualitative, exciting, brand-specific offers and solutions. In many cases, this course of action leads to offering rebates instead of attraction by content, user experiences and values.

There is no doubt that digitalization changes the manner, methods and ways of communication – also communication between company and customer – at nearly every customer touch point. Those real and virtual touch points are the target points for customer focus and brand experience. The new digital mechanisms are causing a shift in the way communication is done today. Customer communication is reduced to customer tracking and tracing on the web and out-of-home (OoH). Only few people realize that the original idea of Customer Centricity is endangered to be turned into its opposite, at least from a customer's point of view. Yet: this way of doing communication hardly generates satisfied customers and long-term customer loyalty. Finally, brand and image are suffering. This is an invaluable loss - for the company and for the customer.

In many cases, the ambition of creating a positive customer experience throughout the customer journey, i.e. pre-sale, point-of-sale, after-sale, exists only at the surface. Product development and marketing concepts are still developed from an internal point of view, driven by a widely accepted make-and-sell attitude. Products and services are launched which were easy to realize because of technological feasibility, for reasons of efficiency or because opinion leaders in the company are pushing the idea. The high rate of unsuccessful products (approx. 70%) shows that these results are far from appealing to the customer and being relevant to him.

New digital technologies can provide new insights of understanding the customer facilitated by a more precise tracking of customer behavior – from first eye contact with the brand until the purchase decision. Those data should be analyzed and considered in conjunction with trends as well as with the framework set by the respective brand. The real motives and emotions behind using a product or service and the in-depth search for the actual "job to be done" [22] must take place. Forward-looking conclusions must be drawn. Those insights must be incorporated into the product development process. But as long as the evaluation of these data is mainly technology-driven, efficiency-driven or make-and-sell-driven, the customer is still at the end of a long process.

Companies ask themselves: What do we have to do to ensure that customers buy our products and services? Instead companies need to raise questions like: Why did a customer choose our offer? For what concrete reasons did people decide to buy other products and not ours? What do people and society need today and tomorrow to fulfil their tasks and challenges more pleasantly, healthier, quickly, effectively, and quali-tatively better - and possibly more cost-effective? How wants the person, who buys our products, be perceived (prestige, values, style, etc.)? And how successful and attractive do our brands make our customers and users? Are there any completely different, novel solutions that no one has ever thought of before - even those that could be developed by new technologies? The process to get those questions answered leading to valuable innovative solutions, is a big challenge and not followed up by many companies.

Digitalization entices people to see technology as the solution to all challenges, problems and wishes. This should be countered by the provocative question of Cedric Price "Technology is the answer, but what was the question?" [31] expressing his general concerns and skepticism in 1966.

This leads us to the **Customer Centricity Paradox**:

Today, nearly everyone agrees that the customer should be in the focus of business considerations and strategies. But, with a more detailed look on the underlying strategies, processes, evaluations and decision filters it becomes clear at a second glance, that - although the customer seems to be in the focus - he is reduced to a set of data points and serves only as a means to an end. The controversial use of face recognition at main traffic hubs or in-store is one example (some companies had to backpedal due to protests). The customer is the "product" (being degraded from subject to object) and not the beneficiary of an offer he intends to use. This trend is reinforced by increasing digitalization and automation. The umpteen questions to be answered in telephone waiting loops, before one is helped, is another example. But: Once the customer himself starts to upgrade his technology as a "defense" against intrusive and unsolicited targeting and tracking (described in more detail in "Gibt es noch Marken in der Zukunft?" [7]), then such a misconceived Customer Centricity risks to develop into an absurdity and will dissolve. More and more customers decide to use, e.g., ad blockers and script blockers to ensure their privacy and to reserve the right to deny and reject invasive promotions. What, if people in the future use bots equipped with AI to react to such invasive persecutions. The technological armament of companies on the one side and counter measures of customers on the other side lead ultimately to an undesirable "machine-to-machine confrontation". This contrasts the goal that brands should be looking for direct but respectful contact to customers, users and fans. It seems that many promises of digital technologies are superimposing the original core idea of Customer Centricity. To prevent this, Customer Centricity must be reflected and rethought. Figure 3 shows the different stages leading to the dilemma of the Customer Centricity Paradox.

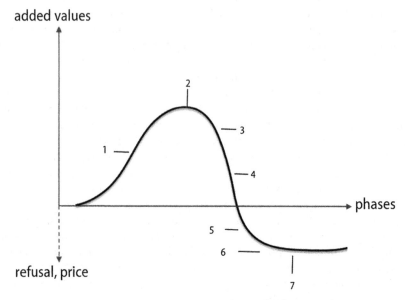

product-centric   customer-centric   company-centric   technology-centric

Fig. 3. The Customer Centricity Paradox: Dilemma, (no 1–7 are explained in the text below). (Source: Graphics by Riedmann-Streitz)

The different stages (Fig. 3) are as follows: 1. First insights: It is the customer who buys and pays for the product. 2. Customer Centricity focusses on "how to get the customer buy our product". 3. Digital technologies are used for massive data collection and tracking & tracing. 4. Technology is widely implemented for cost efficiency. 5. Customers prefer to decide on price & likes. 6. Corporate self-centricity leads to discount war (market), unachieved ROI (company), disloyalty and refusal to buy (customer: ad blockers, dislikes, return deliveries). 7. Technology is the answer with losses on both sides (company, customer).

Make-and-sell-thinking (company-centric) and focusing on efficiency by technology (technology-centric) instead on customer needs, motivation and finally emotional satisfaction fail. Not only that 70% of new products do not reach the customer, three of four companies fail to do reap the benefits of digitalization [32]. Redefining Customer Centricity is key for a viable economy and society in the digital age.

6 Rethinking the Concept of Customer Centricity

6.1 Problems of the Current Customer Centricity Approach

As the Cluetrain Manifestos of 1999 [28] and 2015 [29] reveal, the customer has been made transparent for the company's purposes by employing big data methods. The increasing and widespread use of face recognition and hyper-personalization [7] disregards customer's privacy and freedom of choice. During the described transformation of Customer Centricity, the human being is being developed into a high-performance customer. For efficiency purposes, the customer's wishes are recognized in advance by analyzing the personal profile data and potential purchases are predicted, so that production and logistics can already adapt to it. As soon as the customer orders, the package of the goods he just ordered is ready for delivery. This method is called predictive analytics and is also applied to CRM throughout the customer lifecycle.

In the near future, industry's considerations are aimed at offering customers a new kind of service: based on the outcome of predictive analytics and customer profile data, companies deliver selected products to a customer because the company thinks he would like to buy them. This will happen before he even considered to buy these products, i.e. before he searched for or actually ordered them. If he keeps the product, the amount is debited from his account; if he decides against it, he can, of course, send it back – hopefully free of charge.

We must realize that centering on the customer is necessary, but far from sufficient. The customer has been pushed into a predefined role: he is the one who must pay for what the industry produces. The industry succeeded in designing the Customer Centricity concept purely from the company's point of view – with the help of new technological measures. Precise and ubiquitous tracking methods were optimized and refined to such an extent that the appreciation of the customer, his trust and his well-being in many places is irrelevant. "Understanding the customer" has in many cases experienced a completely new twist. As we have seen, this leads to a total, but restricted focus on customer data, the all-encompassing collection of traces during his customer journey. The persistent tracking allows to detect the exact moment of his purchase likelihood. This is nothing else than a degradation of the customer to a set of data points.

Customer Centricity must be rethought, and redefined and responsible managers must change their mindset. This is not a question of supply, it is a question of value: What does our business proposal offer to customers and how could they benefit from it? Strong brands support their customers in their life and work – including striving for the "best" solution of a problem or an activity or a "job to be done" [22]. The mindset, to take the benefit of the customer as the starting point and make it the core of all considerations, will become a central USP (unique selling proposition) of strong brands, especially in the digital economy.

6.2 Shifting Mindsets and Attitudes

A new perspective is necessary. Not people should adapt to technology, technology must adapt to people! The customer is at the center of the considerations only if he is not considered as a sales volume at the end of the chain, but as a human being and part of the society, who needs offers for today and for the future which enable him to shape his life, his environment and his work in the best possible way – from his perspective. This requires a change of mindset in many industries. The starting point is not the question of what technology could deliver, but what would be desirable for people, for society, for the environment. How do we want to run an economy in the future? How do we want to live and work in the future? And which products and services are needed for this? What do people need and want for a better life, to make their lives more enjoyable and healthy and how could they best benefit from the advantages of new technologies? In turn, businesses have the chance to benefit from sustainable profitability.

According to the findings of Christensen ("job to be done") [22], which are in line with the concept of Hassenzahl ("do-goals"; e.g., buying a bed and "be-goals", e.g., life style, well-being) [16], our new approach focusses on the core objective behind a product purchase. Customers are not looking for bedroom beds, they are looking for deep and refreshing sleep and dreams. Customers, buying at a DIY (do-it-yourself) store, do not want to own a hammer or a drill, but rather wish to hang a picture, shelf, lamp or something else for which they need a hole in the wall. Customers do not want bathroom fittings, but are looking for hygiene, well-being, comfort or a nice inspiring place for self enhancement. Customers are not looking for a dishwasher; they are looking for a solution of coping with the masses of dirty dishes and glasses and getting the job of cleaning done. People are not looking for detergent powder, but they want their family look pretty and neat and get social appreciation. People do not need banks but strong, trustworthy brands and companies to which they can entrust their money. They need a mobile and easygoing but fake-proof secure solution for payment of their private shopping and commercial purchases. Moreover, people do not decide whether they want to do something digitally or not. They see new technologies as instruments, as enablers for participating in the economy and society.

Shifting the Mindset: It is not so much a question of changing processes as of attitude. Attitude, values and visions determine how the process is executed. For Norman, too, the core difference between HCD and ACD (described in Sect. 3.4) is "first and foremost being that of attitude. Attitude? Yes, the mindset of the designer" [26]. Applying this to Customer Centricity, the following is required:

- know your customer (be aware of how he might use your new product or invention: conditions, constraints, habits, preconceptions),
- deeply understand the technology you are applying for the product or service,
- deeply understand the product or service you are creating for your customer,
- deeply understand your customer's reason for this activity (for which you create the solution),
- have a strong transparent vision, clear values and a consistent attitude of how things could be better and what is desirable to fit today's and tomorrow's human needs.

In our approach, Customer Centricity must be grounded in a comprehensive broad perspective – even including the analysis of global social, economic and environmental trends and developments. This is nothing less than trying to find out, create and offer what really matters.

In the literature on marketing and business strategies [33–35], customers are viewed to belong to special and well-defined target groups or peer groups. The analysis could be based on socio-demographic data or on neuromarketing. There are enough data available to know the gender, age, income, job, family and medical situation (e.g., pregnancy), sexual orientation, preferences concerning special products, wishes, motivation and so on. The high performing customer is the full transparent customer. Thinking in terms of target groups or peer groups makes it easy to label the customer and use him as a means to an end. Furthermore, this approach emphasizes primarily past and present behavior. Even predictive analytics makes no difference because it deals with implications of past and present behavior. The customer is reduced to being only a factor in a given formula of Customer Centricity.

In our approach, Customer Centricity must contain a deep understanding of trends and developments and of the problems, hurdles and fears of people when fulfilling their daily tasks. It must be completed by thoughtful purposes, a clear attitude and a strong vision of how things should be – as seen from the user's perspective.

7   Redefining Customer Centricity by Resolving the Paradox

Customer Centricity needs to be redefined so that it respects the human being as it is and adapts technology as supporter, enabler, providing added value to him. The human being, i.e. the customer and user of the products as well as the society which is affected by others using a certain product (e.g., the use of Google® Glasses or WhatsApp® can have implications for other people, although they were not asked for their consent), is the center of thinking and acting. The offer and its benefits as well as the brand relationships must be seen from his point of view, they must be relevant for the addressee. A strong brand could here fulfill the role of a curator, equipped with comprehensive knowledge, a strong attitude and clear vision of how things should be better. It provides orientation and an offer that the customer can identify with.

Therefore, Customer Centricity must be enriched by dimensions known from the concept of UX: the experience of the customer when buying and/or using the product or service, the product's usefulness and benefits seen from his perspective, and the usability, i.e. ease and intuitiveness of use. It has also to be enriched by dimensions known from the concept of brands, i.e. relevance and meaningfulness (seen from the customer's perspective). This is a shift from the focus on target group specifications to the focus on people's needs and activities. Thus, Customer Centricity must be complemented with Activity-Centered Design goals adapted from Norman's plea for ACD [26]. Combining the various aspects, we propose an Activity-oriented approach to Customer Centricity, that we call **ACC**. It includes also motivational aspects and is based on a forward-looking framework and future-oriented thinking. It allows creativity to expand its full potential – for the benefit of the user and in a broader sense of society. The Activity-oriented approach to Customer Centricity leads to a different understanding of what should happen at a customer touch point: it should be much more than an opportunity to deliver triggers to buy. A deep understanding of the customer is the prerequisite. That presupposes the ability of management to find and reframe the customer's problem, maximizing his experience and providing him with an added value – be it rational and emotional, pragmatic and hedonistic.

7.1 Humane Customer Centricity

Given that in the future the focus is really on people and their activities, this has far-reaching consequences. In UX hedonic aspects and well-being gain even greater influence on product and service design [36, 37]. Corporate philosophy and strategy, innovation culture, management culture and KPIs (Key Performance Indicator) must be adapted to the new orientation. This new way of thinking and acting must be anchored in the company's culture and in the behavior of all employees. Correspondingly, the concept of Customer Centricity must be modified and extended. Customer Centricity will only lead to useful solutions that can be applied to people's needs, if it has a humane and philanthropic customer focus. This includes far-sightedness based on clear and transparent values and attitude. Companies take people seriously, respects their needs and privacy. Knowing that this could ensure sustainable profitability for the companies.

That is why we call this new approach: Humane Customer Centricity. The Humane Customer Centricity - including the observation and anticipation of technological and societal developments as well as of the people with their tasks, challenges, problems, dreams and needs in professional and everyday private life - should be in the focus of interest. Applying the Activity-oriented Customer Centricity (ACC) approach is a requirement for Humane Customer Centricity. It will imply a win-win situation for the company and its brands, for customers, users, stakeholders and society in general. The approach of Humane Customer Centricity contradicts the attempt to view human beings as sets of data points that can be used and manipulated or can be spied on using big data, artificial intelligence algorithms and marketing automation.

Referring to the importance of brands, they must evolve to Humane Hybrid Brands [7], upholding the principles and values of a Humane Customer Centricity. This does not happen automatically but must be explicitly initiated and professionally managed and coached. The following aspects distinguish Humane Hybrid Brands: the alignment with Humane Customer Centricity, the respect for privacy and the guarantee that the "Keep the human in the loop" principle is applied (people must be in control and be the final decision-maker in every situation). Streitz [38, 39] argues strongly for "Keep the human in the loop and in control" as the guiding design principle for the 21st century, when being confronted with developments as smart cities, automated driving and related technologies based on artificial intelligence and high degree of automation. In a broader context, this means that Humane Hybrid Brands assume social responsibility, which is not exhausted in declarations of intent, as expressed in many corporate social responsibility reports, but will be experienced by customers, users and society.

Riedmann-Streitz stated [40]: "Focusing on quantity of private data instead on content, wishes, 'jobs to be done' ushers the end of brands: the customer feels upset and annoyed, especially because he entrusted sensitive data to service providers. Digitalization does not solve the problem of understanding and attracting customers." Nor does it solve the challenges of Customer Centricity. "Technology connects people and people with products, but it does not create the branded experience" [40], the user

experience, content and values which inspire, convince, trigger personal recommendation, acceptance, purchase, and loyalty.

Our approach to address the dilemma of the Customer Centricity Paradox described
in Sect. 5 is illustrated by extending the graph in Fig. 3 in the following way (Fig. 4).

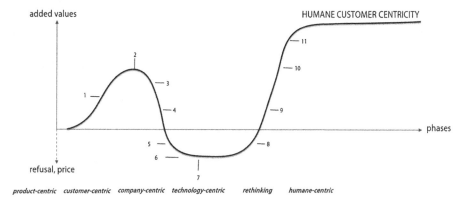

Fig. 4. The Customer Centricity Paradox: Solution, (no 1–7 are explained in Fig. 3, no 8–11 in
the text below). (Source: Graphics by Riedmann-Streitz)

In the technology-centric phase companies find themselves confronted with "losses
on both sides" (7). Ideally, a company achieves an understanding (insight), that this is
because the customer has been degraded from subject to object (8). Rethinking Customer Centricity (9) then leads ideally to a shift of mindsets and attitude (10) which
builds the foundation for the redefinition of Customer Centricity (11) following the
ACC approach. Finally, a company can resolve the Customer Centricity Paradox by
following consequently and consistently the concept of Humane Customer Centricity.

8   Conclusions

Today, we are not faced with a shortage of data or with a lack of information. We suffer
from a lack of causalities as well as qualified, value-oriented, transparent orientation
which allows us to make our personal decisions. Recommendation algorithms allow us
to draw correlations on a global basis wherever and whenever we want - within
milliseconds. It seems to be the perfect condition for a highly elaborated and performing Customer Centricity. But algorithms do not answer the question of the Reason
Why: "Why on earth should we buy a product just because someone else we don't even
know bought it?" [7]. Customer information and customer decision making is driven
by a hyper-personalization, which directs the customer in the direction in which the
company would like to have him. On the other hand, it prevents companies from
establishing a Humane Customer Centricity and the prerequisites for real innovation,
because they lose the basis for understanding the customer, his experiences, emotions,
needs and wishes.

It is essential, that the processing and evaluation of big data is executed with the new mindset in order to arrive at valuable conclusions. It is of key importance to understand the customer's emotional user experience (UX) when searching for and finally "hiring" [41] und then using a product or service to get a "problem" solved or a "job to be done". In combination with the further development of Activity-oriented Customer Centricity (ACC), big data can provide input for the final conclusions and resulting strategies of human experts. Of course, further research is needed to understand the specific mechanisms so that it will be beneficial. Offers are only successful if they contain a relevant future-oriented customer benefit and customer reward. They must help people to perform their daily tasks, small as well as large ones, in the best possible way. And they must fulfill upcoming needs and wishes. Thus, Humane Customer Centricity can provide huge benefit to the company as it discovers valuable hints and impulses for new products and services, new technologies and innovation – aligned to the brand. If companies do not want to misuse the Customer Centricity approach and not turn it against their customers, then they must follow the ACC approach as in the concept of a Humane Customer Centricity. Humane Customer Centricity means thinking and acting consistently from the perspective of people based on a forward-looking human-centered attitude and brand vision. This is a decisive premise, since we do not want to deprive the human being of his freedom and we do not want to subordinate him to technology. Humane Customer Centricity is designed for the benefit of all: company, customers, stakeholders, and society.

Acknowledgements. The author gratefully acknowledges feedback and exchange of ideas with Norbert Streitz on an early version of this paper. Manfred Thüring and Michael Burmester provided valuable feedback during the review process. Nevertheless, the author has the full responsibility for the content of this paper.

References

1. ISO 9241-210. https://www.iso.org/obp/ui/#iso:std:iso:9241:-210d:e-1:v1:en. Accessed 28 Jan 2018
2. Krippendorff, K.: The Semantic Turn: A New Foundation for Design. CRC Press Taylor & Francis Group, Boca Raton (2006)
3. CMO Council, September 2017. https://www.cmocouncil.org/media-center/press-releases/sales-and-marketing-need-to-step-up-and-own-organization-wide-customer-experience-strategy-says-new-cmo-council-study. Accessed 28 Jan 2018
4. Oxford Dictionary: Definition "Customer". https://en.oxforddictionaries.com/definition/customer. Accessed 13 Jan 2018
5. Business Dictionary: Definition "Customer Orientation". http://www.businessdictionary.com/definition/customer-orientation.html. Accessed 28 Jan 2018
6. Freeman, R.E., Reed, D.L.: Stockholders and stakeholders: a new perspective on corporate governance. Calif. Manag. Rev. **25**(3), 88–106 (1983)
7. Riedmann-Streitz, C.: Gibt es noch Marken in der Zukunft? Hybrid Brands – eine Zukunftsvision für starke Marken. Springer Gabler, Wiesbaden (2017). https://doi.org/10.1007/978-3-658-16151-4

8. Müller, W.: Innovationsstrategien - Konzeption und Best Marketing Practices, Fachhochschule Dortmund, FB Wirtschaft, Reihe Forschungspapier, Band 19 (2009)
9. Kelley, T.: The Art of Innovation. Random House, New York (2001)
10. Burmester, M.: Design Thinking – die neue alte Kreativität. https://www.uid.com/de/aktuelles/hcd-design-thinking. Accessed 28 Jan 2018
11. Watzlawick, P., Beavon, J.H., Kackson, D.D.: Menschliche Kommunikation: Formen, Störungen, Paradoxien. Verlag Hans Huber, Bern (1969). http://www.zitate-online.de/sprueche/wissenschaftler/16362/man-kann-nicht-nicht-kommunizieren.html. Accessed 27 Oct 2017
12. Esch, F.-R.: Strategie und Technik der Markenführung, 8. vollständig überarbeitete und erweiterte Auflage. Verlag Franz Vahlen, München (2014)
13. Havas Media: Meaningful Brands. http://www.havasmedia.de/organic-marketing/meaningful-brands/. Accessed 23 Oct 2017
14. Drucker, P.: https://www.brainyquote.com/quotes/peter_drucker_154444. Accessed 31 Oct 2017
15. Drucker, P.: https://www.zitate.eu/author/drucker-peter-ferdinand/zitate/1864. Accessed 31 Oct 2017
16. Hassenzahl, M.: The hedonic/pragmatic model of user experience. In: Hassenzahl et al. (eds.) Towards a UX Manifesto, Lancaster, UK, pp. 10–14 (2007)
17. Christensen, C.M.: The Innovator's Dilemma. Harpers Business, New York (2000)
18. Thüring, M., Mahlke, S.: Usability, aesthetics, and emotions in human-technology interaction. Int. J. Psychol. **42**(4), 253–264 (2007)
19. Minge, M., Thüring, M.: Hedonic and pragmatic halo effects in the course of user experience. Int. J. Hum. Comput. Stud. **109**, 13–25 (2018)
20. Backhaus, N., Trapp, A.K., Thüring, M.: Skeuomorph versus flat design: user experience and age-related preferences. In: Marcus, A., Wang, W. (eds.) DUXU 2018. LNCS, vol. 10918, pp. xx–yy. Springer, Cham (2018)
21. Christensen, C.M., Raynor, M.E.: The Innovator's Solution: Creating and Sustaining Successful Growth. Harvard Business School Press, Boston (2003)
22. Christensen, C.M. et al.: Know your customers "Jobs to be done". Harvard Business Review, September 2016. https://hbr.org/2016/09/know-your-customers-jobs-to-be-done. Accessed 10 Oct 2017
23. Norman, D.A., Design, E.: Why We love (or Hate) Everyday Design. Basic Book, New York (2004)
24. Norman, D.A.: The Design of Future Things. Basic Book, New York (2007)
25. Norman, D.A.: The Design of Everyday Things: Revised and Expanded. Basic Books, New York and MIT Press (UK edition), London (2013)
26. Norman, D.: http://www.jnd.org/dn.mss/human-centered_design_considered_harmful.html. Accessed 30 Oct 2017
27. Hassenzahl, M.: The thing and I: understanding the relationship between user and product. In: Blythe, M.A., Monk, A.F., Overbeeke, K., Wright, P.C. (eds.) Funology: From Usability to Enjoyment, pp. 1–12. Kluwer Academic Publishers (2003)
28. Searls, D., Weinberger, D., Levine, R., Locke, C.: Cluetrain Manifesto (1999). http://www.cluetrain.com/. Accessed 28 Oct 2017
29. Searls, D., Weinberger, D.: Cluetrain Manifesto (2015). http://newclues.cluetrain.com/. Accessed 28 Oct 2017
30. Fader, P.: Customer Centricity. Wharton, Philadelphia (2011)
31. Price, C.: Technology is the answer, but what was the question? Lecture title (1966)

32. Kucher, S.: Mehr Umsatz durch Digitalisierung? Fehlanzeige bei drei von vier Unternehmen. https://www.simon-kucher.com/de/about/media-center/mehr-umsatz-durch-digitalisierung-fehlanzeige-bei-drei-von-vier-unternehmen. Accessed 13 Jan 2018
33. Bruhn, M.: Handbuch des Marketing: Anforderungen an Marketingkonzeptionen aus Wissenschaft und Praxis. Beck, München (1989)
34. Voeth, M., Herbst, U.: Marketing-Management: Grundlagen, Konzeption und Umsetzung, Schäffer Poeschel, Stuttgart (2013)
35. Kotler, P., Keller, K.L.: Marketing Management. Pearson Education, London (2012)
36. Diefenbach, S., Hassenzahl, M., Eckoldt, K., Hartung, L., Lenz, E., Laschke, M.: Designing for well-being: a case study of keeping small secrets. J. Posit. Psychol. **12**(2), 151–158 (2017)
37. Diefenbach, S., Hassenzahl, M.: Psychologie in der nutzerzentrierten Produktgestaltung: Mensch-Technik-Interaktion-Erlebnis. Springer, Heidelberg (2017). https://doi.org/10.1007/978-3-662-53026-9
38. Streitz, N.: Reconciling humans and technology: the role of ambient intelligence. In: Braun, A., Wichert, R., Maña, A. (eds.) AmI 2017. LNCS, vol. 10217, pp. 1–16. Springer, Cham (2017). https://doi.org/10.1007/978-3-319-56997-0_1
39. Streitz, N.: Beyond 'Smart-Only' cities: redefining the 'Smart-Everything' paradigm. Journal of Ambient Intelligence and Humanized Computing (2018, in press). https://doi.org/10.1007/s12652-018-0824-1
40. Riedmann-Streitz, C.: Rethinking ubiquitous digitalization – Do we still need brands in the future? In: Karls Magazine, Rethinking Management, vol. 1, pp. 15–18 (2018). https://karlshochschule.de/fileadmin/files/KarlsMagazine_2018.pdf. Accessed 28 Jan 2018
41. Christensen, C.M.: Customers Don't Simply Buy Products – They Hire Them. https://www.forbes.com/sites/hbsworkingknowledge/2016/10/04/clayton-christensen-customers-dont-simply-buy-products-they-hire-them/2/#76d106b058eb. Accessed 13 Jan 2018

A Roadmap for User Interface Design of Interactive Systems: An Approach Based on a Triad of Patterns

Alexandra Ruíz[1](✉), William J. Giraldo[1], David Geerts[2], and Jose L. Arciniegas[3]

[1] Universidad del Quindío, Armenia, Colombia
{aruiz,wjgiraldo}@uniquindio.edu.co
[2] KU Leuven, Leuven, Belgium
david.geerts@kuleuven.be
[3] Universidad del Cauca, Popayán, Colombia
jlarciniegas@unicauca.edu.co

Abstract. This article presents a Roadmap for user interface designing based on a triad of patterns (data, interaction, and presentation) that comprehends the principles and guidelines from MBUID, HCI, and DCU with the purpose of promoting usability on the final interface. The roadmap is supported by a method, a tool, and languages that allow interface designing. This study is focused on the method only, and it presents the activities and artifacts in detail through its application in a case study in the educational context.

Keywords: User interface design · Patterns · Model driven · Usability

1 Introduction

The User Interface (UI) is considered one of the main components of the development of interactive systems because it connects end users with functionality. Due to its importance and the increasingly demanding requirements to reach to solutions with the quality, usability, and user experience required, the development of the UI has become complex. For this reason, developers and designers must reuse the knowledge already gained by professionals in previous processes, so that they do not have to think about how to solve design problems that have been solved already. For example, certain presentation structures can be common for multiple businesses (sales, purchases, customers), either in the same or different domains. However, a developer who does not have enough experience would have to generate from scratch the interface proto-types and the data modeling that supports them; unless, there is the possibility of using data and UI patterns to generate different proposals of the final interface without much effort.

On the other hand, the complexity of the development of the UI is also due to the heterogeneity of the deployment devices, use contexts, and users, which represent for the software companies more development time of the interactive applications; thus, a greater monetary investment. One of the approaches that have emerged to solve this

© Springer International Publishing AG, part of Springer Nature 2018
A. Marcus and W. Wang (Eds.): DUXU 2018, LNCS 10918, pp. 223–240, 2018.
https://doi.org/10.1007/978-3-319-91797-9_16

problem is the Model Based User Interface Design (MBUID). It is an approach that aims to address the problems of heterogeneity related to devices, users, and use contexts, reducing the necessary effort for the development of the UI.

From the benefits offered by MBUID and the implementation of patterns, the contributions from this article focus on proposing a methodological path that simplifies the work for the developer to generate UI from a triad of patterns (data, interaction, and presentation) that fit the mental model acquired by the user from his own tasks. The proposed path is constructed from a set of proposals that include the principles and the main ideas of the MBUID and the HCI, with the purpose of promoting usability in the final interface. This article is then structured by the following sections: Sect. 2 shows the related works in the context of MBUID and the use of patterns, Sect. 3 presents the fundamentals that characterize the Roadmap, Sect. 4 specifies the Roadmap life cycle and its flow of activities, Sect. 5 presents the application of the Roadmap in a specific case study; and finally, Sect. 6 presents the conclusions and future work.

2 Related Works

The literature reports a variety of approximations based on MBUID, which, according to their characteristics, have been classified into four generations [1]. The first generation is characterized by the development of the UI from a universal model. The second one was characterized by the extension of UI models through the integration of other models. In the third one, developers and designers had to focus on developing user interfaces for different devices with different restrictions. In that generation, MBUID becomes relevant. The fourth generation focuses on the development of context sensitive UI for platforms, devices, and different modalities. Finally, it is observed that as of 2012, more proposals that contemplate the use of patterns have emerged; this way, possibly emanating a fifth generation of MBUID tools. The Fig. 1 presents the MBUID timeline with the most representative proposals of each generation. The graph is an updated version of the one that can be found in [1].

From this wide list of approaches, those that have available information or were current were analyzed. The proposals are: ITS [2], AME [3], MECANO [4], MOBI-D [5], TERESA [6], Supple [7], Maria [8], CIAF/TD_MBUID [9], Cedar [10], MyUI [11], PamGis [12], LIZARD [13] and MODUS [14]. The last four (4) proposals use patterns as a means to provide a certain degree of automation at the usability level. Such is the case of MyUI, a proposal for the generation of individual user interfaces from an interaction model. In this proposal, adaptations are made for different user needs, devices, and environmental conditions, during the execution time. To do this, it uses an extensible repository of design patterns, which includes adaptation rules and modular building blocks for the generation of user interfaces.

On the other hand, PamGis aims to provide a high degree of automation for the generation of artifacts from abstract (UML/XML) and semi-abstract (XML) application models to the source code of the resulting application, through the information inherent to task, user, device, context, and pattern language models.

The central component of the framework is a repository of patterns that contain different types of patterns and pattern languages of different levels of abstraction,

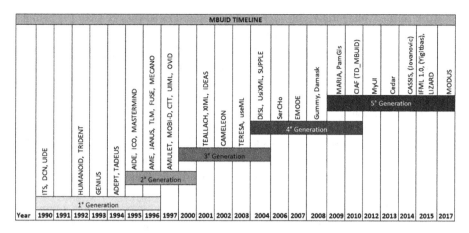

Fig. 1. MBUID [1] proposals timeline, updated version

architecture patterns, design patterns, and HCI patterns. LIZARD allows the definition of applications at a high level of abstraction, based on the specification of domain, task, presentation, device, and data access models. This proposal applies model transformations to generate the target native UI considering the specific features of target platforms. The generated applications follow the UI design guidelines and the architectural design patterns specified by the corresponding operating system manufacturer. Finally, MODUS proposes a tool supported approach for user interface generation directly from the architectural models of the business logic. This proposal transforms the domain model into an ontology in Prolog in order to perform queries to identify data patterns previously stored in a patterns knowledge base. Once the patterns have been selected, the concrete interface is generated and subsequently the final interface, based on transformations of the abstract interface previously associated with each pattern.

The UI development processes of the proposals mentioned have focused on providing a certain degree of usability in the interface through the use of patterns. However, the process is not clear in relation to how integration with the development of other aspects such as functionality is made. In our case, we propose a roadmap for the design of the UI based on a triad of patterns that aims; in addition to promoting usability in the final interface, to the integration with the functionality of the interactive system.

3 Roadmap Fundamentals

The fundamentals according to the Roadmap conception, approach, and principles are presented below.

3.1 How Is the Roadmap Built?

The proposed methodological approach finds its essence in existing proposals in the MBUID and HCI contexts. Due to the degree of contribution of the analyzed proposals, the work of the Collaborative Interactive Application Framework (CIAF) [9] is high-lighted. It proposes a methodological approximation for the development of Model Based User Interfaces in collaborative environments. The proposal is based on the use of several models to represent collaborative and interactive aspects. For this reason, different notations and techniques are used. The integration of three notations is described particularly: 1. CIAN- which involves aspects of human-computer collabo-ration and interaction, 2. UML- which specifies the functionality of computer systems, and 3. usiXML- which describes the user interface for multiple platforms. Additionally, how the model is integrated within the Software Engineering process is described. The process of model development and diagram integration is supported by Eclipse tools. CIAF provides a framework of conceptual, methodological and technological devel-opment for the advance of interactive systems that can be used directly, extended, or customized. This development framework is formally represented. There is a proposal that considers the development of functionality (OpenUP and UML4), group work (CIAM and CIAN5), and user interface (TD-MBUID and usiXML) with languages and tools to obtain user interfaces. These are the three methodological proposals that have been combined to form a single framework, each one managing a different aspect of the development of interactive systems. Each methodological proposal encapsulates its own roles, activities, artifacts, best practices, and tools, allowing being used in isolation.

Relying on the CIAF development framework as the main foundation, we propose a roadmap that expands and customizes the CIAF for the development of the UI from a triad of patterns. Although the roadmap is based on the CIAF, it adds up artifacts, languages, techniques, tools, and models that satisfy the specific necessities of the UI design from a triad of patterns in the context of a specific domain. Thus, a path is obtained which is supported by three essential components: a method, the notation and modelling tools, and code generators for a specific domain.

3.2   What Are the Roadmap's Pillars?

The main pillar of the roadmap is an engineering approach based on a triad of patterns that seeks to simplify to the developer of the interface, the interpretation of the mental models that the expert and the user have, and the way they interact with that data; in order to promote usability in the generated interface through modeling tools and code generators. Through this approach, it is sought that the development of interfaces does not start from scratch, in such a way that it solves the problems of fast functional prototyping and viable minimum product.

Additionally, the proposed roadmap is based on the pillars of the MBUID, the DCU and the design of the UI. The roadmap shares the philosophy of MBUID, in the sense that the models are the essential artifacts in the development process of the UI. Unlike the abstraction levels described in the CAMELEON [15] framework used by some MBUID proposals, the proposed path does not include the abstract user interface (AUI) or modal-independent interface, at least not in an automated way, since the modality is selected at the beginning of the path.

Similarly, the Roadmap shares the DCU [16] principles, such as: (i) the representative users actively participate from early stages and through the whole development process and the entire life cycle of the UI; (ii) the patterns and the UI are built from an iterative and incremental process and (iii) it raises empirical measures of the use of the product based on the evaluation of experts and representative users.

Finally, the roadmap is based on the pillars for UI designing proposed by [17], which argues that the design of the UI must have three elements: processes and guidelines documents (theories and models), software tools of user interface (algorithms and prototypes), and a review by experts and usability tests (controlled experiments). This way, a process is proposed that promotes usability through prototyping and evaluation techniques and that it is supported by model editing tools and automatic code generators for the development of the UI.

What is a Triad of Patterns and How Is it Built?

In the context of this study, a pattern is a model that represents a repetitive solution to a specific problem domain; that is to say, it describes and specifies how a particular problem can be solved, whether it is a model, an implementation, or another abstraction level [18]. In this regard, the triad of patterns is formed by association of a data pattern (domain model), interaction pattern (interaction model), and presentation pattern (presentation model). Their concepts are presented below:

- *Data pattern*: they describe the concepts and data that support the business natural tasks. In this sense, it is sought to specify modelling solutions that simplify the interpreting of mental models by the user [19]. The data pattern is represented by a data model using the UML class diagram notation.
- *Presentation pattern*: it is represented by DataForm model, which allows to express the form semantic (user interface) and the data semantic. The DataForm model is built from how the user structures and perceives the information [20].
- *Interaction pattern*: it is represented by the dialog pattern [9], which preserves the structure and temporary relations of the CTT (*Concur Task Tree*) [21], notation, specifying for each task, the type of Abstract Interaction Components (AIC) associated with the task. These interaction components represent a canonic expression of the rendering and the manipulation of the domain and function concepts in a way of being the most independently possible from the modality (auditive, visual, tactile, etc.) and the informatic platform [22].

The construction of the triad of patterns begins with an exploration of the data patterns for a specific domain. These data have been recognized; assessed by experts that recognize that they have that structure, those elements, and those relationships (expert's mental model), but that it has never been discussed how they must be presented. For this reason, the presentation and interaction patterns (user's mental model) are built from an iterative and incremental process that starts from a user's study, its surroundings, and the task that are done by a specific context and the application of different lab tests with the participation of representative users. Then, the triad of patterns is evaluated by experts and representative users from interface prototypes that are built having in mind different use scenarios, which represent the pattern variability. As a result, a pattern catalog is obtained that can be used for solving design problems for a specific domain.

3.3   Why Those Three Patterns?

In the development of an interactive system, different quality attributes intervene, such as functionality, usability, security, communication, collaboration, etc. Each system attribute requires specific models that describe the information relevant to that attribute. Consequently, a large variety of models are required to develop software.

In our case, we propose an engineering approach that requires only three patterns (models) for the development of the user interface but that uses different models for the construction of each pattern. In this way, the information concerning each quality attribute required is taken into account in that pattern.

The selection of the three types of patterns or models is based on the principles of the development of the functionality and the user interface. Functionality is a process that is developed in parallel with the user interface, which are synchronized. It is related to the domain data (expert opinion), which support the tasks, while the interface is related to how to present and interact with that data but from the user's perspective. In this way, three models (data, presentation and interaction) are required to represent that information.

In the following section, the lifecycle of the proposed methodological roadmap and the main activities of each of its phases are exposed.

4   Proposed Roadmap

4.1   Lifecycle

The Roadmap lifecycle (Fig. 2) is partitioned in the same stages of the software engineering traditional cycle (requirements, analysis and design, implementation, and testing), in such a way that it is easily paired with the development of functionality contemplated in the software engineering conventional methodologies. Likewise, Fig. 2 shows how the user participates actively from early stages and throughout the process, which is iterative and incremental and relies on prototyping and evaluation techniques as one of the mechanisms to promote usability in the final interface.

In the following section, the detailed methodological content of the proposed Roadmap is exposed.

4.2   Detailed Methodological Content

The proposed Roadmap has two main flows: one for creating patterns for a specific domain and the other for the development of the user interface using the created patterns. In Fig. 3 the flow of activities for both cases is observed. According to the stages that make the path, every flow is detailed next.

Flow of Activities for the Creation of Patterns. The flow for the creation of the patterns starts at the plan and research phase and ends at the analysis and design stage. The purpose of this route is to settle the catalog of patterns in such a way that they can be applied to a specific context later. The activities of this flow according to the stages of the Roadmap are presented below.

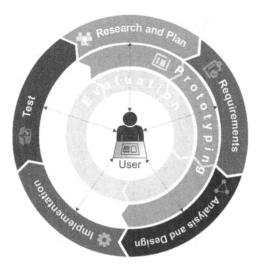

Fig. 2. Roadmap lifecycle

Research and Plan Phase. This stage is aimed at foreseeing the user-centered activities that will be carried out throughout the creation of the patterns and capturing information about the domain of the problem, the user and his tasks, and the product or similar interactive systems. Based on this information, an initial panorama of the context of the type of interactive systems to be designed will be created that will provide information for decision making regarding how the activities of the following stages will be approached. The resulting artifacts of this stage are: usability plan, theoretical frame, data patterns, competitive analysis, user profile, heuristics, and design patterns as presented.

- *Create the usability plan*: it consists of constructing a document that specifies the user-centered activities that will be carried out throughout the construction of the patterns. The plan is a living document that is refined as progress is made in the stages.
- *Know the domain problem*: this activity explores and collects the concepts that characterize the selected domain, in order to identify data patterns that describe the business.
- *Review with experts*: the data patterns found are reviewed with experts, in order to validate domain data in relation to whether they are understandable and complete, both at the concept level and at relationships.
- *Know the product*: tasks that will allow a better understanding of the type of interactive systems to be designed are carried out. For this, there are different techniques that will allow to capture this information such as competitive analysis, literary reviews, user tests, among others. The purpose of conducting activities to get to know the product is to be able to identify main functionalities, design guidelines (e.g. heuristics) and patterns (data, presentation or interaction) already defined for the context of the interactive systems that are being addressed.

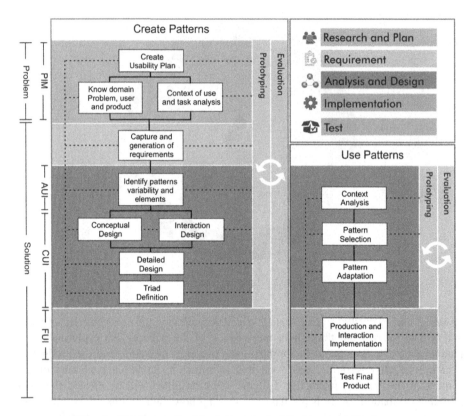

Fig. 3. Detailed methodological content of the proposed Roadmap

- *Know the user*: Finally, once the product is studied, it is necessary to know the potential users of that product. Then, techniques such as interviews, surveys, observation, among others, are applied. The purpose of the application of these techniques is to generate information related to the user's profile, a document that describes and classifies the different potential users in terms of their main characteristics such as skills, limitations, demographic information, appreciations or motivations, etc.
- *Context of use and task analysis*: this activity captures information about the task, how they currently interact with similar systems, what problems they have, what their expectations are, identified needs, etc.

Requirement Phase: As a result of the analysis of the information captured in the previous stage, additional activities are defined or not for the capture of requirements. Subsequently, the information is analyzed and a requirements document containing the user and usability requirements is generated.

Analysis and Design Phase: In this stage, criteria that make the pattern presentation vary are identified. For each variability of the pattern, its Abstract Interface (AUI) is constructed. Afterward, conceptual ideas are generated, and the first prototypes of the pattern presentation are created, which are evaluated to capture the interaction pattern (how the user wishes to interact with the data). Finally, the detailed design is done, and the three patterns are created in the tool: data pattern, presentation pattern (Concrete Interface - CUI) and interaction pattern. The artifacts that are generated in this stage are: validated data, presentation, and interaction patterns, variability tree, sketches, prototypes. The activities of this stage are detailed as follows:

- *Identify patterns variability*: the criteria that can make the pattern vary according to the information related to the use context, task analysis, user profiles, and user requirements are identified. The criteria can be varied and depend on the context that is being addressed.
- *Identify patterns elements*: it corresponds to specify the Abstract User Interface - AUI which is equivalent to identifying the elements that are part of the presentation pattern, according to the selected criteria.
- *Conceptual Design*: in this activity, conceptual ideas are generated for each variability of data pattern. The result can be texts, videos, scenarios, or moodboard. The tasks of this activity are: generate design ideas, create design ideas (images, moodboard, scenarios, sketches, and text documents) and apply metaphors.
- *Interaction Design*: here the first sketches of the data patterns are created, and design patterns are applied if they exist for the context that is being addressed. The evaluation that takes place in this activity is aimed at capturing the interaction pattern and validating the presentation data by the final user. The tasks of this activity are: content and layout design, apply existing design patterns, prototyping, and evaluation.
- *Detailed design presentation*: the detailed design is done here; that is, gestalt laws, heuristics, and other design guides oriented to promote usability in the interface are applied. The evaluation of the prototypes is oriented to evaluate the usability and validate the presentation of the pattern. The tasks of this activity are: apply heuristics or design guidelines, prototyping (digital prototyping), evaluation (usability evaluation, validate patterns presentation).
- *Triad definition for each pattern*: based on the information captured in the previous activities, the triad for each variability of the pattern is created using the model editor. The tasks for this activity are: create data pattern, create interaction pattern, and create presentation pattern.

Flow of Activities Using the Pattern Catalog. The flow for the development of user interfaces using the patterns starts at the analysis and design stage and ends at the testing stage. Below are the activities of this flow according to the Roadmap stages.

Analysis and Design. In this stage, the patterns are selected and adapted according to the business concepts and the context data of the problem. The activities of this stage are:

- *Context Analysis.* The domain of the application is studied to identify the context of the problem; that is to say, to identify the user, the tasks to be performed, and the business concepts and data that are manipulated to execute them. The result of this activity is a general description of the business concepts (Entities) and the context data of the problem.

- *Pattern Selection.* In this activity, the data patterns are selected according to the identified business concepts. The selection of a pattern can be done in different ways: (1) select a pattern from the catalog, (2) create a pattern from the catalog patterns, or (3) create a completely new pattern for the same domain. For the creation of new patterns in the same domain, it is necessary to prototype and evaluate in order to validate the associated presentation of the pattern. Once the data pattern is selected, the variability that fits the problem context is identified for each pattern. Finally, the presentation and interaction pattern associated according with the data that the user requires to perform the task is selected.
- *Pattern Adaptation.* According to their nature, the patterns can be adapted to specific situations of a specific problem; although in the data patterns catalog, possible variations are defined to support different contexts, cases may arise where specific data that were not contemplated are required. Consequently, this activity must validate that the pattern fully supports the user's tasks and data; and if necessary, add or remove data that are not represented, modifying the domain model (initially data pattern) and its respective presentation (CUI) that is obtained from the previous activity.

Implementation Phase. In this stage, the implementation of the productions and the interaction of the CUI is carried out to proceed with its generation. Interaction refers to performing aspects of programming logic that allow exposing functionalities in the prototypes to be generated, which allow defining basic aspects of interaction; for example, autocomplete a text field. Otherwise, the productions refer to generating a set of real data test, instances of the classes of the domain model that supports the interface; which means, generating real data of the business concepts involved. This is done in order to validate the interface with the client early. At the end of this task, the Final Interface (FUI) associated with the selected variability is generated automatically.

Test Phase. In this stage, tests are executed in order to verify the access and interaction to the elements of the screens and the data that are required to carry out each task in the specific context. In other words, the usability of the final interface in the interactive system is evaluated. The resulting information from this evaluation is used as feedback of the triad of patterns.

5   Case Study

As a case study, we propose the development of a web application that assists teachers and students in the teaching-learning process in such a way that it is easy to use by the average teacher and can be paired to a Learning Management System (LMS), specifically to the Moodle platform. The purpose of this application is to provide a didactic strategy model, better known in the jargon of instructional design as "sequence of activities," which allows the teacher to plan their teaching-learning activities in a way that they focus on their work and not in the use of technology. The model allows creating sequences of different didactic activities according to student profiles, previous knowledge, etc. as well as other advantages [23]. The main idea of applying the

Roadmap in this case study is to be able to design the interfaces that will support the didactic activities of the model. As a result, a set of patterns is generated in the educational context that can be used later for the design of interfaces of different interactive systems within the same domain.

Taking into account the interactive system to be developed, we will begin the Roadmap exploration from the activity flow for creating patterns. Later, the created patterns will be used for the development of the interfaces of the proposed interactive system.

5.1 Activity Flow for the Creation of Patterns in the Educational Context

In the next sections, a summary of the information obtained for every single activity of the flow is presented; the emphasis is on the artifacts directly related to triad of patterns.

Create Usability Plan. The flow for the creation of patterns begins with the creation of the usability plan, in which the following activities were considered: (1) literary reviews to identify the relevant concepts (data patterns) around the didactic act, (2) competitive analysis to get to know similar products, (3) application of surveys to get to know the users profile, (4) application of field journals and contextual observation to get to know about the tasks and the use context, (5) implementation of a workshop to define the AUI, and (6) users tests to validate the presentation and interaction of the pattern. Activities 5 and 6 were defined according to the results of the previous activities.

Know Domain Problem. Once the plan was defined, the execution of a literary review began in order to identify the main concepts and their relationships around the didactic act. The main concepts around the subject that originate from the analysis of different conceptual models of the didactic act such as the ones proposed by Marquès [24], Meneses [25], Rodríguez [26], among others are presented below.

According to Marquès [24], teaching is achieved by the means of didactic acts through which the teacher (Role) or trainer proposes multiple activities to students (Role) to aid in the desired learning. These activities, known as learning activities (LearningActivity), are adapted to the characteristics of the students, the available resources, and the contents under study. However, the teaching process is not only composed of learning activities, but also support activities (SupportActivity) [27], which are usually carried out by the teacher to support the students. Marquès suggests that the effectiveness of the teaching resources will depend to a large extent on the way the teacher guides its use within the didactic strategy (DidacticStrategy) framework that he is using. A strategy is an organized procedure oriented towards the attainment of a clearly established goal. In this way, the didactic strategy is the procedure by which the teacher intends to assist learning in students through activities that contemplate the interaction of students with certain content.

As suggested by Conole [28], the learning activities occur in a specific context, in terms of the environment (Environment) where it is developed, the pedagogical approaches adopted, and the institutional procedures and difficulties. For the development of these tasks, students have a series of resources (LearningObject and services). Conole proposes a taxonomy that defines the components that structure a learning activity [28]. One of the most useful aspects of taxonomy is the detailed description of the nature of the task that students will perform as part of the learning activity to achieve the desired objectives. Thus, the types of learning activities according to the nature of the task can be: assimilative, management of information, adaptive, communicative, productive, experiential, and evaluative. All the aforementioned occurs within a learning unit framework (LearningUnit) as a course, a module, a lesson, etc.

From the analysis of the different conceptual models, a business data pattern was generated. The data that compose the pattern were reviewed by experts in pedagogy and instructional design, in order to validate the concepts of the domain. In summary, Fig. 4 presents the data pattern resulting from the analysis of the didactic act applied to an LMS.

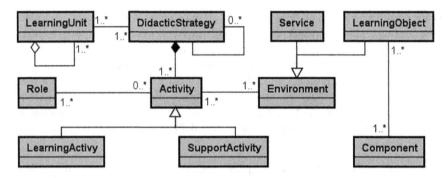

Fig. 4. Didactic act data pattern in an LMS

Know the Users, the Product, and the Tasks. To learn more about potential users, surveys were applied to 50 university students (34 men, 16 women) from different areas of knowledge. Their ages vary between 18 and 54, where 42% have a visual problem. 84% of those surveyed consider themselves to be fast learners and 94% like to work with computers and consider that this tool makes their work easier. 78% have a high experience in the management of computers, but only 12% feel satisfied with the LMS they handle. The most common problems reported with LMS are that their navigation is confusing, unintuitive, and the interface is unfriendly. Finally, 94% consider that the LMS has a high influence on the success of a course.

In order to know more about the LMS, 23 platforms were explored. The exploration was oriented to analyze the main functionalities and the technological components related to the didactic activities. The most common components found were the video player and the document visualizers as the most efficient way to transmit content to the students, the forums and the chat as the way the students discuss the topics learned and contribute to the courses, and Interactive quizzes and online tests as the most common components used to keep track on whether students met the learning objectives or not.

In relation to the tasks and use context, the contextual observation and field journal were used as mechanisms to analyze the didactic activities in the context of a face-to-face class in different university programs. In the contextual observation, the type of didactic activity was analyzed: who performs it, where, when, what resources are used, and the step by step process. In relation to the field journal, it was elaborated by five university students who recorded all their didactic activities inside and outside the university for two weeks. From this information, points of automation were identified in the process in a way that the didactic activity could be taken to a computational environment.

Capture and Generation of Requirement. Once the previous information was obtained, the user and usability requirements that the interfaces that would support the didactic activities must had were defined. The information resulting from this activity will not be described for it is common to most software engineering proposals.

Identify Patterns Variability and Patterns Elements. From the data pattern of the didactic act for an LMS (see Fig. 4), the criteria that make the associated presentation pattern vary in relation to the didactic activities were identified. They are: the type of didactic activity according to the nature of the task [28], synchronous or asynchronous, collaborative or individual, and interactive or passive activities. In accordance with these criteria, the elements that the presentation should have (AUI) associated to a determined variability were defined.

To exemplify the process, we will take the type of assimilative learning activity, according to the types of didactic activity identified in the "Know domain problem" section. An assimilative activity looks for in students to promote their understanding about certain concepts that the teacher presents orally, visually, or written [28]. In this fashion, if we move the environment of a classroom to a computer environment, we can have the video player to present the speech of the teacher, a document viewer to display presentations, or documents that support the speech; and the forum and chat as means of communication between teachers and students or between students. Now, the elements that are part of the interface will depend on the variability in the criteria. For example, if the teacher wishes to carry out an assimilative, asynchronous, individual, and passive activity (without intervention by the student), then he can use the video player and the document viewer. On the contrary, if he makes a variation from passive to interactive (with student intervention) he should use the forum or other asynchronous communication mechanism to receive the student's comments. Table 1 shows some examples of the different elements that the interface must have for an assimilative activity according to the variation in the identified criteria.

Once identified all the variability for each didactic act, the pattern variability tree is obtained as a result.

Conceptual, Interaction, and Detailed Design. From the variability tree, one has to start with the conceptual and interaction design of the presentation pattern for each identified variability. To achieve this, a workshop was held with teachers from different areas of knowledge (including educators) and students. Its purpose was to capture design ideas and obtain the first sketches from the perspective of users and experts. The workshop consisted of forming a scenario based on the variation of the didactic activity. Later, for each scenario, they generated ideas or made a sketch of how the student could interact with the proposed elements. With the results of the workshop, the user and usability requirements were fed back. Likewise, the first prototypes of the

Table 1. Interface elements for an assimilative activity according to the criteria variability

Criteria					
Asynchronous (A) or Synchronous (S)	A	A	A	S	S
Individual (I) or Collaborative (C)	I	I	C	I	C
Interactive (I) o Passive (P)	P	I	I	P	I
Interface elements					
Video player (pre-recorded)	X	X	X		
Video player (live)				X	X
Document viewer	X	X	X	X	X
Chat			X		X
Forum		X	X		

presentation patterns were created, which were evaluated by users in order to identify the way they would interact with each element of the interface in a use context.

Triad Definition. As a result of the previous activities, the triad of patterns is obtained; that is, for each variability of the data pattern, a presentation pattern (CUI) and an interaction pattern are obtained. Each pattern is modeled in the tool and all together contain the pattern catalog for the educational context. In summary, Fig. 6 presents the three patterns for a variability of the assimilative didactic activity. As it is

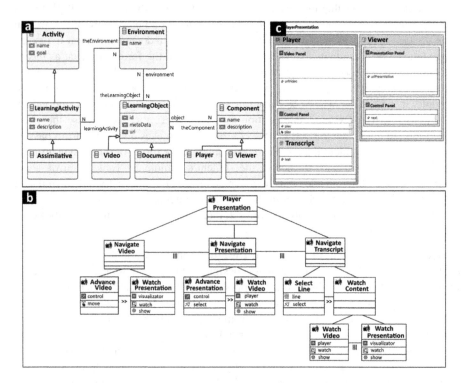

Fig. 5. Triad of patterns for a variability of an assimilative activity

observed, the data pattern (Fig. 5a) only has the data related to the presentation (Fig. 5c), and the interaction pattern (Fig. 5b) only has the actions that the user can perform with the elements of the interface.

The flow for the generation of interfaces from the created patterns is explained next.

5.2   Activity Flow for the Development of Interfaces from Patterns in the Educational Context

The flow for the development of interfaces begins with the analysis of the context, where the information related to the patterns and their different variabilities is analyzed with the purpose of knowing the contexts in which this pattern can be used. Once the patterns that can be used are identified, we select the pattern associated with a didactic activity from the variability tree of the pattern catalog (Fig. 6a). As it is shown, when displaying the selected pattern (Patterns assimilative), their different variabilities appear, which have a data pattern (Data Model), a presentation pattern (Template), and an interaction pattern (Dialog Model) associated. After selecting a certain variability, we proceed to configure the different properties associated with the elements of the interface (Fig. 6b) according to the specific context of use. For example, you can activate or deactivate functionalities (transcription, subtitles, quality, etc.), specify colors, fonts, among others for a video player. Once the interface elements (CUI) have been configured, a production with real test data is created and the programming logic that exposes functionalities in the final interface is implemented. Finally, the FUI is automatically generated. Currently, the tool generates interfaces in HTML5 and JavaScript.

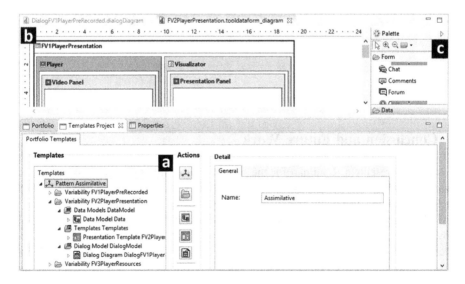

Fig. 6. Development environment of the user interface from patterns

An alternate flow to this procedure is modifying the presentation pattern, adding new widgets or components of the palette (Fig. 6c). To do this, you must bear in mind that changes in the presentation may affect the other models and the usability of the final interface. The interfaces generated in the development environment are proven functional prototypes that can be used in any interactive system in the educational context.

Once the required interfaces were generated, they were integrated into the application as a means to the execution of the didactic activities of the model. In Fig. 7, you can see the model editor integrated in the Moodle platform (Fig. 7a) and the visualization for the student (Fig. 7b). Teachers use the didactic strategy model editor to plan the flow of activities that the student must complete. For each activity, the type of activity, the general data (delivery date, description, etc.), the interface desired for the student to observe, and the resources of the activity (videos, documents, etc.) are specify by teachers in the area of properties. In this way, the teacher focuses on his planning work, and does not have to deal with design or configuration problems of technological components. Likewise, students have an easy-to-use interface that supports them in the tasks they must perform.

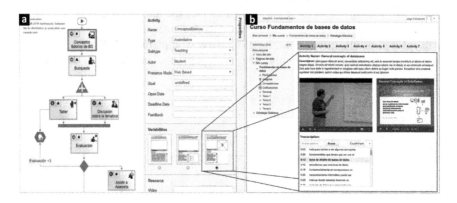

Fig. 7. Didactic strategy model editor and student visualization in the Moodle platform

6   Conclusion and Future Work

This article presents a Roadmap for the design of user interfaces based on a triad of patterns that includes the principles and guidelines of MBUID, HCI, and DCU. The application of the Roadmap in the case study allowed to validate the method as a possible solution towards the automation of the usability in the MBUID tools. Similarly, it shows how it is possible to generate interfaces that although start from the information of three patterns (data, interaction, and presentation), they take into account information from other contexts, namely: from the user and his tasks, the use context, and the experts, as do other MBUID proposals using more models. Finally, this initiative aims for the software industry to apply this approach in such a way that the catalog of created patterns is gradually broadened. In this way, through the use of the catalog, developers and designers can speed up the development process of the user interface and promote usability in the final interface.

As future work, the validation of the Roadmap in other application contexts is proposed, as well as the promotion of this approach in the software industry through the incorporation of the triad of patterns as the main artifact. Additionally, at the tool level that supports the Roadmap, there is an extensive work that can be done such as: creating new code generators, expanding the palette of components and/or widgets, generating databases from data patterns, among others. Likewise, it would be useful to work in a web-based browser that allows the navigation and learning of the Roadmap and the reusing of the methods content for the definition of other process structures that rely on the triad of patterns.

References

1. Meixner, G., Paterno, F., Vanderdonckt, J.: Past present and future of model-based user interface development. iCom **10**, 2–11 (2011)
2. Wiecha, C., Bennett, W., Boies, S., Gould, J., Greene, S.: ITS: a tool for rapidly developing interactive applications. ACM Trans. Inf. Syst. **8**, 204–236 (1990)
3. Märtin, C.: Model-based software engineering for interactive systems. In: Albrecht, R. (ed.) Systems: Theory and Practice, pp. 187–211. Springer, Vienna (1998). https://doi.org/10.1007/978-3-7091-6451-8_9
4. Puerta, A.R.: The MECANO Project: Comprehensive and Integrated Support for Model-Based Interface Development (1996)
5. Puerta, A.R.: A model-based interface development environment. IEEE Softw. **14**, 40–47 (1997)
6. Berti, S., Mori, G., Paternò, F., Santoro, C.: A transformation-based environment for designing multi-device interactive applications. Presented at the Proceedings of the 9th International Conference on Intelligent User Interfaces, Funchal, Madeira, Portugal (2004)
7. Gajos, K.Z., Weld, D.S., Wobbrock, J.O.: Automatically generating personalized user interfaces with SUPPLE. Artif. Intell. **174**, 910–950 (2010)
8. Paterno', F., Santoro, C., Spano, L.D.: MARIA: a universal, declarative, multiple abstraction-level language for service-oriented applications in ubiquitous environments. ACM Trans. Comput.-Hum. Interact. **16**, 1–30 (2009)
9. Giraldo, W.J.: Marco de Desarrollo de Sistemas Groupware Interactivos Basado en la Integración de Procesos y Notaciones – CIAF. Ph.D. Doctoral, Universidad de Castilla - La Mancha (2010)
10. Akiki, P.A., Bandara, A.K., Yu, Y.: Cedar studio: an IDE supporting adaptive model-driven user interfaces for enterprise applications. Presented at the Proceedings of the 5th ACM SIGCHI Symposium on Engineering Interactive Computing Systems, London, United Kingdom (2013)
11. Peissner, M., Häbe, D., Janssen, D., Sellner, T.: MyUI: generating accessible user interfaces from multimodal design patterns. Presented at the Proceedings of the 4th ACM SIGCHI Symposium on Engineering Interactive Computing Systems, Copenhagen, Denmark (2012)
12. Engel, J., Märtin, C.: PaMGIS: a framework for pattern-based modeling and generation of interactive systems. In: Jacko, J.A. (ed.) HCI 2009. LNCS, vol. 5610, pp. 826–835. Springer, Heidelberg (2009). https://doi.org/10.1007/978-3-642-02574-7_92

13. Marin, I., Ortin, F., Pedrosa, G., Rodriguez, J.: Generating native user interfaces for multiple devices by means of model transformation. Front. Inf. Technol. Electron. Eng. **16**, 995–1017 (2015)
14. Machado, M., Couto, R., Campos, J.C.: MODUS: model-based user interfaces prototyping. Presented at the Proceedings of the ACM SIGCHI Symposium on Engineering Interactive Computing Systems, Lisbon, Portugal (2017)
15. Calvary, G., Coutaz, J., Thevenin, D., Limbourg, Q., Bouillon, L., Vanderdonckt, J.: A unifying reference framework for multitarget user interfaces, interacting with computers. Interact. Comput. **15**, 289–308 (2003)
16. Courage, C., Baxter, K.: Understanding Your Users: A Practical Guide to User Requirements Methods, Tools, and Techniques. Morgan Kaufmann Publishers, Burlington (2005)
17. Shneiderman, B., Plaisant, C.: Designing the User Interface: Strategies for Effective Human-Computer Interaction. Pearson Addison Wesley, Boston (2004)
18. Schmidt, D.C., Stal, M., Rohnert, H., Buschmann, F.: Pattern-Oriented Software Architecture, Patterns for Concurrent and Networked Objects, vol. 2. Wiley, Hoboken (2013)
19. Triviño, J.I.: Generación de la interfaz de usuario de negocio a partir de patrones de negocios basada en los fundamentos metodológicos de TD_MBUID. Magister, Informatica Universidad EAFIT (2015)
20. Giraldo, O.W.J., Arias, M.R., Collazos, O.C.A., Molina, A.I., Ortega, C.M., Redondo, M.A.: Fast functional prototyping of user interfaces based on DataForm models, a tool (ToolDataForm). In: 2015 10th Computing Colombian Conference (10CCC), pp. 172–179 (2015)
21. Paternó, F., Mancini, C., Meniconi, S.: ConcurTaskTrees: a diagrammatic notation for specifying task models. Presented at the Proceedings of the IFIP TC13 International Conference on Human-Computer Interaction (1997)
22. Limbourg, Q.: Multi-path development of user interfaces. Ph.D. Université catholique de Louvain, Louvain-la-Neuve, Belgium (2004)
23. Ruiz, A., Giraldo, W.J., Arciniegas, J.: Method for the integration of the didactic strategy model in virtual learning platforms in the university context: a mechanism that takes into account the professor's work. Presented at the 12 Congreso Colombiano de Computación - 12CCC, Cali, Colombia (2017)
24. Marqués, P.: La Enseñanza Buenas Prácticas. La Motivación (2011). http://peremarques.net/
25. Meneses, G.: NTIC, Interacción y Aprendizaje en la Universidad. Doctorado, Departament de Pedagogia, Universitat Rovira I Virgili (2007)
26. Rodríguez, J.L.: Curriculum, acto didáctico y teoría del texto. Anaya, ed España (1985)
27. Koper, R., Olivier, B., Anderson, T.: IMS learning design information model. IMS Global Learning Consortium (2003)
28. Conole, G.: Describing learning activities: tools and resources to guide practice. In: Beetham, H., Sharpe, R. (eds.) Rethinking Pedagogy for a Digital Age: Designing and Delivering E-learning. Routledge, Abingdon (2007)

The Semiotics of Space and Time in Interaction Design

Patricia Search$^{(\boxtimes)}$

Rensselaer Polytechnic Institute, Troy, NY 12180, USA
`searcp@rpi.edu`

Abstract. Since the 1960s artists have been experimenting with the multiple dimensions of electronic art. Their art can inform other disciplines, including interaction design. Digital art has led to new semantic structures that can be applied to human-computer interface design. This paper presents an analysis of the semiotics of the digital image and interaction design, and the new semantic structures that are defined by digital art research and praxis, kinesthetic design, cognitive mapping, and cross-modal perception. The paper also proposes the development of new software tools for designing and visualizing the information architecture, navigation, and cognitive and sensory relationships in a virtual information space. These tools can facilitate the exploration of the unique semantic dimensions that define these interactive environments.

Keywords: HyperGlyphs · Kinesthetic design · Metasyntax · Hyperplanes

1 Introduction

This paper takes a different approach to exploring new ideas for interface design by analyzing interactive semiotics and aesthetics from the perspective of contemporary artists who continually explore ways to use their art to push the boundaries of audiovisual communication. For the past two decades, the international Art of Research conferences have fostered a dialog between artists and design practices [1]. The conferences recognize that artists produce work that challenges the way we see the world around us. Artists use their work to raise questions and prompt reactions and critical thinking about design.

As these conferences point out, art can be a catalyst that expands the horizons of many different types of design practice [1]. In this paper, various types of artwork are highlighted to illustrate semantic and cognitive models for interactive, multimedia design. Interaction design creates opportunities to explore a new syntax for communication and user experience design. In this paper, I show how space and time, kinesthetic design, rhythm, and cross-modal perception define new semantic structures for creating cognitive maps. I also explore some designs concepts for interface designs that challenge traditional approaches to interaction design that use sequential, hierarchical information architectures for content organization and navigation. The examples in the paper that illustrate these concepts include screen captures from interactive art installations where I use art as a catalyst to generate discussion and explore new approaches to interface design.

© Springer International Publishing AG, part of Springer Nature 2018
A. Marcus and W. Wang (Eds.): DUXU 2018, LNCS 10918, pp. 241–255, 2018.
https://doi.org/10.1007/978-3-319-91797-9_17

Unfortunately, it is difficult to demonstrate some of the concepts in this paper. The paper lacks interactivity and sensory stimuli beyond visual information, and it is formatted in a hierarchical, two-dimensional layout that is designed to present information sequentially. As you read this paper, it is important to keep these limitations of print design in mind and envision dynamic, multisensory information spaces that can be accessed in different ways using various types of media and interaction.

2   The Poetics of Space and Time

During the Renaissance, artists used mathematical relationships in space and time to experiment with linear perspective and define three-dimensional space in a two-dimensional plane. Since then, artists have continued to explore ways to define space and time in art and design. Artists like Josef Albers and Frank Stella explored abstract representations of space by using subtle changes in color, line, and form. Jackson Pollock and Willem de Kooning and other abstract expressionists used the physical energy from gestures and body movements to define spontaneous shapes, color combinations, and rhythms in their paintings. Conceptual art and performance art of the 1960s highlighted interaction aesthetics by demonstrating that art can evolve and change over time through audience participation.

Any of these types of art can provide inspiration for interface designs by demonstrating how the innovative use of color, line, form, and human interaction shape the visual message. The field of visual poetry is another area of art that can inspire visual concepts for electronic interfaces. Visual poetry integrates text and forms into a new visual language. Huth [2] points out that these "verbo-visual creations that focus on the textual materiality of language" integrate shape and function [para. 3].

Numerous examples of visual poetry are available online that illustrate how text, form, and space can combine to create this new verbo-visual language. Huth's visual poem titled *jHegaf* [3] and Derek Beaulieu's piece *untitled (for Natalee and Jeremy)* [4] weave letters and areas of white space into rhythmic, integrated wholes. K. S. Ernst and Sheila Murphy create different levels of spatial depth using layers and color gradations in *Vortextique* [5]. In *haiku #62* by Helmes [6], negative space carves into the text and reveals shapes that redefine the meaning of the words.

The individual elements in visual poetry, including the forms, text, and negative space, can be links in an interactive information space. As in the works mentioned above, Fig. 1 illustrates the use of text, space, and form to create a visual language with multiple levels of space and time. The design on the left is the logo for my HyperGlyphs research which is a series of experimental art installations with interface designs that deemphasize hierarchical navigation and content organization [7–10]. Visuals such as the HyperGlyphs logo, or the visual poetry examples mentioned above, could become interface designs in which each element in the design, including the areas of space, are links to the virtual information. In the second version of the HyperGlyphs logo on the right, words have been added to the visual to show how multiple links could be included in the design. While this type of visual integration of positive and negative space has been used in art and design in the past, it has not been adopted as a format for interface designs.

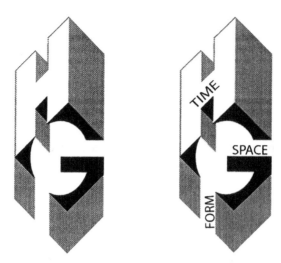

Fig. 1. The designs illustrate how text, form, and space can be integrated into a visual language that becomes the interface for an interactive program. Copyright 2001 Patricia Search. All rights reserved.

3 Digital Art

Computer graphics technology enables artists to define a new type of audiovisual aesthetic and semantic space. Artists create spatial relationships that are mapped to Cartesian grids and highlight the logic of the underlying mathematics and computer programming. Digital tools enable artists to make subtle changes in color, texture, and position that transform two-dimensional lines, forms, and planes into volumetric extensions of space. Artists use algorithms and digital technology to redefine the two-dimensional space using unique shapes and visual effects.

Transparent layers, color gradations, animations, fades, three-dimensional modeling, and viewer participation through interactive technology are just a few additional ways to use this technology to redefine space and bring the element of time into the visual semiotics of the art. Hall's work [11] is an example of the complex new visual language that can be created with digital techniques that integrate layers of text, line, color, and form. Her art creates depth and visual layers of associations that highlight individual elements within the context of a synergistic whole. Examples of her work can be seen on her website at www.debhall.com.

With the addition of interaction design, the ability to reveal information in different configurations brings the element of time into the spatial experience. In Jim Rosenberg's *Intergrams* [12], words layered on top of each other form complex, interactive graphics where the individual words become recognizable as the user removes each layer to reveal the underlying text. His art, which creates texture, depth, and spatiotemporal interaction with text, is an excellent example of Huth's concept of "textual materiality" in verbo-visual forms of expression [2, para.3].

All of these techniques can be incorporated into interface designs to reflect the semantic connections in the program. For example, the ability to use audiovisual layers to represent the semantic structures in the interactive program creates opportunities to define intuitive information spaces that (1) highlight individual elements within the context of the whole; (2) show the perceptual and cognitive networks of associations in the information space; and (3) highlight simultaneous as well as sequential relationships. Although artists have explored these techniques in art and design, few interaction designers have taken advantage of the semiotics of digital art to enhance the interactive experience by visualizing the complex relationships and organization of information in interactive programs.

There will be more discussion of design and semiotics later in this paper. First, it is important to see how perception and cognitive models define the user experience in interaction design.

4 Cognitive Models

Research in cognition can provide insights for designing user interfaces. Most interface designs focus on the hierarchical organization of information. However, research indicates that the cognitive models we create are not limited to this form of organization. Collins and Loftus [13] deemphasized the significance of nodes and links in hierarchical networks and emphasized the role simultaneity plays in constructing semantic models. Research has shown that we use our experiences to build cognitive collages [14]. In a non-linear, multisensory information space, layers of events and time, along with affective domains based on sensory experiences and kinesthetic memory derived from physical actions, enable us to build these cognitive collages.

Research has also shown that the creation of semantic models is a dynamic process that changes over time. Hopfield [15] explored dynamic connectionist models where semantic representations change through interaction with other cognitive processes. These models evolve as an emergent process through learning [16, 17] and contribute to the building of complex schemas and syntactic processing [18]. Schemas and the narratives within them play an important role in knowledge construction, memory, and perception [19, 20] which in turn, contribute to the building of cognitive models. These models identify locations and include information about the way the different areas are connected such as the topology of the space [21].

In the user interface, it is possible to design visual, spatial maps that represent the topology of the space and show layers of simultaneous relationships, as well as hierarchical connections. These maps, which can incorporate references to narratives and schemas to aid memory and knowledge retention, can help the user identify landmarks and build cognitive models for navigation through the dynamic information space. Some visual examples are discussed in Sect. 6 on the Semiotics of Interface Design.

5 Cross-Modal Perception

Perception also plays an important role in building these cognitive associations. Research has shown that we use perception to make cognitive connections, and we integrate current perceptual experiences with past experiences [22, 23].

With multisensory interaction design, it is especially important to consider the role cross-modal perception plays in cognition. Cross-modal perception adds multiple layers of sensory information (stimuli) to the interactive experience that augments the cognitive networks of associations. Cross-modal stimuli can enhance the perception of visual and audio information and impact the perception of spatial and temporal relationships [24]. Freides [25] concluded that perception that involves more than one sensory modality is more accurate than information that is represented with one sense. Brunel et al. [23] cite established research that supports these findings. Specifically, they point to research that shows that with multisensory events it is generally easier to identify [26], detect [27], categorize [28], and recognize [29] information [23, para. 3].

Moreover, we intuitively make connections between specific characteristics in different sensory modalities. For example, a curved shape may evoke a soft tactile experience. We also have "hard" and "soft" sounds in letters and words. Even when an association isn't congruent or intuitive, it is possible to assign connections between sensory modalities that the user will learn and later associate with these modalities [30–32]. Connolly [33] suggests that relationships can be formed by integrating perceptual experiences through an associative learning process called "unitization" which "enables us to 'chunk' the world into multimodal units" [para. 1].

Interaction designers can use these perceptual models and define relationships between information presented in different sensory modalities. Using familiar sensory and cognitive associations in the interface design (e.g., combining curved objects with soft sounds) makes the interface more intuitive. However, it is also possible to assign relationships that the user learns through the associative learning process [33]. This flexibility allows designers to define specific relationships. For example, they can designate unique forms as links to different types of information, images, or sounds.

Connolly [33] notes that it is best for these perceptual systems to be flexible to perform cognitive tasks. He identifies an interactive parallel processing model, such as the one proposed by Townsend and Wenger [34], as a model for associative learning [33]. The concept of parallel processing of sensory information and the ability to make dynamic, flexible connections between information is an interesting concept to incorporate into interface designs. The model presents a flexible way of thinking about cross-modal perception that supports exploration in information design. If the connections between the sensory information are not fixed or permanently integrated through associative learning, the designer has the ability to assign connections that are relevant for a specific application. Alternatively, if a more flexible interactive space is required for the user to explore different relationships, this model provides that flexibility as well. The user can make cognitive assignments that are relevant to specific objectives, and through this process, create cognitive collages that include layers of meaning that are created by perceptually integrating units of information through the associative learning process. Visual, spatial representations of these parallel layers of information in the interface design can highlight simultaneous connections in this cognitive model.

6   Semiotics of Interface Design

Designers can use various techniques in digital technology to visualize the types of cognitive models just discussed. Transparent forms create spatial cues that define simultaneous relationships and show individual elements as well as the integrated whole. Layers of text can be combined or revealed in different configurations and create a new graphic language that integrates the visual semiotics and linguistic syntax.

Figure 2 is a screen capture from the HyperGlyphs research. In this interface design, the words are links, and the user can move the shapes to reveal different layers of text over time. In this example, which illustrates some of the content in this paper, the words *images, sound, kinesthesia*, and *sense*s are visible through transparent layers, and as the user interacts with the design and moves the forms, those words move to the top and are accessible as links.

Figure 3 is another example of an interactive, visual representation of content relationships in an information space. As the user interacts with this interface design, the individual lines of text initially appear as illustrated in the first screen capture, and then move closer together to form a new visual language that symbolizes the integration of the content or ideas (as shown in the second screen capture). Each text link

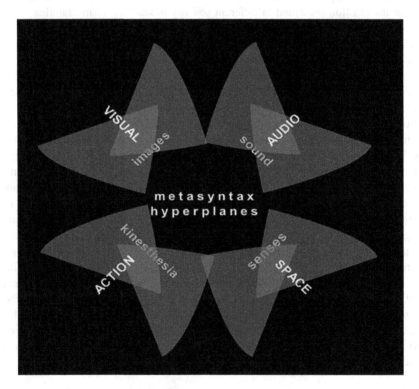

Fig. 2. Design elements in an interface design, such as transparent layers, can show simultaneous networks of associations and multiple dimensions of sensory and cognitive relationships in an interactive program. Copyright 2018 Patricia Search. All rights reserved.

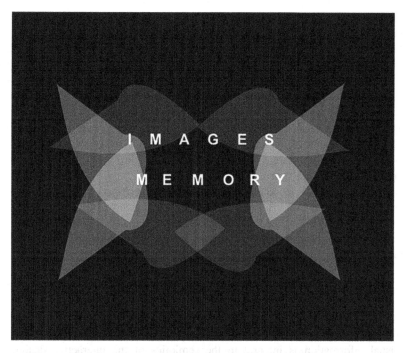

Fig. 3. As the user moves the graphics in this interactive design, the text moves closer together to create a visual language that symbolizes the integration of ideas. Copyright 2018 Patricia Search. All rights reserved.

remains selectable, but the design symbolizes the synthesis of ideas and content into a new visual language and network of cognitive associations or cognitive collage.

This multi-planar environment expands with the addition of sound. Sound defines space in diverse ways depending on the timbre, duration, and rhythm of the sound. Long sounds penetrate space and create depth that intersect with the visual planes and spatial relationships. Short, rhythmic sounds define temporal intervals and add layers of audiovisual syncopation to the information space. Sound also creates an immersive experience in the physical space. Sound can appear to come from different locations in the space and surround the viewer. Sound, like the physical interaction, creates a perceptual and cognitive bridge between the physical space that defines the viewer's real world and the virtual space.

These interactive environments weave layers of multisensory information and diverse media syntaxes into discursive spaces that challenge traditional perspectives of space and time. Layers of sensory information continually change and form new connections and patterns that define a discursive semiotic space. Deterministic logic and fixed networks of associations give way to flexible semantic structures and a symbolic space where causation is all-inclusive, rather than exclusive [35].

As researchers point out, perception is a dynamic process that creates new meanings. In this discursive semantic space, signs take on multiple meanings as new syntactical relationships evolve. Semiotics now means "the logic of signs is the logic of possibilities" [36, p. 76]. In addition, the "space" that defines the links between the audiovisual information is integral to the semiotics of the interactive design. The physical and temporal spaces that define the actions and links are not empty spaces. Space takes on meaning as well, because it is the place where connections evolve into an endless array of associations and relationships.

6.1 Temporal Dynamics

Digital technology makes it possible to add the dimension of time to the semantic relationships. The two-dimensional screen is a dynamic space that continually changes as the user navigates through the information space. The interaction design consists of sequential and simultaneous representations of time. Although navigation itself is a sequential process, the user forms perceptual and cognitive networks of associations that define simultaneous semantic relationships.

Time is also expressed through rhythm—the rhythm of words, images, sound, movement. Rhythm is an important temporal dimension in design that can reflect different types of relationships, while also unifying the diverse layers of information into a coherent whole. For example, the juxtaposition of fluid, organic shapes with mathematical grids creates a unique blend of different types of rhythm. The organic shapes create a dynamic, fluid counterpoint to the quiet rhythm of the grid-like formations. The user's physical interaction with the program also creates a rhythm that defines the aesthetics and semantic meaning of the actions. Djajadiningrat et al. [37] use terms like "interaction choreography" [p. 673] and "semantics of motion" [p. 669] to refer to our physical interaction with products. The rhythm and semantics of motion are integral to kinesthetic design which can help the user define landmarks, create memory, and build cognitive maps. Kinesthetic design and its role in interface design is discussed in more detail in the next section.

Designers can assign meaning to specific types of rhythm to communicate different temporal perspectives and add layers of cognitive associations to the interactive experience. The screen capture in Fig. 4 includes geometric and grid-like forms, as well as fluid, unstructured shapes. The temporal rhythm changes with each type of form. Designers can use different forms like these to represent specific kinds of information in the database. For example, the geometric areas can be links to numerical data, while the fluid forms might link to less structured information such as ambient sounds or diverse perspectives on a topic. Despite these different types of forms, the design still defines an integrated whole that symbolizes the interrelationships in the information space.

The resulting semiosis in interaction design is a combination of sequential and simultaneous representations of time and space. Non-linear, pluralistic concepts of temporality emphasize simultaneity and the multiple ways time can be expressed. Audiovisual rhythms and the rhythm of gestures and other physical movements contribute additional temporal dimensions to the interactive experience.

Fig. 4. In interface designs, forms and space define temporal rhythms that can symbolize different types of information. Copyright 2018 Patricia Search. All rights reserved.

6.2   Kinesthetic Design

The interactive experience can become more tangible with the addition of kinesthetic design which includes the physical movement of the body and gestures. Research has shown that interaction with the physical world helps clarify abstract concepts and aids cognition [38, 39]. Digital technology makes it possible to push the boundaries of embodiment and gesture, and use kinesthetic design to aid cognition and memory in the interactive experience.

With kinesthetic design, there is the movement in the physical space as well as movement in the virtual environment. In large-scale, immersive computing environments, the user can walk around in a space and move to new locations to investigate the virtual world and sound from different angles and perspectives. This experience can lead to new insights and cognitive networks of associations.

Kinesthetic design also includes the gestures or physical movements the user makes to interact with the computer program. This interaction defines patterns of movement in the physical space as well as patterns of movement on the screen. The physical interaction helps define and clarify the conceptual and abstract information in the virtual world by making the abstract concepts more tangible and concrete. Gestures and bodily movements are intuitive forms of communication and learning because they are based on shared experiences [40]. LeBaron and Streeck [40] pointed out that gestures provide a bridge between tactile experiences and the abstract conceptualization of the experiences. Physical movement and interaction with the artifacts and the physical space enable us to define symbolic representations [41] and build cognitive metaphors through image schemas which we derive from our physical orientation, movement, and interaction with the physical world [39].

These physical movements also create muscle memory or implicit memory that helps us learn and remember how to perform actions [42]. In interaction design, the physical movements that build implicit memory include the body movements or gestures that are required to navigate through the program and retrieve information. These movements help us define locations, landmarks, and spatial and temporal relationships that shape our cognitive understanding of the information space [38, 39, 41].

The correlation between these physical movements and the movements in the virtual space defines a network of cognitive metaphors that expands the semantic dimensions of the interactive design. For example, when users move the mouse or other interactive hardware, they create patterns in the physical space in order to select and move objects in the virtual world. These movements create sensory, kinesthetic, and cognitive landmarks for navigation and information synthesis. The user's movements and the movements in the virtual space can be synchronized to have the same movement patterns, directions, and rhythm. The physical and virtual movements can also be different and define a dynamic discourse and syntax that emphasizes change and contrast in the spatial and temporal representations in the semantic models.

As previously mentioned, there is also the space that exists between gestures or body movements as the user selects links and navigates through the environment that is integral to the semiotics of interactive design. It is part of the "interaction choreography" [37, p. 673], and on a conceptual level, the space represents the "space" between ideas where new ideas happen. As illustrated in Fig. 1, visual space is a design element that can be incorporated into the interface design to underscore this potential for new insights and creative exploration.

6.3 Metastructural Dynamics

In multimedia computing, the integration of different media results in a metasyntax and the opportunity for transmodal analysis [43]. A new audiovisual semantic structure integrates the syntax of the media into complex affective and cognitive models. The metasyntax integrates the semantic, spatial, and temporal modalities of words, images, sound, and movements into a holistic, multisensory experience. This pluralism results in a polysemiotic semantic structure that is further enhanced by online collaborations where individuals continually modify information.

The layers of audiovisual information and interactive transitions create mediascapes that transcend the limitations of the two-dimensional screen by weaving a network of sensory, cognitive, and physical associations into spatial patterns that visualize the temporal dynamics of the space. Users can continually redefine relationships and develop new perspectives based on additional information and sensory input. Relationships can be framed within the context of a multidimensional sense of space and time without the perceptual and cognitive restrictions of Western logic and linear causality. This cognitive processing leads to reflective abstraction [44]—a process that promotes the synthesis of diverse perspectives and "leads to constructive generalizations, to genuinely new knowledge, to knowledge at higher levels of development, and to knowledge about knowledge" [45, p. 12].

As users interact with the virtual environment with gestures, body movements, or interactive hardware, they create patterns in the physical space. The patterns define lines and planes that intersect in the user's cognitive map of the relationships. These "hyperplanes" also co-exist with the visual planes in the virtual world [10, 24]. Audio stimuli define additional hyperplanes as layers of sound in the space immerse the viewer with sensory stimuli from different angles and directions.

The hyperplanes create a counterpoint of audio, visual, and rhythmic patterns that define grids of intersecting spatiotemporal planes. The mediascapes and hyperplanes contribute to the development of a sense of place in interaction design by enabling users to weave multisensory landmarks in the physical and virtual environments into semantic maps and cognitive collages.

7   Future Directions

Interaction designers can create visual representations of these spatial and temporal semantic structures in interface designs to help users build cognitive models. However, designing interfaces that visualize the multiple dimensions of this multisensory space can be a challenge with the current software tools that are available for designing the information architecture, content organization, and navigation in an interactive program.

We need software that makes it possible to easily visualize layers of sensory and cognitive relationships. We may need to move beyond two-dimensional design and create three-dimensional visuals to reflect the layers of associations in complex information spaces. There are software packages for interactive, three-dimensional presentations that could serve as models for interface design software that would facilitate the visualization of multidimensional user interfaces [46, 47].

In addition to tools for designers, it will be important to consider interface designs that the user can actually modify to reflect new insights and associations. Interface designs should not remain static, but instead be flexible designs the user can revise to show the multisensory networks that emerge as perception, associative learning, and reflective abstraction contribute to new perspectives and cognitive models.

In database design, there are precedents for creating interactive semantic webs that users can modify to create user-defined information structures. Researchers are expanding the semantic structures in databases by using multimedia metadata (images, video, animations, and sound in addition to text) and allowing users to define relationships between database objects and the metadata [48–50]. These flexible ontologies support user exploration and dynamic revisions that reflect the experiences and perspectives of multiple users who are collaborating on a project. Users can change ontological relationships and discover new connections between ideas and the database content [51]. Srinivasan and Huang [50] created a project called Eventspace for online exhibits that allowed users to change the relationships between nodes in the database. This process leads to a meta-level in the semantic structure of the database that Srinivasan and Huang call "metaviews" [p. 194]. These metaviews evolve when users rearrange the database elements to define different perspectives and create "multiple evolving ontologies" [p. 200]. Paul [52] also noted that meta-narratives emerge from the dynamic reorganization and exploration of the database elements.

Complex semantic structures in interactive multimedia design require new approaches to interface design from the standpoint of the both the design process and the final interface design itself. Both the designer and the user need to be able to explore relationships from different perspectives so they do not limit the possible associations. They should be able to quickly build flexible, dynamic cognitive collages using different sensory stimuli, schemas and narratives, and cognitive models.

There is significant potential for using multimedia in interface designs to define spatial and temporal relationships that represent sensory and cognitive associations in an interactive program. However, there are also design challenges in creating interfaces that encourage exploration and creative input from the user. In particular, we need to consider a new approach to interface design that allows users to modify visual representations of information to reflect the new insights and associations they develop through multisensory perception and associative learning. This approach to flexible, user-centered interface design can become the foundation for the next generation of interaction design.

References

1. Art of Research VI Conference: Catalyses, Inventions, Transformations (2017). http://artofresearch2017.aalto.fi/index.html
2. Huth, G.: Visual poetry today: they are not merely poems, but they are certainly poems (2008). http://www.poetryfoundation.org/poetrymagazine/article/182397

3. Huth, G.: jHegaf (2008). http://www.poetryfoundation.org/poetrymagazine/article/182397
4. Beaulieu, D.: Untitled (for Natalee and Jeremy) (2008). http://www.poetryfoundation.org/poetrymagazine/poems/51811/untitled-for-natalee-and-jeremy
5. Ernst, K.S., Murphy, S.: Vortextique (2008). https://www.poetryfoundation.org/poetryma gazine/poems/51810/vortextique
6. Helmes, S.: haiku #62 (2008). https://www.poetryfoundation.org/poetrymagazine/poems/51815/haiku-62
7. Search, P.: HyperGlyphs: using design and language to define hypermedia navigation. J. Educ. Multimed. Hypermed. **2**(4), 369–380 (1993)
8. Search, P.: HyperGlyphs: new multiliteracy models for interactive computing. In: Cope, B., Kalantzis, M. (eds.) International Journal of Learning 8, pp. 1–19. Common Ground Publishing, Melbourne (2001)
9. Search, P.: The metastructual dynamics of interactive electronic design. Vis. Lang. Cult. Dimens. Vis. Commun. **37**(2), 146–165 (2003)
10. Search, P.: Using new media art and multisensory design for information and data representation. In: Tiradentes Souto, V., Spinillo, C., Portugal, C., Fadel, L. (eds.) Selected Readings of the 7th Information Design International Conference, pp. 179–190. The Brazilian Society of Information Design, Basilia (2016)
11. Hall, D.: Artwork that explores the space between our digital obsession and the natural world (2018). http://www.debhall.com
12. Rosenberg, J.: Intergrams (1988–1992). http://www.inframergence.org/jr/Intergrams_desc.shtml
13. Collins, A.M., Loftus, E.F.: A spreading-activation theory of semantic processing. Psychol. Rev. **82**(6), 407–428 (1975)
14. Tversky, B.: Cognitive maps, cognitive collages, and spatial mental models. In: Frank, Andrew U., Campari, I. (eds.) COSIT 1993. LNCS, vol. 716, pp. 14–24. Springer, Heidelberg (1993). https://doi.org/10.1007/3-540-57207-4_2
15. Hopfield, J.J.: Neural networks and physical systems with emergent collective computational abilities. Proc. Nat. Acad. Sci. **79**(8), 2554–2558 (1982)
16. Rumelhart, D.E., Todd, P.M.: Learning and connectionist representations. In: Meyer, D.E., Kornblum, S. (eds.) Attention and Performance XIV: Synergies in Experimental Psychology, Artificial Intelligence, and Cognitive Neuroscience, pp. 3–30. MIT Press, Cambridge (1993)
17. Jones, M., Willits, J., Dennis, S.: Models of semantic memory. In: Busemeyer, J., Wang, Z., Townsend, J., Eidels, A. (eds.) The Oxford Handbook of Computational and Mathematical Psychology, 232-254. Oxford University Press, New York (2015)
18. Rogers, T.T., McClelland, J.L.: Semantic Cognition. MIT Press, Cambridge (2006)
19. Minsky, M.: The Society of Mind. Simon and Shuster, New York (1988)
20. Bergman, A.: Auditory Scene Analysis. MIT Press, Cambridge (1994)
21. Hartley, T., Burgess, N.: Models of spatial cognition. In: Nadel, L. (ed.) MacMillan Encyclopaedia of Cognitive Science, pp. 111–119. Nature Publishing Group, London (2002)
22. Goldstone, R.L., Landy, D., Brunel, L.C.: Improving the perception to make distant connections closer. Front. Psychol. **2**, 385 (2013). https://doi.org/10.3389/fpsyg.2011.00385
23. Brunel, L., Carvalho, P., Goldstone, R.: It does belong together: cross-modal correspondences influence cross-modal integration during perceptual learning. Front. Psychol. **6**, 358 (2015). https://doi.org/10.3389/fpsyg.2015.00358
24. Search, P.: Multisensory physical environments for data representation. In: Marcus, A. (ed.) DUXU 2016. LNCS, vol. 9748, pp. 202–213. Springer, Cham (2016). https://doi.org/10.1007/978-3-319-40406-6_19

25. Freides, D.: Human information processing and sensory modality: cross-modal functions, information complexity, memory, and deficit. Psychol. Bull. **81**(5), 284–310 (1974)
26. MacLeod, A., Summerfield, Q.: A procedure for measuring auditory and audio-visual speech-reception thresholds for sentences in noise: rationale, evaluation, and recommendations for use. Br. J. Audiol. **24**(1), 29–43 (1990)
27. Stein, B.E., Meredith, M.A.: The Merging of Senses. MIT Press, Cambridge (1993)
28. Chen, Y.-C., Spence, C.: When hearing the bark helps to identify the dog: semantically-congruent sounds modulate the identification of masked pictures. Cognition **114**(3), 389–404 (2010)
29. Molholm, S., Ritter, W., Murray, M.M., Javitt, D.C., Schroeder, C.E., Foxe, J.J.: Multisensory auditory–visual interactions during early sensory processing in humans: a high-density electrical mapping study. Cogn. Brain Res. **14**(1), 115–128 (2002)
30. Brunel, L., Labeye, E., Lesourd, M., Versace, R.: The sensory nature of episodic memory: sensory priming effects due to memory trace activation. J. Exp. Psychol. Learn. Mem. Cogn. **35**(4), 1081–1088 (2009)
31. Brunel, L., Lesourd, M., Labeye, E., Versace, R.: The sensory nature of knowledge: sensory priming effects in semantic categorization. Q. J. Exp. Psychol. **63**(5), 955–964 (2010)
32. Brunel, L., Goldstone, R.L., Vallet, G., Riou, B., Versace, R.: When seeing a dog activates the bark: multisensory generalization and distinctiveness effects. Exp. Psychol. **60**(2), 100–112 (2013)
33. Connolly, K.: Multisensory perception as an associative learning process. Front. Psychol. **5**, 1095 (2014). https://doi.org/10.3389/fpsyg.2014.01095
34. Townsend, J.T., Wenger, M.J.: A theory of interactive parallel processing: new capacity measures and predictions for a response time inequality series. Psychol. Rev. **111**(4), 1003–1035 (2004)
35. Search, P.: Defining a sense of place in interactive multimedia design. In: Avgerinou, M., Chandler, S. (eds.) Visual Literacy in the 21st Century: Trends, Demands, and Capacities, pp. 143–148. International Visual Literacy Association, Chicago (2011)
36. Neiva, E.: Redefining the image: mimesis, convention, and semiotics. Commun. Theory **9**(1), 75–91 (1999)
37. Djajadiningrat, T., Matthews, B., Stienstra, M.: Easy doesn't do it: Skill and expression in tangible aesthetics. Pers. Ubiquit. Comput. **11**(8), 657–676 (2007)
38. Klemmer, S.R., Hartmann, B., Takayama, L.: How bodies matter: five themes for interaction design. In: Proceedings of Designing Interactive Systems, DIS 2006, pp. 140–148. Association for Computing Machinery (ACM), New York (2006)
39. Lakoff, G., Johnson, M.L.: Metaphors We Live By. University of Chicago Press, Chicago (1980)
40. LeBaron, C., Streeck, J.: Gestures, knowledge, and the world. In: McNeill, D. (ed.) Language and Gesture, pp. 118–138. Cambridge University Press, Cambridge (2000)
41. Abrahamson, D., Lindgren, R.: Embodiment and embodied design. In: Sawyer, R.K. (ed.) The Cambridge Handbook of the Learning Sciences, 2nd edn, pp. 357–376. Cambridge University Press, Cambridge (2014)
42. Meister, M.L.R., Buffalo, E.A.: Memory. In: Conn, M. (ed.) Conn's Translational Neuroscience, pp. 693–708. Academic Press, Cambridge (2016)
43. Macken-Horarik, M.: Interacting with the multimodal text: reflections on image and verbiage. Vis. Commun. **3**(1), 5–26 (2004)
44. Piaget, J.: Recherches sur L'abstraction reflechissante, vol. I and II. Presses Universitaires de France, Paris (1977)
45. Campbell, R.: Studies in Reflecting Abstraction. Psychology Press, Philadelphia (2001)
46. Cinector: rapid media production software (2018). http://www.cinector.com

47. Intuilab: create amazing multi-touch applications for any screen. In record time. Without coding (2018). http://www.intuilab.com
48. Christie, M.: Aboriginal knowledge traditions in digital environments. J. Indig. Educ. **34**, 61–66 (2005)
49. Verran, H., Christie, M.: Using/designing digital technologies of representation in Aboriginal Australian knowledge practices. Hum. Technol. **3**(2), 214–227 (2007)
50. Srinivasan, R., Huang, J.: Fluid ontologies for digital museums. Int. J. Digit. Libr. **5**(3), 193–204 (2005)
51. Search, P.: Interactive multisensory data representation. In: Marcus, A. (ed.) DUXU 2015. LNCS, vol. 9187, pp. 363–373. Springer, Cham (2015). https://doi.org/10.1007/978-3-319-20898-5_35
52. Paul, C.: The database as system and cultural form: anatomies of cultural narratives. In: Vesna, V. (ed.) Database Aesthetics: Art in the Age of Information Overflow, pp. 95–109. University of Minnesota Press, Minneapolis (2007)

From Customer Journey to Knowledge Journey: Mapping the Knowledge Journey in Co-design on Public Realm

Di Shi[1(✉)], Rong Deng[1], Xin Xin[2], and Yumei Dong[3]

[1] School of Design, Jiangnan University, Wuxi, China
shidionline@126.com
[2] Beijing Normal University, Beijing, China
[3] School of Design, Tongji University, Shanghai, China

Abstract. The focus of design has recently extended from user and product service systems to public and social service systems. There is a lack of practical studies on what exactly takes place when designing in the public sphere. Whether and how co-design can make a difference when design in public realm? To untangle these problems this paper conducted a comparative study from the knowledge conversion perspective. The first case is design for China village service system without co-design involved while the second case is design for a traditional handicraft service system with co-design approaches included. To get a better understanding, a dynamic model which combined the SECI framework elements with journey mapping format was developed. The analysis and comparison of the two cases through this dynamic model revealed two knowledge journeys which shed light on knowledge conversion in co-design and opened a new direction to study the related fieldworks.

Keywords: Customer journey · Co-design · SECI framework
Public design · Fieldwork study

1 Introduction

The practice of collective creativity in design can be traced back to 1970s, going under the tradition of participatory design (Sanders and Stappers 2008). Participatory Design shared concerns and values with labour unions in emancipating workers at the workplace (Bjerknes et al. 1987; Schuler and Namioka 1993; Lenskjold et al. 2015). Although often used as synonyms co-design as one form of collective creativity in design is not the same as participatory design from 1970s. Co-design as a practice carries perhaps a bit lighter weight on the political agenda but builds on the same mindsets and tools (Mattelmäki and Sleeswijk Visser 2011). The repertoire of co-design tools is huge and well developed including methods such as situated and participative enactment of scenarios (Iacucci et al. 2000), design probes (Mattelmäki 2006; Gaver et al. 1999), design games (Brandt and Messeter 2004; Brandt 2006), make tools (Elizabeth and Dandavate 1999), just to name few.

With the focus of design extending from user and product service system to public and social service system such as design for a more sustainable society (Norman and

A. Marcus and W. Wang (Eds.): DUXU 2018, LNCS 10918, pp. 256–267, 2018.
https://doi.org/10.1007/978-3-319-91797-9_18

Stappers 2016), we as designer and researcher are facing new challenges. Although there are many researches have explored the issue related to design in public realm (Manzini 2014; Manzini and Coad 2015), there still lack of practical studies on what exactly takes place in co-design when designing on public sphere and we lack examples on whether and how co-design can make a difference in this new area.

To deepen our understanding on co-design in public realm, we started by looking at two example cases design for public service. The first one adopted co-design in the design process while the other didn't. We were interested in knowledge exchange in particular. Knowledge plays a role when considering the design as a discipline (Archer 1979; Cross 2001) and when considering the process of design which set out from the ill-structured, open and complex questions (Rittel and Webber 1974; Simon 1973; Cross et al. 1996; Cross et al. 1992; Dorst and Cross 2001). Our analysis of the two cases focus on the knowledge conversion perspective i.e. how the knowledge are shared and changed during the design process in the two cases. However, in our initial analysis we realized that there is a lack of practical tool or method to work with. As a result, we created a new dynamic model which combined the elements in exiting SECI framework with a format of journey mapping. The development and the application of this new dynamic model will be discussed in this study.

This paper is structured in the following order: Firstly, we explained why we choose these two specific cases and how the data are collected from them. Secondly, the article focused on why and how we developed a new analysis approach i.e. the new dynamic model. Thirdly, this study analyse the knowledge conversion process in the two cases through the new model. Fourthly, this paper reflected on what we have learned from this study.

2   The Fieldwork Study of Co-design in Public Realm

The two example cases were projects of design practice for public service system. In the following the two examples are introduced:

2.1   Design for China Village Service System

The first design project named "Design for China Village" aimed to discover the needs and design potentials in Chinese villages and provide novel design concepts for an ideal future. As there are nine hundred millions farmer in China, the development of villages has always been an important issue (Xiaotong 1996; Yangchu 1935). This project is one of the working projects in National Commission of The People's Republic of China for UNESCO (United Nations Educational, Scientific and Cultural Organization). The author was the main designer and coordinator in the design team.

The project was started from June 2014 and it took one year to finish the preliminary investigation. During the investigation, the research team decided to focus on the core unit of a village i.e. a family. One family from a village which located in the centre of China was chosen. 72 h video was documented of this family within each room and the yard of their house. The video was analysed by about twenty students and two teachers in Zhengzhou University of Light Industry which located near this village. The analysis focused on the living routine of different family members in different living space. In June 2015, the results from the video analysis was sent to a design team for further analysis and concepts design. There were four phases within the design process, namely position design, system design, products design and video making which will be compared in detail in the discussion section. The final design concepts were invited to exhibit in the 2015 Gwangju Design Biennale, Korea. The overall project process can be summarized in Fig. 1.

Project stages	Ethnography study	Design				Exhibition
Time line	Jun 2014 Jun 2015	Jul 2015	Sep 2015			Oct 2015
Design process		Position design	System design	Products design	Video making	

Fig. 1. The design for China village project processs.

2.2   Design for Traditional Handicrafts Service System

The second project is a project intended to design a web based tool to be used by various handicraftsmen and customers. The main aim of the project was to provide one business model for the Chinese traditional handicraftsmen. The author coordinated the design process and followed the design process as a participate observer.

Project stages	Data Collecting & analysing	Co-design	
Time line	Apr 2015	Jun 2017	Jul 2017
Design process		Workshop 1	Workshop 2

Fig. 2. The handicrafts project process.

In the project the researcher first collected and analyzed the current situation through interview. After analysing the interviews, a co-design phase including two workshops followed. These will be compared with the first case in the discussion section. The project phases are depicted in Fig. 2.

3 The Fieldwork Study of Co-design in Public Realm

The comparison of the knowledge conversion process within the two cases started by looking at a theory framework to use as a comparison framework. As a result, we created a new dynamic model for the analysis that will be explained in the following.

3.1 Why to Borrow the Elements in the SECI Framework

The main purpose of the analysis approach was to map out the knowledge journey in the two cases, hence we needed a framework for the comparison. In the following we will explain why we decided to create one dynamic model combined the SECI framework elements with mapping format.

Among the existing models in knowledge and information management literatures, the SECI knowledge creation model attracted our attention. Not only because it is widely cited but also because it gives four different "models" of knowledge conversion which facilitate the description the knowledge creation process in a dynamic way.

The SECI framework is proposed by Nonaka in 1990s and has been regard as "most influential" (Choo and Bontis 2002) and "highly respected" (Easterby-Smith and Lyles 2003). In this framework, Nonaka claimed that knowledge is created in the continuous interplay process between tacit knowledge and explicit knowledge through four models of conversion process. The first process is socialization through which new tacit knowledge is converted by sharing experiences. The second process is externalization through which the tacit knowledge are articulated into explicit knowledge. The third process is combination through which the more complex and systematic sets of explicit knowledge is converted. The fourth process is internalization through which the explicit knowledge embodied into new tacit knowledge. It can be the starting point of a new spiral of knowledge creation when it is shared with others through socialisation. The knowledge creation process is depicted in a "spiral". Each "circle" go through the whole four models of knowledge conversion in the framework (Nonaka 1994; Nonaka and Takeuchi 1995a; Nonaka 1991; Nonaka and Takeuchi 1995b; Nonaka et al. 1994; Nonaka 1995; Nonaka et al. 2000; Nonaka and Nishiguchi 2001; Nonaka and Toyama 2003). The "spiral" is treated as the "engine" of the knowledge creation process (Nonaka and Takeuchi 1995b). The four models of knowledge conversion constitue the key elements in this framework and facilitate the description of knowledge creation in a dynamic way (Fig. 3).

Although there are few weighty critics, it is necessary to check them before we decide whether the four models of knowledge conversion are suitable for this study. Some of the critics have identified missing parts in this theory. For example, Jorna criticized Nonaka overlooking the learning theory (Jorna 1998). Generally, these critics does not criticize the four models of knowledge conversion in this framework.

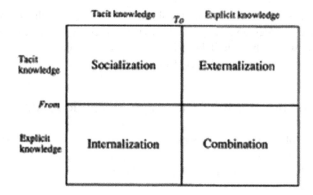

Fig. 3. Models of knowledge creation (from Nonaka, I.: A dynamic theory of organizational knowledge creation. In: Knowledge, Groupware and the Internet, pp. 3–42 (2000)).

Also, there are some critical concerns that the framework emphasizes on "judgment" "belief" and neglects on "truth" (Gourlay 2006). SECI framework was built on the traditional epistemology and adopted a definition of knowledge as "justified true belief" (Nonaka 1994). But there is a difference between the traditional epistemology which focus on the "truthfulness" and emphasize the absolute, static and nonhuman nature of knowledge creation. While this framework emphasizes the dynamic human process of justifying personal beliefs (Nonaka 1994). If there is no "truthfulness" as a knowledge creation base, the process illustrated in this framework will become a knowledge interpretation process not a knowledge creation process (Gourlay 2006). As we focus on how the knowledge are changed or interpreted not how the knowledge are created, these comments were not a challenge to borrow the four models of knowledge conversion into our analysis. What's more, "judgment" and "belief" in design process are considered more valuable than the "truthfulness" which is very important in other discipline such as science. (Cross 2001; Feast 2012)

Gourlay also states that the process of the framework hardly services scrupulous evaluation as this framework comes from theoretical study not from empirical analysis (Gourlay 2003). Stephen Gourlay articulated that there is no evidence to show why the four conversion process start from the socialization of tacit knowledge (Gourlay 2006). Again, this critic does not pointed at the four models of knowledge conversion but the lack of empirical evidence in the knowledge creation process. As we do not analyse the knowledge creation process but the conversion process, it is also not a challenge to use the key elements in this study.

Based on the analysis above, it is clear that the four models of knowledge conversion constructed the key elements in the SECI framework and the key elements facilitate the description of knowledge cration process in a dynamic way. Even though there are some critics on the knowledge creation process in SECI framework, the key elements of this framework has been widely accepted. So it is reasonable to borrow the key elements to analyse the knowledge conversion process in the two cases.

3.2   How to Merge the Elements into a New Model

In design practice, journey is a useful way to visualize a process. For example, customer journey and experience journey are widely used in different situations (Nenonen et al. 2008). Even though the format varies in different context these kind of journeys typical have a timeline developed from left to right and have some elements for analysis developed from top to down. So the new dynamic model which combined the journey mapping and the key elements in SECI framework can be seen in Fig. 4.

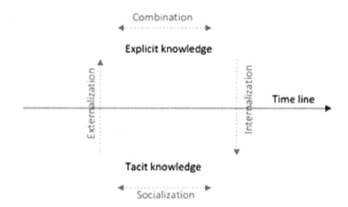

Fig. 4. The adjusted model of knowledge creation (from Nonaka, I.: A dynamic theory of organizational knowledge creation (1994)).

As this study is to analyse the knowledge conversion process not the knowledge creation process which described in the SECI framework, the analysis followed the actual process in the two cases i.e. we merged the above new dynamic model with our projects' processes. To be specific, the timeline will be described with our actual design phases, the documents, tools and images etc. will facilitate the description of explicit knowledge and the citation from the conversations during each design phase will facilitate the analysis of tacit knowledge during each phase. Taking the first case as an example, the specific analysis model for the first case can be seen in Fig. 5.

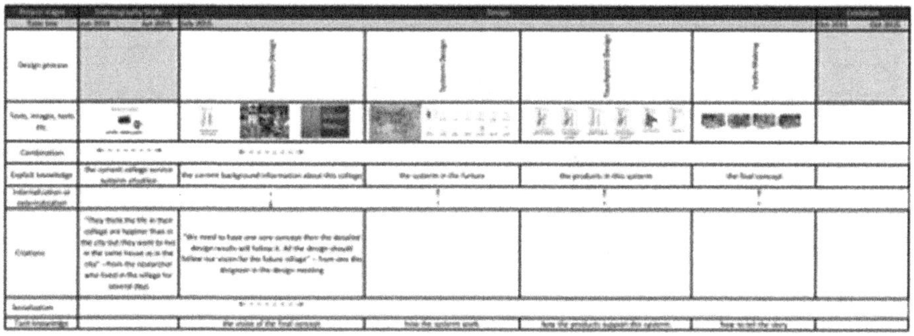

Fig. 5. The analysis model for the first case

As this is the first time to use this new model to the analysis of a knowledge journey, we focus on the general design process. The analysis process can be divided into six phases. First, put all the images, texts, documents from the two cases into corresponding column (the first blank line). Second, summarize what kind of explicit knowledge these images, texts represent then write it down in the "explicit knowledge" column. Third, analyse the conversation during each design phase, pick and put the most dominant content in the "citation" column. Fourth, summarize the main tacit knowledge in each phase then write it down in the "tacit knowledge" column. Fifth, check whether there is combination between explicit knowledge, socialization between tacit knowledge, externalization or internalization between explicit knowledge and tacit knowledge. Sixth, draw a line based on the knowledge conversion analysed through the prior five phases.

4   Discussion

Following the analysis structure, the data that supports the summarizing of explicit knowledge in Design for China Village Project are 72 h video analysis report, texts about the village background, photos that documented the discussion process,

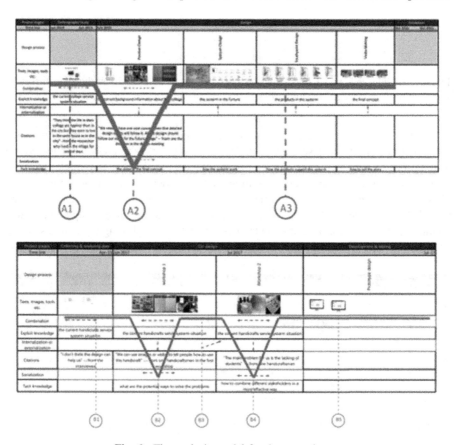

Fig. 6. The analysis model for the second case

documentations during the discussion within the design team, sketches from the system design process, service system design maps, products design sketches and prototypes, design concepts videos. Data that supports the summarizing of tacit knowledge in Design for China Village project are retrospective analysis on the notes during the design process. The data that supports the summarizing of explicit knowledge in handicrafts project are documents from the interviews, photos and workshop materials from the workshop one, photos and workshop materials from the workshop two. The data that supports the summarizing of tacit knowledge in handicrafts project are notes during the whole design process.

After analysing the data in these two cases, we got two different knowledge journeys from the two cases (Fig. 6). Now we will follow these two journeys to compare the two cases and discuss the insights we got from it.

4.1   The Starting Point of the Knowledge Journey

The starting points, A1 and B1, of the two cases are the same. Both of them are started from the combination of explicit knowledge about the context.

In the first case, data analysed from the video was sent to the design team and the designers got a better understanding of the context by combining these data with background information about this village. In the second case, the researcher got a better understanding of the current service context throw the messages gave by the handicraftsmen.

In sum, the starting point of the knowledge journey is the explicit knowledge about the context.

4.2   The Following Process of the Knowledge Journey

The two knowledge journeys followed different trajectory after the same starting point.

In the first case, the design team include seven designers in total. "We need to decide the vision of our design then all the details should be judged by it and follow it" one of the designers emphasized in the second meeting. This is the work strategy of this design team. Even though they are responsible for different parts of the design project, they have shared the same tacit knowledge of the final vision through working together so this tacit knowledge helped them to make a judgement during the whole design process. A2 is the socialized tacit knowledge of the final design vision. A3 is the explicit knowledge of the design concept, such as system diagrams, products sketches and final design video and so on.

In the second case, there is one designer. After the first workshop, the designer already had some tacit knowledge about what can be a design solution to meet the need. B2 is the tacit knowledge about the future design vision. B3 is the explicit knowledge about the second workshop which was carried by the second workshop documents, templates and so on. B4 is the internalized tacit knowledge about the design vision. As the second workshop participant said "Our biggest concern is lacking of students. I think we can combine the power of local companies to meet this need." To combine the power of local companies was considered by the designer before the second workshop, so the tacit knowledge about the design vision has been shared with craftsmen through the socialization with them in the second workshop. B5 is the explicit knowledge on the design concept which has been carried by the manual, documents etc. which explained the concept and prototype of the web based tool.

4.3   Similarities and Differences of the Two Cases

Through comparing the two knowledge journeys, we can realize there is a conversion between different kinds of knowledge throughout the whole design process. Both of the two knowledge journeys begin from the public context knowledge. Then this public context knowledge internalized into personal tacit knowledge which is shared within the designer team. Till this point, the two knowledge journeys are similar.

However, in the first case, the personal tacit knowledge (designer's vision of the new concept) are externalized to explicit knowledge to communicate with others through the system diagram, the products model, the prototypes and the concept video etc. In the second case, the personal tacit knowledge (the designer's vision) are not externalized to final design but externalized to the structure and materials for the second workshop. (B3) During the second workshop the personal tacit knowledge are shared with all the participants. (B4) That is to say, the designer's personal tacit knowledge on the new concept are justified by others personal tacit knowledge. After this process, the designers' personal tacit knowledge are externalized to design concept diagrams, stories, prototypes etc. Through these share and justify process, the designer's personal tacit knowledge about the new concept are shared and adjusted with both service providers and users. This personal tacit knowledge became shared tacit knowledge or pervasive knowledge within the target community.

Through knowledge conversion analysis we realized that there is not only an interplay between "private" and "public" in an explicit way but also an interplay between "personal" and "pervasive" in a tacit way in co-design on public realm. The interplay among "4Ps" can be seen in Fig. 7.

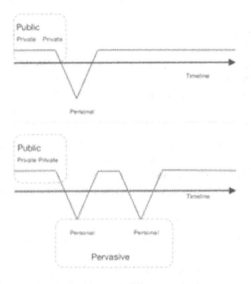

Fig. 7. The similarities and differences in the two cases.

5 Conclusion

The objectives of this paper being twofold: one, it introduces an analysis tool for visualizing knowledge conversion process, and second, it depicts, compares and reflects on two different kind of design processes and their general knowledge conversion journey which facilitate a better understanding of the role of co-design in public realm. Through the development and application of the new dynamic model, we draw the following conclusions from two perspectives.

First, we can draw two conclusions on the model itself. One the one hand, the new dynamic analysis model which combined the elements in SECI framework with the format in journey mapping methods is feasible to analysis the knowledge conversion process in design cases which helped us to get a better understanding on what exactly take place in co-design on public realm. On the other hand, there is a potential to get more fruitful findings if we can use this analysis model on one specific phase within the design process not on the general process.

Second, the analysis of knowledge conversion process shed light on co-design in public realm. As the similarity of the two projects is public realm and the difference is co-design, the similarity of the two knowledge journeys showed how "public realm" can affect the knowledge conversion in design process and the difference of the two knowledge journeys showed how "co-design" can make a difference in knowledge conversion in design process. The similarity of the two knowledge journeys is the starting point which tells us the design process in public realm sets out not from "private" user's knowledge but the "public" system knowledge. The difference of the two knowledge conversion journeys is the socialization of tacit knowledge in the community which tells us it is necessary that not only pay attention to the interplay between "private" and "public" in an explicit way but also pay attention to the interplay between "personal" and "pervasive" in a tacit way in co-design on public realm.

Acknowledgements. The valuable comments and insights from Design for China Village project team and the colleagues at Aalto University is highly appreciated. This paper is supported by The Research and Practice on Progressive Entrepreneurial Talent Cultivation with Intelligent Interactive Lab in the Industrial 4.0 (JG2017101) and Research on The Study on Research Ability Training of Social Sciences Graduate Students based on the Evaluation Index of High-Level Universities.

References

Archer, B.: The three rs. Des. stud. **1**(1), 18–20 (1979)

Bjerknes, G., Ehn, P., Kyng, M., Nygaard, K.: Computers and Democracy: A Scandinavian Challenge. Gower Pub Co, Swansea (1987)

Brandt, E.: Designing exploratory design games: a framework for participation in participatory design? In: Paper Presented at the Proceedings of the Ninth Conference on Participatory Design: Expanding Boundaries in Design-Volume 1 (2006)

Brandt, E., Messeter, J..: Facilitating collaboration through design games. In: Paper presented at the Proceedings of the Eighth Conference on Participatory Design: Artful Integration: Interweaving Media, Materials and Practices-Volume 1 (2004)

Choo, C.W., Bontis, N.: The Strategic Management of Intellectual Capital and Organizational Knowledge. Oxford University Press, Oxford (2002)

Cross, N.: Designerly ways of knowing: design discipline versus design science. Des. Issues **17** (3), 49–55 (2001)

Cross, N., Dorst, K., Christiaans, H.: Analysing Design Activity. Wiley, London (1996)

Cross, N., Dorst, K., Roozenburg, N.: Research in design thinking (1992)

Dorst, K., Cross, N.: Creativity in the design process: co-evolution of problem–solution. Des. Stud. **22**(5), 425–437 (2001)

Easterby-Smith, M., Lyles, M.A.: Handbook of Organizational Learning and Knowledge Management. Blackwell Publishing, Malden (2003)

Elizabeth, B.N.S., Dandavate, U.: Design for experiencing: new tools. In: Paper presented at the First International Conference on Design and Emotion, TU Delft (1999)

Feast, L.: Professional perspectives on collaborative design work. Co-Design **8**(4), 215–230 (2012)

Gaver, B., Dunne, T., Pacenti, E.: Design: cultural probes. Interactions **6**(1), 21–29 (1999)

Gourlay, S.: The SECI model of knowledge creation: some empirical shortcomings (2003)

Gourlay, S.: Conceptualizing knowledge creation: a critique of Nonaka's theory. J. Manag. Stud. **43**(7), 1415–1436 (2006)

Iacucci, G., Kuutti, K. and Ranta, M.: On the move with a magic thing: role playing in concept design of mobile services and devices. In: Paper Presented at the Proceedings of the 3rd Conference on Designing Interactive Systems: Processes, Practices, Methods, and Techniques (2000)

Jorna, R.: Managing knowledge. Semiot. Rev. Books **9**(2), 5–8 (1998)

Lenskjold, T.U., Olander, S., Halse, J.: Minor design activism: prompting change from within. Des. Issues **31**(4), 67–78 (2015)

Manzini, E.: Making things happen: Social innovation and design. Des. Issues **30**(1), 57–66 (2014)

Manzini, E., Coad, R.: Design, When Everybody Designs: An Introduction to Design for Social Innovation. MIT Press, Cambridge (2015)

Mattelmäki, T.: Design probes. Aalto University, Helsinki (2006)

Mattelmäki, T., Sleeswijk Visser, F.: Lost in Co-X: Interpretations of Co-design and Co-creation. In: Paper presented at the 2011 Diversity and Unity, Proceedings of IASDR2011, the 4th World Conference on Design Research (2011)

Nenonen, S., Rasila, H., Junnonen, J.-M., Kärnä, S.: Customer journey–a method to investigate user experience. In: Paper presented at the Proceedings of the Euro FM Conference Manchester (2008)

Nonaka, I., Takeuchi, H.: Knowledge management cycle (1995a). http://www.hubpages.com/hub/htm/Nonaka-and-Takeuchi-knowledge-managementcycle. Accessed 10 Aug 2013

Nonaka, I.: The Knowledge-creating company harvard business review november-december (1991)

Nonaka, I.: A dynamic theory of organizational knowledge creation. Organ. Sci. **5**(1), 14–37 (1994)

Nonaka, I.: Managing innovation as an organizational knowledge creation process. Technol. Manag. Corp. Strat. Tricontinental perspect. (1995)

Nonaka, I., Byosiere, P., Borucki, C.C., Konno, N.: Organizational knowledge creation theory: a first comprehensive test. Int. Bus. Rev. **3**(4), 337–351 (1994)

Nonaka, I., Nishiguchi, T.: Knowledge Emergence: Social, Technical, and Evolutionary Dimensions of Knowledge Creation. Oxford University Press, Oxford (2001)

Nonaka, I., Takeuchi, H.: The Knowledge-Creating Company: How Japanese Companies Create the Dynamics of Innovation. Oxford university press (1995b)

Nonaka, I., Toyama, R.: The knowledge-creating theory revisited: knowledge creation as a synthesizing process. Knowl. Manag. Res. Pract. **1**(1), 2–10 (2003)

Nonaka, I., Toyama, R., Konno, N.: SECI, Ba and leadership: a unified model of dynamic knowledge creation. Long Range Plann. **33**(1), 5–34 (2000)

Norman, D.A., Stappers, P.J.: DesignX: complex sociotechnical systems. She Ji J. Des. Econ. Innov. **1**(2), 83–106 (2016)

Rittel, H., Webber, M.M.: Wicked problems. Man-Made Futures **26**(1), 272–280 (1974)

Sanders, E.B.-N., Stappers, P.J.: Co-creation and the new landscapes of design. Co-Design **4**(1), 5–18 (2008)

Schuler, D., Namioka, A.: Participatory Design: Principles and the Practices. Lawrence Erlabum Associates, Mahwah (1993). ISBN 0-8058-0951-1

Simon, H.A.: The structure of ill structured problems. Artif. Intell. **4**(3–4), 181–201 (1973)

Xiaotong, F.: Re-reading preface to the economy of Jiang Cun. J. Peking Univ. (Hum. Soc. Sci.), **4** (1996)

Yangchu, Y.: The mission of the Rural Campaign. In: Chinese National Association of the Mass Education, Beijing (1935, in Chinese)

Applying Context Awareness Model in Interaction Design Process

Jian Sun[✉] and Jianming Yang

Beijing Institute of Technology, Beijing, China
jeffrey.imagine@gmail.com

Abstract. The traditional process of interaction design includes several parts, such as background analysis, character modeling, scenario analysis, concept stage, and evaluation stage. With the application of context awareness model to design process, more context factors could be considered and the system could actively respond to certain action based on user activity model. In this way, the gap between system behavior and user cognition can largely reduce. This study based on the theory of context awareness, aiming at understanding and describing user context awareness mechanism, providing a reference for the establishment of the corresponding model of context aware systems, meeting user context awareness requirement in the process of the cognitive model. Through user's context aware mechanism modeling, build context perception interaction design model, and explore context aware approach of interaction design.

Keywords: Context awareness · Interaction design · Design methods

1 Introduction

With the development of computer and communication technology, especially mobile technology in the process of rapidly developing, the next generation of mobile technology, pervasive computing has come into being. The rapid development and wide application of pervasive computing technology promotes the maturity of mobile commerce. In recent years, as a new type of mobile business application, context awareness service is obtaining growing concern. Providing users with personalized service which responding to context awareness could bring greater convenience, mobility and security for the people's work and life. Context awareness service has huge market potential.

In the human-computer interaction process, interaction design is aiming to construct an interactive model, through which the users' desire is mapped to the system model. If a system model cannot meet the user's understanding and expectations, users will not be able to correctly understand the system, leading to the user using the system with low efficiency, high error rate and low satisfaction. Context aware systems can provide users with active, adaptive and personalized service and narrow the gap between perception system behavior and user cognitive style, and achieve transition from explicit interaction to implicit interaction.

© Springer International Publishing AG, part of Springer Nature 2018
A. Marcus and W. Wang (Eds.): DUXU 2018, LNCS 10918, pp. 268–276, 2018.
https://doi.org/10.1007/978-3-319-91797-9_19

2   Context Awareness and Context Factors

Schilit and Theimer [1] in 1994 for the first time put forward the concept of context awareness, afterward all the research context aware aspects develop rapidly. Context aware emphasizes the equipment's perception of user's situation and system feedback. Schmidt [2] mentioned that a context describes a situation and environment where the device or user is located, often marked by a specific name. For each context, there is a series of related functions, and the range of each correlation function is determined by the context. Dey and Abowd [3] considered that the context is any information that can be used to represent the entity state. The entity is the person, place or object that interacts with the user and application, and includes the user and the application itself. Context awareness is a system with the basis of the user task requirements, using situational ability to provide relevant information and services to users.

2.1   Context Awareness

Context awareness is the system could actively perceive user context changes provide appropriate information and services according to the needs of the user's current task at the appropriate time. The purpose is to sense and record surrounding people, behavior, and environment context information through the sensor of intelligent equipment and related technologies. By calculating the equipment processing and decomposition ability, appropriate real-time response changes according to the context. Context awareness reflect the important directions of the user experience through appropriate active real-time response from context changes. Perception of user needs, changing tasks and the surrounding scene could influence adaptive changes of interface and function process. In this way, users take the initiative to push service.

2.2   Context Factors

Dey [4] proposed context can be used to describe any information of an entity, the so-called entity refers to anyone associated with the user and application interaction, location, or object, including the user and the application itself. From this definition, the scope of the concept is very wide. All information that is related to entities in the process of the interaction can be considered as the context of the entity. The context includes not only the physical situations, but also the virtual situations. Perception ways of those situations are also different.

From the perspective of human factors and user, Schmidt [5] represented context factors as a model for the context related to human and physical environment. The context related to human includes human information, social environment and user tasks. The context related to physical environment includes location, infrastructure and physical conditions. Gwizdka Jacek [6] divides the context into the internal context and the exterior context. Internal context describes the state of the user; he external context describes the state of the environment. In this study, the context factors were divided into user context, task context and environment context. User context is a description of the user's personal attributes. Task context is the property and state of the object and behavior related to the user to complete the current task. Environmental factor is the description of the user's current environment characteristics (Table 1).

Table 1. Context factors analysis.

Context factors	
User context	Description of the user's personal attributes
Task context	Property and state of the object and behavior related to the user to complete the current task
Environment context	Description of the user's current environment characteristics

3 Context Awareness Mechanism in Human-Computer Interaction

The human-computer interaction focuses on how users interact with the system, the user how to act, perform the task, complete the work. Users how to use the tools and software embodied in the HCI model and research method. This connects computer technology and computer technology, to achieve maximum humanization of computer technology (Fig. 1).

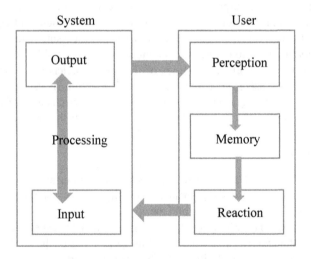

Fig. 1. Information flow of human-computer interaction.

The process of human-computer interaction includes two important participants: user and system. Behavior of the participants is very different due to cognitive complexity. The aim of interaction design is to map interactive user expectations to the system model, so the conceptual model of interaction is very important in interactive design tasks.

In the interaction design model, designer's cognitive structure transform knowledge into information, which is information-coding process. Users' cognition structure absorbs and adapts the information, which is the decoding process of information. When the designer knowledge and user knowledge achieve natural matching, the products of the designer meet the user's expectations. Study of human-computer interaction (HCI) is the interaction methods between people and computers, which are the medium of the user and the computer information exchange. The subjects of human-computer interaction include computer and computer users, graph below represent the information flow of human-computer interaction (Fig. 2).

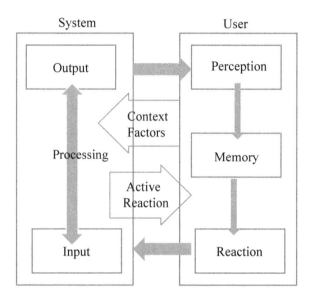

Fig. 2. Information flow of context awareness human-computer interaction.

Context awareness refers to the products and services could actively aware context change around the users, to provide a context based information service according to the needs of individual users. In the process of human-computer interaction, the task of interaction design is to map the user's expectation to the system model. Therefore, the interactive concept model becomes a very important task in interaction design. If we consider the contextual factors in the interaction design, system could actively aware the change of user context. In the process of context aware system, according to the needs of the user current task, system could provide appropriate information and services at appropriate time.

4   Context Awareness Model in Human-Computer Interaction

In human-computer interaction process, each individual interaction process between human and system contains the user behavior. User behavior model theoretical basis is the Russian psychologist, Vygotsk Behaviorism [7], divided the user's behavior into three levels, namely operation, action and activity. At the same time, the three level of behaviors subject to the restriction of condition, goal and motive.

In the study a system could be used as a driven by motivation, which makes the research focus on specific behaviors but not a specific application. It is behavior not the application meet the user's needs and motivation. Although people may use the a same application, it is under the different behavior of the study from the product itself transformed into wider application and background (Fig. 3).

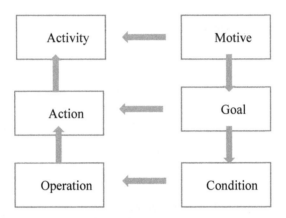

Fig. 3. User behavior model.

Interaction model based on context aware established based on the characteristics of the user's context factors of theoretical foundation, describing the users' judgment of context factors and the understanding process. A more in-depth understanding of context aware mechanisms is established to guide context aware systems design, narrow the gap in human-computer interaction between technology model and user model (Fig. 4).

Human activities occur in a specific context which is composed of individual activities and meaningful context. These activities change with the changing contexts. At the same time, the context cannot exist without the user activities, so the user's activity is the core content of the context, and the study base of the context aware mechanism. Activity is composed of a series of actions, associated with each action with a target, the target and formed the overall goals or motivations. The specific activity stage shows the different active context factors. Some of the user operations provide the rules and the opportunities to set out active context factors, thus triggering the activity of the context awareness. The activity model including activity, action and operation hierarchy is used to establish the relationship between activity and user's context awareness.

In a specific activity, the system can perceive activity may include the context factors, which include user context, task context and environment context. Identification of different context factors constitutes the perception stage of context aware process. By the driver of the target, a series of actions constitutes activity. Different action stages correspond to the corresponding active context factors, and different context factors corresponding to the different trigger rules. Active context factors of

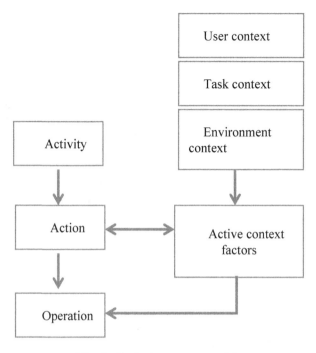

Fig. 4. Context awareness model.

action stages and trigger rules of a context aware process constitute the explanation stage. When certain conditions are met, specific operation is complete, active context factors and the corresponding starting rules provide the appropriate trigger timing, and produce after starting the operation. This is reaction stage of context aware process.

5   Analysis Method and Design Flow Based on Context Awareness Model

The purpose of this study is through the relationship between the user behavior model and context awareness, to establishment of user context aware model, guiding context aware interaction design, and reducing distance between system behavior and users'. expectations. Therefore, improving acceptability and satisfaction in context aware interaction, and through the establishment of the context aware in interaction design, to find a way to explore interaction design methods based on context aware model.

5.1   User Centered Design Process

Interaction design should undergo a complex process from the previous study to the specific design and implementation. User centered design process includes three typical stages: the user analysis stage, design stage and evaluating stage.

(1) User analysis stage

User analysis stage focus on solving the problem is to determine the direction and target of product design. The concept of user-centered design considers that the success of the product depends on the satisfaction with user, to achieve customer satisfaction goals; there should be in-depth and clear understanding of the user, which stage is called description of user characteristics. At the same time, the designer should also clearly understand what is the target users' expectations of the product, including users demanding practical functions and goals, which stage is called demand analysis.

(2) Design stage

In this stage pre-user analysis material is systematically Analysis with refined expression. To map users' expectation with interactive model, designers use the knowledge of object model and gradually transformed it into the concept model and user interface view in different degree, usually low fidelity model and high fidelity model.

(3) Evaluation stage

After the construction of model design, through certain means and methods are used to verify whether the designer for the conceptual model and user model matching. User usability testing and experts' evaluation are common methods User testing is to design a model presented in front of the user, with users' using or discussion to obtain user feedback data. Expert assessment is to invite the authority of the human computer interface design and system function experts, review the design model according to their experience to, and point out the problem of usability.

5.2   User Centered Design Process Based on Context Awareness

The main goal of product interaction design is to create the interaction model between users and products, understanding user needs and improving the user experience. The context aware system interaction process has characteristics of concealment, active service, and personalization, with which traditional product interaction design method also need to adjust, to guide the context aware system interaction design process.

(1) User and environment analysis stage

User analysis based on context awareness focuses on the analysis of user scenario analysis and context analysis, in which stage the user's personal characteristics are described, including a description of the basic features of the user, the description of the life style and behavior preference. Environment context description including the physical environment and social environment, and these factors are classified and collected, which conclude the user needs analysis.

(2) Task analysis stage

At this stage, through the task analysis process, designers decompose behavior of the user into task model. In each model, the task is divided into activity, action and operation phases. At the same time, active context factors and trigger rules are built corresponding with task context analysis (Fig. 5).

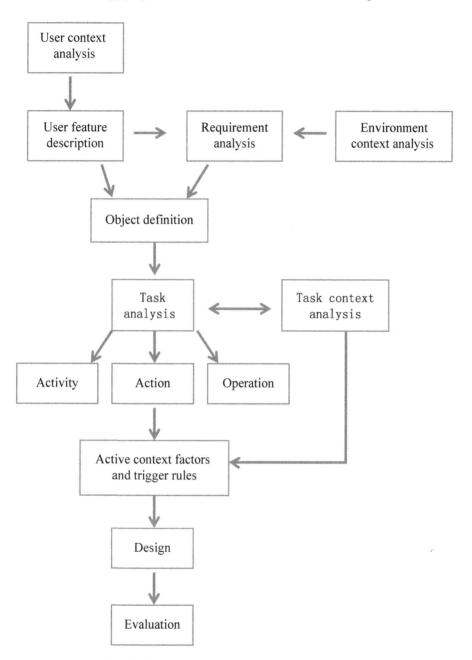

Fig. 5. Context awareness interaction design process.

(3) Design stage

At this stage, designers should not only consider the user and environmental factors, but also consider how under certain circumstance user behavior trigger corresponding active context factors. At the same time, system gives the users certain feedback. Therefore, users' expectation interaction model is mapped to context aware systems. Designers transform user model to different degree of concept model and user interface view, in which way setting up the context aware model of the system.

(4) Evaluation stage

After building design model, certain means and methods are needed to test whether conceptual model could meet the user's goal in certain context, including usability testing and experts' evaluation. Usability testing includes presenting design model user in front of the user, providing corresponding context factor. After simulating user to use, evaluation is made whether the corresponding trigger mechanism can trigger the operation. Expert assessment includes inviting context awareness expert to join the assessment team, according to their experience to review the design model, and point out the problem of the availability.

6   Conclusion

To narrow the distance between users' perception model and design model created by interaction designers, this study get through the theory of context awareness to figure out context factors. After describing information flow of context awareness human-computer interaction model and user behavior model, context awareness model was built. Trying to apply this model to interaction design process needs several adjustments within traditional design process, with was described in the past part of the study. Following new methods and process brought up in the study could let more context factors considered when designing now product and service, and bring users with context awareness system which more adjustable to their perception model.

References

1. Author, F.: Article title. Journal **2**(5), 99–110 (2016)
2. Author, F., Author, S.: Title of a proceedings paper. In: Editor, F., Editor, S. (eds.) CONFERENCE 2016, LNCS, vol. 9999, pp. 1–13. Springer, Heidelberg (2016)
3. Author, F., Author, S., Author, T.: Book title. 2nd edn. Publisher, Location (1999)
4. Author, F.: Contribution title. In: 9th International Proceedings on Proceedings, pp. 1–2. Publisher, Location (2010)
5. LNCS Homepage. http://www.springer.com/lncs. Accessed 21 Nov 2016

Human-Computer Interaction to Human-Computer-Context Interaction: Towards a Conceptual Framework for Conducting User Studies for Shifting Interfaces

Stephanie Van Hove[1]([⊠]), Jolien De Letter[1], Olivia De Ruyck[1],
Peter Conradie[1,2], Anissa All[1], Jelle Saldien[1], and Lieven De Marez[1]

[1] Department of Communication Sciences, imec-mict-UGent,
Ghent University, Ghent, Belgium
stephanie.vanhove@ugent.be
[2] Department of Industrial System and Product Design, Ghent University,
Kortrijk, Belgium

Abstract. Computer interfaces have been diversifying: from mobile and wearable technologies to the human body as an interface. Moreover, new sensing possibilities have allowed input to interfaces to go beyond the traditional mouse- and keyboard. This has resulted in a shift from manifest to latent interactions, where interactions between the human and the computer are becoming less visible. Currently, there is no framework available that fully captures the complexity of the multidimensional, multimodal, often latent interactions with these constantly shifting interfaces. In this manuscript, the Human-Computer-Context Interaction (HCCI) framework is proposed. This framework defines 5 relevant interaction levels to be considered during user research in all stages of the new product development process in order to optimize user experience. More specifically, the interaction context is defined in terms of user-object, user-user, user-content, user-platform and user-context interactions. The HCCI framework serves as a concrete tool to use in a new product development process by HCI researchers, designers, and developers and aims to be technology independent and future-proof. This framework is a preliminary suggestion to be matched against other innovation development projects and needs to be further validated.

Keywords: Human-computer interaction · Ubiquitous computing
Interaction context · User research · Product design · Product evaluation
Framework · User experience

1 Introduction

The level of computer soft- and hardware penetration in our everyday lives has rocketed throughout the recent decades. How we, as humans, interact with these computer-based applications has changed in many ways and has been the focus of

© Springer International Publishing AG, part of Springer Nature 2018
A. Marcus and W. Wang (Eds.): DUXU 2018, LNCS 10918, pp. 277–293, 2018.
https://doi.org/10.1007/978-3-319-91797-9_20

human-computer interaction research. In recent years, we have entered the third wave of computerization called ubiquitous computing [34]. More and more, computer interfaces get completely weaved into the fabric of the everyday lives of users, resulting in interactions outside of the traditional range of human-computer interaction. There has been a shift in objective where computers are not solely performance-oriented, aimed at increasing efficiency of certain tasks. Rather, computers are now also part of leisure, play, culture and art [27].

Concurrently, computer interfaces have been diversifying: while command line interfaces (CLIs) used to be the norm, new and alternative ways of interacting with computers have emerged, including wearable technologies attached to the human body. These new sensing possibilities have allowed input to interfaces to go beyond the traditional mouse- and keyboard [20]. As a consequence, computer interfaces have become multi-modal and embedded in our daily lives. This has resulted in a shift from manifest to latent interactions, where interactions between humans and computer interfaces are becoming less visible [27].

As a result, a complex interplay of interactions defines user experience [10]. In order to identify requirements for new digital products as well as to evaluate user experience, all relevant interactions should be taken into account when conducting user studies. While technology changed rapidly, the focus and methods of HCI research stayed on investigating performance-oriented explicit interactions, often not considering context [33]. The efficiency impact of new system features are, for example, often evaluated in a lab environment, while other external factors that are also important are overlooked. While in some cases increased efficiency and/or effectiveness can directly lead to a positive user experience, this is certainly not always true. Several studies found, for instance, no correlation between efficiency, effectiveness and user satisfaction [33]. Besides assessing a certain impact, it is thus also important to get a grasp on how interactions with a technology are experienced by the user himself. For this purpose, it is important to understand what actually contributes to a worthwhile, valuable experience [16]. In order to achieve this deeper understanding, it is important to identify which interactions are present in the environments where the technology will be used and how these interactions are related to user experience.

Currently, there is no framework available that fully captures the complexity of the multidimensional, multimodal, often latent interactions with these constantly shifting interfaces. Such a framework is, however, necessary as it will help user-centered design studies both in the pre-development stages as in the evaluation stages which ultimately will optimize the technologies. The present article takes a first step towards the development of such a conceptual framework that can serve as a guide for innovation research and is robust against future interfaces.

The development of such a framework is also required in order to develop a suitable methodological toolkit to fully capture interaction dimensions. As the traditional elements of interaction - being the user, the task at hand and the technology - no longer suffice to describe the complex interplay of interactions intrinsic to ubiquitous computing [24], a number of methodological weaknesses can be identified among current HCI frameworks.

Firstly, the ideation stage of innovation development - in which points of pain or goals have yet to be identified - is often very opaque [17]. A more systematic, validated approach grasping the ecosystem of a certain environment would allow for an adequate assessment of points of pain and potential solutions. The challenges associated with ideation are further compounded by the introduction of interfaces beyond the desktop [18].

Secondly, in testing phases to further optimize the technology, researchers always face the experimenter's dilemma in which they have to choose between internal and external validity [25]. Generally, when conducting experimental research the objective is to find an effect or relationship between the dependent variable and the independent variable(s) and generalize findings to a broader population or context [6]. There are two types of validity which contribute to this end-goal. Firstly, internal validity which refers to a controlled experiment design that warrants that changes in the dependent variable are strictly due to the manipulation in the independent variable and not due to extraneous variables (i.e., confounds). Secondly, external validity which is the generalizability of study findings to other populations (population validity), settings (ecological validity), times and measures [5, 6, 14]. Whereas lab experimentation disentangles causal relationships from mere incidental occurrences, field experiments and living lab studies include contextual elements that cannot be simulated in the laboratory. While the former type has high internal validity, due to the fact that the confounding variables are controlled, these do not include all variables influencing the user experience, which ultimately results in low ecological validity. For instance, context is often not taken into account in lab experiments [3, 33]. Field studies, on the other hand, result in higher ecological validity, but in this case, researchers cannot pinpoint what exactly contributed to the overall user experience [25]. While in case of lab studies, researchers know how internal validity can be increased (i.e., by reducing confounding variables), there are no recommendations as to how we could increase ecological validity in more controlled environments. It has, however, been acknowledged that when factors which influence user experience are taken into account in a laboratory setting, ecological validity rises [1, 25].

Hence, a framework that can help researchers and designers pinpoint those factors would allow them to implement a more holistic approach in all stages of a new product development process. This way, a more ecologically valid view on user experience is provided during all iteration stages of development and lab testing, resulting in an optimization of the technologies to be tested in real life environments.

The remainder of this paper is structured as follows. The next chapter will more thoroughly explore the changing nature of computing and, consequently, the changes in HCI theory and practice. Following this, we will introduce our proposed framework, supported with several case studies that illustrate how the framework should be used. We end with concluding remarks.

1.1 Shift from Human-Computer Interaction (HCI) to Human-Computer-Context Interaction (HCCI)

Computing has undergone three waves of transformation. Whereas first, interaction was most prominently through command line interfaces (CLIs), the increase in computing power enabled the introduction of graphical user interfaces (GUIs) that could be manipulated with peripherals such as computer mice [21]. More recently, we have seen the emergence of natural interfaces (NUI), aligning with Ishii's [19] view on tangle bits, where objects in our surroundings become interactive and where users interact with objects using voices and gestures [8]. A specific example of a mainstream NUI is the Kinect, which is a gaming device that reacts to body movement [36]. This shift from CLU to NUI similarly corresponds to the prediction that we are moving from a situation where one computer is used by many people, to where one person has many computing devices which are embedded in the people's daily routine to perform an automation of their environment [35]. This theory is put into practice by, for instance, automatic coffee makers that sense the environment through alarm clock signals and, consequently, start brewing coffee for its owners when the alarm clocks are triggered [23, 34]. According to Weiser [34] ubiquitous computing is meant to be an invisible, 'embodied virtuality' in which the technologies disappear as they weave themselves into the fabric of the everyday lives of users. The end-goal for these technologies, thus, is to become part of users' environments or contexts [34].

These three waves go together with a shift of interaction focus in HCI. In the so called "first wave of HCI" described by Bødker [4], researchers and practitioners focused on usability aspects. Interaction was considered a fairly simple concept: the unique observed user was interacting with one computer in one location, mostly in the context of work. The focus in this era was, thus, more on an interaction with an object or a system, in a controlled environment. In the "second wave", described by Bannon [2], the focus of research was communication and collaboration. This shows a shift towards a more human to human interaction or interactivity as a process rather than interactivity as a product [11]. In the current "third wave of HCI", again described by Bødker [4], the use context and application types are broader and intermixed. In contrary to the first and second waves focusing on the workspace, in the third wave technology has spread to our homes and got woven into the daily lives. This has resulted in a shift in research focus from technology and content to users and context or a shift from Human-Computer Interaction (HCI) to Human-Computer-Context Interaction (HCCI).

1.2   Current Limitations of User Research Methods in the New Product Development Process

The needs of users are an important starting point for HCI research and development. Through an ideation process, user needs can subsequently be translated into products. A variety of methods exist to achieve this, ranging from traditional focus groups [22], to co-creation sessions with end users [29]. However, as noted by Hribernik [18], ideation (in collaboration with users) in these dynamic environments is challenging because of the increasing complexity associated with systems that are used beyond the desktop. This is complicated further when considering that there remain differences between what users say when interviewed, what they do when observed and what they know or feel during a generative session [31].

By conducting an experiment, the effectiveness or efficacy of a new technology feature can be measured or tipping points of a certain technical parameters can be defined (i.e., finding an optimal balance between technological features and cost by pinpointing certain QoS levels that result in a significant increase or decrease in user experience). In HCI, due to the shift in interfaces, we also have witnessed a moving trend in experimentation context. In the past, HCI empirical work has been focused on the laboratory paradigm [24], where the controlled environment minimizes risk of contamination by extraneous variables and the internal validity is high, as explained in the introduction [6, 14, 26]. As the interaction between a user and a computer used to be more manifest, experiments could be confined to the controlled environment of a lab where a subject was given a task, a computer and an interactive system (the interface) [24]. However, as we have now entered the ubiquitous stage of computing where technology becomes an invisible, 'embodied virtuality' and interactions between user and technology have become latent [34], experimenting in the field is being more and more recommended as not all interaction levels with technology are reproducible in a controlled environment [24]. In turn, however, when testing in the field, researchers cannot fully control events. Nonetheless, field experiments or living lab tests should not be treated as 'blackbox' studies, but researchers should try to get a grasp on which contextual factors can influence the user experience when interacting with a certain technology and try to include or assess them in the experimentation environment.

1.3   Defining the Interaction Context

While there are several HCI frameworks available that provide insight in factors to take into account when developing and assessing user experience, these do not sufficiently provide researchers with concrete concepts that can cross-sectionally be used during a user study and be used for a wide range of technologies, let alone for technologies that still have to be developed. For instance, in a lot of frameworks 'context' is considered an important element, but

> "..is often formulated very vaguely or used as a container concept for various intangible aspects of factors influencing product use. Furthermore, context is often analyzed post-hoc, where for measurement purposes we need an upfront view on the specific context" [13].

An interesting framework (see Fig. 1), providing a more holistic view on user experience and especially on context, is the integrated QoE framework by Geerts and colleagues [13]. In this framework, context is divided into three relevant categories which influence the user experience of a technology: the broader socio-cultural context, the situational context of use, and the interaction context. The socio-cultural context refers to the context on a societal level (e.g. the social and cultural background of people). Situational context refers to (the interpretation of) situations and is a more local level of context (e.g., jointly watching a soccer match at home). The interaction context refers to the micro-level of context around the interaction between the user and the product (e.g., interaction of the user with the television, of the user with the other people watching the game and the home environment).

This framework is interesting for the further development of our HCCI framework, as it acknowledges that not only the relationship between the (technical aspects of an) ICT product and the user impact the user experience. The framework states that user experience is the result of an interplay of user characteristics, product characteristics and different contexts. For the purpose of our study, we are especially interested in the interactional context. More specifically, we aim to further specify concrete parameters

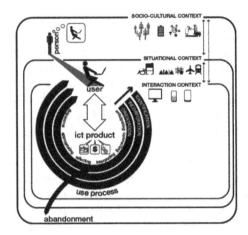

Fig. 1. Integrated QoE framework. Adapted from Geerst et al. [13]

that are part of this interaction context and that impact the user experience. For this purpose, we will develop sensitizing concepts (i.e., concepts that provide direction for research and analysis) in a framework that connect theory and design practice, facilitate idea generation and solution development and can be used by designers and researchers. The framework will fully capture the complexity of the multidimensional, often latent multimodal interactions and should, thus, be able to be implemented in:

- The ideation stage serving as a guide/checklist to analyze the ecosystem of the space in which the technology is being implemented in order to detect points of pain and potential solutions
- The conceptual development stage matching potential ideas against our framework in order to optimize design decisions
- Testing stages (both lab and field tests) serving as a guide to design user studies that are both high in internal and external validity in order to optimize technology before testing it in a real-world environment

For this purpose, we have done a post-hoc analysis of case studies in our research group where user research in the new product development process of ICT is the focus. More specifically, we looked into the issues that emerged during testing phases of mockups, prototypes or finished products due to overlooking relevant factors of the interactional context which influence the user experience from the beginning. Note that the presented concepts and framework is by no means complete or absolute, but rather serves as a preliminary suggestion to be matched against other innovation development projects and to be further validated and extended.

2   Results

Five interaction levels could be distinguished that can be considered relevant to take into account in the new product development process (Fig. 2). First a few remarks about the interactions defining the HCCI framework. In essence, each of the interactions can proceed in a digital or analogue way or with a digital or nondigital object. The motivation to regard both types of objects in the same way is the result of the recent shift to natural interfaces, but also with respect to possible future technologies. Since the line between digital and nondigital interfaces is slowly fading, it is important to enclose both in our framework. Further, an interaction is possible through one of the five senses and is always interpreted from the user's point of view: an interaction with a robot will be a user-user interaction if the user does not notice any difference from a human interaction. Finally, the interaction works both ways: when we talk about user-object interaction, the user can have an impact on an object (i.e., user sets the alarm on a smartphone) but the object can also have an impact on the user (i.e., the alarm wakes the user).

User-Object. Central in HCI research is the interaction between a user and a technology. In our HCCI framework this interaction is called the user-object interaction. Contrary to traditional HCI frameworks that tend to focus on the interaction a user has with a digital technology, in our framework user-object interaction can occur with both digital and nondigital objects (i.e. swiping a screen, or placing a RFID tagged book on a table).

User-User. A second interaction level addresses the interaction between one person, the user, and another nearby or computer-mediated communicator, resulting in a user-user interaction. The outcome of this interaction impacts the interaction with the technology when, for example, the user mutes an incoming call due to an already on-going face-to-face conversation.

User-Content. The next interaction, the user-content interaction, encompasses all the information and feedback the user perceives and processes. This information can either be presented in a digital (e.g., vibrating smart watch that wakes a user) or nondigital format (e.g., reading the wrapping of a chocolate bar). Similar to the user-user interaction, the nondigital content can be relevant for the interaction with the technology. The user-content interaction will always be the outcome of a user-object interaction.

User-Platform. Another interaction is the **user-platform** interaction. A digital object can interact with different types of platforms, i.e., back-end, server or cloud. The user can either directly interact with the platform (e.g., smartphone interface/OS) as indirectly (e.g., automated cloud service). The user-platform interaction plays an important role in the HCCI framework, as it provides a service to the user that is the result of a user-object or user-content interaction. The user-platform interaction will become apparent to the user if it failed to execute the service, or technological parameters (e.g., latency, update rate, accuracy) impacted the positive evaluation of the user-object or user-content interaction.

User-Context. The last interaction is the **user-context** interaction based on the interactional view of Dourish [9]. The context cannot be treated as static information, as it is the result of the user's internal (e.g., values, predispositions) and external characteristics (e.g., temporal, social context) [7]. From this point of view the user-context interaction comprises all contextual elements not central to the interaction, but moderating the interaction to some extent. For instance, when a user arrives home after dark, the light switches automatically on. In case the user arrives home before sunset, the light does not switch on. The context of arriving home after dark plays an important role on the outcome. In the next paragraphs the HCCI framework will be applied to three case studies, each having a different goal; developing a smart shopping cart, developing a festival bracelet, improving air quality awareness and defining a smart home concept.

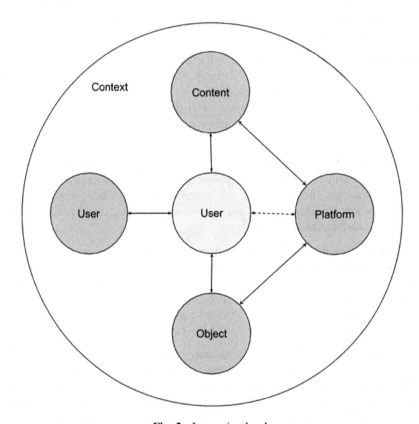

Fig. 2. Interaction levels

3 Case Studies

3.1 Smart Shopping Assistant

A research project in the retail context was directed by a technological and societal challenge. Whereas the technological challenge pointed towards the importance of developing an accurate and scalable solution for the real-time tracking of customers' shopping carts in retail markets, the societal challenge aimed at making the grocery shopping experience more efficient and enjoyable. Eventually, the research project resulted in a smart shopping cart with a touch screen built in the handle. The smart shopping cart guides the customers through the supermarket based on the position of the shopping cart in the supermarket and the customer's shopping list, and serves as an inspiration tool with contextual promotions, which results in a more efficient and enjoyable shopping experience. The project followed a mixed-method approach, consisting of five research steps that constitute the three aforementioned innovation process stages. In the ideation stage, an online survey (1) was conducted to delineate four personas. These personas were substantial to the innovation process since the needs and frustrations of each persona are associated with experience determinants. Thereafter, observations (2) were made in a real supermarket following the mystery shopper approach [30]. The conceptual development stage constituted of three co-creation workshops with customers and retail employees (3) that built on the insights of the observations and the sensitizing personas. Throughout these co-creation workshops we proceeded from an idea longlist over a feature shortlist to a visual concept (Fig. 3). The last testing stage proceeded in two steps. First, the 'smart' shopping cart was evaluated by the end-user using the Wizard of Oz methodology (4) (in this type of testing the researcher (or "Wizard") simulates the user-platform to make the participants believe they are interacting with a working prototype [15], and eye-tracking technology in a real supermarket ($N = 18$) (Fig. 4). After having improved the concept based on the findings of the Wizard of Oz implementation, the concept was implemented and experimentally evaluated in a mockup retail store ($N = 59$) (5). In this field experiment two use cases of the smart shopping cart were evaluated; the display-service of, on the one hand, the location of the users and the products on their shopping list and, on the other hand, the contextual promos (Fig. 5).

Due, but also thanks to the followed mixed-method approach, not all interaction levels emerged in all five research steps. However, as the project proceeded, it became clear that particular interaction levels were more important than others. In general, four relevant interaction levels guided the outcome of the project, but also the constitution of the Human-Computer-Context Interaction Framework. The most remarkable interaction level turned out to be the user-user interaction. Firstly, the observations (2) showed that the social context of grocery shopping could not be ignored. For example a baby or partner often joined the grocery shopping trip. However, none of the co-creation participants (2) mentioned the importance of being accompanied by their significant others, nor the possibility of meeting people in the supermarket due to recall bias. Secondly, in the lab testing step (5) a minority of participants brought a family member with them to co-experience the experiment, although people were personally invited to participate individually in the lab test. The researchers opted for a quasi-experimental design, because they wanted to control as many confounding factors as possible. As a result everyone had to experience the shopping journey individually, without the co-presence of others who could impact their decision-making. Retrospectively, after having established the HCCI framework, the researchers and the designers would have attached more importance to the user-user interaction throughout the entire project. Taking the user research stance, it would have been more beneficial that co-creation participants reflected on the impact of the user-user interaction on the design, also alternative research question should have been addressed in the lab test. However, thanks to the triangulation of multiple methods the user-to-user interaction appeared multiple times. This definitely impacted future versions of the smart shopping cart, e.g., screen won't be integrated in the child seat of the shopping cart and exploration of other interaction types besides touch, such as sound, vibration, ... or more bold and explicit user interface, as people accompanied by others tend to look less to the shopping cart screen.

Another relevant interaction level in the multisensory journey of grocery shopping appeared to be the user-object interaction. This interaction level applies to the interplay between a user on the one hand and a tangible and/or digital object on the other. Firstly, in the observations (2) it appeared that people keep on interacting with physical objects all the time in a supermarket; smelling flowers or herbs, holding shopping list in mouth, meanwhile using smartphone, navigating shopping cart or holding basket, holding two products to compare info, hunting for the freshest vegetables, preparing loyalty cards, cash and bags when queuing at the checkout, etc. This impacted the design of the shopping assistant, resulting in the implementation of the screen in the shopping cart handle and not in the shopper's smartphone as having to carry another item in your hand would negatively impact the user experience. Secondly, once the first proof of concept was developed, it was tested in a real supermarket following the Wizard of Oz approach (3). However, this concept appeared to be too intrusive. The main interaction during this grocery shopping trip was the touch interaction on the shopping cart screen and afterwards people said they were missing out on interacting with the others in the supermarket. This shows that the designers falsely assumed that the user-to-object interaction (i.e., touch screen interaction) could easily replace the user-user interaction. Interaction levels are never isolated, but often directly impact other interaction levels too. As a result, a ranking of the different interaction levels based on their importance in the overall experience should follow each research step and be reexamined afterwards.

A third interaction level, user-context interaction emerged with the triangulation of the personas delineated in the survey (1) on the one hand and the Wizard of Oz implementation (4) and lab test (5) on the other. One persona of the survey (1), Efficient Eden, is most disturbed with the check-out queue, difficult products to find, and the other customers present in the store. It follows that, during the Wizard of Oz test (4), Efficient Eden was more intolerant towards crowdedness in the store or shelf reorganizations, as he could not find a specific product. In contrast, for the lab test (5), participants were invited to a demo supermarket, which is both a controlled research setting, but relevant to the users to interact with [12]. In this demo supermarket, Efficient Eden (a persona within the study) was more tolerant towards the research context of the field experiment than he was in his habitual supermarket. Probably, the difference between the demo supermarket and a real supermarket paved the way for his tolerance; the demo store has a smaller surface than a real supermarket, the supermarket layout is different, and employees are missing.

The forth interaction level, user-platform, sheds light on the technical parameters underlying the concept infrastructure. This type of interaction only appeared in the testing phase. In the Wizard of Oz implementation (4), people were bothered with the delay between the "contextual" promos they received on the shopping cart screen and the actual position of the shopping cart that was already five meters further. This delay was the result of incorrect wizard behavior and system delay. Finding that people are intolerant of delay guided the scope of the lab test (5) to evaluate two latency levels next to features inherent to the concept.

Fig. 3. Participant cutting out the features defining the smart shopping cart in a co-creation workshop

Fig. 4. Wizard of Oz test with the participant wearing eye-tracking glasses and the Wizard (women in black) coordinating the smart shopping cart screen

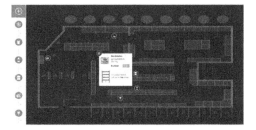

Fig. 5. Printscreen of the smart shopping cart application with the shopping list products positioned on the supermarket map. When the shopping cart (blue dot) gets nearby a product, more information is provided on the price, number and shelf position of the product. (Color figure online)

3.2 Festival Bracelet of the Future

In a study that aimed to develop the festival bracelet of the future, research, technical and commercial partners aimed towards the development of a wearable that enhanced the whole festival experience during the festival, but also resulted in a longer 'post-festival' experience. For this purpose, users were involved in focus groups (ideation) and co-creation sessions (conceptualization) to develop a first prototype. This resulted in a prototype that was tested during the festival. User evaluation on the bracelet and the features were gathered during the festival by means of interviews every 2 h and experience sampling every hour. Six weeks after the festival, a follow-up debriefing sessions was organized. Based on this input, the bracelet was further optimized to again be tested at the festival the next year.

During the ideation phases with participants and conceptualization phases with the partners within the project, the focus was mainly on user-user interaction and user-object interaction. This resulted in 2 main features that were integrated in the first prototype that was tested at the festival: a) a friending feature, connecting festival goers with each other on social media (user-user) by simultaneously clicking on a button on the bracelet and b) cashless payments (user-object) by scanning the bracelet against a pay scanner that can be found at bars or top-up booths. When developing these features in the conceptualization and prototyping phase, an important interaction level that was not taken into account, was user-content. With regard to the friend feature, participants mentioned during the evaluations that they would like to get feedback from the bracelet when the befriending had succeeded by for instance letting the led light integrated in the bracelet turn green. With regard to the cashless payments, participants did not know how much money they were spending or what their balance was, leading to frustration. The only possible way of knowing their balance was to scan their bracelet against the scanners only available at the bar or top-up booths. Therefore, in the next phase the friending feedback mechanism was integrated and an application was linked to the bracelet to check and top up the balance.

With the cashless payments feature, another significant interaction level was overlooked during the ideation and development phase: user-user. More specifically, participants found it very annoying that now, everyone had to get their own drink as it was not possible to transfer drink vouchers to each other, a common user-user interaction which was possible with cash or paper drink vouchers, resulting in large lines at the bar.

If we had used the HCCI framework during the ideation and conceptualization phase for every separate feature, these were issues we would have come across beforehand and would have tackled them before implementing the first prototype at the actual festival. For instance by mapping all interaction levels involved for several situational contexts related to getting a drink at a festival without the cashless feature (ideation phase) and with the cashless feature (conceptualization phase).

One feature that was already present in a previous version of the bracelet (before the project had started) was an integrated led light. The led light was supposed to light up according to the beat of the song that was being played. However, because a festival site is a chaotic environment (large number of people, few network facilities and interference) this did not work very well, leaving users confused and not really understanding the purpose of the led light. Hence, a major goal of this project was to define a latency level between the actual beat and the lighting up of the led light (user-platform) that would still allow for a good user experience of the feature. However, we encountered serious issues when wanting to test this, as a result of not being able to include the user-context interaction level.

In the end, we had to conclude that it was impossible to test this as neither a lab setting nor a field trial could be used. In a lab setting, none of the context variables influencing the experience could be made available, such as a large crowd wearing the same bracelets and thus a large amount of led lights turning on and off again on the beat. In a living lab setting, it was impossible to manipulate latency as the only possible field test we could do, was during the festival itself and this was not something the festival organizers want to experiment with, risking to 'ruin' the user experience when testing with too low latency levels. Even if the festival organizers would allow it, it would have been impossible to assess QoE during several levels of latency as you would want to keep the DJ and song preferably the same when varying latency levels, as content would probably influence QoE. This shows that not only defining relevant interaction levels that can influence user experience is important, but we also need to get insight in which ones are difficult to implement in user studies in order to develop suitable methodologies. For instance, in this case, the solution could be using virtual reality to be able to capture the user-context interaction in order to define optimal latency levels between this user-platform interaction.

3.3 Air Quality Measurement

Our efforts to make buildings more energy-efficient and airtight had a negative effect on the air quality inside the house and pollutants are trapped inside the building. To get a deeper understanding of the different elements which can improve the users' knowledge of air pollution in his home, a multi-method study was set up. An air quality sensor and a smartphone app would be developed to inform the inhabitants of the air quality and how they could improve it.

In the ideation phase, a co-creation session was held to identify the current and future needs around air quality measurement and possible new features. The focus of this workshop laid on the content and the platform of the new tool to inform the inhabitants *(what information should they get?, which type of messages?)*. No attention was given to the interaction with the context *(where do people measure the air? at which moment don't I want to be disturbed?)*; the object *(where will we place the air quality sensor?, how should it look like?)*; nor to the other users *(what will multiple users like to see?, how will they interact?)*.

During the concept phase, a proxy technology study (PTA) with an existing air quality sensor took place in 11 homes over a period of 4 weeks. During this time the families could use an air quality sensor and report their findings in a diary. The study was organized in order to get insights on the interaction with the context *(where do people measure the air?, when?)* and interaction with the object *(Is the display clear to understand?)*. No special attention was given to the interaction with the platform or other users. Qualitative interviews at the end of the test period revealed insights which would not have been obtained when holding this experiment in a lab context instead of in a real home situation.

We see that due to the lack of a methodology to evaluate interactions, several interactions were not taken into account during different development phases. A framework including these 5 interactions would have avoided to overlook them and would create a more user friendly product. For instance, the user-platform interaction was overlooked, which resulted in a sensor which was limited by the availability of sockets and WIFI in the home. A lack of sockets in e.g. the cellar or bedrooms contributed to the lack of knowledge about inferior air quality in these rooms. A final design of the air quality sensor with batteries or modem could solve this problem.

Another missed interaction was the user-context. The app sent push notifications at night which woke up the users who were, as a result, dissatisfied about the product. Designing the app taking the context of the night into account would have created a better product.

4   Discussion

The present article presents a preliminary framework to define interaction contexts of current and future technologies. More specifically, this paper has shown that five relevant interaction levels can be defined that can influence the user experience with a technology: user-user, user-content, user-object, user-platform and user-context. By implementing this framework in all stages of the new product development process, a more holistic approach for conducting user studies will be achieved.

The HCCI framework can be used in three ways. Firstly, it can be used to define the interaction context of existing objects that are the target of innovation. For instance, in order to define users' current points of pain manufacturers who want to develop a smart kitchen use the framework to get insight into which interaction levels are important influencers of how a user interacts with a kitchen hood. Once these points of pain have been established, the framework can be used during idea generation by, for instance, looking for technology-enhanced solutions along all these interaction levels. Secondly, the framework can be used to optimize technology features and design in a concep-tualization and prototyping phase, taking into account all relevant interaction levels when working out certain features. For instance, when designing the cashless payment feature in the festival bracelet, by mapping how it impacts other relevant interaction levels in the situational context of going to a festival with a group of people (e.g., user-user interaction where users give each other money or drinking vouchers so that one person can get drinks for a group of people). Thirdly, the framework can be used to design studies to test and optimize technology in a more controlled environment in order to increase ecological validity. For instance, in our shopping assistant case study, taking into account the impact of shopping together (user-user) on the effectiveness of a pop-up contextual advertisement.

The HCCI framework serves as a concrete tool to use in a new product develop-ment process by HCI researchers, designers, and developers. Our framework aims to be technology independent and future-proof. The decomposition of the object-, user-, content-, platform- and context-interactions can be explored, designed, and evaluated in different technologies (e.g., IoT, virtual and augmented reality, or even innovation triggers such as brain-computer interfaces) [32]. These technologies are expressions of a shift from manifest to latent interfaces and interactions. The HCCI framework helps designers and digital product engineers take relevant interactions into account in order to reveal gaps for new interaction techniques, methods and platforms.

The case studies in the present manuscript have shown that in ideation and concept development stages the focus was primarily on the user-content and/or user-object interaction. However, in the technology evaluation stage, it became apparent that the user-platform, user-user, and user-context interactions were disregarded, yet decisive in the user experience. Furthermore, from the case studies we saw that some methodological issues arose due to the difficulty to simulate all interactions in all innovation stages. Similar to the festival bracelet of the future research project which failed to test the latency levels of the led light in the bracelets on the beat of the music (i.e., user-platform), we expect that simulating user-user and user-context interactions (e.g., large crowds) will be challenging. Lastly, viewing the three case studies through our framework demonstrated that not all interactions are always relevant when using a technology.

5   Limitations and Further Research

Although we believe that this framework serves as a valuable tool throughout the entire new product development process, it certainly has its limitations. Firstly, no systematic analysis of current HCI frameworks and HCI user studies has been conducted in order to initially define certain levels of the interaction context with technological products. Traditionally, HCI frameworks seem to rely on compiled theoretical foundation or on lab-based research [28], but the recent shift in interfaces and interactions (e.g., embodied interactions, sensor-based interactions) complicates this. The interaction levels proposed in this manuscript have been defined bottom-up and inductively by several researchers involved in new product development user research, based on several case studies. The framework is, therefore, only a preliminary suggestion on defining the interaction context with new products and is definitely non-exhaustive. Further validation of this framework is required by systematic implementation in future research projects to provide evidence for the comprehensiveness of the interaction levels, and to address possible vague conceptualizations.

Future research should not only focus on further conceptual validation of the framework, but also search for appropriate methodologies on how to include the interaction levels in different phases of the research process. For instance, investigating opportunities of virtual reality to simulate relevant context variables, such as a large crowd at a festival stage or investigating the use of certain existing technologies such as Alexa in ideation stages to get insight in how user-platform interactions should be defined. In doing this our framework aims to provide guidelines to researchers as well as to designers to be able to use the HCCI framework the appropriate way.

References

1. All, A., Looy, J.V., Castellar, E.N.: Digital game-based learning under the microscope. Development of a procedure for assessing the effectiveness of educational games aimed at cognitive learning outcomes. University Press (2016)

2. Bannon, L.J.: From human factors to human actors: the role of psychology and human-computer interaction studies in system design. In: Readings in Human–Computer Interaction, pp. 205–214 (1995). https://doi.org/10.1016/B978-0-08-051574-8.50024-8

3. Bargas-Avila, J.A., Hornbæk, K.: Old wine in new bottles or novel challenges. In: Proceedings of the 2011 Annual Conference on Human Factors in Computing Systems - CHI 2011, p. 2689 (2011). https://doi.org/10.1145/1978942.1979336

4. Bødker, S.: When second wave HCI meets third wave challenges. In: Proceedings of the 4th Nordic Conference on Human-Computer Interaction Changing Roles - NordiCHI 2006, pp. 1–8 (2006). https://doi.org/10.1145/1182475.1182476

5. Calder, B.J., Phillips, L.W., Tybout, A.M.: The concept of external validity. J. Consum. Res. 9(3), 240 (1982). https://doi.org/10.1086/208920

6. Campbell, D.T., Stanley, J.C.: Experimental and Quasi-Experimental Designs for Research. Houghton Mifflin Company, Boston (1963)

7. Coorevits, L., Jacobs, A.: Taking real-life seriously: an approach to decomposing context beyond " environment" in living labs. Technol. Innov. Manag. Rev. 7(1), 26–36 (2017)

8. van Dam, A.: Post-WIMP user interfaces. Commun. ACM 40(2), 63–67 (1997). https://doi.org/10.1145/253671.253708

9. Dourish, P.: What we talk about when we talk about context. Pers. Ubiquit. Comput. 8(1), 19–30 (2004). https://doi.org/10.1007/s00779-003-0253-8

10. Dubois, E., Celentano, A.: Analysing interaction trajectories in multi-device applications. In: Proceedings of the 9th Nordic Conference on Human-Computer Interaction - NordiCHI 2016, pp. 1–6 (2016). https://doi.org/10.1145/2971485.2996726

11. Egger, S., Reichl, P., Schoenenberg, K.: Quality of experience and interactivity. In: Möller, S., Raake, A. (eds.) Quality of Experience. TSTS, pp. 149–161. Springer, Cham (2014). https://doi.org/10.1007/978-3-319-02681-7_11

12. Evans, D.: In virtual reality, women run the world. http://nymag.com/thecut/2016/09/virtual-reality-women-run-the-world-c-v-r.html?mid=huffpost_women-pubexchange_facebook

13. Geerts, D., De Moor, K., Ketyko, I., Jacobs, A., Van den Bergh, J., Joseph, W., Martens, L., De Marez, L.: Linking an integrated framework with appropriate methods for measuring QoE. In: 2010 Second International Workshop on Quality of Multimedia Experience (QoMEX), pp. 158–163 (2010). https://doi.org/10.1109/QOMEX.2010.5516292

14. Gliner, J.A.: Internal and external validity in two studies that compared treatment methods. Am. J. Occup. Ther. 43(6), 403–407 (1989). https://doi.org/10.5014/ajot.43.6.403. Official Publication of the American Occupational Therapy Association

15. Hanington, B., Martin, B.: Universal methods of design: 100 ways to research complex problems (2012). https://www.iitgn.ac.in/sites/default/files/library_files/2016/04072016.pdf %5Cnpapers3://publication/uuid/FD316216-3845-47B5-B7DA-0E68CD4B3014

16. Hassenzahl, M., Diefenbach, S., Göritz, A.: Needs, affect, and interactive products - facets of user experience. Interact. Comput. 22(5), 353–362 (2010). https://doi.org/10.1016/j.intcom.2010.04.002

17. Hesmer, A., Hribernik, K.A., Baalsrud Hauge, J.M., Thoben, K.D.: Supporting the ideation processes by a collaborative online based toolset. Int. J. Technol. Manag. 55(3/4), 218 (2011). https://doi.org/10.1504/IJTM.2011.041948

18. Hribernik, K.A., Ghrairi, Z., Hans, C., Thoben, K.-D.: Co-creating the internet of things - first experiences in the participatory design of intelligent products with Arduino. In: 2011 17th International Conference on Concurrent Enterprising (ICE), pp. 1–9 (2011)

19. Ishii, H.: The tangible user interface and its evolution. Commun. ACM 51(6), 32 (2008). https://doi.org/10.1145/1349026.1349034

20. Koreshoff, T.L., Leong, T.W., Robertson, T.: Approaching a human-centred internet of things. In: Proceedings of the 25th Australian Computer-Human Interaction Conference on Augmentation, Application, Innovation, Collaboration - OzCHI 2013, pp. 363–366 (2013). https://doi.org/10.1145/2541016.2541093

21. Kortum, P.: HCI Beyond the GUI: Design for Haptic, Speech, Olfactory, and Other Nontraditional Interfaces. Techniques, p. 462 (2008). http://www.amazon.de/dp/0123740177

22. McQuarrie, E.: Focus groups and the development of new products by technologically driven companies: some guidelines. J. Prod. Innov. Manag. 3(1), 40–47 (1986). https://doi.org/10.1016/0737-6782(86)90042-1

23. Mosbergen, D.: This Luxury Alarm Clock Wakes You Up With A Freshly Brewed Cup Of Coffee. The Huffington Post (2014). http://www.huffingtonpost.com/2014/08/05/alarm-clock-coffee-barisieur_n_5651014.html

24. Oulasvirta, A.: Field experiments in HCI: Promises and challenges (2009). https://doi.org/10.1007/978-1-84800-385-9-5

25. Oulasvirta, A., Tamminen, S., Roto, V., Kuorelahti, J.: Interaction in 4-second bursts. In: Proceedings of the SIGCHI Conference on Human Factors in Computing Systems - CHI 2005, p. 919 (2005). https://doi.org/10.1145/1054972.1055101

26. Parsons, T.D.: Virtual reality for enhanced ecological validity and experimental control in the clinical, affective and social neurosciences. Front. Hum. Neurosci. 9, 660 (2015). https://doi.org/10.3389/fnhum.2015.00660

27. Poppe, R., Rienks, R., van Dijk, B.: Evaluating the future of HCI: challenges for the evaluation of emerging applications. In: Huang, Thomas S., Nijholt, A., Pantic, M., Pentland, A. (eds.) Artifical Intelligence for Human Computing. LNCS (LNAI), vol. 4451, pp. 234–250. Springer, Heidelberg (2007). https://doi.org/10.1007/978-3-540-72348-6_12

28. Rogers, Y.: HCI theory: classical, modern, and contemporary. Synth. Lect. Hum.-Centered Inform. 5(2), 1–129 (2012)

29. Sanders, E.B.-N., Stappers, P.J.: Co-creation and the new landscapes of design. CoDesign 4(1), 5–18 (2008). https://doi.org/10.1080/15710880701875068

30. Sinha, P.K., Uniyal, D.P.: Using observational research for behavioural segmentation of shoppers. J. Retail. Consum. Serv. 12(1), 35–48 (2005). https://doi.org/10.1016/j.jretconser.2004.02.003

31. Visser, F.S., Stappers, P.J., van der Lugt, R., Sanders, E.B.-N.: Contextmapping: experiences from practice. CoDesign 1(2), 119–149 (2005). https://doi.org/10.1080/15710880500135987

32. Walker, M.J.: Hype Cycle for Emerging Technologies 2017, July 2017. www.gartner.com

33. Wechsung, I., De Moor, K.: Quality of experience versus user experience. In: Möller, S., Raake, A. (eds.) Quality of Experience. TSTS, pp. 35–54. Springer, Cham (2014). https://doi.org/10.1007/978-3-319-02681-7_3

34. Weiser, M.: The computer for the 21st century. Sci. Am. (Int. Ed.) 265(3), 66–75 (1991). https://doi.org/10.1038/scientificamerican0991-94

35. Weiser, M., Brown, J.S.: The coming age of calm technology. In: Denning, P.J., Metcalfe, R.M. (eds.) Beyond Calculation, pp. 75–85. Springer, New York (1997). https://doi.org/10.1007/978-1-4612-0685-9_6

36. Wenkai, X., Lee, E.-J.: Human-computer natural user interface based on hand motion detection and tracking. J. Korea Multimedia Soci. 15(4), 501–507 (2012). https://doi.org/10.9717/kmms.2012.15.4.501

Experience Design of the Immersive Film: Panoramic View and Interactive Narratives

Feng Ye[(⌧)]

Digital Media School, Beijing Film Academy, Beijing 100088, China
510863715@qq.com

Abstract. When the immersive filmwork is experienced by the audiences with head-mounted display,the interactive experience of immersive images lies in that the audiences (users) need to be part of the story in terms of the visual perception experience and the story emotional experience. Construction of interactive narration and the free perspective of panoramic view creates a new mode of narrative experience. The immersive interactive film provide the audiences with a free moving perspective to observe and experience the story in a natural way. The scene narrative has been main moth of immersive film storytelling. The audio-visual sense and the boundless perspective realize the immersion of sense organs, and achieves the realistic experience of a higher level. And the experience relation among audience, image media and image content are be changed.

Keywords: Immersive · Panoramic view · Interactive narratives

1 Introduction

The immersive filmwork is required to be a panorama video, and the finished work needs to be experienced by the audiences with head-mounted display. Compared with the plane images familiar to us, the immersive film are brand new from the shooting and post production tools to record shooting idea, which shall be explored and thought in terms of technology, expression language and work positioning from a brand new perspective. Undoubtedly, the immersive film with the head-mounted display as the hardware platform is a new audiovisual medium, just as what Frank Rose, the author of the Art of Immersion: How the Digital Generation is Remaking Hollywood, Madison Avenue, and the Way We Tell Stories, thought about, "every new medium brings about a new narrative form" [1], in my opinion, apart from narrative form, the experience appeal of immersive film are also different from those of other media.

The way the story is presented and the form to accept the story change accordingly as the narrative media transforms. The literary narration of the humans has a long history, from dictation to instant communication on the Internet, from frescoes in the temple to book printing and from cave painting to virtual images. For the communication pattern and acceptance experience of the story, the development of the science and technology promotes the transformation of the narrative media. The humans evolve from listening to stories to watching stories and then to experiencing stories. The receivers of the story may cover the listeners, readers and audiences. As far as the

A. Marcus and W. Wang (Eds.): DUXU 2018, LNCS 10918, pp. 294–305, 2018.
https://doi.org/10.1007/978-3-319-91797-9_21

narrative experience of immersive images is concerned, several types of receivers, who provide more comprehensive synthetic perceptual experience or can be said to be the complete experiencers of the priming and undergoing of the story of the virtual world, could be covered.

Reading, listening and watching and other measures to accept the story have their respective experience modes and effects. Relative to reading, the readers unscramble the abstract writing language and proactively motivate their pre-existing life experiences to integrate and imagine the content of the book and their personal affective experience in the brain. However, painting and film with the way of experience based on watching provide the audiences with more intuitive visual effect. Most of the audiences are undergone the passive feedback within the specified content domain of the images. The interactive experience of immersive images lies in that the audiences (users) need to be part of the story in terms of the visual perception experience and the story emotional experience.

2 A Free Perspective Creates a New Mode of Narrative Experience

Immersive image is a kind of new mode of graphic narration, as it provides a free and mobile perspective to observe the world. The tradition painting and images both have the visual boundary, however immersive images attempt to eliminate this boundary, that is, the media is eliminated when the audiences receive the narration and the audiences then obtain the audio visual experience similar to the real world.

The process to experience the immersive interactive film works is characterized by the elimination of the existence of the media.

Comparatively speaking, such narrative media as fresco, book and film fully stress on the existence form of the media itself in terms of the design of narrative experience. The temple frescoes require the decorative design of the temple space, the books would take into account the texture and thickness of the paper for printing and the films would emphasize more on the environmental construction of the cinema. To a large extent, the experience of the design content and effect of the narrative media is an important part of the narrative experience. However, the experience of immersive images prefer to stress on the experience appeal to eliminate the existence of the media itself during the process of narrative experience.

All of the images face a certain problem—how to make the time and space reappear. All the narrative media organize the time and space in an orderly manner, based on which the story is presented to the audiences. Interaction creatively designs the time and space and triggers different narrative structures through the watch and selection of the story-telling scene space. For example, the audiences turn the neck and focus on the content of a certain scene space with the plot development and changes or the scene control of the actor-driven performance. The film may trigger different plots depending on the focus of the audiences on the plot and the time duration, while the maker of the film can lead the audiences to focus on some plots intentionally through the audio-visual elements, so as to push the narration forward according to the director's intentions. The leadership of attention by the maker and the subjective selection of the audiences jointly form the process of the interactive narration. Comprehending from this perspective, the self-directed interactive narration experience space provided by the immersive interactive film is up to the maker to a large extent. The criterion of the spatial scale of the interactive narration that the audiences independently control, the control of the intensity of the leading narration with the maker at its core and the relationship between both of them, namely the treatment of the triadic relation between the audiences and the maker, are the most subtle and best embodiment of the artistic level of the maker on narration by the immersive interactive video art creation.

Hockney, a famous artist, once said [2], "This is the case with all pictures, all of which are drawn from a particular perspective. We view the world in the way of our own, even if it's a small square object. For example, different people have different opinion on a small box. When walking into a room, every one notices different things by his unique feeling, memory and interest."

When we are in the borderless story space as a whole that has not been cut, we would observe this scene and find our own interest point by following our heart, to further build the story world of our own, therefore the story truly lives in our heart. The experience relation among audience, image media and image content have be rebuild in immersive film art.

2.1   Free Perspective of Panoramic View Promote Natural Experience

Generally, immersive images do not edit the time and space in a single plot. Without the picture frame and the directional cutting and combination of montage, it in turn provides a more intense time-space reality. This natural reality, in addition to the real experience of the sense organs in a single vanishing point of perspective on screen texture, light and resolution offered by the traditional painting and 2D images, provides the sense of reality on space-time dimension, more importantly. The immersive images provide the audiences with the time-space dimension that allows them to freely move the perspective to watch the screen and receive the narration in a panoramic image space, and such an experience is closer to the real world.

The realistic perspective is in line with the physiological and psychological characteristics of watching. While looking around and staring, the point of sight (attention) moves with the inner experience and the trigger in the scene, forming the moving first perspective. In 2D video, we watch the screen in the way of focus perspective born with the video camera. However, we may watch in the psychological way in the immersive interactive film works and stay out of the control of field of shooting scale and film editing, thus receiving and promoting the narration from a free perspective. At this time, the image composition changes due to the change of the audience's perspective, forming a mobile experience process. In reality, instead of looking at the world from a fixed point of view like a video camera, we keep turning our eyes and body to search the important and interesting information one after another. Because of the panoramic visual space, the immersive images provide the audiences with the habit to see things, haul the audiences into the story scenes and enhance the sense of immediacy that the audiences experience the story.

The traditional Chinese painting enjoys the way of experiencing the story similar to that provided by immersive film artistic works through a mobile perspective. The picture formed by "cavalier perspective" adopted in the traditional Chinese landscape paintings requires the appreciation of the moving focus. The viewer's eyes move on the picture as if traveling between the landscapes. Like the way we usually look at landscapes, we always look at landscapes in landscapes. Viewers enter in to the scenes of the picture with the unfolding of the Chinese hand-rolled landscape paintings, as if the viewers walk in the mountains and experience a tour crossing time. However, the audiences are always excluded from the scene of the picture, in the paintings and images with a fixed vanishing point of perspective.

The immersive interactive images provide the audiences with a free moving perspective to observe and experience the story in a natural way. The art of video pursues "natural realism" in time and space and creates experiences of specific scenes through narration. Compared to painting and 2D video, the immersive interactive film works is more realistic in terms of the degree of freedom of viewing perspective and the integrity of time and space of the story. As we use the way of perspective to make the spatial performance effects of the picture closer to the real environment that we see with one eye in terms of art of painting, the immersive images pursue the similarity between the sense judgment of the works and the experience of the audiences for the real world as far as possible.

Guo Xi (nearly 1001–1090) pondered over painting completely from the perspective of mountains. In his opinion, the mountains are high and far, meaning "looking up to the top of the mountain from the bottom", deep and far—"peeping the back of the mountain from the front of the mountain" and flat and far—"looking at the distant mountain from the nearby mountain".

Hockney once said [3], "Naturally, there is a problem on what you see first, what you see secondly and what you see thirdly when people look at scenes. For a photo, all things are seen at the first sight, and the camera shoots from a perspective. People do not look at things in this way. It takes time to see, and the space is thus created."

2.2   The Combination of Immersion and Interaction Makes the Experience of Immersive Film Closer to Natural Reality

With the behavioral reality, the users drive the occurrence, change and development of the event and obtain the narration experience in the anticipation and surprise, as the plot logic is in line with the audience's psychological rhythm. The user is placed in the story itself with the trigger of the event and the promotion of the narration. Compared with being an onlooker, it's the best narrative experience to live in it. The synaesthetic experience pursued by interactive design works is realized in the narrative art to the utmost extent. In the process of designing empathy, the artist's design of the experiential relationship between the works and the audience is of great importance. In the interactive experience of the immersive images, synaesthesia is the artistic experience generated by the substituting relation of the interactive design results based on empathy in the audience and works. This kind of sense of synaesthesia close to the elimination of media is just the most unique charm of the immersive interactive images.

The realistic sense of art experience is one of the most important experiences pursued by visual art creation. And the art form that stresses the intuitive expression visually requires the sense of reality in language arts and effects as a matter of course.

The more true the more intuitive, naturally, the stronger the sense of substitution. Visual art, which is characterized by intuitive experience, can only form a complete artistic expression if it's true and thus the audiences can accept and recognize the narration psychologically and be touched, so as to achieve the original intention of the artistic works. In the experience design of video art creation, it is not only the realistic effect of the audio-visual and sensory effects presented by the medium of the works, but also the degree of emotional engagement in the experience process of the works by the audiences, as well as the audio-visual perception, emotion and sentiment experience relationship between the audience and the works of art. In terms of the experience form of the works by the audience, is it the face-to-face relationship between the eyes and screen? Or in terms of the audience's psychology, the individual is in the same entirety of the time and space of the works? The experience form of immersive interactive images realies the latter and the sense of reality achieved by the experience result is far more than other existing narrative media. At the cinema, the mood of the audience will not change the image on the screen anyway. No matter how sad or joyful, the emotion of the reader will not change the changing story and the role behaviors in the book. However, in the immersive interactive artistic works of video, the panorama images with immersion wrap the audience, and the visual boundary of the medium is eliminated and the real environment is replaced by the world of immersive images, while the emotion and reaction of the audience will have a mutual relation and affection with the rhythm and perspective of the plot of the works. The sense of reality, through the language of interaction and immersive images, integrates the audience and the works as a whole and realizes the seamless joint of emotion and the works. The audio-visual sense and the boundless perspective realize the immersion of sense organs, and achieves the realistic experience of a higher level.

The form to experience the works by the audiences is interaction rather than watching. And it's more than watching from a certain distance. Because the audiences will interactively control the works according to the change of the narrative process of the immersive images and the will of subjective emotion, rather than accept the audio-visual information of the works passively, the narrative form and language of immersive interactive images are bound to be different from those of novels and films and other watching and reading narration works. At this time, we need to understand the original significance of narration, that is to say, we try to empathize the audiences through the artistic media and language and achieve the goal that the audiences obtain the thematic affective experience. In the artistic works of immersive interactive images, on the one hand, the audiences accept the elements used for the purpose of empathizing and realize the emotional substitution visually and behaviorally through the interaction via self-behavior, and forget oneself in reality in the immersive image space that is panoramic to be "me" in the narrative plot of the works. This "me" is the art of me, not infected with someone and the "me" in the works. This me is the performance of me in the works context who is formed in real life by life experience and values, and the me defined by the significance of the specific narrative scenes of the works of immersive interactive images. Viewed from the perspective of receiving and feed backing the narrative information of the artistic works, the audiences of the artistic works of immersive interactive images have a meaning different from the audiences of 2D video and paintings.

2.3   Scene—Narrative Space of Immersive Film

In 2D images, the narrative logic and the sense of order of information are formed by field of shooting scale, layout and montage. With specific grammars and audio-visual elements, the audiences can comprehend and receive the narration. How to build the logic of narration in the panoramic immersive images is actually that the immersive images need to conduct a complete narration to build the perfect visual order in the case that the audiences can freely move the point of sight. Just like the traditional Chinese roller landscape paintings and Suzhou Gardens of China, one step makes a difference while the scenes are connected with one another, forming a complete narrative space that is of artistic conception—"scene", which is the scene scheduling of the narrative factors around the point of sight of the audiences.

It has its own uniqueness for the performance of the panoramic space. Panoramic space is a brand new concept of image space for the frame-type shooting scale of image, which is a conversion from plane image to three-dimensional space. This immersion film present of panoramic view space brings about a real immersion experience. The pursuit of immersion experience is exactly our original intention to constantly improve the quality of the cinema and go to the cinema to watch the movies and VR is just a phased step for this original intention. The traditional movie scene, under the constraints of the shooting scale, presents a dynamic picture, and the audiences watch the scene picture face to face, while the VR panoramic presentation provides the audience an audio visual space, and the audiences are just in this space. Both of these are essentially different in the visual representation of narrative.

In the narrative design process of panoramic visual space of immersion film, it is quite necessary to establish the principle of the main view to tell the story with the characteristics of time process. If there is no shooting scale to limit the audiences' attention when watching the movie, the main visual object in the main view range of the panoramic space is the main content carrier to narrate, and what seen from the main view is the design of the narrative content expressed by the creator in the image space, and then the switch connection rule between the main view and the main body content is particularly important, and the main view has become the core content of immersion film audio-visual narrative language.

In addition, as the current mainstream film production process, the scenery, the lighting settings and the actor position are designed around or in front of the lens. The concept of camera lens is weakened when the immersion film are dispatched on the scene. The directly considered is the positional relationship between the panoramic story space and the eyes of the audience, and even the problem of "jump axis" contraindicated in camera stand design emphasized to ensure the smooth narrative for traditional movies is inexistent in the panorama narrative. Therefore, the principle of scene scheduling changes when shooting a VR movie. However, based on the main view narration principle described above, it is necessary to emphasize the connection between the main views and the logical relationship of the camera stands in the entire panoramic space, since the camera stand still represents the view of audiences to watch the entire story, and the audiences are "present" in the immersive experience. The main view is set in the narrative space of the panorama. Since the space is sufficiently close to the real life environment, it is naturally possible to set the secondary views to improve the richness of the narrative in the panoramic space, which is also the unique charm of the panorama view of immersive film narrative.

When the immersion film showing with head-mounted display, the "story" scene will be presented in front of you in depth, and it seems to run across the time and space and reach the event spot. This is the theoretical experience effect of panorama image media and also the objective of the work experience during the creation. The plane image works is realized to edit the story time based on the scene with the features of shooting scale in the expression logic of "looking at here, and look at there…" said by the director to the audiences. For VR head-mounted equipment, the experience brought by the panorama image is closer to "loading" the users on the spot. When the users wear the head-mounted display, the work tells the users that "you are here, and you are here…". In the panorama image, the sense of immediacy and the narrative rhetoric of the immersed experience are corresponding, and the integrity of panorama view is not to realize the integrity of the narration plot through the time-space cutting and recombination. More importantly, the narrative relationship between creators (recorders), works, recorded objects, and audiences is not "peeped" as described in the classic movie theory but "present in scene" the new relationship.

In general, the narrative method of panoramic view in immersive film still needs to follow the narrative as the basic principle of time art and objective physical characteristics of human eyes forward to see things. On the basis of this, how to play the narrative value in "extra" space is one of the directions that creators can explore in immersive film art creation, which is also the key of how to enhance immersion and how to construct the unique experience of immersive film narrative. Immersive film creation provides a different requirement on the director's ability to schedule the scene and the actor's ability to perform from that of the current mainstream movie art creation. The cameraman shall still consider the angle when setting the camera stand and scene sequence, but the relationship between one camera with visual space position and rhythm brought by multiple lens shall be considered, which can be seen that the difficulty of making immersive film art is enhanced, but this is the demand for art experience innovation of immersive film art in creation (Fig. 1).

Fig. 1. Recording and shooting based on panoramic image and panoramic actual sound

3 Construct the Narration of Immersive Imagesz with Interactive Behaviors

3.1 Interactive Narration Is the Key to the Artistic Experience Innovation of Immersive Film

In the works of immersive images, we no longer use the scenes with border and the mode of focus perspective to watch the images, while interaction becomes an important tool to push forward the narration. When the narration is conducted by the combination of immersive images and interaction, the audiences will obtain the artistic experience to enter another time and space from the works. The means of interaction becomes more diverse and mature with the development of technologies. The forms of immersive interaction—spatial gestures, voice and face recognition and even the involvement of AI make the interactive experience more natural. Interaction of the dynamic behaviors of the audiences will bring the fun of experience to the behavior itself, such as the popular VR games. However, the involvement of narrative images requires more abundant interaction fun. The purpose of interaction can be to satisfy the visual senses, music appreciation or emotional experience of joy, anger, sorrow and happiness, and even the judgment and choice of values.

Necessity of interaction as the art experience mode of immersive film.

The immersion film can inevitably prompt to create a totally different artistic experience than the traditional movie art, rather than merely enhancing immersion in hardware. The immersion film can carry a complete rich narrative to express the profound artistic significance, which can be called movie art; otherwise, it still remains in the level of "special movie". On the one hand, this requires an increase in the production equipment, software and playback equipment, on the other hand, the narrative innovation is more important.

From the morphological characteristics of the immersion film, the effect of the immersive experience brought by the panoramic view of the immersion filmspace is not that the audiences watch the lens picture as the spectators, but that the audiences are just in the space of the movie, which must inspire the audiences different experience appeal, therefore it is the best choice to interact with the event in the space. With the interaction, the audiences can experience the give-and-take consciousness narrative rather than the audio visual experience and the audiences are changed from the receivers to the interactors in the narrative space. The interactive narrative is the best experience to promote or match the immersion film, and the sublimation from audiovisual experience of traditional movie to the behavior percipience experience integrating audio visual and operation is bound to further enhance the immersion of the audience in the experience of VR video.

3.2 Construction of Interactive Narration of Immersive Film

In immersive images, the promotion of narration depends on the progress of interaction. But how to promote the narration with interaction? The narration formation of the artistic works of immersive images is totally different from those of paintings and 2D films. The interactive narration forms from the interaction with the film conducted by the audiences in the process of experiencing the works. The audiences play a constructive role in the narration construction of the works of immersive interactive images. It can be said that the formation of interactive narration is formed by the medium of the works and the experience process of the audiences. The process of interactive experience is a story building process. In the artistic works of immersive interactive images, "the story is viewed as a way for the people to build a concept world composed of all kinds of processes. People present as different roles when participating in different processes" [4]. We experience the story and enjoy the wonders when watching the film, enriching the emotion of oneself and creating an artistic me in the works.

Inevitably, the design of interactive narration needs to consider many factors such as narrator, medium of interaction, interaction behavior, and narration structure and narration results. And such factors are based on the audiences as the center, that is, to consider the experience results of the audiences with empathy. In terms of the nodes of interaction, the design of narration conditions (such as "what do I have"), process of thinking (how do I choose), role relationship (who am I), operational behavior (what did I do), language feedback (my suggestion) and feedback results (results obtained) is the main considerations.

With the help of the theoretical methods of cognitive narratology, we can understand what kind of thinking tools, processes and activities make it possible for us to construct and understand the narration. Taking the narration itself as a tool for understanding and experiencing, the cognitive narratology uses the methods of cognitive science, including cognitive psychology, social psychology and other disciplines, to study how the audiences organize and understand the having experiences and the relationship with the narrative plots in the process of narration. "Among many forms of the cognitive narratology, one type puts the emphasis on the importance of frameworks (or schemas) and scripts for readers and authors. The framework is a holistic concept that can be used to edit and limit to include and better understand the experience; scripts are recurring action patterns and sequences" [5]. Like other narrative arts, when we enter the time and space of narration of immersive interactive images, the film tells an overall world outlook and forms an overall narration framework, which is the cognitive base by which the audiences experience the story of interactive narration. Based on the narrative framework and the cognitive life experience of the audiences, the audiences know what can be done or what interaction is required. As we come to a museum, we will appreciate the objects we are interested in carefully and pay more attention to the collection strongly recommended by the museum. As shown in Fig. 2.

Fig. 2. The museum space presented by immersive interactive images, and you can further understand the stories behind the collection by activating the hot spots via interaction.

3.3   Experience Essence of the Interactive Narration of Immersive Images

The illusion of immersion of immersive images allow the audiences to better participate in the narration in the process of experiencing the works, that is, the form of immersion enhances the sense of reality of the interactive narration experience. Interactive narration, based on immersive images, attempts to achieve the same experience in real life to some extent. The story-telling process is the interaction process between the environment and human behaviorally and emotionally; the developing changes of the story is the message sending and message feedback process between the audiences and the objective environment. The difference between real life and works lies in the inconsistency of time and space. Based on realistic space-time and life experience, the perception of the audiences is put into the virtual story world.

The medium form of images decides the form of interactive narration, and the interactive design of narration experience will be made on the content and process of interaction. The design of interactive narration experience of immersive images is unique for being in the virtual story scenes wholeheartedly. As we interact with things and people face to face in the world of real life, we usually use real tools through five sense organs and arms and legs, rather than control the keyboard and touch screen expressionlessly, to hide the emotion and behavior behind the medium. That is to say, the interactive narration of immersive images would, due to the characteristics of immersive medium, naturally lead the audiences to use the means of natural interaction. Of course, due to the limit of technology implementation possibilities in the actual interactive works of immersive images, natural interaction and gamepad interaction will make the move together.

The interaction process that immersive interaction affects the experience of artistic works is a choice, an exploration, a recognition and an acquisition in terms of audience thinking. How this interaction behavior occurs would be influenced by such factors as the interactive experience scene provided by the image works, the life experience, values and aesthetic standard of the audience and so on. The interaction narration experience of immersive images is a kind of virtual practice of the audiences in the time and space with a specific theme in immersive images, and the choice, judgment, analysis, deduction and reasoning of the audiences in the context for the development of the story plots as well. From the perspective of the play of immersive interactive images, the development of the story and the plot changes are related to the audience's feedback.

In the traditional narration media, the audiences, listeners or readers learn a story and get to know its existence through the medium, so as to obtain a kind of satisfaction of seeking novelty. However, knowing a thing or seeking novelty is not the only goal of interactive narration. Its goal is to participate in the wonders and even practical activities to create the wonder. As each behavior tells the story of life in the daily life of the audiences, in the immersive interactive images, the artist offers the audiences a specific environment and thematic scene and the audiences obtain a certain narration experience from it.

On the other hand, Hockney said "Watching uses memory, so it's not the same feeling when looking at strangers and acquaintance" [6]. Moreover, different people have different memory. Even if we stand in the same place, we see a completely different world. Watching is affected by other factors, having never been to this place before and the degree of familiarity of you who have been here before for this place will affect your view here.

The design of interactive narration usually starts the interaction with the audiences from three aspects, namely plot, role and perspective. Because the audiences obtain the possibility and chance to interact with the works in the process of experience, then important evidences to judge whether the works is good or bad are if the design of the interactive narration experience satisfies the audiences, the degree of freedom of interaction provided by the works, the mode of experience of interaction, the presetting of the key points of interaction content and the effect setting of interaction feedback.

In terms of narration, the design elements of immersive interactive images are mainly role, scene and plot. Role interaction mainly refers to the interaction between the audience and the role of the play, or the control of the behavioral expression of the role of the play, or even the replacement of the visual modeling of the role, just as the player's control of the game in the RPG role-playing game. Scene interaction mainly refers to the design of the story scene and the atmosphere control, to achieve the visual atmosphere and spatial structure that the audience can personalize the story scenes, and thus ultimately realize the personalized expression of the story. Plot interaction usually pursues the personalized plot design, so that the audiences can create their own stories. In the present circumstances, it is often the case that several plot clues are designed in a film to provide the audiences with independent or uncertain plot selection possibility on the preset plot points.

Walking in to an artistic works of immersive interactive image is like entering a story world. However, the story hasn't happened yet and awaits the audiences and interaction practice to reconstruct the story world. In such a story world reconstructed by the audiences, who does anything to anyone, when and where, and why and in what way, such interactive factors are the conceptual treatment of the time, space and perspective by the maker of the images, enabling the audience to realize the creation and recognition from experience in the immersive video world.

4   Conclusion

Today, the panoramic view and interactive narrative of immersive film have aroused everyone's interest, the visual experience are shocking us. However, people who have hundreds of years of visual experience in movie have more expectations in the immersive film currently in its infancy. These expectations are just the motivation for immersive film innovation.

In the artistic works of immersive interactive images, Monika Fludernik, a theorist of cognitive narration stands for a generalized narrative theory which can explain the narrative way to construct the story jointly by immersive interactive images and the audience. In his opinion, "the basis of narration does not lie in the narrator or the event sequence, but the so-called experience, namely our practical experience. The key to narration lies in those characters who act and think. In this way, the cognitive framework based on our embodiedness makes the action and thinking become the activities of great importance." [7] These actions and thinking are just the innovation of the artistic experience of immersive interactive image. The immersive images give people a way to observe and experience the world, which is in line with the human kind nature. The interaction behavior of the audiences in the process of experiencing the works reconstructs the story world of immersive images. People get a more natural narrative experience in the new way to observe and display the world, namely immersive interactive images.

Acknowledgments. This research was supported by Beijing social science fund project (17YTB014).

References

1. Rose, F.: The Art of Immersion: How the Digital Generation Is Remaking Hollywood, Madison Avenue, and the Way We Tell Stories. W. W. Norton & Company, New York (2011)
2. Hockney, D., Gayford, M.: History of Drawing - from the Cave Wall to the Computer Screen, p. 22. Zhejiang People's Fine Arts Publishing House, Hangzhou (2017)
3. Hockney, D., Gayford, M.: History of Drawing - from the Cave Wall to the Computer Screen, p. 83. Zhejiang People's Fine Arts Publishing House, Hangzhou (2017)
4. Scholes, R., Phelan, J., Kellogg, R.: The Nature of Narrative: Revised and Expanded, p. 327. Nanjing University Press, Nanjing (2014)
5. Scholes, R., Phelan, J., Kellogg, R.: The Nature of Narrative: Revised and Expanded, p. 291. Nanjing University Press, Nanjing (2014)
6. Hockney, D., Gayford, M.: History of Drawing - from the Cave Wall to the Computer Screen, p. 78. Zhejiang People's Fine Arts Publishing House, Hangzhou (2017)
7. Scholes, R., Phelan, J., Kellogg, R.: The Nature of Narrative: Revised and Expanded, p. 292. Nanjing University Press, Nanjing (2014)

Experience Categories in Specific Contexts – Creating Positive Experiences in Smart Kitchens

Katharina M. Zeiner[(✉)], Julian Henschel, Katharina Schippert, Kristin Haasler, Magdalena Laib, and Michael Burmester

Stuttgart Media University, Nobelstr. 10 70569, Stuttgart, Germany
{zeiner,schippert,haasler,laib,
burmester}@hdm-stuttgart.de, mail@julianhenschel.com

Abstract. Experience categories are a methodology designed to understand existing and create new positive experiences. They describe aspects of positive experiences within a given context, for example work. The aim of this paper is twofold. First, it is intended as a proof-of-concept – we show that experience categories can be applied to new contexts. Second, we describe a design process that focuses on the use of experience categories. Here we explore present positive experiences in kitchens, and how smart kitchens can help us to create and support these. Using Experience Interviews, participants described 94 positive experiences they had around kitchen activities. The analysis yielded 17 experience categories for cooking related activities. Based on these categories, we generated concepts to facilitate new positive experiences in the kitchen before, during, and after cooking. We describe this process as well as five concepts including the generation of rituals, trying new things, and supporting each other.

Keywords: User experience · Cooking · Experience categories

1 Introduction

1.1 Positive User Experience

Following Hassenzahl [1, p. 12] we understand User Experience (UX) as "a momentary, primarily evaluative feeling (good-bad) while interacting with a product or service. […] Good UX is the consequence of fulfilling the human needs for autonomy, competency, stimulation (self-oriented), relatedness, and popularity (others-oriented) through interacting with the product or service (i.e. hedonic quality)." This means, positive experiences through and with a product are achieved by designing for the fulfillment of psychological needs. However, this focus on psychological needs when designing for positive UX can become quite vague – it is easier to say, that a product fulfills the need for popularity about a finished product than it is to design a product that will specifically fulfill the need for popularity.

There are two other approaches which are often used when designing positive experiences, and both have their basis in the framework of Positive Psychology [2], the

© Springer International Publishing AG, part of Springer Nature 2018
A. Marcus and W. Wang (Eds.): DUXU 2018, LNCS 10918, pp. 306–324, 2018.
https://doi.org/10.1007/978-3-319-91797-9_22

study of the different aspects that contribute to a positive emotional state and the strategies that allow us to achieve it (e.g. [3, 4]). Positive Design which was proposed by Desmet and Pohlmeyer [5] addresses three different domains: Pleasure, personal significance and virtue or all three of them. A similar approach was proposed by Calvo and Peters in the form of Positive Computing [6] and combines a number of concepts from Positive Psychology.

The needs-based approach to User Experience, Positive Design and Positive Computing are firmly theory driven. This, in itself is not problematic but can make the application from one context to another quite hard because things have to be contextualized over and over again.

1.2 Experience Categories – Previous Research

In a previous study [7, 8], positive experiences were explored in work environments. Participants repeatedly reported similar experiences that form the basis for experience categories. These experience categories are defined as follows:

- Experience categories describe qualities within positive experiences that occur either in every experience or in a large number of them.
- These qualities are described as activities because experiences are rooted in activities [9] and this description allows for a more direct application.
- Within an experience category there are similarities in the qualities of the facilitating factors (e.g. presence of others, special activities, technology) [7, 8].

In work environments these categories describe themes such as Resonance, Social Support (Challenge, Engagement, Organization, and Communication and New Experiences). A more detailed description of these categories can be found in [7, 8].

The experience categories are extracted from accounts collected using Experience Interviews [7], which can be conducted face-to-face or online. The main focus of that interview is to tell a story from a predefined context (e.g. work or here cooking). This approach is a variation on Flannagan's Critical Incidents method [10] similar to Experience Reports [11] or Experience Narratives [12]. Unlike studies such as Herzberg et al. [13], though, the focus is placed on the experience rather than the underlying factors.

1.3 Aims

The aim of this project was twofold. First, Tuch et al. [14] found that positive (and negative) experiences for work and leisure contexts differ in their need fulfillment. Therefore, we wanted to confirm that experience categories can be applied to a leisure context. Second, we wanted to find out whether and how the categories differ between contexts. Since the original categories [15] were derived from interviews about work contexts some of them might be specific for work contexts. On the other hand, since we assume that the reported experiences are perceived as positive is because they fulfill our needs, there might be significant overlap between the typical positive experiences found in different contexts. To study this, we chose to explore cooking related activities as an example for leisure activities and the related positive experiences.

1.4   Cooking as Example for Leisure Context

Food engages our senses and connects us with other people [16]. This goes as far as that 48% of Millennials described themselves as Foodies (c.f. [16]) in a study from 2013 commissioned by the advertising agency BBDO. Technological advances make everyday and menial tasks in the cooking process easier or even remove them completely. We chose to study cooking rather than other leisure contexts because of the duality of this context. It is, in its nature, analogue and yet we are increasingly adding more and more digital components. Unlike other leisure contexts such as writing letters, however, cooking is unlikely to become completely digitized. What is also striking in this context is a perceived split in the literature. One part of the literature revels only in the potential technological advances and the other part of the literature points out that the user has to be at the focus of the designed technology rather than the technology itself.

1.5   Smart Kitchens and Smart Homes

Life is complex and irregular [17], habits and routines are flexible [18] and often people with different preferences live together [19, 20]. Yet, very often, smart home studies, and smart kitchen research as a sub-field, are driven by simple assumptions, like that life follows habits and routines and if technology could just serve these habits and life becomes more comfortable. Solaimani et al. noted that research on smart homes is very much dominated by research on technological developments. Even the few social science oriented research is more focused on studies eliciting technical requirements [21]. Even usability-oriented research tends to have a technological focus, because the question is mostly about how the existing functions can be accessed and used [19, 22]. Bell and Kaye point out that we should focus on the experience in kitchens rather than the underlying technologies [23] and Grimes and Harper [24] extend this argument even further, suggesting that smart kitchens should support positive experiences.

Within smart kitchen research, cooking support systems are rather prominent. They support by recognizing what the user is doing [25] and e.g. augmenting the kitchen environment with cooking instructions to support cooking processes directly on the working surfaces or cooking related objects [26]. Creating videos for cooking processes by a kitchen with an embedded video authoring system [27] is a special way of supporting others. Smart kitchen systems also focus on behavior change, like calorie-aware cooking by feeding calorie information back while cooking [28]. Another way of supporting people in the cooking process is to facilitate the exchange of recipes in a social community [29].

The interaction with digital enhanced kitchens is another focus of smart kitchen research. Examples are studies on interaction possibilities using gesture based interaction [30, 31] or augmenting the kitchen environment with e.g. projected cooking related information [32].

Aizawa et al. [33] list relevant research topics concerning smart cooking technologies which are dominated by smart support systems, content management, learning and persuasive technologies as well as safety. Just sensing taste, smell and textures is a topic which addresses the experiential side of smart cooking research. Like in research on smart homes, the technology focus is rather strong. There are exceptions such as studies on collaborative cooking behavior by identifying typical physical interaction behavior of people in their kitchen [34] or describing successful collaboration patterns for social cooking situations [35]. However, there is lack of research on creating positive cooking related experiences by using designing technology accordingly.

1.6 Automation at Any Cost?

The focus of technical solutions for smart kitchens on the utility has a drawback. Users are worried that automation will make them passive, lazy, and in the end stupid [19]. A study by Hassenzahl and Klapperich [36] showed that the process of making coffee is perceived as less pleasurable when the process is automated. They argue that even though chores and other household activities take a lot longer when performed manually compared to a (fully) automated process, they offer more possibilities to experience the process, for the senses to get involved, to experience competency. On the other hand, the shorter, automated, situations were perceived as waiting situations with less and weaker positive experiences which, in turn, are crucial for positive User Experience.

2 Positive Experiences While Cooking

With the goal of generating experience- rather than feature-driven scenarios that support positive UX we applied the experience categories [7, 8] to the leisure context cooking in order to generate new context-specific categories. Experience categories describe the essence of clusters of positive experiences. Each experience in a context can be assigned to a category that describes the situation.

The following study aims to answer the following questions:

1. Are the experience categories described in [8, 15] applicable to other contexts? and
2. If not, how do experience categories for cooking contexts differ from those for work contexts? and
3. If the Categories differ - what are the "must have" and "optional" aspects of experience categories for cooking contexts?

2.1 Experience Categories and Cooking - Study

Experience Interviews

Using both the face-to-face and the online version of the Experience Interview [7, 8] participants were asked about a positive experience they recently had while cooking. This was followed by questions about additional information needed to gain a better understanding of the situation such as feelings experienced ("How did you feel?"), activities carried out ("What did you do?"), other people involved ("Who else was there?"), the overall structure of the experience, and environmental factors.

Sample

We collected 87 descriptions of positive experiences from 95 participants. 8 participants were excluded because they either did not finish the online version of the interview or did not describe positive experiences while cooking. Participants were from a variety of age groups (mean = 27.84, min = 18, max = 66, SD = 9.28), living in a number of different sized households (mean = 2.66, min = 1, max = 11, SD = 1.47). 52% reported cooking mostly alone, 27% with one other person, 4% cook in groups and 17% reported 'other' which was mostly clarified as sometimes cooking alone, sometimes in a group.

Out of these 87 experiences, 5 contained more than one experience and were therefore split up into their individual experiences resulting in 94 experiences that were analyzed further. All participants volunteered and gave informed consent.

Analysis

The experiences were first classified by three members of our lab using Mayring's [37] step model for deductive category development and the categories for work contexts [15]. This process is described in more detail in [7, 8, 15] but is described here for completeness.

Using qualitative content analysis [37], the experiences were compared to the experience categories for work contexts and categorized accordingly. Experiences that did not fit the existing categories were clustered and analyzed. New categories were then suggested by the three coders individually and their overlap was compared.

Based on these new categories were decided on and a revised list of categories was assembled by all raters together. The factors (including emotional outcomes) contributing to the positive experiences in these new clusters were isolated. Then all experiences were re-categorized using the revised categories by the raters individually and the pattern with the highest proportion of agreement was chosen (in cases of disagreement the choices were discussed to reach consensus). From this qualitative analysis we compiled a list of reoccurring descriptions and aspects.

Results

For each of these experience categories for cooking we identified a set of "must have" and "optional" attributes that describe this category. 'Must have' are attributes that occur in some form in every experience reported within that category. The 'optional' attributes appear very often and support the description of an experience category. With 'must have' and 'optional' attributes it is possible to understand what describes an experience category and what make a category different from other categories.

Table 1 describes the identified experience categories for cooking. The first column lists the name of the experience category. The proportion in percent of the total number of positive experiences is shown in the second column. The different categories are related and can be grouped into the broader clusters 'Resonance & Support', 'Competence', 'Organization', 'Communication', and 'Atmosphere' listed in the 'Group' column. The "Experiences" columns shows the proportion of experiences in the 'Group' related to all experiences.

We will now go through the different groups and categories for cooking contexts describing their similarities and differences. Each group description is followed by a table (Tables 2, 3, 4, 5 and 6) which lists the must have and optional attributes within the categories and the experiential outcomes reported by participants. Even though

Table 1. Experience categories and experience groups for positive cooking experiences

Experience category	%	Experiences	Group
Receiving personal feedback	7.4%	31 (33.1%)	Resonance and support
Receiving help	1.1%		
Helping others	1.1%		
Learning new skills	17.0%		
Teaching others	1.1%		
Doing something for others	5.3%		
Rising to a challenge	12.8%	23 (24.5%)	Competence
Experiencing creativity	11.7%		
Finishing a task	2.1%	4 (4.2%)	Organization
Keeping track of things	2.1%		
Connecting with others	3.2%	23 (24.5%)	Communication
Experiencing community	6.4%		
Creating something together	13.8%		
Acting according to one's beliefs	1.1%		
Remembering & tradition	3.2%	13 (13.8%)	Atmosphere
Savoring	5.3%		
Experiencing something new	5.3%		
Total	100%	94	

participants were asked about their emotions, these outcomes were not systematically collected. We find, however, that these descriptions can be used to paint a multifaceted picture of the categories. Following this we describe the differences between experience categories for work and cooking contexts (Table 7).

Group: Resonance & Support

The group Resonance & Support is the largest group and combines categories that focus on how we interact with others to grow (Table 2). It includes the categories 'receiving personal feedback', 'receiving help', 'helping others', 'learning new skills', 'teaching others', as well as 'doing something for others'. Typical experiences in these categories include cooking a new dish and receiving positive feedback about the flavor (TN122) for 'receiving personal feedback' or cooking for someone else knowing it will give them joy (TN110) for 'doing something for others'.

Group: Competence

The group Competence is made up of the categories 'rising to a challenge' and 'experiencing creativity' (Table 3). These categories are very similar but bear striking differences. In both the experiences described are those of performing a task that is not trivial. However, when experiencing creativity, skills and demand are in a (perceived) balance. When rising to a challenge, the outcome is less clear. Note that Experiencing Creativity often describes experiences that have striking similarities to Flow [38]. Typical experiences in this group include cooking something new or cooking a dish and having to react to changes in the environment. For example, one participant wrote about making spaetzle on a hiking trip using a cheese grater (TN59) for 'experiencing creativity'.

Table 2. Experience categories of group resonance & support

Must have	Optional	Experiential outcome
Receiving personal feedback		
Positive feedback about performance	Feedback from people who were not involved in the activity	Pride; Validation/affirmation
Receiving help		
Receiving support while performing an activity	Community; Sharing responsibilities; Splitting tasks	Appreciation; Connectedness
Helping others		
Supporting the execution of a task	Community; Sharing responsibilities; Taking over tasks	
Learning new skills		
Active or passive exploration of something new	End result is unclear	Is experienced as enriching; Joy, fun, curiosity
Teaching others		
Acting as a mentor; Sharing experiences and knowledge; Intention: teaching others	Supporting someone in achieving their goals; Showing something new; Giving feedback; Teaching each other	Feeling competent; Pride
Doing something for others		
Positive feedback about performance (afterwards); Doing something for someone else	Making new experiences possible; Letting others participate in experiences	Positive feelings during the activity; Anticipation

Table 3. Experience categories of group competence

Must have	Optional	Experiential outcome
Rising to a challenge		
Completing a difficult task; Positive feedback about performance; Satisfaction with results; Relief if things worked out	Unsure how to solve the problem; Working alone or as a group; Succeeding in something	Pride
Experiencing creativity		
Goal is clear; Road to the goal is open; Competence (skills needed to complete task are present); Cooking freely or tweaking a recipe	Taking unconventional paths Responding flexibly to changing requirements	Flow; Joy and surprise over positive results

Table 4. Categories of group organization

Must have	Optional	Experiential outcome
Finishing a task		
Completing tasks and parts of tasks; Competence (skills needed to complete task are present); Goal is clear; Task is not challenging	Doing something for someone else; Initiating the activity might take some effort; Positive feedback about performance; Intrinsic motivation	Feeling productive
Keeping track of things		
Perceived control over the situation; Perceived competence	Being your own boss	Feeling of security

Table 5. Categories of group communication

Must have	Optional	Experiential outcome
Connecting with others		
Shared activity; Connecting with people that you are not familiar with	Guests; Having something in common	Feeling related to others
Experiencing community		
Working together with people that are liked; Experiencing the atmosphere together	Taking care	Savoring, joy, fun
Creating something together		
Working towards a shared goal; Clearly defined tasks; Agreeing with others on the plan of action	Motivating each other; Learning from each other; Finishing tasks towards the main goal; Relaxed atmosphere; Acquiring new skills	Feeling competent and related
Acting according to one's beliefs		
Doing something meaningful; Acting on one's own principles; Acting of one's own volition	To stand up for something	Confirmation, satisfaction

Group: Organization

The group Organization is made up of the categories 'finishing a task' and 'keeping track of things' (Table 4). They include experiences that involve more mundane tasks such as spring cleaning the kitchen or keeping track of a growing shopping list.

Table 6. Categories of group atmosphere

Must have	Optional	Experiential outcome
Remembering/tradition		
Remembering a past (positive) experience	Clear structures	Feeling secure (through routines)
Savoring		
Experiencing a pleasant atmosphere (food, drink, time in the kitchen)	Community; Enjoying the experience by one's self; Enjoying favorite foods, or drinks	Introspection; Positive feeling during the activity; Anticipation before the activity
Experiencing something new		
Actively or passively experiencing something new	No specific goal or end-result	Joy, fun, surprise

Group: Communication

The group Communication involves activities that foster a feeling of being related to others (Table 5). The category 'connecting with others' involves activities that bring individuals together, allowing them to learn more about each other. 'experiencing community' on the other hand, is experienced with friends and family and the focus moves away from the activity towards the connectedness. 'creating something together' is more active than the previous two categories – here all the exhilarating aspects of teamwork are experienced. Typical experiences in these categories involve enjoying the company of one's peers. For example one participant described getting up really early on Easter Sunday and cooking a coloring eggs with their mother for the entire family (TN103 – 'creating something together') while another participant described being invited over for dinner by their friends and how they chatted for hours over a simple dinner (TN13 – 'experiencing community'). Finally, 'acting according to one's own beliefs' is a more introspective category. Here the focus is on making decisions that are in line with a certain belief or goal, such as healthy eating, dieting, reducing waste, ethical or religious restrictions while experiencing that decision as enriching.

Group: Atmosphere

The group Atmosphere is comprised of more inward looking categories (Table 6). While the experiences can involve others, the focus is on how an individual feels. 'remembering/tradition' looks back to past experiences (either singular ones or reoccurring ones). 'savoring' focuses on the present and 'experiencing something new', which includes experiences with new kitchen equipment that lead to participants speculating on what they could do with them in the future, focuses both on the present experience as well as the future. It is important to note that a lot of cooking experiences center around traditions. The Experiences in this category focus specifically on these traditions rather than just involving them. For example, one participant described a typical holiday dish from her husband's native country that she makes every year for that holiday (TN146).

Table 7. Comparison of the experience categories found for work and cooking contexts.

Experience category	% work	Group work	% cooking	Group cooking
Receiving (personal) feedback	13.5%	Resonance	7.5%	Resonance and Support
Giving feedback	1.1%			
Receiving appreciation	7.7%			
Receiving help	3.4%	Social support	1.1%	Resonance and support
Helping others	5.2%		1.1%	
Teaching others	1.4%		1.1%	
Learning new skills			17.0%	
Doing something for others			5.3%	
Rising to a challenge	21.5%	Challenge	12.8%	Competence
Being given a challenge	3.7%			
Solving a problem	1.7%	Engagement		
Experiencing creativity	2.3%		11.7%	Competence
Finishing a task	4.3%	Organization	2.1%	Organization
Keeping track of things	6.3%		2.1%	
Acting according to one's beliefs			1.1%	Communication
Experiencing community			6.4%	
Connecting with others	4.0%	Communication and new experiences	3.2%	
Creating something together	8.3%		13.8%	
Exchanging ideas	4.6%			
Contributing to something greater	2.6%			
Experiencing something new	5.1%		5.3%	Atmosphere
Remembering & tradition			3.2%	
Savoring			5.3%	
Total number	349		94	

Comparing Experience Categories of Work and Cooking Context

If we compare the categories found in work and cooking contexts there are a number of differences, for example, the actual categories. Table 7 compares the experience categories for work and cooking contexts and their prevalence.

The categories for cooking contexts bear large similarities to the categories previously found for work contexts. We believe this is due to the suspected underlying needs which is currently being studied by our group. However, differences between the two contexts also emerge. Aspects that appear quite crucial for work contexts (such as social hierarchies) are barely mentioned for cooking while other people appear even more important for cooking contexts than for work contexts. Categories also have other aspects that differ from work contexts. For example, generally speaking, the categories for work contexts all show a tendency to involve feedback situations where community and traditions play a much larger role for cooking contexts.

2.2   Discussion of the Experience Categories

What this process showed was: (a) experience categories can be extracted for contexts other than work. (b) 342 experiences were analyzed in the study that extracted the experience categories for work. Here a sample of only 94 experiences allowed us to generate the categories for cooking experiences. While a larger sample would most likely have produced more detailed descriptions of the categories, we believe this lowers possible barriers for the application of the experience categories to contexts where larger samples are hard to find.

Unsurprisingly the categories found for cooking contexts show similarities to previous research. For example, Grimes and Harper [15] describe the fields 'Creativity', 'Pleasure & Nostalgia', 'Gifting', 'Family Connectedness', 'Trend-Seeking', and 'Relaxation'. The experience categories are extracted through a bottom-up approach. Even though the experience categories for cooking context were extracted using the experience categories for work contexts as a basis, if participants do not talk about certain kinds of experiences, we cannot extract an experience category out of thin air.

Differences between work and leisure from the perspective of experience categories:

From all 23 categories 11 can be found in work and leisure context. In work but not in cooking context you can find 'giving feedback', 'receiving appreciation', 'being given a challenge'. 'solving a problem', 'exchanging ideas', and 'contributing to something greater'. Specific cooking categories are 'learning new skills', 'doing something for others', 'experiencing community', 'acting according to one's beliefs', 'remembering & tradition', and 'savoring'.

For cooking contexts community, savoring and rituals are important. For work contexts, on the other hand, challenges, and connections through work are in the foreground. In those situations community is experienced through the work process and cooperation at work. For cooking contexts community is experienced through the results. At work, the focus is on the bigger picture, while cooking the focus is on the involved parties.

It is likely that there is a certain overlap between categories in different contexts because of the needs fulfilled by the experiences in the categories. However there is variation between contexts. Based on the results of several student projects in our department, we assume that there is also variation between different work or leisure contexts. These differences are small enough to allow for one to use categories for work or cooking contexts to design for new positive experiences. However, if one wants to truly understand a given context, it is advisable to establish the specific categories for that context.

3   Designing New Positive Experiences

As we showed for work contexts, experience categories can be used as an inspiration aid to generate new positive experiences [15, 39, 40]. Thus, the categories for cooking related contexts can, for example, be used to design positive experiences in smart kitchens. Note that this does not mean that these types of experiences can only be created for experiences with technology, we simply chose to use smart kitchens as the new context.

We will now describe how we use this approach when generating new concepts. The concepts described here were developed during the ideation phase of the research project SmartKitchen at Stuttgart Media University. As part of this project we ran a series of workshops to use these findings as a basis for new positive experiences. Our focus was on applying what we had learned about experiences while cooking in general to experiences while cooking with smart kitchens. The experience categories served both as the research basis as well as the inspiration for these workshops. In the following sections we describe the design process we used to generate concepts for positive experiences in cooking concepts.

3.1   Design Process

Using the experience categories and groups for cooking we generated activities that represent the categories and clusters within the context. This was done in a variety of brainstorming sessions that included Lego Series Play workshops.

For example, Remembering & Tradition could be supported through an interaction in which the smart kitchen reminds you that tomorrow is your best friend's birthday and that you made a walnut cake for her last year. Without going shopping, it suggests, you could make a madeira cake for tomorrow.

This approach generated a large number of possible interactions. To make this number more manageable, the interactions were clustered using the activities contained in the interactions.

Grouping of the Generated Activities into Activity Clusters
The clustering of the generated ideas was performed using free clustering. For our context (and they will most likely be different for every context) we found the following activity clusters:

- Exploration (of new recipes, techniques, or ideas)
- Do good to others (caring for others or thinking of them)
- Planning (e.g. a menu, an event, or the weekly shop)
- Documentation (of events, recipes, and experiences)
- Atmosphere (savoring an experience, creating a new one)
- Anticipation (e.g. preparing for a dinner party)
- Improvement (e.g. getting better at a cooking technique)
- Rituals (such as celebrating holidays, or pizza night)

Using these activity clusters we then went back to the experience categories to generate ideas for concepts for experiences within a given context (which can then be grouped again and so forth). This means when working on ideas for specific contexts the brief itself does not have to stay as abstract as 'create an experience that will allow the user to establish traditions' but it can be a combination of an activity cluster with an experience category. While it might seem as if this adds complexity to the process, we have found that combining experience categories with previously generated activity clusters allows for very concrete ideas to emerge. In brainstorming sessions within our lab the effect of this combination was similar to the effect of mash ups in a Design Thinking process.

3.2   Concepts

To better explain this design process we will describe two of the concepts generated using the experience categories approach. For each concept we generated a scenario which is described below. We will also show an image that exemplifies how this could be integrated in an interface in a smart kitchen. Note that these concepts are intended to illustrate how the design process with experience categories can work. New technologies create possibilities for new positive experiences. The question is how these experiences can be designed.

Scenario: Remote Cooking (Fig. 1)

In this scenario we wanted to address the activity cluster 'rituals' and the experience categories 'experiencing community', 'receiving help', and 'creating something together'.

Jana loves her mum's signature citrus cake and really wants to bake it for a friend. Even though she has a recipe, Jana feels that her mum has made little tweaks to the recipe that make it "her mum's cake". Jana's kitchen has a remote cooking feature which allows her to call people using the call button (red arrow, this could, for example, be implemented using gesture recognition or on a touch screen) while recording the cooking field and the oven. She contacts her mother in Hamburg over video message, so they can bake the cake together despite the distance. While the cake is in the oven they catch up about what they have been up to and their plans for the weekend. Because they can both check on the progress, her mother can also keep an eye on the cake. Jana feels just like when she was younger and helped her mother in the kitchen.

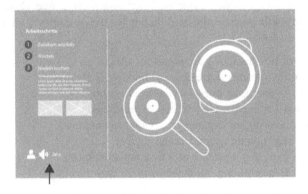

Fig. 1. Scenario - remote cooking: next to the cooking field the kitchen displays the recipe. At the bottom a call button allows Jana to call her mum and ask for help. (Color figure online)

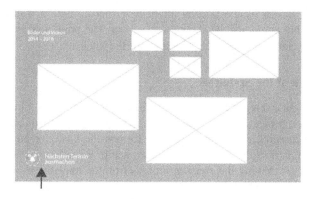

Fig. 2. Scenario - turning experiences into rituals: Next to photos from previous dinners, the kitchen displays a visual reminder that suggest already setting a date for the next get-together. (Color figure online)

Design Rationale
For this scenario several features were specifically designed. These were:

- Both parties can see the work surface and oven and thus the results of the work (receiving help & creating something together)
- Both parties can see each other and their activities (experiencing community and creating something together)
- They can talk to each other (receiving help, experiencing community).

Scenario: Turning Experiences into Rituals (Fig. 2)
In this scenario we wanted to address the activity clusters 'rituals' and 'documentation' and the experience category 'remembering & tradition'.

Every year, Mario and his friends meet for an "asparagus dinner". This year is no exception. They have a great time cooking their meal and eating it, too. While they prepare the food the kitchen takes photo of their food at its various stages of preparation. After dinner, Mario and his friends are in the kitchen with a glass of wine and are reminiscing about past dinners. The kitchen shows a slideshow with photographs from previous dinners (this could be implemented either on a display or projected on any available surface). Mario and his friends are having a lot of fun recalling the stories related to the photos. When the kitchen suggests setting a date for their next get-together (red arrow, this could be implemented using a touch interface or as a visual reminder that is then responded to using voice controls), Mario immediately creates an invite for everybody because they enjoy these evenings so much.

Design Rationale
For this scenario several features were specifically designed. These were:

- The kitchen takes photos of the preparation of the food (documentation)
- Photos from past dinners are shown (remembering & traditions and documentation)
- The kitchen suggests setting a date for the next dinner (remembering & traditions and planning as well as anticipation)
- The kitchen only suggests actions rather than taking them automatically. This was a specific choice to allow for greater autonomy of the user.

The images shown by the kitchen might be projected onto a wall or some other kitchen surface but could also be shown on a screen. The point here is that the images are shown at all and that users can interact with the kitchen.

3.3   Discussion of the Scenarios

Based on experience categories and activity clusters we developed 14 concepts for the use in a research project. Two of them were presented here to illustrate the design process. In the research project the concepts formed the basis for an iterative development of the functionality of a smart kitchen setup. Experience categories and the activity clusters are driving the creation process from an experience perspective.

Requirements like 'visibility of work activities and results' are based on the experience categories 'receiving help' and 'creating something together' in the first scenario. The requirement of continuously taking photos by integrated cameras is based on the experience category of 'remembering & traditions'. The goal of these requirements is not to generate new technological solutions, but they are supposed to support new positive experiences during cooking. This means the technology used is not necessarily innovative (though, innovative solutions could be used) but the interactions with the technology are designed in a different way. The focus is put on the experience which is then 'implemented' in the concept using technological solutions that will support the intended experience and create new possibilities for positive experiences [41] during cooking and in the context of smart kitchens.

4   General Discussion

In this paper we transferred the experience category approach to a leisure context. This allowed us to gain a better understanding of cooking experiences and to apply this understanding to cooking in smart kitchens.

We analyzed 94 experiences that were collected using experience interviews. Qualitative content analysis revealed 17 experience categories. The categories are Receiving personal feedback, Receiving help, Helping others, Learning new skills, Teaching others, Doing something for others, Rising to a challenge, Experiencing creativity, Finishing a task, Keeping track of things, Connecting with others, Experiencing community, Creating something together, Acting according to one's beliefs, Remembering & Tradition, Savoring, Experiencing something new.

The experience category approach was first explored in work contexts. The application to experiences in the kitchen revealed both similarities and differences between the two. For example, "atmosphere" appears as a cluster for experiences in the kitchen which is more-or-less nonexistent in work contexts. Overall all categories are also a lot more social. Work by Tuch and colleagues [14] which explored the differences in need fulfillment between work and leisure activities seems to point in a similar direction. The link between experience categories and needs, however, has to be explored further.

The categories derived from our 94 experiences are sometimes based on only a small number of experiences but we believe that even these less frequent categories have their importance. The fact, that they show up even in this small sample suggests, that using just 94 experiences (compared to 342 for work contexts) provides enough data to form a somewhat representative picture of experiences surrounding a given activity. Furthermore, these less frequent categories point to areas where there is potential for positive experiences that is not fully used which means they are areas where new, less obvious, positive experiences can be created.

This approach explicitly focuses on positive experiences. This means they do not specifically solve problems in kitchens. We believe the experience category approach should be used in conjunction with traditional design approaches such as Contextual Design [42, 43].

The design process described in the second part of this paper shows how experience categories can be used to design new positive experiences in a context for which experience categories already exist or have just been extracted.

A next step might be further exploring the relationship between categories for work and leisure contexts. For example, cooking was treated as a leisure context but needs vary with the roles we have in live so it seems reasonable to propose that a professional chef might describe positive experiences that reflect the experience categories for work contexts rather than those for cooking (as a leisure activity) contexts.

5   Conclusion

In this paper we studied positive experiences in cooking related activities and derived experience categories for this context. Then we described a design process using these categories. In summary, we found:

- Experience categories can be applied to leisure contexts like cooking.
- Experience categories in the leisure context cooking differ from the categories found for work. For example, cooking is more social than work, in that the majority of experiences center around others. The categories also diverge in their hard and soft characteristics. However, there is still a large overlap between the two contexts.
- As with the experience categories for work contexts, the categories derived for cooking contexts can be used to design new positive experiences and support creativity, allowing for a multi-faceted approach to a given context such as smart kitchen environments.
- Experience categories can support the design of context-specific positive experiences across a variety of contexts but they have to be established for each context using qualitative content analysis. Either through inductive content analysis of a larger set of interviews, or through deductive content analysis using experience categories for a different context as a starting point.

Acknowledgments. We would like to thank all participants who described their experiences. This study was conducted as part of the project SmartKitchen which is funded by the Federal Ministry of Education and Research (BMBF), Grant Number: 03FH011PX5.

References

1. Hassenzahl, M.: User experience (UX): towards an experiential perspective on product quality. In: Proceedings of the 20th International Conference of the Association Francophone d'Interaction Homme-Machine, pp. 11–15 (2008)
2. Seligman, M., Csikszentmihalyi, M.: Positive psychology: an introduction. Am. Psychol. **55** (1), 5–14 (2000)
3. Lyubomirsky, S.: The How of Happiness: A Scientific Approach to Getting the Life You Want. Penguin, London (2007)
4. Seligman, M.: Flourish: A Visionary New Understanding of Happiness and Well-being. Free Press, New York (2011)
5. Desmet, P.M.A., Pohlmeyer, A.E., Forlizzi, J.: Special issue editorial: design for subjective well-being. Int. J. Des. **7**(3), 5–7 (2013)
6. Calvo, R.A., Peters, D.: Positive Computing - Technology for Wellbeing and Human Potential. MIT Press, Cambridge (2014)
7. Zeiner, K.M., Laib, M., Schippert, K., Burmester, M.: Das Erlebnisinterview – Methode zum Verständnis positiver Erlebnisse. In: Tagungsband der Mensch und Computer 2016 (2016)
8. Zeiner, K.M., Laib, M., Schippert, K., Burmester, M.: Identifying experience categories to design for positive experiences with technology at work. In: Proceedings of the 2016 CHI Conference, pp. 3013–3020 (2016)
9. Hassenzahl, M., Eckoldt, K., Diefenbach, S., Laschke, M., Lenz, E., Kim, J.: Designing moments of meaning and pleasure. Experience design and happiness understanding experiences. Int. J. Des. **7**(3), 21–31 (2013)
10. Flanagan, J.C.: The critical incident technique. Psychol. Bull. **51**(4), 327–358 (1954)
11. Hassenzahl, M., Diefenbach, S., Göritz, A.: Needs, affect, and interactive products – facets of user experience. Interact. Comput. **22**(5), 353–362 (2010)
12. Tuch, A.N., Trusell, R.N., Hornbæk, K.: Analyzing users' narratives to understand experience with interactive products. In: Proceedings of the CHI 2013, pp. 2079–2088 (2013)
13. Herzberg, F., Mausner, B., Snyderman, B.B.: The Motivation to Work. Transaction Publishers, New Brunswick (1993)
14. Tuch, A.N., van Schaik, P., Hornbæk, K.: Leisure and work, good and bad: the role of activity domain and valence in modeling user experience. ACM Trans. Comput. Interact. **23** (6), 35 (2016)
15. Zeiner, K.M., Burmester, M., Haasler, K., Henschel, J., Laib, M., Schippert, K.: Designing for positive user experience in work contexts – experience categories and their applications. Hum. Technol. (Accepted for Publication)
16. Turrow, E.: A Taste of Generation Yum: How the Millennial Generation's Love for Organic Fare, Celebrity Chefs and Microbrews Will Make or Break the Future of Food. Pronoun, New York (2015)
17. Brush, A.J.B., Lee, B., Mahajan, R., Agarwal, S., Saroiu, S., Dixon, C.: Home automation in the wild: challenges and opportunities. In: CHI Conference on Human Factors in Computing Systems, pp. 2115–2124 (2011)
18. Davidoff, S., Lee, M.K., Yiu, C., Zimmerman, J., Dey, A.K.: Principles of smart home control. In: Proceedings of the 8th International Conference Ubiquitous Computing, pp. 19–34 (2006)
19. Mennicken, S., Vermeulen, J., Huang, E.M.: From today's augmented houses to tomorrow's smart homes: new directions for home automation research. In: Proceedings of 2014 ACM International Joint Conference on Pervasive and Ubiquitous Computing, pp. 105–115 (2014)

20. Chuang, Y., Chen, L.-L., Lee, Y.-H.: Envisioning a smart home that can learn and negotiate the needs of multiple users. In: UbiComp/ISWC 2015 Proceedings of the 2015 ACM International Joint Conference on Pervasive and Ubiquitous Computing and Proceedings of the 2015 ACM International Symposium on Wearable Computers, pp. 237–240 (2015)
21. Solaimani, S., Keijzer-Broers, W., Bouwman, H.: What we do - and don't - know about the smart home: an analysis of the smart home literature. Indoor Built Environ. **24**(3), 370–383 (2015)
22. Väänänen-Vainio-Mattila, K., Koskela, T.: Evolution towards smart home environments: empirical evaluation of three user interfaces. Pers. Ubiquit. Comput. **8**(3–4), 234–240 (2004)
23. Bell, G., Kaye, J.: Designing technology for domestic spaces: a kitchen manifesto. Gastron. J. Crit. Food Stud. **2**(2), 46–62 (2002)
24. Grimes, A., Harper, R.: Celebratory technology. In: Proceeding of the Twenty-Sixth Annual CHI Conference on Human Factors in Computing Systems, CHI 2008, p. 467 (2008)
25. Hashimoto, A., Mori, N., Funatomi, T., Yamakata, Y., Kakusho, K., Minoh, M.: Smart kitchen: a user centric cooking support system. In: Proceedings of the IPMU, pp. 848–854 (2008)
26. Sato, A., Watanabe, K., Rekimoto, J.: MimiCook: a cooking assistant system with situated guidance. In: Proceedings of the 8th International Conference on Tangible, Embedded and Embodied Interaction (TEI 2014), pp. 121–124 (2014)
27. Hayashi, Y., Doman, K., Ide, I., Deguchi, D., Murase, H.: Automatic authoring of a domestic cooking video based on the description of cooking instructions. In: Proceedings of the 5th International Workshop on Multimedia for Cooking and Eating Activities, CEA 2013, pp. 21–26 (2013)
28. Chi, P.-Y., Chen, J.-H., Chu, H.-H., Lo, J.-L.: Enabling calorie-aware cooking in a smart kitchen. In: Oinas-Kukkonen, H., Hasle, P., Harjumaa, M., Segerståhl, K., Øhrstrøm, P. (eds.) PERSUASIVE 2008. LNCS, vol. 5033, pp. 116–127. Springer, Heidelberg (2008). https://doi.org/10.1007/978-3-540-68504-3_11
29. Terrenghi, L., Hilliges, O., Butz, A.: Kitchen stories: sharing recipes with the living cookbook. Pers. Ubiquit. Comput. **11**(5), 409–414 (2007)
30. Neßelrath, R., Lu, C., Schulz, C.H., Frey, J., Alexandersson, J.: A gesture based system for context-sensitive interaction with smart homes. In: Wichert, R., Eberhardt, B. (eds.) Ambient Assisted Living. Springer, Heidelberg (2011). https://doi.org/10.1007/978-3-642-18167-2_15
31. Nansen, B., Davis, H., Vetere, F., Skov, M., Paay, J., Kjeldskov, J.: Kitchen kinesics: situating gestural interaction within the social contexts of family cooking. In: Proceedings of the 26th Australian Computer-Human Interaction Conference on Designing Futures: The Future of Design, pp. 149–158 (2014)
32. Bonanni, L., Lee, C.-H., Selker, T.: Attention-based design of augmented reality interfaces. In: CHI 2005 Extended Abstracts on Human Factors in Computing, CHI 2005, p. 1228 (2005)
33. Aizawa, K., Funatomi, T., Yamakata, Y.: Summary for the workshop on smart technology for cooking and eating activities (CEA 2014). In: ACM Ubicomp Workshop on Smart Technology for Cooking and Eating, pp. 479–485 (2014)
34. Paay, J., Kjeldskov, J., Skov, M.B.: Connecting in the kitchen: an empirical study of physical interactions while cooking together at home. In: CSCW 2015, pp. 276–287 (2015)
35. Isaku, T., Iba, T.: Creative CoCooking patterns: a pattern language for creative collaborative cooking. In: Proceedings for European Conference on Pattern Language of Programs (EuroPLoP 2015), pp. 1–17 (2015)
36. Hassenzahl, M., Klapperich, H.: Convenient, clean, and efficient? The experiential costs of everyday automation. In: Proceedings of the 8th Nordic Conference on Human-Computer Interaction, pp. 21–30 (2014)

37. Mayring, P.: Qualitative Content Analysis. Forum Qual. Sozialforsch./Forum Qual. Soc. Res., **1**(2) (2000)
38. Csikszentmihalyi, M.: Flow: The Psychology of Optimal Experience. Harper and Row, New York (1990)
39. Laib, M., Burmester, M., Zeiner, K.M.: Erlebnispotenzialanalyse – Mit Systematik zu positiven Erlebnissen. In: Mensch und Computer 2017 – Usability Professionals, 10–13 September 2017, Regensburg (2017)
40. Burmester, M., Laib, M., Schippert, K., Zeiner, K., Fronemann, N., Krüger, A.E.: Vom Problemlösen hin zum Entwerfen von Smart Homes für positive Momente und mehr Wohlbefinden. Wiss. trifft Prax. **4**, 38–48 (2016)
41. Desmet, P., Hassenzahl, M.: Towards happiness: possibility-driven design. In: Zacarias, M., de Oliveira, J.V. (eds.) Human-Computer Interaction: The Agency Perspective. SCI, vol. 396, pp. 3–27. Springer, Heidelberg (2012). https://doi.org/10.1007/978-3-642-25691-2_1
42. Beyer, H., Holtzblatt, K.: Contextual Design: Defining Customer-Centered Systems. Morgan Kaufmann, San Francisco (1998)
43. Beyer, H., Holtzblatt, K.: Contextual Design: Design for Life. Morgan Kaufmann, Amsterdam (2017)

Usability and User Experience Evaluation Methods and Tools

A Proposal of Usability Heuristics Oriented to E-Banking Websites

Gloria Baños Díaz and Claudia María del Pilar Zapata Del Río$^{(\boxtimes)}$

Pontificia Universidad Católica del Perú, Lima, Peru
{gloria.banosd, zapata.cmp}@pucp.edu.pe

Abstract. Currently, there has been an increase in the use of Internet Banking, but also cyber-attacks. For this reason, banks invest in physical security mechanisms and provide information to users of their use, since these applications can be accessed by clients with different profiles in experience of using security mechanisms.

So that a banking application does not die in its use, it should be usable and, in addition, safe. Although there are studies that indicate that these concepts are opposed, it is observed that there is a need to balance them in the design of Internet Banking interfaces. To measure the usability of a Web interface design, there are several methods of usability evaluation, but the inspection method is the most used, specifically the heuristic evaluation technique. Nielsen Heuristics are the most used, but according to studies, these heuristics are not complete for the various Web software domains that exist in the market and that does not cover security aspects either.

Given that there are few studies and lack of a formal guide related to the usability and security of Web design of Internet Banking, it is that this paper proposes a set of heuristics for Web sites Internet Banking, based on proposed heuristics in the literature and applied in a case study. Obtaining as a result, Nielsen's heuristics serve as the basis for a usable and safe Web interface design, but there is a need for other heuristics oriented more towards Security, Satisfaction, Personalization and Navigability.

Keywords: Usability heuristics · E-banking

1 Introduction

Due to the rapid extension of the use of the Internet, many industries could improve their operations and provide online services through the use of Web applications [6]. One of the industries that provide online services are banking entities, with the use of Internet Banking.

Currently, many banks provide Internet banking services, offering the confidence of being able to carry out transactions quickly and safely, which is not 100% guaranteed. The growth of the use of these services via Internet brings with it the increase of cyber-attacks, which harms both banks and users. Therefore, banks invest in security mechanisms and provide information to users about the existence of these mechanisms in their systems [19].

© Springer International Publishing AG, part of Springer Nature 2018
A. Marcus and W. Wang (Eds.): DUXU 2018, LNCS 10918, pp. 327–345, 2018.
https://doi.org/10.1007/978-3-319-91797-9_23

If an industry wants its Web application to persist on the Internet, this application should be usable for customers [15]. In the case of Internet banking, where sensitive, private and important customer information is handled, an integration of usability and security in Web interface design should be considered [23]. Although there are studies that indicate that these concepts are opposed, it is observed that there is a need to balance them [4, 6, 19–21, 23].

To measure the usability of a Web interface, there are methods of evaluation of usability, one of the most used being the heuristic evaluation technique [8, 23], which consists of the evaluation developed by expert evaluators based on a set of heuristics. of usability [8]. Nielsen's Heuristics are the most used [13], but according to studies [7] they do not cover all the usability characteristics of specific domains. While [20] it is emphasized that Nielsen's heuristics do not cover security aspects, they are considered as the basis for a usable and safe Web design [23].

While there are few studies of heuristic usability assessments for the Internet Banking domain [7], there is more information from other types of studies that refer to the concept of security as an important characteristic of a Banking Web application design that should be considered without forgetting the features of Usability [23].

For all the above, this article proposes a set of usability heuristics for E-Banking based on the knowledge of heuristics proposed in the literature and information related to usability, always keeping security in mind, as it is an important characteristic of this domain.

1.1 E-Banking

In recent years there has been a rapid development, based on the use of emerging technology, in the way in which banking services are provided. Currently, it is no longer necessary to physically attend the bank to request a service, since now it can be done using other means, such as ATMs, telephone lines or through the Internet with systems called E-Banking [31].

This form of access to the Bank is important because it is a way to reach many customers from anywhere in the world with services such as transfers, payments, credit management, etc. [31].

Internet banking is a type of transactional Web application. A Web application is software that makes use of the Internet and a Web interface, accesses or sends information to a centralized place. This type of application differs from traditional or conventional software by the amount of information it handles and access to millions of users from anywhere in the world [6].

Transactional Web applications, like E-Banking, require an architectural design with an emphasis on security, because when accessed by millions of people from anywhere in the world, them must protect all the information they handle using security mechanisms, to comply with the pillars of information security (CIA): confidentiality, integrity and availability [5].

According to [31] three types of risks can be specified: operational, legal and reputation. We will focus on operational risks due to the context of the project.

Operational risk: It happens due to a failure in the banking system process (either due to system processes or cyber-attacks) or due to human error.

A banking Web application must consider security controls so that it can provide benefits such as [31]:

- Access 24 h a day, from any computer connected to the Internet.
- Avoid long queues to be served at agencies and ATMs.
- Availability in real time of the most relevant information (balances, transactions, etc.).
- Decrease in the time of processing the information (direct from the Database).
- Transparency of information between competitors (the customer can compare prices, services, etc.).

1.2 Usability

According to ISO/IEC 9241-11 [10], usability is defined as "The degree to which a product can be used by certain users to achieve their specific objectives effectively, efficiently and satisfactorily in a given context of use", Whose measurable attributes are: effectiveness, efficiency and satisfaction.

According to ISO/IEC 9126-1 [11], which is being incorporated by ISO/IEC 25000 [34], usability is a quality characteristic of the software product and is defined as "The ability of the software product to be understood, learned, used and attractive when used under specific conditions." The Usability feature has as measurable sub-characteristics [34]: understandable, easy to learn, operable and attractive.

According to ISO/IEC 25000 [34], aligned to the concept defined in ISO/IEC 9241-11, usability is defined as "A subset of quality in use, whose sub-characteristics are efficiency, efficiency and satisfaction" [34].

The definition of usability in ISO/IEC 9241-11 refers to any product that can be used by man. In contrast, in ISO/IEC 9126 it refers to a software product that can be used by man. By orienting these two definitions to the software context, both standards seek that the user can make use of the software product in an easy way, that is understood, that can be used by any user and that is attractive in its use. In this way the user can achieve their objectives effectively, efficiently and satisfying their needs.

According to Jakob Nielsen, usability is a quality attribute that measures how easy it is to use an interface and defines it based on 5 components [15]: ease of learning, efficiency, recall, errors, satisfaction.

1.3 Usability Evaluation Methods

These methods allow determining or measuring the degree of usability of a software product. They are classified into two categories [8]: usability inspection methods and usability test methods.

Inspection Methods
According to Nielsen [25], inspection methods refers to the methods in which an evaluator inspects a user interface. It can be used at an early stage of the software development process, for example in the prototype stage or in the software requirements survey, where tests with users are not required. Compared to the usability test method, it is lower cost and does not require the user.

According to Holzinger [8], these methods are: heuristic evaluation, cognitive walkthroughs and action analysis:

1. Heuristic Evaluation: allows finding more usability problems than other evaluation methods [8]. It is the best-known method, with least formal training, fast, does not require user tests and is widely used as an inspection method [32]. The evaluation process consists in the direct and individual evaluation of the evaluators to a software product, making use of a list of usability heuristics, while the evaluators interact with the software product, inspecting and evaluating each element of this [14].

2. Cognitive Walkthroughs: It is a task-oriented method, which consists of simulating the step by step that users can follow to develop a task in the system. It is predicted the possible actions that users can take or problems they may encounter to reach their goal, by going through the functionalities of the system. Emphasis is placed on cognitive and learning, analyzing the required mental process of users [8]. One version of this method is pluralistic walkthroughs, which consists of a collaborative work in which end users, software developers and experts discuss each element of the system.

3. Action Analysis: Method that allows to quantify the time that it will take to develop a task and to know the behavior that the user may have, it is a slow process method, since everything is in function to what the users do and not to what They say they do, and because all the actions are divided into small tasks. For this type of method, it is required to have users with experience in their journey through the system's functionalities [8].

User Evaluations

According to Nielsen [25], these are methods where evaluations of the user interface are performed through tests with representative users. This method allows a direct communication between developers and users, which will allow the developer to learn more how users perceive the system and if it meets their needs and objectives, and from that, to be able to also know their questions and problems [5].

There are many methods, but the most common are [5]: Pencil and paper test, Thinking aloud, Co-discovery, Formal experiments, Methods of inquiry and Card Sorting.

1.4 Nielsen's Usability Heuristics

The heuristic principles of usability for the evaluation of the design of user interfaces most commonly used and known are the heuristics of Jakob Nielsen [8]. Next, the ten Nielsen principles that are used in the usability evaluation [13]:

1. Visibility of system status
2. Match between system and the real world
3. User control and freedom
4. Consistency and standards
5. Error prevention
6. Recognition rather than recall
7. Flexibility and efficiency of use

8. Aesthetic and minimalist design
9. Help users recognize, diagnose, and recover from errors
10. Help and documentation

1.5 Security

In this article, when talking about security, reference is made to the security of information and the use of security mechanisms to protect this information.

According to ISO/IEC 27002: 2013, the security of information is the "Preservation of confidentiality, integrity and availability of information" [12].

2 Methodology

According to Hermawati [7] there is no formal methodology for the development of usability heuristics but in most of the studies analyzed the authors start with a literature review and then combine methods. Due to this lack of formal methodology, it is that the research conducted by Rusu [29] proposes a methodology for the development of heuristics, this methodology includes a previous review of the literature, related to the subject in question, the development of the proposal of heuristic principles and finally, of a process of validation and refinement of the heuristic proposal.

This methodology was validated by Rusu in his study [29] and used in heuristic proposal studies related to various software domains, such as, in Grid Computing [30], Interactive Television [33], Touchscreen Mobile Devices [9], Transactional Web [15, 27] and in Internet banking [3].

The methodology presents six stages:

- Stage 1 - Exploratory: bibliographical collection related to the subject of study and usability heuristics.
- Stage 2 - Descriptive: Highlight important characteristics of the information collected in stage 1, related to the subject of study.
- Stage 3 - Correlational: Identify the main characteristics that a heuristic usability proposal should consider for the study domain based on traditional heuristics and analyzed case studies.
- Stage 4 - Explicative: formalize the set of proposed heuristic principles, considering a format that describes the heuristic.
- Stage 5 - Validation: this stage consists of the validation of the proposed heuristics, within a real context, in contrast to Nielsen's heuristics. For this, a case study is used to validate the proposed heuristics, in which usability evaluation processes are developed using the Nielsen heuristics and the proposed heuristics, following a protocol scheme modeled for the case.
- Stage 6 - Refinement: Based on the feedback obtained from the evaluators in stage 5, the proposed heuristic principles are refined.

3 Designing the Proposal

3.1 Exploratory Stage

In this stage, the bibliographic collection of current studies of heuristic and usability proposals for the Web Banca Internet domain was carried out, starting in 2012. The methodology followed is based on the one proposed by Kitchenham [17], since it is the most used and validated by different researchers.

After following the steps of the review, three relevant works are selected in the chosen domain, whose summary is shown in Table 1.

Table 1. Papers selected

No	Description
1	**Usability Heuristics for Web Banking** [3]: It proposes a set of 15 heuristics for the evaluation of usability of Internet Banking. The heuristics include principles of usability and security. The heuristics were obtained through an analysis of the literature and a case study developed
2	**Towards a Heuristic Model for Usable and Secure Online Banking** [23]: Pointing to a usable and safe heuristic model for Internet Banking evaluations, this study proposes 16 heuristics. It is based on the studies identified in the literature that contribute to a usable and safe Web design
3	**Usability Heuristics for Transactional Web Sites** [27]: It proposes a set of 13 heuristics for the Web domain of transactional sites, based on the concept that Nielsen's traditional heuristics are not appropriate for measuring usability in new emerging software categories, such as Web transactional

3.2 Descriptive Stage

In this stage the heuristics proposed in the primary studies are described and analyzed, with the purpose of highlighting important characteristics according to the research topic, heuristic principles for Web sites of Internet Banking.

In the selected studies (Fierro [3], Mujinga [23], Paz [27]) a base reference of the Nielsen [13] heuristics is observed to generate new heuristic proposals applicable in the domain. Here is an analysis of the heuristics proposed in the studies, initially focusing on the heuristics of Jakob Nielsen:

Visibility of the State of the System
In visibility of the state of the system, Paz maintains the definition described by Nielsen in the heuristic; However, Mujinga inclines this definition to the concept of security: visibility of the state of the security protection level and the state of connection of the system. On the other hand, Fierro, mentions that the system, apart from, informing the internal state of the system, must inform the state of the security mechanisms, to the user; and in another heuristic, it refers specifically to the state in which a transaction is found: "State of the transaction".

Apart from the definition of the heuristic "Visibility of the state of the system", Paz proposes an additional heuristic, which could be related to this heuristic, and is:

"Feedback on the State of a Transaction", in the first instance it can be understood that this Heuristics could be included in the heuristic of "Visibility of the state of the system", but according to the results obtained by Paz it is defined separately, because in this way it was able to identify more usability problems.

Summary: There is a concern in prevailing that the system must keep the user informed, constant feedback, about what is happening in the system (state), or, in the process of a transaction, of a system's own functionality or of the security mechanisms that it uses.

The System and the Real World

Mujinga refers to it as "User's language", Fierro divides this definition into two heuristics: Clarity and Familiarity, indicating that the security elements must be clear and familiar to the user. Paz relates it to the cultural aspect in which the user develops and interacts with the system.

Summary: there is a concern that the system communicates with the user using a natural language, specific to the user, that is clear and familiar to him. Especially messages related to security.

User Control and Freedom

Paz maintains the definition described by Nielsen in the "Control and user freedom" heuristics. Mujinga refers to the user can easily revoke security actions, if it is possible to perform (Revocability). Fierro refers to the definitions given by Nielsen and by Mujinga for the User Control and Freedom heuristics.

Summary: there is concern that the system provides exit options in situations unwanted for the user. Even in cases of security measures, in this case the revocation is made whenever possible.

Consistency and Standards

Fierro maintains the definition described by Nielsen, in the "Consistency and standards" heuristic, and adds that the system should not only be internally consistent, but also consistent with other similar websites. Meanwhile, Mujinga maintains only what is related to internal consistency.

On the other hand, Paz makes a total separation of these heuristics, which are: "Alignment towards Web design standards" and "Consistency in the design of the system". And in addition, they create a heuristic oriented towards compliance with "standardized symbology" that is often used by the user.

Summary: there is a concern that the design of the system should be aligned to a Web design standard and that it should follow the same style in all its interfaces. In turn, it is observed that the system must use a standardized symbology like other Web environments, which are already part of the user's usual environment.

Error Prevention

Fierro maintains the definition proposed by Nielsen in the "Prevention of error" heuristic, but Fierro adds that the user should know clearly what the consequences would be if a certain security action and whether they are irreversible or not. Paz proposes a new heuristic called "Prevention, recognition and recovery of errors" that covers the concepts defined in the Nielsen heuristics: "Error prevention" and "Help users recognize, diagnose and recover from errors", and is aligned to what was defined by Nielsen. Mujinga, in his "Errors" heuristic mentions that the system must provide messages of security errors, without codes, and how to recover from errors (with simple mechanisms).

Summary: there is a concern that the system prevents the user from a possible error, through messages or other elements. Information that allows the user to identify the consequences of whether he performs a certain action, be it operational or security.

Recognition Rather Than Remembering

Fierro and Paz maintain what Nielsen proposed in the "Recognition rather than remembering" heuristics. On the other hand, Mujinga mentions that security actions must be easy to learn and remember for users (Heuristic "Learning capacity").

Summary: there is a concern that the system allows the user not to retain in memory, for a long time, information that could be provided by the same system, especially when actions are developed where security is involved. The actions to be carried out should be easy to remember, through intuitive interfaces or messages.

Flexibility and Efficiency of Use

Paz and Fierro maintain the definition proposed by Nielsen in the "Flexibility and efficiency of use" heuristic, while Mujinga relates it to the information that must be to obtain a user profile to carry out their task without being harmed (Heuristic "Ideal user").

Summary: there is a concern that the system provides development mechanisms to improve the performance of the user, be it novice or expert, who can carry out their activities without harming each other. Flexibility and efficiency of use is related to both system functionalities and information provided to the user.

Aesthetics and Minimalist Design

Paz maintains the definition proposed by Nielsen in the heuristic "Aesthetics and minimalist design", while Mujinga relates the definition of heuristics to security: show relevant safety information and of the system. Fierro also maintains the proposal by Nielsen, but also adds that this minimalist design must be related to the information of security mechanisms.

Summary: there is a concern that the system provides a design of relevant and necessary information to the user, without overshadowing other important elements for the user such as security.

Helps Users to Recognize, Diagnose and Recover from Errors

Paz maintains the proposal by Nielsen in the heuristic "Help users recognize, diagnose and recover from errors" and defines it within of its proposed heuristic: "Prevention, recognition and recovery of errors". Mujinga, in his "Errors" heuristic, directs him to security error messages and how to get out of it, and Fierro, as described by Nielsen, adds safety concepts.

Summary: there is a concern in providing enough information to the user about how to recognize, diagnose and recover from errors.

Help and Documentation

Paz maintains the definition proposed by Nielsen in the "Help and documentation" heuristic, Fierro also maintains the proposal by Nielsen, but also stresses that there must be documentation related to security, visible and easy to find, for making decisions that the user can make in the face of a security action. Mujinga mentions that the system must aid on how to use the service and security functions, to the user.

Summary: there is a concern that the system provides help and documentation, both system functionalities and the use of security elements, which helps the user to perform certain tasks and to face situations where the user has doubts in what action to perform. This help and documentation should be visible and easy to find.

As we observed, the heuristics proposed by Mujinga and by Fierro are oriented to a system with samples of security elements. Next, heuristic principles are described, which by the definitions presented by the authors can be considered outside the scope of Nielsen's heuristics:

1. Customizable
   According to Mujinga and Fierro the user must be free to customize their interface, including security functions. Mujinga also indicates that if you are given the option to customize the user, you should also provide the reset option to a default configuration. All this will allow the user to be aware of their level of security.
2. Satisfaction
   According to Mujinga the user's experience in interacting with the system and its security mechanisms should be pleasant and satisfactory, otherwise users will be tempted to avoid security features.
3. Navigable
   According to Fierro, the navigation of the site must be logically structured, allowing the user to locate easily from one place to another.
4. Security
   In the case of security, Mujinga mentions two heuristics: Protection of the system, and Security and privacy. In the first, it refers to the veracity of the communication channels between the user and the system, these must be shown to be true and not fraudulent, using security mechanisms, all based on the security principles of Information: confidentiality, integrity, availability, authenticity, non-repudiation and privacy. The second concept refers to the fact that the system must be confidential, complete, available and private. On the other hand, Fierro goes on the perception side, mentions that the user needs to feel the confidence to use the system, that the security measures should be visible, friendly and understandable, for the user.
5. Clarity
   Although Mujinga does not propose a heuristic specifically aimed at the prevention of errors but does pose a "Clarity" heuristic that refers to the prevention of errors in themselves, through clear information, to users, of the consequences of if a certain action is carried out, especially of security or if they are irreversible, and that there must be the option of reversing the action taken.
6. Compliance with Requirement not related to usability
   According to Paz, based on the study conducted, for the Web transactional domain there are three heuristics that cover usability features that are not completely covered by Nielsen's heuristics, which are: "Reliability and Speed of Transactions", "Correct and Expected Functionality" and "Visibility and Clarity of System

Elements", which refer to what the system is expected to perform and return. The first heuristic is related to the fact that the transactions must be reliable and that they be carried out in an adequate manner under any circumstance; the second heuristic is related to the system returning what the user expects, and the last refers to the clarity with which the elements of the system should be viewed, depending on their importance.

On the other hand, Mujinga, proposes two heuristics: "Path of least resistance" and "Minimum authentication delay", where the first refers to the minimum effort that the system must perform to use the security features, and the second, to the waiting time that the system delays in authenticating the user.

In conclusion it is observed that for the usability of Internet Banking it is necessary to give a priority focus to the security aspects in addition to other characteristics that define a Web site as usable, such as, that it is navigable, customizable, satisfactory (at the level of functionalities and use of security elements), secure, clear and that meets the requirements not related to usability.

Adding all the heuristics and characteristics, 16 heuristics were obtained, it is a considerable high number to develop usability tests, this could cause the evaluation process to be longer and perhaps tedious. So first we tried to adapt the concepts identified by the researchers to the traditional heuristics of Nielsen and to add the remaining ones as new heuristics, with the aim of obtaining more complete heuristics that not only point to usability, but also, to security.

3.3   Correlational and Explicative Stages

From the previous section, it is determined that heuristics for Internet banking should not only be usable, but also safe; and that in addition to the heuristics specified by Nielsen, there are other heuristics that are not covered. Therefore, to increase the likelihood that the banking Web design will be more usable, the following characteristics adapted as heuristics should be fulfilled:

1. Customizable: It is a feature that is important for Internet Banking design, because according to Mtimkulu [22], allowing the user to configure their website is already a trend that should be considered in this type of Web design.
2. Navigable: according to Fierro [3] navigability is also important.
3. Satisfaction: it is an important characteristic, because if the system does not satisfy the user, it ceases to be useful for the user [23, 24, 28].
4. Security: because is an important factor that must be present in the Web design of a banking entity [1, 2, 18] is that it is considered an important feature in its design. The presence of security in a Web site provides confidence to the user to continue using the system.
5. Clarity: the definition given by Mujinga [23] in his Heuristic of "Clarity" can be included as part of the definition of the heuristic "Prevention of errors" (clear messages that prevent an error or something related to security); and to the heuristic "Relationship between the system and the real world" (clear information).
6. Functional and Performance: Characteristics better measured by user tests, therefore, will not be used in the proposal.

From what is specified in the correlational stage, we proceed to design the heuristic proposal, which is an extension of Nielsen's heuristics. The first ten heuristics are related to Nielsen's heuristics and the next four to the heuristics identified as characteristics of this Web domain. In Table 2 shows the mapping between Nielsen's heuristics and the proposed heuristics.

Table 2. Heuristics Nielsen (HN) and project proposal (PHB)

ID	Nielsen	ID	Proposal
HN1	Visibility of system status	PHB1	Visibility of system status
HN2	Match between system and the real world	PHB2	Match between system and the real world
HN3	User control and freedom	PHB3	User control and freedom
HN4	Consistency and standards	PHB4	Consistency and standards
HN5	Error prevention	PHB5	Error prevention
HN6	Recognition rather than recall	PHB6	Recognition rather than recall
HN7	Flexibility and efficiency of use	PHB7	Flexibility and efficiency of use
HN8	Aesthetic and minimalist design	PHB8	Aesthetic and minimalist design
HN9	Help users recognize, diagnose, and recover from errors	PHB9	Help users recognize, diagnose, and recover from errors
HN10	Help and documentation	PHB10	Help and documentation
		PHB11	Customizable
		PHB12	Navigable
		PHB13	Satisfaction
		PHB14	Security and privacy

3.4   Validation Stage

For this validation phase we proceeded to develop a case study, from which we intend to explore and know if the Nielsen heuristics or the proposed heuristics are complete for use, under a real context, in usability evaluations of interface design of Internet Banking.

There were two groups of evaluators who reviewed a certain banking website using different heuristic sets, group 1 made use of Nielsen's heuristics and the other of the proposed heuristics.

The comparison of the effectiveness of the proposed heuristics and the Nielsen Heuristics was developed, because they are the most proven through case studies and most recognized in the field of Web domain usability. Furthermore, there is not a group of heuristics in the Internet Banking domain that have been validated with a considerable amount of studies.

The validation phase was applied to the banking website of the study, during the months of January and February of 2017.

Results for Time Invested and Efficiency

According to the results of the survey, the average time invested by the evaluators in developing the evaluation was 32.5 min for Group 1-HN and 71.25 min for Group

2-PHB. The reason for this, according to the answers of the evaluators and that can also be deduced, was due to the time it took them in their understanding and to relate heuristics to identified usability problems, since the proposed heuristics differ a bit from Nielsen's heuristics.

Regarding efficiency, if we relate the time invested with the identified (total) usability problems, Group 1-HN has an efficiency value of 0.67 and Group 2-PHB had 0.39, we observed that Group 1-HN was more efficient than Group 2-PHB, because they did it in less time, although they managed to identify fewer usability problems than the Group 2-PHB group (Table 3).

Table 3. Results for time invested and efficiency

Group	Average time	Problems	Efficiency
Nielsen – Group 1-HN	32.5	22	0.67
Proposal – Group 2-PHB	71.25	28	0.39

Results by Number of Usability Problems

Group 1-HN, using Nielsen's heuristics, identified 22 usability problems, but after reviewing them, eliminating repeated usability problems and validating them, 20 usability problems were obtained. Being the heuristic of "Flexibility and efficiency of use" the one that had more quantity, 6 usability problems (30%), as shown in Fig. 1.

Group 2-PHB, making use of the proposed PHB heuristics, identified 28 usability problems, but after reviewing it eliminating repeated usability problems and validating them, 27 usability problems were obtained. Being the heuristic of "Relationship between the system and the real world" and the heuristic of "Consistency and standards", which had the greatest amount of usability problems. Being 4 the number of usability problems identified (15%) for both cases. As shown in Fig. 2.

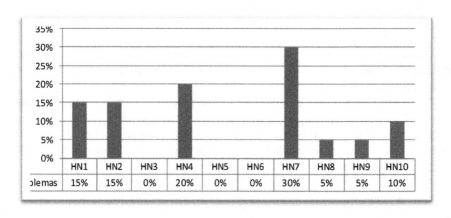

	HN1	HN2	HN3	HN4	HN5	HN6	HN7	HN8	HN9	HN10
olemas	15%	15%	0%	20%	0%	0%	30%	5%	5%	10%

Fig. 1. Percentage of usability problems identified by Group 1-HN - without repeated values

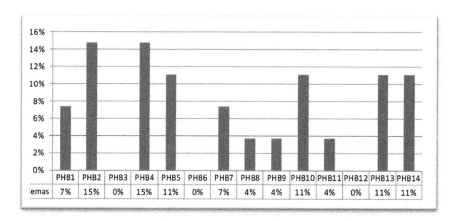

Fig. 2. Percentage of usability problems identified by Group 2-PHB - without repeated values

Analyzing the problems by criteria, it is observed that the number of problems identified only by Group 2-PHB is 25 (56%), the number of problems identified only by Group 1-HN is 18 (40%), and number of problems identified by both groups of evaluators is 2 (4%). See Fig. 3.

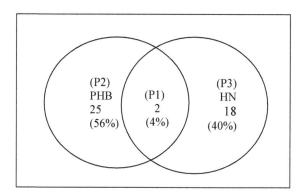

Fig. 3. Problems identified

Results by Severity

From the Table 4, it is observed that the group that made use of the proposed heuristics (Group 2-PHB) obtained more problems of greater degree: 12 major problems and 5 catastrophic problems. On the other hand, the group that made use of the Nielsen heuristics (Group 1-HN) obtained fewer problems of greater degree: 7 major problems and 3 catastrophic problems. In average severity, Group 1-HN obtained 1.83 and Group 2-PHB obtained 2.03, Group 2-PHB has the highest value.

Table 4. Severity of problems

Severity	Group 1 - HN		Group 2 - PHB	
	Problems		Problems	
0 – No problem	0	0%	0	0%
1 – Cosmetic problem	2	10%	3	11%
2 – Minor problem	8	40%	7	26%
3 – Major problem	7	35%	12	44%
4 – Catastrophic problem	3	15%	5	19%
Total	20		27	

Results by Degree of Perception

The objective is to measure the level of perception that evaluators have about each heuristic used. The constructs used were: Ease of use, Utility, Clarity and Need to use a checklist (Checklist) for each proposed heuristic, the model of constructs is based on what was developed by Jiménez [16].

The constructs are:

- Perceived utility: it allows to measure if the heuristics are perceived as useful for a process of usability evaluation in Internet Banking.
- Perceived clarity: it allows to measure if the heuristics are perceived as clear or more specification is necessary to achieve its objective within a process of evaluation of usability in Internet Banking.
- Easy perceived use: it allows to measure if the heuristics are perceived as easy to use in a process of usability evaluation in Internet Banking.
- Need to use a checklist: it allows to measure whether to use the heuristics it is necessary to use a checklist or not, to achieve its objective within a process of usability evaluation in Internet Banking.

The questions of the perception survey are of a closed type, and for its measurement the Likert scale has been used, which includes values from 1 (most negative perception) to 5 (most positive perception). The question form is based on what was developed by Paz in [26].

From Tables 5 and 6 we can see that the heuristics: "Visibility of the state of the system", "Recognition instead of remembering", "Navigability" and "Satisfaction" have more perception, which means that these heuristics are more viable. In contrast, the heuristics "Prevention of errors" and "Help users to recognize, diagnose and recover errors" are those that have a lower degree of perception.

In summary, according to the results obtained in Table 7, it can be seen that PHB heuristics have more validity than Nielsen's heuristics, since they show that a greater number of usability problems can be obtained, and with a greater degree of severity and catastrophic.

Table 5. Nominal results of the survey conducted – Group 1-HN

Id	Heuristic	Easy	Useful	Clear	Checklist
HN1	Visibility of system status	Easy	Useful	Probably yes	Probably yes
HN2	Match between system and the real world	Neutral	Useful	Probably yes	Yes
HN3	User control and freedom	Neutral	Neutral	Neutral	Probably yes
HN4	Consistency and standards	Neutral	Useful	Probably yes	Yes
HN5	Error prevention	Neutral	Useful	Probably yes	Yes
HN6	Recognition rather than recall	Neutral	Useful	Probably yes	Probably yes
HN7	Flexibility and efficiency of use	Easy	Useful	Probably yes	Probably yes
HN8	Aesthetic and minimalist design	Easy	Useful	Probably yes	Probably yes
HN9	Help users recognize, diagnose, and recover from errors	Neutral	Neutral	Neutral	Probably yes
HN10	Help and documentation	Easy	Useful	Probably yes	Probably yes
	Nielsen's Heuristics	Neutral	Useful	Probably yes	Probably yes

Table 6. Nominal results of the survey conducted – Group 2-PHB

Id	Heuristic	Easy	Useful	Clear	Checklist
PHB1	Visibility of system status	Very easy	Useful	Probably yes	Neutral
PHB2	Match between system and the real world	Neutral	Useful	Probably yes	Neutral
PHB3	User control and freedom	easy	Neutral	Probably yes	Neutral
PHB4	Consistency and standards	Neutral	Useful	Probably yes	Neutral
PHB5	Error prevention	Neutral	Useful	Probably yes	Neutral
PHB6	Recognition rather than recall	Easy	Useful	Probably yes	Neutral
PHB7	Flexibility and efficiency of use	Neutral	Useful	Probably yes	Neutral
PHB8	Aesthetic and minimalist design	Neutral	Useful	Probably yes	Neutral
PHB9	Help users recognize, diagnose, and recover from errors	Neutral	Useful	Neutral	Probably yes
PHB10	Help and documentation	Easy	Neutral	Probably yes	Neutral
PHB11	Customize	Easy	Neutral	Probably yes	Neutral
PHB12	Navigability	Easy	Completely Useful	Probably yes	Neutral
PHB13	Satisfaction	Easy	Useful	Probably yes	Neutral
PHB14	Security and privacy	Neutral	Useful	Probably yes	Probably yes
	Proposal	Neutral	Useful	Probably yes	Neutral

Table 7. Summary of results

Criterion	Group 1-HN	Group 2-PHB
Problems found	18	25
Time	32.5 min	71.25 min
Efficiency	0.67	0.39
Severity	07-Major 03-Catastrophic	12-Major 05-Catastrophic
Severity average	1.83	2.03

3.5 Refinement

According to the results obtained, the heuristics that were not clear, easy and useful are refined; and that require a checklist. The definitions and related examples were redefined, focusing more on the security mechanisms, which apparently did not identify themselves.

In addition, because one of the expert evaluators of Group 2-PHB, indicated that these mechanisms are not clear, the concepts of security in the following heuristics are better specified:

- In PHB1: Not only the system must keep the user informed if the access channel is safe or not, but also, must keep informed about the level of security protection, through the visualization of activation states of the mechanisms of security that the banking entity applies.
- In PHB2: it was stressed that the security messages, that the system provides, through different means such as texts, graphics, among others must be clear and be consistent with the real world of the user and must be easy to understand, in this way the user will avoid obviating the security mechanisms that the Bank applies.
- In PHB3: it is indicated that the system allows the user to revoke any unwanted security action, whenever possible.
- PHB6: it is indicated: "For the users, the messages and actions related to security must be easy to understand and learn, not having to resort to the information material in a constant way thanks to the use of metaphors."
- PHB11: includes configurations in the security functions.

In the heuristics PHB4, PHB5, PHB8, PHB9 and PHB14, only the text of the definition was refined to make them clearer and more useful; and for cases PHB10 and PHB7, no change was made, since it is considered that the definition of the text is punctual.

4 Conclusions

Being a bank to analyze, the issue related to errors and help about these are what you want to avoid, Internet banking must be prepared to overcome any internal error, but if it is an error caused by the user, type error number of account, the system will not recognize it as an error, it is considered as a user error.

There are evaluators who indicate that Nielsen's heuristics are complete for this type of Web design, but there are also those who indicate otherwise. After an analysis of the usability problems identified, using Nielsen, it could be identified that some usability problems were better solved using the proposed heuristics such as the case that the system does not return as expected, lack of necessary information or there is an excess of use of security mechanisms; which support the proposed heuristics of Satisfaction, Personalization and Security and data privacy.

From everything analyzed favorable values were obtained using the proposed PHB heuristics, they are not very prominent, but they make the difference. But in this, it must be borne in mind that when judging the Web design based on the criteria and different level of expertise of the evaluators, developed in a single iteration of evaluation processes, it cannot be assured or generalized that the proposed heuristics they are more effective than Nielsen's, for this, several additional evaluation processes are required using refined heuristics. But what can be argued is that Nielsen's heuristics do not fully cover features such as navigability, satisfaction, personalization, and data security and privacy, and that, in addition, the heuristics of Navigability, Satisfaction are well perceived by users. evaluators; and Personalization, and Data security and privacy are currently a necessity, since one is a trend and the other is a factor of adoption in use of Internet Banking, respectively.

References

1. Ojeniyi, A., et al.: Online banking user interface: perception and attitude. In: 2015 International Conference on Computer, Communications, and Control Technology (I4CT), pp. 64–69 (2015)
2. Costante, E., et al.: On-line trust perception: what really matters. In: 2011 1st Workshop on Socio-Technical Aspects in Security and Trust (STAST), pp. 52–59 (2011)
3. Fierro, N., Zapata, C.: Usability heuristics for web banking. In: Marcus, A. (ed.) DUXU 2016. LNCS, vol. 9746, pp. 412–423. Springer, Cham (2016). https://doi.org/10.1007/978-3-319-40409-7_39
4. French, A.M.: A case study on e-banking security-when security becomes too sophisticated for the user to access their information. J. Internet Bank. Commer. **17**(2), 1–14 (2012)
5. Galitz, W.O.: The Essential Guide to User Interface Design: An Introduction to GUI Design Principles and Techniques. Wiley, New York (2007)
6. Ginige, A., Murugesan, S.: Web engineering: an introduction. IEEE Multimed. **8**(1), 14–18 (2001)
7. Hermawati, S., Lawson, G.: Establishing usability heuristics for heuristics evaluation in a specific domain: is there a consensus? Appl. Ergon. **56**, 34–51 (2016)
8. Holzinger, A.: Usability engineering methods for software developers. Commun. ACM **48**(1), 71–74 (2005)
9. Inostroza, R., et al.: Usability heuristics for touchscreen-based mobile devices: update. In: Proceedings of the 2013 Chilean Conference on Human - Computer Interaction, pp. 24–29. ACM, New York (2013)
10. ISO: 9241-11: Ergonomic requirements for office work with visual display terminals (VDT's), Berlin, Germany (1998)
11. ISO: ISO/IEC 9126-1:2001: Software engineering – Product quality – Part 1: Quality model. https://www.iso.org/standard/22749.html

12. ISO: ISO/IEC 27002:2013: Information technology – Security techniques – Code of practice for information security controls. https://www.iso.org/standard/54533.html
13. Jakob Nielsen: 10 Heuristics for User Interface Design. https://www.nngroup.com/articles/ten-usability-heuristics/
14. Jakob Nielsen: Heuristic Evaluation: How-To: Article. https://www.nngroup.com/articles/how-to-conduct-a-heuristic-evaluation/
15. Jakob Nielsen: Usability 101: Introduction to Usability (2012). https://www.nngroup.com/articles/usability-101-introduction-to-usability/
16. Jimenez, C., et al.: Formal specification of usability heuristics: how convenient it is? In: Proceedings of the 2nd International Workshop on Evidential Assessment of Software Technologies, pp. 55–60. ACM, New York (2012)
17. Kitchenham, B., et al.: Systematic literature reviews in software engineering–a tertiary study. Inf. Softw. Technol. **52**(8), 792–805 (2010)
18. Mujinga, M., et al.: Online banking users' perceptions in South Africa: an exploratory empirical study. In: 2016 IST-Africa Week Conference, pp. 1–7 (2016)
19. Mannan, M., van Oorschot, P.C.: Security and usability: the gap in real-world online banking. In: Proceedings of the 2007 Workshop on New Security Paradigms, pp. 1–14. ACM (2008)
20. Mockel, C.: Usability and security in EU E-banking systems - towards an integrated evaluation framework. In: 2011 IEEE/IPSJ 11th International Symposium on Applications and the Internet (SAINT), pp. 230–233 (2011)
21. Moeckel, C.: Human-computer interaction for security research: the case of EU E-banking systems. In: Campos, P., Graham, N., Jorge, J., Nunes, N., Palanque, P., Winckler, M. (eds.) INTERACT 2011. LNCS, vol. 6949, pp. 406–409. Springer, Heidelberg (2011). https://doi.org/10.1007/978-3-642-23768-3_44
22. Mtimkulu, S., van Biljon, J., van Dyk, T.: Designing for the functionality South African internet banking websites should provide to address the needs of Generation-Y users. In: Kotzé, P., Marsden, G., Lindgaard, G., Wesson, J., Winckler, M. (eds.) INTERACT 2013. LNCS, vol. 8120, pp. 366–383. Springer, Heidelberg (2013). https://doi.org/10.1007/978-3-642-40498-6_29
23. Mujinga, M., et al.: Towards a heuristic model for usable and secure online banking. In: 24th Australasian Conference on Information Systems (ACIS), pp. 1–12. RMIT University (2013)
24. Cooharojananone, N., et al.: A study on intention to use factor in the internet banking websites in Thailand. In: 2011 IEEE/IPSJ International Symposium on Applications and the Internet, pp. 556–561 (2011)
25. Nielsen, J.: Usability inspection methods. In: Conference Companion on Human Factors in Computing Systems, pp. 413–414. ACM, New York (1994)
26. Paz, F., Paz, F.A., Pow-Sang, J.A.: Comparing the effectiveness and accuracy of new usability heuristics. In: Nunes, I.L. (ed.) Advances in Human Factors and System Interactions, pp. 163–175. Springer, Cham (2017). https://doi.org/10.1007/978-3-319-41956-5_16
27. Paz, F., et al.: Usability Heuristics for Transactional Web Sites. In: 2014 11th International Conference on Information Technology: New Generations (ITNG), pp. 627–628 (2014)
28. Riffai, M.M.M.A., et al.: Big TAM in Oman: exploring the promise of on-line banking, its adoption by customers and the challenges of banking in Oman. Int. J. Inf. Manag. **32**(3), 239–250 (2012)
29. Rusu, C., et al.: A methodology to establish usability heuristics. In: The Fourth International Conference on Advances in Computer-Human Interactions, ACHI 2011, pp. 59–62 (2011)

30. Roncagliolo, S., et al.: Grid computing usability heuristics in practice. In: 2011 Eighth International Conference on Information Technology: New Generations, pp. 145–150 (2011)
31. SBS: Banca Electrónica: Posibilidades, Riesgos y Lineamientos Regulatorios - Una primera aproximación, (2000)
32. Sears, A.: Heuristic walkthroughs: finding the problems without the noise. Int. J. Hum.-Comput. Interact. **9**(3), 213–234 (1997)
33. Solano, A., et al.: Usability heuristics for interactive digital television. In: The Third International Conference on Advances in Future Internet, pp. 60–63 (2011)
34. ISO/IEC 25000:2014: Systems and software engineering – Systems and software Quality Requirements and Evaluation (SQuaRE) – Guide to SQuaRE. https://www.iso.org/standard/64764.html

Affordable Eye Tracking for Informed Web Design

Jarrett W. Clark[(✉)] and A. Lucas Stephane

Florida Institute of Technology, Melbourne, FL 32901, USA
clarkj2012@my.fit.edu, lstephane@fit.edu

Abstract. Eye tracking hardware and software can be used to analyze and improve websites. If conducting an eye tracking study is too costly, examining mouse movement data can also provide similar insights into user behavior as eye gaze data. Prior research has shown eye gaze and mouse cursor position can strongly correlate. The strength of the correlation, however, depends on the design of the website. It is important to determine if mouse tracking is a reliable substitute for eye tracking as new design patterns emerge. Today, there are low-cost eye tracking solutions available, enabling a wider audience to conduct their own eye-mouse correlation studies. In this paper, we use The Eye Tribe Eye Tracker and the analysis software, EyeProof, to find the relationship between eye gaze and mouse position on the Florida Institute of Technology Human-Centered Design Institute website. The results indicate that mouse tracking data may be a suitable substitute for eye tracking data on the studied website and it may be feasible to use consumer-grade eye tracking products to conduct similar assessments.

Keywords: Eye tracking · Mouse tracking · Web design · Web analytics

1 Introduction

When redeveloping a website, web designers often use web analytics to make decisions to improve the current or next design. Web analytics can provide designers with usage statistics including information about user mouse movements. By examining the mouse movements of website visitors, it is possible to infer which features on a web page attract the most visual attention [2].

The most popular visual elements on a screen can also be determined by recording eye movements with an eye tracker [6]. Eye tracking hardware is now integrated into consumer products such as cell phones and laptops. Standalone eye trackers for consumers are also available. However, data from consumer-grade eye trackers is not yet readily accessible to web authors in aggregate. Instead, designers must trust the data gathered from tracking mouse movements is closely related to eye gaze position.

Prior research has shown that mouse position can strongly correlate with eye gaze position. The strength of the correlation varies, though, based on a number factors such as the arrangement of elements on a user interface [11]. It is important for web designers and researchers to determine if mouse movement patterns provide a fair representation of visual attention on new websites.

In the past, the price of research-grade eye tracking hardware and analysis software could prohibit people from conducting eye tracking studies. With lower-cost, consumer-grade equipment, it is now possible for more people to gather data about eye movements. More web designers and researchers can now determine if eye gaze position correlates with mouse position on a website they are developing.

In this study, the low-cost, standalone Eye Tribe Eye Tracker and companion testing software, EyeProof, were used to determine if a relationship between eye fixations and mouse cursor position existed on the Florida Institute of Technology (FIT) Human-Centered Design Institute (HCDI) website.

Twenty-one participants were recruited and given a search task on three different pages on the HCDI website. Among the participants and on the selected web pages, a strong positive correlation (r > .5) was found between eye fixations and mouse position. The results indicate passively collected mouse movement data from visitors to the website may show where the users were looking on each page. Better informed decisions can in turn be made when redesigning the website in the future. Content and aesthetic elements can be retained, removed, or repositioned based on the estimated visual attraction of each item.

2   Related Work

2.1   Low-Cost Eye Trackers

The accuracy of low-cost, consumer-grade eye trackers has been examined by other authors. Dalmaijer compared the accuracy of The Eye Tribe Eye Tracker with the EyeLink 1000 from SR Research [4]. Dalmaijer determined The Eye Tribe could provide reliable data about eye fixations but warned against using it to track saccades (movements between fixations).

Both Popelka et al. [13], and Ooms et al. [12] tested The Eye Tribe against an SMI RED250. Both groups found the lower-cost system from The Eye Tribe could provide comparable results to the more expensive hardware.

The Tobii EyeX is another low-cost eye tracker available today. Although, primarily intended for video games and interaction, Gibaldi, Vanegas, Bex, and Maiello found the EyeX could track eye fixations with a high degree of accuracy [5].

2.2   Eye-Mouse Coordination

Early research into eye-mouse coordination sought to confirm that a connection existed between gaze and mouse cursor movement. Chen, Anderson, and Sohn allowed users to freely browse a website and found mouse and eye gaze matched 75% of the time [2]. Only one method for defining areas of interest was explored, however. The researchers defined regions around text, images, and additional HTML elements on each page. If both the mouse cursor and user's eye gaze moved into a region, it was considered a match.

Cooke found eye movement and mouse behavior matched 69% of the time in a later study [3]. Cooke's methodology included a wider-range of user behaviors. If a participant visually scanned up and down the page, and used the mouse to vertically scroll the page, it was considered a match.

More recent research focused on eye-mouse coordination on search result pages. Rodden and Fu found mouse movement could be an indicator of which results the user saw and considered clicking on [14]. Rodden et al. identified three distinct mouse movement behaviors on search result pages [15]. They discovered some people used their mouse to mark a potential result that they would click later. Other people moved their mouse horizontally or vertically and kept it near the text they were actively reading.

Guo and Agichtein also looked at search result pages [7]. As eye gaze and mouse cursor position are not always near each other, the researchers sought to automatically predict the areas on the page in which eye and mouse position were most likely to be within 100 pixels of each other.

The relationship between clicks and eye gaze was examined by Buscher et al. [1]. Clicks were not necessary related to visual attention.

Huang, White, and Buscher found that the strength of eye and mouse correlation varies depending on the user's current behavior [9]. The relationship between eye and mouse changed when users were inactive, reading, acting, or examining.

Liebling and Dumais have questioned earlier eye and mouse tracking studies for being too controlled and unrealistic [10]. They found the user's behavior was more complex than reported in other students when the users could work at their own desks and on tasks of their own choosing.

3 Research Method

Twenty-one participants were recruited at FIT for this study. The eye tracking tests were conducted between November 2015 and January 2016.

Prior to administering the eye tracking test, participants were asked to complete a survey. The ages reported by the participants ranged from 22 to 60. The median age was 31. Thirteen users were male and eight were female. The users self-rated familiarity level with the HCDI website is shown in Fig. 1.

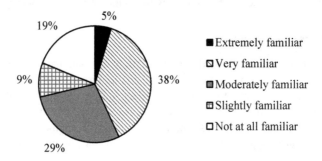

Fig. 1. Responses to the survey question, "how familiar are you with the Human-Centered Design Institute website?"

Participants were also asked about their primary computing device. Three people reported using a cellphone or tablet with a touch screen as their main device. The remaining 18 participants said they used a laptop or desktop with a mouse and keyboard as their primary computer.

Finally, users were asked to rate their confidence in using a keyboard and mouse on a five-point Likert scale. Fourteen of the users indicated they "extremely confident" and seven said they were "quite confident" - the highest and second highest possible ratings.

3.1 Hardware Configuration

The Eye Tribe Eye Tracker was used to record the eye movements of all 21 participants. The Eye Tribe Eye Tracker was released in 2014 for $99 [8].

The eye tracker was set to capture data at 30 Hz. The eye tracker was placed below a 19-in. monitor with a resolution of 1280×1024 pixels. A keyboard and mouse were also provided in front of the eye tracker and monitor. During the test, however, users were instructed to only use the mouse as pressing a key on the keyboard could interrupt the testing software, EyeProof. Participants were also asked to keep their head as still possible, so the system would not lose track of their eyes.

3.2 Scenarios

Three pages on the HCDI website were assessed: the news, courses, and publications pages. While the content varied on each screen, some aesthetic and navigation elements were consistent. Every page on the HCDI site featured a two-column, fixed-width layout and a global horizontal navigation menu at the top.

Due to limitations of the testing tool, EyeProof, only one web page could be presented at a time to the users as a static image. The users were not free to roam the site. The pages were presented in a random order for each test, and the order was determined by the EyeProof software.

Before each page was displayed, users were asked to read a paragraph that provided them with a scenario and search task related to the forthcoming page. All scenarios asked people to imagine they were "a master's student at Florida Institute of Technology." The tasks then required them to find and click a link on the next screen.

On the news page, the participants had to find and click the link to a specific news article among a list of 10 article titles and summaries. On the courses page, the goal was to retrieve a class syllabus among a list of 13 course names and syllabus links. For the publications page, users were asked to find a link to a paper among a reference list of 70 publications.

After clicking on the screen, the users were taken to the next scenario description, or if it was the third and final page, the program exited.

3.3 Analysis

Eye gaze and mouse movement data recorded during each session was stored on the EyeProof website. The EyeProof website also provided tools for analyzing the captured data.

Instead of comparing the raw x, y coordinates of eye and mouse movements, aggregate statistics were generated from areas of interest on each page. The EyeProof site had tools for creating rectangular, round, and irregular shaped areas of interest. However, the system offered no method for drawing shapes with precise dimensions or at exact screen coordinates. To avoid overlapping shapes and inaccuracies due to drawing areas of interest by hand, a user interface automation tool was developed that created shapes with explicitly defined dimensions and coordinates. A result from running this tool can be seen in Fig. 2.

Fig. 2. Screenshot from the EyeProof website where a user interface automation tool was used to create a square grid with each cell measuring 640×640 pixels.

Also, while EyeProof recorded mouse position data and the mouse movement was visible during playback of each session, no statistics were available about mouse movement. For example, the software would not automatically calculate the number of

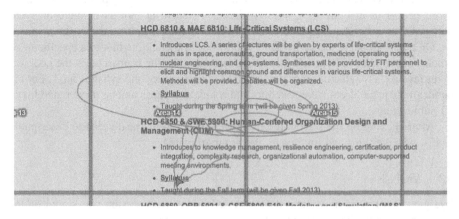

Fig. 3. Screenshot from the EyeProof web tool showing the mouse movement path of a participant. The mouse cursor path is teal colored.

times the users mouse moved into an area. Only metrics about eye movements were provided in EyeProof's data outputs.

To calculate mouse movement statistics, the number of times the participants mouse entered an area of interest was manually counted by playing back each session.

Some users moved the mouse cursor quickly or in complex patterns. Figure 3 shows an example of a complex mouse movement pattern generated by one participant. In these cases, the playback in EyeProof was recorded using a desktop screen recording program and played back in slow motion in an external video player. EyeProof lacked a built-in method for slowing down the session playback.

4   Results

Only 11 of the 21 users completed every task successfully. Seventy-one percent of the participants found the requested article on the publications page. The courses page saw the highest success rate with 86% of the users finding the link to the desired paper. On the news page, 81% clicked on the correct news article link.

A weak relationship existed between the user's familiarity with the HCDI website and successful task completion, although, the results were not statistically significant [$r = .221$, $n = 21$, $p = .336$].

In any case, successful completion of each scenario was not seen as essential in this study. The goal of this research was to find the relationship between eye and mouse movement on the HCDI website. Even when the task was not completed successfully, eye and mouse movement data was still captured and could be evaluated.

The cumulative count of eye fixations and mouse visits were evaluated in areas of interest. Three different methods were used to create areas of interest. On the publications page, a 2×4 grid was created where each area of interest was 640×640 pixels. Another grid was used on the courses page; however, the boxes were reduced to 320×320 pixels each. For the news page, outlines of the HTML elements were created instead of a square grid. A rectangular area of interest was drawn around each paragraph, list item, heading, and link.

A Pearson product-moment correlation coefficient was used to analyze the relationship between mouse visits and eye fixations in the defined areas of interest. The correlation between two sets of variables were examined.

First, the total number of mouse visits was compared to the total number of eye fixations in each area of interest.

The percentage of users who visited an area of interest with their mouse was also compared with the percentage of users who fixated on the area of interest. In other words, mouse visits and eye fixations were only counted once for each user in this measurement.

4.1   Publications Page (640×640 Areas of Interest)

Areas of interest were drawn in a 2×4 square grid on the publications page. Each cell on the grid measured 640×640 pixels. The size of 640 was chosen as it evenly divided the page which had a width of 1280 pixel.

Using a large grid for areas of interest resulted in a strong correlation between the total count of eye fixations and total count of mouse visits [r = .697, n = 8, p = .001]. When comparing the unique or percentage of participants that visited and fixated on area of interest, the relationship was strong between the two variables, however, the result was not statistically significant [r = .931, n = 8, p = .055].

4.2 Courses Page (320 × 320 Areas of Interest)

Smaller areas of interest were created on the courses page. Areas of interest were generated in 4 × 8 square grid where each square was 320 × 320 pixels. Figure 4 shows a scatterplot of the total mouse visits and total eye fixations in each area.

A strong relationship was found on the courses page when comparing the total number of mouse visits and total number of eye fixations [r = .667, n = 32, p = .001]. A strong connection was also found between the percentage of visits and fixations [r = .901, n = 32, p = .001].

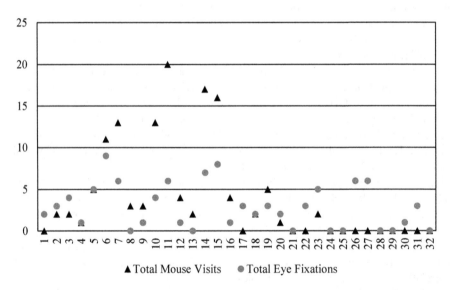

▲ Total Mouse Visits   ● Total Eye Fixations

Fig. 4. The total number of mouse visits and total number of eye fixations in each area of interest on the courses page. The x-axis lists the number assigned to the area of interest and the y-axis shows the number of visits or fixations.

4.3 News Page (HTML Areas of Interest)

A different pattern for the areas of interest was tried on the news page. Rectangles were drawn around the estimated shape of the HTML elements instead of the grid pattern that as was used on the publications and courses page. Fifty-eight HTML elements were marked and tracked on the page. A scatterplot in Fig. 5 shows the data for 29 elements and the percentage of the users who visited or fixated on each element.

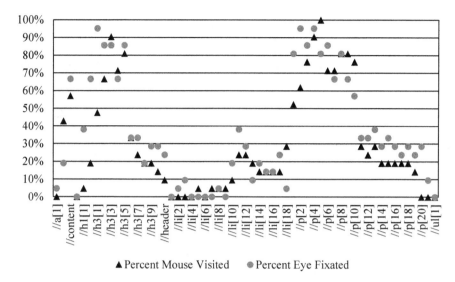

Fig. 5. The percentage of users who visited an area of interest with the mouse at least once or fixated at least once on an area of interest with their eyes. The XPath of the element is displayed on the x-axis.

On the news page and with the HTML element-sized areas of interest, the relationship was strong between the percentage of mouse visits and percentage of eye fixations [r = .889, n = 57, p < .001]. Likewise, a strong correlation existed between the cumulative number of mouse visits and eye fixations [r = .846, n = 57, p < .001].

5   Future Work

This study made use of a single, consumer-grade eye tracker. Because of cost constraints, the results from the low-cost eye tracker were not compared to a research-grade eye tracking solution. In future work, ideally results from consumer products would be confirmed with professional systems.

Because of limitations in EyeProof, mouse visit duration was not measured in each area of interest. Comparing mouse visit duration and fixation duration should be explored in the future with low-cost eye trackers.

Future research should also continue to examine different screen layouts and different types of software. Shifts in interface and product design trends may alter people's behavior, which in turn may affect the strength of the correlation between eye gaze and mouse position.

6   Conclusion

On all three web pages examined and among the 21 participants tested, there was a strong positive correlation between the total number of mouse visits and total number of eye fixations. The correlation was stronger when multiple eye fixations and mouse visits were removed from the data. However, the findings were not statistically significant on the publications page, which used the largest areas of interest.

The findings suggest if eye tracking data is unavailable, mouse tracking data may be a suitable substitute for determining which elements on the HCDI website draw a user's visual attention.

Researchers without access to research-grade eye tracking equipment may be able to use consumer-grade solutions to conduct similar eye and mouse tracking studies. It is important to repeat eye-mouse correlation tests as other research has shown the strength of the relationship between eye and mouse position can vary depending on an interface's design.

References

1. Buscher, G., Dumais, S.T., Cutrell, E.: The good, the bad, and the random: an eye-tracking study of ad quality in web search. In: Proceedings of the 33rd International ACM SIGIR Conference on Research and Development in Information Retrieval (SIGIR 2010), pp. 42–49. ACM, New York (2010)
2. Chen, M.-C., Anderson, J.R., Sohn, M.-H.: What can a mouse cursor tell us more? correlation of eye/mouse movements on web browsing. In: CHI 2001 Extended Abstracts on Human Factors in Computing Systems, pp. 281–282. ACM, New York (2001)
3. Cooke, L.: Is the mouse a "poor man's eye tracker"? In: Proceedings of the 53rd Annual Conference of the Society for Technical Communication, pp. 252–255 (2006)
4. Dalmaijer, E.S.: Is the low-cost EyeTribe eye tracker any good for research? PeerJ PrePrints (2014). https://peerj.com/preprints/585v1.pdf. Accessed 8 Feb 2018
5. Gibaldi, A., Vanegas, M., Bex, P.J., Maiello, G.: Evaluation of the Tobii EyeX Eye tracking controller and Matlab toolkit for research. Behav. Res. Methods 49(3), 923–946 (2017)
6. Goldberg, J.H., Kotval, X.P.: Computer interface evaluation using eye movements: methods and constructs. Int. J. Ind. Ergon. 24(6), 631–645 (1999)
7. Guo, Q., Agichtein, E: Towards predicting web searcher gaze position from mouse movements. In: CHI 2010 Extended Abstracts on Human Factors in Computing Systems, pp. 3601–3606. ACM, New York (2010)
8. Ha, A.: The Eye Tribe says it's shipping its first $99 eye-tracking units, raises another $1M. TechCrunch (2014). https://techcrunch.com/2014/01/08/the-eye-tribe/. Accessed 8 Feb 2018
9. Huang, J., White, R.W., Buscher, G.: User see, user point: Gaze and cursor alignment in web search. In: Proceedings of CHI 2012, pp. 1341–1350. ACM, New York (2012)
10. Liebling, D.J., Dumais, S.T.: Gaze and mouse coordination in everyday work. In: Proceedings of the 2014 ACM International Joint Conference on Pervasive and Ubiquitous Computing, pp. 1141–1150. ACM, New York (2014)
11. Navalpakkam, V., et. al.: Measurement and modeling of eye-mouse behavior in the presence of nonlinear page layouts. In: Proceedings of the 22nd International Conference on World Wide Web (WWW 2013), pp. 953–964. ACM, New York (2013)
12. Ooms, K., Dupont, L., Lapon, L., Popelka, S.: Accuracy and precision of fixation locations recorded with the low-cost Eye Tribe tracker in different experimental setups. J. Eye Mov. Res. 8(1), 1–24 (2015)
13. Popelka, S., Stachoň, Z., Šašinka, Č.: Doležalová1, J.: EyeTribe tracker data accuracy evaluation and its interconnection with hypothesis software for cartographic purposes. Comput. Intell. Neurosci. 2016(1), 1–14 (2016)

14. Rodden, K., Fu, X.: Exploring how mouse movements relate to eye movements on web search results pages. In: Proceedings of ACM SIGIR 2007 Workshop on Web Information Seeking and Interaction, pp. 29–32. ACM, New York (2007)
15. Rodden, K., Fu, X., Aula, A., Spiro, I.: Eye-mouse coordination patterns on web search results pages. In: CHI 2008 Extended Abstracts on Human Factors in Computing Systems, pp. 2997–3002. ACM, New York (2008)

What Does the System Usability Scale (SUS) Measure?

Validation Using Think Aloud Verbalization and Behavioral Metrics

Mandy R. Drew[✉], Brooke Falcone, and Wendy L. Baccus

WeddingWire Inc., Chevy Chase, MD 20815, USA
mdrew@weddingwire.com

Abstract. The System Usability Scale (SUS) is widely used as a quick method for measuring usability; however, past research showed there is only a weak relationship between SUS scores and one behavioral usability measure, and alternatively, SUS corresponds more strongly with user preference. This suggests that the underlying constructs of the SUS may not be well understood. In this study, participants were asked to think aloud while completing a usability test and filling out the SUS. Correlations showed no relationship between behavioral performance and SUS scores. Instead, a relationship was observed between SUS scores and perceived success. Furthermore, participants described a variety of reasons for selecting their SUS responses that were unrelated to the usability of the system, which we have termed *rationalizations*. This suggests that the SUS is constructed of a combination of experiential components, including attitudinal perceptions. Consequently, SUS scores may be more helpful as a tool for comparison (between competitors, iterations, etc.,) or when used in conjunction with formative usability testing methods to provide a holistic view of real and perceived user experience.

Keywords: System Usability Scale · SUS · Think-aloud protocol
Usability testing · User experience

1 Introduction

1.1 Usability Testing

Rooted in ancient principles of ergonomic design, (Marmaras et al. 1999) usability describes how effective, efficient, and satisfying a product is when used to complete the tasks for which it was designed (International Organization for Standardization 1998). While a wide range of attitudinal research methods can be used to understand users' stated beliefs, a large body of evidence shows self-reported claims and speculation are unreliable assessments of usability (Frokjaer et al. 2000; Nielsen and Levy 1994). Asking users to evaluate a product based on whether or not they like it is ineffective because users sometimes prefer designs that actually prevent them from achieving their goals (Andre and Wickens 1995), and requiring users to evaluate an experience

© Springer International Publishing AG, part of Springer Nature 2018
A. Marcus and W. Wang (Eds.): DUXU 2018, LNCS 10918, pp. 356–366, 2018.
https://doi.org/10.1007/978-3-319-91797-9_25

retrospectively is unreliable because users tend to remember and make judgments based on the most recent or intense parts of the experience they encountered (Kahneman et al. 1993). Thus, attitudinal research methods can be effective in measuring user perception but cannot accurately determine usability or pinpoint areas for improvement (Nielsen 1993).

Instead, it is widely agreed that watching participants interact with a product while attempting to use it is a much better measure of overall usability and can also diagnose specific usability problems that exist (Nielsen and Levy 1994). In order to discover users' cognitive processes as they are completing tasks, it is helpful to record them speaking their thoughts aloud during test administration (Ericsson and Simon 1980; Nielsen 1993). Such think-aloud protocol usability studies have proven valuable in identifying design flaws and comprehension gaps users may lack the ability to independently articulate, shedding light on opportunities for improvement (Nielsen and Levy, 1994) without requiring recall on the part of the user.

The implementation of traditional usability studies on digital products has evolved from what was once a fairly complex, expensive process. In the past, studies were conducted in-person with 30–50 participants (Barnum 2002) within the confines of a usability lab outfitted with sophisticated video recording equipment (Nielsen 1993). Modern research reveals testing only 5–7 representative users uncovers about 80% of problems users face, (Nielsen and Landauer 1993) and technological advances have made it possible to reach and test those individuals remotely without the need for a recruiter, moderator, or expensive hardware, decreasing the time and expense it takes to watch target users interact with a system (Bergel et al. 2002). Despite this advance in testing efficiency, increased adoption of the agile software development methodology, which advocates for fast and continuous product delivery, (Beck et al. 2001) may tempt some researchers to forgo even the more streamlined version of remote, unmoderated usability testing available today in favor of self-reported measures, such as the SUS, for speed.

1.2   The System Usability Scale

Over three decades ago, the SUS was developed as a subjective usability measure capable of being administered quickly after users worked through evaluation tasks (Brooke 1996). The questionnaire asks users to rate their level of agreement with statements covering a variety of usability characteristics such as the system's complexity and any support or training participants believe is required to use it effectively. Brooke asserts the simple 10-item post-test questionnaire can quickly assess a product's usability without the need for complicated analysis.

Advantages. The SUS has many benefits that make it a popular choice for usability assessment. In addition to being fast, free, and easy to administer, it is considered fairly simple for participants to answer. This is an important consideration, given participants may have struggled for some time to complete frustrating tasks during the testing process. To account for bias due to fatigue or inattention, the questions alternate between positive and negative, providing a single score which, when translated to a familiar "university grade," is commonly understood and easily shared among project stakeholders (Bangor et al. 2008). Finally, the SUS can be applied to a wide range of technologies and has been used to assess the usability of hardware, software, websites, and mobile devices (Brooke 2013).

Disadvantages. The advantages of SUS coupled with the fast pace of modern product development cycles has made it an industry standard with references in over 1,300 articles and publications (Usability.gov, n.d.), but relying on SUS as a sole measure of usability is problematic for a number of reasons.

First, more recent evidence suggests that the SUS primarily measures subjective user perception. For instance, one study shows that users who give a system a high SUS score also tend to give that same system a high Net Promoter Score (NPS), which indicates that they are very likely to recommend the system to a friend or family member (Sauro 2011). While this means the SUS could be a good indicator of preference, that does not necessarily relate to product usability because users do not always like usable designs (Andre and Wickens 1995). Furthermore, only a very small relationship has been shown between SUS results and the ability to effectively complete usability tasks without making any errors (Peres et al. 2013).

Several studies also highlight how users and researchers can misinterpret items on the SUS. For example, in approximately 13% of questionnaires, the alternating positive and negative items are responsible for incorrect responses and coding errors. (Sauro and Lewis 2011). In addition, the use of the word "cumbersome" in item 8 has been shown to cause confusion for about 10% of all SUS respondents (Bangor et al. 2008; Finstad 2006).

Another notable limitation is that, because SUS questionnaires are administered after the initial test is complete, users may encounter the peak-end effect and evaluate the system based on the most recent or intense parts of their experience (Kahneman et al. 1993). This is problematic because users miss reporting specific events that could be pertinent to the system's overall usability and can result in missed opportunities to pinpoint potential areas for design improvement.

Finally, the assumption that users provide answers to SUS questions based exclusively on the experience they are meant to evaluate has never been validated. In fact, it has been shown that prior experience with a system can lead to more favorable SUS scores (McLellan et al. 2012), which suggests that outside influences can affect how users respond to the questionnaire.

All these factors could potentially explain the negative skew described in a 2008 study which found that the mean scores from SUS questionnaires in over 200 tests were more favorable than the actual test success rates (Bangor et al. 2008).

1.3 Present Study

Previous research suggests that the SUS may better reflect users' perceived success, rather than a system's overall usability (Peres et al. 2013). On the surface, SUS questions appear to cover a variety of aspects essential to usability, such as complexity, learnability, and likelihood of repeat use (Brooke 1996). Thus, the majority of SUS respondents likely recognize the purpose of the survey is to elicit an accurate understanding of their experience with the system in question. However, such "face validity" only concerns judgments made about the survey after it was created but does not necessarily indicate the survey was constructed in such a way as to measure what it asserts (Nunnally 1978). The primary goal of this study is to explore SUS' construct validity; that is, to discover how users justify the SUS responses they choose in order to better understand the disconnect between users' behavior and their perceived success, as reflected by their SUS ratings.

Hypothesis. We expected that participants who exhibited poor behavioral usability measures on a traditional think-aloud protocol usability test but submitted high SUS scores for the same experience would provide verbal rationalizations to explain the SUS answers they chose. Exploring what participants say could provide insights into their cognitive processes in order to better understand how SUS responses relate to task success.

2 Methods

2.1 Participants

Twenty participants from the United States, (17 females, 3 males) with a mean age of 27.1 (SD = 4.06) were recruited from an online panel. All had prior experience with think-aloud protocol and were familiar with the testing platform. Participants were screened for domain-related qualities to ensure they represented real users of the websites in question: (1) engaged to be married or recently married, (2) had never used either of the websites to be evaluated, and (3) had created a wedding registry online. Participants earned a $10 incentive.

2.2 Materials

The study was unmoderated and conducted remotely via Usertesting.com, an online platform that streamlines and automates the recruitment, implementation, and analysis of remote, unmoderated usability studies.

2.3 Procedures

Panelists received invitations to complete a screener survey to determine adherence to the inclusion criteria. The first 20 participants to meet the criteria were prompted to launch the test from their computers and used their system's hardware to record their screen actions and voices as they followed the test tasks.

All twenty participants attempted to complete two tasks on two different websites and the presentation of each website was counterbalanced across participants. In order to measure participants' perception of success, they were asked after each task if they felt they completed it successfully. After testing each website, the SUS questionnaire was administered to evaluate their satisfaction with each system.

The Usertesting.com platform displayed written test instructions and tasks on-screen, and participants' voices and screen actions were recorded throughout test administration. The perceived effectiveness question displayed on-screen after the completion of each task and the SUS questions appeared on-screen after each website was evaluated. Participants selected the appropriate response to the perceived effectiveness and SUS questions from a series of radio buttons. Upon completion of the test, each participant's video, demographic information, and responses to perceived effectiveness and SUS questions were uploaded to the Usertesting.com platform where they were accessed and analyzed by researchers.

2.4 Design

A within-subjects design was used. To mitigate the effects of learning bias and ordering effects, the test was counterbalanced to randomize the order of websites evaluated.

2.5 Measures

In order to gain a holistic understanding of the usability of both experiences, we measured Effectiveness, Efficiency, and Satisfaction (International Organization for Standardization 1998). To understand the reasons why users chose the SUS scores they selected, we created a new metric we called Rationalization.

Behavioral. A previous study calculated the Effectiveness behavioral metric as the percent of test tasks participants completed without making any errors. (Peres et al. 2013). Our study followed the more common practice of assigning a binary value as the Task Success rate (Sauro and Lewis 2005), and also by calculating the total number of Unique Errors each participant made (Sauro and Lewis 2016). This method allowed us to diagnose specific UI problems and also better understand participants' frustration levels with two experiences that were objectively difficult to use. Efficiency (or Time on Task) was calculated by the number of seconds participants spent on each task.

Attitudinal. Satisfaction, or comfort using the system, was determined by tabulating each response submitted to the SUS questionnaire and scoring it according to the methods outlined by John Brooke (Brooke 1996). We measured participants' Perceived Success by asking them whether or not they felt they completed each task successfully and assigning a binary value to their responses. Additionally, we introduced a new metric called Rationalization, in which we observed participants verbally rationalize their decisions for selecting each SUS response.

In order to quantitatively assess the correspondence between user's subjective verbalizations and their SUS ratings, we applied a procedure inspired by the eight-step process for coding verbal data developed by Chi (1997). One researcher independently organized the rationalizations into categories (see Table 2), and another researcher assigned a binary value to indicate in which of the six resulting categories each rationalization best applied: (1) No Rationalization, (2) Blames Self, (3) Minimizes Issues, (4) Good by Comparison, (5) No Basis for Comparison, and (6) Halo Effect. Interrater reliability could not be calculated due to the use of only one rater.

In the event that a participant failed to elaborate on their thought process, the "No Rationalization" category was included. Some participants blamed poor performance on their own unfamiliarity with the subject matter or lack of technological ability, whose responses comprise the "Blames Self" category. This example of social desirability bias stems from the need for social approval and is a common limitation for many user research activities (Nancarrow and Brace 2000). The "Minimizes Issues" category consists of those participants who minimized significant usability issues that caused errors because they considered the overall experience to be positive. The "Good by Comparison" category refers to participants who evaluated the second website in comparison to the first they encountered. The "No Basis for Comparison" category was created to exemplify users that could exhibit a lack of basis for comparison by interpreting an objectively poor experience, such as spending ten or more minutes attempting to complete a task, as adequate. While this rationalization was not observed by the researcher who rated the verbalizations for this study, it should be considered as representative of future samples. Lastly, the halo effect (Berscheid and Walster 1974; Angeli and Hartmann 2006) was observed when participants' valued aesthetics over practicality.

3 Results

3.1 Usability Measures

Correlations for the behavioral and attitudinal usability measures are reported in Table 1. The results indicate that the strongest correlation exists between Time on Task and Errors, such that participants who experienced more errors took longer to complete tasks. Also, there was a strong positive relationship between Task Success and Perceived Success, such that those who experienced more Task Success also scored highly in Perceived Success. Lastly, a weaker, but still moderate relationship was seen between SUS Scores and Perceived Success, indicating that SUS scores increase as perceived success increases.

Table 1. Correlation matrix of behavioral and attitudinal usability measures (N = 40).

	SUS	Errors	Task success	Perc. suc.	ToT
SUS	–				
Errors	.03	–			
Task success[a]	.29	−.07	–		
Perc. suc.[b]	.51**	−.28	.66**	–	
ToT	−.09	.68**	.19	−.13	–

Note: ** $p < .01$, * $p < .05$, n = 40.

3.2 Rationalizations

A Mann-Whitney test indicated that there was not a significant difference in Task Success between those who rationalized and those who did not ($U = 178.00$, p = ns). A Mann-Whitney test indicated that there was not a significant difference in Perceived Success between those who rationalized and those who did not ($U = 182.00$, p = ns).

A MANOVA indicated there was a statistically significant difference in Errors (see Fig. 1) based on whether a user rationalized F $(1, 40) = 4.522$, p < .005. Participants who rationalized committed more errors than participants who did not rationalize.

Table 2. Rationalizations

	Frequency count	% of total	Examples
None	325	.81	
Self-blame	13	.03	"I get confused easily" "My lack of knowledge of wedding registries… makes me inexperienced" "I guess I was doing tasks too fast"
Minimization	10	.10	"Once you learn what you are doing it gets easier. It's just a matter of getting over the first hump which is ridiculous and annoying" "Maybe I could've gotten it with more playing with it" "There were [sic] some weird programming with the buttons, but other than that it was fantastic" "It seemed easy, but I couldn't figure out how to add the registry"
Good by comparison	14	.04	"Easier than [the other website]"
No basis for comparison	0	.00	
Halo effect	10	.03	"Everything matches the beautiful blue color" "I would use the other functions"

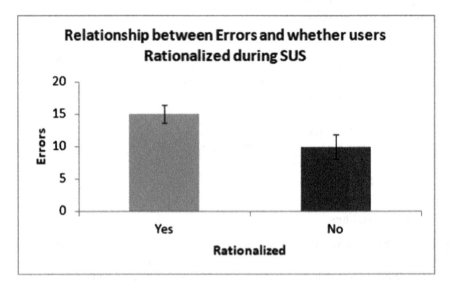

Fig. 1. Average error frequency committed by participants who rationalized and those who did not. Error bars indicate standard error for each group.

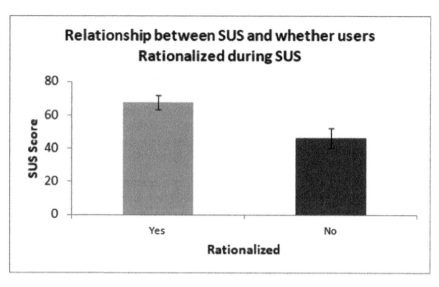

Fig. 2. Average SUS scores reported by participants who rationalized and those who did not. Error bars indicate standard error for each group.

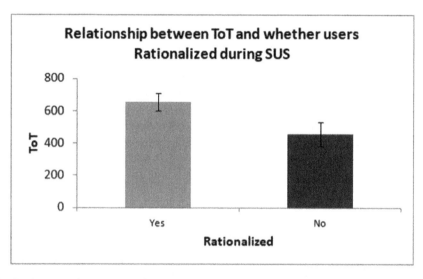

Fig. 3. Average Time on Task of participants who rationalized and those who did not. Error bars indicate standard error for each group.

In addition, there was a statistically significant difference in SUS scores (see Fig. 2) based on whether a user rationalized $F_{(1, 40)} = 8.699$, $p < .005$, where participants who rationalized reported higher SUS scores than those who did not rationalize. There was also a statistically significant difference in ToT based on whether a user rationalized $F_{(1, 40)} = 4.81$, $p < .005$ indicating that those who rationalized spent more time completing tasks than those who did not rationalize (Fig. 3).

4   Discussion

4.1   Interpretation

These findings support previous research that suggests SUS is a measure of user perception, and not actual usability. Regardless of their performance, participants who believed they completed their tasks successfully gave the system a higher SUS score. Participants who struggled to complete their tasks efficiently and effectively often rationalized their performance for reasons unrelated to system usability and gave the system a higher SUS score than an objective review of their experience warranted.

Comparison to Previous Study. The small relationship previously discovered between SUS scores and effectiveness (Peres et al. 2013) is not replicated in these results. That study compared the percent of tasks users completed without any errors to their corresponding SUS scores, and suggested the resulting correlation provided evidence that the SUS could be used to ordinally compare the usability of multiple systems (Peres et al. 2013). That "error-free" method for calculating effectiveness was impractical for this study, given the high level of difficulty users encountered; in fact, none of the tasks for this study were completed without errors. Thus, we determined effectiveness using three different measures: (1) Task Success, (2) Perceived Success, and (3) Unique Errors. No relationship was discovered between Task Success and SUS, but the positive association between SUS scores and Perceived Success suggests that SUS reflects user perception. Participants who believed they completed their tasks successfully gave the system a higher SUS score, regardless of their actual performance. This could explain the relationship described in Peres et al. (2013). Users understood they completed tasks without making mistakes, and thus, chose more favorable SUS responses. Despite the fact that a large proportion of participants did not rationalize while performing the SUS, it is possible that they followed a similar thought process, without verbalizing. Of those who did rationalize, our results demonstrate that SUS scores do not relate to task success; therefore, we recommend it be used in conjunction with standard usability metrics to comprehensively explain the user's experience with a system.

4.2   Practical Applications

The rationalizations observed in this study characterize the type of noise that can cloud objective usability measurement using the SUS and could contribute to the negative skew observed in Bangor et al. (2008). Attempting to gain insight into why users select the SUS responses they choose for each individual study could limit the adverse effects caused by this noise but would diminish the advantages of using SUS as a "quick and dirty" method of usability assessment. Leveraging both formative and summative measures is a commonly recommended best practice (Nielsen and Levy 1994) to gain a holistic understanding of a product's performance, and formative assessments, such as think-aloud protocol usability tests, could mitigate the effects of cognitive bias because researchers can watch what users do with a system while simultaneously discounting what they say about it. However, the effects of employing methods simultaneously on the outcome variables and, ultimately, the conclusions drawn from such research has not been well explored and may introduce interaction effects that could limit the ability to interpret and generalize the results.

A more practical application of SUS scores could be as an instrument of the test-retest reliability method (Carmines and Zeller 1979). The SUS questionnaire could be administered after initial traditional usability testing on the first iteration of a product and the resulting score could be used as a benchmark by which subsequent design iterations could be evaluated. In the event that future product versions garner lower SUS scores, traditional usability testing can again be employed to find out why. This addresses the need for quick product evaluation and continuous delivery while also maintaining research integrity by adhering to industry standard best practices.

4.3 Future Research

It is important to note that the act of recording users during SUS administration could have affected their responses (Macefield 2007), and may cause users to overthink, which John Brooke cautioned against (Brooke 1996). This is beyond the scope of this paper but is an appropriate area for follow-up study.

4.4 Limitations

The present results are exploratory findings uncovered while conducting a larger study aimed to answer an alternative research question. Future studies should explicitly design and test the conclusions incidentally described here.

Future studies employing the Rationalization coding scheme constructed in this study should seek to validate the reliability of the measure between raters using inter-rater reliability (IRR) (Hallgren 2012).

References

Andre, A., Wickens, C.: When users want what's not best for them. Ergon. Des. Q. Hum. Factors Appl. **3**(4), 10–14 (1995)

Angeli, A., Hartmann, J.: Interaction, usability, and aesthetics. In: Proceedings of the 6th Annual ACM Conference on Designing Interactive Systems, pp. 271–280. ACM, New York (2006)

Beck, K., Beedle, M., Bennekum, A., Cockburn, A., Cunningham, W., Fowler, M., Grenning, J., Highsmith, J., Hunt, A., Jeffries, R., Kern, J., Marick, B., Martin, R., Mellor, S., Schwaber, K., Sutherland, J., Thomas, D.: Manifesto for Agile Software Development (2001). http://www.agilemanifesto.org/. Accessed 29 Jan 2018

Bangor, A., Kortum, P.T., Miller, J.T.: An empirical evaluation of the system usability scale. Int. J. Hum.-Comput. Interact. **24**(6), 574–594 (2008)

Barnum, C.M.: Usability Testing and Research. Longman, New York (2002)

Bergel, M., Fleischman, S., McNulty, M., Tullis, T.: An empirical comparison of lab and remote usability testing of web sites. In: Usability Professional Association Conference (2002)

Berscheid, E., Walster, E.: Physical attractiveness. In: Berkowitz, L. (ed.) Advances in Experimental Social Psychology, vol. 7. Academic Press, New York (1974)

Brooke, J.: SUS: a "quick and dirty" usability scale. In: Usability Evaluation in Industry, pp. 189–194. Taylor & Francis, London (1996)

Brooke, J.: SUS: a retrospective. J. Usability Stud. **8**(2), 29–40 (2013)

Carmines, E., Zeller, R.: Reliability and Validity Assessment. SAGE Publications, Thousand Oaks (1979)

Chi, M.: Quantifying qualitative analyses of verbal data: a practical guide. J. Learn. Sci. 6(3), 271–315 (1997)

Ericsson, K., Simon, H.: Verbal reports as data. Psychol. Rev. 87(3), 215–251 (1980)

Finstad, K.: The system usability scale and non-native English speakers. J. Usability Stud. 4(1), 185–188 (2006)

Frokjaer, E., Hertzum, M., Hornbaek, K.: Measuring usability: are effectiveness, efficiency, and satisfaction really correlated? In: Proceedings of the SIGCHI Conference on Human Factors in Computing Systems, pp. 345–352. ACM Press, New York (2000)

Hallgren, K.: Computing inter-rater reliability for observational data: an overview tutorial. Tutor. Qual. Methods Psychol. 8(1), 23–34 (2012)

International Organization for Standardization: ergonomic requirements for office work with visual display terminals (VDTs) – Part 11: guidance on usability (ISO Standard No. 9241-1.) (1998). https://www.iso.org/standard/16883.html. Accessed 29 Jan 2018

Kahneman, D., Fredrickson, B., Schreiber, C., Redelmeier, D.: When more pain is preferred to less: adding a better end. Psychol. Sci. 4(6), 401–405 (1993)

Macefield, R.: Usability studies and the Hawthorne effect. J. Usability Stud. 2(3), 145–154 (2007)

Marmaras, N., Poulakakis, G., Papakostopoulos, V.: Ergonomic design in ancient Greece. Appl. Ergon. 30(4), 361–368 (1999)

McLellan, S., Muddimer, A., Peres, S.: The effect of experience on system usability scale ratings. J. Usability Stud. 7(2), 56–67 (2012)

Nancarrow, C., Brace, I.: Saying the right thing: coping with social desirability bias in marketing research. Bristol Bus. Sch. Teach. Res. Rev. 3(11), 1–11 (2000)

Nielsen, J., Landauer, T.: A mathematical model of the finding of usability problems. In: Proceedings of ACM INTERCHI 1993 Conference, Amsterdam, The Netherlands, pp. 206–213 (1993)

Nielsen, J.: Usability Engineering, 1st edn. Academic Press Inc., Cambridge (1993)

Nielsen, J., Levy, J.: Measuring usability - preference vs. performance. Commun. ACM 37(4), 66–75 (1994)

Nunnally, J.: Psychometric Theory, 2nd edn. McGraw-Hill, New York (1978)

Peres, S., Pham, T., Phillips, R.: Validation of the system usability scale (SUS): SUS in the wild. In: Proceedings of the Human Factors and Ergonomics Society Annual Meeting, vol. 57, no. 1, pp. 192–196 (2013)

Sauro, J.: A Practical Guide to the System Usability Scale: Background, Benchmarks & Best Practices. Measuring Usability LLC, Denver (2011)

Sauro, J., Lewis, J.: Estimating completion rates from small samples using binomial confidence intervals: comparisons and recommendations. In: Proceedings of the Human Factors and Ergonomics Society Annual Meeting, vol. 49, no. 24, pp. 2100–2103 (2005)

Sauro, J., Lewis, J.: Quantifying the User Experience: Practical Statistics for User Research, 2nd edn. Morgan Kaufmann, Cambridge (2016)

Sauro, J., Lewis, J.: When designing usability questionnaires, does it hurt to be positive? In: Proceedings of ACM SIGCHI, pp. 2215–2223. ACM, New York (2011)

Usability.gov: System Usability Scale (SUS). http://www.usability.gov/how-to-and-tools/methods/system-usability-scale.html. Accessed 31 Jan 2018

Considering Users' Different Knowledge About Products to Improve a UX Evaluation Method Based on Mental Models

Stefano Filippi$^{(\boxtimes)}$ and Daniela Barattin

DPIA Department, University of Udine, 33100 Udine, Italy
{stefano.filippi,daniela.barattin}@uniud.it

Abstract. User experience (UX) evaluation and design have become important components of the product development process. The UX describes the users' subjective perceptions, responses and emotional reactions while interacting with products or services, considering users' emotions and cognitive activities as the basic elements of the experience. The emotions encompass physiological, affective, behavioral, and cognitive components; the cognitive activities generate and exploit the mental models that govern the human behavior. The literature offers several methods to evaluate the UX; one of them, the irMMs-based method, considers both users' emotions and mental models to evaluate the quality of the UX. Nevertheless, its current release misses the contribution of users who already know the product under evaluation. This research aims at improving the irMMs-based method by considering also users familiar with those products. The expected benefits of this improvement refer to the completeness of the evaluation results and to the definition of relationships between these results and the evaluation activities that allow them to be discovered. All of this can be useful for both researchers and designers who are willing to increase their knowledge about the generation and exploitation of mental models and to select the most suitable evaluation activities to perform time by time depending on the characteristics of the results they are interested in and on the resources available.

Keywords: User experience · Mental models · UX evaluation

1 Introduction

In recent years, user experience (UX) has gained importance in product development because of the increasing number of functionalities (with the related interface complexity), the development of new interaction paradigms, the availability of innovative technologies and devices, etc. The UX describes the users' subjective perceptions, responses and emotional reactions while interacting with products or services, considering users' emotions and cognitive activities as the basic elements of the experience [1, 2]. Emotions are defined as the responses to events deemed relevant to the needs, goals, or concerns of an individual and encompass physiological, affective, behavioral, and cognitive components [3]. Cognitive activities, highly influenced by emotions, generate and exploit the mental models that govern the human behavior. Mental models

© Springer International Publishing AG, part of Springer Nature 2018
A. Marcus and W. Wang (Eds.): DUXU 2018, LNCS 10918, pp. 367–378, 2018.
https://doi.org/10.1007/978-3-319-91797-9_26

are internal representations of the reality aimed at choosing the best user behaviors respect to foreseen behaviors of products or events [4]. User behaviors aim at overcoming specific, critical situations and at achieving experiences as positive and satisfactory as possible [5].

Product development processes need methods and tools for evaluating the UX. The literature already offers several UX evaluation possibilities, from simple questionnaires like the User Experience Questionnaire - UEQ [6] and the IPTV-UX Questionnaire [7] up to more articulated and complete approaches like the Valence method [8] and the irMMs-based method [9], the starting point of this research. The irMMs-based method considers emotions and mental models to evaluate the quality of the UX. IrMMs means interaction-related mental models. These mental models refer to specific situations of interaction involving meanings and emotions as well as users and products' behaviors. The adoption of the irMMs-based method generates lists of positive and negative UX aspects. The former represent unexpected, surprising and interesting characteristics of the interaction; the latter can refer to bad product transparency during interaction, gaps between the actions expected by the user problem solving process and those allowed by the real products, etc.

Indeed, the UX evaluation cannot deserve the time factor. The literature already demonstrated that the subjective evaluation of products and the related subjective meanings assigned to the experiences with them change after an extended period of usage [10]. In their framework named temporary of experience, Karapanos et al. [11] describe how the UX changes over time and highlight three main forces: the increasing familiarity, the functional dependency and the emotional attachment. Sng et al. [12] exploit the UX lifecycle model ContinUE to demonstrate that the 76% of the needs highlighted by the users after a repeated use of a product are completely new respect to those highlighted by users who get in touch with the same product for the first time.

The current release of the irMMs-based method does not involve users who already know the product under evaluation; therefore, it completely misses possible suggestions about the UX quality coming from extended periods of use. This research aims at filling this gap by improving the irMMs-based method considering also users familiar with the products under evaluation. The expected benefits of this improvement refer to the completeness of the evaluation results and to the definition of relationships between these results and the evaluation activities that allow them to be discovered. All of this can be useful for researchers who are willing to increase their knowledge about the generation and exploitation of mental models by users with different knowledge about the products under evaluation, as well as for designers who can understand and select the most suitable evaluation activities to perform time by time, depending on the characteristics of the results they are interested in and on the resources available.

To achieve this goal, the research analyzes the current release of the irMMs-based method to classify the existing evaluation activities and to add the new ones involving users who already know the products. After that, the new release of the irMMs-based method is adopted in the field. The results of the adoption are then compared to those coming from the old release to evaluate the improvements and analyzed to highlight possible relationships with the evaluation activities.

The paper goes on with the background section describing the current release of the irMMs-based method. The activities section describes the improvement of the irMMs-based method, the first validation of it and the identification of the relationships. The conclusions, together with some perspectives on future work, close the paper.

2 Background: Current Release of the irMMs-Based Method

The irMMs-based method evaluates the UX by exploiting the interaction-related mental models (irMMs). The irMMs consist of lists of users' meanings and emotions along with users' actions and products' reactions/feedback determined by these meanings and emotions [9]. The generation of an irMM comes during the user's attempt to satisfy a specific need in a specific situation of interaction. This process develops through five steps, based on the Norman's model of the seven stages of the action cycle [13]. In the first step, the user perceives and interprets the need. Thanks to this interpretation, in the second step the user recovers existing irMMs from his/her mind and selects those ones that could be suitable to satisfy the need. This selection could be influenced by the presence/consideration of one or more real products. The selected irMMs allow the user to define the goals in the third step. The goals represent intermediate and time-ordered results to achieve; they help in establishing the path to follow to satisfy the need. In the fourth step, the user associates desired meanings and emotions to each goal. These come from the elaboration of the meanings and emotions belonging to the irMMs selected before. Positive meanings and emotions tend to remain as they were; on the contrary, negative ones could be changed into their positive correspondences depending on the number of past experiences that report those negative meanings and emotions. In the fifth step, the user generates the ordered list of actions and the related product reactions/feedback in order to achieve those desired meanings and emotions. This list is generated by elaborating the actions and reactions/feedback present again in the irMMs selected before.

The adoption of the irMMs-based method generates positive and negative UX aspects. This comes by performing tests where real users compare their irMMs, generated before to get in touch with the product as soon as they are told the need to achieve, with the real experience allowed by that product. The irMMs-based method develops through the following four phases.

Phase 1. Input Setting. This phase defines two input. The features of the product to evaluate are the first input; they can be functions, specific procedures to achieve specific goals, physical components, etc. The second input are the users who undergo the tests. Their selection comes by obeying to the rules "the users must not know the product" and "the users must have a specific level of knowledge about the field the product belongs to". Moreover, further rules can apply due to specific characteristics of the evaluations.

Phase 2. Material and Environment Setup. The second phase prepares the material and the environment to perform the tests. The material consists of two documents, one for the users and one for the evaluators. The first document guides the users in generating the irMMs and in performing the interaction with the product. Its first part reports the need to satisfy and the instructions on how to perform each step to generate the irMM, together with examples. The second part shows suggestions on how to perform the interaction and to compare it with the irMM. This document contains tables and empty spaces to describe the irMM and to comment the comparison. The second document allows the evaluators to collect data in specific tables, divided respect to their type (meanings, emotions, etc.); moreover, this document contains instructions on how to conduct the data analysis. Finally, the test execution requires the setup of a suitable environment reflecting the common use of the product under evaluation.

Phase 3. Test Execution. In the third phase, the users generate their irMMs based on a specific need given by the evaluators and, after that, they compare these irMMs to the real experience allowed by the product. The evaluators collect data in the meantime. Before the tests, the users are divided into two groups. The first group do not get in touch with the product before to know the need to satisfy. This group is called absolute. On the contrary, each user belonging to the second group is asked for interacting freely with the product for a short period. This group is labelled as relative. This label comes from the fact that the product will likely influence the users. Once this free interaction comes to the end, the execution of the tests is the same for every member of the two groups. This execution consists of three moments. In the first moment, each user generates his/her irMM by following the guide document. Then, he/she tries to satisfy the need by using the product (second moment). The user must execute the actions as described in his/her irMM and check if his/her actions and the reactions/feedback of the product come as expected. Of course, problems can occur in the meantime; these problems are addressed as gaps. If a gap shows up, the evaluators suggest the way to overcome the problem in terms of user actions allowed by the product and related reactions/feedback. The user reports the reasons for the gap from his/her point of view and judges if the allowed actions and the product reactions/feedback are better or worse than those of his/her irMM. Once the interaction finishes, the third moment consists in a debriefing where the users are called to reason about their experiences and to express further comments about them. In particular, the users are asked to reconsider the meanings and emotions expressed during the generation of the irMMs in order to highlight any change.

Phase 4. Data Analysis. Some rules lead the analysis of the data collected during the tests. These rules allow generating the positive and negative UX aspects starting from the desired meanings and emotions, the real ones, and the gaps between the expected user actions and product reactions/feedback (those of the irMMs) and the real ones. For example, applying one of the rules, a positive UX aspect is generated starting from the desired meaning "temperature" associated to the goal "washing program for delicate clothes set" and the need "washing delicate clothes with the washing machine". The user gives a positive judgment to the desired meaning because of the reason "although I do not know exactly the most suitable temperature for any type of clothes, the washing machine has predefined programs where all parameters are already set, temperature included". This meaning and the related reason allow generating the positive UX aspect "the washing machine offers predefined programs where all the parameters are already set; the user must only select the right program according to the type of clothes to wash".

Once generated the UX aspects, they are compared to each other to delete repetitions. They are placed in an ordered list due to the number of occurrences of each UX aspect, the interaction topics they refer to and their estimated impact. If an UX aspect refers to product characteristics rarely involved in the interaction, its impact will be set to low; on the contrary, if the UX aspect deals with core procedures determining the product cognitive compatibility with the users' problem solving processes, its importance will be higher. The result of the adoption of the irMMs-based method consists of two importance-ordered lists of positive and negative UX aspects.

3   Activities

To achieve the goal of the research, the irMMs-based method (the method, hereafter) must be patched in order to separate the different evaluation activities currently available. This patching makes the method modular and scalable and allows it to be refined by adding the new evaluation activities devoted to the familiar users. We call these activities patching and refining because the former happen at the same level of abstraction while the latter make the abstraction level deeper [14]. At the end, the new release of the method is adopted in the field. This adoption highlights the improvements respect to the old release in terms of quantity and quality of the results and allows identifying the relationships between the UX aspects and the evaluation activities that allowed them to be highlighted.

3.1   Patching the Method

In order to make the different evaluation activities currently available clearly separated, the patching comes by analyzing each phase of the method adoption. Once highlighted, the activities are collected into two separate modules called absolute beginners (AB) and relative beginners (RB) modules, depending on the group of testers involved. This analysis also allows some activities to be revised and optimized. In the following, the peculiarities of these two modules are reported, phase by phase.

Regarding the first phase, concerning the input setting, the AB and RB modules are the same; they share the input in terms of product features and rules to select the users.

The second phase, concerning the material and environment setup, needs more attention. The guide document is the same; nevertheless, it must be diversified between the two modules. The guide document used in the AB module must be made free of references to the product to evaluate to avoid bias. On the contrary, the guide document in the RB module must contain precise information on the characteristics of the product under evaluation to make their attention focusing more on it than on those they could have used in the past. Focusing now on the document for the evaluators, its structure needs some changes in order to integrate the nature of the information (meaning, emotion or gap) with the moment of its generation and the user who finds it, since this is the required information to address the origin of each UX aspect precisely.

In the third phase, where the test execution takes place, the activities in the modules must come as described in the specific guide documents generated in the second phase.

The fourth phase, the data analysis, comes in the same way for both the modules, by filling the documents prepared for the evaluators in the previous phase.

3.2   Refining the Method

The second research activity refines the method by adding the new module devoted to the users familiar with the product. This module is called relative expert (RE) module. This addition makes the method more complete because these users consider the product from a different point of view. For this reason, they could find different UX aspects. What follows describes the peculiarities of the RE module, phase by phase.

In the first phase, the features of the product to evaluate are the same as for the AB and RB modules. On the contrary, the users' characteristics are different; they must know the product and have used it at least for a given period (its duration varies time by time, respect to the product complexity, the required reliability of the evaluation results, etc.). From the point of view of the method structure, the refining requires two more input to introduce, representing the selected modules to adopt time by time and the characteristics of the evaluators, respectively. The new release of the method will be flexible enough to allow the selection of the modules to adopt depending on the specific evaluation. This is the reason for the first new input. Regarding the second new input, although in the case of the AB and RB modules the evaluators can be any, those involved in the RE module must be very skilled and knowledgeable with the product. This is why we need an input to represent the characteristics of the evaluators.

In the second phase, the guide document for the expert users must contain precise references to the product under evaluation in all the activities of the irMM generation (definition of the goals, meanings, emotions, actions and product reactions/feedback). This because the irMMs must focus on the product under evaluation rather than being influenced by past experiences of the users with different products.

In the third phase, the activities of the RE module consist of the same three moments as the AB and RB ones. Thanks to the high level of expertise of the evaluators with the product, the execution of the irMMs can be performed without problems because in case of users running in very specific gaps the evaluators are able to overcome them easily. Finally, during the tests, the evaluators must push the users to stay focused on the specific product features established as input because the high level of knowledge about the product could make the users move to different features.

Finally, the RE module performs the fourth phase by following the same rules as the AB and RB ones by filling its dedicated document and generating the lists of positive and negative UX aspects.

At the end of the refining activities, the new release of the method consists in the three modules, AB, RB and RE. The evaluators can choose any combination of them due to resources available, personal evaluation style, etc. After the selection, the evaluators perform the four phases for each module as described in the previous sections. Since the modules are separated, they can be adopted in parallel, providing that no influences happen among them. At the end, the UX aspects generated by the modules adopted for the evaluation are collected together, compared to each other to delete repetitions and ordered in two lists, one of positive and the other of negative UX aspects.

3.3   Adopting the New Release of the Method

What follows describes the adoption of the new release of the method in the field, phase by phase. This comes to evaluate a state-of-the-art CAD software package developed by a well-known software house working in the engineering research and application fields. This choice comes from the availability of the product for the tests as well as that of the users to involve; moreover, it also comes from the good evaluators' knowledge about the product.

In the first phase, the 3D modeling section of the CAD package is selected as the product feature to evaluate. After that, the users are selected. For the AB and RB modules, the users must not know the selected CAD package; for the RE module, the users must know this product and have used it almost for one month. All of them are students of mechanical engineering courses with good knowledge about 3D modeling since they used one or more CAD packages in the past. In all, thirty users are involved, ten for each module. Finally, all the modules are considered in this first adoption of the new release of the method and three researchers very knowledgeable with the CAD package are selected as reviewers.

In the second phase, the guide documents for the three modules are customized respect to the specific evaluation to perform. The need is set to "generate the 3D model of the socket shown in figure. This model will be used for production. Use the CAD package available on the PC. Please respect the assigned dimensions". Figure 1 shows the drawing of the socket as reported in the guide documents. The documents for the evaluators are used as they are, while a university lab consisting of two separate rooms is selected as the environment to perform the tests. In the first room, the users generate the irMMs; in the second room, a PC with the CAD package running on it allows each user to perform the modeling activities.

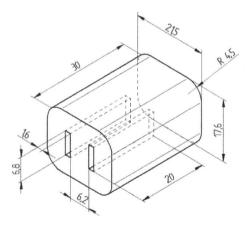

Fig. 1. The drawing of the socket to model (units are millimeters)

Once the material is ready, the tests can start (third phase). Each user associated to the RB module (hereafter, RB user) interacts freely with the CAD package for five minutes. After that, all the users generate their irMMs. It is worth to say that, contrary to what described in the background section, during the definition of the desired meanings and emotions, the users refer them to the need and not to the specific goals. This happens because the need is so simple and immediate that it makes the same meanings and emotions come in mind for every goal. What follows are some examples of goals, meanings and emotions. One of the RE users expresses the two goals "extrusion of the main rectangle shape generated" and "cutting of the two rectangular holes done". In the RB module, a user defines four desired meanings: hobby, job, courses, manufacturing. One of the AB users defines six desired emotions: happy, excited, not engaged, tired, not relaxed and worried. Table 1 collects the excerpt of an irMM generated by one of the RB users referred to the goal "Boolean subtraction done" (please consider the first two columns only, containing the user actions and the product reactions/feedback, respectively).

Table 1. Excerpt of a user's irMM related to the goal "Boolean subtraction done" (first two columns) and evaluation of it against the real interaction (last two columns)

User actions	Product reactions/ feedback	Check	Reason and judgment
Open the menu to perform Boolean operations	The menu to select the Boolean operations is shown	Passed	
Select the command to subtract volumes		Failed	The menu command extrude is unclear. The evaluators show me that it also allows performing subtractions but its label seems to mean the opposite. Negative gap
Select the main prism	The first prism is highlighted	Passed	
Select the prism to subtract	The second prism is highlighted	Passed	
	The preview of the resulting volume is shown	Failed	I was expecting to see only the preview of the resulting volume. Nevertheless, in addition to that, the package shows also the starting prisms as shaded. This allows me verifying if the performed Boolean operation (cut) succeeded. Positive gap
Confirm the operation	The hole in the model is shown	Passed	

Once the users have generated their irMMs, they are called to evaluate the real interaction with the CAD package respect to these irMMs. By carrying on with some examples, consider again Table 1; this time, please focus on the last two columns. During the real interaction, the user highlights two gaps (the two rows with "failed" in the third column). The first one, related to the user action "select the command to subtract volumes", refers to the command extrude and is negative; the second one, related to the product reactions/feedback "the preview of the resulting volume is shown", refers to the richer visualization of the preview of the results and it is positive. The fourth column reports the reasons for the gaps from the user's point of view and the related positive/negative judgment. Once the real interactions come to the end, the users also highlight the changes between the desired meanings and emotions and the real ones. For example, in the AB module, a user defined the desired meaning "software architecture" with the reason "easy understanding and exploiting of the mechanisms that govern the software" and with a positive judgment. After the real interaction, the judgment on the meaning becomes negative and the reason for this is "difficult understanding of the complex mechanisms in using the software". Again, two desired emotions identified by a RB user are happy and quite relaxed. After the interaction, the user changes them into strongly unhappy and not relaxed because she found too many gaps during her test.

The fourth phase generates the lists of positive and negative UX aspects for each module. The AB module generates 4 positive UX aspects and 35 negative ones; the RB module generates 8 positive and 23 negative; finally, the RE module generates 11 positive and 22 negative UX aspects. An example of positive UX aspect, coming from the RE module, is "many different file formats are available to export the model", while one negative UX aspect, coming from the AB module, is "once finished the feature extrude, the window view does not come back to isometric automatically". After that, the UX aspects generated by all the modules are collected and compared to each other to delete repetitions. In the end, the final lists of positive and negative UX aspects contain 16 and 68 items, respectively. The most popular positive UX aspect is "some menu icons are clearer and more intuitive than the classic ones (e.g., coil, hole and rib)", while the most popular negative one is "when users need to generate square holes, they must use the menu command labelled as extrude but extrusion means exactly the opposite".

3.4   First Validation of the New Release of the Method

In order to start validating the new release of the method, the UX of the same CAD package is evaluated using the old release of the method. This comes as described in the background section. Thirty users are selected; they are students coming from the same mechanical engineering courses of the users involved in the previous tests. Considering the same need, the executions of the tests and the analysis of the results highlight the two lists of UX aspects as composed by 6 positive and 52 negative.

The results of the two releases of the method can be compared thanks to the analogies between the two evaluations (same product, same number of users involved, same types of data collected, etc.). This comparison highlights that the new release of the method generated more UX aspects than the old one. This is due to the higher numbers of desired meanings and emotions, gaps and of changes of meanings and emotions in the new release. From the qualitative point of view, the most of the positive and negative UX aspects identified by the new release have been highlighted also by the old one, as for example the negative UX aspects about the feature to create square holes. This correspondence is supported also by the similarities in the desired meanings and emotions from which several UX aspects were generated. Nevertheless, the new release of the method reports UX aspects not highlighted by the old one. These UX aspects refer to gaps (mainly negative ones) identified in specific user actions or product reactions/feedback that only users who know that product quite well can highlight. For example, the "line" command does not remain active if a specific length for the edge is keyed in and confirmed with the enter key instead of defined thanks to mouse movements and clicks only. Moreover, these UX aspects come also from the changes of meanings and emotions because the most of them are generated by RE users. This happened because the users' knowledge about the product allowed them to consider the potentialities of the product in different contexts than those where they currently use the product or used it in the past.

3.5   Identification of the Relationships Between the Results and the Evaluation Activities

The last part of the research aims at identifying relationships between the results of the evaluations and the activities that discover them. This will allow selecting the most suitable modules to adopt time by time depending on the characteristics of the results, on the resources available, on the evaluators' personal style, etc. Different cases are considered; each of them involves a different company that expresses specific requirements about the results. These requirements are translated into the language used by the method and the relationships are defined exploiting the data elaboration happened during the analysis phase. In the following, two examples of relationships are proposed.

The first relationship regards a company interested in the negative emotional impact of one of its products in order to lower it. This requirement can be translated into the consideration of those UX aspects suggested by negative changes of emotions. Analyzing the data collected for each module during the tests, the highest value of these negative changes was generated by the AB module (24), followed by the RB (6) and by the RE (2) ones. Clearly, this was determined by the presence/absence of prior knowledge about the product. AB users must not know the product; therefore, since they based their evaluation exclusively on their experiences with similar products and on what they would like to experience, the product under evaluation could likely make them disappointed. On the contrary, the users associated to the other two modules knew partially (RB) or completely (RE) what to expect from the product; for this reason, the negative emotional impacts were much lower or almost absent, respectively. Therefore, the first relationship can be formulated as "in order to evaluate the negative emotional impact of a product, the AB module is the best choice to adopt, followed by the RB and at the RE ones, in this order".

The second relationship regards a company willing to know the strong pluses about functions and procedures of one of their products in order to emphasize them further. This requirement can be translated into the consideration of the UX aspects deriving from positive gaps. Analyzing again the data collected for each module, this relationship can be formulated as "in order to evaluate the pluses of a product, the RE module is the best choice to adopt, followed by the RB and the AB modules, in this order".

It is worth to say that the relationships have been inferred from just one adoption of the new release of the method and for a specific product; therefore, they need further confirmations before taking them as granted for different products and situations.

4 Conclusions

Aiming at improving the existing irMMs-based UX evaluation method, the research described in this paper kept into consideration the users' knowledge about the product. Users already familiar with the product have been placed side by side to those who never got in touch with it before. This was achieved by patching the existing method in order to split the evaluation activities into two modules, depending on the possibility of the users to interact freely with the product before to start the tests. This made the method modular and allowed its refinement. The refining activities introduced a third module; it involves the users familiar with the product under evaluation. In order to check the improvements and validate the research results, the old and the new releases of the method were adopted to evaluate the UX of a CAD package. The comparison of the results showed that the new release generated more UX aspects, both positive and negative, demonstrating its higher completeness. In addition, the results coming from the three modules were analyzed separately and this analysis allowed highlighting relationships between the results and the modules that generated them. These relationships became suggestions about the best modules to adopt against required characteristics of the results, resources available, evaluators' personal styles, etc.

Some research perspectives could be foreseen too. First, the architecture of the modules should be made as generic as possible to allow adding/modifying them easily and quickly. Second, several activities during the tests should be optimized to avoid time-consuming tests; consequently, users would be more concentrated and the results coming from the evaluation of the real meanings and emotions would be less affected by tiredness and more reliable. Third, new adoptions of the method in the field are required to confirm the effectiveness of the improvements. These adoptions should involve different products and situations, and the needs should be more complex in order to avoid simplifications like the assignment of meanings and emotions to the whole experience - as it happened in the evaluation of the CAD package - rather than to each goal as the definition of the method would require. These further adoptions would be used also to validate the relationships identified in this research and to increase their number. Fourth, these relationships should be generalized to be available in different contexts for evaluating different products. Finally, these relationships should start to be considered not only for evaluation but also for design. In fact, several results of the method adoption, like the lists of user actions and product reactions/feedback (in other words, the irMMs as they are), could be exploited to suggest guidelines to design/redesign products rather than simply to evaluate them. All of this could be the starting point for making the irMMs-based method turn to a UX design aid.

Acknowledgement. The authors would like to thank the students of the Mechanical Engineering courses at the University of Udine who took part of the tests.

References

1. Law, E.L.C., Roto, V., Hassenzahl, M., Vermeeren, A.P.O.S., Kort, J.: Understanding, scoping and defining user experience: a survey approach. In: Conference on Human Factors in Computing Systems, CHI 2009, pp. 719–728 (2009). https://doi.org/10.1145/1518701. 1518813
2. Park, J., Han, S.H., Kim, H.K., Cho, Y., Park, W.: Developing elements of user experience for mobile phones and services: survey, interview, and observation approaches. Hum. Factor. Ergon. Manuf. Serv. Ind. 23(4), 279–293 (2013). https://doi.org/10.1002/hfm.20316
3. Brave, S., Nass, C.: Emotion in human-computer interaction. In: Sears, A., Jacko, J.A.: The Human-Computer Interaction Handbook, pp. 81–96. CRC Press (2012)
4. Gentner, D., Stevens, A.: Mental Models. Lawrence Erlbaum Associates, Hillsdale (1983)
5. Greca, I.M., Moreira, M.A.: Mental models, conceptual models and modelling. Int. J. Sci. Educ. 22(1), 1–11 (2000). https://doi.org/10.1080/095006900289976
6. Rauschenberger, M., Pérez Cota, M., Thomaschewski, J.: Efficient measurement of the user experience of interactive products. How to use the user experience questionnaire (UEQ). Example: spanish language version. Int. J. Artif. Intell. Interact. Multimed. 2(1), 39–45 (2013). https://doi.org/10.9781/ijimai.2013.215
7. Bernhaupt, R., Pirker, M.: Methodological challenges of UX evaluation in the living room: developing the IPTV-UX questionnaire. In: 5th Workshop on Software and Usability Engineering Cross-Pollination, PUX2011, pp. 51–61 (2011)
8. Burmester, M., Mast., M., Kilian, J., Homans, H.: Valence method for formative evaluation of user experience. In: Designing Interactive Systems Conference 2010, DIS 2010, pp. 364–367 (2010). https://doi.org/10.1145/1858171.1858239
9. Filippi, S., Barattin, D.: User experience (UX) evaluation based on interaction-related mental models. In: Ahram, T., Falcão, C. (eds.) AHFE 2017. AISC, vol. 607, pp. 634–645. Springer, Cham (2018). https://doi.org/10.1007/978-3-319-60492-3_60
10. Kujala, S., Vogel, M., Pohlmeyer, A.E., Obrist, M.: Lost in time: the meaning of temporal aspects in user experience. In: 13th Computer-Human Interaction Conference CHI, Extended Abstracts on Human Factors in Computing Systems, pp. 559–564 (2013). https://doi.org/10. 1145/2468356.2468455
11. Karapanos, E., Zimmerman, J., Forlizzi, J., Martens, J.B.: Measuring the dynamics of remembered experience over time. Interact. Comput. 22, 328–335 (2010). https://doi.org/10. 1016/j.intcom.2010.04.003
12. Sng, K.H.E., Raviselvam, S., Anderson, D., Blessing, L., Camburn, B.A., Wood, C.: A design case study: transferring design processes and prototyping principles into industry for rapid response and user impact. In: 21st International Conference on Engineering Design, ICED17, pp. 349–358 (2017)
13. Norman, D.: The Design of Everyday Things: Revised and Expanded Edition. Basic Book, New York (2013)
14. Ullman, D.G.: The Mechanical Design Process, 4th edn. McGraw-Hill, New York (2010)

Improving Usability Evaluation by Automating a Standardized Usability Questionnaire

Priscilla Gonçalves da Silva e Souza and Edna Dias Canedo[✉]

Computer Science Department, University of Brasília (UnB),
Brasília, DF 70910-900, Brazil
priscillagssouzaa@mail.com, ednacanedo@unb.br
http://www.cic.unb.br

Abstract. Usability is one of the factors that determines the success of a software system. Aiming to improve it's usability, it is necessary to evaluate the interfaces using scientific evaluation methods, like questionnaires. Often the results of these evaluations are different when performed by different interface designers, indicating lack of sistematicity of evaluation results. Questionnaires can be automated to support usability evaluation, facilitating the collection and summarization of data. This paper analyzes the automating possibility of a standardized usability questionnaire for further automation. A bibliographical research was carried out about Human-Computer Interaction concepts, usability, usability evaluation methods (including questionnaires) and automation. A systematic review was conducted to identify automated usability questionnaires. The Post-Study Systems Usability Questionnaire (PSSUQ) was chosen to be automated because it is small, free and highly reliable. Analysis of the users and specification of the system requirements and architecture were made.

Keywords: Usability · Usability evaluation · Usability questionnaire
Automation · Mobile devices

1 Introduction

User interface has become more important than in the last decades as a growing number of users perform several tasks with their devices currently [1]. Hugh computer machines used firstly to military and mathematics purposes became smaller, more personal and multitasking [7]. Therefore it is necessary using methods and processes of both Usability Engineering and Human-Computer Interaction (HCI) for design user-centered systems and evaluate them to ensure that [2].

Between these methods, there are the usability evaluation ones, that aim to ensure the systems are suitable and satisfactory for users, helping them to achieve their goals. In the usability test method, for example, interface designers, who conduct the evaluation sessions, observe the users behavior while they use

© Springer International Publishing AG, part of Springer Nature 2018
A. Marcus and W. Wang (Eds.): DUXU 2018, LNCS 10918, pp. 379–395, 2018.
https://doi.org/10.1007/978-3-319-91797-9_27

the system or its prototype, performing designed tasks on it; other method is the questionnaire, used to obtain subjective impressions of the users about the usability of the evaluated system by completing paper forms [3].

However if these evaluations are performed by different designers, studies cited by [4] show usability findings can vary widely and these results will hardly overlap, even if the same evaluation technique is used. This indicates lack of systematicity and predictability of the evaluation results, besides of covering part of the possible actions users may take. Automating some aspects of usability evaluation can be a solution.

This has been done to capture user data mainly [4]. Questionnaires can be automated to reduce evaluation costs and to facilitate data collection and summarization, besides statistics generation to help interface designers, facilitating obtain objective data resume to make better design decisions along the software development process.

Therefore the purpose of this article is to analyze the possibility of automating a standardized usability questionnaire to automate it subsequently. For this, a bibliographic research was carried out on HCI concepts, usability evaluation methods (including usability questionnaires) and their automation.

A systematic review was performed in the literature to identify automated usability questionnaires and how this was made. Some usability questionnaires found are already available in tools. They are standardized (scientifically reliable for usability evaluation), but are paid for use. Others are free, but are not scientific reliable. The Post-Study Usability Questionnaire (PSSUQ) was chosen to be automated because it is free, small, and highly reliable.

Best practices identified in the analyzed studies resulting from the bibliographic research and systematic review were applied on PSSUQ automation process. In this work, were made: the research of the users' context, profile and tasks; low and medium prototypes of the system and specialist evaluation of them; requirements and system architecture specification, and the implementation of the tool. The validation of the PSSUQ implementation will take place through two systems developed in the context of the Brazilian Army.

The remainder of the paper is organized in: Sect. 2, Background, describes the concepts on which this work is based; Sect. 3, Systematic Review of Literature, presents the systematic review conducted to find automated usability questionnaires in the literature; Sect. 4, Tool Specification, describes user analysis, presents the prototypes and its evaluations, requirements and architecture specifications; and Sect. 5, Conclusions, which emphasizes the main ideas and results of this work, and mention future works.

2   Background

This section presents the concepts used as a basis for the development of the work described in this paper.

2.1   Human-Computer Interface (HCI)

HCI is an interdisciplinary field concerned with design, evaluation and development of interactive systems for users, considering its context [3].

2.2   Interface Design Processes

Interface design processes group activities to design systems with user-friendly interfaces. In general, the activities are: user analysis (user profile, tasks and context), create alternative projects (prototyping) and evaluate the interface [3].

2.3   Usability

Usability is a capacity/property of a system [3] that refers to the fact that users make good use of its functionalities [1]. The goal of usability is to ensure that systems are easy to use from the perspective of the users. They must be involved in the whole process of system design and conception, so they can provide information and feedback to improve the system continuously [5].

2.4   Usability Evaluation

Usability evaluation consists of methods to measure aspects of usability of a system, ensuring high quality of the user experience with it [1]. Evaluation methods differ from each other on the objectives and approaches to discover problems, but they should be used complementary in evaluation sessions [4].

2.5   Automation of Usability Evaluation

Automating some aspects of usability evaluation is a trend due to its various benefits, such as saving time and project costs, increasing the consistency of error detection and the coverage of evaluated characteristics, assisting designers who are not experienced in performing evaluations and comparing between alternative designs. It is performed with traditional evaluation methods, automating mainly capture and data analysis [4].

2.6   Standardized Usability Questionnaires

Standardized usability questionnaires are forms with questions which aim to assess user satisfaction with perceived usability of a system. They were made under standards to produce metrics based on the responses obtained from the participants [6]. Their reliability was established scientifically through psychometric tests and are represented by the Alpha coefficient (ranging from 0 to 1, where higher values indicate better reliability) [5].

These questionnaires were made to be used repetitively and to be objective. They are cited in national and international standards (ANSI 2001 and ISO

Table 1. Standardized usability questionnaires

Questionnaire	Quantity of questions	License type	Subject of evaluation	Reliability
QUIS	41	Paid	–	0.94
PSSUQ	16	Free	Computer systems	0.91
SUMI	50	Paid	Software systems	0.92
SUS	10	Free	Any	0.92

1998), such as the post-study ones, applied after the usability tests: Questionnaire for Satisfaction with the User Interface (QUIS), the Measurement Inventory (SUS), the System Usability Scale (SUS) and the System Usability Post-Study Questionnaire (PSSUQ) [5,6].

Some their characteristics are presented in Table 1, showing that two of four questionnaires are free, PSSUQ and SUS. The SUS questionnaire is smaller, with 10 items, while the PSSUQ has 16. But PSSUQ has higher reliability coefficient (0.94), so it was chosen to be automated.

2.7 Mobile Devices

Mobile devices have revolutionized the technology market and also the daily lives of its users, who have many features available only on desktops before. They are very attractive because of their price (these devices became cheaper) and high performance. Many services are delivered in the form of applications focused on specific functions and goals, and can be obtained through delivery mechanisms like Play Store (Google) and Apple Store (Apple Inc.) [7].

A survey conducted in 2012 evaluated the conversion rate - percentage of visitors who complete a desired action - of 100 million visits to the Monetate e-commerce website, for accesses made by computers, tablets and mobile phones. While for Desktop devices the conversion rate was 3.5%, for iPads it was 3.2% and for iPhones only 1.4% [7]. The conversion rates were all low and between the mobile devices, iPad and iPhone, iPad presented higher rate, almost equal to the Desktop rate. For this reason, iPad was chosen platform to develop on the solution for the problem of this work.

3   Systematic Literature Review

This section describes the Systematic Literature Review (SLR) done to identify scientific papers that automated usability questionnaires. SLR is a research technique that uses a rigorous methodology through a pre-defined research protocol aiming to aggregate evidence on a desired research topic to provide background according to the defined strategy [8].

3.1 Systematic Review Protocol

In order to perform an unbiased, objective and systematic approach to collect evidence from software solutions of automated usability questionnaires, researchers defined a mapping study process adapted from [9,10]. It consists of three phases: Planning, Conducting and Documenting the review, according to Fig. 1.

The Planning Phase of the review aims to specify a mapping study protocol describing systematic activities to gather available evidence. The product of this phase is the detailed protocol to support the researchers in the review process. It provides a clear definition of the research questions, search strategy to gather relevant studies, inclusion and exclusion criteria of primary studies, as well as analysis of data extraction and synthesis. All details of the protocol as well as the results of the mapping study are documented in the technical report.

The Conducting Phase of the review involves the application of the research protocol specified to search for primary studies, extract data and synthesize relevant knowledge related to the automated usability questionnaires. The product of this phase is the evidence generated from all the activities of the protocol.

The Documentation Phase of the review reports the findings of the mapping study. The researchers involved consolidate all information, write the technical report, review and publish the results.

Need for This Review. Identify and summarize, in a systematic and unambiguous way, scientific papers that describe software solutions for automated usability questionnaires. There are few studies and most of them propose new questionnaires, but without automating them.

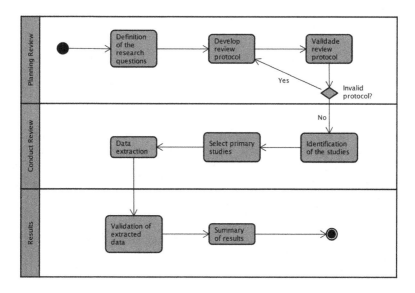

Fig. 1. Mapping study process.

Research Questions. To characterize the evidences on automated usability questionnaires, two questions were formulated addressing different aspects:

- **Question 1:** In the literature, what tools have been developed to automate usability questionnaires?
- **Question 2:** In the group of studies about usability questionnaires identified, how many of them are STANDARDIZED usability questionnaires?

Search Strategy. The search strategy brings together automatic and manual procedures. Before conducting the evaluation of the studies, a pilot study validated the proposed strategy, making changes whenever was necessary. The search strings were constructed combining some terms in English: "questionnaire", "tool", "usability evaluation", "user interface", "user satisfaction" and "automation", also the translation of these terms into Portuguese, since in the pilot study works in Portuguese were identified: "questionário", "ferramenta", "usabilidade", "avaliação", "interface de usuário", "satisfação do usuário" and "automação". After conducting a pilot study with these initial combinations and identifying the inclusion of relevant studies, the search strings were refined and are presented in Table 2 with the initial search results.

Table 2. Search strings and initial results

Search strings	IEEE Xplore	Science Direct	Google Scholar
Usability questionnaire tool	62	37	2
Usability questionnaire automat	39	5	0
User satisfaction questionnaire tool software	30	11	0
Questionnaire measure satisfaction interface user	4	15	0
Questionnaire tool evaluation usability	34	42	0
Ferramenta de avaliacao de usabilidade	0	0	7

Databases. Three digital databases were selected to conduct the research: IEEE Xplore, Science Direct and Google Scholar. They were chosen because they are some of the most relevant databases for Software Engineers [8]. The search strings in Table 2 were applied in the bases using the advanced search options to identify the string terms in the article titles or in the abstracts.

Selection Criteria. To identify relevant primary studies in the research, the following study selection criteria were defined:

Inclusion Criteria (IC)

1. Studies in English or Portuguese on automated usability questionnaires.
2. Studies that contain the following terms in the title: questionnaire or both terms questionnaire and tool, or both terms usability and tool.
3. Studies responding directly to Question 1.

Exclusion Criteria (EC)

1. Studies out of the scope of this research.
2. Studies that do not contain sufficient evidence for this research.
3. Studies describing the conception of new usability questionnaires, but without automating them.
4. Studies describing the automation of questionnaires with different purposes than perform usability evaluation.
5. Studies dealing with the automation of others usability evaluation methods than the questionnaire.
6. Duplicate studies. When a study is published in more than one research source, the most complete version will be used.

Screening Process. One of the main objectives of the mapping study is to determine the relevant papers (primary studies) that correctly address the research questions. According to the search strategy, researchers performed manual and automatic procedures, removing repeated entries. Once the search results were found, the researchers read the titles and abstracts to apply the inclusion criteria. Next, the exclusion criteria were applied during the complete reading of the articles, generating a list of primary studies, as shown in Fig. 2.

Table 3 presents the final research results, after applying the inclusion and exclusion criteria on the initial works. Four relevant studies were identified.

Evaluation of Study Quality. For this study were considered studies present in academic bases appropriated to answer the research questions of this SLR.

Data Extraction. During data extraction process, the researchers carefully read the primary studies. The peer review process was performed and the researchers extracted data for the same study. A pilot data extraction test was conducted to align the researchers' understanding to answer the research questions. The pilot was performed with all primary studies, and disagreements about the individual responses were discussed and resolved. All relevant data from each study were recorded on a form.

Data Summary. The data extracted from the studies were summarized according to the purpose, characteristics and results of use of the tools described in the works.

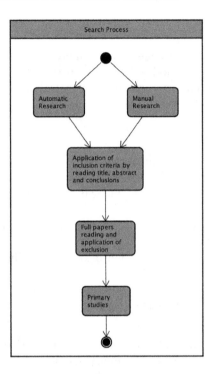

Fig. 2. Search process.

Table 3. Final search results

Database	Results	(IC 1)	(IC 2)	(EC 6)
IEEE Xplore	169	35	7	2
Science Direct	110	5	1	1
Google Scholar	9	4	1	1
Final results	288	44	9	4

3.2   Systematic Review Results

The results of SLR performed are described below:

1. *TOWABE -Usability Assessment Tool for Web Applications:* web tool to evaluate usability of web systems. It automates three evaluation methods: a questionnaire (created based on ISO 9241), inspection and classification of cards. It has two user profiles: Evaluator, who prepares the evaluation, and the Participant, who participates of the evaluation. The 21 items in the questionnaire can be customized, deleted and commented. Each questionnaire is saved with the name of the participant. The results of the evaluations and recommendations for improvement are presented in reports. The case study of the use of the tool showed that users found it practical to receive the invitation by email

to invite for the evaluations. They suggested to include online help and to improve the structure of the questionnaire page, since it did not correspond to their mental model [11].

2. *WQT - Web Questionnaire Tool:* tool to measure usability of interactive systems using questionnaire and video recorder. Developed in PHP language, it allows the creation of a desired questionnaire, by indicating the theme, evaluation criteria, quality factors and items, which can be added or deleted. There are templates of questionnaires already implemented and statistical reports are generated. They can be in textual (HTML or Excel) or graphical format. The results of use of this tool showed that it is robust for users [12].

3. *Mugram:* tool to evaluate usability of mobile systems. For each evaluated system, a project is created. It is possible to create evaluation rounds, for evaluate a version of the system, and compare the results of up to three trial versions. Items are divided into categories and more items can be added. The results of the evaluations are showed in tabs, where the main one shows the total score and the summary of points of the main category; other tabs show the statistical detail for the results of each item. Reports are displayed in diagrams and dashboards. Evaluated by experts, they praised these last two features and found it useful, easy to learn and with clean interface. Suggestions given were: allow exclusion and inclusion of entire categories of items and integrate tool with social networks to share of results [13].

4. *VRUSE:* tool to measure usability of augmented reality systems. It has 100 items divided according to 10 usability factors. Data are collected using a spreadsheet, which facilitates conversion. It is possible to choose the level of expertise of participants regarding the expertise with usage of systems. There is a feedback field at the end of it. The results are displayed on a chart with the score for each usability factor. The case study with the use of VRUSE showed that it has high performance and users felt in control when using it [14].

3.3 Comparative Analysis

To perform a comparative analysis between the works analyzed and described before, the main information about the tools are presented in the Table 4.

Table 4. Questionnaires characteristics

Tool	Platform	System evaluated	Report format
TOWABE	Web	Web	–
WQT	Web	Interactive	Textual/graphical
Mugram	Web	Mobile	Diagram/dashboard
VRUSE	Web	Augmented reality	Chart

Responding to Question 1. All tools run on web platform. Each one evaluates usability of specific systems and most of them allows customization of the questionnaires items. There was concern in evaluating the developed tools, but just Mugram was evaluated by specialists, which has clean design, useful features and very detailed results report. Most of the tools generates graphical reports for easy visualization of them.

Responding to Question 2. None of the analyzed tools automated a standard questionnaire of usability. According to the authors of the articles, standardized questionnaires allow only more general usability assessments, without considering specific characteristics of the systems, such as mobile systems. On the other hand, questionnaires not scientifically tested and accepted, such as the standardized ones, do not have the scientific reliability to perform evaluations. According to [7], only systematic efforts using established methods to evaluate systems can be considered in Usability Engineering. Therefore, the automation of standardized usability questionnaires will allow better analysis and interpretation of the results of the evaluations using a resource of scientific value. Good practices used in the analyzed works will be applied to the work developed in this paper. Based on this research and in the factors in the development of works of this nature, the tool was designed.

4   Tool Specification

This section describes the development and usability processes used, modeling and specification of the requirements and architecture for the proposed tool.

4.1   Software Development Process

A Software Development Process defines a set of necessary activities to develop software with quality. In this work, the process chosen was the Personal Development Process (PSP), which can be used by an individual. Its activities aim to define requirements, design architecture, prototype, generate/test code and verify the effectiveness of the project [15]. The focus of the tool is usability, so an interaction design process Sect. 2 was used with PSP.

4.2   User Analysis

Information about the target users of the tool, its profiles, tasks and context were obtained through bibliographic research and by interviewing professionals who work in the market with consulting and evaluation of system interfaces.

1. *User Profile:* target users are the interface designers, who design user experience and evaluate interfaces. They have knowledge about the usability of several types of systems. Usability evaluations are performed using established methods.

2. *Context:* usability evaluations often occur in laboratories with cameras and tools to record data, such as Google Forms and Excel spreadsheets, that help generate charts. Evaluators instruct participants and then observe them, making records. Usability tests are planned in advance, defining its goal, number of participants recruit, tasks to be performed and schedule for tests. For each completed test scenario the participant fill in a post-task questionnaire, and upon completion of all scenarios, they complete a post-study questionnaire, like PSSUQ, to assess overall system usability [2,16].

3. *User Tasks:* evaluator explains the instructions for participant to complete the questionnaire and deliver it, performing the following steps:
   (a) Participant fills in some information to validate the recruitment, and then, fills in the items and returns the questionnaire to the evaluator;
   (b) Data filled in the questionnaire are validated by the evaluator, who checks it for errors, inconsistencies, blank items, erasures, and the like;
   (c) When completing the usability test, evaluator registers the data in a spreadsheet to generate charts, and
   (d) And generates a report with the classification of the data by punctuation and observations, problems identified and recommendations for improvement for each one. Finally, spreadsheets and reports are stored.

4.3   Functional Requirements

After analyzing the users' profile, their tasks and context, it is possible to define and model the functional requirements of the system in the Use Case Diagram [17] present in Fig. 3.

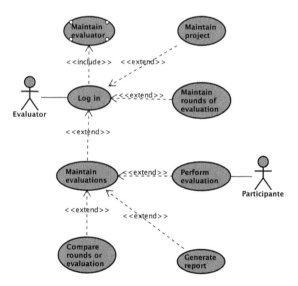

Fig. 3. Functional requirements.

4.4 Low Fidelity Prototypes

The low fidelity prototype of all screens was made on paper and it was evaluated by a interface professional. Just a few screens were shown here.

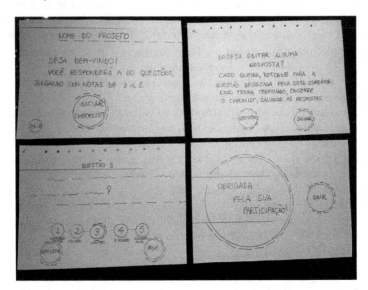

Fig. 4. Questionnaire screen (low fidelity prototype).

Figure 4 shows the process of filling out the questionnaire by a participant, when an individual evaluation is created. On the first screen, quick prompts are given, and after selecting the start option, it answers the questions (one per screen). At the end, participant can return to some question, if wishes, and then finalize the questionnaire.

Prototype Evaluation. System requirements were evaluated through the prototype, that didn't considered the colors choice and icons details for the app. Given recommendations for improvement were: to include messages of feedback for the user for all actions and results of actions performed by participant; to propose a way for evaluator continue his session when participant complete the questionnaire; and the items of the questionnaire should be divided into minor parts.

4.5 Medium Fidelity Prototype

After analyzing the low fidelity prototype, other prototype were made, on a specific tool, with more details, like icons and colors. In Fig. 5 is shown the prototype of the questionnaire screen, with more details in forms, colors, pattern of buttons and actions.

In the Fig. 6 is shown the comparison of project rounds screen.

In these prototype, all recommendations given by the specialist were applied to the previous prototype.

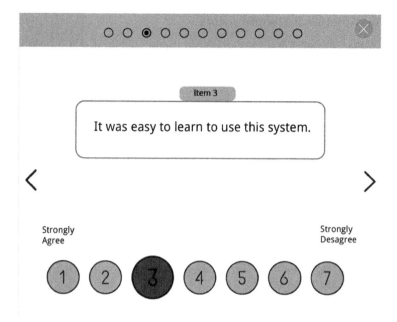

Fig. 5. Questionnaire screen (medium fidelity prototype). (Color figure online)

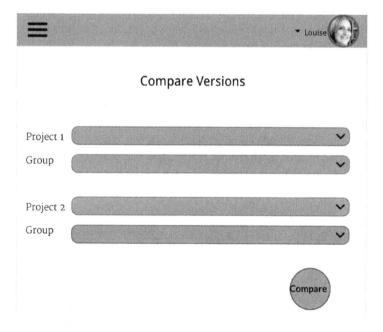

Fig. 6. Comparison screen (medium fidelity prototype).

4.6   Non-functional Requirements

Non-functional requirements express limitations and quality properties of the system [15]. For the tool proposed, the non-functional requirements specified are:

Platform: the system must be developed on the iOS platform - iPad mobile devices.

Security: only users registered as evaluators have access to the features and data.

Installation: the system must be obtained from the Apple Store.

Standard: the system must be developed using the architectural standard Model, Vision and Control (MVC).

4.7   Architecture

The architecture of a system defines the components of its structure. Details of algorithms are not defined here. The architectural style chosen is object-oriented, where the components encapsulate data and operations. Communication occurs by exchanging messages between objects [15].

Architectural patterns address problems in a specific context and serve as the basis for the architectural design. In this project was chosen the standard MVC, suitable for use in mobile applications. The application is separated into three layers: Model, that contains entities and system data; Vision, that contains the logic of data presentation and event capture, and Control, which handles events captured by the Vision and searches the data in the Model to update the Vision [18]. In addition, there is the data layer, that handles the logic to store the application data. In Fig. 7 it is possible to see a simplification of the relationship between the entities of the system.

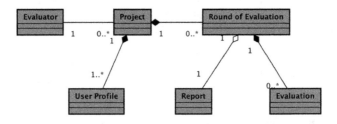

Fig. 7. Entities diagram.

4.8   Implementation

The tool, called iQuest, was implemented according to the defined requirements and the architectural specification made. In the following images, some of the screens of the tool.

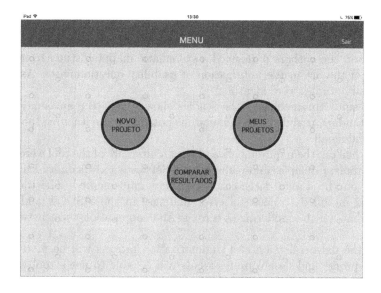

Fig. 8. Menu screen.

Fig. 9. Report screen.

Figure 8 represents the main Menu of the tool with the options offered to the Evaluator (after he/she is logged-in): Register new project, Query registered projects and Compare results of evaluations.

Figure 9 displays the general data in a report for a round of project evaluations.

5   Conclusion

In this work, the authors performed a systematic mapping study to investigate the state of the art in the automation of usability questionnaires. As a result, four primary studies were identified.

The results obtained with the studies showed that the automation of the PSSUQ standard usability questionnaire is possible, since it is free (not licensed for use) and small.

From then on, the requirements and the architecture of the tool were specified using the tools, principles and techniques of Software and Usability Engineering.

Based on the design decisions, iQuest was implemented. The tool will be tested and modified (because of error findings) in the SISDOT and SISBOL projects that will be modernized through the cooperation term between UnB and EB.

Then the data collection and summarization process will be more efficient, less error prone, and design professionals will be able to use a tool with high-quality of usability to perform usability assessments.

Acknowledgments. The authors would like to thank the usability professionals who provided information on interface designers and evaluated the prototype of the system.

References

1. Nielsen, J.: Usability Engineering. Elsevier, New York (1993)
2. Rubin, J., Chisnell, D.: Handbook of Usability Testing: How to Plan, Design and Conduct Effective Tests, 2nd edn. Wiley, Hoboken (2008)
3. Sharp, H., Rogers, Y., Preece, J.: Interaction Design: Beyond Human-Computer Interaction, 4th edn. Wiley, Hoboken (2015)
4. Ivory, M.Y., Hearst, M.A.: The state of the art in automating usability evaluation of user interfaces. ACM Comput. Surv. **33**, 470–516 (2001)
5. Shneiderman, B.: Designing the User Interface: Strategies for Effective Human-Computer Interaction, 5th edn. Pearson Education India, Delhi (2010)
6. Sauro, J., Lewis, J.R.: Quantifying the User Experience: Practical Statistics for User Research, 2nd edn. Morgan Kaufman, Burlington (2016)
7. Nielsen, J., Budiu, R.: Mobile Usability. MITP-Verlags GmbH & Co. KG, Blaufelden (2013)
8. Kitchenham, B., Brereton, O.P., Budgen, D., Turner, M., Bailey, J., Linkman, S.: Systematic literature reviews in software engineering-a systematic literature review. Inf. Softw. Tech. **51**, 7–15 (2009)

9. Galster, M., Weyns, D., Tofan, D., Michalik, B., Avgeriou, P.: Variability in software systems—a systematic literature review. IEEE Trans. Softw. Eng. **40**, 282–306 (2014)
10. Kitchenham, B., Charters, S.: Guidelines for performing systematic literature reviews in software engineering. Technical report TR-001, MIT Research Lab, Keele University and Durham University (2010)
11. Itakura, F.T.: Towabe: uma ferramenta para avaliação de usabilidade de aplicações para web. Universidade Federal do Paraná (2001)
12. Assila, A., Bouhlel, M.S.: A web questionnaire generating tool to aid for interactive systems quality subjective assessment. In: International Conference on Control, Decision and Information Technologies (CoDIT), pp. 815–821. IEEE (2013)
13. Wich, M., Kramer, T.: Enhanced human-computer interaction for business applications on mobile devices: a design-oriented development of a usability evaluation questionnaire. In: 48th Hawaii International Conference on System Sciences (HICSS), pp. 472–481. IEEE (2015)
14. Kalawsky, R.S.: VRUSE - a computerized diagnostic tool: for usability evaluation of virtual/synthetic environment systems. Appl. Ergon. **30**, 11–25 (1999)
15. Pressman, R., Maxim, B.: Engenharia de Software, 8th edn. McGraw Hill Brasil, São Paulo (2016)
16. Lewis, J.R.: Handbook of Human Factors and Ergonomics. Wiley, Hoboken (2006)
17. Larman, C.: Applying UML and Patterns: An Introduction to Object Oriented Analysis and Design and Interative Development. Pearson Education India, Delhi (2012)
18. Barros, T., Silva, M., Espínola, E.: State MVC: Estendendo o padrão MVC para uso no desenvolvimento de aplicações para dispositivos móveis. In: Sexta Conferência Latino-Americana em Linguagens de Padrões para Programação (2007)

Usability Evaluation with Heuristics. New Proposal from Integrating Two Trusted Sources

Toni Granollers[(✉)]

Human-Computer Interaction and Data Integration Research Group (GRIHO),
Polytechnic Institute of Research and Innovation in Sustainability (INSPIRES),
University of Lleida, Lleida, Spain
antoni.granollers@udl.cat

Abstract. The work presented here is born of the huge interest in usability, to be more precise, from the interest in evaluating this aspect in user interfaces. And, to be even more precise, from a substantial experience using one of the most used usability evaluation techniques, the Heuristic Evaluation.

After reasoning about the use of this technique, a substantial improvement is on development and here first stage is presented. In this work we will see a new list of principles for evaluating user interfaces of any interactive system. The reader will see how the list has been achieved and also a set of specific questions to be answered when analyzing every principle.

Keywords: Heuristics · ISO and usability · Usability methods and tools

1 Introduction

Usability heuristics, usually referred to as Heuristic Evaluation (HE), is one of the most widely used methods for evaluating the usability of an interactive system. Heuristic Evaluation became the most popular User Centered Design (UCD) approach in the 1990s, but has become less prominent with the move away from desktop applications [3]. This technique is an effective method to assess user interfaces by taking the recommendations based on UCD principles. These recommendations come in terms of design principles, heuristics, guidelines, best practices or user interface design patterns and standards [1] that are supposed to serve interface designers and evaluators.

Nevertheless, this technique has some pitfalls such as the need for adapting the heuristic set to the specific features of each interactive system. Thus, evaluators must combine different recommendations sources to review the specific application domain. This involves either choosing Nielsen's list [8] (the most well-known and widely used), or a long reviewing process of guideline collections that inevitably causes conflicts between various resources [4]. In addition, each set uses different scoring systems to score the recommendations, so it is necessary to adjust it in the resultant set.

The process of combining different heuristic sets usually finishes up with an extensive list of duplicated recommendations, similar statements using different terms and potentially conflicting guidelines. Then, a clean-up and selection process require to provide a reliable, consistent and easy to use heuristic set [1].

© Springer International Publishing AG, part of Springer Nature 2018
A. Marcus and W. Wang (Eds.): DUXU 2018, LNCS 10918, pp. 396–405, 2018.
https://doi.org/10.1007/978-3-319-91797-9_28

Furthermore, our experience reveals that often (not to say almost always) when someone uses Nielsen's list [8] is due to a lack of (deep) knowledge about it and, most worryingly, about the technique itself. This assertion is based on Nielsen's statement: *"these principles are broad rules of thumb and not specific usability guidelines"* [8], making the list itself impossible to be used to evaluate.

At the same time, even HE is mainly a qualitative technique, some attempts for quantifying have appeared [1, 2, 6, 10, 12], among others. Or, other more ambitious such as work done by Masip et al. [4, 5], who provided a full framework to enable a semi-automatic process to provide the most adequate set of heuristics for each specific situation. It also classifies the heuristics in terms of different constraints (UX-degree) and enables an automatic classification of the problems found (removing the post-evaluation meeting done by the evaluators) for a better full process. Nevertheless, the rigorousness itself of this process makes it so complex that it is not widely used.

In this paper we propose to analyze the usability evaluation as an important technique. After consulting all main related sources, we will put the focus in two of the most known design principles. They will be precisely analyzed and mixed to propose a new list of principles to be used in the future.

2   Combining Common Heuristic Sets

2.1   Main Sources Consulted

Since that Schneiderman, in 1987, established his well-known *Eight Golden Rules of Interface Design* [11], and going via the no less well known Nielsen's *Ten general principles for interaction design* [8] or Tognazzini's *First Principles of Interaction Design* [7], several authors have designed new sets (usually modifying Nielsen's list and/or adding new principles to evaluate specific aspects not covered) to help user interface designers and/or experts in their goal of enhancing usability of any kind of interactive system. A complete review of several sets of usability heuristics created for specific domains by different authors can be found in [10] (specifically in the appendix A of this reference).

Nevertheless, the truth (mainly in private companies) is that when almost everybody refers to evaluate usability or UX with heuristics they refer only to the Nielsen's list.

In our case, after more than twenty years of experience involved in evaluation of interfaces, we decided to take Nielsen's and Tognazzini's lists to do this present work. We selected only these two because both are excellent references. So, there is no need to spend much time refining lists or providing specific new ones when experience evidences that they are not widely used. Nevertheless, as we said before Nielsen's list needed something more to be useful at all and Tognazzini's is too long and detailed to be wide used. It has been confirmed by our own experience, that leads us to complete a new proposal resulting from combining both.

2.2   Methodology

Inspired by recommendations found in Quiñones and Rusu [10] and Quiñones' [9] recommendations, the process followed for deciding our list of proposal principles follows three steps: revision, compare similarities and integration.

Step 1: Revision of the Two Chosen Lists

The first step is to carefully read all the principles of the Nielsen and Tognazzini lists. The revision has been done in terms of understanding the deep meaning of each principle. Tables 1 and 2 shows the revised lists:

Table 1. Nielsen's ten general principles for interaction design [8]

N1	Visibility of system status
N2	Match between system and the real world
N3	User control and freedom
N4	Consistency and standards
N5	Recognition rather than recall
N6	Flexibility and efficiency of use
N7	Help users recognize, diagnose, and recover from errors
N8	Error prevention
N9	Aesthetic and minimalist design
N10	Help and documentation

Table 2. Tognazzi's first principles of interaction design (revised & expanded) [7]

T1	Aesthetics	T11	Human interface objects
T2	Anticipation	T12	Latency reduction
T3	Autonomy	T13	Learnability
T4	Color	T14	Metaphors, use of
T5	Consistency	T15	Protect users' work
T6	Defaults	T16	Readability
T7	Discoverability	T17	Simplicity
T8	Efficiency of the user	T18	State
T9	Explorable interfaces	T19	Visible navigation
T10	Fitts's law		

Step 2: Compare Similarities

As the intention is to get a compact and complete solution for evaluating all kind of user interfaces. The first exercise to be done after the revision is to analyze and compare every principle from both chosen lists. This comparison is done by searching their similarities and try to group as many as possible. Our intention is to generate a new short as possible list that will include all design principles. It will look for all design characteristics, from both authors.

We will start this integration following the order of Nielsen's list. Afterwards, we will continue following the order of Tognazzini's.

The following paragraphs detail the entire reasoning and argumentation of this comparison:

- N1 + T19 + T7 → **H1 - Visibility and system state**[1]

Visibility of system status (N1) means that the system should always keep users informed about what is going on, through appropriate feedback within reasonable time. Feedback that we can assume as actions done to make *navigation visible* (T19).

Moreover, Tognazzini himself already relates *discoverability* (T7) and *visible navigation* (T19) characteristics, then we proposed to group all them into only one.

- N2 + T11 + T14 → **H2 - Connection between the system and the real world, metaphor usage and human objects**

With *match between system and the real world* (N2) Nielsen means that the system capability for speaking the users' language, with words, phrases and concepts familiar to the user, rather than system-oriented terms. Idea that also could be expressed saying that *human interface objects* (T11).

Additionally, Nielsen completes N2 saying that the system should follow real-world conventions, making information appear in a natural and logical order. Conventions that are best represented by the uses metaphors (T14) of the interface because, metaphors generate users' minds strong connections to their world, representing their conceptual model.

- N3 + T9 → **H3 - User control and freedom**

Under the principle of *explorable interfaces* (T9) we find characteristics such as the ability to provide users with well-marked paths and reference points so that they can freely control the interface.

Among its features we can also find the ability to prevent users from choosing system functions by mistake, or find an "emergency exit" clearly marked to leave the unwanted state without having to go through an extended dialogue, which is exactly the Nielsen principle *user control and freedom* (N3). Here, we propose Nielsen's principle name, it is more descriptive.

- N4 + T5 → **H4 - Consistency and standards**

There is no need to argue anything to explain that these two principles can be merged into one: *Consistency* (T5) is part of *consistency and standards* (N4).

- N5 + T2 + T13 → **H5 - Recognition rather than memory, learning and anticipation**

This is a complex case. The heuristic proposed merges three different principles that, in essence, are the same. Nielsen's principle, *recognition rather than recall* (N5) means that minimizing the user's memory load he/she should not have to remember

---

[1] Explanation: every paragraph starts with a sentence like this "*N1 + T19 + T7*→ *H1.- Visibility and system State*" that means that Nielsen number 1 heuristic (N1) plus Tognazzini numbers 19 (T19) and 7 (T7) principles are grouped into our heuristic number 1(H1). All follow the same structure.

information from one part to another. This characteristic facilitates the system's *learnability* (T2) and user's *anticipation* (T13) to all the actions.

Then we propose to merge all them changing "than recall" (from N5) for "than "memory" to strong reinforce the other included characteristics.

- **N6 + T8 ➜ H6 - Flexibility and efficiency of use**

Contrary to the previous case, this is easy to argue: *efficiency of the user* (T8) is clearly included into *flexibility and efficiency of use* (N6). Principles of both authors are looking for the user's productivity, not the computer's. Productivity that is enhanced by means of flexibility elements (i.e. keyboard accelerators) that often speed up the interaction for the user.

- **N9 + T1 + T17 ➜ H9 - Aesthetic and minimalist design**

Aesthetics (T1) is included in first part of *Aesthetic and minimalist design* (N9) principle while *simplicity* (T17) can be assimilated within the second part of N9. Then our proposal here is to use Nielsen's definition integrating these two from Tognazzini.

- **T15 + T18 ➜ H11 - Save the state and protect the work**

Considering the reasoning of Tognazzini, *State* (T18) principle: "make clear what you will store & protect the user's information", it seems clear that to *protect user's work* (T15).

- **T4 & T16 ➜ H12 - Colour and readability**

Tognazzini refers to *colour* (T4) in two aspects: first in terms of accessibility for people that have some form of colour blindness and, second, in terms of vital interface element.

About accessibility he emphasizes about the need for providing secondary cues to convey the information to those who cannot see the colours presented. In the second case he highlights the importance of using colour, but it must be used in clear and readable foreground versus background combinations. Then, we can easily observe that *readability* (T16) is in the essence of both cases.

- **N7 ➜ H7 - Help users recognize, diagnose and recover from errors**
- **N8 ➜ H8 - Error prevention**
- **N10 ➜ H10 - Help and documentation**

In all previous cases, no Tognazzini principle has been identified to be merged with Nielsen's. Then, in these three cases, one Nielsen principle is used directly, without changes.

- **T3 ➜ H13 - Autonomy**
- **T6 ➜ H14 - Defaults**
- **T12 ➜ H15 - Latency reduction**

Here there are those Tognazzini principles that remain alone, so, as before, they are used directly, without changes.

Finally, *Fitts's law* (T10) principle has not been included in the final list. The reason for excluding is because, according to the author's own words, it requires a stop watch users test. That is, like so much in the field of HCI, you must do a timed usability study with users to test for Fitts's Law efficiency. Then, as this list of heuristics is created to be used for evaluators without users, it makes sense to not include it in this proposal.

Step 3: Integrate These Similarities

Previous step enabled us to propose a shorter as possible list of heuristics to be used to evaluate the usability of any user interface. Because it is an integration, the comparison has been done without losing the efficiency of both lists. We have seen that some principles convey to a new one while some others remain the same.

Here, in the integration, there is something as important as the list itself: the questions to be used for analyzing all the principles. Even having a list of principles, without a finite and precise collection of questions for every principle, is quite impossible to make a good usability assessment. For example, many people use Nielsen's principles but, because they are too generalists, when analyzing, same people have misunderstandings about what it is, making lots of mistakes.

Table 3 shows all the principles generated in previous step with their corresponding set of questions needed to be answered when evaluating an interface. All the questions have been obtained from the original sources used, carefully analyzing all the aspects to be assessed underneath every new principle.

Table 3. Heuristic list proposed with all corresponding evaluation questions

H1 - Visibility and system state
- Does the application include a visible title page, section or site?
- Does the user always know where it is located?
- Does the user always know what the system or application is doing?
- Are the links clearly defined?
- Can all actions be visualized directly? (No other actions are required)

H2 - Connection between the system and the real world, metaphor usage and human objects
- Does information appear in a logical order for the user?
- Does the design of the icons correspond to everyday objects?
- Does every icon do the action that you expect?
- Does the system use phrases and concepts familiar to the user?

H3 - User control and freedom
- Is there a link to come back to initial state or homepage?
- Are the functions "undo" and "re-do" implemented?
- Is it easy to come back to an earlier state of the application?

H4 - Consistency and standards
- Do link labels have the same names as their destinations?
- Do the same actions always have the same results?
- Do the icons have the same meaning everywhere?
- Is the information displayed consistently on every page?
- Are the colours of the links standard? If not, are they suitable for its use?
- Do navigation elements follow the standards? (Buttons, check box,...)

(continued)

Table 3. (*continued*)

H5 - Recognition rather than memory, learning and anticipation
- Is it easy to use the system for the first time?
- Is it easy to locate information that has already been searched for before?
- Can you use the system at all times without remembering previous screens?
- Is all content needed for navigation or task found in the "current screen"?
- Is the information organized according to logic familiar to the end user?

H6 - Flexibility and efficiency of use
- Are there keyboard shortcuts for common actions?
- If there are, is it clear how to use them?
- Is it possible to easily perform an action done earlier?
- Does the design adapt to the changes of screen resolution?
- Is the use of accelerators visible to the normal user?
- Does it always keep the user busy? (without unnecessary delays)

H7 - Help users recognize, diagnose and recover from errors
- Does it display a message before taking irreversible actions?
- Are errors shown in real time?
- Is the error message that appears easily interpretable?
- Is some code also used to reference the error?

H8 - Error prevention
- Does a confirmation message appear before taking the action?
- Is it clear what information needs to be entered in each box on a form?
- Does the search engine tolerate typos and spelling errors?

H9 - Aesthetic and minimalist design
- Is used a design without redundancy of information?
- Is the information short, concise and accurate?
- Is each item of information different from the rest and not confused?
- Is the text well organized, with short sentences and quick to interpret?

H10 - Help and documentation
- Is there the "help" option?
- If so, is it visible and easy to access?
- Is the help section aimed at solving problems?
- Is there a section of frequently asked questions (FAQ)?
- Is the help documentation clear, with examples?

H11 - Save the state and protect the work
- Can users continue from a previous state (where they had previously been or from another device)?
- Is "Autosave" implemented?
- Does the system have a good response to external failures? (Power cut, internet not working, …)

H12 - Color and readability
- Do the fonts have an adequate size?
- Do the fonts use colours with sufficient contrast with the background?
- Do background images or patterns allow the content to be read?
- Does it consider people with reduced vision?

(*continued*)

Table 3. (*continued*)

H13 - Autonomy
- Does it keep the user informed of system status?
- Moreover, is the system status visible and updated?
- Can the user take their own decisions? (Personalization)

H14 - Defaults
- Does the system or device give the option to return to factory settings?
- If so, does it clearly indicate the consequences of the action?
- Is the term "Default" used?

H15 - Latency reduction
- Is the execution of heavy work transparent to the user?
- While running heavy tasks, is remaining time or some animation shown?

We can observe **two important aspects** to be considered in all the questions:

a. each question should be able to be answered with a simple "Yes" or "No", and
b. if the answer is "Yes", it will mean good usability for this characteristic and "No" means bad usability.

Both considerations are more significative as it might seem. Answering with a Yes or a No facilitates the evaluator's response, minimizing the meaningless responses that are often done by the "fatigue effect" (as the evaluation is being carried out, due to fatigue of the evaluator, the rigor in the answers decreases).

And, giving the same sense to each answer also minimizes the errors, the evaluator knows from the beginning that a positive or negative answer always means the same.

3   Conclusion and Future Work

In this paper we aim to propose something risky but so ambitious as to propose a new heuristic list to go beyond the famous Nielsen's one. One can think that it is not necessary but, in our opinion, it is necessary at all. With Nielsen' list is not enough to conduct good usability evaluations.

Nielsen' list is very popular because is short, clear and it looks easy to use it. Nevertheless, everyone used to do evaluations knows that this list is not enough, with only the information provided is almost impossible to do a professional job. The list has been unchanged since its creation, twenty-two years ago, nor does it have any specific questions to answer for each principle, making it confusing, completely depending on the evaluators intuition.

Other less popular but more precise and more updated is Tognazzini list. In this case, the list is less known and even less used because its length. Nevertheless, it is much more complete, with more principles and better explanations for every principle. When using this list, it leads to make fewer mistakes, but it is very much more time consuming. In this paper we have analyzed both lists to propose a new one from them.

The obtained list solves all the problems of the previous ones while maintaining all the good characteristics of both. The result is a fifteen principles list that covers all the characteristics enclosed by its predecessors. To be useful in usability evaluations, each principle is accompanied by a set of questions that can be answered with a simple "Yes" or "No", conducting to increase the confidence of the evaluations.

The work here presented is the first one in a list of others that has the goal of providing a complete usability/UX evaluation methodology for modern and future user interfaces (UI). Our aim is to be able to improve the evaluations, making them easier and clearer that current ones.

At the same time, we also aim to be able to quantify the result of every evaluation, providing a number giving some sort of idea about the usability level of the UI evaluated. We want to find a method for obtaining a quantitative value (that can be named as Usability Percentage) that gives a numeric idea about how usable is the evaluated interface.

To achieve it, next steps to be done are: to propose a rating scale for every question, to quantify the values of this rating scale and to find a formula to provide this usability percentage. A sort of experiments will be the final stage to validate all the presented future steps.

References

1. Baker, K., Greenberg, S., Gutwin, C.: Empirical development of a heuristic evaluation methodology for shared workspace groupware. In: Proceedings of Conference on Computer Supported Cooperative Work, pp. 96–105 (2002)
2. Bonastre, L., Granollers, T.: A set of heuristics for user experience evaluation in E-commerce websites. In: Proceedings of the Seventh International Conference on Advances in Computer-Human Interactions, ACHI 2014, pp. 27–34 (2014). ISBN 978-1-61208-325-4
3. Cockton, C.: Usability evaluation, Chap. 15. In: The Encyclopedia of Human-Computer Interaction, 2nd edn. www.interaction-design.org/literature/book/the-encyclopedia-of-human-computer-interaction-2nd-ed/usability-evaluation
4. Masip, L., Martinie, C., Winckler, M., Palanque, P., Granollers, T., Oliva, M.: A design process for exhibiting design choices and trade-offs in (potentially) conflicting user interface guidelines. In: Winckler, M., Forbrig, P., Bernhaupt, R. (eds.) HCSE 2012. LNCS, vol. 7623, pp. 53–71. Springer, Heidelberg (2012). https://doi.org/10.1007/978-3-642-34347-6_4
5. Masip, L., Oliva, M., Granollers, T.: OPEN-HEREDEUX: OPEN HEuristic REsource for Designing and Evaluating User eXperience. In: Campos, P., Graham, N., Jorge, J., Nunes, N., Palanque, P., Winckler, M. (eds.) INTERACT 2011. LNCS, vol. 6949, pp. 418–421. Springer, Heidelberg (2011). https://doi.org/10.1007/978-3-642-23768-3_47
6. Martínez, A.B., Juan, A.A., Álvarez, D., del Carmen Suárez, M.: WAB*: a quantitative metric based on WAB. In: Gaedke, M., Grossniklaus, M., Díaz, O. (eds.) ICWE 2009. LNCS, vol. 5648, pp. 485–488. Springer, Heidelberg (2009). https://doi.org/10.1007/978-3-642-02818-2_44
7. Tognazzini, B.: First Principles, HCI Design, Human Computer Interaction (HCI), Principles of HCI Design, Usability Testing. http://www.asktog.com/basics/firstPrinciples.html. Accessed 5 Mar 2014
8. Nielsen, J.: 10 Usability Heuristics for User Interface Design. https://www.nngroup.com/articles/ten-usability-heuristics. Accessed 1 Jan 1995

9. Quiñones, D.: A methodology to develop usability/user experience heuristics. In: Proceedings of the XVIII International Conference on Human Computer Interaction, Interacción 2017, Article no. 57, p. 2. ACM, New York. https://doi.org/10.1145/3123818.3133832

10. Quiñones, D., Rusu, C.: How to develop usability heuristics: a systematic literature review. Comput. Stand. Interfaces **53**, 89–122 (2017). https://doi.org/10.1016/j.csi.2017.03.009. ISSN 0920-5489

11. Shneiderman, B.: Designing the User Interface: Strategies for Effective Human-Computer Interaction. Addison-Wesley Publ. Co., Reading (1987)

12. Suarez, M.C.: SIRIUS: Sistema de Evaluación de la Usabilidad Web Orientado al Usuario y basado en la Determinación de Tareas Críticas. Doctoral thesis, Oviedo, Spain (2011)

A Method of Evaluating User Visual Attention to Moving Objects in Head Mounted Virtual Reality

Shi Huang[(✉)]

Animation and Digital Arts Academy, Communication University of China,
Dingfuzhuang East Street, Chaoyang, Beijing, China
bit.stone@163.com

Abstract. Virtual reality games/films/applications bring new challenges to conventional film grammar and design principles, due to more spatial freedom available to users in 6-DOF Head-Mounted Display (HMD). This paper introduces a simple model of viewers' visual attention in environment of virtual reality while watching randomly generated moving objects. The model is based on a dataset collected from 10 users in a 50-seconds-long virtual reality experience on HTC Vive. In this paper, we considered three factors as major parameters affecting audiences' attention: the distance between object and the viewer, the speed of objects movement, and the direction of object towards. We hope the research result is useful to immersive film directors and VR game designers in the future.

Keywords: Virtual reality · Focus of attention · Immersive film
VR game · VR experience

1 Introduction

Some business and technology specialists predict that VR (Virtual Reality) will become mainstream by 2020, and that it will eventually be led by non-games applications [1]. They believe that VR technology holds tremendous potential to reshape the future for many industries, from video game, cinema, healthcare, education, arts to engineering. Many film festivals have started VR competitive section or showcase. These events include Cannes Film Festival, Venice Film Festival, Sundance, Tribeca, Toronto, Geneva Intl. Film Festival Tous Ecrans and Dubai fest [2].

However, some film directors regard VR as an immature, somehow dangerous medium for storytelling. Because VR "gives the viewer a lot of latitude not to take direction from the storytellers but make their own choices of where to look [3]." In simulated environment, users may miss the important clue or element when exploring other trivial areas. VR designers must find a way to guide the audiences to look at the right direction, otherwise they may fail to achieve a complete storytelling. How to grab users' visual attention, how to guide the audience's fixation, becomes a very basic and essential technique in VR experience design.

Human visual attention to graphics has been studied for many years. Koch and Ullman presented a computational model of human visual attention in 1987 [4], and

© Springer International Publishing AG, part of Springer Nature 2018
A. Marcus and W. Wang (Eds.): DUXU 2018, LNCS 10918, pp. 406–416, 2018.
https://doi.org/10.1007/978-3-319-91797-9_29

Clark and Ferrier developed a practical implementation in two years later [5]. Recent research includes Judd and Durand in 2012 [6], Borji and Itti in 2013 [7], Borji et al. in 2015 [8], many different computational saliency models have been built to detect salient visual subsets. These studies normally produce saliency map from images and videos by various features, such as brightness, color, shape and other characteristics.

In VR field, visual attention for spherical images/videos has been studied in [9–11]. Bogdanova et al. propose a method to obtain saliency maps from omnidirectional images. Upenik et al. describe a model for head direction trajectories to produce continuous fixation maps. However, these studies are based on spherical VR contents, which are usually shot with VR cameras or pre-rendered on computers. These images/videos compress depth information into a spherical projection, lacking of realistic sense of space.

Current popular VR HMD such as Oculus Rift, HTC Vive or PlayStation VR has 6 DoF (degree of freedom), allowing users to walk and jump within a given space. Many VR experiences are rendered in real-time, for instance, Oculus Story Studio's "*Lost*" (2015) and "*Henry*" (2015), Disney's "*Coco VR*" (2017) and Magnopus' "*Blade Runner 2049: Memory Lab*" (2017). Real-time rendering CG brings the participants more flexibility and interactivity. In these cases, a very effective trick to grab viewer's attention is to place a moving object in the scene. For example, there is a crawling ladybug in the beginning of "*Henry*". The director initially placed various objects with different speeds for test, and finally decided to use a ladybug to direct viewer's attention [12]. Related studies show that human eyes are more likely to focus on moving and near objects than the opposite [13, 14].

In this paper, we propose a simple method to record users' visual attention data in 6-DoF VR environment. We build a virtual space filled with several moving objects. To exclude potential interference of the objects' appearance, we intentionally designed them as white spheres of the same size. Each sphere has a unique speed, generated in a random position towards a random direction in every testing.

Considering users actually observing random scenes in the experiment, we record data of objects instead of users. This is the major difference between our approach and others. When experiment repeated sufficient times, a rough model of users' visual attention to moving objects is concluded.

2 Experimental Settings

In this section we describe the setting of moving objects and virtual environment, the software implemented to record data, as well as the test material and conditions considered during the experiment processing.

2.1 Virtual Environment

Figure 1 shows the virtual environment designed for the experiment. Users are placed in a virtual space, where is empty and dark, existing nothing but an infinite floor lightened by a directional light from the top. The floor within 10 m is illuminated and others fade into the darkness.

In front of the viewer, 20 white spheres are initially generated within a 4 m wide, 2 m high and 4 m deep cubic range. After that, spheres fly away along random directions. Each sphere is in the same color and the same size, precisely, 10 cm in diameter. We apply different velocities to each sphere, from 0.2 m/s to 4 m/s. If a sphere moves out of the given range, it will disappear at the edge and regenerated on the opposite side. As shown in Fig. 2, every sphere moves in a fixed velocity along a random direction. This process will repeat for about 1 min until the experiment finishes.

In order to observe more neatly, all directions are set to be vertical or horizontal, that is to say, there are 6 possible directions in total: top to bottom, bottom to top, left to right, right to left, forward and backward. Depending on the performance of the computer, the loading time can last for 10 to 20 s, and the actual testing time can vary from 50 to 60 s.

Fig. 1. Virtual environment in the experiment

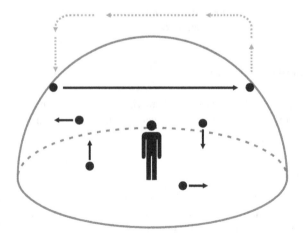

Fig. 2. Objects' movement in VR

2.2   Software

As shown in Fig. 3, we developed a VR application to capture and save to log files the objects' movement every 100 frames or whenever the viewer sees an object in the center of his/her visible range. The major purpose of the software is to associate each attention event to a timestamp and other related information. Once the object is observed by the user (i.e. an attention event), a corresponding log file will add a line, which includes the following data:

- The object's ID (integer)
- Timestamp of the event (float)
- Count of the object being observed (integer)
- Distance between object and the viewer (float)
- Screen position in camera vision (float)
- Whether the object is approaching or leaving (Boolean value)
- Current velocity of the object (float)
- Current direction of the object (3d vector, as described above, there are 6 directions in total).

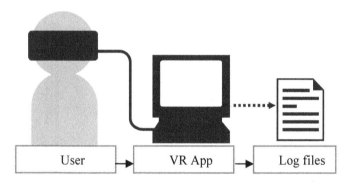

Fig. 3. Workflow of the software

This VR application was developed with game engine Unity in C#, based on the SteamVR Plugin developed by Valve Corporation. This SDK allows developers to target a single interface that will work with all major virtual reality headsets; in this case, the headset was HTC Vive. We performed all tests and the data collection campaign on Windows 10.

2.3   Testing Session

11 subjects participated in the experiment, 9 male and 2 female subjects, between 20 and 39 years old. Most subjects in the sample group are students or staffs from Communication University of China. Some are visitors from other institutes. All subjects have experiences of virtual reality. Before the beginning of the testing, oral instructions were provided to describe the main steps of the testing process. The exact flow is described as following:

1. Before the user puts the HMD on, he/she is asked if they are familiar with HMDs. The instructor records information including gender, age and level of familiarity with VR on HMDs.
2. Before testing starts, the instructor helps user to adjust HMD, such as the fine-tuning of the position and the interpupillary distance.
3. VR application starts and lasts 70 s.
4. At the end of the session, the user is informed that test is over and to remove the HMD.

3 Data Set

Our method respectively records the data of each moving object. Due to the velocity of a certain object is fixed every time, based on the log file name (containing velocity information), we can conveniently evaluate the data for each object.

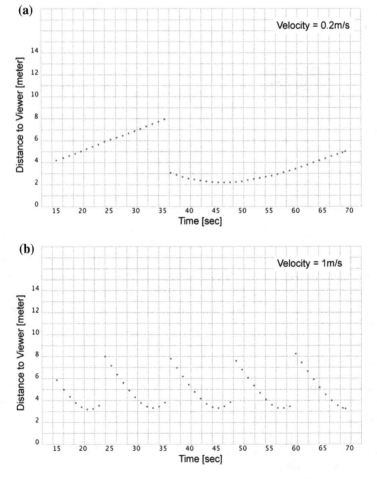

Fig. 4. (a). Object distance to viewer (move at 0.2 m/s) (b). Object distance to viewer (move at 1 m/s) (Color figure online)

3.1   Distance Between Object and Viewer

Distance between a certain object and the viewer is a float, which is recorded every 100 frames (about 1.2 s). Object distances to the viewer are presented as blue dots, as shown in Fig. 4(a) and (b). Because objects move from one side to another repeatedly, the data in Fig. 4 shows a periodic pattern.

During the periodic movement, once the viewer captures the object in view, a data tagged by attention event will be added. These attention events are presented as red dot. And according to the object's proximity to users' visual center (in camera view), we set attention events into different sizes. Object closer to visual center, the size of related red dot is bigger. Figure 5 depicts a typical chart with attention events of an object moving at 0.4 m/s. We can put all experiments data of this object into one figure, as shown in Fig. 6.

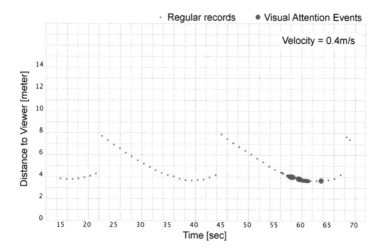

Fig. 5. Distance chart with attention event (Color figure online)

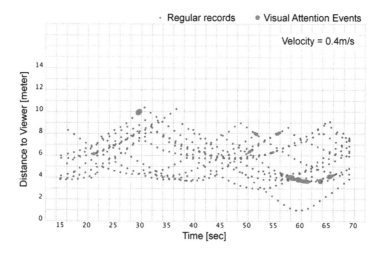

Fig. 6. Summary of all experiment data of an object (Color figure online)

3.2 Velocity

As stated before, each object in the virtual environment moves at a fixed speed, from 0.2 m/s, 0.4 m/s, 0.6 m/s… to 4 m/s. As shown in Fig. 7, each column contains the total attention events of an object (there are 20 objects along x-axis), and y-axis displays the distance between user and object at the moment when this event takes place. To identify potential patterns behind hundreds of dots, we set each dot as a translucent color and set its size based on its position in the camera screen. If a point is small, it means it may have been recorded accidentally.

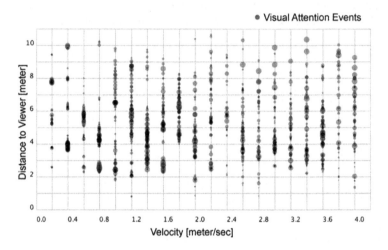

Fig. 7. Attention events distribution of velocity and distance

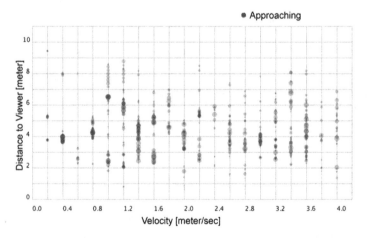

Fig. 8. Distribution of approaching events (Color figure online)

3.3 Approaching and Leaving States

Given that users' responding to approaching objects and leaving objects are different, it is necessary to calculate the motion states of all events to judge whether the object is approaching. Method as below: we save the distance data of target event as d[1], and the distance data of previous second as d[0]. If d[1] greater than d[0], it means the object is leaving the observer; Else if d[1] less than d[0], the object is approaching. As shown in Figs. 8 and 9, we colored approaching and leaving events with different colors, the former with red and the latter with blue. Figure 10 depicts the distribution of these two states, the approaching events appear as circles, and the leaving events appear as rectangles. We find that the distances of these states have significant differences.

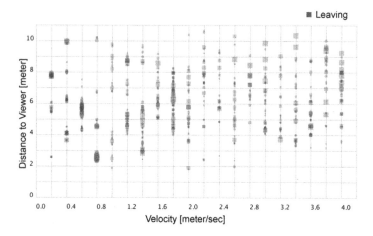

Fig. 9. Distribution of leaving events (Color figure online)

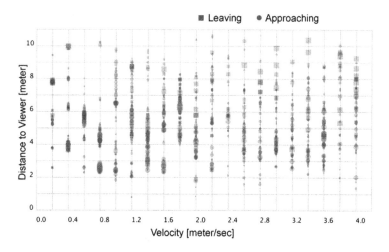

Fig. 10. Colored distribution of attention events (Color figure online)

Distances of leaving events are relatively longer. That means users often gaze at one certain moving object until it disappears far away; but they no longer look at approaching object when it passes by.

3.4 Moving Directions

We classify objects movement into 6 types according to their move directions. Vertical movement has 2 types: rising and rising. Horizontal movement has 2 types: from left to right and from right to left. And other two types are forward and backward. In our dataset, these states are saved as magnitudes of 3d vector. Table 1 shows the statistics of directions and related attention events. Note that the probabilities of each direction shows in experiments are not evenly distributed, which partly explains the reason why some directions get more attentions.

Table 1. Attention events of moving directions

No.	Direction	Magnitude	Attn. events number	Events Pct.	Direction Pct.
1	Rising	(0, 1, 0)	15718	11.30%	12.27%
2	Falling	(0, −1, 0)	35204	25.31%	19.18%
3	Forward	(0, 0, 1)	14860	10.68%	14.00%
4	Backward	(0, 0, −1)	3444	2.48%	10.49%
5	To right	(1, 0, 0)	27106	19.48%	20.49%
6	To left	(−1, 0, 0)	42786	30.76%	23.58%

As shown in Fig. 11, the probability of directions has positive correlation with attention events. And Fig. 12 shows the result of eliminating the influence of probability factor.

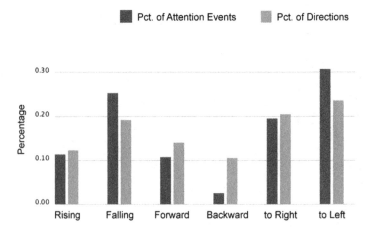

Fig. 11. Percentage of attention events and moving directions

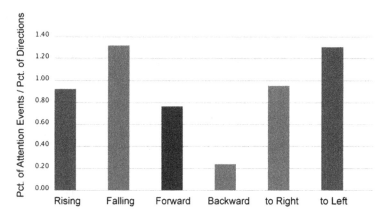

Fig. 12. Users' preference for moving direction

4 Conclusion

In this paper we have described a simple method to record and evaluate users' visual attention to moving objects in 6-Dof virtual reality environment. The method incorporates data analysis of randomly generated objects, which includes moving speed, moving direction, distance to viewer, attention events and timestamps. We imply that in a space filled with multiple moving objects, the speed of the objects has no significant effect on the users' visual attention. In our experiments, users spend less time to object moving along particular directions, such as forward and backward; and users normally watch leaving objects in further distance than approaching objects.

Future work will focus on improving the design of VR environment. More specifically, moving objects will be reduced to 1 or 2, while most objects will remain static. This state is more similar to the actual method of attracting users' attention in VR experiences (for instance, VR film and VR game) and may have more reference value.

References

1. Batchelor, J.: Riccitiello: VR will be mainstream by 2020 (2016). http://www.gamesindustry.biz/articles/2016-12-21-riccitiello-vr-will-be-mainstream-by-2020
2. Vivarelli, N.: Virtual Reality Films Take Hold at Fall's Film Festivals (2017). http://variety.com/2017/film/spotlight/carne-y-arena-venice-virtual-reality-cannes-1202524881/
3. Matyszczyk, C.: Steven Spielberg says VR is a 'dangerous' movie medium (2016). https://www.cnet.com/news/steven-spielberg-says-vr-is-a-dangerous-movie-medium/
4. Koch, C., Ullman, S.: Shifts in selective visual attention: towards the underlying neural circuitry. In: Vaina, L.M. (ed.) Matters of Intelligence. SYLI, vol. 188, pp. 115–141. Springer, Dordrecht (1987). https://doi.org/10.1007/978-94-009-3833-5_5
5. Clark, J.J., Ferrier, N.J.: Modal control of an attentive vision system. In: IEEE International Conference on Computer Vision (1988)
6. Judd, T., Durand, F., Torralba, A.: A benchmark of computational models of saliency to predict human fixations. MIT Technical report (2012)

7. Borji, A., Itti, L.: State-of-the-art in visual attention modeling. IEEE Trans. Pattern Anal. Mach. Intell. **35**(1), 185–207 (2013)
8. Borji, A., Cheng, M.M., Jiang, H., Li, J.: Salient object detection: a benchmark. IEEE Trans. Image Process. **24**(12), 5706–5722 (2015)
9. Bogdanova, I., Bur, A., Hügli, H.: Visual attention on the sphere. IEEE Trans. Image Process. **17**(11), 2000–2014 (2008)
10. Bogdanova, I., Bur, A., Hügli, H., Farine, P.-A.: Dynamic visual attention on the sphere. Comput. Vis. Image Underst. **114**(1), 100–110 (2010)
11. Upenik, E., Ebrahimi, T.: A simple method to obtain visual attention data in head mounted virtual reality. In: IEEE International Conference on Multimedia and Expo 2017, Hong-Kong (2017)
12. Thill, S.: Oculus Creative Director Saschka Unseld: "It Feels Like We're in Film School Again" (2015). http://www.cartoonbrew.com/interactive/oculus-creative-director-saschka-unseld-116773.html
13. Sheng, H., Liu, X.Y., Zhang, S.: Saliency analysis based on depth contrast increased. In: Proceedings of 2016 IEEE International Conference on Acoustics, Speech and Signal Processing, pp. 1347–1351. IEEE, Shanghai (2016). https://doi.org/10.1109/icassp.2016.7471896
14. Park, J., Oh, H., Lee, S., et al.: 3D visual discomfort predictor: analysis of disparity and neural activity statistics. IEEE Trans. Image Process. **24**(3), 1101–1114 (2015). https://doi.org/10.1109/TIP.2014.2383327

Hierarchical Modeling Framework for ICT Application to Measure the User Experience

HyunJae Jo and Chang-Beom Choi[✉]

School of Global Entrepreneurship and ICT, Handong Global University,
558 Handong-ro Buk-gu, Pohang, Gyeongbuk 37554, Republic of Korea
{21600695, cbchoi}@handong.edu

Abstract. In the development and use of applications, the User Interface (UI) and User experience (UX) has become essential. The well-adjusted UI and UX are the key features to assess the completeness of the application. As the importance of the UI and UX increases, formal representation of the UI and UX become essential. This paper proposes a formal representation method for ICT application. The method models an ICT application using the discrete event formalism. By utilizing the hierarchically and modular features of the discrete event formalism, a developer or UX researcher may utilize the modeling method to represent and assess the UI and UX of the ICT application. As a case study, this research illustrates how to model a website by proposed modeling method. The case study shows the modeling method can capture the essential behavior of the ICT application.

Keywords: Hierarchical modeling · UI/UX · ICT application

1 Introduction

As the Information, Communication, and Technology (ICT) become essential in daily life, the importance of ICT application is grown in modern society. In modern society, the ICT application has come a familiar tool to the various fields from agriculture to industry [1, 2], and it has become inevitable. As the growth of the ICT application market increase, application developers or service providers launch their ICT application to the ICT markets. However, as the growth of ICT application market increases, various application developers and service providers may mimic the popular ICT application. Therefore, there is various ICT application exists at the ICT market which has the identical functionalities but has a different design. Thus, the User Interface (UI) and User Experience (UX) have become one of the vital factors to the users to choose proper ICT application among the many similar kinds of applications.

In general, the definition of the UX is the overall experience that the users interact with products, services, and systems. Based on the definition of the UX, the UX can be formed from the interaction between a user and a product which includes the hardware and the software. Therefore, to model or assess the UX, a researcher should model a user and a system. Also, the researcher should consider the UI. The UI is the interface between human and the system. For example, when a user wants to navigate to the previous page on the smartphone, the user should touch a button or give specific

© Springer International Publishing AG, part of Springer Nature 2018
A. Marcus and W. Wang (Eds.): DUXU 2018, LNCS 10918, pp. 417–428, 2018.
https://doi.org/10.1007/978-3-319-91797-9_30

gestures to the device. The UI is the method to trigger event to the ICT system, and the ICT system may react based on the event. During the interaction between the user and the system, the user may accustom to the UI. Therefore, the UX can be considered as accustomed experience from specific software and specific hardware which forms the UI. For instance, a user who uses iOS device may feel difficult when the user uses the Android device. Since the Android device has a physical back button, the UI of the Android device has different form compared to the iOS device. As a result, when the researcher wants to analyze the UX, the researcher should consider the hardware, software and the behavior of the users at the same time.

To model the characteristics of the hardware, software and the behaviors of the users, many researchers proposed various methods [3–5]. To model the characteristics, the researchers may use the natural language or use the graphical representation. For the natural language, researchers describe the characteristics of the UI, hardware specification, or behaviors of the users in the design documents as text or table form. The design documents help a developer and the designers to collaborate with each other to develop the ICT applications. However, the natural language has a critical disadvantage. Since the natural language has ambiguity, the researcher may experience difficulties to analyze the effects of the UI and the behavior of the users. On the other hand, the graphical form utilizes the graphical notations, such as nodes, which represents a state of the system, and arcs, which represents the event trigger. Therefore, the path from an initial state to the given node shows the event sequence of the ICT applications. The problem of the existing method utilizing the graphical notation is that a researcher should model the behavior of a user and the ICT application at the same time. As a result, the researcher should consider the interaction between human and the application and the result of the modeling may be complicated.

This research introduces the hierarchical modeling framework for ICT application to assist measuring the UX using graphical notation. The modeling framework has two components to model the behaviors: the behavior component and association component. The behavior component has two types. The first type of the behavior component models the behavior of the user and other type models the behavior of the application. Each component utilizes the node to represent the state of the system, and the arcs represent the event of the system. For example, when a user wants to navigate to given Uniform Resource Locator (URL) using web browser application on the smartphone, the user may touch the address bar and type the URL. Then, if the user wants to navigate to the previous page, the user may choose to touch the previous icon or the physical back button. To capture the behaviors, the researcher should consider the behavior of the user and the smartphone vendor at the same time. However, the approach of this research separates the hardware behavior and the human behavior. The human behavior of the scenario is that the user triggers the event to navigate to specific URL and navigate back. The physical back button or the previous icon is not essential to the user. The physical back button, the previous icon or the gestures are related to the hardware and the operating system based on the ICT device vendor. Therefore, a researcher may consider the device behaviors based on the hardware and separate them from the graphical notation. Lastly, the association components associate the human behavior model and the system model. The association component simulates the given human behavior model and the system model to analyze the UX. The association component first simulates the human behavior model and send the event to the device model. When the system model receives the event, the device model may choose event transition based on the graphical notation. After that, the device model sends the event to the association component, and the association component relays the events to the human model.

This paper contains five sections. Section 2 describes theoretical backgrounds, UI/UX of ICT application and the Discrete Event System (DEVS) formalism. Section 3 introduces the hierarchical modeling framework based on the DEVS formalism. Section 4 explains how a researcher model the ICT application using the proposed method, and Sect. 5 concludes this paper.

2 Background

2.1 UI/UX of ICT Application

ICT applications have become an essential part of our lives. It includes various types of mobile applications, a personal computer application, and even web services. Since the ICT applications cover various areas, a researcher may not easily define what the ICT application is. However, in general, the ICT application has the following characteristics. First, it is an interactive system; the user and application system exchange and reacts opponent action. Second, ICT applications are made up of segments. Segments work dependently or independently depending on application settings. Third, these segments may or may not respond according to the user input; so, user input is one of the factors considered. Fourth, the segments may or may not respond as time inside changes without input from the user (Fig. 1).

Fig. 1. Example of ICT application

UI and UX are essential factors of an ICT application to differentiate with other ICT application. UX represents the overall experience of the perception, response, and behavior that the user thinks and feels as he or she uses a system or product or service directly or indirectly. That is, the design of UX takes into consideration the feelings and experiences one gain from interacting with objects, machines, and software. Even same ICT application may have different UX based on the hardware platform. Since the UI is a medium that allows interaction between the user and the application, the engineer may choose different implementation method to develop the UI of a system. Therefore, developers should express user-conscious UI and UX designs in their development of ICT applications. Otherwise, the app will be shunned by consumers in the application market.

2.2   Discrete Event System Specification

There are many formal methods to model something that happens in real world [7, 8]. Among them, the Discrete Event System (DEVS) formalism is one of the most popular modeling methods to capture the dynamic transition of system's state by a specific event. The DEVS formalism can describe state transitions as they are transposed through an input event or as time flows internally. This is suitable for modeling ICT applications where the status is transposed by input from the user through the hardware or the status transition by changes in time without input from the user. Second, DEVS formalism decompose a system into small systems using atomic model. When a modeler decomposes a system into non-separable sub-systems, the modeler may use the atomic model to model the non-separable sub-system. The atomic model is used to express the behavior of a system. The coupled model of the DEVS formalism is used to aggregate non-separable sub-system to form a complex system. Therefore, the DEVS formalism is suitable to model a user, the ICT application, and interaction between them [9, 10]. Finally, the DEVS formalism may represent internal state translation based on the time changes, as compared to the Petri-net. The timed transition of the DEVS formalism enables to express state transition by internal time changes without user input, and it is ideal to model ICT application.

The atomic model is a model that describes the behavior characteristics of the system and consists of seven components which are input sets, output sets, status sets, transfer functions that describe the following states of the model, output functions, and time progression functions to produce an output.

DEVS-AM = <X, S, Y, S, δ_{ext}, δ_{int}, λ, ta> where

  X set of internal input events;
  S set of state;
  Y set of external output events;
  δ_{ext} Q × X → S, external transition function specifying state transitions based on the external events;
  δ_{int} Q → S, internal transition function specifying state transitions based on the internal events;
  λ Q → Y, output function generating external events as output;
  ta S → $R_{0,\infty}$, time advance function.
  ❑ Q = {(s, e) | s ⊆ S, 0 ≤ e ≤ ta(s)}

The coupled model consists of multiple component models, which can be the atomic models or coupled models. With these characteristics, the coupled model can be formed by each component model and the external inputs, output, and connections among internal component models.

DEVS-CM = <X, Y, DM, EIC, EIC, EOC, IC, Select>
  X Set of input events
  Y Set of output events
  DM Set of component models of DEVS
  EIC $\subseteq$ X $\times$ $\cup X_i$: Coupling connection of external input
  EOC $\subseteq$ $\cup Y_i \times$ Y: S, Coupling connection of external output
  IC $\subseteq$ $\cup Y_i \times \cup X_i$: Coupling connection of inside
  Select: $2^{\{DM\}} - \phi \rightarrow$ DM: Function of selecting one model of multiple models which generate output simultaneously.

More detailed description of the DEVS formalism and simulation algorithm can be found in [11].

3 Hierarchical Modeling Framework for ICT Application

As the ICT application can be decomposed into several components and may form a hierarchical structure, this research proposes a modeling rule set to model an ICT application and its behavior at the same time. Based on the modeling rules, ICT applications such as the web service or mobile application can be formally modeled. Each component of the ICT application has states to represent the current status of the ICT application. Then, an arc shows the state transition based on the user-generated event or system event, such as animation, sound, and pop-ups.

To model the ICT application, a modeler should characterize the behavior of an ICT application. To represent the application's hierarchical structure, the researcher may divide the application into three categories using the proposed method: (1) full screen of the app, (2) specific region in the app, and (3) segments on a particular screen. The full screen of the app holds every component of the application. A specific region of the app is the component for the full screen. The specific region may have various segments of application. Finally, segments on a specific region are the non-separable component of the ICT application, and it may change the behavior of the ICT application. In summary, the full-screen of the ICT application is the frame that holds every component of the ICT application, and specific region is the group that contains segments. The segment is the behavior component that represents the action of the ICT application. Therefore, full-screen and region of the ICT application are structural components of the ICT application. Figure 2 shows the relationship among full-screen, region, and segments of an ICT application.

As shown in the Fig. 2, the outmost rectangular shows the full-screen that holds four regions, and region may hold one or more segments. As the definition of the segment is the components that changes the behavior, a modeler may model button, link, and animated components as segment. To capture the behavior of the ICT application, a modeler may use modeling rules to model the ICT application. Followings are the

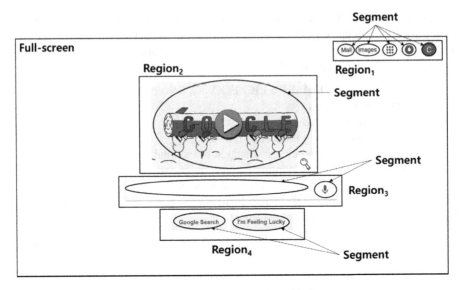

Fig. 2. Example of application hierarchical structure

modeling rules to represent the hierarchical structure and the behavior of the ICT application.

- ICT application should be decomposed into structural components and behavioral components.
- Behavioral components should be modeled as the atomic model of the DEVS formalism, and structural components should be modeled as the coupled model.
- Each behavioral component can be categorized by the functional distinction. Following Fig. 3 shows the classification criteria.

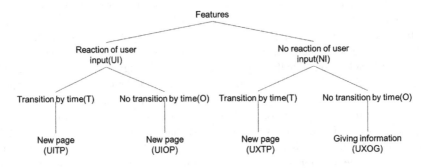

Fig. 3. Classification criteria for segments

Based on the classification criteria, a modeler may select a proper pattern of the DEVS model to model the behavior of the segment. For example, the modeler may select modeling pattern; then the modeler may customize the segment by increasing the number of the states to represent the system state.

For UXOG, there is no transition by external input, and there is no transition of the state by any change in time (Fig. 4).

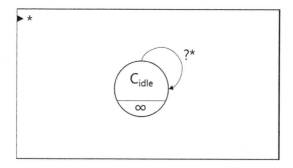

Fig. 4. Function model of UXOG

For UXTP, there is no external transition; however, transition with changes in time occurs, resulting in output (Fig. 5).

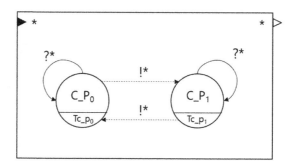

Fig. 5. Function model of UXTP

For UITP, the user input generates a translation. After the occurrence of the user input, the output is processed from the coupled mode, and atomic model takes input after the operation. Based on the input received from the combined mode, atomic model send output to upper model. There is also an internal transition over time (Fig. 6).

For UIOP, the user input generates a translation. After occurrence of the user input, the output is processed from the coupled mode and atomic model takes input after operation. Based on the input received from the Combined mode, atomic model send output to upper model. There is not an internal transition by time changes (Fig. 7).

In this paper, if the other user input entered after the previous user input generates an output, the sequence is expressed by symbol of '→' using feature name.

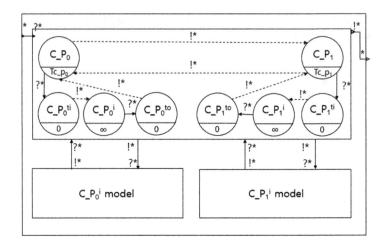

Fig. 6. Feature model of UITP

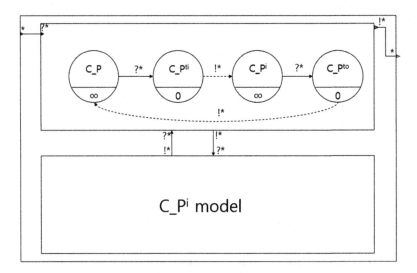

Fig. 7. Feature model of UIOP

4   Case Study

Based on the proposed modeling method, this paper introduces an introductory example, which introduces modeling results of various websites. Two examples of websites will show how to model ICT application. One website is Samsung Display, and the other is Handong Global University. In these cases, they show the modeling results of screen and segment using hierarchical modeling framework (Fig. 8).

The main site of Samsung Display is structured like Fig. 9. Except for ④, ① to ⑧ react to user input. Especially, ② reacts two times continuous reaction and

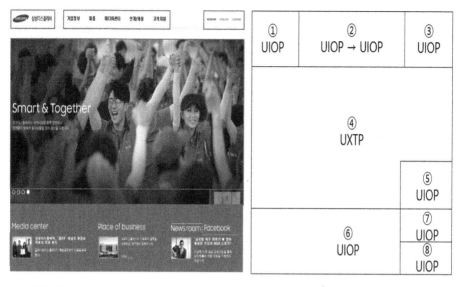

Fig. 8. Main site of Samsung Display

Fig. 9. Regions of Samsung Display main site

Fig. 10. Main site of Handong Global University

Fig. 11. Regions of Handong Global University main site

enumeration can express it. Then, enumeration can show function inheritance of segment (Fig. 10).

Main site of Handong Global University is structured like Fig. 11. Except ④, ① to ⑦ respond to user input. They inherit no user input and react by only one reaction.

The two main sites modelled are listed as Figs. 12 and 13. Looking at the two modeled sites, you can see that the structures of the remaining regions are very similar, with the exception of segment ②. In addition, for Samsung display main page, it can strongly simulate the main page of the Handong Global University.

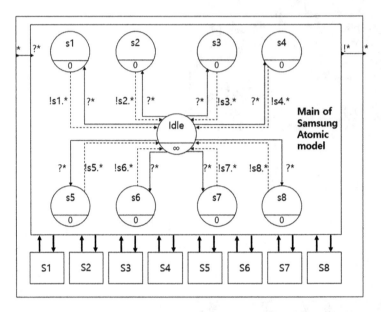

Fig. 12. DEVS model of main site of Samsung Display

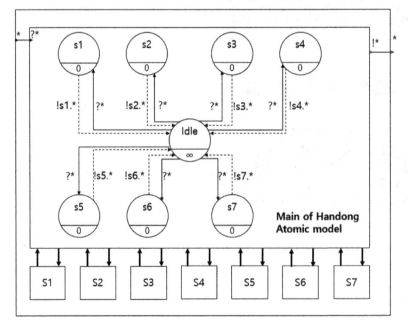

Fig. 13. DEVS model of main site of Handong Global University

The DEVS model of region ② on Samsung display is as follows. There are a total of five segments in region ②. Each segment can be processed on two inputs. That is, within the input model in C1 to C5, there is another model that handles the other inputs. To simplify it visually, it is expressed only on the C1 input model, and the rest of the C2–C5 input models have the same structure as the C1 input model (Fig. 14).

Main site region ⑦ of Handong Global University has 6 segments and segments have each input model. Unlike Samsung displays, each segment only responds one input and release one output (Fig. 15).

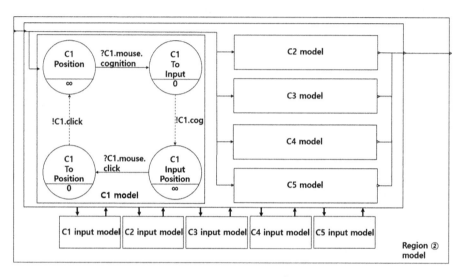

Fig. 14. DEVS model of main site region ② of Samsung Display

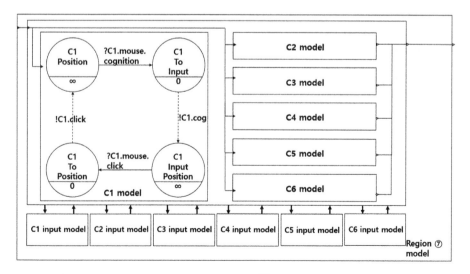

Fig. 15. DEVS model of main site region ⑦ of Handong Global University

5 Conclusion

This paper proposed a modeling method and introduced the relationship between hierarchical representations and ICT applications. A formal representation would allow this modeling method to be applied to a wide variety of ICT applications. Using the above model rules, a modeler can review an ICT application by setting up a UX rule and check the developed application that meets the goals of UX. The method would allow developers to deviate from the way in which they previously asked users to assess applications. This will help reduce the cost of the experiment group and assess as soon as possible whether applications have a good design.

References

1. Chauke, M.: An analysis of the effectiveness/impact of ICTs in dairy production- a case of Zimbabwe's Mashonaland East's Beatrice-Mariranwe Dairy Farmers. Graduate dissertation of University of Zimbabwe (2015)
2. Ghavifekr, S., Afshari, M., Siraj, S., Seger, K.: ICT application for administration and management: a conceptual review. In: 13th International Educational Technology Conference (2013)
3. Blythe, M., Hassenzahl, M., Law, E.L.-C., Vermeeren, A.P.O.S.: An analysis framework for user experience (UX) studies: a green paper. Towards a UX Manifesto (2007)
4. Ardito, C., Costabile, M.F., Lanzilotti, R., Montinaro, F.: Towards the evaluation of UX. Towards a UX Manifesto (2007)
5. Kort, J., Vermeeren, A.P.O.S., Fokker, J.E.: Conceptualizing and measuring UX. Towards a UX Manifesto (2007)
6. Orlova, M.: User experience design (UX design) in a website development: website redesign. Bachelor's thesis Information Technology (2016)
7. Hack, M.: Petri Net Language. Technical report (1976)
8. Zeigler, B.P.: Multifaceted Modeling and Discrete Event Simulation. Academic Press, Orlando (1984)
9. Concepcion, A.I., Zeigler, B.P.: DEVS formalism: a framework for hierarchical model development. IEEE Trans. Softw. Eng. **14**, 228–241 (1988)
10. Kim, T.G.: Hierarchical development of model classes in the DEVS-scheme simulation environment (1991)
11. Zeigler, B.P., Praehofer, H., Kim, T.G.: Theory of Modelling and Simulation, 2nd edn. Academic Press, Cambridge (2000)

A Comparison of User Testing and Heuristic Evaluation Methods for Identifying Website Usability Problems

Martin Maguire[(⊠)] and Paul Isherwood

Design School, Loughborough University Leics, LE11 3TU Loughborough, UK
m.c.maguire@lboro.ac.uk

Abstract. This study compared the effectiveness and efficiency of two usability testing methods, user testing and heuristic evaluation. Thirty two participants took part in the study, sixteen for each of the two methods. Four measures were used to compare their performance: number of problems identified, severity of problems, type of problems and time taken to find problems. It was found that heuristic evaluation found nearly 5 times more individual problems than user testing, so could be seen as more effective. However, user testing found on average slightly more severe problems and took less time to complete than heuristic evaluation. Heuristic evaluation had a faster problem identification rate (number of seconds per problem found), so could also be seen as more efficient. While each method had advantages in the test both methods are seen as complementary to each other in practice.

Keywords: Usability testing · User testing · Heuristic evaluation
Expert review

1 Introduction

User testing is a standard method for identifying usability problems within websites and software applications [1, 2]. This involves observing a number of users performing a pre-defined list of tasks to identify the usability problems they encounter during their interaction. Heuristic evaluation (similar to expert review) is an alternative method for identifying usability problems developed by Jakob Nielsen. Here a small set of evaluators examine a user interface and judge its compliance with recognised usability principles e.g. Nielsen's 10 heuristics for user interface design [3–6] (see Appendix). This study compares the effectiveness and efficiency of these two methods by running an experiment with two websites. This comparison has been researched in the past. However as websites and interaction continually change, it is useful to see whether previous findings still apply.

2 Previous Studies

A comparison of user testing and heuristic evaluation Tan et al. [7] found that heuristic evaluation identified more problems and more severe problems than user testing. However, the authors also discovered that user testing still found problems unidentified

© Springer International Publishing AG, part of Springer Nature 2018
A. Marcus and W. Wang (Eds.): DUXU 2018, LNCS 10918, pp. 429–438, 2018.
https://doi.org/10.1007/978-3-319-91797-9_31

by heuristic evaluation. Hartson et al. [8] found that the heuristic evaluation method finds more problems than any other usability evaluation method. A study conducted by Hasan et al. [9], found that heuristic evaluation found 72% of problems, user testing found only 10% and 18% of the problems were common to both. A further study by Doubleday et al. [10] showed that 40% of problems found were unique to heuristic evaluation, whilst 39% were attributed to user testing.

These studies show that heuristic evaluation seems to highlight more but not all usability problems. This is again seen in a comparative study by Jeffries et al. [11] where heuristic evaluation found approximately three times more problems than user testing; however user testing found additional problems and these tended to be more important. Thankam et al. [12] compared the results of a heuristic evaluation with those of formal user tests in order to determine which usability problems were detected by both methods. Their tests were conducted on four dental computer-based patient record systems. An average of 50% of empirically determined usability problems were identified by the heuristic evaluation which proceeded application of user test. Some statements of heuristic violations were specific enough to identify the actual usability problem that study participants encountered. They concluded that heuristic evaluation can be a useful tool to determine design problems early in the development cycle.

Bailey et al. [13] compared the identification of problems with iterative user testing on a telephone bill inquiry task using two character-based screens with a heuristic evaluation approach. They found that the heuristic evaluation suggested up to 43 potential changes, whereas the usability test demonstrated that only two changes optimized performance.

In a paper by Limin et al. [14], a user interface for a Web-based software program was evaluated with user testing and heuristic evaluation. It was found that heuristic evaluation with human factor experts was more effective in identifying usability problems associated with skill-based and rule-based levels of performance. User testing was more effective in finding usability problems associated with the knowledge-based level of performance.

In terms of organizational costs, heuristic evaluation can provide some quick and relatively inexpensive feedback to designers. However trained usability experts are sometimes hard to find and can be expensive [15]. However user testing is also not cheap to set up, requiring more time to plan and organize and has the expense of recruiting and incentivizing people from the target audience [16].

3   Method

Two commercial websites were used as the user interfaces in this study (one online shopping and the other airline flight booking). A pilot study of these showed that a number of usability problems existed on both sites that could potentially be found.

The study took place in a range of locations, usually in the participant's home or in a university meeting room, both where the participant felt comfortable. The study was conducted on a computer or laptop. Participants used their own computer or laptop, as they would be used to operating it. However, where they could not use their own equipment, a standard laptop computer was provided including the option to use either a mouse or trackpad for input.

A total of 32 participants were recruited for this study — one group of 16 acted as the user in a test study while the other 16 conducted a heuristic evaluation as an expert reviewer. The two sets of participants differed in levels of usability experience. Participants for the heuristic evaluation needed knowledge of one or more of the following: human-computer interaction (HCI), user experience design (UX), user interaction, usability testing, interface design, or human factors. Participants for the user test were regular computer users but without usability knowledge. They were familiar with the internet and having used neither website being tested in the past 12 months. Each method was evaluated using the following measures:

- Number of problems identified
- Severity of problems using Nielsen's 4 level Severity Scale
- Time to find problems or problem per minute rate
- Types of problem (the problems found using both methods were categorized using Nielsen's 10 heuristics for user interface design)

The order of presentation of the two websites were balanced so for each method 8 participants evaluated website 1 first followed by website 2, while the other 8 participants evaluated website 2 then website 1. The participants were directed to the given website's home page and given a set of tasks relevant to that website. The participants were asked to follow the tasks. When they thought they had encountered a usability problem, they would explain and describe the problem to the assessor, who would note it down. The participants were also encouraged to 'think out loud' to understand their mental processes so that all problems could be identified. In addition to this, the assessor would be observing the participant conduct the tasks. When the assessor thought the participant was encountering a problem, even if the participant did not identify it themselves, it would be noted down as a problem. The user test would end when the participant had completed both tasks on both websites and had provided details on any usability problems they had encountered.

The heuristic evaluation method was conducted using another set of 16 participants. These participants had some background knowledge or experience in usability. Again, like in the user test, 8 of those would conduct the evaluation on website 1 first and the other 8 would conduct the evaluation on website 2 first. Before the participants began the evaluation they were asked to review Nielsen's ten heuristics to familiarize themselves with the problem categories. They were given a list of the heuristics, along with possible examples for each one to consult whilst conducting the evaluation. For the purposes of the study, an eleventh 'miscellaneous' category was added to cover any problems that were identified that participants didn't think fitted any of the ten categories. The participants were then directed to the website's home page and asked to explore the website however they wished, with no specific task involved. When the participant thought they had encountered a usability problem, they would identify and describe it to the assessor, who would make a note of it. For this method, the assessor did not observe the participant with the intention of identifying problems for them so the only problems that would be recorded were those the participant had identified. The heuristic evaluation session ended when the participant felt they had covered each websites to a reasonable degree and felt they had found as many problems as they could.

Both methods follow a common and standard process as set out by Maguire [17].

4 Results

Using heuristic evaluation 298 problems were identified in total and 166 individual problems were identified with the removal of duplicates i.e. removing the count if the same problem was identified more than once. In user testing 227 problems were identified in total and 36 individual problems were identified with the removal of duplicates.

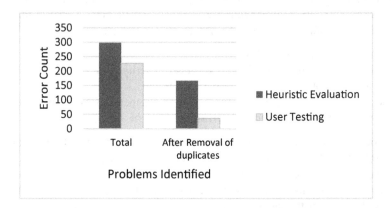

Fig. 1. Number of problems identified by method

Figure 1 shows the number of problems that were identified by each method, showing the total number of problems found and the number of individual problems found after the removal of duplicates. The larger separation between heuristic evaluation and user testing in the two problems identified columns shows that user testing overall finds fewer problems than heuristic evaluation, but also with the problems that user testing does find, it usually finds the same ones' multiple times too, meaning overall, it finds fewer individual problems than heuristic evaluation does.

Figure 2 shows the distribution of the total number of problems found for each method. Heuristic evaluation alone found 90% of the problems whilst user testing only found 19%. 9% of the total problems were common, found with both heuristic evaluation and user testing.

Figure 3 shows that that the largest category of problems found by both methods were 'minor usability problems'. Heuristic evaluation tended to also find quite a few 'cosmetic problems'. Both methods found a number of 'major usability problems' while heuristic evaluation also found some items that were not considered usability problems on Nielsen's severity scale.

Figure 4 shows the time periods taken to conduct both the heuristic evaluation and user testing methods by the 16 participants in each group. The distributions show that user testing tended to take a shorter amount of time to conduct than the heuristic evaluations. User testing times had a low deviation whereas the heuristic evaluations varied quite a lot in the amount of time taken. The standard error of the mean indicates how accurate the observed estimate of the mean is likely to be. A smaller error suggests a more accurate observed mean in relation to the true mean. Calculating the standard error for both methods and with a 95% confidence interval, the sample mean is plus or

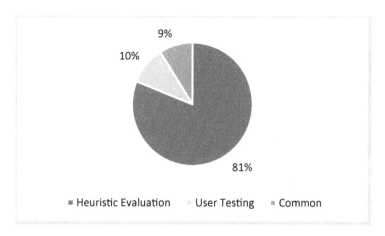

Fig. 2. Percentage of problems found by each method

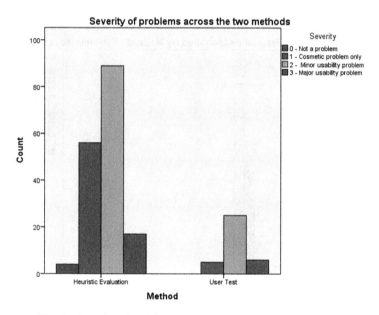

Fig. 3. Severity of problems across the two evaluation methods

minus 16.2 for heuristic evaluation and plus or minus 4.6 for user testing. This indicates that for heuristic evaluation, the true mean is most likely between 25 and 57.4. For user testing, the true mean is likely to be between 16.2 and 25.4. Thus the data collected better represents the true mean for user testing than for heuristic evaluation.

In terms of rate of problem finding, it was found that user testing had an average of 40.3 s per problem identified and heuristic evaluation took 29.1 s per problem identified. With a 95% confidence interval, the observed sample mean is plus or minus 9.3 for heuristic evaluation and plus or minus 6.7 for user testing. This indicates that for heuristic

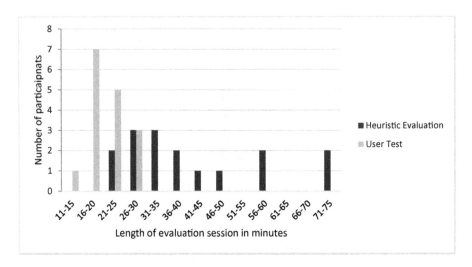

Fig. 4. Distribution of time spent per method

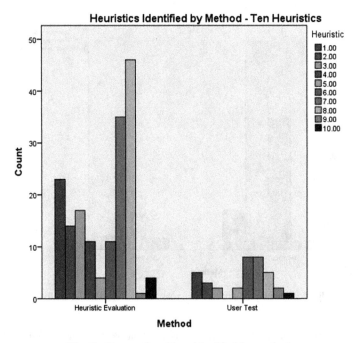

Fig. 5. Types of problem identified by method

evaluation, the true mean is most likely between 19.8 and 38.4. For user testing, the true mean is likely to be between 33.6 and 47. This shows that the data collected better represents the true mean for user testing as there is a smaller standard deviation.

Figure 5 shows the distribution of problem types identified i.e. how many problems within each of the ten heuristics were identified for each method. There is a lot of

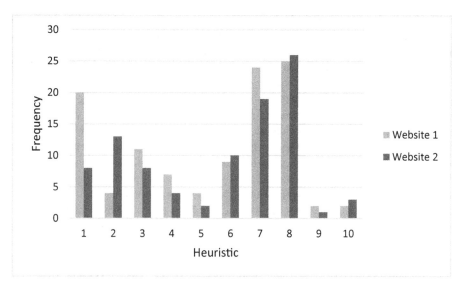

Fig. 6. Frequency of heuristics applied for each website

variation between heuristic categories within the two methods, however, across the methods, there categories 1 (visibility of system status), 7 (flexibility and efficiency of use) and 8 (aesthetic and minimalist design) were all well represented.

Figure 6 shows the distribution of the ten heuristics found on each of the websites. This graph shows that both websites were similar and consistent with the types of problems they found.

5 Discussion

Heuristic evaluation found 31.2% more problems in pure volume than user testing did. Removing duplicates, heuristic evaluation identifies 361% more problems. This shows the user testers identified the same problems multiple times, whereas in the heuristic evaluation, a greater number of unique problems were being identified. This could be due to the fact that in the user testing method, participants were asked to follow a task, limiting the scope to specific parts of both websites. Heuristic evaluation participants were allowed freely explore the websites, meaning a lot more content could be covered and evaluated. User testing however did find some problems that heuristic evaluation did not identify. 10% of the problems were unique to user testing, suggesting to find all usability problems with a website, perhaps multiple methods should be conducted. This finding was consistent with previous studies conducted comparing user testing and heuristic evaluation. Tan et al. [7], Hartson et al. [8], Hasan et al. [9], Doubleday et al. [10] and Jeffries et al. (2001) all found that heuristic evaluation found more problems than user testing. A similar ratio between the numbers of problems found was also common between studies.

Problems from user testing had an average severity rating of 2.02 on the Nielsen's Severity Scale. Heuristic evaluation scored an average of 1.71 which is marginally lower. Tan et al. [7], Jeffries et al. [11] and Archer (2010) were the only previous studies than also took in to consideration the severity of problems or significance of problems found. They all found that user testing overall identified more significant problems.

User testing took a significantly shorter time to conduct at an average of 20.5 min. Heuristic evaluation took an average of 41.1 min. However, the time varied greatly when conducting heuristic evaluation, with a range of 53 min. User testing took consistently a shorter period of time with a time range of only 15 min between longest and shortest. One reason for user testing taking less time to conduct could again be down to the fact that participants had a pre-defined task to follow which is likely to have a more defined and constrained time than the heuristic evaluation method where they could explore the websites for as much or little time as they wanted. Another explanation could be that, seen as experts, participants wanted to take longer and find as many usability problems as possible whereas user testing participants are less likely to have performance in their minds when interacting and just stuck to the task. Hasan et al. [9] and Doubleday et al. [10] found that user testing took longer and total more hours to conduct then heuristic evaluation — the opposite this study.

In this study, user testing may have taken less time to complete overall, but in terms of efficiency and the amount of problems found in the shortest amount of time, heuristic evaluation was more efficient. Heuristic evaluation found a problem, on average, every 29.1 s. User testing found a problem, on average, every 40.3 s. This was due to the much higher frequency of problems that heuristic evaluation identified, even though it took longer to conduct.

In heuristic evaluation and user testing, the types of problems found varied between the two. When assigning all problems to Nielsen's list of ten heuristics, some problem types were most easily identified. For example, 'aesthetics and design' heuristics were present most frequently in both methods, possibly because people are more sensitive to problems that are clearly visible.

6   Conclusion

This study aimed to examine both effectiveness and efficiency with two popular usability testing methods, user testing and heuristic evaluation. It was found that both methods had their advantages over the other. Heuristic evaluation overall found more problems and could identify problems at a quicker rate, therefore being more effective and efficient. However, user testing seemed to find slightly more severe problems and overall took less time to conduct, again showing aspects of effectiveness and efficiency. This suggests both methods have their advantages which may determine whether to choose one method or the other.

In practice, design teams often use expert usability reviews early on to sort out obvious problems design in preparation for usability testing. It is also argued that whilst such expert usability reviews have their place, it is still important to put a developing website in front of users and that the results give a truer picture of the real problems that an end-user may encounter [16].

Given the complementary nature of user testing and heuristic evaluation, the benefits of both methods should be recognized and applied within the design process to gain the maximum benefit from them.

Appendix

Jakob Nielsen's heuristics for user interface design:

1. Visibility of system status
2. Match between system and the real world
3. User control and freedom
4. Consistency and standards
5. Error prevention
6. Recognition rather than recall
7. Flexibility and efficiency of use
8. Aesthetic and minimalist design
9. Help users recognize, diagnose, and recover from errors
10. Help and documentation

References

1. Charlton, S.G., O'Brien, T.G. (eds.): Handbook of Human Factors Testing and Evaluation. CRC Press, Boca Raton (2001)
2. Rubin, J., Chisnell, D.: Handbook of Usability Testing: How to Plan, Design and Conduct Effective Tests. Wiley, Hoboken (2008)
3. Molich, R., Nielsen, J.: Improving a human-computer dialogue. Commun. ACM **33**(10), 338–348 (1990)
4. Nielsen, J.: Finding usability problems through heuristic evaluation. In: Bauersfeld, P., Bennett, J., Lynch, G. (eds.) Proceedings of the SIGCHI Conference on Human Factors in Computing Systems, pp. 373–380. ACM, New York (1992)
5. Nielsen, J.: Heuristic evaluation. In: Nielsen, J., Mack, R.L. (eds.) Usability Inspection Methods. Wiley, New York (1994)
6. Nielsen, J.: 10 Usability Heuristics for User Interface Design (1995). https://www.nngroup.com/articles/ten-usability-heuristics. Accessed 13 Mar 2018
7. Tan, W.S., Liu, D., Bishu, R.: Web evaluation: heuristic evaluation vs. user testing. Int. J. Ind. Ergon. **39**(4), 621–627 (2009)
8. Hartson, H.R., Andre, T.S., Williges, R.C.: Criteria for evaluating usability evaluation methods. Int. J. Hum.-Comput. Interact. **13**(4), 373–410 (2001)
9. Hasan, L., Morris, A., Probets, S.: A comparison of usability evaluation methods for evaluating e-commerce websites. Behav. Inf. Technol. **31**(7), 707–737 (2012)
10. Doubleday, A., Ryan, M., Springett, M., Sutcliffe, A.: A comparison of usability techniques for evaluating design. In: Coles, S. (ed.) Proceedings of the 2nd conference on Designing Interactive Systems: Processes, Practices, Methods, and Techniques, pp. 101–110 (1997)

11. Jeffries, R., Miller, J.R., Wharton, C., Uyeda, K.: User interface evaluation in the real world: a comparison of four techniques. In: Robertson, S.P., Olson, G., Olson, J. (eds.) Proceedings of the SIGCHI Conference on Human Factors in Computing Systems, pp. 119–124. ACM, New York (1991)

12. Thankam, P.T., Monaco, V., Thambuganipalle, H., Schleyer, T.: Comparative study of heuristic evaluation and usability testing methods. Stud. Health Technol. Inform. **143**, 322–327 (2009)

13. Bailey, R.W., Allan, R.W., Raiello, P.: Usability testing vs. heuristic evaluation: a head-to-head comparison, In: Proceedings of the Human Factors and Ergonomics Society Annual Meeting, pp. 409–413. SAGE (1992)

14. Limin, F., Salvendy, G., Turley, L.: Effectiveness of user testing and heuristic evaluation as a function of performance classification. Behav. Inf. Technol. **21**(2), 137–143 (2010)

15. Usability.gov: Heuristic evaluations and expert reviews. https://www.usability.gov/how-to-and-tools/methods/heuristic-evaluation.html. Accessed 13 Mar 2018

16. Halabi, L.: Expert usability review vs. usability testing. https://www.webcredible.com/blog/expert-usability-review-vs-usability-testing. Accessed 13 Mar 2018

17. Maguire, M.: Methods to support human-centred design. Int. J. Hum.-Comput. Stud. **55**(4), 587–634 (2001)

Subjective Preferences Towards Various Conditions of Self-Administered Questionnaires: AHP and Conjoint Analyses

Rafał Michalski[✉] and Marta Staniów

Faculty of Computer Science and Management,
Wrocław University of Science and Technology,
27 Wybrzeże Wyspiańskiego St., 50-370 Wrocław, Poland
rafal.michalski@pwr.edu.pl
http://RafalMichalski.com

Abstract. Using questionnaires for eliciting data from respondents has a long term history. The present paper focuses on subjects' preferences towards specific self-administered questionnaire designs and circumstances in which these experiments are carried out. The paper examines three factors, that is, the assistant presence (yes, no), survey form (paper or electronic), and scale type (visual analogue or Likert). A pairwise comparison technique was employed to obtain participants' opinions. Calculations of the relative preferences were performed according to the Analytic Hierarchy Process (AHP) methodology. The conjoint methodology employed in this study provided partial utilities of the examined factor levels and relative importances for the effects. Apart from verifying the statistical significance of the investigated factors, the analysis of variance revealed also possible interactions between them.

Keywords: Questionnaire design · Subjects' preferences · Survey form
Scale type · Surveyor presence

1 Introduction

Using questionnaires for eliciting subjects' opinions has a long term history. Generally, there are two main approaches for conducting such surveys: personal and self-administered. In the first case, one performs, e.g., a face-to-face structured interview or a telephone survey. In the latter option, data are gathered, e.g., by paper-and-pencil, online, or mail questionnaires. Various examples, detailed description along with advantages and disadvantages of specific modes of conducting surveys can be found, for instance, in the works of Yu and Cooper (1983), Tourangeau et al. (2000), Aldridge and Levine (2001), Bowling (2005), Burns et al. (2008), or Fink (2015). The present paper focuses on self-administered questionnaires that are very popular mostly due to low costs of applying them in comparison with interviews or telephone calls.

There has been an abundance of research on almost every aspect of conducting such studies including technical, physical, and psychological aspects. Many investigations showed differences between various types of self-administered questionnaires

© Springer International Publishing AG, part of Springer Nature 2018
A. Marcus and W. Wang (Eds.): DUXU 2018, LNCS 10918, pp. 439–450, 2018.
https://doi.org/10.1007/978-3-319-91797-9_32

in their effectiveness and efficiency (Dillman 1999; Wright and Ogbuehi 2014). However, much less is known about subjects' preferences towards specific survey designs and circumstances in which these experiments are carried out. Since subjective opinions of respondents may influence the questionnaire results (e.g., Wright and Ogbuehi 2014; Voutilainen 2016), thus, extending the knowledge in this respect is desired both from the methodological as well as practical point of view.

1.1 Assistant Presence

According to Bourque and Fielder (2003, p. 3) the self-administered questionnaires may be characterized on a continuum with one end including cases when the assistant, surveyor, or other supervisory person is present, and the opposite end where no such a supervision exists. There are, naturally, advantages and disadvantages of both extreme approaches. For example, the surveyor may increase the quality of the gathered data by answering participants' questions or explain doubts (Bowling 2005).

Moreover, some general studies show that people prefer direct, face-to-face rather than other ways of communication (e.g., D'Ambra et al. 1998). On the other hand, costs related with self-administered questionnaires filled in without the supervision can be significantly smaller than in the former case (Dillman 1999). Though there have been some studies regarding the influence of the surveyor presence on the subjects' responses, not much is known about participants' preferences in this regard.

1.2 Survey Form

Recently, computer software supports more and more commonly the data collection process. Thus, specific aspects of conducting computer assisted surveys also draw researchers' attention (e.g., Andreadis 2015; Toepoel and Ludtig 2015). The researchers analyzed advantages and drawbacks of traditional and electronic forms of questionnaires. They indicate, among other things, that electronic versions allow for better completeness of the gathered data as compared with the paper based form, however require at least basic computer literacy and access to some electronic devices.

Most of the research dealing with the questionnaire form focuses on their efficiency and effectiveness, still, it is also interesting what the subjects' attitudes towards these two basic forms of questionnaires are. Recently, Wright and Ogbuehi (2014) in their paper about how data collection methodology influences response quality examined, inter alia, respondents' fatigue, boredom, and satisfaction. Though they found no differences between paper and pencil and electronic questionnaires, their experimental design was not focused specifically on the questionnaire form and included many other factors that could have had an impact on the results.

1.3 Scale Type

While designing questionnaires, researchers have to decide what type of scales to use. There are number of possibilities, but among the most common there are Likert (LS) and the visual analogue (VA) scales. The Likert approach allows for selecting one of the specific, commonly odd number of response options, located between two end points, called usually "strongly agree" and "strongly disagree".

The visual analogue scale, in turn, is a line ended with two points between which subjects specify their level of agreement to a statement by placing a mark. There are numerous studies examining various features of these scales (e.g., Lewis and Erdinç 2017), but again little is known about how respondents perceive them. Among few of them there are the works of Laerhoven et al. (2004), or lately, Voutilainen et al. (2016).

1.4   Research Objectives

The current research examines subjects' preferences towards factors differentiating the conditions of conducting self-administered questionnaires. Particularly, three factors are investigated, that is, the assistant presence (present, absent), survey form (paper or electronic), and scale type (visual analogue or Likert scale). As far as we are aware the influence of these effects on subjects' preferences have not been studied simultaneously.

2   Method

A pairwise comparison technique was employed to obtain the participants' subjective opinions. Such an approach allows for acquiring better accuracy than, for example, direct ranking (Koczkodaj 1998). Calculations of the relative preferences were performed according to the Analytic Hierarchy Process (AHP) methodology (Saaty 1977; 1980; Barzilai 1997).

The use of conjoint methodology (Luce and Tukey 1964; Krantz and Tversky 1971; Green and Srinivasan, 1978; 1990; Green et al. 2001) allowed for assessing partial utilities of the examined factor levels and relative importances for the effects. The full factorial analysis of variance apart from verifying the statistical significance of the investigated effects provided, additionally, information on possible interactions between them. Such a multimethod approach gives a fuller picture of subjects' preference structures (Grobelny and Michalski 2011).

2.1   Independent and Dependent Variables

The investigated variants were graphically presented as pictograms along with captions informing both about the factor and its level. The applied images with original Polish captions are demonstrated in Table 1.

2.2   Experimental Design and Procedure

A full factorial design involving the abovementioned effects resulted in eight experimental variants. Participants were asked which survey version they preferred the most. Each subject performed 28 pairwise comparisons of these eight conditions.

The Analytic Hierarchy Process methodology proposed by Saaty (1977; 1980) was used to calculate relative weights for every participant. Overall, the whole procedure took about five minutes, on average.

Table 1. Experimental factors and their levels.

Assistant presence	Survey form	Scale type
Bez ankietera	Elektroniczna	Rodzaj skali — Zdecydowanie nie zgadzam się / Zdecydowanie zgadzam się
Without assistant	Electronic	Likert
Z ankieterem	Papierowa	Rodzaj skali — Zdecydowanie nie zgadzam się / Zdecydowanie zgadzam się
With assistant	Paper	Visual analogue

2.3   Apparatus

A custom made software (see Fig. 1) was applied to present stimuli, gather, store, and process the data. Left/right stimuli locations along with the order of comparisons were randomized by the software. Subjects expressed their opinions by selecting a radio button situated on this side where the preferred survey option appeared. Participants were given the opportunity to freely move forward and backward between comparisons and change their responses as needed. All the results were exported to the *IBM SPSS Statistics 24* statistical software to perform a conjoint analysis.

2.4   Participants

A total of 61 subjects expressed their opinions towards examined variants. Most of them (70%) were at the age range of 20–35 years old, and the rest was older. There were 29 females (48%) and 32 males (52%).

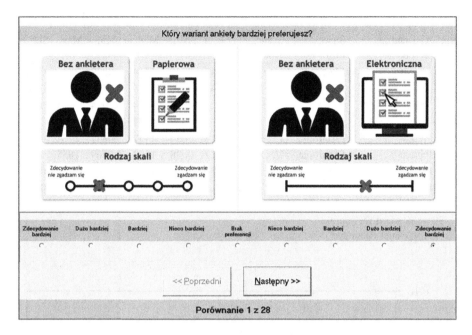

Fig. 1. A graphic software interface for a sample pairwise comparison.

3 Results

3.1 Ahp

Consistency Ratios. All of the consistency ratios (CR) were lower than .1 - the threshold recommended by Saaty (1977; 1980). The lowest value equaled .00476 while the highest - .0281. Therefore, results from all subjects were taken into account in further analyses. The mean value of CR amounted to .0133 (median: .0129) with the standard deviation of .00544. One way analysis of variance was used to check whether the CRs depended on the gender. The results revealed no significant influence of the gender on the inconsistency level (F(1, 59) = 1.8, p = .18).

Basic Statistics. The preferences obtained in a form of relative weights demonstrated that the highest score was attributed to the electronic version of the survey with the Likert scale, conducted without the presence of a survey assistant. The least preferable option was the paper based questionnaire including visual analogue scale, filled in while the survey assistant was present. The full hierarchy along with the computed weights and basic descriptive statistics are put together in Table 2 whereas the graphic illustration of the results are given in Fig. 2.

Table 2. Basic descriptive statistics.

No.	Assistant presence	Survey form	Scale type	Mean	SME*	Median	Min	Max	SD**
1.	Absent	Electronic	Likert	.1447	.0045	.1449	.0829	.2031	.0355
2.	Absent	Electronic	VA***	.1348	.0046	.1345	.0799	.2029	.0358
3.	Absent	Paper	Likert	.1321	.0038	.1279	.0904	.2035	.0298
4.	Absent	Paper	VA	.1190	.0026	.1167	.0804	.1656	.0200
5.	Present	Electronic	Likert	.1218	.0034	.1157	.0847	.2024	.0268
6.	Present	Electronic	VA	.1127	.0028	.1087	.0769	.1835	.0221
7.	Present	Paper	Likert	.1234	.0045	.1125	.0809	.2029	.0354
8.	Present	Paper	VA	.1114	.0038	.1027	.0709	.2026	.0299

* SME – Standard Mean Error,
** SD – Standard Deviation,
*** VA – Visual Analogue

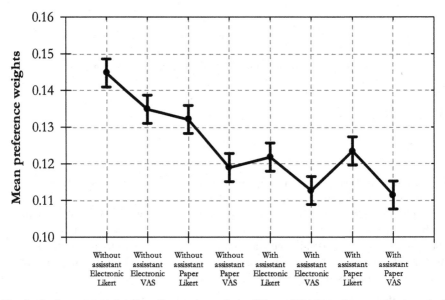

Fig. 2. Preference weights for all experimental conditions. Whiskers denote mean standard errors. ($F(7, 480) = 8.9$, $p < .0001$)

Analysis of Variance. First, a two way analysis of variance was used to check if the examined options influence mean preference weights and whether or not the gathered data depended on the subject gender. The results presented in Table 3 show significant impact of the examined variants irrespective of the participant gender.

Table 3. Two-way Anova results for *Experimental conditions* and *Gender* factors.

Effect	Sum of squares	Degrees of freedom	Mean sum of squares	F	p	η2
Gender	<.0001	1	<.0000	<.0001	1	
Experimental conditions (EC)	.056	7	.00801	8.8	<.0001[*]	.12
Gender × EC	.0026	7	.00038	.42	.89	
Error	.429	472	.00091			

[*] α < .0001

Table 4. Three-way Anova results for *Assistant presence*, *Survey form*, and *Scale type* factors.

Effect	Sum of squares	Degrees of freedom	Mean sum of squares	F	p	η2
Assistant presence (AP)	.029	1	.029	32	<.0001[*]	.062
Survey form (SF)	.0061	1	.0061	6.8	.0096[**]	.014
Scale type (ST)	.015	1	.015	16	<.0001[*]	.033
AP × SF	.0064	1	.0064	7.1	.0080[**]	.014
AP × ST	.000026	1	.000026	.029	.86	.000061
SF × ST	.00028	1	.00028	.32	.57	.00066
AP × SF × ST	.000001	1	.000001	.001	.98	.0000014
Error	.43	480	.000899			

[*] α < .0001
[**] α < .01

Next, to get further insight into obtained preferences, a standard, three way analysis of variance was applied to verify if differences between factor means were statistically significant. The obtained results provided evidence for meaningful influence of all examined factors on mean preference weights. Interestingly, the interaction between Assistant presence and Survey form factors also occurred to be statistically significant. All other interactions were irrelevant. The detailed ANOVA results are given in Table 4.

The mean preference weights for all statistically significant effects are graphically illustrated in Figs. 3, 4, 5 and 6.

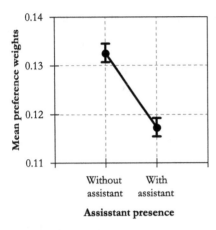

Fig. 3. The influence of *Assistant presence* on mean preference weights. F(1, 480) = 32, p < .0001, η^2 = .062.

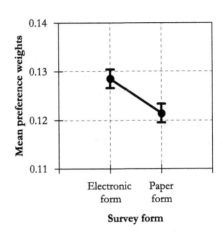

Fig. 4. The influence of *Survey form* on mean preference weights. F(1, 480) = 6.8, p = .0096, η^2 = . 014

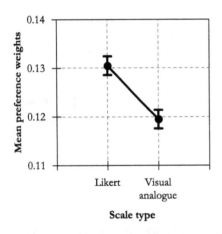

Fig. 5. The influence of *Scale type* on mean preference weights. F(1, 480) = 16, p < .0001, η^2 = .033.

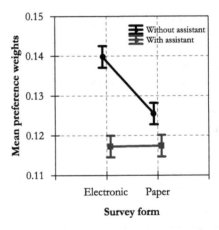

Fig. 6. The influence of *Survey form* × *Assistant presence* interaction on mean preference weights. F(1, 480) = 7.1, p = .0080, η^2 = .014.

3.2   Conjoint

The conjoint analysis, performed in *IBM SPSS Statistics 24*, provided information on partial utilities of the examined factor levels. They are demonstrated in Table 5. Respondents assigned the higher utility to the option without an assistant than when the assistant is present while filling in the questionnaire. Subjects rated the electronic questionnaire better than its classic paper version counterpart, and preferred the Likert over the VA scale type.

Table 5. Conjoint results – partial utilities.

Factor	Level	Partial utility*
Assistant presence	Absent	.00765
	Present	−.00765
Survey form	Electronic	.00353
	Paper	−.00353
Scale type	Likert	.00551
	Visual analogue	−.00551
(Intercept)		.12500

*The standard error for all partial utilities amounted to .00185

Overall importances of the investigated effects amounted to 40.3% for the Assistant presence, the Survey form obtained 35.8% whereas the least significant was the Scale type – 23.9%. The R Pearson correlation between the observed and predicted preferences amounted to .94 while tau Kendall's correlation equaled .786. Both parameters were statistically significant at $\alpha = .005$.

4   Discussion and Conclusion

The presented study examined subjects' preferences towards various conditions concerned with filling in questionnaires. The results, generally, proved that all three investigated factors, that is, Assistant presence, Survey form, and Scale type, significantly differentiated the respondents' subjective ratings. Overall, the analyses revealed that study participants preferred answering survey questions alone than in the presence of an assistant. They liked more the Likert than the visual analogue type of scale. The electronic version of a questionnaire was better perceived than the paper form, however as the significant interaction shows, this is the case only when the assistant is absent. In the condition with present assistant, there is no significant difference in mean preference weights for electronic and paper options.

The conjoint analysis provided evidence that the *Assistant presence* is the most important factor shaping respondents preferences in this study. The second examined factor, *Survey form*, was less important by only 4.5 percentage points. The *Scale type* occurred to be considerably the least significant than the other two effects. The difference in percentages amounted to as much as 16.4% in comparison with *Assistant presence*, and 11.9% as compared with *Survey form*. These outcomes are consistent with magnitudes of partial utilities and only partially correspond with effect sizes from ANOVA where *Scale type* had higher eta-square than *Survey form*. Mean weights obtained by AHP suggest that the most preferred variant is the one without the participation of an assistant, prepared in an electronic form, with Likert scales.

The presence of assistant may be helpful in explaining the purpose of the questionnaire and answering respondents' questions. Some previous studies (e.g., Yu and Cooper 1983) indicated that subjects prefer direct human interaction to other ways of providing information about the questionnaire. The current research, however, does not support it. The explanation of this finding may be related to the specific sample which consisted of mostly young people who probably completed questionnaires in an electronic form without any supervision much often than paper and pencil versions administered by assistants. Another possible reason for lower acceptance of the assistant presence while completing questionnaires is the reluctance of providing sensitive data in such circumstances. Researchers should be aware that perceived greater anonymity while assistants are not present may sometimes prompt subjects to provide fake data.

Studies of Yu and Cooper (1983) and Hox and Leeuw (1994) indicate that there are no differences in paper and electronic forms of questionnaires with regard to the response rate. Our findings may suggest something else. Since preferences in this regard significantly differ, they may influence the response rate as well. The reason may, again, be attributed to the young sample in the present research that have generally bigger experience with electronic devices and computer software than the participants taking part in previous studies. Current experiment respondents are also more accustomed to electronic questionnaires. Furthermore, electronic versions of questionnaires, especially those available on the Internet, may be attractive for respondents because they can freely choose the moment when to provide answers and how much time they can spend to complete them.

From the researcher's perspective it is easier to process data as they are already collected in a digital form and ensure consistency and correctness of the information received (e.g., by validating data during the input of responses). The investigators have also the possibility of embedding audio, video files or some interactive objects into their questionnaires. On the other hand, there is a higher risk of obtaining a bigger number of incomplete data since such questionnaires can be easily interrupted. Moreover, one should not forget that some respondents may still have problems with accessing computers, the Internet or exhibit insufficient computer literacy necessary to complete electronic forms.

The *Scale type* factor influenced the subjects' preferences the least significantly from among investigated factors. They rated the Likert better than the VA scale probably because the Likert scale restricts the number of possible response options to several items while VA allows for selecting any point on a line which may be perceived as a more demanding task. Such an explanation is consistent with the results presented by van Laerhoven et al. (2004) who examined scale type preferences in children's questionnaires. They found that children preferred the Likert over the numeric and simple VA scales and find it easiest to complete while exhibiting similar reliability.

Another possible explanation may result from the fact that Likert type of scale is much more prevalent both in professional scientific questionnaires and in many amateur surveys that often appear on various websites.

As in any scientific research also here there are some limitations in interpreting the findings. First, numerous aspects of conducting self-administered questionnaires were not included in the present research. Usually, the number of factors and their levels needs to be limited to perform the experiment in reasonable time using available resources. In this investigation, the experimental design was additionally restricted due to the employment of the pairwise comparisons based methodology. The number of comparisons in AHP increases, approximately, with the square of the number of options examined.

Thus, a number of other studies on respondents' preferences should involve other possible factors and their interactions. Some other follow-up experiments may be carried out to investigate in a greater detail subjects' preferences towards different modes of questionnaire administration and combine them with completing real questionnaires. A qualitative study on the reasons for reluctance of the assistance presence while completing questionnaires would be very interesting. This effect should also be compared with preferences in different age groups. One should be cautious in generalizing the presented outcomes as the sample size was moderate and included mostly young, white people from a geographically restricted area and uniform social background.

Despite these limitations, the present, preliminary study provides some more insight into how people subjectively perceive various aspects of conducting self-administered questionnaires. Choosing appropriate conditions in this regard can possibly increase the response rate, quality of gathered data, and may have an influence on the overall peoples' attitude towards participation in surveys.

References

Aldridge, A., Levine, K.: Surveying The Social World: Principles and Practice in Survey Research. Open University Press, Buckingham (2001). https://doi.org/10.1046/j.1365-2648. 2002.2138c.x

Andreadis, I.: Web surveys optimized for smartphones: are there differences between computer and smartphone users? Methods Data Anal. **9**(2), 16 (2015). https://doi.org/10.12758/mda. 2015.012

Barzilai, J.: Deriving weights from pairwise comparison matrices. J. Oper. Res. Soc. **48**, 1226–1232 (1997)

Bowling, A.: Mode of questionnaire administration can have serious effects on data quality. J. Public Health **27**(3), 281–291 (2005). https://doi.org/10.1093/pubmed/fdi031

Bourque, L., & Fielder, E. (2003). How to Conduct Self-Administered and Mail Surveys. 2455 Teller Road,Thousand OaksCalifornia 91320 United States of America: SAGE Publications, Inc. https://doi.org/10.4135/9781412984430

Burns, K.E.A., Duffett, M., Kho, M.E., Meade, M.O., Adhikari, N.K.J., Sinuff, T., Cook, D.J.: A guide for the design and conduct of self-administered surveys of clinicians. CMAJ : Can. Med. Assoc. J. **179**(3), 245–252 (2008). https://doi.org/10.1503/cmaj.080372

D'Ambra, J., Rice, R.E., O'Connor, M.: Computer-mediated communication and media preference: an investigation of the dimensionality of perceived task equivocality and media richness. Behav. Inf. Technol. **17**(3), 164–174 (1998). https://doi.org/10.1080/014492998119535

Dillman, D.: Mail and other self-administered surveys in the 21st century: the beginning of a new Era. Gallup Res. J. **2**(1), 121–140 (1999)

Fink, A.: How to conduct surveys: a step-by-step guide, 6th edn. SAGE Publications, Thousand Oaks (2015)

Green, P.E., Srinivasan, V.: Conjoint analysis in consumer research: issues and outlook. J. Consum. Res. **5**, 103–123 (1978)

Green, P.E., Srinivasan, V.: Conjoint analysis in marketing: new developments with implications for research and practice. J. Mark. **54**(4), 3–19 (1990)

Green, P.E., Krieger, A.M., Wind, Y.: Thirty years of conjoint analysis: reflections and prospects. Interfaces **31**(2), 56–73 (2001)

Grobelny, J., Michalski, R.: Various approaches to a human preference analysis in a digital signage display design. Hum. Factors Ergon. Manuf. Serv. Ind. **21**(6), 529–542 (2011). https://doi.org/10.1002/hfm.20295

Hox, J.J., Leeuw, E.D.D.: A comparison of nonresponse in mail, telephone, and face-to-face surveys. Qual. Quant. **28**(4), 329–344 (1994). https://doi.org/10.1007/BF01097014

Koczkodaj, W.: Testing the accuracy enhancement of pairwise comparisons by a Monte Carlo experiment. J. Stat. Plann. Infer. **69**(1), 21–31 (1998)

Krantz, D.H., Tversky, A.: Conjoint measurement analysis of composition rules in psychology. Psychol. Rev. **78**, 151–169 (1971)

van Laerhoven, H., van der Zaag-Loonen, H., Derkx, B.: A comparison of Likert scale and visual analogue scales as response options in children's questionnaires. Acta Paediatr. **93**(6), 830–835 (2004). https://doi.org/10.1111/j.1651-2227.2004.tb03026.x

Luce, D.R., Tukey, J.W.: Simultaneous conjoint measurement: a new type of fundamental measurement. J. Math. Psychol. **1**, 1–27 (1964)

Lewis, J.R., Erdinç, O.: User experience rating scales with 7, 11, or 101 points: does it matter? J. Usability Stud. **12**(2), 73–91 (2017). http://uxpajournal.org/user-experience-rating-scales-points/

Saaty, T.L.: A scaling method for priorities in hierarchical structures. J. Math. Psychol. **15**(3), 234–281 (1977). https://doi.org/10.1016/0022-2496(77)90033-5

Saaty, T.L.: The Analytic Hierarchy Process. McGraw Hill, New York (1980)

Toepoel, V., Ludtig, P.: Online surveys are mixed-device surveys. Issues associated with the use of different (mobile) devices in web surveys. Methods Data Anal. **9**(2), 8 (2015). https://doi.org/10.12758/mda.2015.009

Tourangeau, R., Rips, L.J., Rasinski, K.: The Psychology of Survey Response, pp. 289–312. Cambridge University Press, Cambridge (2000). Chapter 10: Mode of data collection

Voutilainen, A.: Meta-analysis: complex relationships between patient satisfaction, age and item-level response rate. J. Res. Nurs. **21**(8), 611–620 (2016). https://doi.org/10.1177/1744987116655595

Voutilainen, A., Pitkäaho, T., Kvist, T., Vehviläinen-Julkunen, K.: How to ask about patient satisfaction? The visual analogue scale is less vulnerable to confounding factors and ceiling effect than a symmetric Likert scale. J. Adv. Nurs. **72**(4), 946–957 (2016). https://doi.org/10.1111/jan.12875

Wright, B., Ogbuehi, A.:. Surveying adolescents: the impact of data collection methodology on response quality. Electron. J. Bus. Res. Methods **12** (1), 41–53 (2014). http://www.ejbrm.com/issue/download.html?idArticle=333

Yu, J., Cooper, H.: A quantitative review of research design effects on response rates to questionnaires. J. Mark. Res. **20**(1), 36–44 (1983). https://doi.org/10.2307/3151410

The MeCUE Questionnaire (2.0): Meeting Five Basic Requirements for Lean and Standardized UX Assessment

Michael Minge[(✉)] and Manfred Thüring

Cognitive Psychology and Cognitive Ergonomics, Techniche Universität Berlin,
Marchstraße 23, Sekr. MAR 3-2, 10587 Berlin, Germany
{michael.minge,manfred.thuering}@tu-berlin.de

Abstract. Five requirements can be considered as basic for a standardized and lean measurement of user experience (UX): Comprehensiveness of the assessment, efficiency of execution, intelligibility of items and scales, psychometric quality as well as adaptability to different research contexts and types of applications. meCUE is a questionnaire in German and English that was developed to meet these requirements. It is theoretically based on the CUE model (Components of User Experience) and consists of 34 items which cover the components of the model and their sub-constructs: product perceptions (usefulness, usability, visual aesthetics, status, commitment), user emotions (positive, negative), consequences of use (intention to use, product loyalty), and overall evaluation. Items are grouped into four modules which correspond to these components. The modules were separately validated in a series of studies and meCUE has been used in several surveys to assess UX. Insights from this practical use pointed out that items for instrumental product qualities (usefulness, usability) and those for non-instrumental qualities (visual aesthetics, status, commitment) should not be grouped together into the same module. The new version meCUE 2.0 fulfills this demand by splitting up the module for product perceptions into two sub-modules, one for instrumental and one for non-instrumental product qualities. To ensure that this structural change does not impair the psychometric quality of the questionnaire, two data sets were re-analyzed that had formerly been used to validate the German and English version. The results of the analyses confirm that the psychometric quality of both versions remains intact. Due to the modified structure of meCUE 2.0, investigators are no longer obliged to incorporate items for both, instrumental and non-instrumental product qualities into their studies. Hence, the new version of the questionnaire significantly increases efficiency and adaptability and offers more degrees of freedom for combining its modules.

Keywords: Requirements · User experience · Product perceptions
Emotions · Lean assessment · Standardized questionnaire

1   Introduction: Five Basic Requirements for a Standardized Assessment of UX

User Experience (UX) is nowadays regarded as a key factor for the successful development of interactive systems. According to the norm ISO 9241-210 (2010), it covers "all the perceptions and reactions of a user before, during and after interacting with a product or service" [1]. While the traditional view on human-computer interaction has a strong focus on instrumental aspects, such as usability and usefulness, User Experience Design explicitly aims to provide positive experiences and positive user emotions by satisfying psychological needs [2, 3]. The achievement of these objectives requires the assessment of UX already in the early phases of User Centered Design (UCD) and to monitor it throughout the whole development process. In addition to qualitative methods, such as the Valence Method [4] and the Laddering Technique [5], which provide in-depth information about personal needs, values, judgments, and individual meaningfulness, quantitative methods are needed that allow for standardized comparisons [6] and for verifying specific requirements (e.g., benchmarks) with respect to UX. For this purpose, we developed the meCUE[1] questionnaire [7–12]. It aims to fulfill five basic requirements (R_1 to R_5) that we consider as central for a standardized and lean UX measurement and which are only partially met by other UX questionnaires, such as AttrakDiff [13] or the User Experience Questionnaire UEQ [14]:

- R_1 Comprehensiveness: UX is a complex construct and its measurement should be as comprehensive as possible. Hence, the questionnaire should comprise all aspects that are characteristic for experiencing a product, such as the perception of particular product qualities, emotional reactions during usage, behavioral consequences and the forming of an overall opinion about the product.
- R_2 Efficiency: The questionnaire should support a lean and fast assessment of UX. Therefore, it should consist of as few items as possible – but without neglecting relevant UX aspects.
- R_3 Intelligibility: Items of a questionnaire should be short, unambiguous and easy to understand. They should all adhere to the same format to spare respondents the mental effort of switching between different formulations and scales.
- R_4 Psychometric quality: The questionnaire should fulfill the central psychometric quality criteria. Empirical studies should guarantee that it measures UX in a valid, reliable and objective way. Moreover, they should ensure that is suitable for a number of different application domains.
- R_5 Adaptability: Not all UX aspects might be equally relevant for all iteration cycles of the UCD process, or for all kinds of users, systems and application contexts. Therefore, it should be possible to discard parts of the questionnaire which are not adequate for a particular research question or in a particular phase of development. Since the omission of items or scales usually harms the psychometric quality of a questionnaire, adaptability calls for an instrument which consists of modules that

---

[1] meCUE: modular evaluation of key Components of User Experience.

have been validated independently from each other. Such modules could be freely combined, i.e., any module could be left out without harming to psychometric quality of any other module or of the configuration that is chosen for a study.

The development of meCUE questionnaire aimed to account for all five requirements. It started from a theoretical framework which specifies UX key components and offers a sound basis for modularity and adaptability.

2 Theoretical Foundation of the MeCUE Questionnaire and Its Structure

Demanding comprehensiveness (R_1) for assessing a complex construct such as UX, calls for a psychological theory which postulates basic sub-constructs for this construct. The degree of comprehensibility that is achievable by a questionnaire can be judged against this specific theoretical background. A high degree requires that the theoretical concepts are reflected by the dimensional structure of the questionnaire and addressed by its items.

The structure of meCUE is based on the Components model of User Experience (CUE model) by Thüring and Mahlke [15]. This model distinguishes between the perception of instrumental and non-instrumental qualities[2]. While instrumental qualities comprise particular aspects of usability and usefulness, non-instrumental qualities include features like visual aesthetics and identification (compare also [16]). The perception of both types of qualities is directly influenced by interaction characteristics (i.e., product features, user characteristics, and the context of use). It has to be emphasized that the term perception is not only referring to sensation and the forming of a coherent percept, but also includes immediate judgment processes (e.g., goal conduciveness, compatibility with standards). Emotions are an important component of UX, since positive emotions ensure that the overall user experience assumes a positive shape [17]. In the CUE model, their relevance is acknowledged by their central position and their relation to both perceptions of product qualities (see Fig. 1). As the bidirectional relationships indicate, emotions result from these perceptions, but may also react back upon on them.

All three components together (i.e. perception of both qualities and emotions) determine the consequences of use, such as the overall product judgment, acceptance and intentions of future use.

The UX components of the model as well as the consequences of use are reflected by four modules in the meCUE questionnaire (see Fig. 2). The dimensions, which structure the modules in more detail, correspond to selected sub-constructs of the CUE model. Altogether, the questionnaire has 34 items. Each item consists of a statement (e.g., "The product is stylish.") in combination with a 7-point Likert Scale reaching from 1 ("strongly disagree") to 7 ("strongly agree"). The only exception from this format is the single-item of module IV (overall evaluation). It is formulated as a

---

[2] The distinction between perceived 'instrumental' and 'non-instrumental' product qualities shares similarities with Hassenzahl [16] who called them 'pragmatic' and 'hedonic'.

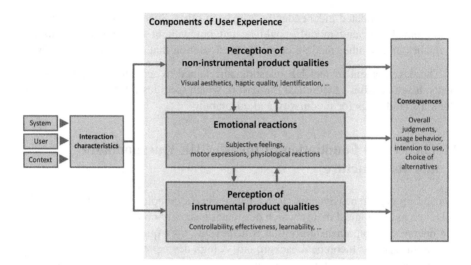

Fig. 1. Components model of User Experience (CUE). Reprinted from [12].

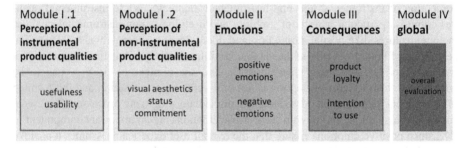

Fig. 2. Modular structure of the meCUE questionnaire.

question at the end of the questionnaire ("Finally, how would you rate the product overall?") and can be answered on a semantic differential, ranging from −5 ("bad") to 5 ("good") with an increment of .5, respectively.

The grouping of dimensions and their associated items into modules addresses the requirement of adaptability (R_5). Depending on the research question, user group, system type, context of use or iteration cycle in the UCD process, it should be possible to choose any combinations of modules that are considered as adequate. The prere-qui-site for this freedom is that the psychometric quality criteria are fulfilled appropriately (R_4). This goal was pursued by validating the modules independently from each other in the course of developing the questionnaire.

3 Development and Validation of MeCUE

The creation of meCUE started with a German version for which a pool of 67 items was initially generated. Item selection and validation of the question-naire were based on five data collections [7–12]. Three surveys were conducted online ($n1 = 238$, $n2 = 238$, $n3 = 237$) and two in a laboratory setting ($n4 = 67$, $n5 = 24$). In all studies, participants rated a wide range of different interactive products (e.g., electronic devices, mobile applications, software, and home appliances). The first two online studies focused on determining those items which loaded high on the scales of the question-naire. Data was analyzed using principle component analyses and resulted in the selection of 33 items measuring nine scales in three different modules. The constructed scales showed a high internal consistency (Cronbach's alpha values between .69 and .83) [7, 11]. Proportions of explained variance were acceptable for all modules (module I: 69.9%, module II: 57.4%, module III: 63.5%). The final set of items and the structure of the questionnaire were replicated under laboratory conditions (Cronbach's alpha values of the scales between .76 and .94, proportions of explained variance for module I: 81.1%, for module II: 74.3%, and for module III: 74.1%) [7, 11]. In order to assess the judgment of a product as a whole, meCUE was supplemented by a fourth module which consists of the single semantic differential described above [9, 11].

The validity of the final version was tested using three different approaches. First, the correlations between meCUE and the dimensions of other questionnaires measuring similar constructs were examined (convergent validity). It was found that meCUE consistently led to comparable values [7, 8, 11]. Strong correlations ($r > .7$) were observed between meCUE's 'usability' and AttrakDiff's 'pragmatic quality' as well as 'perspicuity' and 'dependability' of the UEQ. Ratings of 'visual aesthetics' (meCUE) were highly correlated with 'classical' and 'expressive aesthetics' [18] ($r \geq .7$), whereas correlations between 'visual aesthetics' and 'status', 'commitment' and especially 'pragmatic qualities' were on a more modest level ($.4 < r < .56$). With respect to emotions, strong correlations were obtained between positive affect of PANAS [19] and meCUE ($r = .51$) as well as between the dimensions for negative affect (resp. emotions, $r = .63$). Moreover, valence ratings captured by the Self-Assessment Manikin (SAM [20]) highly correlated with meCUE ($r = .66$ for positive and $r = -.65$ for negative emotions). Finally, the overall evaluation (module IV) was significantly correlated with 'attraction' of AttrakDiff ($r = .559$) [9, 11], AttrakDiff mini ($r = .919$) [10] and UEQ ($r = .887$) [9, 11].

A second approach to test the validity was to correlate subjective ratings with the number of completed tasks within a given time interval of five minutes (TTS = total tasks solved) as external criterion (criterion-related validity). In this study, 67 partici-pants worked with two versions of text-editing software [7, 11]. TTS was significantly correlated with ratings of 'usefulness' ($r = .32$, $p < .01$) and 'usability' ($r = .34$, $p < .01$), whereas non-significant correlations were obtained between TTS and 'visual aesthetics' ($r = .03$, ns), 'status' ($r = .04$, ns) and 'commitment' ($r = .14$, ns).

Finally, it was investigated whether the assessment of UX with the meCUE questionnaire leads to results that are comparable to those of an expert review (dis-criminative validity). The comparison showed that the dimensions of the meCUE questionnaire replicated the results of the experts evaluation very well and even minimal variations of usability and visual aesthetics were consistently captured [11, 12].

Since the evaluations reported so far had demonstrated that the German version of meCUE was well suited for measuring the main components of UX, it was decided to create an English version. Three native speakers who had been working as professional translators or language teachers for several years translated and retranslated the items independently from each other [12]. The factorial structure of the English version was then examined in an online survey. Fifty-eight participants rated their experience with an interactive product of their own choice. For each module of the questionnaire, a principle component analysis was calculated. The results replicate the structure that underlies the German version. Proportions of explained variance were acceptable for all modules (module I: 79.5%, module II: 59.3%, module III: 74.5%) and the scales showed a high internal consistency (Cronbach's alpha values between .76 and .91) [12].

4   Insights from Using MeCUE in Practice

Since its development, the meCUE questionnaire has been successfully used in multiple studies (e.g., measuring UX of consumer products, digital devices, software, mobile applications). For instance, Lebedev et al. [21] implemented the questionnaire to test temporal changes in UX when interacting with a mobile health application. In their study, children with sickle cell disease rated the app regularly over five weeks with an online version of the questionnaire. Klenk et al. [22] employed meCUE to investigate the UX of a fitness app. Even for business software that enables crowd-based requirements engineering, meCUE has been has been successfully applied [23].

However, there are also some limitations and critical remarks that must be regarded. For example, Doria et al. [24] refer to a study that aimed at measuring the subjective quality of lower limb ortheses. For this very special type of device, it was found that meCUE was not able to cover all relevant aspects of product use. Missing issues in this case concerned safety, hardware ergonomics, or wearing comfort. Furthermore, some dimensions of meCUE might get an entirely different meaning in such as medical context and thus call its validity into question. For example, 'status' with respect to medical products might be a problematic scale. It could be argued that the item "By using the product, I would be perceived differently" is rather a measure of stigmatization and social isolation than of social affiliation. There might be other contexts in which specific dimensions of meCUE cannot be clearly evaluated by users, e.g., 'commitment' to industrial software that aims at supporting product development processes [25]. In summary, it must be emphasized that the free combinability of the meCUE modules gives investigators many degrees of freedom. However, it is still their responsibility to check the completeness and the appropriateness of scales' carefully in each individual case.

This requirement is closely linked to the fact that - under some circumstances - non-instrumental product qualities might not be applicable to business applications. In a recent study by Lallemand and Koenig [26], it was reported that a participant raised the question how an intranet could be like a friend to her, when she was about to rate the meCUE item "The product is like a friend to me". At first sight, this remark seems surprising since a low acceptance of such applications often seems to be caused by an insufficient consideration of positive UX. Numerous examples have demonstrated that especially business applications benefit from the creation of hedonic experiences. Barnickel [27], for instance, proposed a number of design solutions for a time tracking tool that aimed at satisfying basic psychological needs, such as autonomy, relatedness, and competence.

Barnickel's work nicely illustrates that the more important issue might be how an intranet can be *designed* that actually feels like a friend to its users. Nevertheless, merging items for instrumental and non-instrumental qualities into a common module is probably a limitation with respect to adaptability (R_5). As a consequence, it seems reasonable to eliminate this restriction by splitting up Module I (product perceptions) into two modules, thus separating the items for instrumental qualities from those for non-instrumental qualities. This separation makes it possible to use the new modules independently from each other, e.g., to refrain from the non-instrumental items when they seem to be inadequate for the system or the usage context under investigation.

To ensure that the change of module I does not impair the psychometric quality of the questionnaire (R_4), two data sets were re-analyzed to validate the new structure – one for the German version, the other one for the English version of meCUE.

5 Re-analyzing the Factorial Structure of the English Version

For the English version, the data of an online survey were processed which had served to validate the prior English version [12]. In this study, fifty-eight native speakers from the United Kingdom and the United States (ages between 23 and 56, $M = 32.6$ years) had rated their experience with an interactive technical product from their personal environment (e.g., mobile devices, laptop, TV, software, mobile application, household appliances). Participants had been free to choose which product they wanted to rate. On average, they had owned the selected device for 9.4 months. Table 1 summarizes the characteristics of the sample. While the four modules of the questionnaire had been presented in a fixed order (i.e., product perceptions, emotions, consequences of use, and overall evaluation), the sequence of items within the respective modules had been randomized.

Based on the Minimum Average Partial (MAP-) Test [28], a principle component analysis was calculated for each module of the questionnaire to check the factor loadings. In contrast to the prior study [12], now two separate component analyses were performed for the items measuring the instrumental and the non-instrumental product qualities.

The analysis of the items measuring instrumental product perceptions revealed two independent components (see Table 2). This finding corresponds to the result that was obtained for the German items.

For the items measuring non-instrumental qualities, the principle component analysis identified the expected three independent components (see Table 3).

Table 1. Characteristics of the sample and the rated products.

Sample

Number of participants	*n* = 58
(female/ male)	*(33/ 25)*
Mean age	32.6
(Age range)	*(23-56)*

Evaluated products	Frequency	Percentage
Mobile phone	27	46,6 %
Laptop/ computer	14	24,1 %
Mobile application	6	10,3 %
Digital camera	3	5,2 %
Mobile audio player	3	5,2 %
Coffee machine	2	3,4 %
Washing machine	2	3,4 %
Software	1	1,7 %
Total	**58**	**100,0 %**

Table 2. Module I (Product perceptions: instrumental qualities). Factor loadings > .4

Item	Usefulness	Usability
With the help of this product, I will achieve my goals	.901	
I consider the product extremely useful	.797	
The functions of the product are exactly right for my goals	.600	
The product is easy to use		.913
The operating procedures of the product are simple to understand		.895
It is quickly apparent how to use the product		.809

The items and factor loadings of module III (User emotions) are listed in Table 4. The analysis showed two independent factors measuring positive and negative emotions.

Finally, a two-dimensional structure was found for module IV (Consequences of use). The pattern of factor loadings is equivalent to the German version with the two dimensions "product loyalty" and "intention to use" (Table 5).

Cronbach's alpha values for each scale were used as a measure of internal consistency (see Table 6). All values are between .76 (acceptable) and .91 (excellent). Table 6 also shows the proportion of explained variance for each scale and the cumulative proportions for each module. All values are comparable to those achieved for the German version.

Table 3. Module II (Product perceptions: non-instrumental qualities). Factor loadings > .4

Item	Visual aesthetics	Social identity: status	Social identity: commitment
The design looks attractive	.889		
The product is creatively designed	.873		
The product is stylish	.859		
By using the product, I would be perceived differently		.884	
The product would enhance my standing among peers		.865	
I would not mind if my friends envied me for this product	.432	.710	
I could not live without the product			.882
The product is like a friend to me			.801
If I ever lost the product, I would be devastated	.512		.553

Table 4. Module III (User emotions). Factor loadings > .4

Item	Positive emotions	Negative emotions
The product relaxes me	.766	
The product exhilarates me	.748	
The product makes me happy	.732	
The product makes me feel euphoric	.723	
The product calms me	.716	
When using the product, I feel cheerful	.623	
The product annoys me		.864
The product angers me		.860
The product frustrates me		.857
When using this product, I feel exhausted		.814
The product makes me tired		.759
The product makes me feel passive		.560

Table 5. Module IV (Consequences of use). Factor loadings > .4

Item	Product loyalty	Intention to use
I would not swap this product for any other	.885	
In comparison to this product, no others come close	.865	
I would get exactly this product for myself (again) at anytime	.826	
I can hardly wait to use the product again		.848
If I could, I would use the product daily		.808
When using this product, I lose track of time.		.757

Table 6. Proportions of explained variance and Cronbach's alpha for all scales.

Modules and scale	Proportions of explained variance	Cronbach's alpha
Product perceptions: Instrumental qualities (Module I)		
Usefulness	33.2	.78
Usability	44.9	.90
Total	**78.1**	
Product perceptions: Non-instrumental qualities (Module II)		
Visual aesthetics	31.9	.91
Social Identity: status	25.0	.84
Social Identity: commitment	21.3	.76
Total	**78.2**	
User emotions (Module III)		
Positive emotions	27.2	.82
Negative emotions	32.1	.88
Total	**59.3**	
Consequences of use (Module IV)		
Product loyalty	39.2	.87
Intention to use	35.3	.78
Total	**74.5**	

6   Re-analyzing the Factorial Structure of the German Version

Analogous to the re-analysis of the English items, data of an online survey were chosen which formerly had been conducted to test the reliability and the validity of the final German meCUE [11]. The procedure of that study had been identical to the procedure of the study validating the English meCUE. Two hundred thirty-seven German native speakers (139 women and 98 men, with an average age of $M = 29.8$ years) had rated their experience with an interactive technical product from their personal environment. Again, participants had been free in their choice of the product. On average, they had owned the selected device for 23.6 months. Table 7 summarizes the detailed characteristics of the sample.

Table 7. Characteristics of the sample and the evaluated products.

Sample

Number of participants	n = 237	
(female/ male)	*(139 / 98)*	
Mean age	29.8	
(Age range)	*(18-70)*	

Evaluated products	Frequency	Percentage
Mobile phone	99	41,8 %
Laptop/ computer	75	31,6 %
Coffee machine	22	9,3 %
Mobile audio player	16	6,8 %
Mobile application	9	3,8 %
Washing machine	7	3,0 %
Digital camera	6	2,5 %
Software	3	1,3 %
Total	**237**	**100,0 %**

In the re-analysis, a principle component analysis based on the Minimum Average Partial (MAP-) Test [28] was calculated for each module of the questionnaire. With regard to product perceptions (module I), two separate component analyses for the items measuring subjective ratings of instrumental and non-instrumental product qualities were calculated. The analysis of the six items measuring the perception of instrumental product qualities revealed the expected two independent components "usefulness" and "usability" (see Table 8).

Table 8. Module I (Product perceptions: instrumental qualities). Factor loadings > .4

Item	Usefulness	Usability
Mithilfe des Produkts kann ich meine Ziele erreichen	.877	
Ich halte das Produkt für absolut nützlich	.794	
Die Funktionen des Produkts sind genau richtig für meine Ziele	.668	
Es wird schnell klar, wie das Produkt zu bedienen ist		.861
Die Bedienung des Produkts ist verständlich		.868
Das Produkt lässt sich einfach benutzen		.856

Items and factor loadings of the items measuring non-instrumental product qualities are displayed in Table 9. Here, the principle component analysis showed the expected three independent components measuring "visual aesthetics", "status", and "commitment".

Table 9. Module II (Product perceptions: non-instrumental qualities). Factor loadings > .4

Item	Visual aesthetics	Social identity: status	Social identity: commitment
Das Design wirkt attraktiv	.889		
Das Produkt ist kreativ gestaltet	.854		
Das Produkt ist stilvoll	.838		
Durch das Produkt werde ich anders wahrgenommen		.881	
Das Produkt verleiht mir ein höheres Ansehen		.835	
Meine Freunde dürfen ruhig neidisch auf das Produkt sein		.576	
Ohne das Produkt kann ich nicht leben			.848
Wenn ich das Produkt verlieren würde, würde für mich eine Welt zusammenbrechen			.849
Das Produkt ist wie ein Freund für mich			.754

Table 10 lists the items and factor loadings of module III (User emotions). The analysis indicated two independent dimensions. According to the corresponding items, these dimensions differ in the quality of emotional reactions, namely negative and positive valence.

Table 10. Module III (User emotions). Factor loadings > .4

Item	Positive emotions	Negative emotions
Das Produkt entspannt mich	.858	
Durch das Produkt fühle ich mich ausgeglichen	.846	
Durch das Produkt fühle ich mich fröhlich	.824	
Das Produkt beruhigt mich	.822	
Das Produkt beschwingt mich	.809	
Das Produkt stimmt mich euphorisch	.805	
Das Produkt frustriert mich		.866
Das Produkt nervt mich		.826
Das Produkt macht mich müde		.818
Das Produkt verärgert mich		.800
Durch das Produkt fühle ich mich erschöpft		.781
Durch das Produkt fühle ich mich passiv		.625

Finally, a two-dimensional structure was found for module IV (Consequences of use). The pattern of factor loadings represents the two expected dimensions "product loyalty" and "intention to use" (Table 11).

Table 11. Module IV (Consequences of use). Factor loadings > .4

Item	Product loyalty	Intention to use
Ich würde das Produkt gegen kein anderes eintauschen	.873	
Im Vergleich zu diesem Produkt wirken andere Produkte unvollkommen	.855	
Ich würde mir genau dieses Produkt jederzeit (wieder) zulegen	.597	.494
Ich kann es kaum erwarten, das Produkt erneut zu verwenden		.840
Wenn ich könnte, würde ich das Produkt täglich nutzen		.755
Wenn ich mit dem Produkt zu tun habe, vergesse ich schon mal die Zeit		.711

As a measure of internal consistency, Cronbach's alpha values were determined for each scale (see Table 12). All values are between .70 (acceptable) and .91 (excellent). Table 12 also shows the proportion of explained variance for each scale and the cumulative proportions for each module.

7 Version 2.0 of the MeCUE Questionnaire

The results of both re-analyses show that the former module I (product perceptions) can be divided into two sub-modules separating the items for measuring the perception of instrumental product qualities (new module I) from those measuring the non-instrumental qualities (new module II) without reducing the psychometric quality of the questionnaire. This applies to both, the German and the English version. Based on our results, we suggest version 2.0 of meCUE with a revised modular structure (see Fig. 3).

In addition to the structural change, we propose to emphasize the phenomenological nature of the questionnaire more explicitly than before. First, this concerns the instruction which precedes the items. Instead of requesting a rating of *product features*, the new instruction explicitly asks to rate how these features are *experienced*. The appendix provides detailed information on the modified instruction. Second, this has also consequences for the single-item of module V. The new item asks "How do you experience the product as a whole?" (In German: "Wie erleben Sie das Product insgesamt?"). As previously, a semantic differential is offered to answer the question. It reaches from "as bad" (−5) to "as good" (5) in the English Version and from "als gut" to "als schlecht" in the German one.

Table 12. Proportions of explained variance and Cronbach's alpha for all scales.

Modules and scale	Proportions of explained variance	Cronbach's alpha
Product perceptions: Instrumental qualities (Module I)		
Usefulness	32.6	.73
Usability	40.3	.86
Total	**72.9**	
Product perceptions: Non-instrumental qualities (Module II)		
Visual aesthetics	26.4	.86
Social Identity: status	22.0	.76
Social Identity: commitment	25.3	.80
Total	**73.7**	
User emotions (Module III)		
Positive emotions	35.0	.91
Negative emotions	31.6	.88
Total	**66.6**	
Consequences of use (Module IV)		
Product loyalty	32.3	.70
Intention to use	33.2	.75
Total	**65.5**	

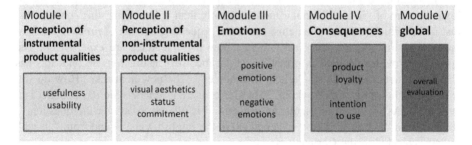

Fig. 3. The structure of the meCUE (2.0) questionnaire.

8 Discussion

To what extent does meCUE 2.0 meet the basic requirements we proposed for a standardized assessment of UX? With respect to the CUE model, both, the old as well as the new version are highly comprehensive (R_1) at the level of UX components. They address all three components postulated by the model as well as the consequences of usage and the user's overall judgment. At the level of sub-constructs, however, not all product qualities are accounted for. Neither items for the perception of the haptic or acoustic quality have been developed so far, nor are all needs addressed which might contribute to a positive user experience when they are satisfied [2, 29]. While accounting for these aspects would certainly increase the comprehensiveness of the questionnaire, it would also decrease its efficiency. Since we aim at providing a lean assessment of UX which is also suitable for practitioners and companies, we had to limit the range of aspects and the number of needs that are covered.

Moreover, a theoretically based questionnaire like meCUE can only be as comprehensive as the theory from which it is derived. At the level below the UX components, perceptions of further product qualities might be relevant that the CUE model does not account for. Three issues seem to be especially important in that respect:

- Safety critical applications might be experienced differently than innocuous ones. Backhaus and Thüring [30], for instance, discussed a number of pros and cons for cloud services from the user perspective. Such services may differ with respect to perceived trustworthiness and thus may induce trust or distrust which in turn may impact emotional reactions, behavioral consequences and overall judgments.
- The CUE model focuses on the experience of users who interact with a technical device in a rather isolated manner. Interpersonal relations and social influences that shape experiences in social media are neither explicitly addressed by the model nor by the questionnaire [31].
- In addition to technical *products*, technology-based *services* are experienced as well. This may shift the focus of research from *user* experience (UX) to *customer* experience (CX). According to Bruhn and Hadwich [32], CX comprises "all individual perceptions, interactions as well as the quality of an offered service that a customer experiences during his interaction with a company" (p. 10). Gentile, Spiller and Noci [33] proposed six dimension of CX. Four of them are sensory, emotional, cognitive and behavioral in nature and thus correspond to UX components as specified by the CUE model. CX, however, is the broader construct since it also incorporates lifestyle characteristics and social features.

Future research has to clarify whether these issues should be accounted for by the CUE model and an extended version of meCUE, or if it were more appropriate to address them in a different framework and by another questionnaire.

Like the first version of meCUE, the second one consists of 34 items in total. At first sight, it therefore appears as less lean than the AttrakDiff questionnaire or the UEQ, with 28 and 26 items, respectively. It must be noted though, that 12 of the meCUE items address users' emotions which are not accounted for in the other two questionnaires. If investigators apply meCUE, they need no additional tool to assess users' emotions. Moreover, they are free to leave out all modules which they consider as irrelevant for their research, thus adapting meCUE to their specific needs and increasing the efficiency of their survey (R_2). In addition to the obvious benefit that adaptability offers for efficiency, the time that is necessary to fill in the questionnaire indicates too that meCUE is a lean assessment tool. On average, it usually takes between 3 and 7 min and thus requires only little effort on behalf of the participants of a study.

To ensure a high degree of intelligibility (R_3), the items of meCUE were formulated in a short and unambiguous way with a clear reference to the product and the respondent of the questionnaire. Compared to the old version, meCUE 2.0 puts special emphasis on the experiential character of the UX assessment. This is reflected by the reformulation of the instruction and by the revised item for the users' overall evaluation. All items – with exception of the single item in module IV – have the same format: a statement combined with a 7-point Likert Scale. This format was chosen to offer an alternative to the semantic differentials of the AttrakDiff questionnaire and the UEQ. Homogeneity of items is no matter of course in UX studies. Investigators who aim to assess a variety of UX aspects must often rely on different types of questionnaires, such as semantic differentials, Likert Scales or grids. Hence, their participants must read and understand several instructions and adapt to a number of divergent formats which might be confusing and requires additional mental effort. For meCUE, this drawback is avoided since its modules cover a wide array of UX components in a uniform way.

The psychometric quality (R_4) of meCUE has been successfully checked in a number of studies for the German as well as for the English version [7–12]. In summary, the results of these studies demonstrated its high internal consistency, its good validity and its ability to explain great proportions of variance. This also applies to meCUE 2.0. As the re-analysis of two datasets showed, the structural change, that was accomplished by splitting module I into two independent parts, does neither harm the internal consistency nor does it impair the factor loadings within any module.

Compared to other UX questionnaires, the modular structure of meCUE is one of its major advantages because it ensures a high degree of efficiency (R_2) and adaptability (R_5). The modified structure of meCUE 2.0 opens up even more possibilities for its future use. It provides more flexibility in combining modules according to a research goal and the kind of product, user group or context of use that is investigated. Moreover, the questionnaire is now more suitable for comparing different design options at all stages of the user-centered design process and for a lean detection of changes in experience during long-term usage.

Although meCUE 2.0 fulfills the basic requirements which we proposed for tools that assess UX, previous experience has demonstrated that investigators still have the responsibility to check carefully whether the subjective perspective of their participants is sufficiently addressed by the questionnaire. In particular, they must decide which of the modules are appropriate for the purpose of their evaluation. A high degree of standardization is a crucial aspect for the quality of any method. However, standardized instruments do not always fit the user group or the system under investigation perfectly [26], and must therefore be carefully selected and handled.

Acknowledgment. The development of meCUE was supported by the German Research Association (DFG) as part of the Research Training Group "Prospective Engineering of Human-Technology Interaction" (prometei; GrK 1013). We would like to thank Laura Riedel and Carina V. Kuhr for their work on the studies. The creation of meCUE 2.0 and the re-analyses of data were supported by the Federal Ministry for Economic Affairs and Energy as part of the project "Mittelstand 4.0 Competence Centre for Usability".

Appendix

Modified instruction of meCUE 2.0 (English version):

This questionnaire serves to assess how you experience the product. On the following pages, there are a number of statements that you can use to judge your experience. Please, express the degree of your agreement with each statement by ticking the according circle. Decide spontaneously and without long contemplation to convey your first impression. Please judge each statement even if you feel that it does not completely match your experience. There are no right or wrong answers – all that counts is your personal opinion!

Modified instruction of meCUE 2.0 (German version):

Dieser Fragebogen dient dazu zu erfassen, wie Sie das Produkt erleben. Auf den folgenden Seiten finden Sie verschiedene Aussagen, die Sie benutzen können, um Ihr Erleben zu bewerten. Bitte geben Sie den Grad Ihrer Zustimmung zu jeder Aussage an, indem Sie das entsprechende Feld ankreuzen. Entscheiden Sie spontan und ohne langes Nachdenken, um Ihren ersten Eindruck mitzuteilen. Bitte beurteilen Sie jede Aussage, selbst wenn Sie meinen, dass sie nicht vollständig zu Ihrem Erleben passt. Es gibt keine "richtigen" oder "falschen" Antworten - nur Ihre persönliche Meinung zählt!

References

1. ISO CD 9241-210: Ergonomics of human-system interaction. Part 210: Human-centered design process for interactive systems. International Standardization Organisation (ISO), Geneva (2010)
2. Hassenzahl, M.: User Experience (UX): towards an experiential perspective on product quality. In: Proceedings of the 20th Conference on Human-Computer-Interaction, pp. 11–15. ACM, New York (2008)
3. Hassenzahl, M.: Experience Design – Technology for All the Right Reasons. Morgan & Claypool, Breiningsville (2010)
4. Burmester, M., Mast, M., Jäger, K., Homas, H.: Valence method for formative evaluation of user experience. In: Halskov, K., Graves Peters, M.G. (eds.) DIS2010 Proceedings, Århus, Denmark, 16–20 August, pp. 364–367. ACM, New York (2010)
5. Vanden Abeele, V., Zaman, B.: Laddering the user experience! In: User Experience Evaluation Methods in Product Development (UXEM 2009) – Workshop. INTERACT, Sweden, 24–28 August 2009

6. Schrepp, M., Hindercks, A., Tomaschewski, J.: User Experience mit Fragebögen evaluieren. In: Hess, S., Fischer, H. (eds.) Mensch und Computer 2016 – Usability Professionals, Aachen, Germany, 4–7 September 2016 (2016)

7. Minge, M., Riedel, L.: meCUE – Ein modularer Fragebogen zur Erfassung des Nutzungserlebens. In: Boll, S., Maaß, S., Malaka, R. (eds.) Mensch und Computer 2013: Interaktive Vielfalt, pp. 125–134. Oldenbourg, Munich (2013)

8. Minge, M., Riedel, L., Thüring, M.: Und ob du wirklich richtig stehst... Zur dis-kriminativen Validität des User Experience Fragebogens "meCUE. In: Boll, S., Maaß, S., Malaka, R. (eds.) Mensch und Computer 2013 – Workshopband, pp. 137–144. Oldenbourg, Munich (2013)

9. Minge, M., Riedel, L., Thüring, M.: Modulare Evaluation von Technik. Entwicklung und Validierung des meCUE Fragebogens zur Messung der User Experience. In: E. Brandenburg, L. Doria, A. Gross, T. Güntzler, H. Smieszek (eds.) Berliner Werkstatt für Mensch-Maschine-Systeme 2013: Grundlagen und Anwendungen der Mensch-Technik-Interaktion, pp. 28–36. Universitätsverlag der TUB, Berlin (2013)

10. Kuhr, C., Minge, M., Thüring, M.: Measuring the user experience of mobile applications – an empirical validation of a quantitative method. In: Schütz, A.C., Drewing, K., Gegenfurtner, K.G. (eds.) Abstracts of the 56th Conference of Experimental Psychologists, TeaP, p. 155. Pabst Science Publishers, Lengerich (2014)

11. Minge, M., Thüring, M., Wagner, I., Kuhr, C.V.: The meCUE questionnaire. a modular evaluation tool for measuring user experience. In: Soares, M., Falcão, C., Ahram, T.Z. (eds.) Advances in Ergonomics Modeling, Usability & Special Populations. Proceedings of the 7th Applied Human Factors and Ergonomics Society Conference 2016, pp. 115–128. International Press, Switzerland (2016)

12. Minge, M., Wagner, I., Thüring, M.: Developing and validating and english version of the meCUE questionnaire for measuring user experience. In: Proceedings of the 60th Annual Meeting of the Human Factors and Ergonomics Society 2016, pp. 2056–2060. Sage Publications, New York (2016)

13. Hassenzahl, M., Burmester, M., Koller, F.: Der User Experience (UX) auf der Spur: Zum Einsatz von www.attrakdiff.de. In: Brau, H., Diefenbach, S., Hassenzahl, M., Koller, F., Peissner, F., Röse, K. (eds.) Usability Professionals 2008, pp. 78–82 (2008)

14. Laugwitz, B., Schrepp, M., Held, T.: Konstruktion eines Fragebogens zur Messung der User Experience von Softwareprodukten. In: Heinecke, A.M., Paul, H. (eds.) Mensch und Computer 2006: Mensch und Computer im Strukturwandel, pp. 125–134. Oldenbourg, Munich (2006)

15. Thüring, M., Mahlke, S.: Usability, aesthetics, and emotions in human-technology interaction. Int. J. Psychol. 42(4), 253–264 (2007)

16. Hassenzahl, M.: Beyond usability – appeal of interactive products. iCom – Usability Emot. 1(1), 32–40 (2002)

17. Tuch, A.N., Van Schaik, P., Hornbæk, C.: Leisure and work, good and bad: the role of activity domain and valence in modeling user experience. ACM Trans. Comput.-Hum. Interact. 23(6), 351–3532 (2016)

18. Lavie, T., Tractinsky, N.: Assessing dimensions of perceived visual aesthetics of web sites. Int. J. Hum.-Comput. Stud. 60, 269–298 (2004)

19. Watson, D., Clark, A., Tellegen, A.: Development and validation of brief measure of positive and negative affect: the PANAS scales. J. Pers. Soc. Psychol. 54(6), 1063–1070 (1988)

20. Bradley, M., Lang, P.: Measuring emotion: the self-assessment Manikin and the semantic differential. J. Behav. Ther. Exp. Psychiatry 25(1), 49–59 (1994)

21. Lebedev, A., Minge, M., Lobitz, S., Thüring, M.: A longitudinal field evaluation of a mobile app for teenagers with sickle cell disease and Thalassemia. In: Goschke, T., Bolte, A., Kirschbaum, C., Fricke, B. (eds.) Abstracts of the 59th Conference of Experimental Psychologists TeaP, p. 119. Pabst Science Publishers, Lengerich (2017)

22. Klenk, S., Reifegerste, D., Renatus, R.: Gender differences in gratifications from fitness app use and implications for health interventions. Mob. Media Commun. 5(2), 178–193 (2017)

23. Stade, M., Oriol, M., Cabrera, O., Schmidt, O.: Providing a user forum is not enough: first experiences of a sofware company with CrowdRE. In: Proceedings of the International Conference on Requirements Engineering (RE) (2017). https://doi.org/10.1109/rew.2017.21

24. Doria, L., Minge, M., Riedel, L., Kraft, M.: User-centred evaluation of lower-limb ortheses: a new approach. Biomed. Eng./Biomedizinische Technik, 58(1). Walter de Gruyter Verlag, Berlin (2013). https://doi.org/10.1515/bmt-2013-4232

25. Sünnetcioglu, A., Brandenburg, E., Rothenburg, U., Stark, R.: ModelTracer: user-friendly traceability for the development of mechatronic products. Procedia Technol. 26, 365–373 (2016)

26. Lallemand, C., Koenig, V.: How could an intranet be like a friend to me? Why standardized UX scales don't always fit. In: Proceedings of ACM ECCE Conference, Umeå, Sweden, September 2017 (ECCE 2017), 8 p. (2017)

27. Barnickel, A.: Blick in die black box: Gestaltung eines Zeiterfassungssystems mit Mehoden des Gameful- und Playful Designs. Unpublished manuscript of a Master thesis at Magdeburg-Stendal University of Applied Sciences (2016)

28. Velicer, W.: Determining the number of components from the matrix of partial correlations. Psychometrika 41(3), 321–327 (1976)

29. Sheldon, K.M., Elliott, A.J., Kim, Y., Kasser, T.: What is satisfying about satisfying events? Testing 10 candidate psychological needs. J. Pers. Soc. Psychol. 80(2), 325–339 (2001)

30. Backhaus, N., Thüring, M.: Trust in cloud computing: pro and contra from the user's point of view. I-com 14(3), 231–243 (2015)

31. Berezan, O., Krishen, A., Agarwal, S., Kachroo, P.: The pursuit of virtual happiness: exploring the social media experience across generations. J. Bus. Res., 6 December 2017 (in press). https://doi.org/10.1016/j.jbusres.2017.11.038

32. Bruhn, M., Hadwich, K.: Customer experience – Eine Einführung in die theoretischen und praktischen Problemstellungen. In: Bruhn, M., Hadwich, K. (eds.) Customer Experience. Forum Dienstleistungsmanagement. Gabler Verlag, Wiesbaden (2012)

33. Gentile, C., Spiller, N., Noci, G.: How to sustain the customer experience: an overview of experience components that co-create value with the customer. Eur. Manag. J. 25(5), 395–410 (2007)

Heuristic Evaluation and Usability Testing as Complementary Methods: A Case Study

Braulio Murillo[1,2]($\boxtimes$), Jose Pow Sang[1], and Freddy Paz[1]

[1] Pontificia Universidad Católica del Perú, Lima 32, Peru
bmurillov@pucp.edu.pe
[2] DHL Express Perú, Callao 01, Peru

Abstract. Given the relevance that is taking the usability evaluation of software systems and especially web-based systems, the present work seeks to provide new evidence in the results obtained by applying combined techniques in usability evaluations. In this work, the process to schedule shipments using a web application was evaluated. First, a heuristic evaluation was performed and then a usability test with user. However, for this specific purpose, both tests will be applied independently to evaluate the results obtained. The evaluations were developed in an academic context.

Keywords: Human-computer interaction · Heuristic evaluation
Usability evaluation · Usability study · Transactional web applications

1 Introduction

Usability is a quality attribute that measures how easy the user interface is to use. It also includes methods to improve ease of use during the software design process [1]. Nowadays on the web, usability is a necessary condition for survival. If a website is difficult to use, people will stop using it. If the page does not clearly state what a company offers and what users can do on the site, people will stop using it. If users get lost on a website, they will stop using it. If the information on a website is difficult to read or does not answer the key questions of users, they will stop using it [2].

The first e-commerce law is that if users cannot find the product, they cannot buy it either [1]. In this paper, we will evaluate the web application of a logistic company using heuristic evaluation and a usability test with users. The results obtained in both tests will be shown to compare them and provide some conclusions.

2 Related Work

There are two types of methods to perform a usability assessment: inspection methods and test methods. The difference between them lies in the person who applies them. In the first case the inspectors perform and in the second the users participate [3].

In the present work, we make the evaluation of usability to a web application using both methods. As an inspection method, a heuristic evaluation is executed. Heuristic

© Springer International Publishing AG, part of Springer Nature 2018
A. Marcus and W. Wang (Eds.): DUXU 2018, LNCS 10918, pp. 470–478, 2018.
https://doi.org/10.1007/978-3-319-91797-9_34

evaluation is a well-known inspection technique that is widely used by usability specialists. It was developed by Nielsen as an alternative to user testing [4].

On the other hand, as a test method the usability test with users is executed. The main purpose of this method is the identification of usability problems during the interaction of users and the system [2].

In previous works, [2, 5], it is argued that applying heuristic and user evaluations as complementary studies provide advantages in the evaluation of usability. The heuristic evaluation and the usability test with users are executed independently. In this way, we seek to avoid any bias in the application of the tests.

The present work has been developed under an academic context. All the participants have developed the tests with professionalism and ethical values.

3 Research Design

In order to test usability in a web application, two methods were used: heuristic evaluations and usability test users. The objective of this test and the selection of the web application were academicals.

3.1 Description of the Web Site

The evaluated web application belongs to a logistics company. This application allows customers to make their schedules of shipments and package pickups, manage contacts and track shipments. As part of the evaluation, only the management of contacts and the scheduling of shipments have been considered.

3.2 Study Design

The purpose of this paper was to compare the results of both, heuristic evaluations and user usability tests based on a web transactional system.

This work was developed in two moments. First a heuristic evaluation was carried out and then a user usability test was developed. Both of them were executed independently.

4 Heuristic Evaluation

4.1 Participants

The heuristic evaluation was performed using the Nielsen's methodology analyzing the ten usability principles "heuristics". The evaluation was performed by three evaluators: one computer engineer, one master of science and one doctoral student.

4.2 Phases

This section describes the steps used to perform the heuristic evaluation. These are described below.

First phase: Each participant carried out the evaluation of the software independently. The results were recorded in their respective reports.

Second phase: A facilitator, arranged a meeting where the evaluators were able to unify the results obtained by briefly explaining the problems they found. A clean and unified listing of the problems encountered was obtained.

Third phase: Each evaluator independently rated the severity and frequency of each problem of the unified listing. With the values of severity and frequency was calculated the criticality: criticality = severity + frequency.

Fourth phase: A facilitator, calculated the averages and standard deviations of the three previously calculated values: severity, frequency and criticality of each problem. Based on the results, was established a ranking of the found problems.

The severity was evaluated according to the rating proposed by Nielsen [6], in which 0 means "I don't agree that this is a usability problem at all" and 4 means "Usability catastrophe: imperative to fix this before product can be released" (see Table 1).

Table 1. Severity ratings

Note	Severity
0	I don't agree that this is a usability problem at all
1	Cosmetic problem: the problem will be fixed unless there is extra time available in the project
2	Minor problem: fixing the problem is of low priority
3	Major problem: it is important to fix the problem, high priority must be established
4	Usability catastrophe: imperative to fix this before product can be released

The frequency was evaluated according the rating of the Table 2.

Table 2. Frequency ratings

Note	**Frequency**
0	<1%
1	1–10%
2	11–50%
3	51–90%
4	>90%

4.3 Data Analysis and Results

A total of twenty one usability problems were identified, which were categorized by the participants who performed the heuristic evaluation. The heuristics "Visibility of system status", "Recognition rather than recall", and "Help users recognize, diagnose, and recover from errors" were not found non-compliance. In Table 3, it can be seen the times that each unfulfilled heuristic.

Table 3. Unfulfilled heuristics

ID	Heuristic	Problems that non-compliance the heuristics	Number the problems that non-compliance the heuristics
N2	Visibility of system status	P2, P3, P4, P11, P13, P15, P17, P18	8
N3	Match between system and the real world	P10, P14	2
N4	User control and freedom	P6, P7, P8, P18, P19, P20, P21	7
N5	Consistency and standards	P1, P9, P10, P12, P16	5
N7	Flexibility and efficiency of use	P21	1
N8	Aesthetic and minimalist design	P1, P5, P9	3
N10	Help and documentation	P3, P15, P17, P18	4

Table 4. Ranking of the most severe problems

ID	Problem	Average severity
P10	The add button disappears when a piece with weight 0.25 is entered in a specific type of packaging	3.33
P4	The options appear in English	2.67
P21	It is not possible to choose more than one type of packaging in the same shipment	2.67

Of all the problems encountered, approximately 15% of them have a severity value greater than 2.50, which tend to be greater or catastrophic. In Table 4, the problems with greater severity are shown.

The evaluators considered that the most severe problem is that when changing the weight in a specific type of packaging, the Add button disappeared, which causes the user not to know how to continue with the process if he wants to add another piece to submit.

Other of the severe problems is that many of the options appear in English, even when the application is in Spanish. This causes that the users in some moments do not know what option to use if they do not dominate the English language.

Another of the severe problems is that you cannot choose more than one type of packaging in the scheduling of a shipment. What causes the user to have to perform another programming for another type of packaging.

On the other hand, Table 5 shows the problems with the highest criticality value (greater than 5). It is important to mention that in the evaluation the maximum criticality value was 5.34 so it can be said that they are not drastic problems that affect the functionality of the web application.

Table 5. Ranking of the most critical problems

ID	Problem	Average severity	Average frequency	Average criticality
P4	The options appear in English	2.67	2.67	5.34
P10	The Add button disappears when a piece with weight 0.25 is entered in a specific type of packaging	3.33	1.67	5.00

5   Usability Testing

5.1   Test Purpose

The purpose of the usability test is for the user to identify problems that arise when executing routine tasks in the web application. The tasks that have been defined are based on two main functionalities of the application: contact management and shipment scheduling.

5.2   Test Design

The tasks were based on two of the most important processes: contact management and shipment scheduling.

As part of the contact management, the tasks focused on the creation of a new contact. In the scheduling of shipments the tasks were focused from the selection of the origin and destination until the data of the package and type of service as well as the delivery times and additional services.

5.3   Participants

Since this is an academic work and in accordance with previous research [7], many participants are not needed to detect many usability issues [9]. For this reason, three professionals from the area of computer science participate in this evaluation. One has a bachelor's degree, another master's degree and the third is a PhD student. Two are male and one female. The age range is from 29 to 35 years.

5.4   Materials

The following materials were developed for the Usability Test:

Confidentiality Agreement: It is a document where the participants show that they agree to participate voluntarily in the usability test.
Previous Indications: Indications are given to participants to be aware of all the stages they will develop as part of the evaluations.
Pre-test Questionnaire: It is a questionnaire to know the demographics of the participants and to classify them, in this way it is possible to contextualize their answers.
Post-test Questionnaire: This questionnaire allows obtaining information complementary to the observations made during the execution of the tests.

Task List: This document details the tasks that participants must perform both for the evaluation of contact management and the scheduling of shipments.

For this evaluation, two scenarios were created: In the first scenario, the user must register a new contact in the application, for which he must record the contact's personal data.

In the second scenario, the user must schedule a shipment for the contact he has created in the previous task. In the scheduling, the user must enter the type of service, shipping information among other necessary information to complete a satisfactory schedule.

Task Compliance Observation Sheet: This document is used by the facilitator to enter the details of the tasks performed by the participants, the time used and any incident that was presented during the evaluation.

5.5   Usability Testing Process

The evaluation is done individually, always with the facilitator attentive to any query of the participant.

At the beginning, each participant is presented with the Confidentiality Agreement and the List of previous indications. After each participant signs the agreement, they initiate the evaluation by answering all the pretest questions [10].

Each participant receives the list of tasks and start the tests with the application. The facilitator records the interaction of the participant with the application and takes note of any incident during the evaluation.

At the end of the tests, each participant fills in the post-test questionnaire and finishes the evaluation.

5.6   Data Analysis and Results

Task 1 Results
Hits presented:

- Users were able to select the options indicated.
- There was not difference in performance executing the task among experimented and not experimented users.
- Users could register a new contact in the website.
- Even when users experience complications, they did not have to seek help from the system.

Inconveniences presented:

- Users have difficulty completing all mandatory fields, as these are not visibly marked as such.

Task 2 Results
Hits presented:

- Users were able to select the options indicated, those who did not have much knowledge of the application were already more familiar.

- There was not difference in performance executing the task among experimented and not experimented users.

Inconveniences presented:

- Users have difficulties placing the weights with two decimals, since the system rounds it to one decimal.
- Users seek help from the system, but it is in English.
- Users can not send more than one piece in the shipment, because the "Add" button disappears after adding the weight of the shipment with two decimals. The users show their discomfort because they have to repeat the process for the second piece.

Data Analysis: Observations. Users use very little help from the system. In Task 1, the main inconvenience that users had was that they could not distinguish whether a field was mandatory. Unlike what was found in the heuristic evaluation, this problem identified as P1, was not evaluated as severe or critical. However, in this usability testing this problem became more relevant. In addition, in Task 2, users do not manage to send two packages in a single schedule, this causes them to do the whole process again. In addition, users can not place the weights of the packages with two decimals.

Data Analysis: Post-test Questionnaire. Table 6 shows that the general appreciation of users with respect to the page evaluated is positive. They emphasize the information is useful, easy to understand and easy to find. Additionally, they agree with using the web application again. The two points that received the lowest rating was the fact that they were not able to complete the tasks because there was poor orientation in the web application.

Table 6. Results of post-test questionnaire

Question		Average result	
1	Fulfill tasks	2.33	Hardly
2	Sufficient and complete information	3.00	Neutral
3	Easy to understand information available	3.67	Easy
4	Required information easy to find	3.67	Easy
5	Information found useful	4.00	Useful
6	Web application easy to navigate	3.33	Neutral
7	Orientation on the web application	2.33	Disagreed
8	Satisfaction with the web application	2.67	Neutral
9	Will use the web application again	3.51	Agreed

6 Result Discussion

In the first part of this work, the results of the heuristic evaluation allowed finding 21 problems. Of these, problems P10, P4 and P21 were the most severe. Additionally, P4 and P10 were the most critical.

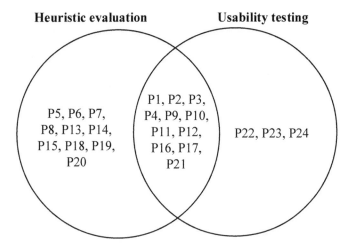

Fig. 1. Identified problems in each stage

On the other hand, in the usability testing some problems obtained in the heuristic evaluation are confirmed. Even some of them in this evaluation are evaluated with greater criticality. Also, in this stage there are new problems that were not identified in the first stage.

In the Fig. 1, the problems found in each evaluation and the problems that were repeated in each stage are summarized.

7 Conclusions

With this work, it is confirmed what was mentioned in a previous one [2], the heuristic evaluation is executed in less time and cost compared to the evaluation of users [8].

In the heuristic evaluation several usability problems were found in the web application. However, there were few problems that really had a high negative impact. Only 15% of problems were considered as very severe and 10% were considered as very critical. In general, under this evaluation it could be said that the web application had a very good result in the evaluation.

However, when the usability testing was performed, a more modest evaluation of the web application was obtained. Additionally, the most critical problems in this evaluation were not considered critical in the heuristic evaluation.

It should be noted that both tests were performed independently, thus there were no biases that could influence the results of the evaluations.

These evaluation methods gave results, since they allowed to make improvements in the web application, achieving an increase in the use of the tool and a better user satisfaction.

In conclusion, it can be affirmed that both tests complement each other, since the results obtained in one are enriched with those of the other test, being able to identify more problems or highlighting problems that an evaluation was not considered critical.

Acknowledgments. This research was carried out thanks to the support of DHL Express Peru, which in its constant search for the excellence of its products and services, is committed to research and innovation of its processes in the IT department. The authors especially thank Hugo Moreno, IT Manager, Adriana Azopardo, Peru Country Manager, Ivan Hay, CIO Central and South America, and Hank Gibson, CIO Americas Region; for their recommendations and their insightful comments to this investigation.

References

1. Nielsen, J.: Usability 101: Introduction to Usability (2012). https://www.nngroup.com/articles/usability-101-introduction-to-usability/. Accessed 29 October 2017
2. Murillo, B., Vargas, S., Moquillaza, A., Fernández, L., Paz, F.: Usability Testing as a Complement of Heuristic Evaluation: A Case Study. In: Marcus, A., Wang, W. (eds.) DUXU 2017. LNCS, vol. 10288, pp. 434–444. Springer, Cham (2017). https://doi.org/10.1007/978-3-319-58634-2_32
3. Holzinger, A.: Usability engineering methods for software developers. Commun. ACM **48**, 71–74 (2005)
4. Paz, F., Asrael Paz, F., Pow-Sang, J.A.: Evaluation of usability heuristics for transactional web sites: a comparative Study. Adv. Intell. Syst. Comput. **448**, 1063–1073 (2016)
5. Paz, F., Villanueva, D., Pow-Sang, J.A.: Heuristic evaluation as a complement to usability testing: a case study in web domain. In: 2014 Tenth International Conference on Information Technology: New Generations (ITNG), pp 546–551, April 2015
6. Nielsen, J.: Severity Ratings for Usability Problems (1995). https://www.nngroup.com/articles/how-to-rate-the-severity-of-usability-problems/. Accessed 02 November 2017
7. Virzi, R.A.: Refining the test phase of usability evaluation: how many subjects is enough? Hum. Factors **34**(4), 457–468 (1992)
8. Jeffries, R., Desurvire, H.: Usability testing vs. heuristic evaluation: was there a contest? ACM SIGCHI Bull. **24**(4), 39–41 (1992)
9. Virzi, R.A.: Streamlining the design process: running fewer subjects. In: Proceedings of the Human Factors Society Annual Meeting, vol. 34, no. 4, pp. 291–294. SAGE Publications, Los Angeles, October 1990
10. Rubin, J., Chisnell, D.: Handbook of Usability Testing: How to Plan, Design, and Conduct Effective Tests. Wiley, Hoboken (2008)

A Web System and Mobile App to Improve the Performance of the Usability Testing Based on Metrics of the ISO/IEC 9126 and Emocards

César Olivera Cokan[✉] and Freddy Paz

Pontificia Universidad Católica del Perú, San Miguel, Lima 32, Peru
{cesar.olivera, fpaz}@pucp.pe

Abstract. A method traditionally used to measure the usability level of software products is the well-known usability testing. In this method, people are employed as participants and usability experts commonly use usability metrics to be able to evaluate participants as they interact with the software product from which they want to measure their level of usability. On the one hand, there is a very wide variety of metrics from the ISO/IEC 9126 standard used to measure software quality. On the other hand, the Emocards allow us to obtain user experience metrics. The traditional usability testing, the metrics of the ISO/IEC 9126 standard and the Emocards can be used together to obtain better results. However, the results of five interviews with usability experts from different contexts and nationalities, who have been part of usability testing teams, allowed identifying a series of problems that arise when performing these methods in a traditional way. Therefore, this paper aims to show the tools called UTWebSystem and UTMobileApp, which pretend to be tools of frequent use to support the usability testing process based on usability metrics and Emocards. It is proposed that these tools solve the problems detected in this research. The collaboration of 30 participants and 6 usability experts was requested in order to carry out experiments and validate the importance of these tools. The results of this study have allowed obtaining promising results that encourage considering the use of these tools.

Keywords: ISO and usability · Usability methods · Tools · Usability testing
Emocards

1 Introduction

There are several interactive software products, which involve the intervention of real users, being these required in different areas, which has given them importance in society. This implies that software products are in constant challenge, which focuses on improving their quality. Usability is one of the main characteristics of the quality of a software product. To evaluate the usability, software developers have the possibility of using the well-known usability evaluation methods, which are diverse and combinations of these can be used [4]. In addition, it is possible to complement said usability evaluation methods with the use of UX evaluation methods.

© Springer International Publishing AG, part of Springer Nature 2018
A. Marcus and W. Wang (Eds.): DUXU 2018, LNCS 10918, pp. 479–495, 2018.
https://doi.org/10.1007/978-3-319-91797-9_35

According to Holzinger, usability evaluation methods are quite diverse, which can be classified into inspection methods and test methods [4]. The present paper focuses on a particular test method and a single variant of it, together with the use of a UX method, which is the use of usability testing process in its "one-to-one" variant, along with the use of usability metrics of the ISO/IEC 9126 standard and Emocards. Usability testing, in its variant "one to one", consist of a process that employs people as test participants, who are representative of the target audience, which are observed, each by a moderator/observer, in order to evaluate the degree to which a software product meets specific usability criteria, such as usability metrics [1].

According to the information gathered from interviews conducted with experts with experience in usability evaluation methods, the traditional usability testing process with users, which includes the use of usability metrics and Emocards, brings some problems due to this process is carried out manually. High rates of time to plan a usability testing session, large volume of material and/or templates, human errors in the calculation for the preparation of reports, significant reduction of the performance of the experts and delays in presenting the results reports to the clients, were the most outstanding problems detected in this research.

In addition, the literature offers descriptions at a high level about the usability testing process [1], usability metrics [2, 5–7] and Emocards [3]. However, the description of the process offered in the literature cannot be applied to the letter, since there are different contexts with different limitations, such as time, the amount of investment available, the number of participating users and experts, among others. This forces test teams to design usability tests with users under different variants. Therefore, in this paper it was necessary to contrast and find points of similarity between the existing literature and cases of real test teams that apply a usability testing process with users adjusted to their context. In this way, we can model a process that can be flexible with the reality of the usability testing teams with users from different environments and contexts.

Several of the usability evaluation and UX evaluation methods can be executed and/or supported by software. In particular, the usability testing`process with users is already being supported by various commercial tools and tools developed in the scientific field, but, as we will see in this research, they have many limitations. In this sense, this paper presents the tools UTWebSystem and UTMobileApp, a web system and a mobile application, which aim to support the execution of the activities that make up the usability testing process with users, which pretend to provide a solution to the previously mentioned problems.

2   Related Works

There are commercial tools that try to support the usability testing process; such is the case of Morae [8]. Morae is a software tool developed by Techsmith corporation, which allows users to capture, analyze, edit and play videos of usability tests sessions remotely or in person. Although this tool provides a way to cover certain steps of the usability testing process, it has a number of limitations that are important to highlight. Firstly, the results of the final reports are based on graphs that are only composed of the combination of three metrics: effectiveness, efficiency and satisfaction. Secondly, there is a limitation when adding new metrics to include them in the usability evaluation, since these can only be based on the movement of the mouse, the clicks that the user gives to the interface, the time to perform a task and the results of the satisfaction questionnaires. Finally, the use of recordings implies an extra effort when performing the usability evaluation, since it implies that usability experts have the task of repeatedly watching the recording of sessions that can take hours.

There are also other commercial tools such as Chalkmark [9], ClickHeat [10], ClickTale [11], Open Hallway [12], Silverback [13] and a variety of software services for usability evaluation, such as Usertesting.com, Userzoom.com, Loop11.com, among others. While these tools are capable of recording usability tests, which allows you to perform the test remotely and produce reports based on cursor tracking, clicks and heat maps, most of these do not allow, at all, develop questionnaires or reports with the most usability metrics based on ISO/IEC 9126 or other standards. All the commercial tools previously presented do not contemplate the combination of usability evaluation methods with the particular user experience evaluation method used by Emocards, which is a limitation that the solution proposed in this paper aims to solve.

With respect to sources of research and/or scientific work, there are software tools, which were found through a systematic search defining a search strategy based on PICOC, according to the guidelines established by Kitchenham and Charters [14]. A search chain (1) was developed considering synonyms and whose publications date from 2013 onwards to analyze the status of the solutions. The search process was carried out using two widely recognized databases to search for primary studies: SCOPUS and IEEE. Gray literature was excluded since it is not peer reviewed.

C: (software OR "support system" OR "support application" OR "collaborative system" OR "collaborative application" OR "support tool" OR "collaborative tool") AND (manual OR "manual process" OR steps OR "manual steps" OR phases OR procedures OR "manual procedures") AND (metrics OR "usability metrics" OR measurements) AND ("usability Testing" OR "usability evaluation" OR "user testing") AND (publication year > 2013) (1).

One of the tools found, through systematic search, that is important to highlight is ECUSI [15], which allows us to plan projects for usability evaluation methods (MEU) according to combinations of more than one MEU, among which are the tests of usability with traditional users. This is based on the use of document templates created in Google Drive for their collaborative work, which, although this tool provides a novel way to solve the problems of disorganization, loss of information and rate of error in the results, this has limitations with respect to the quantity of usability metrics that it contemplates. Added to this, the elaborations of the final reports must be carried out by means of manual calculations, which indicates that there is still the effort and extra time, besides leaving open the possibility of human errors in the calculations. In addition to ECUSI, there are other studies related to the application of usability tests with users remotely, such as, for instance, the use of Surveymonkey [16] and other collaborative tools for recording test sessions, which highlights the effectiveness of these, have to evaluate software products.

In general, and taking into account the current state of literature, the tools that support the traditional usability testing process are lacking. Of the few that were found, it was discovered that they have several limitations, which does not allow us to solve the main problems previously exposed, which are derived from the execution of a traditional usability testing process. Added to the above, there is literature that describes in detail the usability testing process with users, such as the Handbook of Usability Testing [1]; however, this cannot be applied to the letter, since there are different contexts with different limitations, such as time, the amount of investment, the number of participants and experts, among others. This forces test teams to design usability tests with users under different variants. Therefore, it was necessary to contrast and find points of similarity between the existing literature and cases of real test teams that apply a usability testing process with users adjusted to their context.

3   UTWebSystem and UTMobileApp as Tools to Support the Usability Testing Process

Having identified the problems that arise when executing the traditional usability testing process based on metrics of ISO/IEC 9126 and Emocards, the UTWebSystem and UTMobileApp tools were proposed as a solution, which provide support to the usability testing process based on usability metrics of ISO/IEC 9126, leaving the possibility to manage new metrics, and various Emocards proposals. Likewise, UTWebSystem and UTMobileApp are oriented to a process that was modeled as a result of the analysis of the information offered by the literature on usability testing process, usability metrics, Emocards and, on the other hand, the information gathered from the interviews that were conducted as part of the investigation. The objective of the development of these tools is to offer possible benefits for both the evaluators and for the effectiveness of the evaluations, but it should also be noted that there were limitations with respect to the diversity of variants that they can support.

3.1   Supported Process

As will be described later in Sect. 4, interviews were conducted with various usability experts, who have experience performing this type of testing method, in order to contrast the information obtained from the testimony of these experts with information from Literature [1, 17] on the traditional usability testing process.

Having looked for similarities and differences between the information coming from the literature and the information obtained from the interviews with the usability experts, a process was modeled that considers the alternative flows that were identified with the information retrieved from the interviews. The new usability testing process based on usability metrics of the ISO/IEC 9126 standard and Emocards contemplates the stages shown in Fig. 1, from the perspective of the evaluators and the users. Subsequently, a new process model was created in which the same stages are contemplated, but also UTWebSystem and UTMobileApp as tools that support it and allow to overcome the problems that arise when the process is traditionally carried out, which were mentioned in Sect. 1.

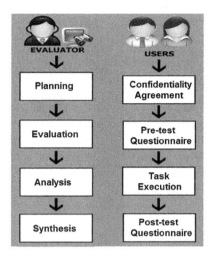

Fig. 1. Stages of usability testing process. Adapted from [18]

3.2 Functionalities

According to the results of the interviews, 100% of the interviewees agreed that it is not a good practice for a usability expert to be involved in more than one stage of the process, except for the Analysis and Synthesis stages because they can be covered by only one role. That is why UTWebSystem has different functionalities that are segregated according to different roles that are based on the stages of the usability testing process. The role "planner" has all the permissions with respect to the tasks of the Planning stage, while the "observer" role and the "participant" role contemplate tasks related to the Evaluation stage. Finally, the "expert-editor" role has all the permissions related to the Analysis and Synthesis stages. It should be noted that there is the role "administrator", which has all the existing permissions, but only had demonstrative purposes on the web system.

UTMobileApp is focused on the evaluation stage from the evaluator's perspective. Consequently, it has functionalities aimed at improving the performance of the evaluators during the observation and the registration of the data collected from the participants.

Planning Stage. In UTWebSystem, users registered in the system with a role "planner" can manage work teams, which can have one or more associated usability testing sessions (see Fig. 2). This means that users have the possibility to configure the test data, select the participants registered in the system according to their profiles and select the evaluators and experts responsible for the analysis and synthesis of results. In addition, users with a "planner" role can manage the Pre-Test and Post-Test questionnaires, the list of tasks for the participants, the list of usability metrics that will be considered in the evaluation and the Emocards. UTWebSystem is designed to reduce the duration of the planning stage, so it allows reusing questionnaires, list of tasks, usability metrics, Emocards or designs of total tests of usability testing projects previously created to be able to create new sessions according to the needs.

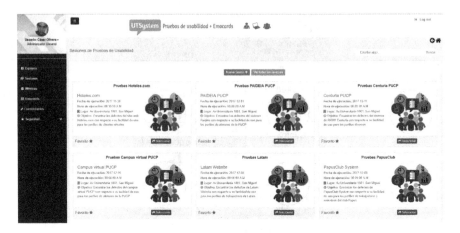

Fig. 2. Interface corresponding to management of usability testing sessions.

Evaluation Stage. In this stage, on the UTWebSystem side, the interaction of the participant with the software product is contemplated. That is why we have the role "participant", which can answer the programmed questionnaires, see the assigned task list and register the user experience through the Emocards. The latter are synchronized according to the progress of the task list.

On the side of UTMobileApp, the corresponding tasks of the observer/moderator are contemplated. UTMobileApp aims to provide functionalities to improve the performance of the observer/moderator in the Evaluation stage (see Fig. 3). That is why only users with observer role can enter the mobile application, which will provide the necessary information for the observer on the dynamics to follow, the metrics to be evaluated and instructions on how to evaluate them. The most outstanding feature of UTMobileApp is that it allows registering, in real time, the input fields of the usability metrics when observing the participants.

Analysis and Synthesis Stages. In the Analysis stage, UTWebSystem will automatically make reports based on the configuration of the test in the Planning stage and the data collected in the Evaluation stage. These reports are known as preliminary reports. Users registered in UTWebSystem who have the role "expert-editor" may consult these preliminary reports. The reports have summaries and statistical graphs of the results of the participants of the test. Its main objective is to provide quick information for the team that developed the software product evaluated to redesign it, if that is necessary.

The report editor of UTWebSystem allows to the usability experts to create detailed final reports. Registered users with the role "expert-editor" have the results to be analyzed (see Fig. 4) and can emit observations on positive and negative aspects. The sections that comprise the final report are editable, allowing you to customize according to the requirements of the clients. Finally, the usability expert can issue a conclusion supported by the results and observations previously detailed in the report.

Fig. 3. Interfaces corresponding to the main functionalities of UTMobileApp.

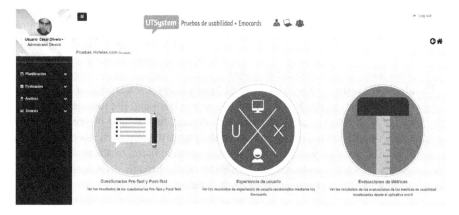

Fig. 4. Interface corresponding to the sample of results for the analysis stage.

4 Development Process

The software development process that was followed to develop the Web system "UTWebSystem" and the mobile application "UTMobileApp" was to use an agile methodology, since it had the collaboration of three usability experts, who took the role of client in all the process. The agile methodology chosen was the XP methodology (Extreme Programming) [19]. This involved going through the stages of Extreme Programming methodology, which are Planning, Design, Codification and Testing.

In the Planning stage, a questionnaire was previously prepared to carry out structured interviews with five usability experts from different contexts. They have the experience of carrying out usability tests in a traditional way. The interviews were useful to collect relevant information about the usability testing process, which allowed us to contrast the theory of the Handbook [1] and it was also possible to abstract generalities to model two processes, under the BPMN standard [20]. On the one hand, the usability testing process with users carried out in a traditional way and, on the other hand, the user usability testing process supported with the solution proposed in this paper.

In the Design stage, an architecture document based on RUP was previously elaborated, which allowed to define the architecture components that will be necessary for the deployment of the applications. In addition, a catalog of user stories was produced because of interviews with customers. It should be noted that these user stories changed throughout the software development process due to the nature of the agile methodology used. Added to the above, prototypes were developed, which the clients in the weekly meetings validated. On the one hand, prototypes were developed with the Mockups tool [21] from Balzamiq for the case of the Web System. On the other hand, prototypes were developed with the Marvel Apps tool [22] for the case of the Mobile Application.

In the Codification stage, the web and mobile application system was developed with the use of two frameworks. On the one hand, the web system was developed with the Laravel framework [23], which allows managing the view-controller model, previously defined in the architecture document. On the other hand, the mobile application was developed with the IONIC framework [24], which allows to build hybrid applications with a high-end aesthetic, in addition, through the Cordova Apache project, it allows building mobile applications for the IOS and Android operating system, which are the most used operating systems to date.

Finally, in the testing stage, a test plan of functionality was carried out based on the user stories that were established for both the web system and the mobile application. The objective of the test plan is to verify the correct functioning of the user stories implemented, in addition to checking whether they meet the requirements of the clients. Based on XP, the test plan was presented in each iteration based on the results obtained. That is, the tests were conducted on a weekly basis through acceptance tests with clients at the end of the presentation of each iteration.

5   Validation Process

Once the solution proposals were implemented, one of the most important questions of the investigation arose. This question was how to validate the ease of use and especially the importance that UTWebSystem and UTMobileApp have in the usability testing process with users based on the usability metrics of the ISO/IEC 9126 and Emocards. As previously mentioned, there are several methods to validate usability, as well as there are other methods to validate the importance of software products that are in a given context.

The environment in which this project was developed was in the Department of Informatics Engineering of the Pontifical Catholic University of Peru (PUCP). Thanks to this, it was possible to count on the support of the UMetSoft research group, which develops research focused on the area of HCI and Software Engineering, in which it has as research topics usability evaluation methods, usability metrics, user experience, usability, among others. The validation process could not have been carried out without the collaboration of the researchers of the UMetSoft group, since they provided the necessary permissions to have a testing laboratory and the attendance of participants that meet the user profile of the web system and mobile application.

5.1   Execution of an Experimental Design

In the first instance, it was decided to evaluate the usability and importance of the web system by means of the research method based on the execution of an experimental design with pre-test-post-test and control group [25]. The experimental design with pre-test-post-test and control group is a type of "pure" experiment, which has two requirements to achieve control and internal validity. On the one hand, they require comparison groups that, in this case, will be two groups. On the other hand, they require that these comparison groups be equivalent; that is, they have similar characteristics. Participants are randomly assigned to the two groups that make up the experiment and pretests are applied simultaneously. Subsequently, one group receives the experimental treatment and the other group does not receive it (control group). Finally, a post-test is applied to both groups [25].

This experiment was adapted to the context of the present research in order to be able to validate later, through a statistical analysis of the results obtained, the usability and the importance that UTWebSystem has in the usability testing process based on usability metrics of ISO/IEC 9126 and Emocards.

Participants. We counted with the collaboration of 30 students of the course of Information Systems 2, which is dictated in undergraduate of the specialty of Informatics Engineering of the Pontifical Catholic University of Peru. The participants fulfilled the profile of users of the web system, since they had the minimum knowledge of the usability testing process with users, usability metrics and user experience.

Materials and Equipment Used. For the use of the web system, a testing laboratory was required with the necessary quantity of equipment. With the help of the UMetSoft research group, it was possible to separate a suitable environment in the facilities of the Pontifical Catholic University of Peru (PUCP).

The pre-test and post-test questionnaires were prepared previously considering the Likert scale from one to five, where one is a negative perception and five is a positive perception.

Use of Questionnaires. On the one hand, the pre-test questionnaire obtained the scores that were used for control purposes in the experiment; that is, it will serve to know how adequate the allocation of the groups that was carried out was. On the other hand, the post-test questionnaire, which will be subject to analysis, consists of 16 items, which collect the data, to determine the perception of the participants, necessary for the validation of the Web System with respect to its ease of use and its importance.

Experiment Design. A total of 30 participants were expected, of which 19 were attended. The design of the experiment consisted of an experimental group and a control group that is why two groups were randomly separated; that is, a group of nine participants and another group of 10 participants. There were two rounds in which, in the first round, a group became the experimental group. In other words, this was the group that supported by UTWebSystem and UTMobileApp to perform the usability testing process based on metrics and Emocards. The other group became the control group; that is, the group that performed the usability test based on metrics and Emocards in a traditional way. In the next round the same thing was done, but in an inverse manner. In short, the group in the previous round was the experimental group became the control group and the group in the previous round was the control group, became the experimental group.

At the beginning of the execution of the experimental design, the pre-test was evaluated to all the participants in order to measure the previous knowledge with the participants and to find out how adequate was the assignment of the groups that was carried out. At the end of the experiment, the post-test questionnaire was evaluated for all participants with the purpose of using the results to perform the statistical analysis.

Both groups (control and experimental) conducted a usability test for a specific software product. The software product that was evaluated was the Hoteles.com website, which offers online accommodation in various hotels around the world.

The usability testing session consisted of a traditional test using questionnaires, usability metrics of the ISO/IEC 9126 Standard, a task list developed by the participants and Emocards to evaluate the user experience. Each group had three members with the role "participant" and the rest with the role of experts (three with the role "observer", a "planner" and an "expert-editor").

Previously the Pre-Test and Post-Test questionnaires were elaborated, a list of predefined tasks for the participants of the experiment was defined, the metrics of the ISO/IEC 9126 standard of usability to be evaluated were selected and the Emocards were designed to collect the experience of the users.

Results of the Experiment. The results of the questionnaires evaluated were collected from the participants who were part of the control and experimental groups, which were analyzed independently of the groups to which they belonged to evaluate the statistical results.

Table 1. Results of the post-test questionnaires.

		Participants																	
		1	2	3	4	5	6	7	8	9	10	11	12	13	14	15	16	17	18	19
ITEMS	1	2	3	5	4	4	4	3	5	5	4	4	4	4	4	3	2	4	5	3
	2	4	3	3	3	5	5	3	5	4	4	3	5	4	3	4	5	3	3	4
	3	3	2	4	3	3	4	4	3	4	3	4	5	4	3	3	5	4	4	5
	4	4	3	4	4	4	4	5	4	5	3	3	5	5	3	4	5	4	4	5
	5	5	5	4	5	5	4	4	5	2	3	4	5	3	5	5	1	5	5	5
	6	4	3	4	5	4	4	4	5	4	4	2	4	4	4	4	1	3	4	4
	7	3	3	4	4	4	4	4	5	4	4	3	5	4	4	3	3	4	4	3
	8	4	4	4	4	5	4	4	5	3	3	4	5	4	5	4	3	4	4	5
	9	5	4	4	4	3	4	4	5	5	4	4	5	4	4	5	4	5	4	5
	10	4	4	4	4	4	3	3	4	4	4	3	4	4	5	4	3	3	5	4
	11	5	5	5	4	5	3	3	4	4	3	3	4	4	4	3	2	4	5	4
	12	4	5	5	3	2	3	4	5	4	3	4	4	4	4	4	3	4	3	4
	13	3	3	4	4	4	4	2	4	4	4	3	4	4	4	4	2	4	3	4
	14	2	4	5	4	3	2	3	3	5	4	4	3	4	5	4	3	3	4	3
	15	2	5	5	4	1	4	4	5	5	4	5	5	4	5	4	4	5	4	5
	16	4	3	4	3	1	4	3	5	5	4	5	5	4	4	5	4	5	4	5

On the one hand, the results obtained from the pre-test allowed confirming that the participants had the prior knowledge required to perform the proposed usability test. In addition, the results allowed knowing that the allocation of the groups was adequate regardless of the rotation shifts that were carried out. On the other hand, the results obtained from the post-test (see Table 1), allowed us to perform a statistical analysis to find out if the general hypothesis is accepted. The hypothesis states that the web system allows usability testing with users and Emocards more easily and efficiently overcoming the problems described in Sect. 1. According to the Likert scale from one to five, the general hypothesis presented is taken only if through the tests that were performed in the statistical analysis it is possible to determine that the average of perceptions exceeds the neutral value 3.0.

Statistical Analysis of the Results. Table 2 shows the descriptive statistical results obtained with the SPSS tool. On the one hand, the average represents the average assigned to UTWebSystem by the participants (3.898026) which is quite good, since it exceeds the neutral value of 3.0, taking into account that 1.0 is considered a totally negative perception and 5.0 a totally positive perception about the Web System. On the other hand, the standard deviation represents how far apart the opinions are among the participants. We find a value of 0.3506, a value below 1.0 and that tends to zero, which indicates that the opinion among the different participants is quite similar. That is, they have the same perception that the Web System would contribute to the development of tests with users and meets the requirements of ease of use.

Although the average results in a value above 3.0, which is a favorable result that serves as a validation of the proposed software, it is necessary to perform a statistical analysis. This analysis has the purpose of determining if the difference between the resulting value (3.898026) and 3.0 is significant; that is, it can be said that the perception of the software product is positive and does not tend to be neutral. Therefore, we proceeded to find out if the distribution of the data is a normal distribution, with

Table 2. Descriptive statistics results. Own elaboration using the SPSS software.

	N	Minimum	Maximum	Mean	Standar Desviation	Variance
Perception	19	3,1250	4,5000	3,898026	,3506012	,123
N valid (per list)	19					

which we propose two hypotheses, the null hypothesis (H0) and the alternative hypothesis (H1), which are described below:

H0: The data come from a normal distribution.
H1: The data do not come from a normal distribution.

To find out which hypothesis is the one that is true, we proceeded to perform the Kolmogorov-Smirnov test [26].

The SPSS software was employed and the result of the Kolmogorov-Smirnov test was obtained, which is detailed in Table 3.

Table 3. Results of Kolmogorov-Smirnov test. Own elaboration using the SPSS software.

	Kolmogorov-Smirnov		
	Statist	gl	Sig.
Perception	,098	19	,200*

*. This is a lower limit of the true significance.

The value of the Kolmogorov-Smirnov statistic is 0.20. Under a confidence level of 95% and a significance of 5%, it was not possible to refuse the null hypothesis, so it was concluded that the data come from a normal distribution.

Finally, due to the reason that the data follow a normal distribution, the most appropriate statistical test to determine if there is a significant difference with 3.0 is the T-Student of a single sample [27]. Again, two hypotheses were proposed, the null hypothesis (H0) and the alternative hypothesis (H1), which are described below:

H0: The average of the perceptions is equal to 3.0
H1: The average of the perceptions is greater than 3.0.

The comparative value used in the T-Student test of a single sample was 3.0. Then, in Table 4, the results of the T-Student test are shown.

As can be seen in Table 5, the value of the T-Student statistic is 0.000. Under a 95% confidence level and a significance of 5%, the null hypothesis was refused. This is because 0.000 is less than 0.05 (5%). Therefore, it was concluded that the average of the

Table 4. T-Student test results from a single sample. Own elaboration using the SPSS software.

| | Test value = 3 | | | | 95% confidence interval of the difference | |
| | | | | Difference of means | | |
	t	gl	Sig. (bilateral)		Lower	Higher
Perception	11,165	18	,000	,8980263	,729042	1,067011

perceptions of the participants is greater than 3.0. In other words, the participants of the experiment had a positive and significant perception in relation to the neutral value (3.0).

Finally, the general hypothesis is true. Therefore, it is stated that the Web System allows usability experts to perform usability tests based on metrics of ISO/IEC 9126 and Emocards more easily and efficiently overcoming the problems described in Sect. 1.

5.2   Expert Judgment

In the second instance, it was decided to jointly evaluate the web system with the mobile application, giving emphasis to the latter in order to validate the usability and the importance it has in the usability testing process based on usability metrics of ISO/IEC 9126 and Emocards. For this reason, the expert judgment method was used, which consists of an informed opinion of people who have experience in the topic of interest, who are recognized by others as qualified experts, and who can provide information, evidence, judgments and assessments [28].

The use of this method opened two important questions to solve. The first question was to know the profile that had the experts who were part of the evaluation. The second question was to know the amount of experts to use. In the context of the present research, factors such as experience and/or publications made in topics related to usability and specifically to methods of usability evaluation were considered for the selection of experts. In addition, it was considered three usability experts who were part of the test. This number of experts was considered adequate because it exceeds the minimum amount required, which is two experts according to the author McGarland et al. [29].

The steps for the execution of the expert judgment method that were considered in the validation of UTMobileApp were based on the Guide for conducting expert judgment of Escobar-Pérez and Cuervo-Martínez [28]. Firstly, the objective of the expert judgment was defined, which was to validate the usability and importance of UTMobileApp, which supports the evaluation stage of the usability testing process with users based on usability metrics of the ISO/IEC 9126 standard and Emocards. Secondly, the experts were contacted, who were given the objective of expert judgment and validation. Thirdly, a list of items was specified, which were separated into two categories. The items related to the ease of use and the items related to the importance of UTMobileApp in the usability testing process with users based on usability metrics of the ISO/IEC 9126 standard and Emocards. With this, a template was developed, which served as a validation instrument since it meets all the characteristics described in the steps previously described. Fourthly, the meeting with the judges was held to carry out the validation by expert judgment. In this meeting, each judge separately used the mobile application together with the web system and qualified the items that were previously specified. The results for the ease-of-use and importance categories of UTMobileApp are shown in Tables 5 and 6 respectively.

Table 5. Expert judgment results regarding the ease of use of UTMobileApp.

	Item N°							Mean	# of observations
	1	2	3	4	5	6	7		
Expert N°1	4	4	5	3	4	3	5	4.00	1
Expert N°2	5	5	5	4	5	4	5	4.71	3
Expert N°3	5	5	5	4	5	4	5	4.71	1

Table 6. Expert judgment results regarding the importance of UTMobileApp.

	Item N°					Mean	# of observations
	1	2	3	4	5		
Expert N°1	5	5	4	4	5	4.60	-
Expert N°2	5	5	4	5	5	4.80	-
Expert N°3	5	5	5	5	5	5	-

Having elaborated the items based on the Likert scale from one to five, where one is the perception in total disagreement and five in total agreement, we obtained means greater than the neutral value 3.0, which is quite positive. To evaluate the concordance of judges, Kappa statistic was used, which had confirmed that agreement in the opinion of the three judges. The judges provided a set of minimum observations and recommendations that, although they did not affect in a decisive way in the validation and in the conclusion of the experts, they served to improve the graphic user interface of UTMobileApp. Finally, the judges came to the mutual agreement that UTMobileApp is easy to use and is important in the usability testing process based on the ISO/IEC 9126 standard and Emocards.

6   Conclusions and Future Works

UTWebSystem and UTMobileApp are tools developed in order to provide a solution to the frequent problems that arise when executing the known usability tests with users along with the use of usability metrics and Emocards. In this sense, they pretend to be tools of frequent use in the field of evaluation of usability and user experience. With the development of these tools, it has also been planned to increase the productivity of the usability experts and/or usability practitioners, since within the agile development methodology that was used, the usability expert has been considered as the client and the development of these tools has focused on these.

Taking into account the results of the systematic search of related works and similar tools in the commercial field, these have many limitations and do not solve most or none of the problems detected in the interviews conducted in this research. In this sense, having developed the solution proposals and having carried out experiments that obtained positive results, encouraging conclusions emerge regarding the UTWebSystem and UTMobileApp tools. With respect to UTWebSystem, it can be concluded that UTWebSystem supports the usability testing process based on usability metrics of ISO/IEC 9126 and Emocards. Firstly, because the experts can have the information centralized in a database, which avoids loss or confusion. Secondly, because it allows collaboration and communication between different usability experts. Thirdly, the web system provides support because it manages to automate the generation of reports, which is no longer manual. Finally, the web system allows working new usability testing sessions based on previous sessions, which greatly facilitates the work of the usability test planner. With respect to the UTMobileApp, it can be concluded that it supports the evaluation stage of the usability testing process with users due to three reasons. Firstly, because it makes the task of the observer simple when entering the observation data to the system. In other words, the well-known observation and compliance sheets in physical format are no longer needed. Secondly, the mobile application was designed to take care of the comfort of the user, since having implemented this module, as a web part would have involved using a larger and heavier equipment. This would make the work of the observer more uncomfortable during the test. Finally, the Mobile Application allows the observer to do his work intuitively without needing to pay all his attention in the handling of this and focus more on the actions of the participants.

Due to the encouraging results, a set of future activities has been proposed. In the first place, since there are several variants of usability tests with users and this solution proposal only addresses the particular case of the "one-to-one" variant, it is proposed as a future work to be able to generalize this solution for all variants of possible usability testing process. This would involve broadening the scope of the research and conducting more interviews with collaborators from different contexts in which traditional usability testing, usability metrics and Emocards are applied. Secondly, another future work to consider is to integrate these tools with the S.I. of a company and evaluate the results obtained. Due to the fact that within the scope of the proposed solution it is contemplated to support usability tests of software products in process or in preliminary versions. This would greatly help to measure the usability of software products giving it a commercial focus. Finally, the last future works to be considered are to refine the graphical user interface of both the web system and the mobile application and, in addition, to be able to control versions of usability testing sessions and apply audit to a greater degree than already It is managed. This will further reduce the risks of human error, which is the main source of problems encountered in the traditional usability testing process.

References

1. Rubin, J., Chisnell, D.: Handbook of Usability Testing: How to Plan, Design, and Conduct Effective Tests, 2nd edn (2008). [electronic resource]
2. ISO/IEC 9126: Software Engineering—Product Quality—Part 1: Quality Model. Security, vol. 2003 (2003)
3. Rivero, L., Conte, T.: Using a study to assess user eXperience evaluation methods from the point of view of users. In: Proceedings of the 17th International Conference on Enterprise Information Systems, pp. 88–95 (2015)
4. Holzinger, A.: Usability engineering methods for software developers. Commun. ACM **48**(1), 71–74 (2005)
5. ISO/IEC 9126: Software Engineering—Product Quality—Part 2: External Metrics. Security, vol. 2003 (2003)
6. ISO/IEC 9126: Software Engineering—Product Quality—Part 3: Internal Metrics. Security, vol. 2003 (2003)
7. ISO/IEC 9126: Software Engineering—Product Quality—Part 4: Quality in Use Metrics. Security, vol. 2003 (2003)
8. Usability Testing - Morae - TechSmith (2017). https://www.techsmith.com/morae.html. Accessed 19 Apr 2017
9. First-Click - Testing Software: Optimal Workshop (2017). https://www.optimalworkshop.com/chalkmark. Accessed 19 Apr 2017
10. ClickHeat (2011). https://www.dugwood.com/clickheat/index.html. Accessed 17 Apr 2017
11. Clicktale: Digital Customer Experience; Website Analytics (2015). https://www.clicktale.com/default.aspx. Accessed 19 Apr 2017
12. OpenHallway (2009). http://www.openhallway.com/. Accessed 19 Apr 2017
13. Silverback 3 (2009). http://silverbackapp.com/. Accessed 17 Apr 2017
14. Charters, S., Kitchenham, B.: Guidelines for performing systematic literature reviews in software engineering. In: International Conference on Software Engineering, vol. 45, no. 4ve, p. 1051 (2007)
15. Solano, A., Ceron, J.C., Collazos, C.A., Fardoun, H.M.: ECUSI: herramienta software para la evaluación colaborativa de la usabilidad de sistemas interactivos. In: 2015 10th Colombian Computing Conference, 10CCC 2015, pp. 157–163 (2015)
16. Symonds, E.: A practical application of SurveyMonkey as a remote usability-testing tool. Libr. Hi Tech **29**(3), 436–445 (2011)
17. Barnum, C., Bevan, N., Cockton, G., Nielsen, J., Spool, J., Wixon, D.: The 'magic number 5': is it enough for web testing?. In: CHI 2003 Extended Abstracts on Human Factors in Computing Systems, CHI 2003, no. 5, p. 698 (2003)
18. Paz, F.A., Villanueva, D., Pow-Sang, J.A.: Heuristic evaluation as a complement to usability testing: a case study in web domain. In: 2015 12th International Conference on Information Technology-New Generations, pp. 546–551 (2015)
19. Beck, K.: Una explicación de la Programación Extrema: aceptar el cambio. Addison-Wesley, Boston (2002)
20. Bizagi: Software BPMN para el modelamiento de procesos (2002). http://www.bizagi.com/es/productos/bpm-suite/modeler. Accessed 07 June 2017
21. L. Balsamiq Studios: Balsamiq Mockups—Balsamiq (2008). https://balsamiq.com/products/mockups/. Accessed 15 Oct 2017
22. Mutlu, M., Moore, B., Siao, J.: Free mobile & web prototyping (iOS, iPhone, Android) for designers – Marvel (2010). https://marvelapp.com/. Accessed 14 Oct 2017

23. Otwell, T.: Laravel - The PHP Framework For Web Artisans (2011). https://laravel.com/. Accessed 07 June 2017
24. Drifty Co: Build Amazing Native Apps and Progressive Web Apps with Ionic Framework and Angular (2013). https://ionicframework.com/. Accessed 20 Nov 2017
25. Hernández, R., Fernández, C., Baptista, P.: Metodología de la investigación. **53**(9) (2014)
26. Ghasemi, A., Zahediasl, S.: Normality tests for statistical analysis: a guide for non-statisticians. Int. J. Endocrinol. Metab. **10**(2), 486–489 (2012)
27. Kim, T.K.: T test as a parametric statistic. Korean J. Anesthesiol. **68**(6), 540–546 (2015)
28. Escobar-Pérez, J., Cuervo-Martínez, Á.: Validez de contenido y juicio de expertos: una aproximación a su utilización. Av. en Medición **6**, 27–36 (2008)
29. McGarland, D., Berg-Weger, M., Tebb, S.S., Lee, E.S., Rauch, S.: Objectifying content validity: conducting a content validity study in social work research. Soc. Work Res. **27**(2), 94–104 (2003)

Quantifying the Usability Through a Variant of the Traditional Heuristic Evaluation Process

Freddy Paz[1]([envelope]), Freddy A. Paz[2], Manuel Sánchez[2], Arturo Moquillaza[1,3], and Luis Collantes[2]

[1] Pontificia Universidad Católica del Perú, Lima 32, Peru
{fpaz,amoquillaza}@pucp.pe
[2] Universidad Nacional Pedro Ruiz Gallo, Lambayeque, Peru
freddypazsifuentes@yahoo.es, manuelsanchezchero@gmail.com,
lcollantes@unprg.edu.pe
[3] Universidad San Ignacio de Loyola, Lima 12, Peru

Abstract. Usability has become in an essential aspect for the success of E-Commerce applications, especially in the current context in which there is high competitiveness because of a large number of websites that are available on the Internet. However, there is little evidence in the literature about the existence of methods that allow specialists to measure the level of usability of the system interfaces through a quantitative approach. The advantage of obtaining a numeric value about the ease of use is the possibility to perform comparisons between different design proposals and determine the best alternative for a specific scenario. Likewise, a quantifying process of the level of usability provide companies with the necessary mechanism to establish the degree in which their web applications are more usable regarding other accessible websites in a highly competitive market. In this paper, we present the results of applying a variant to the traditional heuristic evaluation process to determine the usability degree of two web applications. This case study is intended to serve as a framework for specialists in this field that are interested in retrieving quantitative data in addition to the traditional usability issues that are identified.

Keywords: Human-Computer Interaction · Usability
Heuristic evaluation · Quantitative metrics · Assessment framework

1 Introduction

Nowadays, the usability is a critical success factor for the transcendence of any software product in the global market [6]. This software quality attribute can be a determinant element for people to continue using an application, especially, if the reference is to websites or mobile apps. Given the several alternatives that users have on the Internet, if a website is difficult to use or hard to understand

© Springer International Publishing AG, part of Springer Nature 2018
A. Marcus and W. Wang (Eds.): DUXU 2018, LNCS 10918, pp. 496–508, 2018.
https://doi.org/10.1007/978-3-319-91797-9_36

or fails to clearly state its purpose, users will leave the site and look for similar options that meet all these aspects. In the E-Commerce domain, where there are multiple websites available and the competition between companies is immeasurable, considering criteria to ensure a high level of ease of use can be the decisive feature to stand out in the market.

The relevance of the usability of software products has led to the emergence of several methods which provide specialists with mechanisms to determine if the graphical interfaces of a system are understandable, intuitive and usable [19]. The purpose of most of these techniques is to identify aspects in the proposed design that can affect the usability, and with this information, the development team can be able to fix the interfaces following the recommendations provided by the specialists in HCI or by potential users. However, although these techniques allow the identification of the aspects to be improved, only a reduced percentage of them let specialists obtain a numeric value about the usability of the system. The importance of quantifying the level of usability is the possibility to perform comparisons between software products of the same type. Likewise, a mechanism of this nature provides companies with a systematic procedure for evaluating the best option from several design proposals.

At present, the most recognized methods that quantify in number values the usability of a software system are the questionnaire and the application of usability metrics [17], specifically, the measurements provided by the ISO/IEC 9126 standard [7]. However, both techniques are time-consuming and demanding in human resources, since that the participation of a representative number of users is required [8]. The questionnaires as evaluation tools are based on subjective data and are an attempt for determining the user satisfaction with the current level of usability of the system. The purpose is to measure the participants' opinions concerning their perception of usability. On the contrary, the metrics are based on objective data and are measurements of the participants' performance such as scenario completion time and successful scenario completion rate. The software metrics as well as the usability questionnaires are focused on analyzing the user's perspective or behavior, and can present accurate results only if these are applied to a representative amount of people. Nevertheless, in contrast to these two commonly used user-oriented methods, we propose the adoption of a specialist-oriented inspection technique to quantify the usability. In this study, we describe an experimental case study in which a variant of the heuristic evaluation is applied to a real scenario to obtain quantitative data about the usability of a web application. The advantage of this method in relation to other techniques is that the assessment process is entirely conducted by specialists in the field of HCI and the participation of users is not required. The results establish that this variant of the traditional heuristic evaluation approach provides appropriate feedback about the usability of a software system, and allows the comparison between different design proposals.

The paper is structured as follows. In Sect. 2, we present the new usability methodological assessment process that was adopted for the conduction of this experimental case study. In Sect. 3, we describe the research design of this research. In Sect. 4, we discuss the results of the usability evaluation. Finally, in Sect. 5 the conclusions and future works of this research work are established.

2   A New Heuristic Evaluation Process

The Nielsen's traditional approach [14] to carry out heuristic evaluations does not establish well-defined steps that can guide the usability inspection process. Despite this, some guidelines are indicated in the original proposal [10]:

- Each evaluator must examine the graphical system interfaces individually, to determine if all elements meet certain design principles called "heuristics". In case the established heuristics are not accomplished, the findings must be cataloged as design problems in a predefined template by the inspectors.
- Once the individual evaluations have been performed, the findings must be consolidated in a single list of problems. For this activity, the team must organize a discussion session in which each identified issue is analyzed. According to traditional guidelines, one of the team members must work as a moderator to conduct the meeting and allow specialists to provide their opinion about the problematic aspects of the design that were identified. The purpose of this activity is to define the final list of problems as well as the positive aspects of the proposed graphical system interface.
- Subsequently the evaluation team must proceed to rate the severity of each usability problem that was considered for inclusion in the final list of problems according to the following scale [16] (Table 1):

Table 1. Severity ratings for usability problems

Rating	Description
0	I do not agree that this is a usability problem at all
1	**Cosmetic problem only:** need not be fixed unless extra time is available on project
2	**Minor problem:** fixing this should be given low priority
3	**Major problem:** important to fix, so should be given high priority
4	**Catastrophe:** imperative to fix this before product can be released

In addition to the previous conduction directives, some other considerations are established by the traditional approach:

- Only from three to five specialists are required to identify the greatest number of usability problems that are present in an interface design. According to a statistical study conducted by Nielsen and Landauer [13], the participation of three professionals from the field of HCI is enough to find the 75% of the most critical issues of usability. Based on a comprehensive analysis of several projects in which a software product was developed, Nielsen determined that the optimal number of heuristic evaluators to maintain a positive benefit/cost ratio is between three and five people, considering that each specialist represents a cost for the project, in the same way that the fixes of the interface design, because of the usability problems that were not noticed in early phases. However, in contrast to this theory, there are studies [1,22] that establish that three or five evaluators are still a small and insufficient number to determine the most of all the design issues.

- The participants of the heuristic evaluation process must be specialists in the field of Human-Computer Interaction. According to the traditional approach, this method is cataloged as a usability inspection method [12], in which is required the participation of professionals with a high degree of expertise in usability. The evaluation must be conducted by experts who due to their extensive experience can easily identify real problems in the interface design, without performing a subsequent verification along with representative users of the software system. The accuracy of the results will be strongly related to the profile of the inspectors that are part of the assessment team. For this reason, Nielsen states that only three specialists are required for this evaluations, since they handle a high degree of mastery in the topic that are able to identify by themselves individually the most issues. Many pieces of research that have a critical stance against the optimal number of evaluators proposed by Nielsen, is because of they have not involved in their experimental case studies specialists in HCI. Only from three to five evaluators are required, but as long as these professionals are experienced.

- The heuristic evaluation demands the use of a set of usability principles to identify design problems. Although the assessment methodology does not establish the employment of certain specific list of guidelines, Nielsen has defined ten usability principles for user graphical interfaces [15], which are nowadays the most relevant and used proposal. Nevertheless, some authors [4,18,20] have identified that these heuristics fail to cover relevant aspects when they are used to evaluate emerging categories of software products such as mobile apps, videogames, medical applications, educational systems and others. Despite being widely recognized and used, the original approach of principles was developed with a focus on web and desktop applications. In this sense, there are features that the new types software applications present with significant impact on the usability, but which are not considered by the Nielsen's ten traditional heuristics. For this reason, there are new heuristic proposals in the literature that are oriented to evaluate in a more effective way the usability of the software products from different domains.

In a previous work conducted by Granollers [5], a new approach based on the traditional method was developed. The purpose of this study was to establish a methodological procedure with basis on the heuristic evaluation process with which specialists be able to determine in numerical values the level of usability of a specific software product. In many cases, companies use to request to their development teams, several graphical interface designs to subsequently make a selection of the best option. However, given the original nature of the heuristic technique, there is no way to determine in which degree an interface proposal is better than other for a particular system. Specialists in HCI are in need of a framework whose usage can provide with a measurement (i.e., from 0 to 100) of the ease of use of a graphical user interface. In this way, it would be possible to compare different designs and determine how far is one from another. Until the moment, the questionnaires are the only methods that allow professionals to obtain a numeric value about the level of usability of a software interface [21]. However, these subjective measurement tools have been designed to capture the users' opinion concerning their perception of usability. There is a lack of a mechanism exclusively limited to specialists in HCI for the quantitative estimation of the usability degree of a software product.

The new assessment procedure involves having in addition to the heuristics, a checklist. Unlike the heuristic principles which are broad rules of design, the checklist items are particularly specific to a degree in which the inspectors can quickly identify whether they are met or not, with a simple and fast review of the interface [9]. For this academic scenario, given that the software product to be assessed was a transactional web site, we employed the 64 items of the checklist developed by Granollers to evaluate the usability of E-commerce web applications [2]. Each item of this proposal has been elaborated as a YES/NO question, in which the evaluator would have to answer positively or negatively, depending if the guideline is accomplished or not. The first fourteen items of the entire proposal related to the category of *"Need Recognition and Problem Awareness"* are shown in Table 2. The complete list of heuristic items can be found in the research performed by Bonastre and Granollers [2].

Table 2. Heuristics related to the category of *Need Recognition and Problem Awareness*

ID	Heuristic item
Subcategory: *Search and navigation tools*	
SNT01	Is the navigation obvious enough throughout the related sections?
SNT02	Does the website use a clear user-logical hierarchy of categories to classify products and to find them?
SNT03	Do Category Pages include appropriate filters or facets by features?
SNT04	Does the website provides a search box to locate products and information?
SNT05	Does the search have advanced features that allow for a limit to a great variety of criteria (features, categories, etc.)?
SNT06	Does the search engine provide the customer's expected results?
SNT07	Are there appropriate mechanisms, such as filters or facets to refine the search results?
SNT08	Do the pages and sub-pages provide orientation elements?
SNT09	Does the checkout process includes a progress indicator at the top of the checkout pages?
SNT10	Does the website clearly display the "call to action button"?
SNT11	Does the website includes a site map?
Subcategory: *Stimulating the desire to purchase*	
SNT12	Does the website use elements to draw customer's attention?
SNT13	Are the new products or special offers prominently advertised?
SNT14	Does the website shows the number of current visitors?

Given the nature of the heuristic items, the proposed scoring system establishes that each usability guideline must be rated individually by the evaluators, from 0 to 4 according to the level of achievement of the design rule, in which 0 is referred to a total non-compliance of the heuristic item, and 4 to the opposite scenario, the total accomplishment of the rule. In order to assign a score, the evaluators must attempt to answer to each of the 64 YES/NO questions. If the answer is affirmative, it would mean the guideline is completely fulfilled, and therefore, the proper score for the item would be 4. In the same way, if the answer is negative, it would mean there is a total infringement of the rule, and therefore the score must be 0. In cases in which there is not the possibility to answer YES or NO because of a partial accomplishment of the design rule, the inspector should rate between 1 and 3 according to the level of fulfillment.

Once each evaluator has rated the entire list of heuristic items, all the scores are added with the purpose to obtain a value between 0 and 256. This resulting value must be divided by the number of heuristic items that were considered for the assessment (64 items for this particular scenario), obtaining an final individual value by specialist. Finally, the individual scores must be averaged to

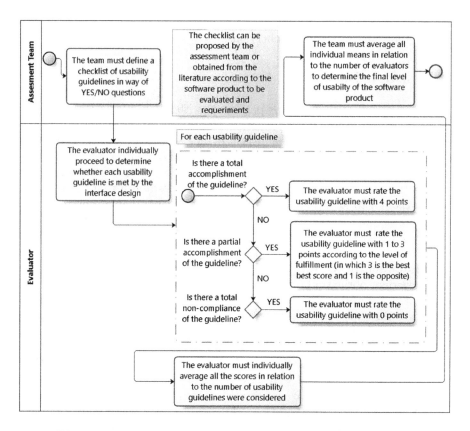

Fig. 1. Heuristic evaluation process to quantify the level of usability

obtain a resulting value. Equation 1 summarizes the way to calculate the level
of usability of a software product.

$$\text{level of usability} = \frac{\sum\limits_{i=1}^{m}\left(\dfrac{\sum\limits_{j=1}^{n} s_{ij}}{n}\right)}{m} \tag{1}$$

where:

- s_{ij} is the assigned score by each evaluator "i" in each heuristic "j".
- n is the number of heuristic items.
- m is the number of evaluators.

The assessment process that quantifies the level of usability is represented in
Fig. 1. In this image, we have defined two organizational entities, the 'assessment
team' and the 'evaluator' in order to divide the collaborative activities from the
individual assignments respectively. The most valued aspect in contrast to the
traditional evaluation approach is the possibility to obtain a global score about
the level of usability of an interface design, which allows specialists to perform
comparisons between versions, or determine in which degree the software product
is better than the competing applications.

3   Research Design

This experimental case study was performed with the participation of six specialists in Human-Computer Interaction (HCI). The professional profiles are
described in Table 3. For the conduction of this study, the general recommendation of Nielsen regarding the proper number of evaluators was taking into
consideration. The specialists were divided into two teams of three members
each, according to the traditional guidelines which establish that three evaluators are enough to identify the most relevant problems that are present in an
interface design [11]. Each team evaluated a different E-Commerce web site with
the purpose to determine if the results from diverse assessments can be compared. Team A employed the quantitative approach of the heuristic evaluation
method to evaluate the usability of Amazon.com. In the same way, Team B
used the variant of the traditional technique to evaluate BestBuy.com. First, the
participants were informed about the new framework that they should follow
to perform the evaluation. Although all the team members were experienced
in the traditional method, they had no prior knowledge about this particular
way of conducting a heuristic evaluation due to this is a recent proposal and
because of the small modifications we have performed to the original methodology. Once the participants were familiar with the new evaluation approach,
they proceeded to evaluate the corresponding web applications according to the
usability guidelines proposed by Granollers for user experience evaluation in E-
Commerce websites [2]. This particular set of design guidelines is structured as a
checklist and consists of YES/NO questions with which a specialist could easily

perform a usability inspection. In addition, this proposal corresponds entirely with the assessment framework in the sense that each principle can be rated with 0 or 4 depending on whether the heuristic is entirely infringed or totally fulfilled, and from 1 to 3 in case it is partially implemented.

Table 3. Profile of the usability specialists

Evaluator	Profile	Team
Evaluator 1	Ph.D. in Informatics Engineering	A
Evaluator 2	Master in Software Engineering	A
Evaluator 3	Student of a Postgraduate Master Program in Informatics	A
Evaluator 4	Ph.D. in Software Engineering	B
Evaluator 5	Master in Computer Systems	B
Evaluator 6	Student of a Postgraduate Master Program in Informatics	B

The set of heuristics proposed by Bonastre and Granollers [2] to evaluate the usability and user experience of E-Commerce web sites is composed of 64 design principles that have been grouped into six categories according to the aspect that the heuristics are addressing:

1. Need Recognition and Problem Awareness [14 guidelines]
2. Information Search [6 guidelines]
3. Purchase Decision Making [13 guidelines]
4. Transaction [10 guidelines]
5. Post-Sales Services Behavior [4 guidelines]
6. Factors that affect UX during the whole purchase process [17 guidelines]

Both inspection teams A and B used this set heuristics together with the assessment framework described in Sect. 2 to determine the level of usability of the assigned software products. The teams were allowed to establish their own organization and distribution of the activities of the entire evaluation process, under the supervision of the authors, that verify all the steps are followed in the correct order and no step is omitted. Finally, once the teams consolidated their findings, the results were exposed to a comparative analysis.

4 Analysis of Results

The usability evaluation was conducted by both teams following the assessment framework as well as the scoring system explained above. It is important to highlight that the purpose of this study is focused on the evaluation process and the way in which this methodological procedure provides support to quantify the level of usability of the web applications. There is no particular intention on the part of the authors to improve the usability of the mentioned systems or to describe in detail the design aspects that must be fixed.

Tables 4 and 5 presents the results of the scoring process for Amazon.com and BestBuy.com respectively. Likewise, Figs. 2 and 3 show the analysis of usability of the web applications for each of the three evaluators.

Table 4. Average of the usability scores assigned in each category to Amazon.com

	1	2	3	4	5	6
Evaluator 1	3.00	3.33	3.08	3.30	3.75	3.43
Evaluator 2	2.93	3.00	3.46	3.40	3.50	3.00
Evaluator 3	2.86	3.50	3.38	3.10	4.00	3.29
Average	**2.93**	**3.28**	**3.31**	**3.27**	**3.75**	**3.24**
Standard deviation	**0.07**	**0.25**	**0.20**	**0.15**	**0.25**	**0.22**

Table 5. Average of the usability scores assigned in each category to BestBuy.com

	1	2	3	4	5	6
Evaluator 1	2.79	3.00	2.31	2.70	3.75	3.00
Evaluator 2	2.71	2.67	2.62	2.50	3.75	2.79
Evaluator 3	2.71	2.83	2.77	2.40	4.00	2.86
Average	**2.74**	**2.83**	**2.56**	**2.53**	**3.83**	**2.88**
Standard deviation	**0.04**	**0.17**	**0.24**	**0.15**	**0.14**	**0.11**

The results establish that the assessment methodology as well as the proposed heuristics together are a reliable tool to evaluate the usability. It is possible to observe that the scoring is uniform. The highest standard deviation in both cases is 0.25 (in the first scenario) and 0.24 (in the second case), which means that overall protocol produces consistent results. From the perspective of the psychometrics [3], a research tool can be considered reliable if it provides similar results under consistent conditions. If the instrument is applied several times over the same subject or object, essentially the same results would be obtained in each attempt.

The global results about the usability of each E-Commerce web site can be calculated by a simple average of all the individual scores. The Fig. 4 is a comparative graph that highlights the usability levels in each aspect that the selected heuristics address. Finally, we averaged the values in each category to determine the final score for the usability for each system (3.29 for Amazon.com and 2.90 for BestBuy.com).

The analysis establishes that both applications present a proper degree of usability given that the reached score is above the median value (2.0). However, in both cases there are opportunities for improvement, especially in the case of BestBuy.com which obtained the lowest score in the qualification. Nevertheless, the current level is appropriate for both systems, and explains in certain degree

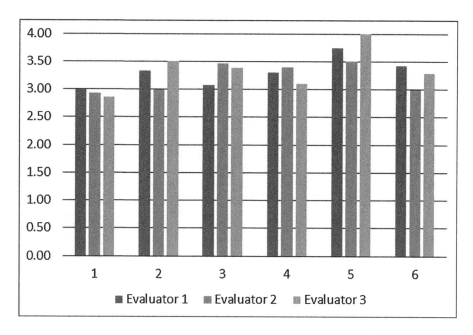

Fig. 2. Results of the evaluation in each category performed to Amazon.com

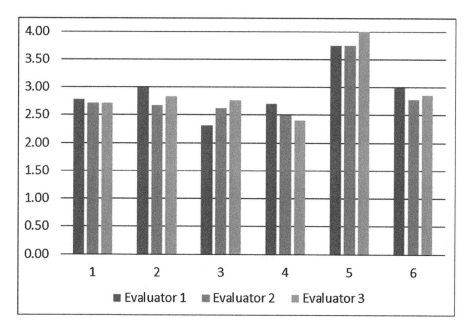

Fig. 3. Results of the evaluation in each category performed to BestBuy.com

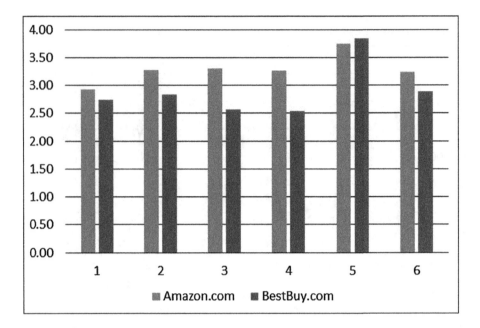

Fig. 4. Comparative analysis of the usability between BestBuy.com and Amazon.com

their success and strong presence in the market. The fact that the heuristics are grouped by aspects is another advantage that the model provides, in the sense that specialists can notice the features that are aligned with the design guidelines and those which need restructuring. The approach also allows comparisons between different design proposals or software systems. In this particular scenario, we determined that Amazon.com is more usable and provides a better user experience than BestBuy.com. Given the proper degree of detail in which the results are offered by the assessment model, the development team can identify immediately the aspects of the interfaces that require of a redesign process to match or exceed the usability level of other software products, and even from the competitors.

5   Conclusions and Future Works

The usability has become an essential quality attribute in which the majority of companies are currently concerned. Nowadays, the success of any technological product that is released to the market, will depend significantly on the degree of ease of use, how intuitive is the artifact to operate, and the level of the users' satisfaction after their first interaction with the product. The field of Software Engineering is not the exception, and the software products have to be usable enough to transcend, especially in the E-Commerce domain, in which there are several web sites for the same purpose.

Given the need for verifying whether a web application meets appropriate levels of usability, some techniques have emerged and are employed to analyze not only the usability, but also the user experience (UX). However, the disadvantage of these evaluation methods is that most of them have a qualitative approach and only allow the identification of usability problems based on personal impressions of specialists or end users about the graphical interfaces. Nevertheless, these methods do not provide a numeric value about the level of usability of the system. The questionnaires and the software metrics are the only approaches which quantify the ease of use, but these methods are time-consuming and demand the participation of a representative sample of people. In this study, we are discussing the results of applying a variant of the traditional heuristic evaluation process to identify the level of usability of E-Commerce web applications. The advantage of using an inspection method to measure the usability according to the literature, is the possibility to obtain accurate results with the involvement of only three specialists in HCI. In this experimental case study, this hypothesis was proven. Six specialists from the academia were requested to evaluate a web site employing a specific approach proposed by Granollers that quantifies from 0 to 4 the global level of usability of a software system. This new methodological proposal establishes the use of a checklist in which each item must be rated to be then averaged with the score of all the heuristics. The analysis establishes this assessment framework is a reliable tool in the sense that all results were uniform. The proposed methodology as well as the selected heuristics allow obtaining consistent results, since that the use of these evaluation tools provide similar scores when the same conditions are met. However, it is still necessary to perform more studies especially when the specialists have a different background or profile. In this research, all the specialists that were involved belonged to the academic field. A future work would be the analysis of the results when a specialist from the software industry are considered in the evaluation. Likewise, it would be important to discuss if there exists a relation between the obtained results and the cultural profile of the evaluators, and if the results are significantly different when more specialists participate of the evaluation. In order to generalize the conclusions, more studies are required. However, this study is intended to demonstrate that the presented methodology is reliable and can provide both quantitative and qualitative results.

References

1. Alroobaea, R., Mayhew, P.: How many participants are really enough for usability studies? In: Proceedings of 2014 Science and Information Conference, SAI 2014, pp. 48–56 (2014)
2. Bonastre, L., Granollers, T.: A set of heuristics for user experience evaluation in e-commerce websites. In: Proceedings of the Seventh International Conference on Advances in Computer-Human Interactions (ACHI 2014), pp. 27–34 (2014)
3. Davis, F.D.: Perceived usefulness, perceived ease of use, and user acceptance of information technology. MIS Q. **13**(3), 319–340 (1989)
4. Díaz, J., Rusu, C., Collazos, C.A.: Experimental validation of a set of cultural-oriented usability heuristics: e-commerce websites evaluation. Comput. Stand. Interfaces **50**, 160–178 (2017)

5. Granollers, T.: Validación experimental de un conjunto heurístico para evaluaciones de ux de sitios web de comercio-e. In: 2016 IEEE 11th Colombian Computing Conference (CCC), pp. 1–8, September 2016
6. Hasan, L., Morris, A., Probets, S.: Using Google analytics to evaluate the usability of e-commerce sites. In: Kurosu, M. (ed.) HCD 2009. LNCS, vol. 5619, pp. 697–706. Springer, Heidelberg (2009). https://doi.org/10.1007/978-3-642-02806-9_81
7. ISO: Software engineering – product quality – part 1: Quality model. Standard ISO 9126–1:2001, International Organization for Standardization, Geneva, Switzerland (2001)
8. Lewis, J.R.: IBM computer usability satisfaction questionnaires: psychometric evaluation and instructions for use. Int. J. Hum.-Comput. Interact. 7(1), 57–78 (1995)
9. de Lima Salgado, A., Agostini do Amaral, L., de Mattos Fortes, R.P., Hortes Nisihara Chagas, M., Joyce, G.: Addressing mobile usability and elderly users: validating contextualized heuristics. In: Marcus, A., Wang, W. (eds.) DUXU 2017. LNCS, vol. 10288, pp. 379–394. Springer, Cham (2017). https://doi.org/10.1007/978-3-319-58634-2_28
10. Nielsen, J.: Finding usability problems through heuristic evaluation. In: Proceedings of the SIGCHI Conference on Human Factors in Computing Systems, CHI 1992, pp. 373–380. ACM, New York (1992)
11. Nielsen, J.: Usability Engineering. Morgan Kaufmann Publishers Inc., San Francisco (1993)
12. Nielsen, J.: Usability inspection methods. In: Conference Companion on Human Factors in Computing Systems, CHI 1994, pp. 413–414. ACM, New York (1994)
13. Nielsen, J., Landauer, T.K.: A mathematical model of the finding of usability problems. In: Proceedings of the INTERACT 1993 and CHI 1993 Conference on Human Factors in Computing Systems, CHI 1993, pp. 206–213. ACM, New York (1993)
14. Nielsen, J., Molich, R.: Heuristic evaluation of user interfaces. In: Proceedings of the SIGCHI Conference on Human Factors in Computing Systems, CHI 1990, pp. 249–256. ACM, New York (1990)
15. Nielsen Norman Group: 10 usability heuristics for user interface design (1995). https://www.nngroup.com/articles/ten-usability-heuristics/. Accessed 14 Jan 2016
16. Nielsen Norman Group: Severity ratings for usability problems (2012). https://www.nngroup.com/articles/how-to-rate-the-severity-of-usability-problems/. Accessed 14 Jan 2016
17. Paz, F., Pow-Sang, J.A.: Current trends in usability evaluation methods: a systematic review. In: 2014 7th International Conference on Advanced Software Engineering and its Applications, pp. 11–15, December 2014
18. Paz, F., Paz, F.A., Pow-Sang, J.A.: Experimental case study of new usability heuristics. In: Marcus, A. (ed.) DUXU 2015. LNCS, vol. 9186, pp. 212–223. Springer, Cham (2015). https://doi.org/10.1007/978-3-319-20886-2_21
19. Paz, F., Pow-Sang, J.A.: A systematic mapping review of usability evaluation methods for software development process. Int. J. Softw. Eng. Appl. 10(1), 165–178 (2016)
20. Quiñones, D., Rusu, C.: How to develop usability heuristics: a systematic literature review. Comput. Stand. Interfaces 53, 89–122 (2017)
21. Sauro, J., Lewis, J.R.: Quantifying the User Experience: Practical Statistics for User Research, 1st edn. Morgan Kaufmann Publishers Inc., San Francisco (2012)
22. Zapata, C., Pow-Sang, J.A.: Sample size in a heuristic evaluation of usability. In: Software Engineering: Methods, Modeling, and Teaching, vol. 37 (2012)

Can We Distinguish Pragmatic from Hedonic User Experience Qualities with Implicit Measures?

Kathrin Pollmann[1(✉)], Victoria Sinram[2], Nora Fronemann[2], and Mathias Vukelić[1]

[1] Institute of Human Factors and Technology Management IAT,
University of Stuttgart, Stuttgart, Germany
kathrin.pollmann@iat.uni-stuttgart.de
[2] Fraunhofer Institute for Industrial Engineering IAO, Stuttgart, Germany

Abstract. User Experience research mainly makes use of self-reported measures to assess the user's experience when using a technical product, especially regarding hedonic product qualities. Our study investigates whether pragmatic and hedonic qualities can be distinguished using two types of implicit measure: behavioural and neurophysiological. Participants interacted with two different software tools designed to emphasize hedonic and pragmatic qualities, respectively. Their implicit evaluations of the two prototypes were examined with the Approach Avoidance Task (AAT) and simultaneous electroencephalographic recordings (EEG), using snapshots from the interaction scenarios. While the AAT showed no differences, the analysis of event-related EEG potentials revealed differences around 300 ms after stimulus presentation. Significant higher cortical activity in the frontal cortex was found for approach tendencies towards snapshots taken from the hedonic prototype interaction. Higher potentials in the parietal (motor) cortex were found for avoidance tendencies towards the pragmatic prototype. The findings show that hedonic and pragmatic user experience qualities can be distinguished based on neuroelectrical data.

Keywords: User Experience · Implicit measures · Approach Avoidance Task Electroencephalography · EEG

1 Introduction

While the early years of research in the field of human-technology interaction (HTI) were spent around terms like 'efficiency' and 'usability of products' in the past two decades a more holistic perspective on the interaction between humans and technical products was established. Summarized under the term "User Experience" (UX) this perspective includes traditional factors, e.g. usability, functionality or task efficiency, as well as additional qualities emphasizing emotional components of the experience with technology [1]. The ISO 9241-210 on human-centered design defines UX as "all the users' emotions, beliefs, preferences, perceptions, physical and psychological responses, behaviors and accomplishments that occur before, during and after use." [2]. Hassenzahl narrows this general definition down, focusing on particular

© Springer International Publishing AG, part of Springer Nature 2018
A. Marcus and W. Wang (Eds.): DUXU 2018, LNCS 10918, pp. 509–527, 2018.
https://doi.org/10.1007/978-3-319-91797-9_37

aspects of emotions and their incorporation into products and devices to promote positive experiences. He defines UX as a "momentary, primarily evaluative feeling (good-bad) while interacting with a product or service" [3]. He adds that a good UX is constituted by the fulfillment of psychological needs [4, 5]. Furthermore he proposes a dichotomous model of UX which "assumes that people perceive interactive products along two different dimensions" [6]: hedonic and pragmatic qualities. Hedonic qualities emphasize the emotional and affective components of a product, such as the enhancement of a person's psychological wellbeing [1, 3, 7]. Pragmatic qualities, on the other hand, describe instrumental, task-related qualities of a product, meaning that the product shall serve as means to an end for the user to manipulate the environment [3, 6, 7].

To assess UX, researchers mainly make use of self-reported measures that rely on introspection, the ability of the user to have explicit access to and be able to verbalize their recently gained experiences with a product. Although these methods can provide valuable insight to the user's perception of a technical product, self-reported data can be distorted by biases. It is questionable whether users can indeed access their experiences through introspection as required by questionnaires, surveys and interviews. According to Nosek et al. [8] humans often lack the motivation, opportunities, abilities or even awareness to report their experiences. This appears to be especially true for hedonic product qualities, as the emotional state constantly changes over time. Emotions are of more subjective nature and therefore more difficult to grasp than pragmatic components of a product. Even if the users are capable of introspection, their answers can still be incorrect in that sense that they do not reflect the true experience [9]. Answers can be distorted either unintentionally or intentionally (faking), due to cognitive biases such as *attribute substitution* [10] and *social desirability* [11]. Self-reported measures could hence benefit from an extension with complementing methods to enable a deeper and more detailed understanding of the user's experience.

Therefore, the present paper investigates the feasibility of using behavioral and neurophysiological implicit measurement tools, as they are commonly used in psychological and neuroscientific research, to obtain additional, valuable information about the UX while interacting with a software tool. On the one hand, this study serves as a feasibility study to examine the value and usefulness of the two approaches (and the combination of both) for UX assessment. On the other hand, the study also investigates whether implicit methods can be used to distinguish hedonic from pragmatic components of UX. The latter is especially relevant in order to draw conclusion about which aspects of a product need to be adjusted to arrive at an overall positive UX. While pragmatic qualities can be assessed with traditional usability methods, measuring the hedonic qualities seems to be a challenge UX researchers are still struggling with. The present study examines whether implicit methods can close this gap.

2   Implicit Methods for UX Assessment

Implicit methods have first been suggested in different fields of psychology as a tool to infer participants' implicit cognitive processes and attitudes based on behavioral measures and without requiring any (self-assessment) effort. In implicit measures the construct is "inferred through a within-subject experimental design: [by] comparing behavioral performance between conditions (e.g. different primes)" [8].

The first prominent tool for implicit assessment was the Implicit Association Test (IAT) by Greenwald et al. [12]. The IAT is based on the assumption that memory content is organized as associative networks in the human brain [13], and that the activation of a certain piece of information automatically results in the activation of associated information within the network. The test requires participants to characterize two different types of target stimuli (e.g. adjectives and pictures of animals) by two categories (e.g. cute/scary, cat/spider) by pressing two different buttons. It is assumed that participants respond faster if two concepts that are strongly associated with each other (e.g. scary and spider) are represented by pressing the same button. The IAT has widely been used to uncover racist tendencies that manifest themselves on fast reaction times (RTs), i.e. fast button presses, for positive adjectives and white people/negative adjectives and black people, respectively (as compared to positive/black, negative/white) [12]. A first attempt to apply the IAT in HTI has been made by Devezas and Giesteira [14] who compared implicit and explicit measures. They assessed the aesthetic judgment (*valence* and *self-identification*) of eight participants for pictures of different interfaces by using the Picture Implicit Association Test (P-IAT). Two bipolar scales were used as explicit measures for valence and self-identification. The authors reported a "medium" correlation ($r = .42$, $p > 0.05$) between implicit and explicit measures and suggest that the IAT can be used as "a complementary or substitutive method for self-report measures" [14] (p. 15).

Another implicit method is the Affect Misattribution Procedure (AMP). In this test participants are briefly (≈ 200 ms) presented with emotionally-loaded prime pictures followed by pictures of Chinese characters [15]. Their task is to rate the Chinese character – and not the picture – as positive or negative via a button press. Chinese characters are assumed to be of no special (emotional) meaning for participants who are not Chinese native speakers. Studies have shown that a participant's attitude towards the preceding prime can be inferred by their response to the Chinese character [16]. The AMP has been applied in an HTI context once to assess participants' implicit attitudes towards robots [9]. In this study, participants were presented with videos of moving or static robots. Afterwards, the participants received a questionnaire as explicit and the AMP as implicit measures. The study revealed a negative tendency towards a certain type of robots, which did not show in the self-reports.

Schmettow et al. [17] investigated participants' implicit associations and attitudes towards technical devices, such as computers or tablets with the Stroop priming task: Participants had to react to colored words of three categories (hedonic, utilitarian and geekism), after seeing a picture of a technical devices. Afterwards, their need-for-cognition level was compared with the latencies retrieved from the task. The study's main aim was to examine the suitability of the Stroop priming task to extend current methods. The authors concluded from the results that "implicit [...] methods [...] may serve to better understand the nature of rating scales in HCI, and give more direct access to users' spontaneous associations and affects" [17].

Lastly, implicit attitudes can be assessed by the Approach-Avoidance Task (AAT) by Rinck and Becker [18]. The task requires participants to respond to a certain picture format (landscape or portrait) by pulling or pushing a joystick. The pictures used for this task are emotionally loaded, i.e. positively or negatively valenced [19, 20]. The test is based on the assumption that pulling (arm flexion) is linked to a positive interpretation of the stimulus (approach tendency), while pushing (arm extension) is related to a negative interpretation of a stimulus (avoidance tendency). Reaction times should hence be shorter for compatible trials (pull positive picture/push negative picture) than for incompatible trials (pull negative/push positive). While it has been shown that the AAT is suitable to assess social anxiety, phobias or alcohol disorders [18, 19], to our knowledge it has never been applied in HTI.

Neurophysiological methods provide another interesting approach to assess implicit information about the user's evaluation of a technical product through monitoring of cognitive and affective processes in the brain. In medical contexts, electroencephalography (EEG) has long been used for this purpose. The method also shows high application potential in HTI research, as EEG devices are portable and allow the user to obtain a rather comfortable position. EEG assesses the temporal and spatial characteristics of brain activity by monitoring electromagnetical processes, i.e. the synchronization processes between populations of thousands of neurons at the cortical surface of the brain [21]. The time course of brain processes can be determined on a millisecond scale, which allows us to study the precise timing of emotional or affective user reactions in the form of event-related potentials (ERPs) [21]. The ERP reflects a stereotypical electrophysiological response to a given stimulus by indicating the latency and amplitude potential of the recorded EEG signal. Thus, with the help of ERPs, the different stages (or components) of emotional stimulus processing and perception can be objectively studied. Generally, the early latency components of the ERPs (N100, P100, N200, i.e. peaks around 100 and 200 ms after stimulus onset) indicate processes, which are involved in the initial perception and automatic evaluation of emotional stimuli. Later ERP components, i.e. later than 300 ms after stimulus presentation, are supposed to reflect higher-level cognitive processes and conscious evaluation of the stimulus. Potential changes around the P300 components are modulated by stimulus-response compatibility [22]. Hence they might play an important role in the evaluation processes taking place in the brain during the behavioural implicit tasks described above.

3   Methods and Materials

Until now, neither of the two implicit measurement approaches, behavioral and neurophysiological, have specifically been used to assess UX in HTI contexts. Our study combines the AAT with EEG recordings to evaluate pragmatic and hedonic qualities of a technical product. This requires dichotomous stimulus material that stimulates the participant's experience of pragmatic and hedonic qualities. We decided to use a simple software tool as the basis of the stimulus material, as the evaluation of software is the most common use case for UX evaluations. Two version of the software tool were developed – one that only provides pragmatic qualities and one that, on top, provides hedonic UX. As proposed by Hassenzahl [3], hedonic qualities presuppose the existence of pragmatic qualities to evolve. It is hence important that the two version of the tool contain the same estimation of pragmatic qualities, but differ in their estimation of hedonic qualities.

As all behavioral implicit tests are based on a prompt response of the participant to a stimulus, it is impossible to carry out these tests with film recordings or even free interaction tasks. Although UX is certainly created through the interaction process and clearly requires some active engagement of the user over a period of time, none of the studies described above feature any interaction with a product. We therefore decided to take a similar approach as Strasser and colleagues [9], but included a prior interaction period instead of video presentation. Participants interact with the two software tools first. Then snapshots from the interaction are used for the implicit test that is carried out immediately after the interaction. Participants' implicit affective reactions to the snapshots of the pragmatic and hedonic software tools, respectively, are recorded through the behavioral response (RTs) and the collateral brain activity (ERPs). It is expected that participants show stronger approach tendencies to the emotionally loaded hedonic software tool than to the solely pragmatic version. Avoidance tendencies are presumed of similar magnitude for both versions, as they provide the same solid level of pragmatic qualities. We presume that the stronger approach tendencies for snapshots taken from the hedonic prototype are also reflected in the event-related electrical potentials accompanying the behavioral response and that, on this basis, implicit reactions to hedonic and pragmatic product qualities can be distinguished on a neuronal level.

3.1 Stimulus Material for Pragmatic and Hedonic UX

The stimulus material was based on the work by Sonnleitner and colleagues [23] who designed different versions of an ideation software to address different human needs, thus increasing the perceived positive UX. While the brainstorming of new ideas is a common task in work environments, the proposed ideation software has some short-comings. It can be assumed that every user has an individual stamping of unfulfilled needs in a certain context and that this needs profile consists of several needs rather than one. A technical product which addresses a single need can thus not fully adhere to the needs of the user. As the focus of the present study lies within the dissociation of pragmatic and hedonic qualities, the original ideation software was redesigned and two prototypes were developed: One that highlights only the pragmatic qualities of the software, and a second one that empathizes the hedonic qualities.

Initial Concept for Pragmatic and Hedonic Prototypes of an Ideation Software.
The two prototypes are note applications that enable and support people in the generation of ideas. The tools provide them with a predetermined set of topics, one after another on individual screens, and guides them through the ideation process like a wizard. On each screen the user is provided with the means to collect up to nine ideas. The prototypes were realized with Axure RP 8 [24], a prototyping tool for web applications.

The pragmatic prototype was created with a clean and clutter-free outer appearance using greyscale color, following the design of an unobtrusive graph paper. The user can write down ideas in designated text boxes and continue by pressing the "next topic"-button. It thus supports an efficient goal achievement, thereby creating good usability estimates, but no other (positive) emotions and experiences.

Table 1. Design elements included in the hedonic prototype and related experience categories.

Experience category	Design elements in the hedonic prototype
Receiving feedback	*Pop-ups:* pop-ups displayed at random during the interaction give feedback on the user's ideas
Appreciation	*Favorite color:* participants can choose their favorite color (personalization) *Greeting:* participants are greeted with their whole name to create a connection between the product and the user *Individual attribute:* participants can choose an individual, motivating attribute to go along with their name ("lateral thinker", "ideator"; "think big") *Thank you message and praise:* in the pop-up they do not only receive general feedback, but also praise for their good work
Prioritizing	*Priority post-its:* participants can prioritize the ideas they generated by coloring the post-its in red, yellow and green for major, medium & lower importance
Exchanging ideas	*Send maps via e-mail:* participants are able to distribute their idea maps via e-mail which enables them to work together with others
Stimulating experience	*Send maps via e-mail:* by means of sending own ideas to others who can work on the same map, it is possible to socialize and to improve ideas through feedback of others
Finishing a task	*Text fields:* these give participants space for their ideas *'Ready' button:* participants are able to tick ideas they are done with and thereby disable the text field

The hedonic prototype can be described as a variant of the pragmatic prototype that includes additional design elements to promote positive emotions and experiences. To arrive at these design elements, the experience categories by Zeiner et al. [25] were used. In their study, they examined the emergence of positive experience in work contexts through experience interviews. The resulting experience reports were grouped into experience categories that describe underlying themes of positive work experiences, e.g. receiving feedback, exchanging ideas or finishing a task. Table 1 describes the design elements included in the hedonic prototype and the related experience categories.

Iterative Development of Pragmatic and Hedonic Prototypes. In order to ensure that the manipulation of hedonic and pragmatic qualities was successful, users and UX experts were involved in the iterative development of the prototypes. Five user tests (3 females, $M_{Age} = 23.8$, $SD = 1.64$) were performed to evaluate the pragmatic and hedonic qualities of the prototypes and they were iteratively changed and improved. Afterwards, four UX experts (1 female; $M_{Age} = 32.8$, $SD = 2.99$) assessed the final versions of both prototypes and their feedback was used to apply the last modifications.

Both, users and experts completed the process of idea generation with the two prototypes and were asked to assess the pragmatic and hedonic qualities of the two prototypes on a quantitative and qualitative level for each prototype individually.

Quantitative feedback was provided by filling in two questionnaires after the interaction with each prototype: the *User Experience Questionnaire*" (UEQ) by Laugwitz et al. [26] and the *meCUE* questionnaire by Minge and Riedel [27]. The UEQ assesses pragmatic and hedonic components of UX through 26 items on a 7-point Likert scale, grouping them into the six factors *attractiveness, perspicuity, efficiency, dependability, stimulation*, and *novelty* [26]. In addition to the UEQ, 2 modules of the meCUE were added to assess positive and negative emotional experience during the interaction in more detail. To collect qualitative feedback, the users were instructed to describe their actions and their experience during the interaction with the prototypes using the *think aloud*-method. Experts completed their review on their own and provided their qualitative feedback through a review report. Moreover, both, users and UX experts, were asked to map the design elements of each prototype to the experience categories. Based on the results of the user tests and expert reviews the initial versions of the two prototypes were iteratively improved (e.g. reduced topics and interaction duration, adjusted design elements) to arrive at the finale stimulus material design.

Selected screenshots of the final versions of the two prototypes are presented in Figs. 1 and 2. In total, 64 snapshots were taken from the interaction with each prototype to serve as stimuli for the AAT.

3.2   Measurement Tools

Behavioral Implicit Measures. To implicitly assess the user's reaction to the two prototypes on a behavioral level the AAT was used [18]. The task requires the participants to respond by pulling or pushing a joystick to a certain picture format, either landscape or portrait. According to Laugwitz and colleagues [19] as well as Wiers et al. [20], every stimulus of this test contains a valence ranging from positive to negative. This notion makes the AAT most suitable for the goal of our study to differentiate between pragmatic and hedonic product qualities. As mentioned earlier, the pragmatic prototype could neither be regarded as negatively valenced stimulus material, nor as as positively valenced as the hedonic prototype. The AAT is the only implicit psychological tests which allows for a differentiation on a valence scale rather than the dichotomous distinction between positive and negative. Rinck and Becker [18] have shown good Spearman-Brown reliability estimates ($r = .71$) for the AAT. The defined time-windows of the trial structures are very suitable for simultaneous event-related EEG recordings.

Two sets of 64 snapshots taken from the interaction with the pragmatic and hedonic prototype, respectively, were used as picture stimuli for the AAT. Each set contained 32 different pictures in both, landscape and portrait format. A pull movement with the joystick increased the size of the snapshot and a push movement decreased the picture size. Each picture remained visible until the joystick was moved to its maximum positions, then it vanished.

Each participant completed two runs of the AAT with this set of in total 128 pictures. In one run participants were instructed to pull portrait and push landscape pictures. In the second run they had to push portrait and pull landscape pictures. Thus, as shown in Table 2, congruent and incongruent trials were created for the pragmatic and hedonic prototype. Congruent trials are all trials were participants had to

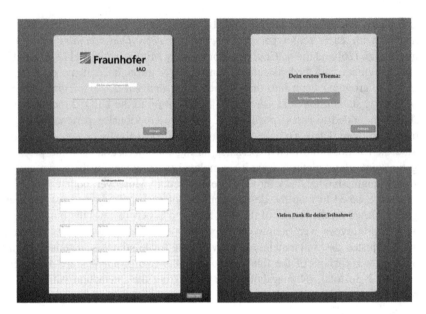

Fig. 1. Screenshots of the pragmatic prototype (from top left to bottom right): Welcome screen and field for entering your name, topic introduction, note pad for ideation, final "thank you"-message.

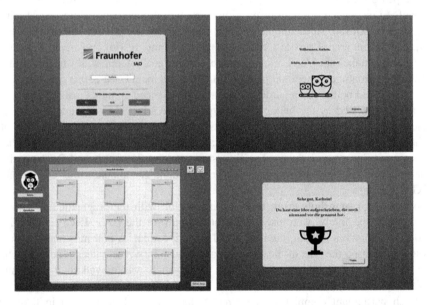

Fig. 2. Screenshots of the hedonic prototype (top left to bottom right): Welcome screen including entering your name and selecting favorite color, personal "welcome"-message, note pad for ideation, feedback pop-up with personalized praise. (Color figure online)

approach/pull the strongly positively valenced snapshots taken from the hedonic prototype or avoid/push the less positively valenced pictures from the pragmatic prototype. Incongruent trials were avoiding/pushing hedonic prototype pictures and approaching/pulling pragmatic prototype pictures. The two runs were counterbalanced across participants.

Neurophysiological Implicit Measures. Scalp EEG potentials were recorded (BrainAmp, [28]) from 32 positions, with Ag/AgCl electrodes (actiCAP, Brainproducts GmbH, Germany) from: Fp1, Fp2, F7, F3, Fz, F4, F8, FC5, FC1, FCz, FC2, FC6, T7, C3, Cz, C4, T8, CP5, CP1, CP2, CP6, TP10, P7, P3, Pz, P4, P8, PO9, O1, Oz, O2, PO10. The left mastoid was used as common reference and EEG was grounded to Cz. All impedances were kept below 20 kΩ at the onset of each session. EEG data was digitized at 1 kHz, high-pass filtered with a time constant of 10 s and stored for off-line data analysis by using the Brain Vision Recorder Software [28]. All EEG data analysis was performed with custom written or adapted scripts in MATLAB®.

Explicit Measures. Besides the implicit methods, two explicit measures were used, mainly to conduct a manipulation check for the two prototypes. We made use of a combination of the meCUE [27] and UEQ [26], as the two questionnaires have already shown to yield good results in the user test during the development of the prototypes.

Table 2. Overview of AAT trials.

| | | Prototype | |
		Hedonic	Pragmatic
AAT trials	Congruent	Approach/pull	Avoidance/push
	Incongruent	Avoidance/push	Approach/pull

3.3 Experimental Design

The experiment was conducted as a within-subject design featuring *prototype* as independent variable and *behavioral implicit evaluation, neuroscientific implicit evaluation*, and *explicit evaluation* as dependent variables with two levels each: *hedonic* and *pragmatic*. The orders of the two prototypes and the two AAT runs were counterbalanced across participants to control for order effects.

3.4 Participants

43 participants were recruited via the participant database of the Fraunhofer Institute for Industrial Engineering IAO in Stuttgart, Germany, as well as via Facebook and flyers. As EEG data was only recorded for 12 participants, we only include the data of those participants in the present paper, in order to guarantee the comparability between behavioral and neurophysiological implicit measures. Participants were between 20 and 29 years old ($M_{Age} = 24.42$ years, $SD_{Age} = 2.93$ years). Participants received a compensation of 15€ for their participation.

3.5   Set-Up and Procedure

Participants had to complete three parts of the experiment: the interaction, the explicit UX evaluation and the AAT (see Fig. 3). At the beginning of the session, participants were briefed about the setup of the EEG and the tasks. After giving their informed consent, participants received the instructions for the 15-min interactions with the prototypes. After each interaction, the participants filled in the UEQ and meCUE questionnaires. Subsequently, they completed the two runs of the AAT. At the end of the study the participants were debriefed about the actual construct assessing, their implicit attitudes on the prototypes.

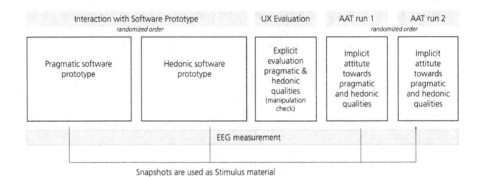

Fig. 3. Experimental procedure.

4   Results

4.1   Subjective Evaluations

For the manipulation check data from both questionnaires were combined. For the analysis of the complete data set an exploratory factor analysis was conducted, in order to obtain clusters of variables among the two merged questionnaires. A principal component analysis was performed with a *Direct Oblimin rotation* and a *Kaiser Normalization*. Eigenvalues equal to or greater than 1 were extracted and yielded six factors accounting for the 32 variables of both questionnaires. The majority of the questionnaire items loaded on the first two factors reflecting *hedonic qualities* and *pragmatic qualities*, which can be deduced by the content of the items they incorporate. Thus, the items were grouped according to these two factors for all further analysis. For the manipulation check the questionnaire ratings on the two defined factors were compared between the pragmatic and hedonic prototype using a Wilcoxon signed-rank test for dependent samples. For all statistical analyses the confidence interval was set to 95%.

The statistical analysis revealed that for both prototypes *pragmatic qualities* were rated significantly higher than *hedonic qualities* (hedonic prototype: $p = .28$, pragmatic prototype: $p = .003$; Fig. 4). It can be noted that *pragmatic quality* ratings were generally rather high, which shows that pragmatic aspects of the prototypes were perceived as intended. While for both prototypes *pragmatic qualities* were rated on a similar level (p = .609), the hedonic prototype received significantly higher ratings for *hedonics qualities* (p = . 008).

4.2 Behavioral Data

Reaction times (RT) were recorded for congruent and incongruent trials for each picture shown in the AAT for the pragmatic and hedonic prototype. RTs smaller than 200 ms (i.e. the minimum of time for humans needed to perceive a stimulus and execute the appropriate action) and >1500 ms (very slow and not intuitive reactions) were removed from the data sets as outliers. We also excluded those trials from the analysis for which participants responded incorrectly.

For the data analysis, we grouped all trial of each of the four conditions (Table 2) together and the mean RTs were calculated. Based on the means, the AAT difference scores were calculated for the pragmatic and hedonic prototype separately. The AAT difference score is calculated by subtracting push-trials from pull-trials. If participants did indeed experience the hedonic prototype as positive, the difference score should be negative, as pull-trials (congruent/approach) are carried out more natural and faster than push-trials (incongruent/avoidance). As no specific approach or avoidance behavior is expected for pragmatic prototype pictures, it can be assumed that participants should be equally fast for congruent (push) and incongruent (pull) trials.

The medians of the calculated difference scores for the hedonic and pragmatic prototype pictures were entered into a Wilcoxon signed-rank test for dependent samples. The statistical analysis did not reveal any difference ($Mdn_{hedonic}$ = 45.5,

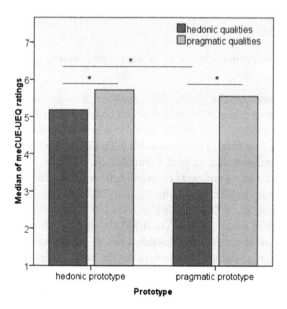

Fig. 4. Comparison between the medians of participants' rating for hedonic and pragmatic qualities of the hedonic and pragmatic prototypes. Statistically significant differences are marked with a *.

Mdn ~pragmatic~ = .5; p = .41). A slightly smaller variance of the difference scores could be observed for pragmatic prototype pictures (compare Fig. 5).

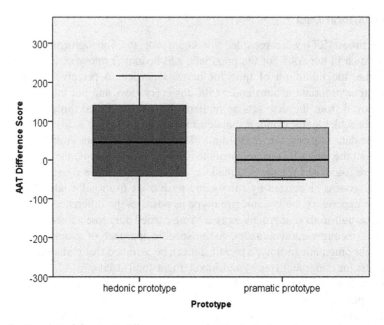

Fig. 5. Boxplot of the AAT difference scores for the hedonic and pragmatic prototypes.

4.3   EEG Data

The ERP analysis investigates the brain processes underlying approach and avoidance tendencies.

EEG Pre-processing. Similar to the AAT analysis, in a first step all congruent and incongruent trials were grouped together for both prototypes. In total, we arrived at four groups of EEG signals. The EEG signals were detrended, zero-padded and re-referenced to mathematically liked mastoids [21]. For the ERP analysis only the time period following the presentation of the stimulus (in our case the picture) is of relevance. Therefore, all trials were cut into several time windows and only the time epochs ranging from −200 ms to 0 ms and from 0 msc to 1000 ms were further analyzed. The 200 ms before the onset of the stimulus provide a baseline which shows the participant's brain activity in a state of rest. The 1000 ms after the stimulus onset is the time window that contains the emotional reaction towards the picture presentation.

Before investigating statistical difference in the data, several pre-processing steps were taken to remove artifacts from the environmental noise or other physiological processes from the data. To do so, we first band-pass filtered the EEG signals between 0.5 to 22 Hz, using a first order zero-phase lag FIR filter. We removed epochs from further analysis when they contained a maximum deviation above 200 μV in any of the frontal EEG channels (Fp1 and Fp2). For the remaining epochs we further performed an independent component analysis (ICA) using the logistic infomax algorithm as implemented in the *EEGlab* toolbox [29]. We removed cardiac, ocular movement and muscular artefacts based on visual inspection of the topography, times course and power spectral intensity of the ICA components [30].

Estimation of ERP Components. To study the dynamical changes of the ERP, artefact-free trials were baseline-corrected by subtracting the mean amplitude during the baseline interval (−200 ms to 0 ms). The result is a signal that only represents the emotional reaction of interest and not the general brain activity as present in the baseline. For each participant we then took all the trials in each of the four groups and calculated the average over all trials. The average provides us with a signal representing the time course of the electrical activity in the 0 ms to 1000 ms time window and at any electrode position on the head (Fig. 6). ERP analysis takes a closer look at the characteristic peaks of these averaged signals, also refered to as *components*. It is of special interest to examine the time points and location in which the peaks occur in order to draw conclusions about the underlying cognitive and emotional processes.

To investigate which time windows of interest (TOIs) are most likely to reveal differences between approach and avoidance tendencies for the hedonic and pragmatic prototype, we computed the signed r^2-value (difference score) as implemented in the *Berlin Brain-Computer Interface (BBCI)* toolbox [31]. The difference score was calculted as an average over all participants for each EEG channel and time point for both prototype picture categories (Figs. 7A and 8A).

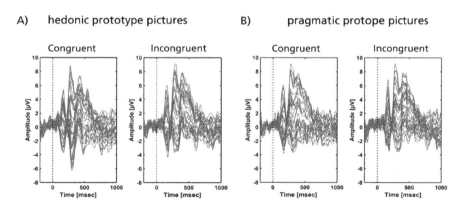

Fig. 6. Temporal dynamics of event-related potentials (ERPs) following the presentation of hedonic (A) and pragmatic prototype pictures (B). The plots show the grand-averaged waveforms (averages across all participants) of ERPs visualized as butterfly plots. Every line represent a single EEG-channel and the dashed black line indicates the beginning of the picture presentation.

For hedonic prototype pictures the strongest difference between congruent and incongruent trials were present at the two TOI, 270 to 400 ms and 410 to 600 ms. Both TOI include a prominent component of the ERP distribution which, in EEG

hedonic prototype pictures

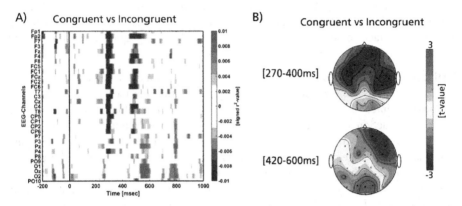

Fig. 7. Spatio-temporal dynamics of event-related potentials (ERPs) during the hedonic picture presentation: (A) The plot shows the spatial distribution of strongest separability between congruent and incongruent trials during the hedonic picture presentation. The 2-D graph represents the grand-averaged signed r^2-values analyzed for every time point (abscissa) for all EEG-channels (ordinate). The vertical black line represents the beginning of the picture presentation. The horizontal color bar indicates the signed r^2-difference between the congruent and incongruent trials. Note that strongest difference between congruent and incongruent trials were present at two time intervals: 270–400 ms and 410–600 ms after picture presentation. (B) The plots represent the t-value topographies differences for the first time interval [270–400 ms] and second time interval [410–600 ms] by comparing the congruent and incongruent trials. Electrode clusters, showing significant differences in the non-parametric randomization test, are indicated by filled black circles. Red color represents increase in negativity while blue represents decrease in negativity. (Color figure online)

research, is known as P300. For pragmatic prototype pictures the TOI of strongest separability were slightly different, but still also in the range of the P300 (300 ms to 390 ms and 410 ms to 490 ms).

Statistical Analysis of ERP Components. Within the defined TOI we statistically examined which EEG-channels show significant modulations due to picture presentation. To do so we compared the congruent and incongruent trials for both hedonic and pragmatic prototype pictures at every EEG position on the head. We used a separate multiple dependent sample t-test with a cluster-based, non-parametric randomization approach including correction for multiple comparisons [32, 33] as implemented in the *FieldTrip* toolbox [34]. The results of the statistical analysis are visualized by heat maps as shown in Figs. 7B and 8B.

For hedonic prototype pictures statistically significant differences between congruent (approach) and incongruent (avoidance) trials were found in the prefrontal and motor cortices during the first TOI, where higher positive activation was observed for avoidance behavior. In the second TOI stronger negativity was observed for congruent trials.

pragmatic prototype pictures

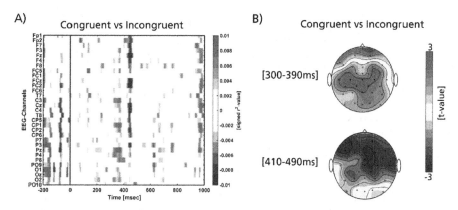

Fig. 8. Spatio-temporal dynamics of event-related potentials (ERPs) during the pragmatic picture presentation: (A) The plot shows the spatial distribution of strongest separability between congruent and incongruent trials during the hedonic picture presentation. The 2-D graph represents the grand-averaged signed r2-values analyzed for every time point (abscissa) for all EEG-channels (ordinate). The vertical black line represents the beginning of the picture presentation. The horizontal color bar indicates the signed r2-difference between the congruent and incongruent trials. Note that strongest difference between congruent and incongruent trials were present at two time intervals: 300–390 ms and 410–490 ms after picture presentation. (B) The plots represent the t-value topographies differences for the first time interval [300–390 ms] and second time interval [410–490 ms] by comparing the congruent and incongruent trials. Electrode clusters, showing significant differences in the non-parametric randomization test, are indicated by filled black circles. Red color represents increase in negativity while blue represents decrease in negativity. (Color figure online)

For pragmatic prototype pictures different activation patterns were revealed: We found a positivity for congruent trials (avoidance) in the motor cortex, followed by a lower negativity in the prefrontal and motor cortex than incongruent trials during the second TOI.

5   Discussion and Future Work

The results indicate that – on a subjective level – our attempt to create a more hedonic experience with the hedonic prototype was successful. The pragmatic prototype was rated as equally pragmatic, but significantly less hedonic. The expected approach and avoidance tendencies towards the hedonic and pragmatic prototype, respectively, could not be demonstrated by the AAT, but were reflected in the neurophysiological data. EEG results provide first indications that different brain processes take place when participants are confronted with snapshots of the two prototypes. Hence it is possible to differentiate the users' reaction to hedonic and pragmatic qualities of a software by statistically comparing the neurophysiological processes underlying approach and avoidance tendencies to hedonic and pragmatic stimuli.

The ERP time course reflects different stages of cognitive information processing starting already at 200 ms after the onset of the picture presentation for both hedonic and pragmatic prototype pictures. Looking at the most discriminative TOIs, we found that hedonic and pragmatic prototype pictures showed highest discrimination during the time window of the P300 component, i.e. around 300 ms after stimulus onset. P300 is sensitive to arousal-related effects of emotional picture processing [35] and is also involved in processing the compatibility between a given stimulus and the performed response [22]. For the congruent hedonic pictures, we found an earlier involvement of the prefrontal cortex which is believed to be involved in the control of emotional or affective behavior in humans [36, 37]. For pragmatic images, only the central brain regions, i.e. the motor cortex, were activated as a first response to the stimuli. Our findings most likely could indicate that for the processing of the hedonic images more higher-order cognitive process are involved for matching the compatibility between a given stimulus and the given movement instruction. It should be noted that the cognitive processing described above takes place before the explicit conscious evaluation of the stimulus and the performance of the pull or push behavior.

While the neurophysiological implicit method yielded promising results, it remains to be discussed why the behavioral measures failed to detect the same differences. It could be argued that the AAT is simply not suitable for UX research. However, the present study does not seem extensive enough to support this claim. In previous studies making use of the AAT the dichotomous stimulus material was always strongly valenced – either positive or negative. The hedonic prototype of our study was clearly on the positive side of the valence spectrum. It is, however, difficult to characterize the pragmatic prototype as negative as it scores high on pragmatic quality, which – even if not as positive as the hedonic prototype – should induce a more or less "neutral" emotional experience. This is in line with Tuch and colleagues who argue that only bad pragmatic qualities causes negative affective reactions [38, 39]. Thus, it is possible that the two prototypes were not different enough from each other to produce distinguishable difference scores for the AAT. Still, the differences we detected in the EEG data suggest that hedonic and pragmatic product features are processed differently in the brain and that this difference just did not manifest itself in all participants' push and pull behavior (also notice the larger standard deviation for the hedonic prototype of the AAT difference scores in Fig. 5 as compared to pragmatic). To clarify this matter, a third prototype should be developed that offers low pragmatic as well as hedonic qualities. Comparing snapshots from the interaction with this new prototype and the hedonic prototype might shed light into whether the AAT is the wrong method for UX assessment or just not sensitive enough to differentiate between implicit attitudes towards hedonic and pragmatic product features.

Overall, the present study can be regarded as a good start to investigate the potential of applying implicit measures in UX research. The results would, however, benefit from a sample size extension. Additional research could also try different stimulus material and possibly also different behavioral implicit tests to widen our understanding of the psychological constructs underlying hedonic and pragmatic product qualities and provide more evidence for the usefulness of implicit measures to assess UX.

References

1. Bargas-Avila, J.A., Hornbæk, K.: Old wine in new bottles or novel challenges: a critical analysis of empirical studies of user experience. In: Proceedings of the 2011 Annual Conference on Human Factors in Computing Systems, pp. 2689–2698. ACM, New York (2011). https://doi.org/10.1145/1978942.1979336
2. ISO: Ergonomics of human-system interaction – Part 210: Human-centered design for interactive systems 2.15 (ISO 9241-210 2.15) (2009)
3. Hassenzahl, M.: The thing and I: understanding the relationship between user and product. In: Blythe, M.A., Monk, A.F., Overbeeke, K., Wright, P.C. (eds.) Funology: From Usability to Enjoyment, pp. 31–42. Kluwer Academic Publishers, Dordrecht (2003)
4. Hassenzahl, M.: User experience (UX): towards an experiential perspective on product quality. In: Proceedings of the 20th International Conference of the Association Francophone d'Interaction Homme-Machine, pp. 11–15. ACM, New York (2008). https://doi.org/10.1145/1512714.1512717
5. Sproll, S., Peissner, M., Sturm, C., Burmester, M.: UX concept testing: integration von user experience in frühen Phasen der Produktentwicklung. In: Brau, H., Diefenbach, S., Göring, K., Peissner, M., Petrovic, K. (eds.) Usability Professionals 2010. Jahresband 2010 der Workshops der German Usability Professionals' Association e.V, pp. 1–6. Fraunhofer Verlag, Stuttgart (2010)
6. Hassenzahl, M.: The hedonic/pragmatic model of user experience. In: Law, E.L.-C., Vermeeren, A., Hassenzahl, M., Blythe, M.A. (eds.) Towards a UX Manifesto. COST294-MAUSE Affiliated Workshop, Lancaster, UK, pp. 10–14 (2007)
7. Väänänen-Vainio-Mattila, K., Roto, V., Hassenzahl, M.: Towards practical user experience evaluation methods. In: Meaningful Measures: Valid Useful User Experience Measurement (VUUM), pp. 19–22 (2008)
8. Nosek, B.A., Hawkins, C.B., Frazier, R.S.: Implicit social cognition: from measures to mechanisms. Trends Cogn. Sci. (2011). https://doi.org/10.1016/j.tics.2011.01.005
9. Strasser, E., Weiss, A., Tscheligi, M. (eds.): Affect misattribution procedure: an implicit technique to measure user experience in HRI. In: Proceedings of the 7th Annual ACM/IEEE International Conference on Human-Robot Interaction – HRI 2012. ACM (2012)
10. Kahneman, D.: Maps of bounded rationality: a perspective on intuitive judgment and choice. In: Frangsmyr, T. (ed.) Les Prix Nobel: The Nobel Prizes, pp. 449–489. Nobel Found, Stockholm (2002)
11. Adams, S.A., Matthews, C.E., Ebbeling, C.B., Moore, C.G., Cunningham, J.E., Fulton, J., Herbert, J.R.: The effect of social desirability and social approval on self-reports of physical activity. Am. J. Epidemiol. **161**(4), 389–398 (2005). https://doi.org/10.1093/aje/kwi054
12. Greenwald, A.G., McGhee, D.E., Schwartz, J.L.K.: Measuring individual differences in implicit cognition. The implicit association test. J. Pers. Soc. Psychol. **74**(6), 1464 (1998)
13. Collins, A.M., Loftus, E.F.: A spreading-activation theory of semantic processing. Psychol. Rev. **82**(6), 407 (1975)
14. Devezas, T., Giesteira, B.: Using the implicit association test for interface-based evaluations. In: ACHI 2014: The Seventh International Conference on Advances in Computer-Human Interactions, pp. 9–16 (2014)
15. Payne, B.K., Cheng, C.M., Govorun, O., Steward, B.D.: An inkblot for attitudes: affect misattribution as implicit measurement. J. Pers. Soc. Psychol. **89**(3), 277 (2005). https://doi.org/10.1037/0022-3514.89.3.277
16. Payne, K., Lundberg, K.: The affect misattribution procedure. Ten years of evidence on reliability, validity, and mechanisms. Soc. Pers. Psychol. Compass **8**(12), 672–686 (2014)

17. Schmettow, M., Noordzij, M.L., Mundt, M. (eds.): An implicit test of UX: individuals differ in what they associate with computers. In: Proceeding of the Thirty-First Annual CHI Conference on Human Factors in Computing Systems - CHI 2013. ACM (2013)

18. Rinck, M., Becker, E.S.: Approach and avoidance in fear of spiders. J. Behav. Ther. Exp. Psychiatry **38**(2), 105–120 (2007). https://doi.org/10.1016/j.jbtep.2006.10.001

19. Heuer, K., Rinck, M., Becker, E.S.: Avoidance of emotional facial expressions in social anxiety: the approach–avoidance task. Behav. Res. Ther. **45**(12), 2990–3001 (2007). https://doi.org/10.1016/j.brat.2007.08.010

20. Wiers, R.W., Rinck, M., Dictus, M., van den Wildenberg, E.: Relatively strong automatic appetitive action-tendencies in male carriers of the OPRM1 G-allele. Genes Brain Behav. **8**(1), 101–106 (2009). https://doi.org/10.1111/j.1601-183X.2008.00454.x

21. Nunez, P.L., Srinivasan, R.: Electric Fields of the Brain: The Neurophysics of EEG. Oxford University Press, New York (2006)

22. Sebanz, N., Knoblich, G., Prinz, W., Wascher, E.: Twin peaks: an ERP study of action planning and control in coacting individuals. J. Cogn. Neurosci. **18**(5), 859–870 (2006)

23. Sonnleitner, A., Pawlowski, M., Kässer, T., Peissner, M.: Experimentally manipulating positive user experience based on the fulfilment of user needs. In: Kotzé, P., Marsden, G., Lindgaard, G., Wesson, J., Winckler, M. (eds.) INTERACT 2013. LNCS, vol. 8120, pp. 555–562. Springer, Heidelberg (2013). https://doi.org/10.1007/978-3-642-40498-6_45

24. Axure: Powerful Prototypes without Coding. https://www.axure.com/. Accessed 13 Dec 2017

25. Zeiner, K.M., Laib, M., Schippert, K., Burmester, M.: Identifying experience categories to design for positive experiences with technology at work. In: CHI 2016. Extended Abstracts (2016)

26. Laugwitz, B., Schrepp, T., Held, M.: Konstruktion eines Fragebogens zur Messung der User Experience von Softwareprodukten. In: Heinecke, A.M., Paul, H. (eds.) Mensch und Computer. im Strukturwandel, pp. 125–134. Oldenbourg Verlag, München (2006)

27. Minge, M., Riedel, L.: meCUE – Ein modularer Fragebogen zur Erfassung des Nutzungserlebens. In: Boll, S., Maaß, S., Malaka, R. (eds.) Mensch und Computer. Interaktive Vielfalt, pp. 89–98. Oldenbourg Verlag, München (2013)

28. Brain Products: Solutions for neurophysiological research. http://www.brainproducts.com/. Accessed 13 Dec 2017

29. Delorme, A., Makeig, S.: EEGLAB. An open source toolbox for analysis of single-trial EEG dynamics including independent component analysis. J. Neurosci. Methods **134**(1), 9–21 (2004)

30. Hipp, J.F., Siegel, M.: Dissociating neuronal gamma-band activity from cranial and ocular muscle activity in EEG. Front. Hum. Neurosci. **7**, 338 (2013)

31. Blankertz, B., Tangermann, M., Vidaurre, C., Fazli, S., Sannelli, C., Haufe, S., Maeder, C., Ramsey, L., Sturm, I., Curio, G.: The Berlin brain–computer interface: non-medical uses of BCI technology. Front. Neurosci. **4**, 198 (2010)

32. Maris, E., Oostenveld, R.: Nonparametric statistical testing of EEG-and MEG-data. J. Neurosci. Methods **164**(1), 177–190 (2007). https://doi.org/10.1016/j.jneumeth.2007.03.024

33. Maris, E., Schoffelen, J.-M., Fries, P.: Nonparametric statistical testing of coherence differences. J. Neurosci. Methods **163**(1), 161–175 (2007). https://doi.org/10.1016/j.jneumeth.2007.02.011

34. Oostenveld, R., Fries, P., Maris, E., Schoffelen, J.-M.: FieldTrip: open source software for advanced analysis of MEG, EEG, and invasive electrophysiological data. Comput. Intell. Neurosci. (2011). https://doi.org/10.1155/2011/156869

35. Foti, D., Hajcak, G.: Deconstructing reappraisal: descriptions preceding arousing pictures modulate the subsequent neural response. J. Cogn. Neurosci. **20**(6), 977–988 (2008)
36. Ernst, L.H., Plichta, M.M., Lutz, E., Zesewitz, A.K., Tupak, S.V., Dresler, T., Ehlis, A.-C., Fallgatter, A.J.: Prefrontal activation patterns of automatic and regulated approach–avoidance reactions–a functional near-infrared spectroscopy (fNIRS) study. Cortex **49**(1), 131–142 (2013)
37. Bechara, A., Tranel, D., Damasio, H., Damasio, A.R.: Failure to respond autonomically to anticipated future outcomes following damage to prefrontal cortex. Cereb. Cortex **6**(2), 215–225 (1996)
38. Tuch, A.N., Hornbæk, K.: Does Herzberg's notion of hygienes and motivators apply to user experience? ACM Trans. Comput.-Hum. Interact. **22**(4), 1–24 (2015)
39. Tuch, A.N., van Schaik, P., Hornbæk, K.: Leisure and work, good and bad. ACM Trans. Comput.-Hum. Interact. (2016). https://doi.org/10.1145/2994147

CHAI: Coding Heuristics for Assessing Intuitive Interaction

Daniel Reinhardt[✉], Jeremias Kuge, and Jörn Hurtienne

Chair of Psychological Ergonomics, University of Würzburg,
Oswald-Külpe-Weg 82, 97074 Würzburg, Germany
daniel.reinhardt@uni-wuerzburg.de

Abstract. An important pragmatic aspect of user experience is intuitive inter-action. Intuitive interaction is defined as the extent to which a product can be used by subconsciously applying prior knowledge, resulting in an effective and satisfying interaction using a minimum of cognitive resources. Despite earlier attempts, it is far from clear how to measure intuitive use on the level of single interactions. This paper reports on the development of CHAI: coding heuristics for assessing intuitive interactions based on observational analysis. An empirical study investigated the validity of the coding scheme in relation to other measures of intuitive use on the task and system levels. The results demonstrate that intuitive interaction assessed with CHAI is significantly related to reduced mental effort and higher perceived subjective consequences of intuitive use. The implications of this finding and plans for future research are discussed.

Keywords: Intuitive interaction · Observational analysis · Evaluation

1 Introduction

In the recent decade, intuitive interaction has been developing from a buzzword used by designers and marketers when talking about interactive technology to a specific field of HCI [1–3]. Due to the increasing digitalization of life and work, people with a wide variety of backgrounds and prior knowledge of technology need to interact with a wide range of electronic products on a daily basis. New electronic products sport advanced technology, and many inbuilt functions and services [4]. Designing for intuitive interaction of products, services and systems is one way of dealing with an aging society and could also be a step towards a more inclusive society. Intuitive interaction occurs when technology is familiar [5], when users do not have to think about their interactions, when they can use a system based on their gut feelings and when they do not have to explicitly learn how to use the system [6]. Formal definitions state that intuitive interaction allows users to effectively use products, services or systems based on the effortless and subconscious use of prior knowledge [7–10]. As intuitive use covers effectiveness, mental efficiency and satisfaction, it clearly describes pragmatic aspects of user experience, but it also includes hedonic aspects, for example, when the interaction is described as "magical" by the users (cf. [11]).

© Springer International Publishing AG, part of Springer Nature 2018
A. Marcus and W. Wang (Eds.): DUXU 2018, LNCS 10918, pp. 528–545, 2018.
https://doi.org/10.1007/978-3-319-91797-9_38

Even though intuitive use itself is difficult to measure because of its subconscious nature, its preconditions and consequences can be measured. Several methods for the evaluation of intuitive interaction have been proposed that examine in what way the interaction with a system is based on the subconscious application of prior knowledge. These methods often involve user observations [12] or the use of questionnaires [12, 13]. Other methods that assess the subconscious prior knowledge include the analyses of product familiarity [4] or image-schematic metaphors [14]. While these approaches are often very detailed, they are cumbersome to apply in practice and do not scale well to using more complex software and larger numbers of participants. To address these problems, his paper introduces CHAI, a simplified coding scheme for assessing intuitive use through user observation. The method is based on the observation method of [12]. To assess the usefulness and validity of CHAI, this paper also reports an empirical study that compares it with other measures of intuitive interaction.

2   Intuitive Interaction

Researchers across the world agree that prior experience is the leading contributor to intuitive use and that it is linked with technology familiarity [6, 8, 15–19]. Originating from an industrial design background, Blackler and colleagues from the Queensland University of Technology (QUT) in Australia stated the following definition based on an extensive review of the literature on creative thinking, intuitive decision making, memory and expertise, consciousness studies and education:

> Intuitive use of products involves utilizing knowledge gained through other experience(s). Therefore, products that people use intuitively are those with features they have encountered before. Intuitive interaction is fast and generally non-conscious, so people may be unable to explain how they made decisions during intuitive interaction [1, 8, 12].

The IUUI (Intuitive Use of User Interfaces) research group in Germany based their definition of intuitive use on a literature review of usability design criteria [20] and a series of interviews and workshops with users, and usability experts as well as an analysis of how software producers describe their products:

> Intuitive use is the extent to which a product can be used by subconsciously applying prior knowledge, resulting in an effective and satisfying interaction using a minimum of cognitive resources [3].

According to Blackler and Hurtienne [21] both definitions have in common that the subconscious use of prior knowledge (although it is phrased differently in each strand of the literature) serves as the prerequisite for intuitive use to happen. The definition of IUUI has additional requirements that relate intuitive use to the international standard ISO 9241-11, which provides criteria for the evaluation of usability: effectiveness, efficiency and satisfaction. Thereby, intuitive use fulfils the requirements of effectiveness, satisfaction and especially focuses on the cognitive (not motoric or temporal) efficiency of interaction. This is in line with recent psychological research in dual-process theories suggesting that the minimal demand on mental effort may be the primary feature to distinguish between system-1 (subconscious, automatic) and system-2 (conscious, controlled) thinking that underlies intuitive and non-intuitive use [22, 23].

The fastness of intuitive interaction as in the definition of [12] is considered as a typical correlate of the minimal demand on cognitive resources and the related enhancement of information processing speed [21, 22]. As a consequence, intuitive use can be assessed by examining the possibility of the subconscious application of prior knowledge when using technology. As this approach focusses on the precondition for intuitive use, another approach would be to focus on the consequences of intuitive use, especially measuring cognitive efficiency as the decisive factor (see Fig. 1).

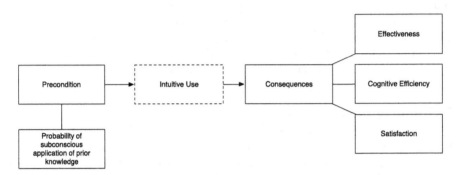

Fig. 1. Preconditions and consequences of intuitive use.

One instrument that measures the subjective consequences of intuitive is the QUESI (QUEStionnaire for the subjective consequences of Intuitive use). It consists of five subscales, which are derived from the above definition of intuitive use by the IUUI group [13]:

- Perceived mental effort (QUESI-M): Items in this subscale were derived from the precondition of the subconscious application of prior knowledge and its consequence of cognitively efficient interaction.
- Perceived achievement of goals (QUESI-G): Items in this subscale were derived from the consequence of effective interaction.
- Perceived effort of learning (QUESI-L): Items in this subscale were derived from the precondition of prior knowledge. When a user interface is based on the prior knowledge of its users, their effort of learning should be low when using the system for the first time.
- Perceived familiarity (QUESI-F): Items in this subscale were derived from the precondition of prior knowledge. When user interfaces are based on prior knowledge, they should lead to a higher familiarity in using the system.
- Perceived error rate (QUESI-E): Items in this subscale were derived from the consequence of effective interaction.

As cognitive efficiency can be seen as the distinctive consequence of intuitive use, mental effort questionnaires like SMEQ "subjective mental effort questionnaire" [24] or its German equivalent, SEA [25], can be used to assess the consequences of intuitive interaction. The SEA questionnaire, for example, consists of a vertical scale, on which users mark their experienced amount of mental workload between 0 and 220. In contrast to QUESI, which is focused on the system level, SEA allows to estimate intuitive use on the system and task levels. Although QUESI and SEA have been successfully applied in different contexts like GUI, gestural interaction and gaming [26–28], these are still subjective measures with all the associated implications like social desirability response bias. In contrast, the observational measure provided by the QUT researchers offers a more objective measure of intuitive use that can be applied on the system and task level alike and focuses on the precondition side of intuitive interaction. Besides video recording of the interaction with a product, the framework requires users to think aloud and a experts to meticulously analyze video recordings to estimate the probability of the subconscious application of prior knowledge [12]. The video coding uses a set of heuristics that we introduce in the following.

3   Development of Intuitive Use Heuristics

This section provides an introduction to the original heuristics of Blackler [12] and demonstrates how these heuristics informed the development of CHAI.

3.1   Original Coding Heuristics for Intuitive Use [12]

Through multiple experiments, the QUT research group developed a coding scheme based on heuristics inspired from the literature. The scheme is designed to assess whether prior knowledge is applied subconsciously and thus whether the precondition for intuitive use is met. For this purpose, users performing a set of tasks with a product and their concurrent thinking aloud is video-recorded [1, 12, 29, 30].

According to Blackler [12], the coding of the observed interactions can be done either feature- or event-based. A feature is a part of a product, which is distinct from others, has its own function, location and appearance and can be designed separately from other features (e.g., a print icon on software, a shutter button on a camera). A task is comprised of a certain number of different events and each event requires one or more interactions to complete. For instance, "entering age" is an event in a greater registration task and it includes multiple button click interactions. It is associated with a certain text box, which represents a feature. Then, all participants' interactions have to be coded either feature- or event-based. The coded variables are the correctness and type of use (see Fig. 2).

Correctness of Use
A "correct use" is considered to be one that is correct for the feature (e.g., shutter button) or event (e.g., button click) and also correct for the associated task or subtask (e.g., to disable an alarm clock via a click on the snooze button). A "correct for feature but inappropriate for task use" is taken as one when it is correct for the feature or event but not for the task or subtask. Or, put another way, a user knew what he wanted to do and used the right feature in doing so, but it was the wrong thing to do at the moment (e.g., the task required the user to set an alarm to wake up early, but he pressed the power-button instead and thus disabled the alarm clock). "Incorrect uses" are wrong for

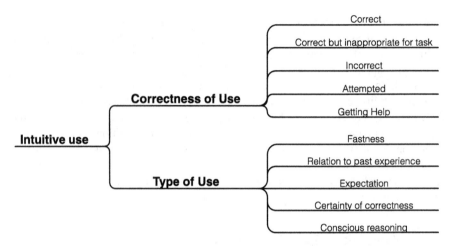

Fig. 2. The original coding heuristics used by Blackler [12].

feature or event, task and subtask. "Attempted uses" are taken when the product did not detect the use due to product failure (e.g., a user's touch that is not registered). When users get help from inbuilt help functions, product labels or the researcher, the use is counted as non-correct as well. However, this large number of graduations seem unnecessary with regard to the definition of intuitive use that only requires to assess whether the interaction was correct or not (see [3]).

Type of Use
As mentioned before, the subconscious application of prior knowledge serves as the precondition for intuitive interaction. In order to determine which uses are associated with the subconscious application of prior knowledge and thereby are likely to be intuitive, a series of main indicators is employed to assess the type of use. These indicators (e.g., fastness) are strongly related to the typical correlates of subconscious processing according to dual-process theories (see [22]).

Fastness
If users are able to locate and use a user interface element moderately fast, the associated feature or event could be coded as an intuitive use. Intuition is correlated with fastness of action initiation and actual interaction [12, 22, 31] and time to make a move can be used as a measure of thinking time [32]. When a user spends too much time in exploring other features that amounts to more than five seconds, that specific step is likely to be non-intuitive – according to Blackler [12].

Relation to Past Experience
During the concurrent thinking aloud, users would sometimes mention that a feature reminds them of something they used or have seen before which shows the evidence of existing prior knowledge. When there is a link to prior experience, it is likely that their action is intuitive.

Expectation

Due to the fact that prior knowledge is the prerequisite for intuitive interaction, it is also used to form expectations [12, 33]. When a user has explicitly worded a clear expectation that a feature would perform a particular function during the concurrent thinking aloud, his or her action is therefore likely to be intuitive.

Certainty of Correctness

Research suggests that intuitive use is accompanied by a certainty of correctness or confidence in a decision [12, 31]. Degree of confidence has been used in experiments as an index of intuition [12, 34, 35]. When participants seem certain about the function of a feature or event (even though they were not always correct) and were not just trying it out, it is likely that their action is intuitive [12].

Conscious Reasoning

Since the application of prior knowledge has to happen without conscious reasoning, the less reasoning was evident for each use, the more likely it can be counted as intuitive. Therefore, participants processing intuitively would not verbalize their reasoning during their actions while thinking aloud [12].

Blackler [12] suggests to code a use only as intuitive when the use was marked as a "correct use" and at least two of the five type-of-use indicators were available. This coding scheme was applied (sometimes with minor adaptions) by experts to code interactions with products such as remote controls, alarm clocks, microwaves, cameras, tangible interfaces and cars [12, 29, 36]. However, even in these systems with a relatively low level of complexity and a small number of possible interactions per task, the effort for coding is quite high. Another concern is that the need to provide a verbal protocol introduces a secondary task, which induced additional cognitive load and thus affect intuitive interaction (cf. [37]). In addition, the original coding scheme is rather vague and might lead to potentially false positives for "intuitive use" when only two indicators out of five are needed to code an event or a feature as "intuitive". For instance, imagine a user who does not speak very much (indicator of conscious reasoning is fulfilled) and is generally fast (<5 s) in clicking during the use of a feature or event (indicator of fastness is fulfilled). Then this feature or event would be mistakenly counted as intuitive, even when other heuristics like certainty of correctness are not fulfilled. For this reason, we suggest an adaptation of the coding scheme to suit more complex systems (e.g., websites, 3D modelling software) and remove uncertainties about the epistemic status of an intuitive use.

Naumann et al. [38] assume that the intuitive use of more complex technical systems is best measureable at the level of single interactions. In accordance with Blackler [12] interactions form the basic parts of an event. Depending on the user interface type, a single interaction can be regarded as a mouse click, touch event or manipulation of a tangible object. Accordingly, technical systems should be perceived as more intuitive, the higher the proportion of intuitive interactions. As the thinking aloud required for the original coding scheme may have an influence on the level of consciousness during the product use and as a secondary task could add to cognitive workload [37] the adapted CHAI heuristics were designed to work without the requirement of thinking aloud.

Inspired by the correctness and type-of-use indicators of Blackler [12], an interaction should be coded as intuitive when it is correct, fast and certain (see Fig. 3). Since the original heuristics of "relation to past experience", "conscious reasoning" and "expectation" are only accessible through verbal protocol, they were not considered in the new set of heuristics. Since a thinking-aloud protocol has not to be analyzed anymore, the overall coding effort is reduced using CHAI. Due to the fact that "fastness" and "certainty of correctness" always need to be present to code an interaction as intuitive, the new coding scheme is more conservative than the original one and might lead to less false positives. The adaptions in detail are explained in the following chapter.

3.2   CHAI: Coding Heuristics for Assessing Intuitive Interaction

Correctness of Use

We slightly simplified the conditions for the correctness of use by reducing the number of categories from five to four. A "correct interaction" is considered to be one that is correct for the user interface element (e.g., menu bar) and also correct for the associated task or subtask. "incorrect interactions" are wrong for the user interface element, task or subtask. "attempted" interactions are taken as ones, when the system does not register the use due to product failure (e.g., a touch event that is not registered). "Getting Help" interactions are, when the users are looking for help in the system or are provided with clues from the researcher. A "correct interaction" is only considered as an intuitive interaction, when the type of use indicators "fastness" and "certainty of correctness" given.

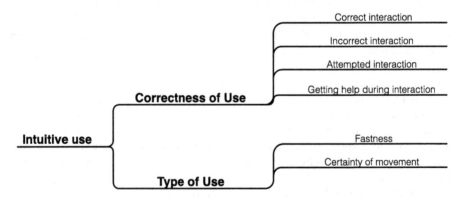

Fig. 3. CHAI: The refined coding heuristics to enable assessment of intuitive interaction.

Type of Use

Fastness

Here, the time interval of five seconds in the original heuristic was shortened to avoid disambiguates in interpreting an interaction as intuitive. We used Keystroke Level Modeling (KLM) to determine a suitable time threshold. KLM is a simple cognitive modeling technique that is used to estimate the times expert users need to accomplish a routine task using an interactive system. The estimations are done on the basis of generalized estimates of the associated cognitive and low-level motor operations. A cognitive operation like the user's decision where to click, for example, is estimated at an average of 1.2 s. The actual pointing of the mouse and clicking is estimated with 1.3 s. Homing the hands between keyboard and mouse is estimated with 0.4 s. Taking all these actions together, a routine click under normal circumstances should not exceed 3 s. Thus, if a user needs more than three seconds for an action, he is likely not acting intuitively based on his prior knowledge [39–42]. Due to the fact that elder adults use technology less intuitively and show in general slowed down perceptive, motoric and cognitive processes the "fastness" heuristic need to be adapted in this case [4]. When the heuristic is used with an another input device (e.g., tangible) the motoric part of the heuristic has to be adapted as well (see [41]).

Certainty of Movement
At this point, the determination of the user's interaction was assessed by an expert via looking at his hand or mouse movements. When participants seemed to move their mouse cursor or hand in a targeted manner towards the user interaction element without inter-ruptions, seeking or circular movements, it is likely that this interaction is intuitive [39].

The above heuristics have been initially applied by Horn [39] on two versions of a ticket machine. Interactions on a touch screen were recorded using a hand camera. The complexity and associated set of required interactions with the ticket machine represent already an increase in contrast to the products that have been evaluated before (e.g., remote control, alarm clock). The results showed significant positive correlations between the proportion of intuitive interactions (intuitive taps) and the total score of QUESI values, $r(26) = .39$, $p < .05$. The correlation shows that the interaction was perceived as more intuitive when there were more intuitive interactions identified by this method, however, the size of the effect was rather small.

The purpose of the following study described here builds on the results of Horn [39] and aims to investigate, whether the refined heuristics can be used to assess intuitive use in a rather complex system (i.e., 3D-modelling software). In this way, the following study examined the construct validity of the refined heuristics as a means to assess intuitive interaction for graphical user interfaces. To test the convergent validity, SEA and QUESI questionnaires were administered. For discriminant validity the total number of mouse clicks were calculated as a measure for motoric (physical) efficiency, which is not associated with the construct of intuitive use [3]. Correlation analyses were then carried out to support the validity of the proportion of intuitive clicks as a measure for intuitive use. Specifically, we expect higher correlations with SEA and QUESI than with number of clicks.

4   Methodology

4.1   Participants

A sample of 20 undergraduates was recruited from a German university campus. Four participants had to be excluded from data analysis due to not completed printed out questionnaires (two participants) and broken video footage (two participants). The remaining sample includes 16 participants (12 women, 4 men). The age of the participants ranged from 18 to 28 years ($M = 21.22$, $SD = 2.39$). All participants were students of human-computer interaction or media communication. None of the participants reported any level of prior experience with 3D modelling tools in general.

4.2 Apparatus and Measures

Participants used SketchUp Make 2017 in this experiment, a 3D modelling software (see Fig. 4). This software was chosen, because we wanted to test the heuristics in contrast to previous studies in a more complex environment covering interaction styles (e.g., clicking) that are widely used in industrial software. According to Akers et al. [43] creation-based software like 3D modelling software is very difficult to test and thus could provide a good benchmark for testing the refined heuristics. The experiment was conducted in a laboratory setting and recorded with the screen capture software Morae Recorder including mouse trajectories and click events. Mouse trajectories needed to be recorded to assess whether the heuristic "certainty of correctness" was given or not. In order to evaluate "fastness", experts judged whether each click (i.e., action is initiated when the cursor starts to move) was within a three second timeframe starting from the last click or pause if no click happened. The very first timeframe was analyzed from the beginning of the task. For the video analysis with the refined heuristics we used Morae Manager. A demographic questionnaire captured gender, age and items on prior experience inspired by the technology familiarity questionnaire of Blackler [12], namely the frequency of using 3D modelling software and the diversity of software features used. The QUESI was completed after each session and participants rated their mental effort using the SEA scale after each task.

4.3 Procedure

Upon arrival at the laboratory, participants were given a brief scripted verbal overview of the session. Then the participants were instructed to fill in the demographic questionnaire. Participants were then instructed not to talk and informed that there will be a retrospective interview utilizing captured video footage.

Then, a 3D model, representing a furnished bedroom, was preloaded in the application. The participants were given a scenario with three tasks. One task included the measurement of the height of a door (measuring task), another dealt with repositioning a bedside lamp (positioning task) and a third task required the rotation of a chair by 180° (rotation task). Thereby, each task required selecting and using basic features for 3D navigation and object manipulation that could be accessed via the toolbar in a logical, independent and goal-oriented manner. Each task consisted of three major parts: the adjustment of the current viewport in order to spot the corresponding object and target, the selection of the correct tool from the menu and, finally, the correct application of the tool.

All tasks were presented one at a time in printed form. The order of tasks was randomized across participants. Each task was designed to be solved within one minute by an expert user. The participants were not informed exactly how long it takes to solve the tasks and were not given any practice. This was necessary to meet our experimental aim to evaluate intuitive interaction using the refined heuristics and thereby allowing us to assess how participants apply their prior knowledge rather than how quickly they could be trained to use the application [12]. Once the participant read a task description and confirmed their understanding, they were asked to start the allocated task. If participants could not solve a task within five minutes, the experimenter asked participants to stop. Participants were then asked to rate their cognitive effort during the task on a SEA scale [25]. Then, participants read the description of the next task and the above process was repeated for the second and third task. After finishing the third task, participants completed the QUESI questionnaire [13]. Finally, participants were debriefed and thanked for their participation. The experiment took about twenty minutes in total.

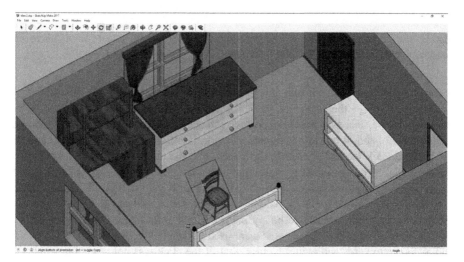

Fig. 4. This screenshot of SketchUp shows the 3D model used in the rotation task, in which participants were instructed to rotate the chair by 180° along its vertical axis.

4.4   Data Analysis

The video footage was coded by two independent raters using the CHAI coding heuristics for assessing intuitive interaction as outlined above. Because our goal was to examine whether the video-recorded interactions were intuitive or not, we also developed a process to apply the heuristics to the videos as efficiently as possible (i.e. the decision tree in Fig. 5). Since interactions with the investigated 3D modelling software were best characterized by mouse events, we focused on mouse clicks (left or right) and mouse movements for our analysis. Figure 6 gives an example of a possible analysis.

As an intuitive interaction requires a quick action interaction and therefore a delay in the performance indicates non-intuitive interaction, we looked at the first timeframe of three seconds to determine whether the participant was inactive (no action initiation; mouse cursor was not moved) or a click happened (see Fig. 5, First decision). The three

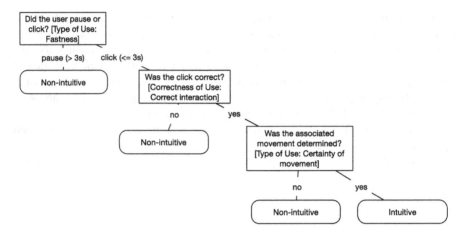

Fig. 5. The decision tree used in the experiment for distinguishing between intuitive and non-intuitive clicks based on the CHAI heuristics.

seconds timeframe was chosen due to KLM estimates for a click interaction as described above in the introduction of the refined heuristics. As a delay in action initiation can be seen as a wasted opportunity to act intuitively and thus the criterion of fastness is violated, it has to be counted as a non-intuitive click every time it happens.

When a click took place within this timeframe, the next step would be to check if the click was correct or not (Fig. 5, second decision). Clicks were registered as correct when their outcome moved the participant closer to a valid system status associated with their task goal while not verbally calling on external assistance. For this purpose, the experimenter identified the "happy path" (cf. [44]), the basic course of action, as well as alternative paths. These paths were used to decide whether a click was targeted and adequate towards achieving the task goal. If the click was not correct in respect of these paths, the click was counted as non-intuitive (Fig. 6A, steps 3 and 4). Finally, if the click was fast and correct, the certainty of the mouse movement was examined (Fig. 5, third decision). When the mouse cursor's path was evaluated as unsteady and serpentine by the experts, the click was not counted as an intuitive click (Fig. 6A, Step 5). If, instead, the cursor was moved in a straight path without major deviations, the certainty heuristic was fulfilled and the click was registered as intuitive (Fig. 6A, Step 6). Once a click was classified as intuitive or non-intuitive, the next three-second timeframe was analyzed and the above process repeated until the end of the recording was reached and all clicks of the participants were classified as intuitive or not.

In this way, all video recordings were coded by the two raters and then each click was discussed whether it was intuitive or non-intuitive. Before the discussion, the inter-rater reliability according to Cohen's kappa was $\kappa = .61$, suggesting a substantial agreement beyond chance [45]. The discussion resolved any disagreements between the raters (e.g., judging the certainty of movement was very difficult sometimes). Finally, the ratio of intuitive clicks to all counted clicks was computed as a proportion on task level. Then these proportions were averaged across the three tasks to obtain a measure for each participant on the system level.

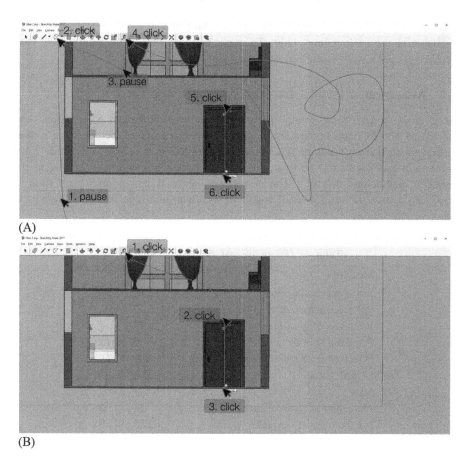

(A)

(B)

Fig. 6. Both pictures show click events for the measuring task. (A) Shows a rather non-intuitive interaction: (1) the user paused for 6 s - one non-intuitive click; (2) the user clicked on an incorrect item within 3 s - one non-intuitive click; (3 & 4) user paused for 2 s and then clicked on the correct icon within 3 s - one intuitive click; (5) user clicked correctly and fast but not targeted - one non-intuitive click; (6) user clicked correctly, fast and targeted - one intuitive click. In total three non-intuitive and two intuitive clicks resulting in 40% intuitive interactions of the overall interaction. (B) Shows an intuitive interaction with the following coding (1) user clicked certainly and correctly within 1 s on the correct button - one intuitive click; (2) user clicked correctly and in a targeted manner on the measurement start point within 2 s - one intuitive click; (3) user performs the measuring task by dragging the cursor top down and then release the mouse button - one intuitive click. In total three intuitive clicks were performed resulting in 100% intuitive interactions of the overall interaction.

5   Results

Intuitive interactions in the form of intuitive mouse clicks were coded as a proportions of the total number of mouse clicks within each user observation and computed on the task and system level. In order to evaluate the convergent validity of the refined coding scheme, SEA values were calculated on the system and task level. QUESI values were available at the system level only. To evaluate the discriminant validity, the total number of clicks were calculated on the system and task level.

5.1   Assessment of Intuitive Interaction on the System Level

An average of QUESI scores, proportions of intuitive clicks and SEA scores were calculated and Pearson correlation coefficients were computed between the system scores obtained from the three instruments. Descriptive data is shown in Table 1 and correlation coefficients can be found in Table 2. All correlation coefficients were statistically significant ($p < .05$). The correlations showed that a high proportion of intuitive clicks resulted in a small cognitive workload and high subjective ratings of intuitive interaction.

Table 1. Descriptive statistics (system level).

Measure	M	SD
Perceived mental effort (QUESI-M)	2.33	.94
Perceived achievement of goals (QUESI-G)	3.25	1.02
Perceived effort of learning (QUESI-L)	2.44	1.28
Perceived familiarity (QUESI-F)	2.56	1.13
Perceived error rate (QUESI-E)	2.41	1.11
QUESI-Total	2.60	1.03
SEA	89.48	23.17
Proportion of intuitive clicks	.33	.30
Number of clicks overall	32.25	14.85

Table 2. Pearson correlation coefficients between the proportion of intuitive clicks, number of clicks overall, QUESI and SEA scores on system level ($*p < .05$; $**p < .01$).

	No. of clicks	SEA	QUESI-M	QUESI-G	QUESI-L	QUESI-F	QUESI-E	QUESI-Total
Intuitive clicks	−.32 (n.s.)	−.61*	.61*	.61*	.65**	.60*	.65**	.67**

5.2   Assessment of Intuitive Interaction on the Task Level

An average of SEA, proportion of intuitive clicks and number of clicks were calculated on the task level (see Table 3). Then, Pearson correlation coefficients were performed between the task scores obtained from SEA, proportion of intuitive clicks and total number of clicks (see Table 4).

Table 3. Descriptive statistics (task level).

Measure	Rotating task		Positioning task		Measuring task	
	M	*SD*	*M*	*SD*	*M*	*SD*
SEA	97.60	40.45	68.02	19.09	102.81	35.16
Proportion of intuitive clicks	.26	.38	.24	.34	.49	.45
Number of clicks	46.06	24.08	36.13	20.03	23.56	19.57
Proportion of tasks solved correctly	.81	.40	.75	.45	.88	.34

Table 4. Pearson correlation coefficients between the proportion of intuitive clicks, number of clicks and SEA scores on task level (*$p < .05$; **$p < .01$).

Measure	Rotating task		Positioning task		Measuring task	
	SEA	No. of clicks	SEA	No. of clicks	SEA	No. of clicks
Proportion of intuitive clicks	−.57*	−.49 (n.s.)	−.56*	−.03 (n.s.)	−.27 (n.s.)	.04 (n.s.)

6 Discussion and Future Work

The main goal of this study was to introduce a refined set of heuristics that can be used to assess the probability of the subconscious application of prior knowledge in relatively complex interactive systems. The findings of this study show that measurements related to intuitive use show similar and acceptable correlations, indicating that the proportion of intuitive interactions as derived from applying the CHAI method shows a good convergent validity. Especially, the correlations between the proportion of intuitive interactions and the precondition-related QUESI scales Familiarity (QUESI-F) and Perceived effort of learning (QUESI-L) were significant supporting the assumption that CHAI can be used for the assessing the probability of the subconscious application of prior knowledge. Furthermore, correlations showed significant relations between the proportion of intuitive interactions and consequences of intuitive use like mental effort, which was measured using the SEA scale and the scale for subjective mental effort of the QUESI (QUESI-M). Regarding effectiveness, the Perceived Error Rate (QUESI-E) and the Perceived Achievement of Goals (QUESI-G) also show a relation to the proportion of intuitive interactions. The absence of correlations between the proportion of intuitive clicks and the total number of clicks suggests that CHAI specifically assesses cognitive efficiency rather than motoric (physical) efficiency. This demonstrates the discriminant validity of CHAI for assessing intuitive use.

Regarding the convergent validity of CHAI on the task level, the correlations with the SEA scores for the positioning and rotation task were positive and acceptable, while the correlations with the SEA scores for the measurement task did not reach significance. However, a general trend can be noted when looking at the effectiveness and the proportion of intuitive clicks (see Table 3). Further studies need to examine whether this trend remains and to find out what was the reason for the non-significant correlation by the use of a multidimensional workload measure like the NASA-TLX [46] instead of the SEA scale. To investigate the discriminant validity at the task level, the correlation analyses between the proportion of intuitive clicks and the number of total clicks showed no significant correlations indicating the discriminant validity of CHAI on the task level as well.

However, as with all experimental studies, there are limitations of this study, which can prompt future research in this area. First, the experiment was carried out using one particular software from one application domain with one input device (mouse). Results from this study should be validated across multiple software in different domains using other input devices (e.g., touch screens, gesture input). It can be expected that the KLM-derived threshold of the fastness criterion would need to be adapted to the specific type of technology used. Second, the manual coding using CHAI is still time-consuming and relies greatly on expert judgment. The inter-rater reliability of $\kappa = .61$ is satisfactory, but both raters coded only if a click was intuitive or not without stating which heuristics led to their decision. It would be interesting to see the inter-rater reliabilities of each of these heuristics. Third, the experiment was conducted in a German context with student participants having no previous experience with the software or similar 3D applications. Thus, the results should not be generalized to other populations before further validation. When designing for older users, we expect that the fastness criterion would need to be adapted as well. Finally, the tasks were simulated in a laboratory setting. Thus, any sense of urgency or other contextual responses that a user may experience in a real-setting may not arise here. A replication of the study in a real-setting should bring further validation.

In summary, with CHAI we introduced a set of coding heuristics for intuitive interaction that unlike previous heuristics [12] do not rely on concurrent thinking aloud and thus do not cause cognitive interference with the actual task. We also reduced the total number of heuristics and developed a more conservative coding scheme which should prevent false positives for intuitive interaction by checking whether all (and not only some of the) heuristics are fulfilled. Besides the effectivity, CHAI promises an enhanced efficiency in contrast to the coding scheme of Blackler [12], because the refined heuristics do not require to analyze the verbal protocol with respect to prior knowledge, conscious reasoning and expectations. Regarding validity, the present results demonstrate that CHAI can be applied to rather complex systems like 3D modelling software and can be used to assess intuitive use both on the system and task level. However, our sample size was too small to draw final conclusions and more studies are needed to confirm the results. Additionally, further work should provide direct comparisons between the original heuristics of Blackler and CHAI, regarding their reliability and validity as well as providing measures of their practicality in research and applied settings.

The future direction of this research should further examine the validity of the approach at the problem level and thereby check the potential of the method for qualitative data analysis as well. Since this work views intuitive interaction mainly from the pragmatic perspective (effectiveness and cognitive efficiency), additional research should check whether CHAI results are also related to hedonic properties of intuitive interaction (gut feeling, magical experience) as suggested by Ulrich and Diefenbach [11]. To conclude, in order to create products that are intuitive to use, designers should be able to not only assess whether a product or a task is intuitive or not, but also get qualitative information at the problem level and an easy way to prioritize these. The proportion of intuitive interactions could offer such an opportunity by enabling designers to spot likely non-intuitive user interface elements on the basis of their non-intuitive interactions across participants. In this way, we are prepared to meet the challenges of digitalization by enabling designers to evaluate the intuitive use with products, which is one step further towards designing interactive systems for users with different backgrounds and prior technology knowledge.

Acknowledgements. The work described in this paper was funded by the German Federal Ministry for Economic Affairs and Energy (#01MU15002C).

References

1. Blackler, A., Popovic, V.: Towards intuitive interaction theory. Interact. Comput. **23**(3), 203–209 (2015)
2. Heskett, J.: Toothpicks and Logos: Design in Everyday Life, vol. 1. Oxford University Press, Oxford (2002)
3. Hurtienne, J.: Image schemas and design for intuitive use. Exploring new guidance for user interface design (Doctoral dissertation). Technische Universität Berlin, Berlin (2011)
4. Lawry, S.G.: Identifying familiarity to facilitate intuitive interaction for older adults (Doctoral dissertation), Queensland University of Technology, Brisbane (2012)
5. Raskin, J.: Intuitive equals familiar. Commun. ACM **37**(9), 17–19 (1994)
6. Mohs, C., Hurtienne, J., Kindsmüller, M.C., Israel, J.H., Meyer, H.A., Group, D.I.R.: IUUI —Intuitive Use of User Interfaces: Auf dem Weg zu einer wissenschaftlichen Basis für das Schlagwort "Intuitivität" [IUUI – Intuitive use of user interfaces: on the way towards a scientific basis for the buzzword "intuitivity"]. MMI-Interaktiv **11**, 75–84 (2006)
7. Hurtienne, J.: How cognitive linguistics inspires HCI: image schemas and image-schematic metaphors. Int. J. Hum.-Comput. Interact. **33**(1), 1–20 (2017)
8. Blackler, A.: Intuitive Interaction with Complex Artefacts: Empirically-Based Research. VDM Verlag, Saarbrücken (2008)
9. Hurtienne, J.: Cognition in HCI: an ongoing story. Hum. Technol. **5**(1), 12–28 (2009)
10. O'Brien, M.A.: Understanding Human-Technology Interactions: The Role of Prior Experience and Age. Georgia Institute of Technology, Atlanta (2010)
11. Ullrich, D., Diefenbach, S.: From magical experience to effortlessness: an exploration of the components of intuitive interaction. In: Proceedings of the 6th Nordic Conference on Human-Computer Interaction: Extending Boundaries, pp. 801–804. ACM, New York (2010)
12. Blackler, A.: Intuitive interaction with complex artefacts (Doctoral dissertation). Queensland University of Technology, Brisbane (2006)
13. Naumann, A., Hurtienne, J.: Benchmarks for intuitive interaction with mobile devices. In: Proceedings of the 12th International Conference on Human Computer Interaction with Mobile Devices and SERvices, pp. 401–402. ACM, Lisbon (2010). https://doi.org/10.1145/1851600.1851685
14. Asikhia, O., Setchi, R., Hicks, Y., Walters, A.: Conceptual framework for evaluating intuitive interaction based on image schemas. Interact. Comput. **27**(3), 287–310 (2015)

15. Hurtienne, J., Blessing, L.: Design for intuitive use—testing image schema theory for user interface design. In: Proceedings of the 16th International Conference on Engineering Design, pp. 1–12. Ecole Centrale, Paris (2007)

16. Hurtienne, J., Israel, J.H.: Image schemas and their metaphorical extensions—intuitive patterns for tangible interaction. In: Ullmer, B., Schmidt, A., Hornecker, E., Hummels, C., Jacob, R.J.K., van den Hoven, E. (eds.) Proceedings of the TEI 2007. 1st International Conference on Tangible and Embedded Interaction, pp. 127–134. ACM, New York (2007)

17. Marsh, A., Setchi, R.: Design for intuitive use: a study of mobile phones. In: Proceedings of the 4th I*PROMS Virtual International Conference. Cardiff University, Cardiff (2008)

18. O'Brien, M.A., Rogers, W.A., Fisk, A.D.: Developing a framework for intuitive human-computer interaction. Proc. Hum. Factors Ergon. Soc. Annu. Meet. **52**(20), 1645–1649 (2008)

19. O'Brien, M.A., Rogers, W.A., Fisk, A.D.: Understanding intuitive technology use in older persons. In: Proceedings of IFA's 9th Global Conference on Ageing & Design, Montreal, Canada (2008)

20. Scholz, D.: Intuitivität von Mensch-Maschine-Systemen aus Benutzersicht [Intuitiveness of human-computer-systems from the user's view] (Diploma thesis). Technische Universität Berlin, Berlin (2006)

21. Blackler, A., Hurtienne, J.: Towards a unified view of intuitive interaction: definitions, models and tools across the world. MMI-Interaktiv **13**, 37–55 (2007)

22. Evans, J.S.B., Stanovich, K.E.: Dual-process theories of higher cognition: advancing the debate. Perspect. Psychol. Sci. **8**(3), 223–241 (2013)

23. Kahneman, D.: Thinking, Fast and Slow. Macmillan, Basingstoke (2011)

24. Zijlstra, F.R.H.: Efficiency in work behaviour: a design approach for modern tools (Doctoral dissertation). Delft University of Technology, Delft (1993)

25. Eilers, K., Nachreiner, F., Hänecke, K.: Entwicklung und Überprüfung einer Skala zur Erfassung subjektiv erlebter Anstrengung [The development and testing of a scale for validating the recording of subjectively experienced effort]. Zeitschrift für Arbeitswissenschaft **4**, 214–224 (1986)

26. Winkler, A., Baumann, K., Huber, S., Tscharn, R., Hurtienne, J.: Evaluation of an application based on conceptual metaphors for social interaction between vehicles. In: Proceedings of the 2016 ACM Conference on Designing Interactive Systems, pp. 1148–1159. ACM, New York (2016)

27. Lugrin, J.L., Latoschik, M.E., Habel, M., Roth, D., Seufert, C., Grafe, S.: Breaking bad behaviors: a new tool for learning classroom management using virtual reality. Front. ICT **3**, 26 (2016)

28. Tscharn, R., Latoschik, M.E., Löffler, D., Hurtienne, J.: "Stop over there": natural gesture and speech interaction for non-critical spontaneous intervention in autonomous driving. In: Proceedings of the 19th ACM International Conference on Multimodal Interaction, pp. 91–100. ACM, New York (2017)

29. Blackler, A., Popovic, V., Lawry, S., Reddy, R.G., Mahar, D., Kraal, B., Chamorro-Koc, M.: Researching intuitive interaction. In: Proceedings of IASDR2011 Diversity and Unity, pp. 1–12. Delft University of Technology, Delft (2011)

30. Lawry, S., Popovic, V., Blackler, A.L.: Diversity in product familiarity across younger and older adults. In: Diversity & Unity, 4th World Conference on Design Research, IASDR2011 (2011)

31. Bastick, T.: Intuition. Evaluating the Construct and its Impact on Creative Thinking. Stoneman and Lang, Kingston (2003)

32. Cockayne, A., Wright, P.C., Fields, B.: Supporting interaction strategies through the externalisation of strategy concepts. In: Sasse, A., Johnson, C. (eds.) Proceedings of INTERACT-1999, pp. 582–588. IOS Press, Bethesda (1999)
33. Klein, G.: Sources of Power: How People Make Decisions. MIT-Press, Cambridge (1998)
34. Eysenck, H.J.: Genius the Natural History of Creativity. Cambridge University Press, Cambridge (1995)
35. Westcott, M.R.: On the measurement of intuitive leaps. Psychol. Rep. **1961**(9), 267–274 (1961)
36. Desai, S., Blackler, A., Popovic, V.: Intuitive interaction in a mixed reality system. In: Lloyd, P., Bohemia, E. (eds.) Proceedings of DRS 2016, Design Research Society 50th Anniversary Conference. Design Research Society, Brighton (2016)
37. Hertzum, M., Hansen, K.D., Andersen, H.H.: Scrutinising usability evaluation: does thinking aloud affect behaviour and mental workload? Behav. Inf. Technol. **28**(2), 165–181 (2009)
38. Naumann, A., Hurtienne, J., Israel, J.H., Mohs, C., Kindsmüller, M.C., Meyer, H.A., Hußlein, S.: Intuitive use of user interfaces: defining a vague concept. In: Harris, D. (ed.) Engineering Psychology and Cognitive Ergonomics, pp. 128–136. Springer, Heidelberg (2007). https://doi.org/10.1007/978-3-540-73331-7_14
39. Horn, A.-M.: Validierung des "Questionnaire for Intuitive Use" am Beispiel der Benutzung zweier Versionen des BVG- Fahrkartenautomaten [Validation of the "Questionnaire for Intuitive Use" by the example of two versions of the BVG- ticketing machine] (Unpublished Master's thesis). Humboldt-Universität zu Berlin, Berlin (2008)
40. Sarodnick, F., Brau, H.: Methoden der Usability Evaluation: Wissenschaftliche Grundlagen und praktische Anwendung [Methods of Usability Evaluation: Scientific Foundations and Practical Application]. Huber, Mannheim (2006)
41. Sauro, J.: Estimating productivity: composite operators for keystroke level modeling. In: Jacko, J.A. (ed.) HCI 2009. LNCS, vol. 5610, pp. 352–361. Springer, Heidelberg (2009). https://doi.org/10.1007/978-3-642-02574-7_40
42. Stanton, N.A., Salmon, P., Walker, G.H., Baber, C., Jenkins, D.P.: Human Factors Methods: A Practical Guide for Engineering and Design. Ashgate Publishing, Burlington (2005)
43. Akers, D., Jeffries, R., Simpson, M., Winograd, T.: Backtracking events as indicators of usability problems in creation-oriented applications. ACM Trans. Comput.-Hum. Interact. (TOCHI) **19**(2), 16 (2012)
44. Chen, Q.: Human Computer Interaction: Issues and Challenges. Idea Group Publishing, Hershey (2001)
45. Field, A.: Discovering Statistics Using IBM SPSS Statistics. Sage Publications, London (2013)
46. Hart, S.G., Staveland, L.E.: Development of NASA-TLX (Task Load Index): results of empirical and theoretical research. Adv. Psychol. **52**, 139–183 (1988)

Towards a Conceptual Framework for the Objective Evaluation of User Experience

Carolina Rico-Olarte[1]($\boxtimes$), Diego M. López[1], and Sara Kepplinger[2]

[1] Universidad del Cauca, Popayán, Colombia
{carolinarico, dmlopez}@unicauca.edu.co
[2] Fraunhofer Institute for Digital Media Technology, Ilmenau, Germany
kpl@idmt.fraunhofer.de

Abstract. Background: The concept of user experience (UX) involves many aspects and different perspectives, making it difficult to evaluate the whole set of what UX represents. Despite existing standards, a clear definition of the UX evaluation concerning the identification of the different aspects to be evaluated according to the perspectives forming the UX (user and system), taking into account a given context of use is missing. Objective: Propose a conceptual framework for identifying differences between the UX evaluation perspectives and their measurable aspects. Methods: We followed a qualitative method for building conceptual frameworks. Results: The proposed conceptual framework identifies and associates the main UX concepts, from the user and system perspectives. The obtained plane of concepts provides a better overview of the phenomenon studied. The built framework led to the definition of an objective UX evaluation method: physiological signals are the convergence point between the physical state of the user and the measurement of emotions. Conclusion: The evaluation of UX is particularly important in ICT solutions for health since users/patients must maintain the motivation to continue using technology, in order to guarantee adherence to their treatments or interventions. The obtained framework and method are the first step towards finding suitable and according-to-context UX evaluation processes allowing an improved interaction between user and system.

Keywords: User experience · Conceptual framework · Evaluation methods
Objective evaluation

1 Introduction

The term user experience (UX) appeared more than a decade ago becoming, after a few years, a phenomenon, a field of study and a practice [1], a core for experts and researchers in the field of Human-Computer Interaction (HCI), and even penetrating other areas of knowledge such as psychology [2], medicine [3], learning [4], and advertisement [5]. At first, researchers and practitioners dedicated a few years to obtain a common definition of what is UX, what does it imply, how is it done, and what is its scope [6–8].

© Springer International Publishing AG, part of Springer Nature 2018
A. Marcus and W. Wang (Eds.): DUXU 2018, LNCS 10918, pp. 546–559, 2018.
https://doi.org/10.1007/978-3-319-91797-9_39

The ISO 9241-210 [9] standardized the concept of UX in 2010. Before this happened, for defining the scope of this emerging area, researchers and practitioners took into account different standpoints, which we can summarize as: (a) usability before UX, (b) UX beyond completing tasks, (c) UX as an emotional aspect, and (d) designing and evaluating for UX. Although there are other considerations on UX approaches, we will not address them in this paper.

(a) *Usability before UX:* the traditional usability framework focused primarily on user's ability to understand (user cognition) and to use (user performance) an 'artifact' in HCI [10]. Usability remained as a necessary condition in the context of interactive products and software, therefore the premise was "it is not sufficient to make a user happy". Positioned in this way, most researchers argue that UX emerged as an extension of usability to accommodate the fuzzy quality attributes of experience such as enjoyment, pleasure or fun, whereas others argue that UX exceeded usability by including it [8].

(b) *UX beyond completing tasks:* the pragmatic/hedonic model from Hassenzahl [11] gave the UX two dimensions for measuring it, differentiating from a focus on the product (pragmatic quality) and a focus on the self (hedonic quality), i.e., on the subjective side of the product [12]. This model links product attributes with human needs (i.e., personal growth, self-expression, and self-maintenance) and values (i.e., increasing knowledge, skills, and memories) [13].

(c) *UX as an emotional aspect:* there is a common understanding of the holistic nature of UX as it makes emphasis on the emotion, motivation, and action, in a given physical and social context. In addition, UX is subjective; it focuses on the "felt experiences" rather than the product attributes [14]. In UX, there are two basic ways in dealing with emotions: one emphasizes the importance of emotions as consequence of product usage; the other line focuses on their importance as previous circumstances of product usage and evaluative judgment [13]. Thüring and Mahlke's framework [15] explicitly defines emotional reactions as an integral component of the user experience and not as a consequence. On the other hand, Mandryk's approach explored physiological data as a direct indication of UX through mathematically modeling emotion [16]. Both models measure physiological reactions; these measures are valued for being unobtrusive and therefore able to monitor, in a constant way, indices of emotion, instead of asking the users to stop their experience, reflect on their emotion, and then disclose it [17].

(d) *Designing and evaluating UX:* both design and evaluation methods have interest in finding ways to evaluate UX of current concept ideas, design details, prototypes, or final products [18]. The primary effort of evaluation methods is to support and help in selecting the best design so development is on the right path, or to measure whether the final product meets and comply with the original UX targets [19]. Kort's framework studies the sense-making process, the UX aspects, and their relationships with design elements intended to create specific experiences [20]. However, this is not an operational framework.

With the arrival of the ISO standard (9241-210) in 2010, and previous work on handling the standard since 2009 (e.g., [21, 22]), researchers and practitioners from the HCI community were divided. There are those who accepted the norm, stuck to it and still do it, and those who, based on their experience in academia and industry, built their own definition and work(ed) around it, always keeping in mind that the concept of UX is complex [1]. New researchers in UX area have seen in the ISO definition a safer way to start walking the long road built to date of what UX is and how we should do it.

According to the ISO 9241-210 standard, which was last reviewed and confirmed in 2015, the UX is defined as a "person's perceptions and responses resulting from the use and/or anticipated use of a product, system or service". This standard also clarifies that: first, the emotions, beliefs, preferences, perceptions, physical and psychological responses, behaviors and accomplishments from users are included in the UX and they can occur before, during and after use. Second, UX is a consequence of three factors:

(i) The interactive system characterized by the brand image, presentation, functionality, system performance, interactive behavior and assistive capabilities.
(ii) The prior experience, attitudes, skills, and personality as causes for the user's internal and physical state.
(iii) The context of use.

Third, usability criteria, interpreted from the perspective of the users' personal goals, can use perceptual and emotional aspects from UX to assess it [9].

As we have demonstrated, UX involves many aspects and different perspectives, so it is difficult to evaluate the whole set of what UX represents. Thus, to the best of our knowledge, there is no clear definition of the UX evaluation concerning the identification of the different evaluative aspects according to the perspectives, and even taking into account the final needs of UX evaluation according to a given context of use.

As a first step towards a clearer definition, we propose a conceptual framework that allows for identifying the difference between the evaluation perspectives and the measurable aspects in each of them. Eventually, this proposal will allow us to settle our measurement needs on those UX aspects that offer a lower risk of bias when carrying out the measurement and evaluation processes.

The remainder of this paper is organized as follows: in the Methods section, we present the qualitative method for building conceptual framework on which our contribution is based on. In the Results section, we highlight the proposed conceptual framework and the description of its usage scenario according to a contextualized problem (namely, the UX evaluation of a video game for children with specific learning disorders). The Discussion section explains the implications of the proposed framework and its comparison with other existing frameworks. Finally, we present the Conclusions section of this paper.

2 Methods

According to [23], a conceptual framework is a plane or a network of interlinked concepts providing a comprehensive understanding of a phenomenon, and it is not a simple collection of concepts; each concept plays a representative role. The proposed methodology follows eight key phases: (1) mapping the data sources, (2) categorizing the selected data, (3) identifying concepts, (4) categorizing concepts, (5) integrating concepts, (6) synthesis and resynthesis, (7) validating the conceptual framework, and (8) rethinking the conceptual framework.

(1) *Mapping the data sources:* in this first part, sources of data were mapped according to the time division created by the ISO appearance:

   - Before ISO: data from workshops and special groups of interest from HCI conferences such as ACM CHI Conference on Human Factors in Computing Systems.
   - After ISO: the standard itself and papers with direct references to it.
   - Scientific databases like Scopus and ACM digital library for reviewing primary studies.
   - Papers on secondary studies [24–28].
   - The SQuaRE (Systems and Software Quality Requirements and Evaluation) series of standards [29].

(2) *Categorizing the selected data:* to categorize the information found in the data sources, four aspects were taken into account:

   - UX design
   - UX evaluation of the user
   - UX evaluation of the system (product or service)
   - Quality evaluation of the system.

(3) *Identifying concepts:* the identification of concepts was made explicitly and implicitly, naming those concepts that were "discovered".

(4) *Categorizing concepts:* in this phase, the main attributes, characteristics, assumptions, and roles from the concepts were identified and organized according to common features.

(5) *Integrating concepts:* the aim of this phase is to integrate and group together concepts that have similarities through association of concepts or relationships.

(6) *Synthesis and resynthesis:* the theorization process of the grouped concepts is iterative and includes repetitive synthesis, in order to recognize a general framework that makes sense.

Regarding phases *(7) validating the conceptual framework* and *(8) rethinking the conceptual framework*, precisely, the scope of this research paper is to validate the presented framework, discuss it with practitioners/researchers, receive feedback, and therefore, rethink the framework knowing that UX as a phenomenon is a dynamic area within the HCI field.

3 Results

In this section, aiming to synthesize the discovered information into one conceptual framework, we analyzed the results of the found data from the selected sources. The section has three parts: first, we define the main concepts in our framework by analyzing the domain of UX evaluation, taking as reference the ISO 9241-210 standard and relating and introducing other concepts derived from psychophysiology. Second, we formalize the conceptual framework relating its main concepts and their associations; third, we introduce a usage scenario for applying the conceptual framework: perform the evaluation of UX from the interaction between a video game for rehabilitation that focuses on memory and concentration therapies and children with specific learning disorders.

3.1 Main Concepts in UX Evaluation

We analyze the UX evaluation domain from two perspectives: (a) the system (product or service) and (b) the person (user).

(a) From the system's perspective, several authors declare to perform UX evaluations when developing usability tests during verification processes of software quality [27]; Miki's evaluation framework of usability and UX [30] tries to separate objective measures represented in effectiveness and efficiency from subjective measures represented in perceptions and satisfaction. The author in [21] discusses, analyzes and conceptualizes in three different ways the relationship between usability and UX. From the software engineering standards, usability reduces UX to a simple aspect of it. Consequently, the pleasure measure in ISO/IEC 25022 [31] is equivalent to UX and the recommended methods to find out user's pleasure are questionnaires.

(b) From the user's perspective, the main categories of the measurement methods to evaluate UX are: observational methods, where an expert estimates the user's reactions; psychometric scales, in which the user evaluates himself/herself; and psychophysiological measures, measuring the body's responses to determine user reactions. In the first two categories, we consider the methods as subjective, while in the third, the methods are objective [28].

Since the analysis of the ISO UX definition will provide us a good basis for a better understanding of UX, we take a deeper look into some of its main concepts, beginning with the "person's perceptions and responses" from the perspective of psychophysiology. As entries of a psychophysiological process, we have the perceptions occurring in the nervous system [32], and the responses being the outcomes of this kind of process.

More precisely, psychophysiology is a research field that tries to understand the underlying mental reactions/functions (psychological responses) connected to the body signals (physiological responses) [33]. The central nervous system (CNS) and the peripheral nervous system (PNS) control the physiological responses: the CNS manages all the information received from the body, whereas the PNS includes all nerve cells external to the CNS. The PNS transmits most of the physical sensations; therefore, on the skin is easier to measure these reactions [34]. On the other side, responses related to emotions and mental workload of the users are the psychological ones, in its most basic definition [16].

3.2   Conceptual Framework for UX Evaluation

As part of the initial thinking of the proposed conceptual framework, the concepts and their associations took part in the plane facilitating the preliminary identification of the basics of the evaluation process in UX (see Fig. 1). Three sources acquired high relevance in the building of the framework: the ISO 9241-210 [9], the SQuaRE standards for Quality Measure Elements [35] and Measurement of quality in use [31]. Additionally, the research field of psychophysiology was relevant.

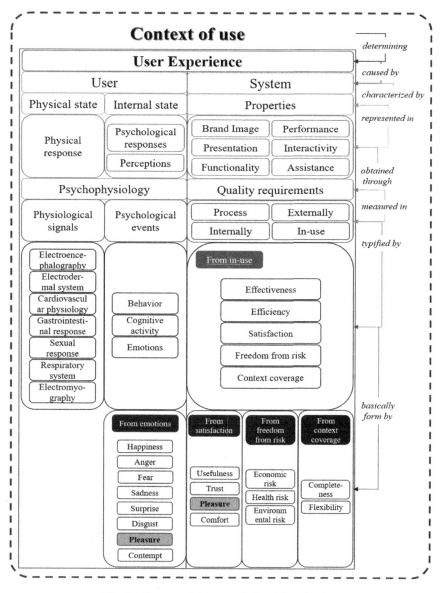

Fig. 1. Conceptual framework for UX evaluation

The clarifying notes given within the definition of UX from the standards mentioned in Sect. 1, helped in the consolidation of the framework, especially in the designation of the causal relationships between the key concepts. Thus, in the first part of the here proposed framework, we declared that user and system are the cause of the UX, particularly the user's states and the properties of the system.

A third cause of the UX comes from the context of use. We omitted this perspective within the conceptual framework, given that we assume the UX evaluation as being made or performed on tangible 'assets', that is, the user and the system, and although the context of use must have the same importance as the other perspectives, we consider it as something intangible and therefore, not measurable over the 'real world'. It is also important to consider that we see the context of use as the interaction (not tangible) therefore as determinant defining the UX. Physical and psychological responses and perceptions represent the user's states (internal and physical) as well as the six properties assigned to the system.

From the user's perspective, psychophysiology collects these states. As psychophysiology is the "scientific study of social, psychological, and behavioral phenomena as related to and revealed through physiological principles and events in functional organisms" [33], we concluded it gathers measures of physiological signals and psychological events separately, in order to obtain its counterpart. Nowadays, psychophysiology emphasizes their research in the map of the relationships between physiological responses and psychological events; the most common case when performing physiological evaluation is where one body response could be associated with two or more mental effects or processes (the many-to-one relationship) [34].

According to Bernhaupt, from an HCI position, the overall goal of UX is to understand the role of affect as an antecedent, a consequence and a mediator of technology, hence, the concept of UX focuses rather on emotional outcomes [36]. Bearing this in mind, from psychological events such as behaviors, cognitive activity and emotions, we approached emotions from their own theory: we represented emotions in our framework inside the set of the 'basic emotions' defined by Izard [37] and Ekman [38]: surprise, sadness, anger, disgust, fear, contempt, pleasure and happiness.

In the case of the perspective from the system, and based on the quality requirements set forth in ISO 25020, we grouped the properties of the system. The measurement of quality requirements includes their assessment in the process, internally and externally, and when the system is in real or simulated use [29]. Based on the effect when a system is actually used, the quality assurance of systems comprises the quality-in-use measures. ISO 25022 typifies the quality requirements in use in terms of effectiveness, efficiency, satisfaction, freedom from risk and context coverage and, in turn, there are quality sub-requirements in three of these requirements; specifically: usefulness, trust, pleasure, and comfort from satisfaction requirement [31].

It is important to highlight that we can also find some of these concepts in the usability definition: "extent to which a system, product or service can be used by specified users to achieve specified goals with effectiveness, efficiency, and satisfaction in a specified context of use" [9], since this concept comes from the HCI.

Finally, in our conceptual framework, we reached a common point between both perspectives; this common point is the emotion and quality sub-characteristic "pleasure": looking at it from the user, it is just another emotion included in a large set of variables to measure from the user and to take into account in the UX evaluation. On the contrary, digging a little deeper into the sub-characteristic from system's perspective, it is the one variable defining all UX.

3.3 Usage Scenario of the Conceptual Framework

HapHop-Physio [39] is a project developed from a technology transfer process to support rehabilitation therapies for children with specific learning disorders in the city of Popayán, Colombia. Through a video game of memory and concentration, we encourage children to complete the therapies while having fun. Evaluation of the UX is particularly important in ICT solutions for health since users/patients must maintain the motivation to continue using the technology, in order to guarantee adherence to their treatments or interventions.

Given that our users are children in cognitive rehabilitation processes, the UX evaluation would become a key factor in understanding the results of the child's therapy sessions. However, the measurement of aspects of UX is a difficult and exhausting task for test participants. With methods such as psychometric scales (like Fun toolkit or This-or-that [40]), children are easily distracted, are not impartial in the evaluation, and their reflection processes are not mature enough which would prevent the externalization of their feelings in a rational way: regarding observational methods, children tend to reject what is intrusive and can inhibit their natural performance.

Therefore, and for our case, we need an evaluation method that takes into account that end users are children, that we need measurements and responses that are as close as possible to objectivity (without risk of bias), and that allows children behave naturally in an environment that is closest to reality. In an extensive search of repositories (e.g., allaboutUX.com) and compilations in the literature of evaluation methods in UX, we found that psychophysiological measures are the closest to cover our needs. Nevertheless, studies using these types of evaluation methods have not done it so with children and the measurements are intrusive and sometimes annoying for users [27].

In the search for an objective evaluation method of the UX, we find in ISO/IEC 25022 [31] a guide that interrelates concepts of quality measurement in a simple and understandable diagram. Starting from this point and without any other method that was suitable for us, the built conceptual framework helped us in the definition of our own objective method (see Fig. 2).

Our method is simplistic: physiological signals are the convergence point between the physical state of the user and the measurement of emotions such as pleasure and happiness. Psychophysiology emphasizes their research in the map of the relationships between signals and emotions, and a convenient way to understand the potential of these relations is to consider a many-to-one relationship, where one body signal could be associated with two or more emotions in our case [33]. Particularly, several studies consider the electrodermal activity and the cardiovascular physiology, as the simplest of the signals and although, providing multiple resources in order to map emotions [41–45].

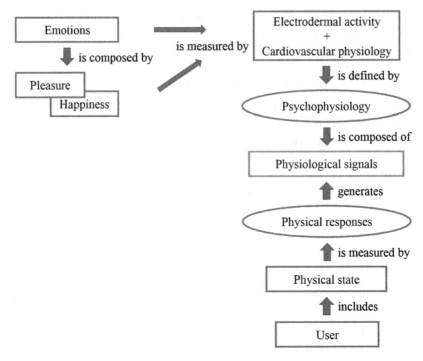

Fig. 2. Objective method for the UX evaluation. Adapted and modified from ISO/IEC 25022.

4   Discussion

In relation to the construction of the conceptual framework, we can argue in the first place that the proposed framework differentiates between the elements involved in an interaction: the user and the system. Additionally, it considers the context of use. Within the HCI community, some researchers and practitioners tend to overlap concepts, which, although they are difficult to separate due to their dependent nature, it is important to recognize their individualities and strengths in their singularity.

Second, this framework relates the different forms of UX evaluation from the user's perspective. We take the process of expansion of the aspects to be evaluated in the UX to its "most basic" form (based on the selected concepts), allowing us to think about a whole lot of exploratory combinations to obtain the desired measurement. We can think about the observation of behavior or analysis of cognitive activity through psychological methods.

Thirdly, it relates the standards to determine the quality of the system from the user's point of view because we base its conception on cascading concepts with general causality relationships. The levels of abstraction of the framework help in the easy connection of concepts of the user with its counterpart in the system to form the sense of the framework. This affirmation is also true with the definition of the objective evaluation method.

The framework also provides clarity regarding the procedure followed to evaluate the UX in a given context. Based on this fourth implication, we support the reason why we do not consider the evaluation of UX from the perspective of the context of use. Everything changes when defining that variable and we complement it with the recognition of the specific needs of each researcher and its project. This is also evident in the proposed evaluation method.

It attends as well as a conceptual and experimental basis for the exploration and subsequent implementation of a measurement procedure that allows obtaining objectively the UX in children with specific learning disorders, by measuring their physiological responses at the usage time of HapHop-Physio. This happening, once we are able to understand in a better way the links to its meanings and its related quality describing causes. We already took the first step towards the procedure by defining the objective method.

In previous sections, we made clear that there is a close relationship between usability and UX, which, according to Bevan, one way to conceptualize it is: "UX can be viewed as an elaboration of the satisfaction component of usability" [21]. Moreover, this is exactly what the ISO standard establishes the UX is, giving to researchers, developers, designers, and practitioners, wrong information about what UX constitutes for the HCI community. We prove that by reaching the common point in the conceptual framework. Correctly, many studies have shown with enough arguments that the relationship between usability and user experience is what Bevan defined as: "the umbrella term for all user's perceptions and responses, whether measured subjectively or objectively" [46].

In comparison with our proposed framework, in the pragmatic/hedonic model of Hassenzahl, the research framework of Turing and Mahlke, the psychophysiological method of Mandryk, and the Kort's framework we find some flaws. In the first place, Hassenzahl's model is quite subjective; there is no room for objective alternatives for measuring the UX aspects. Turing and Mahlke's framework takes into account system properties, user characteristics and context, however, fails in the specification of the causality relationships for the evaluation of the UX measurable aspects. Its framework counts aspects of the user and the system within the components of UX; however, they see the aspects from the user's perspective, so it does not establish a dependency relationship between the user and the system.

In the same way, Mandryk's method is context-dependent, which would not allow its instantiation to satisfy different variables of the context of use, the user context, and the system context. Lastly, Kort's framework encloses UX design and evaluation processes without defining the scope of each one.

Finally, the conceptual framework helped us in the definition of the objective method of UX evaluation thanks to which it allows us to observe more clearly and simply the dynamics of the UX phenomenon, building a method that considers a real application scenario. As part of the future work, we will instantiate the objective method within the described usage scenario, by mapping the electrodermal activity and some cardiovascular physiological measurement with the E4 sensor from Empatica Inc., in order to obtain an objective approximation of the user's internal state.

5   Conclusions

We proposed a conceptual framework in which we see in a more clearly and precisely way, the differences raised in the phenomenon of the UX evaluation seen from the two considered perspectives: the user and the system under consideration of the context. Likewise, the framework organized the most relevant concepts within the UX field, taking as reference several standards (for example, ISO 9241-210, ISO 25022) and relating other areas of knowledge. At the same time, the framework helped in the construction of an objective method of UX evaluation that takes into account our measurement needs and context of use.

We followed a qualitative method for building conceptual frameworks. The method included several steps: the mapping of the information sources, the categorization of the found information, the identification of the most relevant concepts, the organization of the concepts according to their common characteristics and similarities through their associations, and the iteration of synthesis processes. These steps led us to form a "network" or "plane" of concepts that provide a better overview of the phenomenon studied. From the proposed framework, we obtained an objective method, which we consider as a first step towards the validation of the framework.

The conceptual framework has several implications for the UX community: It

(i)   helps in differentiating between the elements involved in an interaction: the user and the system.
(ii) relates the different forms of UX evaluation from the user's perspective.
(iii) relates the standards to determine the quality of the system from the user's point of view.
(iv) provides clarity regarding the procedure followed to evaluate the UX in a given context.

In addition, this approach attends as a conceptual and experimental basis for the exploration and subsequent implementation of a measurement procedure that allows to objectively obtaining the UX in children with specific learning disorders, by measuring their physiological responses at the use time of a video game for cognitive rehabilitation.

Acknowledgments. The General Royalty System (SGR) in Colombia financed this research work under the "InnovAcción Cauca" program and the HapHop-Fisio project (VRI ID 4441).

References

1. Roto, V., Law, E.L.-C., Vermeeren, A., Hoonhout, J.: User Experience White Paper. Presented at the Dagstuhl, Germany (2011)
2. Brezinka, V.: Computer games supporting cognitive behaviour therapy in children. Clin. Child Psychol. Psychiatry **19**, 100–110 (2014). https://doi.org/10.1177/1359104512468288
3. Carrillo, I., Meza-Kubo, V., Morán, A.L., Galindo, G., García-Canseco, E.: Processing EEG signals towards the construction of a user experience assessment method. In: Bravo, J., Hervás, R., Villarreal, V. (eds.) AmIHEALTH 2015. LNCS, vol. 9456, pp. 281–292. Springer, Cham (2015). https://doi.org/10.1007/978-3-319-26508-7_28

4. Colpani, R., Homem, M.R.P.: An innovative augmented reality educational framework with gamification to assist the learning process of children with intellectual disabilities. In: 2015 6th International Conference on Information, Intelligence, Systems and Applications (IISA), pp. 1–6 (2015)

5. Keskinen, T., Hakulinen, J., Heimonen, T., Turunen, M., Sharma, S., Miettinen, T., Luhtala, M.: Evaluating the experiential user experience of public display applications in the wild. In: Proceedings of the 12th International Conference on Mobile and Ubiquitous Multimedia, p. 7. ACM (2013)

6. Law, E., Roto, V., Vermeeren, A.P., Kort, J., Hassenzahl, M.: Towards a shared definition of user experience. In: CHI 2008 extended abstracts on Human factors in computing systems, pp. 2395–2398. ACM (2008)

7. Väänänen-Vainio-Mattila, K., Roto, V., Hassenzahl, M.: Now let's do it in practice: user experience evaluation methods in product development. In: CHI 2008 Extended Abstracts on Human Factors in Computing Systems, pp. 3961–3964. ACM (2008)

8. Law, E.L.-C., Vermeeren, A.P., Hassenzahl, M., Blythe, M.: Towards a UX manifesto. In: Proceedings of the 21st British HCI Group Annual Conference on People and Computers: HCI... but not as We Know it-Volume 2, pp. 205–206. British Computer Society (2007)

9. ISO 9241-210: Ergonomics of human-system interaction—Part 210: Human-centred design for interactive systems (2010). https://www.iso.org/obp/ui/#iso:std:iso:9241:-210:ed-1:v1:en

10. Law, E.L.-C., Roto, V., Hassenzahl, M., Vermeeren, A.P., Kort, J.: Understanding, scoping and defining user experience: a survey approach. In: Proceedings of the SIGCHI Conference on Human Factors in Computing Systems, pp. 719–728. ACM (2009)

11. Hassenzahl, M.: The hedonic/pragmatic model of user experience. In: UX Manifesto, vol. 10, pp. 10–14 (2007)

12. Hassenzahl, M.: User experience (UX): towards an experiential perspective on product quality. In: Proceedings of the 20th Conference on l'Interaction Homme-Machine, pp. 11–15. ACM (2008)

13. Hassenzahl, M., Tractinsky, N.: User experience-a research agenda. Behav. Inf. Technol. **25**, 91–97 (2006)

14. Wiklund-Engblom, A., Hassenzahl, M., Bengs, A., Sperring, S.: What us needs tell about user experience. In: Gross, T., Gulliksen, J., Kotzé, P., Oestreicher, L., Palanque, P., Prates, R.O., Winckler, M. (eds.) INTERACT 2009. LNCS, vol. 5727, pp. 666–669. Springer, Heidelberg (2009). https://doi.org/10.1007/978-3-642-03658-3_71

15. Thüring, M., Mahlke, S.: Usability, aesthetics and emotions in human–technology interaction. Int. J. Psychol. **42**, 253–264 (2007)

16. Mandryk, R.L.: Physiological measures for game evaluation. In: Game Usability: Advice from the Experts for Advancing the Player Experience, pp. 207–235 (2008)

17. Boehner, K., DePaula, R., Dourish, P., Sengers, P.: How emotion is made and measured. Int. J. Hum.-Comput. Stud. **65**, 275–291 (2007)

18. Allam, A., Dahlan, H.M.: User experience: challenges and opportunities. J. Inf. Syst. Res. Innov. **3**, 28–36 (2013)

19. Stone, D., Jarrett, C., Woodroffe, M., Minocha, S.: User Interface Design and Evaluation. Morgan Kaufmann, Burlington (2005)

20. Kort, J., Vermeeren, A., Fokker, J.E.: Conceptualizing and measuring user experience. In: UX Manifesto, p. 57 (2007)

21. Bevan, N.: What is the difference between the purpose of usability and user experience evaluation methods. In: Proceedings of the Workshop UXEM, pp. 1–4 (2009)

22. Bevan, N.: International standards for usability should be more widely used. J. Usability Stud. **4**, 106–113 (2009)

23. Jabareen, Y.: Building a conceptual framework: philosophy, definitions, and procedure. Int. J. Qual. Methods **8**, 49–62 (2009)
24. Rico-Olarte, C., López, D., Kepplinger, S.: User experience evaluation methods in games for children with cognitive disabilities: a systematic review. In: Proceedings of 1st International Young Researcher Summit on Quality of Experience in Emerging Multimedia Services (QEEMS 2017), Erfurt, Germany (2017)
25. Maia, C.L.B., Furtado, E.S.: A systematic review about user experience evaluation. In: Marcus, A. (ed.) DUXU 2016. LNCS, vol. 9746, pp. 445–455. Springer, Cham (2016). https://doi.org/10.1007/978-3-319-40409-7_42
26. Zarour, M., Alharbi, M.: User experience framework that combines aspects, dimensions, and measurement methods. Cogent Eng. Article no. 1421006 (2017)
27. Rico-Olarte, C., López, D., Blobel, B., Kepplinger, S.: User experience evaluations in rehabilitation video games for children: a systematic mapping of the literature. Stud. Health Technol. Inf. **243**, 13 (2017)
28. Maia, C.L.B., Furtado, E.S.: A study about psychophysiological measures in user experience monitoring and evaluation. In: Proceedings of the 15th Brazilian Symposium on Human Factors in Computer Systems, pp. 7:1–7:9. ACM, New York (2016)
29. ISO/IEC 25000: Systems and software engineering - Systems and software Quality Requirements and Evaluation (SQuaRE) - Guide to SQuaRE (2014). https://www.iso.org/obp/ui/#iso:std:iso-iec:25000:ed-2:v1:en
30. Miki, H.: User experience and other people: on user experience evaluation framework for human-centered design. In: Stephanidis, C. (ed.) HCI 2015. CCIS, vol. 528, pp. 55–59. Springer, Cham (2015). https://doi.org/10.1007/978-3-319-21380-4_10
31. ISO/IEC 25022: Systems and software engineering - Systems and software quality requirements and evaluation (SQuaRE) - Measurement of quality in use (2016). https://www.iso.org/obp/ui/#iso:std:iso-iec:25022:ed-1:v1:en
32. ISO 9355-2: Ergonomic requirements for the design of displays and control actuators – Part 2: Displays (1999). https://www.iso.org/standard/21920.html
33. Cacioppo, J.T., Tassinary, L.G., Berntson, G.: Handbook of Psychophysiology. Cambridge University Press, Cambridge (2007)
34. Nacke, L.E.: An introduction to physiological player metrics for evaluating games. In: Seif El-Nasr, M., Drachen, A., Canossa, A. (eds.) Game Analytics, pp. 585–619. Springer, Heidelberg (2013). https://doi.org/10.1007/978-1-4471-4769-5_26
35. ISO/IEC 25021: Systems and software engineering - Systems and software Quality Requirements and Evaluation (SQuaRE) - Quality measure elements (2012). https://www.iso.org/standard/55477.html
36. Bernhaupt, R.: User experience evaluation methods in the games development life cycle. In: Bernhaupt, R. (ed.) Game User Experience Evaluation. HIS, pp. 1–8. Springer, Cham (2015). https://doi.org/10.1007/978-3-319-15985-0_1
37. Izard, C.E.: Basic emotions, relations among emotions, and emotion-cognition relations (1992)
38. Ekman, P.: An argument for basic emotions. Cogn. Emot. **6**, 169–200 (1992)
39. Rico-Olarte, C., Narváez, S., Farinango, C., López, D.M., Pharow, P.S.: HapHop-Physio a computer game to support cognitive therapies in children. Psychol. Res. Behav. Manag. **10**, 1–9 (2017)
40. Sim, G., Horton, M.: Investigating children's opinions of games: fun toolkit vs. this or that. In: Proceedings of the 11th International Conference on Interaction Design and Children, pp. 70–77. ACM, New York (2012)
41. Montañés, M.C.: Psicología de la emoción: el proceso emocional. Universidad de Valencia (2005)

42. Hernandez, J., Riobo, I., Rozga, A., Abowd, G.D., Picard, R.W.: Using electrodermal activity to recognize ease of engagement in children during social interactions. In: Proceedings of the 2014 ACM International Joint Conference on Pervasive and Ubiquitous Computing, pp. 307–317. ACM (2014)
43. Martínez, F., Barraza, C., González, N., González, J.: KAPEAN: understanding affective states of children with ADHD. Educ. Technol. Soc. **19**, 18–28 (2016)
44. Landowska, A., Miler, J.: Limitations of emotion recognition in software user experience evaluation context. In: 2016 Federated Conference on Computer Science and Information Systems (FedCSIS), pp. 1631–1640 (2016)
45. Yao, L., Liu, Y., Li, W., Zhou, L., Ge, Y., Chai, J., Sun, X.: Using physiological measures to evaluate user experience of mobile applications. In: Harris, D. (ed.) EPCE 2014. LNCS (LNAI), vol. 8532, pp. 301–310. Springer, Cham (2014). https://doi.org/10.1007/978-3-319-07515-0_31
46. Roto, V., Vermeeren, A., Väänänen-Vainio-Mattila, K., Law, E.: User Experience Evaluation – Which Method to Choose? In: Campos, P., Graham, N., Jorge, J., Nunes, N., Palanque, P., Winckler, M. (eds.) INTERACT 2011. LNCS, vol. 6949, pp. 714–715. Springer, Heidelberg (2011). https://doi.org/10.1007/978-3-642-23768-3_129

ANTETYPE-PM: An Integrated Approach to Model-Based Evaluation of Interactive Prototypes

Dieter Wallach[1,2(✉)], Sven Fackert[1], Jan Conrad[2], and Toni Steimle[1]

[1] Ergosign GmbH, Saarbrücken, Germany
dieter.wallach@ergosign.de
[2] University of Applied Sciences Kaiserslautern, Kaiserslautern, Germany

Abstract. In this paper, we present an integrated approach to model-based evaluations of interactive prototypes. By combining a state-of-the-art cognitive architecture, ACT-R, with an elaborated prototyping tool, ANTETYPE, we enable UX designers without modeling experience to derive quantitative performance predictions for interactive tasks. Using ANTETYPE-PM, an interface designer creates an interactive prototype and demonstrates the action sequences to complete relevant application scenarios using the *monitoring* and/or *instruction mode* of ANTETYPE-PM. The system learns the interaction paths and predicts the interaction times over trials using ACT-R's symbolic and subsymbolic (i.e. statistical) learning mechanisms. To illustrate the working of ANTETYPE-PM, an example is provided and contrasted with empirical data.

Keywords: Model-based evaluation · Usability evaluation
Cognitive architectures · Quantitative performance prediction

1 Introduction

In this paper we report our progress on an integrated approach to model-based evaluation combining an advanced prototyping tool with a state-of-the-art cognitive architecture to derive quantitative performance predictions for interactive tasks. After first introducing the prototyping tool ANTETYPE, we discuss some limitations of empirical usability testing to motivate the use of model-based evaluation. Given that our approach is based on the cognitive architecture ACT-R, we provide a brief overview of this framework and compare related models to model-based evaluation. Finally, we illustrate the use of our integrated tool, ANTETYPE-PM, and present an example for its application in a real-world task.

1.1 User Interface Prototyping with ANTETYPE

ANTETYPE is a sophisticated design tool to create interactive prototypes for desktop, mobile and web-based applications. ANTETYPE was designed to support a seamless transition from early wireframes defining the layout of an interface, over the creation of visual design alternatives to the creation of complex interactive prototypes. Its layout

© Springer International Publishing AG, part of Springer Nature 2018
A. Marcus and W. Wang (Eds.): DUXU 2018, LNCS 10918, pp. 560–572, 2018.
https://doi.org/10.1007/978-3-319-91797-9_40

engine, advanced features for visual design and elaborated functionality for defining interactions, transitions and animations make ANTETYPE a highly flexible and powerful tool for developing sophisticated interactive prototypes.

Requirements for designing interactive prototypes have become increasingly complex: ANTETYPE's layout engine supports the creation of *responsive designs* that fluidly adapt to different screen dimensions and provide helpful layout declarations for development. Complementing the layout engine, elaborated *visual design functionality* enables designers to work with ANTETYPE from early conceptual wireframes to comprehensive high-fidelity prototypes. Enhancing ANTETYPE prototypes with *transitions and animations* guide users in understanding the consequences of their actions without requiring designers to switch to another tool.

Iteratively modifying and refining a prototype can become a very time-consuming task. Differentiating local and global elements, ANTETYPE's *widget concept* allows the automatic propagation of changes to the visual appearance and behavior of an interface widget—relieving designers from the tedious manual updating of all instances of the widget spread over potentially numerous screens of a prototype. The definition of *state-dependant, hierarchically nested widgets* finally enables the creation of powerful, reusable interface elements to meet the challenges of complex prototypes.

Over the course of a project, ANTETYPE is typically used to iteratively explore and evaluate ongoing design work with stakeholders. A particularly important application of ANTETYPE prototypes is their use in empirical usability tests involving representative participants.

2   Limitations of Empirical Usability Tests

Empirical usability testing is regarded as a hallmark of human-centered design approaches. While usability testing of interactive prototypes in a usability lab allows for the elicitation of valuable feedback from prospective users, several restrictions need to be considered—especially when being interested in *quantitative* performance indicators of an interface.

Predicting the time for the *routine performance* of users dealing with relevant key scenarios, for example, is severely limited when a novel interface is presented in a usability test: participants first need to learn how to operate the new interface. Depending on its complexity, a level of routine interaction will only be reached after significant amounts of practice with the user interface. The time requirements to arrive at such skilled performance might well be outside the practical scope of most usability tests of complex applications. It is, to give an obvious example, not trivial to isolate quantitative measures of *efficiency* from *learnability* metrics of an interface in empirical usability tests—at least for more complex applications.

Instructions in most usability tests typically do not explicitly require participants to complete tasks *as fast as they can.* Given that participants know that their behavior is recorded in a usability test, it is reasonable to assume that their efforts will at least be influenced by the goal to show an *effective, error-free* behavior—which stands in obvious conflict with a focus on time-efficient interaction.

Referring to *quantitative* performance predictions in general, the typical setting and instruction in an empirical usability test—that is often mainly targeted at the elicitation of *qualitative* insights—poses additional complications. To name just one: in most empirical usability tests, participants are asked to *think aloud* while working on test scenarios. Empirical studies (Steimle and Wallach 2018) have shown that concurrent thinking aloud results in significant increases in the time requirements for completing a task, contradicting the goal of valid performance measurement. For what it's worth, the instruction to think aloud can hardly be regarded as a representative characterization of typical working situations.

While we agree that empirical usability testing is an irreplaceable evaluation method, the aforementioned challenges need to be carefully considered when following the goal of deriving quantitative performance predictions for the routine work with an interactive system. Extended practice times with an interface to overcome learning effects in usability tests help to arrive at valid performance predictions for routine interactions. The additional effort, however, inevitably results in even higher costs for conducting empirical usability evaluations—worsening the cost-benefit ratio that inspired Nielsen (1989) to coin empirical usability tests a "deluxe method".

3   Model-Based Evaluation Using Act-R

Model-based evaluations, i.e. using artificial *cognitive crash-test dummies* to simulate user behavior with interactive systems provide a promising and cost-effective approach to overcome at least some of the challenges discussed in the previous section. In the following we will spell out the advantages of combining a powerful prototyping tool like Antetype with model-based evaluation on the grounds of a so-called *cognitive architecture* like Act-R (see Anderson et al. 2004; Laird et al. 2017).

Integrating a model-based evaluation module into Antetype allows quantitative performance predictions for interaction scenarios by simply running "simulated users" with an interface prototype: UX designers can explore the quantitative implications of their design decisions in the very same tool that they are using for the design of user interfaces. In the resulting tool, that we denote Antetype-Pm, UX designers can analyze and compare the performance of different design options for relevant interaction paths through key scenarios. Quantitative performance evaluations do not need to be postponed until the design of a user interface is largely completed—the temporal implications of an interaction path can be explored whenever the part of the user interface to support the respective path is designed, allowing a continuous inspection of performance parameters during the iterative course of interface design activities. Before illustrating how to work with Antetype-Pm, we introduce the Act-R cognitive architecture that forms the theoretical framework underlying the proposed model. After that, we will contrast it with alternative modeling approaches.

The Act-R Cognitive Architecture. A cognitive architecture embodies a comprehensive scientific hypothesis about the structures and mechanisms of the human cognitive system that can be regarded as (relatively) invariant over time. Act-R provides an integrative theoretical framework for explaining and predicting human behavior and is instantiated as a theoretically justified, implemented software system allowing for the computational modeling of a wide range of phenomena. Authors have been discussing the potential benefits of applying cognitive architectures in the domain of Human-Computer Interaction for more than twenty years (Kieras 2007). Their broader use in HCI, however, has been fostered by the extension of architectures with perceptual-motor modules that allow the modeling of perception and interaction with an external world.

ACT-R comprises *symbolic* learning mechanisms to acquire new if-then-rules (so-called *productions)* in procedural memory and declarative facts (so-called *chunks)* in declarative memory, as well as *subsymbolic* mechanism for the statistical tuning of their appropriate application. ACT-R can *perceive* and *manipulate* the external world that is defined, in the case of ANTETYPE-PM, by an interface prototype. Figure 1 depicts a structural overview of ACT-R and its interplay within ANTETYPE-PM.

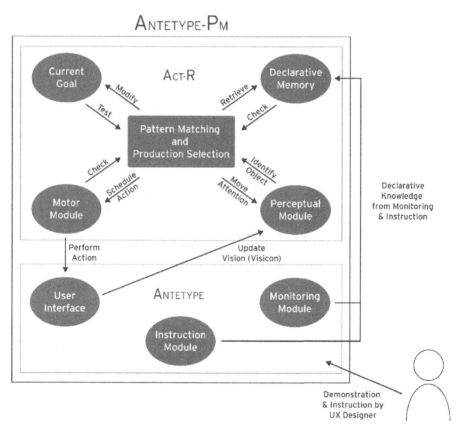

Fig. 1. Interplay of ANTETYPE and the cognitive architecture ACT-R in ANTETYPE-PM

ACT-R provides a theoretical framework that comprises empirically motivated constraints (see Kieras 2007) on the details of models to be written within this framework.

In ANTETYPE-PM we have instantiated a core ACT-R model that provides a set of operators:

- to *perceive* interface objects like buttons or labels on ANTETYPE prototypes,
- to *interact* with ANTETYPE's interface controls,
- to encode declarative and procedural knowledge for *monitoring* and *learning* actions that the model observes,
- to represent basic user-provided *instructions* on the conditional application of actions.

Before illustrating how to work with ANTETYPE-PM, we briefly describe related work in the field.

4   Creating Cognitive Models

Historically, different paths have been taken to arrive at cognitive models for predicting performance in Human-Computer Interaction scenarios. These paths differ, among other criteria, in the required effort for model development, necessary knowledge about the theoretical Cognitive Science underpinnings of a model and prerequisite modeling skills, as well as in the technical support to create models. A brief glance at cognitive modeling in the field of HCI unveils roughly the following approaches:

- *building cognitive models by hand*, which technically requires nothing more than just a pen and piece of paper for establishing an interaction sequence (typically derived from task analysis) and calculating time parameters of hypothetical human cognitive, perceptual and motor operators (see Sect. 4.1 of this paper);
- *using software tools for (more or less) automating* the aforementioned process of calculating the temporal effects of assumed operator sequences underlying the interaction path to be predicted (see Sect. 4.1);
- *utilizing comprehensive cognitive modeling tools* to assist a modeler in both the development and the simulation of a performance model (see Sect. 4.2).

The first two approaches presuppose a basic understanding of Cognitive Science theory to achieve valid results and typically require a serious amount of time for model development. The final approach may seem most promising because of its support in model creation and automating the generation of its predictions. However, without getting deep into the theoretical and syntactic details of the respective modeling tool or cognitive architecture, model development will be limited to very simple tasks. In the next section, we will look at the approaches in more detail.

4.1   Hand-Crafted and Semi-automatic Models

Initially introduced by Card et al. (1980) the *Keystroke-Level Model* (KLM) provides a framework for developing models to predict execution times for expert users completing routine tasks with a given interactive system. The KLM is an example of a (simplified) architecture that forms a foundation for model-based evaluations of design suggestions. Using this approach, a modeler bases his work on a task analysis before then going through the task step by step to translate each identified step into operators declared in the KLM. Each of these operators describes a subpart of the task at the keystroke-level and is associated with a time value. The execution time for an entire task is then calculated as the sum of the individual operators (in the simple case of sequential actions). While modeling is quite straightforward as long as operators only represent motor actions, the situation becomes complicated with cognitive processes. KLM, focusing on the keystroke-level, takes a rather abstract stance on cognitive processes and proposes the insertion of *mental operators*. Mental operators do not have fixed associated time values, but require a modeler to estimate the duration of steps to represent a user's *thinking processes*.

Apart from the time-consuming process of manually analyzing a task and having to write down each step when calculating execution times by hand, the application of KLM is best suited to what its name suggests: modeling at the observable level of key strokes. While it may be necessary to make decisions about underlying cognitive processes at various stages of modeling more complex interactions, KLM fails to provide much guidance on their duration.

Initial steps toward automating the development and simulation of cognitive models have been taken: Computer programs like GLEAN (Kieras et al. 1995) or Cogulator ("Cogulator: A Cognitive Calculator", 2018) provide a graphical user interface for writing cognitive models. Using them, modelers no longer need to manually calculate individual time predictions but are supported by software to compute and output modeling results. While such systems improve the efficiency of developing models and the determination of their temporal consequences, they still lack appropriate support at the cognitive level.

With regard to deriving quantitative predictions, running an ACT-R model can also be classified as a semi-automated way of model-based evaluation. In contrast to the aforementioned approaches, however, the proposed structures and processes of the Act-R cognitive architecture provide a detailed theoretical framework at the cognitive level. This advantage does not come without costs: cognitive architectures have notoriously been known to be hard to learn. Model development in a cognitive architecture is outside the scope for most non-specialists and it is hard to imagine UX designers to include cognitive modeling with ACT-R in their daily toolbox. Automated generation of evaluation models, discussed in the next section, offer a promising step to reduce modeling complexity, thus making cognitive modeling accessible to a larger range of users.

4.2 Automated Generation of Models

The obvious next challenge after automating the simulation of cognitive models is to automate model creation *per se*. A well-known endeavor in this direction is the so-called CogTool – proposed by Bonnie E. John and colleagues. CogTool consists of tools that "allow a UI designer to mock up an interface as an HTML storyboard, demonstrate a task on that storyboard, and automatically produce a consistent, correct KLM of that task that runs in the Act-R cognitive architecture (Anderson and Lebiere 1998) to produce predictions of skilled performance time" (John et al. 2004, p. 462). The advantages of such an approach are obvious: a designer requires no cognitive modeling skills because the model is created automatically while the designer demonstrates the task.

While the reduction in effort and the cost savings using CogTool compared to plain Act-R are without doubt impressive, this approach is still quite limited to the boundaries of KLM. I.e. a model-based evaluation using CogTool still focuses mainly on predicting the total execution *times* for tasks performed by *skilled users* under the assumption that *no errors* occur. In addition, initial versions of CogTool failed to make use of the full potential of the underlying Act-R architecture: cognitive processes were still reduced to the insertion of *mental operators* that only pause model execution for estimated amounts of time (John et al. 2004).

Although a more recent development version of CogTool, called CogTool Explorer (Teo et al. 2012), paved the way for modeling goal-directed user exploration on the cognitive level, the following reasons motivated the need for a tool like Antetype-Pm:

- development of CogTool went into quiescence: at the time of writing this paper, the latest stable release of CogTool dates back to December 2013 using deprecated versions of ACT-R and Java;
- in order to use CogTool, design prototypes need to either be rebuilt within CogTool or imported as HTML files, doubling the amount of work for designers;
- advanced modelers cannot easily elaborate or extend an Act-R model generated by CogTool, giving away options for its refinement.

While the last argument is not without importance, a core objective for developing Antetype-Pm was to create a valuable tool for UX designers without requiring users to have a comprehensive cognitive modeling background. In the next section we present an example for using Antetype-Pm.

5 Using Antetype-Pm: An Example

In order to explain how to apply Antetype-Pm in real world tasks, we present a first example that was targeted at predicting user performance with a new interface for a software-controlled riveting machine for airplanes. Before going into the details of using Antetype-Pm, the following list provides an overview of the necessary working steps, with the final step being optional:

1. Create an interactive prototype using ANTETYPE-PM.
2. Explain the task to ANTETYPE-PM using demonstration and/or instruction.
3. Let ANTETYPE-PM generate the cognitive model for the task.
4. Run an arbitrary number of simulated users on the task.
5. Inspect the predictions and analyze their implications.
6. (Revise your design solution and run the simulation again.)

5.1 Creating Interactive ANTETYPE-PM Prototypes

ANTETYPE-PM interacts directly with design prototypes and thus requires a design proposal to exist that takes the form of an interactive ANTETYPE prototype. As discussed at the beginning of this paper, ANTETYPE assists UX designers throughout the entire design process from wireframes to high-fidelity prototypes. A model-based evaluation using ANTETYPE-PM starts off with the creation of an interactive, low-fidelity prototype (i.e. linked wireframes) of the intended system. This starting point lays the foundation for an iterative design process where the early detection of potential usability short-comings may prevent more expensive alterations of visually elaborated, high-fidelity solutions. Creating the prototype for ANTETYPE-PM does not differ from the usual practice of using ANTETYPE—except that a designer needs to denote which interface objects the underlying ACT-R model can *perceive*. Figure 2 depicts an ANTETYPE prototype of the software-based riveting machine. The interface was designed by an external company to assist users in operating large riveting machines in a complex context of use. Supporting an *efficient* and *error-free* interaction is a mandatory requirement for the machine's user interface. The next section focuses on how to predict the performance of the interface using ANTETYPE-PM.

5.2 Explain the Task Using Demonstration or Instruction

In addition to an interactive prototype that is to be evaluated, a cognitive model in ANTETYPE-PM needs relevant knowledge about the task and its workflow, as well as *generic, task-independent* knowledge about the operation of user interfaces in general. ANTETYPE-PM thus comes with a default set of generic productions that allow interaction with user interfaces, as well as knowledge to encode observed actions. *Task knowledge* and the sequence of involved interaction steps, however, need to be provided to ANTETYPE-PM by the user.

As discussed in Sect. 4.2, ANTETYPE-PM belongs to the category of tools that automate the development of cognitive models. To provide the necessary task knowledge, a user demonstrates the interaction path for a task scenario while ANTETYPE-PM is *observing* and *learning* the respective interaction sequence. There are, of course, dependencies between task steps and decisions that cannot just be derived from observing a designer completing the task with a prototype. An interaction with a check box, for example, may depend on its current state (is it checked or not?), or the next interaction step may depend on the outcome of a comparison of values that are provided by the interface. To resolve the rationale behind such decisions, relevant instructions can be entered into ANTETYPE-PM's instruction module, resulting in the creation of task-specific knowledge in ACT-R's declarative memory.

5.3   Generation of the Cognitive Model

Based on the information collected from demonstration and/or instruction, the cognitive model is generated. Declarative facts are encoded as ACT-R chunks and stored in the declarative memory of the model, whereas procedural knowledge is represented as productions in ACT-R.

The following code shows an example of a chunk type declaration used to store task-specific information about a simple button click interaction. It contains a name for the chunk type, an identifier, the text of the button that should be clicked and the kind of button on the mouse that should be pressed. The name of the chunk type does not have any impact on the model execution. Its main purpose is to improve the readability and clarity of the model. The interaction identifier is used to keep track of the position within an interaction sequence. The last information of this chunk type determines the kind of button that should be clicked. This may be the left or right button of the mouse.

```
(chunk-type button-click-interaction
   interaction-id
   button-text
   mouse-button)
```

This declaration is used to instantiate chunks containing the aforementioned information and is only one example for how task-specific information is delivered to the model. As soon as the model has been generated it is ready for simulating user performance, which is described in the next section.

5.4   Run a Simulation

Running a simulation in ANTETYPE-PM is a straightforward process. A designer just needs to select a task scenario and determine the number of simulation trials that ANTETYPE-PM should work on this scenario. A simulation can be run in *real time* or in *speed mode*. The former will visualize the simulation by highlighting the visual attention and eye movements of a simulated user, as well as showing the respective mouse movements and clicks. A user's visual attention (yellow circle in Fig. 2) and eye movements (blue circle in Fig. 2) are simulated using an ACT-R module called EMMA, developed by Salvucci (2000). Running the simulation in *speed mode* will provide faster results without visualization. The results of the respective modes do not differ, of course.

At this point we need to differentiate between different kinds of potential ANTETYPE-PM users. A typical UX designer without a comprehensive background in Cognitive Science will be able to perform a model-based evaluation by simply following the aforementioned steps. Users with an advanced understanding of ACT-R, however, can inspect and enhance a model's symbolic (declarative and procedural) knowledge or fine-tune its subsymbolic parameters in order to explore the model in an extended scope.

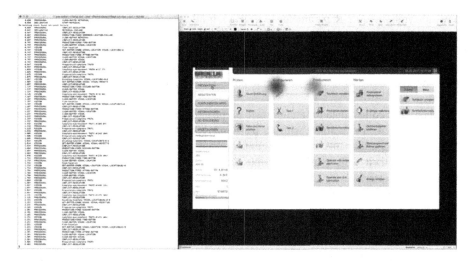

Fig. 2. ANTETYPE-PM showing the ACT-R trace (left) and interaction with a prototype (right) (Color figure online)

5.5 Inspect and Interpret Predictions

After the specified number of simulation runs is completed, results are presented to the user of ANTETYPE-PM. Let us assume that a user is interested in a prediction of the time that it takes for a novice user to achieve a specific task performance with a prototype. Running the simulation for multiple trials will output resulting learning curves that illustrate the transition from novice to more advanced users in terms of their respective time requirements for completing the task. A designer can then utilize this data along with the observations from watching the visualization of the simulation to understanding the time spent in different subparts of the task. Based on an interpretation of these findings, a design solution can then be revised, evaluated again and finally compared to previous solutions.

Repeating this process until the design solution meets a level of desired performance provides designers with constant feedback to derive informed design decisions when iteratively improving an interface. Revising a prototype is straightforward with ANTETYPE-PM and usually does not even require the modeler to configure the task, i.e. to demonstrate/instruct the interaction scenario, again. I.e., altering button positions, sizes, colors or the arrangements of elements will not require the cognitive model to be changed — the implications of the interface changes, however, will be predicted by the model. This enables designers to rapidly try out and compare design variations and to discover potential deficiencies of an interface at a very early stage.

6   Validating the ANTETYPE-PM Model

While it is tempting in the context of writing a paper to present a fine-tuned model that provides impressive fits to available data, we deliberately decided to refrain from such an endeavor. Instead, we report the bare performance of the model without adjusting any subsymbolic ACT-R parameter (e.g. leaving all ACT-R parameters at their default value), not making use of ANTETYPE-PM's instruction module, as well as not adjusting or handcrafting the generated ACT-R model. Formally, this comes down to a *zero parameter model* — and that is exactly what is required given the goal of providing a tool for UX designers without cognitive modelling, or, more specifically, ACT-R experience.

In order to collect data for an interface proposal for the riveting machine modeled in ANTETYPE-PM, we ran a study with 15 participants (8 male, 7 female; mean age: 28.5, SD: 3.8). All participants were very experienced users working professionally with computers in their daily work. After introducing them to the steps of a task scenario with the user interface for the riveting machine, each participant was given a practice trial to clarify questions. After that, all participants were asked to repeat the task scenario for a total of 14 trials.

ANTETPYE-PM was trained for the task scenario by a UX designer who demonstrated the interaction steps while the model observed the respective actions. Then the model was run for a single trial to check its ability to reproduce the interaction path, before simulating a total of 14 runs through the task scenario. I.e., we did not only maintain all ACT-R parameters at their standard values, but also used the very same number of trials that the participants were required to do. Figure 3 shows the mean time trajectories of the participants and the runs of ACT-R over the 14 trials of the task scenario. While the model is clearly significantly slower than the participants in this task, a comparison of the learning trajectories shows an impressive fit with an r^2 of .97 (see Fig. 4).

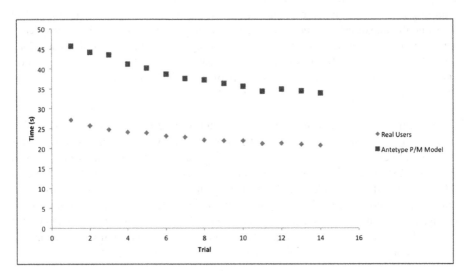

Fig. 3. Performance of the ANTETYPE-PM model in comparison to empirically obtained user performance

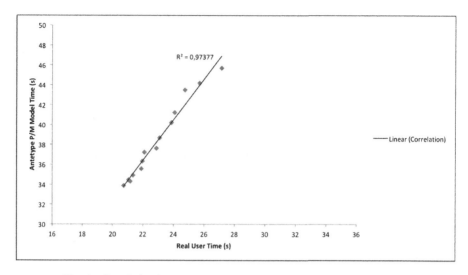

Fig. 4. Correlation between the ANTETYPE-PM model and participant data

While we of course need to explore the model in a broad range of tasks to appropriately judge its practical value, we regard the obtained initial results to be encouraging. Adjusting ACT-R parameters would of course result in a much better correspondence of the absolute values of the model and the empirical data. This, however, would not bring us closer to attaining our goal of developing a tool that is of practical significance. Post-hoc data fitting, although potentially exiting for cognitive modelers, is not of practical interest for a UX designer. Instead, receiving results to derive informed design decisions are needed to speed up iterative development — and such design decisions are to be taken *before* data with a resulting user interface can be collected. This of course does not exclude the exploration of ACT-R parameters that turn out to be more appropriate than the default values in Human-Computer Interaction scenarios.

7 Summary

In this paper we summarized our initial progress on developing a model-based evaluation approach that is combined with an advanced prototyping tool. While an interface created with the prototyping tool provides the external system environment for a human user, a generated model allows UX designers to simulate *artificial users* interacting with this interface. Focusing mainly on UX designers with no or little modeling experience, the resulting system, ANTETYPE-PM, comprises the ACT-R cognitive architecture and allows its use to predict quantitative usability performance parameters. Next research steps will include more detailed analyses to characterize the set of interactive tasks for which the approach is appropriate. While we are currently focusing on quantitatively predicting task times and learning curves with ANTETYPE-PM, initial steps towards the prediction of errors have been undertaken.

Acknowledgements. The authors are thankful to the German Federal Ministry of Education and Research for funding the research reported in the paper in the SiBED project (support code 01IS16037A).

References

Steimle, T., Wallach, D.: Collaborative UX Design. dPunkt, Heidelberg (2018)

Nielsen, J.: Usability engineering at a discount. In: Salvendy, G., Smith, M.J. (eds.) Proceedings of the Third International Conference on Human-Computer Interaction on Designing and Using Human-Computer Interfaces and Knowledge Based Systems, 2nd edn, pp. 394–401. Elsevier, Boston (1989)

Anderson, J.R., Bothell, D., Byrne, M.D., Douglass, S., Lebiere, C., Qin, Y.: An integrated theory of mind. Psychol. Rev. **111**(4), 1036–1060 (2004)

Laird, J.E., Lebiere, C., Rosenbloom, P.S.: A standard model of the mind: toward a common computational framework across artificial intelligence, cognitive science, neuroscience, and robotics. AI Mag. **38**(4), 13–26 (2017)

Kieras, D.E.: Model-based evaluation. In: Jacko, J., Sears, A. (eds.) The Human-Computer Interaction Handbook, 2nd edn, pp. 1139–1151. Lawrence Erlbaum Associates, Mahwah (2007)

Card, S.K., Moran, T.P., Newell, A.: The keystroke-level model for user performance time with interactive systems. Commun. ACM **23**(7), 396–410 (1980)

Kieras, D.E., Wood, S.D., Abotel, K., Hornof, A.: GLEAN: a computer-based tool for rapid GOMS model usability evaluation of user interface designs. In: UIST 1995 Proceedings of the 8th annual ACM Symposium on User Interface and Software Technology, pp. 91–100. ACM, New York (1995)

Cogulator: A Cognitive Calculator. http://cogulator.io/. Accessed 08 Feb 2018

Anderson, J.R., Lebiere, C.: The Atomic Components of Thought. Erlbaum, Mahwah (1998)

John, B.E., Prevas, K., Salvucci, D.D., Koedinger, K.: Predictive human performance modeling made easy. In: CHI 2004 Proceedings of the SIGCHI Conference on Human Factors in Computing Systems, pp. 455–462. ACM, New York (2004)

Teo, L., John, B.E., Blackmon, M.H.: CogTool-Explorer: a model of goal-directed user exploration that considers information layout. In: Proceedings of the SIGCHI Conference on Human Factors in Computing Systems, pp. 2479–2488. ACM, New York (2012)

Salvucci, D.D.: A model of eye movements and visual attention. In: Proceedings of the International Conference on Cognitive Modeling, pp. 252–259. Universal Press, Veenendaal (2000)

Assessing User Experience in Virtual Reality – A Comparison of Different Measurements

Carolin Wienrich[1](✉), Nina Döllinger[2], Simon Kock[2], Kristina Schindler[2], and Ole Traupe[2]

[1] University of Würzburg, Würzburg, Germany
carolin.wienrich@uni-wuerzburg.de
[2] Technische Universität Berlin, Berlin, Germany

Abstract. As other interactive technologies, the promising virtual reality (VR) applications and their success highly depend on the quality of the user's experience. The present study gives first insights into relations between general and VR specific aspects of user experience by: (1) Analyzing the evaluation requirements for a large-scale multi-user use case; (2) relating evaluation concepts from the fields of (2D) user experience (UX) and (3D) VR experiences; (3) testing these relations by incorporating measurements from different research fields, and (4) discussing implications for a holistic evaluation framework. During and after experiencing a multi-user adventure on the Immersive Deck of Illusion Walk, participants rated their experience with respect to various components of general UX as well as other components specific to VR experiences. The results revealed positive correlations of presence and social presence with most of the employed post-experience UX measures. The relations between the post- and in-experience measurements showed some inconsistencies. Overall, the experience was positively appraised. The results encourage further investigations into integrating measurements from different lines of research in order to explore the evaluation space of VR experiences.

Keywords: User experience · Virtual reality · Evaluation framework

1 Introduction

Large-scale virtual reality (VR) experiences have gained importance for location-based entertainment [1]. Companies like Zero Latency [2], the Void [3], or the IMAX Experience Center [4] offer immersive multi-user adventures, which easily supersede the capabilities of typical home VR installations. As with other interactive technologies, promising VR applications and their success highly depend on the quality of the user's experience. While the need for user evaluation is evident, the evaluation procedure itself seems not to be as trivial. The present study performs a user evaluation of a multi-user adventure on the Immersive Deck of Berlin-based Illusion Walk (the first commercial large-scale VR provider in Germany; [5, 6]) by:

(1) Analyzing the evaluation requirements for a large-scale multi-user use case;
(2) relating evaluation concepts from the fields of (2D) user experience (UX) and (3D) VR

© Springer International Publishing AG, part of Springer Nature 2018
A. Marcus and W. Wang (Eds.): DUXU 2018, LNCS 10918, pp. 573–589, 2018.
https://doi.org/10.1007/978-3-319-91797-9_41

experiences; (3) testing these relations by incorporating measurements from different research fields, and (4) discussing implications towards a holistic evaluation framework.

2   Analyzing the Evaluation Requirements

2.1   Situation

The Immersive Deck (Illusion Walk, KG) is a multi-user, multi-room VR installation, which is equipped with a marker-based inside-out tracking technology that allows for the continuous transition between adjacent rooms [5]. Enabling free locomotion, users wear Oculus Rift (Oculus VR, LLC) VR headsets powered by untethered backpack PCs (Intel Core i7 quad-core CPU, NVidia GTX 1070 GPU). In general, Illusion Walk invites users to experience joint adventures, or to collaboratively solve tasks. The basic theme of the story investigated here is a group repair job of a wind turbine in order to restore power to a couple of laser cannons sought to defend Earth's energy supplies against the attack by an alien species. The story requires the participants to move through the VR installation on a predetermined path. Users are virtually represented by avatars based on absolute (6 degrees of freedom; custom built [6]) head and relative (to the head) hand tracking, being rendered from the knees upwards. Hand tracking is achieved using Leap Motion (Leap Motion, Inc.) sensors mounted to the front plates of the VR headsets. Audio stimulation is provided via digital stereo headsets, voice communication is established by means of a custom TeamSpeak server (TeamSpeak Systems GmbH). The virtual environment contains several mixed-reality elements (MRE), in which properties of the real (shape, material, vibration) and the virtual (appearance, sound) world coincide (the walls, a door, a push-button, etc.).

2.2   Evaluation Requirements

Assessing the seemingly trivial perception - similarly desired by VR providers and users - of experiencing and mastering an enjoyable challenge in interaction with others involves the evaluation of various concepts from different research fields on multiple levels of complexity.

2.2.1   Aspects of Evaluation

In the field of *human-computer interaction* this task would be addressed by the evaluation of UX. UX concerns itself with the perception and behavior while interacting with products or technical systems (ISO-Norm BS EN ISO 9241-210). When characterizing UX, the functionality, the content, and the aesthetics of a product, the context of use, and the user's perception of and emotions towards the product must be considered [4, 7–9]. Among others, the following researchers proposed dedicated UX models. The *pragmatic/hedonic model* of UX by Hassenzahl (2007), for example, differentiates between the objective qualities of a product and the user's perception of those [10]. Following this model, pragmatic qualities relate to the degree of how the product enables goal achievement, i.e., to usability and usefulness, while the hedonic quality relates to the psychological needs and the emotional experience of the user.

Similar to Hassenzahl's pragmatic quality, the instrumental quality of the *Components of User Experience* (CUE, [9]) model addresses usability and usefulness. The hedonic quality of the CUE model, however, is divided into different modules: non-instrumental product perception (visual aesthetics, commitment, and status), emotions, and consequences of use (product loyalty, intention to use). Another perspective on UX is described by the ISO 6385, which defines *ergonomics* as the understanding of interactions between humans and other elements of a system in order to optimize human well-being and overall system performance [11]. Three fundamental pillars of ergonomics are described, namely physical, cognitive, and organizational ergonomics. *Physical ergonomics* cover the biomechanical design aspects of the equipment used, while *cognitive ergonomics* address mental processes as they affect interactions among elements of a system. *Organizational ergonomics* concern the optimization of socio-technical systems including communication, teamwork, and cooperative work, among others [11].

As important as for other interactive technologies the described UX components are important, but not sufficient concerning the evaluation of the use case (large-scale, multi-user VR). Thus, evaluation concepts often used in VR contexts might be meaningful additions (e.g., [12, 13]).

VR specific UX, among other aspects, addresses navigation, wayfinding, and object manipulation (detailed discussion in [12]). Additionally, the degree of user engagement (i.e., presence) and the occurrence and severity of simulator sickness are crucial factors (e.g., [12, 14]). The core concept of *presence* describes the user's feelings of actually being in the place provided by VR (place illusion) and reliably and effectively performing certain actions (plausibility) [15]. According to Schubert et al., the construct of presence has three main components: realism, involvement, and spatial presence [16]. Realism is defined as the user's evaluation of how convincing the virtual environment is. Involvement is defined as a facet of presence based on attention. Spatial presence is defined as a component of spatial construction, i.e., spatial encompassment.

Kinetosis is generally described as a physiological reaction to actual or apparent motion, and includes manifestations such as *simulator sickness* [17]. Simulator sickness usually occurs when motion is presented on a screen introducing substantial visual flow (e.g., simulator: [18]). Apart from common symptoms like discomfort, drowsiness, vomiting, and nausea, simulator sickness can cause further visual and visuo-motoric symptoms like eye strain and dizziness. However, the term is also used for similar symptoms of kinetosis in VR (also referred to as cyber sickness) and other negative side effects of VR experiences [19, 20].

A multi-user context imposes additional requirements. The motive of relatedness from the Self-Determination Theory (SDT: [21]), e.g., addresses the meaning of others for one's own actions as well as the importance of one's own actions for others. Many other factors inducing mutual importance are known from a long tradition of social psychology research (e.g., social identity, social interdependence), a detailed introduction to which is beyond the scope of this article. Some of these aspects, however, are incorporated into the concept of *social presence*. It is defined as the sense of being together in a multi-user VR and covers psychological and behavioral involvement as well as affective aspects [22].

2.2.2   Levels of Evaluation

In the field of human-computer interaction evaluation procedures could assess the experience with a whole system (e.g., enjoying the interaction with a smartphone), with individual sub-modules (e.g., enjoying the interaction with a specific app) or with single interactive elements (e.g., enjoying the interaction with the touch display), respectively [23]. Similarly, VR experiences can be evaluated in their entirety (e.g., enjoying an adventure), on a task (e.g., enjoying the mastering of a quest) or element (e.g., enjoying the haptic feeling of mixed reality elements) level. While post-experience questionnaires mainly assess the experience on the system level, observations and in-experience questionnaires can target the experience on system, task or element level, respectively. In the context of a multi-user VR evaluation, in-experience assessments could lead to breaks in presence or story telling. Thus, they cannot be too lengthy and should have plausible ties to the storyline. These requirements raise the question whether (short and adapted to the story) in-experience measurements are valid to assess UX.

The present study investigated general aspects of UX as well as VR specific aspects during and after (i.e., on different levels of) the VR experience described above. Post-experience UX assessment was employed based on the CUE model. In-experience UX was assessed via physical, cognitive, and organizational ergonomics and by assessing affective states. VR specific aspects were assessed through presence, social presence, and health-related issues (e.g., simulator sickness). The study aimed at exploring the relations between these aspects and levels.

3   Relating Evaluation Concepts

The approach of Stanney et al. [16] has already been emphasized to include VR specific constructs for evaluating virtual experiences. However, the main components of UX have rarely been related to additional concepts covering the specifics of VR experiences [14]. Furthermore, connections between different levels (e.g., post- and in-experiences measurements) have previously been neglected. The present article proposes the following relations:

Stanney et al. [12] explicitly include presence as one main factor creating compelling VR experiences [20]. Thus, presence should be related to the UX of the investigated application. Concerning hedonic qualities (particularly affective states), affective responses have been shown to heighten the sense of presence in VR and vice versa (e.g., [24, 25]). Hence, presence should particularly be related to the affective measurements incorporated in UX evaluations (post- and in-experience). Furthermore, the study explores how presence is related to the pragmatic quality (i.e., usability and usefulness), non-instrumental aspects (e.g., aesthetic), and the consequences of use, as well as to mental and physical ergonomics (in-experience).

Previously, it was shown that *social presence* positively impacts on game experience [26], on virtual team performance [27], and on the interaction with virtual agents and avatars in VR [28]. However, a direct connection to the above described aspects of UX has not been drawn yet. Therefore, the present study also explores how social presence is connected to *pragmatic* and *hedonic* (particularly affective states) qualities of UX. In addition, it explores how measurements are related to each other among different levels, particularly to social aspects like the organizational ergonomics (i.e., post- and in-experience).

With respect to VR experiences, *physical ergonomics* might address *pressure points* of the headset or the backpack, as well as distraction by cables and other parts of the equipment limiting the movement of the users. Health-related parameters such as *simulator sickness* might also be important indicators of the specific physical ergonomics of VR systems. As *physical load* (in-experience) is a typical indicator of physical ergonomics (the lack thereof, i.e.), it should be positively related to these VR-specific concepts.

Furthermore, the described in-experience (state affect and ergonomics) and post-experience (CUE model) UX concepts should be tightly connected, as the user experience of individual aspects of the VR experience should clearly affect its overall evaluation. The assessment of affective states during the experience should be related to the emotion module of the CUE model. Mental workload (in-experience), as a typical indicator of cognitive ergonomics, should similarly be related to corresponding post-experience aspects of UX such as negative affects. Organizational ergonomics and physical ergonomics were not connected with post-experience UX.

In sum, the study addressed three goals:

(1) Assessing the assumed relations between the described evaluation concepts originating from the fields of general and VR specific UX.
(2) Exploring relations between the concepts described on different levels (post- and in-experience).
(3) Detecting overlaps, and therefore potential redundancies, in order to work towards an integrated evaluation framework for (large-scale, multi-user) VR applications.

4 Empirical Testing of Relations

The present study puts different evaluation concepts and potential relations between them to the test by evaluating a beta version of the first large-scale, multi-user VR experience of Illusion Walk in Germany [5, 6]. The research questions are explorative. It was assumed that different concepts from different fields of research (general and VR-specific UX) assessed on different levels (post- and in-experience) are related to each other. Correlative analyses examined these relations and proposed conclusions for an evaluation framework of large-scale multi-user VR applications.

Note that the present tests were part of a bigger experimental cycle with additional research questions. To answer these, two experimental conditions were established. In the interdependence condition, (IDP) participants had to solve a series of tasks together with their fellow participants while mutually depending on each other's performance. In the non-interdependence condition (nIDP) participants had to solve a similar control task on their own. In line with the expectations, stronger team affiliation and more cooperation (i.e., mutual importance) were found for participants in the IPD versus the nIPD condition (results presented in detail in [29]).

4.1   Method

4.1.1   Participants

Seventy-two volunteers (n = 12 female; mean age 32.11 years; SD = 8.68 years) with normal or corrected-to-normal vision participated in the study. Participants conducted the experiment in groups of three (n = 4 female experimental groups). None of the participants reported any health problems such as epilepsy or migraine (which could be triggered by VR). A screening questionnaire revealed that the sample was rather highly experienced with VR (M = 3.35, SD = 1.49; poles of scale 1 to 5) and video gaming (M = 3.68, SD = 1.20; poles of scale 1 to 5). Participants also reported a high technical affinity (M = 4.42; SD = .78; poles of scale 1 to 5) and a good tolerance for simulator sickness (M = 4.32; SD = .82; poles of scale 1 to 6). As compensation, participants received a voucher from Illusion Walk for a free VR experience.

4.1.2   Materials

VR Installation and Equipment. The experiment was conducted in the multi-user, multi-room VR installation "Immersive Deck" (Illusion Walk, KG), which is equipped with a marker-based inside-out tracking technology that allows for the continuous transition between adjacent rooms (see Subsect. 2.1). The virtual environment was created and presented with Unity3D (Unity Technologies) running a client-server model over 802.11ac Wi-Fi connections.

Questionnaires. All text-based material for informing, screening, instructing, and assessing the participants outside the experience was presented on tablet devices. To assess the participants' state during different parts of the experience, an in-experience questionnaire was set up (see Fig. 1).

Fig. 1. In-experience questionnaires presented in a pop-up style and operated via the participants' tracked hands; the example shows an item of the PANAS (German version).

Post-experience Assessment. *UX* was assessed by the modules of the *meCUE* questionnaire (*modular evaluation of key Components of User Experience*, [30]). The modules address *product perception* (instrumental - pragmatic subscales: *usability* and *usefulness*; non-instrumental - hedonic subscales: *visual aesthetics, commitment,* and *status*), emotions (subscales: *positive affect* and *negative affect -* hedonic), and *consequences of use* (subscales: *product loyalty, intention to use*), as well as an *overall evaluation* of the experience (one item). In addition, participants were asked: "What are you willing to pay for a similar experience lasting two hours?".

The sense of ***presence*** was measured with the German version of the *iGroup Presence Questionnaire (iPQ,* [16]) entailing subscales for *general presence, realism, involvement,* and *spatial presence.*

Social presence was measured by the *Social Presence Module* of the *Game Experience Questionnaire (GEQ,* [31]). It includes *psychological involvement, behavioral involvement,* and *negative feelings.*

A ***discomfort*** *scale was used* following a model, which assumes that discomfort is influenced by biomechanical design aspects, such as pressure points, and therefore is more relevant to the ergonomic side of design [31]. Since the original discomfort scale was designed to assess seat comfort, the items were slightly adapted to reflect discomfort arising from the VR equipment (i.e., pressure points of the headset, eye strain, etc.).

An itemized analysis is not recommended for the meCUE. Nonetheless, specific items (negative affect subscale) were used assess adverse effects of the experience, such as tiredness.

In-experience Assessment. Complementing post-experience measures, the in-experience assessment contained one team-based item (organizational ergonomics) concerning the importance of the other group members ("At the moment, the experience with the other experts is important for me.").

Physical load (physical ergonomics) and ***mental workload*** (mental ergonomics) were similarly measured by one item, which had been adapted from a scale assessing experienced strain (*SEA,* [33]): "At the moment, how physically strained do you feel?"; "At the moment, how mentally strained do you feel?". Answers could range from "not strained at all" to "extremely strained".

The participants' ***affective state*** was assessed during the experience through the *Positive and Negative Affect Schedule (PANAS,* [32]).

In addition, participants reported their level of ***simulator sickness*** on the *Fast Motion Sickness Scale (FMS,* [33]) before, during, and after the experience.

As mentioned above, the present experiment was part of a bigger experimental cycle with additional research questions. Thus, some further measures were assessed but not referred to here. These include several physiological parameters and behavioral observations, the latter being recorded by a supervisor covertly following the group of participants throughout the tracking space. Furthermore, the Game Experience Questionnaire (GEQ, [31]) was administered. It includes the *In-Game Module* with its subscales *competence, flow, immersion, challenge, tension, negative* and *positive affect,* and the *Post-Game Module* entailing the subscales *positive* and *negative experiences, tiredness,* and *returning to reality.* Moreover, the cooperative module of the *Competitive and Cooperative Presence in Gaming Questionnaire* (CCPIG, [34]), elaborating on cooperative social presence, was administered to investigate the effects of the social interdependence manipulation. Some additional open questions (post-experience) were also not reported in the present article. All details are published in [29].

4.1.3 Procedure

Overall Structure. Each session was structured into a preparation, an experience, and a post-experience phase. The *preparation phase* included usage instructions and safety warnings for the Immersive Deck as well as retrieving the participants' informed consent. Demographic and health data were assessed via a screening questionnaire. The *experience phase* started after putting on the VR equipment followed by a brief technical check-up. The VR experience let the participants move through the virtual scene following the requirements created by a predefined set of events (see below), including a series of tasks and in-experience assessments. Behavioral observations were conducted from outside of the virtual environment. The experience phase ended with unmounting the equipment. The *post-experience phase* included the completion of the post-experimental questionnaires together with a series of open questions.

Detailed Description of the Experience. The experience began with the collective exploration of the virtual starting room, which resembled the physical starting room of the VR installation (MRE) - a measure to facilitate presence via a gradual transition into the virtual environment. The adventure could then be started by any of the participants by pressing a push-button (MRE). This and other elements of the scene could be operated via the virtually represented hands. Immediately following the button press, the first in-experience assessment (pop-up questionnaire; see Fig. 1) was performed establishing a baseline measurement.

The subsequent storyline was structured into three sections, each of them leading to an instance of the task, followed up by a repetition of the in-experience assessment. The task was performed on a graphical user interface, required visuo-motor skills, and had a pronounced speed component. In one condition it also required coordination between participants, conveying an experimental manipulation (nIDP/IDP) in the context of another research question [29].

The basic theme of the story was a collective repair job of a wind turbine to restore power to a set of laser cannons defending Earth's energy supplies against a hostile alien attack. In short, the participants had to enter the wind turbine facility, repair the laser cannons, and - after being abducted by the aliens - activate a spaceship's self-destruction mechanism to ultimately fend off the attack. The story is outlined in greater detail in [29]. To ensure the participants' motivation, the story seemingly depended on task success, with minor contextual workarounds (not detailed here) allowing it to progress even in the case of a failure. The in-experience questionnaires were disguised as a state evaluation within the initially suggested work context.

Task Description. The recurrent task was performed as a minigame linked to a pedestal with identical operating panels on its three side faces (see [29]). The pedestal appeared at pre-designed positions in the scene. Each participant's panel contained three differently shaped and colored buttons (red square, blue circle, green triangle), a graphical timer for the trial time, a numerical timer for the total task time, and a progress bar of stacked triangles on top of the pedestal, its number representing the current sum of successful (positive) and failed (negative) trials. Across the task instances, the difficulty increased to keep the task interesting and challenging.

4.2   Data Analysis

To explore the relations between the different UX measures and components, correlations were computed. In a first step, the items of the standardized questionnaires were aggregated according to the corresponding manuals. Concerning the in-experience questions the average of each scale over the four measurement points were calculated. As most of the resulting scales did not fulfill the requirements for the parametric Pearson correlation coefficient, Spearman's rank correlations were calculated.

5   Results

Due to technical problems in some in-experiment questionnaires, the sample size for in-experience analysis was reduced to N = 38 (9 female, 29 male) participants. Thus, the correlation analyses concerning the post-experience measurements are based on 72 participants; those concerning in-experience measurements included 38 participants. Tables 1 and 2 show descriptive statistics as well as the results of correlation analyses between the post-experience measurements. Figure 2 illustrates the respective correlation patterns.

5.1   Relations Between Presence (VR Specific) and Post-experience UX

In general, the VR experience of Illusion Walk enabled a strong feeling of *presence* (Table 1; caption row). Overall, presence correlated with all aspects of the post-experience UX evaluation (subscales of meCUE) except *usefulness* (see Fig. 2, panel a) at least in one subscale (*involvement*, *realness*, *spatial presence*, or *general presence*). A closer look revealed the correlation with *usability* and *positive affect* was only significant for the *general presence* value (Table 1; column 4; rows 1 and 6). Particularly, *visual aesthetic* and *loyalty* were correlated with *realness* and *spatial presence* (Table 1; columns 2 and 3; rows 3 and 8).

5.2   Relations Between Social Presence (VR Specific) and Post-experience UX

Analogous to the feeling of presence, the VR experience of Illusion Walk enabled a strong feeling of *social presence* (Table 2, caption row). Overall, social presence correlated with all aspects of the post-experience UX evaluation (subscales of meCUE), except u*sefulness* and *negative affect* (see Fig. 2, panel b) at least in one subscale (*involvement*, *realness*, *spatial presence*, or *general presence*). Particularly, the

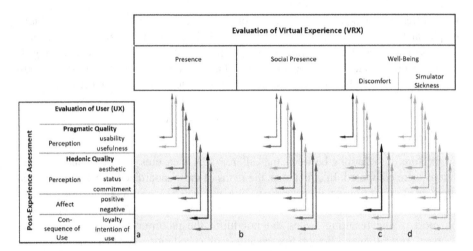

Fig. 2. Arrows depict the correlations between post-experience UX (meCUE) and presence, social presence, discomfort, and simulator sickness (VR specific measurements). Black arrows indicate a significant correlation between each subscale of the VR specific measurement and the subscales of the meCUE. Dark grey arrows indicate a significant correlation between at least one subscale of the VR specific measurement and the subscales of the meCUE. Light grey arrows indicate any significant correlation between subscales of the VR specific measurement and the subscales of the meCUE.

subscale *empathy* was correlated with *pragmatic quality*, *positive affect*, *status*, *commitment*, and *consequences of use* (Table 2; column 1; rows 1, 2, 4, 5, 6, 8, 9). Surprisingly, the subscale *negative feelings* showed positive correlations with *status* and *commitment* (Table 2; column 2; rows 4 and 5). The subscale *behavior* did not show any significant correlation with the subscales of the meCUE (Table 2; column 3).

5.3   Relations Between Health Measures (VR Specific) and Post-experience UX

In general, the VR installation of Illusion Walk caused very low values of *simulator sickness* (M = 1.31; SD = .46) and satisfying levels of *discomfort* (Table 2, caption row and Fig. 2, panel c and d).

   Simulator sickness was not correlated significantly with any subscale of the meCUE questionnaire. Probably, the low variances of its sub-modules are responsible for this observation. Similarly, the *discomfort* scale showed only two significant correlations with the meCUE subscales, namely *usability* (Table 2, column 4; row 1) and *negative affect* (Table 2; column 4; row 7).

5.4   Relations Between Post-experience Measures and In-experience UX

In contrast to the correlation patterns reported above, only two correlations between in- and post-experience UX reached significance (*presence* subscales *spatial* and

Table 1. Means and standard deviations of the different measures and the correlations between presence (iPQ) and post-experience UX (meCUE).

		Presence	Involv.	realness	spatial	general
			(4 6; 1 28)	(3 16; 1 27)	(5 44; 0 86)	(5 97; 0 66)
Pragmatic Quality	**Perception**	**usability** (5.64; 0.9)	$r_s < -.01$, p = .99	$r_s = .12$, p = .32	$r_s = .19$, p = .11	$r_s = .29$, p = .02
		usefulness (5.64; 0.89)	$r_s = -.10$, p = .39	$r_s = .13$, p = .26	$r_s = .08$, p = .48	$r_s = .10$, p = .38
Hedonic Quality	**Perception**	**visual aesthetic**	$r_s = .20$, p = .10	$r_s = .54$, p < .01	$r_s = .38$, p < .01	$r_s = .22$, p = .07
		status (3.69; 1.23)	$r_s = .05$, p = .65	$r_s = .33$, p < .01	$r_s = .07$, p = .58	$r_s = .23$, p = 05
		Commitment	$r_s = -.14$, p = .23	$r_s = .30$, p < .01	$r_s < .01$, p = .98	$r_s = .19$, p = .11
	Affect	**positive** (4.62; 0.83)	$r_s = .13$, p = .27	$r_s = .17$, p = .14	$r_s = .17$, p = .16	$r_s = .25$, p = .04
		negative (2.38; 1.11)	$r_s = -.35$, p < .01	$r_s = -.14$, p = .25	$r_s = -.34$, p < .01	$r_s = -.47$, p < .01
Cons. of Use		**loyalty** (3.68; 1.15)	$r_s = .33$, p = .01	$r_s = .41$, p < .01	$r_s = .23$, p = .05	$r_s = .28$, p = .02
		intention of use	$r_s = .24$, p = .04	$r_s = .22$, p = .06	$r_s = .20$, p = .09	$r_s = .32$, p < .01

Table 2. Means and standard deviations of the different measures and the correlations between social presence (GEQ), well-being (discomfort scale) and post-experience UX (meCUE).

		Social Presence	empathy (3 41; 0 66)	behavior (3 51; 0 83)	feelings (1 94; 0 46)	discomfort (2 37; 1 2)
Pragmatic Quality	Perception	usability (5.64; 0.9)	$r_s = .26,$ $p = .03$	$r_s = .12,$ $p = .33$	$r_s = .08,$ $p = .49$	$r_s = -.28,$ $p = .02$
		usefulness (5.64; 0.89)	$r_s = .28,$ $p = .02$	$r_s = .19,$ $p = .12$	$r_s = .24,$ $p = .05$	$r_s = .48,$ $p = .08$
Hedonic Quality	Perception	visual aesthetic	$r_s = .16,$ $p = .14$	$r_s = .07,$ $p = .54$	$r_s = .06,$ $p = .63$	$r_s = -.21,$ $p = .08$
		status (3.69; 1.23)	$r_s = .36,$ $p = .02$	$r_s = .15,$ $p = .22$	$r_s = .35,$ $p = .01$	$r_s < .01,$ $p = .98$
		commitment (2.24; 1.18)	$r_s = .31,$ $p = .01$	$r_s = .09,$ $p = .46$	$r_s = .24,$ $p = .04$	$r_s = .03,$ $p = .78$
	Affect	positive (4.62; 0.83)	$r_s = .27,$ $p = .02$	$r_s = .11,$ $p = .36$	$r_s = .09,$ $p = .45$	$r_s = -.14,$ $p = .24$
		negative (2.38; 1.11)	$r_s = -.15,$ $p = .19$	$r_s = -.1,$ $p = .41$	$r_s = .08,$ $p = .49$	$r_s = -.04,$ $p = .76$
	Cons. of Use	loyalty (3.68; 1.15)	$r_s = .24,$ $p = .04$	$r_s = .07,$ $p = .64$	$r_s = .22,$ $p = .06$	$r_s = -.03,$ $p = .82$
		intention of use	$r_s = .36,$ $p = .01$	$r_s = .08,$ $p = .51$	$r_s = .05,$ $p = .23$	$r_s = .04,$ $p = .76$

co-presence: $r_s = 0.41$, $p = 0.02$; and *social presence* subscales *behavior* and *co-presence*: $r_s = 0.40$, $p = 0.02$). However, *physical load* (in-experience) correlated positively with *discomfort* (VR specific post-experience) ($r_s = .39$, $p = .01$). Similarly, a positive correlation between *physical workload* and *simulator sickness* (VR specific) was found ($r_s = .31$, $p = .04$). The expected correlations between the post- and in-experience UX measurements (affect module of meCUE and PANAS; *negative affect* subscale of meCUE and *mental workload*) could also be found.

6 Discussing Implications Regarding a Holistic Evaluation Framework

The emerging public perception of VR leads to a growing number of location-based entertainment centers offering multi-user VR experiences (e.g. Zero Latency with currently 12 sites). While the need for user evaluation is evident, the evaluation procedure itself seems not to be as trivial. The present study performs a user evaluation of a multi-user adventure on the Immersive Deck of Berlin's Illusion Walk (the first commercial large-scale VR provider in Germany) [5, 6] by: (1) Analyzing the evaluation requirements for a large-scale multi-user use case; (2) relating evaluation concepts from the fields of (2D) user experience (UX) and (3D) VR experiences; (3) testing these relations by employing measurements from different research fields, and (4) discussing implications for a holistic evaluation framework.

The present study applied UX concepts from the field of human-computer interaction as well as VR specific aspects to appraise the experience of users. The modules of the meCUE (based on the Components of User Experience model, [30]) were related to presence, social presence and health related measurements like simulator sickness (VR specific aspects). The correlation patterns revealed that particularly presence and social presence were related to the components of UX (measured post-experience).

Presence. While the association between presence and affect is well documented (e.g., [24, 25]), the relation between presence and the other UX aspects is mostly unexplored. In the research history of presence, the impact of immersion on presence is well-established (e.g., [15]). Immersion is defined as the degree to which a person can be engrossed in a virtual world, based on objective and quantifiable multisensory stimuli. Hence, immersion describes the extent to which the technological features of the device and the setting can provide the user with the illusion of reality. The higher the degree of immersion, the higher the potential feeling of presence (e.g., [35]). On the one hand, the association between pragmatic aspects of UX and presence might merely mirror the relation between immersion and presence. On the other hand, presence occurs when a mental model is constructed, and attention is allocated to a virtual environment [15, 16]. Hence, the association between pragmatic aspects of UX and presence might also reflect the degree of attention that is deployed to inaccuracies of the systems. Further research is necessary to clarify the causal direction of the association and to transfer the findings on the construct of presence to the field of UX.

Social Presence. Due to the present multi-user context, mutual importance as well as the sense of being together are crucial evaluation aspects. Previously, it was shown that

social presence positively impacts on game experience [26], on virtual team performance [27], and on the interaction with virtual agents and avatars in VR [28]. Further,
it is well known that the presence of others influences cognition and behavior (cf. social
cognition, [36]), which has also been shown in VR (e.g., [37]). These previous results
might indicate a relation between social presence and UX aspects, but a direct connection to the aspects of UX described above has not been drawn yet. The results of the
present study revealed that mainly the subscale of empathy contributed to these relations while particularly the subscale of behavior did not show any relations. However,
this does not justify the conclusion that the other subscales are irrelevant for VR user
evaluations. Rather, the findings might indicate additional information, which is provided by social presence compared to general UX concepts.

The health-related measurements only sporadically showed relations to the UX
aspects. The low values of discomfort and simulator sickness in this study might be
able to explain these findings. Average scores near either end of a scale usually exhibit
only a limited variance, which in turn can only result in limited correlations. Higher
values on health-related measures might have produced stronger correlations with the
more traditional UX concepts, even if the underlying causal relations are unaffected.
Thus, health-related aspect should still be considered in future evaluation processes.

In sum, the present study revealed relations between aspects of UX and VR specific
measures. On the one hand, the results encourage to consider measurements from
different lines of research to explore the evaluation space of VR experiences. On the
other hand, the results motivate to consolidate the spirit of user-centered design processes in commercial VR contexts. However, the present study is just a first step
towards an appropriate evaluation framework. Clearly, more work is needed, which
should include the following steps:

Methods and Theory Building. As the applied methodology was part of a larger
experimental circle, only correlation patterns were calculated to get an impression of
assumed relations. However, causal conclusion could not be drawn. Hence, the proposed relations should be examined in future, experimental studies.

In order to examine the contributions of different UX-concepts to the evaluation of
the experience of users, factorial analyses would reveal variance shared by different
concepts. Such results could indicate measurements addressing the same concepts and
therefore being redundant, and separate them from measurements, which cover different concepts and should be used together. Future theories should conflate these
findings into a model predicting VR-UX, which future research should experimentally
substantiate.

Another question concerns the point of evaluation time. In the context of multi-user
VR evaluation, in-experience assessments could lead to breaks in presence or interaction. Hence, the question occurs whether (short and adapted to the story)
in-experience measurements are valid to assess UX. Our results revealed a satisfying
accordance between the post-experience and in-experience UX measurements. The
health-related measurements (VR specific) and the in-experience UX measurements
also correlated positively. However, presence and social presence were not related to
the in-experience UX measurements. The latter result contrasts with the relation to the
post-experience measurements. Particularly the inconsistencies regarding the affective

measurements are surprising. Previous studies showed strong relations between the feeling of presence and affects [24, 25].

Additional Indicators. Stanny et al. [12] stated wayfinding, navigation, and object manipulation to be important aspects of VR evaluation. In addition, system parameters, particularly latencies, impacted on the experience of users and hence should be evaluated as well. Another very important step are qualitative analyses. VR experiences are often described as journeys. Hence, evaluating the smoothness of the experience would improve the evaluation framework. Benford et al. [38] suggested the analysis of transitions and trajectories. Trajectories reveal the continuity, coherence, and interaction patterns between users and the equipment, as well as between different users. Continuity deals with various transitions within the VR experience itself, but also between the VR experience and the experience in the real world (e.g., transitions of time, space, or roles). Similarly, (2D) UX testing includes qualitative analyses (e.g., think aloud, observation) which should be considered for an evaluation framework. Another related question concerns the point of evaluation time and therewith the level that can be evaluated. Post-experience measurements often assess the holistic experience. In contrast, in-experience evaluations might stress challenges concerning specific tasks or interactions within the experience. However, the in-experience questions should conflate into the story to avoid breaks in presence or interactions [39]. In our opinion, VR in particular might not only be the object of evaluation, but also provide a versatile tool for such analyses. Many parameters can be recorded and controlled - e.g., the trajectories of avatars can be observed without additional camera equipment and easily compared to ideal trajectories.

In sum, the present study put different evaluation tools (general UX and VR specific) and potential associations between them to the test by evaluating the beta version of the first large-scale multi-user VR experience of Illusion Walk in Germany [5, 6]. The tracking and interaction technology of the Immersive Deck seems to have contributed to a general positive evaluation of the experience. High ratings of presence and social presence and low in-experience negative affect indicate the absence of any major constraints due to the equipped VR hardware: Users experienced an enjoyable challenge in interaction with others. The present paper represents a first step towards integrating evaluation concepts from different research fields in order to evaluate large-scale multi-user VR experiences.

References

1. The Future of Virtual Reality isn't Your Living Room - It's The Mall. https://www.forbes.com/sites/charliefink/2017/03/07/the-future-of-virtual-reality-isnt-your-living-room-its-the-mall/1#1e3398502bec. Accessed 22 Dec 2017
2. Zero Latency Madrid: Google Maps (2017). https://zerolatencyvr.com/. Accessed: 22 Dec 2017
3. The void (2007)
4. Understanding, Scoping and Defining User Experience: A survey approach. dl.acm.org. http://dl.acm.org/citation.cfm?id=1518813. Accessed 22 Dec 2017

5. Home—Illusion Walk Berlin the Virtual Reality Immersive Experience Provider. https://www.illusion-walk.com/. Accessed 22 Dec 2017

6. Podkosova, I., Vasylevska, K., Schoenauer, C., Vonach, E., Fikar, P., Bronederk, E., Kaufmann, H.: ImmersiveDeck: a large-scale wireless VR system for multiple users (2016). https://ieeexplore.ieee.org

7. ISO 9241-11: Guidelines for specifying and measuring usability (1993)

8. McCarthy, J., Wright, P.: Technology as experience. Interactions 11(5), 42 (2004)

9. Thüring, M., Mahlke, S.: Usability, aesthetics and emotions in human-technology interaction. Int. J. Psychol. 42(4), 253–264 (2007)

10. Law, E., Vermeeren, A., Hassenzahl, M., Eds, M.B.: Towards a UX manifesto. In: COST294-MAUSE Affiliated Workshop, Structure, September 2007, vol. 2, pp. 205–206 (2007)

11. International Ergonomics Association. http://www.iea.cc/. Accessed 22 Dec 2017

12. Stanney, K.M., Mourant, R.R., Kennedy, R.S.: Human factors issues in virtual environments: a review of the literature. Presence Teleoper. Virtual Environ. 7(4), 327–351 (1998)

13. Tromp, J.G., Steed, A., Wilson, J.R.: Systematic usability evaluation and design issues for collaborative virtual environments. Presence Teleoper. Virtual Environ. 12(3), 241–267 (2003)

14. Wienrich, C., Noller, F., Thüring, M.: Design principles for VR interaction models: an empirical pilot study. In: Virtuelle und erweiterte Realitäten 14. Workshop der GI-Fachgruppe VR/AR, pp. 162–171 (2017)

15. Slater, M.: Place illusion and plausibility can lead to realistic behaviour in immersive virtual environments. Philos. Trans. Roy. Soc. B Biol. Sci. 364(1535), 3549–3557 (2009)

16. Schubert, T., Friedmann, F., Regenbrecht, H.: The experience of presence: factor analytic insights. Presence Teleoper. Virtual Environ. 10(3), 266–281 (2001)

17. Hegemann, S.: Die Entstehung von Kinetosen. In: Plinkert, P.K., Klingmann, C. (eds.) Hören und Gleichgewicht, pp. 185–193. Springer, Vienna (2010). https://doi.org/10.1007/978-3-211-99270-8_19

18. Kennedy, R.S., Drexler, J., Kennedy, R.C.: Research in visually induced motion sickness. Appl. Ergon. 41(4), 494–503 (2010)

19. Burdea, G.C., Coiffet, P.: Virtual Reality Technology. Wiley-IEEE Press, New York (2003)

20. Stanney, K.M., Kennedy, R.S., Drexler, J.M.: Cybersickness is not simulator sickness (1997). http://journals.sagepub.com/

21. Ryan, R.M., Deci, E.L.: Self-determination theory and the facilitation of intrinsic motivation, social development, and well-being. Am. Psychol. 55(1), 68–78 (2000)

22. Ijsselsteijn, W., de Kort, Y., Poels, K., Jurgelionis, A., Bellotti, F.: Characterising and measuring user experiences in digital games. In: ACE Conference 2007, January 2007

23. Reinhardt, D., Kuge, J., Hurtienne, J.: CHAI: coding heuristics for assessing intuitive interaction. In: Marcus, A., Wang, W. (eds.) DUXU 2018. LNCS, vol. 10918, pp. 528–545 (2018)

24. Baños, R., Botella, C., Alcañiz, M., Liaño, V., Guerrero, B., Rey, B.: Immersion and emotion: their impact on the sense of presence. CyberPsychol. Behav. 7(6), 734–741 (2004)

25. Riva, G., et al.: Affective interactions using virtual reality: the link between presence and emotions. CyberPsychol. Behav. 10(1), 45–56 (2007)

26. Ryan, R.M., Rigby, C.S., Przybylski, A.: The motivational pull of video games: a self-determination theory approach. Motiv. Emot. 30(4), 347–363 (2006)

27. Hertel, G., Konradt, U., Orlikowski, B.: Managing distance by interdependence: goal setting, task interdependence, and team-based rewards in virtual teams. Eur. J. Work Organ. Psychol. 13(1), 1–28 (2004)

28. Ellis, J.B., Luther, K., Bessiere, K., Kellogg, W.A.: Games for virtual team building. In: Proceedings of the Designing Interactive Systems, DIS 2008, pp. 295–304 (2008)
29. Wienrich, C., Schindler, K., Döllinger, N., Kock, S., Traupe, O.: Social presence and cooperation in a large-scale, multi-user virtual reality – an empirical evaluation of a location-based adventure. In: IEEE VR (2018)
30. Minge, M., Riedel, L.: meCUE – Ein modularer Fragebogen zur Erfassung des Nutzungserlebens. In: Mensch und Computer, Munich, pp. 89–98 (2013)
31. IJsselsteijn, W.A., de Kort, Y.A.W., Poels, K.: Game Experience Questionnaire. FUGA the fun of gaming: Measuring the human experience of media enjoyment GAME (2015)
32. Krohne, W.H., Egloff, B., Kohlmann, C.-W., Tausch, A.: Untersuchungen mit einer deutschen Version der "Positive and Negative Affect Schedule" (PANAS). Diagnostica **42** (2), 139–156 (1996)
33. Keshavarz, B., Hecht, H.: Validating an efficient method to quantify motion sickness. Hum. Factors **53**(4), 415–426 (2011)
34. Hudson, M., Cairns, P.: Measuring social presence in team-based digital games. In: Interacting with Presence HCI Sense Presence Computer Environments, p. 83 (2014)
35. Dörner, R., Broll, W., Grimm, P., Jung, B. (eds.): Virtual und Augmented Reality (VR/AR). Springer, Heidelberg (2013). https://doi.org/10.1007/978-3-642-28903-3
36. Skarratt, P.A., Cole, G.G., Kingstone, A.: Social inhibition of return. Acta Psychol. (Amst) **134**(1), 48–54 (2010)
37. Wienrich, C., Gross, R., Kretschmer, F., Müller-Plath, G.: Developing and proving a framework for reaction time experiments in VR to objectively measure social interaction with virtual agents. In: IEEE VR (2018)
38. Benford, S., Giannachi, G., Koleva, B., Rodden, T.: From interaction to trajectories: designing coherent journeys through user experiences. In: Chi 2009 Proceedings of the SIGCHI Conference on Human Factors in Computing Systems, vol. 1–4, pp. 709–718 (2009)
39. Freytag, S., Wienrich, C.: Evaluation of a virtual gaming environment designed to access emotional reactions while playing. In: Virtual Worlds and Games for Serious Applications (VS-Games), pp. 145–148. IEEE (2017)

DUXU in Software Development

Agile Web Development with Scrum: A User Experience Based Approach Using Linguistic Metamodel

Daniel Antonio Midena Aguillar[1(✉)] and Plinio Thomaz Aquino Jr.[2(✉)]

[1] Instituto de Pesquisas Tecnológicas de São Paulo,
Av. Prof. Almeida Prado, 532, São Paulo, SP, Brazil
danielaguillar@yahoo.com.br
[2] Centro Universitário FEI – Fundação Educacional Inaciana Pe. Sabóia de Medeiros, Av. Humberto Alencar Castelo Branco, 3972,
São Bernardo do Campo, Brazil
plinio.aquino@fei.edu.br

Abstract. In this work it is proposed an approach based on user experience design for the agile development of web-based software, using the language metamodel. The main motivation was the observation of evidences, in market studies and papers from other researchers, of proportional differences between the usage of agile methods versus methods based on user experience design. This research proposes an approach for the development of web applications using SCRUM, based on UX design, offering the metamodel as a tool to tackle communication problems during this process. The experiments were done in academic and industrial contexts in order to validate and check viability/applicability of the proposed approach: In the academic context, workshops were made for the practical application of the developed approach and information regarding the experiment was collected by means of questionnaires. It was demonstrated that the proposed approach may be viable and may be applied in contexts where it is possible to adopt all stablished recommendations and principles so that the integration between SCRUM and UX happens. It was also used as a facilitating tool, for the integration process, the linguistic metamodel to permeate all existing communication processes, reducing communicational noise related to omission, generalization and distortion of information.

Keywords: UX design · SCRUM · Linguistic metamodel

1 Introduction

The main goal of this research is to propose an approach, based on UX Design, focused on communication, that allows web applications development applying the agile method called SCRUM. The intent is to make UX Design-related tasks compatible with SCRUM-related tasks, generating an agile developed software product that also addresses user's experience.

© Springer International Publishing AG, part of Springer Nature 2018
A. Marcus and W. Wang (Eds.): DUXU 2018, LNCS 10918, pp. 593–607, 2018.
https://doi.org/10.1007/978-3-319-91797-9_42

To help making both cited methods compatible, it will be adopted a communication framework called linguistic metamodel, the goal is to support communication-related activities that will exist throughout the development process. This framework will provide protocols to permeate communication during the application of the proposed approach. Experiments will also take place in order to verify, in a practical manner, the applicability of such approach.

It was verified in some researches a high usage rate of SCRUM method and a low usage rate of UX tools, what led to questionings regarding if the same proportional difference would repeat when dealing with the usage of UX design methods compared to the usage of SCRUM and also if there are studies on how to integrate both. Based on such questionings, papers related to this theme were found, offering clear statements on how small the literature volume on methods or approaches for such integration was and that there was more research on problems found during the integration process and practitioner's experiences. This research proposes an approach for the development of web applications using SCRUM, based on UX design, offering the metamodel as a tool to tackle communication problems during this process. It's also verified the applicability of the proposed approach in both academic and industrial contexts.

The work method used consists on bibliographical research of referenced works as fundaments and base for this research, a systematic review on integration attempts between SCRUM and UX design: During the development of this research technical standards were found along with much work and many studies related to different areas of knowledge, such as computer science, usability, human-computer interaction and neurolinguistics to provide the necessary knowledge base for the consequent creation of an approach that led to the integration of SCRUM and UX design.

After that, also part of the work method, mind maps were created in order to facilitate the process of finding and extracting information to make possible the creation of a comparative analysis table that was used to compare all different researches that 2 were found. Having the comparative table allowed the development and proposal of an approach based on the most used tactics by the found authors, with the application of the metamodel to reduce communication's gaps and flaws. It was also part of the work method a verification on the approach's applicability by means of planning and performing different experiments in different contexts, with data collection and analysis of resulting integration attempts and consequent verification of approach's applicability.

The experiments were done in academic and industrial contexts in order to validate and check viability/applicability of the proposed approach: In the academic context, workshops were made for the practical application of the developed approach and information regarding the experiment was collected by means of questionnaires. In the industrial context, interviews were made with specialists in SCRUM or UX design, collecting their opinions about the presented approach.

The expected contributions of this work are: (a) **Proposal of a formalized and structured approach.** It should unify SCRUM development-related activities with UX Design-related activities; (b) **Usage of communication metamodel within the approach.** The framework should be used in order to reduce communication noise such as omissions, generalizations and distortions that come from interaction between individuals during the development process; (c) **Synthesis of the current knowledge level regarding UX Design x SCRUM integration.** A comparative analysis will be done to investigate related work after a systematic review on the integration topic; and (d) **Demonstration of approach's viability on SCRUM x UX Design integration.** Experiments will take place after the approach's proposal in order to observe and verify its applicability on both industrial and academic contexts.

The paper then includes a section on literature review, that is, agile method, usability and standards, their methods and deliverables, usability engineering. The communication metamodel theory closes the literature review in this work. The research methodology is presented followed by the results obtained.

2 Agile Method: SCRUM

One of the most popular agile methods used nowadays. Its process has adaptive, iterative, rapid, flexible, continuous improvement and feedback characteristics. It was structured in order to help efficient and significant deliveries to users in terms of value proposal during the project [27].

SCRUM has three main roles to make viable its application that will be considered in this research (Fig. 1), they are defined by [27] as follows:

- **Product Owner:** It is the person responsible for achieving the maximum business value for the project. He or she is also responsible for articulating customer requirements and maintaining business justification for the project. The product owner represents the voice of the customer.
- **SCRUM Master:** It is a facilitator who ensures that the SCRUM Team is provided with an environment conducive to complete the project successfully. The SCRUM Master guides, facilitates, and teaches Scrum practices to everyone involved in the project; clears impediments for the team; and, ensures that SCRUM processes are being followed.
- **SCRUM Team:** It is the group of team of people who are responsible for understanding the requirements specified by the Product Owner and creating the Deliverables of the project.

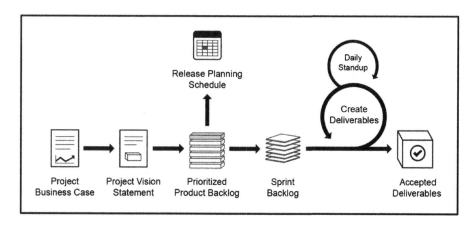

Fig. 1. Typical SCRUM process [27]

SCRUM process involves the following phases: (1) Initiate; (2) Plan and Estimate; (3) Implement; (4) Review and retrospect; (5) Release. The proposed approach will focus on analysis-related phases (1 - Iniciate/2 - Plan and Estimate) and test-related phase (4 - Review and retrospect). Only the cited processes will be considered because they represent moments where there are more interactions between designers and developers, occurring intersection between their work processes. Processes related to development and delivery (3 - Implement and 5 - Release, respectively) do not require any modifications because each team must work on their respective activities following the SCRUM Process.

3 Human-Computer Interaction

3.1 Usability and Standards: ABNT/NBR 9241:2011 e ISO/TR 16982:2014

Both cited standards will be adopted throughout this work [1, 2] because since usability is a widely used term, it may have different interpretations according to the context where it is applied, therefore, it was understood as necessary the adoption of a standardized definition on this term.

Considering the *"Measure in which a product may be used by specific users to reach specific goals with efficacy, efficiency and satisfaction in a specified context"*, such definition from standard [2] was evaluated by UX Design practitioners [19] and was understood as promising. The standard [1] was used in order to understand how to classify available usability methods and select which would be addressed by the approach. The biggest focus on this work lies on project's usability of a product that can be used, seeking to address and respect consolidated recommendations from specialists in the area [22–24]. Analyzing the usability area, it was understood as necessary the definition of a more focused scope of work. Since communication permeates all kinds of interactions [26] it would be desirable to focus on the interaction project during this research.

3.2 Methods and Deliverables

Authors such as [7, 29] describe many methods and deliverables related to the interaction project. Among the cited deliverables, that help defining the interaction project and its usability level, two were select: Personas and User Stories. Both were selected because they are well known methods, largely used that were proven to bring good results on previous integration attempts by other authors [10, 12].

After careful research on both methods, it was found that some improvements were proposed to original user stories [18]. The improvements are related to the reduction of ambiguities on the user story, including the role that does specific tasks in a contextualized way. Its name was also modified to "job story". The structure is defined by [18] as follows: When _____ (Situation), I Want _____ (Motivation), So I can_____ (Expected outcome).

It is also recommended by authors such as [7, 24] the usage of low fidelity prototyping in order to provide mutual understanding between designers and developers, mitigating integration problems. The three selected deliverables were selected in order to provide the approach with tools of different formality levels, in a way that one complements the other and vice versa.

3.3 Usability Engineering

Usability engineering is defined as a discipline that provides, in a multidisciplinary way, a group of methods and activities that generate better user experience when applied during a software's development process [4, 5, 20, 24]. The authors [4, 5, 20, 24] propose a series of activities for the composition of a usability lifecycle, therefore, proposing usability lifecycle models.

When comparing the cited lifecycle models, some degree of similarity was observed. The authors demonstrated the need of defining elements such as user profile, usability goals, prototype design, tests and user feedbacks.

On the other hand, it was also observed some degree of complementarity. The PICAPS project [4, 5] uses the usability engineering process to design the diversity of users in different contexts. In model [24] it is proposed the application of heuristic analysis that complements the activity of interactive prototype evaluation proposed by [20]. Thus, the application of heuristics analysis was considered for this application.

4 Communication Metamodel

Authors such as [7, 9] cite how communication is understood and evaluated in the context of human-computer interaction (HCI). There are four perspectives under which such interactions may occur: Data transmission – in a system; User-system interaction; User using computer as a tool; and Media – communication between users or communication designer-user.

In such cases and scenarios, communication is studied by cognitive and semiotic engineering areas, that characterize a particular case of system-mediated human communication. However, this is not the concept of communication that is being considered. The concept considered in this work involves neuro-linguistic programming (NLP) area, that brings such knowledge to this research.

NLP experts [6] defined that language serves as a representational system for human experience, that is very rich and complex. Given the fact that it is a representational system, therefore, a model, it is inferred that language used in communication only represents a communicator's point of view of what it is observed.

It was also defined that whatever happens inside the human mind regarding an event, is considered as a "map", not being the "territory" is represents. The "map" is something that comes from a perception. On the other hand, the "territory" exists only as an external reality. Such conclusion leads to the understanding that there are two kinds of phenomenon, the factual external reality and the subjective internal reality. It is impossible to represent the world "as it really is" [8].

Based on that, work in the area such as [6] details and classifies communication problems that occur due to such "limitations" on reality's observation and representation, also providing a tool (linguistic metamodel) to help understanding and mitigating communication flaws.

Such communication problems were classified in three categories: Generalization, Omission and Distortion. During the development of this research it was observed that no authors used a tool like this to address communication problems, as an example of [11–13, 15, 25].

The communication metamodel provides a series of "challenge questions" with instructions on how and when to use them, in order to dissolve any sort of generalization, omission and/or distortion in an individual's communication.

5   Research Methodology

The development of this project involved a systematic review based on methods proposed by [16, 17] that were adopted and tailored by the authors as can be seen on the full version of this work [3] (Table 1):

Table 1.   Structure of the research methodology

Research questions definition	Questions were proposed during the systematic review, such as: The disparity between UX Tools and agile methods usage is the same when comparing the use of UX with SCRUM? Is it possible to combine in a single approach an agile method like SCRUM with UX design? Are there studies or other proposals of integration, if so, what approaches exist, and which are them?
Criteria specification for inclusion/exclusion of studies	It was defined and adopted an inclusion and an exclusion criterion to help filtering what was going to be analyzed in order to improve the quality of this research. To be included a study should describe some sort of integration attempt between an agile method and UX Design; Be a systematic review on this subject; or, Propose an integration method. The exclusion criterion was: If a study does not comply to the integration subject – being a false-positive; The publishing year is older than 2011 – excluding theory literature
Research strategy definition	The strategy was: search, date filtering, reading of abstracts, filtering of false-positives and cataloguing in a spreadsheet of reference management program
Definition of data to be extracted from each study, including qualitative data	In order to make viable the comparison between studies, the following data was defined to be extracted: context of work; project's size; related team size; focus of adaptions; if there was training and learning; what activities were done to make compatible both methods; complementary tools, techniques and methods to support the process that were used; and, study results
Maintenance of catalogue	Maintenance of catalogue with included and excluded studies from systematic review. This was done using Microsoft Excel spreadsheet and Zotero, a reference management program
Synthesizing of each study in a mind map	The use of mind maps was done in order to help comparing studies. The previously defined criteria served as base to the creation of mind maps

Within the universe of 60 studies that were found, 33 studies were considered for this research's systematic review. 17 studies were used as theory background and 17 were used for the comparative analysis.

6 UX Design x SCRUM Development Approach

6.1 Comparative Analysis

The 17 studies analyzed helped producing a comparative analysis matrix, available in the full research [3]. The analyzed studies confirmed statements from authors such as [12] that there was little volume of work related to the integration of agile with UX Design. The major part of found work were experimentations or practitioner's reports.

The matrix was built, and it was possible to observe which were the most commonly used techniques, adjustments, most found problems and other information commonly found among the selected research.

Bigger success rates were perceived when teams were put to work together, in the same physical environment, integrating SCRUM and UX teams. Also, personas, low fidelity prototyping and design development with one or more sprints ahead of developers also generated bigger levels of usability and productivity. There was also some evidence that UX training for SCRUM teams and vice versa could enhance both team's productivity and make team work easier. Communication problems seem to be inherent of this process of work, but the approach should address them with the usage of the metamodel. Full matrix available in page 56 of [3].

6.2 Approach Characterization

Studies analyzed during literature review and comparative analysis brought evidence on which would be the best practices to be adopted when characterizing the approach.

In order to simplify the approach's process, it is not recommended to apply a full usability engineering lifecycle, but only to tailor SCRUM process in a way that key-activities from UX are incorporated to the process. This decision was taken due to the low usability maturity level inside organizations as it was observed in other studies [21, 30, 31]. Considering the systematic review that was done and the comparative analysis, it was found that some needs should be addressed by the approach:

- **SCRUM tailoring.** Inclusion of key UX-related activities in the process.
- **Strict control of deadlines.** Designers should define and control deadlines so that there will not be delays in deliveries.
- **Communication improvement.** It should be addressed and made viable between stakeholders, product owner, designers and developers.

This approach should also respect the principles stated in agile manifesto [14] in order to not lose agile's fundamental characteristics. The following key activities from usability standard [2] are addressed by this approach: Identification of use context and its definition; Selection of usability criteria and measures and their definition; and, Usability evaluation. Other activities proposed by the cited standard [2] were not considered due to the fact that SCRUM is a continuous improvement cycle by itself, already having inside its nature criteria evaluation, refactoring and improvement activities.

Key activities were selected from [24] and [20] and a table was created to match standard's activities [2] with usability models [20, 21].

Table 2. Selected key activities for the approach's characterization [3]

Standard activities [2]	Nielsen's usability model [24]	Mayhew's usability model [20]
1 - Identification of use context	Know the user Adopt participative design	Define user profile Analyze tasks Platform characteristics Style guide
2 - Selection of usability criteria and measures	Define usability goals Apply directives and heuristic analysis	Screen patterns
3 - Usability evaluation	Create prototypes Make empirical tests Practice interactive design	Interactive design evaluation User's opinion

The cited approach was developed based on the activities described in Table 2, considering inspection and observation usability methods that may be done without the participation of users, thus, making the evaluation process more complete.

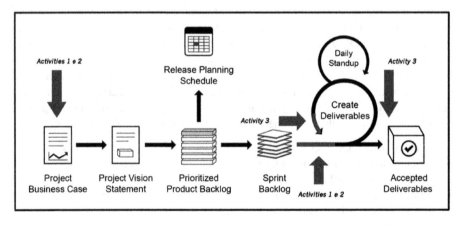

Fig. 2. Tailored SCRUM process with UX activities from Table 1 [3]

Based on what was observed in researches from other authors, there are evidences that the biggest problems for integration between SCRUM x UX Design are related to communication. Ergo, the communication metamodel [6] should be used alongside with the approach as basis of all communication-related activities (written or spoken). Table 3 shows how SCRUM was tailored:

Table 3. Compatibilization of SCRUM process and UX activities.

Phase	SCRUM activities	UX activities
Initiate	1 - Creation of project's vision 2 - Identification of SCRUM Master and stakeholder(s) 3 - Create SCRUM team 4 - Develop Epics 5 - Create prioritized product backlog 6 - Conduct release planning	1 - Identification of use context 2 - Selection of usability criteria and measures
Plane and estimate	7 - Create job stories 8 - Approve, estimate and save 9 - Create tasks 10 - Estimate tasks 11 - Create sprints backlog	
Implement	12 - Create deliverables 13 - Conduct daily standup meetings 14 - Review prioritized backlog	3 - Usability evaluation

The implementation of such approach requires following some premises/principles, they are:

1. **Developers and designers must work in the same place.** That will generate better information exchange and communication between designers and developers.
2. **Developers should have general knowledge on UX design and interaction project and designers should have general knowledge on programming.** That helps generating a bigger degree of mutual recognition and comprehension of each individual's impacts in the work process of others. This may be explored by means of talks and trainings.
3. **Meetings and planning meetings involving the entire team.** Planning, daily, sprint retrospective, release planning, and standup meetings should take place with developers and designers teams, this should guarantee that the backlog always has development and design activities in a parallel or sequential way, planned in a way that deadlines may be attained.
4. **High collaboration level.** Creation of stories, tasks and backlogs are done in a collaborative way, involving designers and developers. This guarantees that all usability and technical aspects are addressed.
5. **Minimal design at the very beginning for documentation.** Designers should help documenting the project developing basic wireframes (low fidelity prototypes), but functional (respecting the minimum viable product concept) so that developers are able to start their work without delays generated by the bigger time that is necessary.

6. **Stablished documentation and conventions respect.** Functions' names, dialog boxes, labels, etc. should be defined and documented between developers and designers before starting the project to avoid rework and consecutive delays.

7. **High communication level.** The communication dynamics should be based on the usage of the proposed metamodel to provide better details on exchanged information between teams, avoiding misunderstandings such as omissions, generalizations or distortions in communication, thus, reducing project's problems. The usage of the metamodel is mandatory in all phases that involve communication. It is also planned that some training will be necessary.

8. **SCRUM + UX.** Incorporation of key usability activities in the SCRUM process as it is shown in Fig. 2.

9. **Guarantee of metamodel use.** SCRUM Master and product owner will have the same roles as defined in [27] and will also have a new responsibility: guarantee that the team is using extensively the communication metamodel in their communications.

10. **Training.** It will be necessary some training on the metamodel for the entire team, except the client.

11. **Shared backlog.** The prioritized backlog must be built addressing both developers and designers activities/tasks. The backlog must be organized in a way that the order/priority of activities considers the time difference to be executed between code implementation and interface design.

12. **Sprint 0.** The initial project's phase must contemplate the development of some basic interfaces following the concept of minimum viable product, in a way that fields, variables, label's names, etc. can be previously defined so that developers may start their work without impediments and designers can continue their UX work.

13. **Equivalent team importance.** SCRUM Master must guarantee that everyone in the team are given the same importance and must be responsible for integrating designers with developers in a collaborative manner, in such a way that everyone is equally listened, and that all prioritization is agreed among all team members. This is very important so that design and development activities have their priorities well defined and respected so that design does not affect development and vice-versa.

Adopting such premises/principles during the approach application, it is expected a successful integration between SCRUM and UX. In order to verify and validate the proposed approach, a small series of experiments have been done in both academic and industrial contexts.

7 Experiments and Approach Validation

Ethical aspects were considered in all cycles of experimentation with volunteers, following ethical recommendations of software engineering and human-computer interaction [28].

7.1   Academic Context

The part of the experiment that took place within an academic context running the following process: 1 - Workshop planning (a workshop was planned in order to teach students how to use the approach); 2 - Definition of web software scope (the software to be built using the approach); 3 - Definition of volunteers requirements (to filter and select volunteers for the experiment); 4 - Selection of place and experiment settings (academic context – labs of graduation/post-graduation institutions); 5 - Invitation of volunteers; 6 - Speech on SCRUM, UX design, communication metamodel and approach (to align the knowledge level of participants); 7 - Experiment application (workshop where students should develop a web software applying the proposed approach); 8 - Collection and analysis of data, and development of result reports.

The experiment took place in 4 different institutions, being 3 graduation institutions and 1 post-graduation institution. Some criteria [3] was applied to filter invalid information given by students that did not have enough participation on the experiment: Iteration 1: 6 students' data was considered; Iteration 2: 16 students' data was considered; Iteration 3: 15 students' data was considered; and, Iteration 4: 6 students' data was considered. One of the biggest challenges of this experiment was to invite volunteers to participate. Unfortunately, it was not possible to find volunteers 100% adherent to the previously defined requirements, therefore, some leveling of knowledge was required during the process.

A total of 63 students participated in the cited experiments, being considered information of 43 of them. A big variation on knowledge levels was noticeable and as previously mentioned, this influenced the experimentation process. Another difficulty that was faced was that most students had never used SCRUM, UX or communication tools like the metamodel before and that affected in a negative way the experiment.

Only 4% of the volunteers (4 people) had some previous experience on integration attempts between SCRUM and UX. Still, their knowledge and opinions enriched this research. The metamodel has shown to be a good communication tool, 86% of participants (36 out of 43) agreed that their communication had improved after learning the metamodel. Only 1 participant disagreed and 5 had a neutral opinion. Such statistics may indicate the viability of using this tool to mitigate communication problems. 90% of the participants agreed that the approach helped improving the development/design process as a whole. Such conclusion suggests that there is some level of efficacy in applying this approach and that it may help developing better software that considers user's experience. 93% of the participants agreed that the approach helped reducing communication problems along in the process. Such data shows evidence of the approach's applicability. 67% of the participants agreed that the integration between SCRUM and UX had been done successfully, what might indicate as valid the proposed approach.

Considering the lack of volunteers' adherence to the requirements, that had a strong impact on the experiment's results, considering the 4 iterations and collected data, there is some indication that this approach is valid and might be tested in other contexts, etc.

7.2   Industrial Context

The industrial context was planned in the same structure as the academic context experiment with one single difference: it would not be possible to make a series of workshops with industry specialists, so it was chosen to perform a series of interviews after explaining how the approach works and how it could be applied.

All interviews were done using Skype's video chat. 6 industry specialists were selected based on their LinkedIn Profile. Unfortunately, only 4 of them accepted being interviewed. 2 of them had 5–7 years of experience in the area and 2 of them had 10–20 years of experience, in both cases, one of them worked with development and the other with UX design.

After explaining the approach and showing data collected in the workshops, 2 of them stated that this approach might be applicable in any context and 2 stated that the approach is definitely applicable in some given contexts.

All of them agreed that the approach helps mitigating communication problems and may result in a successful integration between SCRUM and UX. All interviewees also agreed that this approach is simple and easy to use.

Three of the interviewees mentioned that they had already tried integrating both methods and although they got some level of integration, communication still showed to be a big issue. The good tactics they've learned to try such integration were already considered by the approach.

Also, cited problems they faced were being tackled by the principles defined for this approach.

Although the academic context has provided a good and standardized environment for the execution of the experiment, validating it in the industrial context with experts has exposed this approach to other variables that were not present in the academic context, showing that many could have significant impact on the desired integration process. Certainly all inputs received during these experiments may help improving even more the approach refining it.

8   Conclusion

This research was executed in compliance with what was previously planned in the research methodology. The goals defined for this research can be considered as attained: it was characterized an approach for the web development of applications using SCRUM and UX Design, focusing on communication using the metamodel.

The approach was proposed in a formal and structured way, documenting all compatibilization/unification steps. The metamodel usage had efficacy reducing communication noise that usually comes from processes/activities that involve communication, both inside the same team and between different teams. This was noticed not only by observing the volunteers within workshops, but also by collecting and analyzing their general opinion. The synthesis of knowledge originated in the systematic review related to integrating UX and SCRUM also allowed to have more clarity on the positioning of this work in the area of study. It is believed, therefore, that all expected contributions were generated successfully.

Additionally, it is possible to say that the proposed approach, integrated and made compatible tasks related to the usability engineering lifecycle with software development lifecycle. As previously planned, the metamodel supported communication-related activities, helping to eliminate inherent communication-related problems, as perceived by other authors.

The validation done by means of workshops in the academic context and interviews in the industrial context allowed to verify, in a practical way, how the approach's applicability would be. Both contexts enriched this research by confirming the viability of the approach's application, also bringing contributions for further research on the topic.

It was also found that many factors might be related to the difficulties in integrating SCRUM and UX, for example, the heterogeneity of knowledge in teams, communication, organizational factors, work environment, bureaucracy and processes to which a work environment is subject to. Such factors may impact negatively the desired integration, therefore, it is necessary to plan and organize teams and project before the actual start of the SCRUM process, so that there are no difficulties in the integration, and if they exist, they could be easily solved.

Finally, it is expected that this work has contributed to broaden discussion on the topic, promoting involvement of other knowledge areas to help solving found problems, as an example of the language metamodel.

Critics and problems that occurred during the experiments were registered, serving as inspiration for future work on the matter.

References

1. ABNT: ISO/TR 16982:2014 - Ergonomia da interação humano sistema - métodos de usabilidade que apoiam o projeto centrado no usuário. ABNT–Associação Brasileira de Normas Técnicas (2014)
2. ABNT: NBR 9241-11. Requisitos Ergonômicos para Trabalho de Escritórios com Computadores Parte 11 – Orientações sobre Usabilidade. ABNT–Associação Brasileira de Normas Técnicas (2011)
3. Aguillar, D.A.M.: Desenvolvimento ágil de aplicações Web com SCRUM: uma abordagem baseada na experiência do usuário utilizando metamodelo linguístico. Dissertação de Mestrado, 147 p. Instituto de Pesquisas Tecnológicas do Estado de São Paulo – IPT, São Paulo (2017)
4. Aquino Jr., P.T.: Papéis do Docente em IHC: do conhecimento ao mercado. In: IX Simpósio sobre Fatores Humanos em Sistemas Computacionais. Belo Horizonte, MG. Anais Estendidos do IX Simpósio de Fatores Humanos em Sistemas Computacionais (Volume II). Porto Alegre - RS: Sociedade Brasileira de Computação SBC, IHC 2010, vol. 01, pp. 79–82 (2010)
5. Aquino J., P.T.: PICaP: padrões e personas para expressão da diversidade de usuários no projeto de interação, p. 110. Escola Politécnica, Universidade de São Paulo, São Paulo (2008). https://doi.org/10.11606/t.3.2008.tde-15092008-144412
6. Bandler, R., Grinder, J.: The Structure of Magic I: A Book About Language and Therapy. Science and Behavior Books Inc., Palo Alto (1975)
7. Barbosa, S.D.J., Da Silva, B.S.: Interação Humano-Computador. Elsevier, Rio de Janeiro (2010)

8. Bodenhammer, B.G., Hall, L.M.: The User's Manual for the Brain: The Complete Manual for Neuro-Linguistic Programming Practitioner Certification. Crown House Publishing Limited, Carmarthen (1999)
9. Carroll, J.M.: HCI Models, Theories, and Frameworks: Toward a Multidisciplinary Science. Morgan Kaufmann, Burlington (2003)
10. Choma, J., Zaina, L.A., Da Silva, T.S.: Towards an approach matching CMD and DSR to improve the Academia-Industry software development partnership: a case of agile and UX integration. In: 29th Brazilian Symposium on Software Engineering, SBES, pp. 51–60. IEEE Computer Society (2015)
11. Felker, C., Slamova, R., Davis, J.: Integrating UX with scrum in an undergraduate software development project. In: Proceedings of the 43rd ACM Technical Symposium on Computer Science Education, pp. 301–306. ACM (2012)
12. Ferreira, J., Sharp, H., Robinson, H.: Agile development and user experience design integration as an ongoing achievement in practice. In: Agile Conference, AGILE, pp. 11–20. IEEE Computer Society (2012)
13. Ferreira, J., Sharp, H., Robinson, H.: User experience design and agile development: managing cooperation through articulation work. Softw.: Pract. Exp. **41**(9), 963–974 (2011)
14. Fowler, M., et al.: Agile Manifesto. http://www.agilemanifesto.org. Accessed 13 Feb 2018
15. Jurca, G., Hellmann, T.D., Maurer, F.: Integrating agile and user-centered design: a systematic mapping and review of evaluation and validation studies of agile-UX. In: Agile Conference, AGILE, pp. 24–32. IEEE Computer Society (2014)
16. Kitchenham, B., et al.: Lessons from applying the systematic literature review process within the software engineering domain. J. Syst. Softw. **80**, 571–583 (2007)
17. Kitchenham, B.: Procedures for performing systematic reviews, p. 33. Department of Computer Science, Keele University and National ICT, Australia Ltd. (2004)
18. Klement, A.: Replacing the User Story With The Job Story - Too many assumptions are dangerous. https://jtbd.info/replacing-the-user-story-with-the-job-story-af7cdee10c27#.io e8crn7q. Accessed 13 Feb 2018
19. Law, E.L.-C., et al.: Understanding, scoping and defining user experience: a survey approach. In: Proceedings of the SIGCHI Conference on Human Factors in Computing Systems, pp. 719–728. ACM (2009)
20. Mayhew, D.: The Usability Engineering Lifecycle: A Practitioner's Handbook for User Interface Design. Morgan Kaufmann, San Francisco (1999)
21. Murphy, T.E., Wilson, N., Maritess, S.: Hype Cycle for Application Development. Gartner, Stamford (2014)
22. Nielsen, J.: How to Conduct a Heuristic Evaluation. https://www.nngroup.com/articles/how-to-conduct-a-heuristic-evaluation/. Accessed: 07 Jan 2018
23. Nielsen, J.: The usability engineering life cycle. Computer **25**(3), 12–22 (1992). [5]
24. Nielsen, J.: Usability Engineering. Academic Press, New York (1993)
25. Ovad, T., Larsen, L.B.: The prevalence of UX design in agile development processes in industry. In: Agile Conference, AGILE, pp. 40–49. IEEE Computer Society (2015)
26. Preece, J., Sharp, H., Rogers, Y.: Interaction Design: Beyond Human-Computer Interaction. Wiley, Hoboken (2015)
27. SCRUMstudy: A Guide to the SCRUM Body of Knowledge - SBOK GUIDE. VMEdu, Inc., Phoenix, Arizona, USA (2013)
28. Takahashi, N.M., Aquino, P.T.: Relationship between the scientific and traditional software engineering considering the ethical aspects of human-computer interaction. In: Marcus, A., Wang, W. (eds.) DUXU 2017. LNCS, vol. 10288, pp. 677–696. Springer, Cham (2017). https://doi.org/10.1007/978-3-319-58634-2_49

29. Teixeira, F.: Introdução e boas práticas em UX Design. Casa do Código, São Paulo (2014)
30. Wilson, N., Huizen, V.G., Prentice, B.: Hype Cycle for Application Development. Gartner, Stamford (2013)
31. Wilson, N., Maritess, S.: Hype Cycle for Application Development. Gartner, Stamford (2015). XMind, Hong Kong (2016)

Toward Applying Online Privacy Patterns Based on the Design Problem: A Systematic Review

Maha Aljohani[1([⊠])], James Blustein[1,2], and Kirstie Hawkey[1]

[1] Faculty of Computer Science, Dalhousie University, Halifax, Canada
mh578194@dal.ca, {jamie,hawkey}@cs.dal.ca
[2] School of Information Management, Dalhousie University, Halifax, Canada

Abstract. Privacy patterns are design solutions to common privacy problems—a way to translate "privacy-by-design" into practical advice for software engineering. This paper aims to provide a collection of privacy patterns proposed by previous work through a systematic review. The review identifies 19 research papers on privacy patterns and they were retrieved for full-text analysis based on the type of the privacy pattern, the context, design problem, and the proposed solution. We provide a classification of the privacy patterns by applying a mapping process to the ISO 29100 privacy Framework and the Privacy Enhancing Techniques. We found that the currently available patterns barely reference to privacy legislation or laws. They mostly cover the security-network perspective but not the user interface perspective. This paper presents the results of a systematic, comprehensive review that aims at aiding future IT designers with a collection of privacy patterns to match design contexts and benefit from the proposed privacy design solutions.

Keywords: Privacy patterns · Privacy-by-design
Privacy Enhancing Technologies (PETs)

1 Introduction

Privacy is an emerging design element for interactive systems [1]. Researchers have been studying privacy from different aspects such as privacy-preserving technologies [2–4], e-commerce [5], Healthcare [6, 7]. There are variety of privacy design guidelines to support the integration of privacy in the design lifecycle such as Privacy Impact Assessment (PIA) [8], ISO 29100 Privacy Framework Principles [ISO] [9], Process-Oriented Strategies and Privacy Enhancing Tools (PET) [10]. However, there is a lack of the "end-to-end" solutions to design privacy-preserving systems and the challenge is "in turning these broad guidelines into actionable design solutions" [1].

We are interested in investigating the currently available privacy patterns as privacy design solutions. This paper aims to provide a collection of privacy patterns proposed by previous work through a systematic review. In addition, we discuss how the Privacy Patterns are connected to Privacy Principles and Privacy Enhancing Technologies.

© Springer International Publishing AG, part of Springer Nature 2018
A. Marcus and W. Wang (Eds.): DUXU 2018, LNCS 10918, pp. 608–627, 2018.
https://doi.org/10.1007/978-3-319-91797-9_43

2 Background

In this systematic review, we are analyzing the currently available privacy patterns. As a preliminary to the review, we introduce the Privacy Principles, and Privacy Enhancing Technologies (PETs) to be able to make a comprehensive comparison between these three concepts. Privacy Principles and guidelines are used to describe how organizations handle privacy while Privacy Enhancing Technologies are focused on privacy from a technical point of view. Privacy patterns are in between.

2.1 Privacy Principles

Privacy principles are privacy framework that can be discussed to understand what is privacy and what are the privacy requirements [11]. There are variety of privacy principles around the world such as OECD Privacy Principles which is common in European Union, Asia-Pacific Economic Cooperation (APEC) Privacy Framework which is used in the Asia-Pacific region, the United States Department of Commerce Safe Harbor Privacy Principles, and Generally Accepted Privacy Principles (GAPP) which is popular among Canadian privacy practitioners. They all share basic principles including collection limitation, data quality, purpose specification, use limitation, safeguards, openness, individual participation and accountability principles. ISO 29100 is an example of privacy principles that share the same privacy principles with the previously mentioned privacy frameworks and discussed in the following Table 1.

Table 1. ISO 29100 privacy framework

#	Principle	Definition
1	Consent and choice	Present data subject with choices to obtain consent
2	Purpose legitimacy and specification	Insure following legislations and inform data subjects of the purposes to process the Personal Information
3	Collection limitation	Limit the collection of data to the specified purposes
4	Data minimization	Minimize the amount of data collected and the number of actors involved in processing the data
5	Use, retention and disclosure limitation	Limit the use, retention and disclosure of personal information
6	Accuracy and quality	Ensure data is accurate, up to date, and relevant Periodically check the data
7	Openness, transparency and notice	Provide access to information, inform of the policies in place and provide notices whenever there is a change
8	Individual participation and access	To provide opportunity to access and review personal information
9	Accountability	Inform if there is a privacy breach, apply privacy policy, and provide training
10	Information security	Provide a level of security by applying protocols
11	Privacy compliance	The system meets the legal requirements and applies supervision mechanisms

2.2   Privacy Enhancing Technologies (PETs)

Borking and Raab [12] defined PET as a "system of ICT [Information and Communication Technology] measures protecting informational privacy by eliminating or minimizing personal data thereby preventing unnecessary or unwanted processing of personal data, without the loss of the functionality of the information system." The European Commission adopted the same definition in 2007. The purpose of developing new privacy enhancing technologies is to protect the privacy of users and at the same time allowing them to still share and communicate through the Internet. Some examples of these technologies are summarized next.

Anonymizer is a type of PETs that remove all personal information to preserve users' privacy; it helps users to browse the Internet without their identity being disclosed. Such systems use one of the following mechanisms to ensure anonymity: anonymous proxies, anonymous/pseudonymous servers and firewalls [13]. One such system is available at <URL: https://www.anonymizer.com/>. The idea of using proxies is to create an account with a "trusted" Internet Service Provider in which both the user and the organization trust. One type is location anonymizer, which works in a way that it hides users' information and replaces pseudo-identifier [14]. For example, if the user wants to go visit Google, he/she does not send a request to the Google server. Instead, the request is made through the anonymizer server, which connects to Google server and forwards the information to the user. It has many advantages including not sending a user's IP address, not forwarding the user's email as an identifier, and eliminating all cookies that might be stored in the user device. Another PET example that uses the same concept is iProxy, which is available at iProxy.net.iProxyanonymizer service http://iproxy.net/.

Crowds is a system that helps users to browse the Internet while protecting their privacy by grouping users into diverse crowds to hide personal information. This prevents attackers from tracking the source of information and requests [14]. The anonymizer relies on using a proxy that it is installed in a local machine or online; the primary objective of Crowds is to browse anonymously by hiding the information about both the user and the information shared from servers and third parties [15]. The idea of crowds relies on hiding individual actions with actions of other individuals [15]. For example, if user A sends a message to a server, Crowds sends the message as it is from a random member which prevents the server from detecting the real sender [15].

Platform for Privacy Preferences (P3P). P3P was initially proposed and developed by The World Wide Web Consortium [16]. The platform is designed in a way that helps users understand how their personal information is used by websites. It compares a website privacy policy and a user's privacy policy to help the user to decide whether to share their information or not. However, it does not alert the user, nor set minimum standards for privacy. The tool should be tested to measure the success of using P3P in solving privacy problems [16]. There are a variety of tools that were developed and implemented based on P3P summarized from [13] including:

- Netscape 7.0 which disclose the privacy policy of the website and inform the user about the cookies used.

- JRC P3P Version 2.0, which controls access to servers according to privacy preferences that are initially set up by the user.
- AT&T Privacy Bird helps users to be informed about how their personal information is collected and used.

There are a variety of PETs that serve the same goal of protecting users' privacy over the Internet which include GUIDES (EU Data Protection Directive (95/46/EC)—DPD.), Privacy Incorporated Software Agent PISA (http://www.tno.nl/instit/fel/pisa.), and GAP [17]. There are variety of examples of PETs such as 'onion routing' [18].

2.3   Definitions of Actors

We adopted the classification of the European Directive on Data Protection (2007) and the Italian privacy authority portal (2005) that defined different actors who would be involved in data processing including:

- Data Subject (DS): an individual or a person who has the rights to share, manage and control personal information
- Data Controller (DC): the person who decides in which and how data are processed
- Data Processor (DP): a person or an individual who process data on behalf of the data controller.

These definitions were used to identify different roles in the process of proposed solutions to the privacy patterns.

3   Research Objectives

Privacy designers face challenges in applying privacy-preserving techniques. The main goal of the study is to support the concept of Privacy-By-Design (PbD) [19] by providing privacy designers and developers with currently available privacy preserving patterns to apply in early design lifecycle. A supporting goal is to validate whether the proposed Privacy Patterns can be mapped to worldwide standards-based methodologies (e.g., ISO 29100) [9] to answer the questions: What privacy principles are guaranteed if the system design followed the privacy patterns from the literature? We want to compare the privacy patterns and Privacy Enhancing Techniques (PETs) to identify how they are intertwined and what aspects of privacy patterns are covered by the PETs.

4   Method and Analysis

A systematic review was conducted using ACM, IEEE, Science Direct, and Springer libraries to identify proposed privacy patterns that propose solutions for privacy design problems. A total of 200 references were screened. The papers that were candidate for inclusion in the systematics review were read more comprehensively to decide to include them. After applying exclusion criteria, 19 were retrieved for full-text analysis.

We adopted the format of the POSA2 on all collected patterns because it includes all elements that designers and developers need when they search for solutions to solve design problems. Following one structure will help designers and developers to adopt and use these patterns when they share the same context, problem, solution, and will help to understand the consequences and challenges they would face. The patterns are formatted using the order: context, problem, solution, known uses, and consequences. We added the related or similar patterns section because we believe that patterns should not contradict, and they are connected to each other to provide solutions to the same problem, and by draw connections between patterns in the literature, we provide richness and increase comprehension level to designers in case they want to apply the patterns to their contexts. We list the patterns that share the same or part of the solution which provides useful classification in our literature review according to the solution.

5   Results and Discussion

We have listed 19 privacy patterns. They are included because they are the most popular and have well-known uses. Privacy patterns are: Informed Consent for Web-Based [20], Masked Online Traffic [20], Obtaining Explicit Consent Pattern [21], Access Control to Sensitive Data Based on Purpose [21], Minimal Information Asymmetry [20], Privacy Dashboards [22], Instant User Interface for Information about Personal Identification Information [23], Non-repudiation Pattern [25], Data abstraction [23], Ambient notice and Private link [22], Outsourcing [24], Notification, and limit disclosure [26]. Privacy patterns are "design solutions to common privacy problems—a way to translate "privacy-by-design" into practical advice for software engineering". In typical design lifecycle, privacy patterns are implemented in the design and implementation and recommended to be applied in the early during requirement analysis and architectural design [27]. Some of the patterns can be linked to the privacy from the legal perspective as discussed in Sects. (5.12, 5.13, and 5.14). However, the literature lacks in this domain and a few number of patterns were found to cover the legal perspective. The results of the systematic review include the following privacy patterns and the relationship between them is shown in Fig. 1.

5.1   Informed Consent for Web-Based Transaction Pattern

The pattern is proposed by Romanosky et al. [20]:

Context. A web designer or developer wants to create a website that collects personal information for surveys and registration. The Data Controller wants to protect the DSs' personal information because laws and it is under the US regulation.

Problem. When collecting personal information, websites usually use cookies. DSs are concerned that their personal information would be collected and used without their consent or do not want to share their personal information. The problem relies on how the designers would communicate their goals of using the information without ignoring the DSs' concerns.

Solution. To solve the problem, the web designer should provide the DS with the following elements:

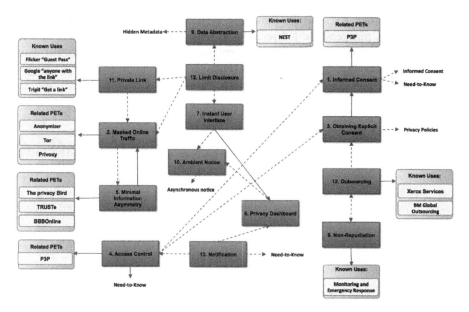

Fig. 1. The relationship between the privacy patterns, their known uses and related PETs

Disclosure. To help DSs know how the information will be collected: explicitly by asking DSs to provide the information or implicitly by their IP address or cookies.

Agreement. To be able to opt-out at any time without being concerned that the information will be used without permission or maintained for a longer time.

Comprehension. To ensure that DSs know how this information would be collected, what are cookies, and for what purpose the information is collected.

Voluntariness. To not manipulate the DS by not offering a certain service unless they provide their personal information and provide the DS with other alternative options in case they have some questions about being asked to provide the information (e.g., online chat-center or telephone number to contact a representative).

Competence. The DS is eligible (e.g., age restrictions) to provide the information that is being collected.

Minimal Distraction. To not distract the DS from completing the main task.

Known Uses. The pattern has been used in many well-known websites, (i.e., Yahoo, Google, and ehealthinsurance.com) during the filling of the registration form. The form explains to the DS why specific information needs to be filled. For example, Yahoo has an informative box near to the birthday selection to explain to the DS why the website needs to have the DS's birthdate, which will be used in the future for account verification as shown in Fig. 1.

This pattern matches the Fair Information Practices (FIP) deployed by many website privacy policies and laws (Federal Trade Commission Report 2000). It is consistent with using P3P as an automated platform to match between the website privacy policies practices and DS preferences. Another use is by developers or technical support of desktop applications that require DSs' information for further assistance about installation or other activities (Fig. 2).

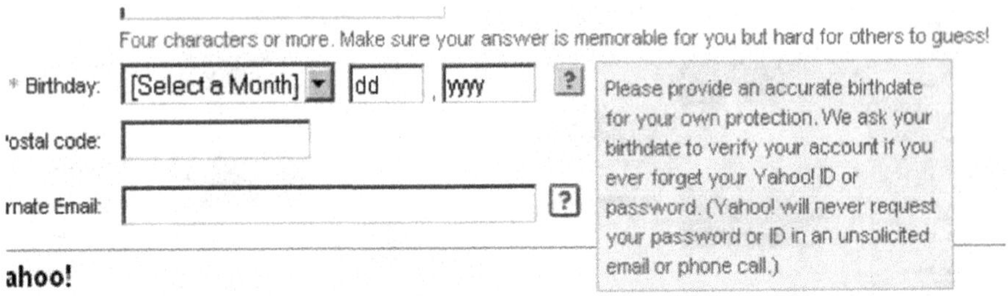

Fig. 2. Yahoo registration adopted form (yahoo.com)

Consequences. The pattern has two benefits: it helps in reducing the amount of information collected from the user (Data Subject) by the organization (Data Controller), and it helps in building trust between them by providing explanations about why their information is being collected. The pattern suffers from limitations that include: it does not help DSs to stop the use of the information at any time (opting-out). Some websites do not want to explain why they collect the information to allow them to use it. The website budgets might not cover all the expenses to cover every element in the pattern.

Related/Similar Patterns

- Informed Consent (Fischer-Hübnner et al. 2010) and [24]. Both patterns are related in one aspect because they focus on providing the Data Subject with a consent stating purposes of collecting the PI.
- Need-to-Know pattern [24] focus on limiting the access to the PI by Data Processors (third parties) for only specified permission.

Therefore, the Informed Consent for Web-Based Transaction Pattern covers more than stating the purposes and access by permission. It covers opting in and out from an agreement by understanding how the information is collected with minimal distraction from the main task.

5.2 Masked Online Traffic

The pattern is proposed by Romanosky et al. [20]:

Context. The Data Subject want to browse the Internet but does not want to reveal more personal information than necessary. The DS is concerned about the information privacy. DSs are aware of some applications and technologies that would protect their privacy but are not sure when and how to use them.

Problem. How the Data Subject can minimize the amount of personal information sent over a public network. The following forces should be considered:

- The message sent by DS might not be revealed, but information associated with it would reveal information about the DS.
- The DSs do not have to be a network or technology expert to hide their information over the network.
- The DS wants to have a solution that is easy to use.

Solution. To use one of following techniques:

Anonymity Techniques. To help the DS to communicate but still be unidentified. Two types of systems can be used: anonymizing systems, which help DSs to be completely anonymized to parties; and pseudonymous systems, which help DSs to not be identified as individuals.

Blocked Requests. Software tools can block cookies and web bugs that are used to track users.

Known Uses. One popular PET applications that ensure anonymity include:

- Anonymizer (www.anonymizer.com). The application offers a launching connection to other websites on behalf of the DSs without revealing of any personal information.
- Tor (https://www.torproject.org) applies Onion Routing protocol, which uses many routers to encrypt the requests and process it in many layers.
- Privoxy (www.privoxy.com). It acts as a virtual server that prevents cookies, and banners ads.

Consequences. The pattern includes many benefits: the applications offered as solutions are not complicated, and do not require technical knowledge. They require only a basic knowledge of how to install and configure a desktop application. Another benefit is that DSs can interact with online websites and still be anonymized. The pattern suffers from limitations that include: using anonymizing proxies to interact on behalf of the DS means that these proxies collect and monitor the DS's communication through the network. Using Tor offers extra layers and routers over the network to process the request, which might decrease the interaction performance. Some websites require identification information (i.e., online banking) in which a use anonymizing protocols would not be suitable.

Related Patterns. Minimal Information Asymmetry [20] is related to the aspect of providing the DS with enough information about a service or a tool that will collect the information to help the DS make decisions to allow or deny the collection (Sect. 5.5).

5.3 Obtaining Explicit Consent Pattern

The pattern is proposed by Porekar et al. [21]:

Context. DSs want to use an industrial medical application that collects sensitive data about patients and which is regulated by the organization privacy policy.

Problem. How can the organization collect the information without disclosing patients' information without gaining DSs' permission?

Solution. Agreement between the Data Subject (user) and Data Controller (organization) needs to be accomplished by implementing three elements:

Agreed Privacy Policy. After forming the privacy policy, the DS can negotiate the content either automatically or in person.

Signatures of Both Parties. Once the DS agrees on the privacy policy, both sign the agreement.

Timestamp. Once it is signed, a time stamp is created in case the organization wants to change/edit some parts, DSs are informed and the process starts again.

Known Uses. No known uses.

Consequences. The application employs a *Certificate-of-Liability* that explains the converge and limitation of the consent, which allows DSs to sue the organization in case of misuse of the sensitive information.

Related Patterns that Deal with Privacy Policies [21]

- Constructing Privacy Policy-building the terms and conditions of the privacy policy
- Maintaining Privacy Policy-explaining the reasons for these conditions and terms and maintaining agreements over longer periods of time
- Privacy Policy Negotiation-negotiation between the two actors who use and apply the policy.

Similar Patterns. Informed consent [24] patterns are related in the aspect of the need of providing consent to collect the information. The pattern differs in adding details to the consent (i.e., signature and timestamp).

5.4   Access Control to Sensitive Data Based on Purpose

The pattern is proposed by Porekar et al. [21]:

Context. The organization is collecting the sensitive data according to a specific purpose that should be clear to the DS.

Problem. How can the organization make the purpose clear to the DS and allow the DS to have a level of control over what is collected? The DS determines the amount of personal data that will be collected. The DS can decide which part of information a third party can access and hide the other part of the information.

Solution. The pattern applies the *"Need-to-know"* technique to limit the amount of sensitive information transmitted to third parties. The pattern provides access to only the data for which the DS gives permission to be shared and the third party does not have the right to access the information that the DS wants to hide. This pattern depends on an agreement between DS and organization about what to make available to third parties and what to hide.

Known Uses. Platform for Privacy Preferences (P3P) [16].

Consequences. The pattern supports the benefit of giving the DS a level of control over what they want to share over the internet by third parties according to an agreed privacy policy. However, how the DS would know if the organization allowed a third party to collect the information and use them? What would guarantee that they do not do so?

Related Patterns that Deal with the Agreement Are

- Obtaining Explicit Consent [20] is related in one aspect, which is providing consent, but it takes the solution further to cover extra aspects (i.e., signature and timestamp).
- Informed consent [24].

Similar Patterns. Need-to-know pattern [24] is the same pattern that provides the same solution.

5.5   Minimal Information Asymmetry

The pattern is proposed by Romanosky et al. [20]:

Context. The Data Subject is in some online services to buy products or services, and wants to register to be able to access the services. These services include subscriptions to local news, events, online banking, and health insurance. The Data Subject is interested in having feedback on the process of the information collection and the agreement statement on the Data Controller's websites. The Data Subject is discouraged to start using the website due to the lack of information.

Problem. The problems associated with this context are as follows: the DS wants to perform a purchasing task and wants to have a feedback about the privacy policy before inserting any personal information. Second, the DS is concerned about future privacy violations after the purchase is completed, and the transaction should be safe and accomplished easily. Third, the DS does not want to provide more sensitive information than necessary while following the purchase steps.

Solution. The DS can acquire more information about the websites that apply both *Informed Consent* and *Signals*.

Informed Consent. Websites that apply the "Informed Consent for Web-Based Transaction" can provide the DS with all the information they need and provide the ability to opt-in and out from the website services.

Signals. Signals are messages that are provided by the business to inform the DS about either the product or the agreement. The DS must recognize these signals and use them to gather the information. Examples of such signals include money-back guarantees, warnings, and privacy policies.

Known Uses.

- The privacy Bird (search.privacybird.com)
- TRUSTe (www.truste.org)
- BBBOnline (www.bbbonline.org).

Consequences. Benefits of this pattern include reducing the risk of privacy violations by helping the Data Subject to make the right decisions after getting proper feedback about privacy policy of the websites and services.

Related/Similar Patterns. Masked Online Traffic- to reduce the amount of information transmitted to others [20]. It is discussed in detail in Sect. 5.2. This pattern is used as the first part of the solution along with the signals for the Minimal Information Asymmetry.

5.6   Privacy Dashboards

The pattern is proposed by Privacypattern.org [22]:

Context. There is an organization that collects personal information about DSs and these information changes over time. The methods used by the organization to collect the information are unexpected or invisible. The pattern allows DSs to access and browse the information.

Problem. DSs are asked to enter personal information without an explanation provided to them on how these data will be collected and used. DSs are not confident or sometimes are overwhelmed. DSs need to understand what is going behind the scene regarding data collection.

Solution. An informational privacy dashboard to provide DSs with information about what is collected and how their information is processed. It can be used to provide a visual representation of the personal information and how it is handled. This gives DSs the ability to view, correct, and delete their personal information. Privacy Dashboards answer the DS's question "what do you know about me?".

Known Uses. Google Privacy Dashboards (https://www.google.com/dashboard) as shown in Fig. 3.

 Latitude

Location: Updated automatically ⚙
Most recent: Berkeley, CA, USA at 12:50 AM

Google Location History: Enabled
Distance Traveled: 46746170 meters

Google Talk Location Status (beta) Disabled

Manage privacy
Manage applications
Location History Dashboard

Latitude privacy policy

Fig. 3. Google privacy dashboard (https://www.google.com/dashboard)

Consequences. Using this pattern might create new privacy issues such as providing personal information to others (i.e., other users, third parties, stalkers). Designers should balance between showing information to the user and ensuring that the personal information refers only to that user.

Related/Similar Patterns. Ambient notice [22] is discussed in Sect. 5.10.

5.7   Instant User Interface for Information About Personal Identification Information

The pattern is proposed by Bier and Krempel [23]:

Context. The personal information is collected and processed by the online technology service. The data Subject should understand enough of the system design to be informed about how the system collects and processes the personal information.

Problem. The system collects and processes the personal data through complex transactions. It is difficult for a typical user to understand when and why the data is collected. The system stores personal information in sensors and these sensors (servers) might not be in one place.

Solution. Informing the Data Subject about the sensor that collects and processes the data during the communication. It would help the DSs to understand that the information is placed in a sensor, and they can access the information anytime for any reason.

Known Uses. Privacy Dashboard such as Google Privacy Dashboards (https://www.google.com/dashboard) but the Instant User Interface pattern focuses on informing the DSs about the location where their information is stored.

Related/Similar Patterns. Ambient Notice [22] is related to the concept of providing a DS with a feedback, which is discussed in Sect. 5.10.

5.8   Non-repudiation Pattern

The pattern is proposed by Compagna et al. [25]:

Context. When the Data Controller performs its own tasks by dividing the tasks into subtasks and relays the responsibilities of DSs information protection/processing to parties or actors according to predefined relations. The DC (organization) needs a commitment from the Data Processor (third party/agent) to preserve DS's privacy but the Data Controller does not have any guarantee that the supplier takes the responsibility to achieve and provide commitment.

Problem. The Data Controller must have evidence that the Data Processor cannot repudiate the pre-defined commitments.

Solution. The solution is to gain this commitment through two parts:

- Part 1: is a proof of commitment when the data controller delegates the responsibility to the data supplier.

- Part 2: is a trust that is initiated between the two actors and any failure of fulfillment can be returned to the proof presented by the supplier in the first part.

Known Uses. Monitoring and Emergency Response Centre (MERC) in any healthcare system.

Related/Similar Patterns. The Outsourcing Pattern [24] is related to the pattern in the aspect of the agreement to process information with DP as discussed in Sect. 5.12.

5.9   Data Abstraction

The pattern is proposed by Bier and Krempel [23]:

Context. The data processing occurs in different levels of abstraction and data storage varies in different forms.

Problem. The second use of data (personal information) is a great threat of DSs' privacy. Who is allowed to access the data when it is stored?

Solution. To perform data abstraction, which helps in reducing the amount of information stored and collected. Data abstract can help in revealing only what is needed for specific tasks.

Known Uses. NEST video abstraction & fusion [30].

Related/Similar Patterns. Hidden Metadata [31] is related in the aspect of network encryption method by hiding the personal information transmitted over the network.

5.10   Ambient Notice

The pattern is proposed by [22]:

Context. When the DC performs ongoing tracking of DS's locations or can access DSs' location at any time.

Problem. When the DS's location information is used as a repeated model dialog with or without the DSs' permission. How can DSs get a notice about every time a service is using location information?

Solution. The solution is an ambient notice that appears instantly when location information is retrieved. The notice should provide an opportunity to interact with the permissions.

Known Uses. Location-based services icons used in Mac OS.X. It is shown as a compass arrow that appears in the taskbar every time an application is used to track the DS's location as shown in Fig. 4.

Fig. 4. Ambient location services icon in Mac OS X [22] (privacypattern.org, 2014)

Consequences. Providing the DS with overwhelming details is a disadvantage of this pattern and notices might be annoying.

Related/Similar Patterns. Asynchronous notice [22] which shares the same context and solution.

5.11   Private Link

The pattern is proposed by [22] Privacypattern.org (2014):

Context. When the DS wants to share content to a group of users (public, or part of the public), and the private content can be accessed regularly.

Problem. The DS wants to limit the number of people who can access the private content available online.

Solution. The DS is provided with a private link or un-guessable Uniform Resource Locator (URL). Only a pre-authorized DS who has the link can access the personal information. The DS decides on who can access the information.

Known Uses

- Flicker "Guest Pass" (https://help.yahoo.com/kb/SLN13039.html)
- Google "anyone with the link" sharing (https://support.google.com/drive/answer/2494893?hl=en)
- Tripit "Get a link" (https://www.tripit.com).

Consequences. Security requirements should be implemented to ensure that only the authorized group can access the content.

Related/Similar Patterns. The Masked Online Traffic [20] is discussed in Sect. 5.2.

5.12   Outsourcing

The pattern is proposed by Compagna et al. [24]:

Context. The Data Controller (organization or a website owner) outsources the data processing practices to a Data Processor (third party).

Problem. Only the DC is responsible to perform the data processing. How can the organization transfer the rights to the Data Processor (DP) without provoking DS's privacy?

Solution. The outsourcing can be legal if the DP agrees to a data processing contract, which must be signed by both the DC and the DP (third party). This means that the DC has to inform the DS about which data will be shared or processed with other parties.

Known Uses

- Xerox Services "IT Outsourcing" (http://services.xerox.com/it-outsourcing/enus. html)
- BM Global Outsourcing Services (http://www-935.ibm.com/services/us/en/it-services/outsourcing.html).

Consequences. The DSs need to be informed and their consents need to be gained before applying the pattern. In some cases, the DS's consent is not gained and the DP still can access without permission. Another issue might arise which is what is the case would be if the DP rejected to agree on the data processing agreement. The solution is to associate this pattern with the Non-Repudiation Pattern [25].

Related Patterns

- Obtaining Explicit Consent [20] and Informed consent [24] are related to this pattern in the need to provide a consent whenever sensitive data is processed.
- Non-repudiation Pattern [25] is related in one aspect by defining the tasks and subtasks that should be accomplished by DP according to an agreement to process DS personal information.

5.13   Limit Disclosure Privacy Pattern

The pattern is proposed by Aljohani et al. [26].

Context. The DS has the right to get access to a list of activities carried out on their information (have a list of who accessed the information) and can to request to not disclose information (choose from the list).

The pattern is applied in healthcare applications and personal health information. The DS agrees on sharing the information with some health agents and organizations and to limit the access to a well-identified list of agents.

Problem. The DS wants to balance between what is shared and who can gain access. The secondary use of information shared between organizations without consent concerns the DSs.

Solution. By being able to limit the organizations that can access the information the privacy pattern protects DS's health information. It allows for limiting the information shared over organizations as follows:

Access Control. The DS requests a record of activities that have been done on the PHI regarding the list of agents who accessed the information. The DC retrieves the information either from a third party, which should be gained from an earlier agreement or from the organization server. The DS has the ability to: agree on the list, or; limit the list by choosing from the list (blocking some), and request not to disclose at all to any of them. Individuals would be able to choose the information that they decide they would like to reveal and mask the rest by providing levels of disclosure.

Authentication. The system applies two-steps identity clarification technique to lock out unauthorized access and/or modification as a security measures.

Consent. The DSs have to sign a consent on the responsibilities associated with not disclosing information because it is associated with personal health information. The DC has to confirm changes and provide feedback.

Feedback. The feedback feature should be applied to inform and notify DSs of the ongoing changes in case there is a new setting.

Related Patterns

- The Masked online traffic pattern by [20] allows users to control what information to reveal and minimize the amount of personal information shared (Sect. 5.2).
- Data abstraction pattern by [23] allows individuals to control whom to reveal the information and provide feedback on who has access to the information (Sect. 5.9).
- Private link pattern by [22] works in limiting who can see the personal health information (Sect. 5.11).
- Instant user Interface by [23] allows individuals to opt in or opt out (Sect. 5.7).

5.14   Notification Privacy Pattern

The pattern is proposed by Aljohani et al. [26].

Context. The individual under this right is being notified of unauthorized activities performed on his/her personal health information.

Problem. The collected information should be used for the purpose that it was collected for and should not be accessed/and or processed for other purposes. The DS wants to be informed instantly in case of secondary use of information, which includes stolen information, lost or subjected to unauthorized access, use, disclosure, copying, or modification.

Solution. To design a privacy-preserving application, two aspects should be investigated: the system-server aspect and user-system aspect. In case of the system-server, the system should apply the Secure Socket Layer (SSL) to protect it from unauthorized access. In case of the user-system, to prevent unauthorized modification the system should apply two-step identification process.

Notification and Consent. The DS is notified in different situations classified according to the type of the practice, which includes; information is stolen or lost as one type, information use, disclosure, copy, and modified as another type. The last type is being subjective to unauthorized access.

Consequences. The DS is informed about the list of activities and agents who are performing these activities and the DS has to agree on collecting the information before the collection with an indication of clear purposes. A challenge of the pattern is that it does not prevent the unauthorized access before it occurs. It focuses on providing feedback when it occurs to help the DS make decisions on next steps to recover the breach. Some security measures should be already installed by the organizational.

Related Patterns

- Need-to-know informs users about recent activities done on the personal health information [24].
- Access control by [21] informs users about the requests to access the information (Sect. 5.4).
- Privacy dashboard and ambient notice by [22] allows users to be informed on how and why the information is collected (Sect. 5.6).

5.15   Mapping Privacy Patterns to ISO Privacy Framework

It is important to identify the difference between Privacy Enhancing Technologies (PETs) and privacy patterns. PETs solve only one specific privacy problem in already implemented software while privacy patterns are design frameworks and guidelines that can be used in similar contexts [28]. Because the there is a lack of methods to validate privacy patterns, we evaluate the proposed privacy patterns according to ISO29100 privacy framework and Privacy Enhancing Techniques. Privacy patterns that are based on a legal framework and focuses on the design of UI are rare.

Only two papers were based on privacy from a legal perspective [24, 26]. Therefore, there is a need to translate privacy from a legal perspective into privacy in the IT perspective. The literature review lacks in this domain. The current state of severe problems around the world in managing personal information has created a gap between the privacy regulation requirements and Information Technology designers [29]. To bridge the gap, designers need to evolve data protection practices throughout the system design process, which relates to the concept of Privacy by Design (PbD) [19] and privacy patterns (Table 2).

Table 2. Mapping privacy patterns to ISO privacy framework

Patterns	ISO 29100 privacy principles								
	Consent and choice	Purpose legitimacy and specification	Collection limitation	Data minimization	Use, retention and disclosure limitation	Accuracy and quality	Openness, transparency and notice	Individual participation and access	Accountability
1.	✓	✓	✓	×	✓	×	✓	✓	✓
2.		✓	✓	✓	×	✓		✓	✓
3.	✓	✓	✓	×	×	✓	✓		✓
4.		✓	×	×	✓	×	✓	✓	×
5.	✓	✓	×	×	✓	×	✓	✓	×
6.	×	✓	×	×	×	×	✓	✓	×
7.	×	×	×	×	✓	✓	✓	×	✓
8.	×	✓	✓	×	✓	✓		×	×
9.	×	×	✓	×	✓	✓	✓	✓	×
10.	×	✓	×	×		×	✓	×	×
11.	×	✓	✓	×	✓	×	✓	×	✓
12.	✓	✓	✓	×	✓	×	✓	✓	×
13.	✓	✓	✓	×	✓	×	✓	✓	×
14.	✓	✓	✓	✓	×	×	✓	✓	✓

5.16   Privacy Patterns Categorization

The privacy patterns are classified according to two concepts: the stakeholder for which the problem was described (a user, organization developer, and/ or system designer); and into which privacy principle they belong. The classification adds to the literature by shedding the lights on the patterns that propose solutions to solve the privacy design problem from the user's perspective, not the security-network perspective. In the following table, we summarize the categorization of the privacy patterns in Table 3.

Table 3. Privacy patterns classification

Privacy pattern	Problem according to	Privacy principle
Informed consent for web-based transaction pattern	Designer	Access, transparency, and feedback
Masked online traffic	End users	Encryption
Obtaining explicit consent pattern	Organization developer	Notice
Access control to sensitive data based on purpose	Organization developer	Access
Minimal information asymmetry	End users	Minimization and user control
Outsourcing	Organization developer	
Privacy dashboards	End users	Access, transparency, and feedback
Instant user interface for information about personal identification information	End users	User interface and transparency
Non-repudiation Pattern	Organization developer	Access
Data abstraction	Designer and organization developer	Minimization
Ambient notice	End users and organization developer	Transparency and user control
Private link	End users	User control

6   Conclusion

We presented a systematic review of the currently available privacy patterns mapped to IDO privacy principles and PETs. The currently available patterns focus on proposing implementation solutions for privacy problems in specific contexts. They barely reference to the legal legislation or laws on which they are based. They focus on how to implement privacy through a security-network perspective and they do not address privacy from the end user's perspective. We believe conducting the systematic review of currently available privacy patterns will provide Information Technology (IT) and UI designers and developers with a privacy framework to help them to apply according to their matching design contexts.

Acknowledgments. This work has been funded by the University of Jeddah in Saudi Arabia, with the support of the Saudi Cultural Bureau in Canada.

References

1. Iachello, G., Hong, J.: End-user privacy in human–computer interaction. Found. Trends® Hum.-Comput. Interact. **1**(1), 1–137 (2007)
2. Yang, J.J., Li, J.Q., Niu, Y.: A hybrid solution for privacy preserving medical data sharing in the cloud environment. Future Gener. Comput. Syst. **43**, 74–86 (2015)
3. Liu, X.Y., Wang, B., Yang, X.C.: Survey on privacy preserving techniques for publishing social network data. J. Softw. **25**(3), 576–590 (2014)
4. Bao, L., Zhang, D.Y., Wu, J.B.: Internet of things and privacy preserving technologies. Electron. Sci. Technol. **23**(7), 110–112 (2010)
5. Aïmeur, E., Brassard, G., Fernandez, J.M., Onana, F.S.M.: A lambic: a privacy-preserving recommender system for electronic commerce. Int. J. Inf. Secur. **7**(5), 307–334 (2008)
6. Lu, R., Lin, X., Shen, X.: SPOC: a secure and privacy-preserving opportunistic computing framework for mobile-healthcare emergency. IEEE Trans. Parallel Distrib. Syst. **24**(3), 614–624 (2013)
7. Anderson, C., Agarwal, R.: The digitization of healthcare: boundary risks, emotion, and consumer willingness to disclose personal health information. Inf. Syst. Res. **22**(3), 469–490 (2011)
8. Clarke, R.: Privacy impact assessment: its origins and development. Comput. Law Secur. Rev. **25**(2), 123–135 (2009)
9. ISO/IEC 29100: Information technology – Security techniques – Privacy framework. Technical report, ISO JTC 1/SC 27
10. Hoepman, J.-H.: Privacy design strategies. In: Cuppens-Boulahia, N., Cuppens, F., Jajodia, S., Abou El Kalam, A., Sans, T. (eds.) SEC 2014. IAICT, vol. 428, pp. 446–459. Springer, Heidelberg (2014). https://doi.org/10.1007/978-3-642-55415-5_38
11. OECD: Excerpts from Annex to the Recommendation of the Council of 23rd September 1980: Guidelines Governing The Protection of Privacy and Transborder Flows of Personal Data are © OECD 1980 (1980)
12. Borking, J.J., Raab, C.D.: Laws, PETs and other technologies for privacy protection. J. Inf. Law Technol. **1**, 1–14 (2001)
13. Seničar, V., Jerman-Blažič, B., Klobučar, T.: Privacy-enhancing technologies—approaches and development. Comput. Stand. Interfaces **25**(2), 147–158 (2003)
14. Damiani, M.L.: Privacy enhancing techniques for the protection of mobility patterns in LBS: research issues and trends. In: Gutwirth, S., Leenes, R., de Hert, P., Poullet, Y. (eds.) European Data Protection: Coming of Age, pp. 223–239. Springer, Dordrecht (2013). https://doi.org/10.1007/978-94-007-5170-5_10
15. Reiter, M.K., Rubin, A.D.: Crowds: anonymity for web transactions. ACM Trans. Inf. Syst. Secur. (TISSEC) **1**(1), 66–92 (1998)
16. W3C: Platform for Privacy Preferences, P3P 1.0 (2002). http://www.w3.org/P3P/

17. Bennett, K., Grothoff, C.: GAP – practical anonymous networking. In: Dingledine, R. (ed.) PET 2003. LNCS, vol. 2760, pp. 141–160. Springer, Heidelberg (2003). https://doi.org/10.1007/978-3-540-40956-4_10

18. Communication COM: 228 from the Commission to the European Parliament and the Council. On Promoting Data Protection by Privacy Enhancing Technologies (PETs) (2007)

19. Cavoukian, A.: Privacy by design: leadership, methods, and results. In: Gutwirth, S., Leenes, R., de Hert, P., Poullet, Y. (eds.) European Data Protection: Coming of Age, pp. 175–202. Springer, Dordrecht (2013). https://doi.org/10.1007/978-94-007-5170-5_8

20. Romanosky, S., Acquisti, A., Hong, J., Cranor, L.F., Friedman, B.: Privacy patterns for online interactions. In: Proceedings of the 2006 Conference on Pattern Languages of Programs, p. 12. ACM, October 2006

21. Porekar, J., Jerman-Blazic, A., Klobucar, T.: Towards organizational privacy patterns. In: 2008 Second International Conference on the Digital Society, pp. 15–19. IEEE, February 2008

22. Privacypattern.org

23. Bier, C., Krempel, E.: Common privacy patterns in video surveillance and smart energy. In: 2012 7th International Conference on Computing and Convergence Technology (ICCCT), pp. 610–615. IEEE, December 2012

24. Compagna, L., El Khoury, P., Krausová, A., Massacci, F., Zannone, N.: How to integrate legal requirements into a requirements engineering methodology for the development of security and privacy patterns. Artif. Intell. Law 17(1), 1–30 (2009)

25. Compagna, L., Khoury, P.E., Massacci, F., Thomas, R., Zannone, N.: How to capture, model, and verify the knowledge of legal, security, and privacy experts: a pattern-based approach. In: Proceedings of the 11th International Conference on Artificial Intelligence and Law, pp. 149–153. ACM, June 2007

26. Aljohani, M., Hawkey, K., Blustein, J.: Proposed privacy patterns for privacy preserving healthcare systems in accord with nova scotia's personal health information act. In: Tryfonas, T. (ed.) HAS 2016. LNCS, vol. 9750, pp. 91–102. Springer, Cham (2016). https://doi.org/10.1007/978-3-319-39381-0_9

27. Bösch, C., Erb, B., Kargl, F., Kopp, H., Pfattheicher, S.: Tales from the dark side: privacy dark strategies and privacy dark patterns. Proc. Priv. Enhanc. Technol. 2016(4), 237–254 (2016)

28. Chung, E.S., Hong, J.I., Lin, J., Prabaker, M.K., Landay, J.A., Liu, A.L.: Development and evaluation of emerging design patterns for ubiquitous computing. In: Proceedings of the 5th Conference on Designing Interactive Systems: Processes, Practices, Methods, and Techniques, pp. 233–242. ACM, August 2004

29. Aljohani, M., Blustein, J., Hawkey, K.: Participatory design research to understand the legal and technological perspectives in designing health information technology. In: Proceedings of the 35th ACM International Conference on the Design of Communication, p. 39. ACM, August 2017

30. Moßgraber, J., Reinert, F., Vagts, H.: An architecture for a task-oriented surveillance system: a service-and event-based approach. In: 2010 Fifth International Conference on Systems (ICONS), pp. 146–151. IEEE, April 2010

31. Hafiz, M.: A collection of privacy design patterns. In: Proceedings of the 2006 Conference on Pattern Languages of Programs, p. 7. ACM, October 2006

Merging the Cultures of Design and Engineering: A Case Study

Julie Baca[1](✉), Daniel Carruth[2], Elijah Davis[2], and Daniel Waddell[2]

[1] U.S. Army Corps of Engineers, Engineering Research and Development Center,
Vicksburg, MS 39180, USA
julie.a.baca@usace.army.mil
[2] Center for Advanced Vehicular Systems, Mississippi State University,
Starkville, MS 39759, USA
{dcarruth, ecdl57, dmw277}@msstate.edu

Abstract. This paper presents a case study of a web application development project, in which user-centered design (UCD) was successfully integrated in an environment with strong historical and cultural roots in traditional engineering. The case study details the key factors that led to the success of the project in a deeply traditional risk-averse engineering culture, and how the lessons learned apply beyond its scope. Key factors included a design team with experience in the worlds of both design and engineering, a careful selection of UCD methods, and finally a management structure that embraced cultural change.

Keywords: User-centered design · Usability · Prototyping

1 Introduction

In the revised edition of his classic text, *The Design of Everyday Things*, Donald Norman added an entire chapter devoted to "Design Thinking" and another to "Design in the World of Business" [1]. In these additions, from the vantage point of over 30 years of experience since the original text, he explores anew the fundamental differences between the goals and practices of design culture and those of the cultures of traditional engineering and business. Design thinking, he contends, is by nature iterative, exploratory, circular, open-ended, and most importantly, human-centered, with a focus on meeting human needs and desires. A human must always be in the exploratory loop to quickly test and refine ideas as they are generated. This approach inherently embraces risk, and the likelihood of failure in early design iterations.

In contrast, traditional engineering and business methods are linear and unidirectional with clearer beginnings and endings, a more limited ability to backtrack and refine ideas, and, of critical importance, are risk-averse and far less human-centered, focused instead on product qualities such as reliability and verifiability. Successful product design, Norman argues, requires a marriage of the best of both of these cultures. These ideas have been well understood and followed by researchers and practitioners in the fields of user interface (UI) and user experience (UX) design for decades. Why, then,

A. Marcus and W. Wang (Eds.): DUXU 2018, LNCS 10918, pp. 628–641, 2018.
https://doi.org/10.1007/978-3-319-91797-9_44

should we still be discussing them? The answer lies in a statement Norman makes in the final chapter of the book:

"Technology changes rapidly; people and cultures change slowly."

Although the need for human-centered design in software development has been understood in the design community for over 30 years, its inclusion in actual practice remains, at best, hit or miss. Software continues to be developed predominantly from within the cultures of traditional engineering and business, and, cultural change, as Norman points out, is grindingly slow. Beyond simply changing methods or practices, it requires a fundamental shift in thinking, or at the very least, loosening the grip of deeply held beliefs about the appropriateness of the underlying paradigm for all aspects of product design. Ideally, it is an evolutionary shift that does not discard traditional engineering methods where appropriate, but includes and integrates those of human-centered design where needed.

This paper presents a case study of a web application development project, in which user-centered design (UCD) was successfully integrated in an environment with strong historical and cultural roots in traditional engineering. Although the methods and techniques used are not novel in the UCD world, the effort merits study to gain insight into why it succeeded in such a deeply traditional, risk-averse engineering culture, and how the lessons learned apply beyond that scope. In overview, its success can be attributed to three key factors: (1) the "multicultural" composition of the design team, i.e., all with prior experience in or exposure to the methods of both design and engineering, (2) the particular choice of UCD methods used in the project, and finally, (3) a management structure that embraced cultural change.

2   Case Study

2.1   Design Team

This case study examines the integration of UCD in the software lifecycle for a product called the Ground Vehicle Interface (GVI), developed by the U.S. Army Corps of Engineers (USACE) Engineering Research and Development Center (ERDC). GVI was unusual from the outset in that it was conceived by management with the specific goal of providing intuitive web access to a suite of analytical tools for a wide range of high performance computing users, with no requirement for extensive knowledge of the underlying modeling and simulation capabilities. The leadership focus on the needs of users exhibited a major advance in cultural understanding over previous generations, regarding the importance of ease of use to product acceptance. That emphasis alone set the course of the project in a successful direction. Attaining this goal, however, would further challenge and ultimately alter the established software culture and practices. The first steps toward change began when the development team created an initial version of the software. While it was functionally robust, both developers and leadership recognized the need to include available expertise in user-centered design and usability.

The UCD team was led by a trained usability specialist with over a decade of experience in User Interface (UI) and User experience (UX) design, as well as a strong previous working background in software development. The team also included a cognitive scientist with dual training and experience in both cognitive science and computer engineering, a graphic designer experienced in delivering designs in an engineering environment, and a computer science graduate student, focusing on human-computer interaction. The multidisciplinary nature of the team embodied an atypical blend of design thinking and skills with experience in an engineering culture. This created a team mindset that could adapt to existing cultural practices without compromising core design values.

Critical to the success of the project were the selection of UCD methods and the specific manner in which they were applied that recognized the limitations of the culture while seeking to push beyond them. These included: (1) usability walkthrough, (2) user advisory panel, (3) iterative prototype review with formative usability testing, and (4) summative usability testing.

2.2   Usability Walkthrough

Ideally, UCD teams begin to gather usability requirements simultaneous to the development team gathering functional requirements. In traditional engineering cultures, however, UCD teams are rarely included in a software project in the earliest stages. In this case, again, the support of management enabled the inclusion to occur relatively early in the lifecycle. Although its inclusion occurred after an initial UI had been developed, it was still well before any testing or production cycles were eminent.

Once included, the design team had to determine the best course of action to set the foundation for a good UI design. In theory, restarting the cycle to gather usability requirements with a representative set of users might seem the best choice. But this ignores several unspoken cultural issues that can present barriers to acceptance of the design team by the developers. Requirements gathering is time-consuming, does not offer a rapid actionable result, and thus, developers can quickly lose patience as their own deadlines loom. Also, while they may recognize deficiencies in the existing UI, developers are not educated in UCD, so do not fully understand why, and thus how, to get from point A (the existing UI) to point B (the improved UI). Frustration builds over the unknown and the unpredictable, both anathema to the traditional linear deadline-driven model; in an iterative UCD design process friction with the design team can result. It is a classic example of the conflict between the linear thinking necessary for sound engineering, and the cyclical nature of UI design.

Therefore, the first action of the design team was to simply conduct a usability evaluation of the initial UI. This action was chosen because it can be done fairly quickly, i.e., as little as 1–2 weeks rather than months, and yields immediate visible and tangible results. More importantly, it rapidly educates the development team and offers insight about the nature of the problems and how to solve them. The evaluation was conducted using a variant of a heuristic method, the "usability walkthrough" [2–5]. This technique typically identifies potential usability problems in a user interface in the design stage. It entails a usability specialist (or a team of specialists) who "walk through" a set of interactive exercises with a user interface to identify potential problems, based on known usability heuristics and principles. The technique has been reported to identify a significant percentage of usability problems in the design stage [5]. This does not replace formal testing with users, which can be conducted later in the development cycle. Of particular importance to this effort, it also helps developers to see the possible need to revisit requirements gathering with users with respect to usability. Also significant, the UCD team employed mockups and sketches to show possible solutions to the problems, tangibly illustrating a "Point B" goal for the linear developer mindset to target. *Understanding and insight reduce frustration and thereby, increase developer patience with the process.*

Heuristics. A set of general usability heuristics, such as those defined in [6], are considered in an evaluation of any user interface. Since GVI is a web application, a more specific set of heuristics and guidelines were also considered. Those for general websites are first, followed by those specific to web applications. A comprehensive set of web usability guidelines are given in [7–13]. Those relevant to GVI include:

(1) Clearly establish identity and purpose on the home or opening page [7, 8, 10]
(2) Place all critical information and interactions "above the fold" before the user must scroll [7–10]
(3) Use strong focal points and a hierarchy of visual cues to draw the user into the site or application and guide the user through the interaction space [8, 14]
(4) Provide persistent or "sticky" navigation allowing users access to the main site navigation bar from anywhere within the site [8, 10, 15].

Distinctions between websites and applications that have important usability implications are described in [16–18]. The main purpose of a website is to present content to the user with limited interactivity beyond search engines or contact forms. In other words, the overall purpose of a website is more informational than interactive. Conversely, the purpose of a web application is to support users interactively performing frequent and/or repetitive complex tasks. This latter distinction requires a greater emphasis on the following elements and activities:

• Simplicity in visual design to counterbalance complexity of interactions
• Clearly defined user profiles, including novice and expert roles
• Detailed task analyses for each category of user profiled.

Walkthrough Results. Highlights of issues noted on the home page that intersect both the website and web application usability heuristics are presented here. Detailed results of the walkthrough are given in [19].

Home Page Analysis. The home page is the entry point into the site and thus critical to establishing ease of use. The walkthrough identified three main usability issues on the home page, shown below in Fig. 1, in regard to guidelines 1–3 above. These pertained to identity, purpose, and the use of visual cues.

First, many strong, but similar visual elements are positioned on the screen. Without proper focal points and visual hierarchy, these elements compete for the user's attention. This makes it more difficult for the user to focus, discern the identity and purpose of the application, and choose an interaction. Figure 2 shows the issues in more detail. Note the dark grey headers are the strongest individual visual elements on the page.

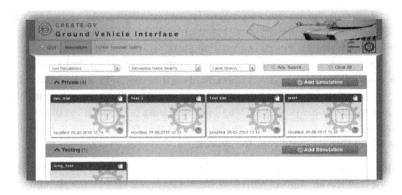

Fig. 1. GVI home page

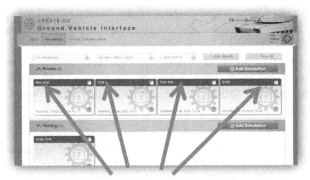

Split focal points

Fig. 2. Home page usability issues

The horizontal listing of simulations is the strongest *group* element on the page, as shown in Fig. 3. However, it isn't clear what these elements contain or the interaction they offer the user. Each simulation rectangle is fairly large; taken together as a group in the horizontal listing, these act almost like "bars" on the page pushing users away visually, rather than inviting them to delve further. In addition, the number of these elements renders other key interactions inaccessible "above the fold" before the user must scroll.

This illustrates highlights of the major issues identified in the walkthrough. To summarize, the main issues identified related to identity and purpose, use of proper visual hierarchy, and navigation.

Walkthrough Recommendations. As a final step to solidify developer acceptance and confidence, the UCD team presented mockups of possible solutions to key problems noted in the walkthrough. As noted, this technique offers critical appeal to the linear thought process of the development team, by illustrating a visible path from "Point A" to "Point B." Figure 3 shows a mockup of a refined home page that

Fig. 3. Redesigned home page mockup

addresses key issues identified in the walkthrough. A more detailed discussion of this page is given in Sect. 2.4.

Subsequent to presenting the walkthrough results and mockups, recommendations for further actions were provided to the development team. The recommendations emphasized that the software provided rich, complex, and greatly needed functionality to users in the HPC M&S community. This acknowledged the effort and skill of the developers, another aspect of the overall process critical to success, but often overlooked by UCD teams without experience in both design and engineering cultures. To fully tap the potential of the software, however, it was recommended that representative users be included in the usability design process. As noted in [16, 17], since GVI is a web application, particular emphasis would need to be given to two activities:

1. Clearly defining user profiles, including novice and expert roles
2. Performing detailed task analyses for each category of user profiled.

These activities would need to be conducted iteratively with the development of an increasingly interactive series of mockups and prototypes which users and developers would review and test. This would require: (1) assembling a properly composed user advisory panel, and (2) executing an appropriately detailed prototyping process. These are described further in the sections below.

2.3   User Advisory Panel

The rationale and methods for assembling user advisory panels (roughly 2–5 users) is argued in a variety of sources, including [19, 20]. Studies have shown that, if properly composed, a group of this approximate size can be very effective for conducting user-centered design [20]. This diverges from conventional software development methods in that it focuses on eliciting user needs, rather than developer concerns, to drive the UI design [19]. Therefore, panelists would be chosen to provide the widest representation of typical user needs. To achieve this goal, members of the user advisory panel (UAP) would be selected along at least two criteria, (1) organizational representation, and (2) diversity of experience, i.e., novice versus expert.

GVI would be available to users in three different organizations, The U.S. Army Tank Automotive Research, Development and Engineering Center (TARDEC), the U.S. Marine Corps, and the U.S. Navy. The final composition of the panel included 3 TARDEC users, 2 Marines users, and 1 Navy user. From within this overall mix, 4 users identified themselves as experienced in the use of modeling and simulation (M&S) software tools, while 2 users considered themselves novices.

2.4   Prototyping

The visual, interactive nature of a user interface, particularly for a web application, makes it impossible to capture all usability requirements through verbal interviews with users [14, 16, 18]. User review of interactive prototypes allows design and development teams to iteratively refine, adjust, and "get it right" before moving to a final deployment. The UCD team had created a first phase non-interactive set of mockups to capture the functionality and look and feel of the enhanced design features. The mockups were used as a starting point for the prototyping process. A mixture of horizontal (overall system organization) and vertical (specific feature) prototyping would be used [20–22]. Periodic reviews by the UAP of these prototype designs would be scheduled as they became available. The prototypes would incrementally evolve into a fully functional interface, with more comprehensive usability and error testing scheduled in the latter half of the project lifecycle.

Iterative Prototype Review. The UAP participated in 3 cycles of prototype review, each of which led to refinements that were then evaluated in subsequent review. The first prototype review used a set of non-interactive screen designs, arranged in sequences to simulate interactions. Users were asked to evaluate the screen designs for overall look and feel, i.e., color scheme, layout, and organization and for how well they captured potential interactions that would support user goals. The screens reviewed were not comprehensive, but selected to represent interactions that were either critical or would likely occur frequently in the regular use of the GVI application.

Follow-up phone interviews were also conducted in which users further clarified comments regarding any aspects of GVI, including their goals and needs, how well the screen designs reflected those needs, and suggestions for enhancements. Screens and interactions evaluated included those for the home page, adding simulations and vehicles, and an interactive tutorial for new or novice users, "New to GVI?" The redesigned home page is shown with comments in Fig. 4.

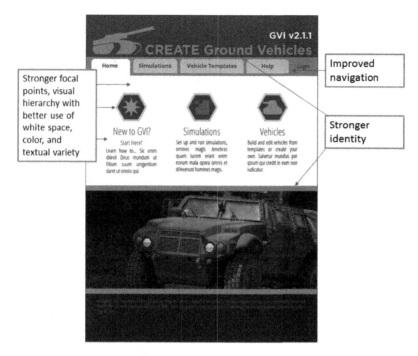

Fig. 4. Redesigned home page

Discussions with the UAP prior to beginning the prototyping process uncovered the need to provide a path through the application for new or novice users. The option "New to GVI?" shown in Fig. 4 on the redesigned home page was designed to meet this requirement. If selected by the user, the screen shown in Fig. 5 begins an inter-action sequence that walk new users through the application. Several options for the initial screen were presented for review. The final design for this screen chosen by the UAP is shown in Fig. 5.

From this initial screen, multiple design options for the first 3 steps, 'Add a new simulation,' 'Add tests,' and 'Add a vehicle,' were again presented to the UAP for review. The initial screen in the sequence of the final options chosen by the UAP for 'Add tests,' and 'Add a vehicle,'' are shown in Figs. 6 and 7.

Results of Review 1. While many important details were gathered from the first review, the critical overall issues, determined from all UAP discussion, both online and via phone, are listed below in order of priority order:

1. Unanimous support for a "project management" option: The UAP requested a method to organize and store all related information regarding a set of vehicles, simulation test conditions, and results in a single location.
2. More emphasis on the concept of "vehicle" over "simulation" as an organizing theme and metaphor. The first prototype focused on a simulation as the central organizing theme. This initial focus made sense as the driving concept of the application was to support advanced simulation tools. However, users all agreed

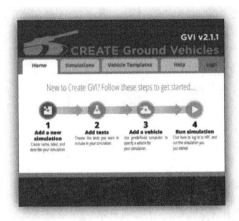

Fig. 5. 'New to GVI' initial screen

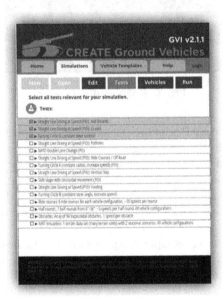

Fig. 6. 'Add tests' option

that in their mental processes, the vehicle was first and foremost in their workflow, followed by the operating or test conditions under which they would run simulations. In subsequent prototypes we attempted to better reflect that order in multiple aspects of the designs.

3. Confusion resulting from use of the term "test" to denote the events or conditions in which a vehicle would be evaluated for performance during a simulation. Opinions conflicted on the appropriate candidate, but the following were offered: Test event,

Fig. 7. 'Add a vehicle' option

Operating conditions, Test conditions, Universal agreement that "metric" is not the correct language for this concept.

For the second prototype, we chose the term "test conditions" for these designs since it contained elements of multiple comments, expecting the need for further possible refinement. Again, users have ideas in discussion or on paper that need refining once they experience them interactively.

4. Need for a menu option for vehicle editing that provided maximum information in minimal space. Our second prototype design sought to better fit that need, with refinements expected.

Figures 8, 9 and 10 show highlights of the critical refinements.

Many other screens and interaction sequences were refined to better capture user requirements and preferences resulting from Review 1. These screens show only highlights of critical refinements to the second prototype.

Results of Prototype Review 2. Highlights of the second prototype review by the UAP included the following: (1) Project management option remained unanimously supported with refinements needed for *adding test conditions* and *adding vehicles* to a project in the areas of interactivity and level of detail; (2) A new 'Vehicle Builder' option was positively received with refinements needed in organization/flow; (3) A 'Simulation Builder' option was positively received with requests to match the general design of 'Vehicle Builder' as it develops. Once the refinements identified in Review 2 were complete, the UAP was asked to perform one final review before summative usability testing.

Results of Prototype Review 3. Highlights of the third prototype review by the UAP included the following: (1) Further refinements requested in the 'New to GVI' option for both interactivity and layout; (2) Refinements in aspects of interactivity were requested for 'Project Manager' and 'Vehicle Builder.'

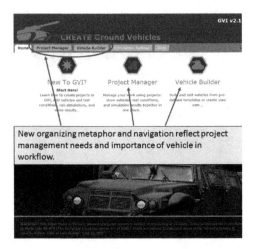

Fig. 8. Refined home page showing new organization and navigation

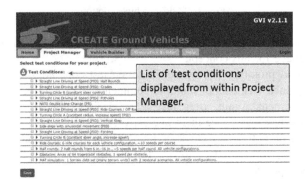

Fig. 9. Use of new terminology and navigation for 'test conditions

2.5   Summative Usability Testing

Following the iterative cycle of prototype design, implementation, UAP review, developer review, and refinement, the interactive prototype was presented to naïve users for a summative usability evaluation.

Participants (N = 13) were recruited from the general population to provide the perspective of a naïve user. Each participant was asked to complete five data entry and modification tasks using the GVI. In one task, the participants were asked to use the 'New to GVI' interface to define a new project and run a simulation. In other tasks, the participants were asked to add or modify projects or vehicles without the 'New to GVI' interface. After each task, the participants were asked to complete the 10-question System Usability Survey (SUS) [23]. The SUS provides a quick but reliable evaluation of the usability of a system. It is a 10-item Likert questionnaire.

Overall SUS scores were calculated and responses to each of the 10 items were also analyzed. An SUS score above 68 is considered above average. The average overall

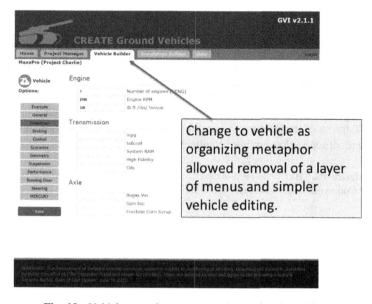

Fig. 10. Vehicle central to user mental model and workflow

SUS score for the GVI was 88.4 (SD = 9.6) indicating that the final design was well received. The mean and standard deviation for overall scores and individual SUS items for the 3 major interface areas are listed in Table 1.

Table 1. Mean and standard deviation for the individual items in the SUS survey by interface.

SUS score/item	New to GVI		Project manager		Vehicle builder	
	M	SD	M	SD	M	SD
Overall SUS	84.0	10.4	88.9	10.2	90.0	9.8
Would use frequently	2.9	0.9	2.8	0.6	2.9	0.6
Too complex*	3.5	0.8	3.7	0.8	3.7	0.9
Easy to use	3.5	1.0	3.7	0.5	3.7	0.5
Need support to use*	3.7	0.5	3.7	0.4	3.8	0.4
Well integrated	3.0	0.7	3.3	0.6	3.4	0.7
Too inconsistent*	3.5	0.8	3.7	0.5	3.7	0.5
Quick to learn to use	3.6	0.7	3.6	0.5	3.7	0.4
Cumbersome to use*	3.5	0.9	3.6	0.9	3.6	0.7
Confident when using	3.0	0.8	3.7	0.4	3.8	0.5
Need to learn a lot*	3.5	0.7	3.7	0.6	3.8	0.4

Note: * Scores adjusted so higher number indicates positive feeling across all SUS items.

3 Conclusions

Engineering and design cultures are inherently opposite in their approaches, the former linear and risk-averse, the latter cyclical, iterative and risk-embracing. This case study has examined how these two cultures can be merged to produce successful software products and how lessons learned may be applied beyond its scope. The key factors contributing to its success factors included a design team with experience in the worlds of both design and engineering, a careful selection of UCD methods, and finally a management structure that embraced cultural change.

Acknowledgements. This material is based upon work supported by the U.S. Army TACOM Life Cycle Command under Contract No. W56HZV-08-C-0236.

References

1. Norman, D.: The Design of Everyday Things Revised and Expanded, pp. 217–293. Basic Books, New York City (2013)
2. Nielsen, J.: Heuristic evaluation. In: Nielsen, J., Mack, R.L. (eds.) Usability Inspection Methods. Wiley, New York (1994)
3. Nielsen, J., Mack, R.L.: Usability Inspection Methods. Wiley, New York (1994)
4. Bias, R.G.: The pluralistic usability walkthrough-coordinated empathies. In: Nielsen, J., Mack, R.L. (eds.) Usability Inspection Methods. Wiley, New York (1994)
5. Spencer, R.: The streamlined cognitive walkthrough method: working around social constraints encountered in a software development company. In: Proceedings of CHI 2000, pp. 253–259 (2000)
6. Nielsen, J.: 10 Usability Heuristics for User Interface Design. NN/G Nielsen Norman Group, 1 January 1995
7. Nielsen, J.: Designing Web Usability. New Riders Publishing, Indianapolis (2000)
8. Nielsen, J., Loranger, H.: Prioritizing Web Usability. New Riders, Berkeley (2006)
9. Van Duyne, D.K., Landay, J.A., Hong, J.I.: The Design of Sites: Patterns, Principles, and Processes for Crafting a Customer-Centered Web Experience. Addison-Wesley, Boston (2002)
10. Nielsen, J., Tahir, M.: Home Page Usability: 50 Sites Deconstructed. New Riders, Berkeley (2007)
11. Pirolli, P., Card, S.: Information foraging. Psychol. Rev. **106**(4), 643–675 (1999)
12. Pirolli, P.: Information foraging on the web: rational analyses of human-information interaction. Cogn. Sci. (2004)
13. Brinck, T., Gergle, D., Wood, S.: Designing Sites that Work: Usability for the Web. Morgan Kaufman, San Francisco (2000)
14. McIntire, P.: Visual Design for the Modern Web. New Riders, Berkeley (2008)
15. Denney, H.: Navigation issues: sticky menus are quicker to navigate. Smashing Mag. (2012)
16. Jovanovic, J.: Designing User Interfaces for Business Web Applications. Smashing Mag. (2010)
17. Nielsen, J.: Best Application Designs. NN/G Nielsen Norman Group, 23 April 2012
18. Beier, B., Vaughn, M.W.: The bulls-eye: a framework for web application user interface design guidelines. In Proceedings of CHI 2003, pp. 489–496 (2003)
19. Baca, J.: GV1 Usability Evaluation and Recommendations, 29 July 2015

20. Preece, J., Rogers, Y., Sharp, H.: Interaction Design: Beyond Human-Computer Interaction. Wiley, New York (2002)
21. Norman, D.A., Draper, S.W.: User Centered System Design: New Perspectives on Human Computer Interaction. Erlbaum, Hillsdale (1986)
22. McCurdy, M., Conners, C., Pyrzak, G., Kanefsky, B., Vera, A.: Breaking the fidelity barrier: an examination of current prototypes and an example of mixed-fidelity success. In: Proceedings of CHI 2006, pp. 1233–1242 (2006)
23. Brooke, J.: SUS: a quick and dirty usability scale. Usability Eval. Ind. **189**(194), 4–7 (1995)

The Use of Design Thinking in Agile Software Requirements Survey: A Case Study

Edna Dias Canedo$^{(\boxtimes)}$ and Ruyther Parente da Costa

Computer Science Department, University of Brasília (UnB),
70910-900 Brasília, DF, Brazil
ednacanedo@unb.br, ruyther@me.com
http://www.cic.unb.br

Abstract. This work presents an experience report using the technique of Designer Thinking applied in the modernization of two real systems. We used software development in this modernization. In addition, it describes a the participation of a Designer throughout the development process and what the perceptions of project participants are in relation to the benefits of this professional's involvement in the whole development process cycle. The evaluation of the perception of those involved was carried out through a survey in the form of a questionnaire to analyze the results. The Project has 29 participants and of these 24 responded to the questionnaire. 75% of the participants stated that the prototypes proposed by the Designer were important for carrying out their activities in the project and 92% consider the experience of using prototypes to support the system development functionalities positive.

Keywords: Designer · Prototype · Requirements elicitation
Micro scenarios · Agile methodology · Design Thinking

1 Introduction

The recent literature in the field of Human-Computer Interaction (HCI) and Software Engineering clearly shows that there is a growing research interest on integration of Design Thinking (DT) design and agile software development.

Often these studies begin with time-consuming up-front activities such as contextual enquiries, interviews, definition of requirements and usability goals, among other activities, resulting in extensive documentation. On the other hand, Agile Software Development is light-weight, customer-oriented and a highly collaborative approach that follows a continual exploration of the business need as the basis to gather and refine software requirements to develop quality software.

Requirements engineering is the step of system development that treats about discovering, defining, documenting and maintaining it requirements. It produces a set of system requirements which is the most complete, consistent and relevant it can be to mirror what customer wants and actually solve his problems [1].

© Springer International Publishing AG, part of Springer Nature 2018
A. Marcus and W. Wang (Eds.): DUXU 2018, LNCS 10918, pp. 642–657, 2018.
https://doi.org/10.1007/978-3-319-91797-9_45

In some models, requirements engineering consists of the first phase of the development process and ends with the guideline delivered to the team of developers, who proceed alone from that point [2].

In this article, we will deal with a development model where the requirements engineering permeates all its stages, being responsible for organizing new requirements that arise during the development and keeping the previous requests met or replaced by the best possible solutions.

Designers are involved from the outset and are responsible for defining and monitoring the solutions. Along with developers, they conduct all requirements survey steps by merging design field methodologies with software engineering practices. It results in a iterative methodology [3]. The steps are:

- **Requirements elicitation:** designers, developers, and stakeholders meet to discuss the issues that must be resolved with the implementation of new software.
- **Requirements analysis and discussion:** requirements are identified and there is consensus among stakeholders. Use cases and graphical representations are used to represent the solutions found. As the design team is present from the beginning, at that moment prototyping is already under way. As an iterative process, the approval of the requirements with the client permeates the entire project and is done with the presentation of prototypes.
- **System modeling:** as the requirements arose, prototypes equivalent to the definitions were made, becoming a new instrument of validation and survey of new requirements. Because the agile method was used, this action was repeated several times concomitant to the development, but the prototype was released to the developers only after a certain level of maturity, when it was considered very close to the state expected for the software.
- **Requirements specification and validation:** it results in a formal artifact called Requirements Specification (RS). At this point, The documented requirements and models had to be checked if they are consistent and fit the needs of the stakeholder.
- **Requirements management:** as the system was developed, the requirements team supervisioned all the activities since elicitation until to put into use.

These steps are not in sequence. In practice there is considerable interleaving of these activities as doubts and new definitions are considered to find the best solution that combines development and customer needs.

The principal perceived problems observed in general in requirement engineering are **incomplete requirements, moving targets, and time boxing, with lesser problems being communications flaws, lack of traceability, terminological problems, and unclear responsibilities**. We will observe the contribution of the design methodologies for this phase of the project, its positive and negative additions to the progress and consequent result.

Design means changing situations [4]. To do this, it molds and deploys artifacts transforming realities and solving problems by delivering the means for that to happen. Its focus is on seeing possible future solutions and broadening the spectrum of results. Analytical and critical studies focus on what already exists, but the design team is concerned about what can be created from what is presented as a need. Because of its exploratory nature, it is often necessary to spend a little more time in the initial stages, involving users as well as developers and stakeholders to constantly evaluate the possibilities found.

These possibilities are the result of research and evaluation of what is already practiced, of the positive and negative scenario for innovation and the best combinations with the available technology.

Exploring possible future solutions implies problems changing. Since with each new sketch is presented, situations mentioned above become irrelevant or invalid and are replaced by new ones. For the practice of contemporary interaction design, this has implications such as reconsidering notions of exhaustive specifications before building in favor of final approaches.

A consequence of this characteristic is that the traditional systems development and engineering processes, where the goal is to finalize the descriptive analysis for a requirements specification before the entry of the designer, end up not exploring the potential of continuous and joint construction of requirements to the quality of the final solution.

Another important contribution of the designer's participation is the use of graphical resources to represent micro scenarios, which generate important insights and complements to the conclusions, becoming smaller parts of a larger construction and allowing problems to be solved gradually [5]. This feature optimizes the arrival to the most accurate and coherent conclusions with the reality, since it goes beyond the memory or previous experience of the stakeholders for the verbal presentation of the situations. Therefore, it makes sense the progress of the project need to be followed in all its instances, since the technical decisions influence the aesthetic qualities of the resulting interaction, the instrumental choices on the resources to offer have ethical repercussions, and so on. Every steps are linked.

The goal of this work is to describe an experience in the design thinking usage applied in the development process of two real projects. Thus, the main contributions of the paper are:

- A experience report using the design thinking in the agile software development;
- Report of the importance of the Designer participation in the development process;
- A survey applied together with project developers and stakeholders on what are the teams perceptions involved in the project with the adoption of the adopted approach.

The remainder of this paper is organized as follows. Section 2 presents the background. Section 3 presents a brief overview of Design Thinking, Design Thinking Process Models and Tools contexts in Design Thinking. Section 4 presents the characterization of the case study. Section 5 presents an analysis of the results obtained with the survey application. Section 6 has the final remarks and paths for future work.

2   Background

The main objective of the agile software development is to deliver quality software products in a cost and time effective manner through a series of short iterative and incremental development cycles. Each iteration of the agile software development produces a version of working software that emphasizes a business value to the customer ensuring that all agreed requirements have been met.

Software requirements are customer needs expressed in sentences and condition the software quality, describing which services, constraints and characteristics a system must provide, obey and possess, and specify the knowledge needed to develop it. Its obtaining is done through a systematic process that involves several tasks, such as elicitation, analysis and negotiation, besides documentation, validation and requirements management, this process is known as Requirements Engineering [6].

One of the problems that Requirements Engineering has tried to solve, is how to turn a problem into possible solutions with a methodological orientation [7]. The lack or the little involvement of users/stakeholders during the software development process may be one of the causes of this problem. According to [8], the involvement of users/stakeholders throughout software development is one of the criteria that contribute to the project success. Understanding the users/stakeholders is essential to designing software that meets your needs and expectations [9].

One way to keep the focus on the users/stakeholders during agile software development is to use the Design Thinking (DT) methodology [10]. The integration of Design Thinking (DT) into agile software development has been widely discussed in the literature.

Design Thinking can be defined as a methodology used by designers when approaching problems and can be applied in all areas of knowledge, with the goal of achieving innovation [11]. According to [12], Design Thinking presents an alternative to traditional approaches to solving organizational problems, which consist of several steps, which include: **Problem definition and Generation and testing of solutions**.

In the context of Requirements engineering, Design Thinking provides a methodology for eliciting user needs and produces a series of prototypes that normally converge to innovative solutions [7].

There are techniques and tools that support the methodology of Design Thinking (DT). These techniques and tools facilitate the Design Thinking innovation process and the selection of the correct methods is important, especially in the early stages of software development. Knowing what these methods are and how they are applied in Software Engineering makes possible the knowledge of new alternatives for the development process and can involve the user and the stakeholders more effectively in the stages of software development [13].

3 Design Thinking

Design Thinking (DT) is how designers think and apply their mental processes to design objects, services, or systems. DT combines approaches and method solvers used by Designers with insights and practices of technology and business [14].

Design Thinking practices help organizations solve complex problems, encourage innovation, and support the creative process [14]. Therefore, DT is presented as an appropriate methodology to encourage innovation and economic growth [14]. The innovation results from the elaboration of a creative solution that is desirable for the user/stakeholder and economically and technologically viable [11].

3.1 Design Thinking Models and Its Phases

We analyze some designs thinking models reported in the literature to highlight the similarities between these models and how they relate to problem solving leading to creativity and innovation in agile software development projects. The Thinking Design models analyzed adopt phases for their execution. For example, the model presented by [15] has seven phases. This model is adapted for real-time applications and presents as phases: define, explore, idealize, prototype, choose, implement and revise. Figure 1 presents DT models and their respective phases.

There are models that use Design Thinking associated with other technologies or development processes, such as Agile methodology and Lean Startup. The work [16] presents the Nordstrom model. This model initially used Design Thinking only at the beginning of the model and then added the phases of the Agile Development and Lean Startup. After some modifications they proposed a new Nordstrom model, which expanded Design Thinking to the entire development process.

The paper [17] presents the DrivingBoard, which is a component of Design Thinking that makes up a framework called Speedplay. In addition to Design Thinking, this framework uses Participatory Design and Agile Development. The DrivingBoard is a DT model that comprises the following phases: approach, develop, present and provoke, explore, reflect and escape.

The model proposed by [11] identified as Converge model, combines Design Thinking, Lean Startup and Agile Development. The Design Thinking used in the Convergent model is from Stanford University's D-School. Figure 1 presents the design thinking models analyzed in this paper, as well as their respective phases.

The prototyping phase is present in almost all models found in the literature. This work uses the Adobe Illustrator tool (available at: http://www.adobe.com/products/illustrator.html) to build prototypes during the requirements elicitation phase. In addition, the model proposed by [15] was used during the software development process.

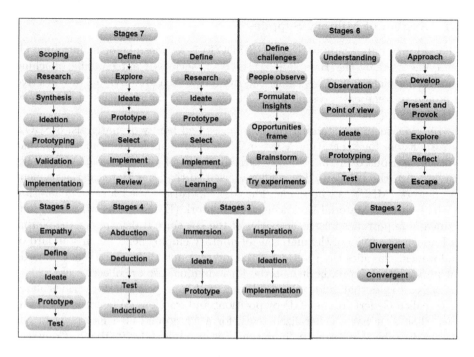

Fig. 1. Design thinking process models and its stages [15, 16, 18–22].

4   Case Study

This work presents an experience report using the technique of Design Thinking during the process of modernization of two legacy systems in the Brazilian army. A legacy system is software written over a period of time using obsolete techniques, but it still performs important work within an organization [23]. The same is difficult to maintain, evolve and/or modified and has a high need for modernization.

Modernization takes place when maintenance is not enough to keep the system up to date and aligned with the business goals. According to [23, 24] modernization entails more significant changes, such as implementing a novel and relevant functional requirement, a modification on the software architecture, or a system migration to a new software platform. Therefore, as pointed in [23], modernization is more pervasive than maintenance, and this is one of the main aspects in their difference. The work for modernization should preserve the data and the functionalities of a system, as it would otherwise be characterized as a replacement [24].

The Brazilian Army (BA) has a Systems Development Center (CDS) through which various software systems are developed, maintained and modernized.

This work applied Design Thinking in the process of modernization of two current systems of BA, namely: System of Endowment of Military Jobs (Sect. 4.1) and System of Bulletins (Sect. 4.2).

4.1   System of Military Supplies

The Military Labor Supply System (SISDOT) is responsible for maintaining all materials used by the Brazilian Army (BA), such as Canteen, rifle, machine gun, fuel, vehicles, etc. These materials are most often of individual or collective use, and in some cases essential for the exercise of the activities of a Military Organization (MO).

In addition to maintaining the type, class and family of materials, SISDOT is responsible for generating a list of all military employment materials that will be distributed in the Military Organizations of the Brazilian Army. This list is called the "Caller". The Caller is used so that the Material Endowment Framework (MEF) can be made. The MEF in turn is used for the generation of the Expected Material Endowment Framework (EMEF). The MEF is of fundamental importance for the activities of the BA since it determines the Norms of Endowment (NE) of the materials of military employment, i.e., a standard of endowment classifies the position of the military and the material that it needs for perform their work, be it material for individual use or collective use.

NEs are rules that guide the establishment of appropriations for various materials (called Generic Items - GI) by positions and fractions. When it is standardized, that is, it has a generalized reach for a Cargo and or a Fraction, an NE should describe that property/intention. For example, GI (10201009 - Complete Individual Use Equipment) - NE = 1 per soldier in an Operational Type MO. In this case, it is verified that the reach of the NE that operates in all military of the Operational MOs.

The modernization of SISDOT comprises new functionalities, as well as improvements in functionalities existing in the current system.

The main functionalities of SISDOT are:

– Register Type of Material; Register Material Class; Register Material Family; Register for Military Jobs; Generate Caller – Edit, Clone, and Delete; Generate MEF – Edit, Clone, Validate, Revoke, or Delete; Generate EMEF – Edit, Clone, Validate, Revoke, or Delete; Register Provisional Allocation Standard; Generate Allocation Standard from the Caller; Register Observation; Register Note; Register Synthesis; Generate Reports – Materials, Caller, Distribution Standard, MEF and EMEF.

4.2   Bulletin System

The Bulletin System (SISBOL) developed during this work aims to replace its legacy version, which is currently used by all Military Organizations belonging to the Brazilian Army. In this way, the modernization of SISBOL is based on the scope of the legacy version, adding some improvements.

The scope of the new SISBOL involves 30 functionalities, which were divided into Legacy Features (23) and New Features (07). Legacy features are:

1. Maintain Military Qualification; 2. Maintain MO Binding; 3. Maintain Military Organization; 4. Maintain Post/Graduate; 5. Keep Bulletin Parts; 6.

Keep Bulletin Sections; 7. Maintain Function; 8. Maintain Category; 9. Maintain Document Type; 10. Maintain Section; 11. Maintain General Subject; 12. Maintain Subject Specific; 13. Maintain Military; 14. Maintain Bulletin Types; 15. Maintain Note; 16. Maintain Bulletin; 17. Generate Note PDF; 18. Generate Bulletin PDF; 19. Maintain Notes in the Bulletin; 20. Maintain Service Time; 21. Approve Changes; 22. Generate Changes and 23. Generate Identification Card.

The new features are:

1. Maintain Workflow Processing; 2. Trafficking Entity in Workflow; 3. Track Quotes; 4. Maintain Note History; 5. Maintain Bulletin History; 6. Search Information in the Bulletin; 7. Present Pendencies (Inbox).

4.3 Development Team

The two systems are being developed in parallel. The development team consists of:

- 03 professors from University de Brasília – (UnB);
- 03 software architect;
- 01 Designer and 01 trainee of the course of Industrial Designer of UnB;
- 04 master's students;
- 01 project manager and;
- 16 trainees who are students of the courses of Computer Science, Mechatronics and Software Engineering of UnB.

4.4 Integrated Design Thinking Framework for Agile Software Development

During the conduction of the works, we initially defined the user stories with the purpose of reflecting the need expected by the user/stakeholder. From the user stories we have completed the Define phase of the model and we were able to explore the functionality of the respective systems, SISDOT and SISBOL, on a more detailed level.

An accurate understanding of the problem enables the development of more accurate solutions. In this phase we use interview techniques and the 5 whys.

The Explore phase gathers information about what will be worked on, such as identifying potential users and their needs, besides observation of previous solutions related to the same problem. This stage gave the team very important information for the future generation of ideas, as it helped ensure that the ideas are oriented toward the needs of the project.

During the stage Ideate, is important to identify the things that are relevant to the people involved in the activity and to generate as many ideas as possible for meeting those needs. Brainstorming is the core of this stage, but it is also important to consider other ways of getting insights for the future design. In this work, it is used a Brainstorming technique to conduct the work during this phase.

The ideas generated in the Ideate phase were transformed into prototypes. Design Thinking promotes prototyping from the beginning stages of the design process. Furthermore, early prototyping of software design is recommended in order to help users/stakeholders identify their needs in order to make them part of the process, among other reasons. According to the Design Thinking methodology, the prototypes do not usually need to be detailed or working prototypes in the early stages of the process. The tool selected for this stage was: Adobe Illustrator (Available in: http://www.adobe.com/products/illustrator.html).

All user stories were prototyped and presented initially to users/stakeholders, in order to validate the system needs. With prototyping it was possible to better understand the users' needs and identify various improvements in system requirements. All improvements identified and suggested were again with prototyped and homologated with the users/stakeholders. A number of user stories required a number of discussions and approvals to ensure that there was no doubt about the correct functioning of the functionality. After the acceptance by the users/stakeholders, the prototypes were delivered to the development team for implementation.

Select and Implement are merged since the tool that is most suitable for both stages is the same, and its application is based on the analysis of the reality that is being developed. When this information becomes available, the development of the software can begin, using both the results of the activity analysis and the requirements from the briefing. In the Select and Implement phase, we reviewed all proposed solutions and implemented those that were in accordance with the project objective.

The prototypes developed for each functionality comprised all the instructions necessary for the development team to implement them, from the detailed detailing of the business rules of the features to the types and sizes of fonts, buttons and messages that should be used, among other details.

Once the project was finished, Review phase, the design team had to keep track of how the product was introduced to the users whether it really fits the purposes it was conceived for, and identified possible areas of improvement and collected information from the people that benefit from the application.

5   Result

In order to evaluate the perception of project participants regarding the importance of the participation of the Designer and the use of the Thinking Design Technique (Prototyping), we conducted a survey in a questionnaire format, which contains 13 questions.

A survey is not just the instrument (the questionnaire or checklist) for gathering information. It is a comprehensive research method for collecting information to describe, compare or explain knowledge, attitudes and behavior. The purpose of a survey is to produce statistics, that is, quantitative or numerical descriptions of some aspects of the study population. The main way of collecting information is by asking questions; their answers constitute the data to be analyzed.

Generally information is to be collected from only a fraction of the population, that is a sample, rather than from every member of the population [25].

Most questions have 5 alternative answers: I strongly disagree; I disagree; Neutral; Strongly Agree and Agree. In addition, the questionnaire has a descriptive question so that the participant can write some comment or suggestion regarding the Participation of the Design Professional in the project.

5.1 Analysis of Results

The project has 29 participants and 24 respond to the questionnaire. Figure 2 shows the distribution of participants per project. 25% of participants work in SISBOL, 42% in SISDOT and 33% are developing activities in both projects.

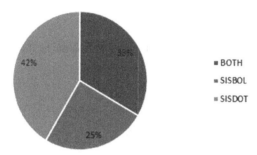

Fig. 2. Number of participants per project

In Fig. 3 it is presented the results obtained with the response of the participants in relation to what activity they carry out within the project. 50% of respondents participate in the software development phase, 13% participate in software development and testing, 8% participate in requirements survey, 13% are project managers, 8% are responsible for modeling data and systems development, and 8% are responsible for the software architecture.

46% of the participants already worked on other projects where a Designer was involved in the requirements survey phase and 48% of them had already worked on the development of system functionalities from prototyping.

In the question related to the prototypes proposed by Designer were important for the project activities to be carried out by the participants, 33% agreed completely and 42% agreed that the prototypes were important. 25% of the respondents were neutral in relation to the proposed prototypes, as shown in Fig. 4.

Regarding the role of the Designer in an agile software development process, 83% of the participants fully agree that it is to propose an interface and 63% affirm that it is to propose a functional interface, according to the version in Fig. 5.

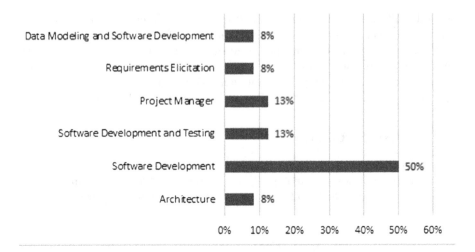

Fig. 3. Activity exercised by the participant in the projects

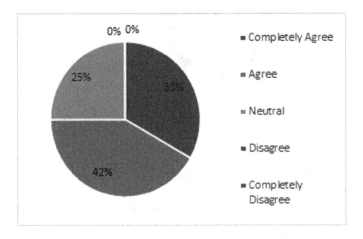

Fig. 4. Importance of prototypes in the execution of the project participants activities

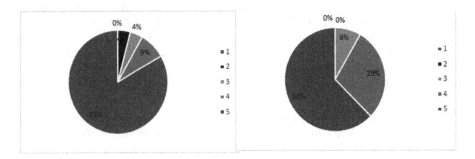

Fig. 5. Designer's role

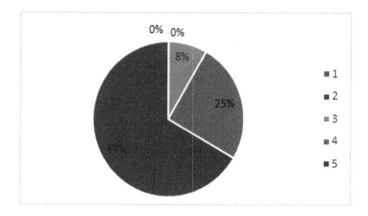

Fig. 6. To propose an interface of easy memorization

67% of survey participants replied that they fully agree that it is Designer's role to propose an easy-to-memorize interface. 25% agree and 8% of the respondents were neutral in relation to this responsibility by the Designer, as it can be seen in Fig. 6.

54% of survey participants agree completely on the positive experience of using prototypes to support the development of project features. 42% agreed and 4% positioned themselves as neutral, as shown in Fig. 7.

Regarding the questioning if the participant considers the visualization of the components, buttons and screens of the system positive, through prototypes in relation to the efficiency of their deliveries in the project, 54% agree completely and 38% agree that it is positive. 8% of the respondents were neutral in the response, as shown in Fig. 8.

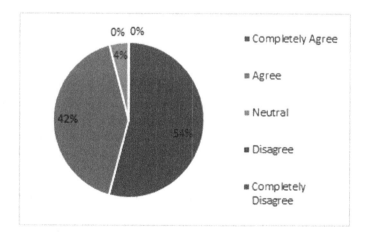

Fig. 7. Use of prototypes to support the development of system functionalities

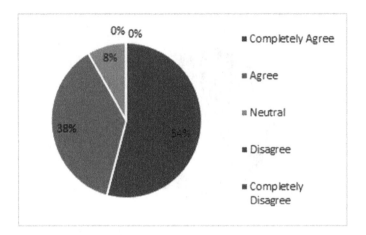

Fig. 8. Visualization of components, buttons and screens of the system through prototypes

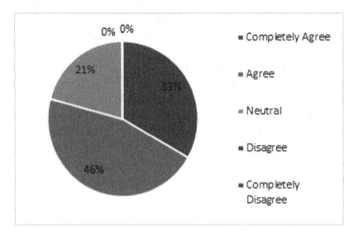

Fig. 9. Quality of the instructions contained in the prototypes delivered by the Project Designer

Regarding the quality of the instructions contained in the prototypes delivered by the Project Designer, 33% of participants agree completely that it is of quality, 46% agree and 21% were neutral in this response, as shown in Fig. 9.

Concerning the suggestions of the Designer participation in an agile software development project, the discursive answers that have been received are:

1. I think Designer needs to be more present at meetings with developers to heal doubts.
2. Most of the answers were neutral, since prototyping was not actually used in the SISBOL system, only in SISDOT. So I did not have so much contact with the technique.

3. No good prototyping was proposed for the specific screens that the Brazilian army needs for SISBOL. From my point of view, even without much experience, there was a bit more interaction between the Designer and the project development teams.
4. The Designer should propose an interface using the html language, since this would facilitate the development process. The proposal made by the Designer in "pdf" format does not contribute to the development of the functionalities.
5. The Designer should hold a meeting every 15 days at least with the project development team. In addition, providing an email or phone to contact for questions and send suggestions would be important. The interaction with *Designer* was difficult and complicated.

6   Conclusion

The use of the Thinking Design technique in the agile development process has been widely used, according to the literature. Although there are not many practical examples of the application of the technique, as well as the positive and negative results of its use in real software systems.

This work validated the use of the design thinking technique applied to two real projects, using prototyping and in addition, the participation of a Designer, graduated in the Industrial Designer course of the University of Brasília (UnB) throughout the development life cycle software.

The results make us reflect on the importance of the role of the Designer, as well as on the quality of the proposed prototypes.

As future work it would be important to replicate the use of the technique and the participation of the Designer in large scale systems, evaluating through a parameterized process the benefits of this participation with the members of the project team and incorporating the improvements suggested by the survey carried out in this work.

Acknowledgements. The authors would like to thank the Systems Development Center (CDS) and the 4ª Deputy Chief of Staff of the Brazilian Army (BA) for their support of this work (FUB / CIC 6138/2016).

References

1. De Lucia, A., Qusef, A.: Requirements engineering in agile software development. J. Emerg. Technol. Web Intell. **2**(3), 212–220 (2010)
2. Wiegers, K., Beatty, J.: Software Requirements. Pearson Education, London (2013)
3. Grau, R.: Requirements engineering in agile software development. In: Maedche, A., Botzenhardt, A., Neer, L. (eds.) Software for People, pp. 97–119. Springer, Heidelberg (2012). https://doi.org/10.1007/978-3-642-31371-4_6
4. Stickdorn, M., Schneider, J., Andrews, K., Lawrence, A.: This is Service Design Thinking: Basics, Tools, Cases. Wiley, Hoboken (2011)
5. Ehn, P.: Participation in design things. In: Proceedings of the Tenth Anniversary Conference on Participatory Design 2008, Indiana University, pp. 92–101 (2008)

6. Kotonya, G., Sommerville, I.: Requirements Engineering: Processes and Techniques. Wiley, Hoboken (1998)
7. Vetterli, C., Brenner, W., Uebernickel, F., Petrie, C.: From palaces to yurts: why requirements engineering needs design thinking. IEEE Internet Comput. **17**(2), 91–94 (2013)
8. Kaur, R., Sengupta, J.: Software process models and analysis on failure of software development projects. arXiv preprint arXiv:1306.1068 (2013)
9. Castro, J.W., Acuña, S.T., Juristo Juzgado, N.: Enriching requirements analysis with the personas technique (2008)
10. Ostrowski, S., Rolczyński, R., Pniewska, J., Garnik, I.: User-friendly e-learning platform: a case study of a design thinking approach use. In: Proceedings of the Mulitimedia, Interaction, Design and Innnovation, p. 19. ACM (2015)
11. Ximenes, B.H., Alves, I.N., Araújo, C.C.: Software project management combining agile, lean startup and design thinking. In: Marcus, A. (ed.) DUXU 2015. LNCS, vol. 9186, pp. 356–367. Springer, Cham (2015). https://doi.org/10.1007/978-3-319-20886-2_34
12. Paula, D., Cormican, K.: Understanding design thinking in design studies (2006–2015): a systematic mapping study. In: DS 84: Proceedings of the DESIGN 2016 14th International Design Conference (2016)
13. Chasanidou, D., Gasparini, A.A., Lee, E.: Design thinking methods and tools for innovation. In: Marcus, A. (ed.) DUXU 2015. LNCS, vol. 9186, pp. 12–23. Springer, Cham (2015). https://doi.org/10.1007/978-3-319-20886-2_2
14. Learning to use design thinking tools for successful innovation
15. Sandino, D., Matey, L.M., Vélez, G.: Design thinking methodology for the design of interactive real-time applications. In: Marcus, A. (ed.) DUXU 2013. LNCS, vol. 8012, pp. 583–592. Springer, Heidelberg (2013). https://doi.org/10.1007/978-3-642-39229-0_62
16. de Paula, D.F.O., Araújo, C.C.: Pet empires: combining design thinking, lean startup and agile to learn from failure and develop a successful game in an undergraduate environment. In: Stephanidis, C. (ed.) HCI 2016. CCIS, vol. 617, pp. 30–34. Springer, Cham (2016). https://doi.org/10.1007/978-3-319-40548-3_5
17. Newman, P., Ferrario, M.A., Simm, W., Forshaw, S., Friday, A., Whittle, J.: The role of design thinking and physical prototyping in social software engineering. In: Proceedings of the 37th International Conference on Software Engineering, vol. 2, pp. 487–496. IEEE Press (2015)
18. Hiremath, M., Sathiyam, V.: Fast train to DT: a practical guide to coach design thinking in software industry. In: Kotzé, P., Marsden, G., Lindgaard, G., Wesson, J., Winckler, M. (eds.) INTERACT 2013. LNCS, vol. 8119, pp. 780–787. Springer, Heidelberg (2013). https://doi.org/10.1007/978-3-642-40477-1_53
19. Coutinho, E.F., Gomes, G.A.M., José, M.A.: Applying design thinking in disciplines of systems development. In: 2016 8th Euro American Conference on Telematics and Information Systems (EATIS), pp. 1–8. IEEE (2016)
20. Dunne, D., Martin, R.: Design thinking and how it will change management education: an interview and discussion. Acad. Manag. Learn. Educ. **5**(4), 512–523 (2006)
21. de Carvalho Souza, C.L., Silva, C.: Uso do design thinking na elicitação de requisitos de ambientes virtuais de aprendizagem móvel. In: WER (2014)
22. Adikari, S., McDonald, C., Campbell, J.: Reframed contexts: design thinking for agile user experience design. In: Marcus, A. (ed.) DUXU 2013. LNCS, vol. 8012, pp. 3–12. Springer, Heidelberg (2013). https://doi.org/10.1007/978-3-642-39229-0_1

23. Bennett, K.: Legacy systems: coping with success. IEEE Softw. **12**(1), 19–23 (1995)
24. Weiderman, N.H., Bergey, J.K., Smith, D.B., Tilley, S.R.: Approaches to legacy system evolution. Technical report, Carnegie-Mellon University, Pittsburgh, PA, Software Engineering Institute (1997)
25. Kitchenham, B.A., Pfleeger, S.L.: Personal opinion surveys. In: Shull, F., Singer, J., Sjøberg, D.I.K. (eds.) Guide to Advanced Empirical Software Engineering, pp. 63–92. Springer, London (2008). https://doi.org/10.1007/978-1-84800-044-5_3

How to Include Users in the Design and Development of Cyberinfrastructures?

Hashim Iqbal Chunpir[1,2,3(✉)]

[1] Department of Computer Science, Universidade Federal de São Carlos,
São Carlos, SP, Brazil
[2] Faculty of Informatics, University of Hamburg,
Vogt-Kölln-str. 30, Hamburg, Germany
[3] German Climate Computing Centre (DKRZ),
Bundesstraße 45a, Hamburg, Germany
hashim.chunpir@gmail.com

Abstract. Cyberinfrastructures have reached their production level as far as their capability to serve researchers and connect big data is concerned. However, users face difficulties while they perform complex operations via cyberinfrastructures by using their user interfaces (UIs), for big data analysis and research. Using these infrastructures users perform operations such as data access, data visualization to complete their research activities. Unfortunately, there are not enough studies and projects conducted so far that provides guidelines to developers to design and develop interfaces that meet user requirements in cyberinfrastructures. These infrastructures are also known as e-infrastructures, big data infrastructures, open data infrastructures, virtual research environments. In this work, guidelines are recommended so that user requirements can directly be incorporated into the design and development of cyberinfrastructure applications serving a particular target audience. In this paper, an example of a cyberinfrastructure is given, using which users can be involved in its design and the development. These techniques can then also be transferred to the designers and developers of other cyberinfrastructures to improve the user experience as well as usability of UIs and associated services. Furthermore, these techniques can be enhanced even further and generalized to meet the requirements of users of applications other than cyberinfrastructures.

Keywords: e-Research · e-Science · User experience (UX)
Human computer interaction (HCI) · Open data · Cyberinfrastructure (CI)
e-Infrastructures · Usability · Big data infrastructures · Citizen science

1 Introduction

The cyberinfrastructures (CIs) enable digitalization of data, access to data, communication and collaboration amongst the users i.e. researchers. They impact the social, material, technical, political relations of research and enable knowledge production of research communities. The acts of performing science through Information and Communication Technologies (ICTs) have been set under several labels such as big science, data-driven science, networked science, open science, digital humanities and

© Springer International Publishing AG, part of Springer Nature 2018
A. Marcus and W. Wang (Eds.): DUXU 2018, LNCS 10918, pp. 658–672, 2018.
https://doi.org/10.1007/978-3-319-91797-9_46

Science 2.0. Other terms used are: e-Science, e-Social Science, e-Research, e-infrastructure, e-Science infrastructures and CIs [1]. Yet other terms used for these infrastructures are: Science Data Infrastructures (SDI) [2], open data infrastructures [3], big data infrastructures, digital science, collaboratories, virtual science, Virtual Research Environments (VREs) and big data science [4]. E-Science domains include medicine, earth sciences, climate sciences, particle physics, bio-informatics, social sciences and other fields [5]. In this work e-infrastructures and cyberinfrastructures have been used interchangeably.

Since e-Science initiatives are funded by public money, the idea is to create, maintain and provide access to knowledge that is open to all scientific communities including general public. There are various communities that directly interact with the CIs, these are: Users of CIs, developers of e-infrastructures, service providers of CIs, funding agencies of data projects, research projects and other stakeholders [6]. The users interacting with the CIs are of different types and they have different needs, technical abilities and capabilities [6, 7]. These stakeholders not only use tangible and intangible resources e.g. hardware and software but they also develop tangible and intangible resources e.g. data, software, information and knowledge for other stakeholders.

Users need an interface to access resources offered by CIs, usually data and computation power. It is essential to know how these infrastructures are used in reality and who the users are. While there can be thousands of users of a CI, the users who use the infrastructure extensively can be very few [8]. The interface to access CI resources includes command line tools, web portals and Graphical User Interface (GUI) to access data assets; which are the main resources hosted. These interfaces provided by a CI are the key to perform operations facilitated by a CI such as: Creating data, collecting data, storing data, sharing data, publishing data, searching data sets, visualizing data and processing data. The UIs of a CI are designed and implemented normally by the developers.

The future work and research directions for the enterprises especially related to cloud and grid computing technologies can be guided by a greater research objective. Specifically, the objective of making software developers aware, particularly those who design UIs of applications (mobile applications as well as others), to design interfaces that meet users' requirements so that users are able to interact with applications without any trouble. It is suggested to focus the future research in this direction, related to CI based applications because users daily access many terabytes of data through these applications to do science and enable access to these data. In this context, the future research projects and collaborations are proposed to be based on five fundamental research questions:

I. To what extent the concepts of service orientation and meeting users' needs are incorporated into the business models of big data enterprises especially based on grid and cloud technologies?

II. How are the developers of the interactive UIs of applications (on mobile, web and desktop) capturing users' information about the user's interaction, and are addressing users' needs, especially the development of UI components of non CI applications whether mobile applications, web-based or desktop?

III. How are the developers of the interactive UIs of a CI capturing the user's information about the user's interaction and are addressing the user needs, especially the development of UI components of CIs?

IV. Are there any similarities or differences between the user requirements of general-purpose applications and the applications for data infrastructures, i.e. comparing and contrasting research question I and II?

V. What techniques or Human Computer Interaction (HCI) artefacts[1] (e.g. user scenarios, user stories or others) can be utilized in the software engineering process to capture users' requirements to provide better usability and UX to the users of non CI applications as well as applications for CIs?

Answering these research questions by initiating future projects will help users to enhance the user experience (UX) and the usability features in the projects, services and products offered by cloud based enterprises and its industrial partners. For instance, in the field of e-Science this research will help researchers to get the required data and information to perform e-Research using the UI interfaces of a particular CI, thus, encouraging user interaction with the CIs.

It is indeed needed to incorporate user's point of view in the process of development of software and interfaces, whether related to e-Science or not, in such a form that the developers can address users' UI requirements. Since there are different types of users of CIs, it is important to consider all groups of users [6]. Most of the stakeholders, e.g. in e-Science and ICT infrastructures include data scientists, data curators, computer scientists, domain experts, managers and most importantly interface designers as well as software engineers. All can provide input to enable better usability to the users. Usability is always associated with technology design with an aim of getting job done efficiently with satisfaction [9, p. 588]. Observing UX aspects allow developers incorporation of the fundamental design issues but these UX aspects are more about being amazed, having fun and experiencing emotional responses and creating interest [9, p. 588]. These attributes can incite more interest of scientists as well as other practitioners and can act as a catalyst to increase their participation in using scientific data through CIs. All users have different capabilities, the incorporation of user stories can make life easier of many scientists (users) to increase usability, data search and understanding of data sets.

Earlier, the UK e-Science Task Force has also explicitly indicated to consider broad set of user perspectives in studying a user, a support staff, an administrator and a CI developer [10]. This is because incorporating user perspectives in the form of user stories can maximise the use of e-Science technologies and applications to support new forms of scientific community and can be a source of boom of scientific discoveries. Providing better usability via new interfaces and representation of scientific concepts can directly increase the effectiveness of e-Science researchers [10].

In this work, I take a case study of a CI: Earth System Grid Federation (ESGF) to further explain the research directions and the research methodology as an example to

---

[1] Artefacts (also spelled as artifacts) are the objects modified by humans as opposed to objects that exist in nature. In HCI or interaction design terminology they mean a *tool* or even *activities* in a process, e.g. user stories, scenarios, use cases etc. [47]

guide future research in this field. This research methodology to involve users and designers has been illustrated in Sect. 4. ESGF is an international collaboration with a purpose to develop the software infrastructure needed to study climate change at a global scale. The background about CI and the knowledge gap is given in Sect. 2. The rationale and justification to do such type of research is provided in Sect. 3.

2   Background on ICT Infrastructures and the Knowledge Gap

In the last decades, the ways to conduct research and produce knowledge has been evolving and the traditional ways to perform science has been challenged. The acts of performing research nowadays have been closely related to the use of information and communication technology (ICT) infrastructures [1]. The CIs are pulling people together, allowing collaboration amongst people, facilitating joint initiatives across various cross disciplinary fields, institutions and geographies in the fields of science and humanities. These infrastructures offer new opportunities for sharing and connecting resources such as data, code, publications, computing power, laboratories, instruments and major equipment to generate meaningful information to enable discoveries in science. Infrastructures that have been deployed to access and share the scientific knowledge, data, computing resources and even human resources to facilitate the intra- and inter-disciplinary research are called e-Science infrastructures or e-infrastructures.

The underlying infrastructures that enable e-Science to take place are popularly known as "e-Science infrastructures" in Europe and "cyberinfrastructures" in the US [11]. In this paper we use the term CIs. Moreover, CIs have been widely deployed to share the knowledge by accessing the scientific data, computing resources with joint efforts of other human resources to facilitate the intra- and inter-disciplinary research called e-Science [12]. Other names connected to the concept of e-Science include e-Research, digital science, collaboratories, virtual science and big data science [4]. E-Science domains include medicine, earth sciences, climate sciences, particle physics, bio-informatics, social sciences, humanities and other fields.

There are number of challenges in the arena of open science and CIs. Dealing with the data generated in massive amounts is itself a big challenge [13]. Once the data are generated there are issues of storing this data in data archives [14]. Around 90% of the data that is produced during research projects are lost and not saved [2, 14]. The original raw data is not made accessible and only processed data is published to open data platforms [15, 16]. There are multiple platforms and not a single platform to fetch data. The scientists can easily lose the track of the fragmented sources of data behind the platforms [16]. At times data are temporarily not available on the platforms and some data are only partly available [16]. Some data is only available without relevant information [15]. The use of fragmented software applications, legacy systems complicate the publicizing and processing of data [15].

Besides, there is a resistance amongst scientists to make data public for number of reasons [14, 15]. Uncontrolled use of data, abuse of data and fear that the research results will be published by other scientists are some of the reasons behind this resistance [2, 14, 15]. There are also number of technical concerns related to data replication amongst data centre sites and distribution of data to data centres [14].

There have been some recent achievements in the last couple of years, these include: automation in data management, re-use, re-publish, global data availability, wide public access including existence of infrastructure components as well as improved security and access control providing trusted environments [2]. With these recent developments some of the challenges mentioned before are in an attempt to be resolved. However, it has been observed that the open data that is obtained from the scientific research institutions and organisations has no value in itself; it only becomes valuable when used [15, p. 266]. Yet, it is predominantly the case that the users' view is largely unfortunately neglected and the benefits of scientific data might not realise to full extent [15, p. 266]. Moreover, the use of open data might not be easy [15, p. 266]. In order to use open-data in Science the focus on service orientation cannot be ignored [17]. Moreover, a business model or a vision that provides an efficient user support process is inevitable accompanied with suitable UIs for researchers to enable better UX of CI to get the data and information that they need in a required format.

The barriers associated to the use of open science data via CIs are classified under the following categories as reported by Zuiderwijk et al. (2012) and Schulte et al. (2016) using literature review as well empirical evidence from interviews and discussion forums: (1) availability and access to data, (2) find ability of data, (3) usability, (4) understand ability, (5) quality, (6) linking and combining data, (7) comparability and compatibility, (8) metadata, (9) interaction with the data provider, and (10) opening and uploading [16, 18]. Most of these barriers are pertaining to the access and the use of scientific data via CI interfaces. A search on Google, Scopus, Web of Science with the keywords "e-Science", "e-Research", "user experience", "usability" and their combinations show that there are unfortunately fewer studies conducted that evaluates the current UIs provided by the CIs or analyses the techniques the developers use to incorporate user's perspectives while designing UIs of CIs. Fewer previous studies in this direction in which the author was involved were [19–24].

E-Science UI portals provide web-based or desktop tools to access and run scientific applications and data as well as searching data or linking these applications. The types of UIs used in CI can be categorized into four main categories: desktop utilities, smartphone clients, workflow wrappers and integrated research platforms [25]. There have been initiatives to provide better UI in all these categories, for example; e-Science initiatives in USA such as ESGF. In ESGF project, the new UI web platform powered by ESGF COG (www.earthsystemcog.org), was developed by a UI development team headed by scientists from University of Colorado and NASA.

Desktop utilities are GUIs; an alternate to command line interfaces that help users to run applications and launch commands on remote supercomputers. They provide features such as drag and drop. They hide complexity but at the same time they may limit access to certain features of applications [25]. According to the current ESGF management team, the new UI is user friendlier and provides more features for users than the previous one. These features include better data search, data download, navigation and data visualization facilities. Similarly, in FP7 ENGAGE CI project, advanced search functionality for data is provided via UI. Moreover, ENGAGE claims that data results that the user is looking for, is made easier [3, p. 263]. Navigation of the portal has been improved by providing clear buttons and breadcrumbs. Appropriate UI has been provided in ENGAGE based on state of the art technology using Spring Model-View-Controller (MVC) project [3, p. 263].

Handheld UIs for e-Science also exist e.g. in UK e-Science RealityGrid project, two handheld *smart phone clients* were developed which include features of real-time computational steering and interactive 3D visualisation [26]. Features offered were generic pan, zoom, rotate etc. *Workflow wrappers* are a collection of tools to automate common operations regarding a scientific workflow. Examples include KEPLER, or more recently in the bioinformatics domain, BIOCONDUCTOR or GENEPATTERN [25]. *Integrated research platforms* are tools that allow users to combine and/or explore several tools and perform data observations. Such tools are not mature and are currently hot research areas [25]. An example of such a platform is the Kidneyome portal. Other notable achievements in the UI of CIs include the development of friendly interfaces for life scientists, specifically for the community of human genetic researchers in the project Hope [27]. However, the user rating of the GUIs of any of these platforms has not been done. Moreover, there is no evidence that while offering UIs to the users the picture of different types of users is kept in mind by the developers during the development and design of UI of a CI. It is important to capture users' mental model of using the UI of a particular application. An interesting work in this area for the further reading and background in mental models is [28].

There is a substantial progress in development of user friendly UI for CIs. This notable advancement in the UI development has been achieved due to use of state of the art technologies that supports better UI development for users. Yet, it is important to note that the effectiveness of UI from the end-users or other stakeholder's point of view has not been studied.

In order to provide better usability to the users of CIs, the proposed research directions will contribute in producing Human Computer Interaction (HCI) artefacts that shall be used by developers of the software part of a CI to enable better usability and UX to the users. These artefacts will be used as a supporting tool for developers to discover and formalize the issues related to the interaction of the end-users with the CI. Furthermore, the purpose of these artefacts is to support developers of the software components of a CI, in meeting the user needs in order to provide suitable interaction possibilities for the users to interact with CIs to fulfil the needs of users. Better user experiences as a result can attract more and more scientists to perform e-Research; hence, discoveries can be made easier and faster due to user friendly interfaces provided by CIs. Similar HCI artefacts can also be used to capture user requirements of other general purpose ICT applications as well.

3 Justification and the Rationale

The data offered by a CI using cloud and grid technologies must not just be seen as a product [29] but as an ongoing movement to utilize this data as well as the infrastructure capacities by the users to come up with new scientific discoveries. The software applications that provide an interface to CI are the doors to get the required data and to transform this data into information, knowledge and create a shared understanding of a scientific observation or a concept thus contributing to wisdom. Key to these doors is providing better usability, UX and accessibility to the infrastructures. In essence, these e-Science applications can contribute to Data, Information, Knowledge, Wisdom (DIKW) hierarchy. This research agenda and pathway shown in this work will help all the stakeholders especially data users, data providers to search, fetch, download, visualize, re-use, annotate, re-analyse and perform computing operations on data. In this way, more value from the data can be derived that can benefit the data publishing as well as data users community by making their life easier.

Many studies claim the benefits that can be realized by the open data and open data infrastructures [13, 16]. However, to realize the benefits and creating a public value one needs to overcome the barriers, especially the barriers to use the CIs and their associated applications. Unfortunately, there is hardly a work already found in literature search that incorporates user perspectives in the form of artefacts for developing UIs for CIs. The proposed research direction is a first attempt to create value for users in ICT infrastructures.

Previously, the user support process of a well-established CI: Earth System Grid Federation (ESGF) was analyzed by collecting data from various sources such as interviews, survey questionnaire, field study from the stakeholders, thus enabling data triangulation [7, 22]. ESGF comprises of geographically distributed peer nodes that are independently administered, yet united by common federation protocols and application interfaces [30].

The data analysis from various sources provided the information about the view and the understanding of the previous user support process in ESGF. Based on this analysis, the problems were identified and the solutions were suggested in the form of a recommendation framework; Federated User Support Enhancement (FeUSE) framework was compiled [6, pp. 231–299]. Finally, based on the findings, the user support process in ESGF evolved. A significant outcome of that study was the identification of end-users and the separation of end-users from the other stakeholders [22, 31]. It was furthermore emphasized after studying the user support process of ESGF that the CI is made for the users i.e. researchers who want to find, access, download and process data and therefore the users are needed to be supported actively. Based on the user interaction with the CI in the form of e-mail queries, the categories of user problems, the workarounds and solutions were suggested. The detailed findings and the contribution can be found in [6, 7, 17, 22–24, 31–33].

This work in the form of a research agenda aims to further deepen this topic and initiate further projects and collaborations with new industrial partners. Furthermore, it intends to include the usability aspects especially in the form of introducing artefacts to the developers of the UIs of CI software applications and other domains to provide better usability and UX features. In order to study the UIs and the development of UIs of CIs, a strong partnership is recommended to be planned with the participating institutions of CIs. It is claimed that the UIs for the users in CIs like ESGF, ENGAGE and others are present and with the passage of time, there have been attempts to improve them [3, 34]. However, these interfaces have not been evaluated and secondly, there exists no aid mechanisms for developers in the form of HCI artefacts to incorporate user's point of view.

4   Research Methods and Research Plan

A case study method is selected to explore the concept of user's involvement, UX and the usability of ICT facilities in a CI. In future research, each relevant project with the UX and usability aspects that organisations may undertake can be seen as a single case, eventually each case can be compared later on. A case study focuses on understanding the dynamics present within single settings [35]. It can also be defined as an empirical inquiry that investigates a contemporary phenomenon within its real-life context [36]. ESGF[2], along with its all partner institutions and its associated data projects is chosen as a case study to explain this research agenda with the help of a study design i.e. research method. Furthermore, it is explained how the software UIs, that already exist, can be further designed and developed by the development team of ESGF. ESGF is one of the major peer-to-peer international federated CI effort in climate science research [37, 38]. It has elements similar to other CIs and that's why chosen as an example in this work.

The main research goal of this proposed future research agenda is to see how the user's requirements shall be integrated in the design process of UI and how the needs of users shall be met by the developers of the CI's software interface. To address this research goal, firstly, it is important to investigate what methods, techniques are currently being used by the developers to incorporate users' needs in the UIs of a CI and secondly, how the developers meet user requirements when they design and build tools for users. In order to accomplish this in this exposé; Design Science Research (DSR) approach combined with Cooperative Method Development (CMD) is chosen in the form of Software Cooperative Design Research (SoftCoDer) approach as proposed by Choma et al. (2015). CMD is an adaptation of Action Research (AR) [39] (see Fig. 1).

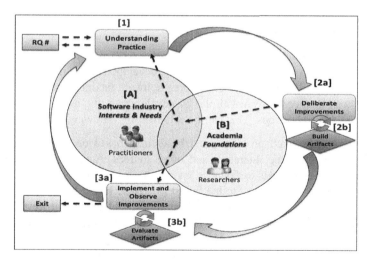

Fig. 1. The SoftCoDer approach [39].

---

[2] www.esgf.llnl.gov.

DSR is based on building artefacts and evaluating them based on an observation and a prior knowledge about a particular business setting. According to Hevner, the major purpose of DSR is achieving knowledge to understand the problem domain by designing an artefact [40]. Therefore, in DSR process artefacts are built to suite the business needs in a particular context. DSR is commonly used in Information Systems (IS) as well as in Software Engineering [41]. DSR combined with CMD in the form of SoftCoDer approach is well suited for this proposed future agenda because of its relevance with the social settings, software engineering context, artefacts development and improvement and incorporation of the user's perspectives. Moreover, it helps to improve techniques and processes in problem-oriented social settings [39]. Another reason for the choice of SoftCoDer approach is because it is based on systematic body of evidence and is aimed at understanding and improving human performance [39]. The researchers need to look at the practitioners approach in the industrial projects about developing Software GUIs for the users that is why SoftCoDer approach is deemed suitable. The phases are suggested to the researchers as an example who would like to pursue research in this direction, keeping with the guidelines of the SoftCoDer approach.

5   Phases Suggested to the Researchers as an Example

The following phases are suggested to the researchers who would like to involve users in the design and development of a CI. Here ESGF CI is given as an example. These phases are illustrated in the form of guidelines to the researchers who would like to pursue research in embedding users in the design and development of CIs, keeping with the steps of the SoftCoDer approach:

5.1   Phase 1 - Understanding the Practice

In this proposed research, understanding the current process of UI development in CIs is needed to be observed by studying the ways, developers are currently meeting user requirements of the UI design and developing software facilities for users in CI. The researchers can then compare it with the UI development of general purpose applications i.e. non CI applications. This can be achieved by following steps:

Step 1:   First a research problem must be defined based on the prior knowledge about this topic, literature and other sources. According to the literature review conducted so far, it is known that users are not able to exploit the potential of open data to the fullest [3]. There have been problems found in ICT facilities of CIs such as registration problems, data access and download problems [6]. These problems are related to the UI of applications of a CI directly or indirectly. Moreover, as according to Zuiderwijk et al. (2013): services for the use of open data towards end-users are often lacking. Keeping with the evidence present in the literature, the problem definition has already been done to some extent.

Step 2: In the second step, in order to achieve the research objectives, data should be collected from different sources in order to understand the current practices (also known as *"as-is"*) of the developers involved in designing and developing of UI, as indicated in the SoftCoDer approach. The following sub-steps are suggested to capture *as-is*:

    (a) Reviewing the literature of the use of methods, software engineering techniques, HCI artefacts being used by developers and designers in industry or other sectors to incorporate user's requirements in UIs of information systems will be the foundation.

    (b) A web-based survey questionnaire is proposed to be designed to get the current picture of UX of applications, keeping with the guidelines provided by Usability Metric for User eXperience (UMUX) [42–45] and System Usability Scale (SUS) [46]. After conducting the survey-questionnaire, the data shall be collected and then analysed. The target respondents of the survey-questionnaire shall be the stakeholders; mainly the users of a particular ICT infrastructure, for instance; ESGF and ESGF-related global projects. It is estimated that the total users of ESGF are 25,000 out of which only few hundreds are active. The responses from the users could provide the current picture of usability of ESGF.

    (c) Semi-structured interviews shall be conducted with the stakeholders of organisations participating in ESGF e.g. about the current techniques the stakeholders apply to capture user requirements for UI of CI software applications. For instance, interviewing 20 stakeholders, especially developers out of the population of 55 active employees in ESGF is a good option. It is estimated that the people involved in the development of software of ESGF are not more than 20.

From these sub-steps of the first phase of SoftCoDer approach, the current UX and usability of UI of the applications offered by ESGF to select and download big data shall be gauged. Moreover, from these sub-steps the current methods to capture user requirements can be known. The problem statement shall be re-visited and re-defined. From the data gathered from these steps, proposed above; an overall-picture of the usability and user requirements in ESGF as well as associated projects shall be portrayed in the form of a report describing major features, strengths, weaknesses and the problems found in the aspects of usability and UX in e-Science. Moreover, the methods, techniques, artefacts suggested in literature and other software engineering projects to capture requirements of users must be studied and selected. Thus, in this way in the business model of e-Science organisation, user service orientation can be focussed on.

These methods, techniques, artefacts can be suggested to the developers in the next step called deliberate improvements, so that the developers and designers of UI could use them in the development process.

5.2   Phase 2a - Deliberate Improvements

Based on the observation of the current practices and theoretical groundings emanating from the first phase, the possible improvements in the process of development of UI for users in e-infrastructures shall be suggested. Furthermore, based on this analysis, recommendations shall be made to the developers to use the techniques, methods or artefacts that help to improve the usability features of UIs of CIs.

Moreover, it shall then be instructed to use these suggested HCI artefacts or techniques by the ESGF management that the developers agree upon to incorporate users' points of view in the CI. The HCI artefacts and techniques are intended to contribute to enhance the overall usability and UX of CIs and to make the UIs more usable and pleasurable.

5.3   Phase 2b - Building Artefacts

The suggested recommendations of the artefacts from the last phase shall be presented to the ESGF project stakeholder's committee and demonstrated to the developers. In fact, in this phase, the actual implementation of artefacts will be made in the UI development process and artefacts will be created in collaboration with the researchers as well as the development team of the collaborating partners e.g. in this case ESGF. These artefacts will then be used in the development of UI for users in CIs with the help of practitioners of ESGF.

5.4   Phase 3a - Implement and Observe Improvements

An online questionnaire shall be carefully designed to create a common agreement and consensus amongst the researchers as well as the practitioners of ESGF about the implementation of the recommended artefacts in the development process of UIs. Furthermore, these suggestions in the form of artefacts shall be put into practice under the guidance from the ESGF management.

In this phase, the researchers will observe the implementation of using artefacts in the development process of UIs of the desktop or web applications of a CI. From the group that used artefacts or other techniques, multiple sub-groups of developers, will be instructed to create a UI prototype for users using a single artefact. The other group (control group) will create a UI prototype for users without using any artefact.

Moreover, after the implementation, a discussion in the form of a workshop with the practitioners will be organised to see each other's UI prototype, rate it and suggest possible improvements. This step will be conducted with the help of ESGF management. The researchers shall guide ESGF management in this aspect to take appropriate decisions.

5.5   Phase 3b - Evaluate Artefacts

The UI prototype based on each artefact shall then be rated by the users via an online questionnaire. At the same time, the suggested artefacts must be rated by the UI developers from ESGF and outside ESGF. From the users and the practitioners involved in this evaluation and rating process the lessons can then be drawn.

5.6 Phase 4 - Communication and Dissemination of Results

The communication of the results of the project shall take place after every 6 months from the initiation of the project with the ESGF and its partner institutions. Finally, the lessons learned and the final results of the project and the artefacts will be communicated to the whole ESGF team in a meeting. Moreover these results and artefacts can then be communicated in the final report of the proposed project, technical reports, journal papers and conference proceedings.

A validation of results and evaluation of the outcome can be made with the help of focused groups again. Moreover, future directions can be given to other collaborating CI projects so that the results can then be generalized with other CI and non CI projects.

6 Expected Future Outcomes

The aim of this work is to provide recommendations in the form of artefacts to developers and the policy makers of big data enterprises especially from the government sector that fund CI projects, so that they are able to develop and design UI in CIs that are eventually usable by the users and offer better UX for future. The recommendations in the form of artefacts can be bundled in a proposed framework called *e-Science UI usability (eUIu) model* and then it can be compared with the usability guidelines for non CI applications. This model can provide significant input to the enterprise model and the business model of CIs and other enterprises. With this model both the developers of CI and developers of other infrastructures will benefit. Moreover, they will be able to enable better UX and usability for users in various domains of data science such as climate science, medical science, physics and others. Besides, a set of proposed web-based UI prototypes and visualization environments shall be created by the developers to support better UX in CIs. Furthermore, it is expected that a shared understanding amongst developers about the user's point of view will be developed, facilitated by the artefacts. As a result of better interfaces the open science data will be made easily accessible to the public and most predominantly to the researchers using CIs.

The eventual outcome of these future research directions is improvement in the usability and the UX of the UIs provided by a CI, e.g. ESGF. If the UX and usability is enhanced, there can be a significant boom in e-Research, scientific discoveries and more interest in the research community in using CIs. Consequently, this work is intended to start a usability movement combined with software development derived towards providing better UX and fulfilling users' needs. It can initiate some pioneer projects within and across the domains offered by CIs that can contribute to the age of easy to use e-Science in the form of reducing usability problems and promoting an open e-Research that in turn encourages collaboration amongst scientists, other practitioners and even public i.e. citizens at a later stage.

References

1. Karasti, H., Millerand, F., Hine, C.M.: Knowledge infrastructures: part I. Sci. Technol. Stud. **29**(1), 2–12 (2016)
2. Demchenko, Y., Zhao, Z., Grosso, P., Wibisono, A., De Laat, C.: 2012 IEEE 4th International Conference on Cloud Computing Technology and Science Addressing Big Data Challenges for Scientific Data Infrastructure, pp. 614–617 (2012)
3. Zuiderwijk, A., Janssen, M., Jaffery, K.: Towards an e-infrastructure to support the provision and use of open data. In: Conference for eDemocracy and Open Government, pp. 259–275 (2013)
4. Hey, T., Trefethen, A.E.: Cyberinfrastructure for e-science. Science **308**(5723), 817–821 (2005)
5. Chunpir, H., Moll, A.: Analysis of marine ecosystems: usability, visualization and community collaboration challenges. Procedia Manuf. **3**, 3262–3265 (2015)
6. Chunpir, H.I.: Enhancing User Support Process in Federated E-Science. University of Hamburg (2015)
7. Chunpir, H.I., Ludwig, T., Badewi, A.A.: Using soft systems methodology (SSM) in understanding current user-support scenario in the climate science domain of cyber-infrastructures. In: Marcus, A. (ed.) DUXU 2014. LNCS, vol. 8519, pp. 495–506. Springer, Cham (2014). https://doi.org/10.1007/978-3-319-07635-5_48
8. Freeman, P.A.: Is it possible to define cyberinfrastructure ? First Monday 6(12) (2007)
9. Preece, J.: Citizen science: new research challenges for human – computer interaction. Int. J. Hum. Comput. Interact. **32**(8), 585–612 (2016)
10. UK e-Science Usability Task Force. Usability Research Challenges in e-Science (2009). http://www.cs.nott.ac.uk/ ~ psztar/UTF.pdf. Accessed 19 Sept 2016
11. Jirotka, M., Lee, C.P., Olson, G.M.: Supporting scientific collaboration: methods, tools and concepts. Comput. Support. Coop. Work **22**(4), 667–715 (2013)
12. Chunpir, H.I., Zaina, L.: Assisting users in open data infrastructures: a management perspective. In: 15th Internationa Conference WWW/Internet 2016, pp. 27–34 (2016)
13. Chen, J., et al.: Big data challenge: a data management perspective. Front. Comput. Sci. **7**(2), 157–164 (2013)
14. Rudolph, D., Thoring, A., Vogl, R.: Research data management: wishful thinking or reality? PIK – Prax. der Informationsverarbeitung und Kommun. **38**(3–4), 113–120 (2015)
15. Janssen, M., Charalabidis, Y., Zuiderwijk, A.: Benefits, adoption barriers and myths of open data and open government. Inf. Syst. Manag. **29**(4), 258–268 (2012)
16. Zuiderwijk, A., Janssen, M., Choenni, S., Meijer, R., Alibaks, R.S.: Socio-technical impediments of open data. Electron. J. e-Gov. **10**(2), 156–172 (2012)
17. Chunpir, H.I., Ludwig, T., Williams, D.N.: Evolution of e-Research?: from infrastructure development to service orientation. In: DUXU 2015, Part III, LNCS, vol. 9188, pp. 25–35. Springer, Cham (2015)
18. Schulte, F., Chunpir, H.I., Voß, S.: Open data evolution in information systems research: considering cases of data-intensive transportation and grid systems. In: Proceedings of 5th International Conference, DUXU 2016, Held as Part of HCI International 2016, Part III, Toronto, Canada, 17–22 July 2016, pp. 193–201 (2016)
19. Chunpir, H.I., Curri, E., Zaina, L., Ludwig, T.: Improving user interfaces for a request tracking system: best practical RT. In: Yamamoto, S. (ed.) HIMI 2016. LNCS, vol. 9735, pp. 391–401. Springer, Cham (2016). https://doi.org/10.1007/978-3-319-40397-7_37

20. Chunpir, H.I.: Prioritizing tasks using user-support-worker's activity model (USWAM). In: Yamamoto, S. (ed.) HIMI 2016. LNCS, vol. 9735, pp. 379–390. Springer, Cham (2016). https://doi.org/10.1007/978-3-319-40397-7_36

21. Chunpir, H.I., Williams, D., Ludwig, T.: User experience (UX) of a big data infrastructure. In: Yamamoto, S. (ed.) HIMI 2017. LNCS, vol. 10274, pp. 467–474. Springer, Cham (2017). https://doi.org/10.1007/978-3-319-58524-6_37

22. Chunpir, H.I., Ludwig, T., Badewi, A.: A snap-shot of user support services in Earth System Grid Federation (ESGF): a use case of climate cyber-infrastructures. In: Proceedings of the 5th Applied Human Factors and Ergonomics (AHFE) Conference, July 2014

23. Chunpir, H.I., Rathmann, T., Ludwig, T.: The need for a tool to support users of e-science infrastructures in a virtual laboratory environment. Procedia Manuf. **3**, 3375–3382 (2015)

24. Chunpir, H.I., Badewi, A.A., Ludwig, T.: User support system in the complex environment. In: Marcus, A. (ed.) DUXU 2014. LNCS, vol. 8520, pp. 392–402. Springer, Cham (2014). https://doi.org/10.1007/978-3-319-07638-6_38

25. Harris, P.J., et al.: The virtual kidney: an eScience interface and Grid portal. Philos. Trans. R. Soc. London Ser. A Math. Phys. Eng. Sci. **367**, 2141–2159 (2009)

26. Mancini, E.P., et al.: Simulation in the cloud using handheld devices to cite this version: simulation in the cloud using handheld devices (2012)

27. Venselaar, H., Ah, T., Kuipers, R.K.P., Hekkelman, M.L., Vriend, G.: Protein structure analysis of mutations causing inheritable diseases. An e-Science approach with life scientist friendly interfaces. BMC Bioinform. **11**, 548 (2010)

28. Chunpir, H.I., Ludwig, T.: A software to capture mental models. In: Antona, M., Stephanidis, C. (eds.) UAHCI 2017. LNCS, vol. 10279, pp. 393–409. Springer, Cham (2017). https://doi.org/10.1007/978-3-319-58700-4_32

29. Zuiderwijk A., Janssen, M.: A comparison of open data policies and their implementation in two dutch ministries. In: ACM 13th Annual International Conference on Digital Government Research (Dg.O 2012) (2012)

30. Williams, D.N.: ESGF project overview (2015)

31. Chunpir, H.I., Ludwig, T.: Reviewing the governance structure of end-user support in e-Science infrastructures. In: Informatik 2014 Proceedings on Mastering Big Data Complexity. Lecture Notes in Informatics (LNI), vol. 232 (2014)

32. Chunpir, H.I., Ludwig, T., Curri, E.: Improving processes for user support in e-Science. In: IEEE 10th International Conference on e-Science (e-Science), vol. 2, pp. 87–90 (2014)

33. Chunpir, H.I.: Prioritizing Tasks Using User-Support-Worker's Activity Model (USWAM). In: Yamamoto, S. (ed.) HIMI 2016. LNCS, vol. 9735, pp. 379–390. Springer, Cham (2016). https://doi.org/10.1007/978-3-319-40397-7_36

34. Chunpir, H., Williams, D., Cinquini, L., Kindermann, S.: Third annual ESGF and ultrascale visualization climate data analysis tools face-to-face meeting report. Livermore, CA (2013)

35. Yin, R.: Case Study Research: Design and Methods, 5th edn. Sage Publishing, Thousand Oaks (2013)

36. Eisenhardt, K.: Building theories from case study research. Acad. Manag. Rev. **14**(4), 532–550 (1989)

37. Cinquini, L., et al.: The Earth System Grid Federation (ESGF): an open infrastructure for access to distributed geospatial data. In: 8th IEEE International Conference on E-Science, pp. 1–10 (2012)

38. Williams, D.N., Bell, G., Cinquini, L., Fox, P., Harney, J., Goldstone, R.: ESGF: federated and integrated climate data from multiple sources. In: Hiller, W., Budich, R., Redler, R. (eds.) Earth System Modelling, vol. 6, pp. 61–77. Springer, Heidelberg (2013). https://doi.org/10.1007/978-3-642-37244-5_7

39. Choma, J., Zaina, L., Silva Da Silva, T.: Towards an approach matching CMD and DSR to improve the Academia-Industry software development partnership. In: 29th Brazilian Symposium on Software Engineering, pp. 51–60 (2015)
40. Hevner, A.R., March, S.T., Park, J., Ram, S.: Design science in information systems research. MIS Q. **28**(1), 75–105 (2004)
41. Livari, J., Venable, J.: Action research and design science research seemingly similar but decisively dissimilar. In: Proceedings of ECIS 2009 European Conference on Information Systems (2009)
42. Finstad, K.: The system usability scale and non-native English speakers. English **1**, 185–188 (2006)
43. Finstad, K.: Interacting with computers the usability metric for user experience. Interact. Comput. **22**, 323–327 (2010)
44. Finstad, K.: Response interpolation and scale sensitivity: evidence against 5-point scales. J. Usability Stud. **5**, 104–110 (2010)
45. Finstad, K.: Response to commentaries on 'The usability metric for user experience'. Interact. Comput. **25**, 327–330 (2013)
46. Sauro, J.: Measuring Usability With The System Usability Scale (SUS) Measuring Usability (2011)
47. Papantoniou, B., et al.: The Glossary of Human Computer Interaction. Interaction Design Foundation. https://www.interaction-design.org/literature/book/the-glossary-of-human-computer-interaction/artifact. Accessed 22 Feb 2018

A New Software Development Model: Innovation Through Mobile Application with UCD

Jorge Espinoza[1]([⊠]), Pamela Loarte[1], Carlos Espinoza[2], Freddy Paz[1], and Juan Arenas[1]

[1] Pontificia Universidad Católica del Perú, Lima 32, Peru
{jeespinozam, Ploarte, fpaz}@pucp.pe,
jjarenas@pucp.edu.pe
[2] Universidad Peruana de Ciencias Aplicadas, Lima 32, Peru
u201621874@upc.edu.pe

Abstract. Pursuit of innovation projects with the absent of a methodology to follow hampers the development of the software product as its complexity grows since the freedom of its own advancement is confused with the lack of order on it. Traditional and agile methodologies do not adapt to this kind of projects therefore, in this paper we aim to design a model that incorporates characteristics of both of them to get a solution of a need found in society. In this study, we focus on the construction of a mobile application that answer to the lack of a system that integrates pharmaceutical products from different establishment through the appliance of usability concept with the UCD (User centered design) approach. In this case we only detail about four of the seven stages proposed in the model developed with its techniques, tools and activities conducted. Results obtained show that the model proposed achieve the expectative and its use is not limited to just mobile applications but to any kind of software project.

Keywords: Innovation · Model · User-centered design · Mobile application
Usability

1 Introduction

Computer science allows new working methods and with the growth of IT, commercial and business activities have completely changed. These changes did not only happen at a technological level, Internet transformed the means by which products and services are bought and sold, which caused organizations to be reformed in order to incorporate electronic commerce [25]. As a result, the consumer today has the ability to purchase anything at any time with the click of a mouse or the tap of a finger [28].

Electronic commerce (e-commerce) can then be defined, according to Dimitrios Buhalis, as the secure trading of information, products and services via computer networks and the exchange of online value, as well as the support of commercial transactions over a digital infrastructure [7].

© Springer International Publishing AG, part of Springer Nature 2018
A. Marcus and W. Wang (Eds.): DUXU 2018, LNCS 10918, pp. 673–692, 2018.
https://doi.org/10.1007/978-3-319-91797-9_47

The number of e-commerce websites and mobile applications have increased considerably, becoming an increasingly competitive environment where value streams become the basis of business models and strategy development, but what about the user's satisfaction? The acceptance of the user, in addition to the economic impact, plays a fundamental role in the widespread adoption of e-commerce applications, so it is important for users to interact with usable, safe and reliable applications and websites that are not affected by factors such as the time it takes to find the desired information, efficiency and security when carrying out the transaction, reliability of the delivery service behind the website, etc. [8, 9]. Concepts as usability and user experience become into essential quality attributes and the user centered design (UCD) works as the approach applied to achieve a good level of usability in web or mobile software development [12].

In this paper, we aim to analyze usability and user experience in order to provide a model that can carry out an innovation process to solve a problem and need presented in society using the approach of User centered design (UCD), specifically in the construction of a mobile platform related to the commercial sector that allows the comparison, purchase and delivery of pharmaceutical products. Current fundamental research considers the model used based on traditional and agile software product design methodology necessary to achieve a quality process that meets the requirements of end users in all stages of development. Finally, the results obtained are shown and discussed for future work.

2 Background

2.1 Concepts

Usability: It is the efficiency, effectiveness and satisfaction by which specific users achieve a set of specific tasks in particular environments [16]. These three components cannot be evaluated independently; while the effectiveness is related to the accuracy and completeness, the efficiency is given by the speed by which users can complete their tasks that may cause or not the satisfaction of the user [3].

In mobile development, the concept of usability according to Nielsen has as its main point that "When you are writing for mobile users, focus on the essential content." This is because the small screen reduces comprehension and usually people do not want to deal with secondary texts but only with the main points [19].

Nielsen in [20] mentions the following stages as part of the lifecycle model of usability engineering: Know the user, competitive analysis, set goals (establish performance levels for usability attributes), parallel design (different designs of an interface in a parallel process), participatory design (involve the user in the design process), coordinated design of the entire user interface (consistency of the entire interface), guides and heuristic evaluation, prototyping, empirical tests and iterative Design.

However, the development of a mobile application, which cover a social necessity and has not a specific client who could delimit the requirements, cannot cover all stages mentioned above. The participatory design, either through surveys or a direct intervention of the users, will always remain as a small group of people, and this perspective will not always be the best option to make decisions, this is called the coverage error in surveys in [26]. In this situation, an approach like finding experts can facilitate the process, because they do know their fields and trends to achieve the goals without neither continuous user validation processes nor massive. This is called the heuristic method of usability [18], which is different from an empiric one that requires the participation of users.

The concept of usability becomes independent of our platform, since Ionic (app platform) was used instead of making a native application. Fling B. states that native applications are not viable in the long term, since the loss of incrementally improve the application, loss control and therefore decrease profits, as well as adding the problem of device fragmentation. Besides that, for the first time the device manufacturers are all working to achieve the same standards [13].

Importance of User-Centered Design (UCD): The term UCD was born in the Donald A. Norman Research Laboratory at the University of California, San Diego [21] and it has allowed developers, innovators and more to make products that the end-user can understand and feel confident using them. Ritter, Baxter and Churchill define in [23] that User-centered design involves paying particular attention to the user's needs, allowing to carry out an activity/task analysis as well as a general requirements analysis, performing early testing and evaluation, and designing with iterations.

It is important to take into account the interests of the wide range of stakeholders. This does not mean they must be in the design team, but should be considered in order to design an effective and suitable product [2]. A set of questions thus are provided in [10] as a road map in the development of product and services

- Who are the users of the product?
- What are the tasks and objectives of the users?
- What is the level of knowledge and prior experience of users with technology?
- What is the user experience with the product or with similar products?
- What features do users expect from the product?
- What product information may users need? In what way will they need it?
- How do users think the product works?
- How can the product design facilitate the cognitive processes of the users?

These questions allow a clear focus on what shall be done, so the obtained product may satisfy the user's needs, limitations and/or solve their difficulties [10], and lead to a vital reduction in development time and costs. by doing so, the user experience will be pleasant and generate confidence and efficiency allowing a growth of users who make use of the product.

2.2   Case of Study

Problem to Solve: In search for specific medications or products related to hygiene and personal care the consumer finds itself disorientated about prices, places of purchase, available stocks and more, in addition to the time and money that imply all above.

Nowadays the pharmaceutical system works independently. Some pharmacies have their own mobile platform and delivery, but limit the consumer to a small offer and variety of products. Furthermore, the quality standards are low and the interface is slow, confusing and does not inspire confidence to the user.

Px Pharmacy: It is the name of the application that seeks to centralize the service and facilitate the acquisition of products through a virtual payment system and cash post acquisition.

The application allows to identify possible nearby pharmacies according to geographical location or other point of interest, choose the best monetary amount among a large variety of pharmacies, make a delivery order and manage the payment.

3 Adopted Model

In order to develop an application, is very common to find traditional and agile methodologies concepts. The stages of the process of a traditional software development, described in the waterfall model and the agile method, explained in an iterative cycle, are shown down below in Figs. 1 and 2 respectively.

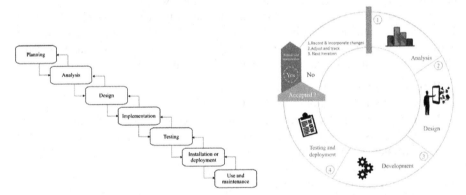

Fig. 1. Software development life cycle - Waterfall Model

Fig. 2. Software development life cycle - Agile Methodology

Traditional methodologies are based on planning with an intense stage of analysis and design before the development, which leads to a low risk management [22]. Based on this, Abrahamsson mentions that the challenge of a dynamic environment must be confronted, with frequent modifications in the needs and expectations of the client, (…) with approaches oriented to relatively short development cycles, typical of agile methodologies for software development.

On the other hand, an agile methodology is defined by being incremental (incremental advances), cooperative (between client and developers), simple and adaptable (allows changes in the last moment) [1].

In our case, both traditional and agile methodology, did not meet the criteria. As an innovation, it is required to respond to changes. This opposes to the strong planning of a traditional method, and not having a client to consecutively cooperate with during the development of the software is different from the definition of a "Product Owner" (The one who defines what must be done) in the agile methods. From this analysis, a model was defined to integrate the best of both methods. Figure 3 introduces us to the approach of the adopted model.

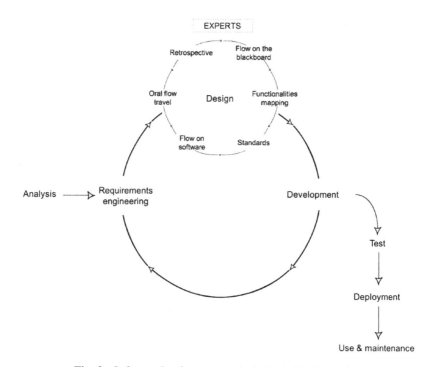

Fig. 3. Software development method adopted in the project

This model is divided into seven stages:

1. Analysis
2. Requirements Engineering
3. Design
   a. Oral flow travel
   b. Retrospective
   c. Flow on the blackboard
   d. Functionalities mapping
   e. Standards
   f. Flow on software

4. Development
5. Test
6. Deployment
7. Use & maintenance

Each iteration from 2 to 4 stages could work as a release of the application. In the Design stage, another iterative cycle is defined and concepts as user-centered design and usability are critical. A bad definition of them leads to a launch destined to failure, which is why a transversal element is present: the experts, who function as the equivalence of a "Product Owner" of the agile method. These are the ones who determine a level of acceptance to continue with the development stage.

It is important to mention that in this study we only focus on the first four stages of the model previously presented:

1. Analysis: Establishes the user's profile.
2. Requirements Engineering: Settle what is needed and priorities each requirement obtained.
3. Design: Defines the standards and structure the solution through a diagram or scheme of the interface.
4. Development: Implement the design as software product.

In addition, the questions previously defined for a "User-centered design" were taken as a reference in the Analysis and Requirements Engineering stages. It should be stressed that by adopting part of both methods (traditional and agile), unique aspects incorporated can be applied in similar projects that aim to solve a society problem through innovation (development of an application) considering a user-centered design and the usability it entails.

3.1 Analysis

This stage make use of the "persona" technique, which implies identification of a user profile for the app (choose the pharmaceutical products, compare prices and make a delivery order) by means of information search. This profile must be precise, to identify what the flow expected by the user will be like.

Ming-Hui Wen, quoting Nielsen, reaffirms that the main factor to define a profile is demographic, which includes, according to him nationality, race, age, date of birth, blood type, gender, education, income, occupation, family patterns, geographical location, urban living, family life cycle, marital status, and other variables [27].

In addition, some of the previously defined questions for UCD were taken as a reference:

- Who are the users of the product?
- What is the level of knowledge and prior experience of users with technology?
- What is the user experience with the product or with similar products?

3.2   Requirement Engineering

At this stage, the first thing made was a brainstorming over the functionalities that the developer team should consider necessary, then a survey was conducted with a sample group of people who fits the profile obtained in Analysis, to validate the proposed main functionalities.

The survey was divided into three sections: basic data, about the service and testing (Table 1).

Table 1. Survey questionnaire

Section	Questions
Basic data	- How old are you?
About the service	- How often do you use the delivery service? - Would you like to compare the different prices of a product in different pharmacies? (Y/N) - Would you like to have a Chabot that offers you pharmaceutical products according to your symptoms? (Y/N) - Would you like to find product categories? (Y/N) - Do you think it is important to know the location of your order during the delivery service? (Y/N) - What other functionalities would you like to find in a pharmacy delivery application?
Testing	- Would you like to be a beta tester of Px Pharmacy and enjoy it for free? (Y/N) - If the previous answer was "Yes", please enter your email

It is necessary that the result of this stage meets certain characteristics defined by Arias Chaves in [4]: Concise, complete, consistent and unambiguous. These allow the developer to focus on clear and fixed objectives, in such a way that they do not incur in steps or processes that may cause delay or confuse them in the software development.

Moreover, part of the UCD questions used were:

- What are the tasks and objectives of the users?
- How can the product design facilitate the cognitive processes of the users?
- What product information may users need? In what way will they need it?
- What features do users expect from the product?
- How do users think the product works?

Based on the results of the brainstorming, the survey and the solution of part of the UCD questionnaire, a software requirements specification (SRS) was proposed, divided into functional (software) and non-functional (hardware) requirements and an assignment of priorities. It is worth highlighting that if there were a bad definition of priorities, too much time would be invested into functionalities that would not be used or would not be necessary costs to assume on launching. Part of the process of developing through innovation lies in saving time, since human resources are limited [6].

3.3   Design

The purpose was to define the functioning of the application. The iterative stage has the following sub stages:

1. Oral flow route: A complete interaction of the steps the user will make from the beginning of the session until the end of the purchase order was mentioned aloud. This step is important to avoid inconsistencies.
2. Retrospective: All points in favor and against the result obtained were mentioned to reformulate and adapt the flow.
3. Flow on the blackboard: The idea was diagrammed and the flow was indicated through arrows between buttons or links and mobile views.
4. Functionalities mapping: A detailed writing of the components of each mobile view was made and therefore new features were discovered to be detailed.
5. Standards: Color, iconography and typography were defined.
6. Flow on software: Mockups were made using designing tools (Justinmind and Sketch).

The first iteration defines the base flow and the next iterations will try to give a detailed solution to the rest of functionalities that will be discovered in step 4.

3.4   Development

The early definition of a good architecture will enable the idea of innovation to achieve the general and functional purpose of the software [17]; in such a way that the abstraction in the first iterations of the proposed model does not limit the software development to a single functionality, but that it may grow over the time [24]. A scalable database and an ordered code allow innovation not to be more complicated as it grows (more iterations). If not it will leave a legacy-code with time and cost losses to solve or improve functionalities.

Over time some technologies become obsoletes and new ones appear with better results and easier use when working. For this reason, an analysis must be done to identify which of them are best suited. The technologies we used allow an abstraction of Front and Back End. These were:

- Ionic (Front End): Framework that allows the development of hybrid mobile applications, which means that it is not restricted to an operating system. It is based on HTML5, CSS and JS and optimized with Sass and TypeScript.
- NodeJS (Back End): Uses Javascript (JS), same as Ionic. Express was used as its application framework.
- PostgreSQL: Open source object-relational database system.
- Gitlab: Version managing system.

4   Results

4.1   Analysis

The objective of this stage was to define the profile of the user of the mobile application by seeking specific information, understanding the demographic factor and integrating the concept of "User centered design" through a set of specific questions.

The user age of the mobile application ranges from 18 to 60 since is necessary to reach the legal age because of the responsibility that implies the purchase of pharmaceutical products, besides it has been constrained to the age of 60 approximately due to elderly people fear and rejection over e-commerce and that only the 9% of them make use of internet, according to the INEI [14].

It is worth highlighting that Ipsos Apoyo sets that the predominant online consumer age ranges from 25 to 35, with average age of 31. This one is constantly active in social networks and more than the 50% is already banked.

On the other side, it is claimed that the online consumer profile belongs to A (High), B (medium high) and C (Medium) socioeconomic levels. Furthermore, the last report of the world bank (WB) defines that medium socioeconomic category perceive incomes from 10 to 50 USD per day [5]. People in this or a higher socioeconomic level have the acquisitive economic power to buy through electronic media [11, 15].

It should be pointed out that due to available information limitation at first stage, the use of the mobile application was restricted to a local framework: Lima, Peru. Likewise, the answers to the first part of the questionnaire of User-centered design are shown below:

- Who are the users of the product?
  Consumers who seek to purchase pharmaceutical products through mobile devices.
- What is the level of knowledge and prior experience of users with technology?
  People who use and handle mobile applications and are familiar with e-commerce.
- What is the user experience with the product or with similar products?
  Use of mobile applications for sales and delivery.

With all above Table 2 was defined:

Table 2. User profile

Characteristic	Definition
Age	18–55 years old (Average: 31), based on Ipsos Apoyo
Gender	No limitations specified
Job/occupation	No limitations specified
Education	No limitations specified
Localization	Anywhere in Lima Peru
Incomes	More than 10 USD per day, according to the World Bank
Technology	People who use and handle mobile applications and are familiar with e-commerce
Family	No limitations specified
Marital status	No limitations specified

4.2   Requirement Engineering

The purpose of this stage was to establish a set of requirements and priorities for the app. A brainstorming and a survey based on a test group were carried out. Furthermore, the second part of the User Centered design questionnaire was answered and finally the software requirements specification (ERS) were made.

Relevant results from the survey, shown in Fig. 4 and summed up in a set of graphics, served to validate the proposed functionalities by the development team.

In the other hand, the answers of the second part of the User centered design questionnaire are shown below:

- What are the tasks and objectives of the users?
  - Search medicine
  - Buy medicine
  - Seek offers/discounts
- How can the product design facilitate the cognitive processes of the users?
  Easier, faster, safer and more organized processes. Simple and understandable flow.
- What product information may users need? In what way will they need it?
  A tutorial presented by videos or slides.
- What features do users expect from the product?
  - Search system
  - Catalog of products
  - Product information
  - Offers/discounts search
  - Real time tracking of the order
  - Request delivery service
- How do users think the product works?
  Search and add products to the cart according to the consumer's preferences. Verification of the order, select payment method and add localization for the delivery service.

In our case, we just made one iterative cycle in accordance with the model presented in Fig. 3, which means that the requirement engineering was made just once. Some of the functional requirements and the non-functional are shown below (Tables 3 and 4).

4.3   Design

In this stage, we determine the mockups of the mobile application through a set of sub stages raised in the model proposed. The documented results belong from sub stage 3 to 6 of the flow of the model:

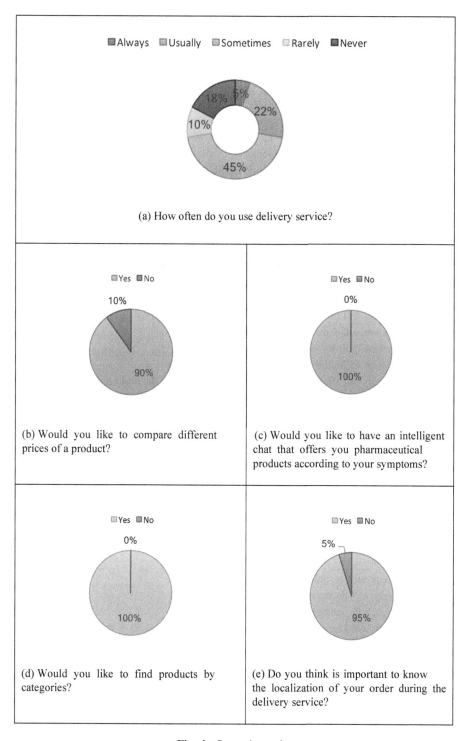

(a) How often do you use delivery service?

(b) Would you like to compare different prices of a product?

(c) Would you like to have an intelligent chat that offers you pharmaceutical products according to your symptoms?

(d) Would you like to find products by categories?

(e) Do you think is important to know the localization of your order during the delivery service?

Fig. 4. Survey's results

Table 3. Functional requirements

	Description	Priority
1.	The system will allow the register/access through social networks or a username and password	High
2.	The system will check the ID provided for accounts which are not previously registered	High
3.	The system will show the terms and conditions in order to use the app	High
4.	The system will have a lateral menu that will show available settings	High
5.	The system must have a user profile	High
6.	The system will allow to add products to the shopping cart	High
7.	The system will allow the search by name	High
8.	The system will have a product catalog	High
9.	The system will show information about the selected product (description, precautions, contraindications, etc.)	High
10.	The system must show the order state	High
11.	The system must ask for confirmation before the checkout	High
12.	The system will show the best total amount accumulated by the selected products	High
13.	The system will provide a tutorial about the main functionalities	Medium
14.	The system will show the order tracking	Medium
15.	The system must have an order history	Medium
16.	The system will allow to add products to the favorites list	Medium
17.	The system will allow the user to define the amount of the desire product	Medium
18.	The system will allow to filter the product catalog in categories	Medium
19.	The system will allow to order the search by filters (alphabetic, relevance, most purchased items, etc.)	Medium
20.	The system will show products suggestions related to the selected product	Low
21.	The system will allow the user to choose the payment method	Low
22.	The system will ask for user's information like the address if necessary	Low

Table 4. Non-functional requirements

	Description	Priority
1.	The system must be able 24 h the 7 days of the week	Not-functional
2.	The system will be developed for Android and IOS	Not-functional
3.	The system will manage PostgreSQL database	Not-functional
4.	The system will keep all users' information confidential	Not-functional
5.	The system will follow MVC architecture (Model – View-Controller)	Not-functional

Blackboard Flow: Draw of the main views that compose the base flow (Fig. 5).

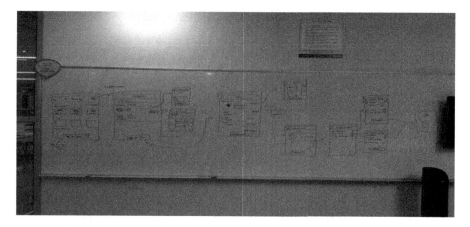

Fig. 5. Base flow

Functionalities Mapping: List of the considered views and their components: buttons (B), fields (F), lists (L) and inputs (I) (Table 5).

Table 5. Description of components on each view

1. Pre Start	7. Cart or my order
• Log in (B)	• Back arrow (B)
• Enter as guess (B)	• Products list (L)
• New user/Sign in (B)	• Total monetary amounts of the list of products proposed. (F)
2. Login	8. Make the order
• Email (B)	• Choose pharmacy
• Password (B)	• Pharmacies listed from cheapest to the most expensive total
• Facebook and Google (B)	monetary amounts of products (L)
3. Sign in	• Payment method
• Name and last name (F)	• Cash (B)
• ID (F)	• Visa (B)
• Email (F)	• MasterCard (B)
• Password (F)	• Confirmation view
• Phone (F)	9. Orders History
• Facebook and Google (F)	10. Pending order (Tracking)
4. Profile	• Estimated time (F)
5. Home	11. My favorites
• Hamburger menu (B)	12. My places (Addresses)
• Shopping Cart (B)	• Saved addresses list (L)
• Search bar (I)	• Complete address (F)
6. Product details	• Shortcut name (F)
• Product name (F)	13. System configurations
• Add to favorites (B)	
• Add to cart (B)	

Standards (Tables 6 and 7):

Table 6. Font standards

Font	Typeface	Weight	Size
Title	**.SF NS Text**	Semibold	18px
Subtitle	.SF NS Text	Regular	15px
Text	.SF NS Text	Light	13px

Table 7. Color standards

Colors	Hex	RGB	Sample
Primary	277BC3	39,123195	
Secondary	F9FAFD	249,250,253	
Link Button	434343	67,67,67	
Alert Button	F5F5F5	245,245,245	

Software Flow: Table 8 resumes some results of the last iterations of the design stage compared to the last participation of the experts.

From the results, we can observe that the experts/specialist perspective contributes to a vision toward the standard.

4.4   Development

The architecture developed for the mobile application directed to final users is shown in Fig. 6.

The abstraction of the Front and the Backend have been observed along with the integration of technologies mentioned before.

– Mobile client: Mobile device by which the user access to Px Pharmacy mobile application.
– Platform: Front End, Interface by which the user interacts.
– API/REST: Back End, which defines methods and functions that access the database.

Table 8. Results comparison

Last iteration	Post result after experts' participation	Comments
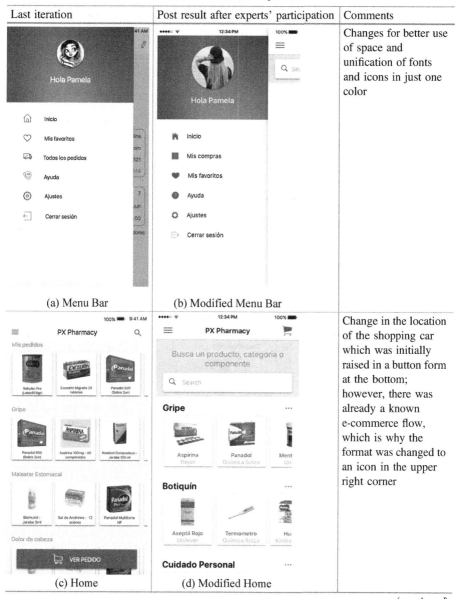		Changes for better use of space and unification of fonts and icons in just one color
(a) Menu Bar	(b) Modified Menu Bar	
(c) Home	(d) Modified Home	Change in the location of the shopping car which was initially raised in a button form at the bottom; however, there was already a known e-commerce flow, which is why the format was changed to an icon in the upper right corner

(*continued*)

Table 8. (*continued*)

Last iteration	Post result after experts' participation	Comments
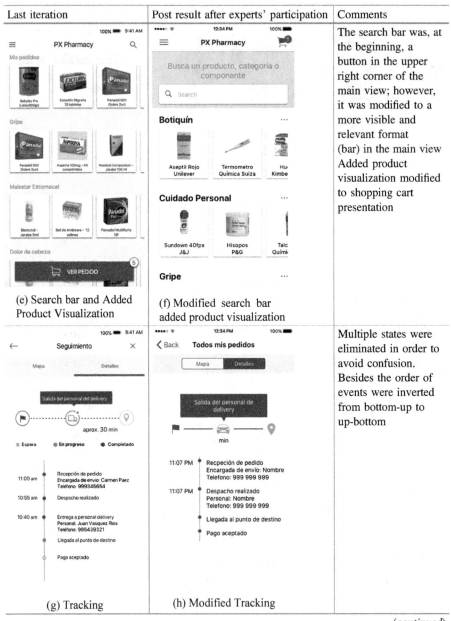		The search bar was, at the beginning, a button in the upper right corner of the main view; however, it was modified to a more visible and relevant format (bar) in the main view. Added product visualization modified to shopping cart presentation
(e) Search bar and Added Product Visualization	(f) Modified search bar added product visualization	
(g) Tracking	(h) Modified Tracking	Multiple states were eliminated in order to avoid confusion. Besides the order of events were inverted from bottom-up to up-bottom

(*continued*)

Table 8. (*continued*)

Last iteration	Post result after experts' participation	Comments
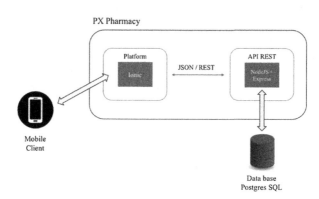		Tags were removed to consolidate a search engine as the best search option because of the simplicity it represents, Additionally, the "I like" (Heart) button was clarified
(i) Favorites	(j) Modified Favorites	

PX Pharmacy

Platform
Ionic

JSON / REST

API REST
NodeJS + Express

Mobile Client

Data base
Postgres SQL

Fig. 6. Px pharmacy mobile application architecture

5 Conclusions

Traditional and agile methodologies did not adapt well in the development of this project. Although their use is the most common and sophisticated for different software developments, a new model was established in order to integrate the best of them. From this approach, it was possible to continue progressively and effectively with an innovation process through the project, which sought to find a solution to a problem of the society considering the user-centered design (UCD) that helped in the definition of several stages of the model presented.

The first stage, Analysis, made use of the "persona" technique to define a user profile, taking into account the demographic factor. Based on it, the development of the next stages was focused on achieving a personalized, simple and enjoyable user experience. Requirements Engineering defined a guide to follow. Concise, complete, consistent and unambiguous characteristics of requirements allowed their subsequent prioritization to avoid the incorrect or overuse of resources. Design was the main stage to consolidate the achievement of the requirement goals. Following the sub stages on it, we were allowed to design a coherent flow that was optimized with each iteration and the participation of the experts.

It is interesting to know new tools of programming, which are increasingly better and more revolutionary. Managing these tools, in Development stage, allowed to build an architecture with simplicity, flexibility, extensibility, maintainability and efficiency in the use of resources.

6   Future Works

Although the results, there are still many aspects to cover. Related to the mobile application development process, it would be proper to complete the stages of testing, deployment, use and maintenance, since they all require an specific treatment and research and they results would help in the consolidation of the proposed model. In regard to the system, the first step is to build the web platform for pharmacies that will work as a means by which products will be entered and inventories, handled.

Nowadays, the analysis of information allows to take actions, based on the user's behavior and preferences. This is the reason why data mining with the collected data, through the application, is planned, but considering all privacy aspects and conditions. In addition, we will seek to establish a financial projection, to know the different growth scenarios and therefore know how to direct the economic focus of the business plan and what adjustments need to be done.

References

1. Abrahamsson, P., Salo, O., Ronkainen, J., Warsta, J.: Agile Software Development Methods: Review and Analysis. VTT (2002)
2. Abras, C., Maloney-Krichmar, D., Preece, J.: User-centered design. In: Bainbridge, W. (ed.) Encyclopedia of Human-Computer Interaction, vol. 37, no. 4, pp. 445–456. Sage Publications, Thousand Oaks (2004)
3. Arellano, P., Bochinski, J., Elias, B., Houser, S., Martin, T., Head, H.: Selecting a mobile app: evaluating the usability of medical applications (2012). http://s3.amazonaws.com/rdcms-himss/files/production/public/HIMSSguidetoappusabilityv1mHIMSS.pdf. Accessed 28 Dec 2017
4. Arias Chaves, M.: La ingeniería de requerimientos y su importancia en el desarrollo de proyectos de software. InterSedes: Revista de las Sedes Regionales, vol. 6, no. 10, pp. 1–13 (2005). http://www.redalyc.org/html/666/66612870011/. Accessed 09 Jan 2018

5. Peñaranda, C.: La clase vulnerable alcanza al 34% de la población peruana. La cámara, Revista de la CCL. no. 786, pp. 6–8 (2017). https://www.camaralima.org.pe/RepositorioAPS/0/0/par/EDICION786/ED_DIG_786.pdf. Accessed 15 Aug 2017

6. Berra, M., Velázquez, A.G.: Innovación tecnológica e innovación social: nuevos modelos organizativos. Revista Gestión y estrategia, no. 6, pp. 114–120 (1994). http://gestionyestrategia.azc.uam.mx/index.php/rge/article/view/470/465. Accessed 21 Jan 2018

7. Buhalis, D.: eCommerce, tourism. In: Jafari, J., Xiao, H. (eds.) Encyclopedia of Tourism. Springer, Heidelberg (2014). https://doi.org/10.1007/978-3-319-01669-6_473-1

8. Buzzi, M.C., Buzzi, M., Leporini, B., Akhter, F.: User trust of eCommerce services: perception via screen reader. In: Proceedings of 3rd International Conference on New Trends in Information and Service Science, (NISS 2009), pp. 1166–1171 (2009)

9. Clarke, I.: Emerging value propositions for m-commerce. J. Bus. Strat. **18**(2), 133–149 (2001)

10. Domingo, M.G., Pera, E.M.: Diseño centrado en el usuario. Exabyte Informatica (2010). https://www.exabyteinformatica.com/uoc/Informatica/Interaccion_persona_ordenador/Interaccion_persona_ordenador_(Modulo_3).pdf. Accessed 28 Dec 2017

11. Falcon, D.: Comercio electrónico en el Perú (2017). Gestión. https://gestion.pe/blog/innovaciondisrupcion/2017/03/comercio-electronico-en-el-peru-2017.html. Accessed 15 Aug 2017

12. Ferre, X., Villalba, E., Julio, H., Zhu, H.: Extending mobile app analytics for usability test logging. In: Bernhaupt, R., Dalvi, G., Joshi, A., K. Balkrishan, D., O'Neill, J., Winckler, M. (eds.) INTERACT 2017. LNCS, vol. 10515, pp. 114–131. Springer, Cham (2017). https://doi.org/10.1007/978-3-319-67687-6_9

13. Fling, B.: Mobile Design & Development: Practical Concepts and Techniques for Creating Mobile Sites and Web Apps, p. 151. O'Reilly Media, Newton (2009)

14. Instituto Nacional de Estadística e Informática: Población que utiliza internet incrementó frecuencia de uso (2015). INEI: https://www.inei.gob.pe/prensa/noticias/poblacion-que-utiliza-internet-incremento-frecuencia-de-uso-8275/. Accessed 15 Aug 2017

15. Ipsos: Comprador en línea 2017 (2017). Ipsos: https://www.ipsos.com/sites/default/files/2017-03/EComerce.pdf. Accessed 15 Aug 2017

16. ISO: ISO 9241-1 (1992)

17. Losavio, F., Chirinos, L., Lévy, N., Ramdane-Cherif, A.: Quality characteristics for software architecture. J. Object Technol. **2**(2), 133–150 (2003). http://www.jot.fm/issues/issue_2003_03/article2.pdf. Accessed 26 Aug 2018

18. Mascheroni, M., Greiner, C., Petris, R., Dapozo, G., Estayno, M.: Calidad de software e Ingeniería de Usabilidad (2012). SEDICI: http://sedici.unlp.edu.ar/bitstream/handle/10915/19202/Documento_completo.pdf%3Fsequence%3D1. Accessed 28 Dec 2017

19. Nielsen, J., Budiu, R.: Mobile Usability. MITP-Verlags GmbH & Co. KG, Frechen (2013)

20. Nielsen, J.: Usability Engineering. Elsevier, New York (1994)

21. Norman, D.A., Draper, S.W.: User-Centered System Design: New Perspectives on Human-Computer Interaction. Lawrence Earlbaum Associates, Hillsdale (1986)

22. Letelier, P: Proceso de desarrollo de software. Universidad Politécnica de Valencia, Department of Information System

23. Ritter, F.E., Baxter, G.D., Churchill, E.F.: User-centered systems design: a brief history. In: Ritter, F.E., Baxter, G.D., Churchill, E.F. (eds.) Foundations for Designing User-Centered Systems, pp. 33–54. Springer, London (2014). https://doi.org/10.1007/978-1-4471-5134-0_2

24. Serna, E.: La importancia de la abstracción en la informática. Scientia et technica, vol. 16, no. 48, pp. 122–126 (2011). http://www.redalyc.org/pdf/849/84922622022.pdf. Accessed 26 Jan 2018

25. Van Limburg, A.H.M., van Gemert-Pijnen, J.: Towards innovative business modeling for sustainable eHealth applications. In: Second International Conference on eHealth, Telemedicine, and Social Medicine, ETELEMED 2010, pp. 11–16 (2010)
26. Vissbr, P., Krosnick, J., Lavraws, P.: Survey Research. Stanford University (2013). http://web.stanford.edu/dept/communication/faculty/krosnick/Survey_Research.pdf. Accessed 28 Dec 2017
27. Wen, M.-H.: The 100,000 participant laboratory - a crowd-centered approach to design and evaluate the usability of mobile apps. In: Marcus, A. (ed.) DUXU 2016. LNCS, vol. 9746, pp. 377–384. Springer, Cham (2016). https://doi.org/10.1007/978-3-319-40409-7_36
28. Wong, W., Bartels, M., Chrobot, N.: Practical eye tracking of the ecommerce website user experience. In: Stephanidis, C., Antona, M. (eds.) UAHCI 2014. LNCS, vol. 8516, pp. 109–118. Springer, Cham (2014). https://doi.org/10.1007/978-3-319-07509-9_11

Comparing Human Against Computer Generated Designs: New Possibilities for Design Activity Within Agile Projects

Farley Fernandes[1(✉)], Ernesto Filgueiras[2,3], and André Neves[4]

[1] UNIDCOM, Beira Interior University, Covilhã, Portugal
fmmf@ubi.pt
[2] LabCOM, Beira Interior University, Covilhã, Portugal
evf@ubi.pt
[3] Centre for Architecture, Urbanism and Design (CIAUD),
University of Lisbon (FA/Ulisboa), Lisbon, Portugal
[4] Universidade Federal de Pernambuco, Recife, Brazil
andremneves@gmail.com

Abstract. Our research explores the possibility of using intelligent agents to automate some of the design activity and evaluate if this kind of tool can perform as good as a human designer would. Thus, we present an app called Design Thinking Canvas Autonomus that supports and automates the creation of design concepts. The justification to do so comes from the context of design activity being executed within agile projects. From the most prominent themes of this conjunction, Little Design Up-Front stands outs as one of the most important. It corresponds to agile projects' need of defining a clear objective, while avoiding unnecessary waste in the long run. In order to test if Autonomus could help addressing this need, we tested its performance against a human designer. The results showed that there was not a statistically significant difference between Design Thinking Canvas Autonomus and its human counterpart in all considered criteria. Actually, for suitability factor, Autonomus had a statistically proven advantage compared to human designs (p-value of 0.037), according to specialist designers' evaluation. It establishes a new frame of reference for agile projects, as the cost and effort to execute Autonomus is significantly lower than a human process.

Keywords: Design automation · Design methodology · Little design up-front
Agile · Design thinking · Design process aid

1 Introduction

Regarding design activity, computational tools to support it have been around for quite some time. The most popular set is what is called CAD (computer-aided design) tools which are usually applied in advanced stages to help materialization of products and its representations when the scope of the project is already fairly defined. The difficulty for technological tools to delve into conceptual stages in design process comes from the need for human intervention on these. "There is a real challenge in this field to open up

© Springer International Publishing AG, part of Springer Nature 2018
A. Marcus and W. Wang (Eds.): DUXU 2018, LNCS 10918, pp. 693–710, 2018.
https://doi.org/10.1007/978-3-319-91797-9_48

to more exploration based tools and processes", according to Peschl and Fundneider [1]. It requires a constant exploration of the problem space and creative inputs to define an initial solution. In this paper, we set out to investigate whether an intelligent system can help in diminishing this gap while maintaining the same efficacy as a human would provide. Our main focus is to evaluate how this new kind of interaction with a computational machine changes a designer's relationship to its own work.

This type of approach is of particular interest for agile projects as they aim to bring higher rates of collaboration and communication through a more decentralized project structure [2]. Amongst the most relevant topics in the conjunction of design and agile paradigm, currently one of the foremost concerns is Little Design Up-front (LDUF), whereby the design work should be conducted in small portions throughout the project, especially in the beginning of the project [3, 4]. This is a conflicting issue, because, on the one hand, design activity classically expects to generate all or most of its specifications early on a project [5–8]. On the other hand, the expectation of agile methodologies with Little Design Up-Front is to minimize waste generation during project execution – large amount of designs being discarded in the future –, so it is expected that all of product development processes, including design activities, to be conducted in an emerging way.

The need to properly address Little Design Up-Front is especially relevant for startup companies as they usually lack resources to make big investments. Issues related to LDUF, such as lack of up-front planning or unpredictability, are among the greatest worries for companies adopting agile [9]. In order to address this, our contribution will be the evaluation of the impact made by conceptual design automation on designers' activity. Moreover, can computational machines alone be as efficient as humans aided by software while proposing design concepts? We discuss these initial results to elicit possible effects on human designer-computer relationship.

2   Related Works: Agile Context and Design Activity Support by Technological Tools

Design activity can happen in several contexts, but the one of our interest is within agile projects due to its relevance and large application nowadays. As we previously stated, our focus is on the phenomena of Little Design Up-Front. The amount of time and effort to be spent on LDUF is still an issue presented as open by Silva [10] and similarly by Gunst [11], as there are many ways to handle this question, one can interpret it as a need for process optimization (design's one, in our case). Albeit being conflicting with a more traditional view of design's disposition, the theme of Little Design Up-Front is very relevant with regard to the implementation of design activities in agile context (see Fig. 1), similar relevance is also shown by [4, 8].

On the one hand some researchers report that there should not be room for much design at the outset [13, 14], while others making the case where a certain amount of design should be conducted earlier in the project [15, 16], and others bringing a combination of the two, with design going a cycle ahead of development [17]. Alternatively, our take will be through the integration of a computational tool to

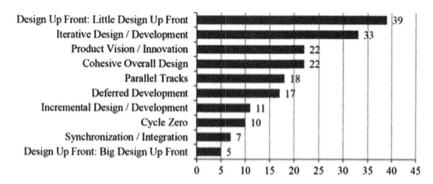

Fig. 1. Most important themes elicited from design activity in agile projects [12]

support and automate conceptual design process. Thus, we evaluate and discuss this integration to see its future implications for designer-computer relationship.

There is no need to restate the importance of computational tools for contemporary work environment, but computational thinking has been reported as being strongly correlated to problem-solving ability [18]. This is especially important considering that amongst the most relevant digital skills for the 21st century are: creativity, critical thinking and problem solving [19]. This represents the capacity to employ techno-logical tools to come up with new ideas, make better reasoning with data and provide solutions, respectively.

Automated systems' accuracy has serious effects on its reliability, as even improvements leads to lower gains in this aspects in the future [20]. For instance, chatterbots are tools that employs artificial intelligence techniques in order to establish natural communication with human beings. They been recently applied to work on unstructured environments like social media, for example. In a study focused on Twitter social network it was found that, regarding communication with a chatterbot, people had equivalent levels of learning capabilities when compared to a human agent [21]. In the hardware domain, some research has been conducted to model the inter-action between human operators and automated robots [22]. Considering human-agent teamwork, our focus of interest, the fact of being led by an agent was not a factor of team abandonment by humans [23]. This clearly indicates possibilities of using this type of tools to aid design process in collaboration between humans and computational agents.

Specifically considering design activity, it is important to note that introducing computational tools to aid or support its process should not happen without acknowledging and controlling unwanted effects already identified, namely: circum-scribed thinking, premature fixation and bounded ideation [24, 25]. Liddament [26] states that computational tools usually materializes an "ontological reduction" in the sense that in only approximates reality while design is most of the time dealing with real-world entities or objects. A natural conflict comes from that.

Designers' tacit knowledge, as unstructured as it is, has found very weak support in terms of computational tools and they have mostly been "design-centric" instead of "designer-centric", in the sense that supporting product development usually overrides designer's needs, as a user [24]. These researchers have also shown that agent-based computations (our research focus) have not yet addressed important designer's actions such as: forming analogies, co-evolving problem and solution, recalling conceptual structures and recalling recognizable problems.

Baxter et al. [27] argue that knowledge management should indeed expand itself towards design activity, as it can potentially free up companies' resources in the search for innovation in competitive markets. They identified five types of approaches for classifying design knowledge management: computer-aided design (CAD) models' retrieval, methodology, function, ontology and process. Likewise, Kitamura and Mizoguchi [28] proposed a framework for device ontology as a way of achieving interoperable and consistent models among designs. They have applied it for functional decomposition of devices in very specific domains (e.g. fluid-related plants), and acknowledge that others are still to be developed. Also referring to engineering design, an interesting finding from Ahmed [29] was that the experience of a designer affects how they express themselves about their activity and consequently the formulation of an ontology.

Considering the whole spectrum of design process, it is interesting to be able to convert functional mappings in configuration representations [30]. These researches did so through a software program that receives a functional model as input, processes possible combinations and generates configuration-based outputs, but still as a model. Nevertheless, their analysis showed that these configuration models helped designers during concept generation considering the metrics of: completeness, novelty and variety. These findings counterpose some of the worries reported in the beginning of this section.

After reviewing these works, we can see that, albeit having already achieved relevant results, automating or supporting designers' activity through computational has plenty room for contribution. Our approach is based on a specific design methodology which represents a work model for designers. Our objective is to evaluate this automation and support for designer's activities, sticking to the "attitude of enabling and emergence" [1] as this is needed across time by agile methodologies.

3   Methodology – Design Thinking Canvas

Design Thinking Canvas (DTC) methodology [31] is our design framework that represents the computational concepts discussed in this work. This Design Thinking (DT) methodology was created and has been maintained by GDRLab research group at Universidade Federal de Pernambuco. Inspired by Osterwalder's Business Model Canvas [32] and Maurya's Lean Canvas [33], DTC also employs a canvas as a basic structure to register all of its information (see Fig. 2). The difference is that DTC, as a design methodology, besides the "what" it also defines "how" designers should develop such information by applying its methods [34]. Several scientific works have been developed using DTC as their foundation, which helped to develop the methodology itself across domains, for example: sustainability [35], game development [36, 37] and business models [38].

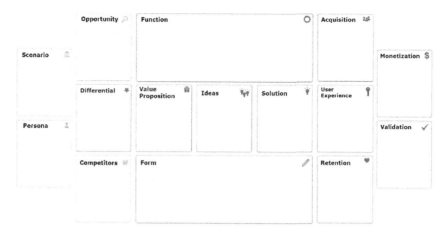

Fig. 2. Canvas blocks from DTC [31]

To do so, the methodology is comprised of four sequential phases: Observation; Conception; Configuration and Publication. During its execution, designers are able to rigorously develop the information for each of the fifteen blocks in the canvas as they have design methods associated to them.

During Observation phase, the methods applied to complete its blocks are: direct and indirect observation [39], persona [40] and desk research [41]. *Scenario* stands for a description of environment where the problem observed takes place, it might be a physical, virtual or conceptual space. The *persona* block aggregates all of profiles to be considered in addressing the problem as they might convert into users of the solution to be developed. It materializes raw data in a more personal relatable perspective as fictitious characters are created. *Opportunities* summarizes the open gaps that can possibly be explored by the solution yet to be developed. They are inferred from the problems identified from personas' context. As a way to benchmark and differentiate itself, the *Competitors* block lists all of the existing solutions that compete direct or indirectly in the same market.

Conception phase is the stage mostly associated with creative work in the methodology, it applies specific adaptions of the following methods: Brain Writing [42], Heuristics [43], Value Curve [44] and Storyboard [40]. In *differential* block, it is supposed that design team make explicit what makes the solution unique in terms of technology, domain or market aspects. A natural derivation from this block is *value proposition* one, where the team states what values does this solution adds to its users' life visualizing it through a comparative curve. The *ideas* block comes from all the concepts generated from the divergence that is collaboratively developed by all team member through Brain Writing, the objective is to achieve diversity by a large number of ideas. From this previous block, *solution* stands to the selection of the best concepts in a collaborative way through the application of heuristics. They must be balanced from desirability, feasibility and viability dimensions. As we have a group of concepts to me merged, the design team can develop a storyboard that maps out the *experience* as a user journey.

Next, there is the Configuration phase when the solution is materialized. As DTC is normally associated with technological artifacts, so in this phase we have the development of user interface layouts (*form* block) and main functionalities specification (*function* block).

Finally, DTC has the Publication phase where we define the strategy for the product in three main dimensions: user acquisition, retention and monetization, a simplification from Pirate Metrics framework [45]. *Acquisition* stands for the tactics applied to bring new users to the product, while *retention* aggregates the ones responsible to retain the existing user. *Monetization* by its turn refers to the channels explored where users can generate financial results from their activity. The *validation* block reflects a set of six heuristics to test user acceptance for the proposed solution.

3.1 Design Thinking Canvas Autonomus

In this paper, in order to assess the implications of inserting automation within design activity, we evaluate a computational intelligent agent that makes decisions and automatically proposes innovative artifacts. It is materialized as an iOS app named Design Thinking Canvas Autonomus reflecting its related design methodology, described previously. It is intended that most of the app users will be designers interested in a support for conceptual stages of their projects.

This type of system has to implement a computational structure named ontology, which enables its data to be processed automatically. Ontologies are "a formal, explicit specification of a shared conceptualization" [46]. Creating an ontology is a way of making knowledge explicit and serves as a crucial step to make it machine readable [47]. This kind of structure might prove useful in order to map design's process for a specific domain.

Besides the academic context, Design Thinking Canvas has already been applied within several Brazilian companies aiming the creation of innovative products for the last 10 years. Therefore, by executing its "offline" design methods, it was possible to historically collect and digitally index several validated data points, which reflects design knowledge around: desirability (user profile and needs), feasibility (technological capabilities) and viability (business strategy). Ontologies can be created following three approaches: bottom-up, top-down and middle out [47]. As those several data points from previous iterations and a well-structured concept framework already existed from Design Thinking Canvas, Autonomus' ontology was constructed through a 'bottom-up approach'. It is a way of doing so by starting from existing concepts and later classifying (or generalizing) them [47]. As of today, Autonomus' ontology is focused only on software apps and its database is composed by four XML files [48]:

- *personas.xml*: contains customers' profiles represented as fictional people with information like: name, region, social class, age, etc. It has initially ten personas entries.
- *activities.xml*: enlist information about daily activities from personas' life. The initial database has thirty-four activities and links back to its possible personas.

- *features.xml*: list of app features that links back to the activities. The features are categorized through Four Actions framework [44], regarding if it can keep, raise or create factors for value in this activity. The database has three hundred and eighty-six features.
- *arm.xml*: has three lists of business strategies. One list with user's acquisition strategies, another with user's retention strategies and other with monetization strategies. There are sixty-four business strategies entries in this database.

Using the structure previously described, Design Thinking Canvas Autonomus can combine several of these data in order to conceive mobile apps within its correspondent design methodology's framework. The main blocks shown in the canvas are related to the *opportunity* to be explored, *features* to be developed and *strategies* to be adopted. All of the basic information for each of these canvas blocks can be automatically generated by Autonomus (see Fig. 3). Alternatively, the designer can also go step by step deciding which information to pick (see Fig. 4), this can be done for all of the blocks and respective sub-blocks. Later, the designer can evaluate through heuristics if these suggestions are adequate for the problem to be addressed or not before moving to the subsequent block.

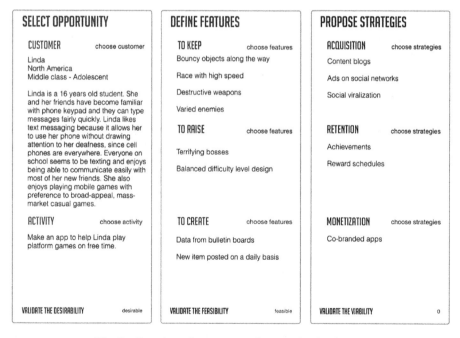

Fig. 3. Overview of an automated suggestion by the app

Although it does not provide detailed information, this type of visual representation in a canvas is particularly useful for agile projects in their first iterations. In their pursuit for Little Design Up-Front, these projects can set a common vision for all of its teams

Fig. 4. Choosing a persona from its specific database

regarding what the product to be developed must achieve. At the same time, design details or refinements can be done in emergent way across time, as the team becomes more aware of the problem to be solved.

4   Procedures

Our main objective is to compare human versus computer proposed designs in terms of their quality and discuss further implications for human designer-computer relationship. Inspired by Turing's classical experiment [49] to check whether a computational machine can sufficiently making itself indistinguishable from another human being, ours sets out to explore if a machine can provide conceptual design inputs to a level that is equivalent to what a human designer could do itself. We do so by comparing projects developed by a machine and projects developed with human intervention through a multiple-criteria evaluation. The parallel here is that if a machine can fool human beings into making its designs as relevant as human ones, it can certainly provide enormous contributions to design process and Design as a scientific domain.

4.1   Experiment

For our experiment, we used Design Thinking Canvas Autonomus to conceive four apps, each one related to a different opportunity. In two of these projects (A and B) a human assisted the computational agent by editing some information and in the other two (C and D) the app worked by itself to propose these concepts (see Figs. 5, 6, 7 and 8). Trust among human beings and automated systems is an enormously relevant theme and has multiple perspectives to be considered [50]. Thus, it is important to note that all of the evaluators did not have any knowledge which of these four concepts were automatically developed by a machine or not in order to avoid any bias.

For each of the four projects, all of the evaluators were given Likert scales [51] from 1 and 5 to score the strength of the following pre-defined list of criteria:

- Creativity: the level of novelty and differentiation in the approach to solve the problem in focus.
- Feasibility: the level of technical capability to develop the product for the market.
- Viability: the level of business sustainability and interest for the concept presented.
- Suitability: the level of alignment regarding all the elements presented for solving the problem under consideration.

In order to answer our research question, we had to group and compare automated (C and D) and non-automated (A and B) results to check if they had any statistically relevant difference between them. Consequently we had these two independent samples being scored in an ordinal scale, thus the statistical test used to verify this previous condition was Wilcoxon-Mann-Whitney [52].

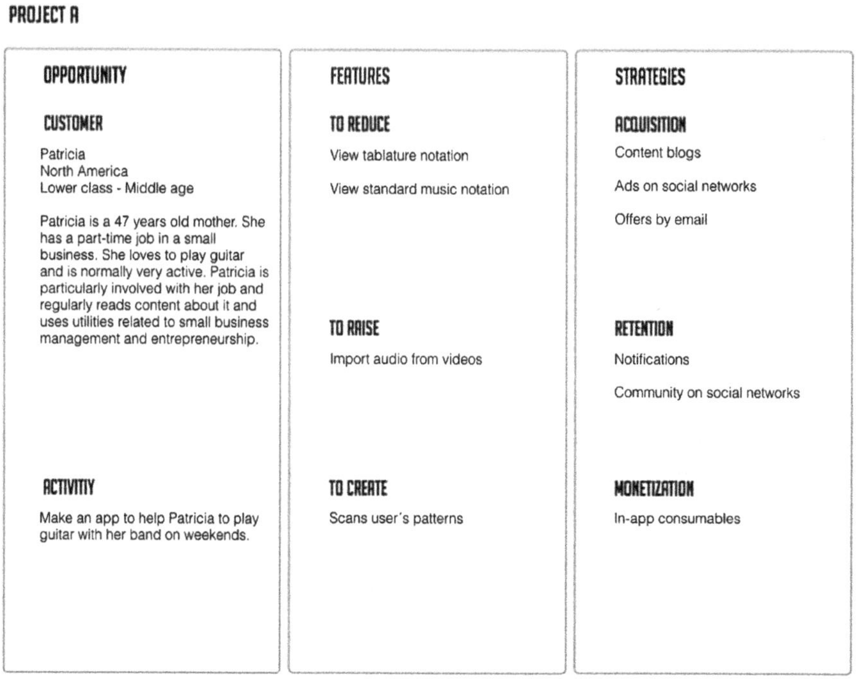

PROJECT A

OPPORTUNITY	FEATURES	STRATEGIES
CUSTOMER	**TO REDUCE**	**ACQUISITION**
Patricia	View tablature notation	Content blogs
North America		
Lower class - Middle age	View standard music notation	Ads on social networks
		Offers by email
Patricia is a 47 years old mother. She has a part-time job in a small business. She loves to play guitar and is normally very active. Patricia is particularly involved with her job and regularly reads content about it and uses utilities related to small business management and entrepreneurship.		
	TO RAISE	**RETENTION**
	Import audio from videos	Notifications
		Community on social networks
ACTIVITIY	**TO CREATE**	**MONETIZATION**
Make an app to help Patricia to play guitar with her band on weekends.	Scans user's patterns	In-app consumables

Fig. 5. Project A created by human designer in the app

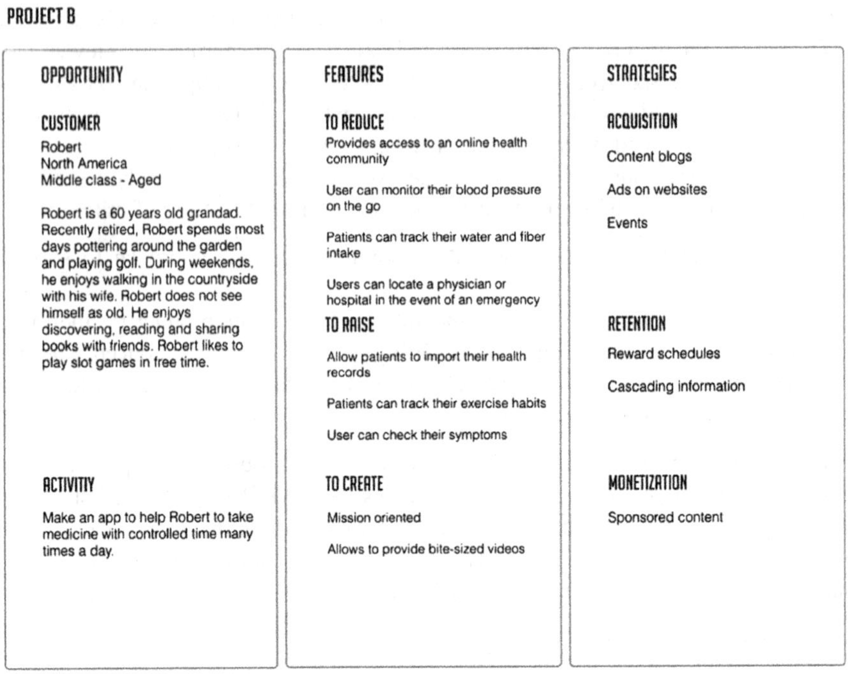

PROJECT B

OPPORTUNITY	FEATURES	STRATEGIES
CUSTOMER Robert North America Middle class - Aged Robert is a 60 years old grandad. Recently retired, Robert spends most days pottering around the garden and playing golf. During weekends, he enjoys walking in the countryside with his wife. Robert does not see himself as old. He enjoys discovering, reading and sharing books with friends. Robert likes to play slot games in free time.	**TO REDUCE** Provides access to an online health community User can monitor their blood pressure on the go Patients can track their water and fiber intake Users can locate a physician or hospital in the event of an emergency **TO RAISE** Allow patients to import their health records Patients can track their exercise habits User can check their symptoms	**ACQUISITION** Content blogs Ads on websites Events **RETENTION** Reward schedules Cascading information
ACTIVITIY Make an app to help Robert to take medicine with controlled time many times a day.	**TO CREATE** Mission oriented Allows to provide bite-sized videos	**MONETIZATION** Sponsored content

Fig. 6. Project B created by human designer in the app

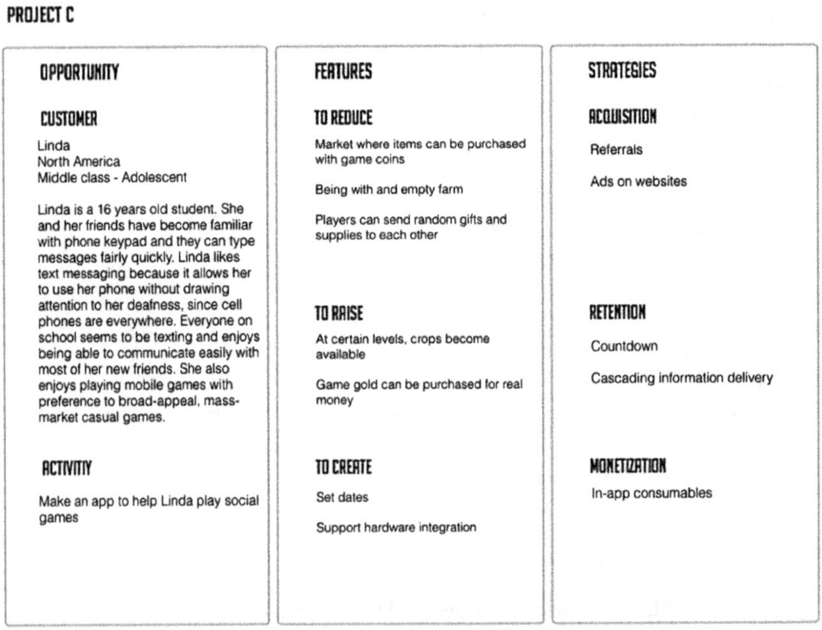

PROJECT C

OPPORTUNITY	FEATURES	STRATEGIES
CUSTOMER Linda North America Middle class - Adolescent Linda is a 16 years old student. She and her friends have become familiar with phone keypad and they can type messages fairly quickly. Linda likes text messaging because it allows her to use her phone without drawing attention to her deafness, since cell phones are everywhere. Everyone on school seems to be texting and enjoys being able to communicate easily with most of her new friends. She also enjoys playing mobile games with preference to broad-appeal, mass-market casual games.	**TO REDUCE** Market where items can be purchased with game coins Being with and empty farm Players can send random gifts and supplies to each other **TO RAISE** At certain levels, crops become available Game gold can be purchased for real money	**ACQUISITION** Referrals Ads on websites **RETENTION** Countdown Cascading information delivery
ACTIVITIY Make an app to help Linda play social games	**TO CREATE** Set dates Support hardware integration	**MONETIZATION** In-app consumables

Fig. 7. Project C automatically created by Autonomus

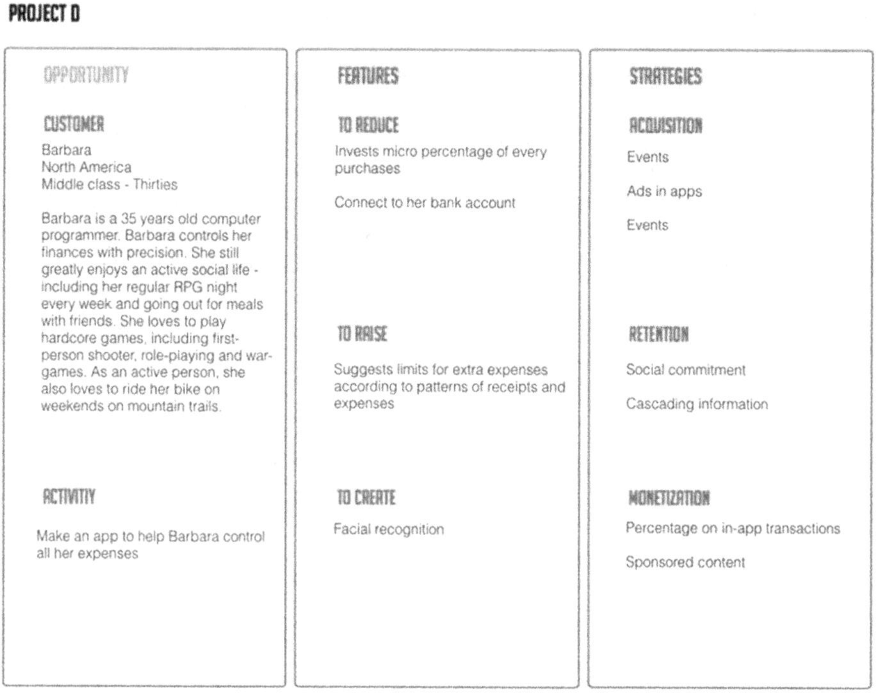

PROJECT D

OPPORTUNITY	FEATURES	STRATEGIES
CUSTOMER	**TO REDUCE**	**ACQUISITION**
Barbara	Invests micro percentage of every	Events
North America	purchases	
Middle class - Thirties		Ads in apps
	Connect to her bank account	
Barbara is a 35 years old computer		Events
programmer. Barbara controls her		
finances with precision. She still		
greatly enjoys an active social life -		
including her regular RPG night		
every week and going out for meals	**TO RAISE**	**RETENTION**
with friends. She loves to play		
hardcore games, including first-	Suggests limits for extra expenses	Social commitment
person shooter, role-playing and war-	according to patterns of receipts and	
games. As an active person, she	expenses	Cascading information
also loves to ride her bike on		
weekends on mountain trails.		
ACTIVITY	**TO CREATE**	**MONETIZATION**
Make an app to help Barbara control	Facial recognition	Percentage on in-app transactions
all her expenses		
		Sponsored content

Fig. 8. Project D automatically created by Autonomus

4.2   Sample

These four projects were sent to a total of twenty-one evaluators. Our sample was basically comprised by two different groups of evaluators: six digital artifact designers with at least five years of professional experience; and fifteen spontaneous participants from an open call on Design Thinking Canvas' Facebook community. All evaluations were obtained for 42 days, from July 18th to August 31st in 2015. Besides developing an overall analysis, our intention was also to delve into the perspectives of experienced design specialists and a more general public, reflecting possibly real-world users of Autonomus' app.

5   Results and Discussion

In this section, we present and discuss the results from Wilcoxon-Mann-Whitney statistical test regarding the criteria previously presented: creativity, feasibility, viability and suitability. We will first see the overall results considering the total sample and later we focus on the analysis from design specialists.

Can machines "imitate" humans while developing conceptual designs in Design Thinking Canvas? To answer our research question, we need to check whether the samples show statistical equivalent groups or not. As we stated before, this study intends to compare the performance of an intelligent machine in proposing conceptual designs to a human designer.

So as hypothesis for our experiment, we say that there is no difference between the scores for computer proposed designs and human ones. To conduct our analysis we used IBM SPSS Statistics software, version 24 [53]. To use the non-parametric test of Wilcoxon-Mann-Whitney, we rewrote our hypothesis in terms of the distribution of the scores between human designs group (X_h) and computer designs group (X_c) for $\alpha = 0.05$ as significance level for a two-tailed test. Thus, we have the following null (H_0) and alternative hypothesis (H_1) for all the considered criteria:

$$
\begin{aligned}
H0: F(Xh) &= F(Xc) \\
H1: F(Xh) &\neq F(Xc)
\end{aligned}
\tag{1}
$$

In the results presented, the row for the grouping variable "Designer" is comprised of the values: *Computer* (aggregates results for projects C and D) and *Human* (aggregates results for projects A and B) to designate both groups of projects, automated and non-automated respectively. Table 1 summarizes the results for all considered criteria which we discuss later individually.

Table 1. Comparison for DTC variations under Creativity, Suitability, Viability and Feasibility criteria

Wilcoxon-Mann-Whitney test results		Creativity	Suitability	Viability	Feasibility
Mean ranks for designer	Human	46.85	39.10	41.12	42.69
	Computer	38.15	45.90	43.88	42.31
Mann-Whitney U		699.500	739.000	824.000	874.000
Wilcoxon W		1602.500	1642.000	1727.000	1777.000
Z		−1.681	−1.327	−.539	−.075
Asymp. sig. (2-tailed)		.093	.184	.590	.941
Exact sig. (2-tailed)		.093	.188	.601	.947
Exact sig. (1-tailed)		.046	.094	.301	.473
Point probability		.000	.002	.008	.004

(N = 42)

5.1   Creativity

What we found for creativity was that the mean rank is consistent with our alternative hypothesis as machine designs value (38.15) is lower than human ones (46.85) (see ranks table below). But in the test report we can see that the p-value for two-tail is 0.093 which is higher than our significance level (0.05), then we fail to reject our null hypothesis.

From the results, we noticed that we cannot sustain the difference as being statistically significant, although they were borderline, this means that the novelty proposed by both automated and non-automated concepts were equivalent for the evaluators. This is an interesting finding as creativity is usually associated to human factors, especially within design activity, but in this case machine performed as good as them.

5.2   Feasibility

Regarding Feasibility, we found that the mean rank is also consistent with our alternative hypothesis as machine designs have lower value (42.31) than human ones (42.69). But in this case the report also show us that the p-value is 0.947 which is higher than our significance level (0.05). In this case, we also fail to reject the null hypothesis.

Again, due to the absence of statistical strength we cannot support the difference between human and non-human designs. Feasibility is a dimension of utter importance for agile projects as teams usually defers important decisions as late as possible in order to avoid unnecessary commitments early on [54]. Thus, having the notion of a proper level of confidence in feasibility factor is key to project success.

5.3   Viability

In Viability for its turn, the mean rank is consistent with our alternative hypothesis as machine designs has greater value (43.88) than human ones (41.12). The report shows us that the p-value is 0.601 which is higher than our significance level (0.05). Again, we also retain the null hypothesis, and again we cannot find enough statistical evidence for the difference between human and non-human designs.

Deriving from a Design Thinking, products developed through our target methodology must be created also aiming for its own market sustainability among other dimensions [55]. So, it is important to have this factor in place for both human and non-human designs, which indeed happens as they are equivalent in this experiment. This finding is especially relevant to the objective of addressing Little Design Up-Front as it means that the business vision established by the automated concepts are clear enough to be pursued.

5.4   Suitability

Finally, for Suitability the mean rank is also consistent with our alternative hypothesis: machine designs have greater value (45.90) than human ones (39.10). The report shows us that the p-value is 0.188 which is higher than our significance level (0.05). Due to a lack of statistical evidence, we again retain our null hypothesis.

As stated previously, suitability factor represents a balance of the elements presented on DTC's canvas while addressing a specific problem. It is not necessary to restate the relevance of the findings of equivalence between human and computer designs for agile project teams. Although they are commonly multidisciplinary, these teams might lack a specific competence or at least have fewer experience in a certain area (e.g. business). Thus, finding that computer designs are as suitable as human ones brings a great possibility of employing this type of aid for design process in the future.

5.5   Specialist Designers' Evaluation

In order to have a particular perspective for comparison, we have repeated the same analysis but this time considering only the cases where we have design specialists as evaluators within our overall sample. We did so as this group reflect evaluations from those that have more specialized experience in design practice. Table 2 summarizes all results for this group. The objective was to check if there is any significant difference from the previous results, which considered all the cases regardless of this segmentation.

Table 2. Evaluations of DTC variations by specialist designers

Wilcoxon-Mann-Whitney test results		Creativity	Suitability	Viability	Feasibility
Mean ranks for designer	Human	12.46	9.54	11.42	12.00
	Computer	12.54	**15.46**	13.58	13.00
Mann-Whitney U		71.500	36.500	59.000	66.000
Wilcoxon W		149.500	114.500	137.000	144.000
Z		−.030	−2.167	−.775	−.359
Asymp. sig. (2-tailed)		.976	.030	.438	.719
Exact sig. (2-tailed)		.986	.037	.478	.763
Exact sig. (1-tailed)		.493	**.018**	.239	.381
Point probability		.000	.003	.035	.035

(N = 12)

Creativity. Regarding creativity factor, we found the mean rank comparison consistent with our alternative hypothesis as machine designs value (12.54) is higher than human ones (12.46), but the p-value is 0.986 which is higher than our significance level (0.05). Thus, we retain the null hypothesis.

This again represents an interesting finding for design activity. Specialist designers are usually rigorous with the creative factor as this usually represents one of the most notorious aspects of their work. From the results, we can see that they were "fooled" by Autonomus automatic performance regarding creativity as well. This might represent an initial recognition of the support that computational machines can provide for creative processes.

Feasibilty. For this factor, the mean rank comparison is again consistent with our alternative hypothesis as computer designs score (13.00) is higher than human ones (12.00), but the p-value is 0.763 which is higher than our significance level (0.05). So again, we could not reject the null hypothesis.

Considering the reported experience of the specialist designers (5 or more years in digital product segment), they are clearly suitable to evaluate the feasibility of the proposed concepts. Thus, it is indeed revealing the findings of equivalence among automated and non-automated designs, possibly meaning that they trust indistinctly on the completion or realization of the proposed products.

Viability. In viability, the mean rank is for computer designs is again higher (13.58) than human ones (11.42), but the p-value is 0.478 which is higher than our significance level (0.05). This time again we fail to reject the null hypothesis, meaning we did not find statistical strength to defend otherwise.

As previously stated in Sect. 5.3, business dimension is collaboratively constructed and evaluated within Design Thinking process. Although it is not classically expected that designers do so, it is important that they participate in this process, especially experienced ones as in this segment of our sample. Again, this group of designers could not differentiate automated and non-automated designs in terms of their market prospects.

Suitability. Lastly, for suitability the mean rank for computer produced designs is also higher (15.46) than human ones (9.54) and the p-value is 0.037 which is lower than our significance level (0.05). In this case, we are able to reject the null hypothesis due to statistical evidence which states that the distribution between the groups are indeed different, with machine automated designs scoring better than human ones.

This was indeed the most notorious finding of our study as the groups of automated and non-automated designs could indeed could be differentiated, meaning that one of them could perform statistically better than the other. To our surprise, the most suitable ones were automated designs. This is especially relevant considering these evaluators' experience in design field. We hypothesize that this happened due to the unbiased behavior of Autonomus' algorithm in balancing all of the dimensions from Design Thinking Canvas framework, which does not seem to happen with human intervention. The difference from the overall evaluation (presented in 5.4) is possibly explained by the fact that design specialists, as being more experienced, are more sensitive to a general congruence of the elements from the methodology.

6   Conclusion

We introduced our work by contextualizing the conjunction of agile and design activity to identify the most important themes from it. Accordingly, Little Design Up-Front is the most mentioned and debated topic which makes it important to further investigate. It was also shown the importance and related works regarding the application of technological tools to aid design process as we set out to explore this possibility to address Little Design Up-Front.

From this justification, we proposed an experiment using an established DT methodology, Design Thinking Canvas, which has been implemented as a conceptual design automation app (Design Thinking Canvas Autonomus). So, it was created two automated projects and two projects with human intervention. These projects were evaluated under four criteria and the evaluators did not have any knowledge that some of them were developed automatically by a computational app.

In summary, we could not find enough statistical evidence to support any difference between computer automated designs and human ones. It means that Design Thinking Canvas Autonomus system was at least as efficient as a human being using the same framework. This finding is especially relevant to our main objective of addressing Little Design Up-Front as a clear objective for agile teams' developing product is set up early on, while being effective in the long run at the same time.

In practical terms, for agile design projects this is an important fact to consider as the overall costs and efforts to develop each set of design concepts by a non-human agent would be significantly lower. In this case, design teams can focus their attention or resources on more complex problems or tasks that machines cannot conduct within design projects. For instance, a higher number of sketches produced through critiques is already reported to enhance creativity in collaborative digital environments [56], so it would be beneficial for design process to free up some time to focus on this type of activity.

According to design specialists' evaluation, we found a marginal advantage for automated designs, as in suitability evaluation computer designs scored even better than human ones. We think this happened due to the fact that computational processing tends to avoid bias by balancing all the elements which favors this factor. Even considering that the group of specialist designers would be more rigorous as evaluators, the results also showed that computer generated designs are at least equivalent to human developed ones. Although we could not find enough statistical evidence to support it, something that stands out and must be commented is the fact that computer generated designs had better mean ranks in all of the four criteria considered in our study. This presents an excellent opportunity for future studies to further investigation.

Having clear goals is a factor that have significant impact on team performance [57]. As stated before, the previously presented findings mean that Design Thinking Canvas Autonomus can possibly help design teams in setting a specific goal for their agile projects earlier, saving resources and shortening the phase of product conception, while still delivering at least the same results as human beings would do.

References

1. Peschl, M.F., Fundneider, T.: Designing and enabling spaces for collaborative knowledge creation and innovation: from managing to enabling innovation as socio-epistemological technology. Comput. Hum. Behav. **37**, 346–359 (2014)
2. Inayat, I., Salim, S.S.: A framework to study requirements-driven collaboration among agile teams: findings from two case studies. Comput. Hum. Behav. Part B **51**, 1367–1379 (2015)
3. Adikari, S., McDonald, C., Campbell, J.: Little design up-front: a design science approach to integrating usability into agile requirements engineering. In: Jacko, J.A. (ed.) HCI 2009. LNCS, vol. 5610, pp. 549–558. Springer, Heidelberg (2009). https://doi.org/10.1007/978-3-642-02574-7_62
4. Silva, T., Martin, A., Maurer, F., Silveira, M.: User-centered design and agile methods: a systematic review. Presented at the August (2011)
5. Baxter, M.: Projetos de Produtos. Guia Prático Para o Design de Novos Produtos. Edgard Blucher (2000)
6. Cross, N.: Engineering Design Methods: Strategies for Product Design. Wiley, Chichester (2000)
7. Pahl, G., Beitz, W.: Engineering Design: A Systematic Approach. Springer Science & Business Media, Heidelberg (2013). https://doi.org/10.1007/978-1-84628-319-2
8. Sohaib, O., Khan, K.: Integrating usability engineering and agile software development: a literature review. In: 2010 International Conference on Computer Design and Applications, (ICCDA), pp. V2–32. IEEE (2010)
9. Melo, C., Santos, V., Katayama, E., Corbucci, H., Prikladnicki, R., Goldman, A., Kon, F.: The evolution of agile software development in Brazil: education, research, and the state-of-the-practice. J. Braz. Comput. Soc. **19**, 523–552 (2013)

10. Silva, T.S.: A framework for integrating interaction design and agile methods (2012). http://tede.pucrs.br/tde_busca/processaArquivo.php?codArquivo=4176

11. Gunst, J.: Introducing interaction design in agile software development (2012)

12. Brhel, M., Meth, H., Maedche, A., Werder, K.: Exploring principles of user-centered agile software development: a literature review. Inf. Softw. Technol. **61**, 163–181 (2015)

13. Lindvall, M., et al.: Empirical findings in agile methods. In: Wells, D., Williams, L. (eds.) XP/Agile Universe 2002. LNCS, vol. 2418, pp. 197–207. Springer, Heidelberg (2002). https://doi.org/10.1007/3-540-45672-4_19

14. Ungar, J., White, J.: Agile user centered design: enter the design studio-a case study. In: Extended Abstracts on Human Factors in Computing Systems, CHI 2008, pp. 2167–2178. ACM (2008)

15. Ferreira, J., Noble, J., Biddle, R.: Agile development iterations and UI design. In: Agile Conference, (AGILE), pp. 50–58. IEEE (2007)

16. Ferreira, J., Noble, J., Biddle, R.: Up-front interaction design in agile development. In: Concas, G., Damiani, E., Scotto, M., Succi, G. (eds.) XP 2007. LNCS, vol. 4536, pp. 9–16. Springer, Heidelberg (2007). https://doi.org/10.1007/978-3-540-73101-6_2

17. Sy, D.: Adapting usability investigations for agile user-centered design. J. Usability Stud. **2**, 112–132 (2007)

18. Román-González, M., Pérez-González, J.-C., Jiménez-Fernández, C.: Which cognitive abilities underlie computational thinking? Criterion validity of the computational thinking test. Comput. Hum. Behav. **72**, 678–691 (2017)

19. van Laar, E., van Deursen, A.J.A.M., van Dijk, J.A.G.M., de Haan, J.: The relation between 21st-century skills and digital skills: a systematic literature review. Comput. Hum. Behav. **72**, 577–588 (2017)

20. Madhavan, P., Phillips, R.R.: Effects of computer self-efficacy and system reliability on user interaction with decision support systems. Comput. Hum. Behav. **26**, 199–204 (2010)

21. Edwards, C., Beattie, A.J., Edwards, A., Spence, P.R.: Differences in perceptions of communication quality between a Twitterbot and human agent for information seeking and learning. Comput. Hum. Behav. **65**, 666–671 (2016)

22. Yagoda, R.E., Coovert, M.D.: How to work and play with robots: an approach to modeling human–robot interaction. Comput. Hum. Behav. **28**, 60–68 (2012)

23. van Wissen, A., Gal, Y., Kamphorst, B.A., Dignum, M.V.: Human–agent teamwork in dynamic environments. Comput. Hum. Behav. **28**, 23–33 (2012)

24. Bernal, M., Haymaker, J.R., Eastman, C.: On the role of computational support for designers in action. Des. Stud. **41**, 163–182 (2015)

25. Robertson, B.F., Radcliffe, D.F.: Impact of CAD tools on creative problem solving in engineering design. Comput.-Aided Des. **41**, 136–146 (2009)

26. Liddament, T.: The computationalist paradigm in design research. Des. Stud. **20**, 41–56 (1999)

27. Baxter, D., Gao, J., Case, K., Harding, J., Young, B., Cochrane, S., Dani, S.: A framework to integrate design knowledge reuse and requirements management in engineering design. Robot. Comput.-Integr. Manuf. **24**, 585–593 (2008)

28. Kitamura, Y., Mizoguchi, R.: Ontology-based description of functional design knowledge and its use in a functional way server. Expert Syst. Appl. **24**, 153–166 (2003)

29. Ahmed, S.: Encouraging reuse of design knowledge: a method to index knowledge. Des. Stud. **26**, 565–592 (2005)

30. Kurtoglu, T., Campbell, M.I., Linsey, J.S.: An experimental study on the effects of a computational design tool on concept generation. Des. Stud. **30**, 676–703 (2009)

31. Neves, A.: Design Thinking Canvas (2014). https://dl.dropboxusercontent.com/u/1889427/designthinkingcanvasV2.pdf

32. Osterwalder, A., Pigneur, Y.: Business Model Generation: A Handbook for Visionaries, Game Changers, and Challengers. Wiley, Hoboken (2010)
33. Maurya, A.: Running Lean: Iterate from Plan A to a Plan that Works. O'Reilly Media, Inc., Newton (2012)
34. Araújo, A.: Métodos de design como instrumento para construção de modelos de negócio (2013)
35. Sóter, C., Vilar, E.: O FATOR VERDE NO DESIGN THINKING CANVAS: USO DE CARTAS E HEURÍSTICAS PARA INFLUENCIAR DESIGNERS A TEREM IDEIAS SUSTENTÁVEIS. Presented at the December (2016)
36. Filho, M.B.M.: Utilização da Metodologia Design Card Game na Configuração de Mecânicas para Jogos Digitais (2014)
37. de Oliveira, B.S.: Engenharia reversa como ferramenta de suporte à especificação de jogos digitais de baixa e média complexidade (2015)
38. Vargas, V.C.L.: Uma extensão do Design Thinking Canvas com foco em Modelos de Negócios para a Indústria de Games (2015). http://repositorio.ufpe.br/handle/123456789/16490
39. Berg, B.L.: Qualitative Research Methods for the Social Sciences. Allyn and Bacon, Boston (2001)
40. Hanington, B., Martin, B.: Universal Methods of Design: 100 Ways to Research Complex Problems, Develop Innovative Ideas, and Design Effective Solutions. Rockport Publishers (2012)
41. Crouch, S., Housden, M.: Marketing Research for Managers. Butterworth-Heinemann, Oxford (2003)
42. VanGundy, A.B.: Brain writing for new product ideas: an alternative to brainstorming. J. Consum. Mark. 1, 67–74 (1984)
43. Breyer, F.B.: Avaliação heurística para protótipos de jogos digitais (2008). http://repositorio.ufpe.br/handle/123456789/3103
44. Kim, W.C., Mauborgne, R.: Blue ocean strategy. You Read Nothing Strategy Read Thesebest-Sell. Article no. 71 (2004)
45. McClure, D.: Startup Metrics for Pirates. Saatavilla (2007)
46. Gruber, T.R.: A translation approach to portable ontology specifications. Knowl. Acquis. 5, 199–220 (1993)
47. Cristani, M., Cuel, R.: A survey on ontology creation methodologies. Int J. Semantic Web Inf. Syst. 1, 49–69 (2005)
48. XML (2016). https://en.wikipedia.org/w/index.php?title=XML&oldid=717949842
49. Turing, A.M.: Computing machinery and intelligence. Mind 59, 433–460 (1950)
50. Culley, K.E., Madhavan, P.: Trust in automation and automation designers: implications for HCI and HMI. Comput. Hum. Behav. 6, 2208–2210 (2013)
51. Allen, I.E., Seaman, C.A.: Likert scales and data analyses. Qual. Prog. 40, 64 (2007)
52. Marôco, J.: Análise estatística com o SPSS Statistics. ReportNumber, Lda (2011)
53. IBM SPSS Statistics. https://www.ibm.com/us-en/marketplace/spss-statistics
54. Poppendieck, M., Poppendieck, T.: Lean Software Development: An Agile Toolkit. Addison-Wesley Professional, Boston (2003)
55. Brown, T.: Change by Design: How Design Thinking Transforms Organizations and Inspires Innovation. Harper Collins Publisher Inc., New York (2009)
56. Karakaya, A.F., Demirkan, H.: Collaborative digital environments to enhance the creativity of designers. Comput. Hum. Behav. 42, 176–186 (2015)
57. Lu, Y., Xiang, C., Wang, B., Wang, X.: What affects information systems development team performance? An exploratory study from the perspective of combined socio-technical theory and coordination theory. Comput. Hum. Behav. 27, 811–822 (2011)

A Canvas Method to Foster Interdisciplinary Discussions on Digital Assistance Systems

Holger Fischer$^{(\boxtimes)}$, Björn Senft, Florian Rittmeier, and Stefan Sauer

Paderborn University, SICP, Fürstenallee 11, 33102 Paderborn, Germany
{h.fischer,b.senft,f.rittmeier,s.sauer}@sicp.upb.de

Abstract. Meaningful and usable digital assistance systems that support the employees in their everyday tasks seems to be a challenge for many organizations in terms of individual and organizational acceptance including usability, UX, or Work 4.0 issues. Existing software engineering methods are insufficient to integrate employees in the design and development, and to discuss solution concepts of such systems at eye level. In this paper, a lightweight canvas method is presented that shall address these challenges. It includes the human, the business as well as the technological perspective in one communication instrument. First evaluations show that participants appreciate the canvas concept and that the method is versatile in different scenarios. Several questions enrich the discussions about new systems and improve the acceptance as well as the mindset at early stages in the design and development process.

Keywords: Digital assistance systems · Canvas method
Acceptance · Organizational communication
Human-centered software engineering
Requirements engineering · Software quality · Work 4.0

1 Motivation

In Germany, the term "Arbeit 4.0" (en. Work 4.0) as a part of digitization addresses the direct and indirect interaction between digital technologies and all processes of work design, organization of work, and working conditions [1].

Software solutions especially digital assistance systems (DigASys) are increasing within the professional work context [2], e.g. cooperative robots in industrial manufacturing or augmented reality glasses in the commissioning. We understand a *digital assistance system* as follows:

Definition 1. *A digital assistance system is a software solution (e.g. apps) as well as a combined software and hardware solution (e.g. smart glasses, augmented reality, drones), with which people interact via a user interface and thus are supported in their work situation. Excluded are hardware solutions with embedded software (e.g. autonomous industrial trucks, robots) that do not have a direct user interface.*

© Springer International Publishing AG, part of Springer Nature 2018
A. Marcus and W. Wang (Eds.): DUXU 2018, LNCS 10918, pp. 711–724, 2018.
https://doi.org/10.1007/978-3-319-91797-9_49

The possibilities are versatile and also encourage further discussions about the impacts on the human working life.

The employees' as well as the organizational acceptance of these systems is crucial and includes quality aspects of usability, user experience, and Work 4.0 as well as of the business perspective [3].

In addition, we can observe five big trends affecting work in the future [4]: New behaviors due to social media, millennials in the workplace, mobility, globalization, and new technologies. These developments change the expectations regarding software solutions like they are part of the organizations today.

Despite all efforts, today's software products have quality gaps in terms of functionality and usability [5,6]. Organizations spend lots of money to develop digital assistance systems, which are not accepted by employees or works councils (employee representative committees) after their rollout. Software solutions increase in their complexity or expectations, and user needs are often out of focus. Project managers and software developer cannot cope with the challenges on their own. The active involvement of employees in the software development process has become essential.

Current software engineering (SE) methods are insufficient. Methods do not focus on users – the employees working with the software – in terms of active involvement during the development process. Human-centered design (HCD) methods address the active involvement of users, but do not take the business strategy into account, which is important for the organizational acceptance.

A lightweight method to foster the communication and discussion between all stakeholders starting from the beginning of an assistance system project is necessary to include all three perspectives: The human, the business and the technology. Such a method can create an overview and address critical issues right from the start.

In this paper we present an approach that is based on a canvas concept. Our aim is to create a lightweight method that is easy to use, quick to conduct and accepted by both management and employees. Therefore, we sum up canvas-based methods as related work, introduce our "Digital Assistance System Canvas", and conclude with our experiences.

2   Canvas-Based Methods

To achieve the goal of a lightweight and management-accepted method, we have adopted the concept of the *Business Model Canvas* (BMC) [7]. Osterwalder and Pigneur published their BMC in 2010 and challenged the way to *"systematically invent, design, and implement [...] powerful new business models"*. With their method, they addressed questions like *"How can we question, challenge, and transform old, outmoded [business models]?"* and *"How can we turn visionary ideas into game-changing business models that challenge the establishment – or rejuvenate it if we ourselves are the incumbents?"*.

The BMC addresses the business perspective of an organization and *"describes the rationale of how an organization creates, delivers, and captures value"*. Therefore, Osterwalder and Pigneur specified nine basic building blocks categorized into three main areas of business – the customers (customer segments; customer relationships; communication, distribution, and sales channels) and the offer (value propositions), the infrastructure (key resources; key activities; key partnerships), and the financial viability (revenue streams; cost structure).

As described, the BMC is focussed on the business value of an organization. It merely takes the employees of an organization into account as a key resources and does not model the working processes that shall be supported with a digital assistance system. Nevertheless, the canvas concept is highly accepted by managers, academics, and practitioners around the world and seems to be a good starting point for innovation projects [8].

While the BMC is focussed on the whole business strategy of an organization, Patton [9] adopted the BMC concept in his *Opportunity Canvas* and aims on facilitating discussions about new features or capabilities. He assumes that a product already exists within an organization and eliminates the operational or revenue building blocks. Patton puts the focus on the user's problems instead as there are too many ideas for features that could be added. With the Opportunity Canvas, he encourage the participants to think about how the users would use the solution to solve their problems and how this can either hurts or helps the business.

The advantage of this canvas lies in the focus on the users' problems. Concerning the development of new digital assistance systems, this would be an adequate starting point to support employees in their work. Nevertheless, Patton only addresses features of already existing systems and neglect issues like the working context, the work design, or possible impacts of a system. Furthermore, he only makes assumptions about users' problems instead of involving actual employees in the discussion.

Another adoption of the BMC and Opportunity Canvas is the *Lean UX Canvas* presented by Gothelf [10]. The aim of this canvas is to *"help teams frame their work as a business problem to solve (rather than a solution to implement) and then dissect that business problem into its core assumptions"*. Therefore, Gothelf established building blocks to describe the users and customers, the users' benefits, and hypotheses as well as questions what shall be learned to validate the hypotheses.

The focus on validation of hypotheses is an advantage towards the Opportunity Canvas and reduces the risks to not only build a system on assumptions and to get rejected by employees or works councils. Nevertheless, the Lean UX Canvas focusses on business problems and does not take account of the working context, the work design, etc. to build assistance systems that support working processes in an adequate way.

To sum up, all three canvases contain worthwhile concepts to address business problems and to discuss business outcomes. None of the canvases puts a focus on the working context or the task that shall be supported, let alone looking at impacts on the users and needs of the users of the system. Therefore, we adopted these canvases and changed the focus towards work, acceptances criteria and active user involvement.

3   The Digital Assistance System Canvas

The working context of an organization is very important. Every organization needs satisfied employees in order to be innovative and to create values for customers of its products and services.

Due to new technological possibilities and new work concepts, the way we work is continually changing. Digital software-based assistance systems support the employees who can focus on their core tasks again.

In order to build meaningful assistances systems, it is necessary to foster a communication culture within organizations. The acceptance of such systems is not only created by the systems themselves, but also by the way employees are valued and involved during the development process. We base these assumptions on our observations that we have made in several projects with business partners.

To create a lightweight method that is easy to use, quick to implement and accepted by both management and employees, we have done research on existing canvas concepts (cp. Sect. 2). Furthermore, we have analyzed several projects with our business partners concerning questions about what behavior we observed among the various stakeholders and which activities have led to more acceptance of the final solution (Sect. 3.1). Based on that, we have defined objectives to be achieved with our canvas (Sect. 3.2) and have developed a structure as well as questions for every building block of our canvas (Sect. 3.3). In addition, we have created a short practical guide to apply the canvas, which is based on human-centered design following ISO 9241-210 [11] (Sect. 3.4). Finally, the concept of the canvas has been evaluated with focus groups of practitioners (Sect. 3.5).

3.1   Observations Within Business Projects

In the last three years, we have been supporting various companies in the design and implementation of digital assistance systems in their working environments. Three of the projects are described below to illustrate the differences in their thematic orientation and their company structure:

- *Project 1: Energy-efficiency installation.* The organization of this case advises, installs and maintains combined heat and power (CHP) units of all sizes for various properties. Therefore, they are kind of responsible for the energy-saving result. However, the decision for an optimal CHP is very complex and depends on the interaction of all the energy consumers of a property as well as the people working there. In order to demonstrate the actual energy savings as well as to interpret deviations in the behavior and to plan maintenance work ahead, it is necessary to analyze and interpret a large number of energy data. The aim of the project was to introduce an assistance system to support all actors from the craftsman through the energy engineer to the owner of the property. During the project, we had access to all stakeholders and were able to validate assumptions with them.

- *Project 2: Facade engineering.* The organization of this case is active within the context of building construction and supports their customers (e.g. architects, engineers, constructors) with free of charge services in order to convince them to buy their building elements later on. Some stand-alone solutions exist that supports the involved people with some assistance. With the aim to improve the overall construction planning and coordination process and to connect existing solutions, a project has been set up to analyze the context of use within the company (sales, engineering, consulting) as well as with the users of their services. During the project, we did interviews with all internal stakeholders and we were able to talk to several customers of the company.
- *Project 3: ATM assembly.* The organization of this case produce all different kinds of self-service systems, e.g. automated teller machines (ATM). The automated production of the parts needed is followed by a manual assembly line. Multiple quality gates within this assembly line ensure the quality of the products. As the number of produced machines is low within each order due to individualization by the customer, quality problems are reported at a time when they cannot be fixed anymore. A project has been set up to identify possibilities for digitalization of paper-based documentation and quality assistance for the worker. This was the most complex of the three projects described. Due to the size of the company and the nature of the project, we had to involve the works council as well as the union in order to talk to the workers in the assembly line. We had to conduct many interviews to keep everyone involved and validate findings as well as concepts in regular meetings.

Within the different projects we observed that mixed teams in an organization started to talk to each other in the past only after new software solutions were unsuccessfully introduced or developed.

For example, a developed enterprise social network was stopped by the works council just before the start due to data privacy issues that have not be considered before and have not been a problem in other countries. As a result, the start was postponed by two years.

Another example is a tablet-based commissioning system that failed after usage by a test user. The test user had been unsatisfied by the solutions and influenced his colleagues in not using it. The company had to rework the whole system in order to restore the acceptance with the system.

We claim that a digital assistance system should be discussed within an organization right from the beginning including three crucial perspectives: A solution should be strategized for the impact it has on the *business* and on the organization. It should be designed for the outcome that is generated by the *employees* and that can change their workflow. And it should be built for output using *technologies* that fit to the business goals as well as users? expectations.

Otherwise, we observed that crucial questions regarding digital assistance systems were asked late in the development process. For example, some of our business partners bought multiple smart glasses and tablet computers because they were interested in the technology. Only then did they ask in what scenarios they could use them. After spending lots of money and implementing first applications, the people in the project teams started to learn what they are doing and to ask crucial questions that did not come up before the implementation due to communications issues, e.g.:

- Is it fine to have shared smart glasses for augmented reality due to sanitation issues?
- How long is it suitable to wear smart glasses due to ergonomic aspects (e.g. neck muscular)?
- What about the liability of mobile devices in case of damages?
- Shall mobile devices be locked during breaks or after work?
- Shall we have a personal mobile devices or shall it be shared by the employees?
- How is accident protection organized, e.g. while using tablets or smart glasses in areas of forklift trucks or autonomous vehicles?

All these questions are able to interrupt or even to stop a project, but could have been avoided if people would have started earlier to talk and to discuss with each other. To enrich the communication between different people within a project or within an organization, we started to develop our canvas method, which shall also address further objectives.

3.2 Objectives

The authors present a method to foster the communication in early stages before buying or developing new software solutions: The Digital Assistance System Canvas. The canvas shall be a living document. It shall foster the discussion within multidisciplinary project teams (managers, works council, union workers, employees, IT, etc.) to uncover critical questions as well as crucial impacts on the workflow (e.g. changes on task responsibilities) as early as possible, and to remember the overall vision and these findings during the ongoing design and development. Therefore, we would like to address different objectives with the canvas:

- *Communication* is a crucial aspect in every organization and also when thinking about digital assistance of human workflows. The method shall foster the communications within teams to build the right system.
- *Participation* of all stakeholders (employee directly interacting with the system; employee that are affected by the system; employee that perceive itself to be affected by a decision, activity, or outcome) shall be supported. Stakeholders shall participate in every development stage starting with requirements elicitation in order to ensure an appropriate workplace design and individual acceptance. Human-centeredness shall be an integrated aspect in the design and development of assistance systems.
- *Interdisciplinary teams* shall be introduced comprising managers as well as workers, works council, etc. to deploy an appropriate digitization and to enable innovations through the employee. It shall support the organizational

change within the software-using organization and shall create a feeling of participation and decision on the employee level likewise. The decision-makers within an organization shall decide, which workflows they would like to digitize and in which way they would like to do this. They shall balance different perspectives with different objectives for a digitization. All perspectives shall be taken into account, to foresee possible impacts and to formulate a strategy, including key performance indicators (KPI) to ensure individual and organizational acceptance.

- *Acceptance* of digital assistance systems can be established in two ways. One way is to build a system that is suitable for the tasks. The more important one is to create acceptance through the process of participation. Both aspects shall be fostered by the method.
- *User needs elicitation* shall be enriched by the method through communication and visualization, since lots of implicit needs can only be communicated when the idea becomes tangible.
- A *shared vision* shall be created with the canvas concept and shall guide the team through the project so that the usability and user experience of the system can lead to more acceptance and usefulness.
- A *big picture* of dependencies of human workflows, organizational processes and existing systems shall be identified in advance to achieve a broader view of the organization and to enable an appropriate interaction and user experience of digitized assistance services.
- *Consolidated goals* shall be specified through the method so that they are visible for every stakeholder.
- As a *"companion"*, the canvas shall be used through the whole design and development process, and shall foster an ongoing reflection of assumptions made.

3.3   The Canvas Structure

The Digital Assistance System Canvas shall take three perspectives into account: Human (H), business (B), and technology (T). Therefore, it is structured into three parts (see Fig. 1).

Furthermore, the canvas is divided into five areas (see Fig. 2). Essentially, the canvas focusses on the employees that are the domain experts of their tasks as well as the users of assistance systems. They have to work with the systems every day and are crucial for the acceptance of digital assistance systems.

Following the framework of human-centered design for interactive systems [11], the part *Human* is divided in three areas, which focus on the employees (I), the working context with the tasks (II), and solution concepts with its impacts on work (III). The business investments and outcomes for the organization (IV) is focussed in the part *Business*, and the technological settings (V) are discussed in the part *Technology*.

Behind the three perspectives with its five areas, nine building blocks enriched with supporting questions represent the actual content of the canvas:

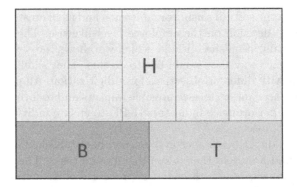

Fig. 1. Three perspectives: human, business, and technology

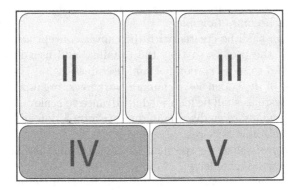

Fig. 2. Five areas of the canvas

1. *Employees/Users:* The employees of an organization and therefore the *users* of the digital assistance systems are represented in the first building block. There are a variety of characters when designing interactive systems in a work context. They have a different technology affinity and also different competencies or experiences. To increase the acceptance of interactive systems, it is necessary to think about what kinds of people work in the organization, who will be affected by the digitization project, what are their personal motivations and goals, or if there are any cultural challenges. In a manufacturing context, this could be, for example, workers, foremen, operations managers, the works councils, or even IT manager responsible for system integration.
2. *Work Context:* After identifying potentially relevant stakeholders, it is necessary to analyze the problem space and take a look at their job. Questions for discussions can be how a typical working day looks, which tasks have to be done, what kind of unplanned work influences the normal tasks, which particular behavior can be observed, if there are any workarounds used, or what current pain points are.

3. *Physical Environment:* In addition to the tasks, it is worthwhile to look at the physical environment in which the tasks are performed. Designing interactive systems, it is necessary to analyze the workplace and ask questions like how the workplace is structured, if the people have to walk between different workplaces, if there are any occupational safety requirements like gloves, protective goggles, or if their are any noise or light impairments. These information can be crucial in later technological considerations, e.g. is it possible to use touch interaction due to gloves, to use voice interaction due to noisy surroundings, or to use tablets in places without tray areas.

4. *Social Relationships:* Certain workflows require, for example, the release of supervisors or make collusion with colleagues necessary. Therefore, it is important to analyze social relations as well. Which employees have to work together, how does the kind of communication look like (e.g. direct interaction, information providing, reporting, approval procedures, work instructions), or how does the manner towards other employees look like, shall be questions of interest.

5. *Solution Idea:* Having analyzed the problem space, possible alternative solution concepts can be discussed. Therefore, it is necessary to decide on the tasks that should be supported by a system and to think about necessary preconditions, potential or natural inhibitors of the solutions, or if the solutions help to meet the core needs of the employees.

6. *Acceptance Criteria:* After sketching solution alternatives, a crucial step is to think about criteria that have to be addressed in order to create solutions that will be accepted by the employees. A possible model of acceptance criteria can be found in Fischer et al. [3].

7. *Impacts:* When deciding about systems that influence or change the work context, it is necessary to analyze the impacts of the solution ideas. Questions might be how activities or responsibilities will change, if there are other workplaces that will be affected by the solution as well, or if there might be any communication impacts.

8. *Business Invest & Revenue:* In addition to substantive questions, it is also necessary to consider what this means for the organization due to the organizational acceptance of the system. A major discussion point might be the financial invest as well as the expected added value (e.g. time saving, effectiveness, quality improvement, or flexibility). But also other questions about necessary or caused changes have to be considered: Do we have to change some mindsets first? Do we need to adapt the organizational culture? Do we need to change our business processes?

9. *Technology Setting:* Last but not least, the technological feasibility is crucial before starting the implementation of the solution. Therefore, decisions have to be made about technologies that can be used and how these technologies might fit to the overall system infrastructure. It is necessary to analyze which information are needed, from where the information can be obtained, and if the data quality is sufficient for the solution concepts.

3.4   Usage of the Canvas

The Digital Assistance System Canvas (see Fig. 3) is meant to be a communication instrument within workshops to bring together all relevant people and perspectives of an organization and project. It can be used in multiple ways:

1. *Initial Workshop:* This kind of workshop takes place in the early beginning of a project and lasts at least about four hours. The canvas can either be used to map the entire organization depending on its size or as commonly used to look at a defined area. There should be people with any experience levels participating from the trainee to the professional and from the shop floor to the management. Especially in larger organizations, it is recommended to involve the works council as well. The canvas is meant to be plotted on a large poster format (DIN A0 or 46.8 × 33.1 in.). Sticky notes are used to put the information on the canvas. One sticky note color shall be used for each modeled employee type. This way the colors can be used in the other building block to visualize the dependencies to employees of the first building block. They are flexible and can be moved over the poster during the workshop. If there are more then approx. ten people in the workshop, multiple canvases can be worked out in parallel in smaller groups with around 5–6 people. The canvases have to compared and merged at the end of the workshop to get an overall picture. The building blocks of the canvas have numbers from one to nine printed in the background. They define the journey of the participants during the workshop.

2. *Follow-up Workshops:* The canvas is meant to be a living instrument. Hanging in the meeting or project room, it can be continuously enriched with further details or even specific models of the different perspectives. Techniques from usability engineering can be used to analyze and specify the context of use, e.g. personas [12] detail the employees building block, context models [13] or flow models [14] detail the work context and the social relationships. Techniques from the business domain can be used to analyze and specify the business invest, risks and outcome, e.g. SWOT analysis [15], key performance indicators [16], etc. Techniques from software engineering can be used to specify the technology setting, e.g. UML [17], IFML [18], software architectures, etc. The new findings can then be discussed in further workshops from time to time having the overall big picture visible all the time.

3. *Comparative Workshops:* The project team will learn while doing the project. At some point it might be helpful to hang the existing canvas aside and to start with a blank canvas and an initial workshop to see how the ideas and assumptions have changed over time.

As shown, the digital assistance system canvas is versatile and foster the communication with the organization. Especially the idea of a comparative workshop with a blank canvas came up during one of our workshop sessions.

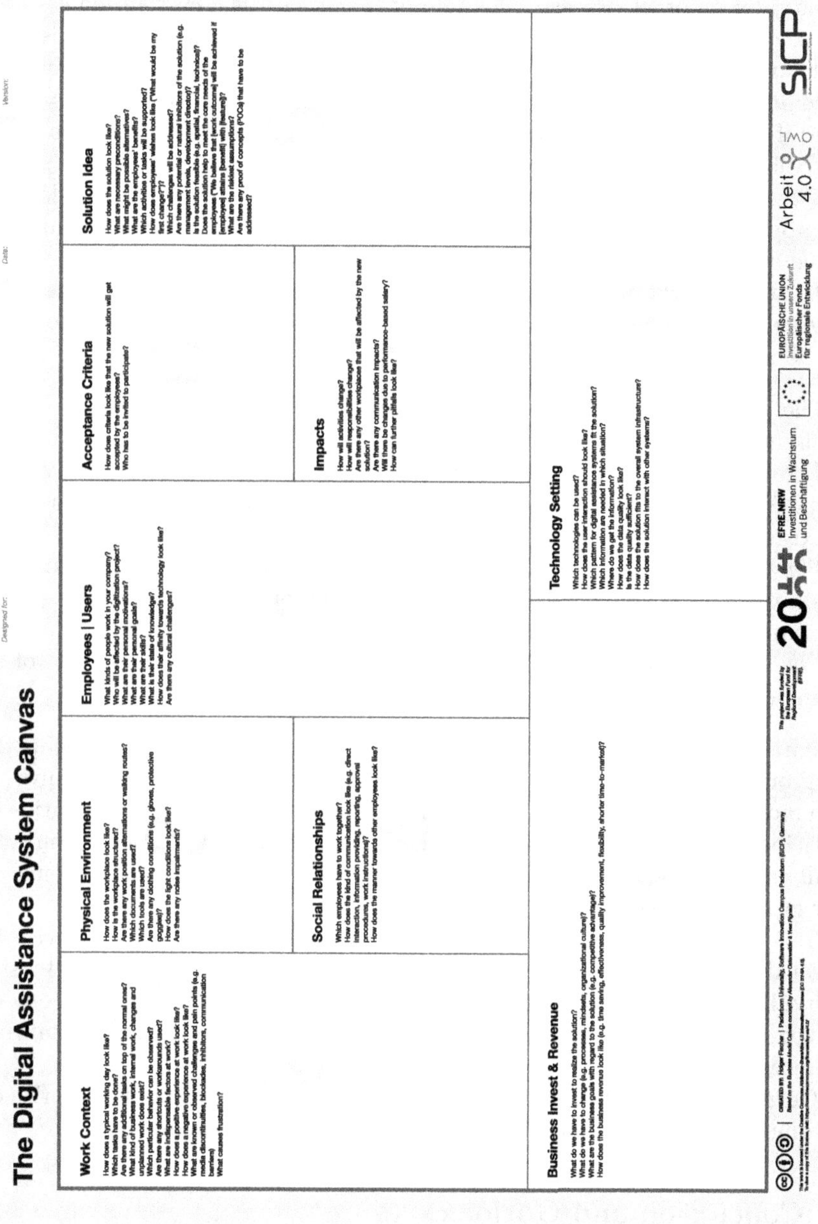

Fig. 3. Digital assistance system canvas (download: http://bit.ly/DASCanvas)

3.5 Evaluation

So far we have evaluated the concept of the canvas within focus group workshops with about ten practitioners each. Thereby, we described an easy to understand scenario for an order process. The item of the order was a customized cake at a cake shop. The story was told to the workshop participants and they discussed digitization potentials and impacts on the work. We observed their discussions while performing an initial two hours canvas workshop. We asked them to think aloud if any questions occur concerning the canvas. Afterwards, we did a review and collected feedback of the group of participants.

Overall, the canvas was very well received and all participants understood and appreciated the idea. The participants started to discuss the scenario and placed sticky notes all over the canvas without having obvious problems.

In addition, the participants started to develop further use scenarios of the canvas during the review part of the workshops. They figured out that the canvas can be used in various situations:

1. The problem is clearly understood and defined and the canvas is used to discuss the solution ideas.
2. The solution idea is already existing and the canvas is used to detail or validate the feasibility of the solution, or to check if better alternative solutions might exist.
3. The canvas is used to identify the work space that the organization would like to digitally support. Therefore, multiple potential solutions exists and are compared with each other.
4. The canvas is used to identify overall digitization potentials of an organization.

Furthermore, the participants discussed if only one canvas should be used in the group or if multiple canvases would be helpful to either have one canvas for each modeled employee or for each identified solution idea. As an alternative the participants discussed to improve the method by starting with the identification of all employees and edit all other building blocks step by step with only one user group after another.

Talking about iterations of the canvas, the participants came up with the above described concept of a comparative workshop. Their idea was to start with a blank canvas and review the result with the previous canvas. The newly worked-out knowledge either might lead to further ideas or it might confirmed the already existing ones.

Currently, the applicability of the canvas is evaluated using it in workshops with multidisciplinary teams within manufacturing companies.

4 Conclusion and Outlook

Summing up, the aim of this paper is to enrich the communication among the project team and the quality when designing and developing digital assistance systems. Current established requirements techniques like observations or contextual interviews seems to be insufficient. People as well as hierarchies in larger organization shall learn from each other to create individual as well as organizational acceptance during the project and not afterwards.

Therefore, the concept of the digital assistance system canvas has been presented. It shall foster the envisioning, the big picture as well as the visible concept during the ongoing project, and ensure the participation of the people that have to work the system. The canvas equally addresses the human, the organizational and the technological perspective. It discusses the employees, their tasks, their work environment and the social relations, and contrasts it with the solutions ideas and their acceptance criteria as well as impacts.

Existing canvas concepts have been analyzed regarding their focus on human-centered quality characteristics. Several finished projects have been reviewed to identify important questions and crucial pitfalls. The canvas has been created based on these findings. Focus group workshops with practitioners have been carried out to evaluate the concept of the canvas. Overall, the results show that the canvas was received by the participants very well and that participants communicated at eye level.

Future work will contain further evaluations to validate the practical feasibility within digitization projects. The canvas is thought of as an agile companion within the project which continuously reflects the mindset. As it can only be enriched by the use of further techniques, it has to be proven if the visibility of the solution concepts during the project will be supported by the canvas.

The canvas addresses software solutions in the B2B area that focus on assistance in work situations. It has not been developed to address software solutions in the B2C area, e.g. e-commerce web applications. It would be interesting to evaluate if the canvas can be used for such solutions, too.

Acknowledgement. This work was partially funded by the European Fund for Regional Development (EFRE) within the projects "Arbeit 4.0 - Lösungen für die Arbeitswelt der Zukunft" (en. "Work 4.0 - Solutions for the future workplace") (funding code: *34.EFRE-0300029*) and "Business 4.0 - Neue Geschäftsmodelle und Wertschöpfungsketten mit IKT" (en. "Business 4.0 - New business models and value chains with ICT.") (funding code: *34.EFRE-0300028*).

References

1. German Federal Ministry of Labour and Social Affairs (BMAS): Re-Imagining Work - Green Paper Work 4.0 (2015). http://www.bmas.de/SharedDocs/Down loads/DE/PDF-Publikationen/arbeiten-4-0-green-paper.pdf. Accessed February 2018
2. German Federal Ministry for Economic Affairs and Energy (BMWi): Monitoring Report Digital Economy (2014). www.bmwi.de/EN/Service/publications, did=686950.html. Accessed February 2018
3. Fischer, H., Engler, M., Sauer, S.: A human-centered perspective on software quality: acceptance criteria for work 4.0. In: Marcus, A., Wang, W. (eds.) DUXU 2017. LNCS, vol. 10288, pp. 570–583. Springer, Cham (2017). https://doi.org/10.1007/978-3-319-58634-2_42

4. Morgan, J.: The Future of Work - Attract New Talent, Build Better Leaders, and Create a Competitive Organization. Wiley, Hoboken (2014)
5. Johnson, J.: CHAOS 2014. The Standish Group, New York (2014)
6. Sage Software GmbH: Independent Study on IT investments (2014). http://goo.gl/qy0eM0. Accessed February 2018
7. Osterwalder, A., Pigneur, Y.: Business Model Generation-A Handbook for Visionaries, Game Changers, and Challengers. Wiley, Hoboken (2010)
8. Stampfl, G.: The Process of Business Model Innovation - An Empirical Exploration. Springer, Wiesbaden (2016). https://doi.org/10.1007/978-3-658-11266-0
9. Patton, J.: Opportunity canvas (2016). http://jpattonassociates.com/opportunity-canvas/ Accessed February 2018
10. Gothelf, J.: The Lean UX canvas (2016). http://www.jeffgothelf.com/blog/leanuxcanvas/. Accessed February 2018
11. ISO 9241–210: Ergonomics of human-system interaction - Part 210: Human-centred design for interactive systems (2010)
12. Cooper, A.: The Inmates are Running the Asylum. Macmillan Publishing Co., Inc., Indianapolis (1998)
13. Holtzblatt, K., Beyer, H.: Contextual Design - Design for Life, 2nd edn. Morgan Kaufmann, Cambridge (2017)
14. Fischer, H., Rose, M., Yigitbas, E.: Towards a task driven approach enabling continuous user requirements engineering. In: Joint Proceedings of the REFSQ 2016 Co-Located Events, 2nd Workshop on Continuous Requirements Engineering (CRE), vol. 1564. CEUR-WS (2016)
15. Kotler, P., Berger, R., Rickhoff, N.: The Quintessence of Strategic Management. Springer, Berlin (2010). https://doi.org/10.1007/978-3-642-14544-5
16. Kaplan, R.S., Norton, D.P.: The Balanced Scorecard - Measures That Drive Performance, pp. 71–79. Harvard Business Review, Boston (1992). issue January–February
17. Object Management Group (OMG): Unified Modeling Language (UML). http://www.omg.org/spec/UML/. Accessed February 2018
18. Object Management Group (OMG): Interaction Flow Modeling Language (IFML). https://www.omg.org/spec/IFML/. Accessed February 2018

A Systematic Literature Review
for Human-Computer Interaction and Design
Thinking Process Integration

Hye Park[(✉)] and Seda McKilligan

Iowa State University, Ames, IA, USA
{hjpark, seda}@iastate.edu

Abstract. Human-computer interaction (HCI) has been challenged in recent years because of advanced technology requiring adoption of new applications and investigations of connection with other disciplines, to enhance its theoretical knowledge. Design thinking (DT), an innovative and creative problem solving process, provides potential answers to the kind of knowledge and techniques designers can bring into HCI. This paper reports a systematic review of comparison between HCI design process and DT process. A total of 72 peer-reviewed research papers were reviewed published between 1972 and 2017 towards answering the following question: *How do HCI and DT processes overlap, differ, and can learn from each other?* Synthesizing the findings revealed a description and taxonomy of the variations, success factors, and practices between the two problem solving processes. The review highlights shared process phases with different goals in each suggesting that the two domains could complement each other in various ways, for applications in academia and industry.

Keywords: Human-computer interaction · Design thinking
Systematic review

1 Introduction

Human-computer interaction (HCI) has been considered as computer-related cross-disciplinary domain that is strongly associated with design for information, interaction, and communication and technology [6, 16, 25, 26, 42, 51, 62]. Researchers in HCI are frequently involved in designing research prototypes based on theories from the cognitive and social sciences, anthropology, and sociology in addition to computer science. They equally focus on HCI research [25] and the analytic approaches and techniques in design practice [6, 7, 29, 60]. However, there is a lack of clarity regarding the nature of design processes involved in this influential field and the role of design and design thinking in HCI research and practice.

HCI education and practice have been facing many challenges triggered by the rapid advancement of technology [17]. Fast changing interface and interaction systems require new processes that allow for rapidly developed designs, evaluations, and interaction strategies facilitating efficient and unique user interactions with computer systems [65]. This emphasizes the continuous change that the HCI discipline has to go

© Springer International Publishing AG, part of Springer Nature 2018
A. Marcus and W. Wang (Eds.): DUXU 2018, LNCS 10918, pp. 725–740, 2018.
https://doi.org/10.1007/978-3-319-91797-9_50

through to adopt the challenge of 'speed' [17, 32]. How can HCI design process be morphed into a more flexible process allowing for creative design explorations, in a rapid manner? One approach to address this question might be an integration with a process valued for its effective problem-solution exploration [14, 21, 27, 52, 61]: Design thinking.

Design thinking (DT) has gained increased interest in the past decade [12, 38, 47, 48]. According to Brown [10], DT is a "human-centered, creative, iterative, and practical approach to finding the best ideas and ultimate solutions" with innovative activities, proving itself as an effective strategy for organizational changes [10]. These character-istics allow DT to be used widely in diverse contexts [44, 45, 49, 57] as well as creating and making choices [49]. Also, DT allows involving various disciplines to address complex problems and enhance user experience [8, 46, 69] emphasizing human values [16].

This paper describes a systematic literature review conducted on potential DT and HCI process integration. The objective of this review is to focus on where the varia-tions between the two processes exist and why, with the goal of proposing how these variations could be translated and transformed into each other. This work provides a considerable body of literature that is of great potential importance to design research in both HCI and other design domains. The research questions are: (1) How do HCI and DT design processes overlap? (2) How does the HCI design process differ from DT design process? and (3) What are the lessons HCI and DT could learn from each other's processes?

2   Human-Computer Interaction Process

HCI is concerned with methods and tools for the development of human-computer interfaces, assessing the usability of computer systems [56] and with broader human-centric issues including how people interact with computers [19]. It is based on theories about how humans process information and interact with technology and other people in social contexts where computers are used, placing HCI designers at the heart of a system interaction between human and machine [31, 37]. This interaction also brings design knowledge into the context, such as visual hierarchy, color, and typography [71].

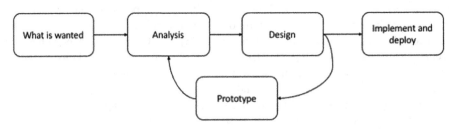

Fig. 1. HCI design process [19].

The first step in the HCI process, what is wanted, focuses on investigating user's needs and their lifestyles to provide insights on how the HCI designers can generate interactive solutions to match the user's needs [19, 62]. Some suggested tools for this exploration phase are interviewing the user, recording the user's behavior, observing user's world directly, and analyzing existing documents [19].

Analysis step emphasizes synthesizing the main issues coming from the first step and provides directions to the next step, design [19]. The main goal of this phase is to solve problems while bringing usability factors and practices into the process [19]. As designers' progress towards the goal of the ideal solution, they develop prototypes to analyze the quality of their solutions using guidelines such as Shneiderman's eight golden rules, guidelines like heuristics, and Norman's seven and Nielsen's 10 design principles. These guidelines are used to enhance the solution's usability and interaction with the targeted users [19]. Paper-based designs, storyboards, video presentation, and cardboard mockup are created as early forms of prototypes [19, 62]. Next step is integrating physical device and software where HCI researchers rely on guidelines to assess design violations while users interact with the solutions in their own environment [19]. Prototypes are often treated as restricted presentations of a design and used for testing the solutions effectiveness with the users [62]. This design evaluation phase helps the HCI designers to find problems and gives them an opportunity to address it in early steps of development [19]. Once the prototype is proven to be effective and functional, the design is implemented and deployed to market [19].

3 Design Thinking Process

Design thinking (DT) offers a systematic, exciting direction for creative problem solution, by integrating human, business and technical factors [11, 16, 22, 23, 58] with a focus on building innovative solutions relying on user-centered perspective [9, 10, 52, 65, 67]. An increasing number of companies and institutions, from industry giants like IBM to startups like Airbnb, have adopted this user-centric innovation method, along with accompanying mindsets and toolkits.

Design thinking originated from processes used by designers, such as user understanding and user experience. In recent years, its application has been extended to address wider problems – ways for companies and other groups to identify new strategic directions, innovate new service possibilities, or implement procedural change. DT has a non-linear process steps with iterative loops [9, 20, 35, 55, 67], and each step includes various tools that achieve each goal [55, 67]. Although these principles, perspectives and general outline of the process are similar across different visual representations, because DT adopts Simon's [63] model widely [35], specific steps including tools might differ [9, 21, 35, 54, 68].

Design thinking rests on defining different stages of innovation - discovering and describing problems via processes to connect with users and frame challenges. This inspiration evolves into stages of ideation and prototyping; opportunities for solution

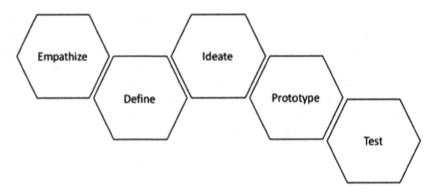

Fig. 2. Design thinking process [55].

can then be tested and refined, to result in final implementation. Five-steps including empathize, define, ideate, prototype, and test introduced by the Hasso-Plattner Institute of Design at Stanford (d.school) [55]. Empathy is the key principle for this process as it builds on understanding users, their needs, motivations, emotions, and experiences [35, 50, 55, 68], through observations and contextual inquiries [35] and interviewing activities [50].

The aim of define step is to generate meaningful problem statements [55] based on the information and insights gathered and built through the empathize stage, and analyzed and framed to reflect the objective [35, 50]. The ideate step is often referred to as the "creative" step [68] where many alternative ideas are generated [9] through brainstorming, brainwriting, and visualization activities [35, 68].

Generated ideas (solutions) are then transferred into quick prototypes [50, 68]. This step is an experimental phase, and to goal is to investigate what works and doesn't work to inform the ideate phase once again [50]. Through inexpensive or downscaled versions of the prototypes [10, 35, 55] designers derive useful feedback [55]. Prototypes can take various forms, such as videos, role-playing activities, post-it notes, or storyboards to communicate the message to the user, to observe their interaction with the proposed solutions in different ways and to refine the solutions [35, 55].

In the test step, real users evaluate the prototypes and provide feedback about why the prototype is satisfactory and not satisfactory [50, 68]. This is another chance to understand users and improve provided solutions [5, 55]. These feedback loops allow designers to go back to previous steps [68]. Design thinking, in nature, is iterative, rather than a linear process. Although these five steps are practiced; the order changes based on the context of the problem and in many cases designers go back to collecting additional insights or reframing their problem statements based on what they observe in the interaction with the prototypes. In this paper, our goal is to describe specific features practiced in the two user-centered design processes and identify the touch-points they can interact and complement.

4   Research Methodology

The role of systematic review is to investigate, evaluate, and interpret all potential researches related to specific research questions, interests, or themes [40]. Our approach for a systematic review in HCI and DT processes was informed by the three stages suggested by Kitchenham [40]: (1) planning, (2) execution and (3) results analysis. This review was conducted by a researcher with a background in visual design and HCI, with input from a design thinking researcher.

4.1   Planning

As stated previously, the review focused on the how the human-computer interaction design process was practiced compared to the design thinking process. Only studies focusing on these two topics were included. In the initial 'planning' phase, we reviewed 14 articles that focused on systematic literature review of concepts close to HCI and DT, including engineering design, design education, and interaction design. Our goal with this phase was to identify the selection and exclusion criteria commonly that would be most suitable for our purposes of a comparative review analysis. Table 1 shows the synthesis of this review process, each paper's extraction criteria, keywords used for inclusion, number of papers reviewed, and process of finding the papers.

Table 1. Reviewed papers.

Author(s)	Discipline(s) reviewed	Keywords used to identify papers for review	Number of papers reviewed	Process of finding the papers
Agrawal et al. [2]	HCI and IS	HCI, computer-mediated communication, and literature review	32	EBSCO and publisher databases were used with keyword search to identify appropriate papers
Akoumianakis and Stephanidis [3]	HCI and universal design	Namely, guidelines, user interface development frameworks and architectures, user interface software technologies, and support actions	N/A	N/A
Aryana and Øritsland [4]	HCI and science	Culture, mobile HCI, design, and review	40	Concept-matrix, which make category with presented concepts of papers was used
Baines et al. [5]	Lean, product design, engineering, and development	Lean, new product development, review, and design	24	Keywords and phrases search were used, and then reviewed every article
Carter et al. [13]	HCI and player-computer interaction (PCI)	HCI, game studies, and paradigms	178	Open and axial coding processes were used to examine number of papers with PCI domain. Then, focused on discovered papers' methodological and conceptual approaches introduced at CHI conference

(*continued*)

Table 1. (*continued*)

Author(s)	Discipline(s) reviewed	Keywords used to identify papers for review	Number of papers reviewed	Process of finding the papers
de Almeida Neris et al. [18]	Sustainability and HCI	Sustainability, systematic review, and HCI	51	Systematic review was applied to discover relative papers of a research question
Eng et al. [24]	Engineering design	Hypermedia, graph, diagram, complexity, design flow, and visual literacy	N/A	Qualitative perspective with mixed methods like observation and interview was considered to gather relative papers
Hayes and Games [30]	Computer software, computer games, education, and design thinking	Video games, learning, thinking, game design, and software	N/A	N/A
Insfran and Fernandez [34]	Usability evaluation	Usability evaluation methods, web development, and systematic review	51	Systematic review was applied to discover relative papers of a research question
Johansson-Sköldberg et al. [38]	Design thinking	Design thinking, design, and thinking	168	Keyword search was used to collect papers. Then, organized papers with list: academic and practitioner journal articles, refereed conference papers associated with DT. Frequently mentioned papers were also considered
Kjeldskov and Paay [41]	HCI and interaction design	Research methods, research purpose literature survey, introductory and survey, design, and human factors	55	The literature survey method was adopted
Li [43]	HCI	Affective state assessment, user modeling, intelligent assistance, and HCI	N/A	N/A
Rosli et al. [59]	HCI and interaction design	Interaction design, design issues, and HCI	32	Coding process including content analysis process, words, concepts, themes, phrases, characters or sentences were applied
Ugras et al. [70]	Usability and website	Usability, user experience, website, systematic review, research trends, and web design	199	Systematic review was applied to discover relative papers of a research question. keyword search was used to collect papers

The 14 reviewed papers demonstrated that HCI and DT have been adopted in various disciplines particularly in designing games, products, systems and other user experiences. Additionally, the articles guided us in exploring strategies to find and analyze relevant papers in literature; the reviewed articles used similar processes where majority of them adopted "keywords search" to search for papers and applied systematic review method for analysis articles. Therefore, our search strategy and article selection process replicated the 14 publications we reviewed, following a "keywords search" methodology [2, 5, 13, 38, 70].

4.2 Execution

Literature was initially gathered through searches of major design, engineering, and computer science databases (e.g., ACM Digital Library, Technology Research Database) conducted between September 5, 2017 and December 5, 2017. Search terms are presented are presented below. Table 1 shows the eligibility assessment of the chosen articles against four inclusion criteria.

- HCI/ Human-Computer Interaction and Design thinking;
- HCI/ Human-Computer Interaction and Design thinking review;
- HCI/ Human-Computer Interaction review;
- Design thinking review;
- HCI/ Human-Computer Interaction design process;
- Design thinking process;
- Design process;
- Comparison of HCI/ Human-Computer Interaction and Design thinking process.

Table 2. Inclusion criteria.

No.	Criteria
1	Article must be published in English
2	If a conference paper, article must be published in 10 years
3	Article must report original research
4	Article must focus on HCI, DT, engineering design, interaction design, design approaches, or user-centered design
5	Article must either focus on processes of HCI, or DT, or both

Articles included in the review are denoted with * in the reference list at the end of the paper. Key characteristics of the articles are summarized below:

- The oldest article was published in 1972, and the newest in 2017. Seventy-eight percent of the reviewed articles were published in the last 10 years.
- The rate of HCI related papers were 46% and DT related articles were 51% for this study.
- Half of HCI papers (61%) were focused on design research and practice, and Majority of DT articles (92%) reporting the design thinking process and its impact and value were published in the last 30 years.
- Only 5.5% of studies focused on both HCI and DT in the last 10 years.
- Eighteen percent of the articles reported studies on *process* either HCI or DT.

In total, 72 papers published between 1972 and 2017 were considered in this study. Our major journal resources included Design Studies, Design Issues, and Computers in Human Behavior. We also included HCII and CHI papers, which are well-known international conferences in the HCI domain. In this study, 22 published journals, 26 peer-reviewed conference papers, 15 books, 3 magazine articles, 5 articles from design and HCI research organizations, and 1 technical report were involved. In results analysis phase, 72 studies were reviewed again and categorized based on their major themes or issues.

4.3   Results Analysis

Collectively, articles were found to reflect on design viewpoints on the nature of design processes taking place in the two domains: engineering, design, education, healthcare, etc.

Understanding of HCI design process is critical as it is becoming core aspect of system development process to improve and enhance systems and to satisfy users' needs and necessities. Having a clarity about this process will likely allow the stakeholders to be on the same page regarding the criteria to follow and the setting the expected outcomes from the HCI design team. Table 3 presents HCI process steps and the keywords used to define each phase, from the paper reviewed in this study. A description and taxonomy of the variations, success factors, and practices were reported. Some process models are focused on engineering design [14, 64] whereas others' emphasis is more on interaction design [62], and user-centered design process.

Table 3. A comparison of HCI design process models.

Models	Step 1	Step 2	Step 3	Step 4	Step 5	Step 6
Cross [15]	**Exploration**	**Generation**	**Evaluation**	**Communication**		
Dix et al. [19]	**What is wanted** (requirements) • Find out what is currently happening • Interviewing • Videotaping • Looking at documents, objects that they work with • Observing directly	**Analysis** • The result of observation and interview • Scenarios • Rich stories of interaction	**Design** • Rules • Guidelines • Design principles • Modeling and describing interaction	**Prototype** • Evaluate design	**Implement & deploy** • Writing code • Making hardware • Writing documentation and manuals	
ISO 9241-210 [36]	**Identifying the need** • System must encompass the specified: functional, organizational, and user requirements	**Observe & analysis** • Understand and specify the user context	**Design** • Specify the user requirements	**Prototype** • Produce design solutions to meet user requirements	**User feedback** • Evaluate designs against requirements	
Sharp et al. [62]	**Identifying needs & establishing requirements** for the UX	**Developing alternative designs** that meet those requirements	**Building interactive versions of the designs** so that they can be communicated and assessed	**Evaluating** what is being built throughout the process and the user experience it offers		
Tayal [64]	**Understand the need** • Detecting problem • Understanding project requirements • Detecting limitations • Understanding users • Establishing goal • Gathering information and conducting research • Involving people from different backgrounds	**Imagine** • Brainstorming • Being creative • Investigating existing technologies and methods to use • Exploring, comparing, and analyzing possible solutions	**Select a design** • Selecting the most promising idea	**Plan** • Planning for how to evaluate, analysis, and test	**Create** • Building a prototype and test • Analyzing and finding what could be improved	**Improve** • Revision • Iteration

There were notable findings from the six models in Table 1. The models suggested to understand requirements, generate designs that reach the requirements, and evaluate selected design. These commonalities among the models emphasizes designing computer systems that support people so that they can carry out their activities productively and safely, and understanding and creating software and other technology that people will want to use, will be able to use, and will find effective when used [37]. In other words, HCI process supports users in terms of achieving their goals successfully [37]. Although the process titles across the models vary, when looked at the descriptions and key purposes, the objective to achieve in each step were alike.

Table 4. A comparison of design thinking process models.

Models	Step 1	Step 2	Step 3	Step 4	Step 5
Adams and Nash [1]	**Empathize & define** • Understanding users		**Ideate** • Brainstorming	**Prototype** • Building and testing	
Brown [10]	**Inspiration** • Problem framing • Contextual observations • Involves diverse disciplines		**Ideate** • Sketches • Scenarios • Involving customers • Prototype • Test	**Implementation** • Spread across the world	
Culén [17]	**Empathy/context**	**Define**	**Ideate**	**Prototype**	**Evaluate**
Dam and Siang [35]	**Empathize** • Empathic understanding of the problem • Observing	**Define** • Defining the problem • Synthesizing observations	**Ideate** • Brainstorming • Brainwriting	**Prototype** • Adopting a hands-on approach in prototyping	**Test** • Developing a prototype/solution to the problem
Gibbons [50]	**Understand (empathize & define)** • Developing knowledge • Talking with users • Observing users		**Explore (ideate & prototype)** • Brainstorming • Creative ideas	**Materialize (test & implement)** • Transform an aspect of the end user's life	
IDEO (n. d.) [33]	**Gather inspiration** • Discovering what people really need		**Generate ideas** • Push past obvious solutions	**Make ideas tangible** • Build rough prototypes	**Share the story** • Craft a human story to inspire others toward action
Pandey [53]	**Problem identification**	**Problem & context discovery** • Ecosystem mapping • Design ethnography	**Synthesis** • Affinity mapping (grouping data)	**Ideation** • Sketching	**Prototype** • Storyboarding • Rapid prototyping
Plattner [55]	**Empathize** • Observing • Engaging • Watching and listening	**Define** • Provide focus and frames the problem • Inspire team • Inform criteria for evaluating competing ideas	**Ideate** • Generate the broadest range of possibilities • Step beyond obvious solutions and thus increase the innovation potential of solution set • Uncover unexpected areas of exploration	**Prototype** • Build to think and test to learn • To ideate and problem-solve • Communicate and conversation • Fail quickly and cheaply	**Test** • Refine prototypes and solutions • Refine point-of-view

Table 4 shows the eight models commonly referred to in the literature when DT process was applied or described. Some models grouped several steps [1, 10, 50] instead of listing all phases, but the basic purposes and concept of steps were the same. The eight models demonstrated that DT not only focuses on user-centeredness through understanding users with empathy but also pursues possible solutions with creative and innovative approaches. Creative design activities like abstraction laddering, mapping techniques including journey mapping and concept mapping, low-fidelity prototyping and various visualization and communication techniques were suggested to generate and explore solutions. Although only three models [10, 33, 50] described *Implement* phase, they highlighted the importance of translating ideas (solutions) into the user's world, successfully (Fig. 1), (Table 2).

5 Commonalities, Differences, and Lessons Between HCI and DT Processes

We detailed the results of the systematic review analysis regarding our three research questions, as follows. The notable findings from the result were reported in Table 5.

Overall, the two processes showed similarities to discover and solve the problem with iterative process. Particularly, *prototype* phase presented the same purpose to change idea (solution) into interactive systems. Although there are commonalities, the two domains illustrated dissimilarities that HCI and DT processes pursued different perspectives to approach their goals in each phase excepting *prototype*. Commonalities and differences of two processes showed potential possibilities to integrate and support each other (Fig. 2).

Table 5. Commonalities, differences, and lessons between HCI and DT processes.

	HCI	DT
Commonalities	• Similar concepts and principles in each step: understanding users with observing and interviewing techniques, defining issues from analysis, designing/generating ideas (solutions), prototyping, and testing • Iterative process • Purpose of prototype	
Differences	• Understanding users as requirements • Analysis for further interpretation • Design with rules, guidelines, design principles • Implementation for 'real' system	• Understanding users with empathy • Define for interpretation of insights gathered from users • Ideation with creative design activities • Implementation (testing) for translating the solution into user's life
Lessons	• Potential to learn DT's empathy • Potential to learn DT's design ethnography and mapping technology to detect issues and context • Potential to learn DT's design activities to generate creative solutions • Potential to learn DT's holistic approach	• Potential to learn HCI's systematic ideation steps through rules, guidelines, and principles

5.1   How Do HCI and DT Design Processes Overlap?

HCI design and DT processes shared similar goals and steps in their processes: understanding and observing users to determine problems, ideation, and prototyping and testing as well as pursuing iteration process for refining ideas [16, 72]. Figure 3 presents a visualized diagram of the steps that are involved in overlapped HCI and DT processes. Although HCI and DT's concepts of the first step were different, recommended techniques were rather close to each other: observing users directly and indirectly, conducting field studies, interviewing, video-recording to understand users, discovering user's needs, developing relevant knowledge, and detecting problems [10, 19, 33, 35, 50, 55].

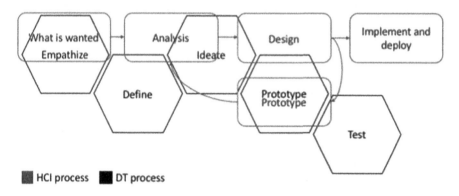

Fig. 3. Overlapped HCI and DT processes.

Particularly, the *prototype* step targeted the same objective for both HCI and DT: transferring ideas or concept solutions into tangible forms [33]. The major goal of prototype is to discover the best ideas that can be a solution of problem and respond to the users' needs through evaluating a design [19, 35]. Early prototyping is achieved through inexpensive and simple materials to communicate the concept [10, 19, 35, 55] then, software version was considered if it is necessary [19].

5.2   How Does the HCI Design Process Differ from DT Design Process?

Although overall processes of HCI and DT showed similarities, each step described different principles. The first phase in HCI process is often referred to as the process to *understand users as requirements* [19, 62]. However, DT process stressed *building empathy* with the users, rather than using the knowledge built to create requirements to inform the rest of the process [1, 17, 35, 50, 55]. The second step of HCI is *analysis* [19, 62] while this phase is often referred to as *define* in DT process [1, 17, 35, 50, 55]. Although first phases function alike, *analysis* is described as detailed examination of the elements as a basis for further interpretation, whereas *define* phase includes problem framing-structuring-iterating activities in order to interpret the insights gathered from the user.

HCI used term *design* as the third step, which can be considered as a main stage to move from what is wanted to how to do it [19]. To build interactive design, HCI as a profession requires to follow rules and guidelines, including Shneiderman's eight golden rules, Norman's seven and Nielsen's 10 design principles, and heuristics [19]. On the other hand, DT uses the term *ideate* [1, 10, 35, 50, 53] which facilitates design iterations encouraging to search for possible solutions through creative design thinking tools to explore the solution space in full capacity [1, 10, 35, 50, 53, 55]. *Prototype* step did not show any differences between the two domains.

The last step, *implementation*, in HCI calls for preparing code, hardware, and relevant documents and manuals that'd go into a 'real' system [19]. DT refers to this phase as *testing* for transforming the design solution to user's life (human) [50] through marketplace [10]. In summary, although the process steps are very much alike between the two domains, the emphasis for HCI process is on analyzing, evaluating and testing the solutions, DT process relies heavily on users' perceptions of the artefact through deep observation and inquiries [10] with holistic view and innovative approaches [16, 52, 65, 72].

5.3   What Are the Lessons HCI and DT Could Learn from Each Other's Process?

HCI and DT's similar and different process (see Fig. 3) perspectives allow to integrate and support each other. As an initial step of *what is wanted, empathize, and define* from HCI and DT process share the similar techniques such as interviewing and observing [19, 35, 50, 55] to understand their target users and current problems. However, they have different concepts to study their users. This gap can provide opportunity to support each other. HCI can learn from DT as it places the user in the center and heavily relies on building empathy. Since empathy can bring creative ideas and input various experiences into different user groups, it would support HCI design, which focuses on collecting data as requirement [39] to have creative approach.

Analysis step of HCI would be interrelated with *define* step as well. The role of *analysis* in HCI and *define* in DT is to analyze the result of user observations and interviews and other contextual data gathered to define and discover insights and the issues [19, 35, 53, 55] to understand user group. *Analysis* in HCI can learn from DT's focus on design ethnography and mapping technology [53] discovering problems and context, method of encouraging and inspiring teams, and building criteria for selecting best ideas to evaluate [55].

Design phase of HCI and *ideate* stage of DT could easily be morphed into each other. *Design* phase in HCI requires following the principles and guidelines that are standardized for HCI process across diverse practitioners [19]. Whereas *ideate* phase in DT doesn't follow guidelines; however, it focuses on exploring the solution space in depth while generating many alternatives as potential solutions to the problem at hand, without evaluating [55]. In this scenario, the design phase in HCI could practice similar creative approaches with the goal of generating diverse solutions instead of heavily relying on principles and standards, and DT could practice systematic ideation steps and potentially explore principles to follow for certain design cases, through adopting guidelines and standards.

For the overall design process, HCI and DT considered different aspects to solve problems. DT's non-linear process allows to refine diverse set of concepts [72] while promoting innovativeness [16]. In addition, the holistic approach of DT offers possibilities to generate several potential solutions with broad perspectives in different ways, whereas non-holistic aspect of HCI is restricted to generate solutions in various viewpoints [65, 66]. These different perspectives can encourage HCI to learn DT's innovative non-linear process-oriented method with holistic approach [9, 10, 20, 35, 52, 55, 65, 67] to enhance entire HCI design process.

6 Conclusion

Human-computer interaction, as a discipline, addresses human-centeredness and collaboration of cross-disciplinary fields [6, 16, 25, 26, 42, 51, 62] to understand users and contextual use of solutions [16, 62]. However, rapidly changing technology generates challenges to HCI practice such as fail to introduce updated design for new product [16, 17, 28]. Design Thinking process has been widely used as an innovative and user-oriented approach [9, 10, 67] to solve wicked problems with many diverse applications [11, 12, 16, 38, 58]. Overall, HCI and DT shared similar steps with iterative process: understanding and observing users to determine problems, designing/ideation, prototyping and testing. However, each step has specific principles, determining the tools to use, and the goals to achieve. HCI requires understanding users to build requirements, applying design rules and principles for design, and focuses largely on designing software. On the contrary, DT highlights building empathy to understand users, design activities to generate ideas/solutions, and encourages the solutions to be translated into user's life. This study suggests that although the two disciplines follows alike procedures, there are lessons each can take and apply from the other.

References

1. Adams, C., Nash, J.B.: Exploring design thinking practices in evaluation. J. Multi. Eval. **12** (26), 12–17 (2016). *
2. Agrawal, A., Boese, M.J., Sarker, S.: A review of the HCI literature in IS: the missing links of computer-mediated communication, culture, and interaction. In: AMCIS, p. 523 (2010). *
3. Akoumianakis, D., Stephanidis, C.: Universal design in HCI: a critical review of current research and practice. In: Engineering and Construction, p. 754 (1989)
4. Aryana, B., Øritsland, T.A.: Culture and mobile HCI: a review. In: Norddesign 2010 Conference, pp. 217–226 (2010). *
5. Baines, T., Lightfoot, H., Williams, G.M., Greenough, R.: State-of-the-art in lean design engineering: a literature review on white collar lean. Proc. Inst. Mech. Eng. Part B: J. Eng. Manuf. **220**(9), 1539–1547 (2006). *
6. Bellotti, V., Shum, S.B., MacLean, A., Hammond, N.: Multidisciplinary modelling in HCI design… in theory and in practice. In: Proceedings of the SIGCHI Conference on Human Factors in Computing Systems, pp. 146–153. ACM Press/Addison-Wesley Publishing Co. (1995). *

7. Bellotti, V.: Implications of current design practice for the use of HCI techniques. In: Proceedings of the Fourth Conference of the British Computer Society on People and Computers IV, pp. 13–34. Cambridge University Press (1988). *

8. Brooks, F.P.: The Design of Design: Essays from A Computer Scientist. Person Education, London (2010)

9. Brown, T.: Change by Design: How Design Thinking Transforms Organizations and Inspires Innovation. Harper Business, New York (2009). *

10. Brown, T.: Harvard Business Review: Design Thinking. Harvard Business School Publishing Corporation, vol. 86, pp. 84–92 (2008). *

11. Buchanan, R.: Wicked problems in design thinking. Des. Issues 8(2), 5–21 (1992). *

12. Carlgren, L.: Design thinking in innovation, in practice: the case of Kaiser Permanente. In: EURAM Conference Proceedings. European Academy of Management (2016). *

13. Carter, M., Downs, J., Nansen, B., Harrop, M., Gibbs, M.: Paradigms of games research in HCI: a review of 10 years of research at CHI. In: Proceedings of the First ACM SIGCHI Annual Symposium on Computer-Human Interaction in Play, pp. 27–36. ACM (2014). *

14. Cross, N.: Design Thinking: Understanding How Designers Think and Work. Berg, New York (2011). *

15. Cross, N.: Engineering Design Methods Strategies for Product Design. Wiley, Chichester (2000). *

16. Culén, A.L., Følstad, A.: Innovation in HCI: what can we learn from design thinking?. In: Proceedings of the 8th Nordic Conference on Human-Computer Interaction: Fun, Fast, Foundational, pp. 849–852. ACM (2014). *

17. Culén, A.L.: HCI education: innovation, creativity and design thinking. In: International Conferences on Advances in Computer-Human Interactions, pp. 125–130 (2015). *

18. de Almeida Neris, V.P., da Hora Rodrigues, K.R., Lima, R.F.: A systematic review of sustainability and aspects of human-computer interaction. In: Kurosu, M. (ed.) HCI 2014. LNCS, vol. 8512, pp. 742–753. Springer, Cham (2014). https://doi.org/10.1007/978-3-319-07227-2_71. *

19. Dix, A., Finlay, J., Abowd, G.D., Beale, R.: Human-Computer Interaction. Pearson Prentice, New York (2004). *

20. Dorst, K.: Frame Innovation: Create New Thinking by Design. The MIT Press, Cambridge (2015). *

21. Dorst, K.: The nature of design thinking. In: Paper Presented at the 8th Design Thinking Research Symposium (DTRS8) (2010). *

22. Dunne, D., Martin, R.: Design thinking and how it will change management education: an interview and discussion. Acad. Manag. Learn. Educ. 5(4), 512–523 (2006). *

23. Efeoglu, A., Møller, C., Sérié, M., Boer, H.: Design thinking: characteristics and promises. In: 14th International CINet Conference on Business Development and Co-creation, pp. 241–256 (2013). *

24. Eng, N.L., Bracewell, R. H., Clarkson, P.J.: Concept diagramming software for engineering design support: a review and synthesis of studies. In: ASME 2009 International Design Engineering Technical Conferences and Computers and Information in Engineering Conference, pp. 1221–1234. American Society of Mechanical Engineers (2009). *

25. Fallman, D.: Design-oriented human-computer interaction. In: Proceedings of the SIGCHI Conference on Human Factors in Computing Systems, pp. 225–232. ACM (2003). *

26. Giacominc, J.: What Is Human Centred Design? Des. J. 17(4), 606–623 (2014)

27. Gray, C.M., Seifert, C.M., Yilmaz, S., Daly, S.R., Gonzalez, R.: What is the context of "Design Thinking"? Design Heuristics as conceptual repertoire. Int. J. Eng. Educ. 32(2) (2015). *

28. Greenberg, S., Buxton, B.: Usability evaluation considered harmful (some of the time), In: CHI 2008, pp. 111–120. ACM, New York (2008)
29. Gugerty, L.: The use of analytical models in human-computer-interface design. Int. J. Man-Mach. Stud. **38**(4), 625–660 (1993)
30. Hayes, E.R., Games, I.A.: Making computer games and design thinking: a review of current software and strategies. Games Cult. **3**(3-4), 309–332 (2008). *
31. Head, A.J.: Design Wise. Thomas H Hogan Sr, Medford (1999)
32. Hornbæk, K.: Current practice in measuring usability: challenges to usability studies and research. Int. J. Hum.-Comput. Stud. **64**(2), 79–102 (2006)
33. IDEOU Homepage. https://www.ideou.com/pages/design-thinking. Accessed 08 Feb 2018. *
34. Insfran, E., Fernandez, A.: A systematic review of usability evaluation in web development. In: Hartmann, S., Zhou, X., Kirchberg, M. (eds.) WISE 2008. LNCS, vol. 5176, pp. 81–91. Springer, Heidelberg (2008). https://doi.org/10.1007/978-3-540-85200-1_10. *
35. Interaction Design Foundation Homepage. https://www.interaction-design.org/literature/article/5-stages-in-the-design-thinking-process. Accessed 08 Feb 2018. *
36. ISO 9241-210: Ergonomics of human-system interaction - part 210: human-centered design for interactive systems, p. 32. International Organization for Standardization (2010). *
37. Issa, T., Isaias, P.: Usability and human computer interaction (HCI). Sustainable Design, pp. 19–36. Springer, London (2015). https://doi.org/10.1007/978-1-4471-6753-2_2
38. Johansson Sköldberg, U., Woodilla, J., Çetinkaya, M.: Design thinking: past, present and possible futures. Creat. Innov. Manag. **22**(2), 121–146 (2013). *
39. Karahasanović, A., Culén, A.L.: Can HCI education benefit from design thinking? In: NordiCHI 2014 Workshop Innovation in HCI: What Can We Learn from Design Thinking? Helsinki, Finland (2004). *
40. Kitchenham, B.: Procedures for performing systematic reviews. Keele University, Keele, UK, vol. 33, pp. 1–26 – Technical report (2004)
41. Kjeldskov, J., Paay, J.: A longitudinal review of mobile HCI research methods. In: Proceedings of the 14th International Conference on Human-Computer Interaction with Mobile Devices and Services, pp. 69–78. ACM (2012). *
42. Binder, T., Löwgren, J., Malmborg, L.: Karri Kuutti. In: Binder, T., Löwgren, J., Malmborg, L. (eds.) (Re)Searching The Digital Bauhaus. HCIS. Springer, London (2009). https://doi.org/10.1007/978-1-84800-350-7_3. *
43. Li, X.: Integrating user affective state assessment in enhancing HCI: review and proposition. Open Cyber. Syst. J. **2**, 192–205 (2008). *
44. Liedtka, J., Azer, D., Salzman, R.: Design Thinking for the Greater Good: Innovation in the Social Sector. Columbia University Press, New York City (2017). *
45. Lin, T.S., Yi, M.-Z.: The categorization of document for design thinking. In: Marcus, A., Wang, W. (eds.) DUXU 2017. LNCS, vol. 10288, pp. 100–113. Springer, Cham (2017). https://doi.org/10.1007/978-3-319-58634-2_8. *
46. Martin, R.L.: The Design of Business: Why Design Thinking is the Next Competitive Advantage. Harvard Business Press, Boston (2009). *
47. McKilligan, S., Dhadphale, T., Ringholz, D.: Speed dating with design thinking. In: Paper Presented at the International Association of Societies of Design Research Conference, Cincinnati, OH (2017). *
48. McKilligan, S., Fila, N., Rover, D., Mina, M.: Insights on using design thinking as a process to changing pedagogical practices in engineering. In: Paper Presented at the Frontiers in Education, Indianapolis, IN (2017). *
49. Mulder, I.: A pedagogical framework and a transdisciplinary design approach to innovate HCI education. IxD&A **27**, 115–128 (2015). *

50. Nielsen Norman Group Homepage. https://www.nngroup.com/articles/design-thinking. Accessed 08 Feb 2018. *
51. Norman, D.A., Verganti, R.: Incremental and radical innovation: Design research vs. technology and meaning change. Des. Issues **30**(1), 78–96 (2014). *
52. Owen, C.: Design thinking: notes on its nature and use. Des. Res. Q. **2**(1), 16–27 (2007). *
53. Pandey, S.: Proto design practice: translating design thinking practices to organizational settings. IxD&A **27**, 129–158 (2015). *
54. Plattner, H., Meinel, C., Leifer, L.: Design Thinking. Springer, Berlin (2011). https://doi.org/10.1007/978-3-642-13757-0. *
55. Plattner, H.: An introduction to design thinking process guide. The Institute of Design at Stanford, Stanford (2010). *
56. Preece, J., Rombach, H.D.: A taxonomy for combining software engineering and human-computer interaction measurement approaches: towards a common framework. Int. J. Hum.-Comput. Stud. **41**(4), 553–583 (1994)
57. Razzouk, R., Shute, V.: What is design thinking and why is it important? Rev. Educ. Res. **82**(3), 330–348 (2012). *
58. Rittel, H.: On the planning crisis: systems analysis of the 'first and second generations'. Bedriftskonomen **8**, 390–396 (1972)
59. Rosli, D.I., Alias, R.A., Rahman, A.A.: Interaction design issues: a literature review. In: 2010 International Conference on User Science and Engineering (i-USEr), pp. 133–138. IEEE (2010). *
60. Rosson, M.B., Kellogg, W., Maass, S.: The designer as user: building requirements for design tools from design practice. Commun. ACM **31**(11), 1288–1298 (1988)
61. Rowe, P.: Design Thinking. MIT Press, Cambridge (1987)
62. Sharp, H., Rogers, Y., Preece, J.: Interaction Design: Beyond Human-Computer Interaction, 2nd edn. Wiley, Hoboken (2007). *
63. Simon, H.A.: The Sciences of the Artificial. MIT press, Cambridge (1996)
64. Tayal, S.P.: Engineering design process. Int. J. Comput. Sci. Commun. Eng. 1–5 (2013)
65. Thies, A., Ljungblad, S., Claesson, I.S.: Beyond ICT: how industrial design could contribute to HCI research. Swed. Des. Res. J. **13**(1), 22–29 (2015)
66. Thies, A.: On the value of design thinking for innovation in complex contexts: a case from healthcare. IxD&A **27**, 159–171 (2015). *
67. Thoring, K., Müller, R.M.: Understanding design thinking: a process model based on method engineering. In: DS 69: Proceedings of E&PDE 2011, The 13th International Conference on Engineering and Product Design Education, London, UK, 08–09 September 2011 (2011a). *
68. Thoring, K., Müller, R.M.: Understanding the creative mechanisms of design thinking: an evolutionary approach. In: Proceedings of the Second Conference on Creativity and Innovation in Design, pp. 137–147. ACM (2011b). *
69. Uehira, T., Kay, C.: Using design thinking to improve patient experiences in Japanese hospitals: a case study. J. Bus. Strategy **30**(2), 6–12 (2009). *
70. Ugras, T., Gülseçen, S., Çubukçu, C., İli Erdoğmuş, İ., Gashi, V., Bedir, M.: Research trends in web site usability: a systematic review. In: Marcus, A. (ed.) DUXU 2016. LNCS, vol. 9746, pp. 517–528. Springer, Cham (2016). https://doi.org/10.1007/978-3-319-40409-7_49
71. Wright, P., Blythe, M., McCarthy, J.: User experience and the idea of design in HCI. In: Gilroy, S.W., Harrison, M.D. (eds.) DSV-IS 2005. LNCS, vol. 3941, pp. 1–14. Springer, Heidelberg (2006). https://doi.org/10.1007/11752707_1
72. Zimmerman, J., Forlizzi, J., Evenson, S.: Research through design as a method for interaction design research in HCI. In: Proceedings of the SIGCHI Conference on Human Factors in Computing Systems, pp. 493–502. ACM (2007)

Below the Interface: Evaluation of PLM Software Usability and User Self-efficacy

Michael Saenz[(⊠)], Marlen Promann, Alaina Creager,
and Nancy Rasche

Purdue University, West Lafayette, IN 47906, USA
saenz1@purdue.edu

Abstract. In this paper, we discussed a case study on the user experience of a new PLM software system run in a Fortune 500 company. We list the common use cases and made guidelines to solve user experience errors of the software. Each guideline explains the context of the problem with title, explanation, and example included with direction for development improvement.

Keywords: Corporate culture · Enterprise UX structure and process
Product Lifecycle Management

1 Introduction

User experience (UX) design has received a generous amount of attention within the Product Lifecycle Management (PLM) field in the past several years. In this paper, we will use Don Norman and Jakob Nielson's definitions of user experience. ""User experience" encompasses all aspects of the end-user's interaction with the company, its services, and its products" [1]. Researchers have suggested that incorporating UX within software design and development will increase user's performance in the software. While applying UX design principles should enhance the user's efficiency within the PLM systems, there are drawbacks associated with the way it has been applied in new web-based, thin-client, PLM systems. The changes in new software have been focused solely on the graphic user interface (GUI) and not the holistic experience. Due to this and the reputation of poor usability in PLM software, users lack confidence in their self-efficacy [2] of adopting new PLM software. In this paper, we discuss how we evaluated PLM legacy software systems and a web-based, user interface PLM software, which we will refer to as thin-client PLM software. The research was conducted for a Fortune 500 company, whom we will refer to as Company A to protect their confidentiality. By following a user-centered design process and leveraging interview and contextual inquiry methods with a focus on usability, we list and describe user experience issues found with the thin-client software. We discuss these issues through the lens of self-efficacy and how it can affect user's perception of their potential adoption and their performance with a new PLM software. Lastly, we propose design considerations for software developers at Company A that should be considered when designing a new PLM system. These recommendations may also be applicable to other PLM software redesigns in general. The design consideration should help with common errors found in the software and in turn help users with low self-efficacy.

© Springer International Publishing AG, part of Springer Nature 2018
A. Marcus and W. Wang (Eds.): DUXU 2018, LNCS 10918, pp. 741–757, 2018.
https://doi.org/10.1007/978-3-319-91797-9_51

To understand the problem, we researched the market, usability and current trends of PLM software, as well as, user perception of PLM systems and their self-efficacy regarding software changes. PLM is "the process of managing the entire lifecycle of a product from its conception, through design and manufacture, to service and disposal. PLM integrates people, data, processes and business systems and provides a product information backbone for companies and their extended enterprise." [3] PLM systems are stated to improve a company's efficiency and reduce manufacturing time and costs [4]. In turn, companies that sell PLM software solutions use this as a means to increase the marketability appeal of the software. According to Transparency Market Research, the global PLM market will reach a value of US$ 75.87 billion in 2020 [5]. Even with such a large market, PLM software has a reputation of being difficult to learn and to use by all stakeholders who are part of the product life cycle. Thus, many engineers' opinions of new PLM software systems, even ones they have not used, is that they will be complex, unmanageable, and difficult to adopt.

In recent years, the need to make PLM systems user-friendly and digestible to all stakeholders in the product life cycle has been emphasized. Although, based on the evaluation of PLM systems, most of the updates have not been focused on improving the user experience, but instead on aesthetic changes to a more metaphoric interface and in the development of a more accessible web-based, thin-client [6]. While this type of work may influence users' performance, preliminary work must still be done on defining engineers' attitudes on why they find PLM systems to be cumbersome and to investigate the fundamental UX issues with the current legacy systems that impede adoption of new systems. Before proposing solutions to improve the user experience, we must first understand the user's concerns with existing systems and their low self-efficacy regarding the adoption of new systems.

We ran an empirical user study where we investigated usability and user experience issues with legacy software systems for PLM. We examined how these user experiences with the current complicated legacy systems may affect engineer's confidence in the adoption of new software systems. To do this, we worked with engineers from Company A to evaluate the usability and the user experience of their current legacy PLM systems to analyze the engineer's perception of the software and of the proposed new PLM thin-client. We collected daily practice data from surveys, observations, interviews and contextual inquiries. We used qualitative research and user experience methods to analyze our data; such as data coding, affinity diagramming, and experience mapping. In our findings, we list common errors found in the thin-client system. In our discussion section, we propose guidelines to increase the usability and experience of the PLM software for this use case. We also relate how the lack of user-centered design research and development in PLM systems has affected engineer's self-efficacy of new PLM systems. We used our qualitative data to show how they perceive the software will continue to be difficult to use and how new design guidelines, based on their needs and goals, may affect this thought process. The results of the study can be used as a starting point for a protocol for companies using PLM software and for UX industry professionals to collaboratively develop software that is more user-centered. In turn, the stakeholders who were involved with the user experience design research will see the emphasis on their needs and can improve their perception of new PLM software as being easier to use and adopt.

2 Literature Review

In order to form a deeper understanding of PLM software the team reviewed existing academic and industry literature on PLM development and usability. The PLM software topics researched included the PLM market and current trends, usability of PLM software, and user perception and self-efficacy in relation to software changes. The following literature reviews showed us deeper information into what the PLM market looks like today through the eyes of software developers and users as well as what PLM movements expected in the years to come.

2.1 PLM Market and Current Trends of PLM

According to Twenty years of PLM The Good, the Bad and the Ugly for the past 20 years PLM software has always been complex [7]. This is partially due to the great deal of functionality required for users to carry out their work functions within these applications. Now, more than ever, the complexity of collaboration between both employees and additional applications is necessary in business. Today's PLM market expects software to reflect the in-house work processes and allow for the same amount of communication between systems and individuals. However, this sense of collaboration is not easily implemented into PLM software. "This increase in system complexity, does not coincide with the increase of complexity of enterprises, which is mainly driven by growing organizational complexity (collaboration, decentralization) and increasing product complexity" [7]. Technology adds to this complexity as well. Products now contain smarter technology and much more safety restrictions than what PLM companies have seen in the past [7]. These types of factors feed to the expectations of PLM and can inadvertently cause the systems to be increasingly more complex. In Meier, Fischli, Sohrweide, and Nyffenegger words, "PLM projects get more complex, time to production becomes longer, and the need for IT infrastructure has increased drastically" [7]. These factors along with collaboration are what weigh down the PLM lifecycle and add complexity to the correlating software. In Meier, Fischli, Sohrweide, and Nyffenegger's [7] study on PLM over the past 20 years, they found that the main factors that have a negative effect on PLM have been present since its initial release. The delay in system update, is what is primarily setting PLM software back. As PLM complexities arise, companies look to solve the PLM process itself and leave the PLM software as is. "System upgrades result in large scale projects, that might throw a company back for years instead of continuously developing their PLM maturity" [7]. These process changes could be reflected in the software as well. This could potentially assure that process and software expectations coincide and that there is a constant iteration on the tools being used by PLM employees. In the long run this could eventually aid time on task, learning curve, and usability issues.

According to Kreis [8] PLM is actually quite generic when considered how it is applied over certain fields. They primarily discuss automotive, aerospace and machinery industries as being within the general outline of how typical PLM works.

However, in the future they believe that many other sectors will be able to have their own templates of PLM such as construction, pharmaceutical, textile, chemical, and medical technologies. With the possibility of templates for these sectors there is also the potential of PLM breaking into non-industrial sectors. These templates would serve as standardized formats for each PLM market type that could be customized and edited to serve a certain work process based on a company's preferences. Kreis, believes that with a templated approach that allows for more specialized opportunity businesses such as hospitals, insurance, and service-companies could all have the potential to utilize PLM strategies and software in the years to come.

According to Patrick Waurzyniak, Senior Editor of www.advancedmanufacturing. com, PLM will require great advances in order to keep up with the impact of big data and the internet of things. www.advancedmanufacturing.com is a PLM research site that releases research and analysis on manufacturing standards and processes in the United Kingdom. He believes that the only way to do this is by finding new ways to employ key tools through the comparison of CAD based PLM and the manufacturing process behind creating products and services. He even sites the "Aerospace and Defense Industry PLM Value Gap Survey," when stating that there is a significant gap between PLM tools (CAD, CAM, CAE) and the digital manufacturing factory layout software [9]. He concludes that when companies do not reach the full potential of their PLM that they are behind. We live in a world that is thriving with smart technology that has a potential to make a difference in the world of PLM. Waurzyniak believes that through expansion of the configuration management and inclusion of certain smart technologies design validation can be reached at a quicker pace [9]. However, in order to reach this expectation organizations will need to form a developed understanding of where "factory" ends and maintenance of products begins. This differentiating presents a change in the way that PLM systems have traditionally been implemented. According to Peter Schroer, CEO and founder of Aras Corporation, PLM is utilized only through design phases, with more recent inclusion of product configuration through manufacturing, but for PLM to reach its full potential is will need to handle the entire product life span [9].

2.2   Usability

According to the Nielsen Norman Group, "usability is a quality attribute that assesses how easy user interfaces are to use. The word 'usability' also refers to methods for improving ease-of-use during the design process" [10]. When it comes to PLM software, usability refers to the ease of use of engineers and additional stakeholders of the software. Usability contains many factors including learnability, efficiency, memorability, errors and satisfaction. In the field, user experience researchers and designers evaluate and create products and services based on these criteria. There are a variety of research methods and user tests that may be conducted in order to measure the success of the various metrics within each criteria method. For example, if engineers are struggling to carry out their daily work tasks a usability test may be conducted with them to determine the amount of errors the user runs into and what is causing the given issues. The more success a user has within a system, the more usable it is. This is especially important in PLM software where users are working with files and information that can affect an entire organization.

OpenBOM CEO and PLM blogger, Oleg Shilovitsky, states that many enterprise level PLM systems have been created with wrong goal in mind [11]. He believes that many software engineers have developed products by focusing on product features instead of the ultimate task or goal result that the user needs to achieve. This relates directly to adding features overtime, but not considering how it affects the whole of the system. As these products age they become layered in functionality and design patterns that eventually stray from a cohesive and involved system. Shilovitsky recommends three approaches to fixing this issue. His first concern is that speed is the ultimate factor that contributes to the effectiveness of performance. Carrying out processes should be instantaneous and waiting should be eliminated. Second, he states that "management" tasks such as involved approvals as well as check-ins and outs should be removed. In many cases this formal approval is defined by the movement of files from central locations to working spaces for the entire team to utilize and build off of. His primary solution for minimizing usability issues includes cloud-based software that allows for collaboration and universal file storage. Third, configuration and set-up should be eliminated. Shilovitsky does not believe that there should be extra code required to configure databases with PLM software. Instead these systems should allow for retrieval from these systems in a blended and efficient way. All in all, Shilovitsky references simplicity as the primary characteristic of an ideal dominant PLM system.

Hollie Farrahi, marketing manager at Selerant, has compared the usability and functionality of different PLM software including entire resource planning (ERP) and general PLM. [12] Selerant has over 25 years of experience in designing and developing this software and find usability to be a severely important trait in order to make it more accessible to non-expert users. Their company has recently created a team of usability experts and interaction designers to improve versions of their systems. One of the methods these creators have taken include a push, don't pull method. This push notification model supplies information to users depending on their location within the system. This aids users in reducing information overload and supplied them with what they need in a contextual manner. What Selerant focuses on most is assuring that users of their system do not have to hunt for information. This factor is so relevant to their company because "with a single PLM implementation supporting anywhere from a few to thousands of users, organizations must consider the various demands and needs of each unique user profile" [12]. In order to make the initial discovery simpler for new and experienced users the company assures that, necessary information and functionalities are placed in front of them, easing the user journey.

Alain Bernard, Lous Rivest, and Debasish Dutta, authors of Product Lifecycle Management for Society propose that integrating an ergonomic approach will improve the usability of PLM interfaces. This method focused on efficiency and comfort as primary metrics for success, while this will aid usability it does not solve all issues. PLM usability can be integrated through the application of agile methodology. They state that "many problems found by PLM software users are complexity or lack of flexibility of the system can be solved by including usability features" [12]. Not only this, but they also believe that these systems are under-utilized, and a great deal of management expect employees to be able to navigate these systems, despite the complexity and lack of intuitive design. Management's primary goal is to reduce cost, improve efficiency and avoid delay of production. What they may not realize is that creating more user-friendly software could aid all three of these goals. Considering these factors and the approach suggested by Bernard, Rivest, and Dutta the usability of software should be a main priority to PLM management teams.

2.3   User Perception and Self Efficacy

According to Self-Efficacy in the Workplace, "self-efficacy (also known as social cognitive theory or social learning theory) is a person's belief that she is capable of performing a particular task successfully. [13] Think of self-efficacy as a kind of self-confidence [14] or a task specific version of self-esteem [15]" [2]. Manoj K Rasad and Professor J. Gajendra Naidu of the Pacific Academy or High Education and Research University ran a study titled, Managing Software Adoption by Employees with the goal of identifying assessing and understanding user reception of PLM software adoption based on its benefits and ease of usage and its relationship with variables [2]. These variables included culture, attitudes, values, beliefs, habits, emotions, and norms of employees. Their study emphasized the role champions and catalysts play in ensuring the success of employees. Their main finding identified that culture of retail organization was positive and progressive, but needed effective involvement and engagement of managers and employees during rollout phases. However, in the adoption phase active commitment and enforcement of leaders is what determined success. In order to ensure this adoption employees needed to be included in early stages of rollout and be a part of a structured and planned change that allowed them to see how this implementation would benefit them and be introduced. From this study it was evident that management and leadership played a large part in ensuring that employees felt comfortable with transitions and that change management was handled in an intentional, effective manner. Not only were leadership teams responsible for the employee readiness for implementation, but they also had to identify risks and mitigation. Rasad and Naidu concluded their study with a recommendation of a (1) plan, (2) lead, (3) sustain tactic for managers to ensure the success of adoption and fluent implementation into their organizations.

Oleg Shilovitsky, PLM blogger and OpenBOM CEO, believes that in order to improve the employee adoption rate for PLM software you need to look at the company's deployment strategies. Today's practice of full enterprise deployment is typically slow and require a great deal of synchronization between not only divisions, but entire departments. Within PLM, many parts of the organization utilize and have access to the data in these systems and this is what can cause pain points. From deployment software engineers wait for approval from all and expect all parts of an organization to be happy with changes. However, Shilovitsky feels that this satisfaction can be met and still be not only deployed but also adopted at a quicker rate if organizations utilize agile software development methodology. This would allow for minor changes overtime and for frequent updates to the system as opposed to the timely creation of a one size fits all software that contains outdated design by the time of its implementation. Shilovitsky believes that the PLM industry can learn a great deal from IT companies and their ability to add functionality in a timely manner [12]. With the adoption of agile methods and effective change management Shilovitsky states that this new production format could be in high demand in recent years to come [12]. Tech Clarity's Preside, Jim Brown, reflects of the user perception of PLM software in his article, What do Users Really Think about their PLM Software [12]? Brown ran a study on PLM User Satisfaction where he surveyed over 500 PLM users. In his findings he was able to identify two main viewpoints. These viewpoints were "Yeah, I'm pretty much satisfied" and

"Please Change Everything." According to Brown, "we analyzed the survey responses related to different categories of questions including usage, support, ease of use, quality, performance, stability, and performing various functional tasks. The results were all about the same." This showed more specifically that when it came to satisfaction 23% of respondents loved their software, 35% liked it, and 27% were neutral in their views. This totaled out at 85% of respondents with primary differentiation due to organizational level and departmental function. The "Please Change Everything" viewpoint was analyzed from written responses only where respondents utilized a great deal of capital letters and exclamation points to identify their hatred for certain aspects of their experiences with PLM. Brown reflected on the study by saying that he was not surprised by the results stating that most users have very low expectations of their PLM software and for this reason stated that they were mostly satisfied. He also identified that fear was evident in many responses. Many users identified that they were afraid of change when it came to software. Many users are comfortable with their software because they've finally mastered their workflow and don't want to face confusion again. He believes that with the rise in expected user experience that exists with several IT companies today, the growth of expectation will also adapt to the PLM market.

3   Methodology

Our data collection process was split into 3 phases, each phase directly informed the following stages, allowing for a generative process. The completed phases in order were a survey, contextual inquiries, and interviews with the Company A engineers across its different PLM lifecycle stages. This data allowed us to detail the PLM pipeline for the engineering processes of our participants at Company A.

3.1   Survey

The goal of the survey was to aggregate user groups, understand current work practices, and identify common use-cases when using PLM software for manufacturing at Company A. The survey questions were constructed using information from a co-design with Company A's PLM employees and the research team. The survey contained 24 questions, divided into three sections. The first section, demographics, included questions about the user's age and work experiences. This allowed us to see what type of worker was using the PLM systems and for how long. An example question from this section included, "How long have you been working for the company?" The second section of questions focused on understanding the engineer's current work practices and their sentiments for them. This section asked for information such as, "what kind of information do you typically need to update and manage in your job role?" and "are there any critical problems that you face in your current information export and use process?" These types of questions allowed us to understand user's typical workflows in using PLM software and identify issues they currently have with their workflow. The third section of questions focused on the user's thoughts of the PLM system. Primarily, understanding their current experiences and their self-perception of the advantages and limitations of the system in relation to their current work practices. The survey was sent out via email and received 24 responses.

3.2   Contextual Inquiries

Using the information from the survey such as the use-cases and common tasks, we conducted an on-site contextual inquiry with eight engineers. This was conducted on the participant's personal laptop computer in a conference room that simulated the participant's most typical office environment. Within the space, the facilitator ran the usability test while the observer took notes of each participant's actions. A video camera faced the computer screen to document the workflow. The facilitator briefed the participants on the testing procedure and instructed them based on a script. Participants signed informed consent documents that acknowledged: the participation was voluntary, and they could cease at any time, the session was videotaped, and their privacy of identification was safeguarded. The facilitator asked the participants if they had any questions before beginning each session.

Participants answered a pre-test demographic and background information questionnaire. The facilitator explained that the test was a qualitative contextual inquiry into how they achieve their daily work goals. The amount of time taken to complete the test task was noted and any exploratory behavior outside the task flow did not occur until after task completion. The facilitator instructed the participant to "think aloud" so that a verbal record existed of their interactions with the applications they used to achieve their work goals. At the start of each task, the facilitator asked a leading question and the participant explained the work goal based off of the question from the script. Then the participant began the task. Time-on-task measurement began when the participant started each task, but the think aloud was taken into factor in our analysis. The researchers observed and entered user behavior, user comments, and system actions in the notes and later reviewed the videos in Morae software to mark and annotate the results for further analysis. The advantage of this type of interview was that it was done within the context of the user's typical work environment. As we discussed, during each use-case the user was able to physically show us how they perform tasks within their existing tools on their workstation. For example, we asked each user how they edit a specific type of information within a tool. During this process, we asked users to think aloud. This meant that they would verbalize each interaction and their reasoning as it was performed, which allowed us to grasp their mental processes. In addition, we allowed the users to provide their opinion on the software.

3.3   Interview

The last step of data collection was an interview that was conducted after testing the thin-client PLM software. Our research team was able to use information from the survey and the contextual inquiries to develop a semi-structured interview. After each use case and with a post-test questionnaire, the test observer asked each participant to answer questions about their experience with the thin-client software. The questions pertained to user needs, hopes, fears, problems, process, and sentiment that were identified during the survey and contextual inquiries. These were open-ended questions, and the participants were free to answer questions as they saw fit. The goal was to allow the users to elaborate about their personal PLM experiences and perception of new tools. This allowed the research team to gather the user's thoughts on the thin-client and specifically, how it compares to Company A's legacy system. We also ran a usability test of the thin-client with nine engineers. They were asked to do tasks within the 3 the use cases that are listed in the results section and complete a post survey that due to space will not discussed it in this paper.

4 Results

Each of the conducted research methods provided ample amounts of data that allowed us to understand the inner workings of PLM work practices within Company A. The team worked as a unit to code the data and extract valid information from each method. The information below is representative of the analysis performed by the team and the main takeaways from each of the research methods conducted.

4.1 Survey

The survey respondents sampled were 90% male and 76% were between 30–59 years old. Two-thirds of the respondents were in product area A (38%), product area B (29%), product area C (9%), and (28%) other less represented areas. Two-thirds of the respondents identified as foundation Engineers (67%), application Engineers (28%), and other (5%). 48% of the respondents had more than 6 years' experience at Company A while the largest group was 38% at 3–5 years of experience. The data collected about current work practices helped us create common tasks within three use cases categories; finding, editing, and reporting information. There were three user groups aggregated based on jog role. Use cases were developed to match each of the group's current practices to structure the contextual inquiry.

4.2 Contextual Inquiries

The contextual inquiry results from the 9 participants provided knowledge that was summarized into user personas, daily workflow processes and performance measures for comparison with the thin-client PLM. User personas identified the representative user background, expectations, goals, and pain points Performance measures collected included issue markers, time on task, and sentiment. The issue markers represented are Q (Step failure: Could not finish intent), X (Error: Deviated from expected intent), A (PLM Thin-client comment), N (Negative comment), P (Positive comment), F (Features that are novel), O (Observations), S (Software company has internalized), and M (Microsoft Software). There were 1,165 annotated issue markers for the contextual inquiry. The largest average task time was editing information with finding information as a close second. Reporting information had a relatively short average task time. Both editing and finding information tasks required the most steps and had the most errors.

4.3   Interview

The interview showed the participants' sentiment of the thin-client PLM software's ease of use in comparison to their current work practices software tools. Comments about negative experiences were higher compared to positive comments. Users stated that editing tasks were the most difficult. The most common struggle was to find the correct process to edit items. They also had difficulty in finding information due to confusing terminology, action selection, and hidden information.

Use Case. A use case, as represented in this project, is a breakdown of the most commonly performed tasks by engineers at Company A. We determined these use cases based on information retrieved from our survey and contextual inquiries of current work practices. We were able to identify the most common use cases performed by the respondents in their job responsibilities as finding, editing and reporting. These cases are the overarching categories for which we placed specific job tasks. This allowed us to identify different portions of engineers' work as pertaining to each use case during discussions. These use cases can be used by designers to test new software. The use cases are as listed below.

Finding Information. The user mostly looked for information about requirements and their program. The most common tools were internal company software, Microsoft software, and "asking a colleague" to find necessary information. The key issue in the this use case was that data is dispersed instead of inter-linked. Other issues pertained to version control, current information, non-intuitive interfaces, unclear help, poor search system, and too many different software systems.

Editing Information. The users most common editing task was to edit and manage design rules. The most common tools to edit were commercial software such as Excel, Sharepoint, Word, and Powerpoint. The key issue with editing is that there was no standard updating processes, so there was a large quantity of programs that could be used. This resulted in many versions of the files that were unidentifiable as the "master" file which increased confusion and reduced productivity.

Reporting Information. The respondents most commonly used their information for reporting, compliance, and/or approvals. The most common process for reporting information was to export information from Company A's internal software into Microsoft software to visualize and then share by email. The key issues were that the sharing of information was unnecessarily manual, that information was not in one location, and the process was not standardized.

5   Discussion

In our Discussion section, we suggest why some of the current solutions are not working for the PLM thin-client software development in Company A. All findings are directly influenced by the research and data retrieved from the research methods. The primary takeaways from this study represent user experience issues and recommendations for usability improvements. Issues/errors that were identified during the evaluation process were organized based on web heuristics [16]. We used these heuristics because the computer software is being transitioned into a new thin-client (i.e. a web-based PLM alternative). The six web heuristics that were used to organize errors can be seen in Fig. 1.

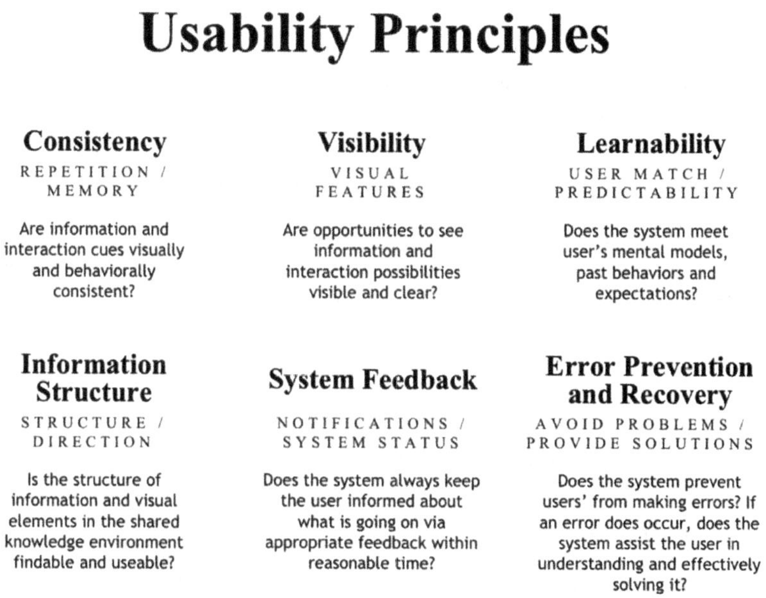

Usability Principles

Consistency REPETITION / MEMORY Are information and interaction cues visually and behaviorally consistent?	**Visibility** VISUAL FEATURES Are opportunities to see information and interaction possibilities visible and clear?	**Learnability** USER MATCH / PREDICTABILITY Does the system meet user's mental models, past behaviors and expectations?
Information Structure STRUCTURE / DIRECTION Is the structure of information and visual elements in the shared knowledge environment findable and useable?	**System Feedback** NOTIFICATIONS / SYSTEM STATUS Does the system always keep the user informed about what is going on via appropriate feedback within reasonable time?	**Error Prevention and Recovery** AVOID PROBLEMS / PROVIDE SOLUTIONS Does the system prevent users' from making errors? If an error does occur, does the system assist the user in understanding and effectively solving it?

Fig. 1. Usability principle categorization

The 1,165 markers from the data collected were consolidated and sorted into 4 categories; (1) current issues, (2) what works, (3) what doesn't work, and (4) hopes for thin-client. 124 issues in the (3) what doesn't work category were prioritized as the most important to address as areas of improvement. The development of the user experience issues & design considerations used information from the 3 phases of study. It should be noted that high priority was given to any error observations that were a roadblock and any issues observed over 5 times during our study (even if it did not cause an error). The guidelines include the title, the problem, an example, the context, and the solution. The user experience issues and solutions for the guidelines are below.

5.1 Make All Interactive Elements Visible

Problem: Unclear interactive elements: visibility
Compartmentalized interactive elements (buttons) within items provided unclear indications of actions because they were not visible. All context on items looked like information and the hover effect highlighted the entire item, so many users just clicked in the center of the item. 67% of the users missed the Open Icon in the upper right corner of the item.

Example: Users needed to know that you must click on the "L" during searching to open it. There are three clickable options, and none are intuitive as to what action they will accomplish.

This feature has 3 possible interactive elements, yet hover is shown as one element. Context: Visibility/Learnability/Feedback: Interactive elements should be easy to distinguish by visual cues that predict their action and are behaviorally consistent throughout the software.

Solution: All interactive elements should have a consistent visual cue to indicate action and must stand alone. Modify hover effect to highlight only one interactive element at a time.

5.2   Develop Consistent Content Library, Terminology

Problem: Confusing terminology: learnability
Terminology of elements, features, and actions confused users because they were different from the other programs used at Company A and they do not match the task they expected to be doing.

Example: System A is incomprehensible to users. If users remember they need to open context, they would often open the reference item instead and then fail to find the diagrams as a result. This is because they don't know what the context of System A is and how it is different or necessary for the task.

> Quote: "I feel like you used the word context, but I don't remember. Or open in context, I'm not even sure what that means."

Context: Learnability: Terminology of elements, features, and actions that are not unique to the software function should follow as closely as possible to what the user already understands to improve adoption of software and reduce relearn. This can be taught during training, it is unnecessary and can be avoided by capitalizing on the users' current mental model. All new terminology should be reserved for new elements, features, and actions that are unique to the software program because they will require a learning curve.

Solution: Use terminology and actions that match the users' mental model of the system's software programs whenever possible. Removing unnecessary steps and reducing options will help prevent errors when introducing new terminology.

5.3   Improve Sense of Feedback

Problem: Unintuitive interface layout: learnability, system feedback
When searching the interface for information and status, the users were unsure where to look. The structure and layout of content was cluttered, too complex, and lacked consistency.

Example: Users struggled to find the interactive element to move to the next step. They did not know where to look to find their status.

> Quotes: "Finding info was difficult, most of this is still not intuitive for me. Still not knowing that I'm looking in the right spot for things."

> "Finding info was difficult. It is only because I have seen some people click through some of this that I know some things should be available, and roughly how. But most of this is still not intuitive for me. Knowing that I'm looking in the right spot for things."

Context: Learnability/system feedback: Users struggled to figure out where they were and what they need to do next because the layout, icons, and actions were cluttered and would change as they moved through steps in the process. The breadcrumb navigation history was not in one consistent location and the horizontal orientation required abbreviation of the steps and content.

Solution: Use a consistent interface layout that is the same throughout the entire task process with visible system feedback of status. Clustering icons by function will reduce clutter and complexity. This will also improve learnability of their location. The interface should provide one location for system status that will cascade to allow for complete viewing without abbreviation.

5.4   Provide Shortcuts to Improve Efficiency

Problem: Lack of shortcuts: learnability, consistency, system feedback
Users attempted to use the typical mouse and keyboard shortcuts. They were frustrated when they did not work as expected and they had to search the interface for interactive elements specific to the task they were trying to complete. These extra steps reduced efficiency and increased frustration.

Example: Many tried to use the mouse right-click to see options to edit items in the diagram.

> Quotes: "One of these clicks should allow for alt changes, but the system seems to need to refresh from the last edit."
> "I want to be able to Right-Click and Drag and Drop."

Context: Learnability/consistency/system feedback: Users tried to use shortcuts throughout the testing process with varying success. They usually attempted to use the mouse shortcuts in the editing tasks (ex. Right-click for options) and tried to use the keyboard shortcuts (ex. Ctrl+S) during the sharing or reporting use cases.

Solution: The interface should meet user expectations for conventional shortcuts. Utilize the users' knowledge of shortcuts in Windows OS to improve efficiency and reduce steps and document all shortcuts in a quick reference guide.

5.5   Develop Workflow Editing Guidelines and Include System Mode Status

Problem: Lack of consistent workflow procedure: error prevention, system feedback
Users did not follow a consistent procedure and/or order of steps in the workflow. They often had to start over. They were confused about how to start a task. The lack of visibility of system feedback of selected items or actions further reduced learnability of the workflow.

Example: Users failed to select the item before generating the interface matrix.

Context: Error prevention/system feedback: Users were unsure how to start steps in the use cases. They would question whether they should select the authored item first or select the action of authoring first. It is important that users understand the editing workflow. If both options are available, then the system should provide the user with feedback about the mode status.

Solution: Be consistent in development to encourage a consistent workflow and provide system feedback for mode status to help with error prevention, recovery, and learnability. If users expect to start every task by having to select item (feedback: item is highlighted) then select action (feedback: changes mouse or action highlighted), it will help them consistently follow that procedure. It is important to support their understanding of the status of the system with visual feedback.

5.6   Improve Action Selection with Reduced Options and System Feedback

Problem: Too many options: error prevention, system status

Users were slowed down and frustrated because there are too many options to find, select, and/or open items. (e.g. contexts, parent assemblies, references). Users struggled to know where they should be in the system and therefore were unsure about what, how, when, and where to open items.

Example: Users were confused by the options available in the TABS because they changed depending on what item you have selected. They were also confused about which to open.

Quote: "I guess I always get lost between LH (parent assemblies) and L (references)."

Context: Error prevention/system feedback

Solution: Be consistent in the information structure and reduce the options for actions based on where the user is in the system. Be careful not to remove actions but make them inactive. Deleting or moving actions (icons, buttons, links, etc.) reduces learnability and increases frustration. Again, it is important to support their understanding of the status of the system with visual feedback.

5.7   Enhance Item Selection for Editing

Problem: It is difficult to tell when a port or a connection is selected.

The system did not provide adequate feedback to the user when an item was selected. Many users tried to use the mouse right-click to see options.

Example: Users repeatedly attempted to select ports and connections without noticing that they already been selected. Users thought connection was selected, but it wasn't.

Quote: "I thought I picked that one, but..."

Context: Information structure: This issue relates back to #5 Develop workflow guidelines and include system status. Consistent feedback needs to be supported by a consistent workflow.

Solution: Increase the size and/or appearance of the items when selected. Allow right clicks to view options. Follow a consistent editing workflow for all contexts.

5.8   Improve Search and Filtering

Problem: Too many similar search results: information structure
Users were confused by similar items in the search results and could not distinguish them by the information that was displayed. Users wanted to see dates or an indication of most recent or last edited. Users mentioned Google, struggled to know where they should be in the system and therefore were unsure about what, how, when, and where to open items.

Example: Search results were too many and the users were confused by the information shown in the items. They did not know what L, LH, etc. meant, thus they were confused about which to open.

Quote: "so I don't know how to tell these two apart: CONTROLS vs. Controls."

Context: Information structure/visibility: Searching for the correct item to complete a task required the user to do a lot of trial and error because there was a lack of visibility of the needed information.

Solution: Improve the way that information is displayed in the search results. Consider a search setup like common systems used at Company A that the users think work well, such as nested search. Or implement a search system that provides more necessary information in a more organized manner and is nested or cascading. Implement a post search filter/sort to organize or further reduce options (most recent, user name, user role, dates, etc.).

5.9   Recover at Same Location or Save Last Location and Remind

Problem: Refreshing the thin-client often canceled previous log in, role and use context selection. Users that refreshed the system did not realize that they were no longer logged in. The system did not ask for them to re-enter this information, so the user assumed that they were still in the same context.

Example: Once inside the thin-client, users forget to re-select these options during a refresh of the system. Users went to start searching again and did not realize that they were no longer logged in.

Context: System feedback, error, and recovery: When the system is refreshed, the panel disappeared, the use context was canceled, and the logical in the search results were gone. This was because it did not retain their login information.

Solution: Automate to re-select last choices and location or if login is required again, make it obvious with a pop-up or revert to the home screen.

6   Low Self-efficacy Effects of Adopting New Software

Within this section, we will discuss how self-efficacy may affect user's perception, adoption rate and performance of new PLM software. Furthermore, we reiterate user experience issues found and discuss how these issues are affecting the user self-efficacy of software adoption. During our data analysis phase, we were interested in why users openly display a disdain for a new software adoption. Thus, we re-coded our data with a low self-efficacy lens. We found two major themes in relationship to adopting systems for PLM, positive and negative. People who feel in to positive theme were either willing to change or try new software, while the users in the negative did not want to change current practices and learn any new software. The users that did not want to adopt new software fell into two categories, the first category being lack of self-efficacy (1) in learning the software and (2) in aversion to anything new. Those in the (1) first category, believed they would not be able to master a new software system and were scared to even try. For example, a participant who was editing a document stated, "I think software is absolutely horrible for search. Whereas people who have been here five more years have enough intuition about the naming conventions that they will know I need to put in (here)." Participants who fell into this category may adopt the new PLM software, but in a slower manner or with caution.

They would hastily quit a task if something went wrong. For example, a participant who was doing an editing task stated, "I don't think this will work. I cannot drag and drop." The software did not fit into the users' mental model, causing apprehension with adjusting to the new software. Those in the (2) second category simply didn't want to change or learn anything new. These users believe they've learned and mastered current software and don't need to change. When new software is introduced to them, they believe it will lower their performance. For example, a participant who fell into this category stated, that "always having new technologies with new requirements, I have to keep learning all the time" and "I do not want to learn another system." This user's self-efficacy was so low that it reflected in animosity to any new software system or changes to existing systems. Our work suggests that users who have low self-efficacy will adopt software slowly or/and will reject software change. Thus, we propose the guidelines that we set will help improve the user's experiences and transition more smoothly to new software adoption for users with low self-effect because the goal is to improve usability by capitalizing on existing mental models.

For example, people who fell into categories one will benefit from guidelines two, three and four because these guidelines will help with the user's learnability of the software. Users that fell into categories two will benefit from guidelines two, five and nine because they try to match users' mental models to the software.

7   Conclusion and Future Work

In this paper, we discussed a case study on the user experience of a new PLM software system run in a Fortune 500 company. We list the common use cases and made guidelines to solve user experience errors of the software. The guidelines include the title, the problem, an example, the context, and the solution to frame the issues and provide direction for improvement. Lastly, we recorded our data with a low self-efficacy lens and found two major categories in relationship to adopting systems for PLM for people with low self-efficacy. In future work, we would like to study users who fall into the category of low self-efficacy and try to model how they adopted new software.

References

1. Norman, D., Nielsen, J.: The definition of User Experience (UX) (2012). https://www.nngroup.com/articles/definition-user-experience/. Accessed 18 Jan 2018
2. Lunenburg, C.: Self-efficacy in the workplace: implications for motivation and performance. Int. J. Manag. Bus. Adm. **14**(1), 1–6 (2011)
3. Saaksvuori, A., Immonen, A.: Product Lifecycle Management. Springer, Berlin (2008)
4. Schuh, G., Rozenfeld, H., Assmus, D., Zancul, E.: Process oriented framework to support PLM implementation. Comput. Ind. **59**, 210–218 (2008). https://doi.org/10.1016/j.compind.2007.06.015
5. Vadoudi, K., Allais, R., Reyes, T., Troussier, N.: Sustainable Product Lifecycle Management and Territoriality: New Structure for PLM. IFIP Advances in Information and Communication Technology Product Lifecycle Management for a Global Market, pp. 475–484 (2014). https://doi.org/10.1007/978-3-662-45937-9_47
6. Hidajat, R.: Active Workspace Making PLM Accessible for All (2016). https://community.plm.automation.siemens.com/t5/Teamcenter-Blog/Active-Workspace-Making-PLM-Accessible-for-All/ba-p/319560. Accessed 13 Oct 2017
7. Meier, U., Fischli, F., Sohrweide, A., Nyffenegger, F.: Twenty Years of PLM – the Good, the Bad and the Ugly. In: Ríos, J., Bernard, A., Bouras, A., Foufou, S. (eds.) PLM 2017. IAICT, vol. 517, pp. 69–77. Springer, Cham (2017). https://doi.org/10.1007/978-3-319-72905-3_7
8. Kreis, B.: The future of product development. CIRP Des. Conf. **17**, 37–47 (2007)
9. Roche, J.: PLM Value Gap Emerges (2014). http://www.aerospacemanufac-turinganddesign.com/article/amd0214-plm-value-survey/. Accessed 2 Jan 2018
10. Nielsen, J.: Usability 101: Introduction to Usability (2012). https://www.nngroup.com/articles/usability-101-introduction-to-usability/. Accessed 15 Dec 2017
11. Shilovitsky, O.: Nobody Wants to Use PLM Products and It's Okay (2016). http://beyondplm.com/2016/01/18/nobody-wants-to-use-plm-products-and-its-okay/. Accessed 10 Jan 2018
12. Farrahi, H.: Build a Strong Business Case Without Sacrificing User Needs (2016). http://resources.selerant.com/product-lifecycle-management/the-usability-vs.-functionality-dilemma-in-plm-software. Accessed 20 Sept 2017
13. Shilovitsky, O.: 3 PLM Deployment and Adoption Challenges (2015). http://beyondplm.com/2015/01/09/3-plm-deployment-and-adoption-challenges/. Accessed 10 Jan 2018
14. Bandura, A.: Self-Efficacy: The Exercise of Control. Macmillan, Basingstoke (1997)
15. Kanter, R.: Confidence: How Winning and Losing Streaks begin and End. Crown Random House, New York (2006)
16. Brockner, J.: Self-Esteem at Work (1988)
17. Nielsen, J.: 10 Usability Heuristics for User Interface Design (1995). https://www.nngroup.com/articles/ten-usability-heuristics/. Accessed 10 Oct 2017

Assist Users to Straightaway Suggest and Describe Experienced Problems

Björn Senft[(⊠)], Holger Fischer, Simon Oberthür, and Nitish Patkar

Paderborn University, SICP, Fürstenallee 11, 33102 Paderborn, Germany
{b.senft,h.fischer,s.oberthuer}@sicp.upb.de

Abstract. Requirements elicitation plays a vital role in building effective software. Incorrect or incomplete requirements lead to erroneous software and costs a huge amount of rework. Rework costs in terms of money and efforts are usually higher than the early detection of potential flaws in the requirements. This happens because most of the techniques employed to extract requirements fail to understand end user goals. Understanding your users and their goals is important to build a capable, viable and desirable product or software system. This paper attempts to suggest and evaluate an alternative approach to understand your potential users and their goals so that correct and complete requirements can be formulated resulting in a successful software. We introduce the concept of a tool-guided elicitation process, classify elicitation techniques in term of their suitability in such a tool-guided process, and present an initial study of the usability und usefulness of our prototype called *Vision Backlog*.

Keywords: Agile development · Requirements elicitation · Vision Backlog
Tool-guided elicitation process · Participation · Understanding users

1 Introduction

As a response to an increasingly dynamic world (new and uncertain contexts, complexity, competition, updatability, and user feedback) software is developed like an evolutionary system, e.g. in a DevOps approach (cf. [1] or Netflix[1]). During the diffusion process of software innovations, the users start to change and evolve the initial idea of the software and re-invent it [2]. This makes it necessary to frequently observe the users for changed behavior and requirements. Furthermore, the focus of software becomes more and more experts/highly skilled users that shall be supported in their work [3]. They possess specialized knowledge and experience-based knowledge that is indispensable for a successful software development, but usually this knowledge is only activated if they are in their specific work context (cf. [4]). Hence, the question arises how we can get aware of changes and new ideas as well as challenges in such contexts, where we must update our understanding continuously.

---

[1] https://www.nginx.com/blog/microservices-at-netflix-architectural-best-practices/, https://medium.com/netflix-techblog/its-all-a-bout-testing-the-netflix-experimentation-platform-4e1ca458c15.

© Springer International Publishing AG, part of Springer Nature 2018
A. Marcus and W. Wang (Eds.): DUXU 2018, LNCS 10918, pp. 758–770, 2018.
https://doi.org/10.1007/978-3-319-91797-9_52

We tackle this question in one of our projects called ZenMEM[2] where we are developing software tools supporting musicologists in their work. In an initial project phase, it has become clear that besides a phase-oriented requirements elicitation and evaluation, we needed means of getting continuously feedback on our results as well as the vision. Unfortunately, traditional approaches to user participation like lead users working closely with the developers are not feasible for scarce resources on both sides (users and developers) and the spatial distance.

Hence, the idea arose that we require additional structures for feedback and wishes of the users. It should be made possible for them to asynchronously give us feedback on insights they gained during their work, problems they encounter, and visions they have for further developments. Our users are not developers or requirements engineers and solutions such as feature requests via e-mail or ticketing systems like *Jira* only take unstructured information. Therefore, we inevitable run into problems such as incomplete or hidden requirements and stakeholders with difficulties in separating requirements from known solution design [5].

Our solution for this challenge is to empower the users to participate independently and asynchronously in the requirements elicitation process via an assisting system that helps them to structure their thoughts so that they can straightaway suggest and describe experienced problems as well as new ideas and changes. The main contribution of this paper is to discuss and evaluate the possibility of such a tool-guided elicitation process. For that we present

- the details of the idea of a tool guided elicitation process (cf. Sect. 3),
- a classification of requirements elicitation techniques regarding their usability and usefulness to locate and scope problems and be applied by users independently from requirements engineers (cf. Sect. 4),
- how we integrated selected elicitation techniques in our software prototype called *Vision Backlog* as a proof of concept that such a tool is technical feasible (cf. Sect. 5),
- and the results of an initial study regarding the usability of the tool as well as the usefulness of the results (cf. Sect. 6).

2 ZenMEM: Context and Problem of Our Use Case

The project ZenMEM contains all the mentioned challenges addressed in the introduction. There is a team of three developers with no one dedicated solely to do usability and requirements engineering. The field of digital music editions is quite novel, and the de-facto standard is still paper-based music editions. Hence, everything that is done equates to an innovation if not revolution for the potential user base with approximately 500 users worldwide. A 30-min car drive away are based a handful musicologists that we are eager to work more closely with the developers. They are

---

[2] http://www.zenmem.de.

very limited due to a strict schedule within their other projects. Another 50 musicologists are scattered all around in an eight-hour car drive radius.

Because of their current work style, they have many routines that are not described formally but are based on their experiences and become topic if they actively need it. For that reason, we regularly miss important requirements. On top of that, the tool support we introduce, represent emerging practices that still must proof to be good or best practices in the field of digital music editions. Hence, the work style and requirements will change over the time and the regular feedback from the users is needed without interfering too much in their work and having them on-site.

There are different challenges for the requirements elicitation process. Naive stakeholders have very little knowledge of the elicitation process, so either they must learn it or must keep depending on the requirements and usability engineer. Both solutions are not feasible considering the stringent time constraints.

Elicitation requires specific skills. Among all the stakeholders, only requirements engineers are familiar with those [6]. If stakeholders must depend on this role for elicitation all the time, the requirements engineer can become a bottleneck. Furthermore, in small organizations as well as in this project the requirements engineer is a relatively busy resource.

Typically, naive stakeholders focus more on the suspected solution rather than the actual problem they are facing. Often, they are not even aware of the actual problem. But identifying the core of the stakeholder's problem is an almost necessary step to quality requirements [7].

Additionally, notes, lists, sketches which are mostly used to record needs or expectations of stakeholders are not efficient ways, as they cannot naturally be tied to actual requirements [6]. Formal meetings are not feasible enough to thoroughly extract stakeholder's needs, expectations, etc. [6]. Stakeholders can get *insights* about their needs literally any time, especially when they are working on it. It could be hard during formal meetings to point out or recollect specific things [7–9].

3   Towards a Tool-Guided Elicitation Process

Requirements elicitation is described as learning, uncovering, extracting, surfacing, or discovering needs of customers, users, and other potential stakeholders by Hickey and Davis [10]. In the requirements engineering process, elicitation is one activity besides analysis, triage, specification, and verification. Although most existing models show these activities in an ordered sequence, Hickey and Davis state that in reality, requirements activities are not performed sequentially, but iteratively and in parallel. This is an important insight for a tool-guided elicitation process, as it emphasizes that elicitation will never be unidirectional and must be conducted continuously.

Hence, a tool-guided elicitation process for users will never be a complete substitute for user researcher and requirements engineers as analysts. Instead, the activity of requirements elicitation will be shared among stakeholders and analysts with feedback mechanism between these two groups. A tool-guided process would not replace requirements analysts, but it will ease their work by reducing efforts and time spent on eliciting correct and complete requirements. Because of our use case, a tool-guided process must support and connect both stakeholders and analysts.

Just as much, the tool must support a learning process over the time like it is normal in approaches as Design Thinking, DevOps and Lean UX. This is especially reasonable for the context of digital music editions (cf. Sect. 2) as it is distinguished by innovations and complex as well as chaotic problem domains. Innovations are not adopted immediately by everyone at once but need time to prove their advantages. Usually they are adapted during the adoption process in a way that was not intended by the originators [2]. Complex and chaotic problem domains need to be handled with a strategy that involves probing/acting as starting point to sense the effects and react accordingly to it [11]. Thus, we are safe to assume that the initial requests made by the tool need to be adapted and refined over the time.

To sum up, a tool-guided requirements elicitation process should capture the stakeholder's exact needs and expectations in the form of goals with associated context and always be available so that stakeholders can benefit from it at any time. The captured knowledge/information through this system shall help requirements engineers to extract tacit knowledge and to formulate more accurate and complete requirements. All the stakeholders shall actively participate in understanding the underlying problem to collectively reach an appropriate solution.

Besides the tool approach and its potential users, it must be defined which techniques should be incorporated. According to Maiden [12], the primary function of requirements work is to locate and scope problems, then create and describe solutions. Hall [40] once stated that the first rule of user research is to never ask anyone what they want. Nielsen [41] goes into the same direction and states that to design the best UX, pay attention to what users do, not what they say. Adding the 'I can't tell you what I want, but I'll know it when I see it' [13] dilemma, it gets obvious that for user participation we should start with techniques that focus on locating and scoping problems instead of on creating and describing solutions. In the following, possible elicitation techniques are classified for a potential use in a tool-guided elicitation process.

4 Classification of Elicitation Techniques

Based on a literature research, we gathered requirements elicitation techniques from different disciplines like social science, design, usability engineering and requirements engineering (cf. Table 1 for the gathered techniques). These techniques need to be classified in accordance to their usefulness for our goals.

This classification can be done in many ways. One way is to classify them according to the means of communication they involve: conversational, observational, analytic and synthetic [14]. The conversational method is based on verbal communication between two or more people. Methods in this category are called verbal methods. The best example is interviews. The observational method is based on understanding problem domain by observing human activities. There are requirements which people cannot verbally articulate properly. Those are acquired through observational methods, for example protocol analysis. Analytic methods provide ways to

Table 1. Classification criterion for elicitation techniques

Technique	Locating and scoping problems	Suitable for autarkic execution	Practicable for both stakeholder and analyst	Representable in software
Interview [18]	✓	✓	✓	✓
Questionnaire [16, 21]	✓	✓	✓	✓
Task analysis [16, 22, 23]	✓	✓	✓	✓
Domain analysis [24]	✓	✓	✓	✓
Observation [16]	✓	✓		
Protocol analysis [16, 25]	✓	✓		
Prototyping [26]			✓	
Brainstorming [16, 27]			✓	✓
Card sorting [16]		✓	✓	✓
Joint application development [28]			✓	
Scenarios [16]		✓		
Viewpoints [16]		✓		
SWOT analysis [29]	✓	✓	✓	✓
Theory of change [30]	✓	✓	✓	✓
Problem definition [31, 32]	✓	✓	✓	✓
Repertory grids [33, 34]		✓	✓	✓
Laddering [35–37]		✓	✓	✓
Literature review [38]	✓	✓		
Persona [19, 32]	✓	✓	✓	✓

explore the existing documentation of the product or knowledge and acquire requirements from a series of deductions which help analysis capture information about application domain, workflow and product features. Examples include card sorting. Synthetic methods systematically combine conversational, observational and analytical methods into a single method. They provide models to explore product features and interaction possibilities. An example is prototyping with storyboards.

Although the techniques mentioned above make sense, these schemes are not much of a help considering our goals. The primary concern is that the stakeholders should focus on the problems they are facing and should not get distracted by solution or implementation details. Another challenge is that a technique should be representable in a software. Examining the literature that describes these techniques [15, 16], following classification criteria are established:

- **Locating and scoping problems**:
  Is the technique intended to locate and scope problem and not solution oriented?
- **Suitable for autarkic execution**:
  Can techniques be used individually, and it is not performed as a group activity?
- **Practicable for both stakeholder and analyst**:
  Can the technique be used by both stakeholder and analysts?

- **Representable in software**:
  Can the technique be imitated as a software?

Direct answers to *locating and scoping problems* and *suitable for autarkic execution* can be found in the above-mentioned literature. Considering how much in-depth knowledge is required to use a specific elicitation technique, whether it can be used by stakeholders is indicated by *practicable for both stakeholder and analyst*, keeping in mind that stakeholders must not learn anything new. *Representable in software* classifies techniques as per their ability to be imitated as software. There already exist software which implement certain techniques [17–20]. Other techniques are included in our prototype and the usage is described in Sect. 5. Techniques which fulfill a specific criterion are marked in Table 1.

5   Vision Backlog – A Prototype for a Tool-Guided Elicitation Process

Based on this classification, the elicitation techniques listed in Table 2 have been selected to be implemented in our prototype that we call *Vision Backlog*. The selected elicitation techniques intend to gather diverse information at different stages of the elicitation process. These techniques are practiced in different formats with different surrounding environment settings.

To be usable in *Vision Backlog*, we analyzed these techniques for common factors and found one in *questioning*. Based on this insight we created in total 34 questions corresponding to the purpose of the different selected techniques. The questions are intended to ask information about stakeholder goals, activities, aptitudes, attitudes, and skills. These questions have been integrated in the stakeholder view of *Vision Backlog*.

The stakeholder view is intended for stakeholders (like users) to be able to enter data about the task they perform, and more contextual data like why they perform this task, what tools or knowledge they require to perform it, and if there are any alternatives to this task. Along with these information, they provide personal information like education they have had, job designation, and skills they possess. That is why the stakeholder view mainly separates in the two areas tasks and user profile.

The user profile area (cf. Fig. 1) is presented on the very first login with a help pop-up that explains the purpose of the application and the different functionalities including their importance. In this area the stakeholders create a personal profile. The questions we ask are based on Cooper's suggestions for Personas [19] and generalized categorization for the adopter categories on how innovations are adopted by different groups of people from Rogers [2].

In the task area (cf. Fig. 2), the stakeholder can create tasks as they perform them as part of their job. They can provide details about how frequently and how important the task is, the reason behind performing this task, and any improvements he can think of. This area is divided into four steps *Quick intro*, *Think about it*, *Supporting details*, and *Finishing details*. Within each step a description is given what this step is about. It is also possible to suspend doing the steps and continue them afterwards.

Table 2. Selected elicitation techniques and their purpose in *Vision Backlog*

No	Technique	Purpose
1	Interview	Structured stakeholder interviews are used to gather information about their personal attributes, their goals, business drivers behind them, underlying contexts and the domain
2	Questionnaire	Similar to the interview
3	Domain analysis	Used along with interview to gather domain specific information like vocabulary, specific terms used during execution of a specific process or a task
4	Task analysis	Used to gather information about the tasks stakeholders perform, subtasks and concrete steps, with contextual information like specific skills required
5	Problem definition	Used along with questionnaire to gather information about stakeholder's problems with current processes or tasks along with possible alternatives
6	Theory of change	Used along with interview to make stakeholder think about their high-level goals with tasks those help them achieve the goal, and potential risks etc.
7	SWOT analysis	Used to gather information about possible improvements, challenges and alternatives to the tasks stakeholders performs
8	Persona	Provide all the project stakeholders with a common understanding of their target user

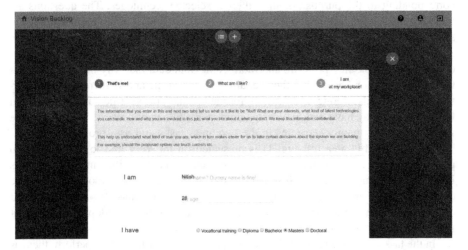

Fig. 1. User profile creation

Within the step *Quick intro* the user shall give an overview of the task, he wants to tell the analyst more about. The questions in this step are about a short description of the task, frequency, importance, his role, and an overview of the steps necessary in this task. In the next step *Think about it* a short rationale for this task shall be given before

Fig. 2. *Vision Backlog* – stakeholder view: task creation

getting to the *Supporting details* step. In this step information regarding the context and the impacts of this task is given. In the last step *Finishing details* additional information about other involved people are given as well as possible factors for improvements.

Besides the stakeholder view with the user profile and task area, we implemented an analyst view (cf. Fig. 3). This view is dedicated to the usability/requirements engineer to explore and discover inputs from the stakeholders. It has various filter and sorting options in this view. Additionally, it can structure the task descriptions from the stakeholders into features for the further development. Besides these functionalities for sorting the created task descriptions, this view also includes a dashboard presenting the users with their attributes for creating personas as well as an overview of the system.

Select	Id	Title	How often	How important	How important in improvement	Why important in improvement	Feature	Stakeholder
	1	Nitish task one	Daily once	Extremely important	Rather important	Saves time	1	1
	2	Nitish task two	Couple of many times ...	Extremely important	Extremely important	Saves extra efforts	1	1
	3	Mihir task one	Weekly once	Rather important	Less important	Saves time	1	2
	4	Mihir task two	Daily once	Extremely important	Extremely important	Saves extra efforts	1	2

Total Tasks: 7   Limit: 4   Page: 1

TASKS   FEATURES   USERS   BEHAVIORAL VARIABLES   ADD TO FEATURE

Fig. 3. *Vision Backlog* – analyst view: task list screen

6   Evaluation

We evaluated *Vision Backlog* with an initial two levels study consisting of a usability test and an expert review on the content quality. These two evaluations have been conducted non-consecutively. The entered data from the usability tests have been used for the expert reviews on the content quality.

The goal of the usability test was to show that stakeholders can understand the tasks presented in *Vision Backlog* and are able to use the tool for the selected elicitation techniques. We have been using the single evaluation from *AttrakDiff* [39] to survey the usability and attractiveness of our tool with a total of five participants. The usability test itself was done remotely and asynchronously. The summed-up results of the survey are presented in Fig. 4. The meaning of the terms used in the diagram are as followed:

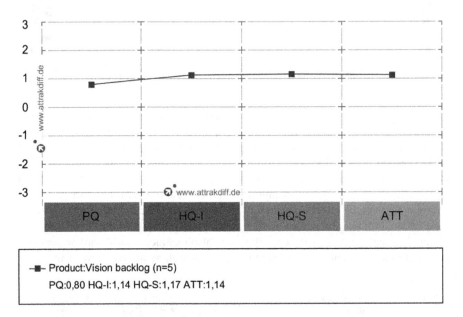

Fig. 4. Usability evaluation results

- *Pragmatic Quality (PQ)* indicates how successful users are in achieving their goals with the product,
- *Hedonic Quality-stimulation (HQ-S)* indicates to what extent the product supports human needs of developing something new in terms of novel, interesting and stimulating functions, contents, interaction and presentation styles,
- *Hedonic Quality-identity (HQ-I)* indicates to what extent the product allows user to identify with it and,
- *Attractiveness (ATT)* is the global value of the product to which Hedonic and pragmatic qualities contribute equally

The results indicate that *Vision Backlog* is rated positive, but the confidence level for PQ (1,62) and HQ (0,95) are quite huge, meaning that the participants evaluated the application differently. Overall, the participants have been successful in achieving their goals and rated the application attractive, but there is still room for improvement.

We had three participants for the expert review on the content quality. All participants had a background in computer science and experiences in requirements elicitation. They used the analyst's view and had to answer five questions afterwards in an online form with a four-point scale for the answers (cf. Table 3). Overall, the participants rated that the utilized techniques have been explained properly and how they are related to requirements elicitation. They strongly agreed that the analytics provided by *Vision Backlog* were helpful but showed a differentiated picture regarding the representation of the analytics.

Table 3. Usefulness evaluation results

	Strongly agree	Agree	Disagree	Strongly disagree
The concepts vision-analytics uses i.e. Persona, behavior variables are explained properly	66.7%	33.3%	0%	0%
The application explains how the concepts used can be used for eliciting requirements	66.7%	33.3%	0%	0%
The semantic segregation of the data is helpful	66.7%	33.3%	0%	0%
The analytics provided are helpful	100%	0%	0%	0%
The structure used i.e. lists etc. to represent the analytics are helpful	33.3%	33.3%	33.3%	0%

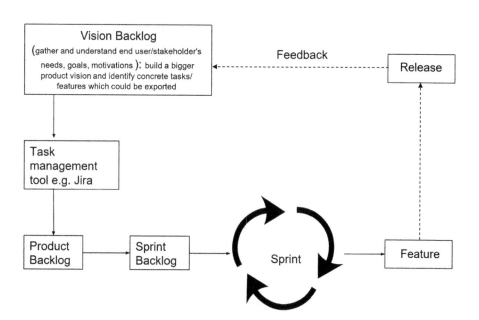

Fig. 5. Future work

7 Conclusion and Outlook

In this paper we presented the idea of a tool-guided elicitation process that empowers users and other stakeholders to actively participate in the requirements elicitation process without being dependent on a usability or requirements engineer. To implement this idea, we created a classification for requirements elicitation techniques and realized it with a prototype called *Vision Backlog*, which is also presented in this paper. In a first study, *Vision Backlog* was evaluated regarding its usability and usefulness.

Vision Backlog concentrated on requirements elicitation in general without focusing on any specific software development methodology. As the concept *Vision Backlog* itself is agile in nature i.e. it encourages stakeholders to iterate over their own vision repeatedly to refine it, it would be interesting to figure out and demonstrate how such an approach can be extended and integrated into an Agile methodology (e.g. into Scrum). By doing this, stakeholder needs can be managed and monitored since their inception until they are developed, typically in a span of a sprint. This would help to measure stakeholder involvement into elicitation activities and give feedback on how much rework is avoided in the presence of *Vision Backlog*. The same approach can be used as well for reducing technical debt. The general idea is depicted in Fig. 5.

Vision Backlog would serve as a starting point which will be used to build a broader product vision and through which potential tasks concerning a specific product feature can be extracted. Such tasks could potentially correspond to tasks in tools like *Jira*. This should form an initial product or even smaller sprint backlog. Once the development work is over for a sprint, a retrospection provides feedback to *Vision Backlog* so that stakeholders or end users can refine their vision if the developed solution do not match sufficient enough with their ideas. Ideally, rework costs while practicing scrum without *Vision Backlog* should be higher than when *Vision Backlog* is integrated into scrum.

Acknowledgement. This work was partially funded by the German Federal Ministry of Education and Research (BMBF) within the project "Zentrum Musik – Edition – Medien" (funding code: **01UG1714A–B**).

References

1. Denning, P.J., Gunderson, C., Hayes-Roth, R.: The profession of IT evolutionary system development. Commun. ACM **51**(12), 29–31 (2008)
2. Rogers, E.M.: Diffusion of Innovations, p. 551. Free Press, New York (2003)
3. Pfeiffer, S., Suphan, A.: The labouring capacity index: living labouring capacity and experience as resources on the road to industry 4.0 (2015)
4. Benner, P.: From Novice to Expert. Addison-Wesley, Menlo Park (1984)
5. Fernández, D.M., Wagner, S., Kalinowski, M., Felderer, M., Mafra, P., Vetrò, A., Conte, T., Christiansson, M.T., Greer, D., Lassenius, C., Männistö, T.: Naming the pain in requirements engineering. Empirical Softw. Eng. **22**(5), 2298–2338 (2017)
6. Yozgyur, K.: A proposal for a requirements elicitation tool to increase stakeholder involvement. In: 2014 5th IEEE International Conference on Software Engineering and Service Science (ICSESS), pp. 145–148. IEEE, June 2014

7. Browne, G.J., Rogich, M.B.: An empirical investigation of user requirements elicitation: comparing the effectiveness of prompting techniques. J. Manag. Inf. Syst. **17**(4), 223–249 (2001)
8. Batool, A., Motla, Y.H., Hamid, B., Asghar, S., Riaz, M., Mukhtar, M., Ahmed, M.: Comparative study of traditional requirement engineering and agile requirement engineering. In: 2013 15th International Conference on Advanced Communication Technology (ICACT), pp. 1006–1014. IEEE, January 2013
9. Maiden, N., Jones, S., Karlsen, K., Neill, R., Zachos, K., Milne, A.: Requirements engineering as creative problem solving: a research agenda for idea finding. In: 2010 18th IEEE International Requirements Engineering Conference (RE), pp. 57–66. IEEE, September 2010
10. Hickey, A.M., Davis, A.M.: A unified model of requirements elicitation. J. Manag. Inf. Syst. **20**(4), 65–84 (2004)
11. Snowden, D.: Cynefin: a sense of time and space, the social ecology of knowledge management (2000)
12. Maiden, N.: So, what is requirements work? IEEE Softw. **30**(2), 14–15 (2013)
13. Boehm, B.W.: A spiral model of software development and enhancement. Computer **21**(5), 61–72 (1988)
14. Zhang, Z.: Effective requirements development-A comparison of requirements elicitation techniques. In: Berki, E., Nummenmaa, J., Sunley, I., Ross, M., Staples, G. (eds.) Software Quality Management XV: Software Quality in the Knowledge Society, pp. 225–240. British Computer Society (2007)
15. McManus, J.: A stakeholder perspective within software engineering projects. In: Proceedings of 2004 IEEE International Conference on Engineering Management Conference, vol. 2, pp. 880–884. IEEE, October 2004
16. Zowghi, D., Coulin, C.: Requirements elicitation: a survey of techniques, approaches, and tools. In: Aurum, A., Wohlin, C. (eds.) Engineering and Managing Software Requirements, pp. 19–46. Springer, Heidelberg (2005). https://doi.org/10.1007/3-540-28244-0_2
17. Card Sorting Tools for Surveying Information Architecture (IA). https://dynomapper.com/blog/19-ux/428-card-sorting-tools. Accessed 20 Oct 2017
18. Cooke, N.J.: Varieties of knowledge elicitation techniques. Int. J. Hum.-Comput. Stud. **41**(6), 801–849 (1994)
19. Cooper, A., Reimann, R., Cronin, D.: About Face 3: the Essentials of Interaction Design. Wiley, Hoboken (2007)
20. Atukorala, N.L., Chang, C.K., Oyama, K.: Situation-oriented requirements elicitation. In: 2016 IEEE 40th Annual Conference on Computer Software and Applications Conference (COMPSAC), vol. 1, pp. 233–238. IEEE, June 2016
21. Foddy, W.: Constructing Questions for Interviews and Questionnaires: Theory and Practice in Social Research. Cambridge University Press, Cambridge (1994)
22. Wilson, M.: Task models for knowledge elicitation. In: Knowledge Elicitation: Principles, Techniques and Applications, pp. 197–220 (1989)
23. Carlshamre, P., Karlsson, J.: A usability-oriented approach to requirements engineering. In: Proceedings of the Second International Conference on Requirements Engineering, pp. 145–152. IEEE, April 1996
24. Prieto Díaz, R.: Domain analysis: an introduction. ACM SIGSOFT Softw. Eng. Notes **15**(2), 47–54 (1990)
25. Goguen, J.A., Linde, C.: Techniques for requirements elicitation. In: Proceedings of IEEE International Symposium on, Requirements Engineering, pp. 152–164. IEEE, January 1993
26. Sommerville, I., Sawyer, P.: Requirements Engineering: A Good Practice Guide. Wiley, Hoboken (1997)

27. Osborn, A.F.: Applied Imagination; Principles and Procedures of Creative Problem-Solving: Principles and Procedures of Creative Problem-Solving. Scribner, New York City (1963)
28. Wood, J., Silver, D.: Joint Application Development. Wiley, Hoboken (1995)
29. Pickton, D.W., Wright, S.: What's swot in strategic analysis? Strateg. Change **7**(2), 101–109 (1998)
30. Taplin, D.H., Clark, H.: Theory of Change Basics: A Primer on Theory of Change. Actknowledge, New York (2012)
31. Kimbell, L., Julier, J.: The Social Design Methods Menu. Fieldstudio Ltd., London (2012)
32. Tools – Development Impact and You. http://diytoolkit.org/tools/. Accessed 20 Oct 2017
33. Kelly, G.: The Psychology of Personal Constructs: Volume Two: Clinical Diagnosis and Psychotherapy. Routledge, Abingdon (2003)
34. Fransella, F., Bell, R., Bannister, D.: A Manual for Repertory Grid Technique. Wiley, Hoboken (2004)
35. Vanden Abeele, V., Zaman, B.: Laddering the user experience! In: User Experience Evaluation Methods in Product Development (UXEM 2009)-Workshop, August 2009
36. Hinkle, D.N.: The change of personal constructs from the viewpoint of a theory of construct implications (Doctoral dissertation, The Ohio State University) (1965)
37. Gutman, J.: A means-end chain model based on consumer categorization processes. J. Mark. **46**, 60–72 (1982)
38. Greener, S.: Business Research Methods. BookBoon, London (2008)
39. Hassenzahl, M., Burmester, M., Koller, F.: AttrakDiff: Ein Fragebogen zur Messung wahrgenommener hedonischer und pragmatischer Qualität. In: Mensch & Computer 2003, pp. 187–196. Vieweg+Teubner Verlag (2003)
40. Hall, E., Zeldman, J.: Just Enough Research. A Book Apart, New York (2013)
41. First Rule of Usability? Don't Listen to Users. https://www.nngroup.com/articles/first-rule-of-usability-dont-listen-to-users/. Accessed 20 Oct 2017

Music at Your Fingertips: Designing Mobile Interaction Interfaces for Runners

Susanne Koch Stigberg$^{(\boxtimes)}$

IT Department, Østfold University College, Halden, Norway
susanne.k.stigberg@hiof.no

Abstract. This paper presents a technique to simplify the making of mobile interaction interfaces. We often use smartphones while moving, resulting in non-optimal or even unsafe mobile interactions. Better interactions need to be created with locomotion in mind and experienced in context. Consequently interactive behavior of mobile devices cannot be sketched, but must be made to be experienced. Making mobile prototypes is time-consuming and requires programming literacy. It often involves the making of an input artifact; establishing a connection between artifact and mobile phone; and implementing an application on the mobile phone for exploring the interactive behavior. The use of commercial smartphone automation tool eliminates the need for re-implementing available smartphone functionalities, and invites non-programmers into the process of making mobile interaction interfaces. To illustrate the proposed technique I present a case study of a wearable prototype to control music on the mobile phone by tapping one's fingertips.

Keywords: Mobile interaction interfaces · Interaction design
Rapid prototyping · Automation tools

1 Introduction

Research in mobile interaction design is concerned with the use of technology while being mobile. So far most mobile systems request the user to "stop-to-interact", designed for interaction only when a user is standing still, paying visual and mental attention to the device [1]. Research has shown that the user's ability to interact with technology in motion is decreased even for simple activities like walking [2, 3]. Lumsden and Brewster [4] requested "a paradigm shift in terms of interaction techniques for mobile technology" already in 2003. Since then mobile technology has been an important theme in HCI research. Liu et al. [5] published a review focusing on keyword analysis of CHI publications to understand how the landscape of the HCI field has evolved. They list mobile phone as the most frequently used keyword between 2004–2013. Still ten years later Marshall and Tennent [1] claim that mobile interaction does not exist. They highlight four challenges designing interactions for mobile devices: cognitive load, physical constraints, terrain and other people.

Recognizing these challenges, interaction designers must explore mobile interfaces and users' experiences with these interfaces in their anticipated context. User experience is often described with the "why", "what" and "how" of device use. The "why"

© Springer International Publishing AG, part of Springer Nature 2018
A. Marcus and W. Wang (Eds.): DUXU 2018, LNCS 10918, pp. 771–781, 2018.
https://doi.org/10.1007/978-3-319-91797-9_53

involves the users' motivation, their meaning construction and value of interaction; the "what" addresses the device functionality; the "how" relates to the style of interaction. To understand and design for mobile interactions, we need working prototypes ("what") that have interactive behavior ("how") and are adaptable to users' needs ("why"). This paper proposes a rapid prototyping technique to create novel interaction interfaces to explore mobile interactions, enabling users to experience two-way inter-actions with devices while in motion. The technique allows to:

- Re-use smartphone functionalities available from installed applications;
- Create customizable interaction interfaces that can be altered easily during use.

To demonstrate the technique I present FingerTap, a wearable prototype to control Spotify[1] on a smartphone by tapping one's fingertips. The concept was generated in a bachelor thesis in industrial design. The students mapped out problem areas around smartphone usage in sports and designed smartphone accessories that could simplify usage while exercising. One design sketch illustrated how Apple's EarPods[2] func-tionalities could be mapped onto one's fingertips (Fig. 1). The article continues in Sect. 2 with an overview of current research and theories in mobile interaction design. Section 3 discusses making in interaction design in general. I review mobile proto-typing tools in the HCI literature and present my rapid prototyping technique. The FingerTap case study is presented in Sect. 4. The article ends with a discussion and a conclusion in Sects. 5 and 6.

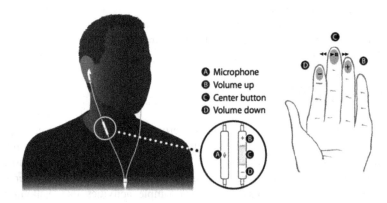

Fig. 1. FingerTap concept sketch

2   Mobile Interaction Design Research

The research community has focused on probing alternative interaction interfaces by implementing high-fidelity prototypes for pre-defined functionalities and evaluating their ease-of-use [6]. Several active mobile interaction interfaces [7–9] have been

---

[1] http://www.spotify.com/.

[2] https://www.apple.com/shop/product/MNHF2AM/A/earpods-with-35-mm-headphone-plug.

developed to demonstrate possible alternatives. Hands-free and non-visual alternatives to remotely control mobile devices such as the PocketMenu [10] or the Gesture RSS Reader Study [11] show promising results. Marshall et al. [12] propose a taxonomy of mobile interactions based on two dimensions: inhibition of interaction and relation to locomotion, where inhibition of interaction looks at how much an interaction with technology is constraint by an activity, and where relation describes how much the interaction is integrated and encouraged for the activity. While this framework helps researchers to describe mobile interactions with technology and offers general design strategies, it does not provide an account on how to actually design for them.

Mobile interactions need to be experienced. Researchers have to create prototypes with working interactive behavior to study their user experience and use qualities [13]. Situatedness, embodiment, the particularity of each context of use, meaning construction, and values are themes for mobile interaction design. Svanæs [14] refers to Merleau-Ponty's theories to understand interaction as embodied perception. He describes the feel dimension of a user experience as the user's perception of the object's interactive behavior. This mindset requires active participation and kinaesthetic creativity to be used in interaction design research [14]. Kinaesthetic creativity as defined by Svanæs [14] is "the body's ability to relate in a direct and creative fashion with the feel dimension of interactive products during the design process". Moen [15] argues that movement-based interactions shall be designed from a non-technological, people-centered point of view in order to create embodied and engaging interaction experiences. Similar, Zhao expects an interaction shift from device-centric to human-and-environment-centric. Turning from a focus in technology invention to an interest in participation, kinaesthetic creativity and performance requires methods, not common in present mobile HCI research. In a meta-study [6], Stigberg reports on user participation and design methods in mobile interaction design research between 2012–2017. She concludes that the typical mobile HCI study is device-centric, developing a prototype and evaluating its usability with 14 students. Only 12% of the analyzed studies had a more human-centered focus including participants throughout the design process. These findings open up for exploring further tools and techniques to support a people-and-environment-centric design of mobile interactions.

3 Making Mobile Interaction Interfaces

Making novel mobile interaction interfaces often involves three steps:

- Making a new interaction artifact;
- Integrating the artifact and the smartphone;
- Implementing a smartphone application for coupling artifact input to desired functionalities.

Such a process is presented in [16], there we use a glove-based gesture input coupled to video recording and social media functionalities.

Making prototypes to understand a problem and evaluate a possible solution is a central part in the traditional design process. The process of design is often described as a sequence of divergent steps, where ideas are produced; and convergent steps, where ideas are eliminated. Sketching and lo-fi prototyping are used early in the process to open up the design space and allow for diversity and participation with low cost and low technology threshold. Making hi-fi prototypes on the other hand is used later in the design process during converging, implementing one idea for evaluation, often a time consuming activity that requires programming literacy.

However interactive behavior of mobile devices cannot be sketched, but must be made [17]. Hi-fi prototypes in mobile interaction design are more than "a representation of a design, made before the final solution exists" [18]. They are also used in the early phases of design for exploration and demonstration [19], as tools for gaining empathy [20] or as learning vehicles [21]. Lim et al. [21] try to give a different perspective on prototypes and they present two prototyping principles: fundamental prototyping principle and economic principle of prototyping. Prototypes should be as simple as possible to explore qualities of interest "without distorting the understanding of the whole" and they should in the most efficient way, make "the possibilities and limitations of a design idea visible and measurable". Following these principles and simplifying the making of hi-fi prototypes early in the design process, I present a rapid prototyping technique to explore and evaluate design ideas with people. The created prototypes have configurable working interactive behavior and are made using simple prototyping tools, rather than high-fidelity materials.

3.1   Mobile Prototyping Tools

There exist a number of making tools available to support mobile prototyping in the HCI literature. AWARE [22] is an Android framework for handling extensive mobile context information. Programmers can access, create and share context information through plugins when creating new applications. An early prototyping platform for context-aware mobile applications is ContextPhone [23], offering phone resources and context information to application programmers. Both frameworks provide support primarily for programmers during the development of new applications.

iStuff Mobile [24] is a rapid prototyping framework aimed for interaction designers, supporting exploration of new sensor-based interfaces for mobile phones. The framework uses a combination of desktop and mobile phone applications communicating via Bluetooth to create and evaluate new interaction interfaces, making it unpractical for evaluation in the wild. Mogeste [25] is a mobile phone tool for users to create rapid, in-situ mobile gestures, however the tool does not support working interaction interfaces, since gestures cannot be coupled to phone functionalities. Prototyping tools that enable non-programmers to design and experience novel interaction interfaces are not yet commonplace.

3.2   Simplifying the Making of Mobile Interfaces Using Tasker

From previous projects I noticed two areas in the process of making that could be simplified:

- Functionalities are re-implemented for each new interaction device even though there are plenty of smartphone applications available offering ready-made functionalities.

- Functionalities are defined by the researcher during the design process and cannot be changed during use by the participants.

Automation tools can be used to create and adapt mobile interaction interfaces using ready-made functionalities from installed smartphone applications. *Automate*, *AutomateIt* and *Tasker* are commercially available automation tools for Android that trigger actions based on user-defined setup rules. Here I present a technique based on *Tasker* to reuse and reconfigure smartphone functionalities for new interaction devices as illustrated in Fig. 2. *Tasker* executes *tasks* (sets of actions) based on *contexts* (application, time, date, location, event, gesture) in user-defined *profiles* [26]. For my purpose *Tasker* provides a way of coupling user input to smartphone functionalities for rapid prototyping of new mobile interaction interfaces in three steps:

- Creating an event plugin for new interaction devices,
- Creating *Tasks* using ready-made functionalities,
- Coupling input events and tasks by creating *Profiles*.

This approach eliminates the need to implement a smartphone application with desired functionalities. Instead designers and non-programmers can customize the coupling of functionalities to input in *Tasker* throughout the design process.

Creating Tasks. Tasks are sequences of actions that control built-in smartphone functionalities such as handling calls, display on/off or volume up/down, as well as third-party application functionalities. A task can be of varied complexity, run stand-alone or be called by another task. *Volume Up* (Fig. 4) is an example of a simple task with only one action, raising the media volume of the device by one step. *Tasks* can be extended by additional utility apps e.g. *SecureSettings* to unlock the screen, or *AutoInput* to simulate touch input.

Creating Profiles. Tasks can be triggered by events. These couplings are defined as *Profiles*. Input events from new interaction devices can be included in *Tasker* as *Event Plugins*. For example the *FingerTap* plugin has three possible events: *index finger tapped*, *middle finger tapped* and *ring finger tapped* (Fig. 4). A *Profile* could be defined as: *Index finger tapped* entails *Volume down* task. Profiles can be *active* or *passive* and *Profile* status is updated automatically when *Tasker* is closed.

Tasker Plugin. *Tasker* supports standard Android automation plugins [27]. Any input device can be integrated in *Tasker* as an *Event Plugin*. Off-the-shelf input devices, such as the Myo Gesture Control Armband[3] and the Flic button[4] implement this standard and are available in *Tasker*. The *FingerTap* prototype demonstrates a plugin implementation. Tasker provides a tutorial and example project for developing a plugin[5].

Benefits. I noticed four major benefits using *Tasker* for rapid prototyping mobile interaction interfaces:

---

[3] https://www.myo.com.

[4] https://flic.io.

[5] http://tasker.dinglisch.net/plugins.html.

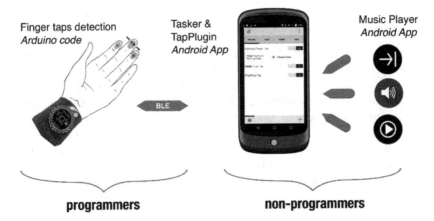

Fig. 2. Simplifying the making of mobile interaction interfaces using tasker

- It allows an easy integration of novel interaction devices and ready-made smartphone functionalities through *plugins*.
- It supports the reuse of smartphone functionalities for different interaction devices as stored *tasks*.
- It enables to alter mappings of input and smartphone functionalities throughout the entire design process in *profiles*.
- It provides a mean to co-design mobile interaction interfaces with non-programmers.

4 Case Study

Lisa is a recreational runner. She likes to run longer distances and enjoys listening to music. She uses her phone as a music player during her runs. She has a favorite playlist, which she starts before running. She puts the phone in her jacket pocket or in a phone belt around her waist and goes for a run. Sometimes the current song does not fit her mood and she likes to switch to the next song. She listens to the song anyway because it is bothersome to take up the phone and select the next song via touchscreen. Sometimes she meets a friend and likes to stop the music during conversation. Instead she takes off her headphones, stopping the music takes too long when meeting a friend. Lisa would love an easy way to control her music during her runs without the hassle of touchscreen interaction.

Lisa's story inspired three bachelor students in industrial design to come with the FingerTap, a wearable prototype to control Spotify on a smartphone by tapping one's fingertips. In a design sketch the students illustrated how Apple's EarPods functionalities could be mapped onto one's fingertips (Fig. 1) to help Lisa. I created a working artifact using the proposed prototyping technique, to provide means to explore their concept in use.

Making the Artifact. The FingerTap prototype is based on a *LilyPad Simblee BLE Board* connected to 110mAh lithium battery for e-textiles hidden inside a sweatband (Fig. 3). Index, middle and ring finger are connected to digital ports using a line of conductive paint from wrist to finger. The thumb is connected to VCC in the same way. I used pull-down resistors to read the digital state of the fingers as low when inactive and high when tapping thumb on finger. An alternative solution utilizes copper tape as means of connecting the fingertips to the *LilyPad*. The Arduino code is an adaption of the *LedButton* example provided by *Simblee*. The making of the artifact took a total of 2 days.

Programming the Plugin. The plugin implementation on the phone was time-intensive (about 4 days). The core functionality enables communication between prototype and smartphone based on Bluetooth Low Energy (BLE) built upon the BluetoothLE example [28] available in Android Studio. I added the Locale API project [27] and created new *EditActivity* and *QueryReceiver* classes. *Tasker* calls *EditActivity* when creating a new *Profile* in *Tasker* and choosing the plugin from the *Add Event* dialog. The *QueryReceiver* is called whenever the plugin notifies *Tasker* that an event has occurred. *Tasker Event Plugin* is a special type of Android automation plugin and I included a *TaskerPlugin.java* file to the Android project and made some minor changes in the project files as described in [26]. To make the plugin reusable for further interaction artifacts I mapped the three different finger-tapped input events to generic labels (*first, second, third*).

Creating Profiles and Tasks. After 6 working days of making the interaction artifact and programming the plugin I met with the bachelor students to create the mobile interaction interface. We defined three profiles (Fig. 4): Indexfinger Tapped, where index finger lowers the volume by one; Middelfinger Tapped, where middle finger toggles playback; and Ringfinger Tapped, where ring finger raises the volume by one.

Exploring FingerTap Interaction Interfaces. After defining the profiles we put on the prototype. First we used conductive paint to connect the interaction artifact with the fingertips. The paint took around 20 min to dry properly before it could be used. In another meeting we used thin copper tape (5 mm) to connect the fingertips with the interaction artifact. This was much faster than using the paint. Second we powered up the interaction artifact and connected it to the mobile phone via BLE. During the two meetings we explored three dimensions of the prototype:

- Exploration on the material used for the interaction
- Exploration on the form of the interaction.
- Exploration on the functionality of the interaction.

The Interaction Material. Both conductive paint and copper tape were used to connect the fingertips to the artifact. Conductive paint became fragile when dry and broke easily when moving the hand. The paint was water-soluble and not a reliable solution for outdoors and sports, exposed to rain and sweat. Copper tape was easy to apply but not elastic to cope with the moving hand. Both alternatives aren't practical solutions for outdoor use. We are interested in testing conductive tattoos as alternative interaction material [29].

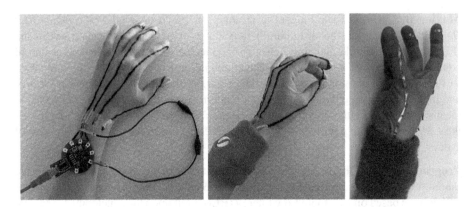

Fig. 3. FingerTap interaction artifact

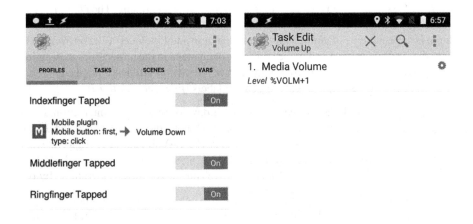

Fig. 4. Screenshots: tasker profiles (left) and volume up task (right)

The Interaction Form. The students explored different finger tapping scenarios; index, middle and ring finger were selected as favorable tapping gestures. They explored, left-hand, right-hand and two-handed tapping. The prototype is flexible to adapt its interaction form to their liking.

The Interaction Functionality. The students created new tasks and changed profiles to adapt to different running scenarios, such as handling calls while running, managing activity tracking, or taking pictures and videos of the activity. The prototype is flexible to adapt its interaction functionality to different scenarios.

5 Discussion

The FingerTap case study illustrates how to support active participation and kinaesthetic creativity in mobile interaction design [14]. Using an automation tool reduces the need for programming literacy when designing the interface and enables non-programmers to join the process of making as anticipated by Sanders and Stappers [30]. The technique supports designers to rapidly prototype working interactive behavior early in the design process, opening up the design space to explore the "why", "what" and "how" of user experience.

The FingerTap prototype evolved through exploring alternatives and enacting future scenarios together with the design students. We reused music player functionalities to investigate possibilities and limitations of a design idea in a simple and efficient way, following the economic and fundamental principles of prototyping as defined by Lim et al. [21]. The prototype was adapted to the needs of runners to provide meaningful interactions ("why") by defining profiles. Tasks were defined as functionalities of the prototype ("what"). Finger tapping as form of the interaction ("how") was altered to explore different gesture interfaces.

However the design space is limited through the technique itself. In the FingerTap case, we could only add available smartphone functionalities as tasks. Moreover, the artifact had just three tapping events, a convergent design choice made early in the process. Researchers need to be aware about the limitations and choose carefully where to open up the design space to support the research interest and where to converge the design space to enable non-programmers to participate. Used thoughtfully automation tool enable exploration of interaction concepts in a simple and rapid way, and acknowledge non-programmers in the process of making these interfaces.

6 Conclusion

To understand an object's interactive behavior Svanaes [14] proposes designing with active participation and kinaesthetic creativity. Using an automation tool, I proposed a technique to create prototypes with working interactive behavior early in the design process. I presented FingerTap, a wearable prototype to control music on the mobile phone by tapping one's fingertips. The case study with three bachelor students in industrial design described how the prototyping technique allows non-programmers to be involved in the making of mobile interaction interfaces. First, the students were able to explore different materials used for the interaction artifact. Second, they were able to modify the interaction form of the interface and third, they were able to adapt the functionality coupled to the interaction interface. Overall the presented technique is an effort to support a more people-and-environment-centric design of mobile interactions.

In my opinion, rethinking the tools and techniques for mobile interaction design can open up for a paradigm shift in the field. Hopefully, my work will inspire the research community to explore further approaches for this shift.

References

1. Marshall, J., Tennent, P.: Mobile interaction does not exist. In: CHI 2013 Extended Abstracts on Human Factors in Computing Systems, New York, NY, USA, pp. 2069–2078 (2013)
2. Bergstrom-Lehtovirta, J., Oulasvirta, A., Brewster, S.: The effects of walking speed on target acquisition on a touchscreen interface. In: Proceedings of the 13th International Conference on Human Computer Interaction with Mobile Devices and Services, New York, NY, USA, pp. 143–146 (2011)
3. Schildbach, B., Rukzio, E.: Investigating selection and reading performance on a mobile phone while walking. In: Proceedings of the 12th International Conference on Human Computer Interaction with Mobile Devices and Services, New York, NY, USA, pp. 93–102 (2010)
4. Lumsden, J., Brewster, S.: A paradigm shift: alternative interaction techniques for use with mobile & wearable devices. In: Proceedings of the 2003 Conference of the Centre for Advanced Studies on Collaborative Research, Toronto, Ontario, Canada, pp. 197–210 (2003)
5. Liu, Y., et al.: CHI 1994–2013: mapping two decades of intellectual progress through co-word analysis. In: Presented at the Proceedings of the SIGCHI Conference on Human Factors in Computing Systems, Proceedings of the 32nd Annual ACM Conference on Human Factors in Computing Systems, pp. 3553–3562 (2014)
6. Stigberg, S.K.: A critical review on participation in mobile interaction design research. In: MUM 2017: The 16th International Conference on Mobile and Ubiquitous Multimedia, 26–29 November, Stuttgart, Germany, New York, NY, USA, 2017, pp. 161–166 (2017)
7. Dancu, A., et al.: Gesture bike: examining projection surfaces and turn signal systems for urban cycling. In: Proceedings of the 2015 International Conference on Interactive Tabletops & Surfaces, New York, NY, USA, pp. 151–159 (2015)
8. Kim, K., Joo, D., Lee, K.-P.: Wearable-object-based interaction for a mobile audio device. In: CHI 2010 Extended Abstracts on Human Factors in Computing Systems, New York, NY, USA, pp. 3865–3870 (2010)
9. Mueller, F.F., O'Brien, S., Thorogood, A.: Jogging over a distance: supporting a 'jogging together' experience although being apart. In: CHI 2007 Extended Abstracts on Human Factors in Computing Systems, New York, NY, USA, pp. 2579–2584 (2007)
10. Pielot, M., Kazakova, A., Hesselmann, T., Heuten, W., Boll, S.: PocketMenu: non-visual menus for touch screen devices. In: Proceedings of the 14th International Conference on Human-computer Interaction with Mobile Devices and Services, New York, NY, USA, pp. 327–330 (2012)
11. Wiliamson, J.R., Crossan, A., Brewster, S.: Multimodal mobile interactions: usability studies in real world settings. In: Proceedings of the 13th International Conference on Multimodal Interfaces, New York, NY, USA, pp. 361–368 (2011)
12. Marshall, J., Dancu, A., Mueller, F.F.: Interaction in motion: designing truly mobile interaction. In: Proceedings of the 2016 ACM Conference on Designing Interactive Systems, New York, NY, USA, pp. 215–228 (2016)

13. Löwgren, J.: Articulating the use qualities of digital designs. In: Fishwick, P.A. (ed.) Aesthetic Computing, pp. 383–403. MIT Press (2008). https://books.google.no/books?id= M-qjYktThEMC&lpg=PA383&ots=ICzWeqaxVn&dq=Articulating%20the%20use%20qua lities%20of%20digital%20designs&hl=sv&pg=PP1#v=onepage&q=Articulating%20the% 20use%20qualities%20of%20digital%20designs&f=false. ISBN 0262562375, 97802625 62379

14. Svanæs, D.: Interaction design for and with the lived body: some implications of merleau-ponty's phenomenology. ACM Trans. Comput.-Hum. Interact. **20**(1), 8:1–8:30 (2013)

15. Moen, J.: From hand-held to body-worn: embodied experiences of the design and use of a wearable movement-based interaction concept. In: Proceedings of the 1st International Conference on Tangible and Embedded Interaction, New York, NY, USA, pp. 251–258 (2007)

16. Karlsen, J., Stigberg, S.K., Herstad, J.: Probing privacy in practice: privacy regulation and instant sharing of video in social media when running. In: Proceedings of the 2016 International Conference on Advances in Computer-Human Interactions, Venice, Italy, pp. 29–36 (2016)

17. Löwgren, J.: On the significance of making in interaction design research. Interactions **23**(3), 26–33 (2016)

18. Moggridge, B., Atkinson, B.: Designing Interactions, vol. 17. MIT Press, Cambridge (2007)

19. Houde, S., Hill, C.: Chapter 16 - What do prototypes prototype? In: Helander, M.G., Landauer, T.K., Prabhu, P.V. (eds.) Handbook of Human-Computer Interaction (Second Edition), pp. 367–381. North-Holland, Amsterdam (1997)

20. Buchenau, M., Suri, J.F.: Experience prototyping. In: Proceedings of the 3rd Conference on Designing Interactive Systems: Processes, Practices, Methods, and Techniques, New York, NY, USA, pp. 424–433 (2000)

21. Lim, Y.-K., Stolterman, E., Tenenberg, J.: The anatomy of prototypes: prototypes as filters, prototypes as manifestations of design ideas. ACM Trans. Comput.-Hum. Interact. **15**(2), 7:1–7:27 (2008)

22. Ferreira, D., Kostakos, V., Dey, A.K.: AWARE: mobile context instrumentation framework. Front. ICT **2**, 6 (2015)

23. Raento, M., Oulasvirta, A., Petit, R., Toivonen, H.: ContextPhone: a prototyping platform for context-aware mobile applications. IEEE Pervasive Comput. **4**(2), 51–59 (2005)

24. Ballagas, R., Memon, F., Reiners, R., Borchers, J.: iStuff mobile: rapidly prototyping new mobile phone interfaces for ubiquitous computing. In: Proceedings of the SIGCHI Conference on Human Factors in Computing Systems, New York, NY, USA, pp. 1107–1116 (2007)

25. Parnami, A., Gupta, A., Reyes, G., Sadana, R., Li, Y., Abowd, G.: Mogeste: mobile tool for in-situ motion gesture design. In: Proceedings of the 2016 ACM International Joint Conference on Pervasive and Ubiquitous Computing: Adjunct, New York, NY, USA, pp. 345–348 (2016)

26. Tasker for Android. http://tasker.dinglisch.net/. Accessed 20 Mar 2017

27. Developer, Locale for Android. https://www.twofortyfouram.com/developer/. Accessed 12 May 2017

28. BluetoothLeGatt|Android Developers. https://developer.android.com/samples/ BluetoothLeGatt/index.html. Accessed 12 May 2017

29. Kao, H.-L.C., Holz, C., Roseway, A., Calvo, A., Schmandt, C.: DuoSkin: rapidly prototyping on-skin user interfaces using skin-friendly materials. In: Proceedings of the 2016 ACM International Symposium on Wearable Computers, New York, NY, USA, pp. 16–23 (2016)

30. Sanders, E.B.-N., Stappers, P.J.: Probes, toolkits and prototypes: three approaches to making in codesigning. CoDesign **10**(1), 5–14 (2014)

Application of Agile Development Methodology and User-Centered Design for the Interdisciplinary Project Zuku

Max Vilcapoma[✉] and Freddy Paz

Pontificia Universidad Católica Del Perú, Av. Universitaria 1801, San Miguel, Lima 32, Peru
{christian.vilcapomag, fpaz}@pucp.pe

Abstract. The user-centered design allows the creative teams to focus on the real needs avoiding investing effort in features that will not add value to the product to be elaborated, this also reduces the rework that may result from not being clear about the requirements and assuming the that our experience dictates as a truth as to what may be useful to the end user. Within a multidisciplinary development project in which different specialties are part of the creative process and its implementation, the team members' skills and experience in each of the involved areas are exploited, for the project to be developed will be a result of the sum of all the parts and not individual work. In consequence, the application of a user-centered methodology with agile development is presented in which the point of view of the different team members can contribute to the development of the software product. This paper describes what the Zuku project consists of, the context in which it was developed, methodologies involved, phases of the project and final results of the implementation.

Keywords: User-centered design · Agile development
Multidisciplinary development project · Design sprint · Design thinking

1 Introduction

The interdisciplinary projects allow to carry out all the knowledge acquired during the study stage. The great challenge of this type of projects is to identify what kind of methodology allows the different specialties involved to cooperate in the creation process without falling into the error of doing an isolated job and thinking that during the process the advances can be combined without generating compatibility problem. The challenge to raise a working methodology, to apply it and face the different barriers that arise along the way is what prompted the development of this document. In the following document, the context of the proposed project, the ideation phase to select the work methodology, the obstacles that were presented along the way and finally the lessons learned so far will be described [13].

© Springer International Publishing AG, part of Springer Nature 2018
A. Marcus and W. Wang (Eds.): DUXU 2018, LNCS 10918, pp. 782–794, 2018.
https://doi.org/10.1007/978-3-319-91797-9_54

2   Context

The Pontifical Catholic University of Peru as part of the specialty of computer engineering's course curriculum presents in the tenth semester the course Development of Programs 2. In this course, seeks to apply the knowledge acquired throughout the career in the development of a software product. In comparison to other semesters, the structure of this course varied, trying to integrate computer knowledge with the innovative talent of the specialties of Industrial Design and Electronic Engineering. Thus, the interdisciplinary project "Zuku" was born, which is presented as a proposal of a solution to the current problems of service and attention in the cafeterias of the campus, developing an integral redesign of the service that improves the processes of food purchase and the user's experience in that process.

The problems that usually occur in these canteens are the congestion of queues, delays when paying and lack of signaling in the place. In addition, the delay in the replenishment is the problem that arises for the concessionaire.

3   Work Methodology

3.1   Concepts

In the present project, the teams of the different specialties arrived with their own work methodologies used in previous projects. The specialty of industrial design worked under the guidance of Bruno Munari, an Italian artist who provided much knowledge in that field, laying the foundations of design work methodologies in his many publications in which highlights "How objects are born" (1989) [1]. In this book, the author presents the foundations on the design process called "project method" which is based on the problems' solution. Referring to the following figure (Fig. 1).

On the other hand, from a computer perspective, the methodologies or processes of software development have been categorized into two groups based on their work principles and philosophies, these are traditional methodologies and agile methodologies.

The traditional methodology like Unified Software Development Process (USDP) is based on the study of cases, which uses the UML notation to define its structures [2]. This methodology, extended by Rational Software Inc. gives rise to the traditional framework Rational Unified Process (RUP). The framework is oriented to uses cases, has an iterative and incremental process and focuses on architecture. The framework is made up of four phases and the activities carried out during the process can be classified into nine disciplines. Referring to the following figure (Fig. 2).

The agile methodologies, which were popularized within the software development industry, follow an iterative, adaptive and cooperative development line with constant feedback in order to be able to respond to unpredictable scenarios that may arise during the project. It is based on twelve principles which are called Agile Manifesto [3].

The CHAOS REPORT demonstrates the growing success of agile methodologies in projects compared to traditional methodologies [4]. Referring to the following figure (Fig. 3).

Fig. 1. Bruno Munari design method [1].

In the current academic semester, the specialty of Industrial Design, as part of the study topics covered during the cycle, adopted Design Thinking as a work methodology. Design Thinking is a design methodology that takes as tools such as empathy and experimentation to propose innovative solutions. In this design process, the final user is always present as the center of everything. In 1969, Herbert Simon raised one of the first formal models of Design Thinking in his publication "The Sciences of the Artificial" in which he considered seven stages of the process [5]. Today there are

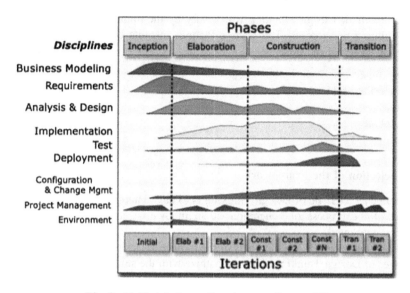

Fig. 2. Unified Software Development Process [2]

SIZE	METHOD	SUCCESSFUL	CHALLENGED	FAILED
All Size Projects	Agile	39%	52%	9%
	Waterfall	11%	60%	29%
Large Size Projects	Agile	18%	59%	23%
	Waterfall	3%	55%	42%
Medium Size Projects	Agile	27%	62%	11%
	Waterfall	7%	68%	25%
Small Size Projects	Agile	58%	38%	4%
	Waterfall	44%	45%	11%

CHAOS RESOLUTION BY AGILE VERSUS WATERFALL

The resolution of all software projects from FY2011–2015 within the new CHAOS database, segmented by the agile process and waterfall method. The total number of software projects is over 10,000.

Fig. 3. Chaos Report 2015 [4]

many variants of Design Thinking which vary by the number of stages that are considered during the process. The Hansso-Plattner Institute of Design at Stanford proposes five stages of the process:

- Empathise
- Define the problem
- Ideate
- Prototype
- Test

3.2   Selection of the Framework

The main characteristic of Design Thinking is to have interdisciplinary groups that can be part of the process of concretion of an innovative solution that can solve the problems presented.

During the semester, the members of the Industrial Design team carried out each of the stages of Design Thinking. They empathize with the student in the daily activity of going to the university canteens to make the purchase in person and later pick up, define the problem (which consisted in the discomfort of the service of buying and distributing food); devised solutions that can reduce that dissatisfaction of students by the work involved in acquiring food in the dining rooms, prototyping solutions such as devising many variants of sales flows and planning the design of new furnishings that provide a satisfactory shopping experience.

In the team of the specialty of informatic engineering, it was clear from the beginning that a web tool and mobile application that can support the new flow raised by the specialty of Industrial Design should be developed, in which it was considered as part of the flow the implementation of RFID modules that would be elaborated by the electronic engineering team.

Being aware that the computer solution was the one described above, it would not be applicable to use Design Thinking in the creation process since the solution was already known. Instead, what this methodology seeks is to find an unknown solution based on a problem. Consequently, the need to propose a work methodology that allows to involve all the specialties for the ideation of said IT solution, taking into consideration a design stage and a development one was determined [15].

A research stage was carried out in which the studies of Doctor Toni Granollers on the integration of the software development process and the user-centered design were taken as a basis [6]. Based on his research, a hybrid development model was proposed, which integrated characteristics of agile development methodologies with a collaborative work form for the iterative stage of design based on a variant of Design Thinking proposed by Google Ventures called Design Sprint.

Among the characteristics of agile development, the following were taken into consideration [11]:

From Scrum:

- Sprint: basic development unit in Scrum, lasting from one to two weeks, which is composed of a list of features or requirements to be implemented in the sprint, known as Sprint Backlog, which is defined at the beginning of each sprint.
- Daily meetings: daily meetings of short duration (15 min) to discuss the progress in the project, the difficulties encountered and the plans for the future.
- Sprint retrospective: meeting after the completion of each sprint to discuss what can be changed so that the next sprint is more productive.
- Burndown chart: graphic representation of the remaining work versus time, with the objective of making estimates about when the work will be completed.

From Kanban:

- Kanban board: workflow visualization tool composed of cards that represent tasks located in different columns of a board (in its simplest form: 'To do', 'Doing', 'Done') to communicate the status and progress of those tasks.
- Work in progress: section of the Kanban Board that represents work in progress. To optimize workflow, the goal of a Kanban system is to limit the amount of work in progress and minimize it as much as possible.

From XP:

- Refactoring: a process that consists of, once the functionality is already implemented, making adjustments or internal restructuring of the code without changing its external behavior to guarantee its maintainability.

Regarding the design process that was considered as part of the proposed methodology, Design Sprint was taken as an activity to be carried out in the Spike of the development cycle. Spikes are small cycles that are not considered as development but are activities that help solve a problem encountered or add value to the sprint in its course.

Design Sprint uses the concept of Sprints that is part of the development cycles of agile methodologies. The Design Sprint phases are aligned to the five phases of Design Thinking, but it has its own five-day activity structure. The first day consists of **mapping**, during which it seeks to understand the needs of users, technological capabilities and business objectives and define the central route desired for the user. On the second day, it is carried out the outlined which consists in diverging generating a rain of individual **sketches** that represent ideas of solution. The third day is for **deciding**, for it is reviewed all the ideas and converges among the main ideas. On the fourth day, the solution chosen the day before is **prototyped**. On the fifth day, the **validations** are made with potential users to obtain feedback [7]. Referring to the following figure (Fig. 4).

Within the main deliverables were considered notes, user journey maps, prototypes, reports of findings found in user tests and plans for the following steps.

Based on the previously proposed characteristics, the Sprint model was presented during the development of the software. Referring to the following figure (Fig. 5).

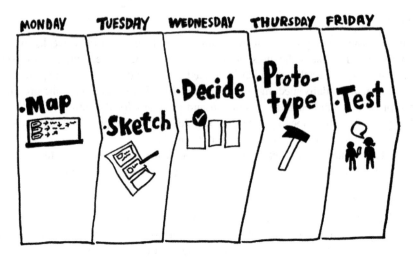

Fig. 4. Design sprint process [7].

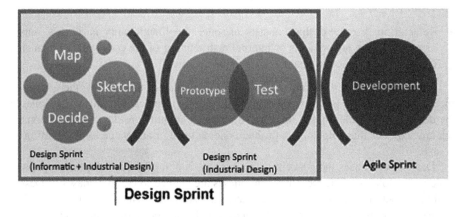

Fig. 5. Stages of the cycle of the proposed methodology

The weekly sprint starts with the Spike's Design Sprint, which must generate a tested prototype and become part of the next week's development sprint. At the beginning of the following week, as it unfolds the first Sprint code, the second Sprint Design will take place. This result will be implemented in development sprint 2. Referring to the following figure (Fig. 6).

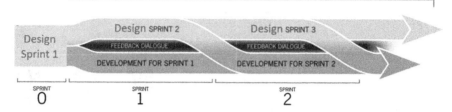

Fig. 6. Workflow of proposed methodology

4   Results of the Application

During the life of the project the team were carried out the activities of the proposed methodology.

4.1   Map

During the mapping stage, activities were carried out to understand what the user's needs were and which could be solved with the computer tool to be developed (Fig. 7).

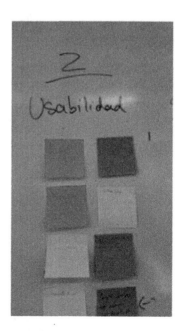

Fig. 7. Map process

4.2   Sketch

In this stage, individual sketches were made on the screens to be presented to the user (Fig. 8).

Fig. 8. Sketch process

4.3   Decide

During this stage the feasibility of the elaborated proposals is evaluated and was decided for those that added more value to the user (Fig. 9).

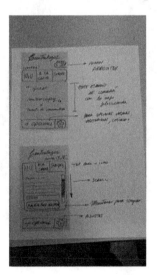

Fig. 9. Decide process

4.4   Prototype

The stage of prototyping at high level was a job that was made by the specialty of Industrial Design with its extensive knowledge of prototyping tools and color theory (Fig. 10).

Fig. 10. Prototype process

4.5   Test

Tests were carried out with users for the mobile application, recording the feedback they expressed during the user test [14] (Fig. 11).

Fig. 11. Test process

4.6   Barriers to the Project in Progress

During the Zuku project, barriers that were found led to the modifying of work form initially proposed without losing the essence of it.

One of the major limitations was the availability of team members to carry out the Sprint designs; this led to a reduction of the activities planned for five days to only two days. An adjustment of time was made in activities taking on the first day the process of understanding, outlining and deciding and, on the second day, prototyping and testing.

It is not against the plan to reduce the time since Frans Stijnman, member of the Digital Strategy & Customer Engagement team of Osudio, expresses in his article "It will be more effective with the 3-day design sprint" that it is feasible to reduce the number of days of design sprint, obtaining results that are as valid as in a five-day process [8] (Fig. 12).

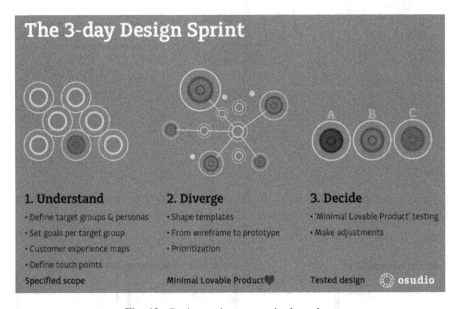

Fig. 12. Design sprint process in three days

Another barrier that arose was the little experience of the group at implementing methodologies of development and user-centered design. The members of the Industrial Design team had knowledge of Design Thinking which was an important contribution. In electronic engineering, they had not experienced a work methodology as the proposal and, in the computer engineering team, two members were part of a Design Sprint project with Priority, with which they were responsible for guiding the entire group in learning this methodology.

Finally, it was expected that this concretion process will be enriched thanks to the participation of members from different specialties and it was expected that the approaches would be different and some cases generating debate in the design of a prototype, finally agreements were reached based on the which was the final prototype.

5 Conclusions

As part of the computer engineering specialty team, promoting the implementation of methodologies not used in previous software development projects was a risky but very enriching proposal when it came to reality. The impact that it could have on the development of the project was initially evaluated since they spent an important amount of time during the week to carry out these activities and this required commitment from all the members of the Zuku project team.

The interdisciplinary project was presented as the perfect opportunity to experiment with new ways of working with which we learn the importance of developing a product from different perspectives.

To conclude this document, we thank the Industrial Design and Electronic Engineering team for the contribution from a different approach which could add considerably to the process of Designate Sprint development of the Zuku project.

References

1. Munari, B.: Cómo nacen los objetos?, 3rd edn. Gustavo Gilli, Barcelona (1983)
2. Choudhary, B., Rakesh, S.: An approach using agile method for software development. In: International Conference on Innovation and Challenges in Cyber Security (2016)
3. de Souza Carvalho, W., Rosa, P., dos Santos Soares, M., Teixeira da Cunha Jr., M., Buiatte, L.: A comparative analysis of the agile and traditional software development processes productivity. In: 30th International Conference of the Chilean Computer Science Society (2011)
4. 2015 Chaos Report on Software Development. https://www.linkedin.com/pulse/2015-chaos-report-software-development-steve-dean. Accessed 06 July 2017
5. Simon, H.: The Sciences of the Artificial, 3rd edn. MIT Press, Cambridge (1996)
6. Villegas, M., Giraldo, W., Collazos, C., Granollers, T.: Software process implementation method with eclipse process framework composer: MPiu+a case. In: 8th Computing Colombian Conference (2013)
7. Knapp, J., Zeratsky, J., Kowitz, B.: Sprint: How to Solve Big Problems and Test New Ideas in Just Five Days. Simon & Schuster, New York (2016)
8. Become more effective with the 3-day design sprint. https://www.osudio.com/en/blog/postings/how-to-the-3-day-design-sprint. Accessed 06 July 2017
9. Trender, M.: Ux Design for Startups, United States (2013)
10. Nielsen, J.: Iterative user-interface design. Computer 26, 32–41 (1993)
11. Smith, R.: Scrum Guide: Agile Project Management Guide for Scrum Master and Software Development Team. Createspace Independent Publishing (2016)
12. McInerney, P., Maurer, F.: UCD in agile projects: dream team or odd couple? Interactions 12, 19–23 (2005)

13. Mental Health Commission: Multidisciplinary Team Working, Ireland (2016)
14. Afonso, A., Reis, J., Pérez, M.: Usability assessment of web interfaces – user testing. Int. J. Inf. Sci. **3**(3), 57–62 (2013)
15. Galli, F., Suteu, I.: Design thinking as a disruptive discourse embracing conflict as a creative factor, Milano, Italy (2013)

Deep Learning Model and Its Application in Big Data

Yuanming Zhou[1], Shifeng Zhao[1(✉)], Xuesong Wang[1], and Wei Liu[2]

[1] College of Information Science and Technology,
Beijing Normal University, Beijing, China
zhao_shifeng@bnu.edu.cn
[2] Department of Psychology, Beijing Normal University, Beijing, China

Abstract. In the era of big data, many of the data that previously seemed hard to collect and use began to be utilized, resulting in an increase of millions of the data to be processed. In order to obtain valuable information, large-scale data can be processed and analyzed using a well-developed deep learning framework. This study introduces the concept of deep learning and three common deep learning models - Multilayer Perceptron, Convolutional Neural Network and Recurrent Neural Network, and analyzes the improvement of the model in dealing with large-scale data and gives the capacity and diversity analysis. Introducing the innovative application of deep learning in various fields under big data. Looking forward to the development of deep learning in the era of big data, the integration of big data and in-depth learning will make breakthroughs in various fields. Through constant innovation, they will gradually create more value for mankind.

Keywords: Big data · Deep learning · Multilayer Perceptron
Convolutional neural network · Recurrent neural network

1 Introduction

Big data or huge amounts of data, as the name implies, refers to a large amount of information. Big data is called big data when it is huge enough that the database system can not store, calculate, process and analyze information that can be interpreted within a reasonable time. There is a wealth of information in these huge amounts of information, such as relevance, unexplained patterns, market trends, may be buried with unprecedented knowledge and application waiting for us to discover. However, the traditional methods do not work because the data volume is too large and the flow rate is too fast. Therefore, promoting us to continue to develop a new generation of data storage devices and technology, hope we can extract from the big data that valuable information. Deep learning is the key to unlocking the big data era [1].

Deep learning is a sub-area of machine learning that simulates the human brain to analyze, interpret and manipulate text, images [2], and voice [3] messages. It builds a learning model with multiple hidden layers to train massive data through supervised/unsupervised training. After training, it can automatically learn features and improve classification or prediction accuracy. The advantages of the deep learning

© Springer International Publishing AG, part of Springer Nature 2018
A. Marcus and W. Wang (Eds.): DUXU 2018, LNCS 10918, pp. 795–806, 2018.
https://doi.org/10.1007/978-3-319-91797-9_55

model are the next two sides. The first is the ability to extract features. The resulting feature data is more representative of the original data, which will greatly facilitate the classification and visualization issues. The second is the combinatorial ability of features. Because deep learning has a more complicated network structure and has many non-linear parts, its feature combination ability is very strong.

At the same time, the evolution of big data has spawned the upgrade of hardware and software systems. The distributed architecture makes the performance of the algorithm no longer have a bottleneck, parallel framework and training methods to speed up the deep learning more efficient. Deep learning has transformed the mindset of problem solving and is the best partner for big data [4]. This study describes three typical deep learning models and their applications.

2   The Main Model of Deep Learning

Although the concept of deep learning [5] has been short-lived since its introduction, the algorithm model has rich research achievements and has also performed well in an era of rapid data growth. Deep learning algorithms often involve large-scale hidden neurons and millions of parameters that can process vast amounts of data and handle complex models. This section presents three depth models: Multilayer Perceptron, Convolutional Neural Networks, and Recurrent Neural Networks, as well as algorithmic and model improvements when working with large-scale data.

2.1   Multilayer Perceptron

Multilayer perceptron [6, 7] is a feedforward artificial neural network model, which contains multiple neurons arranged in multiple layers. Adjacent layers have nodes or edges and connections are provided with random weights. Usually they are the random numbers which between [−0.5, 0.5]. The principle is to map multiple input data sets to a single output data set. In statistical analysis, pattern recognition, optical symbol recognition, multi-layer perceptron is a powerful tool (Fig. 1).

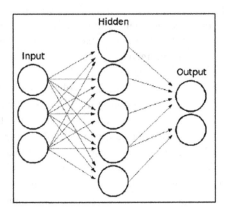

Fig. 1. Multilayer perception machine model

At every layer of neural network output, the trigger value of each neuron is calculated. The trigger value is the sum of the product of the value of all the neurons connected to the previous level of this neuron and the corresponding weights. The activation function is used to normalize the output of each neuron. For a K-layer multi-layer perceptron machine, the matrix is expressed as follows:

$$y(x) = f_K(\ldots f_2(w_2^T f_1(w_1^T x + b1) + b2)\ldots + b_{K-1}) \tag{1}$$

The backtracking algorithm uses delta rules to compute a local gradient drop from the output neuron back to each neuron in the input layer. First get the error of each output neuron

$$e_j(n) = d_j(n) - o_j(n) \tag{2}$$

The j-th neuron for the output layer l is then calculated

$$delta_j^{(L)}(n) = e_j^{(L)}(n) * f'(u_j^{(L)}(n)) \tag{3}$$

Finally calculate there j-th neuron for hidden layer

$$delta_j^{(l)}(n) = f'(u_j^{(l)}(n)) \sum_k (delta_k^{(l+1)}(n) * w_{kj}^{l+1}(n)) \tag{4}$$

After getting the delta for all the neurons, adjust the weight according to the following formula:

$$w_{ij}^l(n+1) = w_{ij}^{(l)}(n) + \alpha * [w_{ij}^{(l)}(n) - w_{ij}^{(l)}(n-1)] + \eta * delta_j^{(l)}(n)y_i^{(l-1)}(n) \tag{5}$$

For layer l, the new weight is the current weight plus a potential coefficient α and the learning coefficient η multiplied by the layer l's delta and the output of the neurons of the previous layer $l - 1$. The implementation of the delta rule is usually also an approximation of the gradient of the error sum. If there is a sufficiently small learning rate, the delta rule will find a set of weight-minimization error equations.

The research [8] shows that the multi-layer perceptron model neural network has the ability of parallel processing and self-learning. When the neural network has more than two hidden neural nodes, it can approximate the nonlinear function with arbitrary precision. Zen et al. [9] proposed a speech synthesis model based on multi-layer perceptrons using the algorithm in literature [10]. The model uses the input feature sequence to represent the input text. Each frame of the input feature sequence is mapped to the respective output features through multiple layers of perceptrons to generate speech parameters. Finally, the speech is synthesized through voiceprint. The training data consists of 33,000 segments of voice material recorded in US English by a female professional speaker. The results of this model are superior to those of the Hidden Markov Model method under a large number of data tests.

Large scale data will undoubtedly lead to slow training, in order to improve the problem, Cheng et al. [11] proposed a Learning-NEAT (LNEAT), a grid training method for large-scale data classification problems, which simplifies network evolution by splitting a problem into several subtasks. Learning subtasks is accomplished by applying Back Propagation rules in the NEAT algorithm. The LNEAT algorithm takes into account the advantages of the NEAT algorithm and the BP algorithm in topology and weight search, and overcomes the problems caused by the use of the NEAT algorithm. LNEAT algorithm has got satisfactory results in speech recognition, and has greatly improved the speed of network training.

2.2   Convolutional Neural Networks

Convolutional neural network [12] is a deep machine learning method from artificial neural network. In recent years, it has achieved great success in the field of image recognition. Convolutional neural network retains the deep structure of the network because of using local connection and weight sharing, and at the same time greatly reduces the network parameters so that the model has good generalization ability and is easier to train. A convolutional neural network is mainly composed of the following four parts: convolutional layer, pooling layer, fully connected layer and loss function. In the process of concatenation of different layers, the feature extraction and feature combination of image features are realized (Fig. 2).

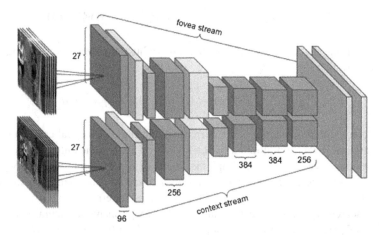

Fig. 2. Convolution neural network model

Convolution layer is used for feature extraction. Usually, multi-layer convolution layer is used to get deeper feature maps. Low-level convolution layer performs edge detection on the image. Higher-level convolution layer extracts Feature map for further feature extraction. Each convolution layer contains a number of convolution kernels, through different convolution kernel to complete the extraction of different features, the public expression is:

$$x_j^l = f(\sum_{i \in M_j} x_i^{l-1} * k_{ij} + b_j^l)$$ (6)

The activation function f is used to increase the nonlinear factors to enhance the system's ability to express. Commonly used activation functions are as follows:

$$Sigmoid(x) = \frac{1}{1 + e^x}$$ (7)

$$TanH(x) = \frac{e^x - e^{-x}}{e^x + e^{-x}}$$ (8)

$$ReLU(x) = \max(0, x)$$ (9)

After the features are obtained by the convolution layer, the features need to be sorted by the pooling layer [13]. The pooling layer aggregates the features of different locations. Common collection methods are the largest collection and average collection

$$O_{i,jk} = \underset{0 \le x \le m, 0 \le y \le m}{MAX} (I_{im + x, jm + y, k})$$ (10)

$$O_{i,jk} = \underset{0 \le x \le m, 0 \le y \le m}{AVE} (I_{im + x, jm + y, k})$$ (11)

The fully connected layer acts as a "classifier" throughout the convolutional neural network [14]. If the operations such as convolutional layer, pooling layer and activation function layer map the original data to hidden layer feature space, then the fully connected layer serves to map the learned "distributed feature representation" to the sample markup space. In practice, the fully connected layer can be implemented by a convolution operation: the fully connected layer to the front layer can be transformed into a convolution kernel with a 1 the "fully coated feature representation" to the sample markup space follows: of different features, the public expression is the global convolution of $h \times w$, h and w are respectively the height and width of the convolution results of the previous layer. Usually fully connected layer is located at the top of the network.

The loss function can continuously compare the output characteristic distance with the target, and use the backward conduction algorithm to continuously adjust the parameters in the whole network so as to achieve the goal of continuously optimizing the network structure and making the network develop in the expected direction. The European distance loss function [15] and softMax loss function are commonly used. The Euclidean distance loss function is a fundamental loss function aimed at reducing the Euclidean distance between the system output and a given label. The objective function of softMax can be written as

$$J(\theta) = -\frac{1}{m}[\sum_{i=1}^{m} 1 - y^{(i)} \log(1 - h_\theta(x^{(i)})) + y^{(i)} \log h_\theta(x^{(i)})]$$ (12)

The use of convolutional neural networks in large-scale data requires the use of multicore GPUs. The number of threads required for training depends on the size of the filter selected. Researchers at Microsoft Research Asia [16] used a network of depths up to 100 in the ImageNet Challenge, winning at an error rate as low as 3.57%. The number of layers in this network is more than 5 times that of any neural network that has been successfully used in the past, and has achieved good results in dealing with large-scale images.

When the required space in the GPU exceeds the available memory, the data needs to be copied into the CPU memory, but the transfer rate between the GPU and the CPU is relatively slow. Satish et al. [17] modulated data transmission into integer linear programs and improved simulated annealing algorithms/mixed integer linear programming algorithms significantly reduce the data transfer between the GPU and the CPU. Compared with the non-optimized method, the 30-fold reduction in data throughput is obtained, which provides important support for convolutional neural network processing large-scale data and parallel computing.

2.3   Recurrent Neural Networks

Recurrent neural networks (RNN) are neural networks with fixed weights [18], external inputs, and internal states that can be thought of as behavior dynamics of internal states with weights and external inputs as parameters. According to the basic variables is the neuron state or local field state can be divided into static field neural network model and local field neural network model. According to different ways of processing signals, the neural network can be divided into continuous system and discrete system.

Figure 3 is example of a fully deployed RNN network [19]. x_t represents the t-step input. s_t is the state of the t-step hidden layer, which is the memory unit of the network. s_t Calculate based on the output of the current input layer and the state of the hidden layer in the previous step

$$S_t = f(Ux_t + Ws_{t-1}) \tag{13}$$

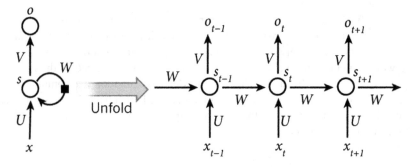

Fig. 3. Expanding recurrent neural network model

f is generally a non-linear activation function such as tanh or $RELU.s_{-1}$, the hidden state of the first word, is needed to calculate s_0, but it does not exist and is usually set to o in the implementation. o_t is the output of the step t, expressed in vector as

$$o_t = soft\max(Vs_t) \tag{14}$$

The recursive neural network introduces the ring structure, so the output at a certain time is not only related to the input of the current time, but also related to the state of the previous moment, and it can be used to deal with the variable length sequence problem through the weight sharing so that the recursive neural network can enhance its robustness.

However, the recursive neural network is more complicated than the feedforward neural network and has more computation and decoding speed. Which limits the application of recurrent neural network in the task of high real-time and large amount of data. In order to achieve the purpose of accelerating computation, Zhang et al. [20] proposed a method of frame skipping computation, which can reduce computational overhead by regularly dropping overlapping frames and directly reducing the number of frames to be calculated in the neural network. It can be applied directly to the recursive neural network model by adding the necessary cross-state transitions to the HMM in the Hidden Markov Model and the network structure itself does not change. The method can get 2–4 times speedup with less loss of accuracy.

Yosuke et al. [21] proposed a performance model for a distributed Deep Neural Network (DNN) training system called SPRINT, as Fig. 4, which takes DNN architecture and machine specifications as input parameters, taking into account the low-volume and gradient probability distributions that are core parameters of asynchronous SGD training (ASGD Training). Using asynchronous GPU processing based on the smallest batch SGD, the average error time was estimated as 5%, 9%, and 19%, respectively, in the processing of the entire dataset on supercomputers on thousands of GPUs. Progress has been made in dealing with the speed of large-scale data.

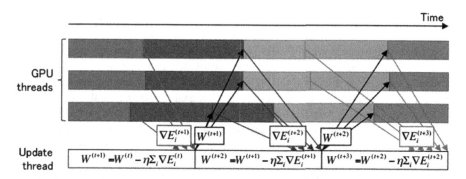

Fig. 4. Timeline of ASGD training [21]

3 Deep Learning Application in Big Data

This section will introduce some applications of deep learning under large-scale data. The results of the integration of big data and deep learning in engineering applications are mainly reflected in intelligent voice systems and machine vision images. As learning progresses and technology grows, it also begins to take advantage of the following areas.

3.1 Multi-function Network

Although the combination of deep learning and big data already has a lot of flexibility, the combination of the two can only do one problem at a time. For example, training a network or only recognize the picture, or only recognize the voice, they can not be identified at the same time. There is not yet a network that recognizes objects both visually and audibly. Despite the multitasking learning technology, the web can identify profiles, gestures, shades, texts, and more while recognizing image categories, but today's deep neural networks can be very low-energy compared to our human-versatile brain.

At present, if an application needs different capabilities, multiple networks must be combined, which is not only a huge consumption for computing resources but also difficult to form an effective interaction between different networks. How to enable them to achieve multiple goals at the same time, the current enlightenment from the human brain is that, in some way, it may be possible to connect the networks responsible for different functions to form a larger network. Noam et al. [22] introduced a decentralized gated mixed-expert layer (MOE) consisting of up to thousands of feedforward subnets, using a trainable gated network to determine the sparse combination of these experts, then present model architectures in which a MOE with up to 137 billion parameters is applied convolutionally between stacked LSTM layers. On large language modeling and machine translation benchmarks, these models achieve significantly better results than state-of-the-art at lower computational cost.

3.2 Medical System

Medical institutions, whether pathological reports, cure programs or drug reports and so on are relatively large data industries, the face of many viruses, tumor cells are in the process of evolution, the diagnosis will find the diagnosis of the disease and treatment programs to determine is very difficult. This can be based on the pain points in the medical field, building a deep learning model, the use of big data analysis to solve medical problems, such as users can use the big data acquisition behavior analysis, visual query and analysis, multidimensional analysis, retention analysis, funnel analysis, return visit analysis, etc., to build a deep learning model, the depth of the patient's various problems.

Google's DeepMind and IBM's Watson are active in this area, especially Watson, in some specific areas, its diagnostic accuracy has exceeded human experts. Because the majority of medical cases are unstructured textual data, the deep belief networks stacked by multi-layer limiting Boltzmann machine could automatically extract features from textual cases and learning knowledge in the medical records effectively, and can be efficiently diagnosed.

3.3   Translation

Real-time machine translation [23, 24] is one of the most promising directions for deep learning technology to use under big data. From the machine translation approach originally based on rules based on human compilation to the later statistical-based statistical machine translation (SMT) approach to the present neuro-machined translation (NMT), translation technology has been continuously updated over the past six decades, especially in 2012. The deep learning technology get into people's perspective, the machine translation accuracy constantly updated. Based on the deep learning technology, translation technology adopts an end-to-end structure, does not require human to abstract features and network structure design is simple, does not require word segmentation, alignment, syntax tree design and other complex design work, is very suitable for work under a lot of data.

Dzmitry and Yoshua [25] mapped an original language sentence into an implicit vector of a fixed length through an encoder, which is the bottleneck to improve the translation effect of NMT. Actually, when the decoder decodes the target language sentence, it only correlates with a part of the input source sentence. Based on this, they put forward a mechanism of "attention mechanism" that allows the model to automatically find the key correspondence between the source language sentence and the target language sentence word and the word, without limiting the length of the hidden vector. A set of content-based attention calculation method is given. The essence is to use a two-way Long Short-Term Memory (LSTM) to learn the importance of none of the words in the source language. This method is very effective and can also be used to study deeply in many other fields under large scale of data, for example Q & A, large-based number of sentence reasoning, entity extraction, huge document generation and so on (Fig. 5).

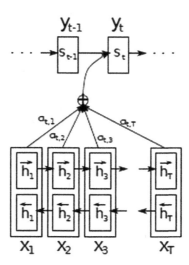

Fig. 5. The graphical illustration of the proposed model trying to generate the t-th target word y_t given a source sentence $(x_1, x_2, \ldots, x_T)$ [25]

3.4   Playing Strategic Games

When people are still shocked by the impact of ALPHAGO, DeepMind team non-stop brought a new surprise. London local time on October 18, DeepMind [26] team announced the most powerful version of AlphaGo, code-named AlphaGo Zero. AlphaGo Zero Intensive learning self-play. After several days of training, AlphaGo Zero completed almost 5 million self-game, has been able to surpass humans and beat all previous versions of AlphaGo. The neural network takes the checkerboard position s as an input, outputs a vector of the movement probability p for the component $p\_a = P\_r(a|s)$ for each action a, and scalar value $v \approx E[z|s]$ for estimating the expected result z from the position s. AlphaZero learns the probability of winning these steps entirely from self-play; these results are then used to guide the search of the program.

DeepMind team said in the official blog, Zero with the updated neural network and search algorithm reorganization, as the training deepened, the performance of the system a little bit of progress, through a powerful neural network search algorithm, after the self-game obtained The results are getting better and better, while the neural network has become more accurate.

4   Opportunities and Challenges

Current deep learning algorithms and big data technologies perform far less well than their theoretically achievable performance. Unsupervised learning can solve the real-world identification of very large objects, learn the rules, patterns and features of large-scale data without the intervention of artificial models through direct training using unlabeled data, and understand that ordinary human beings The problem that the brain can not be directly extracted and extracted is used by mankind to solve practical problems. To fully tap the hidden value in big data can serve human life.

Although the existing data volume is already large, it is still not enough. The complexity, dimensions and diversity of common data are not enough to cover all possible boundary conditions in the real world. In the existing distributed system, a large amount of data and parameters need to be transmitted between nodes, and the communication cost is too high. When the number of nodes exceeds a certain number, a continuous acceleration ratio can not be obtained. How to design a distributed system requires DNN algorithm experts and system experts to work together to solve the problem. The solution may need to modify the algorithm to match the underlying hardware architecture, but also requires the system expert to design a powerful computing single machine, but also design high-density Integrated, efficient communication server. Secondly, the model of deep learning in big data, its data volume and computational volume are very large, often need a few weeks or even months of training time, bound to require parallel training to improve training speed, but when training different data between multiple nodes, how to coordinate and synchronize may need to be redesigned from an algorithmic perspective.

5   Conclusion

This study introduces three models of deep learning, and introduces the challenges and applications of each model in big data environments. In this era of massive growth of data, the first issue to be considered in dealing with vast amounts of data is how to effectively analyze and process the data and mine the value of the data. Deep learning methods play a key role in processing big data by adaptively extracting their internal representations from data, minimizing human involvement, and providing greater generalization. If the analogy of artificial intelligence as a rocket, then the deep learning is the rocket engine, big data is the rocket fuel, two parts get together at the same time could be able to successfully launch the rocket into space. In the context of big data, with the continuous deepening of deep learning research, the efficient combination of the two will surely make the computer more intelligent so as to assist human decision-making and bring good news to mankind.

Acknowledgements. This work was supported by Beijing Natural Science Foundation (Grant No. 4174094).

References

1. Yu, B., Li, S., et al.: Deep learning: a key of stepping into the era of big data. J. Eng. Stud. 20–45 (2014)
2. Wu, M., Chen, L.: Image recognition based on deep learning. In: Chinese Automation Congress, Wuhan, China, pp. 542–546 (2015)
3. Zhao, Y., Xu, Y.M., Sun, M.J., et al.: Cross-language transfer speech recognition using deep learning. In: Proceedings of the 11th IEEE International Conference of Control & Automation (ICCA), Munich, Germany, pp. 1422–1426 (2014)
4. Wang, J., Chen, H., Liu, Q.: The study of deep learning under big data. Chin. High Technol. Lett. **1**, 005 (2017)
5. Hinton, G.E., Osindero, S., Ten, Y.W.: A fast learning algorithm for deep belief nets. Neural Comput. **18**(7), 1527–1554 (2006)
6. Bengio, Y., Lamblin, P., Popovici, D., et al.: Greedy layer-wise training of deep networks. In: Advances in Neural Information Processing Systems, pp. 153–160. MIT Press, Cambridge (2007)
7. Zeiler, M.D., Krishnan, D., Taylor, G.W., et al.: Deconvolutional networks. In: 2010 IEEE Conference on Computer Vision and Pattern Recognition (CVPR), pp. 2528–2535. IEEE, Piscataway (2010)
8. Sagar, G.V.R., Venkata, C.S.: Simultaneous evolution of architecture and connection weights in artificial neural network. Int. J. Comput. Appl. **53**(4), 23–28 (2012)
9. Zen, H., Senior, A., Schuster, M.: Statistical parametric speech synthesis using deep neural networks. In: 2013 IEEE International Conference on Acoustics, Speech and Signal Processing (ICASSP), pp. 7962–7966. IEEE, Piscataway (2013)
10. Tokuda, K., Yoshimura, T., Masuko, T., et al.: Speech parameter generation algorithms for HMM-based speech synthesis. In: Proceedings of 2000 IEEE International Conference on Acoustics, Speech, and Signal Processing, pp. 1315–1318. IEEE, Piscataway (2000)
11. Cheng, Z.: Research and Application of Large Scale Multi-layer Perceptron Neural Network Jilin University, vol. 6 (2017)

12. Harley, A.W.: An interactive node-link visualization of convolutional neural networks. In: ISVC, pp. 867–877 (2015)
13. He, K., Zhang, X., Ren, S., et al.: Spatial pyramid pooling in deep convolutional networks for visual recognition. IEEE Trans. Pattern Anal. Mach. Intell. **37**(9), 1904–1916 (2014)
14. Simard, P., Steinkraus, D., Platt, J.C.: Best practices for convolutional neural networks applied to visual document analysis. In: Seventh International Conference on Document Analysis and Recognition (ICDAR 2003), vol. 2, pp. 958–962. IEEE (2003)
15. Lecun, Y., BottouL, B.Y., et al.: Gradient-based learning applied to document recognition. Proc. IEEE **86**(11), 2278–2324 (1998)
16. Sun, J., He, K.M., Zhang, X.Y., et al.: Delving deep into rectifiers: surpassing human-level performance on imagenet classification (2015)
17. Satish, N., Sundaram, N., Keutzer, K.: Optimizing the use of GPU memory in applications with large data sets. In: Proceedings of the 16th International Conference on High Performance Computing, Kochi, India, pp. 408–418 (2009)
18. Bengio, Y., Lamblin, P., Popovici, D., et al.: Greedy layer-wise training of deep networks. In: Advances in Neural Information Processing Systems 19, p. 153. Neural Information Processing Systems Foundation, Inc. (2006)
19. Sak, H., Senior, A., Beaufays, F.: Long short-term memory recurrent neural network architectures for large scale acoustic modeling. In: 15th Annual Conference of the International Speech Communication Association (Interspeech 2014), Singapore, pp. 338–342 (2014)
20. Zhang, G., Zhang, P.Y., Pan, J., et al.: Fast decoding algorithm for automatic speech recognition based on recurrent neural networks. J. Electron. Inf. Technol. **4** (2017)
21. Yosuke, O., Akihiro, N.: Predicting statistics of asynchronous SGD parameters for a large-scale distributed deep learning system on GPU supercomputers, pp. 306–331 (2016)
22. Noam, S., Azalia, M., Krzysztof, M., et al.: Outrageously large neural networks: the sparsely-gated mixture-of-experts layer, pp. 204–220 (2017)
23. Ciresan, D.C., Meier, U., Gamarde lla, L.M., et al.: Deep, big, simple neural nets for handwritten digit recognition. Neural Comput. **22**(12), 3207–3220 (2010)
24. Ranzato, M., Poultney, C., Chopra, S., et al.: Efficient learning of sparse representations with an energy-based model. In: Advances in Neural Information Processing Systems Foundations, Inc., pp. 379–420 (2006)
25. Dzmitry, B.,Yoshua, B.: Neural machine translation by jointly learning to align translate. Published as a Conference Paper at ICLR 2015, pp. 167–190 (2015)
26. David, S., Julian, S., Karen, S., et al.: Mastering the game of go without human knowledge. Nature **550**, 354–359 (2017)

Author Index